DATE DUE FOR RETURN

THE COLLECTED SCIENTIFIC PAPERS OF
PAUL A. SAMUELSON

VOLUME III

THE COLLECTED SCIENTIFIC PAPERS OF
PAUL A. SAMUELSON

Edited by Robert C. Merton

THE M.I.T. PRESS
Massachusetts Institute of Technology
Cambridge, Massachusetts, and London, England

See pages 909–914 for acknowledgments of previously published material.

Library of Congress Cataloging in Publication Data

Samuelson, Paul Anthony, 1915–
    The collected scientific papers of Paul A. Samuelson.

    Vol. 3–   edited by Robert C. Merton.
    Includes bibliographies.
    1.   Economics — Collected works.
HB33.S2   330.08   65–28408
ISBN 0 262 19080 X

AUTHOR'S PREFACE

The first two volumes of my *Collected Scientific Papers* having apparently served a useful purpose, I am happy to see gathered into a third volume the harvest of the half dozen years since 1965. Once again I have been blessed by having a young and brilliant economist serve as editor, leaving me to my new harvestings. Robert C. Merton carries on in a tradition begun by Joseph E. Stiglitz, and I am grateful.

Dr. Merton has exercised his judgment as to what should be included. His general rule has been to include *all* scientific and scholarly papers, but generally not to include ephemeral financial and other writings. Otherwise what threatens to exceed a couple of hundred items could become several times as numerous. In a few cases, however, in which he has thought to discern some scientific merit or spark, the editor has included samples of these more fugitive writings. Wisely, as I believe, the original paging has been preserved in the reproduction, with occasional correction of obvious misprints by the editor and rare second thoughts — identified as such — by the author.

I owe thanks both to The M.I.T. Press and to the National Science Foundation, but most of all to Professor Merton.

Paul A. Samuelson

Cambridge, Massachusetts
February, 1972

v

EDITOR'S PREFACE

The third volume contains seventy-eight chapters representing all the scientific papers written by Paul A. Samuelson from mid-1964 through 1970, and many of his papers for the year 1971. Most of the articles were collected from scientific journals, festschrifts, and professional books, although I have not hesitated to include articles of a scientific nature from nonprofessional sources.

The articles are arranged by subject in nineteen parts, and they are grouped within each part by their relationship to one another. Eighteen of the parts are titled as in the previous volumes and represent a continuation of Professor Samuelson's research in these areas. The nineteenth contains his first contributions to the theories of portfolio selection, warrant pricing, and speculative markets under uncertainty. A complete chronological listing appears at the end of the volume.

While an attempt has been made to eliminate all mechanical errors in the articles, there were no changes of substance, even when Professor Samuelson's opinion on the topic has subsequently changed.

I started collecting these papers in 1968 and each time I was prepared to publish the volume, Dr. Samuelson would write another paper which I wanted to include. In 1971, the pipeline is still full and with no end in sight, I take my wife's advice and reluctantly close the third volume.

ROBERT C. MERTON

Cambridge, Massachusetts
January, 1972

CONTENTS

Volume III

Book One
Problems in Pure Theory: The Theory of Consumer's Behavior and Capital Theory

Contents

Part IV. On Ricardo and Marx

Book Two

Topics in Mathematical Economics

Book Three

Trade, Welfare and Fiscal Policy

Contents

Book Four

Economics and Public Policy

Part XII.   Pure Theory of Public Expenditure

Part XIII.   Principles of Fiscal and Monetary Policy

Part XIV.   The Individual and the State

Book Five

Economics—Past and Present

Contents

BOOK ONE

Problems in Pure Theory:
The Theory of Consumer's Behavior and Capital Theory

PART I

The Theory of Revealed Preference and Other Topics in
Nonstochastic Consumption Theory

MAXIMUM PRINCIPLES IN ANALYTICAL ECONOMICS

PAUL A. SAMUELSON

Massachusetts Institute of Technology, Cambridge, Massachusetts

Nobel Memorial Lecture, December 11, 1970

The very name of my subject, economics, suggests economizing or maximizing. But Political Economy has gone a long way beyond home economics. Indeed, it is only in the last third of the century, within my own lifetime as a scholar, that economic theory has had many pretensions to being *itself* useful to the practical businessman or bureaucrat. I seem to recall that a great economist of the last generation, A. C. Pigou of Cambridge University, once asked the rhetorical question, "Who would ever think of employing an economist to run a brewery?" Well, today, under the guise of operational research and managerial economics, the fanciest of our economic tools are being utilized in enterprises both public and private.

So at the very foundations of our subject maximization is involved. My old teacher, Joseph Schumpeter, went much farther. Instead of being content to say economics must borrow from logic and rational empirical enquiry, Schumpeter made the remarkable claim that man's ability to operate as a logical animal capable of systematic empirical induction was itself the direct outcome of the Darwinian struggle for survival. Just as man's thumb evolved in the struggle to make a living—to meet his economic problem—so did man's brain evolve in response to the economic problem. Coming forty years before the latest findings in ethology by Konrad Lorenz and Nikolaas Tinbergen, this is a rather remarkable insight. It would take me away from my present subject to more than mention the further view enunciated by Schumpeter [1] in launching the new subject of econometrics. Quantity, he said, is studied by the physicist or other natural scientist at a fairly late and sophisticated stage of the subject. Since a quantitative approach is, so to speak, at the discretion of the investigator, all the more credit to the followers of Galileo and Newton for taking the mathematical approach. But in economics, said Schumpeter, the very subject matter presents itself in quantitative form: take away the numerical magnitude of price or barter exchange-ratio and you have nothing left. Accounting does not benefit from arithmetic; it is arithmetic—and in its early stages, according to Schumpeter, arithmetic is accounting, just as geometry in its early stages is surveying.

I must not leave you with the impression that analytical economics is concerned with maximization principles primarily in connection with providing vocational handbooks for the practising decision maker. Even back in the last generation, before economics had pretensions toward being itself useful to practitioners, we economists were occupied with maxima and minima. Alfred Marshall's *Principles of Economics*, the dominating treatise in the forty years after 1890, dealt much with optimal output at the point of maximum net profit. And long before Marshall, A. A. Cournot's 1838 classic, *Researches into the Mathematical Principles of the Theory of Wealth*, put the differential calculus to work in the study of maximum-profit output. Concern for minimization of cost goes back a good deal more than a century, at least back to the marginal productivity notions of von Thünen.

It is fashionable these days to speak of identity crises. One must not make the mistake attributed to Edward Gibbon when he wrote his *Decline and Fall of the Roman Empire*. Gibbon, it was said, sometimes confused himself and the Roman Empire. I know in these days of the living theater—and I ought to add on this occasion, of the theories of quantum mechanics—the distinction often becomes blurred between observing audience and acting players, between the observing scientist and the guinea pigs or atoms under observation. As I shall discuss in connection with the role of maximum principles in natural science, the plumb-line trajectory of a falling apple and the elliptical orbit of a wandering planet may be capable of being described by the optimizing solution for a specifiable programming problem. But no one will be tempted to fall into a reverse version of the Pathetic Fallacy and attribute to the apple or the planet freedom of choice and consciously deliberative minimizing. Nonetheless, to say "Galileo's ball rolls down the inclined plane *as if* to minimize the integral of action, or to minimize Hamilton's integral," does prove to be useful to the observing physicists, eager to formulate predictable uniformities of nature.

What is it that the scientist finds useful in being able to relate a positive description of behaviour to the solution of a maximizing problem? That is what a good deal of my own early work was about. From the time of my first papers on "Revealed Preference" [2] through the completion of *Foundations of Economic Analysis*, I found this a fascinating subject. The scientist, as with the housewife, finds his work is really never done. Just in these last weeks I have been working on the very difficult problem of understanding stochastic speculative price—e.g. how cocoa prices fluctuate on the London and New York exchanges. [3] When confronted with an unmanageable system of nonlinear difference equalities and inequalities, I could have despaired of finding in the mathematical literature a proof of even the existence of a solution. But suddenly the problem became solvable in a flash, when out of the strata of memory, I dredged up the recollection that my positive descriptive relations could be interpreted as the necessary and sufficient conditions of a well defined maximum problem. But I run ahead of my story if I give you the impression that maximum principles are valuable merely as a convenience and crutch to the less-than-omniscient analyst.

Seventy years ago, when the Nobel Foundation was first established, the me-

3

thodological views of Ernst Mach enjoyed a popularity they no longer possess.[1] Mach you will remember, said that what the scientist seeks is an "economical" description of nature. By this he did not mean that the navigation needs of traders decreed that Newton's system of the world had to get born. He meant rather that a good explanation is a simple one that is easy to remember and one which fits a great variety of the observable facts. It would be a Gibbonlike fallacy to illustrate this by the deistic view of Maupertuis that the laws of nature are the working out of a simple teleological purpose. Mach is not saying that Mother Nature is an economist; what he is saying is that the scientist who formulates laws of observed empirical phenomena is essentially an economist or economizer.

Nonetheless, I must point out that these distinct roles are, almost by coincidence so to speak, closely related. Often the physicist gets a better, a more economical, description of nature if he is able to formulate the observed laws by a maximum principle. Often the economist is able to get a better, a more economical, description of economic behaviour from the same device.

Let me illustrate this by some very simple examples. Newton's falling apple can be described in either of two ways: its acceleration toward the earth is a constant; or its position as a function of time follows that arc which minimizes the integral, taken from its moment of release to the terminal time at which it is observed, of an integrand which can be written as the square of its instantaneous velocity minus a linear function of its position. "What?" you will say, "can you seriously regard the second explanation as the simple one?" I will not argue the point, except to point out that simplicity is in the eye of the beholder, and that if I were to write out for the mathematical physicist the expression

$$\delta \int_0^T \left(\frac{1}{2} x^2 - gx \right) dt = 0$$

he would not consider it less simple than $\ddot{x} = -g$; and he would know that the Hamilton principle formulation in variational terms has great mnemonic properties when it comes to transforming from one coordinate system to another.

Although I am not a physicist and do not suppose that many of my audience are either, let me give a clearer example of the usefulness of a minimum principle in physics. Light travels between two points in the air before me along a straight line. Alternatively like the apple's fall, this arc can be defined as the solution to a minimization problem in the calculus of variations. But now let us consider how light is reflected when it hits a mirror. You may observe and memorize the rule that the angle of reflection is equal to the angle of incidence. A neater way of understanding this fact is by the least-time principle of Fermat, which was already known to Hero and other Greek

---

[1] Whatever their ultimate worth, we must be grateful to Mach's concepts for their influence on the young Einstein's formulation of special relativity theory. Although an older Einstein rebelled against this same methodology, this cannot rob them of their just credit.

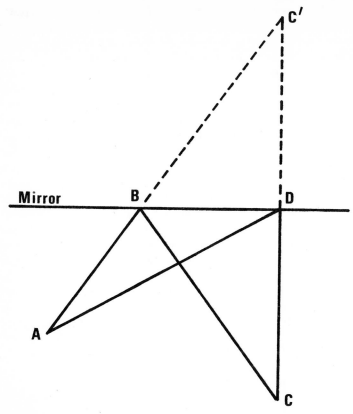

scientists. The accompanying diagram with its indicated similar triangles can be self-explanatory.

If ABC' is clearly shorter in length than ADC', it is evident that the similar ABC path is shorter and involves less time than any other path such as ADC.

You could validly argue that the minimum formulation is neat, but really no better than the other formulation. However, move from this lecture room to your bathtub and observe your big toe in the water. Your limbs no longer appear straight because the velocity of light in water differs from that in air. The least-time principle tells you how to formulate behaviour under such conditions and the memorizing of Snell's Law about angles does not. Who can doubt which is the better scientific explanation?

An Illustrative Economic Example

Let me illustrate the same thing in economics as a simplest imaginable case. Consider a profit-maximizing firm that sells its output along a demand curve in which the price received is a non-increasing function of the amount sold. Suppose further that output is producible by two, three, or ninety-nine different inputs. To keep the example simple, suppose that the production function relating outputs to inputs is smooth and concave.

As a positivistic scientist interested merely in cataloguing the observable facts, a Machian economist could in principle record on punch cards ninety-nine demand functions relating the quantity of each input bought by the firm to the ninety-nine variables depicting the input prices. What a colossal task it would be to store bits of information defining ninety-nine distinct surfaces in a one hundred dimensional space! But the ninety-nine surfaces are not really independent. In actuality, it is enough to have knowledge of a single parent surface in order to be able to calculate the exact information about the ninety-nine children. How is this tremendous economy of description possible? It is by virtue of the fact that the observed demand curves, which that great Swedish economist of the generation before last, Gustav Cassel, would have taken as the irreducible atoms of the economists' theory, are actually themselves solutions to a maximum-profit problem. Under simple regularity conditions of the calculus, they are the inverse functions of a family of partial derivatives of the Total Revenue function, where revenue is given by the output producible by any specified quantities of all inputs times the determinate demand price at which that output will sell. When smooth and strongly concave, this parent revenue function has as its children a ninety-nine by ninety-nine matrix of second partial derivatives which is symmetric and negative definite. It is an exercise in algebra to show that these functions can be uniquely inverted to form a new family of children with the same properties; and ninety-nine such children cannot fail to have a parent function which, so to speak, if it had never existed we should have to invent in a Pygmalion fashion.

Mathematically we have

$$\underset{\{v_i\}}{\text{Max}}[R(v_1, ..., v_{99}) - \sum_1^{99} p_j v_j] = R(v_1{}^*, ..., v_{99}{}^*) - \sum_1^{99} p_j v_j{}^*$$
$$= -H(p_1, ... p_{99}), \qquad (1)$$

where
$$R(v_1, ..., v_{99}) = Q(v_1, ..., v_{99}) \, P[Q(v_1, ..., v_{99})]$$

is a smooth, strongly concave "regular" revenue function. Necessary conditions for the maximum are

$$\partial R(v_1{}^*, ..., v_{99}{}^*)/\partial v_i = p_i, \quad (i = 1, ..., 99) \qquad (2)$$

If in addition the Hessian matrix of second partial derivatives, $[\partial^2 R/\partial v_i \partial v_j]$, is negative definite, Equations (2) are sufficient for the maximum. This implies inverse relations that can be interpreted as partial derivatives of a Hotelling-Roy dual function, H, namely

$$v_i{}^* = \partial H(p_1, ... p_n)/\partial p_i, \quad (i = 1, ..., 99) \qquad (3)$$

It follows that for

$$\sum \Delta v_j{}^2 \neq 0 \neq \sum \Delta p_j{}^2,$$

our variables satisfy the inequality

$$\Delta p_1 \, \Delta v_1 + \Delta p_2 \, \Delta v_2 + ... + \Delta p_{99} \, \Delta v_{99} < 0 \qquad (4)$$

More can be said. Although my intuition is poor enough in three dimensional space, I can assert with confidence on the basis of the above that raising any input's price while holding all remaining inputs' prices constant will definitely reduce the amount demanded of that input by the firm—i.e. $\partial v_i / \partial p_i < 0$: Such a commonsense result might be expected by anyone who performed an act of empathetic introspection, "Suppose I were a jack-ass of an entrepreneur, what would I do to adjust to the dearness of an input in order to conserve as much profit as possible?"

Here the commonsense and advanced mathematics happen to agree. But we all know the Giffen pathology according to which an increase in the price of potatoes to Irish peasants, who must depend heavily on potatoes when they are poor, may itself impoverish them so as to force them into buying more rather than less potatoes. In this case common sense recognizes itself only under the search-light of mathematics.

With the assistance of mathematics, I can see a property of the ninety-nine dimensional surfaces hidden from the naked eye. If an increase in the price of fertilizer alone always increases the amount the firm buys of caviar, from that fact alone I can predict the answer to the following experiment which I have never seen performed and upon which I have no observations: an increase in the price of caviar alone will increase the amount the firm buys of fertilizer. In thermodynamics such reciprocity or integrability conditions are known as Maxwell Conditions; in economics they are known as Hotelling conditions in honor of Harold Hotelling's 1932 work [4].

One of the pleasing things about science is that we do all climb towards the heavens on the shoulders of our predecessors. Economics, like physics has its heros, and the letter "H" that I used in my mathematical equations was not there to honor Sir William Hamilton, but rather Harold Hotelling. For it was his work that I found so stimulating when I came on the scene, at about the same time that the late Henry Schultz [5] was trying by econometric methods to verify the empirical validity of the Hotelling integrability conditions.

There are still other predictable conditions of definiteness relating to how weak these "cross effects" must be in comparison with "own effects," but I will spare my audience discussion of them, except for mention of the condition that all principal minors have to oscillate in sign.

As a last illustration of the black magic by which a maximum formulation permits one to make clearcut inferences about a complicated system involving a large number of variables, let me recall the work I have done in formulating clearly and generalizing what is known in physics as LeChatelier's Principle [6]. This Principle was enunciated almost one hundred years ago by a French physicist interested in Gibbs-like thermodynamics. It is a vague principle. A third of a century ago when I thumbed through different physics treatises, my mathematical ear could not discern what tune was being played. If you pick up most physics books today, perhaps your luck will be no better. Usually the argument is obscurely teleological, reading something like the following: If you put an external constraint on an equilibrium system, the equilibrium shifts to "absorb" or "resist" or "adjust to" or "minimize" the change. I was struck by a remark made by an old teacher of mine at Harvard, Edwin Bidwell Wilson. Wilson was the last student of J. Willard Gibbs' at Yale and had worked creatively in many fields of mathematics and physics: his advanced calculus was a standard text for decades; his was the definitive writeup of Gibb's lectures on vectors; he wrote one of the earliest texts on aerodynamics; he was a friend of R. A. Fisher and an expert on mathematical statistics and demography; finally, he had become interested early in the work of Pareto and gave lectures in mathematical economics at Harvard. My earlier formulation of the inequality in equation (4) owed much to Wilson's lectures on thermodynamics. In particular I was struck by his statement that the fact that an increase in pressure is accompanied by a decrease in volume is not so much a theorem about a thermodynamic equilibrium system as it is a mathematical theorem about surfaces that are concave from below or about negative definite quadratic forms. Armed with this clue I set out to make sense of the LeChatelier Principle.

Let me now enunciate a valid formulation of that Principle. "Squeeze a balloon and its volume will contract. But compare how its volume contracts under two different experimental conditions. First, imagine that its surface is insulated from the rest of the world so that none of the so-called heat engendered can escape. In the second alternative administer the same increase in pressure in the balloon, but let it come into temperature equilibrium with the unchanged temperature of the room. Then according to LeChatelier Principle the increase in volume when the insulation constraint is placed on the system will be *less* than when the temperature is constrained to end up constant." The steeper light curve in Figure 2 (see a later page) shows the relationship between the pressure on the vertical axis and volume on the horizontal axis that prevails for the insulated increase. The less steep curve going through the same point "A" shows the pressure-volume relationship for an iso-thermal change. It is the essence of LeChatelier's Principle that the light curve must be more steep than the heavy curve or, in usual thermodynamic notation

$$(\partial v / \partial p)_t \leqslant (\partial v / \partial p)_s \leqslant 0 \qquad (5)$$

where t stands for temperature held constant, and s stands for the insulated (or adiabatic or isentropic) change.

Now what in the world has all this to do with economics? There is really nothing more pathetic than to have an economist or a retired engineer try to force analogies between the concepts of physics and the concepts of economics. How many dreary papers have I had to referee in which the author is looking for something that corresponds to entropy or to one or another form of energy. Nonsensical laws, such as the law of conservation of purchasing power, represent spurious social science imitations of the important physical law of the conservation of energy; and when an economist makes reference to a Heisenberg Principle of indeterminacy in the social world, at best this must be regarded as a figure of speech or a play on words, rather than a valid application of the relations of quantum mechanics.

However, if you look upon the monopolistic firm hiring ninety-nine inputs as an example of a maximum system, you can connect up its structural relations with those that prevail for an entropy-maximizing thermodynamic system. Pressure and volume, and for that matter absolute temperature and entropy, have to each other the same conjugate or dualistic relation that the wage rate has to labor or the land rent has to acres of land. Figure 2 can now do double duty, depicting the economic relationships as well as the thermodynamic ones. Now on the vertical axis goes p_1, the price of the first input. On the horizontal axis goes v_1, its quantity. The story can be told of a ninety-nine variable system but I think you will forgive me if I discuss the simpler case of two variables, say labor and land.

As in the case of the balloon we perform an experiment under two alternative sets of specified conditions. In the first case, we raise p_1, the price of the first input labor, while holding constant the quantity of the second input, land or v_2—as for example in the Marshallian short-run when only labor can be varied. The rise in p_1 must lower v_1 as shown by the negative slope of the light curve through A.

Now, in the second alternative experiment we raise p_1 by the same amount but hold the price of v_2, p_2, constant. Again, for a profit maximizing monopolist there can be but one qualitative answer: less of v_1 will now be bought, as shown by the negative slope of the heavy curve through A. Now one can state what perhaps might be called the LeChatelier—Samuelson Principle: The heavy curve of longer-run adjustment, with other price constant (and other quantity of course thereby itself adjusting *mutatis mutandis* to restore the maximum-profit equilibrium), must be less steep or more elastic than the light curve depicting the demand reaction when the other input is held constant. Mathematically now

$$(\partial v_1 / \partial p_1)_{p_2} \leqslant (\partial v_1 / \partial p_1)_{v_2} \leqslant 0 \qquad (6)$$

I have included the equality signs to allow for the case where two inputs might be quite independent in production. What is remarkable about the relation is that the indicated inequalities will hold whether the two inputs are complements such as pumps and insecticides or substitutes such as organic and inorganic fertilizers. The interested listener might try to work out the intuitive verification of this in those opposite cases.

Not only in the theory of production but also in the general theory of constrained rationing does the LeChatelier Principle have various economic applications.

CONSUMER DEMAND THEORY

This brings me to the theory of consumer demand. Unlike the maximizing profit situation that has been discussed up to this time, now we have a budgetary constraint within which maximizing has to occur. Prior to the mid-1930's, utility theory showed signs of degenerating into a sterile tautology. Psychic utility or satisfaction could scarely be defined, let alone be measured. Austrian economists would insist that people acted to maximize their utility, but when challenged as to what that was, they found themselves replying circularly that however people behaved, they would presumably not have done so unless it maximized their satisfaction. Just as we can cancel two from the ratio of even numbers, so one could use Occam's Razor to cut utility completely from the argument, ending one up with the fatuity: people do what they do.

I exaggerate only a little. It is true that the Russian Slutsky [7] had in 1915 gone beyond this, but his work, published in an Italian journal, was forgotten in the backwash of the First World War. The better known work of Pareto [8] lacked the mathematical technique of the Weierstrass theory of constrained extrema. Two dimensional analysis of indifference curves had been worked out by W. E. Johnson [9], a Cambridge logician who had studied with Marshall and Whitehead and who is thought to have influenced the probability researches of J. M. Keynes [10], Frank Ramsey [11], and Sir Harold Jeffreys [12]. However just before I arrived on the scene, when Sir Roy Allen and Sir John Hicks [13] at the London School, and Henry Schultz in Chicago, were pioneering the theory of consumers' behaviour, the contributions of Slutsky were unknown.

From the beginning I was concerned to find out what *refutable* hypotheses on the observable facts on price and quantity demanded were implied by the assumption that the consumer spends his limited income at given prices in order to maximize his ordinal utility (i.e., his better-or-worse situation without regard to any numerical indication of how much better or worse). To make a long story short, the flash of inspiration for "Revealed Preference" came to me in argument with one of my teachers, as so many of my best ideas have done. Having learned about indifference curves from Leontief, I put them to use next year in Haberler's international trade course. When he objected to my postulating convex indifference curves, I heard myself replying: "Well, if they are concave, then the Laspeyres-Paasche index-numbers of your doctoral thesis are no good."[2] Far from being a *reductio ad absurdum*, this proposition, upon reflection suggested how a scientific investigator could refute the hypothesis of maximizing behaviour by a test on two price-quantity observed situations. All that remained was to work out the details of the theory of revealed preference.

My early theory of revealed preference was by itself perfectly adequate to handle the problems of two consumption goods. I went on to conjecture that if we ruled out similar contradictions for choices of more than two situations,[3] then the phenomenon of "non-integrability" of the indifference field could be ruled out.

[2]In explanation, suppose you are maximizing the utility of your consumptions of $(Q_x, Q_y, ...)$, at prices $(P_x, P_y, ...)$, spending positive income of $P_x Q_x + ... = \sum PQ$. Then in two situations, $(P^1, Q^1, \sum P^1 Q^1)$ and $(P^2, Q^2, \sum P^2 Q^2)$, it is a contradiction to maximization of ordinal utility to be able to observe both $\sum P^1 Q^2 / \sum P^1 Q^1 < 1$, and $\sum P^2 Q^1 / \sum P^2 Q^2 < 1$. With variants of $\leq$ for $<$, denying this possibility is one form of the Weak Axiom of Revealed Preference.

[3]Using the notation of the previous situation, I conjectured that non-integrability could be ruled out by the axiom "$\sum P^i Q^i > \sum P^i Q^{i+1}$ for all of $i = 1, ..., n-1 \geq 1$ rules out $\sum P^n Q^n > \sum P^n Q^1$" for $n = 2$, this merely repeats the Weak Axiom; for all $n > 2$, it becomes the Strong Axiom of Houthakker.

Especially on occasions like this when one is only too likely to reminiscence about scientific victories, one ought to pause frequently along the way to express some lamentations over defeats and failures. Even with the aid of some of the world's leading mathematicians I was not able to verify and prove the truth of the previous footnote's conjecture, and I was persuaded to omit that material from the published version of "Revealed Preference". All the more credit therefore must go to Hendrik Houthakker [14] who on his maiden venture into economics formulated the Strong Axiom and proved that it did exclude nonintegrability.

How shall I in a morning lecture explain in words what non-integrable indifference fields are all about? In 1950 I [15] gave a review of the integrability discussion, going back to Pareto in the early years of this century and before that to Irving Fisher's 1892 classic thesis [16], and even before that to resurrected work of the rather unknown Antonelli [17]. How obscure the status of the integrability problem was in the mid-1930's when I arrived on the scene can be indicated by the fact that two close collaborators already cited, Sir John Hicks and Sir Roy Allen, seemed actually to be at odds in their views on the subject. Now that the empirical implications of non-integrability are understood, most theorists are inclined to postulate integrability. How to make clear its meanings? My good friend Nicholas Georgescu-Roegen, from whose classic 1935 paper I gleaned so many insights into the integrability problem, would argue that it is impossible to state such complicated mathematical relations in mere words. I am on record with the contrary view, namely that mathematics is language and in principle what one fool can comprehend so can another. Let me therefore refer you to Figure 2 in which I am able to present an in-the-large interpretation of integrability conditions for our earlier profit maximizing firm with its hiring of ninety-nine inputs.

The steep curves in the diagram represent the demand functions for the first input v_1, in terms of its price p_1, when all other inputs are held constrained as in a Marshallian short-run. The heavier and less steep curves also represent demand functions for v_1 in terms of p_1, but with all other factor prices frozen. If someone challenged me to explain what the existence of integrability implies, but refused to let me use the language of partial derivatives, I could illustrate by an equi-proportional-area property in Fig. 2 that meaning of integrability. I may say that the idea for this proposition in economics came to me in connection with some amateurish researches in the field of thermodynamics. While reading Clerk Maxwell's charming introduction to thermodynamics, I [19] found that his explanation of the existence of the same absolute temperature scale in every body could be true only if on the p-v diagram that I earlier referred to in connection with LeChatelier's Principle, the two families of curves—steep and light or less-steep and heavy—formed parallelograms like a, b, c, d in Fig. 2 which everywhere have the property area a/ area b = area c/ area d. And so it is with the two different economic curves. It is a consequence of the Hotelling integrability conditions which link together the ninety-nine different demand functions for factors that the areas shown have this proportionality property. In leaving this interesting result, let me mention that it holds even when—as in linear programming—the relevant surfaces have corners and edges along which unique partial derivatives are not defined. Finally, this illustrates that once we know one of the demand functions everywhere, the other function only needs to be known along one razor's edge in space in order for it to be determined everywhere.

I should not leave the analytics of maximizing functions without mentioning that all of this is not an idle exercise in logic and mathematics. Debates rage in economics as to whether corporations maximize their profits. Yet neither side of the debate pauses to ask what difference it ought to make for observables if there is or there is not some function that is being maximized. And if I depart from the narrow field of economics, I must confess that the writings of sociologists like Talcott Parsons [20] seem to me to be seriously empty because they never seem even to ask the question of what difference it makes to have social action part of a maximizing value system, or just what is implied by "functionalist" interpretations of the observed phenomena.

NON-MAXIMUM PROBLEMS

I must not be too imperialistic in making claims for the applicability of maximum principles in theoretical economics. There are plenty of areas in

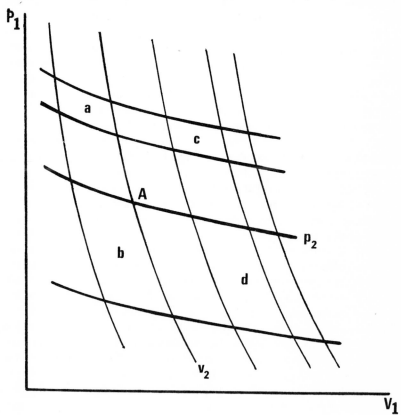

which they simply do not apply. Take for example my early paper dealing with the interactions of the accelerator and the multiplier [21]. This is an important topic in macroeconomic analysis. Indeed, as I have recorded elsewhere this paper brought me a disproportionate amount of reputation. True the topic was a fundamental one, and mathematical analysis of stability conditions was able to give it a neat solution at a level that could be understood both by the intelligent beginner and the virtuoso in mathematical economics. But the original specification of the model had been made by my Harvard teacher Alvin Hansen, and the works of Sir Roy Harrod [22] and Erik Lundberg [23] clearly pointed the way to the setting up of this model.

My point in bringing up the accelerator-multiplier here is that it provides a typical example of a dynamic system that can in no useful sense be related to a maximum problem. By examining the sick we learn something about those who are well; and by examining those who are well we may also learn something about the sick. The fact that the accelerator-multiplier *cannot be* related to maximizing takes its toll in terms of the intractability of the analysis. Thus when my colleague, Professor Richard Eckaus, was a younger man, he wrote a doctoral dissertation [24] under my direction on generalizing the accelerator-multiplier analysis to many sectors and countries. It was an excellent piece of scholarship; Dr. Eckaus, with great ingenuity and elegance, extracted everything from the model that could be extracted. Yet he would be the first to assert that, in a sense, the ratio of useful output to high grade input was somewhat disappointing. Few grand simplicities emerged. The conscientious investigator had to point out a great range of possibilities that could happen, and had to use up much of his intelligence in taxonomy and classification of those possibilities. To illustrate the intrinsic intractability of such a problem, let me recall to you a remarkable difficulty. Suppose Europe in 1970 is a seventeen sector multiplier-accelerator complex that is stable—i.e., we can show that all of its characteristic roots are damped and decaying rather than being anti-damped and explosive. Now go back in history to 1950. The coefficients of the Europe model will be somewhat different, but suppose again that they gave rise to a stable system. Now let me give you this exact bit of information. In 1960, which is a simple mean of 1950 and 1970, by miraculous coincidence it proved to be the case that the coefficients of the model were in each and every case the exact arithmetic mean of the 1950 and 1970 coefficients. What would you predict about the stability of the 1960 system?

If my asking the question had not alerted you to a paradox, I'm sure your first temptation would be to say that it is a stable system, being literally halfway between two stable systems. But that would not be consistent with Dr. Eckaus' findings. You can make the paradox evaporate when you realize that the determinantal conditions for stability of a system [25] do not define a stability region in terms of the coefficients of the system that is a convex region. Hence a point half-way between two points in the region may itself fall outside that region. This sort of thing does not arise in the case of well-behaved maximum systems.

I think I have said enough to demonstrate why perhaps the hardest part of my 1947 *Foundations of Economic Analysis* had to deal with the statics and dynamics of non-maximum systems.

DYNAMICS AND MAXIMIZING

Naturally this does not deny that there is a rich dynamics which can be related to maximizing. Thus consider the dynamic algorithm for finding the top of a mountain which consists of the "gradient method": this says to make your velocity in the direction of any coordinate proportional to the slope of the mountain in its direction. Such a method cannot be counted on to get you to the highest point in the Alps from any initial spot in Europe. But it is bound to converge to the maximum point of any concave surfaces that appear in the Santa Claus examples of the class-room textbooks.

Like the light rays of physics that I mentioned earlier, the optimal growth paths of the theories that have grown out of Frank Ramsey's pioneering work [26] of more than forty years ago, themselves provide a rich dynamics. Such a dynamics is quite different from that of say a positivistic accelerator-multiplier analysis. You may recall that Sir William Hamilton spent a great many years trying to generalize to more than two dimensions the notion of a complex number. The story is told that his family sympathized with his earnest quest for the quaternion, and each night his children would greet him on his return from the astronomical observatory with the question: "Poppa, can you multiply your quaternions?"—only to be sadly told, "I can make my quaternions add but I can't make them multiply." Back in the 1930's if Lloyd Metzler and I had had any children, they would have asked each night: "Did all your characteristic roots turn out nicely stable?" For in those days, impressed by the stubborness of the American Depression and its resistance to transitory pump-priming, we more or less embraced the dogma of stability.

How different were my preoccupations during the 1950's when I was on the fruitless search for a proof of the so-called "Turnpike Theorem" [27]. Here one does deal with a maximizing model, at least in the sense of inter-temporal efficiency. When you study a von Neumann input-output model, it becomes the case of a min-max, or saddle-point problem like that of von Neumann's theory of games; and this destroys the possibility that your dynamic characteristic roots could all be damped. So, if my children did not treat my scholarly work with what can only be called "benign neglect," in the 1950's they would have had to ask me: "Daddy, did your characteristic roots come in reciprocal or opposite-signed pairs, as befits a catenary motion around a saddlepoint turnpike?"

May I crave your indulgence to digress and tell an anecdote? I do so with some trepidation because when I was invited to give this lecture I was warned by Professor Lundberg that it must be a serious one. Although it is said I was a brash young man, I had only one encounter with the formidable John von Neumann, who of course was a giant of modern mathematics and who in addition proved himself to be a genius in his work on the hydrogen bomb, game theory, and the foundations of quantum mechanics. To illustrate his stature, I will defy Professor Lundberg even more shamelessly and tell an anecdote within an anecdote. Someone once asked Yale's great mathematician, Kakutani: "Are you a great mathematician?" Kakutani modestly replied, "Oh, not at all. I am a nothing, a mediocre plodder after truth." "Well if you're not a great mathematician, who would you name as one?" he was asked.

Kakutani thought and he thought and he thought, and then according to the story he finally said—"Johnny von Neumann."

This sets the stage for my encounter with Goliath. Sometime around 1945 von Neumann gave a lecture at Harvard on his model of general equilibrium. He asserted that it involved new kinds of mathematics which had no relation to the conventional mathematics of physics and maximization. I piped up from the back of the room that I thought it was not all that different from the concept we have in economics of the opportunity-cost-frontier, in which for specified amounts of all inputs and all but one output society seeks the maximum of the remaining output. Von Neumann replied at that lightning speed which was characteristic of him: "Would you bet a cigar on that?" I am ashamed to report that for once little David retired from the field with his tail between his legs. And yet some day when I pass through Saint Peter's Gates I do think I have half a cigar still coming to me—only half because von Neumann also had a valid point.

A glance through modern journals and texts will show that, whereas the student of classical mechanics deals often with vibrations around an equilibrium, as in the case of a pendulum, the student of economics deals more often with motions around a saddlepoint of catenary shape: i.e., just as a rope suspended between two nails will hang in the shape of a catenary, leaning toward the groundlevel, so will the economic motions hang in the shape of a catenary toward the turnpike. I might mention how the turnpike got its name. All Americans are used to the notion that in going from Boston to Los Angeles, the fastest way is to move quickly to a major highway and only at the end of your voyage depart to your local goal. So in economics: to develop a country most efficiently, under certain circumstances it should proceed rather quickly toward the configuration of maximum balanced growth, catch a ride so to speak on this fast turnpike, and then at the end of the twenty year plan move off to its final goal. An interesting triple limit is involved: as the horizon becomes *large*, you spend an indefinitely *large* fraction of your time within a *small* distance of the turnpike. I shall not spell out this tongue-twister further.

FINALE

I have not been able in one lecture even to scratch the surface of the role of maximum principles in analytic economics. Nor have I even been able to present a representative sample of my own research interests in economics, or for that matter in the narrower area of maximization theory. Thus, one of my abiding concerns over the years has been the field of *welfare economics*.

Along with my close friend, Abram Bergson of Harvard, I have tried to understand what it is that Adam Smith's "invisible hand" is supposed to be maximizing. Thus, consider the concept which we today call Pareto-optimality —and which might with equal propriety be called Bergson-optimality, since it was Bergson [28] who, back in 1938, read sense into what Pareto was groping to say and who related that narrow concept to the broader concept of social norms and a welfare function. Just recently I was reading an article by a writer of the New Left. It was written in blank verse, which turns out to be an extremely inefficient medium for communication but which a dedicated scholar must be prepared to struggle through in the interest of science. The writer was scathing on the notion of Pareto-optimality. Yet as I digested his message, it seemed to me that precisely in a society grown affluent, where dissident groups are called toward a way of life of their own, there arises an especial importance to the notion of giving people what *they* want. An Old Left writer dealing with a socialist economy on the verge of subsistence has surely less need for the concept of Pareto-optimality than does the modern social observer in the United States or Sweden.

Moreover, it has been a special source of satisfaction to me that the calculus of modern welfare economics [29] was able to elucidate the old problem of Knut Wicksell [30] and Erik Lindahl [31], the analysis of public goods.

An American economist of two generations ago, H. J. Davenport, who was the best friend Thorstein Veblen ever had (Veblen actually lived for a time in Davenport's coal cellar) once said: "There is no reason why theoretical economics should be a monopoly of the reactionaries." All my life I have tried to take this warning to heart, and I dare call it to your favorable attention.

REFERENCES

1. J. A. Schumpeter, *Econometrica*, 1, 5 (1933)
2. P. A. Samuelson, *Economica*, N.S. 5, 61 and 353 (1938), reproduced in P. A. Samuelson, *Collected Scientific Papers*, ed., J. E. Stiglitz, Vol., I (M.I.T. Press, Cambridge, Mass., 1965) Ch. 1. Cf., also Chs. 3, 9, 11.
3. P. A. Samuelson, *Proc. Nat. Acad. Sci.* U.S., 68 (1971)
4. H. Hotelling, *Jour. Polit. Econ.*, 40, 577 (1932)
5. H. Schultz, *Theory and Measurement of Demand,* (University of Chicago Press, Chicago, Ill., 1938)
6. P. A. Samuelson, *Foundations of Economic Analysis* (Harvard University Press, Cambridge, Mass., 1947) Chs. 3, 6; see also *Collected Scientific Papers, II,* op.cit., Chs. 42, 43, 35.
7. E. Slutsky, *Gior. Degli. Econ.*, 51, 1 (1915)
8. V. Pareto, *Manuele di economie politica* (Societa Editrice Libaria, Milan, 1907)
   —, *Manuel d'economie politique* (V. Giard and E. Briere, Paris, 1909)
9. W. E. Johnson, *Econ. Jour.*, 23, 483 (1913)
10. J. M. Keynes, *A Treatise on Probability* (Macmillan, London 1921)
11. F. P. Ramsey, *Foundations of Mathematics,* (Kegan Paul, London, 1931)
12. H. Jeffreys, *Theory of Probability* (Clarendon Press, Oxford, 1939)
13. J. R. Hicks, and R.G.D. Allen, *Economica*, 14, 52 and 196 (1934)
14. H. Houthakker, *Economica*, 17, 159 (1950)
15. P. A. Samuelson, *Collected Scientific Papers*, I, op. cit., Ch. 10.

16. I. Fisher, *Mathematical Investigations in the Theory of Value and Prices* (Yale Press, New Haven, Conn., 1925, reprint)

17. G. B. Antonelli, *Teoria matematica della economica politica* (Pisa, 1886)

18. N. Georgescu-Roegen, *Quart. Jour. Econ.*, 49, 545 (1935)

19. P. A. Samuelson, *Collected Scientific Papers* I, op. cit., Ch. 44 (Appendix)

20. T. Parsons, *Structure of Social Action* (Free Press, Glencoe, Ill., second edition, 1949)

21. P. A. Samuelson, *Collected Scientific Papers,* II, op. cit., Ch. 83.

22. R. F. Harrod, *The Trade Cycle* (Clarendon Press, Oxford, 1936)

23. E. Lundberg, *Studies in the Theory of Economic Expansion* (P. S. King, London, 1937)

24. R. S. Eckaus, *Dynamic Models of Domestic and International Trade* (unpublished Doctoral dissertation, M.I.T., 1954)

25. P. A. Samuelson, *Foundations of Economic Analysis,* op. cit., 436.

26. F. P. Ramsey, *Econ, Jour.*, 38, 543 (1928)

27. P. A. Samuelson, *Collected Scientific Papers,* I, op. cit., Chs. 33 III, 25, 26, and *West. Ec. Jour.*, 6, 85 and 90 (1968), and R. Dorfman, R. M. Solow, and P. A. Samuelson, *Linear Programming and Economic Analysis* (McGraw-Hill, New York, 1958)

28. A. Bergson (Burk), *Quart. Jour. Econ.*, 52, 310 (1938)

29. P. A. Samuelson, *Collected Scientific Papers,* II, op. cit., Chs., 92, 93; also P. A. Samuelson in *Public Economics,* ed. J. Margolis (Macmillan, London, 1969) Ch. 5.

30. K. Wicksell, *Finanztheoretische Untersuchungen* (Jena, 1896)

31. E. Lindahl, *Die Gerechtigkeit der Besteuerung* (Lund, 1919)

KUNGL. BOKTR. STHLM 1971

131

The Monopolistic Competition Revolution

by Paul A. Samuelson

Some Sociology of Knowledge

No historian of science would be surprised to learn that Edward Chamberlin and Joan Robinson[1] had written in the same year separate books that break definitively with the assumptions of perfect competition. Newton and Leibniz both discovered the calculus because that subject was then in the air, waiting to be discovered. Similarly, 1933, the year of *The Theory of Monopolistic Competition* and of *The Economics of Imperfect Competition*, followed a decade of intense discussion concerning the nature of competition, the so-called "cost controversy" initiated by Clapham's famous complaint about the "empty boxes" of economic theory.

Many of the great names of the day were involved in that controversy: Allyn Young, Knight, J. M. Clark, Dennis Robertson, Robbins, Viner, Shove, Harrod, Schumpeter, Yntema, Hotelling, Sraffa, Pigou, J. Robinson, Kahn, and many others.[2] In retrospect I judge it

---

Grateful acknowledgment is made to the Carnegie Corporation for granting me a reflective year, to Harvard University for providing the fulcrum on which to place my lever, and to Mrs. F. Skidmore for research assistance.

[1] E. H. Chamberlin, *The Theory of Monopolistic Competition*, Harvard University Press, Cambridge, Mass., first edition, 1933; eighth edition, 1962; J. Robinson, *Economics of Imperfect Competition*, Macmillan, London, 1933.

[2] For a sampling, see G. J. Stigler and K. E. Boulding, eds., *Reading in Price Theory*, Irwin, Homewood, Ill., 1952, which contains articles by J. H. Clapham (1922), A. C. Pigou (1922), D. H. Robertson (1924), F. H. Knight (1924), P. Sraffa (1926), and J. Viner (1931); cf. also J. M. Clark, *Economics of Overhead Costs*, University of Chicago Press, Chicago, 1923. Aside from preparing the way for theories of monopolistic and imperfect competition, the cost controversy did result in a better understanding of competitive theory.

to have been rather a sterile debate, as will appear from what follows. But experience with the history of science amply testifies that the journey between two points is not a straight line. Having made detours and been caught in *culs-de-sac*, a subject must make progress by the negative act of dumping ballast.

The keen historian of science will not be surprised, either, to learn that simultaneous discoveries that appear to be substantially similar turn out, on careful examination, to be substantively different. In our own field of economics, it is customary to bracket Jevons, Menger, and Walras as independent discoverers of the subjective theory of value and of utility; but with the hindsight of a century we see that Walras's formulation of general equilibrium quite overshadows the brilliant work of his contemporaries and he might have been spared the pain of discovery that Jevons had beaten him to what both thought was the important Pole.

With cogency and pertinacity, Chamberlin has always insisted on differentiating his product from that of Mrs. Robinson. Posterity will agree. But in its typical wayward manner, posterity will amalgamate into an optimal package what it conceives to be the best of the various systems. Thus, when Chamberlin tells us that his work did not find its inspiration in the cost controversy, we find strong corroboration in the historical documents denoting his journey along the road to Damascus, from 1921 through 1927 and beyond, as well as in the structure and texture of his 1933 classic. But, again, as the sociologist of science knows, there is a feedback reaction between the readers of a seminal work and its author. Most of Chamberlin's readers, in America as well as in England, were exercised by the cost controversy. Allyn Young, Chamberlin's thesis supervisor and teacher of Frank Knight, who in turn taught Chamberlin, was an important participant in the controversy. Although we have abundant evidence, after 1933 as well as before, that Edward Chamberlin was a lone-wolf scholar with infinite capacity for formulating and pushing a problem to solution in his own way, still, no man is an island unto himself. If A has any sort of communication with B who has any communication with $C, \ldots$, there is no way to rule out mutual interaction between A and Z even if they have never met or had any direct contact.

As an illustration of mutual dependence, consider Mrs. Robinson and J. M. Clark's *Economics of Overhead Costs*. There is no reason to think she had ever heard of this stimulating 1923 book. But if Robertson, Pigou, Shove, Austin Robinson, Kahn, or any other member of the Cambridge set had ever read the work, then some degree of influence cannot be ruled out by the historian of science even though he can never hope to measure its degree. Or consider Sraffa's December 1926 article. Without doubting that an April 1927 thesis could have been written completely independently of it, we are still not surprised that Chamberlin's 1933 book should take notice of the great similarity between the *Weltanschauung* of Sraffa's final part with the perfected theory of monopolistic competition. In rereading Sraffa for the present essay, I was struck by, and marked, certain lines that seemed to me to be in the Chamberlin spirit; and it was, therefore, with interest that I subsequently noted some of them quoted at the beginning of Chamberlin's book.

A final illustration of the virtual impossibility of ruling out truly independent simultaneous scientific discovery can be taken from the combined field of international trade and welfare economics. At the London School of Economics in the 1930's, brilliant young economists such as Lerner, Hicks, and Kaldor worked out graphical models of international exchange and what we would today call Pareto-optimality necessary conditions for welfare. References to Vilfredo Pareto will be sought in vain, even though his books were known to the more widely-read members of that circle. The reason? Pareto is an obscure enough writer, the subject is a sufficiently subtle one, and the men involved are sufficiently creative and self-stimulating for me to think that Pareto's influence was at best subconscious. But a quite different influencing is that which I would associate with the name of Viner. In January 1931, Viner gave a public lecture at L.S.E. on international trade, in which he married Haberler's production-possibility frontier to consumer indifference curves. Everyone, including the lecturer, may have forgotten the very fact that the lecture was given. But nothing can change the fact that independent rediscovery of this bit of analysis became impossible in that environment after that date. Even if only Victor Edelberg understood Viner. . .[3]

The Theoretical Shortcomings of Perfect Competition

My purpose in this essay is not to isolate the peculiar contributions to price theory made by Edward Chamberlin. He has done that job superlatively well and we can take it for granted. Indeed the time has

---

[3] That the compensation principle as applied to losers from free trade should have been enunciated in the late 1930's using the same kind of example that Viner had used earlier shows a similar indirect influence of Viner on the London School, but it would take a more tedious detective operation to trace through its unconscious contacts. See J. Viner, *Studies in the Theory of International Trade*, Harper, New York, 1937, p. 521.

come when we may permit ourselves to use the terms monopolistic competition and imperfect competition interchangeably, emancipating them from their first associations with the different conceptions of Chamberlin and Mrs. Robinson, and using them as convenient names for the best current models of price theory.[4]

My purpose here is to discuss some of the *theoretical* reasons why perfect competition provides an empirically inadequate model of the real world. This forces us to work with some versions of monopolistic or imperfect competition. Chicago economists can continue to shout until they are blue in the face that there is no elegant alternative to the theory of perfect competition.[5] If not, the proper moral is, "So much

[4] Admittedly, impure competition might be a better name than imperfect competition, in consideration of Chamberlin's point that denying perfect knowledge can still leave the firm a pure competitor facing a price at which it can sell all it wishes; but impure competition sounds dirty, just as monopolistic competition sounds evil, and so we find convenience in the label *imperfect competition*.

[5] G. J. Stigler, *Five Lectures on Economic Problems,* Macmillan, London, 1950, in particular Lecture 2, "Monopolistic Competition in Retrospect"; M. Friedman, *Essays in Positive Economics,* University of Chicago Press, Chicago, 1953, Ch. 1; E. H. Chamberlin, *Toward a More General Theory of Value,* Oxford University Press, New York, 1957, Ch. 15; G. C. Archibald, "Chamberlin *versus* Chicago," *Review of Economic Studies,* XXIX (1961), pp. 2-28; G. J. Stigler, "Archibald *versus* Chicago," *Review of Economic Studies,* XXX (1963), pp. 63-64; M. Friedman, "More on Archibald *versus* Chicago," *Review of Economic Studies,* XXX (1963), pp. 65-67; G. C. Archibald, "Reply to Chicago," *Review of Economic Studies* XXX (1963), pp. 68-71. First, I must emphasize that, despite some ambiguity in Chamberlin's own writing, the symmetric large group of Chamberlin must not be taken to be the content of the words "monopolistic competition" or even to constitute the significant content of the theoretical revolution. Second, although I personally emphasized in my *Foundations of Economic Analysis,* Harvard University Press, Cambridge, Mass., 1947, the importance of the empirically testable implications of second-order maximization inequalities, I must dissociate myself from Archibald's criticism of the Chicago criticism, which consists of Archibald's demonstration that the Chamberlin theory has few unambiguously signed implications of my *Foundations* type. If the real world displays the variety of behavior that the Chamberlin-Robinson models permit—and I believe the Chicago writers are simply wrong in denying that these important empirical deviations exist—then reality will falsify *many* of the important qualitative and quantitative *predictions* of the competitive model. Hence, by the pragmatic test of prediction adequacy, the perfect-competition model fails to be an adequate approximation. When Friedman claims (*Essays*, pp. 36-37) that a tax will have the type of incidence on the cigarette industry that it would on a competitive industry, he is at most showing that *some* predictions of the latter theory are adequate. To the degree that other predictions are falsified—consumer price approximately equal to marginal cost, advertising cost equal to zero—the competitive model fails the pragmatic predictive test.

The fact that the Chamberlin-Robinson model is "empty," in the sense of

the worse for elegance" rather than, "Economists of the world, unite in proclaiming that the Emperor has almost no clothes, and in pretending that the model of perfect competition does a good enough job in fitting the real world." More than once I shall have to report that we theorists, quite removed from Cook County, have retrogressed in the last quarter of a century, taking the coward's way of avoiding the important questions thrown up by the real economic world and fobbing off in their place nice answers to less interesting easy questions.

Exorcizing the Marshallian Incubus

The ambiguities of Alfred Marshall paralyzed the best brains in the Anglo-Saxon branch of our profession for three decades. By 1930 the profession had just about reattained the understanding of the pure theory of monopoly that Cournot had achieved in 1838; and it had yet to reattain the understanding of the theory of competitive general equilibrium that Walras had achieved by 1878 or 1896.

Although Marshall was a great economist, we must remember in appraising his originality that he knew well the work of Mill, Cournot, Dupuit, and Mangoldt. Even if we accept at face value his claim that he owed little or nothing to such contemporaries as Jevons and Walras —and I for one think the only appropriate answer to that claim is: the

---

ruling out few empirical configurations and being capable of providing only formalistic descriptions, is not the slightest reason for abandoning it in favor of a "full" model of the competitive type *if reality is similarly* "empty" and "non-full." In 1960, elementary particle theory was similarly "empty" and Newtonian mechanics similarly "full"; but only an idiot would have tried in 1960 to use Newton's model to describe high-energy physics. To reach retroactively into the urn of monopoly to explain advertising expense and into that of the competitive model to explain some case of tax incidence is to advance not a step, and, as the wastes of free entry under imperfectly competitive conditions cannot be predicted by any blend of items selected from each urn, illustrates the indispensability of the 1933 revolution. Cf. R. L. Bishop, "Monopolistic Competition after Thirty Years: the Impact on General Theory," *American Economic Review, Papers and Proceedings,* LIV (1964), pp. 33-43.

As a final instance, consider the notion that many business firms set price on some kind of a "full-cost mark-up" over some kind of cost (R. L. Hall and C. J. Hitch, "Price Theory and Business Behavior," *Oxford Economic Papers,* II (1939), pp. 12-45). It might be argued that this is an empty formulation, because, depending on alternative estimates of demand elasticity and alternative specifications of entry of rivals, this model can lead to price above marginal cost to any percentage degree. Granted, but by what logic does that permit anyone to replace the vacuum by asserting the competitive outcome of P equals one times M.C., or P equals one-plus-epsilon times M.C.?

more fool he—we must realize that there was precious little in the theory of partial equilibrium under perfect competition to be developed by anyone unlucky enough to have been born as an economist *after* Cournot, Mill, Dupuit, and Mangoldt.[6]

Unfortunately, because of his unwillingness to make sharp distinctions between perfect and less-than-perfect competition, Marshall managed to set back the clock both on competitive theory and on the theory of monopoly. Edgeworth was almost an exact contemporary of Marshall, but seems to have been scared to death of that eminent Victorian. The profound researches of Edgeworth on bilateral monopoly and various forms of oligopoly received little attention from the Marshallian tradition. And it was not until 1934 with the work of von Stackelberg, and indeed 1944 with the *Theory of Games* of von Neumann and Morgenstern, that the modern literature reattained the depth of Edgeworth's analysis.[7]

Let us make no mistake about it. The theory of simple monopoly is child's play. That grown men argued seriously in 1930 about who had first used or named the curve that we now call "marginal revenue" is a joke. Cournot had settled all that a century earlier and in a completely modern manner, so that the reader who picks up the English translation of his book and has to guess at the date of its authorship merely on the basis of an understanding of the cost-controversy literature ought to guess 1927 or 1933. Chamberlin always used to insist that the essence of his contribution to the subject had nothing particularly to do with

[6] Testifying to the cogency of my *a priori* reasoning on this point is the fact that both Fleeming Jenkin (1870) and Auspitz and Lieben (1889) developed partial-equilibrium theory in all of its fundamentals before Marshall's 1890 *Principles of Economics;* neither could have been helped in this regard by Marshall's 1879 tract, *The Pure Theory of Domestic and International Values,* which deals hardly at all with partial equilibrium and deserves high praise thereby.

[7] H. von Stackelberg, *Marktform und Gleichgewicht,* Springer, Berlin, 1934; W. Fellner, *Competition Among the Few,* Knopf, New York, 1949; J. von Neumann and O. Morgenstern, *Theory of Games and Economic Behavior,* Princeton University Press, Princeton, New Jersey, 1944. Chamberlin's Chapter 23 and Appendix A provide a valuable but far-from-adequate history and analysis of the problems of bilateral monopoly, duopoly, and general game-theoretic problems. In particular the 1929 notion that Edgeworth was principally to be known for his "oscillatory" solution to duopoly is a sad understatement. By 1897 Edgeworth already had a full appreciation of the game-theoretic indeterminacy: his Arctic explorers already trace out 1934 von Stackelberg solutions and much else. F. Y. Edgeworth, *Papers Relating to Political Economy,* Royal Economic Society, London, 1925. Indeed, in his *Mathematical Psychics,* Paul, London, 1881, pp. 35-39, 139-148, Edgeworth had already anticipated the modern concept of the "core" of a game, in its relation to large numbers of sellers. See also footnote 17 below.

the rediscovery and naming of the simple marginal curves. We can readily agree with him. Whether it is correct to go on and say, as some have said, that Mrs. Robinson's book differs from his in that hers is primarily a book on monopoly, I find a more difficult question to answer. To a considerable extent her book is that, and we feel that the reviewer of it had a small point when he said that the time spent in reading her work might with better profit be spent on studying Irving Fisher's little textbook on the infinitesimal calculus.[8] For it is true that simple monopoly theory consists of little other than elementary calculus, in which ordinary and partial derivatives are to be set equal to zero whereas higher derivatives are required to be nonpositive. Marshall was so enamored of his silly little unitary-elasticity hyperbolas that he omitted a straightforward treatment of simple monopoly, leaving room in the first third of this century for quasi-independent rediscovery by literary economists of these rudiments.

Retrogression in Monopoly Theory

But where Marshall threw off two generations of scholars was in his insistence on having his cake and eating it too. He would try to treat at the same time cases of less-than-perfect and of perfect competition. He would try to achieve a spurious verisimilitude by talking about vague biological dynamics, and by failing to distinguish between reversible and irreversible developments. He would insist on confusing the issue of external economies and diseconomies—which played an important role in the work of such pre-Marshallian writers as Henry Sidgwick—with the entirely separable (and separate!) issue of varying laws of returns. Marshall was so afraid of being unrealistic that he merely ends up being fuzzy and confusing—and confused.

Although harsh, these are my well-considered judgments on the matter, and I mention them only because no one can understand the history of the subject if he does not realize that much of the work from 1920 to 1933 was merely the negative task of getting Marshall out of the way. I shall not document these opinions but shall merely give single examples of what I have in mind.

First, that part of simple monopoly theory which consists of neat theorems—such as that a lump-sum tax or a tax on net profits will have no effect on monopoly output, whereas a tax on gross revenues or

---

[8] A. J. Nichol, "Robinson's Economics of Imperfect Competition," *Journal of Political Economy*, XLII (1934), pp. 257-259. Actually, when Mrs. Robinson comes to discuss a world of monopolies and other issues, she does go far beyond simple monopoly theory.

on output will lower output and raise prices—was well known to any reader of Cournot and involves little more than the calculus of a single variable.

Second, which of us has not been brought up short in his reading of Marshall when suddenly, in the midst of what was thought to be a discussion of "competition," it turns out that some entrepreneur fails to do something because of his "fear of spoiling the market," a sure sign of some kind of imperfection of competition? Such aberrations as these, to which I point in horror, are taken by some modern writers as signs of Marshall's genius and erudite wisdom about the facts of life. "It's all in Marshall," they say, failing to add, "All the words of economics are in Webster's dictionary or in the fingertips of monkeys in the British Museum." But just as it takes more than monkeys to find the Michaelangelo statues that lurk in any old cube of marble, so it takes more than can be learned in Marshall to isolate the good sense that is embalmed therein. Marshall's crime is to pretend to handle imperfect competition with tools only applicable to perfect competition.

Third, Marshall was a victim of what the modern Freudians call self-hate. He was a good chess player who was ashamed of playing chess, a good analytical economist who was ashamed of analysis. He well understood Cournot's insistence that the marginal cost curve must not be falling for any maximizing pure competitor, but balked at simple acceptance of the fact. All of his prattle about the biological method in economics—and the last decades' genuine progress in biology through the techniques of physics has confirmed my dictum of 20 years ago that talk of a unique biological method does mostly represent prattle—cannot change this fact: any price taker who can sell more at the going price than he is now selling and who has falling marginal cost will not be in equilibrium. Talk of birds and bees, giant trees in the forest, and declining entrepreneurial dynasties is all very well, but why blink at such an elementary point?

Fourth, this leads to the further confusion by Marshall of *external* effects with increasing *returns* phenomena. Because Marshall (*Principles,* Book V, Ch. XIII, pp. 467-470) made an elementary mistake in his graphical reckoning of consumers' surplus, forgetting to take into account producers' surplus—an odd omission for a chap who always insisted correctly that there are two blades in the scissors of supply and demand— he came up with what seems like an exciting policy theorem: *Tax to contract increasing cost industries; subsidize to expand decreasing cost industries.*

As we congratulate ourselves that commonsense economics has for once produced fruit, we are brought up short by the realization that this is quite wrong. It merely sounds like a couple of other things that are right. Increasing returns industries are likely to be somehow monopolized, and a monopoly markup of price over marginal cost does create a *prima facie* case for public expansion of that industry. Futhermore, under increasing returns, marginal cost is below average cost; and hence marginal cost pricing would require a state subsidy. But wait: it was a *competitive* decreasing cost industry we were talking about, a contradiction in terms if the increasing returns are *internal* to the firm. So Marshallians hasten to say that it must be, of course, decreasing cost due to *external economies* that was meant, and which ought to be subsidized. Subsidizing external economies is indeed correct but, unfortunately for the false theorem of Marshall, external economies ought to be subsidized even when they occur in industries strongly subject to increasing cost; and external diseconomies require penalty even when they occur in decreasing cost industries. The point is that Marshall was simply wrong in focusing on the effect of external diseconomies and economies on the trend of industry *unit* costs. It took Pigou years to extricate his welfare economics from their Marshallian origins and misconceptions.[9]

Retrogression in Perfect Competition Theory

At the same time that Marshall was doing a disservice to the theory of monopoly and less-than-perfect competition, he was inadvertently delaying the understanding of general equilibrium. (I might have written Walrasian general equilibrium but there is only one general equilibrium, whatever its name.) Ironically, it was not until after World War II that economists generally began to think in terms of general equilibrium. As will be seen in a moment, this represents an advance in logical clarity but something of a retreat in terms of realistic appraisal of actual imperfectly competitive market structures.

If there is a proper understanding of general equilibrium, it is possible to attain for the first time an understanding of partial equilibrium. The studies by Chamberlin and the contemporaries involved in the cost

---

[9] Allyn Young in his original review of Pigou's 1912 *Wealth and Welfare* pointed out Pigou's error in thinking that the upward bidding of rents in an industry whose output expands represents anything other than a transfer item that ought to be allowed to take place. Later Knight and Robertson made the same point and Pigou finally capitulated. For an historical recapitulation and summary, see H. S. Ellis and W. Fellner, "External Economies and Diseconomies," *American Economic Review*, XXXIII (1943), pp. 493-511, reprinted in Stigler and Boulding eds., *op. cit.*, pp. 242-263. My generally critical view of Marshall is not universally shared, but a trend is discernible, and it is significant that Marshall's remaining defenders among theorists tend to be those satisfied with perfect competition as an approximatation to reality.

controversy had, along with the task of developing an analysis of monopolistic or imperfect competition, the task of developing for the first time a proper analysis of the relationship between firms and industry. This task, neglected by Marshall, was not needed by Walras for his ideal model of general equilibrium. For, as we shall see, perfect competition proceeds most smoothly when the extreme assumption of *constant returns to scale* is firmly adhered to. And yet it is precisely under strict constant returns to scale that the theory of the firm evaporates.

If scale does not matter it is immaterial where we draw the boundaries of the firm or whether we draw them at all. So to speak, the proportions of labor and fertilizer to land are determined at the same ratio everywhere on the homogeneous Iowa plain; and it is industry demand that sets the total output to be produced with these factor proportions. Or as Wicksell so well put the matter, under constant returns to scale and statical conditions of certainty, it is immaterial which factor hires which. Like Topsy, they all spontaneously come together under Darwinian competition in the proper amounts, with any deviations lacking survival value. Labor as much hires capital goods and land as capital hires labor and land. (As we shall see, the situation is a little changed if strict constant returns to scale is relaxed in favor of replicable quanta of least-unit-cost combinations.)

This euthanasia of the concept of the firm under most-perfect competition—which is actually an odd way of putting the matter since what need never exist cannot very well be said to wither away— paradoxically bothered writers of the 1920's and 1930's. Writers like Kaldor and Hicks seemed to agree with Schumpeter that pushing perfect competition to its extreme assumptions led ultimately to the blowup of perfect competition. Thus a constant unit cost curve coinciding with a horizontal firm demand curve would make each pure competitor's output quite indeterminate. (The mathematical economists encountered the same phenomenon in the shape of a singular Hessian matrix associated with homogeneous functions and semidefinite quadratic forms.) My example of the Iowa plain shows that this concern over the firm's indeterminacy was misplaced, for the reason that it is inessential under strict constant returns just how industry's (determinate!) output is allocated among firms. These writers erred in supposing that with every firm in neutral equilibrium, there would be no penalty to having one expand indefinitely until it "monopolized" the industry. Actually, as pointed out elsewhere,[10] even if a firm has 99 or 100 percent of the output, it has

[10] P. A. Samuelson, *Foundations of Economic Analysis,* Harvard University Press, Cambridge, Mass., 1947, pp. 78-79.

under the stipulated returns condition *zero* long-run monopoly power: the net long-run demand curve to it is derived by subtracting from the industry curve the horizontal supply curve of actual and *potential* suppliers, leaving it with a horizontal long-run personal demand curve; like a constitutional monarch, it is left to reign only so long as it does not rule.[11]

The Revolution Beckons

The empty boxes that Clapham should have been asking to be filled in the 1920's were thus not the Marshallian categories of increasing, constant, and diminishing cost under competition. The empty boxes were those of market description and classification, involving all the possible patterns of oligopoly, monopoly, duopoly, differentiation of products with numbers large and numbers small, and so forth. But Chamberlin had not yet created this new theoretical vision of the economic world.

Piero Sraffa's justly famous 1926 article takes on a new light in terms of this analysis of the Marshallian influence. Truly reversible decreasing cost industries associated with external economies are perhaps a *curiosum*. If a competitive industry is small, and to the degree that it uses no specialized factors in intensities different from that of the bulk of the rest of industry, it does tend to fall in the category of *constant* costs. We can agree with Sraffa on this.

But this constant cost case is of no intrinsic difference for policy or other purposes from the case that Sraffa needlessly plays down—the case in which the industry uses some factors of special advantage to it alone or in which it uses the various factors of production of society in proportions significantly different from the rest of industry. In this case, and particularly where we add the realistic consideration that almost any product you can name is something of a joint product produced along with and in partial competition with certain by-products, increases in demand for the products of the industry *will* result in increas-

---

[11] Even within the constant returns technology, we shall see that there are possible advantages (and no disadvantages!) to be derived from having the owners of any unique factor of production, e.g., land suitable for mulberry growing, form a coalition that exploits its monopoly power. We should not wonder that the calculating self-interest on which Adam Smith relies to move the Invisible Hand of perfect competition should motivate people to utilize the ballot box of democracy to institute crop control and other public programs interfering with perfect competition. To a psychologist, Bentham's individualism and Webb's Fabianism are one in motive and appeal.

ing costs and relative prices. Such cases create absolutely no complications for general equilibrium, even though Sraffa may be right in thinking they do for partial equilibrium (in which case, so much the worse for partial equilibrium analysis, Marshallian or otherwise!). The point needing emphasis for Sraffa's readers is that *these* phenomena and complications do not themselves create a need for monopolistic competition theory. Where that theory is needed is in handling genuine empirical deviations from perfect competition. Mere interdependence of essentially competitive industries should have led Sraffa merely to a plea for abandonment of Marshallian partial-equilibrium models in favor of Walrasian general-equilibrium models.

Today, as a result of quite other historical influences and developments, general-equilibrium thinking has swept the field of analytical economics. A modern theorist would say that the box diagram analysis of optimal allocation of inputs among industries is just the tool to handle this standard instance of increasing cost. The production possibility frontier, or so-called opportunity cost transformation frontier, captures the essence of the phenomena. But remember that this frontier was first introduced, and then in connection with Haberler's analysis of international trade, only in 1930. It was *after* the 1930's that Stolper and Samuelson, Joan Robinson, and Viner clarified the increasing cost case by considering it in its general-equilibrium context by use of the factor box diagram or equivalent verbal reasonings.[12]

Fortunately, Sraffa's failure to realize that the Walrasian model would supply many of the deficiencies of the Marshallian partial equilibrium served the useful function of pushing him down the road toward Chamberlinian monopolistic competition theory. Because of realistic market conditions that standard theory had been forced to gloss over, ignore, or deny, economics was long overdue for a movement in that direction. If anyone doubts that Sraffa, Mrs. Robinson,

---

[12] See W. F. Stolper and P. A. Samuelson, "Protection and Real Wages," *Review of Economic Studies,* IX (1941), pp. 58-74, reprinted in H. S. Ellis and L. A. Metzler, eds., *Readings in the Theory of International Trade,* Irwin, Homewood, Ill., 1949; J. Robinson, "Rising Supply Price," *Economica,* VIII (1941), pp. 1-8, reprinted in Stigler and Boulding, *Readings in Price Theory,* pp. 233-241; J. Viner, Supplement to 1931 *Zeitschrift für Nationalökonomie,* appearing in *Readings in Price Theory,* pp. 198-232. For Haberler's first paper using the frontier, see G. Haberler, "Die Theorie der komparativen Kosten und ihre Auswertung für die Begründung des Freihandels," *Weltwirtschaftliches Archiv,* XXXII (1930), which gave rise to the well-known expository articles by A. P. Lerner in the 1932 and 1934 *Economica* and by W. W. Leontief in the 1934 *Quarterly Journal of Economics.* Irving Fisher had used a transformation curve in connection with the trade-off between present and future consumption early in this century; Frederic Benham and R. F. Harrod had anticipated in the 1930's a number of the critical relationships involved in the factor-price box diagrams.

and Chamberlin had a useful task to perform, let him only compare the contribution to the cost controversy by Dennis Robertson in 1924 (Stigler and Boulding, *op. cit.,* pp. 143-149) with the Sraffa contribution of 1926. Robertson was one of the world's leading economists, a Marshallian expert if ever there was one, and at the prime of his scholarly life. Yet he still enmeshed himself in mystical falling cost curves of a competitive industry, conjuring up group identities that have no existence, and failed completely to relate the behavior of the trees to that of the forest. Robertson's realistic instinct was right— costs do *not* behave as if generated by constant-returns-to-scale production functions—but he failed to follow through and drop the incompatible assumption of perfect competition, thereby forcing himself into logical contradiction and ambiguity. In Sraffa's world of monopolies, each with its own market but checked by overlapping substitutes, we are clearly on the way to Robert Triffin's 1940 *Monopolistic Competition and General Equilibrium Theory,* and hence on the way to *The Theory of Monopolistic Competition.*

The Breakdown of Perfect Competition

Perfect competition theory had to be jettisoned in favor of some alternative theory, primarily in the decreasing cost case. J. M. Clark sensed this and gave as title to his too-little appreciated classic of the 1920's, *The Economics of Overhead Costs.* This is a good title, but it would be a better one still if it had been named *The Economics of Increasing Returns.* Returns rather than costs are the relevant phenomena because costs can depend on pecuniary changes in factor prices that have no distorting effects on competitive equilibrium.

It is hardly an exaggeration to assert:

Increasing returns is the prime case of deviations from perfect competition.

Its corollary is this:

Universal constant returns to scale (in every thing, including the effective acquisition and communication of knowledge) is practically certain to convert laissez-faire *or free enterprise into perfect competition.*

I must not overstate my case. Let me digress to recognize that there are other causes of monopolistic imperfection than deviations from constant returns.

(i) There are of course patents, trademarks, and other government-created or "institutional" monopolies. But notice even here that the

King does not give the princely gift of being permitted to compete with a million other farmers for a living; his franchise often, though not always, refers to an industry with some monopoly feature to begin with.

(ii) Then there are self-serving scarcities of knowledge. I ought to share my profitable secrets on how to produce competitive corn more efficiently with other farmers, but why should I? It might eventually depress the price of corn, and inhibit me from expanding the scale of my profitable operations. In a utopian world, one man need not give up his fertilizer to another because in doing so he is deprived of its use; but when one man gives up knowledge to another he is still left with as much useful knowledge for himself, and an optimally running society would ensure that this external economy be extended beyond the point that the private pecuniary calculus would motivate. Still, we must not confuse the issue by classifying any departure from the optimum due to externalities as itself necessarily coming under the heading of monopolistic competition.

(iii) The old-fashioned notion of *contrived* scarcity, as distinguished from *natural* scarcity, deserves mention.[13] Reformers used to speak of the "land monopoly," meaning no more than that land is scarce, and earns very high incomes for the few people who happen to own much of it. Fabians like Shaw and Webb also used such terms, and extended this concept of monopoly to all private property (at the same time making what we would call the Austrian assumption that all factors of production can be regarded as being fairly inelastic in supply to society and hence can be viewed as "rent-earning"). Often they joined with Marxians in regarding human labor as being exploited in the sense of getting less than 100 percent of the national product, having to give up too large a fraction to undeserving owners of property.[14]

Of course to modern theorists such usage of the nomenclature of *monopoly* is only confusing. All the phenomena of exploitation described are completely compatible with the most pure competition. The Duke of Liverpool may earn tens of millions of pounds a year by rent-

---

[13] See the chapter on profit in any of the recent editions of P. A. Samuelson, *Economics,* McGraw-Hill, New York, 1964.

[14] In the 1930's, Oskar Lange urged Marxists to look at the problem of exploitation in this way and not to waste time on the orthodox Marxian labor theory of value. O. Lange, "Marxian Economics and Modern Economic Theory," *Review of Economic Studies,* II (1935), pp. 189-201. For essentially the same view, see J. Robinson, *An Essay on Marxian Economics,* Macmillan, London, 1942. For a diagnosis of property income that neglects the identification made by such reformers of nonland property with land property, see G. J. Stigler, "Bernard Shaw, Sidney Webb, and the Theory of Fabian Socialism," *Proceedings of the American Philosophical Society,* CIII (1959), pp. 469-475.

ing his vast acres of land in perfectly competitive markets. The demand curve for his factors of production could conceivably be perfectly horizontal and still he would not be receiving from society according to his needs. The most simplified J. B. Clark model of perfectly competitive equilibrium would be subject to all of the reformers' criticisms.

Monopolistic or imperfect competition enters in genuinely only when the owner of a factor of production perceives that he faces a derived demand curve for his factor whose slope is appreciably negative. It then pays him to withhold some of his supply lest the last bit affect adversely the terms of trade of the whole supply. This means merely that he always equates marginal revenue product, which deviates from value of marginal product, to his marginal disutility; and the resulting discrepancy leads to a deviation from Pareto-optimality, with the consequence that it would be possible to find a movement that would make each and every person better off. Whatever ethical criticism may be made of the perfectly competitive imputation of rents to the so-called land monopoly, that configuration is assuredly Pareto-optimal. So to speak, what the exploited lose in material terms, the exploiters gain.[15]

(iv) This instance of monopolistic competition, associated with the

---

[15] The ancient antipathy toward interest and usury represents a beautiful mingling of elements of imperfect competition and ethical abhorrence of purely competitive imputations. The Bible, Aristotle, the Medieval Schoolmen, and the man in the street abhor usury for any or all of the following reasons. (1) The man who borrows is usually poorer and in greater distress than the man who lends. (We should for the same reason criticize the purchase of bread for cash by a low-income consumer from a prosperous baker.) (2) The curse of the poor is their ignorance and, ignorant or not, many debtors have traditionally had to borrow in monopolistically competitive markets. (3) A man may be tempted to borrow even though society and he himself in retrospect or in tranquil contemplation may deem the full consequences of such actions personally and socially harmful. (In the same way *laissez-faire* could lead to opium, cigarette, and unaesthetic-automobile purchases, which some or all of the electorate might deem better prohibited by self-imposed democratic fiat, unanimous or of lesser majority. There would be more such legislation but for the realization that many such fiats are practically unenforceable and end up doing more harm than good. This does not affect the principle.) (4) Simple failure to see through the monetary veil covering the true production and time-phasing-of-consumption implications of money borrowing. (I have in mind here a statement we would consider ridiculous if not attributed to Aristotle: money is barren, hence interest *verboten*. One who believes it legitimate to pay rabbits for the borrowing of gravid rabbits, or pay twenty-years-purchase for permanently fertile land, ought not to cavil at the same operations performed with the device of money.) See Thomas F. Divine, *Interest, an Historical and Analytical Study in Economics and Modern Ethics*, Marquette, Milwaukee, 1959, for a Jesuit's view, which seems to argue that, today, interest transactions should be regarded as legitimate if arising in truly competitive markets.

ownership under one direction of a unique productive factor, can certainly persist even in the presence of universal constant returns to scale. When is such concentration of decision making to be expected? If we think in oversimplified terms of social output as being produced by the few broad categories of homogeneous land, homogeneous labor, and the capital goods ultimately producible out of these primary factors, and if these primary factors are under the dispersed ownership of millions of different individuals, then contrived scarcity would seem out of the question. Each small factor owner faces a derived demand curve of virtually infinite elasticity: there is no discrepancy betwen marginal revenue and price to cause deadweight loss.

But even here the competitive configuration is vulnerable. Unless we invoke a significant real cost to the formation of collusive communications, pushing the theory of games to its logical limits will lead to the following paradox. Let everyone in the system act like a pure competitor except the owners of one factor, say the owners of homogeneous land. Now let two small land owners collude, acting tacitly or explicitly in common. Ending up still small relative to the whole, they will reap no advantage, but it is important to realize there will be no *dis*advantage in their colluding—and this can be said about the colluding of 100,000 land owners or 90 or even 100 percent of all land owners. With respect to incipient collusion, then, the *laissez-faire* system is under a kind of neutral equilibrium even in universal constant returns to scale. But when millions of land owners act in concert, they do face a tilted demand curve and benefit by taking into account the discrepancy between their marginal and average revenues. This can be summarized.

THEOREM. *Even under universal constant returns to scale, the competitive configuration is unstable with respect to (costless) collusion of owners of factors of production.*

It will be said that the above result depends critically on assuming away all costs of organizing and policing collusions. And so it does. Realistically, there are always some costs to organizing concerted action—the basic costs of communication and persuasion, and the important costs of overcoming or adjusting to antitrust and common-law prohibitions against such collusions. Perhaps we are lucky that people are so dispersed, perverse, cantankerous, and deaf to communication, for otherwise our world of not-very-workable competition could be far more imperfectly competitive indeed. That is the moral of the story of the Tower of Babel. Easy communication can add to knowledge; it can also add to deadweight loss!

Anyone who had tried to coordinate two people on the dance floor or eleven people on the playing field will appreciate how difficult it is to coordinate hundreds of millions of producers. There is safety in numbers. (And we shall see that it is the deviations from constant returns to scale that seriously deprive society of that safety.) It is precisely here, though, that the competitive configuration becomes vulnerable to a new threat—*the use of government itself to coerce collusive action.* A million farmers cannot persuade each other to withhold wheat from the market, but—speaking luridly—the pistol in the hands of the U.S. marshal and the threat of bars of the Leavenworth penitentiary work miraculously toward orderly marketing.

It was Gunnar Myrdal, in his 1950 Manchester lectures[16], who stressed the fundamental fact that the same self-interest on which economists rely to keep atomistic competitors minimizing costs and maximizing profits can be expected in a modern democracy to lead to class legislation that is destructive of *laissez-faire* and competitive equilibrium. How could it be otherwise? You breed me a race of individualistic Benthamites, and after a century of democratic development I have to confront you with a race of Fabian interventionists. It will be said that coercion is involved. Precisely.[17]

Thus far I have been talking about an idealized aggregative model with only a few homogeneous categories of inputs. From the standpoint of coercion by government, this homogeneity or symmetry of factor owners is a boon, making the attractiveness of a common rule and its enforcement all the easier. But in real life, factors of production are not homogeneous. No two acres of land, no two pairs of hands, are really alike. When we put away our telescope and look at economic

---

[16] G. Myrdal, "The Trend towards Economic Planning," *Manchester School of Economic and Social Studies,* XIX (1951), pp. 1-42.

[17] A question in the theory of games poses itself. In the absence of government coercion, once all n owners formed a monopolistic collusion, could not one of them hope to benefit by breaking away and refusing to withhold part of his supply? More specifically, is such a collusion therefore unstable and can we prove that, as $n \rightarrow \infty$, perfect competition is immune to the collusions I have been talking about? Yes, in the following formal sense: let land be equally divided among n identical landlords, and let there be m identical propertyless laborers. Modern game theory, following Edgeworth, defines the "core" of the resulting game as the set of final imputations with the property that they are immune to being upset by some new coalitions among a subset of the $m + n$ participants. Then it is a theorem that as n and m both go to infinity, the core of the game shrinks to the purely competitive imputation. Cf. G. Debreu and H. Scarf, "A Limit Theorem on the Core of an Economy," *International Economic Review,* IV (1963), pp. 235-246, where references to the work of R. J. Aumann, M. Shubik, and H. Scarf are given. I have benefited from oral conversation with Professor Scarf.

reality with a microscope we see that the occurrence of contrived scarcities becomes locally almost universal.

Here is a strong example. Withholding one of two one-hundred-acre Iowa corn farms will not increase the pecuniary marginal product gained from the other. But suppose we divide any one such farm into a consecutively numbered checkerboard of one-inch squares. Give me ownership of all the odd-numbered squares and my identical twin ownership of the even. We have now created for ourselves a fine problem in bilateral monopoly, and it is a problem that, despite all the brave symbolism of game theory, is indeterminate in its solution. Without my plot, my twin's land is useless. Conceivably I might contrive my scarcity so as to get up to 100 percent of the joint pecuniary product. Conceivably he might get up to 100 percent or any figure in between. Ultimately, there is no way to tell. Because we happen to be identical twins, a facile mind will come up with the principle of insufficient reason and suggest a 50 percent split or even an imputation based on the toss of a fair coin. But why need that be the outcome? He needs me, I need him. If stubborn enough, either one can inflict total damage on the other and on both.

Of course many will say that the farm ought to be cultivated as an organic whole regardless of the ultimate distribution of the thereby maximized product. And actually a court of equity would probably so rule. Indeed, our jurisprudence evolves traditions and principles that serve to rule out transparently obvious deadweight loss. I could devise a contract to bequeath every other square of a checkered farm to one of my two sons; but I would have to be explicit in drawing up such a will and my executor might have difficulty in proving that I was of sound mind while doing so. In the absence of unmistakable specification, the prudent court will act to ensure that the whole plot of land can be "prudently" used.

Let us be clear, though, that the rational self-interest of each of two free wills does not necessitate that there will emerge, even in the most idealized game-theoretic situation, a Pareto-optimal solution that maximizes the sum of the two opponents' profits, *in advance of and without regard to how that maximized profit is to be divided up among them.* Except by fiat of the economic analyst or by his tautologically redefining what constitutes "nonrational" behavior, we cannot rule out a non-Pareto-optimal outcome. We can rule it out only by Humpty-Dumptyism.

This microscopic prevalence of contrived scarcity and indeterminate bilateral monopoly is obvious, because I have selected a transparently obvious case of artificially numbered checkerboard plots of land. It is not so obvious, but it is true, that a similar problem is ubiquitous in real life at the microscopic level. If my secretary has been trained to my ways and I have been trained to hers, there is a range of indeterminacy to the imputation of our joint product. Without her I can find some kind of a substitute but not necessarily, per dollar of cost, a close substitute. On the other hand, were I to turn tomorrow to a career in plumbing, her considerable investment in mastering the vocabulary of my peculiar kind of economics might become totally valueless. If I were poised on the margin of indifference it might pay her to make me side payments to tempt me to eschew a career with the monkey wrench.

Again, this is a fanciful example. But as Gerald Shove of Cambridge used to insist, actual commercial life is at one level more like a jig-saw puzzle than like an equilibrium of homogeneous substances. This Shovian insight is well known to every personnel director and real-estate agent.[18]

(v) Probability or uncertainty phenomena are another breeder of bigness and possible monopolistic imperfections. This can be considered an alternative to "increasing returns" as a cause of monopoly; or, if we wish to alter our terminology, stochastic phenomena can be said to be a cause of increasing returns and decreasing costs. What is involved here is the fact, basic to the "law of large numbers" and the "central limit" theorems of statistics, that the sum of two identical independent variates does not have twice the standard deviation of each but only 40 percent more than each. Since $\sqrt{2} = 1.4+$, we see that a $\sqrt{N}$ law is involved for total cost or $1/\sqrt{N}$ for average costs; this implies for returns, instead of a homogeneous function of degree one, a homogeneous function of degree two.

Thus if two power grids are side by side it always pays to convert them in order to take advantage of noncoincidence of peak loads. General Motors can borrow at a lower interest rate as a result of its being able to cancel Pontiac variations against those of Oldsmobile and Chevrolet—a fact that should give pause to those critics of government who feel it is somehow unfair or inefficient for it to borrow large sums at low interest rates to allocate among diverse public projects. Indeed,

[18] Some readers have interpreted R. H. Coase, "The Problem of Social Cost," *Journal of Law and Economics*, III (1960), pp. 1-44, as having shown how *laissez-faire* pricing can solve the problem of "externalities" and "public goods" harmoniously. The above analysis shows that a problem of pricing two or more inputs that can be used in common is not solved by reducing it to a determinate maximized total whose allocation among the parts is an indeterminate problem in multilateral monopoly. It should come as news to no economist or game theorist that duopoly, oligopoly, bilateral and multilateral monopoly are indeterminate in their solution.

in a world of stochastic risk, where technology itself can be made to follow constant returns to scale, the ultimate state would seem to be one in which all enterprise is owned by one large mutual fund, with maximum diversification of risk enjoyed by its security owners. If this seems like a Leviathan monopoly, we can alternatively think of it as benevolent-government ownership, under the control of all of us as citizens.

It is important to realize that reduction of relative risk takes place only to the degree that the contingent events pooled are *not* perfectly positively correlated. Thus the tendency toward merger and monopoly is not so harmful if it is merely a case of pooling *independent* risks: if Tri-Continental Investment Company owns both a Montana ranch and a Florida Ford agency, it pools risks without creating monopoly power itself. However, in real life the fact that largeness permits reduced riskiness is only too likely to reinforce *other* increasing returns factors making for bigness *and* imperfection of competition.

Before turning to increasing returns proper, the Hamlet of the drama involving imperfect competition, I ought to point out some interaction between stochastic uncertainty and quasi-geometrical deviation from constant returns.

Consider the case of oil drilling. A homogeneous field is best drilled by wells located in hexagons with an optimal grid distance between wells. Under *laissez-faire* this does not happen: I drill at the boundary of my property to "rob" my neighbor, and he does the same to rob me. Here then is a case of an "external diseconomy." But when we analyze the reasons for it, we see that drilling oil on two acres of land involves essentially a joint productive phenomenon, not intrinsically different from joint production of wool and mutton. But joint production is not itself a sufficient condition to kill off perfect competition. Farming, our most competitive industry, always involves joint production. I have heard of sheep farmers, but never of separate wool and separate mutton farmers. As long as the joint production of sheep (i.e., wool-*cum*-mutton) can be replicated at constant returns, competition remains perfect among multiproduct firms.

The same *almost* applies to an oil field (or to an orchard, which needs bees to cross-fertilize it but which may find its bees flying off to fertilize some other orchard). As one firm grows in size to encompass many oil wells, it is a geometric fact that the ratio of its perimeter declines relative to its area. Hence, with each firm very large, the oil field will be exploited mostly by optimal hexagons: the joint production phenomena will be mostly internalized and the external diseconomy held down to a minimum. Even if you own a county in Texas, you still have negligible monopoly power in the oil markets of the world.

But here is where uncertainty enters in. No one can know in advance how much oil will be found in any region of Texas. Even the largest oil companies will prefer to buy up only part of any new region, in order to diversify their risks. Hence uncertainty phenomena help, under *laissez-faire*, to pulverize the optimal size arrangements that ought to prevail.

We are back to the fact that perfect knowledge is not producible and capable of being optimally allocated according to first-degree homogeneous production functions. Impurity of competition is a mighty breeder of imperfection of knowledge and foresight—as every small-town banker knows, and for which he is grateful.

Before returning to increasing returns, we may digress to discuss some geometric instances in which imperfect competition could produce inefficiencies not present in either (a) perfect competition, or (b) "perfect" monopoly. (The impatient reader may skip the next section at a first reading.)

Wastes of Freedom under Imperfect Spatial Competition

To illustrate that free enterprise can lead to greater inefficiency than either monopoly or ideal planning or a perfectly competitive configuration, I take a spatial example like that of Chamberlin's Appendix C. Rival stores or plants locate on a circle along which customers are distributed evenly. The farther goods must be transported the greater the real costs. Furthermore, true cost is assumed to increase more than proportionally with distance: hence, for two units each to go two miles is better than for one to go three miles and one to go one mile.

Figure 5-1 shows the pattern that would be optimal if there are $n = 1, 2, 3, 4, 5, 6, 7, 8$ stores or factories. They should, of course, be symmetrically placed to minimize cost, as in the upper circles of Figure 5-1a. The halfway point between centers is the watershed between markets, and the median person in each market encounters a distance to the center of half of the market length.

By contrast the lower row of circles, Figure 5-1b, shows what will happen under higgledy-piggledy *laissez-faire*. A single monopoly has the same pattern as that utopian planning. A second seller then moves to the antipodal point, again producing the same pattern as ideal planning. But for $n = 3$, there is asymmetry and waste: the third man can do no better, in the short run when the others are located, than toss a coin and go halfway between the existing two sellers. Now one quarter of the customers get their distances reduced, the rest are left with unchanged distances, and the maximum distance traveled by any customer is $0.5\pi R$: this contrasts with the efficient pattern that cuts the maximum

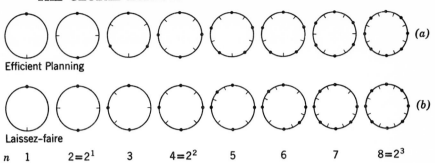

Figure 5-1 The symmetric, efficient pattern of planning is duplicated where $n = 2^m$, $m = 0,1,2,3, \ldots$; but, in the remaining half of the instances where $n \neq 2^m$, the pattern compares unfavorably with the oligopoly pattern that results when each new man finds it most profitable to settle halfway between the most separated—but neighboring—established centers.

distance a consumer must travel from $0.5\pi R$ to $0.33\pi R$, or by one third.

Paradoxically, oligopoly leads again to the ideal when $n=4$; similarly, for $n = 8$ and generally for $n = 2^m$, where m denotes an integer. But between 2^m and $(2^m)2$, no matter how large n (and m) become, we are half the time in the unbalanced, asymmetric, inefficient pattern. No wonder cities need planning: the random walk of history does not know where it is heading, and its past wandering prejudices the efficiency of each new increment. Inefficient reality is not a blend of efficient monopoly and Pareto-optimal competition.[19]

The Paradox of Adam Smith

After the last digression, let us go back to the relation between laws of return and market perfection. Increasing returns is the enemy of perfect competition. And therefore it is the enemy of the optimality conditions that perfect competition can ensure. How ironic it thus is that Adam Smith, the founding father of the doctrine of the beneficent Invisible Hand, should also be the progenitor of the doctrine that "spe-

---

[19] If society moves permanently from $n=2$ to $n=3$, the seller at 6 o'clock might well ultimately move toward 4, drawing the middle seller half as far in the same direction. But under dynamic growth, in passing through the efficient 1, 2, 4, 8, . . . , 2^m, points, the firms need have no incentive to avoid spending half the time in unbalanced states. Similarly, in two-dimensional space, an initial pattern of squares gives a less efficient grid than hexagons. Given stationary conditions, squares might get transformed into hexagons; but given *laissez-faire* growth, each new man has a short-run advantage in placing himself inside the largest market left, so that increased numbers lead to another grid of smaller squares or diamonds—still not efficient hexagons.

cialization is limited by the extent of the market." A *leitmotiv* in the *Wealth of Nations* is the concept of *division of labor*. Even if Smith did not realize it, we dwarfs who can stand on his gigantic shoulders should:

As long as the specialization is still being limited by the division of labor, competition cannot be working perfectly.

To this consideration should be added another. We have seen that constant returns to scale is the condition most perfectly constituted to produce perfect competition. But it is precisely the conditions of deviation from constant returns to scale that are the essence of the division of labor.

I must not overstate the case. There are certain kinds of specialization and division of labor that are compatible with constant returns: Ricardian comparative advantage in international trade gives us an example; the Heckscher-Ohlin analysis of international trade in terms of differences in *relative* factor endowments is another. But, and this is the point, the kind of division of labor that is limited, or could be limited, by the extent of the market is precisely the kind that is nonexistent under constant returns to scale.[20]

Number Growth and Perfection of Competition

Because I have repeatedly related perfection of competition to strict constant returns, I have by logical implication been relating imperfection of competition to deviations from constant returns. This requires me, in an essay glorifying the Chamberlinian revolution, to take sides in a long-standing controversy between Chamberlin and Kaldor. Kaldor[21]

[20] Ohlin's now classic *Interregional and International Trade,* Harvard University Press, Cambridge, Mass., 1933, shows this same dualism. The Heckscher-Ohlin relative-factor-endowment theory is quite different from the other Ohlin theory, which in effect attributes trade to the advantages of specializing to reap the advantages of large-scale operations. In this second theory, Ohlin is being Smithian and plunging us into a Chamberlin universe. In his first theory, Ohlin is generalizing Ricardo. It is worthy of note that Smith, the great critic of mercantilistic protectionism, did not present so sophisticated a monetary mechanism of trade-balance equalization as did his friend and predecessor, David Hume; nor does he anticipate the conclusive Ricardo-Torrens arithmetic of comparative advantage. What does he give us free traders besides commonsense—I mean rhetoric? Merely the parable and symbol of the Invisible Hand, a metatheorem at best—and one not understood until the present generation of economists.

[21] See N. Kaldor, "Market Imperfection and Excess Capacity," *Economica,* II (1935), pp. 33-50, reprinted in G. Stigler and K. Boulding, eds., *Readings in Price Theory,* pp. 384-403; and *Theory of Monopolistic Competition,* particularly Appendix G and Chapter IX.

long maintained that much of market imperfection would disappear if all production functions obeyed strict constant returns to scale—that is, if they were strictly homogeneous of degree one. This Chamberlin has always denied. Wording the issue as I have carefully done, my verdict must be for Kaldor in this matter—but with the warning that Chamberlin is instinctively right in his concern that we must not extrapolate new significances into such a verdict.

Logically, our syllogisms can be set out as follows.

THEOREM: *In the absence of institutional elements of monopoly, production functions that are universally of strict first-degree homogeneity lead under* laissez-faire *to perfect (or pure) competition no matter how "differentiated" are the products consumers demand.*

COROLLARY: *In the absence of institutional elements of monopoly, imperfection of competition presupposes some deviations from constancy of returns. The terribly important welfare and market problem of differentiation of product arises only because of these deviations (which are inevitable in the real world, because at small enough output, first-degree homogeneity is an empirical absurdity). All degrees of sourness of cider could be produced and enjoyed under constant returns. But as soon as we abandon this strong returns case, product differentiation becomes an acute problem and one with "public good" aspects.*[22]

I don't see why any Chamberlinian should deny the literal truth of my carefully worded propositions. They do not say (i) imperfect competition is unimportant; (ii) product differentiation is irrational; or (iii) the use of the word "indivisibility" is mandatory or helpful in describing (or "explaining"!) unit cost curves that decline in some short or long period. My propositions do not imply, but I admit they do tempt one to accept, the extrapolation that says:

CONJECTURE: *As the size of the market grows relative to the size of the minimum scale at which unit costs are at their lowest, the system approaches the perfectly competitive equilibrium.*

This last conjecture Chamberlin has stoutly denied on a variety of grounds. Thus, assuming zero costs and a homogeneous product, he points out (in Appendix G) that for any number of sellers—whether $N = 1$ or some large number—firm equilibrium is at the point of maxi-

---

[22] P. A. Samuelson, "The Pure Theory of Public Expenditure," *Review of Economics and Statistics,* XXXVI (1954), pp. 387-389; "Diagrammatic Exposition of Public Expenditure," *Review of Economics and Statistics,* XXXVII (1955), pp. 350-356; "Aspects of Public Expenditure Theories," *Review of Economics and Statistics,* XL (1958), pp. 332-338.

mum gross (and net) revenue where elasticity of demand $E_N = -1$. Hence as $N \to \infty$, $E_N = -1 \neq -\infty$. We can grant Chamberlin this, and sidestep the issue of whether, in calculating a typical firm's E_N as $p(\Sigma q_j)/p'(\Sigma q_j)q_i$, we should hold $p(q_1 + \cdots + q_N)$ constant as we take the limit $N \to \infty$, or hold q_i constant. But Chamberlin's is an empty victory, once we introduce ever-so-little positive marginal cost for each firm. Thus, if every firm has constant M.C. equal to $m > 0$, the equilibrium condition $p + q_ip' = m$ leads, as $N \to \infty$, to $E_N = -\infty$, the competitive result. Geometrically, how can free entry result in tangency of a downward sloping firm demand curve to a horizontal non-U-shaped cost curve? The answer is, only when $N = \infty$ and the firm's demand has its intercept touching but not crossing the horizontal cost curve. Although, as $N \to \infty$, $q_i = Q/N \to 0$, we find industry $Q = Nq_i \to Q^*$ the root of the competitive equilibrium M.C. $= m = p(Q)$.[23]

Chamberlin cannot seem to admit the logic of Kaldor's result because his imagination will simply not let him envisage anything so unrealistic as strict constant returns to scale. His subconscious keeps reminding him that at very small scales such an assumption is empirically preposterous. Granting that the point is a purely logical one, reminiscent of Scholastic quarrels over how many angels can stand on the point of a pin, we must insist that under the ideal conditions postulated, each consumer could have produced to his own order any differentiated product at minimum cost, and hence Chamberlin ought to concede absence of the slightest monopolistic imperfections.

Quantum-Theory Economics and Asymptotic Homogeneity

The "new math" has infected mathematical economics. Inequalities, convex sets, and the theories of cones have made modern formulations

---

[23] I must defend Chamberlin from having, in his Chapter 5 large-group case, become enmeshed in Zeno's Paradox, in which an infinite number of infinitesimals are wrongly summed to zero rather than a positive finite case. Stigler (*op. cit.*, pp. 15-17) wrongly treats such a symmetric case of heterogeneous substitutes as *logically* self-contradictory; questions of realism aside, Stigler simply has not used his mathematical imagination strongly enough. Let $q_i = D^i(p_1, \ldots, p_n, \ldots)$ $= D(p_i; p_1, \ldots,)$, a function symmetric in the (p_j) variables where $j \neq i$. Suppose $\partial q_i/\partial p_i = -A$, independently of n and $\partial q_i/\partial p_j = -B/(n-1)$ for $j \neq i$. Then the effect of a change in p_i on any p_j does indeed go to zero as $n \to \infty$. The effect, however, on the sum of the *increasing* (!) number of such other price changes does add up to a finite positive number, namely $B/(2A - B)$. But the resulting effect of *all* such changes on q_i, which is what is relevant for testing the legitimacy of Chamberlin's *ceteris paribus* dd curve, nevertheless does go to zero as Chamberlin says, being equal to $B^2/(2A - B)(N - 1)$.

more elegant and easier. Unfortunately, if we look at modern treatises[24] we find that often they score easy victories and represent a retrogression where realism in dealing with market imperfections is concerned. Thus the nice necessary and sufficient conditions for a maximum in linear programming, or in more general Kuhn-Tucker concave programming, come after ruling out increasing returns and varying returns phenomena—in which things often get worse before they get better, and for which there is a formidable search problem for the *maximum maximorum* among a large number of local maxima.

Because the convexity conditions of the modern formulations of competition are rarely met in real life, I propose in this section to state and prove some asymptotic theorems according to which we approach, in the limit as replicable numbers become indefinitely large, an approximation to the convexity conditions needed for competition.

Whether or not we care to use the terminology of "indivisibilities," we can agree with Chamberlin that, at the smallest scales of production, unit cost curves are falling; hence, production functions, $Q = F(V_1, \ldots, V_n)$, act at small enough scales as if they possessed homogeneity of greater than degree one, as measured locally by the scale elasticity coefficient $R = \Sigma_1^n V_j (\partial F / \partial V_j)/F$. In principle there is no reason why this stage should not prevail forever, with the unit cost function $c(Q) = C(Q)/Q$, forever having a negative slope. In some such cases, as where $R \leq 1 - \epsilon$ always, no matter how great the demand grows for the homogeneous product a regime of perfect competition can never be attained.

Suppose, however, that there is a level c^* of unit cost below which $c(Q)$ can never fall. Then asymptotically, $c(Q)$ must approach as a limit the horizontal curve $c(Q) \equiv c^*$; and along with unit cost, marginal cost $c'(Q) = C(Q) + QC'(Q)$ must approach the same horizontal asymptote, c^*. Asymptotically, a near approach to perfect competition is then possible, with $R \to 1$, the constant returns case suitable for perfect competition.

A third of a century ago M. F. W. Joseph[25] indicated how U-shaped cost curves, belonging to replicable plants or (under free entry) to replicable firms, lead asymptotically to *horizontal* unit cost curves for the

[24] For example, R. Dorfman, P. A. Samuelson, and R. Solow, *Linear Programming and Economic Analysis,* McGraw-Hill, New York, 1958; G. Debreu, *Theory of Value,* Wiley, New York, 1959.

[25] M. F. W. Joseph, "A Discontinuous Cost Curve and the Tendency to Increasing Returns," *Economic Journal,* XLIII (1938), pp. 390-398.

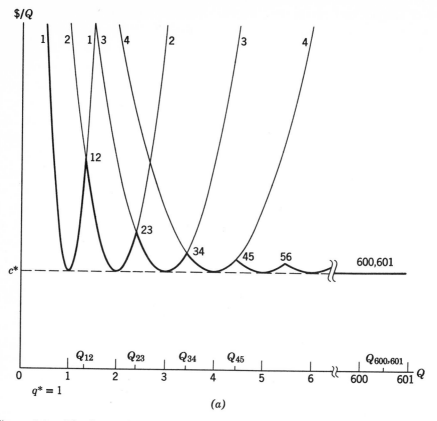

Figure 5-2a The heavy lower envelope goes along 1-1 to its 12 intersection with 2-2, to its 23 intersection with 3-3, . . ., until asymptotically it is the horizontal line at the $c^* = c(q^*) = \text{Min } c(q)$ level.

industry and multiplant firms. After elucidating this analysis, I shall show that the possibility of replication leads to "asymptotic-first-degree-homogeneity" of the production function.

Figure 5-2a constructs the lower-envelope unit cost curve attainable from 1, 2, . . . , N , . . . replicable plants. The basic curve 1-1 is shown U-shaped in Figures 5-2a and 5-2b. The curve 2-2 shows U-shaped unit costs when output is divided *equally* among 2 plants; similarly in 3-3, output is divided equally among 3 plants. Geometrically, 2-2 is the same as the 1-1 curve but with the horizontal scale doubled; 3-3 is the same as 1-1 curve but with the horizontal scale tripled; and so forth. To keep unit, and hence total, costs as low as possble, follow 1-1 to its intersection point with 2-2, marked 12, corresponding to Q_{12}; then follow 2-2 until it intersects with 3-3 at 23; and so forth.

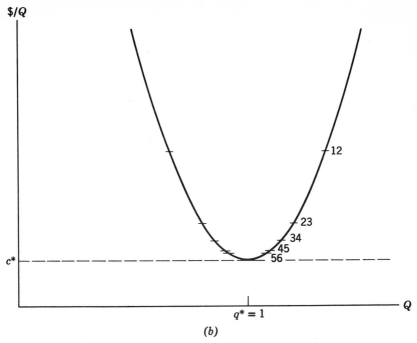

(b)

Figure 5-2*b* Each of the identical plants cuts back its output when one new plant is brought in. The rearrangements, from the right of q^* to the left, become smaller and smaller as the switch points (12;23; . . .) approach the (q^*, c^*) bottom-of-the-U as a limit.

Thus we generate the scalloped or curved heavy curve. But, as is shown in the enlarged horizontal scale of Figure 5-2*b*, depicting what happens in each and every identical plant, the height of the switch points (12; 23; 34; . . . ; N; $N + 1$) moves east and south to the level of minimum unit costs, $c^* = c(q^*)$. Asymptotically, the heavy envelope approaches the horizontal level c^*, and the sharpness of its corners becomes less and less. Within each of the identical plants, when N becomes so large that its difference with $N + 1$ becomes of negligible relative importance, each of the identical plants has its outputs remaining ever closer to the optimum scale q^*, corresponding to the bottom of the U.

To pave the way for asymptotic homogeneity, I present briefly the mathematics of the Joseph analysis.

Let $c(q) = C(q)/q$ = unit cost of 1 replicable plant; $c(q^*) < c(q)$, $q \neq q^*$. Then unit costs when N plants are being used equally are given by

$$\frac{NC(Q/N)}{Q} = \frac{C(Q/N)}{Q/N} = c\left(\frac{Q}{N}\right) = \text{unit costs with } N \text{ plants} \quad (5\text{-}1)$$

The envelope is given by

$$\operatorname*{Min}_{\{N\}} c\left(\frac{Q}{N}\right) = \Phi(Q) \geq \operatorname*{Min}_{\{q\}} c(q) = c(q^*) = c^* \qquad (5\text{-}2)$$

Obviously,

$$\Phi(Q) = c^* \qquad \text{for } Q = Nq^*, \qquad N \text{ integral} \qquad (5\text{-}3)$$

The successive switchpoints are the unique roots of

$$c\left(\frac{Q_{12}}{1}\right) = c\left(\frac{Q_{12}}{2}\right), \ c\left(\frac{Q_{23}}{2}\right) = c\left(\frac{Q_{23}}{3}\right), \ \ldots, \ c\left(\frac{Q_{N,N+1}}{N}\right)$$
$$= c\left(\frac{Q_{N,N+1}}{N+1}\right) \quad (5\text{-}4)$$

Asymptotically, if $c''(q^*) > 0$, it can be shown that

$$Q_{N,N+1} \approx Nq^*\left(1 + \frac{1}{2N+1}\right) \qquad (5\text{-}5)$$

Necessarily

$$\lim_{N \to \infty} \Phi(Q) = c^* \qquad (5\text{-}6)$$

which is the Joseph theorem on asymptotic constant costs.
Now consider a replicable production function

$$Q = F(V_1, V_2, \ldots, V_n) \qquad (5\text{-}7)$$
$$= F\left(V_1, \frac{V_2}{V_1} V_1, \ldots, \frac{V_n}{V_1} V_1\right) = F(V_1, v_2 V_1, \ldots, v_n V_1) = F(V_1)$$

For fixed factor ratios, $(V_2/V_1, \ldots, V_n/V_1)$, let

$$\operatorname*{Max}_{\{V_1\}} \frac{F(V_1)}{V_1} = \frac{F(V_1^*)}{V_1^*} = f^*(v_2, \ldots, v_n) \qquad (5\text{-}\mathcal{E})$$

THEOREM OF ASYMPTOTIC HOMOGENEITY. *The maximum output obtainable from optimally replicated production processes is given by*

$$\operatorname*{Max}_{\{N\}} NF\left(\frac{V_1}{N}, \frac{V_2}{N}, \ldots, \frac{V_n}{N}\right) = \operatorname*{Max}_{\{N\}} NF\left(\frac{V_1}{N}\right)$$
$$= \psi(V_1, V_2, \ldots, V_n) = \psi(V_1) \geq f^* V_1,$$

with equality sign[26] *holding for* $V_1 = NV_1^*$; *and*

$$\lim_{\substack{V_1 \to \infty \\ V_i/V_1 = v_i}} \left[\frac{\psi(V_1, \ldots, V_n)}{V_1 f^*(V_2/V_1, \ldots, V_n/V_1)} \right] = 1. \qquad (5\text{-}9)$$

This is an important formalization of the Smithian dictum that widening the extent of the market will, after it can result in no further extension of the division of labor and exploitation of increasing returns, create conditions suitable for workably perfect competition.

One way to apply this is to hold technology of an industry constant, and also factor prices to it, while widening the demand curve for its homogeneous product (where there is such a thing!).

Thus, let

$$\Sigma q = Q = M \cdot D(p), \quad M \text{ being a parameter of widening}$$
$$(5\text{-}10)$$

Then, as $M \to \infty$, the industry and firm equilibrium will approach that of perfect competition.

An alternative application of the asymptotic theorem comes from holding industry demand constant, $\Sigma q = Q = D(p)$ but imagining a technological change that reduces q^*, the bottom-of-the-U scale. Thus, write $c(q/\lambda q^*)$, and let $\lambda \to 0$ to attain perfect competition.

These asymptotic theorems must be used with great caution. Often they merely say, "If the world were different (in range and density, ...) from what it is, competition might be more perfect than it now is."[27] On the other hand, Bain, Sylos–Labini, and Modigliani have rightly emphasized that the conditions for replication and entry are impor-

---

[26] In the cases I have considered, the minimal asymptote is actually realized in the quantum states $(q^*, 2q^*, \ldots, Nq^*, \ldots)$, or $(V_1^*, 2V_1^*, \ldots, NV_1^*, \ldots)$. It is easy to construct cases in which this does not happen. Thus, consider two distinct elements of cost $[c_1(q), \Phi_1(q); c_2(q), \Phi_2(q)]$. If q_1^* and q_2^* are incommensurable numbers, like $(1, \sqrt{2},)$ their sum $\Phi_1(q) + \Phi_2(q)$ will still have the asymptotic property of approaching $c_1^* + c_2^*$, but $\Phi_1(q) + \Phi_2(q) > c_1(q) + c_2(q)$ for all finite q.

Even if q_1^* and q_2^* are commensurable, but like 100 and 101 have a least common multiple that is very large (namely 10,100), then only for $q^* = (10,100, 20,200, \ldots N\ 10,100)$, truly gigantic scales, will the minimum c^* be fully achieved. For the auto industry to be perfectly perfectly competitive, it must attain the optimum scale of that component with largest minimal scale.

[27] But where applicable, the asymptotic theorems are crucial. Thus most of the "successful solutions" to the public goods problem referred to in footnote 22 come in cases—like those where traffic is heavy enough to require numerous parallel roads, in which marginal cost pricing will just recover full cost—in which sufficient replication is possible.

tant in determining and limiting the degree of imperfection of competition.[28]

The Proliferation of Differentiation

We now have the equipment to analyze and appraise Chamberlin's contention that proliferation of numbers alone need not lead to perfection of competition. No one will dispute his contention that merely doubling the areas containing, say, imperfectly competing barber shops need not reduce monopolistic elements. But of course it is an increase, in some sense, of the *density* of numbers that everybody recognizes to be the relevant situation that needs to be appraised.

Chamberlin (Appendix G, p. 288) is willing to meet head on the case

---

[28] J. S. Bain, *Barriers to New Competition,* Harvard University Press, Cambridge, Mass., 1956; P. Sylos-Labini, *Oligopoly and Technical Progress,* Harvard University Press, Cambridge, Mass., 1962; F. Modigliani, "New Developments on the Oligopoly Front," *Journal of Political Economy,* LXVI (1958), pp. 215-252. This asymptotic theorem is relevant to the discussion of M. J. Farrell, "The Convexity Assumption in the Theory of Competitive Markets," *Journal of Political Economy,* LXVII (1959), pp. 377-391, with later contributions by F. Bator, T. C. Koopmans, S. Reiter, and M. J. Farrell in the 1961 *Journal of Political Economy.*

In (5-2) and my theorem it is important that N be integral. If N is unrealistically treated as any real number, (5-2) becomes $\Phi(Q) \equiv c^*Q$, since Min $c(Q/N) = c(q^*)$ is attained by setting $N = Q/q^*$, even where the latter ratio is not integral. This gives us our asymptotic result from the beginning! But, as Solomon knew when he ironically ordered the baby to be divided into halves for division between rival mothers, babies and plants come in integral numbers and it makes no sense to speak of $\sqrt{2}$ babies or even p/q babies where p and q are integers, $q \neq 1$.

I recall discussion by my old teacher, Paul Douglas, of a dubious demonstration by Wicksell that all production functions must be homogeneous of degree $R = 1$. For if R were greater than 1, we would have one single firm—an empirical absurdity. And if R were less than 1, we would have an infinite number of firms, each producing an infinitesimal—also, an empirical absurdity. Ergo, $R \equiv 1!$ Actually, if $R > 1$ always, in the limit you could produce output with vanishingly small inputs per unit—perhaps an absurdity, but no man has ever been to the horizon to report back on its plentitude. And, if $R < 1$ always, with no integral or quantum restrictions on inputs, the expression $Nf(V^1/N, \ldots, V_n/N) \to \infty$ as $N \to \infty$, so you could get an *infinite* output from an iota of inputs—a neat trick if you can bring it off. The absurdity is in thinking that all functions can be divided into three categories: those with R *always* equal to, greater than, or less than unity. Given such an absurd Hobson's choice, perhaps $R = 1$ would win. But who needs accept such a specified choice, when R can be a variable magnitude, varying with scale for each set of proportions and going through the U-shaped pattern of this section.

where numbers, and hence density, increase along a spatial line. He indicates, rightly, that if the sellers double and each remains sovereign in his halved market area, there is no presumed increase in each seller's elasticity of demand. (If transport costs diminished, so that each seller serves a larger exclusive domain, the same would be true, a conclusion that might give us pause.) But, when the number (and density) of sellers increases, will there not be a greater temptation on the part of some to cut prices—not merely to gain business from the next seller down the line, but in order to draw price-conscious customers from more remote areas? Within a large city, a niche develops for discount houses, which live in symbiosis with full-price stores. Within a hamlet, or even medium-size city, no similar opportunity for small-markup stores exists.

Admirers of perfect-competition theory like to point to large-volume, "competitive" sellers who provide a safety valve for the price-conscious consumers and who come into viable existence because of the existence of a sizable number of such consumers. To borrow a term from the unconventional wisdom, such consumers exercise in concert their "countervailing power." But, at best, this only establishes the existence of pockets of near-perfect competition.

A story is told about an oriental student who was asked, on his General Examination at Harvard by Professor Leontief, about integrability conditions and violations of transitivity of choice in consumer-preference theory. He was supposed to have replied airily, "Who cares about clazy people?" Well, God cares about price-insensitive consumers and the wastes involved in imperfectly competitive markets that experience the deadweight losses of non-Pareto-optimality. An ideal system is one that serves well the interests of ordinary man and not just those of *homo economicus*.

One of the beauties of perfect competition is that—if conditions suitable to it prevailed universally—under it most of us could relax our pursuit of self-interest, knowing that the existence of a margin of eager beavers sufficed to produce the price uniformity and other optimality conditions that we would all enjoy. A market system of imperfect competition that provides a competitive escape valve only to those ready to pay the price of perpetual vigilance is not an ideal system. To say, "Those who buy at prices well above marginal cost (including, of course, the extra costs of convenience services and differentiation of product) have made their beds. Let them lie in them—they could have chosen otherwise," is to express an attitude: it does not demonstrate that the wastes of imperfect competition under *laissez-faire* are small, or preferable to what would result from some government interferences.

All my fine theorems about asymptotic homogeneity of the functions producing a homogeneous output, where the quantities of product of different sellers can be meaningfully added as $q_1 + q_2 + \cdots + q_N$, cannot negate the Chamberlinian insight that wider markets (more ultimate similar consumers) or reduced technical optimal scales (of the q_i^* type discussed above) are likely to permit, and hence induce, further differentiation of products. If electric power permits shorter runs of mousetrap production, consumers with a yen for diverse types of mousetraps will find someone providing a greater variety. Thus larger N may result merely in a finer grid of differentiated products, but without $N \to \infty$ leading to perfect competition.

I personally suspect that increases in N will generally, even *after* they induce the Chamberlinian pulverization of markets, tend to reduce market imperfections on balance. But that does not mean that the limit as $N \to \infty$ is zero market imperfection. Instead the limit may be at an irreducible positive degree of imperfection.

Staying, for metaphorical purposes only, with the spatial analogy, the proper Chamberlinian vision treats enlarged numbers and densities in the following way. As N grows, sellers (say doctors) become more frequent and tighter spaced. Specialists develop—internists, obstetricians, kidney specialists, left-kidney specialists, and so forth. Along a line, the beads or nodes of specialists—or of department stores versus local shops—are more sparse than the beads of general practitioners. On a uniform plane—as Lösch theorized [29]—the fine hexagonal grid of high-markup local stores will be contained in a coarser grid of high-volume stores.

Under free entry it is possible that new complexes of differentiated products can be created at constant costs or better. Investing enough money in advertising and other activities, a group of soap, cigarette, or cosmetic companies can come into existence at no worse than constant returns. After the rents are bid up of factors uniquely gifted to promotion—television networks or station licensees, world champion athletes, golden-voiced announcers—there may appear no extraordinary profits anywhere. Yet this is not to be identified with perfect competition, nor are we justified in regarding the differentiation of product as lacking in intrinsic utility. Most, if not all of the items, are being sold at an excess over marginal cost, such that it would add to the welfare of the universe if an extra item were somehow sold and consumed at less than market price. Nothing like this would occur in the conventional models of perfect competition, or, for that matter, of monopoly.

As the universe is seen to have more and more solar systems like ours,

[29] A. Lösch, *The Economics of Location,* Yale University Press, New Haven, 1954.

Nature contrives to perform more and more experiments with varied—or as we might say—differentiated outcomes. That is Chamberlin's imperishable vision.

Conclusion

In speaking of theories of monopolistic or imperfect competition as "revolutions," I know in advance that I shall provoke dissent. There are minds that by temperament will define away every proposed revolution. For them it is enough to point out that Keynes in 1936 had some partial anticipator in 1836. Newton is just a guy getting too much credit for the accretion of knowledge that covered centuries. A mountain is just a high hill; a hill, merely a bulging plain. Such people remind me of the grammar-school teacher we all had, who would never give 100 to a paper on the ground that "No one is perfect."

With such semantics, I have no quarrel—provided its rules-of-the-game are clearly understood. However, to those familiar with the history of sciences—how they develop, the role of new and altered modes of thinking in marking their growth, the role even of myth in the autobiography of a science—revolutions are a useful way of describing accelerations in the path of growth. An old theory—or model; or, to use Kuhn's terminology,[30] "paradigm"—is never killed off, as it should be, by a new set of facts. Being prisoners of their own *Gestalts*, scientists (like lovers) abandon an old theory only when they have found a new theory in which to clothe their beliefs. Chamberlin, Sraffa, Robinson, and their contemporaries have led economists into a new land from which their critics will never evict us.

---

[30] T. S. Kuhn, *The Anatomy of Scientific Revolutions,* University of Chicago Press, Chicago, 1962.

132

REPLY *

PAUL A. SAMUELSON

In the Chamberlin *Festchrift*, I noted that total transport costs are minimized if n sellers are distributed equidistantly to serve customers evenly spread on a circle; but that under laissez faire the arrival of one new seller would tend to result in his locating halfway between the pair of existing sellers who are farthest apart. Hence, when A and B are at opposite poles of a circle, the arrival of C will be followed — not by all three ending up equidistant — but by C's being halfway between A and B, which is an asymmetric and inefficient result. As sellers grow to become $n = 1, 2, \ldots, 2^m - 1$, $2^m, 2^m+1, \ldots$, it is only at the (rare) points where n is an integral power of 2 that the symmetric efficient pattern is achieved.

Mr. Grace raises two objections. The first can be easily disposed of. The second poses genuine problems.

I

Grace criticizes my assumption that transport costs grow more than proportionally to distance. So let me withdraw that assumption: all of my analysis is *unchanged* if we replace this assumption by the weaker assumption that "cost merely increases with distance."

For the theory of city centralization, it does matter whether cost as a function of distance, $C(x)$, is a convex (from below) function, as I assumed, or a concave function. For example: to serve two equally large city markets, I minimize total costs by settling halfway between them if $C(x)$ is convex; I settle at one of them if $C(x)$ is concave; if $C(x)$ is linear, and I agree with Grace that there is merit in this case, location is indifferent (just as the median of two observations is *anywhere* between them).

My problem of evenly spaced consumers, on the other hand, always has lowest total transport costs at a mid-location whatever $C(x)$'s curvature, providing only that $C(x)$ increases with x. To see this, you need only consider the case of three customers evenly spaced on a line. If the sellers locate at the midpoint, one customer pays for zero distance and each of two pays for a distance of one.

* Aid from the National Science Foundation is thankfully acknowledged.

Were the seller to move to either extreme, there will still be one customer at zero distance; but in effect one customer will be shifted from a distance of one to a distance of two, which is definitely a net loss.

The same argument applies to customers spread evenly on a line or arc between fixed left and right neighbor sellers. If transport costs increase with distance (no matter how), each customer buys from the plant nearest him. So at equal F.O.B. prices, wherever you settle in the interval, your market area goes from the point halfway to your left neighbor over to the point halfway to your right neighbor. And as far as this whole arc is concerned, each neighbor has exactly the same number of customers, similarly situated, as you do on his side. Now suppose you were to move off a bit from dead center — say, to the right. This shortens both market intervals on the right, losing their longest hauls. But you lengthen both market intervals on the left and, so to speak, the long hauls lost on the right now appear as *still longer* hauls on the left. With cost rising as the haul rises, that substitution resulting from a non-midpoint location must force up total transport costs. Q.E.D.[1]

This shows that total costs can be reduced when any triad of plants is not equally spaced, and therefore that equal spacing around the rim is the efficient locational pattern. My fault for introducing an unnecessary and obfuscating assumption.

1. Defining, by choice of distance unit, the length of the total arc as unity, we can write total transport costs for all customers on the interval as a function of a, the fraction of the arc (measured from the left neighbor) at which you locate, with $1 - a$ being the fraction measured from the right neighbor. Then $c(a) = 2 \int_0^{a/2} C(x)dx + 2 \int_0^{1-a/2} C(x)dx$. For a minimum, $c'(a)$

$= 0$, or $C(\frac{a}{2}) = C(\frac{1-a}{2})$, which for $C(x)$ monotone implies $a=1-a=\frac{1}{2}$, the midpoint. Since $c''(a) = \frac{1}{2}C'(\frac{a}{2}) + \frac{1}{2}C'(\frac{1-a}{2}) > 0$, a minimum is assured at the midpoint independently of the curvature of $C(x)$. To dispense with differentiability or even continuity assumptions, we can write $c(a)$ above in the symmetric form $c(a, 1 - a) = c(1 - a, a)$, the sum of two convex functions. Any symmetric function subject to a symmetric constraint must take on an extremum at its symmetry axis, and if convex its extremum must be a minimum. Hence, the midpoint with $a=1-a$ is the optimum. Finally, to duplicate the logical argument of the text above, it suffices to concentrate on $a < \frac{1}{2}$ and write

$$c(a) = 2[\int_0^{1/4} C(x)dx - \int_{a/2}^{1/4} C(x)dx] + 2[\int_0^{1/4} C(x)dx + \int_{1/4}^{(1-a)/2} C(x)dx]$$

$$= c(\frac{1}{2}) + 2\int_{a/2}^{1/4} \{C(x + \frac{1}{4} - \frac{a}{2}) - C(x)\} dx = c(\frac{1}{2}) + a \text{ positive number,}$$

by virtue of the fact that monotonicity on $C(x)$ makes the last integrand and integral positive for all $a < \frac{1}{2}$.

II

Now to Grace's main point: in a dynamic economy, where the number of sellers is growing, how would an ideal planner specify the proper locational program? And how would this compare with the result under laissez faire?

In framing my example, I had been struck by the baleful influence of the dead hand of the past. August Lösch, Walter Christaller, Walter Isard, and locational theorists [2] have shown that you cover space most effectively by *hexagons*, not by squares. (So to speak, a circle is the most perfect market area, but a circular cookie cutter always leaves dough at the edges; and a hexagon is the nearest thing to a circle among regular polygons, namely, among triangles, squares, and hexagons, capable of covering the plane.) Yet when I fly over Iowa, I see square townships and a checkerboard pattern of roads. And it is no one small person's business to change this frozen pattern. Since space examples are hard to describe and line examples are easy, I dramatized this conundrum by using a circle model.

Perhaps if laissez faire possessed perfect *futures* markets, in which all subsequent states of the world were rationally appraised, in the Arrow-Debreu manner, it might achieve whatever an ideal planner — governmental or belonging to a, hopefully regulated, monopolist — could achieve. But I was faced with the imperfect, impure world of Chamberlin's small merchants and gasoline stations and not with an omniscient bourse.

Rather than press my earlier contrast between planning and laissez faire, let me join with Grace and stress some qualifications. If the costs of relocating A and B are minor, then the arrival of C between them will, even under laissez faire, tend to push them both away from C until the ideal *equidistant* pattern is achieved.[3]

The same holds in space whenever markets areas are nonhexagonal. Suppose everyone sells on an Iowa checkerboard with square-shaped markets. If all of us in one row were to move laterally collusively, we could hope to increase our profits at the expense of the sellers above and below us (as Isard has shown in the cited 1953 article). But one seller alone has no such motives to move toward

2. August Lösch, *The Economics of Location* (New Haven, Conn.: Yale University Press, 1954) is a definitive reference on these matters. See also Walter Isard, "Some Remarks on the Marginal Rate of Substitution between Distance Inputs and Location Theory," *Metroeconomica*, V (April 1953), 11–21, particularly Fig. 1.
3. Let me mention here that the drafting error in my Figure 5–1a that Grace points out should be corrected in the manner indicated by him.

this more efficient hexagonal pattern, which is the only pattern from which no one would be motivated to move.

But suppose relocation costs are heavy. Then, for the planner too, there is a formidable problem in dynamic discrete programming to determine what is the best locational program *over time*. Such an optimal program will look inefficient if one imagines freezing it permanently!

In conclusion,[4] what should be emphasized is the need for *information* about the future — a problem in what Chamberlin would call "imperfection" and not merely "impurity" of competition. Since information involves externalities and does not generally obey laws of constant returns to scale, there is a *prima facie* case that the Invisible Hand of Smithian competition does itself need some kind of a helping hand.

Addendum: Demand Curves, Welfare, and Location

If at each point demand is given by $q = D[P + C(x)]$, the arguments in note 1 apply once we substitute $D[P + C(x)] \cdot C(x)$ for $C(x)$. But even with $C'(x) > 0$, because $D' < 0$, the new function may not be monotone increasing. Hence the midpoint location may *maximize* locally rather than minimize total transport costs, and indeed as far as lowering transport costs is alone concerned it might pay to locate in clusters and abandon some markets completely. At a less superficial level of welfare maximizing, if the consumer's surpluses of the different consumers are ethically commensurable and addable, we can write that utility surplus at each point as $U^*[P + C(x)]$, where in the normal case this indirect utility function is monotone decreasing in its argument. Now in all the integrals above we substitute U^* for C and maximize instead of minimizing. And the fact that U^* is a declining function of distance x suffices to show that equal spacing is more than merely technocratically optimal. The same mathematics will show that a seller is motivated to locate at the midpoint. If his profit on each unit sold is $(P - MC)q$, and $q = D[P + C(X)]$, then the integrand in

---

4. Grace's penultimate paragraph can be briefly commented on. In discussing the Kaldor-Chamberlin debate as to whether increase in numbers leads to perfection of competition, my conclusion was not that Kaldor is logically correct but that Chamberlin has merit in terms of realism. I was trying to say that the Kaldor result *is not mandatory as a matter of logic* — since added numbers *could* be offset (without logical contradiction) by intensification of product differentiation.

his profit integrals is a declining function of X, and the above kind of proof goes through smoothly. (If AC is a rising function the situation could be more complicated.) Even without assuming ethical commensurability of different people, we can prove optimality of equal spacing by probability argument. If your utility is an inverse function of your distance from a supplier, and if you have an equal chance of finding yourself anywhere on the arc, then you will join in a unanimous vote to insist upon midpoint location of the plant in question, for that will maximize the average or expected value of *your* utility.

MASSACHUSETTS INSTITUTE OF TECHNOLOGY

133

Two Generalizations of the Elasticity of Substitution

Paul A. Samuelson

I. *One Good and Multiple Factors*

Review. In 1932 Hicks defined the useful concept called the elasticity of substitution, in the form

$$\sigma = \sigma_{12} = \frac{F_1 F_2}{F F_{12}} = \sigma_{21} , \tag{1}$$

where $F(V_1, V_2)$ is a homogeneous first-degree neoclassical production function and where subscripts depict partial differentiation with respect to the indicated variable (such as $F_i = \partial F(V_1, V_2)/\partial V_i$, etc.). In 1933, Joan Robinson defined a related concept, designed to serve as a criterion of change in relative shares:

$$\sigma^{(R)} = - \frac{d(V_1/V_2)/(V_1/V_2)}{d(W_1/W_2)/(W_1/W_2)} , \tag{2}$$

where W_i refers to the price of the V_i factor. And it was soon demonstrated that these are identical coefficients when applied to a two-variable neo-classical production function, whose partial derivatives provide the marginal-productivity determinants of factor prices.

When more than two inputs are involved, the problem of generalizing the Hicks σ coefficient becomes complex. Champernowne, Pigou, and others, in pursuit of the question of how the change in a factor price, W_i, affects the amount demanded of a different factor, V_j, have moved in the direction of defining a square matrix of partial-elasticities of substitution, of the type $[F_i F_j / F F_{ij}]$. Aside from being complex, this approach has led to little in the way of definite results and has moved away from the task of providing a criterion of change in relative factor shares.

New Approach. I have long found it convenient in lectures to generalize σ to more than two variables by moving in a different direction. Thus, for a homogeneous first-degree production function $F(V_1, V_2, \ldots, V_n)$, $n \geqslant 2$, I define different σ's, of the form $(\sigma_1, \ldots, \sigma_n)$, with the property that each σ_i provides a criterion of change in the relative share of the ith factor as V_i increases with other V_j held constant—or, what is the same thing, as every V_j/V_i diminishes in the same proportion.

One natural way of approaching my concept is to rewrite the $n = 2$ Hicks coefficient, σ_{12}, in asymmetric notations:

$$\sigma_{12} = \frac{F_1 F_2}{F F_{12}} = -\frac{F_1 F_2}{F} \frac{V_2}{V_1 F_{11}} = -\frac{F_1}{V_1 F_{11}}\left(1 - \frac{F_1 V_1}{F}\right)$$

or, for $i = 1, 2$,

$$\sigma_i = -\left(\frac{F_i}{V_i F_{ii}}\right)\left(1 - \frac{F_i V_i}{F}\right) = \frac{\partial \log V_i}{\partial \log F_i}(1 - \alpha_i) = -E_{V_i F_i}(1 - \alpha_i), \quad (3)$$

where $(E_{V_i F_i})$ is the elasticity of the *ceteris paribus* marginal-product demand curve for the ith factor, α_i is the relative factor share of the ith factor, and $1 - \alpha_i$ is the relative share of the rest of the factors.

It is evident that this formula can hold for any one of three or more factors. Thus, I end up defining

$$\sigma_1 = -E_{V_1 F_1}(1 - \alpha_1)$$
$$\sigma_2 = -E_{V_2 F_2}(1 - \alpha_2)$$
$$\sigma_3 = -E_{V_3 F_3}(1 - \alpha_3) \qquad\qquad (4)$$
$$\cdots \cdots \cdots \cdots$$
$$\sigma_n = -E_{V_n F_n}(1 - \alpha_n).$$

Criterion of Relative Shares. I can now easily prove the theorem that σ_i does provide an indicator of relative shares.

Theorem 1: If $Q = F(V_1, \ldots, V_n) \equiv \lambda^{-1} F(\lambda V_1, \ldots, \lambda V_n)$
$$W_i = \partial F(V_1, \ldots, V_n)/\partial V_i \qquad (i = 1, \ldots, n),$$
$$\alpha_i = W_i V_i/Q = F_i V_i/F$$

then $\quad \dfrac{\partial \alpha_i}{\partial V_i} \gtreqless 0$ depending on whether

$$\sigma_i = -\frac{F_i}{V_i F_{ii}}\left(1 - \frac{F_i V_i}{F}\right) = -E_{V_i F_i}(1 - \alpha_i) \gtreqless 1$$

To prove this, note that the algebraic sign of

$$\frac{\partial \log \alpha_i}{\partial \log V_i} = \frac{\partial \log F_i}{\partial \log V_i} + 1 - \frac{\partial \log F}{\partial \log V_i}$$

$$= \frac{1}{E_{V_i F_i}} + 1 - \alpha_i = \frac{1}{E_{V_i F_i}} [1 + E_{V_i F_i}(1 - \alpha_i)] \qquad (5)$$

is plus, zero, or minus depending on which of these signs the last bracket has, which directly proves the theorem.

Equality of Generalized Hicks and Robinson Coefficients. More specifically, let us rewrite Robinson's definition

$$\sigma^{(R)} = -\frac{d(V_1/V_2)/(V_1/V_2)}{d(W_1/W_2)/(W_1/W_2)}$$

$$= -\frac{\partial \log (V_1/V_2)/\partial V_1}{\partial \log (W_1/W_2)/\partial V_1}$$

$$= -\frac{1}{\dfrac{\partial \log \left(\dfrac{W_1 \, V_1}{W_2 \, V_2}\right)}{\partial \log V_1} - 1}$$

$$= \frac{1}{1 - \dfrac{\partial \log \left(\dfrac{\alpha_1}{1 - \alpha_1}\right)}{\partial \log V_1}}. \qquad (6)$$

I now generalize this to $n \geqslant 2$, in the form

Theorem 2. $\quad \sigma_i^{(R)} = \dfrac{1}{1 - \dfrac{\partial \log \dfrac{\alpha_i}{1 - \alpha_i}}{\partial \log V_i}}$

$$= \frac{1}{1 - \dfrac{1}{1 - \alpha_i} \dfrac{\partial \log \alpha_i}{\partial \log V_i}} = \frac{1}{1 - \dfrac{1}{1 - \alpha_i}\left[\dfrac{1}{E_{V_i F_i}} + 1 - \alpha_i\right]}$$

$$= \frac{1}{1/\sigma_i} = \sigma_i.$$

This proves the identity of my n-dimensional generalization of the 1932 Hicks coefficient with my n-dimensional generalization of the 1933 Robinson coefficient.

Some Cases of Constant σ_i. This completes my first generalization. Some simple applications can now be indicated.

First, consider the n-dimensional Cobb-Douglas case. For

$$F(V_1, \ldots, V_n) = aV_1^{k_1}V_2^{k_2}\ldots V_n^{k_n}, \quad \sum_1^n k_j = 1$$

$$\sigma_i = -\frac{F_i}{V_i F_{ii}}\left(1 - \frac{F_i V_i}{F}\right)$$

$$= -\frac{1}{k_i - 1}(1 - k_i) = 1. \tag{7}$$

Hence, for the C-D case, the new coefficient is identically unity, as anyone would wish it to be.

Second, consider the obvious n-dimensional analogue of the Solow-Champernowne-Bergson so-called constant-elasticity-of-substitution function

$$Q = [a_1 V_1^{(\sigma-1)/\sigma} + \ldots + a_n V_n^{(\sigma-1)/\sigma}]^{\sigma/(\sigma-1)}.$$

For this

$$\sigma_i = -\frac{F_i}{V_i F_{ii}}\left(1 - \frac{F_i V_i}{F}\right) \tag{8}$$

$$= -\frac{1}{\left(\dfrac{\sigma-1}{\sigma}-1\right)(1-\alpha_i)}(1-\alpha_i) = \sigma \quad (i = 1, \ldots, n).$$

Hence, this n-dimensional CES function does indeed have a constant σ_i that is the same for all factors.

This raises an interesting question. What n-dimensional $F(V_1, \ldots, V_n)$ has constant but unequal values for $(\sigma_1, \ldots, \sigma_n)$? For $n = 2$, we know there exists no such function since, by definition $\sigma_1 \equiv \sigma_2$ when $n = 2$. This alerts us to the fact that, for any $n > 2$, not all the $(\sigma_1, \ldots, \sigma_n)$ can be independently constant. Thus, if

$$\sigma_2 = \sigma_3 = \ldots = \sigma_n \equiv 1,$$

it is quite evident that we must be in the Cobb-Douglas case with σ_1 also unity. Likewise, if

$$\sigma_2 = \sigma_3 = \ldots = \sigma_n = \sigma \neq 1,$$

we must be in the generalized CES family with σ_1 also equal to σ.

Certainly the $(\sigma_1, \ldots, \sigma_n)$ must be connected by the relation

$$\alpha_1 + \ldots + \alpha_n = 1 = \sum_1^n \left(1 + \frac{\sigma_i}{E_{V_i F_i}}\right) = n + \sum_{i=1}^n \frac{\sigma_i}{E_{V_i F_i}}. \tag{9}$$

Suppose we try to impose constancy on $(n-1)$ of the σ's, say $(\sigma_2, \ldots, \sigma_n)$. Then we impose on the $(n-1)$ dimensional function

$$F(1, V_2/V_1, \ldots, V_n/V_1),$$

$(n-1)$ partial differential equations of the form

$$-\frac{\partial F(1, v_2, \ldots, v_n)/\partial v_i}{v_i \partial^2 F(1, v_2, \ldots, v_n)/\partial v_i^2}\left[1 - \frac{v_i \partial F(1, v_2, \ldots, v_n)/\partial v_i}{F(1, v_2, \ldots, v_n)}\right] \equiv \bar{\sigma}_i$$

$$(i = 2, \ldots, n). \quad (10)$$

Whatever the most general solution, $F(1, v_2, \ldots, v_n)$, to these equations may be, it is too much to expect that, for arbitrary $\bar{\sigma}_2, \ldots, \bar{\sigma}_n$,

$$\sigma_1 = -\frac{\partial F(1, V_2/V_1, \ldots, V_n/V_1)/\partial V_1}{V_1 \partial^2 F(1, V_2/V_1, \ldots, V_n/V_1)/\partial V_1^2}$$

$$\left[1 - \frac{V_1 \partial F(1, V_2/V_1, \ldots, V_n/V_1)/\partial V_1}{F(1, V_2/V_1, \ldots, V_n/V_1)}\right] \quad (11)$$

should turn out also to be a constant. I omit proof of this assertion.

Equivalent Approach via Leontief Physical-Composite Factor. The present σ_i involves the ith factor against all the rest. Thus, in computing σ_1, we change V_1, above, holding $(V_2, \ldots, V_n)$ constant. Holding any such inputs constant ought to be capable of being regarded as a case of holding some single *composite* physical factor bundle constant, and thus should be capable of being handled by the old $n = 2$ definition of 1932. In 1936, Leontief defined physical composite goods in connection with the economic theory of index numbers. Thus, consider the homogeneous function

$$Q = F(V_1, V_2, V_3, \ldots, V_n).$$

Subject the inputs to the new restrictions

$$V_1 = V_I$$
$$V_2 = \bar{V}_2 V_{II} \quad\quad\quad\quad\quad\quad (12)$$
$$\ldots$$
$$V_n = \bar{V}_n V_{II}$$

to get
$$Q = F(V_I, \bar{V}_2 V_{II}, \ldots, \bar{V}_n V_{II})$$
$$= F(V_I, V_{II}; \bar{V}_2, \ldots, \bar{V}_n) \quad\quad (13)$$
$$= \Phi(V_I, V_{II}) \text{ for short.}$$

Now it is easy to verify that Φ has all the properties of a well-behaved concave homogeneous-first-degree neoclassical production function in 2 variables. We can apply the old 1932 definition, $\sigma_{I,II}$, to it. Obviously, we get the same coefficient as in my new definition of σ_1.

Theorem 3. If $\Phi(V_I, V_{II}) \equiv F(V_I, \overline{V}_2 V_{II}, \ldots, \overline{V}_n V_{II})$,

$$\sigma_{I,II} = -\frac{\Phi_I \Phi_{II}}{\Phi \Phi_{I,II}} = -\frac{F_1}{V_1 F_{11}}\left(1 - \frac{F_1 V_1}{F}\right) = \sigma_1$$

at any initial point $(V_I, V_{II}; V_1, \ldots, V_n) = (V_1, 1; V_1, \overline{V}_2, \ldots, \overline{V}_n)$.

To prove this, merely note that $1 - \alpha_1$ and $1 - \alpha_I$ are the same thing, and so are the *ceteris paribus* marginal-productivity elasticities $E_{V_1 F_1}$ and $E_{V_I F_I}$.

Alternative Approach via Hicks Price-composite Factor. One of Sir John's most interesting contributions to economic theory has been the use of price-composite commodities. These are in a certain sense dual to the Leontief-Ricardo physical doses of commodities, and also have well-behaved properties. This approach leads to a somewhat different set of E-of-S coefficients $(\sigma_1^*, \sigma_2^*, \ldots, \sigma_n^*)$, and to various intermediate coefficients.

Mechanically, we can abruptly define any one of the new set of coefficients simply as follows:

$$\sigma_i^* = -\left(\frac{\partial \log V_i}{\partial \log W_i}\right)_{\substack{\text{certain other } V\text{'s constant} \\ \text{certain other } W\text{'s constant}}} (1 - \alpha_i) \tag{14}$$

The first term on the right represents a factor-demand elasticity. Which factor demand? That depends on what our *ceteris paribus* assumptions are. Thus, let $i = 1$ and suppose we decide to hold $V_2, \ldots, V_r$ constant and hold $W_{r+1}, \ldots, W_n$ constant, thereby letting

$$(W_2, \ldots, W_r, V_{r+1}, \ldots, V_n)$$

vary *mutatis mutandis* as W_1 and V_1 vary, varying as they will and must to maintain the optimizing marginal product-conditions

$$W_1 = \frac{\partial F(V_1, \ldots, V_n)}{\partial V_1}$$

$$W_2 = \frac{\partial F(V_1, \ldots, V_n)}{\partial V_2}$$

$$\cdots\cdots\cdots\cdots$$

$$W_n = \frac{\partial F(V_1, \ldots, V_n)}{\partial V_n}. \tag{15}$$

Clearly, for $r = n$, we are holding *all* other physical inputs constant and we are back in my original (Leontief equivalent) case. This could be considered the extreme short-run case, where no other factors adjust.

At the other extreme is the hypothetical long-run in which a (small) industry can hire all other factors at constant factor prices. (This is hypothetical, because in many situations the ironical remark, 'You should live so long!' is indicated.) For this extreme and a homogeneous production function, *all* the elasticities end up infinite! Why? Because any last real factor price is completely determined–along a horizontal, infinitely-elastic demand curve–once *all* other real factor prices are stipulated, as the recent concept of the Factor-Price Frontier makes evident.

Between the extreme short run and the extreme long run, we can define a whole set of intermediate runs. And by the Le Chatelier principle, it is easy to show that

$$0 \leqslant \sigma_1 = [\sigma_1^*]_{r=n} \leqslant [\sigma_1^*]_{r=n-1} \leqslant \cdots \leqslant [\sigma_1^*]_{r=2} \leqslant [\sigma_1^*]_{r=1} = \infty . \qquad (16)$$

It is gratifying that all these various approaches end up in general agreement with Sir John's recent afterthoughts on his seminal *Theory of Wages* (Hicks, 1932).

II. *Intercommodity Substitution and Homothetic General Equilibrium*

The Multi-commodity Problem. From the beginning of his 1932 discussion, Sir John Hicks had clearly in mind that an increased scarcity of one factor would result in less of a rise in its price if people can shift away from consuming goods which use much of it in favor of consuming now-relatively-cheapened goods that use little of it. Since Machlup's 1935 discussion of this problem, it has tended to be eclipsed by more technical analysis of single commodity cases (like my Part I).

It is no joke to have to analyze the incidence of anything, a tax change or a factor-supply change, in a full general equilibrium model. What I propose to do here, very briefly, is to exhibit a beautifully simple special case of general equilibrium where intercommodity substitutions become transparently obvious.

Uniform, Homothetic Tastes. Heroically, assume with me that all people have the same tastes whether rich or poor, so that every dollar gets spent always in the same way. This is known to require uniform, homothetic indifference contours, which can be summarized by a cardinal utility function that is homogeneous of the first degree, and which will be concave in the well-behaved case. Thus

$$u = u[Q_1, Q_2, \ldots, Q_m] \equiv \lambda^{-1} u[\lambda Q_1, \lambda Q_2, \ldots, \lambda Q_m], \qquad (17)$$

where Q_j represents the total amount produced and consumed of the jth commodity. u has all the properties of a neoclassical production function and, as will be seen, plays the role of real social output (or real-dollar output), being able by virtue of the homotheticity axiom to solve rigorously the traditional index-number problem.

Each commodity Q_j is assumed to be produced by a concave, homogeneous-of-first-degree production function, that depends on the

$$[V_{1j}, V_{2j}, \ldots, V_{nj}] = [V_{ij}]$$

inputs devoted to its industry; and of course the total V_i of the ith factor is allocated among the m commodity industries: hence

$$Q_j = F^j(V_{1j}, \ldots, V_{nj}). \qquad (j = 1, 2, \ldots, m) \qquad (18)$$

$$V_i \geqslant V_{i1} + V_{i2} + \ldots + V_{im}, \qquad (i = 1, 2, \ldots, n) \qquad (19)$$

Competitive equilibrium is led, as if by an Invisible Hand, to solve the following maximum problem:

Subject to $V_i \geqslant V_{i1} + \ldots + V_{im}$

$$\underset{\{V_{ij}\}}{\text{Max }} u[F_1(V_{11}, \ldots, V_{n1}), \ldots, F_m(V_{1m}, \ldots, V_{nm})] = U(V_1, V_2, \ldots, V_n).$$
$$(20)$$

This last function, which depicts (maximized) real social output as being (optimally) manufactured out of available factor-input aggregates, is easily seen to have *all* the properties of a neoclassical physical production function. Thus, all of the single-good analysis of Part I's $F(V_1, \ldots, V_n)$ can be applied without qualification to $U(V_1, \ldots, V_n)$.

In particular, I can define total elasticity-of-substitution coefficients $(\bar{\sigma}_1, \ldots, \bar{\sigma}_n)$ that already take into account inter-commodity as well as intra-commodity substitutions, namely

$$\bar{\sigma}_i = -\left[\frac{U_i}{V_i U_{ii}}\right]\left[1 - \frac{V_i U_i}{U}\right] = -E_{V_i U_i}[1 - \alpha_i] \quad (i = 1, \ldots, n) \quad (21)$$

where the subscript notation writes $\partial U / \partial V_i$ as U_i, etc.

Intuition tells us that these total $\bar{\sigma}$'s will tend to be (if anything) more elastic than the single-good technical E-of-S applied to a single industry production factor $F^j(\cdot)$. Thus, suppose there were no technical substitutions possible, so that every production function were of the fixed-coefficient form

$$Q_j = \text{Min}\left[\frac{V_{1j}}{a_{1j}}, \ldots, \frac{V_{nj}}{a_{nj}}\right]. \tag{22}$$

Then, provided the input-requirements vectors $[a_{1j}, \ldots, a_{nj}]$ were not all proportional (and thus of equal factor intensity), the fact that

$$u(Q_1, \ldots, Q_m)$$

permits some smooth inter-commodity substitution would permit $(\bar{\sigma}_1, \ldots, \bar{\sigma}_n)$ to be positive rather than zero. Of course, if all industry production functions were of the same factor intensities, with

$$F_1(x_1, \ldots, x_n) \equiv F_2(x_1, \ldots, x_n) \equiv \ldots \equiv F_m(x_1, \ldots, x_n), \tag{23}$$

changes in a factor total, like V_1, would have no effect on relative commodity prices and induce no inter-commodity substitutions. In such a singular case, my total $\bar{\sigma}_i$ would be identical with, and not greater than, the common intra-industry technical σ_i.

Intuitive Conclusions. If one works out the algebra of total $\bar{\sigma}_i$ of $U(V_1, \ldots, V_m)$ in terms of the technical σ's of the component

$$F^j(V_{1j}, \ldots, V_{nj})$$

functions and the consumer substitution properties of the $u(Q_1, \ldots, Q_m)$ function, then common sense rules will be verified:

Total elasticity of substitution is greater

(1) the greater is intra-industry technical substitutability in the $F^j(\cdot)$ functions;

(2) the greater is consumer substitutability in the $u(\cdot)$ function;

(3) the greater is the difference in factor intensities among industries.

To highlight the final factor-intensity point, consider the singular case where each industry uses a single input unique to itself, or

$$Q_j = F^j(V_{jj}) = \frac{V_j}{a_{jj}} = 1 \cdot V_j \text{ by convention .}$$

Then only inter-commodity substitutions by consumer come into play, and all of the substitutability comes from the consumer side. In this limiting case

$$U(V_1, \ldots, V_m) \equiv u(V_1, \ldots, V_m) \tag{24}$$

and the total elasticity of substitution

$$\bar{\sigma}_i = -\frac{u_i}{V_i U_{ii}}\left[1 - \frac{V_i u_i}{u}\right] \tag{25}$$

becomes purely a consumption coefficient.

Equilibrium Conditions. All of the 1932 and 1963 Hicksian insights were confirmed by the analysis. For completeness, I write down the optimality conditions that enable us to define the $U(V_1, \ldots, V_m)$ function of (20). We solve the indicated Kuhn-Tucker problem in (concave) non-linear programming, by attaining the saddle-point conditions for

$$u[F^1(V_{11}, \ldots, V_{n1}), \ldots, F^m(V_{1m}, \ldots, V_{nm})] + \sum_{i=1}^{n} w_i\left[V_i - \sum_{j=1}^{m} V_{ij}\right]. \tag{26}$$

Necessary and sufficient conditions for this are that the non-negative primal variable (V_{ij}) and dual variables (w_i) satisfy the inequalities

$$\frac{\partial u}{\partial Q_j}\frac{\partial F^j}{\partial V_{ij}} - w_i \leqslant 0, (i = 1, \ldots, n; j = 1, \ldots, m) \tag{27}$$

$$V_i - \sum_{j=1}^{m} V_{ij} \geqslant 0$$

$$\sum_{1}^{n}\left(V_i - \sum_{j=1}^{m} V_{ij}\right)w_j + \sum_{i=1}^{n}\sum_{j=1}^{m}\left(w_i - \frac{\partial u}{\partial Q_j}\frac{\partial F^j}{\partial V_{ij}}\right)V_{ij} = 0$$

$$w_i \geqslant 0, V_{ij} \geqslant 0.$$

In the regular, smooth case of classical interior maximization, this becomes equivalent to

$$\frac{\partial u}{\partial Q_j}\frac{\partial F^j}{\partial V_{ij}} - w_i = 0 \qquad (i = 1, \ldots, n; j = 1, \ldots, m) \tag{28}$$

$$V_i - \sum_{j=1}^{m} V_{ij} = 0$$

and $\qquad \dfrac{\partial U}{\partial V_i} = w_i.$ \hfill (29)

My uniform-homothetic case is manageable in general equilibrium form because all income effects are nicely balanced out. As soon as we permit different individuals to have different tastes and factor endowments, income effects enormously complicate the general equilibrium analysis. Thus, it is well known that the demand for a factor may be positively sloped when income effects are sufficiently badly-behaved. Indeed if the owners of a factor happen to have particularly strong tastes for commodities that require this factor in great intensity, we can easily encounter multiplicity of equilibria and instability: 'bootstrap operations' are then possible in which it pays much for owners of a factor to shift their demands a little toward goods requiring themselves. (This can provide an economic rationale for campaigns by Negroes or other minority groups to spend money 'among your own people'.) One must not ignore hard problems, or call them non-statical, just because they are hard.

I shall mention only one extreme case of unbalanced income effects. Suppose each factor spent all its money on a single good and that this happened in every case to be produced by that factor alone. Then the conditions of equilibrium would degenerate into $m = n$ entirely independent markets: that is, equilibrium would simply entail

$$Q_i = \frac{V_i}{a_{ii}} \qquad (i = 1, \ldots, n = m). \tag{30}$$

Relative prices and relative social shares are quite indeterminate. Although the intra-industry technical elasticity of substitution is in every case infinite, a total elasticity of substitution will be undefined.

I conclude with the observation that unrestricted general equilibrium is very complicated. And if you ask a very complicated question you must expect its answer to involve a very complicated analysis.

III. *Historical Postscript*

J. R. Hicks (1932, pp. 117–20, 241–7) presents the original definition of σ for the two-factor case, both as an indicator of relative shares and as a component of elasticity of derived factor demand. Joan Robinson (1933, pp. 256–62, 330) gives the definition of $\sigma^{(R)}$ for the two-factor case, and proves that a monopolist will have $\partial V_2 / \partial w_1 \gtreqless 0$ depending on whether product demand elasticity is greater or less than the elasticity of substitution. A. C. Pigou (1934) and D. G. Champernowne (1935) show how complicated becomes the incidence of a factor price change in an n-variable model of partial elasticities of substitution. See R. G. D. Allen (1938, pp. 341–5, 372–4, 504–5, 512–13, 520) for n-variable generalization in terms of partial elasticities of substitution $[\sigma_{ij}]$, along with reference to Hicks-Allen consumption measures. R. F. Kahn (1933) proves the equivalence of the two definitions in the case of 2-factor constant returns. J. R. Hicks (1963, p. 373) provides a compact proof.

The formulas for $(\sigma_1, \ldots, \sigma_n)$ of my lectures come close to Hicks's (1963, pp. 339–40, 378–81, 293–5) discussions. For $n = 2$, equation (8) of p. 379 is identical with my (3), and below (8) of p. 379 appears the equivalent to my (4), which is obviously derivable from 1932 formulas on pp. 244 and 246 when elasticities of product demand and of other factor supply are set respectively equal to infinity and zero. Applying his (8) definition to $\Phi(V_I, V_{II}) = F(V_I, V_{II}\bar{V}_2, \ldots, V_{II}\bar{V}_n)$, Hicks will arrive at the same as my (σ_i). To get $[\sigma_1^*]_r$ we apply (8) or my (3) to $\psi_r(V_I, V_{II})$ defined as

$$\text{Subject to } w_{r+}V_{r+1} + \ldots + w_n V_n \leqslant V_{II}$$

$$\underset{V_{r+1}, \ldots, V_n}{\text{Max}} \quad F(V_I, V_{II}\bar{V}_2, \ldots, V_{II}\bar{V}_r, V_{r+1}, \ldots, V_n)$$

$$= \psi(V_I, V_{II}; \bar{V}_2, \ldots, \bar{V}_r; w_{r+1}, \ldots, w_n)$$

$$= \psi_r(V_I, V_{II}).$$

The discussion of pp. 377–81 is couched in terms suggesting that

$$\Phi(V_I, V_{II}) \equiv F[V_1, V_{II}(V_2, \ldots, V_n)],$$

which would presuppose a special 'tree' property on F; but I doubt that such an implication is intended. For discussion of the Le Chatelier principle see P. A. Samuelson (1947, pp. 36, 38, 81, 168; 1966, chapters 42–4).

For intercommodity substitution of my Part II, see Hicks (1932, p. 120; 1963, pp. 297–9, 340–1, 381–4). F. Machlup (1935) has also emphasized this general equilibrium approach. Incidentally, my strong case of uniform-homothetic tastes (or of every dollar spent in the same way, anywhere) is known to be the only case where 'collective indifference curves' can *rigorously* generate observed market equilibria involving multiple individuals. (Samuelson, 1966, chapter 78). From the non-classical writings on the economic theory of index numbers, by Könus, Staehle, Frisch, Leontief, and others, it is known that unitary income elasticities are mandatory if there is to be a price index holding for all income levels.

Rather than burden the text with the algebra of computing my total $\bar{\sigma}_i$, I present here a brief summary that ought to be relatable to the 1963 algebra of pp. 381–4.

At a critical point where

$$\frac{\partial F(x_1, \ldots, x_n; \alpha)}{\partial x_i} = 0, \tag{31}$$

we can evaluate the total change in F due to a parameter α, $F(\alpha)$, by the simplifying formulas (Samuelson, 1947, pp. 34–5).

$$F'(\alpha) = F_x\frac{dx}{d\alpha} + F_\alpha = 0 + F_\alpha \tag{32}$$

$$F''(\alpha) = \frac{d}{d\alpha}\left[F_x\frac{dx}{d\alpha}\right] + F_{\alpha\alpha} + F_{\alpha x}\frac{dx}{d\alpha} = 0 + F_{\alpha\alpha} - F_{\alpha x}F_{xx}^{-1}F_{x\alpha}, \tag{33}$$

where $[f_x, f_\alpha] = [\partial f/\partial x_i, \partial f/\partial\alpha]$

$$\begin{bmatrix} f_{xx} & f_{x\alpha} \\ f_{\alpha x} & f_{\alpha\alpha} \end{bmatrix} = \begin{bmatrix} \dfrac{\partial^2 f}{\partial x_i\partial x_j} & \dfrac{\partial^2 f}{\partial x_i\partial\alpha} \\ \dfrac{\partial^2 f}{\partial\alpha\partial x_j} & \dfrac{\partial^2 f}{\partial\alpha^2} \end{bmatrix}.$$

If f is identified with the Lagrangian saddlepoint expression of (26), we can calculate

$$[\partial^2 U/\partial V_i\partial V_j] = [\partial w_i/\partial V_j]$$

expression by the above kinds of formulas; this will involve square matrices of no less than $nm+n$ columns.

To reduce the problem to matrices of only $n+m$ columns I write the equilibrium conditions with the help of the minimum-unit-cost-of-pioduction functions $A^j(w_1, \ldots, w_m)$, which are dual to the $F^j(V_{1j}\ldots, V_{nj})$ production functions, being concave and homogeneous of the first degree and known to have as partial derivatives

$$\frac{\partial A^j}{\partial w_i} = A_i^j = a_{ij}. \tag{34}$$

Equilibrium is defined by

$$V_i = \sum_{k=1}^{m} A_i^k(w_1, \ldots, w_n)Q_k \qquad (i = 1, \ldots, n) \tag{35}$$

$$0 = A^j(w_1, \ldots, w_n) - \partial u[Q_1, \ldots, Q_m]/\partial Q_j \qquad (j = 1, \ldots, m),$$

with

$$\begin{bmatrix} \partial w_i \\ \partial V_j \end{bmatrix} = \begin{bmatrix} \sum_k A_{ij}^k Q_k & a_{ij} \\ a_{ji} & -u_{ij} \end{bmatrix}^{-1} \begin{bmatrix} I \\ 0 \end{bmatrix},$$

a negative semi-definite matrix by virtue of $[u_{ij}]$ and $[A_{ij}^k]$ all having that property.

For the special case where $m = n$, and $[a_{ij}]$ is a non-singular matrix of constants (the fixed-coefficient case), with an inverse $[a_{ij}]^{-1} = [a^{(ij)}]$, we can compute directly

$$\left[\frac{\partial^2 U}{\partial V_i \partial V_j}\right] = \left[\sum_{r=1}^{m} \sum_{s=1}^{m} \frac{\partial^2 u}{\partial Q_r \partial Q_s} a^{(ir)} a^{(js)}\right]. \tag{36}$$

This shows that total $\bar{\sigma}_t$ is finite and positive, even when every technical production function involves zero substitutability; it is the $[\partial^2 u / \partial Q_r \partial Q_s]$ inter-commodity substitution that produces the over-all elasticity of factor demand, in confirmation of economic intuition. (It will be noted that I have not found it useful to handle the homothetic case by separating out income and substitution effects. A direct approach seems more helpful.)

ACKNOWLEDGMENTS

I should like to thank my colleagues and former students Eytan Sheshinski and David Levhari for helpful criticisms of this paper and acknowledge financial aid from the National Science Foundation.

134

USING FULL DUALITY TO SHOW THAT SIMULTANEOUSLY ADDITIVE DIRECT AND INDIRECT UTILITIES IMPLIES UNITARY PRICE ELASTICITY OF DEMAND

By Paul A. Samuelson[1]

The "indirect utility function," a concept associated with Hotelling, Roy, Houthakker, and others, gives the maximized value of consumer's ordinal utility in function of the prices and income of his budget constraint: namely, $\phi^*(p_1/I, \ldots, P_n/I) =$ Max $\phi(x_1, \ldots, x_n)$ with respect to x's satisfying the budget constraint $\sum_1^n (p_j/I)x_j = 1$. Writing $p_j/I = y_j$, $\Phi(Y) = -\phi^*(Y)$, it follows that $N(X; Y) = \phi(X) + \Phi(Y) \le 0$ along $\sum_1^n x_j y_j = 1$, equalling zero only along the equilibrium demand relations $X = X(Y)$, $Y = Y(X) \equiv X^{-1}(X)$. It is shown that $\phi(X)$ and $\Phi(Y)$ are completely dual functions, one possessing *all* the general properties of the other. Just as ϕ's partial derivatives give $\phi_i/\phi_j = y_i/y_j$, Φ's give $\Phi_i/\Phi_j = x_i/x_j$, etc. Numerous theorems are proved, such as: if either of ϕ and Φ has homothetic contours, so does the other; if both can be stretched into an additive form, they are both homothetic and belong to the so-called constant-elasticity – of-substitution family of Solow *et al.*, a result already anticipated by Bergson in 1936; if the above can hold with no stretching required, we are in the "pure Bernoulli-Marshall" or Cobb-Douglas case of unitary own-elasticity and other demonstrated equivalent properties. Finally, dual functions of mixed variables, $\phi(y_1, \ldots, y_r; x_{r+1}, \ldots, x_n)$ and $\Phi(x_1, \ldots, y_r; y_{r+1}, \ldots, y_n)$, are defined by Legendre transformations and the properties of "demand under rationing" are deduced from them.

1. summary

In an interesting paper[2] Houthakker has investigated some of the empirical implications of ordinal utility that can be written as a sum of independent functions of each commodity. In addition to this familiar case of "direct additivity," he has investigated the statistically convenient case of "indirect additivity" in which the indirect utility function, which records the maximized amount of attainable (ordinal) utility that a consumer can achieve for prescribed prices and income, can be written as a sum of independent functions of the ratios of prices to income. The present paper will show the limited compatibility of direct and indirect additivity: for them to hold *simultaneously* implies the special demand function $x_i p_i = k_i I$; for them both to hold, "non-simultaneously," implies demand belongs to the special Bergson family. These results may be of some limited interest for their own sake. Of perhaps greater interest, is the exploitation of the full duality properties of the direct and indirect utility functions, which demonstrates a technique that can be useful in a great number of more difficult problems, such as, a summarization of all kinds of mixed utility functions that are intermediate be-

[1] I must gladly acknowledge financial aid from the Ford Foundation, and over the years priceless intellectual aid from Hendrik S. Houthakker, with whom I have had innumerable oral discussions that have added much to my understanding of the subject.

[2] H. S. Houthakker, "Additive Preferences," *Econometrica*: An Issue in Honor of Ragnar Frisch, Vol. 28, No. 2, April, 1960, pp. 244–257.

tween the direct and the indirect polar cases and that summarize conveniently the properties of demand functions under rationing.

2. REGULARITY ASSUMPTIONS

Let $U=\phi(x_1, \ldots, x_n)=\phi(X)$ be a *regular* utility indicator function of the non-negative goods X with the following convenient properties. (1) The set of points which are at least as good as a given level of utility are to form a *strictly* convex set, i.e., $\phi(X) \geqslant \overline{U}$ defines a strictly convex set in the X space. (2) Increasing any good alone insures that the level of satisfaction goes up, i.e., $\phi(X)$ is a strictly monotonic increasing function of each of its arguments. These first two assumptions guarantee that an individual who is subject to the budget constraint $\Sigma p_i x_i \equiv P'X=I>0$, will attain his maximum feasible level of satisfaction at a point X that is a single-valued homogeneous function of degree zero in prices and income: $X=X(P; I)$.

We can add further regularity assumptions to insure that these demand functions can be uniquely inverted to give all p_i/p_j price ratios as single-valued functions of quantities. (3) All ordinal indicators of utility are to be everywhere continuously twice differentiable so as to form a "smooth" preference field and to ensure the differentiability of the $X(P; I)$ demand functions. (4) To avoid boundary maxima with the implication that several equilibrium price ratios can correspond to a boundary point, any utility indicator $\phi(X)$ must be less when any good is zero than when all goods are positive (however small), i.e., $\phi(A) > \phi(B)$ if A represents a point with all goods positive and B another point in which at least one good is zero.

Needless to say, these regularity assumptions can be lightened if appropriate modifications in the arguments are made. But they do provide a convenient way to avoid various complications initially.

3. DUALITY

The demand functions $X(P; I)$ provide the unique solution to the following problem:

(1) $$\max_{\{P'X\leqslant I\}} \phi(X)=\phi^*(P; I)=\phi(X(P; I)),$$

where ϕ^* is the "indirect utility function." Under our regularity assumptions, the demand functions are the unique solutions to the familiar Gossen relations:

(2) $$\frac{\phi_1(x_1, \ldots, x_n)}{p_1} = \frac{\phi_2(x_1, \ldots, x_n)}{p_2} = \ldots = \frac{\phi_n(x_1, \ldots, x_n)}{p_n}$$

$$= \frac{\sum\limits_{1}^{n} \phi_i(x_1, \ldots, x_n)x_i}{I},$$

where the subscript in ϕ_j denotes the partial derivatives with respect to the jth variable and where in (1) we can drop the inequality sign in recognition of the fact that all income will be assuredly spent on the desirable goods. Note too that from now on we need only consider *positive* p's and x's. These n equations determine the n optimal x's as single-valued demand functions of the prescribed income and price parameters, even though the common value of (2)'s ratios is not invariant to the choice of ordinal indicator of utility.

Using the convenient new relative price variables, $y_i = p_i/I$, and the notation $X(Y; 1) \equiv X(Y)$, $\phi^*(Y; 1) \equiv \phi^*(Y)$ we can rewrite (1) and (2) as

(1')
$$\underset{\{Y'X=1\}}{\text{Max}} \ \phi(X) = \phi^*(Y) = \phi(X(Y)),$$

(2')
$$\frac{\phi_1(X)}{y_1} = \frac{\phi_2(X)}{y_2} = \ldots = \frac{\phi_n(X)}{y_n} = \sum_1^n \phi_i(X)x_i.$$

Now define a new fundamental function of both x's and y's,

$$N(x_1, \ldots, x_n; y_1, \ldots, y_n) = N(X; Y) = \phi(X) - \phi^*(Y).$$

Although its exact form will depend upon which indicator of ordinal utility is used, this "excess utility" has the property that it is always negative unless you have achieved the optimal x's for the prescribed y's. *And* vice versa! Thus, for $Y'X = X'Y = 1$,

(3)
$$N = \phi(X) - \phi^*(Y) \leqslant \underset{\{Y'X=1\}}{\text{Max}} \ [\phi(X) - \phi^*(Y)] \quad \equiv \quad 0.$$
$$ \{ \underset{Y'X=1}{X,Y} \}$$

Note that all this is true for *any* prescribed Y, so that an equilibrium configuration of quantities and prices (X^*, Y^*), which belongs to the n dimensional equilibrium subspace of the $2n$ dimensional space of all x's and y's is defined by solutions of the symmetric formulations

$$\underset{\{\underset{Y'X=1}{X,Y}\}}{\text{Max}} \ N(X, Y) \quad \text{or} \quad N(X, Y) = 0, \ Y'X = 1 \ ;$$

or by either of the following dual problems admitting of a unique solution

$$\underset{\{Y'X=1\}}{\text{Max}} \ N(X, Y) \quad \text{or} \quad \underset{\{X'Y=1\}}{\text{Max}} \ N(X, Y).$$

Because of the noticeable complete symmetry between $\phi(X)$ and $-\phi^*(Y)$, it will be convenient from now on[3] to work with the dual functions

$$\phi(X) \text{ and } \Phi(Y) \equiv -\phi^*(Y), \text{ with } N \equiv \phi(X) + \Phi(Y).$$

By using the negative of the indirect utility function, we keep both problems a maximum problem enjoying perfect symmetry.

[3] Houthakker function $\psi(Z_1, \ldots, Z_n) \equiv \psi(I/p_1, \ldots, I/p_n)$ is related to my Φ by the identity $-\Phi(y_1, \ldots, y_n) \equiv \psi(1/y_1, \ldots, 1/y_n)$. In statistical analysis of budget data, ψ is very convenient; for theoretical purposes of duality, Φ is useful.

Hence, the equilibrium set of variables is defined by solutions to *either* of the dual problems:

$$(1'') \qquad \operatorname*{Max}_{\{Y'X=1\}} \phi(X) \quad \text{or} \quad \operatorname*{Max}_{\{X'Y=1\}} \Phi(Y),$$

where it is evident that Φ has exactly the same regularity properties postulated for ϕ. (Thus, Φ's smoothness follows from the differentiability properties of ϕ and of the demand functions; Φ's monotonicity from that of ϕ; etc.)

The complete duality of (ϕ, X) and (Φ, Y) having been established, we can at once write down the dual relations to $(2')$:

$$(2'') \qquad \frac{\Phi_1(Y)}{x_1} = \frac{\Phi_2(Y)}{x_2} = \ldots = \frac{\Phi_n(Y)}{x_n} = \sum_1^n \Phi_i(Y) y_i \,.$$

It is true, but perhaps not obvious, that at any equilibrium point the common value of the ratios in $(2'')$ is precisely the same as the common value of the ratios in $(2')$, each being the marginal utility of a *percentage* increase in income, $\partial \phi^*(P; I)/\partial \log I$. Later we shall derive a more general result that contains this one as a special case.

Just as $(2')$ led to the demand functions $X = X(Y)$ relating quantities to relative prices, $(2'')$ demonstrates the existence of single-valued "inverse" demand functions relating relative prices to quantities, $Y = Y(X)$. So

$$X = X(Y) \text{ and } Y = Y(X) \text{ imply } Y(X) \equiv X^{-1}(X) \text{ and } X(Y) \equiv Y^{-1}(Y) \,.$$

It is of interest that the invertability of these demand functions can be deduced without reference to the Jacobians of implicit function theory; also that invertability implies smoothness of ϕ and Φ, and vice versa.

The content of $(2')$ and $(2'')$ for equilibrium configurations can also be summed up in familiar dual relations:

$$(4) \qquad \frac{\phi_i(X)}{\phi_j(X)} = \frac{y_i}{y_j}, \quad \sum_1^n y_k x_k = 1, \quad \frac{\Phi_i(Y)}{\Phi_j(Y)} = \frac{x_i}{x_j}\,.$$

4. DIRECT AND INDIRECT HOMOGENEITY

Some necessary relations between ϕ and Φ can be directly derived. Thus, consider the theoretically interesting, but alas empirically untrue, case where the consumer facing given prices always divides his expenditure among goods in the same way at low as he does at high incomes. In this special case of unitary income elasticities, doubling income doubles all the quantities. The indifference surfaces are known to be "homothetic," i.e., each surface is just a radial blowup of any other surface. And it is intuitively obvious that there is a way of numbering these indifference surfaces so that the indicator of utility, $g(X)$, can be written as a homogeneous function of degree one in the quantities, doubling when all quantities double. In this case doubling income is just like halving all the Y variables; so halving all the Y variables, which corresponds to doubling direct utility, does double indirect utility g^* and the dual G. Hence, G is a homogeneous function of degree minus one in its arguments Y. Being homogeneous of some degree, its iso-contours are also homothetic.

Hence, when either ϕ or Φ is homothetic, so is its dual. "Direct homogeneity" implies "indirect homogeneity" and vice versa. If ϕ is homogeneous of degree m, Φ is homogeneous of degree $-m$.

It is instructive to prove this commonsense conclusion mathematically. Any one contour of ϕ can always be written in the form

$$x_1 + R(x_2, \ldots, x_n) = 0$$

where R_i represents the positive marginal rate of substitution between good i and the *numeraire* good 1, and where $[R_{ij}]$ has the regularity convexity property of being negative definite.

In the homothetic case we can call this arbitrary contour unity and get the indicator of utility $g(X)$ that is homogeneous of the first degree by solving the following implicit equation for g as a unique homogeneous function of all the x's

$$\frac{x_1}{g} + R\left(\frac{x_2}{g}, \ldots, \frac{x_n}{g}\right) = 0 .$$

For convenience work with $\phi(X) = \log g(X)$ and write out (2′)

$$\frac{\phi_i(X)}{y_i} = \sum_1^n \phi_j(X) x_j, \quad \text{or} \quad \frac{g_i(X)}{g(X) y_i} = \frac{\sum_1^n g_i x_i}{g} = \frac{g}{g} = 1 .$$

Hence, we can eliminate any proportionality constants and immediately write down our demand functions as partial derivatives of the function ϕ and of a function which will soon be recognized as its dual Φ:

$$y_i = \frac{\partial \phi(x_1, \ldots, x_n)}{\partial x_i}$$

(5) $\hspace{4cm}$ $(i = 1, \ldots, n)$

$$x_i = \frac{\partial \Phi(y_1, \ldots, y_n)}{\partial y_i}$$

where the latter functions are the inverse of the former, being connected by $[\phi_{ij}]^{-1} = [\Phi_{ij}]$. It can be verified that these Hessian matrices are both negative definite and that all the functions in (5) are homogeneous of degree minus one in their arguments. This homogeneity property of $\partial \phi / \partial x_i$ follows directly from ϕ's definition. The similar property of $\partial \Phi / \partial y_i$ can be verified by inversion, or more simply as follows. Unitary income elasticities imply our demand functions can be written

$$x_i = X^i(p_1, \ldots, p_n; I) = X^i\left(\frac{p_1}{I}, \ldots, \frac{p_n}{I}; 1\right)$$

$$= If^i(p_1, \ldots, p_n) = f^i\left(\frac{p_1}{I}, \ldots, \frac{p_n}{I}\right),$$

where the new f functions have to be homogeneous of degree minus one in all their arguments if the X functions are to be homogeneous of degree zero in all their arguments. By calculating the symmetric Slutsky matrix $[X_j^i + X^i X_I^i]$ we can easily verify that $f_j^i \equiv f_i^j$ and the f's are indeed the partial derivatives of some existent function, as we have already seen. By duality, if the $Y(X)$ functions are derivatives of ϕ, then the $X(Y)$ functions must be derivatives of Φ, a fact that can be independently verified by showing that the line integral $\Sigma_1^n \int f^i(y_1, \ldots, y_n) dy_i$ satisfies integrability conditions which make it a function that, for proper choice of integration constant, is identical with $\Phi = \log G(Y)$, where G and g are duals.

5. DIRECT AND INDIRECT ADDITIVITY

Homogeneity is a severe restriction in that it converts a problem which depends upon arbitrary function of n variables into one that depends only upon an arbitrary function of $(n-1)$ variables. A much more severe restriction is that of direct additivity. Direct additivity, by definition, means ϕ can be written as a sum of n functions of single variable only as $\phi(x_1, \ldots, x_n) = \phi_1(x_1) + \phi_2(x_2) + \cdots + \phi_n(x_n)$.

Houthakker's "indirect additivity" is similarly to mean that $\Phi(y_1, \ldots, y_n) = \Phi_1(y_1) + \Phi_2(y_2) + \cdots + \Phi_n(y_n)$.

Although homogeneity of ϕ did imply homogeneity of Φ, it is easy from one of an infinity of counterexamples to verify Houthakker's assertion that direct additivity does not imply indirect additivity; by duality, indirect additivity does not imply direct additivity.

But, are direct and indirect additivity simultaneously compatible? Houthakker implies they are, but shows that a severe necessary condition for this is that one of the dual pair (ϕ, Φ), and hence both by our previous demonstration, has to be homogeneous. Still this does not dispose of the matter since it could be that other necessary conditions for compatibility have to be satisfied and that they are inconsistent with this condition specified by Houthakker. Indeed, unless we can find at least one case where direct and indirect homogeneity and direct and indirect additivity are simultaneously compatible, direct additivity would exclude indirect additivity and vice versa.

The present discussion will clarify this whole matter. In particular, it will answer in the negative Houthakker's open question: granted that direct and indirect additivity imply homogeneity, does homogeneity imply direct and indirect additivity? A single counterexample, such as $\phi = x_1^{\frac{2}{3}} x_2^{\frac{1}{3}} + x_1^{\frac{1}{3}} x_2^{\frac{2}{3}}$, shows this to be false—since for no $f(\phi)$ do we get the sum of independent functions. More precise conditions for compatibility will be demonstrated and they will be seen to be highly restrictive.

Here though, I must make a subtle distinction. We must carefully distinguish between two kinds of compatibility. First, by "*simultaneous* direct and indirect additivity" I shall mean that both ϕ and *its* Φ are to be of additive form:

$$\phi(X) = \sum_1^n a_i \phi_i(x_i), \quad \Phi(Y) = \sum_1^n A_i \Phi_i(y_i) \text{ with } -\phi(X(Y)) = \Phi(Y).$$

As my title indicates, it turns out that the only case that can satisfy this stringent requirement is the special case where the demand functions all have unitary price elasticities: $x_i = k_i(p_i/I)^{-1}, \Sigma_1^n k_i = 1$.

Second, there exists the possible case where ϕ can be written in an additive form, and where Φ, while not itself of additive form, could be put in that form by an admissible monotonic stretching $F(\Phi)$. By duality, the same statements could then be said about Φ and $f(\phi)$. This second wider definition contains, but is not contained in, my first definition. It could be called the case of "direct and indirect additivity" without any use of the word simultaneous. A close reading of Houthakker's paper does not make certain which of these two concepts he may have had in mind. Suffice it to say that while much of his discussion would seem to be in terms of *simultaneous* direct and indirect additivity, his fundamental result in his equation (26)—that homogeneity is implied—can be shown to hold valid for both cases. And, at the very least, I think it can be suggested that most students who prefer ordinal utilities to particular cardinal utilities will find the second wider concept of considerable interest.

6. THE BERGSON FAMILY

At a first glance, or perhaps in view of the complexity of the subject matter I ought to say second glance, it might appear that simultaneous direct and indirect additivity are quite impossible in view of the following three theorems. First, Houthakker's theorem shows that direct and indirect additivity together imply unitary income elasticities or "homogeneity." Second, a well-known theorem of Abram Bergson[4] shows that homogeneity plus additivity means the direct (or

---

[4] Abram Bergson, "Real Income, Expenditure Proportionality, and Frisch's 'New Methods of Measuring Marginal Utility'," *Review of Economic Studies,* Vol. IV, No. 1, October, 1936, pp. 33–52. This Bergson family of functions has been rediscovered in recent years in the field of macroeconomic production functions. It is the "mean value" family of homogeneous production functions of the first degree characterized by constant elasticity of substitution, and includes the Cobb-Douglas as the special case where that elasticity is unity. Cf. R. M. Solow, "A Contribution to the Theory of Economic Growth," *Quarterly Journal of Economics,* LXV (1956), pp. 65–94, especially p. 77; K. Arrow, H. Chenery, B. Minhas, and R. Solow, "Capital-Labor Substitution and Economic Efficiency," *Review of Economics and Statistics,* XLIII (1961), pp. 225–250, especially Part II.

indirect) utility function can be written as a sum of powers of the variables: or in our notation as

$$f(\phi) = b + \sum_1^n a_i x_i^m = \sum_1^n a_i \frac{(x_i^m - 1)}{m}, \quad m < 1$$

(6)

$$F(\Phi) = B + \sum_1^n A_i y_i^M = \sum_1^n A_i \frac{(y_i^M - 1)}{M}, \quad M < 1.$$

Third, I stated above the theorem that if ϕ is homogeneous of degree m, then the corresponding Φ is homogeneous of degree $-m$. Now if ϕ and Φ are *simultaneously* additive, they must then be of the form

$$\phi = \sum_1^n a_i \frac{x_i^m}{m} + b,$$

$$\Phi = \sum A_i \frac{y_i^{-m}}{-m} + B.$$

However, if we calculate the demand functions $X(Y)$ for this Bergson case, we do not find $\phi(X(Y))$ expressible as a power series with $-m$ as exponent. (Example: $\phi = x_1^{\frac{1}{2}} + x_2^{\frac{1}{2}}$, $\Phi = \sqrt{(y_1 + y_2)/y_1 y_2}$.)

Nevertheless, the above argument is misleading in that it blithely ignores the case where $m = 0 = -m$. Years ago, Bergson authorized me to remove a minor blemish from his 1936 formulation so as to blanket in the case where $m = 0$, or more precisely the limit function that holds as $m \to 0$. Because anything raised to the zero power is unity, we must take our limit carefully in (6), namely,

$$(7) \quad \lim_{m \to 0} \sum_1^n a_i \frac{(x_i^m - 1)}{m} = \frac{0}{0} = \sum_1^n a_i \frac{\frac{d}{dm}(x_i^m - 1)}{\frac{d}{dm} m} = \sum_1^n a_i \log_e x_i.$$

In this limiting Bergson case we have lost the power series representation but achieved an even simpler logarithmic formulation, and this gives us, at the end of our digression, the hope that at a third glance there may be found a case—but only a single case!—in which simultaneous direct and indirect additivity are compatible.

7. THE SPECIAL CASE

Actually, Houthakker is perfectly right that direct additivity does not exclude indirect additivity because we can indeed specify an obvious case where both are satisfied. This case happens to be so strongly special as to be interesting from a theoretical viewpoint but trivial for empirical applications. As my title indicates, it is the case of (1) unitary (own) price elasticities; or alternatively, it can be characterized as the case of (2) zero cross-elasticities; or as the case (3) where the proportionate expenditures on the respective goods are everywhere constant regardless of prices and income; or it could be called (4) the Cobb-Douglas consumption case or (5) the Bernoulli case of additive logarithmic utilities; or, as I have elsewhere shown, (6) the "purest Marshallian case" where utilities are independent and the marginal utility of income is strictly constant with respect to any price changes. So severe are its restrictions that all arbitrary functions have disappeared from the problem and only $(n-1)$ expenditure fractions are independently prescribable.

Since each of the above six properties implies all of the others, one could begin in various alternative ways. I propose to begin with what might be observed—the homogeneous of degree zero demand functions

$$(8) \qquad x_i = \frac{k_i I}{p_i}, \quad k_i > 0, \quad \sum_1^n k_i = 1.$$

But are they demand functions derivable from a transitive preference field? We calculate the Slutsky matrix,

$$S = \left[\frac{\partial x_i}{\partial p_j} + x_j \frac{\partial x_i}{\partial I}\right] \equiv \left[-\frac{k_i I}{p_i^2}\delta_{ij} + \frac{k_j k_i}{p_j p_i}I\right],$$

which is indeed symmetric, assuring us that integrability conditions are satisfied. S is also singular with $[p_i, \ldots, p_n]S \equiv 0$ for all (p, I), and every $(n-1)^2$ principal minor is indeed negative definite. As I once proved, this guarantees us the existence of well-behaved indifference contours.

We can rewrite (8) in the completely dual form $x_i y_i = k_i$, and from now on anything I say about the x's could equally well have been said about the y's. In particular,

$$\frac{p_i}{p_1} = \frac{\phi_i(X)}{\phi_1(X)} = \frac{k_i x_i^{-1}}{k_1 x_1^{-1}},$$

and we can write the Pfaffian differential expression and an exact differential and its integral as follows:

$$dx_1 + \frac{k_2 x_2^{-1}}{k_1 x_1^{-1}} dx_2 + \ldots \quad \text{and} \quad \frac{k_1}{x_1} dx_1 + \frac{k_2}{x_2} dx_2 + \ldots = d\phi,$$

$$\phi = k_1 \log x_1 + k_2 \log x_2 + \ldots + k_n \log x_n + c$$
$$= k_1 \log x_1 + k_2 \log x_2 + \ldots + k_n \log x_n - \tfrac{1}{2}(k_1 \log k_1 + \ldots + k_n \log x_n),$$

where the particular constant of integration has been chosen so that ϕ and Φ are exactly self-dual, i.e.,

$$\phi = \sum_1^n k_i \log x_i - \tfrac{1}{2}\sum_1^n k_i \log k_i = \sum_1^n k_i \log (x_i/k_i^{\frac{1}{2}}) \log x_i/k_i^{\frac{1}{2}}$$

and

$$\Phi = \sum_1^n k_i \log y_i - \tfrac{1}{2} \sum_1^n k_i \log k_i = \sum_1^n k_i \log (y_i/k_i^{\frac{1}{2}}) \log y_i/k_i^{\frac{1}{2}} .$$

These utilities are recognizably of the Bernoulli logarithmic form. By setting $f(\phi) = e^\phi$ and $f(\Phi) = e^\Phi$, we easily recognize the Cobb-Douglas forms

$$e^\phi = \prod_1^n \left(\frac{x_i}{k_i^{\frac{1}{2}}}\right)^{k_i} \quad \text{and} \quad e^\Phi = \prod_1^n \left(\frac{y_i}{k_i^{\frac{1}{2}}}\right)^{k_i}, \quad \sum_1^n k_i = 1 .$$

It is easily verified from the demand function that all cross-elasticities are everywhere zero and that all own price elasticities are everywhere unity. (It is also evident that all income elasticities are everywhere unity, but unlike the others this is a necessary but not a sufficient condition.) From the Bernoulli ϕ, we get for the marginal utility of income

$$\lambda_\phi (p_1, \ldots, p_n, I) = \frac{\phi_i(X)}{p_i} = \frac{k_i}{x_i p_i} = \frac{1}{I} ,$$

which is independent of all prices. Finally, relative expenditures $x_i p_i/I$ are from (8) strict constants.

To work backward and prove that any one of these properties implies, as well as is implied by, all the rest is straightforward but time consuming, leading to a variety of solvable functional equations. Let us briefly sketch the derivations.

Constant expenditure proportionalities are directly equivalent to (8) and so all of (8)'s demonstrated consequences do follow from this assumption.

If cross-elasticities are all zero, $x^i(p_1, \ldots, p_n, I)$ evidently take the form $x^i(Y; 1) \equiv R^i(y_i)$. But $\Sigma_1^n y_i R^i(y_i) \equiv 1$ implies $y_i R^i(y_i) = k_i$, and hence $R^i(y_i) = k_i y_i^{-1}$.

If own price elasticities are all unity, $y_i x_i = c_i$, which must be a function of all other y's alone. The functional equation

$$c_1(y_2, \ldots, y_n) + c_2(y_1, y_3, \ldots, y_n) + \ldots + c_n(y_1, \ldots, y_{n-1}) \equiv 1$$

can be easily proved, in the 2-good case, to have the unique solution $c_i \equiv$ constants, k_i, which again leads back to (8). In the 3-good or n-good case, as Professor W. M. Gorman has privately warned me, one has to stipulate integrability conditions on the c's and use their nonnegative property to prove them constants. I omit my proof.

Instead of demonstrating again that $\lambda_\phi = 1/I$ and direct additivity do together imply unitary price and income elasticities, I need only refer to my 1939 proof of this.[5]

8. MIXED UTILITY FUNCTIONS

From the proof that only a member of the Bergson family is eligible for the class

[5] Oscar R. Lange (ed.), *Studies in Mathematical Economics and Econometrics*: in Memory of Henry Schultz, (Chicago, 1942), pp. 75–91.

of simultaneously direct and indirect additivity functions, I have demonstrated by elimination that only the logarithmic form involving unitary price elasticities can have this property. A more direct proof will be of interest, particularly because it involves important new utility functions that are neither direct nor indirect, but which have the more general property of involving *both* quantities and prices. I have used these new "utility potentials" in some unpublished researches unifying the economic theory of rationing; more recently in the Hotelling *Festschrift*,[6] I elucidated the general properties of such Legendre transforms in thermodynamics, economics, or any minimum system. The present exposition involves an appropriate modification of this earlier analysis.

Consider

$$N(X; Y) = N(x, \bar{x}; \bar{y}, y) = \phi(x_1, \ldots, x_r, \bar{x}_{r+1}, \ldots, \bar{x}_n)$$
$$+ \Phi(\bar{y}_1, \ldots, \bar{y}_r, y_{r+1}, \ldots, y_n),$$

where instead of considering either the quantity set $(x_1, \ldots, x_n)$, or the relative price set $(y_1, \ldots, y_n)$ as arbitrarily prescribed, we instead prescribe a mixed set $(\bar{y}_1, \ldots, \bar{y}_r; \bar{x}_{r+1}, \ldots, \bar{x}_n)$, where for each $(i = 1, 2, \ldots, n)$ we pick either a price *or* a quantity. Clearly, for $r = n$, we have the special case of a pure price set, and for $r = 0$ we have a pure quantity set; equally clearly, by a suitable renumbering of variables, every one of the possible 2^n prescribed sets consisting at each stage of either a p_i or its conjugate x_i can be written in the above form.

By earlier arguments, it is evident that the equilibrium n dimensional locus of the $2n$ dimensional total space, can be found by maximizing N with respect to the free variables as of properly prescribed values of $(\bar{y}_1, \ldots, \bar{y}_i; \bar{x}_{r+1}, \ldots, \bar{x}_n)$; i.e., subject to $Y'X = 1$,

$$\underset{\{x, y\}}{\text{Max}} \, N(x, \bar{x}; \bar{y}, y) = 0$$

defines the mixed demand functions

$$x_i = x^i(\bar{y}_1, \ldots, \bar{y}_r; \bar{x}_{r+1}, \ldots, \bar{x}_n) \quad (i = 1, \ldots, r),$$

(9)

$$y_i = y^i(\bar{y}_1, \ldots, \bar{y}_r; \bar{x}_{r+1}, \ldots, \bar{x}_n) \quad (i = r+1, \ldots, n),$$

which of course satisfy the budget identity $\bar{y}'x + \bar{x}'y \equiv 1$.

It may be mentioned that, because of the Giffen's phenomenon inherent in a constrained maximum problem of this type, it may not be possible for the barred quantities to take on completely arbitrary values; and when such phenomena arise, the demand functions may not be single-valued, instead involving various different branches. We shall need only to work with admissible points $(x, \bar{x}; \bar{y}, y)$ belonging to the $[X, Y(X)]$ or $[X(Y), Y]$ equilibrium subspace and shall for sim-

---

[6] Ralph W. Pfouts (ed.), *Essays in Economics and Econometrics*: A Volume in Honor of Harold Hotelling (Chapel Hill), pp. 1–33.

plicity of exposition treat the easier case where the above mixed-demand functions happen all to be single-valued.

It is natural then to introduce the $(n+1)$ utility functions $\phi(\bar{x}_1, \ldots, \bar{x}_n)$, $\phi(\bar{y}_1; \bar{x}_2,$ $\ldots, \bar{x}_n)$, $\phi(\bar{y}_1, \bar{y}_2; \bar{x}_3, \ldots, \bar{x}_n)$, $\ldots$, $\phi(\bar{y}_1, \ldots, \bar{y}_{n-1}; \bar{x}_n)$, $\phi(\bar{y}_1, \ldots, \bar{y}_n) \equiv \phi^*(\bar{y}_1, \ldots,$ $\bar{y}_n) \equiv -\Phi(\bar{y}_1, \ldots, \bar{y}_n)$. In every case the position of the semicolon serves to distinguish among and identify the different functions. Evidently, an exactly dual $(n+1)$ family of functions based upon Φ can be defined and they can be paired with these ϕ functions so as to be identical except with respect to the reversal of sign.

That any ϕ can be interpreted as the utility actually enjoyed by the maximizing individual for the prescribed $(\bar{y}; \bar{x})$ levels can be seen from its definition,

$$\phi(\bar{y}; \bar{x}) \equiv \phi(x^1(\bar{y}; \bar{x}), \ldots, x^r(\bar{y}; \bar{x}), \bar{x}_{r+1}, \ldots, \bar{x}_n), \text{ etc.}$$

From the fact that each ϕ is the maximized utility

$$\underset{(x_1, \ldots, x_r; y_{r+1}, \ldots, y_n)}{\text{Max}} \quad [N(x, \bar{x}; \bar{y}, y) = \phi(x, \bar{x}) + \Phi(\bar{y}, y)] \quad \text{subject to } \sum_1^n y_i x_i = 1$$

we have

$$(10) \qquad \frac{\dfrac{\partial \phi(x, \bar{x})}{\partial x_1}}{\bar{y}_1} = \ldots = \frac{\dfrac{\partial \phi(x, \bar{x})}{\partial x_r}}{\bar{y}_r} = \frac{\dfrac{\partial \Phi(\bar{y}, y)}{\partial y_{r+1}}}{\bar{x}_{r+1}} = \ldots = \frac{\dfrac{\partial \Phi(\bar{y}, y)}{\partial y_n}}{\bar{x}_n} = \lambda,$$

where λ at any equilibrium point is independent of r and can there be written as

$$(11) \qquad \lambda = \sum_1^r \frac{\partial \phi(x, \bar{x})}{\partial x_i} x_i + \sum_{r+1}^n \frac{\partial \Phi(\bar{y}, y)}{\partial y_i} y_i.$$

From a known theorem involving Lagrangean multiplier expressions, $\partial \phi(\bar{y}; \bar{x}) / \partial \bar{x}_{r+i}$ is exactly the same as $\partial L / \partial \bar{x}_{r+i}$ where the Lagrangean L defined by

$$L(x, \bar{x}; \bar{y}, y; \lambda) = \phi(x, \bar{x}) + \Phi(\bar{y}, y) - \lambda \left(\sum_1^r \bar{y}_i x_i + \sum_{r+1}^n \bar{x}_i y_i - 1 \right)$$

is at a stationary value with respect to all unbarred variables. Hence, combining all this with (10), we get

$$\frac{\partial \phi(\bar{y}; \bar{x})}{\partial \bar{x}_{r+i}} = \frac{\partial L}{\partial \bar{x}_{r+1}} = \frac{\partial \phi(x, \bar{x})}{\partial \bar{x}_{r+1}}, \quad \frac{\partial \phi(\bar{y}; \bar{x})}{\partial \bar{y}_i} = \frac{\partial L}{\partial \bar{y}_i} = \frac{\partial \Phi(\bar{y}, y)}{\partial \bar{y}_i},$$

and by symmetry we establish the following generalization of (2), (2″), and (4)'s dual relations

$$(12) \qquad \begin{aligned} \frac{\partial \phi(\bar{y}; \bar{x})}{\partial \bar{x}_{r+i}} &= \lambda y_{r+i}, & \frac{\partial \phi(\bar{y}; \bar{x})}{\partial \bar{y}_i} &= -\lambda x_i, \\[2ex] \frac{\partial \Phi(\bar{y}; \bar{x})}{\partial \bar{x}_{r+i}} &= -\lambda y_i, & \frac{\partial \Phi(\bar{y}; \bar{x})}{\partial \bar{y}_i} &= \lambda x_i, \end{aligned}$$

where λ is as defined by (10).

Let us now apply these findings to the case of simultaneous direct and indirect additivity, where

$$N = \sum_1^n \phi_i(x_i) + \sum_1^n \Phi_i(y_i) .$$

From the variety of relations in (12), we can write

$$\frac{\phi_1'(x_1)}{y_1} = \ldots = \frac{\phi_1'(x_n)}{y_n} = \frac{\Phi_1'(y_1)}{x_1} = \ldots = \frac{\Phi_n'(y_n)}{x_n} ;$$

and we can select any paired relationship

$$(13) \qquad \frac{\phi_i'(x_i)}{y_i} = \frac{\Phi_i'(y_i)}{x_i} .$$

If (13) is to be a valid identity for x_i and y_i independently varied, albeit with equilibrium relations satisfied, clearly the functional equation

$$x_i \phi_i'(x_i) \equiv y_i \Phi_i'(y_i)$$

can be satisfied only with each side of this identity strictly constant. Hence

$$\phi_i'(x_i) = \frac{k_i}{x_i}, \quad \Phi_i'(y_i) = \frac{k_i}{y_i} ;$$

and we verify directly that the only possible case of simultaneous direct and indirect additivity is when[7]

$$\phi = \sum_1^n k_i \log x_i + c , \quad \Phi = \sum k_i \log y_i + C$$

9. NON-SIMULTANEOUS DIRECT AND INDIRECT ADDITIVITY

I have now proved that only in one special case is simultaneous direct and indirect additivity possible. I now consider the less stringent requirement in which there is to exist non-simultaneous direct and indirect additivity, i.e., where ϕ and

---

[7] By setting $c = C = -\frac{1}{2}\Sigma k_i \log k_i$, we actually have ϕ and Φ self-dual, in the sense that $\phi(Z) \equiv \Phi(Z)$. Is there any other case of self-duality possible? Writing the demand equations

$$x_i = f^i(y_1, \ldots, y_n) \qquad (i = 1, \ldots, n)$$

in compact form $x = f(Y)$, we have to determine whether the following functional equations have any solution other than $f^i(Y) \equiv k_i/y_i$:

$$Y \equiv f(f(Y)), \qquad Y'f(Y) \equiv 1$$

and with $f(Y)$ satisfying the integrability conditions

$$\frac{\partial f^i}{\partial y_j} - f^j \sum_1^n \frac{\partial f^i}{\partial y_k} y_k \equiv \frac{\partial f^j}{\partial y_i} - f^i \sum_1^n \frac{\partial f^j}{\partial y_k} y_k$$

for all i and j. I must leave this as an open question.

$f(\Phi)$ may both be written as sums of independent functions. Our previous analysis has established the requirement that it is a necessary condition for direct and indirect additivity that ϕ be a member of the Bergson family. It will now be shown that there is no other requirement; in short, that every member of the Bergson family does have the non-simultaneous direct and indirect additivity property.

This will be shown by direct substitution. However, in case we did not already know the theorem to be proved, I shall first present a line of argument by which one could be led to formulate it.

Suppose $\phi = \Sigma a_i x_i^m$ is a member of the Bergson family. Then the first part of (4) becomes

$$(14) \qquad \frac{\phi_i(X)}{\phi_j(X)} = \frac{a_i x_i^{m-1}}{a_j x_j^{m-1}} = \frac{p_i}{p_j}.$$

This leads, even before we have any knowledge of Φ or $f(\Phi)$, to the remaining relation of (4)

$$(15) \qquad \frac{x_i}{x_j} = \left(\frac{a_i}{a_j}\right)^{1/(1-m)} \left(\frac{p_i}{p_j}\right)^{1/(m-1)} = \frac{f'(\phi)}{f'(\phi)} \frac{\dfrac{\partial \Phi}{\partial p_i}}{\dfrac{\partial \Phi}{\partial p_j}}$$

for arbitrary positive $f'(\phi)$. Examining (15) and (14), we see that with respect to the dual variables, they are exactly of the same mathematical form, but with $(m-1)^{-1}$ playing the role of $(m-1)$. Hence, by setting up the exact differential expression $\Sigma(\pm a_i)^{1/(1-m)} p_i^{1/(1-m)} dp_i$, we see that there does exist a particular $f(\Phi)$ which is of the Bergson family but with exponent equal to $(m-1)^{-1}+1$.

Instead of the above proof, we can derive the explicit demand functions for a Bergson ϕ of degree m and show by substitution that there exists a particular $f(\Phi)$ which is a member of the Bergson family of degree $(m-1)^{-1}+1$. Since exactly one of m or $(m-1)^{-1}+1$ will be a positive fraction, there will be seen to be no real loss of generality in assuming $0 < m < 1$ and positive a's. From (15) we deduce at sight the Bergson demand functions

$$(16) \qquad x_i = \frac{a_i^{1/(1-m)} y_i^{m/(m-1)}}{\displaystyle\sum_{j=1}^{n} a_j^{1/(1-m)} y_j^{m/(m-1)}}.$$

Substitute these into ϕ to get

$$\Phi = -\phi(X(Y)) = -\frac{\left(\sum_1^n a_i a_i^{m/(1-m)} y_i^{m/(m-1)}\right)}{\left(\sum_1^n a_j^{1/(1-m)} y_j^{m/(m-1)}\right)^m}$$

$$= -\left(\sum_1^n a_j^{1/(1-m)} y_j^{m/(m-1)}\right)^{1-m},$$

which is seen to be indeed a homogeneous function of degree $-m$, but which is not itself of additive form. However, if $f(\Phi) = -(-\Phi)^{1/(1-m)}$, then

$$f(\Phi) = -\sum_1^n a_j^{1/(1-m)} y_j^{m/(m-1)}$$

does display indirect additivity. By duality the argument holds equally well to go from Bergson indirect additivity to a case of Bergson direct additivity. Note that in the special case where $m=0$, $f(\Phi) \equiv \Phi$ and we have simultaneous direct and indirect additivity; and if we write $M = (m-1)^{-1} + 1 = m(m-1)^{-1}$, then M and m are connected by the perfectly symmetric relation $mM - m - M = 0$, a fact predictable from duality itself.

[Example: if $\phi(X) = x_1^{\frac{1}{2}} + x_2^{\frac{1}{2}}$, $\Phi(Y) = -\sqrt{y_1^{-1} + Y_2^{-1}}, -\Phi(y)^2$
$$= -(y_1^{-1} + y_2^{-1}).]$$

10. CONCLUSION

I have by no means exhausted the implications of duality. But enough has been said to show that this principle does give you two for the price of one, so to speak: whatever you prove about a suitably limited direct utility function must have a counterpart that can be proved about a similarly limited indirect utility function. This would suggest to me that Houthakker's sentence, "Indirect Additivity is not as rich in consequences as direct additivity" must be construed very carefully. More important than this minor emendation is the following insight yielded by duality: If the important implications of Houthakker's Theorem I on direct additivity are expressed in terms of the partial derivatives of my $X(Y)$ functions, it will be obvious that exactly similar results will be implied for $Y(X)$ by indirect additivity. Similarly, his Theorem II implications of indirect additivity expressed in terms of the partial derivatives of $X(Y)$ have a formal counterpart in similar implications of direct additivity on the partial derivatives of $Y(X)$.

I hope at some future date to relate my *Foundations of Economics* analysis to recent discussions of utility trees and additivity. Let me merely express the hope here that some of the statistical users of these hypotheses will subject them to stringent empirical validation or refutation. Thus, if direct additivity were strictly true, Houthakker's Theorem I shows that $n^2 - n$ certain complementarity coefficients must vanish, and that $(n-1)$ further conditions should be realized. In terms of the partial derivatives of my $X(P; I)$ functions, these could be written as

$$h_{ij} = \left(1 - p_i \frac{\partial x_i}{\partial I}\right) \left(\frac{\partial x_i}{\partial p_j} + x_j \frac{\partial x_i}{\partial I}\right) - \left(\frac{\partial x_i}{\partial p_i} + x_i \frac{\partial x_i}{\partial I}\right) \equiv 0, \quad i \neq j,$$

$$h_{11} \equiv h_{22} \equiv \ldots \equiv h_{nn}, \quad \text{where } h_{ii} = \frac{\dfrac{\partial x_i}{\partial I}\left(1 - p_i \dfrac{\partial x_i}{\partial I}\right)}{\dfrac{\partial x_i}{\partial p_i} + x_i \dfrac{\partial x_i}{\partial I}}.$$

In what sense do empirical calculations of h_{ij} turn out to approximate to these ideal values; in what sense do they fail to approximate to these implications of direct additivity? To the economist this, after all, is the important question.

Massachusetts Institute of Technology

135

Econometrica, Vol. 37, No. 2 (April, 1969)

CORRECTED FORMULATION OF DIRECT AND INDIRECT ADDITIVITY[1]

By Paul A. Samuelson

1

Sir John Hicks [1] is right. My corrected theorem should read as follows.

THEOREM: *Direct and indirect additivity imply all goods have unitary price elasticity with the exception of (at most) one good.*

The exceptional Hicks case

(1) $U = u_1(x_1) + \alpha_2 \log x_2,$

where $u_1(x_1)$ is an arbitrary monotone increasing concave function, refutes my 1965 theorem as stated [4] and refutes the basic 1960 Theorem of Houthakker [2] upon which my extension was based.

To elucidate the nature of the exception, let me perform a post mortem on the 1960 and 1965 discussions. I employ my earlier notations: $x_1, x_2, \ldots,$ for goods; $p_1, p_2, \ldots,$ for their prices; I for income; $p_1/I, p_2/I, \ldots,$ for standardized prices; U or ϕ for direct utility; and U^* or $-\Phi$ for (maximized) indirect utility, in function of p_i/I.

2

Houthakker's basic theorem [Theorem 3 of p. 252, 2] follows.

THEOREM: *Direct and indirect additivity imply unitary income elasticities [or a so-called "homothetic" preference field].*

Houthakker proves this by combining the following implication of direct additivity

$$\frac{\partial x_i/\partial p_K}{\partial x_j/\partial p_K} = \frac{\partial x_i/\partial I}{\partial x_j/\partial I}, \quad i \neq k \neq j \neq i,$$

(equation (10) of Houthakker) with the following implication which he has deduced for indirect additivity:

$$\frac{\partial x_i/\partial p_K}{\partial x_j/\partial p_K} = \frac{x_i}{x_j}, \quad i \neq j$$

(equation (21) of Houthakker).

Equating equals, he deduces for any i and j that

$$\frac{\partial x_i/\partial I}{\partial x_j/\partial I\cdot} = \frac{x_i}{x_j}, \quad \text{or} \quad \frac{\partial x_i}{\partial I}\frac{I}{x_i} = \frac{\partial x_j}{\partial I}\frac{I}{x_j}$$

(equation (26) of Houthakker). Since all income elasticities average out to unity by definition, equality of them all can be possible only if all are equal to unity. I accepted this reasoning and theorem and took over from there.

3

As written above, the Hicks exception involves but two goods. For such a case, Houthakker's equation (10) becomes vacuous and no deductions can be built upon it. This suggests, at first

[1] I wish to thank the Carnegie Corporation for a reflective year and F. Skidmore for research assistance.

glance, that the Houthakker theorem and my extension of it are valid if only we carefully add the words "for three goods or more." It is well known [3, Ch. 7] that independent additivity has a quite different meaning in the two-good case from that in the three-or-more good case. So one would, retrospectively, not be surprised that something singular might arise in the $n = 2$ case.

However, as Sir John's subsequent discussion points to, for $n \geqslant 3$ we do have the following exception to the stated theorems:

$$(2) \qquad U = u_1(x_1) + \alpha_2 \log x_2 + \alpha_3 \log x_3 + \ldots + \alpha_n \log x_n.$$

To verify that this is an exception, write out the optimality requirement that marginal utilities be proportional to price at the configuration which best spends total income, in the form $(2')$ of my paper,

$$(3) \qquad \frac{u_1'(x_1)}{p_1/I} = \frac{\alpha_2}{(p_2/I)x_2} = \ldots = \frac{\alpha_n}{(p_n/I)x_n} = u_1'(x_1)x_1 + \alpha_2 + \ldots + \alpha_n.$$

Equating the first and the last of these gives an implicit expression for x_1 in terms of p_1/I alone, independently of other p_i/I; this can be solved explicitly for $x_1 = X_1(p_1/I)$. Substituting this into the last expression just above makes that expression a function of p_1/I alone. Then each of the middle expressions can be equated to the last to acquire their explicit demand functions as a function of their own p_i/I and of p_1/I alone. In detail, we end up with

$$x_1 = X_1(p_1/I),$$

$$(4) \qquad x_2 = \frac{\alpha_2}{\alpha_2 + \ldots + \alpha_n} \frac{[1 - p_1 X_1(p_1/I)]}{p_2/I}$$

$$\ldots \qquad \ldots \qquad \ldots$$

$$x_n = \frac{\alpha_n}{\alpha_2 + \ldots + \alpha_n} \frac{1}{(p_n/I)}[1 - p_1 X_1(p_1/I)].$$

All this has an intuitive explanation. The logarithmic utilities for goods 2 to n cause any money spent on them to be allocated in the familiar fixed proportions, with unitary own-price elasticities and zero cross-price-elasticities on *other* goods when one of their prices changes. The allocation between good 1 and the remaining group follows exactly the same analysis as for the two-good Hicks exceptional case.

As a final step to show indirect additivity, we substitute these special demand functions into U, to eliminate all x's in favor of (p/I)'s, to get

$$(5) \qquad U^* = u_1[X_1(p_1/I)] + \sum_2^n \alpha_j \log \frac{\alpha_j}{\sum_2^n \alpha_K}[1 - p_1 X_1(p_1/I)] - \sum_2^n \alpha_j \log (p_j/I)$$

$$= u_1^*(p_1/I) - \sum_2^n \alpha_j \log (p_j/I).$$

It is reassuring that the dual function $-U^*$ is of exactly the Hicks exceptional logarithmic form. Were this not so, we could deduce from the principle of duality that there were still other exceptional cases.

An easy generalization of (1) and (2) is worth recording.

THEOREM: *If, and only if*

$$U = u(x_1, \ldots, x_r) + \sum_{r+1}^n \alpha_j \log x_j, \qquad 1 \leqslant r \leqslant n,$$

then

$$U^* = u^*(p_1/I, \ldots, p_r/I) - \sum_{r+1}^n \alpha_j \log (p_j/I).$$

To prove this, write the optimality conditions

(6)
$$\frac{\partial u(x_1,\ldots,x_r)/\partial x_i}{p_i/I} = \sum_1^r x_i \,\partial u(x_1,\ldots,x_n)/\partial x_i + \sum_{r+1}^n \alpha_j, \qquad i \leqslant r,$$

$$\frac{\alpha_k}{(p_j/I)x_k} = \sum_1^r x_i \,\partial u(x_1,\ldots,x_n)/\partial x_i + \sum_{r+1}^n \alpha_j, \qquad r < k \leqslant n.$$

These first r equations can be solved to give

(7a) $\qquad x_i = X_i(p_1/I,\ldots,p_r/I)$ $\hfill (i = 1,\ldots,r).$

Then the final $n - r$ equations can be solved in the form

(7b) $\qquad x_k = \dfrac{\alpha_k\left[1 - \sum_1^r (p_i/I)X_i(p_1/I,\ldots,p_r/I)\right]}{\sum_{r+1}^n \alpha_j p_k/I}$ $\hfill (k = r+1,\ldots,n).$

Substitution into U then gives the desired U^* as in (5).

4

If, as we have just seen, the Houthakker theorem needs modification even in the $n \geqslant 3$ case, we are still left with the puzzle of where the syllogism, "(10) and (21) imply unitary income elasticities," runs into troublesome exceptions. Whenever algebra produces paradox, experience suggests we look for division by zero. And that does prove to be the key to the mystery. The Hicks singular case, as mentioned above, does lead to zero cross elasticities which gives rise to the following form of Houthakker's equation (10):

$$\frac{\partial x_1/\partial p_n}{\partial x_2/\partial p_n} = \frac{0}{0}, \quad \frac{\partial x_i/\partial p_k}{\partial x_j/\partial p_k} = \frac{0}{0}, \quad k > 1, \ i \neq k \neq j.$$

These are indeterminate forms, and one cannot legitimately manipulate their equalities as if they were regular numbers. This can be verified by writing out (10) and (21) in safer determinental form.

(8)
$$\begin{vmatrix} \partial x_i/\partial p_k & \partial x_i/\partial I \\ \partial x_j/\partial p_k & \partial x_j/\partial I \end{vmatrix} = 0, \quad \begin{vmatrix} \partial x_i/\partial p_k & x_i \\ \partial x_j/\partial p_k & x_j \end{vmatrix} = 0.$$

Take $n = 3$ and notice that if these all have zero first columns for $k = 2, 3$, you cannot deduce the elasticity equalities $E_{11} = E_{21}$, $E_{11} = E_{31}$, even though you can deduce $E_{21} = E_{31}$.

Having isolated the source of the logical pathology, we are in a position to verify that the Hicks exception is indeed the only one in the $n \geqslant 3$ case. The 0/0 trouble arises only when $n - 1$ goods (or more) have the property of prices that do not affect any other good, i.e., when they have the unitary price elasticity needed to produce zero cross elasticity in the independent utility case. This confirms the fact that my very first reformulation takes care of all admissible cases.

5

There remains only to verify for the $n = 2$ case that the Hicks exception is the only one. It is convenient to combine my *dual* optimality relation, (2′) and (2″) to get directly

(9) $\qquad \dfrac{u_1'(x_1)}{p_1/I} = \dfrac{u_2'(x_2)}{p_2/I} = \dfrac{-u_1^{*\prime}(p_1/I)}{x_1} = \dfrac{-u_2^{*\prime}(p_2/I)}{x_2}.$

By cross-multiplication, this gives

(10) $x_i U_i'(x_i) \equiv -(p_i/I)u_i^{*\prime}(p_i/I),$ $(i = 1, 2).$

As Hicks points out, such an identity can hold if each side is constant—the logarithmic case; or it can hold if x_i depends only on its own p_i/I, a kind of independence possible only if the other good has the log form needed for unitary price elasticity. (My discussion, [4, p. 793] had failed to note this exception.)

6

One error in an argument renders all its parts suspect. Therefore, I have reexamined the whole of my 1965 paper and of Houthakker's 1960 paper. As far as I can tell, Houthakker's paper receives a clean bill of health: no result, other than his Theorem 3, involves 0/0 complications; his Theorem 3, restricted to three-or-more goods, is subject only to the general Hicks exception of (2) above.

My own discussion of non-simultaneous additivity—which concluded that if U and U^* can be stretched into additivity, they can be stretched into the Bergson-Solow constant elasticity of substitution form—must be subject to the same Hicksian exception. For $n \geqslant 3$, there would appear to be no other exception, since the Houthakker theorem upon which my discussion of non-simultaneous activity was based, has been shown to be subject to no other exception.

We see, however, that the $n = 2$ case of non-simultaneous additivity is left uncovered, and completeness requires that we examine it. We seek implications of

(11) $U = u_1(x_1) + u_2(x_2)$ and $U^* = f[\Phi_1(p_1/I) + \Phi_2(p_2/I)]$

where f is an arbitrary, monotone decreasing stretching. Using y_i as an abbreviation for standardized prices p_i/I, this implies the dual optimality relations,

(12) $\dfrac{u_1'(x_1)}{y_1} = \dfrac{u_2'(x_2)}{y_2} = \sum_1^2 x_j u_j'(x_j) = -f'[\Phi_1(y_1) + \Phi_2(y_2)]\dfrac{\Phi_i'(y_i)}{x_i}$

$= -f'[\Phi_1(y_1) + \Phi_2(y_2)] \sum_1^2 y_j \Phi'(y_j)$ $(i = 1, 2).$

Equating each of the first two expressions separately to the last expression gives, after inverting the function $u_i'(x_i)$, the following explicit demand functions and their inverses

(13) $\begin{aligned} x_i &= X_i(y_1, y_2), \\ y_i &= Y_i(x_1, x_2), \end{aligned}$ $(i = 1, 2).$

As shown in [3, p. 176], the necessary and sufficient conditions for two-good additivity are

(14′) $\dfrac{\partial^2 \log \dfrac{X_1(y_1, y_2)}{X_2(y_1, y_2)}}{\partial y_1 \, \partial y_2} \equiv \dfrac{\partial^2 \log \dfrac{\Phi_1'(y_1)}{\Phi_2'(y_2)}}{\partial y_1 \, \partial y_2} \equiv 0,$

(14″) $\dfrac{\partial^2 \log \dfrac{Y_1(x_1, x_2)}{Y_2(x_1, x_2)}}{\partial x_1 \, \partial x_2} \equiv \dfrac{\partial^2 \log \dfrac{u_1'(x_1)}{u_2'(x_2)}}{\partial x_1 \, \partial x_2} \equiv 0.$

Whether these partial differential equations have any solutions other than

$U = A + \alpha_1 \log x_1 + \alpha_2 \log x_2,$

$U = A + \alpha_1 x_1^m + \alpha_2 x_2^m, \quad m < 1,$

$U = u_1(x_1) + \alpha_2 \log x_2,$

is a formidable problem that I must still leave open.[2]

Massachusetts Institute of Technology

REFERENCES

[1] HICKS, J. R.: "Direct and Indirect Additivity," *Econometrica*, 37, 1969, pp. 353–354.
[2] HOUTHAKKER, H. S.: "Additive Preferences," *Econometrica: An Issue in Honor of Ragnar Frisch*, 28, 1960, pp. 244–257.
[3] SAMUELSON, P. A.: *Foundations of Economic Analysis*. Harvard University Press, Cambridge, Mass., 1947.
[4] ———: "Using Full Duality to Show that Simultaneously Additive Direct and Indirect Utilities Implies Elasticity of Demand," *Econometrica*, 33, 1965, pp. 781–796.

---

[2] In partial atonement, I shall help answer Houthakker's open question of when $U \equiv -U^*$ in functional form, and $x = X(y) \equiv X(X(x))$ with $X(\cdot) \equiv Y(\cdot)$. By following up a lead of Dr. Subramanian Swamy of Harvard, I have proved, for $n = 2$, and preference homothetic, that my $x_i = c_i(I/p_i)$ is the only possible case. For $n \geqslant 3$ and U homothetic, I suspect the same can be proved. For general non-homothetic U, the question is still open.

PART III

The Pure Theory of Capital and Growth

136

A Catenary Turnpike Theorem Involving Consumption and the Golden Rule

Catenaries One Meets

A rope will hang in the shape of a catenary, $y(x) = a_1 e^{\lambda x} + a_2 e^{-\lambda x}$, because even a dumb rope knows that such a shape will minimize its center of gravity. The young man on the flying trapeze, when he approaches the vertical in his swing, goes through catenary motions. The essence of the Turnpike Theorem in modern economics is the catenary property of efficient paths in closed von Neumann or neoclassical models.[1]

Although the catenary is met less frequently in physics and economics than its antipodal concept, sinusoidal vibrations, I know of two other places in economic theory where the catenary is involved. One is in the pure theory of intertemporal speculative price equilibrium.[2] The other is in connection with the famous Ramsey problem of optimal saving. This aspect of the Ramsey problem, which seems not to have been commented on in the literature, was actually one clue back in 1949 to formulating the Turnpike Theorem, even though that theorem explicitly excludes the enjoyment of consumption as the goal for maximizing (by virtue of the Neumann assumption that *all* output is reinvested in the closed system).

Here I shall briefly sketch a new kind of Turnpike Theorem in which the utility of consumption represents the *desideratum* for the problem.

[1] This theorem was first conjectured in the RAND memo, *Market Mechanisms and Maximization*, Pt. III (1949). See R. Dorfman, P. A. Samuelson, R. M. Solow, *Linear Programming and Economic Analysis*, New York 1958, Ch. 12; P. A. Samuelson, "Efficient Paths of Capital Accumulation in terms of the Calculus of Variations," in K. J. Arrow, S. Karlin, and P. Suppes, eds., *Mathematical Methods in the Social Sciences, 1959*, Proceedings of the First Stanford Symposium, Stanford 1960, pp. 77–88; R. Radner, "Paths of Economic Growth That are Optimal with Regard Only to Final States: A Turnpike Theorem," *Rev. Econ. Stud.*, Feb. 1961, *28*, 98–104; M. Morishima, "Proof of a Turnpike Theorem: The 'No Joint Production Case'," *Rev. Econ. Stud.*, Feb. 1961, *28*, 89–97, and *Equilibrium, Stability and Growth*, Oxford 1964, Ch. 6; T. C. Koopmans, "Economic Growth at a Maximal Rate," *Quart. Jour. Econ.*, Aug. 1964, *78*, 355–94; L. W. McKenzie, "Turnpike Theorems for a Generalized Leontief Model," *Econometrica*, Jan.–April 1963, *31*, 165–80, and "The Dorfman-Samuelson-Solow Turnpike Theorem," *Internat. Econ. Rev.*, Jan.1963, *4*, 29–43.

[2] For a complete treatment of the simplest ideal model, see P. A. Samuelson, "Intertemporal Price Equilibrium: A Prologue to the Theory of Speculation," *Weltwirtschaftliches* Archiv, Band 79 (1957), pp. 181–221, particularly p. 217 of the Mathematical Appendix where equations (4) and (5) possess the catenary property in the neighborhood of equilibrium. Actually, catenaries have a great future in economics. For a theorem of Poincaré guarantees that the characteristic roots near an equilibrium motion of a Hamiltonian maximum problem come in pairs with opposite signs: half the time, so to speak, a time-reversible system will have pure imaginary roots and give rise to sinusoidal vibrations and half the time will have the real roots of a catenary.

COMMUNICATIONS

How the World Ends

Frank Ramsey, living in a happier age and being a Cambridge philosopher, assumed society would last forever and seek to maximize the utility of its consumption over all infinite time.[3] With a fixed population, his problem was the following:

$$
(1) \quad \underset{\{k(t)\}}{\text{Max}} \int_0^\infty u[c(t)]dt = \int_0^\infty u[f(k(t)) - \dot{k}(t)]dt
$$

$$
\text{subject to } k(0) = k^0
$$

where

$u(c) =$ utility of consumption, a concave function with $u' \geq 0$, $u'' \leq 0$,

$f(k) =$ annual output, producible by capital and (fixed) labor,

$\dot{k} =$ net capital formation (after depreciation), equal to $f(k) - c$.

In order that the infinite integral be convergent, Ramsey must stipulate some "Bliss" saturation assumptions. For the present catenary theory, I shall concentrate on the Schumpeter case where capital gets saturated at a finite level, producing a zero own-rate-of interest. Mathematically, I assume

$f(k)$ a concave, nonnegative function, $f''(k) < 0$

(2) $f(k^*)$ a unique maximum for $0 < k^* < \infty$, where $f'(k^*) = 0$

$u(c)$ an increasing concave function for $0 \leq c \leq c^* = f(k^*)$.

Since $u(c) \leq u(c^*)$, I can set $u(c^*) = 0$ and ensure $u(c) < 0$, $c < c^*$, thereby avoiding the need to speak of minimizing the divergence from Bliss. An alternative Bliss assumption would involve saturation of $u(c)$ or asymptotic saturation of $f(k)$. But, by a simple device,[4] the Ramsey analysis can be put on a per capita basis to handle the Golden-Rule problem; and positive exponential population growth leads to Bliss-convergence conditions like those of (2).

Figure 1 plots the concave production function $f(k)$, showing for fixed labor its Bliss maximum b at k^*. (The upper curves should be ignored at this reading.) Figure 2 plots the concave utility function $u(c)$. Note that its origin constant has been adjusted so that, at its Bliss level $c^* = f(k^*)$, $u(c^*) = 0$, with $u(c) < 0$ for all other feasible consumption levels. By this device, we ensure that the maximum of our integral is finite, being equal or less than zero. (At this stage, ignore the per capita symbols C/L.)

The solution to Ramsey's problem is well known. If society's initial k^0 is at the Bliss level k^*, it will consume all its income and stay there indefinitely. If it begins with $k^0 < k^*$, it will engage in positive capital formation

[3] F. Ramsey, "A Mathematical Theory of Saving," *Econ. Jour.*, Dec. 1928, *38*, 543–59.

[4] The year 1962–63 was a golden year for Golden-Rules at M.I.T. In the seminar of Robert Solow and Edmund Phelps (visiting from Yale), Christian von Weizsäcker (of Basel, Hamburg, and Berlin), Christopher Bliss (of Cambridge), and others proved all kinds of theorems. Professor Phelps reminds me that Weizsäcker and T. Koopmans had independently developed this device, as did S. Chakravarty (of Delhi) during his 1963–64 stay at M.I.T.

$\dot{k}$ at a rate which is ever an increasing function of the k^*-k discrepancy of each moment. Actually, the optimal decision rule is given by $\dot{k}=D(k^*-k)$, where $D(x)$ has the sign of x. This rule comes from the familiar energy-integral condition of the calculus of variations

$$(3) \qquad H(\dot{k},\, k) = \dot{k}\,\frac{\partial u[f(k) - \dot{k}]}{\partial \dot{k}} - u[f(k) - \dot{k}] \equiv \text{constant}.$$

The constant is seen to be zero if we put $\dot{k}=0$ and $k=k^*$ into this relation. This implicit relation can be solved to give $\dot{k}$ in terms of k because of the curvature conditions on u and f that ensure a maximum (namely, the good old laws of diminishing returns and of diminishing marginal utility).

Note this. If we call the Bliss level a "turnpike," a Ramsey *optimal saving program does spend most of its time in a close neighborhood of the turnpike.*

Now let us assume the world (or the program or the Monarchy) may come to an end at finite time T. As before we begin with initial capital stock k^0. But now we either assume that there must be a prescribed terminal capital stock k^T, or (if it really is the end of the world and we couldn't care

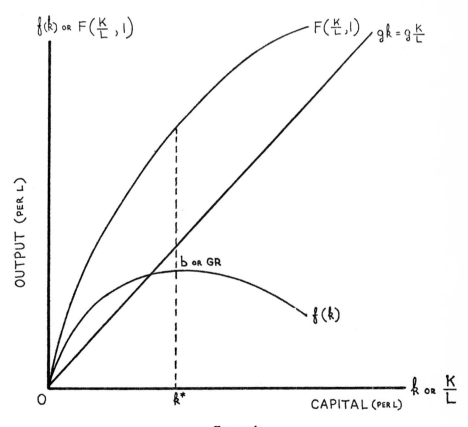

FIGURE 1

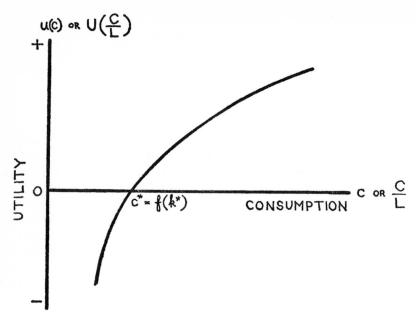

FIGURE 2

less what the *après-déluge* posterity inherits) that k^T can be allowed to be zero.

Now we have the two-point problem:

$$(4) \qquad \text{Max}_{\{k(t)\}} \int_0^T u[f(k) - \dot{k}]dt \quad \text{for} \quad k(0) \leq k^0, \; k(T) \geq k^T \geq 0.$$

The standard first-variation necessary condition for a maximum is that of Euler,

$$\frac{d}{dt} \frac{\partial u}{\partial \dot{k}} - \frac{\partial u}{\partial k} \equiv 0 \quad \text{or}$$

$$(5) \qquad -\frac{d}{dt} u'[f(k) - \dot{k}] - u'[f(k) - \dot{k}]f'(k) \equiv 0$$

$$u''[f(k) - \dot{k}][\ddot{k} - f'(k)\dot{k}] - u'[f(k) - \dot{k}]f'(k) = 0.$$

Since u does not involve t explicitly, it is well known that the energy relations (3) can be directly deduced from (5).

This second-order differential equation is sufficient as well as necessary for a maximum, since u is a strictly concave function in terms of the variables $(\dot{k}, k)$. This remark rules out conjugate points and assures us of a unique solution satisfying the end condition $[k^0, k^T]$ for all T.

Figure 3 shows some optimal programs. The horizontal line bb represents the Bliss level, which is itself an optimal path if we start and end on it. Starting from limited capital at A, the path AR depicts the optimal Ram-

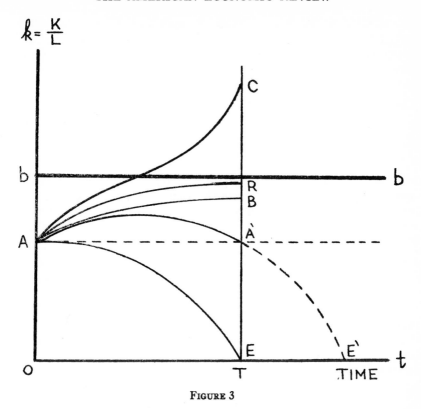

FIGURE 3

sey program, which will approach closer and closer to the *bb* turnpike as time increases. The path *AB* is optimal if we are to end up at *B*: society consumes more and saves less than in the Ramsey path, because it bequeathes less. The path *AC* proceeds on the opposite assumption, namely that the terminal k^T exceeds that of the Bliss k^*. It is no accident that *AC* has a inflection point where it crosses the turnpike, since all extremals are convex to the turnpike. The path *AA'* actually ends up at the same k^T level as k^0, where it begins. Not accidental is the fact that it *must* arch toward the turnpike with a somewhat symmetric arch. (Why? Because a positive technical interest rate faces a zero subjective rate of time preference, making it optimal to abstain now from some consumption in order to get more later and, of course, to dissave later.) Finally, *AE* gives the maximum of utility for the finite interval (O, T), ending up like a feckless annuitant with zero terminal capital. For it the world ends neither in a bang nor a whimper, but on an upbeat of consumption.

We can summarize Figure 3's contents in the aphorism:

> Just as a rope hangs toward the ground in a catenary, the optimal path arches toward the Bliss turnpike.

The Theorem Stated

Now in Figure 3, merely increase the time span T, holding in every case the terminal k^T at the same A, B, C, A', and E levels as before. Economic intuition tells us that *all* the paths will then have to arch closer to the Ramsey path or, what is the same thing, to the Bliss turnpike itself. E.g. in Figure 3 the branch $A'E'$ already hinted that AE will veer toward the turnpike if T is made large enough.

The Consumption Turnpike Theorem. An extremal to

$$\underset{\{k(t)\}}{\text{Max}} \int_0^T u[f(k) - \dot{k}]dt \quad \text{for} \quad k(0) = k^0, \ k(T) = k^T$$

will, as T becomes sufficiently large, spend an arbitrarily large portion of the time arbitrarily near the turnpike. I.e., $1 - \epsilon$ of the time interval will be spent within a neighborhood η of the Bliss turnpike, where ϵ and η can be made as small as we like provided we stipulate T sufficiently large.

I shall first give a proof to the theorem along the lines of my 1959 Stanford discussion of the usual Turnpike Theorem, and the Samuelson-Solow 1956 generalization of the Ramsey problem.[5]

Stability analysis of the behavior of the differential equation (5) in the neighborhood of the Bliss point where $(k, \dot{k}) = (k^*, 0)$ requires examination of the linear first-degree terms in (5)'s Taylor's expansion around that origin. As with conventional small vibration analysis, this leads to the associated linear system for $k - k^* = y$

(6) $$L_{11}\ddot{y} - L_{22}y = 0$$

where

$$L_{11} = \left.\frac{\partial^2 u}{\partial \dot{k}^2}\right|_{\substack{k=k^* \\ \dot{k}=0}} = + u''[f(k^*) - 0] < 0$$

$$L_{22} = \left.\frac{\partial^2 u}{\partial k^2}\right|_{\substack{k=k^* \\ \dot{k}=0}} = + u'[f(k^*)]f''(k^*) < 0$$

$$L_{12} - L_{21} = 0 = \text{coefficient of the } \dot{y} \text{ term.}$$

[5] P. A. Samuelson, "Efficient Paths of Capital Accumulation," in K. J. Arrow, S. Karlin, and P. Suppes, eds., *Mathematical Methods in the Social Sciences, 1959* (Stanford 1960), pp. 77–88. P. A. Samuelson and R. M. Solow, "A Complete Capital Model Involving Heterogeneous Capital Goods," *Quart. Jour. Econ.*, Nov. 1956, 537–62. In the errata slip of the Stanford book, it was pointed out that only in the one-degree-of-freedom case does the $(L_{12} - L_{21})$ coefficient of the velocity $\dot{y}$ cancel out. As Professor Morishima pointed out to me, in the n-variable case the $\dot{y}$ of p. 88 equation (34) vector is premultiplied by a nonzero matrix. Fortunately, however, it is a skew-symmetric matrix which preserves the essential catenary property—that all roots come in pairs with opposite-signs. Professor Morishima has also kindly pointed out that some errors are contained in the pp. 333–34 discussion of R. Dorfman, P. A. Samuelson, and R. M. Solow, *Linear Programming and Economic Analysis*, New York 1958; still the saddlepoint analysis there of Fig. 12-9 can be recast along the lines of Figure 4 here.

The solution to (6) is seen to be the catenary

(7) $y(t) = A_1 e^{\lambda t} + A_2 e^{-\lambda t}$ where $\lambda = + \sqrt{L_{22}/L_{11}}$, a real number.

Figure 4 shows the contours of motion, $H(\dot{k}, k) = \overline{H}$ from (3), in the important phase space $(k, \dot{k})$. In most physics problems, as in the conservative oscillations of a trapeze star around the *bottom* of his pendulum-like swing, the trajectories are along closed energy contours (being concentric ellipses for small, sinusoidal vibrations). But here, and for the trapeze star near

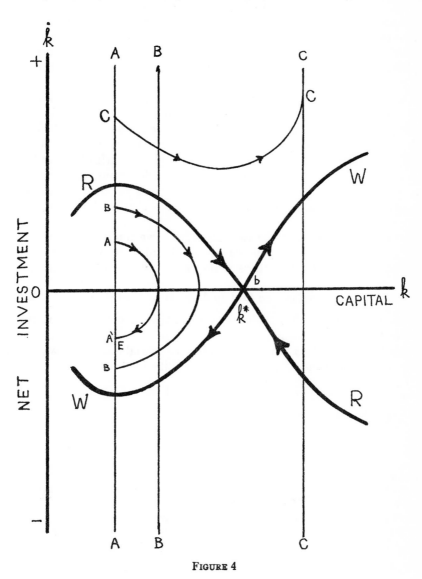

FIGURE 4

the *top* of his swings, the catenaries give rise to saddlepoint contours.

The point b represents Ramsey's equilibrium Bliss point. It is at the intersection of the heavy curve RbR, which represents the AR optimal Ramsey path of Figure 3 and WbW, which represents a Ramsey path that has been departing from Bliss since time immemorial (and which has no simple economic interpretation).

All of the paths that began at A in Figure 3 begin on vertical line AA in Figure 4. And each ends on the vertical line that corresponds to its terminal k^T. Thus the old path AB in Figure 3 appears as BB in Figure 4. And AC, AD, AE become respectively the paths CC, DD, and EE.

Time is not shown directly on Figure 3. Obviously, near the equilibrium point b the motions all slow down and it takes longer and longer to traverse the indicated paths. Indeed one never quite gets from R to b, since as b is approached speed slows down. Now the essence of the turnpike theorem is this:

If we go between any two vertical lines in Figure 4 and specify that it shall take us a longer and longer time to do so, we must begin and end nearer and nearer to the intersections of those lines with RbR or WbW. Thus, AA' must approach R and W along the vertical line AA. While the "small vibration" analysis by which I deduced catenaries here and in the 1959 Stanford paper involve only "local" considerations, the reasoning is valid globally: our strong concavity assumptions makes the saddlepoint topologically invariant and makes analysis in-the-small congruent with analysis in-the-large.

Instead of working with the variables $(\dot{k}, k)$, we could work with Hamilton's canonical variables $(p = \partial u/\partial \dot{k} = -u', k)$ and verify the same catenary, saddlepoint properties. But there is no need to do so on this occasion.

Generalization to Any Number of Variables

While I have here followed Ramsey in talking of only one consumption and one capital good, Solow and I have shown in the cited 1956 paper how the analysis generalizes to any number of variables. Now we replace $c + \dot{k} = f(k)$ by the general production-possibility frontier

(8) $$c_1 + \dot{k}_1 = f(k_1, k_2, \cdots ; c_2 + \dot{k}_2, \cdots)$$

with a saturation $p - p$ frontier

$$c_1^* = f(k_1^*, k_2^*, \cdots, k_n^*; c_2^*, \cdots)$$

and

(9) $$\text{Max } u[c_1, c_2, \cdots] = u[c_1^*, c_2^*, \cdots] = 0 \geq u(c_1, \cdots, c_n).$$

The system will stay arbitrarily close to this c^* turnpike most of the time if we let $T \to \infty$ and hold terminal k's constant. This provides the easy generalization of the new turnpike theorem. Its proof need only be sketched here.

As in our 1956 paper define

$$\underset{\{c_1,\ldots,c_n\}}{\text{Max}} \quad u[f(k_1, k_2, \cdots ; c_2 + \dot{k}_2, \cdots) - \dot{k}_1, c_2, \cdots]$$

$$= U(k_1, k_2, \cdots ; \dot{k}_1, \dot{k}_2, \cdots)$$

a concave function with negative-definite matrix of second partial derivatives. Note $U(k_1^*, k_2^*, \cdots ; 0, 0, \cdots) \geq U(k_1, k_2, \cdots ; 0, 0, \cdots)$. The optimal Euler extremals are

$$\frac{d}{dt} \frac{\partial U}{\partial \dot{k}_i} - \frac{\partial U}{\partial k_i} = 0$$

and the catenary property of the notion around the Bliss-turnpike $(k_1^*, k_2^*, \cdots)$ is assured by the fact the roots of the characteristic polynomial

$$(10) \qquad \det \left[\frac{\partial^2 U^*}{\partial \dot{k}_i \partial \dot{k}_j} \lambda^2 + \left(\frac{\partial^2 U^*}{\partial \dot{k}_i \partial k_j} - \frac{\partial^2 U^*}{\partial k_i \partial \dot{k}_j} \right) \lambda + \frac{\partial^2 U^*}{\partial k_i \partial k_j} \right] = 0$$

come in pairs of opposite sign (and which cannot be pure imaginaries because of the concavity-definiteness condition on U).[6]

Application to Golden Ages[7]

Until now I have followed Ramsey and kept population and labor constant. With $L(t) = $ constant, mention of it in $f(k)$ could be suppressed. Now, following Chakravarty and others, I assume the neoclassical production function

$$(11) \qquad C + \dot{K} = F(K, L) = LF\left(\frac{K}{L}, 1 \right)$$

$L(t) = L^0 e^{gt}$, an exponential growth for labor where g is the natural rate of population growth.

There are many possible integrals that might be maximized when L grows and choosing among them is not easy. I follow the crowd and posit

[6] Cf. Samuelson-Solow, *op. cit.* Section V. The small vibrations of physics there omit the middle skew-matrix, as is proper where the $\dot{S}_j$ velocities enter quadratically; but we erred in the economics case in not including a nonzero skew-symmetric matrix of the Morishima type. I am indebted to Professor Morishima for an example of a knife-edge case of semi-definite Hessian matrix of a concave U, for which (10) has pure imaginary roots, requiring us to go to nonlinear analysis to confirm the general catenary property. Also, he has produced a direct proof of this Consumption Turnpike Theorem that does not involve stability analysis.

[7] T. W. Swan, "Of Golden Ages and Production Functions," presented at the Round Table on Economic Development in East Asia (International Economic Association), Gamagori, Japan, April 1960 [revised 1962]. mimeo., 18 pp.; E. S. Phelps, "The Golden Rule of Accumulation," *Am. Econ. Rev.*, Sept. 1961, *51*, 638–43; J. Robinson, "A Neoclassical Theorem," *Rev. Econ. Stud.*, June 1962, *29*, 219–26, with Comments by R. M. Solow, P. A. Samuelson, J. E. Meade, *et al.*; C. C. von Weizsäcker, *Wachstum, Zins und Optimale Investitionsquote*, (Kyklos Verlag, Basel, 1962), 96 pp.

(12) Max $\displaystyle\int_0^T U\left(\frac{C}{L}\right) dt$, where $U\left(\dfrac{C}{L}\right)$ is utility of the representative man.

With minor changes in notation, we can now throw this problem into the Ramsey form, the only difference being that we interpret k, c, and u as per capita terms. Definitionally,

$$k = \frac{K}{L}, \quad \frac{\dot{K}}{K} - \frac{\dot{L}}{L} = \frac{\dot{K}}{K} - g = \frac{\dot{k}}{k}$$

$$\frac{C}{L} = c, \quad U\left(\frac{C}{L}\right) = u(c)$$

Dividing (11) by L and subtracting $g(K/L) = gk$, we rearrange to get

(13) $\qquad c + \dot{k} = f\left(\dfrac{K}{L}\right) - g\,\dfrac{K}{L} = f(k) - gk \equiv \psi(k)$

Note that (13) looks to be exactly like our original Ramsey production relation in (1) and Figure 1, which was the special case of (13) when $g = 0$ and labor is fixed.

We must now reinterpret the Ramsey Bliss convergence conditions. With labor growing exponentially at the rate g, the counterpart of Bliss is the Phelps-Swan-Robinson Golden-Rule state of maximum *per capita* consumption, defined by

(14) $\qquad\qquad \operatorname*{Max}_{\{k\}} \psi(k) = \operatorname*{Max}_{\{k\}} f(k) - gk = \psi(k^*)$

where

(15) $f'(k^*) = $ interest rate $= g$, the system's natural rate of growth.

Turn back to Figure 1 to verify that the maximum vertical distance of $F(K/L)$ above $g(K/L)$ comes at the point k^*.

Now the integral of (12) will become convergent for infinite T if we measure utility as a (negative) divergence from the Golden-Rule state $c^* = f(k^*)$, at which we set $u(c^*) = 0$.

All the rest of the new turnpike theorem goes exactly as before: per capita catenaries, saddlepoint, etc. We may state it briefly as follows.

Per Capita Consumption Turnpike Theorem. Let a system with exponentially growing labor begin and end with specified per capita capital stock $(k^0, k^T) = (K^0/L^0, K^T/L^T)$. If the time that elapses becomes sufficiently large, the system will spend an indefinitely large fraction of its time as near as one wishes to the Golden-Rule turnpike configuration of maximum maintainable per capita consumption. And exactly the same holds if k and c are interpreted as vectors of diverse capital goods and consumption items per capita, $(k_1, k_2, \cdots)$ and $(c_1, c_2, \cdots)$.

Loosely, one might say, even if we do not know when the world will end, if only we can expect that date to be indefinitely far in the future, we should prudently emulate the Puritan Ethic or the Law of Moses and the Prophets: Accumulate! Accumulate! Accumulate! But *not* faster than Ramsey's Law and only if you share the philosophy of no time preference.[8] Actually, though, no loose statement can do justice to the Theorem, which says what it says, not more and not less.

PAUL A. SAMUELSON*

[8] Suppose society has a systematic subjective rate of time preference ρ, so that the integrand of (1), $u(c)$, is replaced by $u(c)e^{-\rho t}$. Then a new "turnpike" is given by the root of $f'(k) = \rho$ rather than equal zero. Call this k^{**}. Then for T sufficiently large, for all (k^0, k^T), the optimal path $k(t)$ will remain indefinitely near to k^{**} an indefinitely large fraction of the time. The motions are not quite balanced catenaries, instead approximating to $k(t) = a_1 e^{\lambda_1 t} + a_2 e^{-\lambda_2 t}$, $\lambda_1 > \lambda_2$. (When $g > 0$, we of course find the root of $f'(k) - g = \rho$.) This constitutes an even more general Turnpike Theorem than the one elaborated here, and it reminds us that correct saving must depend on what is assumed about social time preference. Professor Karl Shell, now of M.I.T., and Dr. David Cass, now at the Cowles Foundation, have unpublished work dealing with similar problems.

* The author is professor of economics at the Massachusetts Institute of Technology. Acknowledgment is made to the Carnegie Corporation for research aid, and to Felicity Skidmore for valuable assistance.

137

A Turnpike Refutation of the Golden Rule in a Welfare-Maximizing Many-Year Plan

PAUL A. SAMUELSON

Massachusetts Institute of Technology

1. Introduction

In 1958 I showed [8] that, in a model of exponential population growth without capital, the golden rule consumption configuration among different age groups that will maximize the representative man's *ex ante* and *ex post* lifetime utility is that which would be realized if every man faced a competitive interest rate equal to the biological rate of population growth.

In 1965 Peter Diamond [2] added productive (neoclassical) capital to this model and showed that, along with the consumption golden rule, maximization of the representative man's utility requires that the Swan-Phelps (production) golden rule be satisfied, in which the marginal productivity of capital is also equal to the rate of population growth [5, 10].

In 1966, A. Asimakopulos [1] pointed out that Diamond had not mentioned the A. P. Lerner [4] objection to the Samuelson maximum-representative-man biological optimum. Lerner proposed the alternative Benthamite criterion of maximizing a social welfare function that consisted of the sum of the utilities of all individuals in every age period, and concluded that its optimum would be achieved for a capital-less model by an interest rate of zero. Asimakopulos went on to show that this same paradoxical discrepancy was called for even with real capital in the model: for the optimal Lerner-Asimakopulos consumption allocation, a zero rate of interest, $r = 0$, would be called for even if the system were, in terms of production, in a Swan-Phelps golden age—with marginal productivity of capital equal to population growth, $f'(k) = r = n > 0$.[1]

2. Paradox Upon Paradox

It is indeed paradoxical that the policy which maximizes social utility in every period should, when applied to a permanently growing exponential, result in a configuration such that every man who ever lives is worse off. This paradox, like most paradoxes,[2] arises from the infinity assumption involved in the concept of a *permanently* growing exponential. Lerner presumably would bypass the pitfalls of divergent geometric series by insisting that the assumption of a permanently growing exponential is an absurd and monstrous one, involving a Ponzi-game or chain-letter swindle. (If golden-age assumptions are successfully ruled out by Lerner as monstrous, he will in one swoop kill off a sizable fraction of the modern growth-theory literature.)

Presumably Asimakopulos would let the production golden rule, $r = n$, stand in order to maximize the total of consumption to be allocated among all living generations, but would achieve by redistributional intervention of the state the $r = 0$ lifetime allocation of the maximized total. Within the tyranny of a golden-age exponential that had been agreed upon this might be deemed optimal. But many will argue that a limited universe cannot tolerate such a permanently growing state.

Suppose we are to be for a very long time in such an exponential state—say a billion or a trillion years. Is not the indicated optimum of a Bentham-Lerner social welfare function achieved by straddling both stools, equating $f'(k) = r = n$ in terms of production and allocating lifetime consumption as if $r = 0$, thereby getting the best of both worlds? The answer, surprisingly I think, is no.

3. An Odd Result

CATENARY TURNPIKE THEOREM. Even if society starts out with the capital-labor ratio of the Swan-Phelps golden rule age k^* such that $f'(k^*) = n$, and after a long period of time T is to end up in that same k^* configuration, the

---

[1] In this regard, Asimakopulos is almost out-Lernering Lerner, since the latter had said: "The Samuelson plan *would* be optimal if one could really get $2 for $1 [i.e., $1 + f'(k) > 1$] by postponing consumption and reaping the rewards of a positive marginal efficiency of investment." (A. P. Lerner, [4], p. 525.)

[2] Canceling out, so to speak, the above paradox that seems to tell in favor of the Samuelson-Diamond state rather than the Lerner-Asimakopulos one, is the following. Up to *any* instant of time, the L-A state has produced more social utility than the S-D state. And departing from an ever held S-D state in favor of an L-A state leads to an increase in social utility in *every* subsequent period.

path that optimizes Bentham-Lerner social welfare must have k arch above k^*, approaching the Schumpeter zero-interest level k^{**} at which $f'(k^{**}) = 0$, remaining long in the neighborhood of this saturation level, and penultimately reverting back to the S-P golden rule state. Most of the time, so to speak, society must be indefinitely near a zero rate of interest, which means most of the time definitely away from the golden rule state.

Paradoxically, this turnpike theorem requires the system to be most of the (very long) time definitely in the region where Phelps and Koopmans [6] forbid it to be permanently!

To demonstrate this odd result I employ the analysis of my 1965 catenary turnpike discussion [9]. Before generalizing it to discrete time and to lifetime optimization, I shall briefly review its contents.

4. Review of Catenary Turnpike Analysis

Frank Ramsey [7] taught us how to maximize undiscounted utility in a population with stationary population, by having capital grow from its initial limited level to the "bliss" or "turnpike" level k^{**} at which the interest rate is zero,

$$f'(k^{**}) = 0. \tag{1}$$

If population grows exponentially at rate n and society acts to maximize utility per capita, the turnpike becomes the golden rule state at which the interest rate equals population growth, or

$$f'(k^*) = n. \tag{2}$$

Now let society aim to maximize a discounted integral of per capita utility, of the form

$$\int_0^\infty e^{-\rho t} U(c) \, dt.$$

Then the turnpike shifts once again to the level where

$$f'(k^*) - n = \rho. \tag{3}$$

Usually the time-preference rate is considered to favor present over future, with $\rho > 0$ and the infinite integral finite. However, the catenary turnpike theorem deals with long, finite times and applies for $\rho \lessgtr 0$. Figure 1 illustrates the alternative cases where $\rho > 0$ and $\rho < 0$ in the special situation where beginning and ending capital is at the golden rule level.

To prepare us for the Bentham-Lerner optimum, suppose in Figure 1 we set $\rho = -n$ and drop the interpretation of it as reflecting subjective time preference by anyone. Instead let $\int e^{nt} U(c) \, dt = \int L(t) U(c) \, dt$ be the total of social utility accruing to the absolute number of all individuals over time.

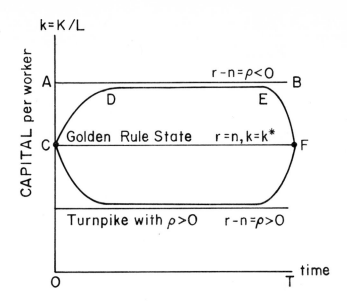

FIGURE 1. Starting and ending the system at the golden rule level of capital, the optimal path arches toward a lower turnpike with positive time preference and toward a higher turnpike with negative time preference.

This means that e^{nt} or $L(t)$ are weighting factors which make it desirable to have more consumption *at a later date* when there are more people and, hence, when less diminishing marginal utility will have been reached for each total of consumption. And now we understand why it pays to go from C to F via the roundabout path through D and E: the path of greater capital deepening makes more consumption *possible in toto* and gives more of it at a later date when there are more people and hence more social need.[3]

The necessary Euler-Lagrange condition for an optimizing extremal to

$$\underset{k(t)}{\text{Max}} \int_0^T e^{nt} U[f(k) - nk - \dot{k}] \, dt \qquad \text{for } k(0) = k_0, k(T) = k_T \qquad (4)$$

---

[3] If we let $T \to \infty$, the optimizing path will approach the upper horizontal asymptote. This limiting path is easily seen to be worse, in terms of individual *and* social utility, than the golden rule path through CF, and is dominated in terms of consumption by the latter, being in this sense Phelps-Koopmans "inefficient." The reason is clear: the limiting path never harvests the late-stage surplus of consumption: it is a case of no jam today and no jam tomorrow, because jam is being put in the bank forever. Needless to say, the integral $\int_0^\infty e^{nt} U(c) \, dt$ is divergent and infinite even when $U(c^*)$ by convention is set equal to zero. Along the Lerner optimizing extremal, $C_T(t)$,

$$\int_0^T e^{nt} U[C_T(t)] \, dt > 0;$$

and

$$\lim T \to \infty, \quad \int_0^T e^{nt} U[C_T(t)] \, dt \to \infty \neq \int_0^\infty e^{nt} U[\lim_{T \to \infty} C_T(t)] \, dt = -\infty.$$

107

is

$$0 \equiv E_t[\ddot{k}, k, k] \equiv \frac{d}{dt} \frac{\partial}{\partial k} \{e^{nt} U[f(k) - nk - \dot{k}]\}$$

$$- \frac{\partial}{\partial k} \{e^{nt} U[f(k) - nk - \dot{k}]\}, \tag{5}$$

with the sole stationary turnpike solution, like that of Schumpeter or Ramsey in Equation 1,

$$E_t(0, 0, k^{**}) \equiv 0, \quad \text{where } f'(k^{**}) - n = -n \quad \text{or} \quad f'(k^{**}) = 0. \tag{6}$$

In Figure 1, with the proviso that $\rho = -n$, the higher AB turnpike can be identified as the Ramsey-Schumpeter bliss level, where $r = 0$.

5. Discrete Analogue to Calculus of Variations

I shall sketch rapidly the parallelism between the continuous-time differential equation model of a maximized integral and the discrete-time difference equation of a maximized sum. First, I write down a self-explanatory glossary of correspondences for the traditional one-sector neoclassical growth model.[4]

$$C_t + \dot{K}_t = G(K_t, L_t) - \delta K_t \qquad\qquad C_t + (K_{t+1} - K_t) = G(K_t, L_t) - \delta K_t$$

$$= F(K_t, L_t) \qquad\qquad\qquad = F(K_t, L_t)$$

$$= L_t F\left(\frac{K_t}{L_t}, 1\right) \qquad\qquad\qquad = L_t F\left(\frac{K_t}{L_t}, 1\right)$$

$$= L_t f(k_t), \; f'' < 0 \qquad\qquad\qquad = L_t f(k_t), \; f'' < 0$$

$$\frac{K_t}{L_t} = k_t, \quad \frac{C_t}{L_t} = c_t \tag{7}$$

$$\frac{\dot{L}}{L} \equiv n, \quad \frac{\dot{k}_t}{k_t} = \frac{\dot{K}_t}{K_t} - n \qquad\qquad \frac{L_{t+1} - L_t}{L_t} \equiv n$$

$$\frac{C_t}{L_t} + \frac{\dot{K}_t}{K_t}\frac{K_t}{L_t} = f(k_t) \qquad\qquad \frac{C_t}{L_t} + \frac{K_{t+1}}{K_t}\frac{L_{t+1}}{L_t} - \frac{K_t}{L_t} = f(k_t)$$

$$c_t = f(k_t) - nk_t - \dot{k}_t \qquad\qquad c_t = f(k_t) + k_t - (1 + n)k_{t+1}$$

$$\underset{c_t}{\text{Max}} \int_0^T e^{-\rho t} U(c_t) \, dt \qquad\qquad \underset{c_t}{\text{Max}} \sum_0^T \lambda^{-t} U(c_t)$$

---

[4] Note that the same symbol n is used in both cases but with a small difference of meaning, and likewise for the symbol F and G.

Now consider the discrete analogue of maximizing an integral of the form $\int L(x, dx/dt, t)\, dt$, which is the sum

$$\text{Max} \sum_{x_t}^{T} L(x_{t+1}, x_t, t) \qquad \text{subject to } (x_0, x_{T+1}) \text{ prescribed.} \qquad (8)$$

Ordinary partial differentiation gives the standard calculus conditions for an extremum

$$0 \equiv E(x_{t+1}, x_t, x_{t-1}, t) \equiv L_2(x_{t+1}, x_t, t) + L_1(x_t, x_{t-1}, t-1), \qquad (9)$$

where subscripts L_i indicate partial derivatives with respect to the indicated argument. If the conditions of Equation 9 are all satisfied, and the L functions are concave, Equation 9 represents sufficient as well as necessary conditions for the maximum.[5]

The generalized Ramsey problem now becomes in discrete form

$$\text{Max} \sum_{c_t}^{T} \lambda^{-t} U(c_t) = \max_{k_t} \sum_{0}^{T} \lambda^{-t} U[f(k_t) + k_t - (1+n)k_{t+1}], \qquad (10)$$

$$(k_0, k_{T+1}) \text{ prescribed.}$$

This entails the extremal condition

$$0 \equiv \lambda^t E(k_{t+1}, k_t, k_{t-1}, t) \equiv U'(c_t)[1 + f'(k_t)] - (1+n)\lambda U'(c_{t-1}). \qquad (11)$$

A stationary turnpike exists for Equation 11 when

$$\lambda^t E(k, k, k, t) = e(k^*, k^*, k^*) = 0,$$

or

$$1 + f'(k^*) = (1+n)\lambda. \qquad (12)$$

This corresponds to the general Equation 3 of the continuous-time model.

For the Ramsey special case, where $n = 0$, $\lambda = 1$, we have the bliss level corresponding to Equation 1,

$$1 + f'(k^{**}) = 1, \quad \text{or} \quad f' = r = 0. \qquad (13)$$

For the golden rule state of Phelps-Swan with $\lambda = 1$, corresponding to Equation 2 we have

$$1 + f'(k^*) = 1 + n, \quad f' = r = n. \qquad (14)$$

---

[5] If x_{t+1} is replaced by x_{t+h} and we properly let $h \to 0$, we can rearrange the terms of Equation 9 to get the standard Euler differential equation for an extremal in the calculus of variations. Actually it was by such a limit process that Euler first derived his equation.

For the Bentham-Lerner welfare turnpike, where $\lambda^{-1} = 1 + n$, we have corresponding to Equation 6 the Schumpeter-Ramsey bliss level (but with a growing population),

$$1 + f'(k^{**}) = \frac{1 + n}{1 + n} = 1, \qquad f'(k^{**}) = r = 0. \tag{15}$$

Note that the extremals of Equation 11 become for this special Lerner case, where $\lambda^{-1} = 1 + n$ and we maximize the absolute total of all persons' utilities,

$$\operatorname*{Max}_{c_t} \frac{1}{L_0} \sum_0^T L_t U(c_t) = \max_{c_t} \sum_0^T (1 + n)^t U(c_t), \tag{16}$$

the customary Fisher [3] relation between marginal utilities and the interest rate,

$$\frac{U'(c_{t-1})}{U'(c_t)} = 1 + f'(k_t) = 1 + r_t. \tag{17}$$

The continuous analogue to Equation 17, derivable from the extremal condition of Equation 5, is

$$\frac{-(d/dt)U'(c_t)}{U'(c_t)} = \frac{-d \log U'(c_t)}{dt} = r_t. \tag{18}$$

In completing this brief sketch of the discrete case, I mention (but do not give the proofs) that all the catenary turnpike theorems (and local stability analysis) of the continuous-time case hold without essential modifications in the discrete-time case. Specifically, as in Samuelson [9], we have:

GENERALIZED CATENARY TURNPIKE THEOREM. If a system is given specified initial and terminal per capita capitals, and maximizes over a long period of time a discounted sum of per capita utilities, it will arch toward the turnpike defined in Equation 11 and spend most of its time in a near neighborhood of that turnpike, before finally moving to the prescribed terminal capital stock.

6. Welfare Optimum of Life-Cycle Consumption

With the analysis of the discrete case in hand, the intralife allocation of consumption can be treated definitely. As in the Samuelson-Diamond model, the persons L_t born (as economic units) at time t consume in the first, working stage of their lives per capita consumption of c_t^1 units, their total consumption in time t being $L_t c_t^1 = C_t^1$. At time t the number of people in the second, retirement stage of life is L_{t-1}, the number born one period earlier; their per capita consumption at time t is denoted by c_t^2, and their total consumption is $L_{t-1}c_t^2 = C_t^2$. The total of all consumption at time t is $C_t^1 + C_t^2 = C_t = L_t c_t$, where the c's without superscripts are precisely the consumptions dealt with in this essay until now.

The utility of any man born at time t is given by $u(c_t^1, c_{t+1}^2)$. Utility *ex ante*, as seen at the beginning of life, might differ from that *ex post*, as evaluated upon retrospective reflection. The difference might be Böhm-Bawerkian subjective-time preference, as for example

$$u = v(c_t^1) + .9v(c_{t+1}^2), \qquad ex\ ante,$$

$$u = v(c_t^1) + v(c_{t+1}^2), \qquad ex\ post.$$

My 1958 model was content to work with *ex ante* utility. However, if *ex ante* and *ex post* utility differ for the individual, a problem is created for the Bentham-Lerner social welfare function. Which shall an ethical observer respect and add up for his social total? To bypass this complication and also the complication if u is a joint function of consumptions in the different stages of life, I shall stick to the hypothesis that individual utility—both *ex ante* and *ex post*—is the sum of identical, independent—and hence time-symmetric—utility functions for each life stage. Always,

$$u(c_t^1, c_{t+1}^2) = v(c_t^1) + v(c_{t+1}^2), \qquad v' \geq 0,\quad v'' < 0. \tag{19}$$

Now, if labor grows exponentially with $L_t = (1 + n)L_{t-1}$, in each golden age when capital does likewise, with $K_t/L_t = k_t$ frozen to constancy, the Samuelson-Diamond maximum utility enjoyed by each and every man is given by

$$\underset{c^t}{\text{Max}}\ u(c^1, c^2)$$

subject to

$$C_t^1 + C_t^2 = C_t = \gamma L_t, \qquad \text{where } \gamma \text{ depends on } k \text{ as in Equations 7,}$$

$$L_t c_t^1 + L_{t-1}c_t^2 = \gamma L_t, \tag{20}$$

$$c^1 + \frac{c^2}{1 + n} = \gamma,$$

which entails

$$\frac{\partial u(c^1, c^2)/\partial c^1}{\partial u(c^1, c^2)/\partial c^2} = 1 + n = 1 + r. \tag{21}$$

This is the consumption golden rule of the biological interest rate, where, for consumption purposes, $r = n$.

But now let us turn to the Bentham-Lerner social sum of individual utilities, defined at time t as the sum of utilities enjoyed by all (identical) people alive in all stages of life:

$$W_t = L_t v(c_t^1) + L_{t-1}v(c_t^2). \tag{22}$$

For each available total of consumption,

$$C_t = C_t^1 + C_t^2 = L_t c_t^1 + L_{t-1} c_t^2, \tag{23}$$

Bentham-Lerner require

$$\text{Max}_{c_t^i} [L_t v(c_t^1) + L_{t-1} v(c_t^2)], \tag{24}$$

and, hence, equal[6] marginal utilities everywhere of the transferable consumption goods

$$v'(c_t^1) = v'(c_t^2). \tag{25}$$

Once this good rule is followed, the maximized social welfare becomes a function of the available c_t total, and of course the amounts of population. Specifically, Expressions 22, 23, and 24 lead to

$$\text{Max}_{c_t 1, c_t 2} W_t = L_t w\left(\frac{C_t}{L_t}, \frac{L_t}{L_{t-1}}\right),$$

$$= L_t w(c_t, 1 + n), \tag{26}$$

$$= L_t w(c_t), \qquad \text{if } n \text{ is frozen, with } w' \geq 0, w'' < 0.$$

But note this remarkable fact: the social welfare function $w(c_t)$ has *all* the properties of the $U(c_t)$ individual per capita functions used earlier in the Ramsey-type maximized integrals $\int e^{-\rho t} U(c_t)\, dt$ or sums $\sum \lambda^{-t} U(c_t)$. All of the apparatus of the catenary turnpike can be put at the disposal of Lerner, and his calculated optima can be compared with those of Samuelson, Diamond, Phelps, and others. I shall do so, assuming that the ethical hedonist has no telescopic time preference, knowing that the experienced reader will be able to introduce in a straightforward way such e^{-Pt} and Λ^{-t} functions of social time preference.

We set up the definitive Lerner problem

$$\text{Max}_{c_t} \frac{1}{L_0} \sum_0^T L_t w(c_t) = \max_{k_t} \sum_0^T (1 + n)^t w[f(k_t) + k_t - (1 + n)k_{t+1}] \tag{27}$$

for fixed (k_0, k_{T+1}), ending up with the extremum conditions of the type of Equation 11:

$$0 = E(k_{t+1}, k_t, k_{t-1}, t)$$
$$= (1 + n)^t \{w'(c_t)[1 + f'(k_t)] - (1 + n)^{-1} w'(c_{t-1})(1 + n)\}, \tag{28}$$

---

[6] If older people systematically, *ex ante* and *ex post*, individually, and as seen by the ethical observer, had a greater or lesser utility—as, for instance, $v_2(c_t^2) = .8 v_1(c_t^1)$ now that wine and song have lost 20 per cent of their charm—the analysis would be changed only trivially, since $v_2' = v_1'$ is still implied but with $c_t^1 \neq c_t^2$.

with a unique stationary turnpike defined by the Schumpeter-Ramsey bliss level

$$1 + f'(k^{**}) = 1 + r = 1 + 0. \tag{29}$$

Our knowledge of demonstrated results about catenary turnpike theorems tells us that those who plan for a long period of time T will want to move close to the zero-interest-rate turnpike and stay near it most of the time.

Figure 2 shows, on semilogarithmic paper where golden-age motions appear as straight lines of slope n, optimal paths of total capital (not per capita capital as in Figure 1) as heavy curves. Note that the light CF Swan-Phelps golden

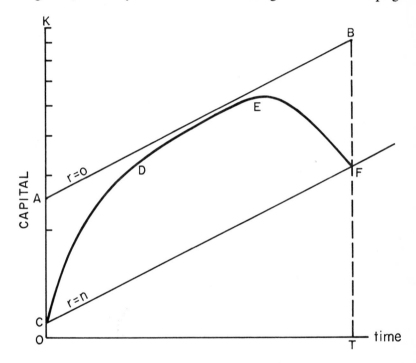

FIGURE 2. To go from C in the Phelps golden rule configuration to F in that same state, social utility is maximized by departing from the golden rule golden-age path CF: instead, if T is large, one should arch (as in AD) toward the zero-interest-rate bliss turnpike, staying near it for most of the time (as in DE), and finally arching down (along EF) back to F. Thus, any golden-age path that differs from the AB golden-age path—like CF, the golden rule path—can definitely be bettered. This is in no conflict with the truth that social (and individual) utility along "efficient" AB is *less* than it would be along "inefficient" CF; it is this last odd fact that explains why *permanent* movement along the "finite-time-efficient" AB path is "Phelps-Koopmans inefficient" in comparison with *permanent* movement along the "finite-time inefficient" CF path. (The reader will realize that the best path from A to F, which he can draw between AB and $ADEF$, involves more utility than either.)

113

rule golden age is *not* optimal under the hedonist criterion, and this remains true no matter how long T is—a day, a year, a century, or a trillion millennia.[7]

An alternative direct solution to the welfare maximization of Equations 25 through 27 can be given as follows:

$$\underset{c_t1,\, c_t2}{\text{Max}} \frac{1}{L_0} \sum_0^T [L_t v(c_t^1) + L_{t-1} v(c_t^2)]$$

$$= \underset{k_t,\, c_t2}{\max} (1 + n)^t \sum_0^T \left\{ v\left[f(k_t) + k_t - (1 + n)k_{t+1} - \frac{c_t^2}{1 + n} \right] + \frac{v(c_t^2)}{1 + n} \right\},$$

$$(30)$$

with extremal conditions

$$v'(c_t^1) = v'(c_t^2), \qquad (30a)$$

$$\frac{v'(c_{t-1}^1)}{v'(c_t^1)} = 1 + f'(k_t) = 1 + r_t. \qquad (30b)$$

Laissez faire will *not* lead to satisfaction of these conditions, even under perfect competition. From these two sets of equations, we can derive a third set that will be satisfied under perfect competition, namely,

$$\frac{v'(c_{t-1}^1)}{v'(c_t^2)} = 1 + f'(k_t) = 1 + r_t. \qquad (30c)$$

Together Equations 30c and 30a would produce the optimum; but perfect competition by consumers who maximize only over their own lifetimes provides only Equation 30c and not Equation 30a. The latter presupposes direct intervention by the state to redistribute consumptions by lump-sum taxation.

7. Conclusion

Even if one rejects the Samuelson-Diamond representative-man criterion in favor of the Bentham-Lerner criterion, one must be grateful to Diamond for his positive analysis of the incidence of internal and external public debt. However, the normative interpretation of debt incidence must be modified under the new criterion.

Thus, Diamond shows that larger internal debt impinging on a situation in which the competitive market produces a golden age with interest less than the rate of population growth, will raise the interest rate. By his criterion, this is a good thing in that it moves r toward the golden rule identity with n.

---

[7] This shows how limited and precise must be the claims for the Phelps-Koopmans notion of (permanent!) dynamic inefficiency, as footnote 3 on divergent limits had warned.

But a Lernerite would have to disagree. Anything that raises the interest rate for a very long period (but not forever) stands to lessen the total of social utility.

Indeed since Lerner himself disbelieves in the relevance of exponentials that grow over infinite time, he would ask Diamond to elaborate his analysis of debt incidence. Instead of asking, "What new golden age will result from this new element of per capita debt?" we ask, "If new debt is created now and maintained afterward at such and such a time profile, what will be the resulting change in total and intrageneration consumption, and in the cumulative total of social utility?" I shall not enter into this matter here.

References

1. Asimakopulos, A., unpublished, Massachusetts Institute of Technology, 1966.
2. Diamond, P., "National Debt in a Neoclassical Growth Model," *American Economic Review*, Vol. 55 (1965), pp. 1126–1150.
3. Fisher, I., *The Theory of Interest*, New York: The Macmillan Company, 1930.
4. Lerner, A. P., "Consumption-Loan Interest and Money" (Reply), *Journal of Political Economy*, Vol. 67 (1959), pp. 512–518; P. A. Samuelson, "Reply," *Ibid.*, pp. 518–522; A. P. Lerner, "Rejoinder," *Ibid.*, pp. 523–525.
5. Phelps, E. S., "The Golden Rule of Accumulation: A Fable for Growthmen," *American Economic Review*, Vol. 51 (1961), pp. 638–643.
6. Phelps, E. S., "Second Essay on the Golden Rule of Accumulation," *American Economic Review*, Vol. 55 (1965), pp. 793–814.
7. Ramsey, F. P., "A Mathematical Theory of Saving," *Economic Journal*, Vol. 38 (1928), pp. 543–559.
8. Samuelson, P. A., "An Exact Consumption-Loan Model of Interest with or without the Social Contrivance of Money," *Journal of Political Economy*, Vol. 66 (1958), pp. 467–482; reproduced in J. Stiglitz (ed.), *The Collected Scientific Papers of Paul A. Samuelson*, Cambridge, Mass.: The M.I.T. Press, 1966, Vol. I, pp. 219–234.
9. Samuelson, P. A., "A Catenary Turnpike Theorem Involving Consumption and the Golden Rule," *American Economic Review*, Vol. 55 (1965), pp. 486–496.
10. Swan, T. W., "Of Golden Ages and Production Functions," 1960 Gamagori *IEA* paper published in K. Berrill (ed.), *Economic Development with Special Reference to East Asia*, New York: International Economic Association, 1964, pp. 3–16.

138

THE TWO-PART GOLDEN RULE DEDUCED AS THE ASYMPTOTIC TURNPIKE OF CATENARY MOTIONS

PAUL A. SAMUELSON[*]

MASSACHUSETTS INSTITUTE OF TECHNOLOGY

1. *Introduction.* What is the optimal capital formation and lifetime allocation of consumption in the Good Society? These are vital questions for investment planning, social security, fiscal, and monetary policy. The present paper provides the following answers:

> 1. Capital must be accumulated so that, most of the time, the interest rate nearly equals the (assumed constant) rate of population growth — the Swan-Phelps production Golden Rule;
>
> 2. Goods must be allocated among the generations of different ages as if the consumption-loan interest rate nearly equals, most of the time, the natural rate of growth of the population — the Samuelson biological-interest-rate Golden Rule of consumption.

Using a Ramsey-Solow optimizing model, I shall deduce this two-part Golden Rule as a steady-state equilibrium and show how longtime optimal dynamic programs approach the Turnpike so defined and then veer away from it, in accordance with the catenary-like stability properties of a saddle-point equilibrium.[1]

2. *Assumptions.* In a one-sector neoclassical model,[2] let consumption plus net capital formation (i.e. NNP) be producible by exponentially-growing labor and homogeneous capital under classical returns (i.e. constant returns to scale and diminishing returns to varying factor proportions):

---

[*]Financial assistance of the National Science Foundation is gratefully acknowledged.

[1]For the production Golden Rule, see T. W. Swan, "Of Golden Ages and Production Functions," in K. Berrill, ed., *Economic Development with Special Reference to East Asia: Proceedings of a 1960 Conference Held by the International Economic Association* (New York, 1964); E. S. Phelps, *Golden Rule of Economic Growth* (New York, 1966), which contains references to his original 1960 *American Economic Review* article and to related discoveries by von Weizsäcker, Desrousseaux, Joan Robinson, Allais, and Solow. For the biological interest rate, see P. A. Samuelson, "An Exact Consumption-Loan Model of Interest with or without the Social Contrivance of Money" (*Jour. Pol. Econ.*, Dec. 1958, 66, 467-82) reproduced in *Collected Scientific Papers* of Paul A. Samuelson (Cambridge, 1966) as Chapter 21 along with replies to comments by A. P. Lerner and W. H. Meckling that appeared in the 1959 and 1960 *Journal of Political Economy*; see also, Peter Diamond, "National Debt in a Neoclassical Growth Model" (*Amer. Econ. Rev.*, Dec. 1965, 55, 1126-50), P. A. Samuelson, "A Catenary Turnpike Theorem Involving Consumption and the Golden Rule" (*Am. Econ. Rev.*, June 1965, 55, 486-96), and "A Turnpike Refutation of the Golden Rule in a Welfare Maximizing Many-Year Model," in K. Shell, ed., *Essays in the Theory of Optimal Economic Growth* (Cambridge, 1967), and finally A. Asimakopulos, "Biological Interest Rate and the Social Utility Function" (*Am. Econ. Rev.*, March 1967, 57, 185-89).

[2]My notation parallels that of my 1967 paper in the cited Shell volume, and differs from that of Diamond trivially after one translates his e's into my c's.

(1) $\qquad C_t + (K_{t+1} - K_t) = f(K_t, L_t) = L_t f(K_t/L_t), \qquad f'' < 0$

In terms of per capita variables $(c_t, k_t) = (C_t/L_t, K_t/L_t)$, this becomes

(2) $\qquad c_t = f(k_t) + k_t - (L_{t+1}/L_t) k_{t+1}$

$\qquad\qquad\qquad = f(k_t) + k_t - (1+n) k_{t+1}$

if labor grows exponentially like $(1+n)^t$.

For simplicity, assume that current consumption can be allocated among the two living generations, C^1_t going to those in the first working period of life, and C^2_t going to those in the second retirement period of life. If all men of each generation are alike and if none of the L_t born as workers dies before the end of the retirement period, we have

(3) $\qquad\qquad C_t = C^1_t + C^2_t$

$\qquad\qquad\qquad = c^1_t L_t + c^2_t L_{t-1}$

$\qquad\qquad\qquad = L_t [c^1_t + (1+n)^{-1} c^2_t]$

where c^i_t represents the per capita consumption of the i-th generation at the time t.

Finally, let $u[c^1_t, c^2_{t+1}]$ represent the concave lifetime utility, *ex ante* and *ex post*, of the representative man born as a worker at time t.

3. *The generalized Ramsey problem.* Our optimization problem is to maximize over an interval of time, from now to T years from now, the following sum

(4) $\qquad$ Maximize $S_T = u[c^1_0, c^2_1] + u[c^1_1, c^2_2] + \ldots + u[c^1_T, c^2_{T+1}]$

$$= \sum_{t=0}^{T} u[c^1_t, c^2_{t+1}]$$

subject to[5] prescribed initial and terminal values $(k_0, c^2_0; k_{T+1}, c^2_{T+1})$ and the production-possibility restriction of (2) and (3)

$$c^1_t = f(k_t) + k_t - (1+n) k_{t+1} - (1+n)^{-1} c^2_t$$

Substituting this last relationship into (4) to get rid of the (c^1_t) variables, we end up with

(4') Maximize $S_T = \sum_0^T u[\, f(k_t) + k_t - (1+n) k_{t+1} - (1+n)^{-1} c^2_t, c^2_{t+1}\,]$

4. *Dynamic optimality conditions.* To get the conditions for optimal programs, we differentiate our maximand with respect to each of the decision variables to get

[5]If the planner really cares nothing about the periods after $T+1$, k_{T+1} could be set as small as is optimal and c^2_{T+1} could be determined by optimality conditions with $c^1_t = 0, t > T + 1.$

$$(5a) \qquad \frac{\partial S_T}{\partial k_t} = 0 = \frac{\partial u[c_t^1, c_{t+1}^2]}{\partial c_t^1} [f'(k_t) + 1] - \frac{\partial u[c_{t-1}^1, c_t^2]}{\partial c_{t-1}^1} (1 + n)$$

$$(5b) \qquad \frac{\partial S_T}{\partial c_t^2} = 0 = -(1 + n)^{-1} \frac{\partial u[c_t^1, c_{t+1}^2]}{\partial c_t^1} + \frac{\partial u[c_{t-1}^1, c_t^2]}{\partial c_t^2}$$

These correspond to the Euler extremal conditions in the calculus of variations involving continuous time. For discrete time, these are a set of second-order difference equations in the unknown time profile of capitals and of generation consumptions. With our prescribed initial and terminal conditions, we can always find a solution. Alternatively, if we are given two initial periods' values for our unknowns, we define an optimal path or motion through time (except for singular cases).

5. *Stationary Turnpikes.* Upon inspection of our dynamic equations we see that they do have stationary equilibrium solutions for the Turnpike $(k_t, c_t^1, c_t^2) = (k_*, c_*^1, c_*^2)$, the roots of (5a)'s implied interest-rate-equals-growth-rate relation

$$(6a) \qquad\qquad r_* = f'(k_*) = n \qquad \text{Production Golden Rule}$$

and of (5b)'s implied

$$(6b) \qquad \frac{\partial u[c_*^1, c_*^2]/\partial c^1}{\partial u[c_*^1, c_*^2]/\partial c^2} = 1 + n \qquad \text{Biological Interest Rate}$$

That these two Golden Rules are analytically independent is seen from freezing k at any non-optimal level, say at k_{**} ,thereby losing the optimality conditions (5a) and (6a). But still the set (5b) and its implied (6b) require the consumption-loan interest rate to be $n \neq f'(k_{**})$. Alternatively, freeze the fractional allocations of output among generations at some non-optimal level (say by a poorly contrived social security system); we then lose the optimality set (5b) and (6b). But still we determine from (5a) the production Turnpike k_* of (6a).

6. *Dynamic instability.* Will all dynamic optimizing paths satisfying the extremal difference equations (5) approach asymptotically, for large T, the Double-Golden Turnpike defined by (6)? As I showed in the papers dealing with consumption Turnpikes, the answer is "Definitely no." The optimal trajectories are (generalized) catenaries, arching close to the Turnpike and then ultimately moving indefinitely far away from them (and actually terminating as efficient paths in finite time.

If, however, we maximize over infinite time (selecting our origin for cardinal utility so that the Turnpike level is zero), we have the convergent sum

$$(7) \qquad\qquad S_\infty = \overset{\infty}{\Sigma} [u(c_t^1, c_{t+1}^2) - u(c_*^1, c_*^2)]$$

It then must be the case that we select from each initial point that singular Ramsey solution of (5) that does approach the Turnpike asymptotically. This is the only permanently-extendable solution to (5)'s extremal conditions that satisfies the prescribed initial conditions; any other solution eventually hits a boundary and terminates in finite time. That explains the logic of any Turnpike theorem: if T gets large, in order to avoid dead-end inefficiency we must hug ever closer to the Turnpike.

Thus we have made clear the general truth of the Consumption Turnpike Theorem (Samuelson-Cass), which says that for T large enough and fixed initial and terminal values for k and c^i, all paths move indefinitely close to the Double-Golden Turnpike and stay indefinitely close to it an indefinitely large fraction of the time.

7. *Catenary property of reciprocal roots.* Specifically, the small divergence of a typical variable, such as k_t, from its Turnpike value k_*, is locally of the form

$$(8) \qquad k_t - k_* = a_1 q_1^t + a_2 (q_1^{-1})^t + a_3 q_2^t + a_4 (q_2^{-1})^t + \text{Remainder}$$

where the remainder depends upon the squares and higher cross-products of the divergences. Only for the asymptotic Ramsey path will the coefficients of the q's that exceed one in absolute value all vanish. All other efficient paths will be locally anti-damped and ultimately divergent.[4]

8. *Systematic time preference and Bentham-Lerner hedonism.* Cass and I have independently shown that the Golden Turnpike can be generalized to a whole set of Turnpikes each appropriate to any preassigned constant rate of time preference. We derive this by introducing into our maximand a discount factor $(1+R)^{-t} = \lambda^{-t}$, to get

$$(4'') \qquad \text{Maximize } S_T(\lambda) = \sum_0^T \lambda^{-t} u[c^1{}_t, c^2{}_{t+1}]$$

Then (5a) and (5b) become

$$(5a') \qquad \frac{\partial u[c^1{}_t, c^2{}_{t+1}]}{\partial c^1{}_t} [1+f'(k_t)] - \frac{\partial u[c^1{}_{t-1}, c^2{}_t]}{\partial c^1{}_{t-1}} (1+n)\lambda = 0$$

$$(5b') \qquad -(1+n)^{-1} \frac{\partial u[c^1{}_t, c^2{}_{t+1}]}{\partial c^1{}_t} + \frac{\partial u[c^1{}_{t-1}, c^2{}_t]}{\partial c^2{}_t} \lambda = 0$$

Their generalized Turnpike is now given by $(k_{**}, c^1{}_{**}, c^2{}_{**})$, the roots of

$$(6a') \qquad 1 + r_{**} = 1 + f'(k_{**}) = (1+n)\lambda = (1+n)(1+R)$$

$$(6b') \qquad \frac{\partial u[c^1{}_{**}, c^2{}_{**}]/\partial c^1}{\partial u[c^1{}_{**}, c^2{}_{**}]/\partial c^2} = (1+n)(1+R)$$

[4]These propositions are developed in P. A. Samuelson, "Reciprocal Characteristic Root Property of Discrete-Time Maxima," which is appearing simultaneously in this Journal.

The commonsense of this is clear: if population is stationary, the long-term interest rate equals the subjective rate of (planner's) time preference; if population is growing, the equilibrium interest rate must exceed the subjective rate by enough to coax out the widening of capital needed to equip the growing labor force; and of course the same interest rate appropriate to production is appropriate for consumption-loan transactions.

A remarkable feature of this long-run equilibrium deserves notice. The normative long-run equilibrium is quite independent of the subjective time preference of the representative individual during *his* own lifetime. Thus suppose we imagine two quite different societies, one consisting of Puritans with no biased underestimation of future psychological utilities, and the other of feckless hedonists. Their respective utility functions might be

$$u = F(c^1) + F(c^2) \text{ and } u = F(c^1) + \tfrac{1}{4}F(c^2)$$

Yet if they collectively should decide on the same planning discount rate R, they will end up near the same $(1+R)(1+n)$ Turnpike. Of course it is possible that their political voting behavior will display differences in choice among planning discounts that somehow reflect their private fecklessness or foresight. But this might not be the case. We are confronted here again with the paradox that I pointed out in my original 1958 paper, that there is no presumption that *laissez faire* will end society up at or near the described optimum. Some will say, "So much the worse for *laissez faire*"; and others have said, "So much the worse for any so-called optimum," but without telling us in terms of what norm (other than itself) such a statement can be made.

It is interesting to note that if R is negative, corresponding to reverse time preference, the generalized Turnpike Theorem says that the system must for most of the time definitely be beyond the Golden-Rule state, which is where Phelps-Koopmans have proved it must not *permanently* be. I have already called attention to this paradox.

A case of particular interest occurs when $\lambda^{-1} = 1 + n$, which will prevail under the Bentham-Lerner proposal to maximize the sum total of utilities of everybody who ever lives, with the growing population introducing a growing weighting of per capita utilities of the form $(1 + n)^t$. In this case the Turnpike is the Schumpeter zero-interest configuration, showing that such a state does have a special normative significance regardless of a constant positive rate of population change and its shifting of the Swan-Phelps interest rate.

In the case where time enters explicitly into the maximand even if in the ideal exponential form, we lose the reciprocal-root property of the motions. But for small discount factors, the roots will still come in pairs that are damped and anti-damped and catenary-like motions around a saddlepoint will be assured.

139

LOCAL PROOF OF THE TURNPIKE THEOREM

PAUL A. SAMUELSON*
MASSACHUSETTS INSTITUTE OF TECHNOLOGY

    1.   Turnpike theorems first appeared in print in the RAND 1958 Dorfman-Samuelson-Solow, *Linear Programming and Economic Analysis*. Since Roy Radner's first rigorous proof in 1960, Lionel McKenzie, Michio Morishima, Tjalling Koopmans, Sir John Hicks, myself and numerous others[1] have extended economic analysis of these relations; and Consumption Turnpike theorems of the generalized Ramsey type have been developed by David Cass, Cass and Yaari, Karl Shell, myself, and other writers on optimal control theory.[2]

    However, the original heuristic proof in Dorfman-Samuelson-Solow (hereafter referred to as D-S-S) that the efficient motion around the turnpike had the saddlepoint property needed for the Turnpike theorem has long been known to be marred by computational errors. In his second cited paper of 1963, Professor McKenzie provided the needed corrections of the D-S-S proof (and at the same time essentially established the important fact that the characteristic roots associated with stationary solutions of discrete-time maximum problems occur in reciprocal pairs). The present paper provides a slightly different treatment of the problem, paralleling my 1959 calculus-of-variations treatment at Stanford and achieving various simplifications by converting the problem into one involving an unconstrained integral over time that is expressible in terms of factor ratios alone. Some slight generalizations of the D-S-S model are given.

    2.   As in D-S-S Chapter 12, I assume an efficient one-period transformation function relating the period's consumptions $(C^1_t, C^2_t, \ldots, C^n_t)$, C_t for short, to its initial and terminal capital stocks, $(S^1_t, S^2_t, \ldots, S^n_t) = S_t$ and S_{t+1}: namely

(1) $S^1_{t+1} = F[S^1_t, \ldots, S^n_t; S^2_{t+1}, \ldots, S^n_{t+1}; C^1_t, \ldots, C^r_t]$

where F is a concave, homogeneous-first-degree function.[3]

    Since the original Turnpike theorem referred to closed systems without exogenous consumption, we need only consider

(2) $S^1_{t+1} = F[S^1_t, \ldots, S^n_t; S^2_{t+1}, \ldots, S^n_{t+1}; 0, 0, \ldots, 0]$

            $= F[S^1_t, \ldots, S^n_t; S^2_{t+1} \ldots, S^n_{t+1}]$ for short

*I thank Robert Merton of M.I.T. for scientific assistance and the National Science Foundation for financial assistance.

[1] See [14], [8], [9], [10], [6], [7], [18], [21], [3], [12]. Also see books by M. Morishima [10, pp. 154-99] and J. R. Hicks [5, pp. 208-50].

[2] See [15], [16], [1], [2], [13]. Following a seminal article [4], I in [20] and K. Shell and J. Stiglitz in [23] have studied dynamical systems with saddlepoint properties.

[3] In D-S-S, this was written in the slightly less general form

$$S^1_{t+1} = F^1[S^1_t, \ldots, S^n_t; S^2_{t+1} + C^2_t, \ldots, S^n_{t+1} + C^n_t] - C^1_t$$

and for $r = n = 2$. Also S^2 rather than S^1 was taken as *numeraire* good.

where again F is a concave, homogeneous-first-degree function.

Intertemporal efficiency requires solution, with respect to $(S^2_{t+1}, \ldots, S^n_{t+1})$, of the maximum problem:

(3) $\quad \text{Max } S^1_{t+2} = \text{Max } F[F[S^1_t, \ldots, S^n_t; S^2_{t+1}, \ldots, S^n_{t+1}],$

$$S^2_{t+1}, \ldots, S^n_{t+1}; S^2_{t+2}, \ldots, S^n_{t+2}]$$

$$= F_2[S^1_t, \ldots, S^n_t; S^2_{t+2}, \ldots, S^n_{t+2}]$$

If all the maxima are smooth and interior, this requires

(4) $\quad \dfrac{\partial S^1_{t+2}}{\partial S^j_{t+1}} = 0 = \dfrac{\partial F[S^1_{t+1}, \ldots, S^n_{t+1}; S^2_{t+2}, \ldots, S^n_{t+2}]}{\partial S^1_{t+1}}.$

$$\dfrac{\partial F[S^1_t, \ldots, S^n_t; S^2_{t+1}, \ldots, S^n_{t+1}]}{\partial S^j_{t+1}} + \dfrac{\partial F[S^1_{t+1}, \ldots, S^n_{t+1}; S^2_{t+2}, \ldots, S^n_{t+2}],}{\partial S^j_{t+1}}$$

$$(j = 2, \ldots, n)$$

the fundamental envelope conditions for intertemporal efficiency.

For $T > 2$ periods ahead, we have the recursive maximum problems solved with respect to $(S^n_{t+T-1}, \ldots)$:

(5) $\quad \text{Max } S^1_T = \text{Max } F[F_{T-1}[S^1_t, \ldots, S^n_t; S^2_{t+T-1}, \ldots, S^n_{t+T-1}],$

$$S^2_{t+T-1}, \ldots, S^n_{t+T-1}; S^2_{t+T}, \ldots, S^n_{t+T}]$$

$$= F_T[S^1_t, \ldots, S^n_t; S^2_{t+T}, \ldots, S^n_{t+T}] \; T = 1,2,3, \ldots.$$

with $F_1[S^1_t, \ldots, S^n_t; S^2_{t+1}, \ldots, S^n_{t+1}] \equiv F[S^1_t, \ldots, S^n_t; S^2_{t+1}, \ldots, S^n_{t+1}]$

It is easy to verify that this goes back inductively to the envelope conditions of (4) for all intermediate times and to no new conditions.

The Turnpike theorem is a statement about some of the properties of the F_T functions as $T \to \infty$ or becomes large.

3. Alternatively, we can think of (2) and (4) as a set of difference equations determining the efficient trajectories of the $[S^j_t]$. In particular, it is easy to verify that a von Neumann balanced growth (or "turnpike") configuration satisfies these equations, with

(6) $\quad S^j_t/S^1_t = s^j_*$, a constant, $\quad (j = 2, \ldots, n)$

$$S^j_t = S^1_0 s^j_*(\gamma_*)^t$$

where γ_* is the von Neumann maximum rate of balanced growth of the system.

What D-S-S tried to prove in Chapters 12-2-10 and 12-2-11 was that the linearized difference equations for the S^j_t/S^1_t ratios, which are associated with the system (2)-(4), have characteristic roots which necessarily appear in reciprocal pairs. This property ensures that the diagram of the phase space does approximate the saddlepoint form shown in Figure 12-9 of D-S-S.

4. Taking advantage of the homogeneity properties of the system, which are basic to all production Turnpike theorems, I shall reformulate the problem in terms of ratios, namely:

$$(7) \qquad s^j{}_t = S^j{}_t/S^1{}_t, \qquad (j = 2, \ldots, n)$$

$$\gamma^1{}_t = S^1{}_{t+1}/S^1{}_t$$

Dividing our homogeneous transformation function of (2) through by $S^1{}_t$, we rearrange terms to get the (per capita of S^1) relation

$$(8) \qquad \gamma^1{}_t = S^1{}_{t+1}/S^1{}_t = F[1, s^2{}_t, \ldots, s^n{}_t; s^2{}_{t+1}\gamma^1{}_t, \ldots, s^n{}_{t+1}\, \gamma^1{}_t]$$

Now it is easy to see, economically and mathematically, that this implicit equation can be solved uniquely for $\gamma^1{}_t$, namely:

$$(9) \qquad \gamma^1{}_t = f(s^2{}_t, \ldots, s^n{}_t; s^2{}_{t+1}, \ldots, s^n{}_{t+1})$$

Intertemporal efficiency can now be formulated as the following maximum problem:

$$(10) \quad \text{Max} \log (S^1{}_T/S^1{}_0) = \text{Max} \log [(S^1{}_T/S^1{}_{T-1})(S^1{}_{T-1}/S^1{}_{T-2}) \ldots (S^1{}_1/S^1{}_0)]$$

$$= \text{Max} \log [\prod_{j=1}^{T} (S^1{}_{T-j+1}/S^1{}_{T-j})]$$

$$= \text{Max} \sum_{j=1}^{T} \log (\gamma^1{}_{T-j}) \qquad \text{from (7)}$$

$$= \text{Max} \sum_{t=1}^{T-1} \log (\gamma^1{}_{t-1})$$

$$= \underset{\{s^i{}_t\}}{\text{Max}} \sum_{t=1}^{T-1} \Phi(s_{t-1}, s_t) \qquad \text{from (9)}$$

where

$$(11) \qquad \Phi(s_t, s_{t+1}) \equiv \log [f(s^2{}_t, \ldots, s^n{}_t; s^2{}_{t+1}, \ldots, s^n{}_{t+1})].$$

Now we have a standard unconstrained problem in discrete-time programming, with prescribed terminal conditions (s_0, s_T). Elsewhere,[4] I have recently proved the general theorem that all motions around a stationary point of such a variational system must possess the desired ("generalized catenary") property of having associated characteristic roots that appear in reciprocal pairs.

[4] [22]. A still more general analogue for difference equations of the Poincaré stability analysis for periodic motions is given in [17].

The efficiency conditions of optimality are the Euler-like variational relations for (10):

$$(12) \qquad \frac{\partial [\log (S^1{}_T/S^1{}_0)]}{\partial s^j{}_t} = 0 = \frac{\partial \Phi(s_t, s_{t+1})}{\partial s^j{}_t} + \frac{\partial \Phi(s_{t-1}, s_t)}{\partial s^j{}_t}$$

$$(j = 2, \ldots, n), \quad (t = 1, \ldots, T-1)$$

It is straightforward to show the equivalence of these to (4)'s envelope relations of efficiency, and that these equations have a stationary solution at the von Neumann Turnpike, namely that $s_t \equiv s_*$ does satisfy (12).

Because Φ is not necessarily concave in all its variables, first-order necessary conditions need to be supplemented by secondary conditions sufficient to ensure a maximum and not a minimum or mere stationary value. Actually, the concavity of the original F rules out Jacobi conjugate points and other pathologies. Similar remarks are in order concerning f in (9') later and its relation to the F of (1').

Associated with the $n-1$ second-order non-linear difference equations (12) are the linear equations:

$$(13) \qquad 0 \equiv \phi^{12} y_{t+2} + (\phi^{11} + \phi^{22}) y_{t+1} + \phi^{21} y_t$$

where

$$y_t \equiv [s^i{}_t - s^i{}_*] \qquad\qquad (i = 2, \ldots, n)$$

$$\phi^{11} = \left[\frac{\partial^2 \phi(s_*, s_*)}{\partial s^i{}_t \partial s^j{}_t} \right]; \quad \phi^{22} = \left[\frac{\partial^2 \phi(s_*, s_*)}{\partial s^i{}_{t+1} \partial s^j{}_{t+1}} \right]$$

$$\phi^{12} = \left[\frac{\partial^2 \phi(s_*, s_*)}{\partial s^i{}_t \partial s^j{}_{t+1}} \right]; \quad \phi^{21} = \left[\frac{\partial^2 \phi(s_*, s_*)}{\partial s^i{}_{t+1} \partial s^j{}_t} \right]$$

In the case $n = 2$, (13) becomes a single difference equation:

$$(14) \qquad a y_{t+2} + b y_{t+1} + a y_t = 0$$

Its solution is of the form:

$$y_t = C_1 \lambda_1{}^t + C_2 \lambda_2{}^t$$

where (λ_i) are roots of the characteristic quadratic:

$$(15) \qquad a\lambda^2 + b\lambda + a = a(\lambda - \lambda_1)(\lambda - \lambda_1{}^{-1}) = 0$$

where

$$\lambda_1 = \frac{-b}{2a} + \frac{(b^2 - 4a^2)^{1/2}}{2a}$$

Except for singular initial conditions,

$$(16) \qquad \lim_{t \to \pm \infty} y_t = \lim_{t \to \pm \infty} [C_1 \lambda_1{}^t + C_2 \lambda_1{}^{-t}] = \pm \infty$$

For $|\lambda_1| > 0$ and singular initial conditions that make $C_1 = 0$, we have

(17)
$$\text{limit } y_t = 0$$
$$t \to \infty$$

the razor's-edge case that represents approach to the turnpike.

In D-S-S Figure 12-9, the phase space was incorrectly framed in terms of the variables here written as (γ_t, s_t). Actually, the equations for these variables are shown there to be of the form:

$$s_{t+1} - s_t = \triangle s_t = M(s_t, \gamma_t)$$

$$\gamma_t - \gamma_{t-1} = \bigtriangledown \gamma_t = N(s_t, \gamma_t)$$

These are *not* explicitly in causal form since both receding and advancing differences are involved. As I have shown in a paper [19] on Hamiltonian canonical equations for a discrete-time system, this is no accident: generally receding and advancing differences will be involved. For small time intervals, the discrepancy will not matter much.

By solving some implicit equations, or by redefining new phase variables —such as (s_t, s_{t+1})—we can plot the vectors of motion as we go from (s_t, s_{t+1}) to $(s_t + \triangle s_t, s_{t+1} + \triangle s_{t+1})$. These approximate the smooth curves of D-S-S Figure 12-9 and the saddlepoint form shown there when $n = 2$.

For $n > 2$, the characteristic roots are given by the determinantal polynomial of $(2n-2)^{th}$ degree:

(18)
$$\triangle (\lambda) = \det[\phi^{12}\lambda^2 + (\phi^{11} + \phi^{22})\lambda + \phi^{21}]$$

$$= \lambda^{2n-2}\det[\phi^{12} + (\phi^{11} + \phi^{22})\lambda^{-1} + \phi^{21}\lambda^{-2}]$$

$$= \lambda^{2n-2}\det[\phi^{21} + (\phi^{11} + \phi^{22})\lambda^{-1} + \phi^{12}\lambda^{-2}]'$$

$$= \lambda^{2n-2} \triangle(\lambda^{-1})$$

Hence, except for the singular case where $\lambda = 0$, λ_j^{-1} is a root where λ_j is, and all roots do come in reciprocal pairs.

For $n > 2$, there may be complex roots, and so our catenaries and saddlepoints are really generalizations of these simple concepts.

5. This completes our corrected proof. Because the calculus of variations is better known than discrete-time maximization, I shall quickly sketch the parallel treatment of the continuous-time case, amplifying slightly my 1959 Stanford-symposium treatment. By using a parallel notation, the exposition should be self-explanatory.

Corresponding to (1) and (2), we now have:

(1') $\quad \dot{S^1} = F(S^1, S^2, \ldots, S^n; \dot{S^2}, \ldots, \dot{S^n}; C_1, \ldots, C_r)$

(2') $\quad \dot{S}^1 = F(S^1, S^2, \ldots, S^n, \dot{S}^2, \ldots, \dot{S}^n) = F(S^1, S^2, \ldots, S^n, \dot{S}^2, \ldots, \dot{S}^n;$

$$0, 0, \ldots, 0)$$

where F is a concave, homogeneous-first-degree function.[5]

Corresponding to (4)'s envelope relation, we have the Euler external equations:

(4') $\quad \dfrac{d}{dt} \dfrac{\partial F}{\partial \dot{S}^i} = \dfrac{\partial F}{\partial S^i} + \dfrac{\partial F}{\partial S^1} \cdot \dfrac{\partial F}{\partial \dot{S}^i} \qquad (i = 2, \ldots, n)$

which are derived from the constrained Lagrangian expression:

$$\delta \int_0^T L dt = \delta \int_0^T \left\{ \dot{S}^1 + \lambda(t)[F(S^1, \ldots, S^n, \dot{S}^2, \ldots, \dot{S}^n) - \dot{S}^1] \right\} dt = 0$$

As in (7), we define new variables $s^j(t) = S^j(t)/S^1(t)$ and convert (2') into:

(8') $\quad \dot{S}^1/S^1 = F(1, s^2, \ldots, s^n, \dot{s}^2 + s^2(\dot{S}^1/S^1), \ldots, \dot{s}^n + s^n(\dot{S}^1/S^1))$

(9') $\qquad = f(s^2, \ldots, s^n, \dot{s}^2, \ldots, \dot{s}^n)$, by Implicit Function Theorem.

Now efficiency is equivalent to the simple maximum problem:

(10') $\quad$ Max $\displaystyle\int_0^T \dfrac{d}{dt} [\log S^1] dt =$ Max $\displaystyle\int_0^T f(s^2, \ldots, s^n, \dot{s}^2, \ldots, \dot{s}^n) \, dt$

$$\{s^i(t)\}$$

This implies the Euler differential equations

(12') $\quad \dfrac{d}{dt} \left[\dfrac{\partial f(s; \dot{s})}{\partial \dot{s}^i} \right] - \dfrac{\partial f(s; \dot{s})}{\partial s^i} = 0 \qquad (i = 2, \ldots, n)$

These have stationary turnpike solutions (which are actually maximum steady-state values)

$$0 - \dfrac{\partial f(s^*; 0)}{\partial s^i} = 0 \qquad (i = 2, \ldots, n)$$

[5]In my 1959 paper [18], equation (1) is written in the more special form:

$$\dot{S}^1 = f[S^1, \ldots, S^n, \dot{S}^2 + C_2, \ldots, \dot{S}^n + C_n] - C_1, \qquad r = n$$

where the $[S^j]$ here are written there as $[S_j]$.

Associated with the non-linear equations (12′) are the linear equations:

(13′)
$$f^{22}\ddot{y} + (f^{21} - f^{12})\dot{y} - f^{11}y = 0$$

where

$$
\begin{bmatrix} f^{11} & f^{12} \\ f^{21} & f^{22} \end{bmatrix} =
\begin{bmatrix}
\dfrac{\partial^2 f(s^*;0)}{\partial s \, \partial s} & \dfrac{\partial^2 f(s^*;0)}{\partial s \, \partial \dot{s}} \\[2ex]
\dfrac{\partial^2 f(s^*;0)}{\partial \dot{s} \, \partial s} & \dfrac{\partial^2 f(s^*;0)}{\partial \dot{s} \, \partial \dot{s}}
\end{bmatrix}
$$

$$
= \begin{bmatrix} f^{11} & f^{21} \\ f^{12} & f^{22} \end{bmatrix}' \quad ; \quad (f^{12} - f^{21}) = (f^{21} - f^{12})'
$$

$$y(t) = [s^i(t) - s^i_*] \qquad (i = 2, \ldots, n)$$

The general solution of (13′) consists of sums of terms of the form C_k exp $(\lambda_k t)$, where λ_k are characteristic roots of the characteristic polynomial and C_k is, at worst, a polynomial in t:

$$
\Delta(\lambda) = \det[f^{22}\lambda^2 + (f^{21} - f^{12})\lambda - f^{11}]
$$
$$
= \det[f^{22}\lambda^2 + (f^{12} - f^{21})\lambda - f^{11}]' \text{ by above symmetry relations}
$$
$$
= \det[f^{22}(-\lambda)^2 + (f^{21} - f^{12})(-\lambda) - f^{11}]
$$
$$
= \Delta(-\lambda)
$$

This proves a classical Poincaré theorem which asserts that the characteristic roots associated with the stationary solutions of a Hamiltonian system occur in opposite-signed pairs. This confirms the generalized catenary or saddle-point property of the turnpike. Now the phase diagram, Figure 12-9 of D-S-S, becomes exact.

When $n = 2$, $f^{12} - f^{21} = 0$, and the roots are real and opposite in sign; a simple saddlepoint is then assured. (If f were convex in $\dot{s}$ and concave in s, as in the pendulum problems of classical mechanics, the roots would be opposite-signed pure imaginaries, $\lambda_j = \pm i(|f^{11}|/|f^{22}|)^{1/2}$, giving rise to sinusoidal oscillations. If f is quadratic in the velocities, as in mechanical problems involving no gyroscopic terms, we have $f = \sum_p \sum_q a^{pq}(s^*)\dot{s}^p\dot{s}^q - V(s)$ and $f^{12} \equiv 0 \equiv f^{21}$. If $V(s^*)$ is a minimum of potential energy, and $[a^{pq}(s)]$ is positive definite, then all the roots will be pure imaginaries of opposite signs, and the fluctuations will be conservatively stable. In economics, when $n > 2$, we may have, as Morishima [11] has observed, opposite-signed complex roots, $u + iv$ and $-u - iv$, resulting in oscillations anti-damped for large

$\pm$ t. In 4 or more dimensional phase space, we have generalizations of saddlepoints and catenaries, but the Turnpike theorem remains valid.[6]

[6]In [18, p. 298], I first omitted the $f^{21} - f^{12}$ term and had to add an *erratum* slip to the published Stanford book. Unfortunately, this correction was not made in the *Collected Scientific Papers*. In both cases, equations (34) and (35) should respectively have added in them middle terms, reading as:

$$0 = \sum_{j=2}^{n} \left\{ \frac{\partial^2 F^*}{\partial x_i{'}\partial x_j{'}} (x_j - x_j*)'' + [\frac{\partial^2 F^*}{\partial x_i{'}\partial x_j} - \frac{\partial^2 F^*}{\partial x_i\partial x_j{'}}](x_j - x_j*)' - \frac{\partial^2 F^*}{\partial x_i\partial x_j} (x_j - x_j*) \right\}$$

$$det [\frac{\partial^2 F^*}{\partial x_i{'}\partial x_j{'}}\lambda^2 + (\frac{\partial^2 F^*}{\partial x_i{'}\partial x_j} - \frac{\partial^2 F^*}{\partial x_i\partial x_j{'}}) \lambda - \frac{\partial^2 F^*}{\partial x_i\partial x_j}] = 0$$

For $n > 2$, it will not be the case that λ^2 is necessarily real. Actually, opposite-signed complex roots can definitely occur, as Professor Morishima had pointed out to me.

REFERENCES

1. D. Cass, "Optimum Growth in an Aggregation Model of Capital Accumulation: A Turnpike Theorem," *Econometrica*, Oct. 1966, 34, 833-50.
2. _____ and M. Yaari, "Individual Saving, Aggregate Capital Accumulation, and Efficient Growth," in *Essays on the Theory of Optimal Economic Growth*, ed., K. Shell, Cambridge 1967, 269-80.
3. H. Furuya and K. Inada, "Balanced Growth and Intertemporal Efficiency in Capital Accumulation," *Internat. Econ. Rev.*, Jan. 1962, 3, 94-107.
4. F. Hahn, "Equilibrium Dynamics with Heterogeneous Capital Goods," *Quart. Jour. Econ.*, Nov. 1966, 80, 633-46.
5. J. R. Hicks, *Capital and Growth*. Oxford 1965.
6. _____, "Prices and the Turnpike (I) The Story of a Mare's Nest," *Rev. Econ. Stud.*, Feb. 1961, 28, 77-88.
7. T. C. Koopmans, "Economic Growth at a Maximal Rate," *Quart. Jour. Econ.*, Aug. 1964, 78, 355-94.
8. L. W. McKenzie, "The Dorfman-Samuelson-Solow Turnpike Theorem," *Internat. Econ Rev.*, Jan. 1963, 4, 29-43.
9. _____, "Turnpike Theorems for a Generalized Leontief Model," *Econometrica*, Jan. 1963, 31, 165-80.
10. M. Morishima, *Equilibrium Stability and Growth*. Oxford 1964.
11. _____, "Proof of a Turnpike Theorem: The 'No Joint Production Case,'" *Rev. Econ. Stud.*, Feb. 1961, 28, 89-97.
12. H. Nikaido, "Persistence of Continual Growth near the von Neumann Ray: A Strong Version of the Radner Turnpike Theorem, *Econometrica*, Jan.-Apr. 1964, 32, 151-62.
13. E. S. Phelps, *Golden Rules of Economic Growth*. New York 1966.
14. R. Radner, "Paths of Economic Growth that are Optimal with Regard Only to Final States: A Turnpike Theorem," *Rev. Econ. Stud.*, Feb. 1961, 28, 98-104.
15. P. A. Samuelson, "A Catenary Turnpike Theorem Involving Consumption and the Golden Rule," *Am. Econ. Rev.*, June 1965, 55, 486-96.
16. _____, "A Turnpike Refutation of the Golden Rule in a Welfare-Maximizing Many-Year Plan," in *Essays on the Theory of Optimal Economic Growth*, ed., K. Shell, Cambridge 1967, 269-80.
17. _____, *Classical Orbital Stability Deduced for Discrete-Time Maximum Systems*, Jan. 1968, unpublished.
18. _____, "Efficient Paths of Capital Accumulation in Terms of the Calculus of Variations," in *Mathematical Methods in Social Sciences, 1959*, eds., K. J. Arrow, S. Karlin, and P. Suppes, Stanford 1960, 77-88; also in *The Collected Scientific Papers of Paul A. Samuelson*, Vol. 1, ed., J. Stiglitz, Cambridge 1966, 287-98.
19. _____, *Hamilton's Canonical Equations for Discrete-Time Variational Systems*, Jan. 1968, unpublished.
20. _____, "Indeterminacy of Development in a Heterogeneous-Capital Model with Constant Saving Propensity," in *Essays on the Theory of Optimal Economic Growth*, ed., K. Shell, Cambridge 1967, 219-32.
21. _____, "Market Mechanisms and Maximization (III) Dynamics and Linear Programming," a 1949 RAND memo reproduced in *Essays on the Theory of Optimal Economic Growth*, ed., K. Shell, Cambridge 1967, 489-92.
22. _____, "Reciprocal Characteristic Root Property of Discrete-Time Maxima," *Western Econ. Jour.*, 6, 90-93.
23. K. Shell and J. Stiglitz, "The Allocation of Investment in a Dynamic Economy," *Quart. Jour. Econ.*, Nov. 1967, 81, 592-609.

140

TURNPIKE THEOREMS EVEN THOUGH TASTES ARE INTERTEMPORALLY DEPENDENT

PAUL A. SAMUELSON*

Massachusetts Institute of Technology

1. *Summary.* Post-Ramsey optimal-growth theory usually involves an additive maximand, such as $\int_0^T U[C(t)]dt$ or $\sum_0^T U[C_t]$. This assumes a kind of "independence" of tastes between periods — such as that my tastes for lobster today are unaffected by yesterday's consumption of lobster, or that my palate's ability to enjoy good wine is unaffected by years of wine drinking. Such independence is a definite limitation on the empirical facts of life;[1] yet most known results in theoretical growth theory — such as asymptotic approach to a saddlepoint "turnpike" or "bliss" level — have been derived by variational methods appropriate only to additive maximands.

The present paper shows that one can relax the independence assumptions somewhat and still derive the usual known results.[2] Concretely, it is assumed that consumption in one period can affect tastes for some *finite* time into the future.

*I owe thanks to the National Science Foundation for financial aid, and to M.I.T. graduate student Katsuhito Iwai for letting me see his valuable paper on Koopmans' separable utility, entitled *Stationary Utility and Optimal Economic Growth.*

1. Dissatisfaction with this independence straight-jacket has often been expressed, as for example in my own first published paper, "A Note on the Measurement of Utility," *Review of Economic Studies*, IV (1937), pp. 155-161. Uneasiness on this score underlay some of the unenthusiastic remarks about Ramsey's model, which reviewers of my *Collected Scientific Papers* have commented on, as was explained in my Foreword to S. Chakravarty, *Capital and Development Planning* (Cambridge, Mass.: M.I.T. Press, 1969), p. viii. See also similar doubts in John Hicks, *Capital and Growth* (Oxford, U.K.: Oxford University Press, 1965), pp. 265-263. The present paper shows that much of growth theory can be rescued from this doubtful assumption.

2. Credit should be given to my old student and coworker, Henry Y. Wan, Jr., now of Cornell University, for having first demonstrated several years ago that the turnpike properties will hold so long as we assume "asymptotic independence," in which interdependence of tastes gradually fades over long enough periods of time. Credit should also be given for independent derivation of similar results by K. Iwai in the paper already acknowledged. Mr. Iwai assumes that utility, $U[C_0, C_1, \ldots, C_t, \ldots]$ takes the Koopmans separable form:

$$U[C_0, C_1, \ldots, C_t] \equiv V(C_0, U[C_1, C_2, \ldots, C_t, \ldots]),$$

referring to work in the mid-1960s by T. C. Koopmans and by Koopmans-Diamond-Williamson. Between equation (4) and (5), I later comment further on the relationship of the present paper to Iwai's model. I should add that Iwai's model is shown to lead to a nice 2-dimensional Fisher diagram of development, an innovation which Mr. Iwai discovered independently of Nissan Liviatan's discovery of that technique as applied to the conventional additive maximand. Cf. N. Liviatan, "A Diagrammatic Exposition of Optimal Growth," *American Economic Review*, LX (June, 1970), pp. 302-309.

2. *Finite-time interdependence of tastes.* Instead of maximizing

$$U_1(C_1) + U_2(C_2) + \dots + U_t(C_t) + \dots$$

where C_t may be a single consumption good or a vector of goods, I assume a maximand of the form

(1) $\quad U_0[C_0; C_{-1}, \dots, C_{-N}] + U_1[C_1; C_0, \dots, C_{1-N}] + \dots + U_t[C_t; C_{t-1}, \dots, C_{t-N}] + \dots$

Thus, the marginal rate of substitution at, say $t = T$, between tea and coffee, as measured by $(\partial U_T/\partial C_T^{tea})/\partial U_T/\partial C_T^{coffee})$ will be affected by tea or salt consumed at an earlier period, namely by C_{T-1}^{tea} or C_{T-1}^{salt}.

For the present purpose, there will be no genuine loss in generality to set $N = 1$ and consider taste contamination only between adjacent periods. The argument is easily qualified for the general case. A more important specialization is that of stationary tastes with constant systematic time discount, so that (1) becomes

(2) $\quad U = u[C_0; C_{-1}] + Bu[C_1; C_0] + B^2u[C_2; C_1] + \dots + B^tu[C_t; C_{t-1}] + \dots$

where $B = 1/(1 + \rho)$, ρ being the systematic rate of subjective time preference; and where u is assumed strictly concave in its arguments, with $u(C; C)$ a strictly increasing function not subject to satiation.

As in simple Ramsey-Solow theory, let technology be given by a one-sector neoclassical production function

(3) $\qquad\qquad C_{t+1} + K_{t+1} - K_t = f(K_t) - \delta K_t \qquad\qquad K_t, C_t \geqslant 0$

where the concave function f has derivative $f'(K_t)$ subject to the usual Inada conditions, $f'' < 0$, $f'(0+) = \infty$, $f'(\infty) = 0$.

We may now state the principal growth-theory results.

THEOREM 1:

Given arbitrary K_{-1}, C_{-1}, an optimal infinite-time program will have the property of approaching asymptotically the (generalized) turnpike K^*, defined in the next section and independent of the form of the $u(C_t; C_{t-1})$ function.

THEOREM 2:

Given K_{-1}, C_{-1}, and fixed $K_T = A$, as the time of the program T becomes indefinitely large, its optimal program must spend an indefinitely large fraction of the time arbitrarily near to the turnpike level K^*.

These will be recognized as the usual Ramsey gradual approach to (modified) bliss, and as the usual consumption-turnpike theorem.[3] And essentially the same result holds when there is interdependence of tastes over N periods, $N \geqslant 1$.

3. *Proof.* I shall not try here to give globally rigorous proofs, but shall sketch a local proof for regular cases that do not involve multiplicity of turnpikes and other complications.

First, replace (2) by the most general form and consider solving the optimal-growth program

$$\text{Max } U[\ldots, C_{-1}, C_0, C_1, \ldots, C_t, \ldots] =$$
$$\underset{K_t}{\text{Max }} U[\ldots, C_{-1}, g(K_{-1}) - K_0, g(K_0) - K_1, \ldots, g(K_{t-1}) - K_t, \ldots]$$

subject to prescribed $[, \ldots, C_{-1}]$ and K_{-1}, and where $g(K)$ is short for $f(K) + K - \delta K$.

A necessary first-order condition for a regular maximum is

$$-\partial U[\ldots]/\partial C_{t-1} + g'(K_{t-1}) \partial U[\ldots]/\partial C_t = 0, \text{ or}$$

(4) $$g'(K_{t-1}) = [\partial U/\partial C_{t-1}]/[\partial U/C_t]$$

This states the equivalence of the technological rate of interest, $g' = f' + 1 - \delta$, to the subjective marginal rate of substitution, a familiar result from Fisher's theory of interest.

---

3. For a convenient summary of post-Ramsey consumption turnpike theory involving discrete time, see P. A. Samuelson, "A Turnpike Refutation of the Golden Rule ...," in K. Shell, ed., *Essays on the Theory of Optimal Growth* (Cambridge, Mass.: M.I.T. Press, 1967), Ch. 24, which gives references to my 1965 *AER* paper; D. Cass has also independently done similar analysis.

However, in general, the right side of (4) could involve the K's of *all* periods and could depend on time. Only when we impose some "separability" or "tree" requirement on $U[\ ]$ can we hope to convert (4) into the finite-time difference equation we need to derive the conventional results. Ramsey's additivity is a strong form of separability. Iwai's use of Koopman's separable utility, as cited earlier, is a weaker form. My (1) and (2) are in some ways weaker and in some ways stronger than Iwai's: weaker because it does permit "contamination" of future marginal rates of substitution; stronger because my functions are additive.

For my specialization in (2), (4) becomes

$$(5)\quad g'(K_{t-1}) = B\,\frac{u_1[g(K_{t-2}) - K_{t-1};\, g(K_{t-3}) - K_{t-2}] + Bu_2[g(K_{t-1}) - K_t;\, g(K_{t-2}) - K_{t-1}]}{u_1[g(K_{t-1}) - K_t;\, g(K_{t-2}) - K_{t-1}] + Bu_2[g(K_t) - K_{t+1};\, g(K_{t-1}) - K_t]}$$

where $u_i[X_1, X_2]$ is short for $\partial u[X_1, X_2]/\partial X_i$.

Equation (5) is a non-linear fourth-order difference equation.[4] It will have a stationary solution, $K_{t-3} \equiv K_{t-2} \equiv K_{t-1} \equiv K_t \equiv K_{t+1} \ldots \equiv K^*$, at the turnpike K^* defined as the root of

$$(6)\qquad g'(K) = f'(K) - \delta + 1 = 1/(1 + \rho) = B$$

This is seen to be the usual generalized turnpike, defined as that level where the technological and subjective rates of interest are equal to a common market rate. (Note: (6)'s turnpike is independent of the form of $u[\ \ldots\ ]$, a remarkable fact!) For $\delta = 0$ and no time discount, we have the Ramsey-Schumpeter bliss level at a zero rate of interest.

Vibration analysis, by means of the *linear* difference equation associated with (5) in the small neighborhood around the K^* stationary point, can be applied to determine the stability behavior in a local region around

---

4. For $N \geqslant 1$, (5) would become a difference equation of order $2N$, with the same left-hand side but with the right-hand side replaced by

$$B\sum_1^{N+1} B^j u_j\, [E^{j-1} C_t, E^{j-2} C_t] \Big/ \sum_1^{N+1} B^j u_j\, [E^{j-2} C_t, E^{j-3} C_t]$$

where $C_t = g(K_{t-1}) - K_t$ and $EC_t = C_{t+1}, E^2 C_t = C_{t+2}, E^{-1} C_t = C_{t-1}$.

Equation (6) is unchanged and the polynomial associated with (7) will be of the 2^{nth} degree and for sufficiently small δ will be "near" to $0 = (X - X_1)(X - X_1^{-1}) \ldots (X - X_n)(X - X_n^{-1})$, so that all qualitative results are independent of N.

the K^* turnpike. We expand the non-linear relation (5) in the neighborhood of K^* and, retaining terms of the first degree only, determine an associated linear fourth-order difference equation in terms of divergences from equilibrium, $K_t - K^* \cong y_t$, namely

$$(7) \qquad a_0 y(t+4) + a_1 y(t+3) + a_2(t+2) + a_3 y(t+1) + a_4 y(t) = 0$$

where the a_j coefficients are computable from the partial derivatives of $u[\dots]$ evaluated at the C^* levels corresponding to K^*.

In the time-free case where there is no time discount and $\delta = 0$, we can invoke a fundamental Poincaré theorem on variational systems[5] to prove that the K^* bliss level is a saddlepoint in phase space. For in that case $a_0 = a_4 = 1$, and the characteristic polynomial associated with (7) takes the form

$$(8) \qquad 0 = a_0 X^4 + a_1 X^3 + a_2 X^2 + a_3 X + a_4$$

$$= (X - x_1)(X - x_1^{-1})(X - x_2)(X - x_2^{-1})$$

Now if we rule out, as we can from concavity, save in singular cases, the case where the characteristic roots are of unit modulus, it will follow that the x_i roots in function of δ will, for sufficiently small δ, by continuity, continue to fall into pairs, each member of which is above and below one in absolute value. And thus, only for that razor's edge of initial conditions in which half the roots, those which are above one in absolute value, are suppressed, will the optimal infinite-time motion approach the turnpike asymptotically. Hence, it should be possible to prove the general saddlepoint, turnpike, catenary features of the solution just as in the Ramsey independence case.

This heuristic proof needs, of course, to be supplemented by rigorous topological discussion in the large.

---

5. Strictly speaking, it is my generalization to difference-equation systems of the Poincaré result on differential equations that is needed. See P. A. Samuelson, "Reciprocal Characteristic Root Property of Discrete-Time Maxima," *Western Economic Journal*, VI, (1968), pp. 90-93. For details of vibration analysis see, for example, P. A. Samuelson, "Local Proof of the Turnpike Theorem," *Western Edonomic Journal*, VII (1969), pp. 1-8.

EDITOR'S NOTE

Lacking poets and musicians, economists have little means to celebrate an important event. Would that we could compose a "March for a Nobel Prize Winner"!

The inclusion of this article in this issue represents the *Journal's* attempt to celebrate and to send Professor Samuelson our congratulations. Surely his taste for an *expected publication* has become intertemporally jaded after a quarter century of perpetual expectations. So we tender him a new product, called a *surprise article*, published seven days after the manuscript surprised *us* in the morning mail.

Since we didn't dare edit so much as a comma, any remaining errors are either the typesetter's—or Samuelson's.

141

Notes on Turnpikes:
Stable and Unstable

NISSAN LIVIATAN

AND

PAUL A. SAMUELSON

Massachusetts Institute of Technology, Cambridge
Massachusetts 02139

1. INTRODUCTION

Forty years ago Ramsey demonstrated that an optimum saving model approaches a Bliss, or Golden Rule, Turnpike. As has been shown by various writers [1], this turnpike represents a *saddlepoint*. The motions in the neighborhood of the saddlepoint are of *catenary type*, in accordance with the classical Poincaré theorem that characteristic roots at a stationary point of a time-free variational system come in opposite-signed pairs. This turnpike can also be easily generalized to take account of a constant rate of population growth with everything expressed in per-capita magnitudes; and then it becomes a Golden Rule state, but with a positive (rather than zero) interest rate equal to the rate of population growth.

A further generalization is to assume a non-negative rate of time preference [2], which has the effect of reducing the (asymptotic) turnpike levels of consumption and capital. Here too, in simple models, the turnpike is unique and stable in the saddlepoint sense. But now the motions become *unbalanced* catenaries inasmuch as the Poincaré theorem has to be modified to yield, in regular systems, pairs of opposite-signed roots of different magnitudes.

In a generalization of the Poincaré theorem [3], Professor Kurz [4] has recently raised the possibility of variational systems with a positive subjective rate of time preference that are completely unstable (i.e., with all characteristic roots having *positive* real parts) at a stationary point. Since in growth models one usually expects to deal with a *single* turnpike, the foregoing possibility may seem odd since it suggests that an asymptotic motion into the turnpike is impossible and, hence, that no infinite-time optimal program exists!

This apparent paradox can be dissolved if we consider the case where the system has more than one regular turnpike. In another paper, Professor Kurz [5] shows that in an optimal control problem we may have multiple optimal steady states both of the stable and unstable kind as a result of introducing capital as an argument in the utility function [6].

In the present paper, we pursue this subject further, showing how the phenomenon of multiple turnpikes can arise even in the ordinary growth models where direct utility is derived only from consumption, and not from wealth, and where utility is not satiable at any consumption level. For, when *joint* production is possible, even a one capital, one consumption-good growth model, maximizing a discounted integral of utility of consumption, can display multiple turnpikes, alternately stable and unstable. In addition, we shall analyze the razor-edge phenomenon of turnpikes which have one-sided stability. We shall also display the qualitative in-the-large topology of the motions in phase space under some regularity conditions. In particular, we assume that boundary inequalities are not binding, leaving these complications for a possible later study.

A related topic taken up in this paper is the generalization of the Consumption Turnpike Theorem [7] to the case of multiple saddlepoints. In particular, we show how to determine which saddlepoint constitutes the relevant turnpike for a finite-horizon problem with fixed initial and terminal capital stocks.

Finally, we shall supplement our analysis of stable and unstable turnpikes with the examination of a turnpike which is *too stable*. By this we mean the *inefficient turnpike* that exists *beyond* the Golden Rule state, at the point where stationary consumption is zero, towards which *all* nearby motions go (as is depicted in the phase diagram of Koopman's study [8]). This is, of course, in sharp contrast to the motions around a saddlepoint where all motions, except those on a razor's edge, are divergent. We shall resolve this apparent contradiction to the Poincaré theorem and explain the irrelevance of the zero-consumption state as a true turnpike for finite-horizon problems.

2. MULTIPLICITY OF TURNPIKES UNDER JOINT PRODUCTION

Consider a neo-classical model involving one consumption good (C) industry and many capital good industries under nonjoint production, in which

$$\int_0^\infty e^{-\delta t}U[c]dt$$

is maximized (with $\delta > 0$), where c denotes consumption per capita. In this case, any arbitrary rate of return r (r is defined net of depreciation and population growth, so that $r =$ interest rate minus growth rate, and equals all net own-rates) determines a unique (efficient) steady-state configuration of the capital stocks [9]. This optimal stationary state (OSS) is then uniquely determined by equating r to the social discount rate δ (as can be deduced from the Euler optimality equations). The OSS state is approached asymptotically by all optimal programs based on an infinite-horizon and starting from arbitrary initial capital stocks. The OSS is also known [10] to possess the usual Turnpike property for finite-horizon programs.

To simplify matters, and to enable the use of phase diagrams, we shall concentrate on a two-commodity model with one consumption good, C, and one capital good, K. Under steady-state conditions, with $dk/dt = 0$, the net rate of return r is a function of capital per capita (k) only, say $r = r(k)$. Under nonjoint production $r(k)$ can be shown to be a monotonically decreasing function of k. The stationary optimal value of k is then determined at the intersection of $r(k)$ with the horizontal line $r = \delta$.

However, under conditions of joint production, the $r(k)$ curve need not be monotonic and may behave like the curve in Fig. 1, which displays three

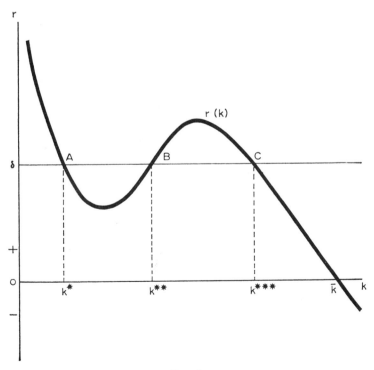

Fig. 1.

OSS turnpikes at the intersection points of the wavy $r(k)$ with $r = \delta$. It will be shown that these points are not all of the same nature: while A and C do represent asymptotes to optimal programs (with infinite horizon) for arbitrary nearby initial condition, this is not true of B. In fact, k^{**} corresponding to B is shown to be the watershed for all optimal growth programs: All those with initial capital k_0 satisfying $0 < k_0 < k^{**}$ converge to k^*, while those with $k^{**} < k_0$ converge to k^{***}. In this sense, A and C represent stable OSS while B represents an unstable OSS. A condition sufficient for stability is that $r'(k) < 0$ at the OSS, and conversely $r'(k) > 0$ implies instability. Generally, therefore, stable and unstable OSS will come alternately on the k axis. We turn now to establish this result.

3. STABLE AND UNSTABLE TURNPIKES

We assume a production function

$$c(t) = f[\dot{k}(t), k(t)], \tag{1}$$

where $c(t)$ and $k(t)$ represent, respectively, consumption and capital per capita at time t and $\dot{k}(t) = dk(t)/dt$. It is understood that f specifies the *maximum* c for a given k and $\dot{k}$, and that it already incorporates the parameters of exponential depreciation and population growth. We assume $f_1 < 0$, (f_i and f_{ij} being partial derivatives in the usual notation) and strict concavity of f, i.e., $f_{ii} < 0$ ($i = 1, 2$) and $f_{11} f_{22} - f_{12}^2 > 0$ for all k and $\dot{k}$.

As usual, we also assume the existence of a golden rule, i.e., $\overset{\max}{k} f(0, k)$ at $k = \bar{k}$. We then have $f_2(0, k) \gtreqless 0$ as $k \lesseqgtr \bar{k}$. Now the net own rate of return r (the interest rate minus the growth rate) is given by

$$r = r(\dot{k}, k) = -f_2(\dot{k}, k)/f_1(\dot{k}, k).$$

Hence, the sign of r follows the same rule as the sign of f_2. From considerations of diminishing returns, it is plausible to posit that there exist a value of k, say $\hat{k}$, beyond which $\dot{k}$ must be negative (in view of the nonnegativity of c). This implies the boundedness of $k(t)$ for any feasible program.

As mentioned, the welfare function is assumed to be of the form

$$\int_0^\infty e^{-\delta t} U[c(t)] dt, \qquad \delta > 0, \tag{2}$$

where U is a concave utility function satisfying $U' > 0$, $U'' < 0$ for $c > 0$. Usually we shall assume $\lim_{c \to 0} U'(c) = +\infty$. The integral in (2) is to be maximized subject to (1) and to $c_t, k_t \geq 0$ for all t, given initial capital k_0. Under the foregoing conditions we may assume that, for any k_0, there exists an optimal program based on an infinite horizon.

For notational simplicity define $F(\dot{k}, k) \equiv U[f(\dot{k}, k)]$, where F is of course a strictly concave function, with F_1 and F_2 obeying the same rules as f_1 and f_2. The Euler conditions for an extremum of (2) then yields (after cancellation of $e^{-\delta t}$ terms)

$$F_2 + \delta F_1 = (d/dt)F_1. \qquad (3)$$

For an OSS, the condition of stationariness yields

$$\delta = -\frac{F_2(0, k)}{F_1(0, k)} \left(= -\frac{f_2(0, k)}{f_1(0, k)} \right), \qquad (4)$$

i.e., $r(0, k) = \delta$. The slope of r, i.e., $\partial r(0, k)/\partial k = r_2(0, k)$ is given by

$$r_2(0, k) = -\frac{1}{F_1} (F_{22} + rF_{12}). \qquad (5)$$

Since the concavity of F does not restrict the sign of F_{12}, we cannot rule out $r_2(0, k) > 0$. At an OSS, (5) becomes

$$r_2(0, k) = -\frac{1}{F_1} (F_{22} + \delta F_{12}) = -\frac{1}{f_1} (f_{22} + \delta f_{12}), \qquad (6)$$

which can very well be positive, as we shall later illustrate by a numerical example.

The nature of the production function, which can give rise to the oscillatory behavior of $r_2(0, k)$ depicted in Fig. 1, is illustrated in Fig. 2's depiction of isoconsumption contours. The slope of the contours $f(\dot{k}, k) = \text{const}$ is equal to r, so that a decreasing r along the horizontal axis of $\dot{k} = 0$ represents $r_2(0, k) < 0$. At A we have a normal stable OSS with $\delta = r_2(0, k)$. Alternatively, the case of $r_2(0, k) < 0$ can be described (for $\delta > 0$) by a negatively sloped expansion path EE' [11]. There is, however, nothing in the property of the concavity of $f(\dot{k}, k)$ which prohibits EE' from turning upward and crossing $\dot{k} = 0$ again at B. Indeed, if we consider $Z = -\dot{k}$ as an input and turn the $\dot{k}$ axis upside down, we find that $r_2(0, k) < 0$ corresponds to the concept of Z being a normal input, while $r_2(0, k) > 0$ corresponds to Z being an inferior or regressive input in the theory of production [12]. As is well known, *regressivity* is perfectly consistent with the concavity of f. Hence, multiplicity of turnpikes is clearly possible.

Suppose that $r(0, k)$ intersects $r = \delta$ repeatedly as in Fig. 1. What can be said about the nature of the intersection points? To answer this, write out (3) in full as

$$F_{11}\ddot{k} + F_{12}\dot{k} - (F_2 + \delta F_1) = 0. \qquad (7)$$

Expanding this second-order differential equation linearly around an OSS,

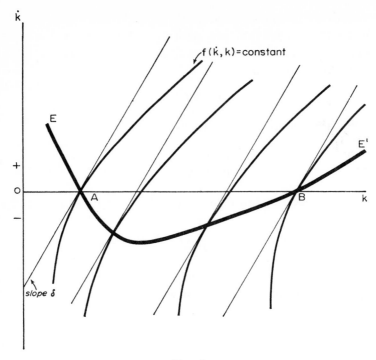

FIG. 2.

and neglecting higher-order terms in the discrepancies of k from equilibrium, we have the strictly linear equation

$$\ddot{y} - \delta\dot{y} - \left(\frac{F_{22} + \delta F_{12}}{F_{11}}\right) y = 0, \qquad (8)$$

where $y = k$ minus equilibrium k and all F_{ij} coefficients are evaluated at $(\dot{k}, k) = (0, \text{equilibrium } k)$.

Write (8) as $\ddot{y} + a\dot{y} + by = 0$ and denote the characteristic roots corresponding to this equation by $\lambda_i(i = 1, 2)$, so that $X^2 + aX + b = (X - \lambda_1)(X - \lambda_2)$. Then

$$\lambda_{1,2} = \frac{\delta \pm \sqrt{\delta^2 - 4b}}{2}$$

$$b = -\frac{(F_{22} + \delta F_{12})}{F_{11}}. \qquad (9)$$

If at an OSS we have $r_2(0, k^*) < 0$, then by (6), $F_{22} + \delta F_{12} < 0$ and, hence, $b < 0$. It then follows from (9) that the λ_i are real and have opposite signs, which ensures that we have a local saddlepoint in the $(\dot{k}, k)$ phase space.

Alternatively, if $r_2(0, k) > 0$, then $F_{22} + \delta F_{12} > 0$; therefore, $\lambda_1 \lambda_2 = b > 0$, and we *cannot* have a saddlepoint. It then follows from (8) and (9), that we must have a completely unstable OSS, with all real parts of the λ_i positive. Because of concavity and the fact that we have a single capital good these roots can be shown to be real.[1]

We shall describe later the motions around the various OSS points. However to complete our analysis, we must also justify the treatment of points which satisfy $r_2(0, k) = \delta$ (i.e., the necessary condition for an OSS) as *optimal* ones, i.e., as ones which actually do maximize the utility integral. This, however, follows essentially from the concavity of F. Indeed under the concavity and other regularity assumptions with $U' > 0$ and k_i bounded, one can prove the following:

THEOREM A. *If a feasible (infinite horizon) program satisfies the Euler condition and in addition*

$$\lim_{t \to \infty} e^{-\delta t} F_1 = 0,$$

then the program is uniquely optimal.

This theorem has been proved in various versions in the literature[2] and it certainly ensures the optimality of our stationary points regardless of whether the point is stable or unstable in the saddlepoint sense.

Finally, it must be noted that our characterization of saddlepoint stability in terms of the behavior of the own rate r cannot, without considerable elaboration, be carried over to the case of more than one capital good where the own-rates are $r_i = -F_{k_i}/F_{\dot{k}_i}$. In general, the form of the characteristic determinant is, in matrix notation,

$$\Delta(\lambda) = \left| F_{\dot{k}_i \dot{k}_j} \lambda^2 + (F_{\dot{k}_i k_j} - \delta F_{k_i \dot{k}_j})\lambda - (F_{k_i k_j} + \delta F_{k_i \dot{k}_j}) \right| = 0,$$

[1] *Proof.* We have

$$b = -\frac{(F_{22} + \delta F_{12})}{F_{11}} = \frac{(F_{22}/F_{12} + \delta)}{-F_{11}/F_{12}}, \quad (F_{12} > 0 \text{ since } r_2 > 0).$$

Define $Z_1 = -F_{11}/F_{12}$ and $Z_2 = -F_{22}/F_{12}$ so that

$$b = \frac{-Z_2 + \delta}{Z_1}, \quad (Z_i > 0).$$

Concavity of F implies $Z_1 Z_2 > 1$. Hence,

$$b = \frac{-Z_1 Z_2 + \delta Z_1}{Z_1^2} < \frac{-1 + \delta Z_1}{Z_1^2} = \phi(Z_1; \delta).$$

But ϕ has a maximum w.r.t. Z_1 at $Z_1 = 2/\delta$. Hence, $0 < b < (\delta/2)^2$. It then follows from (9) that $\lambda_i (i = 1, 2)$ are real and positive.

[2] See, e.g., D. CASS, Ref. 2, which utilizes the transversality condition

$$\lim_{t \to \infty} e^{-\delta t} U'(c_t) = 0.$$

Since $\dot{k} \equiv 0$ at any turnpike, the Euler condition is satisfied and with concavity this ensures the turnpike's optimality for any duration of time however long.

where the matrix $F_{k_ik_j} + \delta F_{k_ik_j}$ is related to the rates of return matrix by

$$\partial r_i / \partial k_j = -(F_{k_ik_j} + \delta F_{k_ik_j})/F_{k_i}.$$

In the case of a single capital good, the sign of $\partial r / \partial k$ is sufficient to determine whether the roots come in opposite pairs, i.e., the saddlepoint stability, but in general the properties of the matrix $F_{k_ik_j} + \delta F_{k_ik_j}$ alone are not sufficient to determine stability once δ becomes large.

4. A NUMERICAL EXAMPLE

To illustrate the possibility of multiple OSS let the following function[3] represent f in the relevant range

$$f(\dot{k}, k) = Q(k)\dot{k} + \tfrac{1}{2}A\dot{k}^2 + B_0 k + B_1 k^2 \tag{10}$$

where $Q(k) = \alpha_0 + \alpha_1 k + \alpha_2 k^2 + \alpha_3 k^3$ with the following values for the parameters

$$B_0 = 0.148, \qquad B_1 = -0.037$$

$$\alpha_0 = -0.037, \qquad \alpha_1 = -1, \qquad \alpha_2 = 2, \qquad \alpha_3 = -1$$

with $A < 0$.

Consider Eq. (4) with $\delta = 1$ so that $f_2(0, k) = -f_1(0, k)$. In Fig. 3, we plot the foregoing functions which are represented in our example by $B_0 + 2B_1 k$ and $-Q(k)$, respectively. The intersection points of the curves represent OSS levels. In our case, we have three roots given approximately by $k_1 = 0.14$, $k_2 = 0.71$ and $k_3 = 1.15$. Note that k_1 and k_3 correspond to $r_2(0, k) < 0$ while $r_2(0, k_2) > 0$.

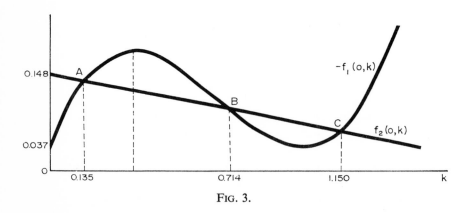

FIG. 3.

---

[3] If one insists that k appear only in the form $\dot{k} + nk$ (where $n = \lambda + g$ represents depreciation and population growth), one could replace $\dot{k}$ in (10) by $\dot{k} + nk$; then this will have all the properties of (10) when n is sufficiently small.

It can be seen from the diagram that in the relevant range of $f_1(0, k) < 0$ and $f_2(0, k) > 0$, as one postulates. We also have $f_{11} = A < 0$ and $f_{22} = 2B_1 < 0$. Finally, for concavity of f we also need

$$f_{11}f_{22} - f_{12}^2 = 2B_1 A - Q'(k)^2 > 0,$$

which is also seen to be satisfied in the relevant range once we set $|A|$ sufficiently large.[4] We cannot of course use (10) everywhere without violating the foregoing restrictions, but we may assume that (10) changes its form smoothly to one which has all the required properties everywhere.

5. THE (k, k) PHASE SPACE AND THE ACCUMULATION RULE

We turn now to consider the motions of the system in the close neighborhood of the OSS points and in the large. Using the transformation $\dot{y} = z$, we may write (8) as a system of differential equations

$$\dot{y} = z. \tag{11}$$

$$\dot{z} = -az - by. \tag{12}$$

Let $\lambda_i(i = 1, 2)$ be a root of the characteristic polynomial which corresponds to this system and let (h_i^1, h_i^2) be its corresponding eigenvector. Then, because of the special form of (11) we have $h_i^2 = \lambda_i h_i^1$ for the case of real nonzero roots.[5] It follows that the equations of the asymptotes (characteristic lines) in the (z, y) phase space are given by (Pontryagin, ibid.)

$$z = \lambda_i y \qquad (i = 1, 2). \tag{13}$$

We have seen earlier that the OSS points occur with opposite signed λ_i for A and C and with positive λ_i for B. Hence, the motions of the system in a small neighborhood of the OSS points corresponding to Fig. 1 take the form depicted by the trajectories in Fig. 4. (We shall elaborate on these motions later.)

In the neighborhood of a saddlepoint A, the motion along the characteristic line $A'A''$ toward A does (up to the accuracy of linear approximation) represent an optimal path. This is a consequence of the earlier Theorem A. The same sufficiency conditions are satisfied for the trajectories $C'C$ and $C''C$ going into C. On the other hand, for the point B

[4] For example, if $A = -540$, then $2B_1 A = 40$, while the maximal value of $(Q')^2$ in the range $0 \le k \le 2$ is only 25.

[5] See, e.g., L. S. PONTRYAGIN, "Ordinary Differential Equations," pp. 124–125, Addison–Wesley, Reading, Mass., 1969.

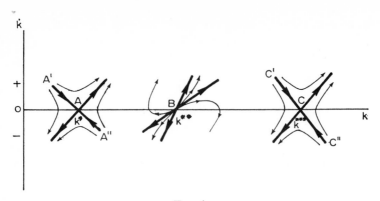

FIG. 4.

all trajectories move in the outward direction, so that starting with $k_0 \neq k^{**}$, the ensuing optimal path (which must, of course, correspond to some Euler trajectory), moves away from k^{**}. For $k_0 = k^{**}$ itself, the path $k_t = k^{**}$ is seen to be optimal by virtue of its satisfying Theorem A.

To consider the motion of the system in the large we note first that $\dot{k}$ is bounded from above for each k because of the nonnegativity of c. The maximal value of $\dot{k}$ is given by solving $0 = f(\dot{k}, k)$, which yields say max $\dot{k} = G(k)$ as in Fig. 5. We denoted earlier by $\hat{k}$ the maximal value of k for which $G \geq 0$. To avoid having to consider some unusual cases, we shall also assume that for an *optimal* path $\dot{k}$ is bounded from *below*. (Alternatively, we may suppose that there is a smooth limit on useful disinvestment such that $f_1(\dot{k}, k) \equiv 0$ for $\dot{k} \leq g(k) > -\infty$).

Consider the locus of $(\dot{k}_t, k_t)$ that corresponds to optimal infinite horizon programs. Call it the *optimal locus*. Clearly, the optimal locus can intersect the k axis only at OSS points. Further, we know by the optimality aspect of Theorem A that the trajectories going into the stable points A and C (to be called the *optimal trajectories*) must correspond to the optimal locus. Finally, by the uniqueness assertion of Theorem A, we know that a vertical line, k constant, can be intersected by one, and only one, optimal trajectory. Piecing together the foregoing facts we may conclude, by topological continuity, that the optimal locus has the general shape of the continuous heavy line $OABC$ in Fig. 5.

It follows from this phase diagram that A, B, and C subdivide the k axis into segments where the optimal $\dot{k}$ is intermittantly positive and negative. These segments correspond to $r(0, k)$ being respectively greater or smaller than δ. The remarkably simple rule is

$$\dot{k}_{\text{opt}} \gtreqless 0 \quad \text{as} \quad r(0, k) \gtreqless \delta. \tag{14}$$

That is, the decision function, for optimal $\dot{k}$ in terms of k, has the form

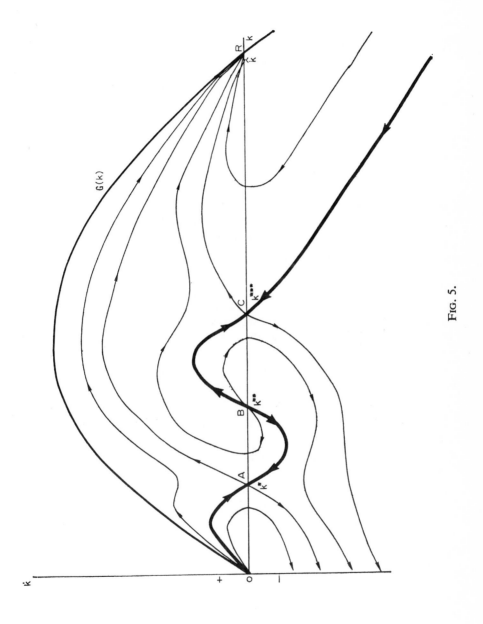

Fig. 5.

$\overset{*}{k} = [r(0, k) - \delta]A(k)$, $A(k) \geq 0$. This is somewhat surprising since the criterion for nonsteady-state behavior depends only on steady-state measures! It seems, however, that this rule is applicable only to the case of a single capital good, becoming more complex in the case of vectors of capital goods.

6. ONE-SIDED STABILITY OF TURNPIKES

We have seen that whether $\partial r(0, k)/\partial k < 0$ or > 0, we can prove a saddlepoint in phase space is stable or unstable. There remains the singular case where, at

$$\delta = r(0, k^\dagger), \quad \partial r(0, k^\dagger)/\partial k = 0, \quad \partial^2 r(0, k^\dagger)/\partial k^2 > 0.$$

Here, local linearized analysis cannot be relied on to give the correct qualitative analysis of the motions near the stationary point. At such a singular stationary point, along with the normal characteristic root $\lambda_1 > 0$, we have a vanishing root $\lambda_2 = 0$; stability properties depend on higher-degree nonlinear terms. Intuitively, from the economics of the situation and the accompanying Fig. 6, one can deduce that this singular case corresponds to a left-sided turnpike—stable from the left, but unstable from the right.

In Fig. 6a, at the large δ^* shown, we have the usual three turnpikes, with unstable B being surrounded by stable A and C. Fig. 6b shows the usual three OSS, with the unstable B having both characteristic vectors of positive slope. Fig. 6c shows the corresponding asymptotic motion in the time domain. Now, as we lower δ^* toward $\bar{\delta}$, B and A ultimately coalesce and we lose in Fig. 6c the region between B and A. In Fig. 6b, the heavily-drawn contours, $A'A$ and $B'B$ join at the now common point A and B, $A^\dagger$. Fig. 6d shows that, aside from the normal positive characteristic vector with slope λ_1, the new one must enter the origin like a parabola, having zero slope there and making high contact. To the left, the arrow points inward toward the singular turnpike; to the right, the arrow of motion points outward, since for $k > k^\dagger$, all infinite-time optimal motions go asymptotically to the stable $C^\dagger$ turnpike.

To prove the one-sided property let us transform the Euler Equation

$$F_{11}\ddot{k} = -F_{12}\dot{k} + F_2 + \delta F_1$$

into a system

$$k = e \tag{15}$$

and

$$\dot{e} = -\frac{F_{12}}{F_{11}} e + \frac{F_2 + \delta F_1}{F_{11}} \equiv g(e, k) \tag{16}$$

31

146

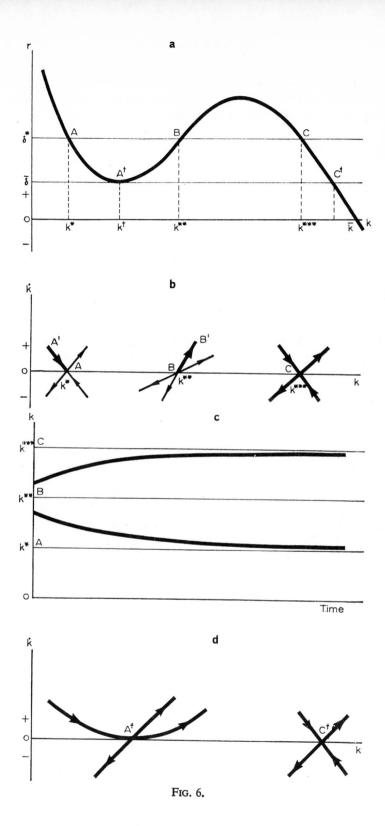

FIG. 6.

with the arguments of F being e and k. Consider the curve defined by $g(e, k) = 0$ with e being treated as a function of k, say $e = e(k)$. The derivatives of e, computed from the identity $g[e(k), k] \equiv 0$, are given by

$$e' = -\frac{g_2}{g_1}, \quad e'' = -\frac{[g_1(g_{22} + e'g_{21}) - g_2(g_{11}e' + g_{12})]}{g_1^2} \tag{17}$$

At the point $(e, k) = (0, k^\dagger)$ we find that $g_1(k^\dagger) = \delta$ and $g_2(k^\dagger) = 0$, so that $e'(k^\dagger) = 0$.

To compute e'', we use the facts that at $(e, k) = (0, k^\dagger)$ we have $r_2(0, k^\dagger) = 0$ and $r_{22}(0, k^\dagger) > 0$, which implies that $F_{22} + \delta F_{12} = 0$ and $F_{222} + \delta F_{122} > 0$. This in turn implies that, at the foregoing point, we have $g_{22} = (F_{222} + \delta F_{122})/F_{11} < 0$. Combining these results, we deduce that, at $(e, k) = (0, k^\dagger)$, we have

$$e' = 0, \quad e'' = -(g_{22}/\delta) > 0. \tag{18}$$

It follows from the foregoing calculations that in the neighborhood of $(0, k^\dagger)$ the curve $\dot{e} = g(e, k) = 0$ takes the form depicted in Fig. 7. Further,

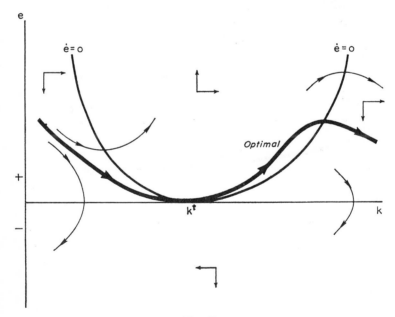

FIG. 7.

at $(0, k^\dagger)$ we have $g_1 > 0$ and, therefore, by continuity, the sign of this derivative will remain positive in some neighborhood of this point. We see, therefore, that the arrows of motion of the system (15)–(16) in the neighborhood $(0, k^\dagger)$ follow the pattern depicted in Fig. 7. It is seen that the optimal path (heavy line) must come in from the left into $k^\dagger$, representing a left-sided turnpike, and leaving $k^\dagger$ to the right.

Analytically, one can verify by the calculus that there are two trajectories passing smoothly through the $(0, k^\dagger)$ origin—one positively sloped and corresponding to the unstable eigenvector of the earlier nonsingular cases, and the other a parabola-like singular path with zero slope as indicated in Fig. 6's one-sided stability path. This will confirm the above geometry.

The method we use is rarely encountered in the literature but consists of straightforward repeated differentiations: This will give us, for first derivatives, the equivalent to the eigenvectors of associated linear systems; but, for higher derivatives, we can in principle get as accurate relations as we like in the case of analytical functions, or in other cases, as accurate results as the postulated number of existent derivatives permits.

The slope of any trajectory in phase space $(\dot{k}, k) = (e, k)$ is given by

$$\frac{de}{dk} = \frac{d\dot{k}}{dk} = \frac{d\dot{k}/dt}{dk/dt} = \frac{\dot{e}}{e} = \frac{g(e, k)}{e}, \tag{19}$$

where g is defined by our earlier Euler equation. Denoting this slope for short as e' (but taking care not to confuse e', e'', e''' along a trajectory with those same symbols denoting the slope of the $g(e, k) = \dot{k} = 0$ locus just studied) we write the identity, $g(e, k) - ee' \equiv 0$. We can differentiate this totally with respect to k, treating e as a function of k, to get identities involving e', e'', e''', ..., etc., namely

$$g_1 e' + g_2 - \{(e')^2 + ee''\} = 0, \tag{20a}$$

$$g_{11}(e')^2 + 2g_{12}e' + g_{22} + g_1 e'' - \{3e'e'' + ee'''\} = 0, \tag{20b}$$

$$e'[\psi] + g_{222} + g_{11}e'e'' + g_{12}e'' + g_1 e''' - \{3(e'')^2 + 4e'e''' + ee''''\} = 0, \tag{20c}$$

where ψ stands for a collection of terms involving k, e, and possibly e'.

We are interested in evaluating these derivatives at the singular point $(0, k^\dagger)$ where $e = 0 = g$. Hence, the first of the above relations becomes a quadratic equation for e', namely the characteristic polynomial already met in connection with the associated linearized system near $(0, k^\dagger)$. Thus, $(e')^2 - g_1 e' - g_2 = (e')^2 - g_1 e' - 0 = (e' - \lambda_2)(e' - \lambda_1)$, where $\lambda_1 = g_1(0, k^\dagger) > 0$ and $\lambda_2 = 0$ when $g_2(0, k^\dagger) = 0$ as in the singular case. Corresponding to the positive eigenvalue, we have the usual unstable characteristic vector. Hence, from now on, we concentrate on the zero λ_2 root with $e' = 0$ as well as $g = 0 = e$.

Now our second relation above has all expressions in its curly brackets vanish, leaving us with the same $e'' = -g_{22}/g_1 > 0$ conditions as for the parabola-like $\dot{k} = g(e, k) = 0$ locus just analyzed above.

But to verify that our singular one-sided motion through the origin does lie below the $g = 0$ locus to the left of the turnpike and above it to the right, as shown in Fig. 7, we merely have to prove that e''' there is greater on the trajectory than on the $g = 0$ locus. But our last relation does demonstrate this, since for $e = 0 = e'$, it becomes $0 = g_1 e''' - \{3(e'')^2\} +$ same expression as for $g = 0$ locus.

Since, the expression in brackets is positive and g_1 is positive, it is evident that the bracket term does make the e''' of the trajectory greater than the e''' of the $g(e, k) = 0$ locus. Hence we have verified analytically the correctness of Fig. 7's topological assertions.

When we face the foregoing borderline case $\ddot{y} - \delta\dot{y} + 0y = 0$, with $y = k - k^\dagger$, the Liapunov linear analysis fails to reflect the true topological properties of the original nonlinear motions. The higher-order terms in the Taylor's expansion are no longer dominated and ignorable, and there is no substitute for nonlinear analysis.

Yet the linear analysis is, so to speak, still trying to tell us something. In the $(\dot{y}, y)$ phase space, there is no longer a unique stationary point at the $(0, 0)$ origin. Every $(0, y)$ point along the horizontal y axis is a stationary point. The trajectories traced out by the family of parametric equations, $\dot{y}(t) = \dot{y}_0 e^{\delta t}$, $y(t) = y_0 + (\dot{y}_0/\delta)(e^{\delta t} - 1)$ are parallel straight lines with slope $\delta > 0$. Thus, from $y_0 \neq 0$, *no motion* can return to the origin.

In the actual nonlinear system, where $(\dot{k}, k - k^\dagger)$ approaches the origin from the left side with high or parabolic contact, the approach of $k - k^\dagger$ to zero with high t is infinitely slow in terms of number of decimal places of accuracy reached. This qualitative feature can be summarized in terms of the 1st order differential equation for $\dot{k}$ in terms of k relevant for an optimal infinite program. Thus, as mentioned earlier,

$$\dot{k} = [r(0, k) - \delta]A(k) = (k - k^\dagger)^m[a + B(k)], \quad B(k^\dagger) \neq 0.$$

If $r_2(0, k^\dagger) \neq 0$, $m = 1$. But if $r_2(0, k^\dagger) = 0$, m is an integer greater than 1, and the convergence is asymptotically infinitely slower. Normally, for left-sided stability, the asymptotic rate of convergence is like that of

$$\dot{k} = (k - k^\dagger)^2,$$

rather than $\dot{k} = (k - k^\dagger)$, and its linear counterpart $\dot{y} \equiv 0$ is nearer to the former case than the latter.

By applying the same kind of analysis to a case where $r(0, k^{\dagger\dagger}) = \delta$, $r_2(0, k^{\dagger\dagger}) = 0$, and $r_{22}(0, k^{\dagger\dagger}) < 0$, one finds that it yields a right-sided turnpike. Note that the accumulation rule in (14) is preserved under one-sided stability.

A final dramatic form of one-sided stability is provided by the switch-point between two activities in models like those of Joan Robinson and linear programmers. Suppose $r(0, k)$ is monotone decreasing but at $r = \delta^{\dagger\dagger\dagger}$ has a *finite* horizontal branch between $k = k_a^{\dagger\dagger\dagger}$ and $k = k_b^{\dagger\dagger\dagger}$. Then every point on this *open* interval obviously has, as far as infinite-time optimal programs are concerned, a kind of neutral stability. The left point $k_a^{\dagger\dagger\dagger}$ is obviously stable from the left with $k_b^{\dagger\dagger\dagger}$ being similarly stable from the right. To the right of $k_a^{\dagger\dagger\dagger}$ the motion is, so to speak, neutrally stable like that of any interior point. (Suppose in the left neighborhood of $k_a^{\dagger\dagger\dagger}$, $r = \delta^{\dagger\dagger\dagger} + (k - k_a^{\dagger\dagger\dagger})^3$, while in the right neighborhood of $k_b^{\dagger\dagger\dagger}$, $r = \delta^{\dagger\dagger\dagger} - (k - k_b^{\dagger\dagger\dagger})^3$. Then $r(0, k)$ has continuous first and second derivatives and the calculus methods used above can prove these asserted properties.)

7. THE CONSUMPTION TURNPIKE THEOREM

Consider now an optimal program with a *finite* horizon, a given initial k_0 and prescribed terminal capital $k(T) = k_T$. Suppose, we let T increase indefinitely holding k_0 and k_T constant. Near which of the OSS Turnpikes will the program spend most of its time after T has become indefinitely large?

After reflection, one would expect that the finite-horizon program will approach that unique OSS which is the asymptote for the infinite-horizon program starting from the same k_0. In other words, the (far-away!) terminal condition should be irrelevant for the determination of the catenary-asymptotic behavior. We shall now indicate that this result can indeed be established. It should be noted that our argument can be generalized to any number of capital and consumption goods.

The finite time horizon problem is:

$$\max \int_0^T e^{-\delta t} U[c(t; T)] dt \quad \text{given} \quad k(0; T) = k_0 \quad \text{and} \quad k(T; T) = k_T,$$

provided of course the terminal condition is feasible. Denote the optimal finite horizon path by $c'(t; T)$, $k'(t; T)$ and let

$$J'(T) = \int_0^T e^{-\delta t} U[c'(t; T)] dt. \tag{21}$$

We assume that there exists for the same k_0 an optimal infinite-horizon program denoted by $c^*(t)$, $k^*(t)$. Essentially what we have to show is $k'(t; T) \to k^*(t)$ as $T \to \infty$ for every t and regardless of k_T $(= \text{const})$. If $k'(t; T) \to k^*(t)$, and since we know to what asymptote the path $k^*(t)$

converges, the same relevant turnpike is seen to be determined for the long-time finite-horizon program.

To establish this important correspondence we construct an auxiliary feasible path for any finite horizon. Let $\tilde{c}(t; T)$, $\tilde{k}(t; T)$ represent a feasible program which coincides with $c^*(t)$, $k^*(t)$ over the interval $(0, \hat{T})$, $0 \le \hat{T}(T) \le T$, where $\hat{T}$ is made as large as possible subject to the following constraints

$$\tilde{k}(T; T) = k_T \quad \text{and} \quad \underline{U} \le U[\tilde{c}(t; T)] \le \overline{U}, \, t \in [\hat{T}, T] \tag{22}$$

where $\underline{U}$ and $\overline{U}$ are, respectively, arbitrarily small and large fixed numbers.

Intuition tells us, as one can prove rigorously, that we can find $\underline{U}$ and $\overline{U}$ which will make the auxiliary path feasible for any k_0 and k_T in the appropriate range, provided T is sufficiently large. Moreover, we certainly expect $\hat{T}(T) \to \infty$ as $T \to \infty$.[6] Define

$$\tilde{J}(T) = \int_0^{\hat{T}} e^{-\delta t} U[\tilde{c}(t; T)] dt + \int_{\hat{T}}^T e^{-\delta t} U[\tilde{c}(t; T)] dt. \tag{23}$$

Then, since in the first integral on the *RHS* $\tilde{c}(t; T) = c^*(t)$ and in the second integral $U(\tilde{c})$ is bounded by (22), it follows, using the fact that $\hat{T}(T) \to \infty$ with T, that

$$\tilde{J}(\infty) = J^* + 0 = \int_0^\infty e^{-\delta t} U[c^*(t)] dt + 0. \tag{24}$$

Note however, that, for any T, $\tilde{J}(T)$ and $J'(T)$ have the same initial and terminal conditions, so that by definition of the latter as optimal we must have $J'(T) \ge \tilde{J}(T)$.

However, as $T \to \infty$, $J'(\infty)$ cannot exceed J^*, the latter being unconditionally optimal over the infinite horizon regardless of any ultimate $k(T; T) = k$ restriction. Hence, taking into account (24), we have

$$J^* \ge J'(\infty) \ge \tilde{J}(\infty) = J^*, \tag{25}$$

which implies $J'(\infty) = J^*$. Since the program (*) is uniquely optimal it follows that the program $c'(t; \infty)$, $k'(t; \infty)$ must be identical with $c^*(t)$, $k^*(t)$. This shows that it is only the initial conditions that determine the relevant turnpike for long-time finite-horizon programs.

---

[6] One can verify these statements rigorously by noting that if T is made sufficiently large, we can reach in finite time any k_T from any k_0 over the range $0 \le \underline{k} < k_0$, $k_T < k < \hat{k}$, where $\underline{k}$ and $\hat{k}$ are fixed numbers arbitrarily close to zero and $\hat{k}$ respectively, with the only constraint on c being $c \ge 0$. The same will be true for a constraint of the form $0 < \underline{c} \le c \le \bar{c}$ with the fixed numbers $\underline{c}$ and $\bar{c}$ appropriately chosen. We then let $\underline{U} = U(\underline{c})$ and $\overline{U} = U(\bar{c})$. The constraint (22) will then be satisfied. By the maximal nature of $\hat{T}$, we shall have $\hat{T}(T) \to \infty$ as $T \to \infty$.

8. THE INEFFICIENT TURNPIKE

A regular optimal program for an infinite horizon satisfies the Euler Condition for all t. Is the converse statement also true? If a motion permanently satisfies the Euler condition, does it maximize

$$\int_0^\infty e^{-\delta t} U(c) dt?$$

In connection with the related problems of intertemporal efficiency of production and the *Hahn problem* of efficient allocation of aggregate savings, there is the Furuya–Inada and Stiglitz–Shell demonstration that all Euler paths ultimately terminate in finite time except for the unique *Ramsey solution* to the infinite-time integral maximization problem that approaches the von Neumann Turnpike. Somewhat surprisingly, no similar result applies in the consumption realm. As has been noted for example by Koopmans,[7] and as is clear from Fig. 5, all motions in the $\dot{k} > 0$ region beyond C go asymptotically into R (where consumption is zero). Why does not such a permanent, efficient motion represent an optimal program for maximizing the infinite-horizon integral? First, the established uniqueness of the infinite-horizon path shows that there is only one that goes into a stable saddlepoint. More basically, it is evident that a path going into R is inefficient in the Phelps–Koopmans [*13*] sense (although not inefficient in a finite-horizon sense).

It follows from Theorem A, that an infinite-time extremal, which goes into R, the inefficient turnpike, cannot satisfy the transversality condition $e^{-\delta t}F_1 \to 0$, since if it did, the foregoing turnpike would be optimal—which we know to be incorrect. This must mean that $-F_1$, which can be interpreted as the current shadow price of terminal capital must tend to plus infinity. Thus, a planner may indeed be enticed to follow permanently the motion into the inefficient turnpike if he is faced with an ever increasing price for the terminal capital stock.[8]

Let us now apply the usual vibration analysis of linearization to verify that the inefficient turnpike represents a strongly-damped stationary point [*14*], in apparent defiance of the Poincaré Theorems about opposite-signed roots

---

[7] T. KOOPMANS, Ref. 2. In a (k, t) diagram with one stable k^*, consider the extremals emanating from a k_0 point on the $t = 0$ vertical axis. One such motion will be ∞-time optimum and approach a stable k^* asymptotically. All those below it, ultimately turn back and intersect the $k = 0$ axis, terminating and being succeeded by inefficiency. All extremals *above* the one asymptotic to k^* will, perhaps surprisingly overshoot k^* and converge on to the inefficient turnpike at which $c = 0$.

[8] In writing the following paragraphs we have greatly benefited from the valuable discussion by J. S. CHIPMAN in his forthcoming book, "Notes on the Theory of Optimal Growth."

for variational systems and of the Kurz extension, which says that $\delta > 0$ rules out both roots with negative real parts.

If $U'(c) \to \infty$ as $c \to 0$, in $F(\hat{k}, k) \equiv U[f(\hat{k}, k)]$ we have $F_k \to \infty$ and $F_{\hat{k}} \to -\infty$ as $c \to 0$. Similarly, $F_{\hat{k}\hat{k}} \to -\infty$, $F_{kk} \to -\infty$, $F_{\hat{k}k} \to \pm \infty$; it is this singularity of $F_{\hat{k}k}$ that vitiates the hypotheses used to prove the Poincaré theorem.

Examination of some simple cases, such as $U(c) = \log c$ or $\log(c/c^*)$, c^* some suitable bliss constant in the $\delta = 0$ case, reveals that the way $U'(c) \to \infty$ as $c \to 0$ is important. Hence, we postulate that

$$\lim_{c \to 0} E(c) = \lim_{c \to 0} \frac{U'(c)}{cU''(c)} = -h > -\infty, h > 0. \tag{26}$$

Actually, if $U'(c)$ became infinite at some positive subsistence c_1 level, we could easily replace the $c = 0$ level by that c_1 level and leave the properties of the point R.

The Euler condition now becomes

$$0 = \frac{d}{dt}(f_1 U') - (f_2 + \delta f_1)U'$$

$$= (f_{11}\hat{k} + f_{12}k)U' + f_1(f_1\hat{k} + f_2k)U'' - (f_2 + \delta f_1)U'$$

$$= \left\{ \frac{U'}{U''}[f_{11}\hat{k} + f_{12}k - f_2 - \delta f_1] + f_1^2\hat{k} + f_1 f_2 k \right\} U''. \tag{27}$$

Clearly, the expression in curly brackets must vanish almost everywhere, or

$$[f_1^2 + E(f)ff_{11}]\hat{k} + [f_2 f_1 + E(f)ff_{12}]k - E(f)f[f_2 + \delta f_1] = 0 \tag{28}$$

This, like (27), has an ordinary stationary point where

$$f_2(0, k^*) + \delta f_1(0, k^*) = 0,$$

as before. But since (28) has also a stationary point—i.e., it does vanish—at $(\hat{k}, k, f) = (0, \hat{k}, 0)$, we wish to examine (28)'s behavior near that point. The associated linear system near there, in terms of $y = k - \hat{k}$, becomes

$$\hat{f}_1^2 \ddot{y} + [\hat{f}_1 \hat{f}_2 + h\hat{f}_1 \hat{f}_2 + \delta \hat{f}_1^2]\dot{y} + h[\hat{f}_2 + \delta \hat{f}_1]\hat{f}_2 y = 0, \tag{29}$$

where $\hat{f}_i = f_i(0, \hat{k}) < 0 < h$. [Remember $\hat{k}$ is so large that $\partial c/\partial k < 0$.]

We see that all coefficients in (29) are positive, which are the Routh–Hurwitz conditions for damped stability of the $(0, \hat{k})$ stationary point, implying

$$0 > \text{real part of } \lambda_i \qquad (i = 1, 2).$$

This denies that in the $\delta = 0$ case $0 < \lambda_1 = -\lambda_2$, as the Poincaré theorem would require; it also denies that for $\delta > 0$, not all real $\lambda_i < 0$, as Kurz's extension would require.

To illustrate the general analysis above, consider $\delta = 0$ and

$$\max \int_0^T \log (c/c^*)dt = \max \int_0^T \log cdt, \qquad c^* = 1,$$

where

and

$$c = 2k - k^2 - \dot{k}$$

$$c^* = \max_k [2k - k^2] = 2 - 1 = 1.$$

To maximize

$$\int_0^T \log (2k - k^2 - \dot{k})dt$$

Euler requires

$$0 = \frac{d}{dt}\left(\frac{1}{\dot{k} - 2k + k^2}\right) + \frac{2(1-k)}{\dot{k} - 2k + k^2}$$

$$= \frac{-\ddot{k} + 2\dot{k} - 2k\dot{k}}{(\dot{k} - 2k + k^2)^2} + \frac{2(1-k)(\dot{k} - 2k + k^2)}{(\dot{k} - 2k + k^2)^2}. \tag{30}$$

Almost everywhere, this implies

$$0 = \ddot{k} - 2\dot{k} + 2k\dot{k} + 2(k-1)(\dot{k} - 2k + k^2)$$

$$= \ddot{k} + 2(k-1)\dot{k} - 2(k-1)c. \tag{31}$$

Evidently, $k^* \equiv 1$ and $(c, \dot{k}, k) = (0, 0, \hat{k} = 2)$ provide stationary solutions. The linear system associated with $y = k - 2$ is

$$\ddot{y} + 4\dot{y} + 4y = 0 \tag{32}$$

This has characteristic roots

$$X^2 + 4X + 4 = (X - \lambda_1)(X - \lambda_2) = (X + 2)(X + 2).$$

Its general solution is

$$y(t) = C_1 e^{-2t} + C_2 t e^{-2t},$$

with

$$\lim_{t \to \infty} y(t) = 0.$$

Finally, consider the point R in Fig. 5 from the point of view of the consumption turnpike theorem which relates to *finite* horizon problems. Thus fix k_0 and k_T and let T increase. Can any program approach $\hat{k}$? As is verified from Fig. 5 the answer is clearly no! In order to make a finite horizon program approach $\hat{k}$ along an inefficient turnpike, we must keep varying not only T but also k_T, which is not the type of experiment to which the Turnpike Theorem refers.

ACKNOWLEDGMENTS

The authors acknowledge National Science Foundation grants to the MIT Economics Department. N. Liviatan, on leave from Jerusalem University, acknowledges a Ford Foundation Fellowship for 1968–69.

Thanks go to Robert C. Merton of MIT.

REFERENCES

1. See, for example, P. A. SAMUELSON, A catenary turnpike theorem involving consumption and the golden rule, *Amer. Economic Rev.* **55** (1965).

2. D. CASS, Optimum growth in an aggregative model of capital accumulation, *Rev. Economic Studies* **32** (1965); T. C. KOOPMANS, On the concept of optimal economic growth, *Pontif. Acad. Sci.* (1965).

3. H. POINCARÉ, "Les Méthodes nouvelle de la Mécanique céleste," Vol. 1, Chap. 4, 1892; G. D. BIRKHOFF, "Dynamical Systems," 1927, Chap 3; E. WHITTAKER, "Analytical Dynamics," 1937, 4th ed., Chap. 15; P. A. SAMUELSON, Reciprocal characteristic root property of discrete-time maxima, *Western Economic Journal* **6** (1968), 90–93; P. A. SAMUELSON, "Classical Orbital Stability Deduced for Discrete-Time Maximum Systems," (1968) (to be published) handles motions near a periodic solution.

4. M. KURZ, The general instability of a class of competitive growth processes, *Rev. Economic Studies* **35** (1968), 155–174.

5. M. KURZ, Optimal economic growth and wealth effects, *Int. Economic Review* **9** (1968), 348–357.

6. The paradox cannot so easily be dissolved if only one (regular) turnpike exists. And Kurz's 1968 *RES* paper does analyze such a case based on an example due to Professor Arrow: This is a case of a quadratic utility function and a linear one-sector production constraint; in it, for time preference greater than the constant rate of interest, there is only one regular turnpike—that one located at utility satiation—and it is quite unstable! Here, as the Kurz–Arrow analysis shows, we must bring in the economic inequalities implicit in the problem to define a second (irregular) turnpike at the point where capital and, hence, consumption and investment are all zero. In a later paper, the present authors hope to write up notes on how inequalities supplement the analysis of the present study.

7. P. A. SAMUELSON, Ref. 3.

8. T. C. KOOPMANS, Ref. 2, p. 277. We have benefited too from seeing JOHN CHIPMAN'S, "Lectures on Optimal Growth Theory," given at Harvard in 1967 and to appear soon in book form.

9. The usual regularity conditions of smoothness, Inada conditions, etc. are postulated here. For proof of this monotonicity, familiar to readers of Sraffa and Joan Robinson, see P. A. SAMUELSON, Equalization by Trade of the Interest Rate Along with the Real Wage, in "Trade, Growth and the Balance of Payments," in honor of Gottfried Haberler, Rand McNally, 1965.

10. P. A. SAMUELSON, Ref. 1.

11. This assumes k increases along the expansion path.

12. See, e.g., J. R. HICKS, "Value and Capital," 2nd ed., pp. 92–94, Oxford University Press, New York/London, 1946.

13. E. S. PHELPS, Second essay on the golden rule of accumulation, *Amer. Economic Rev.* **55** (1961).

14. This is reminiscent of the Tulip-mania, stock market boom, or Ponzi game problems at infinity discussed in P. A. SAMUELSON, "Intertemporal Price Equilibrium: A Prologue to the Theory of Speculation," "Weltwirtschaftliches Archiv," Band 79, Heft 2 (December, 1957), pp. 181–219, reprinted as Chap. 73, pp. 946–984 in SAMUELSON, "Collected Scientific Papers," Vol. II .See particularly pp. 979–988, or 214–215 in the original.

RECEIVED: October 31, 1969

142

Law of Conservation of the Capital-Output Ratio*

Paul A. Samuelson

MASSACHUSETTS INSTITUTE OF TECHNOLOGY, CAMBRIDGE, MASSACHUSETTS 02139

Communicated September 1, 1970

Abstract. Just as simple harmonic motion, definable by a variational condition, $\delta \int (\frac{1}{2} \dot{x}^2 - \frac{1}{2} x^2) \, dt = 0$, has motions which must conserve the sum of kinetic and potential energies, $\frac{1}{2} \dot{x}^2 + \frac{1}{2} x^2 \equiv$ constant, so in a neoclassical von Neumann economy, where all output is saved to provide capital formation for the system's growth, it will be true that there exists a conservation law—namely the constancy along any intertemporally-efficient motion of the capital-output ratio $\Sigma P_t^j K_t^j / \Sigma P_t^j \dot{K}_t^j$. This is derived as an "energy" integral of a time-free integrand[1] in an optimal-control problem of variational type.

Assumptions. A transformation function relates the vector of n capital goods, $K_t = (K_t^j)$, and the contemporaneous vector of net capital formations, $\dot{K}_t = (dK_t^j/dt)$, namely

$$F(K_t, \dot{K}_t) = 0 \tag{1}$$

where F is assumed to be homogeneous-first-degree, concave, and smoothly differentiable. An optimal control program of intertemporal efficiency requires that, for assigned initial $(K_0^1, K_0^2, \ldots, K_0^n)$ and terminal $(K_T^2, \ldots, K_T^n)$ at time $T > 0$, we must maximize K_T^1. This defines the variational problem

$$\text{Max} \int_0^T \dot{K}_t^1 \, dt \text{ subject to } F(K_t, \dot{K}_t) = 0$$

and assigned boundary conditions. (2)

The Euler-Lagrange necessary conditions for this constrained-maximum problem are known to be given by

$$0 = \delta \int (\dot{K}_t^1 + \lambda_t F) dt = \delta \int L(K_t, \dot{K}_t, \lambda_t) dt \tag{3}$$

where the integrand L does not involve t explicitly. In consequence, any motion must satisfy the "energy integral"

$$L - \sum_{j=1}^n \dot{K}^j \partial L / \partial \dot{K}^j \underset{t}{\equiv} \text{constant} = c \tag{4}$$

$$\dot{K}^1 + 0 - \dot{K}^1 - \lambda_t \sum_1^n \dot{K}^j \partial F / \partial \dot{K}^j \underset{t}{\equiv} c$$

Economic Interpretation. We can now give an interpretation of this conservation law. We define in the usual fashion[2]

$$-\partial F/\partial \dot{K}^i = P^i, \text{ the cost-price of the } i\text{th capital good} \qquad (5)$$

$$\partial F/\partial K^i = R^i, \text{ the net rental of the } i\text{th capital good}$$

$$Y_t = \sum_1^n P^j \dot{K}^j = \sum_1^n R^j K^j, \text{ national income}$$

$$W_t = \sum_1^n P^j K^j, \text{ national wealth}$$

$$\begin{aligned}
r_t &= \dot{W}_t/W_t, \text{ the interest rate} \\
&= (\Sigma P^j \dot{K}^j/\Sigma P^j K^j) + (\Sigma \dot{P}^j K^j/\Sigma P^j K^j) \\
&= [\Sigma R^j K^j/\Sigma P^j K^j] + [\Sigma(\dot{P}^j/P^j)P^j K^j]/\Sigma P^j K^j \\
&= \Sigma[(R^j/P^j) + (\dot{P}^j/P^j)]P^j K^j/\Sigma P^j K^j
\end{aligned}$$

But the Euler variational conditions for a maximum can be shown to imply that *every* bracketed factor in the last expression is a constant independent of j, and therefore equal to r_t itself. For $\delta \int L dt = 0$, Euler-Lagrange conditions[3] are

$$\partial L/\partial K^i - d/dt\, \partial L/\partial \dot{K}^i = 0 = \lambda \partial F/\partial K^i - \dot{\lambda}\partial F/\partial \dot{K}^i - \lambda d/dt\, \partial F/\partial \dot{K}^i,$$
$$(i = 1, 2, \ldots . n)$$

Or

$$\begin{aligned}
-\dot{\lambda}/\lambda &= (\partial F/\partial K^i)/(-\partial F/\partial \dot{K}^i) + \\
&\qquad\qquad (d/dt\, \partial F/\partial \dot{K}^i)/(\partial F/\partial \dot{K}^i), \qquad (i = 1, \ldots, n) \quad (6) \\
&= (R^i/P^i) + (\dot{P}^i/P^i) \\
&= r_t, \text{ if the last relation of (5) is to hold.}
\end{aligned}$$

Thus, from the definition of W_t and r_t and (6), we have

$$W_t = W_0 \int_0^t \exp r_s ds = W_0 \lambda_0/\lambda_t \qquad (7)$$

But, recalling the definition of P^i and Y in (5), our energy integral also takes the form

$$\lambda_t Y_t \underset{t}{\equiv} \lambda_0 Y_0 \qquad (4')$$

Combining (4') and (7), we arrive at our fundamental economic law of conservation of the capital-output ratio, $W_t/Y_t \equiv W_0/Y_0$, which I have deduced elsewhere[4] as the energy integral of an equivalent unconstrained minimum-time problem.

For efficient balanced growth, or for the unique path through any initial K_v that approaches that von Neumann turnpike asymptotically, the constant ratio will be the reciprocal of the von Neumann interest rate or of the equivalent maximal rate of balanced growth, $g = r^*$.

* Aid from the National Science Foundation is gratefully acknowledged.

[1] Whittaker, E., *Analytical Dynamics* (Cambridge, U.K.: Cambridge University Press, 1937).

[2] Dorfman, R., P. Samuelson, and R. Solow, *Linear Programming and Economic Analysis* (New York: McGraw-Hill, 1958).

[3] Samuelson, P., *Collected Scientific Papers, I* (Cambridge, Mass.: M.I.T. Press, 1965), Chs. 17 (1937), 20 (1959).

[4] Samuelson, P., "Two Conservation Laws in Theoretical Economics," to be published, in the *Journal of Economic Theory*, and in which it is shown that the present-discounted value of both capital and income are time-invariants for any efficient program in a closed von Neumann model.

143

A THEORY OF INDUCED INNOVATION
ALONG KENNEDY–WEIZSÄCKER LINES*

Paul A. Samuelson

1. For 30 years economists have toyed with the notion that innovation, along with its purely random component, has a bias toward being labor saving in some sense. Very little definite has been demonstrated in this area, suggesting that the subject can use more careful economic analysis.

Suppose we have a neoclassical production function in two factors subject to technical change. Its general form will be $F(V_1,V_2;t)$. A special ("factor-augmenting") form will be $F[V_1/\lambda_1(t),V_2/\lambda_2(t)]$, where a decrease in λ_i means a saving of the amount of the V_i factor needed to produce any given output. (Think of V_1 as "labor" and V_2 as "capital.")

Presumably a limited amount of resources available for research and development can be used to get a larger decrease in $\lambda_1(t)$ only at the expense of a slower decrease in $\lambda_2(t)$. Thus, we might experiment with the hypothesis that the rates of improvement; $-\dfrac{1}{\lambda_i}(d\lambda_i/dt) = -\dot{\lambda}_i/\lambda_i = q_i$, are related by a transformation function with the usual convexity properties of

---

* Although the formulation here is my own, the original idea was given to me by Dr. Christian Weizsäcker during his 1962–1963 sojourn at M.I.T., and by an informal seminar paper given at M.I.T. on May 28, 1964 by Professor Charles Kennedy of the University of the West Indies, a preview of C. Kennedy, "Induced Bias in Innovation and the Theory of Distribution," *Economic Journal*, LXXIV (Sept. 1964), 541–547. What the theories of Weizsäcker and Kennedy have in common is a transformation trade-off relating the technical improvements in input requirements of the respective factors of production. A similar idea, but not so explicit, can be found in the writings of many modern writers, most notably Professor William Fellner of Yale in W. Fellner, "Two Propositions in the Theory of Induced Innovations," *Economic Journal*, LXXI (June 1961), 305–308.

Finally, I should like to acknowledge financial aid from the Carnegie Corporation and the research assistance of Mrs. Felicity Skidmore.

a production possibility frontier as shown in figure 1

$$q_2 = f(q_1), \; f'(q_1) < 0, \; f''(q_1) < 0. \tag{1}$$

For each set of factor prices (W_1,W_2), at any stage there will be a minimum unit cost of production, which can be written in the form

$$M[W_1\lambda_1(t),W_2\lambda_2(t)]$$

where

$$M(W_1,W_2) = \underset{[V_j]}{\text{Min}} \; \overset{2}{\underset{1}{\Sigma}} \; W_j V_j \text{ subject to}$$
$$F(V_1,V_2) = 1 \tag{2}$$

and the partial derivatives of M, $M_i(W_1,W_2)$, are proportional to the V_i's, being equal to the $V_i/F = a_i$ input requirements per unit of product. (The $M(W_1,W_2)$ function is completely "dual" to $F(V_1,V_2)$ having the same homogeneous concavity;[1] $1 = M(W_1,W_2)$ defines the important factor-price frontier, giving the trade-off between one real factor price in terms of another; the dual relations, $(\partial F/\partial V_i)/(\partial F/\partial V_j) = + W_i/W_j$ and $(\partial M/\partial W_i)/(\partial M/\partial W_j) = + V_i/V_j$ hold.)

2. The instantaneous rate of reduction in unit cost is given by differentiating M to get

$$-\frac{\dot{M}}{M} = -\left(a_1\frac{\dot{\lambda}_1}{\lambda} + a_2\frac{\dot{\lambda}_2}{\lambda}\right) + \text{terms involving}$$
$$W \text{ changes} \tag{3}$$
$$= a_1 q_1 + a_2 q_2 + \cdots$$

where the relative shares of the factors are defined by marginal productivities

$$\frac{W_i V_i}{MF} = a_i = \frac{W_i}{M}\frac{\partial M(W_1\lambda_1,W_2\lambda_2)}{\partial W_i}$$
$$= \frac{V_i}{F}\frac{\partial F(V_1/\lambda_1,V_2/\lambda_2)}{\partial V_i}. \tag{4}$$

Provided the f transformation function is

---

[1] See P. A. Samuelson, "Parable and Realism in Capital Theory: The Surrogate Production Function," *Review of Economic Studies*, XXIX, No. 3 (1962), 193–206.

FIGURE 1. — The heavy concave technical frontier, $q_2 = f(q_1)$, is tangential to the equi-unit-cost contours of $-(\dot{M}/M) = a_1 q_1 + a_2 q_2$ at A, whose tangency gives $-f'(q_1) = a_1/a_2$.

SHORT-RUN EQUILIBRIUM

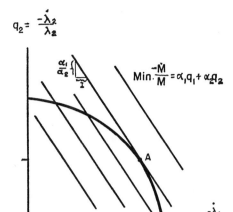

suitably concave (like a quarter circle or the usual production-possibility frontier of economics), the firm maximizes its instantaneous rate of cost reduction in (3), subject to (1), by finding a tangency position at which

$$\frac{a_1}{a_2} = -f'(q_1). \tag{5}$$

(Figure 1 shows the short-term equilibrium tangency.) But for fixed (W_i) or (V_i) ratios, the a's themselves depend on the λ_1/λ_2 ratio in accordance with the formulas in (4) or (2). Making the necessary substitution of (4) into the inversion of (5) leads us ultimately to the differential equations of the simple Weizsäcker-Kennedy (W-K) process

$$\frac{-\dot{\lambda}_1}{\lambda_1} = g\left[\frac{\lambda_1}{\lambda_2}\frac{W_1}{W_2}\right] \tag{6}$$

$$\frac{-\dot{\lambda}_2}{\lambda_2} = f\left[\frac{-\dot{\lambda}_1}{\lambda_1}\right]$$

where the sign of $g'(\cdot)$ can be shown to depend on the relation of the elasticity of substitution to unity, namely

$$g' \underset{<}{\overset{>}{=}} 0 \longleftrightarrow \sigma \underset{>}{\overset{<}{=}} 1. \tag{7}$$

3. The condition that $\lambda_1(t)/\lambda_2(t)$ remains

constant, with both factors being "augmented" by innovation in equal degree and thereby being Hicks-neutral, is that we find the following q^* root of (6) or (1)

$$\frac{-\dot{\lambda}_1}{\lambda_1} = \frac{-\dot{\lambda}_2}{\lambda_2} = q^* = f(q^*). \tag{8}$$

If it be the case that (8) hold and

$$\lambda_i(t) = \lambda_i(t_0)e^{-q^*t}, \tag{9}$$

either asymptotically or from the beginning, then from (5) we deduce the corresponding asymptotic (or invariant, equilibrium) value for relative shares

$$\frac{a_1^*}{a_2^*} = -f'(q^*). \tag{10}$$

Equations (8) and (10) constitute a "theory of relative shares" (described in figure 2), but the marginal productivity equation, (4), above, warns us that this is in no genuine sense an "alternative theory" of distribution to the neoclassical one. Nor have we yet established the fact that the states defined by (8)–(10) will in fact be realized initially or asymptotically. We must now analyze the dynamic properties of (6).

4. Let us first look briefly at the Cobb-Douglas (C-D) case where relative shares are constant and $\sigma \equiv 1$. In this case there is no unique way of splitting change into its labor-augmenting and capital-augmenting components, since the $\lambda_i(t)$ function can be factored out of the C-D expressions and divorced from either input. Specifically, either of the following are equivalent

$$F(V_1, V_2; t) = b\left(\frac{V_1}{\lambda_1}\right)^{\frac{3}{4}}\left(\frac{V_2}{\lambda_2}\right)^{\frac{1}{4}}$$
$$= b\left(\frac{V_1}{\gamma_1}\right)^{\frac{3}{4}}\left(\frac{V_2}{\gamma_2}\right)^{\frac{1}{4}}, \tag{11}$$

$\lambda_i \neq \gamma_i$, but $\gamma_1^{\frac{3}{4}}\gamma_2^{\frac{1}{4}} = \lambda_1^{\frac{3}{4}}\lambda_2^{\frac{1}{4}}$.

None the less a technical constraint like (1) could hold for a particular choice of $[\lambda_1(t), \lambda_2(t)]$. A director of research and development, who had to make a decision about innovational effort, would find it valuable to know about the feasible effects on $-\dot{\lambda}_i/\lambda_i$. So let us examine the implications of (6) for C-D functions.

In this singular case, where the relative shares, a_i, are strict constants independent of the λ's, W's, or V's, $g' \equiv 0$ and $g(\cdot)$ is a strict

FIGURE 2. — In the long run, if $q_1{}^* = q_2{}^* = q^*$ at E, Hicks-neutral technical change will persist, with relative shares given by $a_1{}^*/a_2{}^* = - f'(q^*)$.

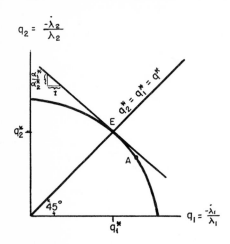

LONG-RUN EQUILIBRIUM

$$q_2 = \frac{-\dot{\lambda}_2}{\lambda_2}$$

$$q_1 = \frac{-\dot{\lambda}_1}{\lambda_1}$$

constant. Hence, (6) leads, in general, to endless divergence of the rates of improvement of the λ's, namely

$$-\frac{\dot{\lambda}_1}{\lambda_1} = \beta_1 \neq \beta_2 = -\frac{\dot{\lambda}_2}{\lambda_2} \qquad (12)$$

so that the ratio (λ_2/λ_1) is proportional to $\exp(\beta_1 - \beta_2)t$, which goes to zero or infinity depending on whether β_2 exceeds or falls short of β_1.

There seems to be no *a priori* presumption that β_2 be greater or less than β_1. However, if we get tempted into making the "equal-ignorance" assumption that f in (1) is a *symmetric* transformation function

$$q_2 = f(q_1) \longleftrightarrow q_1 = f(q_2) \qquad (13)$$
$$q^* = f(q^*) \longleftrightarrow - f'(q^*) = 1,$$

then the factor with the highest relative share (say $a_1 = \frac{3}{4}$, labor's share) will have its requirement-per-unit improving faster than will the capital factor whose $a_2 < \frac{1}{2}$. However, the steady augmentation of labor, even if it exceeds the rate at which capital (in efficiency units) is being deepened relative to labor population, cannot make labor's relative share deteriorate, because nothing can in the Cobb-Douglas case.

The C-D case is significant because in it the alleged Kennedy distribution-of-income condition given in my equation (10) has no relevance to actual income determination. Except by fluke, the actual $(\frac{3}{4}, \frac{1}{4})$ income distribution dictated by C-D marginal productivity will differ from the Kennedy distribution of $(\frac{1}{2}, \frac{1}{2})$ given by equation (13)'s symmetric specification of (10).

5. Equations (6) by themselves constitute an incomplete system, unless like Kennedy we are content to consider the W's, or their ratio, as constants.

Even though each small entrepreneur may take the factor prices W_i as given parameters subject to time trends he cannot appreciably affect, for the system as a whole, relative factor supplies V_i and the effectiveness factors λ_i are prime determinants of factor prices. Still, let us examine the general properties of (6) on the assumption that the W's or their ratio can be treated as constants (or on the less monstrous assumption that their ratio changes very slowly compared to λ_i/λ_j changes). Subtract (6)'s second equation from its first, to get

$$\frac{1}{(\lambda_2/\lambda_1)} \frac{d(\lambda_2/\lambda_1)}{dt} = \frac{-\dot{\lambda}_1}{\lambda_1} - \frac{-\dot{\lambda}_2}{\lambda_2}$$

$$= \frac{-\dot{\lambda}_1}{\lambda_1} - f\left(\frac{-\dot{\lambda}_1}{\lambda_1}\right) = \phi\left(\frac{-\dot{\lambda}_1}{\lambda_1}\right)$$

$$= \phi\left[g\left(\frac{\lambda_2}{\lambda_1} \frac{W_2}{W_1}\right) \right] = \psi(\lambda_2/\lambda_1);$$

or

$$\frac{1}{(\lambda_2/\lambda_1)} \frac{d(\lambda_2/\lambda_1)}{dt} = \psi(\lambda_2/\lambda_1), \text{ for fixed } W_2/W_1,$$
$$(14)$$

where

$$\text{sign } \psi' = \text{sign } (1 - f') \text{ sign } g'$$
$$= \text{sign } (\sigma - 1). \qquad (15)$$

Equation (14) is a first-order differential equation for λ_2/λ_1. If its left-hand side vanishes at $(\lambda_2/\lambda_1)^*$, where

$$\psi\left(\frac{\lambda_2}{\lambda_1}\right)^* = 0,$$

there is a possible state of Hicks-neutral technical progress at which both factors have equal-percentage augmentation, with $\lambda_i(t)$ proportional to $\exp\text{-}q^*t$. This Kennedy configuration may or may not be stable, depending on whether

$$\psi'(\lambda_2*/\lambda_1*) \lessgtr 0 \longleftrightarrow g'\left(\frac{\lambda_2*}{\lambda_1}\frac{W_2}{W_1}\right)$$

$$\lessgtr 0 \longleftrightarrow (\sigma* - 1) \lessgtr 0. \qquad (16)$$

Theorem: If for fixed W_2/W_1 a Kennedy neutral-change state exists, at it

$$\frac{-\dot{\lambda}_1}{\lambda_1} = \frac{-\dot{\lambda}_2}{\lambda_2} = q*, \ \lambda_2/\lambda_1 = \frac{c_1 e^{q*t}}{c_2 e^{q*t}} = (\lambda_2/\lambda_1)*;$$

it will be stable (unstable) if the elasticity of substitution there is less than (greater than) unity.

6. I conclude this section with two warnings. First, it is not legitimate to neglect the *induced* changes in factor prices W_2/W_1. (Thus, my (6) was deduced using (4)'s imputation equations, which imply that the W's are variables determined by relative effective factor scarcities $(V_1,V_2,\lambda_1,\lambda_2)$ and are not parameters.)

Waiving this fundamental objection, we must recognize that there may be no equilibrium configuration compatible with the Kennedy condition (10) and the competitive market imputation (4). We saw this in the C-D case, but there are other counter-examples even when $\sigma \neq 1$. (For example, let $q_2 = f(q_1)$ be a symmetric function, calling in the Kennedy theory for $-f'(q*) = a_1*/a_2* = 1$, or equal factor shares. But suppose $F(V_1,V_2) = V_1{}^{.8}V_2{}^{.2} + V_1{}^{.7}V_2{}^{.3}$, with factor shares always between 70 and 80 per cent for labor. Then Kennedy will find endlessly divergent rates of growth for the λ's and no Hicks-neutral equilibrium state. We shall see that the Solow constant-elasticity-of-substitution family, $F(V_1,V_2) = [(a_1V_1)^b + (a_2V_2)^b]^{1/b}$, whose σ can always be bounded *away* from unity, avoids this paradox; but economists should not emancipate themselves from the tyranny of Cobb-Douglas only to enchain themselves in a new Solow *CES* tyranny.)

II

7. It is time now to drop the assumption that factor prices are constant. Instead they are deducible, as will be relative shares, from the marginal productivities of the factors, being dependent only upon the effective factor supplies $(V_1,V_2,\lambda_1,\lambda_2)$. Hence, our earlier differential equations of (1) and (5) will enable us to express the percentage rate of change of the ratio (λ_2/λ_1) in terms of this ratio itself, or more precisely in the form

$$\frac{d(\lambda_2/\lambda_1)}{(\lambda_2/\lambda_1)dt} = G\left[\frac{\lambda_2}{\lambda_1}\frac{V_1}{V_2}\right],$$

$$\text{sign } G' = \text{sign } (\sigma - 1). \qquad (17)$$

To derive this, use (4) to express a_2/a_1 in terms of $(V_2/\lambda_2)/(V_1/\lambda_1)$ and substitute this into the inversion of (5).

If the factors in natural units are constant, or grow in the same ratio, we can look for a fixed ratio λ_2/λ_1 that will satisfy this equation. In such a regime, the induced inventions will have become neutral in the 1932 sense of Hicks, augmenting both factors at the same percentage rate. Equation (17) is a logical, and needed, fulfillment of the Kennedy-Weizsäcker theories.

8. Now in the case of assumed symmetry of the $q_i = f(q_j)$ technical-improvement frontier (which might be called the case of a "neutral" technical-improvement frontier), it is evident from the symmetry of equation (8), that (5) can be rewritten as

$$q_1* = q_2* = q* \longleftrightarrow \frac{a_2*}{a_1*} = -f'(q*) = 1 = \frac{a_1*}{a_2*}.$$

Hence, only for relative shares equal to one-half (or to 1/n in the case of n factors) can the system with a neutral technical-improvement frontier settle down to a steady state of balanced technical change.

I call this paradoxical tendency for factor shares to become absolutely equal the Kindleberger Effect, because my colleague Professor Charles P. Kindleberger conjectured that this empirically bizarre result was implied by the present theory.

9. Until we are told something about the determination of V_1/V_2, (17) constitutes an incomplete system for the unknowns $(\lambda_2/\lambda_1,V_1/V_2)$. If the V's are assumed constant as in a stationary state, or if they grow always in the same proportion so that their ratio stays constant at $(V_1/V_2)*$, (17) becomes a complete system. A stationary solution for $(\lambda_2/\lambda_1)*$, in which both factors are augmented in accordance with Hicks-neutral change, is possible wherever

$$0 = G\left(\frac{\lambda_2*}{\lambda_1}\frac{V_1*}{V_2}\right) = G(X*), \qquad (18)$$

an equation which may have no roots at all (as in the C-D and related cases), which may have exactly one root (as in the CES case, $\sigma \neq 1$), or may have multiple roots (as in cases where

σ varies above and below unity as factor proportions change).

10. A well-behaved example would be a CES function with $1 > \sigma = 1/(1 - b)$, $b < 0$, say $b = -1$:

$$F(V_1,V_2) = [(a_1V_1)^{-1} + (a_2V_2)^{-1}]^{-1}, \quad (19)$$

a weighted "harmonic mean" of the inputs. For it,

$$G(X^*) = 0 \quad (20)$$

will have the single root X^*, with $G' < 0$. Hence, for all initial conditions with $(V_1/V_2)^*$ constant, the system will approach ultimately an asymptotic state

$$\lim_{t \to \infty} \frac{\lambda_2(t)}{\lambda_1(t)} = \frac{X^*}{(V_1/V_2)^*}, \quad (21)$$

and induced technical change becomes asymptotically Hicks-neutral.

11. Now consider a CES case with $\sigma > 1$, say $\sigma = 2$, $b = \frac{1}{2}$,

$$F(V_1,V_2) = [(a_1V_1)^{\frac{1}{2}} + (a_2V_2)^{\frac{1}{2}}]^2. \quad (22)$$

As did (19), with $\sigma \neq 1$, (20) has a unique root X^*, but now $G'(X^*) > 0$. Hence, $X^*/(V_1/V_2)^*$ is an equilibrium state that will persist forever if not at all perturbed. However, for the slightest deflection of the system from equilibrium, the system will move ever further away in a cumulative self-reinforcing flight from equilibrium. Using the convention that initially $\lambda_i(0) = 1$, we consider the two cases where $(\lambda_2/\lambda_1)^* > 1$ or < 1. If the former holds, the unstably-diverging system must move ever further from equilibrium with $\lambda_1/\lambda_2 \to 0$: if only λ_1 is being reduced, we have purely labor-augmenting technical change of the Harrod-neutral variety; because $\sigma > 1$, this Harrod-neutral change is definitely Hicks capital-saving with labor's share of product going to *100* per cent and the profit rate going to zero! The reader can work out the opposite case where the system diverges on the other side of $(\lambda_2/\lambda_1)^*$ and approaches pure capital-augmentation.

If σ oscillates around unity for different values of $(V_2/\lambda_2)/(V_1/\lambda_1)$, there may be multiple equilibrium values for X^* and $(\lambda_2^*/\lambda_1^*)$. These will be alternately stable and unstable, depending on the negatives of the sign of $G'(X^*)$, which in turn depends upon the sign of $\sigma(X^*) - 1$. (If for $\sigma(X^*) = 1$ there should happen to be an equilibrium, it will be stable

(unstable) on any side where σ turns less (more) than unity.)

We can now state the correct version of our previous theorem, removing the blemish of self-contradiction in assuming factor prices as parameters of the problem.

Basic Theorem: If $(V_2/V_1)^*$ is constant, the process of selecting among alternative inventions,

$$\frac{-\dot{\lambda}_2}{\lambda_2} = f\left(\frac{-\dot{\lambda}_1}{\lambda_1}\right), f' < 0, f'' < 0,$$

the optimal combination that minimizes instantaneous unit costs (of consumption and capital goods interchangeably) will involve

$$\frac{a_1}{a_2} = -f'\left(\frac{-\dot{\lambda}_1}{\lambda_1}\right)$$

and (expressing relative shares a_1/a_2 in terms of effective factor ratios)

$$\frac{1}{(\lambda_2/\lambda_1)} \frac{d(\lambda_2/\lambda_1)}{dt} = G\left[\frac{\lambda_2}{\lambda_1} \frac{V_2^*}{V_1}\right] = G(X),$$

where

sign $[G'(X)] =$ sign $[\sigma(X) - 1]$.

Then if $\sigma(X)$ is sufficiently bounded away from unity (or some other sufficient conditions are postulated),

$$0 = G(X^*)$$

may have one (or more) equilibrium roots at which the system undergoes Hicks-neutral technical change, with

$$\left(\frac{\lambda_2}{\lambda_1}\right)^* = \frac{X^*}{(V_2/V_1)^*}, \frac{-\dot{\lambda}_1^*}{\lambda_1^*} = q^* = \frac{-\dot{\lambda}_2^*}{\lambda_2},$$

$$\lambda_i(t)^* = c_i e^{-q^* t}$$

$$q^* = f(q^*), \frac{a_1^*}{a_2^*} = \frac{a_1^*}{1 - a_1^*} = -f'(q^*).$$

Each equilibrium state will be stable (or unstable) depending upon whether $\sigma(X^*) < $ (or $>$) 1. However, the multiplicity of X^* does not imply any multiplicity of relative shares (a_1^*, a_2^*) since q^* is always unique. Should $\sigma > 1$ always, as in the CES case, it is virtually certain that the system will diverge from the (a_1^*, a_2^*) equilibrium toward a pure capital- or pure labor-augmenting state where one factor gets all the product and the other has a zero price.

For the symmetric $f(\cdot)$ frontier, we have the Kindleberg Paradox.

Corollary: If by the Principle of Insufficient Reason, we posit that the technology of labor augmentation is likely to be symmetric with that of capital augmentation so that

$$q_2 = f(q_1) \longleftrightarrow q_1 = f(q_2) \longleftrightarrow -f'(q^*)$$
$$= 1 \text{ where } q^* = f(q^*)$$

Kennedy-Weizsäcker induced technical change will be in a permanent Hicks-neutral state only when labor and property incomes have become equalized (or, if we call male labor, female labor, and property the three factors, when their shares are all $a_i = 1/3$ — or $a_i = 1/n$ in the general case of n specified factors). But only if the E of S departs sufficiently from unity need there even exist such an equilibrium state, and if one or more such equilibrium states does exist, only for $\sigma^* < 1$ will a particular state be (locally) stable and be asymptotically approached from near-by initial conditions.

12. We ought now to drop the assumption of fixed factor ratio V_1/V_2, replacing it by the more realistic recognition that capital is "deepening relative to labor," with the $K/L = V_2/V_1$ ratio growing exponentially at around two or three per cent per year. Indeed, the rate of technical progress has to be postulated to have been just enough to offset neoclassical diminishing returns if we are to be consistent with a fairly constant profit or interest rate and a fairly constant capital-output ratio.

What does this imply for the (λ_1, λ_2) model? Unless the production function of that model is Cobb-Douglas, we know that realism requires that the technical change be Harrod-neutral and nothing else. There is no other way of ensuring a constant profit rate and constant capital-output ratio. But Harrod Neutrality implies for the (λ_1, λ_2) model that λ_1 only changes! Only an invention that can be regarded as purely labor-augmenting can be persistently Harrod Neutral.[2]

I conclude from this that the (λ_1, λ_2) theory outlined in this paper fails to account for one of the stylized facts of modern development, namely that the interest or profit rates show no clear trend upward or downward.[3]

[2] Of course, the C-D case requires separate formulation. Here the distinction between Harrod and Hicks evaporates along with the possibility of distinguishing between the amount of augmentation of specific factors.

[3] Both Kennedy and Weizsäcker have variant models which do deduce an ultimate state that is purely labor-augmenting (and, with $\sigma < 1$, is Hicks labor-saving). In Kennedy's case, this is supposed to come about when he drops his assumption (which has *not* been mine) that technical progress takes place only in the consumption goods sector, and replaces it by the ". . . much-analysed one-product model in which the single product can be used equally well as a consumption good or as a capital good." This model, which I would write after conventional change

13. I shall now give an extension of the Kennedy theory that helps bring it into agreement with the Hicks and Fellner emphasis on labor saving rather than neutral invention.

Assuming a constant V_2/V_1 ratio ignores the fundamental fact that historical development has involved an accumulation of capital relative to labor. If V_2/V_1 grows exponentially as capital "deepens," there will be a powerful tendency to lower interest rates and raise real wages even in the absence of technical change. Moreover, as Marx, Hicks, and Fellner have argued, this very fact should bias technical change in some kind of a labor-saving (or factor-that-can-be-expected-to-become-dear) direction. Can my basic equation (17) justify any such conclusion? The answer is a qualified yes.

The intuitive explanation of my theory would run as follows. How could relative shares remain constant as capital deepens relative to labor even when the elasticity of substitution is less than unity and is tending to raise labor's relative shares? Answer: If, and only if, the induced technical change is relatively labor-augmenting in comparison with capital-augmentation — so that λ_2/λ_1 moves in the same direction as V_2/V_1, ensuring that the ratio of effective factor supplies, in "efficiency units" as measured by $(V_2/\lambda_2)/(V_1/\lambda_1)$, remains unchanged. For all this to be the case, we must have

$$\frac{-\dot{\lambda}_1}{\lambda_1} - \frac{-\dot{\lambda}_2}{\lambda_2} = q_1^{**} - q_2^{**} = \gamma$$
$$= \frac{d(V_2/V_1)}{(V_2/V_1)dt}, \qquad (23)$$

or

$$f(q_1^{**}) = q_1^{**} - \gamma, \quad \frac{a_1^{**}}{a_2^{**}} = -f'(q_1^{**}). \quad (24)$$

Figure 3 shows how the Hicks-neutral equilibrium of Kennedy, corresponding to q_1^* and $\gamma = 0$, is displaced southeast in the labor-saving direction by the capital-deepening factor $\gamma > 0$. This moves labor's equilibrium share, a_1^{**}/a_2^{**}, upward, and, hence, in the equal-ignorance case of $f(\cdot)$ symmetry, it pushes the share of the factor that is showing most rapid

of units in the Ramsey-Solow form, $dV_2/dt = F(t; V_1, V_2)$ — Consumption Output, is the one I have been analyzing, and for it I do not reach the Kennedy conclusion $-\lambda_2/\lambda_2 = q_2 = 0$, corresponding to Harrod-neutrality.

165

FIGURE 3. — If capital grows relative to labor (in natural units) at 2 per cent per year or at rate $\gamma = .02$, any long-run equilibrium has to be at E', where $f(q_1^{**}) = q_1^{**} - \gamma$ and $a_1^{**}/a_2^{**} = - f'(q_1^{**})$ and technical change is persistently "relatively labor-augmenting." If, at E', $\sigma < 1$, change will be Hicks labor saving and E' will be the stable equilibrium asymptote. But the interest rate will be ever-rising.

BIASED INVENTION

$$q_2 = \frac{-\dot{\lambda}_2}{\lambda_2}$$

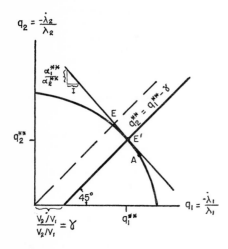

$$\frac{V_2/V_1}{V_2/V_1} = \gamma$$

relative growth (i.e., capital) down below $\frac{1}{2}$. Qualitatively, this agrees with the fact that property gets only about 20 rather than 50 per cent of total product. But one must reserve doubt that so severe a reduction could be attributable to the rather mild secular rate of capital deepening.

Substitute $V_1/V_2 = C \exp - \gamma t$ into (17), to get

$$\frac{d(\lambda_2/\lambda_1)}{(\lambda_2/\lambda_1)dt} = G\left[\frac{\lambda_2}{\lambda_1} Ce^{-\gamma t} \right]; \qquad (25)$$

and try for a possible solution of the form $\lambda_2/\lambda_1 = Y \exp + \gamma t$, to get

$$\frac{\dot{Y}}{Y} = G[CY] - \gamma \qquad (26)$$

the steady state of which is given by $Y = Y^{**}$ in

$$\gamma = G(CY^{**}) = G(X^{**}). \qquad (27)$$

Just as (18) can be solved uniquely for X^* if σ is always bounded away from unity, so can (27) be solved for a unique X^{**} under these

conditions.[4] If $\sigma < 1$, as in the CES case, this "equilibrium state" — in which the bias of induced technical factor augmentation just offsets the bias toward capital/labor accumulation — will in fact be approached asymptotically from any initial conditions.

14. The time has come to summarize the results. In the end, even in a model where no one looks forward to future increases in wages relative to interest or capital rents, we have been able to develop a model in which the accumulation of capital relative to labor does, with the help of a Kennedy-Weizsäcker technical change frontier, generate a steady state of induced labor-saving (or, more precisely, relative labor-augmenting) invention.

Be it noted that the argument does not rest upon wages being in some sense "high." High compared to what? Compared to marginal physical productivity? Obviously not, since in least-cost equilibrium all factors are equally productive, dear, or cheap, per dollar spent at the margin. Nor does the argument apply to a land-rich country like America, which is alleged to have higher wages than those it sees abroad, and is supposed, therefore, to have some special inducement to introduce labor-saving inventions. (Actually, if America is self-sufficient in the products in question, why should it look abroad and be interested in lower wage rates abroad? And if it is not self-sufficient, why should comparative advantage leave it producing goods with high labor content?) To repeat, the Fellner emphasis, upon a reasonable expectation on the part of non-myopic entrepreneurs that wage rates will be rising in the future (which we shall touch on in the next sections), is not at all involved in the present model.

Only the following elements are involved:

A. The explicit assumption, for which evidence is not at all copious, that the elasticity of substitution is less than unity, so that an increase in capital relative to labor would tend, statistically, to raise labor's relative share.

[4] The usual multiplicity (stable and unstable) on non-existence of solution can hold for (27) if σ is not bounded away from unity. However, the a_1^{**}/a_2^{**} level is unique by virtue of the uniqueness of (24)'s solution. But unless it is compatible with (4)'s marginal productivity relations, (27) will have no root and my K-W model fails to give a theory of long-run distribution.

B. A factual assumption that capital, in natural units, is accumulating relative to labor in natural units.

C. A hypothetical assumption that, other things being equal, the larger the fraction of costs going to a factor, the more it will pay inventors to work to reduce the physical requirement of that input in production. This is what is involved in the time-invariant technical progress frontier as specified in equation (1).

Then the content of figure 3 and the equations leading up to (26) can be stated intuitively, as follows.

The accumulation of capital tends to raise labor's share. The increased labor share accelerates the successful search for labor-saving inventions. The process reaches steady-state equilibrium when the increase in the capital/labor ratio in natural units is just being offset by relatively labor-augmenting or labor-saving invention at a pace that makes the effective requirements ratio λ_1/λ_2 grow exactly as fast as V_2/V_1.

III

15. I shall now give a natural generalization to the problem. Why should we want to maximize the *instantaneous* rate of unit cost reduction? This could appear to be a rather myopic procedure. Instead of maximizing $-\dot{M}$, suppose we sought to act now to minimize unit cost at some future date, say five years from now. Or more generally, act to take account of the effect that alternative choices of present $\dot{\lambda}_i/\lambda_i$ will have on some weighted average of future unit costs. Thus, instead of maximizing $-\dot{M}$ at each instant, we set up the calculus of variations problem

$$\text{Maximize} \; -\int_{t_0}^{t_1} J[M(W_1\lambda_1, W_2\lambda_2)]dt \quad (28)$$

subject to (1)

$$-\frac{\dot{\lambda}_2}{\lambda_2} = f\left(-\frac{\dot{\lambda}_1}{\lambda_1}\right).$$

By the usual technique of Lagrange multipliers, this leads to the Euler differential equations for an optimal path. I leave this to the reader, and work out only the special case where we aim to minimize unit cost at a time T periods from now. Our problem can be written

$$\text{Maximize} \int_0^T -\frac{d\log M}{dt}dt = \int_0^T -\frac{\dot{M}}{M}dt$$

$$= -\int_0^T \sum_1^2 \frac{\dot{\lambda}_j}{\lambda_j}a_j dt \quad (29)$$

subject to the above constraint on the $\dot{\lambda}_j/\lambda_j$.

We write down the usual variation condition on the Lagrangian integrand, using the more convenient variables $-\dot{\lambda}_i/\lambda_i = d\log\lambda_i/dt = \dot{y}_i$

$$L = \sum_1^2 \dot{y}_j a_j + \mu[f(\dot{y}_1) - (\dot{y}_2)]. \quad (30)$$

The resulting Euler equations

$$\frac{d}{dt}\frac{\partial L}{\partial \dot{y}_i} - \frac{\partial L}{\partial y_i} = 0$$

become

$$\frac{d}{dt}[a_1 + \mu f'(\dot{y}_1)] = \dot{y}_1\frac{\partial a_1}{\partial y_1} + \dot{y}_2\frac{\partial a_2}{\partial y_1}$$

$$\frac{d}{dt}[a_2 - \mu] = \dot{y}_1\frac{\partial a_2}{\partial y_1} + \dot{y}_2\frac{\partial a_2}{\partial y_2} \quad (31)$$

$$\dot{y}_2 - f(\dot{y}_1) = 0.$$

To these extremal conditions must be adjoined transversality conditions to determine the terminal values of (y_i) which maximize $-M(T)$. These can be written as

$$\frac{-\partial M}{\partial y_1(T)} = \frac{\partial L}{\partial \dot{y}_1}\Big]_T = a_1 + \mu f' = 0$$

$$\frac{-\partial M}{\partial y_2(T)} = \frac{\partial L}{\partial \dot{y}_2}\Big]_T = a_2 - \mu = 0. \quad (32)$$

It is evident that eliminating μ gives the optimality tangency condition (5) of the myopic theory. This is as it should be since, at the end of the period planned for, it pays to be myopic!

In the special Cobb-Douglas case where the a's are constants, the right-hand side of (31) vanishes and the left-hand side integrates to

$$a_1 + \mu f'(\dot{y}_1) = c_1, \text{ a constant}$$

$$a_2 - \mu = c_2, \text{ a constant.}$$

The terminal condition (32) assures us that these constants are zero.

Thus, in the C-D case, myopia has no penalty and farsightedness confers no advantages. Again, this is as it should be. For, wherein lies the advantage of planning ahead? Obviously, if we know that present decisions concerning the direction of research effort will affect the weight of labor costs relative to other costs in the future, we should prudently take into account that influence and not operate, as in the simplest W-K theory, completely in terms of curent a weights.

The general theory sketched here would seem distinctly superior to the myopic theory if it were really a question of managerial planning by a single monopoly firm. But, in the context of Darwinian perfect competition, there is something to be said for the myopic theory. Each competitor must minimize cost for the moment because it is only in the transient moment when he has a cost advantage that he can make any profit above the competitive minimum. The competitive system as a whole then gives the appearance of being run by an *Invisible Hand* which acts in the manner postulated by the myopic model.

Until we redo the problem, as we did the myopic version, in terms of a growing $V_2(t)/V_1(t)$ ratio and deduce from this fact the expected decline in W_2/W_1, our general formulation is still symmetric in its formulation of the variables. Hence, it is still subject to the defect of displaying the Kindleberger Effect, a tendency for relative shares to become absolutely equal (or, in the case where $\sigma > 1$, for one factor to gobble all the totals). But taking account of an expected rise in real wage will tend (with $\sigma < 1$ and an unchanged frontier) to bias the final equilibrium in the labor-saving direction.[5]

IV

16. The situation is not changed in essentials if we study more than two factors. If the transformation function of (1) is written as a symmetric function of many variables

$$T(q_1, q_2, \ldots, q_n) = 0, \qquad (33)$$

and if there are no systematic changes in V_i/V_j proportions, the Kindleberger Effect will continue to hold, with $a_i = 1/n$ the ultimate steady state.[6]

Again, if every elasticity of substitution has $\sigma_i < 1$, an accumulation of any factor or subset of factors relative to the rest will tend to lower its relative share a_i.**

17. I shall not attempt here an extended

[5] In W. Fellner's cited 1961 *Economic Journal* paper, his Figure 1 shows that an expected rise in the wage relative to the interest rate will cause firms, other things being equal, to choose of two improvements the one with relatively low labor requirements. This somewhat reinforces the previous section's non-expectational results.

[6] Even if we deem it more realistic to put into the transformation function, along with λ_i/λ_i, the attained levels of the λ_i themselves, the equal-ignorance assumption of the Principle of (In)Sufficient Reason will still imply the Kindleberger Effect — both in the myopic theory and the version involving the calculus of variations.

critique of the theories under discussion. A few dogmatic remarks must suffice. In situations involving imperfect knowledge there is a danger in thinking up new concepts. Definition should be harmless, but the human tendency to presuppose constancy in some new brain child puts the scientist at the mercy of the random walk of his thoughts.

Once I write down a transformation function between improvements in input requirements, I forget to make it so general as to be compatible with all behavior. It would be all right, indeed salutary, to put restrictions on behavior if such restrictions grew out of empirical observations, but if they grow merely out of the happenstance of definition, the result can be harmful.

18. To be sure, altering the specification of the transformation function can undo the harm, at the possible cost of introducing new arbitrary errors. Suppose, for example, that employers have learned from experience that any dollar of costs is as promising an object for research improvement as any other dollar. Then the boss may wisely decree that mobile research resources will be allocated to each input *ex ante* in direct proportion to its cost. This means that a factor like labor, or like unskilled female labor, will get the same research and development *per dollar of cost* that any other factor gets. Such a theory seems fatal to any simple notion of induced and biased technical change.

This is what the late W. E. G. Salter of Australia seems to have had in mind in his valuable *Productivity and Technical Change* (Cambridge University Press, 1960), when he put matters thus:

> The entrepreneur is interested in reducing costs in total, not particular costs such as labour costs or capital costs. When labour costs rise any advance that reduces total cost is welcome, and whether this is achieved by saving labour or capital is irrelevant. There is no reason to assume that attention should be concentrated on labour-saving techniques.
>
>   . . .
>
> The above arguments make it difficult to accept any *a priori* reason for labour-saving biases. . . . (pp. 43–44).

It is certainly what I had in mind in the latest edition of my text, *Economics*, 6th Edition (McGraw-Hill, 1964):

. . . we must recognize that *any* invention which lowers cost of production can benefit the first competitor who introduces it. Furthermore, since the relative share of wages in total costs has been approximately constant for a century, any employer who is planning his research expenditures over the coming years will reasonably take this into account and will do well to spend now the same number of pennies on experimentation designed to save a dollar of future cost, whatever its source. (pp. 738–739).

Kennedy, recognizing that the Salter argument is inconsistent with his own, regards his own argument as so ". . . indisputable that it is difficult to see how Mr. Salter, in the passage quoted above, persuaded himself otherwise. . . . reaching a conclusion that conflicts with common sense. For if the reduction in unit costs is the same whatever the character of the innovation, then there is no reason why the entrepreneur should search for one type of improvement rather than another." [7]

As is argued in the last footnote, this misinterprets the nature of the argument that ". . . in the absence of specific knowledge about possible innovation, any dollar of expenditure is as likely a candidate for innovational economy as any other." We embody this in-

[7] Kennedy, *op. cit.*, p. 543. Kennedy goes on to interpret, in his equation (3), Salter as having to assume that the transformation schedules or in my diagrams or in my (1) have to be a straight line with slope that happens to be the same as the relative shares. This would indeed make the entrepreneur *indifferent* to the degree of q_1 augmentation chosen. But Kennedy has not understood the nature of the common-sense argument made by Salter and me. It is not that we assume straight-line transformation schedules and indifference, but rather that the entrepreneur, by the principle of Sufficient Reason and in the absence of some special knowledge about exogenously given trends of innovation, has no reason to expect that the tangency equation of my diagrams and equation (5) comes with $q_2 > q_1$ rather than with $q_1 < q_2$. To render this fundamental insight mathematically, we assume that the form of the transformation function itself depends upon relative shares, a_1/a_2, and in such a way that at the root $q_1 = q_2 = q$, the slope equals the ratio of relative shares. All this is embodied in my subsequent equations and in figure 4. That common sense lies in this direction is made more clear when we realize that redefinition of what we specify as "a factor of production," so that unskilled, male labor becomes a different factor from a violin player and from a carpenter, leaves the Salter-Samuelson formation invariant, while it seems to make nonsense of the Kennedy-Weizsäcker formulation. The objection I have made here is the familiar one that probability theorists have always made to the lack of invariance of *a priori* probabilities to changes in what is specified as equally-likely. A modern Bayes approach avoids fallacy but achieves results only by stipulation of believed knowledge, not of ignorance.

sight, and emasculate the Kennedy-Weizsäcker formulations, by rewriting the transformation function (1) so that it *involves relative shares directly*

$$q_2 = f(q_1; a_1) \tag{34}$$

subject to the specific property that at $q_1 = q_2 = q$, we have the slope property

$$\frac{a_1}{1 - a_1} \equiv -\frac{\partial f(q; a_1)}{\partial q_1}, \quad q = f(q; a_1)$$
$$= q(a_1). \tag{35}$$

The whole point of this reformulation is to get away from the implicit theorizing by which one assumes that the entrepreneur can have knowledge that the transformation function remains invariant over time and has naught to do with the costs and shares of the factors themselves. There is no necessity to agree with my formulation. (If there were, this would be an empty tautology. Indeed, if it were the case, as engineers tell me it is not, that innovational research aimed at reducing labor costs could concentrate on improving processes that are inherently human, and that have a transfer value for all laborers whether they be violin players or typists, one would not want to specify a transformation function with (34)'s properties.)

By virtue of (35)'s definition, the minimization of unit costs is achieved at the following tangency point, which represents a simple generalization of the Kennedy condition (5)

$$\frac{-\dot{M}}{M} \text{ is at a minimum where } q_1 = q_2 = q \text{ and}$$
$$\frac{a_1}{a_2} = \frac{-\partial f(q; a_1)}{\partial q_1}. \tag{36}$$

This says that, in the absence of special knowledge, induced technical change is presumably Hicks-neutral. Note that the common q is not q^*, an asymptotic state, but rather one that holds all the time.

What are the fundamental equations of dynamic development of this Samuelson-Salter process? When we substitute (36) into (34) we get the following counterpart to (6) and (17)

$$\frac{-\dot{\lambda}_1}{\lambda_1} = \frac{-\dot{\lambda}_2}{\lambda_2} = q(a_1)$$
$$a_1 = \frac{\partial F[1, V_2(t)/V_1(t)]}{\partial V_1} F[1, V_2(t)/V_1(t)]^{-1}.$$

169

FIGURE 4. — If the firm's best policy is to spend on research equal sums to reduce each dollar of expense, the (q_1, q_2) transformation function depends on relative share a_1 in such a way as to make the slope at E always equal to $- a_1/a_2$. No bias results.

UNBIASED EQUILIBRIUM

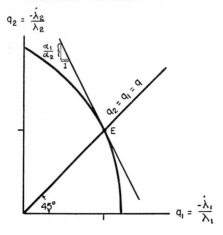

$$q_2 = \frac{-\dot{\lambda}_2}{\lambda_2}$$

$$q_1 = \frac{-\dot{\lambda}_1}{\lambda_1}$$

This says that, in the absence of special knowledge about technical change, labor's relative share develops in dependence upon relative factor supplies, going with capital deepening up (or down) if $\sigma < 1$ (or > 1), and with induced technical change *not* being presumed to alter the probabilities.

19. Until now, I have gone along with the assumption that there are no discernible exogenous trends in technical development. This is of course not true. Any scientist can tell you, after some breakthrough has been made, that there is likely to be "pay-dirt" in pursuing a certain line of invention rather than another. Indeed, the whole art of decision-making in creative science is to discern such promising developments. Nor is there, as has sometimes been argued by means of shallow semantics, a contradiction in terms in being able to know in advance of the development or discovery of as yet unknown phenomena. What we have in advance are probability judgments about the general character of promising findings. To know the answer to a question is, of course, to deny that it is still a question. But to have a flair for asking the right question at the right

time is part of what is meant by being a creative scientist.

Hence, it is not realistic to assume that new discoveries are "random." Indeed, as in the theory of Darwinian evolution that is supposed to take place by virtue of "random mutation conditioned by selective survival," one finds on deeper analysis that one cannot even define the notion of random mutation precisely. (This does not drive one to the alternative of believing that if I play tennis hard my offspring will be better tennis players, but it does recognize that if I play with X-rays my children may be likely to have certain forms of pathology predictable in advance.)

We might in a formal way allow for a "natural drift" of technical change by introducing exogenous functions $\lambda_i^\dagger(t)$, with certain specifiable properties, and then rewrite (1) or (34) in the form

$$\frac{-\lambda_2/\lambda_2}{-\lambda_2^\dagger/\lambda_2^\dagger} = f\left[\frac{-\lambda_1/\lambda_1}{-\lambda_1^\dagger/\lambda_1^\dagger}; a_1\right]. \qquad (37)$$

Then certain patterns of $-\dot{\lambda}_i/\lambda_i$ become more profitable than others, depending on what is known about $\lambda_i^\dagger(t)$. (An interesting hypothesis might make the latter neutrally exponential.) I shall not explore this important matter of natural drift of technology further.[8]

V

After these extensive researches, some historical conclusions can be briefly summarized:

i. Ricardo, to the disgust of some of his disciples (such as McCulloch), noted that invention of machines might hurt wages. Wicksell corrected what appears to be one of Ricardo's rare outright errors — namely the view that an invention might harm all of a competitive society. In resurrecting Ricardo's discussion of invention, Wicksell called attention to the passages in which Ricardo is all but recognizing that labor's share is affected in accordance with what today would be described as how the relative shift and twist in labor's Clarkian marginal-product diagram ends up changing the ratio of its marginal-product rectangle to its residual-rent triangle.[9]

[8] The absence of zero serial correlation in innovation gives this notion of natural drift operational content.

[9] K. Wicksell, *Lectures on Political Economy, Vol. I: General Theory* (London: Routledge & Kegan Paul, 1934),

ii. Wicksell gives the first modern discussion of technical change and distribution, although applied primarily to labor and land rather than to land and capital. Hick's 1932 treatment is more like that of Wicksell than anybody else, but the influence of Edwin Cannan and of Pigou is also evident.[10]

iii. Hicks, like Marx before him, ends up with a vague notion that innovation tends to be biased in a labor-saving direction. Numerous authors, including economic historians, have pursued this vague line of reasoning.[11] But in what sense any factor price can be said to be "high" was insufficiently explored. Fellner, at least, tried to make the Hicks analysis dynamic and expectational, utilizing (as Kennedy never does) the Hicksian insight that capital tends to grow (in some kind of natural units) relative to labor. All that Fellner seems to end up showing is that, if two improvements seem equally easy to make, the one which involves the least labor will tend to be introduced with greater probability the greater is the expectation of the entrepreneur that wage rates will rise relative to other factors. This near tautology, by itself, conveys little to my mind.

iv. Kennedy, although he thinks he is fulfilling the Hicks program of labor-saving bias, in fact deduces an asymptotic state of Hicks-neutral technical change [12] (which I show to be stable if, and only if, the elasticity of substitution can be assumed to be less than unity). This is not a theory of constant relative shares

so much as a theory that technical change itself will not ultimately contribute toward a change in relative shares when the ratio of factor prices or of factor supplies is not exogenously changing.

v. When I postulate a deepening of capital relative to labor, so that V_2/V_1 tends to rise and to raise labor's relative share (if the elasticity of substitution is presumed to be less than unity), I am able to deduce an asymptotic steady state of induced labor-augmenting (and also, with $\sigma < 1$, Hicks labor-saving) technical change, by virtue of the fact that every increase in labor's relative share increases the inducement to augment its technical effectiveness by purposive invention.

This is demonstrated in my basic theorem of section 11. In the special case of assumed symmetry, my corollary shows that we can avoid the Kindleberger paradox of equal relative shares as the deepening of capital induces labor-saving invention at a rate large enough to cause labor to have the larger relative share. While this agrees with broad facts, the model cannot explain the approximate constancy of the rate of profit over long periods of time.

Having entrepreneurs show prevision and minimize costs over a future period of time in which wage rates can be presumed to rise does give a Fellner reinforcement to the above conclusion.

vi. However, all of the above is emasculated if we should postulate that a rational entrepreneur will, other things being equal, have no reason to expend more effort to reduce one dollar of expenditure than another. As soon as we make the technical transformation function of (1) depend upon factor shares in the way stipulated in (35), so that cost minimization is as likely to take place with either factor augmented more than the other, the Principle of Sufficient Reason makes induced technical change Hicks-neutral at every instant no matter what the relative shares. Hence, induced invention has no systematic bias, and the drift of relative shares depends upon the drift of exogenous technical changes and upon the change of factor proportions (as affected by the relevant elasticity of substitution).

vii. Final analysis shows factor shares free to drift as the wind listeth. As a matter of his-

---

143–144; David Ricardo, *Principles of Political Economy* (Sraffa edition), Chapter XXXI; N. Kaldor, "A Case Against Technical Progress?" *Economica*, 12 (1932), 180–196; P. A. Samuelson, "Wages and Interest: A Modern Dissection of Marxian Economic Models," *American Economic Review*, 47 (1957), 884–912, particularly 894.

[10] J. R. Hicks, *The Theory of Wages* (London: Macmillan, 1932 and 1963), Chapter 5; E. Cannan, *The Economic Outlook*, p. 215ff; A. C. Pigou, *Economics of Welfare*, 4th ed. (London: Macmillan, 1960), Part IV, Chapter IV; W. Fellner, *op. cit.*

[11] Cf. E. Rothbarth, "Causes of the Superior Efficiency of U.S.A. Industry as Compared with British Industry," *Economic Journal*, 56 (Sept. 1946), 383–390, and H. J. Habakkuk, *American and British Technology in the Nineteenth Century* (Cambridge University Press, 1962). Professor Kindleberger is correct is his famous quotation that economic history is great fun but [often] can not be taken seriously. It is even more comical when it degenerates into inconclusive anecdotes purporting to verify ill-formulated economic theorizing.

[12] See however, my qualification in footnote 3.

torical fact and reasonable expectation, the purely exogenous drift of invention need not be "random" in any easily defined sense. Informed technologists in any era and area have good hunches concerning the natural drift of productive invention, all of which can be formally embodied in the basic technical transformation functions.

viii. For the most part, labor-saving innovation has a spurious attractiveness to economists because of a fortuitous verbal muddle. When writers list inventions, they find it easy to list labor-saving ones and exceedingly difficult to list capital-saving ones. (Cannan is much quoted for his brilliance in being able to think up wire*less* as a capital-saving invention, the syllable "less" apparently being a guarantee that it does save capital!) That this is all fallacious becomes apparent when one examines a mathematical production function and tries to decide in advance whether a particular described invention changes the partial-derivatives of marginal productivity imputation one way or another.

Thus, consider a locomotive. It is big and heavy. So the literary mind thinks that it must correspond to a capital-using invention and hence to a labor-saving invention. Or think of a complex Rube Goldberg-like modern contraption. It is intricate and round about. So it must be regarded as labor saving and capital using. And yet there is not the slightest pretext for such an inference. In the steady state, when human labor is organized through time with locomotives rather than without them, there is no way to tell in advance whether the relative share of labor in comparison with property has gone up or down in the steady state with production at all the stages vertically integrated.

We have the unfortunate tendency to use labor as the denominator in making productivity statements. *Any* invention, whether capital saving or labor saving, just by virtue of its definition as an invention rather than a disimprovement will, other things being equal, result in more output with the same labor or the same output with less labor. *That* could be said with *any* factor substituted for labor. But we know how difficult it is in a changing technology to get commensurable non-labor factors

to put in the denominator of a productivity comparison. So we tend to concentrate on labor. and then we fall for the pun, or play on words, which infers a labor-saving invention whenever there is an invention! [13]

Thus, consider a simple case where output acts as if it were produced by a Cobb-Douglas function with coefficients $\frac{3}{4}$ and $\frac{1}{4}$. Now let the locomotive, or the wheel, or fire, or the calculus be invented. Now can one have the least idea whether the function is merely increased in scale as against being twisted one way or the other in terms of its C-D coefficients? And when one considers embodied technical change, and changing elasticities of substitution, as one must be prepared to do, how far from intuitive inference the problem becomes.

VI

The following summary may help the understanding of this intricate analysis.

Since the 1932 publication of J. R. Hicks' *Theory of Wages* there has been the vague notion that high wages somehow induce "labor-saving" inventions. Rothbarth, Kaldor, and Habakkuk have attempted to use this theory to interpret the history of American prosperity. Since at minimum-cost equilibrium, all inputs are equally marginally dear and productive, the simplest interpretation of the high-wage theory of induced innovation is ill-founded. Fellner has added the dynamic consideration that, the steady accumulation of capital (somehow defined) relative to labor can be expected to continue in the future as in the past. It is reasonable for firms, therefore, to extrapolate a rising trend of (money and real) wage rates, and not unreasonable for them to extrapolate the historical lack of trend of the profit rate, and the concomitant downward trend in rental rates for equipment of the same technical type. This dynamic expectational effect of relatively high wage rates should, other things equal, pro-

[13] Even Pigou (p. 675) is capable of this gem: "Probably, however, the majority of inventions in the narrower sense would have to be reckoned as 'labor-saving,' because as Cassel has observed, 'almost all the efforts of inventors are directed toward finding durable instruments to do work which has hitherto been done by hand'." As if inventors wanted durability for its own sake, or that one could legitimately make inferences about labor share from the natural desire to economize on payrolls.

mote inventions designed to lower labor-input requirements.

The present paper carries the analysis further. Based upon the Kennedy-Weizsäcker notion of a (time-invariant) trade-off frontier between innovational reductions in labor versus capital-input requirements, then the theorem is proved that a long-run equilibrium of constant relative shares will exist, and that, provided the elasticity of substitution is less than unity, the equilibrium will be stably approached i.e., any initial tendency for the share of labor to drift upward will make it especially profitable to introduce relatively labor-augmenting innovations, thereby (with $\sigma < 1$) bringing labor's share back to the equilibrium level. If factor supplies remain in balance, my theory deduces an equilibrium of Hicks-neutral technical change. (Under a special symmetry assumption, the model would lead to equal factor shares for two factors or for n factors, a rather bizarre result.) Then the theorem is proved that steady growth of the capital/labor ratio will lead to a long-run equilibrium in which there is induced relatively greater labor-augmenting or labor-saving inventions to just the degree needed to keep the ratio of capital (in efficiency units) to labor (in efficiency units) constant. This equilibrium, which would be unstable if the elasticity of substitution were greater than one, provides a theory of stable relative shares with the testable implication that an increase in thrift relative to labor growth will increase the share of labor relative to property. This conclusion is independent of Fellner expectational effects, but reinforced by them. The model leading to this conclusion is shown to be only one of a number of economically important models — as, for example, the simple view that each dollar of cost tends to merit an equal research effort toward cost reduction, with *no* implied bias of innovation.

173

144

REJOINDER: AGREEMENTS, DISAGREEMENTS, DOUBTS, AND THE CASE OF INDUCED HARROD-NEUTRAL TECHNICAL CHANGE *

Paul A. Samuelson

I

1) Nietzsche once complained of the offensive clarity of Mill's style, and Kennedy [1] complains of the blinding light which my analysis throws on the problem of technical change — an indictment that induces no complaint from me. But if I was guilty of over-differentiating my product, I shall here try to make amends by showing constructively how my analysis can deduce the Harrod-neutral golden age of Kennedy and Weizsäcker.

While this does have ". . . the gratifying result of reconciling the Samuelson and Kennedy models, and even permitting, possibly, a Samuelson-Kennedy hyphenation," I shall be glad to settle for a Kennedy-Weizsäcker-Samuelson hyphenation. But before we have a merger of minds, there had better first be a meeting of minds.

2) First, I do divorce myself from Kennedy's Kaldoristic hope that ". . . the innovation-possibility frontier might be able to swallow up the tradi-

tional production function and replace it altogether." Until the laws of thermodynamics are repealed, I shall continue to relate outputs to inputs — i.e., to believe in production functions. Until factors cease to have their rewards determined by bidding in quasi-competitive markets, I shall adhere to (generalized) neoclassical approximations in which relative factor supplies are important in explaining their market remunerations. One can accept with appreciation various Kaldor insights — e.g., learning by doing — without swallowing his protean macroeconomic models of full-employment equilibrium through induced changes in factor shares and thriftiness.

But all that is another story. Let me merely say here that a many-sectored neoclassical model with heterogeneous capital goods and somewhat limited factor substitutions can fail to have some of the simple properties of the idealized J. B. Clark neoclassical models.[2] Recognizing these complications

* My thanks go to the Carnegie Corporation for providing me with a reflective year, and to Mrs. F. Skidmore for research assistance.

[1] Charles Kennedy, "Samuelson on Induced Innovation," this REVIEW, XLVIII (Nov. 1966).

[2] In my model below, although marginal productivity relations are not explicitly mentioned and although Chamberlinian imperfections are not ruled out, I do confine myself to well-behaved properties in which the capital-output ratio rises with increases in the ratio of capital to labor and

does not justify nihilism or refuge in theories that neglect short-term microeconomic pricing. In any case, the present discussion has the constructive purpose of showing how compatible are existing models with mechanisms of innovation.

3) To narrow the area of disagreement, let me state agreement that the innovation-possibility frontier can extend some distance into the quadrants of negative factor-augmentation, and that nothing hangs on my drawings having been confined to the positive quadrant.

How far into the negative quadrant can $-\dot\lambda_i\lambda_i$ go? A technical change must be an *improvement* if it is to win its way under competition. So, holding $(V_1, V_2, \ldots)$ constant, the change in λ's over time must increase output F, or

$$0 \leqslant \frac{dF}{dt} = \overset{2}{\underset{1}{\Sigma}}(\lambda_i V_i) \frac{\partial F\left[\dfrac{V_1}{\lambda_1(t)} \quad \dfrac{V_2}{\lambda_2(t)}\right]}{\partial \lambda_i} \left(\dfrac{\dot\lambda_i}{\lambda_i}\right)$$

$$= \Sigma_i (W_i V_i)\, (-\dot\lambda_i/\lambda_i)$$

$$= [a_1(-\dot\lambda_1/\lambda_1) + a_2(-\dot\lambda_2/\lambda_2)]F \quad (1)$$

where a_1 is relative share of labor $= 1 - a_2$.

Figure 1 shows that the admissible distance into

FIGURE 1

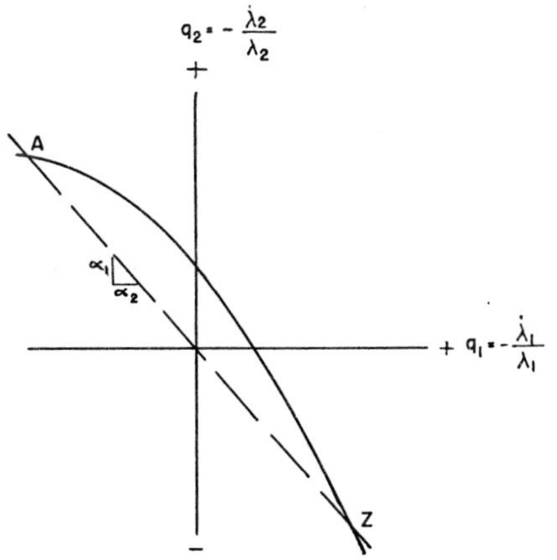

One factor augmentation can go negative if the invention makes the other factor augmentation sufficiently positive. However, if the change is to be a viable cost-reducing improvement, it must be on the range AZ cut off by a line through the origin with the slope determined by current short-term factor shares, a_1/a_2. (If we were at Z with a's slope corresponding to Z's slope, we could currently move southeast of Z to a new limit.)

in which the relative share of factors does depend on relative factor supplies.

the negative quadrant must change as factor supplies move and change relative shares.

4) Note that the case of simple factor augmentation is only a special case, which probably is valid at best only for local approximations to the general case of $F(V_1,V_2;t)$, where t is the true parameter of technical change. As many other writers have pointed out,[3] the following identity is a restrictive one:

$$F(V_1,V_2;t) \equiv F[V_1/\lambda_1(t),V_2/\lambda_2(t)]. \quad (2)$$

Among other things, it implies that the invention shifts each isoquant so that, by a change in scales on each axis, they can be made to coincide. What is the same thing, the shift of an isoquant plotted on double-log paper must be a perfectly parallel one in some direction, the degree of bias of that direction from a 45° southwest direction depicting whether the invention is neutral or relatively labor- or capital-saving.[4]

5) Since my purpose here is to throw light rather than shadow-box, let me state that Kennedy's first two sections do shake me somewhat in my skepticism concerning the invariance of the innovation frontier. A holder of the Salter-Samuelson view is indeed given pause by Kennedy's sentences:

Suppose there is a change in the price of one factor but no other change in the situation. A transformation function that involves relative shares then commits us to the view that the entrepreneur believes the change to have altered the technological innovation possibilities. I cannot see how such a view can be reconciled with common sense, or even rationality.

[3] Dr. Eytan Sheshinski, now of Harvard, in an M.I.T. term paper and E. S. Phelps in a privately circulated paper.
[4] The isoquant's absolute slope on the double-log plot represents relative shares a_1/a_2, being constant for the Cobb-Douglas straight-line case. For elasticity of substitution less than one $\sigma < 1$, the isoquant is a concave (from below) arch. If the direction of parallelism is more west than south — the relatively labor-augmenting case — the invention will be seen to be Hicks labor-saving, reducing the slope of the isoquant to the exact southwest and, therefore, deteriorating labor's relative share at unchanged V_2/V_1 ratio. A parallel interpretation holds for relative capital augmentation; of course, if $\sigma > 1$, these directions have to be reversed.

Consider two time periods, $t + \Delta t > t$. If an innovation-possibility frontier holds invariantly regardless of V_i or attained $\lambda_i(t)$, of the form

$$\frac{F[V_1/\lambda_1(t + \Delta t), V_2/\lambda_2(t + \Delta t)]}{F[V_1/\lambda_1(t), V_2/\lambda_2(t)]}$$

$$\equiv T\left[\frac{\lambda_1(t + \Delta t)}{\lambda_1(t)}, \frac{\lambda_2(t + \Delta t)}{\lambda_2(t)}\right] \equiv c$$

then F can be shown to be necessarily Cobb-Douglas — a result arrived at I believe by Professor S. Ahmad of Khartoum in a forthcoming 1966 *Economic Journal* article. To prove this fact, note that $f(x)/f(y) \equiv \psi(x/y)$ implies that $f(x) \equiv cx^k$. Paradoxically, the Kennedy frontier would in this case be convex rather than concave, exactly like a Cobb-Douglas isoquant on non-log paper.

If further reflection on this argument should cause me to recant some of my skepticism, I must warn against some possible misunderstandings.

a) Research experimentation to innovate must involve probabilities about uncertain future events. The innovational frontier envisaged by the inventive decision-maker is very much an *ex ante* concept. Without regard to whether the specific productive contribution of one factor can be isolated from that of another — at the margin by marginal-productivity partial derivatives, or nowhere because of fixed-and-joint proportions — it makes sense for an important user of a factor (such as copper or skilled female labor) to ask whether he can spend time and money to lower his requirements of that factor. Mathematically, even if $F[V_1/\lambda_1, V_2/\lambda_2]$ is of fixed-coefficient type without smooth substitution, lowering a λ_i has operational meaning.

This explanation, while not intended to controvert the quoted sentences from Kennedy, may help clarify some of his earlier queries as to what I meant by ". . . research resources allocated to an input [such as copper or female labor]," or by ". . . a factor will get research and development."

b) To repeat, my extending the frontiers into the negative quadrants is not germane to any of these issues.

Now to my attempt to grapple with Kennedy's quoted lines. It is not my thought that a mere change in the price quoted for a factor will alter the technical possibility of innovating ways of learning how to use less of the factor. Rather, it is that when effective factor proportions have changed — whether by changes in natural supply or past changes in efficiency-unit content of the factor — we will be in a different part of the production function and, therefore, that this change in the physical position might well alter the prospect for *further* innovational savings in the use of that factor.

At these changed factor-ratio positions, we shall be at changed relative shares, a_1, and it is in this sense that changes in a_1 may be associated with changes in the Kennedy — or must I now say Samuelson? — innovational frontier.

Concretely, with Fellner, let me consider going from production function $F(V_1, V_2; t)$ at time t to a better one $F(V_1, V_2; t + \Delta t)$, by spending some optimal amount of money and energy on innovation during the intervening time Δt. To an approximation, describe this by the factor-augmenting form of (2). Hence, the unit-isoquant

$$1 = F(V_1, V_2) = F(V_1, V_2; t) \tag{3}$$

goes over into

$$F[V_1(1 + q_1), V_2(1 + q_2)] = 1. \tag{3'}$$

Since relative factor share ends up dependent upon V_2/V_1 and $V_2(1 + q_2)/V_1(1 + q_1)$, why should not the q's in (3') be related by a transformation function which depends on (a) the position of V_1/V_2 and hence of relative shares a_i, and for that matter on (b) the length of time elapsed since previous innovation had utilized the store of accumulating knowledge of new scientific discoveries?

Cannot my proposal to write, as in (equation 34, p. 352)

$$q_2 = f(q_1; a_1)$$

or

$$\frac{q_2}{q_2^\dagger} = f\left[\frac{q_1}{q_1^\dagger}; a_1\right]$$

where the $q_i^\dagger$ are the trend factors described in (equation 37, p. 353), be reconciled with "rationality" by the above argument? Even if the answer is yes, there remains the burden of showing that there is some reason to expect a particular bias of shifting of the (q_2, q_1) frontier.

Let me try to make an argument, with no claim for its finality. Consider the case deduced in the last part of the present comment: persistent labor-augmenting innovation with zero capital-augmentation. Can this go on long without improving the prospects for profitable capital-augmentation? I doubt it. Anyone who believes in diminishing returns as applied to continued innovational exertions in one direction within a limited time period, and who believes in hysteresis effects of the past pattern of innovation on present prospects for successful innovation, will perhaps share my doubts.

II

For the rest of this note, bury the above doubts and work out the agreement of my analysis with the Kennedy case of induced Harrod-neutral labor augmentation.

Kennedy's exogenous assumption was that of a constant interest or profit rate. Mine was of an exogenous accumulation of capital relative to labor — a growth of K/L or in my notation of V_2/V_1. Neither is necessarily an assumption superior to the other, nor to some third assumption — such as a constant percentage, s, of income saved. To show that my complete model can handle any of the alternatives, and to bring it closer to the Harrod-neutral technical change state of Kennedy and Weizsäcker, I shall here [5] give a brief analysis of

[5] See Kennedy's references to the papers by Fellner and by Phelps and Drandakis. Several graduate students at M.I.T., and I daresay elsewhere, have independently arrived at similar results and I claim no originality for the following demonstration.

the third case, deducing the following interesting result.

Theorem. If labor grows exponentially in natural units at a growth rate of n per year, and if a constant fraction of income, s, is always saved, then a standard system with elasticity of substitution less than one and subject to a Kennedy technical change transformation frontier will have an asymptotic generalized golden-age state with

  i) Harrod-neutral technical change.

  ii) Asymptotically constant relative factor share that is independent of s and n, depending only on the slope of the Kennedy frontier at the horizontal intercept of pure labor augmentation.

  iii) Asymptotically constant interest rate, which rises with rate of population growth and declines with rate of saving.

  iv) Real wage that is asymptotically growing at the rate of labor augmentation, N^∞, which is independent of n and s as in the case of relative shares, but whose level is affected by n and s in a way opposite to that of the interest rate.

  v) Output and capital stock will asymptotically grow at the rate of population growth plus rate of ultimate labor-augmentation (and real wage increase), which is independent of s. The capital-output ratio will be asymptotically constant at a level that increases with s and declines with n, being dependent on the ultimate relative share and the once-and-for-all level of capital augmentation that gets achieved before pure labor-augmentation sets in.

  vi) All the above asymptotic states are stable if $\sigma < 1$ and the golden age will reassert itself if locally perturbed.

Figure 2 illustrates these relations on a semi-log diagram.

To set up the model, employ my previous notation but with L and K substituted for V_1 and V_2, to get

$$\dot{L}/L = n \ , \ L = e^{nt} \tag{4}$$

$$\dot{K} = sY = sF(L/\lambda_1, K/\lambda_2) \tag{5}$$

$$-\dot{\lambda}_2/\lambda_2 = f(-\dot{\lambda}_1/\lambda_1) \tag{6}$$

$$a_1/a_2 = -f'(-\dot{\lambda}_1/\lambda_1) \tag{7}$$

$$a_1 = 1 - a_2 = WL/Y \tag{8}$$
$$= H[(K/\lambda_2)/(L/\lambda_1)],$$

with $H' > 0$ if the elasticity of substitution, σ, satisfies $\sigma \leqslant k < 1$.

For assigned initial values of $(K, L, \lambda_1, \lambda_2)$, the

FIGURE 2

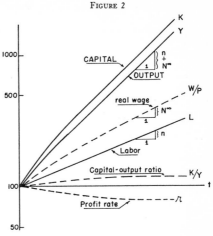

Constant saving ratio leads initially to falling interest rate and profit share, thereby encouraging labor-augmentation relative to capital-augmentation until asymptotically Harrod-neutral technical change is great enough to keep labor, in efficiency units, growing at the same rate as output and capital (in natural units) growth. Constancy of relative shares, profit rate, and capital-output ratio emerges asymptotically.

system (4) through (8) generates its own determinate development. To study its behavior, initially and asymptotically, concentrate on the key variable, relative factor proportions in terms of efficiency (not natural) units, $(K/\lambda_2)/(L/\lambda_1)$, which I call x. Labor's relative factor share a_1 depends on it as in (8) for marginal-product reasons not here discussed. From the short-run tangency conditions of optimal induced innovation of (6) and (7), we can solve to get labor augmentation, capital augmentation, and their relative augmentation in terms of x alone. Once we know this relative augmentation in terms of x and know from (4) and (5) the accumulation of capital relative to labor in terms of x, we have a complete two-by-two system for determining the rate of growth of x and λ_2 in terms of themselves alone. In short (4) through (8) can be reduced to the simple system

$$-\dot{\lambda}_2/\lambda_2 = M(x) \ , \ M' < 0 \tag{I}$$

$$\dot{x}/x = \frac{s}{\lambda_2} A(x) - n - N(x), \ A' < 0, \ N' > 0. \tag{II}$$

From familiar Solow-Harrod analysis, $A(x)$ is found to be the reciprocal of the capital-output ratio; $N(x)$ is the relative rate of labor and capital augmentation, $[d(\lambda_1/\lambda_2)/dt]/(\lambda_1/\lambda_2)$, depicting how an increase in the capital-labor ratio will raise labor's relative cost and encourage labor-augmenting invention at the expense of capital-augmenting, in accordance with the tangency analysis of my Kennedy diagrams; $M(x)$ depicts how much a rise in x lowers capital's share and lowers the rate of capital augmentation. Finally, equation (II) says that the growth in x, written as $(K/L)(\lambda_1/\lambda_2)$ comes from (5)'s saving ratio operating on K, from (4)'s postulated labor growth operating as the subtraction of n, and finally the subtraction of N comes from the change in λ_1/λ_2 as deduced from the Kennedy-Weizsäcker tangency conditions (6) through (8) already described.

To find a golden age for our system or equilibrium point $(x^\infty,\lambda_2^\infty)$, we equate the left-hand sides to zero. This enables us to solve (I) for the Harrod-neutral intercept's factor share a_1^∞ and concommitant factor-ratio root x^∞. Knowing asymptotic x^∞, we solve (II) for the asymptotic level of (no longer growing) capital augmentation

$$\lambda_2^\infty = \frac{sA(x^\infty)}{n + N^\infty}$$

where $N^\infty = N(x^\infty)$ is the rate of ultimate Harrod-neutral labor augmentation, as measured by the horizontal intersect itself of any of my earlier paper's Kennedy-transformation curves. Thus, our system (I) (II) is solved for its asymptotic state, and we can go back to (4) through (8) to get the associated values for all the variables, of which a few key ones are:

$$(K/Y)^\infty = \frac{f(x^\infty)}{x^\infty \lambda_2^\infty} = \frac{s}{n + N^\infty}$$

$$r^\infty = \frac{f'(x^\infty)}{\lambda_2^\infty} = a^\infty \frac{n + N^\infty}{S}$$

where $f(x) \equiv f(1,x)$.

Standard stability analysis for the unique equilibrium point of such a differential equation system shows that the asymptotic golden age is indeed locally stable, and will be reapproached if the system is perturbed to a neighborhood of it. Thus, the characteristic polynomial associated with the system is

$$0 = m^2 + [\ + x^\infty N'(x^\infty) -$$
$$+ [\ - x^\infty M'(x^\infty)A(\infty)s/\lambda_2^\infty].$$

Because the bracketed coefficients are assuredly positive, the characteristic roots are damped with real parts definitely negative, ensuring local stability. If a so-called limit cycle could be ruled out, global stability would be assured as well.

The reader will note that I have deduced, not assumed, Harrod-neutrality and constant profit rate. The challenge to explain the stylized facts of capitalism — as described for example in the growth chapter of my *Economics* (sixth edition, chapter 35) — has been successfully met by this model. This says much for it, but of course does not settle the question of whether a time-invariant technical progress frontier is realistic.[6]

[6] If $\sigma \to 1$ in some region, so that factor share cannot run the whole gamut of values, there will be no stationary root to (I) — (II) and the model describes its own dynamic development.

145

THE FUNDAMENTAL SINGULARITY THEOREM
FOR NON-JOINT PRODUCTION*

By Paul A. Samuelson[1]

1. THE TECHNOLOGY for a society can be summarized by its Production Possibility-Frontier

$$(1) \qquad Q_1 = T(V_1, \cdots, V_m; Q_2, \cdots, Q_n) ,$$

where the m factor inputs are denoted by V_j and the n goods by Q_i, and where any one of the goods could have been called Q_1 and be regarded as being maximized for prescribed totals of the remaining variables. The partial derivatives of this transformation function provide the shadow or actual prices so important for efficiency and for positive market descriptions, namely

$$(2) \qquad \begin{aligned} \frac{W_j}{P_1} &= \frac{\partial T}{\partial V_j} & (j = 1, 2, \cdots, m) , \\[2mm] \frac{P_i}{P_1} &= - \frac{\partial T}{\partial Q_i} & (i = 2, 3, \cdots, m) . \end{aligned}$$

In the special case of a neo-neoclassical technology, where the feasible production set is both convex and subject to constant-returns-to-scale, T will be a homogeneous function of first degree and a concave function in terms of the variables Q_i and V_j. Where it has smooth partial derivatives, its Hessian matrix of second partial derivatives, H, must be singular and negative semi-definite.

2. An example of a possible P-P Frontier would be

$$(3) \qquad \sqrt{Q_1^2 + Q_2^2} = \sqrt{V_1 V_2} \quad \text{or} \quad Q_1 = \sqrt{V_1 V_2 - Q_2^2} .$$

If we had two countries with this same function and we let them trade freely, you might think from the famous factor-price equalization theorem that for near-enough endowments (and waiving certain patterns of specialization and peculiar factor intensities) they would come to have identical real wages and factor returns. But you would be wrong to think so. For that theorem depends upon ruling out *joint production*, as do the non-substitution theorems of 1949 and 1961 and various forms of the Turnpike Theorem[2]. It will by no means

---

* Manuscript received January 7, 1965, revised May 6, 1965.

[1] Grateful acknowledgement is made to the Carnegie Corporation for a research grant.

[2] P. A. Samuelson, "Abstract of a Theorem Concerning Substitutability in Open Leontief Models," *Activity Analysis of Production and Allocation*; Tjalling C. Koop-

(Continued on next page)

be obvious that the example in (3) does intrinsically involve joint production. Indeed, I wish, for contrast with (3), I could write down an analytic expression for T which comes definitely from a technology which involves no joint production. But also, even though modern and older economists spend most of their time in talking about the case where joint production is not permitted, I do know an analytic expression for only one non-trivial case, that in which one good uses but one of the factors. Thus $Q_1 = V_1^{1/4}(V_2 - Q_2)^{3/4}$ is an admissible case for a non-joint-production model, as would be $Q_1 = V_1 f[(V_2 - aQ_2)/V_1]$ where $f[\cdot]$ is any concave function.

Nevertheless, I know that (3) must have involved joint production. How do I know this? For one thing, I might work backward and show that non-factor-price-equalization leads to a contradiction to the assumption of non-jointness. But that is backing into the problem in an awkward way. I propose to follow a different method, one which I have used in lectures for many years but which I have never seen referred to in the literature.

3. If each single good can be thought of as being produced in its own industry with its own factors, we have in the background of (1)'s T, the industry production functions

$$(4) \qquad Q_i = Q^i(V_{1i}, V_{2i}, \cdots, V_{mi}) \qquad (i = 1, 2, \cdots, n)$$

where Q^i is a concave, homogeneous function of the first degree, and V_{ji} is the amount of the j-th factor allocated to the i-th industry. As I have shown elsewhere[3], there must necessarily exist a fundamental

mans, editor (New York: John Wiley & Sons Inc. 1951), chapter VII, 142.

P. A. Samuelson, "A New Theorem on Nonsubstitution", Festchrift Johan Akerman, *Money, Growth and Methodology*; Hugo Hegeland, editor (Lund, Sweden: CWK Gleerup, 1961), 407-23. In the 1965 Haberler Festchrift, I prove a nonsubstitution theorem involving durable capital goods.

Robert Dorfman, P. A. Samuelson and R. M. Solow, *Linear Programming and Economic Analysis* (New-York: McGraw-Hill, 1958), Chapter 12.

Michio Morishima, *Equilibrium, Stability and Growth* (Oxford: Oxford University Press, 1964), 156-71.

Hirofumi Uzawa, "Prices of the Factors of Production in International Trade," *Econometrica*, XXVII (July 1959), 448-68, erred in deducing necessarily-incomplete factor-price equalization by failing to note that the T function is such as not to lead to single-valued linear excess demand functions.

[3] P. A. Samuelson, "Parable and Realism in Capital Theory: The Surrogate Production Function", *The Review of Economic Studies*, XXIX (June 1962), 193-206. To avoid obvious, but uninteresting degeneracy cases, I shall assume that the Hessian matrix of second partial derivatives of Q^i is not decomposable, thus ruling out $Q^i(x, y, z) = f(x, y) + g(z)$, or $f(x, y) + 0$, etc.

Factor-Price Frontier connecting the factor returns

(5) $$\frac{W_j}{P_i} = \frac{\partial Q^i(V_{1i}, \cdots, V_{mi})}{\partial V_{ji}} , \qquad (i = 1, \cdots, n; j = 1, \cdots, m)$$

in such an industry, namely

(6) $$\frac{W_1}{P_i} = f^i\left(\frac{W_2}{P_i}, \frac{W_3}{P_i}, \cdots, \frac{W_m}{P_i}\right), \text{ or}$$

$$A^i\left(\frac{W_1}{P_i}, \frac{W_2}{P_i}, \cdots, \frac{W_m}{P_i}\right) = 1 \qquad (i = 1, 2, \cdots, n)$$

where A^i is a unit-cost-of-production function which is *dual* to the production function Q^i and has *all* the qualitative mathematical properties it has (namely, homogeneity of degree 1 and concavity).

4. We can now substitute the F-P Frontier relations of (6) into the general pricing relations of (2), to get the following severe restrictions on (1)'s T function if it is to have come from the non-joint production case

(7) $$A^1\left(\frac{\partial T}{\partial V_1}, \cdots, \frac{\partial T}{\partial V_m}\right) \equiv 1$$

$$A^i\left(-\frac{\partial T/\partial V_1}{\partial T/\partial Q_i}, \cdots, -\frac{\partial T/\partial V_m}{\partial T/\partial Q_i}\right) \equiv 1 \qquad (i = 2, 3, \cdots, n)$$

As will be shown, not all of these restrictions are independent, since the first can be deduced from the rest.

5. Before exploring further the implications of these basic relations, I can now apply the test to the function in (3) to show that it does violate the non-jointness conditions. For this negative purpose, it is enough to show that two different values of W_2/P_1 can be found to correspond with the same value of W_1/P_1, in violation of the condition that there is a single-valued F-P Frontier for the first industry. Routine differentiation of (3) as indicated in (2) reveals that the following values can coexist:

$$\left(\frac{W_1}{P_1}, \frac{W_2}{P_2}\right) = \left(\frac{1}{\sqrt{2}}, \frac{1}{\sqrt{2}}\right), \text{ or}$$

$$\left(\frac{1}{\sqrt{2}}, \frac{2}{\sqrt{2}}\right) \text{ or } \left(\frac{1}{\sqrt{2}}, \frac{V_2}{\sqrt{2}}\right)$$

where V_2 is arbitrary. This is a clear contradiction.

Common sense confirms that (3) does involve joint production. For, the first version of it shows that a Cobb-Douglas function involving the inputs produces an intermediate good, which we might call Y.

This intermediate good can then be "cracked" to make various alternative amounts of good Q_1 and good Q_2, just as crude oil is cracked to make variable proportions of gasoline and kerosene.

6. The relations (7) involve existent functions whose form we may not directly know from knowledge of T in the neighborhood of actual empirical observations. So it will be useful to derive the logical implications of (7) for T in any neighborhood of the surface. Implicit function theory tells us that if there is to exist a functional relationship between a number of functions of a common set of variables, certain critical Jacobian matrices must be identically singular. To simplify the writing of the implied relations, I shall from now on employ a subscript notation to indicate partial differentiation.

$$\frac{\partial T}{\partial V_j} = T_j, \quad \frac{\partial^2 T}{\partial V_i \partial V_j} = T_{ij}, \quad \frac{\partial T}{\partial Q_i} = T_{m-1+i}, \text{ etc.}$$

Now consider the first relation of (7), $A^1 = 1$. Since each of the m T_j functions involve the common variables $(V_1, V_2, \cdots, V_m, Q_2, \cdots, Q_n)$, this is known to imply that the following Jacobian matrix

$$(8) \qquad J^1 = \begin{bmatrix} T_{11} \cdots T_{1m} & \cdot & T_{1,m+1} \cdots T_{1,m-1+n} \\ \vdots & \vdots & \vdots & \vdots \\ T_{m1} \cdots T_{mm} & \cdot & T_{m,m+1} \cdots T_{m,m-1+n} \end{bmatrix} \text{ be of rank } m-1.$$

Similarly, if we designate

$$-\frac{\partial(T_j/T_{m-1+i})}{\partial V_k} = {}^i a_{jk}, \quad -\frac{\partial(T_j/T_{m-1+i})}{\partial Q_r} = {}^i a_{j,m-1+r}$$

the remaining relations of (7) require that

$$(9) \qquad J^i = \begin{bmatrix} {}^i a_{11} \cdots {}^i a_{1m} \cdots {}^i a_{1,m-1+n} \\ \vdots & \vdots \\ {}^i a_{m1} \cdots {}^i a_{mm} \cdots {}^i a_{m,m-1+n} \end{bmatrix} \begin{matrix} \text{be of rank } m-1 \\ \text{for } i = 1, 2, \cdots, n. \end{matrix}$$

Note that (9) is written to include (8) if we adopt the convention that ${}^1 a_{jk} = T_{jk}$. Note, too, that the rank could be less than $m-1$ if we do not rule out degeneracy within the industry.

Intuition tells us that if all industries but the last each have their own-real-factor-prices constrained by an industry Factor-Price Frontier, then the last industry's factor prices must satisfy its similar relation. Mathematically, if all the $(J^2, \cdots, J^n)$ satisfy the indicated rank criteria, then so must J^1. This follows from the homogeneity property of T, which is well known to require *singularity* of its negative semi-definite Hessian matrix of cross derivatives

$$(9') \qquad H = \begin{bmatrix} T_{11} & \cdots & T_{1m} & \cdots & T_{1,m-1+n} \\ \vdots & & \vdots & & \vdots \\ T_{m1} & \cdots & T_{mm} & \cdots & T_{m,m-1+n} \\ \hline \vdots & & & & \vdots \\ T_{m-1+n,1} & \cdots & T_{m-1+n,m} & \cdots & T_{m-1+n,\,m-1+n} \end{bmatrix} \quad \text{be singular .}$$

I shall leave it as an exercise in determinants for the zealous reader to prove that the rank conditions on $J^1, \cdots, J^n$ are not all independent.

7. If we have knowledge of the $T(V; Q)$ function *everywhere*, we can immediately identify the separate industry production functions if they really exist. For, by definition,

$$Q^1(x_1, \cdots, x_m) = T(x_1, \cdots, x_m, 0, \cdots, 0) ,$$

$0 = Q^2(x_1, \cdots, x_m) - Q_2$ is equivalent to

(10)
$$0 = T(x_1, \cdots, x_m, Q_2, 0, \cdots, 0) ,$$

$0 = Q^n(x_1, \cdots, x_m) - Q_n$ is equivalent to

$$0 = T(x_1, \cdots, x_m, 0, 0, \cdots, Q_n) .$$

From these Q^i functions, we can derive in my indicated fashion the corresponding dual $A^i(W_1/P_i, \cdots, W_m/P_i) = 1$ functions explicitly (and vice versa). One can then make the indicated substitutions of (7), to see whether T does indeed possess the non-jointness property that was hypothesized. This procedure obviates the need to calculate (9)'s J^i matrices and test their rank conditions.

8. Still another test procedure can be applied. For *any* T, by setting every Q_i but one equal to zero, we can identify uniquely a genuine or pseudo-industry production function $Q^i(V_{1i}, \cdots, V_{mi})^*$. These are always, by the usual additivity, free-disposability and convexity assumptions, *feasibly* open to us. Then we can get the maximal social transformation that corresponds to these $Q^i(\cdots)^*$ functions. Call it T^* to distinguish it conceptually from our original observed T.

Now if T^* is exactly of the same form as T, we can speak of our economy as *not* involving intrinsic joint production. But if $T^* < T$, we know that intrinsic joint production was somewhere involved in T.

9. The example of (3) can illustrate this procedure. Applying the procedure of (9) to the case (3) obviously yields pseudo-industry functions

(11)
$$Q^1(V_{11}, V_{21})^* = \sqrt{V_{11} V_{21}} ,$$
$$Q^2(V_{12}, V_{22})^* = \sqrt{V_{12} V_{22}} .$$

Solving the maximal problem

$$\max_{\{r_{ij}\}} Q^2(V_{11}, V_{21})^* \text{ subject to } Q^2(V_{12}, V_{22}) \geqq Q_2, \sum_{i=1}^{2} V_{ji} \leqq V_j, (j = 1, 2)$$

can be shown, from the symmetry of (3) to give

(12) $$Q_1 = T(V_1, V_2, Q_2)^* = \sqrt{V_1 V_2} - Q_2 < \sqrt{V_1 V_2 - Q_2^2},$$

the inequality being an obvious one from the identity

$$V_1 V_2 - Q_2^2 = (\sqrt{V_1 V_2} + Q_2)(\sqrt{V_1 V_2} - Q_2).$$

10. The 2-factor 2-good case is most beloved by economists. A complete characterization for it to involve no joint production is that its negative semi-definite Hessian matrix

(13) $$H = H^T = \begin{bmatrix} T_{11} & T_{12} & T_{13} \\ T_{21} & T_{22} & T_{23} \\ T_{31} & T_{32} & T_{33} \end{bmatrix} \text{ be of rank 1 and negative semi-definite.}$$

A necessary and sufficient condition for this which exhausts the content of (8) is that

(13′) $$\begin{bmatrix} T_{11} & T_{12} \\ T_{21} & T_{22} \end{bmatrix} \text{ be singular, with } \begin{bmatrix} V_1 \\ V_2 \end{bmatrix} \text{ an eigenvector.}$$

Of course, there are other equivalent conditions, such as that any other 2×2 principal minor vanish identically, or that non-principal minors like $T_{11} T_{23} - T_{21} T_{13} \equiv 0$, but it would be (harmlessly) redundant to specify them.

We can use (13′) to test the example of (3). For it we find

$$\text{det. } [4Q_1^3 H] = \begin{vmatrix} -V_2^2 & V_1 V_2 - Q_2^2 & 2Q_2 V_2 \\ V_1 V_2 - Q_2^2 & -V_1^2 & 2Q_2 V_1 \\ 2Q_2 V_2 & 2Q_2 V_1 & -4V_1 V_2 \end{vmatrix} \equiv 0$$

$$\text{det. } \begin{bmatrix} -V_2^2 & V_1 V_2 - Q_2^2 \\ V_1 V_2 - Q_2^2 & -V_1^2 \end{bmatrix} = -4Q_2^2(Q_2^2 - V_1 V_2) = -4Q_1^2 Q_2^2 \not\equiv 0$$

Since (13′) is not satisfied, we verify again that (3) does involve joint production.

11. The 2-factor 3-or-more-good case is known to involve straight-line rulings on the $(Q_1, \cdots, Q_n)$ surface derived from T when we freeze the V's; hence it has an infinity of indifferent production responses to certain critical price ratios. Our analysis confirms this degeneracy property for any case where the number of independently-produced goods exceeds the number of factors, $n > m$. Such degeneracy in the

(Q_i) surface implies that H has rank less than $n - 1$; since our analysis requires the rank to be $m - 1$ at most, $m < n$ does imply and confirms this important property.

12. Although the 2-factor 2-good case conditions can be expressed simply in terms of the rank of H alone, one must not infer that the rank of H is sufficient in the general case. Thus, if Q_1 is produced non-jointly and Q_1 and Q_3 are produced jointly, H will have rank $m - 1 = 1$, if there are but 2 factors. It is only when $n = 2$ that we have the accidental feature that non-jointness in one good means non-jointness in all but one good; hence non-jointness in all.

13. In modern neo-neoclassical economics, it is admissable to deny the smooth substitutability of conventional neoclassical economics. Thus, v. Neumann, Leontief and modern programmers may assume fixity of proportions for one or a number of alternative activities. For such cases, there may be lacking the partial derivatives needed for the Jacobian conditions of (9). Nevertheless, our criteria of (7) will still apply to suitably defined dual prices, as the following brief sketch will indicate.

Now let us rewrite (1) so that the feasible set of non-negative inputs and outputs (Q, V) is given by

$$(14) \qquad F(Q_1, Q_2, \cdots, Q_n; V_1, \cdots, V_m) \geqq 0$$

where F is concave and homogeneous of degree 1. We may consider "normalized" sets of (Q, V) which satisfy

$$(15) \qquad Q_1 + \cdots + Q_n + V_1 + \cdots + V_m = 1$$

Consider now a set of optimal (Q, V) which ensure

$$(16) \qquad \max_{\{Q, V\}} Z = \sum_{i=1}^{n} P_i Q_i - \sum_{j=1}^{m} W_j V_j$$

for certain prescribed non-negative (P, W). In particular, consider a normalized set (P^*, W^*, Q^*, V^*) for which $\max Z = 0$. Now corresponding to (2), let us define for any such given (Q^*, V^*) its correlated (P^*, W^*) dual-variable ratios as "generalized partial derivatives." This definition will agree with the conventional definition of (2) wherever true partial derivatives exist. At corners where they do not exist, there will be a cone of supporting hyperplanes to the F surface, and our definition will include all the slopes of such supporting planes.

Now we can characterize the non-joint-production case by the requirement that

$$(17) \qquad A^i \left(\frac{W_1^*}{P_i^*}, \frac{W_2^*}{P_i^*}, \cdots, \frac{W_m^*}{P_i^*} \right) \equiv 1 \qquad (i = 1, 2, \cdots, n)$$

exactly as in (7) above.

14. There is an alternative way of summarizing all the above conditions for non-jointness. In such a model, knowledge of all factor-prices certainly makes determinate each and every commodity price, since these latter must, under competition, equal minimized unit costs of production. In particular, expressing all factor and goods prices in terms of Q_1 as *numeraire*, knowledge of the partial derivatives $(T_1, T_2, \cdots, T_m)$ determines each and every $(- T_{m-1+i})$. But actually we can do even better than that. Not all of the $(T_1, \cdots, T_m)$ are independently prescribable because of industry 1's factor-price frontier. Pursuing this line of thought, we can end up with the conclusion: In general, specifying any $m - 1$ of the following $m + n - 1$ functions $(T_1, \cdots, T_{m-1+n})$ must make the remaining functions determinate. When it is recalled that each of these functions depends upon the $m + n - 1$ variables $(V_1, \cdots, V_m, Q_2, \cdots, Q_n)$, and if we posit smooth differentiability, we are led by the ordinary calculus of implicit function theory to the following *numeraire* Jacobian conditions on submatrices of the Hessian matrix—namely:

$$(18) \qquad H = \begin{bmatrix} T_{11} & \cdots & T_{1m} & \cdots & T_{1,m-1+n} \\ \vdots & & \vdots & & \vdots \\ T_{m-1+n,1} & \cdots & T_{m-1+n,m} & \cdots & T_{m-1+n,\,m-1+n} \end{bmatrix}$$

to be rank $(m - 1)$ at most.

These necessary conditions seem to be equivalent to the extended set (9).

15. In conclusion, it will be obvious that certain mixed cases where only a subset of industries involve jointness or where only an intermediate capital good that is exclusive to one industry involves jointness, could be characterized by methods similar to this paper.

Massachusetts Institute of Technology, U.S.A.

146

P. A. SAMUELSON AND F. MODIGLIANI

The Pasinetti Paradox in Neoclassical and More General Models [1]

I. INTRODUCTION

In 1962 Dr Pasinetti [2] enunciated a remarkable result.

Pasinetti's Theorem:

Consider a system in which the labour force grows at some exponential rate n', technological progress is Harrod-neutral and occurs at a constant rate n'', and therefore the " effective " labour supply, measured in " efficiency " units, rises at the rate $n = n' + n''$.[3] Suppose further that one can meaningfully identify a class of income receivers—the " capitalists "—whose *sole* source of income is earnings from capital, and suppose that this group has a propensity to save (average and marginal) equal to s_c. Call the remainder of the community " workers " and assume they save the fraction s_w of their wage or interest income.

Then, if the system is capable of generating a " golden-age " growth path along which income, consumption and capital all grow exponentially at the " natural rate " n, this equilibrium growth path has the following remarkable properties:

1. The steady-state rate of return to capital or rate of interest, r^*, depends only on the rate of growth n and on s_c according to the simple formula $r^* = n/s_c$; it is therefore *completely independent* of the workers' saving propensity s_w or of the form of the production function.

2. The steady-state capital output ratio $(K/Y)^*$, the capital labour ratio $(K/L)^*$ and the share of income going to capital $\alpha_k^* = (rK/Y)^*$ are also independent of s_w; again, they depend on n/s_c, but also on the *form* of the production function.

From this surprising theorem come other remarkable corollaries such as: if s_c is unity, a situation that Pasinetti associates (pp. 277-278) in particular with a socialist state —although the association is questionable, as indicated below—then it follows from (1) that r will tend to the natural rate of growth n, and saving will approach the Swan-Phelps [4] golden rule of accumulation $S = I = P$, where $P = rK$ is total income from capital.

A result of this generality puts us all in debt to Dr Pasinetti, and is worthy of further study and elucidation, which is what we offer in this paper.

[1] We should like to acknowledge helful research assistance from Felicity Skidmore, and financial aid from the Ford Foundation and the Carnegie Foundation. Helpful comments were received from the Harvard-M.I.T. mathematical economics colloquium. In particular we are indebted to R. Solow and G. LaMalfa for helpful criticism.

[2] Luigi L. Pasinetti, " Rate of Profit and Income Distribution in Relation to the Rate of Economic Growth ", *Review of Economic Studies*, 29 (1962), 267-279, a seminal paper.

[3] To sidestep the complications that come in when K/L goes asymptotically to zero or infinity (when capital is incapable of being widened fast enough or slow enough), we first posit that positive labour is needed to produce positive output, and that n is positive but not too large. We remove this simplifying restriction in the Appendix which gives an exhaustive analysis of possible pathological divergences.

[4] T. W. Swan, " Of Golden Ages and Production Functions ", presented at the Round Table on Economic Development in East Asia (International Economic Association), Gamagori, Japan, April 1960 (revised 1962), mimeo., 18 pp.; E. S. Phelps, " The Golden Rule of Accumulation ", *American Economic Review*, 51 (1961) 628-643; J. Robinson, " A Neoclassical Theorem ", *Review of Economic Studies*, 29 (1962), 219-226, with Comments by R. M. Solow, P. A. Samuelson, J. E. Meade *et al.*; C. C. von Weizsäcker, *Wachstum, Zins und Optimale Investitionsquote* (Kyklos, Verlag, Basel, 1962), 96 pp.

(a) First, we shall show the limited range of the workers and capitalists saving co-efficients within which the above formulation of the Pasinetti Theorem is valid. Outside that range we formulate a theorem that is dual to it and of the same generality. It too involves a paradox, namely that the average product of capital—the reciprocal of the capital output ratio—to which the system settles is, this time, equal to n/s_w and completely independent of the s_c propensity to save out of profit or of the form of the production function. All the other golden-age variables of the system depend only upon n/s_w and on the form of the production functions. The complete duality of all this with the Pasinetti theorem is notable and we state the general case that covers all contingencies.

(b) A second, though relatively minor purpose, is to help dispel the notion, which seems to have been entertained by some readers, that Pasinetti's analysis has some peculiar relevance to a Kaldorian *alternative* theory of distribution, of the type presented by Kaldor in 1955, 1957, 1961, and 1962, or to some version of a " Cambridge " theory of distribution.[1] The following lead sentence of Pasinetti (and indeed his whole lead paragraph) might predispose the reader in the street to this view.

" One of the most exciting results of the macro-economic theories which have recently been elaborated in Cambridge is a very simple relation connecting the rate of profit and the distribution of income to the rate of economic growth, through the interaction of the different propensities to save " (p. 267).

Other passages may give the impression that the major accomplishment of his analysis is to remove " a logical slip " (p. 270) in the Kaldorian formulation which allowed for some saving by workers but did not permit these savings to accumulate and produce income.[2]

Actually, as Dr Pasinetti makes clear at many places (and in particular in the long footnote on p. 276) his analysis is one of the greatest generality. His theorem applies in fact to any system capable of a golden-age growth path. But, precisely because of this great generality, his analysis can in no way help us to discriminate between alternative theories of income distribution. In order to make this point perfectly clear, and for its own sake, our own analysis shall deal primarily with a neoclassical production function capable of smooth factor substitution and with the case of perfectly competitive markets. Later we shall provide some indications of how the analysis might be extended if either of these conditions fails.

(c) Finally, we shall investigate, and prove, the stability of the Pasinetti golden-age in the case where it is valid. That is, we shall prove that the system will asymptotically approach the steady-state from arbitrary initial conditions, at least in a local neighbour-hood of that unique state. And where our anti-Pasinetti golden age holds, in which the workers' saving propensity is all important, we demonstrate its global asymptotic stability.

Our asymptotic stability analysis, which can be extended in considerable measure to certain cases of fixed-proportions and distribution theories different from that of

---

[1] N. Kaldor, " Alternative Theories of Distribution ", *Review of Economic Studies*, **23** (1955), 83-100 (reprinted in *Essays on Value and Distribution*, pp. 228-236); " A Model of Economic Growth ", *Economic Journal*, **67** (1957), 591-624 (reprinted in *Essays in Economic Stability and Growth*, pp. 256-300); F. Lutz and D. C. Hague (eds.), *The Theory of Capital* (1961), pp. 177-220, from the 1958 Corfu I.E.A. Conference; with J. A. Mirrlees, " A New Model of Economic Growth," *Review of Economic Studies*, **29** (1962), 174-192. Cambridge writings related to Kaldorism, but not necessarily identical with it, are J. Robinson, *Accumulation of Capital* (1956) and *Collected Economic Papers*, **2** (1960), particularly pp. 145-158, " The Theory of Distribution"; *Exercises in Economic Analysis* (Macmillan, London, 1960), *Essays in the Theory of Economic Growth* (Macmillan, London, 1962); D. G. Champernowne, " Capital Accumulation and the Maintenance of Full Employment ", *Economic Journal*, **67** (1958), 211-244; R. F. Kahn, " Exercises in the Analysis of Growth ", *Oxford Economic Papers*, New Series, **10** (1958), 143-156.

[2] Actually, it might be argued that there need not be a " logical slip " in the Kaldorian model, if it will merely assume that the propensity to save out of income from capital is s_c whether that income is received by capitalists or by workers. This hypothesis, which may or may not be empirically sound, is certainly not *logically* self-contradictory—as our colleague Professor Solow has pointed out to us. Actually, such a model has been extensively studied by many writers as can be seen by looking up the references Uzawa (1961), Solow (1961), Inada (1963), Drandakis (1963) and still others in the valuable bibliography to F. H. Hahn and R. C. O. Matthews, " The Theory of Economic Growth: A Survey ", *Economic Journal*, **74** (1964), 779-902.

marginal productivity, must not be confused with the problem of stability of the instantaneous differential equations of capital formation and growth at continuous full employment (or at any other posited level of employment). Dr Pasinetti's stability analysis seems to be related to the instantaneous rather than asymptotic state. In the context of fixed-coefficient models, such stability analysis becomes very intricate indeed. We shall not here attempt to clarify the real and formidable problems posed by such a model for theories of distribution (and/or full employment) of macroeconomic type.

Our general analysis is shown to apply even though capitalists and workers may be divided into any number of subcategories each with a different propensity to save. On this growth path the rate of interest, the capital-output and the capital-labour ratio always depend at most on but one of the various capitalists' propensities to save (the maximum one), and are completely independent of all the others.

In view of the many nice properties sketched out above which hold for an economy satisfying the saving assumptions of the present model, it is with some regret that we must confess to most serious qualms over the empirical relevance of these assumptions—notably that relating to the existence of identifiable classes of capitalists and workers with "permanent membership"—even as rough first approximation. These qualms and the grounds on which they rest are set forth in the concluding section.

II. THE NEOCLASSICAL FORMULATION OF THE MODEL

Let total real output be produced by labour L and by total physical homogeneous capital K.[1] Total K is split into two parts, K_c the capital of the "capitalist" class, and K_w, the capital of the class which receives at least part of its income from labour.

For simplicity, the production of consumption output C and of net capital formation $\dot{K} = dK/dt$ is assumed to involve the same capital-labour factor intensities; this conventional Ramsey-Solow simplification means that total real net output Y can be split up into real consumption C plus real net capital formation $\dot{K}$, and for proper choice of units can be written as $Y = C + \dot{K}$. All this is summarized in the relation

$Y = C + \dot{K} = F(K_c + K_w, L)$, a constant-returns-to-scale function [2]

$$K = K_c + K_w, \quad \dot{K} = \dot{K}_c + \dot{K}_w. \quad ...(1)$$

For analytical purposes we find it frequently convenient to deal with variables expressed per head of the "effective" labour force L; variables so expressed will be denoted with the same letter as the corresponding aggregates but in lower case. Thus $y = Y/L$, $k = K/L$, $k_c = K_c/L$, etc. With this notation, equation (1) in view of its first-degree homogeneity property, can be rewritten as

$$y = F(k, 1) = f(k), \quad \frac{\partial F(k, 1)}{\partial k} = f'(k) > 0 \quad ...(1')$$

with $\dfrac{d^2f(k)}{dk^2} = f''(k) < 0$ in consequence of "diminishing returns". We shall posit neoclassical smoothness and substitutability and perfect markets, under which conditions competition will *enforce* at all times equality of factor prices to factor marginal productivities,[3] namely,

---

[1] Heterogeneity of capital goods can, under certain special assumptions like those underlying surrogate capital models, be introduced without necessarily vitiating the results.

[2] The assumption of constant returns to scale is essential both to Pasinetti's and our own analysis, for otherwise the concept of a golden age steady state becomes self-contradictory. If depreciation is mK, then $F(K, L) + mK$ is the function for *gross* national product.

[3] Of course w is the wage rate per efficiency unit if Harrod-neutral technical change is going on. As we shall see in Section 10 below, for most of our results it is not necessary that r and w be equal to the marginal product of capital and labour.

$$\text{interest or profit rate} = r = \frac{\text{Total Profits}}{\text{Total Capital}} = \frac{P}{K} = \frac{P_c + P_w}{K}$$

$$= \text{marginal product of capital} = \frac{\partial F(K, L)}{\partial K} = f'(k)$$

$$\text{real wage rate} = w = \frac{\text{Total Wages}}{\text{Labour}} = \frac{W}{L} = \frac{Y - rK}{L}$$

$$= f(k) - kf'(k). \qquad \qquad ...(2)$$

We shall also denote the average product of capital $Y/K = f(k)/k$ by $A(k)$, which is the reciprocal of the capital-output ratio K/Y, and note for later reference that, with a well-behaved production function, i.e. with concave $f(k)$ having the properties $f'(k) > 0$, $f''(k) < 0$, k is a monotonic decreasing function of r, while the average product $A(k)$ is a decreasing function of k, i.e. $A'(k) < 0$. Finally we shall use the symbol $\alpha(k)$ to denote the share of income accruing to capital, for given k, i.e. $\alpha(k) = rk/f(k)$, which reduces, when marginal productivity relations are valid, to the ratio of marginal to average product $f'(k)/A(k)$.

Now, the basic savings-investment equations for the two classes—which hold for all time periods, short or long—can be written down:

$$\dot{K}_c = s_c P_c = s_c(rK_c) = s_c K_c \frac{\partial F(K_c + K_w, L)}{\partial K}$$

$$\dot{K}_w = s_w(W + P_w) = s_w(W + rK_w) = s_w(Y - rK + rK_w) = s_w(Y - rK_c)$$

$$= s_w \left[F(K_c + K_w, L) - K_c \frac{\partial F(K_c + K_w, L)}{\partial K} \right]. \qquad \qquad ...(3)$$

The first equation says that the total saving of the capitalist class, and hence the rate of growth of their capital K_c, equals s_c times their total profits. The second equation says that workers savings, and hence the rate of growth of their capital K_w, is a fraction of s_w of their total income, consisting of wages W and income from their capital, rK_w, or equivalently of total income less capitalists income.

Equations (1), (2) and (3), or the equations (3) alone in their final form, give us a determinate growth system in (K_c, K_w) once we are given the time profile of labour employment $L(t)$. Now we posit the usual exponential growth of the labour force, which we equate with labour input $L(t)$, implying $L(t) = L_0 e^{nt}$ (with the understanding that the natural rate of growth n could include Harrod-neutral technical change, in which case L must be given an efficiency-unit interpretation). Hence

$$L = L(t) = L_0 e^{nt}, \quad \frac{\dot{L}}{L} = n$$

$$\frac{\dot{k}}{k} = \frac{(K/L)}{K/L} = \frac{\dot{K}}{K} - \frac{\dot{L}}{L} = \frac{\dot{K}}{K} - n \qquad \qquad ...(4)$$

$$\frac{\dot{k}_c}{k_c} = \frac{\dot{K}_c}{K_c} - n, \quad \frac{\dot{k}_w}{k_w} = \frac{\dot{K}_w}{K_w} - n.$$

Using the equations (3) to substitute for $\dot{K}_c/K_c$ and $\dot{K}_w/K_w$ in the right-hand side of the last two equations and writing k as short for $k_c + k_w$, we obtain

$$\frac{\dot{k}_c}{k_c} = s_c r - n = s_c f'(k) - n$$

$$\frac{\dot{k}_w}{k_w} = s_w \frac{Y - rK + rK_w}{K_w} - n = s_w \frac{f(k) - rk}{k_w} + (s_w r - n)$$

$$= s_w \frac{A(k) - f'(k)}{k_w} k + \left[s_w f'(k) - n\right] = s_w \frac{f(k) - k_c f'(k)}{k_w} - n, \qquad \ldots(5)$$

a system of two simultaneous differential equations in the intensive variables k_c and k_w, and not explicitly containing any dependence on time.

For convenient future reference, we can combine the equations of (5) to show, after various substitutions, that

$$\frac{\dot{k}_c}{k_c} - \frac{\dot{k}_w}{k_w} = \frac{(k_c/k_w)^{\cdot}}{(k_c/k_w)} \gtreqless 0$$

depending upon whether $\qquad \ldots(5')$

$$\frac{k_c}{k_w} \lesseqgtr \frac{\alpha(k)s_c - s_w}{[1 - \alpha(k)]s_w}.$$

This criterion is remarkable in that it does not contain n explicitly.

III. POSITIVE STEADY STATE SOLUTION

To find the steady state equilibrium values of k, k_w and k_c, say (k^*, k_w^*, k_c^*), we set $\dot{k}_c$ and $\dot{k}_w$ equal to zero in (5) and solve the static equations

$$s_c f'(k) - n = 0$$

$$s_w[f(k) - rk] + (s_w r - n)k_w = 0,$$

or

$$f'(k^*) = r^* = \frac{n}{s_c}$$

$$k_w^* = s_w \frac{A(k^*) - f'(k^*)}{n - s_w f'(k^*)} k^* = \frac{\text{av. product of capital} - \text{marg. product of capital}}{\dfrac{n}{s_w} - \dfrac{n}{s_c}} k^*$$

$$k_c^* = k^* - k_w^* = \frac{n - s_w A(k^*)}{n - s_w f'(k^*)} k^* = \frac{\dfrac{n}{s_w} - A(k^*)}{\dfrac{n}{s_w} - \dfrac{n}{s_c}} k^* \qquad \ldots(6)$$

$$\frac{k_c^*}{k_w^*} = \frac{\alpha(k^*)s_c - s_w}{[1 - \alpha(k^*)]s_w}.$$

The first of these equations (6) will be recognized as Pasinetti's Theorem: on the equilibrium growth path (where $\dot{K}/K = \dot{K}_c/K_c = \dot{K}_w/K_w = n$), the rate of interest is determined by n and s_c only. To this value of r^* there corresponds in turn the unique capital-labour ratio k^*, the unique average product of capital $A(k^*)$, and its unique reciprocal, the capital output ratio $k^*/f(k^*)$. Hence these ratios are also independent of s_w; but still they do depend on the form of the production function F or f. Note also that all solutions of (6) depend on (n, s_w, s_c) only in the ratio form $(s_c/n, s_w/n)$.

However for the solution (6) to be economically meaningful it must satisfy the non-negativity condition $k_w \geqq 0$, $k_c \geqq 0$. The implication of the first inequality can be inferred from the second of the equations (6). Since the numerator of the expression on the right-hand side is the difference between the average and the marginal product of capital, which is necessarily non-negative, the denominator of the fraction must be positive if k_w is to be non-negative and finite or,

$$s_w < s_c. \qquad \qquad ...(7)$$

i.e. the workers' saving propensity must be smaller than that of the capitalists if Pasinetti's theorem is to hold. This same inequality is implicit in Pasinetti's inequality conditions (6) and (7). But we must hasten to add that, though (7) is necessary for Pasinetti's theorem (as we have characterized it) to apply, and though (7) is necessary for many versions of the Kaldorian theory of income distribution to yield economically meaningful results, (7) has in general nothing to do with the existence and stability of a steady-state full employment equilibrium, as we shall presently show explicitly.

As for the second non-negativity condition $k_c \geqq 0$, we can see from (6)'s last equation, derivable from (6)'s other equation or from the criterion at the end of the last section, that

$$s_w \leqq \alpha(k^*)s_c = n\frac{k^*}{f(k^*)}. \qquad \qquad ...(8)$$

This inequality is seen to be more stringent than (7) since the capital share $\alpha(k)$ is generally less than one, and empirically very much less than one. Thus if $\alpha(k^*) = \frac{1}{4}$, and $s_c = \frac{1}{5}$, Pasinetti's theorem could not hold for s_w any higher than a modest 0·05.[1]

Inequality (8) has some correspondence to Pasinetti's (6), which says $s_w < \dfrac{I}{Y}$, since

in steady-state equilibrium when $I/K = \dot{K}/K = \dot{L}/L = n$, we have $I/Y = nK/Y = n\dfrac{k}{f(k)}$. However, Pasinetti's simple inequality[2] is ill-defined, since outside of the steady-state equilibrium, I/Y could take any value whatever; and even on the equilibrium growth

---

[1] These numbers are econometrically reasonable for a mixed economy like the U.S., U.K., or Western Europe. Rather different-appearing numbers would seem to come from an argument like the following. " Suppose corporations pay out in dividends only $\frac{2}{3}$ of their earnings (which constitute most of the earnings of capital) and individuals all save about one-twelfth of their disposable incomes. (Such numbers are econometrically not too unrealistic.) Then identify $s_c = 1 - \frac{2}{3} = \frac{1}{3}$, $s_w = \frac{1}{12}$, and find that we can stay in the Pasinetti regime if α_K is about one-fourth." Actually, of course, the above behaviour equations would lead to the old Kaldor model whose logical consistency is criticized by Pasinetti and defended, as a possibility in our footnote 6. So, sticking to the notion that only one saving propensity applies to the worker class regardless of type of income, we would have to reinterpret the above data as follows. If people know that along with each \$2 of dividends they receive, there is saved for them \$1 in ploughed-back corporate earnings and that this can with reasonable confidence be deemed to yield them equivalent (and lightly taxed!) capital gains, they will (and there is some econometric evidence that they actually do) include their share of imputed corporate income in their true income and will adjust accordingly (although perhaps not on a 100 per cent basis) their saving out of so-called disposable personal income. Hence, a pure capitalist may prudently spend $\frac{6}{5}$ of his dividends and still end up saving $\frac{1}{5}$ of his true imputed income. If workers are stubbornly to end up with the same s_w for their share of capital income—a somewhat implausible hypothesis—they must spend $\frac{47}{40}$ of their dividends to keep $s_w = \frac{1}{20}$. Who will buy the stock that some people are liquidating? Anyone who fully understands the meaning of equation (3) will know the answer: the saving out of wages will be just enough in the model to match the overspending out of dividends. Repeatedly we give our reservations about the realism of the strict Pasinetti assumptions. (Warning: if one tries to oversimplify reality by forcing it into the mould of simple propensities to save of people and corporations, one should realize that a corporate propensity to save of $\frac{1}{4}$ reflects in real life Kuh-Meyer effects in which—to oversimplify reality again—all of corporate investment is not autonomous with corporate saving independent of it. E.g., if a corporation has a marginal-propensity-to-invest its " cash " earnings of $\frac{1}{4}$ and a marginal-propensity-to-save of $\frac{1}{3}$, then in all Keynesian multiplier formulas for effective demand, the relevant marginal leakage coefficient is not $\frac{1}{3}$ but rather $\frac{1}{3} - \frac{1}{6}$. One gets bad realistic prediction about comparative statics of mixed capitalism if one fails to take these interconnections into account—preferably in a less crude manner than described here.)

[2] After further discussion of the crucial limits on s_w/s_c, footnote 11 will return to the meaning of Pasinetti's (6).

path $f(k)/k$ is not a given of the problem but a characteristic of the solution, if any, except possibly in the very special case of fixed production coefficients, where K/Y might be identified with the technologically determined (minimum) capital coefficient. Our (8) has the merit of making explicit what must not be left ill-defined, namely that the inequality $s_w < \alpha(k^*)s_c$ must hold precisely at $k = k^*$, the k that corresponds to $r^* = n/s_c$. In what follows by r^*, k^* and other starred symbols we always mean the magnitude that corresponds to the root of Pasinetti's equation $f'(k) = n/s_c$, an equation that must be distinguished from the theorems that can sometimes be related to it.

IV. LIMITS ON THE PASINETTI THEOREM

To understand a theorem you must understand its limitations. The numerical range of the parameter s_w for which Pasinetti's theorem is applicable is severely limited, as indicated by (8). Let us see why, in terms of the comparative static properties of equations (6).

First consider s_c positive and s_w zero. Then freeze n and s_c, and consider the implication of higher values of the parameter s_w. For s_w zero, since both (7) and (8) are satisfied, we shall have $r^* = n/s_c$ and $k = k^*$ corresponding to r^*. Furthermore, $k_w^* = 0$ if $s_w = 0$, and hence $k_c^*/k^* = 1$.

Now let workers become thrifty. At first positive s_w will continue to satisfy (7) and (8) and therefore r^* and k^* will be unchanged. That is Pasinetti's remarkable theorem. Clearly k_w^* has become positive, showing that k_c^* must at first be forced down by rising s_w. Thrift on the part of workers, as long as s_w is sufficiently small, gives society no lasting appreciable *per capita* benefit; it merely causes capitalists of unchanged thriftiness to end up with less of the unchanged *per capita* wealth.

How does this come about dynamically? Start out in (r^*, k^*) equilibrium with $s_w = 0$. Now let s_w suddenly move to a permanent positive level, though still small enough to satisfy (8). The new flow of workers' saving will transiently increase k above k^*, decreasing r below r^*. Even though Y begins transiently to grow faster than n so that y rises, the lower interest rate means that the capitalists' K_c grows more slowly than before, which means more slowly than n. Hence, k_c initially drops *below* the old $k_c^* = k^*$. Once this is understood, it is easy to see that k_c will not continue *permanently* to fall but will instead approach the new critical level for k_c^* given by the next-to-the-last equation (6). It will have permanently declined to this level only when k_w^* has permanently risen to its new appointed level as given by the proper equation of (6). (Note: there could be damped oscillation around the new equilibrium, as will be shown later.)

Fig. 1 illustrates this by exhibiting the behaviour of k^∞ and k_c^∞—the values of k and k_c on the golden age path to which the system tends as $t \to \infty$—in function of s_w, and for a fixed value of n and of s_c. For concreteness, we have frozen s_c at $\frac{1}{5}$ and assumed $\alpha(k^*) = \frac{1}{4}$. The dashed locus, beginning as a straight line parallel to the abscissa is the graph of k^∞. Within the range of applicability of Pasinetti's theorem, i.e. $s_w < \alpha(k^*)s_c = 0.05$, we know k^∞ is a constant k^*. The behaviour of k_c^∞ is shown by the declining solid curve starting at k^* on the abscissa. Within the range of validity of Pasinetti's theorem we know that $k_c^\infty = k_c^*$ and hence the equation of its locus is given by the second of equations (6), which can be conveniently rewritten as

$$k_c^* = \frac{1 - s_w \alpha(k^*)^{-1} s_c^{-1}}{1 - s_w s_c^{-1}} k^* = \frac{1 - 20 s_w}{1 - 5 s_w} k^*.$$

For $s_\omega = 0$, $k_c^* = k^*$. But as s_ω rises k_c^* becomes a smaller and smaller fraction (and k_w^* becomes a growing fraction) of the unchanging k^*, until for $s_w = 0.05$ k^* reduces to zero and $k_w^* = k^*$. Here the applicability of Pasinetti's theorem and hence of equations (6) ends. The dotted continuation of the graph of the second equation (6) into the negative quadrant is of no economic significance. Instead, as we shall presently see, the valid extension of the k_c^∞ curve is the heavily-shaded horizontal axis itself. Similarly we will see that for $s_w > \alpha(k^*)s_c$, $k^\infty = k_w^\infty$ will rise above k^*, increasing monotonically with s_w, as shown by the rising portion of the dashed curve labelled k^{**}. It will be presently shown that the behaviour of k^∞, k_c^∞ and k_w^∞ in this range is covered by a theorem complementary to Pasinetti's theorem, its dual. The general theorem which covers both cases will demonstrate the remarkable duality results: for s_w on the left of the dividing line, $k^\infty = k^*$,

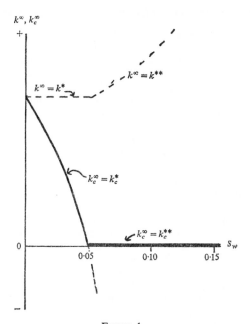

FIGURE 1

Behaviour of k^∞ and k_c^∞ for fixed n (assuming $\alpha(k^*) = \frac{1}{4}$; $s_c = \frac{1}{2}$).

the value determined by the condition that the *marginal product of capital must be equal to n/s_c* (and hence k^∞ is totally independent of s_w). But, on the other side of the dividing line $k^\infty = k^{**}$, the value determined by the condition that the *average product of capital must be equal to n/s_w* (and hence k^∞ is quite independent of s_c). The system in its wisdom will pick out of the dual regimes the one that gives it *most per capita* income and capital.

V. THE FUNDAMENTAL DUALITY THEOREM

To establish these results let us examine closely just what happens when condition (8) fails to hold, i.e. when

$$s_w > n \frac{k^*}{f(k^*)} = \frac{n}{A(k^*)} = \alpha(k^*)s_c. \qquad \qquad ...(9)$$

Dr Pasinetti has not explored this case although several passages in his paper suggest that the system would not tend to a steady state and in fact might even be incapable of maintaining full employment.[1] It should be immediately apparent that, as long as the production function is well behaved, failure of (8) or even of (7) to hold cannot interfere with full employment, which is insured by conditions (2). What happens instead is that, eventually the rate of growth of capitalists' assets will become and remain smaller than the rate of growth of workers' assets and also smaller than n. This in turn means that, asymptotically, k_c as well as K_c/K, the capitalists' share of total wealth, will approach zero while the workers' share, K_w/K will approach unity.

This conclusion may be seen in many ways, the most conclusive involving examination of the mathematical differential equations (5). The economic common sense is also very clear. For we have seen that as s_w rises from zero through small positive values, k_c^* is forced down to make room for growing k_w^*. What happens when k_c^* has been forced down to zero, which (6) shows takes place at the critical limit where (8)'s inequality begins to take over?

An increase in s_w beyond $\alpha(k^*)s_c$ must inevitably result in a decline of K_c/K and k_c toward zero. This is seen immediately in the extreme case where s_w exceeds s_c, since then the workers' savings out of profits *alone* will grow at a faster rate than can the total of all capitalists' savings. In the intermediate case where s_w is between s_c and $\alpha(k^*)s_c$, the same result can be demonstrated as follows. Begin in the Pasinetti k^* point with some positive k_c: then K_c is growing exactly as fast as n by definition of that point. However, it is now impossible that K_w and K should be growing as slowly as n at this point; the criterion (5')'s numerator shows that, for any positive K_c/K_w level, (9) implies that K_w is growing faster than K_c, and hence both K_w and K are growing faster than n at the Pasinetti point. Hence, k grows beyond k^*, and r falls below r^*, now dictating a definite falling off of k_c toward zero. But despite the decline in k_c, total capital k must continue to grow past k^*. This conclusion can be established from the following equation for $\dot{k}$ which is implied by the two equations (5):

$$\dot{k} = \left(\frac{s_w}{n} - \frac{k}{f(k)}\right) nf(k) + rk_c(s_c - s_w). \qquad ...(5'')$$

In the first place this equation confirms that, when (9) holds, $\dot{k}$ is positive at k^* since

$$\frac{s_w}{n} > \frac{k^*}{f(k^*)} = \alpha(k^*)\frac{s_c}{n}.$$

It also shows that $\dot{k}$ must remain positive and hence k must continue to grow at least until it has become large enough for the first term to vanish, i.e. until $\dfrac{k}{f(k)} = \dfrac{s_w}{n} > \dfrac{k^*}{f(k^*)}$. But since for $k > k^*$ we must have $r < r^*$, k_c must continue to fall indefinitely, fading toward zero. The limiting value to which k tends, say k^{**}, can then be inferred from (5'') by setting $\dot{k}$ equal to zero and disregarding the last term. We thus find that k^{**} must satisfy the condition $\dfrac{k^{**}}{f(k^{**})} = \dfrac{s_w}{n}$. Or, as we prefer to express it in order to bring out the duality of our theorem to Pasinetti's, the system must approach the equilibrium $k \to k^\infty = k^{**}$

---

[1] " . . . if (6) [the equivalent of our (8)] were not satisfied the system would enter a situation of chronic Keynesian unemployment. Similarly if (7) were not satisfied the system would enter a situation of chronic inflation " (p. 269). Actually all that one can say is that I/Y must always be a weighted mean of the non-negative (s_c, s_w) coefficients, never lying outside their range because neither factor share can be negative. $I/Y = s_c \neq s_w$ would imply zero wage share, and $I/Y = s_w \neq s_c$ would imply zero profit share. But that is as far as mere arithmetic can take us. To infer inflation from $s_c < I/Y$ and unemployment from $s_w > I/Y$ requires behaviour hypotheses of a particular and special sort. Thus, in some of our neoclassical models characterized by inflationless full employment, golden ages emerge with $s_w = I/Y > s_c$.

where k^{**} is the root of the dual relation

$$A(k^{**}) = \frac{f(k^{**})}{k^{**}} = \frac{n}{s_w}. \qquad \text{...(10)}$$

This result is readily understandable by noting that, with k_c tending to vanish, the limiting behaviour of our system reduces to the familiar Solow process with a single class of savers, namely the workers. It is well known that such a process deepens capital to an asymptotic limit given by the Harrod-Domar equation $\dfrac{K}{Y} = \dfrac{k}{f(k)} = \dfrac{s}{n}$, which agrees with our result above.

In summary, a system with $s_w > \alpha_k(r^*)s_c$ is bound to have the following asymptotic properties [1]

$$\lim_{t \to \infty} \frac{K_w}{K} = 1, \; \lim_{t \to \infty} \frac{K_c}{K} = 0$$

$$\lim_{t \to \infty} \frac{\dot{K}_w}{K_w} = \lim_{t \to \infty} \frac{\dot{K}}{K} = n > \lim_{t \to \infty} \frac{\dot{K}_c}{K_c}$$

$$\lim_{t \to \infty} (k_c, k_w) = (0, k^{**})$$

$$\lim_{t \to \infty} k = k^{**}, \text{ the root of } \frac{f(k^{**})}{k^{**}} = \frac{n}{s_w} \qquad \text{...(11)}$$

$$k^{**} > k^*, \text{ the root of Pasinetti's } f'(k^*) = \frac{n}{s_c}$$

$$\lim_{t \to \infty} r = r^{**} = f'(k^{**}) < f'(k^*) = r^* = \frac{n}{s_c}$$

$$\lim_{t \to \infty} \frac{\dot{K}_c}{K_c} = r^{**}s_c < r^*s_c = n, \text{ or } \lim_{t \to \infty} \frac{\dot{k}_c}{k_c} < 0.$$

To reinforce our common sense proof, suppose the system has come into the k^* configuration defined by Pasinetti's $f'(k^*) = n/s_c$. Fig. 1 shows it will pass out of that state when $s_w > \alpha(k^*)s_c$. Why? Because for any positive division of k^* between k_c and k_w we shall be at the vertical level of some definite point on the descending curve of Fig. 1. On that line k_c and k_w would grow in balance; but now take notice that s_w has increased, moving us rightward of the curve (*due eastward!*); if lower s_w would keep K_w growing in balance with the unchanged rate of growth of K_c, then higher s_w means K_w grows *faster* at k^* than does K_c. Hence, we are on our way to a new equilibrium point—the one we have called k^{**}, identifiable by considering workers as the only (that is, as the overwhelmingly only) source of asymptotic saving.

This leads to another, perhaps more sophisticated way, of understanding the two cases—Pasinetti's and its dual opposite. Consider the artificial condition where the capitalist class never gets a chance to do its Marxian " primitive accumulation ": set K_c initially zero. The resulting steady state is the familiar one of Solow et al., in which the uniform s_w of the single class determines the golden age we have denoted by k^{**}, the root of $f(k^{**})/k^{**} = n/s_w$. Now, is this special steady-state *stable* when we test it by bringing

---

[1] F. H. Hahn and R. C. O. Matthews, op cit., devote a page of their masterly review to the Pasinetti analysis. After describing the Pasinetti regime, they correctly mention in a footnote the possibility of the Dual regime in which $k_c \to 0$; but they incorrectly state the possibility of a third regime where " the assets of wage-earners, while not growing at the same rate as those of capitalists have become a negligible fraction of the latter " (p. 799, n. 1). Actually, if s_w is positive, our general theorem shows that it is impossible for $k_w \to 0$ in the manner alleged.

an iota of positive K_c into existence? The answer is clearly Yes, if we are in the range of the dual theorem where (9) holds. For a little K_c will initially grow at the rate $s_c r^{**}$. Now, since by definition $\dfrac{k^{**}}{f(k^{**})} = \dfrac{s_w}{n}$ and $\dfrac{k^*}{f(k^*)} = \dfrac{\alpha(k^*)s_c}{n}$, (9) implies $\dfrac{k^{**}}{f(k^{**})} > \dfrac{k^*}{f(k^*)}$ and therefore $r^{**} < r^*$. Thus $s_c r^{**} < s_c r^* = n$, and K_c will grow slower than L, so that $k_c = K_c/L$ will tend to vanish again, moving us back toward the initial solution. On the other hand, if we are in the Pasinetti range, $s_w < \alpha(k^*)s_c$, then, by the same token, $s_c r^{**} > s_c r^* = n$ and hence the initial k_c will grow displacing the initial equilibrium to a new equilibrium with $r = r^*$ and hence $k = k^*$, the Pasinetti solution.

Fig. 2 illustrates the critical boundary of the Pasinetti range and of the range of the dual theorem. The heavy n/s_c line intersects the marginal-product curve $f'(k)$ at the k^* abscissa. If s_w is very small, the n/s_w line marked 1 will intersect the average product curve $f(k)/k$ at a k_1^{**} level lower than k^*. So Pasinetti's theorem will apply. Alternatively, let s_w be so large as to bring the n/w line down to 3, which intersects the AP curve at $k_3^{**} > k^*$. Then workers' saving will dominate (and ultimately completely dominate) and we are in the domain of the anti-Pasinetti dual theorem. Evidently, the critical watershed is at 2, where n/s_w intersects AP at the same k^* level where n/s_c intersects MP. The critical ratio for s_w/s_c is where it equals $(MP/AP)^*$; but this last is precisely the definition of relative capital share $\alpha(k^*)$.[1] (The aesthetic eye will resent our always writing $s_w \gtreqless \alpha(k^*)s_c$ and not its dual $s_w \gtreqless \alpha(k^{**})s_c$; but careful study of Fig. 2 will show that these are equivalent criteria.)

From equations (10) and the above discussion, we conclude that when s_w exceeds a modest critical level, Pasinetti's theorem must be replaced by the following:

Dual Theorem. When $s_w \geq \alpha(k^*)s_c = nf(k^*)/k^*$, the steady-state growth path to which the system tends has the following characteristics:

(i) The rate of interest, the capital-labour and capital-output ratio and therefore also the distribution of income between wages and profits are completely independent of the capitalist propensity to save s_c.

(ii) The average-product-of-capital (and its reciprocal the capital-output ratio) are independent even of the form of the production function, depending only on the rate of growth n and the workers' saving propensity according to the formula $(Y/K)^{**} = n/s_w$.

(iii) The remaining ratios and the rate of interest depend on s_w/n and on the form of the production function.

(iv) If K_c is ever positive, its ultimate growth rate will be less than that of the system as a whole.

---

[1] Why did Dr Pasinetti's mathematics not warn him that his was only a fraction of the story? Well, it did. But it whispered rather than shouted. In his equation (13), p. 272, he notes that the factor $(I - s_w Y)$ must not be zero if he is to be able to cancel it out and arrive at his final formulas. Who can be blamed for thinking such vanishing to be an unimportant singular case of razor's-edge width? Unfortunately, it is the content of our Dual theorem that the above expression will asymptotically vanish for all $s_w \geq \alpha(k^*)s_c$, as will be evident if only k_w^{**} counts asymptotically there. $P/K = r^{**}$ is still determinate, but not from the p. 272 equations. Our Dual theorem corrects the absurdities implied by an attempt to confine reality to the Pasinetti theorem's consequences. Thus, suppose the last capitalist went permanently to work for a minute a day: the careful reader of pp. 272-274 might be forgiven for concluding that economic in-determinacy would suddenly result, as he ponders over the words . . . " the behavioural relation $(s_c P_c)$ determining the rate of profit drops out of the picture altogether and the rate of profit becomes indeterminate. . . . (The parameter s_w, which remains cannot determine the rate of profit!) " (p. 274). Once our Dual theorem is understood, no cataclysmic indeterminacy sets in: the determinate asymptote for P/K becomes $r^{**} = \alpha(k^{**})n/s_w$, where k^{**} is defined above in terms of n/s_w alone. Economic intuition is vindicated.
In Dr Pasinetti's important footnote on p. 216, the differential equation $s_c[F(K, L) - W] = knL + Lk$ is erroneous, being patently inconsistent with our (3), (5) and later (5''); an asymptotic identity was wrongly used in deriving this differential equation purporting to be valid at all times. The correct formula, which together with (3) or (5) will lead to all valid cases, is given by our equation (5'').

The general formulae that cover both theorems can be stated as follows. For any variable X, let X^∞ denote the limit which that variable approaches as $t \to \infty$.

General Theorem. Then: (i)

$$k^\infty = \text{Max}\,(k^*, k^{**}), \text{ where } \begin{cases} k^* = \text{root of } f'(k^*) = \dfrac{n}{s_c} \\[2mm] k^{**} = \text{root of} \dfrac{f(k^{**})}{k^{**}} = \dfrac{n}{s_w} \end{cases}$$

...(12)

$$r^\infty = \text{Min}\,(r^*, r^{**}) = \text{Min}\,[f'(k^*), f'(k^{**})] = \text{Min}\left[\left(\frac{s_c}{n}, f'(k^{**})\right)\right].$$

$$(Y/K)^\infty = \text{Min}\,[A(r^*), A(r^{**})] = \text{Min}\left[A(r^*), \frac{s_w}{n}\right].$$

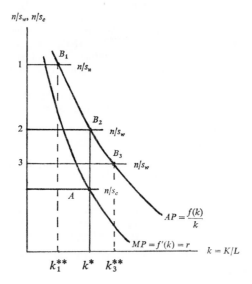

FIGURE 2

The intersection of n/s_c with the MP curve of interest at A determines the Pasinetti equilibrium. It is the actual asymptote for the system if, and only if, s_w is small enough to make the n/s_w intersection with the average product curve occur to the right of A, as at B_3. If s_w exceeds the product of s_c and capitalists' relative share α_k, the k_3^{**} Anti-Pasinetti point becomes the asymptotic equilibrium.

(ii) The ultimate allocation of k^∞ between (k_c^∞, k_w^∞) is given by $(0, k^{**}) = (0,$ function of s_w/n alone) if $s_w \geqq \alpha(k^*)s_c$; and, if $s_w < \alpha(k^*)s_c$, by positive numbers $(\beta_1 k^*, \beta_2 k^*)$, where k^* depends only on s_c/n and where the fractions β_j depend (for fixed k^*) only on s_w.[1]

[1] The reader can construct a diagram dual to Fig. 1. Now s_c is on the horizontal axis, with s_w fixed. On the vertical axis, k^∞ is a horizontal line marked k^{**} and k_w^{**} up to the critical $s_c = s_w/\alpha(k^*)$ level. In this same dual range $k_c^\infty = k_c^{**} = 0$, the horizontal axis. For larger s_c, we are in the Pasinetti range: k^∞ now rises in a convex-from-below broad market k^*; k_c^∞ rises from zero to positive levels along the k_c^* branch, but could eventually decline with s_c if diminishing returns were strong enough; k_w^∞, on the other hand, must be helped by an increase in s_c, just as it is by an increase in s_w.

VI. STABILITY ANALYSIS

Now we revert back to the neoclassical model to show that our golden-age equilibria, (k_c^*, k_w^*) or $(0, k^{**})$, are stable in the sense that when the s_w/s_c is appropriate for each it will in fact be approached asymptotically from all sufficiently nearby values (k_c, k_w). We use standard *local* stability analysis to prove that any small disturbance from equilibrium will be followed by an asymptotic return to it. We are unable to state a global stability theorem in the Pasinetti case because we are not able to rule out the possibility of limit cycles. If they could be ruled out, our unqualified local stability conditions would entail global stability for all positive K's.

Begin with Pasinetti's (k_c^*, k_w^*). Around this positive level, expand the differential equations (5) in a Taylor's series, retaining only the first-degree terms in the divergences $(k_c - k_c^*, k_w - k_w^*) = (x_1, x_2)$, deriving *linear* differential equations for (x_1, x_2). For notational convenience, replace the subscripts c and w by 1 and 2, to get

$$\begin{bmatrix} \dot{x}_1 \\ \dot{x}_2 \end{bmatrix} = \begin{bmatrix} \dfrac{\partial k_i}{\partial k_j} \end{bmatrix}^* \begin{bmatrix} x_1 \\ x_2 \end{bmatrix} \qquad \text{...(13)}$$

where the * outside the matrix indicates that we evaluate its elements as the partial derivatives of (5) at the equilibrium levels (k_c^*, k_w^*). [In a moment, we shall perform similar stability analysis of our anti-Pasinetti equilibrium $(0, k^{**})$, putting ** on the related matrix of partial derivatives.]

The calculated result is

$$\begin{bmatrix} \dfrac{\partial k_i}{\partial k_j} \end{bmatrix}^* = \begin{bmatrix} s_c f'' k_c & s_c f'' k_c \\ -s_w f'' k_c & -s_w f'' k_c + (s_w f' - n) \end{bmatrix}. \qquad \text{...(14)}$$

Putting $-\lambda$ in the diagonal of the matrix, we calculate its characteristic polynomial

$$\Delta(\lambda) = \lambda^2 + [(s_c - s_w)(-f'')k_c + (-s_w f' + n)]\lambda + [(-s_w f' + n)(-f'')k s_c]$$
$$= (\lambda - \lambda_1)(\lambda - \lambda_2) = 0. \qquad \text{...(15)}$$

The bracketed coefficients of this polynomial are seen to be both positive, because every factor in every term is assuredly positive for $s_w < \alpha(k^*)s_c < s_c$, $f'' < 0$, $s_w f' < s_c f' = n$. And the positiveness of these coefficients are the known necessary and sufficient conditions that the real parts of both λ roots be negative—which does assure the local stability property.

How local is local? That is never easy to specify. However, if initially (or, equivalently, ever) $K_c = 0$, obviously it is forever zero and the motion will approach the $(0, k^{**})$ asymptote. However, the slightest positive perturbation of k_c will send the system away from that point so long as $s_w < \alpha(k^*)s_c$. And our analysis confirms that there exists no locally unstable equilibrium point in the positive quadrant.

Will the ultimate approach to (k_c^*, k_w^*) be by means of damped oscillations or be monotonic? That depends on whether the λ_i roots are complex or real. Either case is possible. Thus rewrite the characteristic polynomial in the self-defining notation

$$\lambda^2 + [\alpha_1 \alpha_2 + \alpha_3]\lambda + \alpha_3 \alpha_2 = 0.$$

Then by making the discriminant $(\alpha_1 \alpha_2 + \alpha_3)^2 - 4\alpha_3 \alpha_2$ negative, we get damped oscillations of the focus type; and by making it positive, we get monotonic stability of the nodal type. The numerical cases $(\alpha_1, \alpha_2, \alpha_3) = (1, \frac{1}{2}, 1)$ or $(1, \frac{1}{2}, 0\cdot01)$, both of which appear to be admissible, lead respectively to damped oscillations and simple decay.

Let us now test the local stability of our dual equilibrium $(0, k^{**})$, which prevails when $s_w > \alpha(k^*)s_c$. Now our linear approximation has the matrix

$$\begin{bmatrix} \dfrac{\partial k_i}{\partial k_j} \end{bmatrix}^{**} = \begin{bmatrix} s_c f'(k^{**}) - n & 0 \\ 0 & s_w f'(k^{**}) - n \end{bmatrix} \qquad \text{...(16)}$$

whose λ roots will both be clearly negative because of the relations

$$0 = s_w \frac{f(k^{**})}{k^{**}} - n > s_c f'(k^*) - n > j_w s_c f'(k^{**}) - n$$

$$0 = s_w \frac{f(k^{**})}{k^{**}} - n > s_w f'(k^{**}) - n. \qquad \text{...(17)}$$

With local stability assured, what about global stability? A phase diagram can verify that our dual equilibrium is stable no matter what non-negative values (k_c, k_w) are perturbed to take on initially. For now the locally stable point $(k_w^{**}, k_c^{**}) = (k_w^{**}, 0)$ falls on the horizontal axis, so that for a limit cycle to surround it the variables would have to become negative, which is a contradiction. Thus, our dual-theorem equilibrium has true stability in the large.

It is remarkable that this general system has both a unique equilibrium and unconditional local stability. To emphasize this recall that a similar system in which all profits are saved at an s_c rate and all wages at an s_w rate can, even in the well-behaved neoclassical case, easily (for $s_w > s_c$) have multiple equilibria (of which some are unstable).[1]

VII. CONCEPT OF A GENERALIZED GOLDEN AGE

This is perhaps the place to dispose of a terminological ambiguity. A person unsophisticated in the conventions of mathematics might be inclined at first to expect *everything* in a " golden age " to be growing at *exactly* the same percentage rate. And in the case where one of the variables, say K_c, were zero, he might be puzzled over how to interpret its $\dot{K}_c/K_c = 0/0$ rate of growth. The applied mathematician is used to singular cases, where nice distinctions must be made between things being non-negative and positive. To avoid sterile controversy over semantics, he will define a " generalized golden age " as a state which, including the standard one as a special case, goes on to include steady-state configurations in which some of the equilibrium ratios are zero.

Our dual-theorem case is an example in point. K_c, if once positive, grows forever, never approaching zero. But the ratio $k_c \rightarrow 0$ because L grows faster than K_c. Now consider two situations, one where $K_c^1 \equiv 0$ and $k_c^1 \equiv 0$, and two where $K_c^2 > 0$ and $k_c^2 \rightarrow 0$. Although $k_c^2 \rightarrow k_c^1$, the divergence between K_c^2 and $K_c^1 \rightarrow \infty$! The mathematician, with his concepts of " relative stability " of ratios like $(K_c/K_w, K_c/K, K_c/L)$ is not at all perturbed that some different extensive variables show infinitely-divergent behaviour. And actually, once the literary economist has thought the matter through, he should not be perturbed either. For the phenomenon has already been occurring unnoticed in the standard Pasinetti case and is not peculiar to the dual-theorem case.

To see this let $s_w < \alpha(k^*)s_c$, and suppose the system starts out on the equilibrium path, with $[K_c(t), K_w(t), K(t)] = [K_c^*(t), K_w^*(t), K^*(t)] \equiv [k_c^* e^{nt}, k_w^* e^{nt}, k^* e^{nt}]$. Now suppose that at some date t_0 we bomb out of existence some capital, say some K_c. After t_0 the system follows a path $[K_c^1(t), K_w^1(t), K_c^1(t)]$ different from the equilibrium path, because of the initial disturbance $K_c^*(t_0) - K_c^1(t_0) > 0$. As we know from the stability analysis, all divergences of *per capita* magnitudes from equilibrium must go to zero in the limit: $(k_c^1, k_w^1) \rightarrow (k_c^*, k_w^*)$. But does this " relative stability " also imply " absolute stability ", namely that $|K_c^1(t) - K_c^*(t)|$ and $|K_w^1(t) - K_w^*(t)|$ tend to zero? The answer is, not necessarily, surprising as this may seem to the literary intuition. It is easy to show by numerical illustrations and by generalized stability analysis that the absolute divergence,

$$|K_c^1(t) - K_c^*(t)| = \delta(t)$$

[1] See the papers by Uzawa, *et al.* of the Hahn-Matthews bibliography cited in footnote 2, p. 270. Mr Edwin Burmeister, in a current MIT Ph.D. thesis, has contributed to this same subject. We leave as an open research question the problem of whether the Pasinetti equilibrium can fail to be globally stable because of the existence of a limit cycle.

need not approach zero, but may instead *increase without bound*; in fact when plotted on semi-log paper (as in Fig. 3*a*) the absolute discrepancy may approach asymptotically a *positively* sloped straight line with a slope smaller than *n*, the system's natural rate of growth. In other words the discrepancy can grow exponentially, though at a rate smaller than *n*.[1]

Thus, we have already had in the Pasinetti range the same infinite divergence of absolute magnitudes that is apparent in the Dual range. Why not? When on *semi-log paper* one curve approaches a positive-sloped straight line asymptotically, the eye sees a vanishing divergence; but when we translate into absolute numbers the magnitudes of the divergence, it can often be shown to become infinite. The sophisticated eye knows how one must allow for the properties of exponentials and ratios.

Fig. 3*a* shows how $(K_c, K_w, K) \rightarrow (k_c^* L, k_w^* L, k^* L)$ in a Pasinetti case, as indicated by the fact that all their curves end up paralleling *L*'s growth rate. The broken lines show that no lasting *per capita* improvement will result for society from a small increase in s_w alone: the new *K* path approaches the old asymptote, as K_c comes to lose what K_w gains.

At the bottom of Fig. 3*a* we have plotted the absolute divergence from the equilibrium path discussed above, namely $\delta(t) = K_c^*(t) - K_c^1(t)$. Note that $\delta(t) \rightarrow$ a straight-line growth path with slope $< n$.

Fig. 3*b* shows the asymptotic behaviour in our dual case. K_w approaches the curve of total *K*, which ends up parallel to the growth of *L*. But K_c ends up with the slower growth rate $s_c f'(k^{**}) < n$, and becomes of vanishing relative importance in the limit. Now if s_w is increased a little more, the broken-lines show that *K* and K_w end up *permanently* higher, with *per capita* product permanently higher even though ultimate growth rate is the same. The capitalists end up permanently worse off, with an ultimate growth rate that is definitely lower. [The reader can show that an increase in s_c alone would, in this case of 3*b*, raise capitalists' ultimate growth rate but have a negligible ultimate effect on society's growth rate or *per capita* magnitudes. In Fig. 3*a*, the reader can show that an increase in s_c will permanently raise the *per capita* ratios k^* and k_w^*, but k_c^* can actually be lowered if the elasticity of substitution is low enough.][2]

VIII. GENERALIZATION TO MANY CAPITALIST OR WORKER CLASSES

Now that we have given a rigorous analysis of the Pasinetti and Dual theorems, we can rapidly consider various generalizations. Dr Pasinetti indicated in his paper that his theorem could be applied to a world in which " the non-capitalists might be divided into any number of sub-categories one likes " (p. 274), each having a different saving propensity, say $s_w^1 > s_w^2 > \ldots > s_w^M$, provided, of course, $s_w^1 < \alpha(k^*) s_c$. He has not, however, investigated the case in detail nor the case where there are also any number of subcategories of capitalists, having different saving propensities $s_c^1 > s_c^2 > \ldots > s_c^N$. Clearly, the simple formula $r = n/s_c$ cannot then hold, since it would give *N* different (and inconsistent) values for *r*. The correct solution is found by examining the following extension of (5)'s saving equations, where *k* is short for $k_c^1 + \ldots + k_c^N + k_w^1 + \ldots + k_w^M$, and $\lambda_j = L_j/L$, the constant relative fraction

---

[1] Mathematically, previous stability analysis showed that $k_c(t) = k_c^* + a_1 \exp(\lambda_1 t) + a_2 \exp(\lambda_2 t) + R$, where the remainder term *R* is dominated by $\exp[t \max(\text{real part of } \lambda_1, \text{real part of } \lambda_2)] = \exp(tm)$, for short. Perturbations affect only the a_i coefficients. Hence, the divergence defined above can be written as

$$\delta(t) = be^{(n+m)t}[1 + \rho(t)]$$

where $\rho(t) \rightarrow \rho(\infty) = 0$. Provided $n > -m = -\text{Max}[\text{real part of } \lambda_i]$, we have infinite absolute divergence. One instance suffices to show that this condition is easily possible. Let $f(k) = \alpha^{-1} k^\alpha$, $s_w = 0$ (or " small "), $s_c > \alpha s_w$. Then, we find from (15) above, $m = \text{Max}[-n, s_c f'' k_c] = \text{Max}[-n, -n(1-\alpha)] = -n(1-\alpha)$. Hence, $n > (1-\alpha)n = -m$ because $1 - \alpha$ must be a positive fraction. Q.E.D.

[2] At this point, the interested reader can be referred to the Appendix, which brings to completion the above analysis by considering explicitly the problems that arise when K/L tends either to zero or infinity.

of labourers who belong permanently in the jth non-capitalist category:

$$k_c^i = [s_c^i f'(k) - n]k_c^i \qquad\qquad (i = 1, 2, ..., N)$$

$$k_w^j = s_w^j [f(k) - kf'(k)]\lambda_j + [s_w^j f'(k) - n]k_w^j \quad (j = 1, ..., M) \qquad ...(18)$$

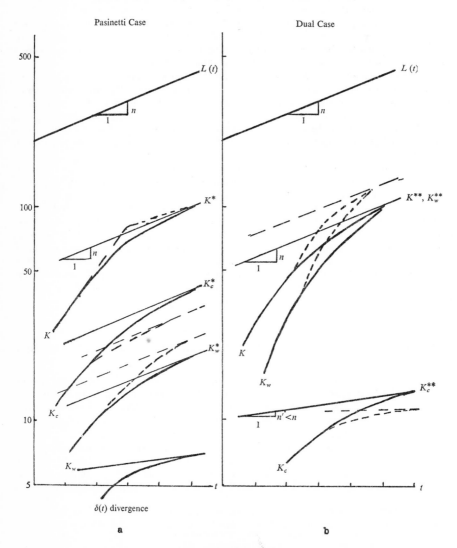

Pasinetti Case

Dual Case

$\delta(t)$ divergence

a

b

FIGURE 3

In the Pasinetti regime, K, K_c and K_w all approach the asymptotic growth rate of labour. The broken lines in 3a show the effects of a small increase in s_w, with ultimate K trend unchanged, as K_c loses what K_w gains. $\delta(t)$ plots the absolute divergence from the equilibrium path attributable to an initial reduction in K_c, a divergence that goes to infinity, but becomes negligible relative to K or L.

In the Dual regime of 3b, K and K_w approach the growth rate of L; K_c grows toward infinity, but at an asymptotic rate lower than K_w and K, so that the generalized golden age is dominated by K_w.

Quite obviously setting $(k_c^1, ..., k_c^N)$ simultaneously equal to zero will lead to a self-contradiction unless

$$s_c^1 f'(k^*) - n = 0$$

$$0 = k_c^2 = ... = k_c^N.$$

Inevitably K_c^1 will grow faster than K_c^i; at best, k_c^1 can become a positive constant with all other k_c^i diminishing to zero, since $\dot{K}_c^i/K_c^i < \dot{K}_c^1/K_c^1$.

There are then only two possibilities for

$$[k_c^1(\infty), k_c^2(\infty), ..., k_c^N(\infty); k_w^1(\infty), ..., k_w^M(\infty)],$$

namely

$$[a_1^*, 0, ..., 0; b_1^*, ..., b_M^*]$$

where the positive b_j^* and a_1^* add up to k^*, the Pasinetti root of $f'(k^*) = n/s_c$; or

$$[0, 0, ..., 0; b_1^{**}, ..., b_n^{**}]$$

where $\Sigma b_j^{**} > k^*$. These Pasinetti and Dual-Theorem extensions can be summarized in a third general theorem that includes all previous theorems as special cases.

General Theorem. Let k^* be the root of $f'(k^*) = n/\text{Max}_i(s_c^i)$ and designate the respective extended Pasinetti and extended Dual cases according to whether

$$s_w^1 = \text{Max}\,[s_w^1, ..., s_w^M] \lessgtr \alpha(k^*)\,\text{Max}\,[s_c^1, ..., s_c^N]. \qquad ...(19)$$

(i) In the extended Pasinetti case, all

$$(k_c^i;\ k_w^j) \rightarrow (a_1^*, 0, ..., 0;\ b_1^*, ..., b_M^*), \text{ with}$$

$$f'(a_1^* + b_1^* + ... + b_M^*) = r^* = \frac{n}{s_c^1}. \qquad ...(20)$$

While the interest rate is independent of the form of the production function, the ultimate values for other starred equilibrium magnitudes depend on n/s_c^1 according to the form of the production function. [See Equation 22 below.]

(ii) In the extended dual case $(k_c^i;\ k_w^j) \rightarrow (0, ..., 0;\ b_1^{**}, ..., b_M^{**})$, where

$$k^{**} = b_1^{**} + ... + b_M^{**}$$

exceeds k^*, and is the root of

$$\sum_{j=1}^{M} \frac{[f(k^{**}) - k^{**}f'(k^{**})]s_w^j \lambda_j}{n - s_w^j f'(k^{**})} - k^{**} = 0. \qquad ...(21)$$

Now r^{**} is below r^* and, like all equilibrium double-starred magnitudes is a function of n, all the (s_w^j) and (λ_j), and depends on the form of the production function.

(iii) In every case, the relative magnitudes of b_j^* or b_j^{**} are increasing functions of the respective s_w^j: the workers' group with the highest saving propensity ends up with the largest capital *per capita*, which in the extended Pasinetti case is completely at the expense of the other groups in society.

(iv) There is a fundamental asymmetry between a worker and capitalist category. Thus, if one of two capitalists with the same s_c^1 starts out with more wealth, he " ends up " permanently ahead by a finite " *per capita* " amount of k_c^*. Indeed " his " extra k_c^* forces an equivalent reduction in the k_c^* of his class colleagues, since the *total* k_c^* of the class is unchanged and hence the k_w^* of all workers is left unchanged. This last conclusion holds even in the dual case, except that of course *all* k_c^* end up zero in that case.

However, suppose some one worker or subgroup of workers should somehow begin with more k_w^j (or more k_w^j/λ_j), the ultimate *per capita* effect upon other workers in the same jth category, upon other workers in a different category, or on the ultimate k_c^∞ of any capitalist group is null in *every* case. High initial k_w^j/λ_j gets washed out in the end since always equation (18) ends up with

$$\frac{k_w^j(\infty)}{\lambda_j} = \frac{f(k^\infty)-k^\infty f'(k^\infty)}{\frac{n}{s_w^j}-f'(k^\infty)}$$

$$k_c^1(\infty) = k^\infty - \sum_{j=1}^{n} k_w^j(\infty)$$

...(22)

independently of any initial or penultimate conditions.

[As in our earlier Section VII discussion, the effects on absolute (K_c, K_w, K) magnitudes must be distinguished from effects on relative (k_c, k_w, k) magnitudes. If one member of the s_c^1 capitalist class has some of "his" K_c^1 destroyed by fire, in enough time his absolute wealth will have fallen infinitely behind that of his colleagues, even though his (diminished) principal grows at the same rate as theirs and though his share of $k_c^1(\infty)$ declines by only a finite amount. Suppose a cohort of workers lose some K_w^j to fire. We have seen that time washes out this effect as far as their ultimate *per capita* $k_w^j(\infty)/\lambda_j$ is concerned. But the absolute effect of the fire on their $K_w^j(t)$, which is given by the $\delta(t)$ divergence of $k_w^j(t) \exp(nt)$, can be shown by an extension of footnote 11c's mathematics to be capable of growing like $\exp(n+m)t$ where $n+m>0$, and m is the maximum real part of the λ roots appropriate to the linear stability analysis of (18).]

The proof of all these statements comes from putting all the k terms on the left-hand side of (18) equal to zero, and then searching the resulting statical relations for relevant non-negative solutions. Stability analysis is not presented here, but would represent a straightforward extension of our earlier discussion.

IX. SOME IMPLICATIONS FOR THE GOLDEN RULE AND ITS ALLEGED RELATION TO SOCIALISM

Our General Theorem has one interesting corollary that Dr Pasinetti has commented on, and somewhat surprisingly linked with a "socialist system". (Section VIII, pp. 277-278.)

Corollary. If there is one capitalist who *permanently* succeeds in saving *all* his income (and if Max $[s_w^j] < \alpha(k^*)$ where k^* is the root of $f'(k^*) = n$), then in enough centuries the system will—independently of all other saving propensities s_w^j and s_c^j—approach the Golden-Rule state of Swan-Phelps, that golden age characterized by maximum *per capita* consumption, in which $r^* = n$ and $I = P$.

Dr Pasinetti has associated this case of $s_c^1 = 1$ with socialism on the ground that "the state as such cannot consume" (p. 277) and hence must have a propensity to save equal to unity. However, since the government uses resources to provide many kinds of current services which it could finance with its property income in lieu of taxes and since it could always distribute some of its property income by gratuitous transfers, it would seem that socialism, in the usual sense of the term as involving public *ownership* and *management* of (some or all) means of production, is neither sufficient nor necessary for the analytic result enunciated. This is of course not to deny that government policy can be an important determinant of the rate accumulation in socialist as well as mixed economies.

We emphasize the centuries that may be involved to stress that we are talking here and everywhere of hypothetical steady-states which will *never* quite be reached from other states and which may be closely approximated only after such long periods of time as to make the models' realism questionable. Of course, this is no more a point against Dr. Pasinetti than against Solow, Harrod, Joan Robinson, Meade, Samuelson-Modigliani and other golden-age mongers.

X. NEOCLASSICAL DISTRIBUTION THEORY ABANDONED OR GENERALIZED

Most of the above seem to rest on marginal productivity notions of the Clark-Wicksteed-Solow-Meade type. But if one examines the basic Equations (3) and all the steps leading up to (5) and beyond,[1] it will be found that no direct use has been made of equation (2)'s marginal productivity relations. There is no necessity to identify the interest rate relations $r = f'(k)$ with the partial derivative symbol $\partial F(k, 1)/\partial k$ or with $df(k)/dk$! All we need is that r should be a determinate function of K/L, but that function need not be the above derivative. Thus, even if there are not smooth substitutability properties posited for (1)'s production function or even if Chamberlinian imperfect competition intervenes in factor or commodity markets, our analysis can still be applied. If Kalecki, or Boulding, or Hahn, or Kaldor, or Schneider, or Walter Reuther, or Thünen come forward with some alternative theory of distribution, provided only that the profit rate is a declining function of the ratio of capital to labour—call it $r = \phi(K/L)$ [2]—both the Pasinetti formalism and our various duals and generalizations of them remain valid.[3]

Now the positive wage rate becomes $f(k) - k\phi(k)$ rather than $f(k) - kf'(k)$ and $\alpha(k)$ becomes $k\phi(k)/f(k)$ rather than $kf'(k)/f(k)$. The basic equations are now

$$k_c = [s_c\phi(k) - n]k_c$$
$$k_w = s_w[f(k) - k\phi(k)] + (s_w\phi(k) - n)k_w.$$

As before, we are in the Pasinetti or Dual anti-Pasinetti range depending upon whether

$$k^{**} < k^* \text{ or } k^{**} > k^*$$

where

$$k^* \text{ is root of } \phi(k^*) = \frac{n}{s_c}$$

$$k^{**} \text{ is root of } \frac{f(k^{**})}{k^{**}} = \frac{n}{s_w}.$$

[1] The stability matrix (14) and (16) is a minor exception to this. See footnote 1, p. 289 for modifications in our stability analysis when marginal productivity relations are dropped. The Appendix discussion of pathology would also require some minor modifications.

[2] For an excellent survey of these diverse theories see K. W. Rothschild, " Some Recent Contributions to a Macro-economic Theory of Income Distribution," *Scottish Journal of Political Economy*, **8** (1961), 173-179. [Warning: many macroeconomic theories, e.g. Kaldor's, exclude the existence of a $\phi(k)$ function].

[3] After we had completed this analysis, our attention was called to the valuable paper, J. E. Meade, " The Rate of Profit in a Growing Economy ", *Economic Journal*, **73** (1963), 665-674, which gives many of the results for the case of a Cobb-Douglas function that we had also arrived at. While we find much to admire in this paper, we think unfortunate the impression that many readers will get from Professor Meade's words " . . . the ' neo-classical ' result will be true in its simplest form if $s_w > \alpha(k^*)s_c$ [our notation] while the ' neo-Keynesian ' will be true in its simplest form if $s_w < \alpha(k^*)s_c$." (p. 669). If the term " neo-classical " is used as we use it, merely to indicate existence of smooth derivatives $\partial F/\partial K$, $\partial^2 F/\partial K^2$, and competitive imputation of factor prices, then the range of validity of the Pasinetti theorem as against our Dual (and General theorems) has nothing peculiarly to do with this smooth differentiability issue—as our earlier analysis showed and as this section further illuminates. This remark of ours would seem to apply too to Dr Pasinetti's " Comments " on Meade's paper, *Economic Journal*, **74** (1964), 488-489; but it should be interpreted in the context of our later Section 12's discussion. If neo-Keynesian is used merely as an O.K. word for valid arithmetic identities—such as the implications of $\dot{Y}/Y = \dot{K}/K = \dot{L}/L = n$—we are all neo-Keynesians. Along with rejecting the notion that some particular range of the s_w/s_c parameters has a neo-Keynesian as against neoclassical significance, we question the imperialistic notion that the " neo-Keynesian results hold in general " if the words " neo-Keynesian " are here interpreted to involve any or all of the following notions: I must be thought of as in some sense autonomous; marginalism is a modern irrelevancy; effective demand problems are always vital; income shares alter (in the long or short run) to equilibrate full employment; causation of interest or profit determination runs from growth rates of labour and not from impatience, thirftiness, and " technical productivity ". Many of these elements enter into certain models that we often choose to analyse, but there is nothing universal about such behaviour equations.

This presupposes that more capital relative to labour means lower r, so that $\phi'(k) < 0$ even if $\phi'(k) \neq f''(k)$. We shall again have as watershed between the two regimes

$$s_w < \alpha(k^*)s_c \quad \text{Pasinetti}$$
$$s_w > \alpha(k^*)s_c \quad \text{Dual.}$$

Fig. 2 still applies, but now with the MP curve no longer having a marginal productivity interpretation. The AP curve still does have an average product interpretation.

Let us illustrate by a " bargaining power or a just-wage or Kalecki markup theory of distribution ". A stringent example will be the case of fixed-coefficients of production à la Leontief and early Walras. Suspending our disbelief in the realism of such a model, we write

$$C + \dot{K} = \text{Min}\left(\frac{K}{k^\dagger}, \frac{L}{1}\right) = Lf(k) = L\,\text{Min}\left(\frac{k}{k^\dagger}, 1\right) \qquad ...(1')$$

where L has been defined in units such that $1\,L$ is needed to produce 1 unit of C or of $\dot{K}$, and where $k^\dagger$ is the minimal capital-output ratio (measured in years). In this special neo-neoclassical model, capital and labour are " needed " in fixed proportion, and whichever happens to exceed this critical balance is redundant from a current technical point of view. (I.e., $f'(k) = d\,\text{Min}\,(k/k^\dagger, 1)/dk = 1/k^\dagger$ for $k < k^\dagger$; $= 0$ for $k > k^\dagger$; and is indeterminately defined as anywhere inbetween for $k = k^\dagger$.) Marginal productivity can certainly not determine $\alpha(k^\dagger)$ because of the kinked corner that $f(k)$ has at $k = k^\dagger$.

Jettisoning marginal productivity, suppose collective bargaining, the State, or Kalecki-Chamberlin markup always gives wages three-fourths the total product, giving the remaining one-fourth as profit or interest to owners of capital (in proportion to the quantity of capital they own). This is a fairly bizarre theory since, for all but a razor's edge of $K/L = k^\dagger$, one or the other of K and L is quite redundant and would become a free good under any regime of ruthless competitive price flexibility. (Thus, it is here implied that, even if total K were redundant, a small private owner who brings into existence some further K is able to command the same r profit as existing capital. There is then a great divergence between private pecuniary return from K and " the true social return "). The constancy of relative shares sounds, in one aspect, like a pseudo Cobb-Douglas function with coefficients $(\frac{3}{4}, \frac{1}{4})$. But why bother with Cobb-Douglas terminology? Instead, define r as

$$r = \phi(k) = \frac{\frac{1}{4}Y}{K} = \frac{1}{4}A(k) = \frac{1}{4}\frac{\text{Min}\,(k/k^\dagger, 1)}{k} = \frac{1}{4}\,\text{Min}\left(\frac{1}{k^\dagger}, \frac{1}{k}\right) \qquad ...(23)$$

and just carry on. In this example, both $\phi(k)$ and $A(k)$ have finite maxima:

$$\text{Max}\,\phi(k) \equiv r_m = (\tfrac{1}{4})(1/k^\dagger), \quad \text{Max}\,A(k) \equiv A_m = 1/k^\dagger.$$

It is shown in the Appendix that under these conditions, if n is sufficiently large relative to s_c and s_w, then accumulation will prove insufficient to keep up with the growth of labour (in efficiency units) and $k \to 0$. The specific condition for this to happen is that

$$n > \text{Max}\,[s_c r_m, s_w A_m] = \text{Max}\,[\tfrac{1}{4}s_c, s_w]\frac{1}{k^\dagger}. \qquad ...(24)$$

When this inequality holds, *labour* will eventually tend to become technically redundant, $(k, y, w) \to (0, 0, 0)$, while $r \to r_m$. If, on the other hand, the above inequality is reversed, then *capital* will eventually become technically redundant, although r, not being related to capital's marginal productivity, will not tend to zero. We have two possible cases here:

(i) The Pasinetti Case, where $s_w < \tfrac{1}{4}s_c$. Here $k^\infty = k^*$, the root of

$$\phi(k^*) = \tfrac{1}{4}\,\text{Min}\left(\frac{1}{k^\dagger}, \frac{1}{k^*}\right) = \frac{n}{s_c},$$

which is satisfied by $k^* = \frac{1}{4}\frac{s_c}{n} > k^\dagger$ in view of (24). Also from (6),

$$k_w^\infty = k_w^* = \frac{3}{4}\frac{1}{\frac{n}{s_w} - \frac{n}{s_c}} > 0, \quad k_c^* = \frac{\frac{1}{4}s_c}{s_w} - 1}{\frac{n}{s_w} - \frac{n}{s_c}} > 0$$

$(y^\infty, w^\infty) = (1, \frac{3}{4})$.

(ii) The Dual Case, where $s_w \geqq \frac{1}{4}s_c$. Here $k^\infty = k^{**}$, the root of

$$A(k^{**}) = \text{Min}\left(\frac{1}{k^\dagger}, \frac{1}{k^{**}}\right) = \frac{n}{s_w},$$

which is satisfied by $k^{**} = \frac{s_w^{\text{?}}}{n} > k^\dagger$ (by 24). Also,

$$k_c^\infty = k_c^{**} = 0; \quad k_w^\infty = k_w^{**} = k^{**} = \frac{s_w}{n}$$

$$r^\infty = r^{**} = \phi(k^{**}) = \frac{1}{4}\frac{n}{s_w} \leqq \frac{n}{s_c} = r^*;$$

$(y^\infty, w^\infty) = (1, \frac{3}{4})$.

There remains the hairline case:

$$n = \text{Max}\left[s_c r_m, s_w A_m\right] = \text{Max}\left[\frac{1}{4}s_c, s_w\right]\frac{1}{k^\dagger}.$$

Here we have again $r = r^*$ if $s_w < \frac{1}{4}s_c$, and $r = r^{**}$ otherwise. However, k can end up anywhere in the interval $(0, k^\dagger)$. If k ends up smaller than $k^\dagger$, labour is again technically redundant and $(y, w) \to (0, 0)$; while if $k = k^\dagger$, neither capital nor labour are redundant and $(y, w) \to (1, \frac{3}{4})$.

The above illustration, in which distribution of income was fully specified from the outset, should help to bring home clearly the basic fact that Pasinetti's theorem and our general theorem about golden age identities have nothing to do *per se* with any " alternative theory of income distribution ".

In general, however, there is no need to postulate constancy of shares as in the above example. Let, in a general model, the $\alpha(k)$ share be specified as some determinate function of factor proportions $k = K/L$, say $\alpha(k)$. Then $r = \alpha(k)F(k, 1)/k = \phi(k)$ gives the profit rate.

Recall that one of Kalecki's two theories about profits makes $\alpha(k)$ depend on the " average degree of monopoly or imperfection of competition " in the economy. Subject to the above stipulations, this is an admissable determinant of our $r = \phi(k)$ function. Or consider a theory of the " just wage ". On Thünen's gravestone was the formula for the " natural wage ", which in our notation becomes $[f(k)\partial F/\partial L]^{\frac{1}{2}} = T(k)$. Hence, $(Y - LT)/K = [f(k) - T(k)]/k$ will serve to define our $\phi(k)$.[1]

XI. A FURTHER NOTE ON FIXED COEFFICIENTS AND KALDORIAN DISTRIBUTION THEORIES

In the last section we have shown that, even if one discards competitive theory involving smooth neoclassical production functions, any model in which the profit rate r is a declining

---

[1] It will conduce toward stability if $\phi'(k) < 0$ in the diminishing returns case. If $f'(k) - \phi(k) = h(k)$ our differential equation (5) must everywhere have $f'(k)$ replaced by $f'(k) - h(k)$. This introduces into the stability matrixes (14) and (16), and into the coefficients of their characteristic polynomial, terms proportional to the factors $h(k)$ and $h'(k) = f''(k) - \phi'(k)$. For $|h|$ sufficiently small, stability is assured in every case. However, for large h divergences, it is possible to produce instances of instability. One conjectures, from diminishing returns considerations, that stability is always assured for $|-\phi'|$ sufficiently large. [Note: if wages and interest are to be positive and $\phi'(k) < 0$, $\alpha(k)$ must be fractional and obey the elasticity restriction: $E\alpha(k)/Ek < 1 - Ef(k)/Ek$.]

function of the K/L ratio will obey our general theorems of Pasinetti and Dual type. One such model, involving fixed coefficients, was just exhibited by way of illustration. On the other hand, macroeconomic distribution theories of the Kaldor type which provided the springboard for Pasinetti's general analysis, must now be given brief notice here.

Such models fare best under the assumption of fixed coefficients, for if smooth marginal productivities were well defined one would have no need for a genuinely alternative theory of distribution.[1] So recognizing the empirical oddity of the postulate, we posit last

---

[1] This sentence is worded cryptically and could be misunderstood. Marginal productivity, properly understood, provides some of the equations needed in a smooth neoclassical model for a complete theory of (factor and goods) pricing. Depending upon the time run, parameters of population growth (like n) and saving propensities (like s_c or s_w) also contribute blades of the scissors needed to determine equilibrium. The model defined by our equations (1)-(4), precisely because it possesses some simplifications of a neo-classical model (effectively one-sector, effectively one capital good, etc.), is useful to contrast with what appear to be some Cambridge attributions of causation. To test the cogency of a line of logic and the universality of an hypothesized direction of causation, it is valuable to apply them to *both* our neoclassical model *and* the fixed coefficient model of this section—and to certain intermediate cases involving a finite number of alternative activities or blueprints.

Specifically, assume s_w/s_c small, and consider $f'(k^*) = r^* = n/s_c$. Then, in our model, marginal productivity does " determine " the profit or interest rate at every instant of time, but that doesn't deny that n/s_c also does " determine " the interest rate in the long run. Both blades of the long-run scissors count. When we have two long-run unknowns—k^* and r^*—the presence of two independent equations is not an inconsistency; it is a necessity. Because the long-run " supply curve " is given by the *horizontal* level n/s_c, while the long-run demand curve is the varying function $f'(k^*)$, there is a genuine sense of long-run causation, which we share and also neoclassical writers share with Cambridge writers (like Kahn quoted below), that says: $n/s_c \rightarrow$ long-run r^*.

But all of the above is quite consistent with short-run causation that runs in quite the opposite direction. In each short run, let $k(t) = K/L$ be given by past history. This provides us with a *vertical* short-run supply schedule, which intersects the $f'(k)$ schedule of demand. In the short run, for the model of (1)-(4), the " true " causation seen, in every instant of time, $k(t) \rightarrow f'[k(t)] = r(t)$. For this model, *capital scarcity relative to labour is the key to the level of the rate of interest.* Given the saving-investment propensities of (3), it is deduced that positive $[r(t) - n/s_c] \rightarrow$ positive $\dot{k}$ (or, more exactly, $\dot{k}_c$ if $s_w \neq 0$) in every run of time, so that if initially $k < k^*$ and therefore $r > n/s_c$, $\dot{k}$ will be positive and k will grow, and if k ever attains k^*—the level of capital scarcity where $[f'(k^*) - n/s_c] = 0$—then $\dot{k} = 0$, and we stay in the k^* golden age. (If one wants to trace short-run effective demand sequences, the Central Bank ensures that the market interest rate, R, is put above and below the $f'(k) = r$ level, just enough to induce full-employment investment without inflationary or deflationary gaps.) The full-employment growth path of the system as determined by its differential equations is causal, in the same sense that the trajectories of the planets around the sun, following their Newtonian differential equations, are termed causal. This is a third meaning of causality in the present context, alongside the long term causal chain $n/s_c \rightarrow r^*$ and the short-run chain $\dot{k} \rightarrow f'(k) = r$.

Warning: in a two-sector neoclassical model, where the sectors have different intensities and with production-possibility frontier $\dot{K} = T(K, L; C)$, $k(t) \rightarrow f'[k(t)] = r(t)$, would be replaced by

$$[k_c(t), k_w(t); s_c, s_w] \rightarrow [c, k_c, k_w, r = \partial T/\partial K = \partial \dot{K}/\partial K]$$

and where we would have to take into account the possibility of multiplicity of short-run equilibria (as e.g. in the anti-Pasinetti case where $s_c = s_w$ and capital goods production is sufficiently more relatively capital-intensive than consumption goods production) and of long run equilibria (as in the case just mentioned, where the ratio of the value of capital to output might *fall* while r falls).

In a general, neo-neoclassical model involving a great number of heterogeneous capital goods and processes, let $[k_1, k_2, ...]$ stand for a vector of per capita capital goods. Then in every short run, the " scarcity " of this " supply " of physical capital goods, taken together with the saving-investment demand-composition condition of the model, is an important determinant of the quasi-rents of all capital goods and of the spread of (own) rates of profit and interest $[r_1, r_2, ...]$. Thus, subject again to the possibility of multiple equilibria, $[k_1(t), k_2(t), ..., s_c, s_w] \rightarrow [r_1(t), r_2(t), ...]$. Under fixed saving propensities, steady-trend technology and population, middling-good foresight by entrepreneurs who are not in regions of liquidity-traps or profit-uncertainty regions, and certain nudges from fiscal and monetary authorities, such models

often evolve into a golden age. *i.e.* $[r_1^\infty, r_2^\infty, ...] = [r^*, r^*, ...]$ where $r^* = n/s_c$; but still the general causality in each short run is from capital-good supply and demand conditions to the level and spread of profits; and in the longest run r^* is achieved only because the system has brought into being through capital-goods changes, and has kept into being through replacement and capital widening, the needed plentitude and

variety and composition of the capital goods vector $[k_1^\infty, k_2^\infty, ...] = [k_1^*, k_2^*, ...]$. [See P. A. Samuelson and R. M. Solow, " A Complete Capital Model Involving Heterogeneous Capital Goods ", *Quarterly Journal of Economics*, **70** (1956), 537-662.

As the present section shows, if $f(k)$ is characterized by fixed-coefficients, marginal productivity is undefined at $k^\dagger$ and there is both room for and need for a short-run *alternative* theory of distribution.

Suppose now that many, but only a finite number of, alternative pages of mechanized blue prints are possible. If the alternatives are many and varied, putting r^* in different narrow intervals will cause the processes used to be different (and will usually involve differences in the calculated aggregate ratio of the value of capital to output). Any particular short-run r can prevail only if the proper plentitude and scarcity of diverse physical capital goods is available per capita. Given reasonable, but not perfect foresight,

section's (1)′, in which $k^†$ represents the minimum capital-output ratio, beyond which output expands not at all and k is technically redundant and before which labour is technically redundant. When output *per capita* is given by $y = \text{Min} (k/k^†, 1)$, the capital-output ratio equals $k^†$ for $k \leq k^†$ and equals k itself for $k > k^†$.

The Kaldorian analysis concentrates on the case where k is at $k^†$, neither factor being technically redundant. It does not seem to tell us what $r = \phi(k)$ is away from $k^†$, and hence we must work out the conditions under which the system could stay at $k^†$.

As both Kaldor and Pasinetti explicitly insist, the theory has a need to stipulate the inequality

$$s_w < nk^† < s_c. \qquad \qquad ...(25)$$

We shall now *deduce* this condition as a requirement for the system's being capable of staying at $K/L = k = k^†$. Our treatment is different in deducing (25) from dynamic stability analysis of the differential equation of growth; but more important, it differs in that Kaldorians seem to think (25) must hold lest some factor share become negative or lest some regime of inflation or of unemployment become chronic. For us (25) must hold only if the system is to be capable of staying at $k^†$; if (25) is violated, the system merely moves, in the manner already studied in section X and analyzed in more detail in the Appendix, toward $k = 0$ or toward technically redundant $k > k^†$.

investors will start new physical capital goods and abandon old ones at a rate determined by the over-all (s_w, s_c) ratios and the inherited composition of physical capital goods. The result can be an approach toward a new golden age, with (the vector of) " capital scarcity and plenty " thought of as determining at each time the steadily evolving profile of own rates of interest, with no great surprises occurring but with some people experiencing good luck and some bad, and with most prudently remaking their plans as new experience warrants. In moving from a higher to a lower interest rate, any new golden age we come to is assuredly characterized by definitely higher real wages. And the lower interest rate does reflect a lower trade-off between consumption today and consumption next year. (Or, more precisely, one gets not more than $1+r$ of next-period C for sacrifice of each current C; and one gives up not less than $1+r$ of next-period C to get one more current C; the more varied and numerous the pattern of alternative blueprints, the more these inequalities narrow down toward the Fisher equality $| \partial C_{t+1}/\partial C_t | = 1+r$.) Because multiplicity of equilibria is possible, and " Wicksell effects " of market revaluation of capital can take place in any direction, one cannot be sure that a lower r^∞ always corresponds to a higher ratio of the value of capital to output or even to a higher plateau of maintainable total consumption for a fixed population; in possible, so-called perverse cases, society might move from a high to a low interest rate state without having to abstain from current consumption goods, instead actually being splashed with a transient increase in consumption. Empirically, one expects the blueprints of technology to be such that at a lower interest rate, not only are wages higher because of less discounting of gross productivities, but also because the size of the social pie has gone up, and along with it the size of labour's undiscounted " productivity "; but exceptions to this are logically possible.

Given the above version of a useful pragmatic model, let us examine the Cambridge view expressed well by R. F. Kahn (op. cit.). He says: " Thrift is important, however, because it determines the real wage-rate in a Golden Age" (p. 151). We would say, " In our model certainly, and in most realistic models we suspect with great probability, past abstention from consumption was necessary to build up the stock of capital goods approriate to the high-real-wage-rate Golden Age; and continued abstention from utilizing resources for additional consumption goods is needed to replace and maintain the *per capita* supply of capital goods of that Golden Age. In our model, with interest low, real wages are two ways higher: output $f(k)$ is higher and, for each *same* level of k, less r means a lower subtraction of profit from $f(k)$ to get w; and, of course, the effects of K/L on absolute and relative profit shares depend on the (generalized) ordinary elasticity and on the (generalized) elasticity of substitution for k." Kahn says (p. 153): " If two different Golden Ages are compared, with the same saving coefficients but different rates of growth, the higher rate of growth is associated with the higher rate of profit. This higher rate of profit is to be attributed to the higher rate of growth of capital rather than the other way around." We say: " The unobjectionable first sentence does not logically (or empirically) imply the second. In our model the higher rate of profit persists in the higher-rate-of-growth regime because the stipulated limited thrift will, when L grows so fast, provide capital formation that will preserve only a low and scarce K/L ratio (or *per capita* vector of heterogeneous capital goods); and the resulting capital scarcity " explains " the high r. This is true not only in the simple model (1)-(4), but also in many models with tens-of-thousands of heterogeneous physical capital goods and technologies and with a large number of alternative blueprints. (Again, there are exceptions. And if Kahn and we drop the assumption that s_w is small, we can for some such exceptional cases find that a rise in the rate of population growth ends us up, for a long time or even permanently, with a lower rather than higher interest rate. This odd effect is inconsistent with simple neoclassical parables but not with the general market conditions of neo-neoclassical models.) The cited Champernowne article, precisely because it is mathematical, shows that some of what is considered different about Cambridge or macroeconomic theories of distribution is compatible with complete models of general-equilibrium pricing that we would espouse.

REVIEW OF ECONOMIC STUDIES

Begin by supposing $s_w > nk^\dagger$. There are two cases of this: $s_w > s_c$ or $s_w < s_c$. In the first, we know from previous discussion that our Dual analysis must hold and necessarily $k_c \to 0$ with $k_w \to k$. With capitalists' saving being ignorable, the familiar Harrod-Domar-Solow formula for a golden-age becomes applicable, namely $s/n = (k/y)$, where s and s_w are now the same. Since $s_w/n > k^\dagger$ by hypothesis, the equilibrium capital-output ratio must obviously end up at $k > k^\dagger$. So $k^\dagger$ is not viable.

In the second case, we have $s_c \geqq s_w > nk^\dagger$, and the ultimate saving ratio s, averaged over both classes, must satisfy: $s > nk^\dagger$, and $(k/y) = s/n > k^\dagger$ must be the equilibrium capital-output ratio. Again $k^\dagger$ is not viable.

To complete our derivation of (25), examine the remaining case where

$$\text{Max} (s_c, s_w) < nk^\dagger.$$

Any average of (s_c, s_w) must satisfy $s < nk^\dagger$. Therefore, we find for all K/L that $\dot{K}/K < n$ and $k \to 0$. Proof:

$$\frac{\dot{K}}{K} = s\left(\frac{Y}{K}\right) < nk^\dagger\left(\frac{Y}{K}\right) = nk^\dagger \text{Min}\left(\frac{1}{k^\dagger}, \frac{1}{k}\right) = n \text{Min}\left(1, \frac{k^\dagger}{k}\right) \leqq n.$$

Hence, $k^\dagger$ is again not viable.

By examining all cases, we have shown that unless (25) is satisfied $k^\dagger$ will not be viable. Regardless of the distribution of income α, either saving will be insufficient to widen capital in balance with L growth, or it will be so great as to deepen capital beyond the knife-edge $k^\dagger$. If (25) is satisfied, there is still no guarantee that $k^\dagger$ will be maintained and certainly no guarantee that from $k \neq k^\dagger$ the system will move in a stable way to $k \to k^\dagger$.

If (25) is satisfied and if we start the system with values of k_c and k_w that add up to $k^\dagger$ (and if, as will be soon discussed below, k_c is not too small), there will exist one distribution of income $\alpha^\dagger$ and concomitant $r^\dagger$—call it the Kaldor-Pasinetti one—which will make $\dot{k} = 0$ and hence maintain k momentarily at $k^\dagger$. While k remains at $k^\dagger$, its composition between k_c and k_w will generally be changed at the next moment; but if $\alpha^\dagger$ is always kept adjusted to the resulting $(k_c^\dagger, k_w^\dagger = k^\dagger - k_c^\dagger)$ so as to keep $\dot{k} \equiv 0$, we shall prove that $\alpha^\dagger \to \alpha^{\dagger\dagger}$, a unique Cambridge distribution of income for which $(\dot{k}_c, \dot{k}_w, \dot{k}) = (0, 0, 0)$ and at which $r^\dagger \to r^{\dagger\dagger} = n/s_c$ in good Pasinetti fashion. Just why any actual economic system should go to $k^\dagger$, and more importantly, being there should neatly settle into the $(\alpha^\dagger, r^\dagger)$ configuration is a topic that appears not to have been adequately discussed in the Kaldorian literature. And it is not discussed here. We merely state the conditions for the existence of $\alpha^\dagger$ and prove the asymptotic stability of $\alpha^{\dagger\dagger}$ if $\alpha^\dagger$ somehow is made always to prevail.

Theorem of Kaldor-Pasinetti type. If

$$C + \dot{K} = \text{Min}\left(\frac{K}{k^\dagger}, L\right) = L\text{Min}\left(\frac{k}{k^\dagger}, 1\right),$$

$$s_w < nk^{\dagger\dagger} < s_c$$

$$k = k^\dagger = k_c^\dagger + k_w^\dagger, \quad k_c^\dagger \geqq \frac{nk^\dagger - s_w}{s_c - s_w} k^\dagger, \quad \quad \ldots(25')$$

then

(i) there will exist an $(r^\dagger, \alpha^\dagger)$, given below, that will keep $\dot{k}$ in (5″) of Section V zero

$$\dot{k} = \left(\frac{s_w}{n} - k^\dagger\right) n + r^\dagger k_c^\dagger(s_c - s_w) = 0, \text{ or}$$

$$r^\dagger = \frac{nk^\dagger - s_w}{(s_c - s_w)k_c^\dagger}, \quad \alpha^\dagger = \frac{r^\dagger k^\dagger}{y^\dagger} = \frac{nk^\dagger - s_w}{(s_c - s_w)} \frac{k^\dagger}{k_c^\dagger} \quad \ldots(26)$$

(ii) there will exist a golden age $(r^{\dagger\dagger}, \alpha^{\dagger\dagger})$

$$r^{\dagger\dagger} = \frac{n}{s_c}, \quad \alpha^{\dagger\dagger} = \frac{r^{\dagger\dagger}k^{\dagger}}{y^{\dagger}} = \frac{n}{s_c}k^{\dagger} \qquad \qquad \ldots(27)$$

with $(k_c^{\dagger\dagger}, k_w^{\dagger\dagger})$ satisfying (26) and (27) and

$$k_c^{\dagger\dagger} = \frac{nk^{\dagger} - s_w}{(s_c - s_w)r^{\dagger\dagger}} = \frac{(nk^{\dagger} - s_w)s_c}{(s_c - s_w)n}, \quad k_w^{\dagger\dagger} = k^{\dagger} - k_c^{\dagger\dagger} \qquad \ldots(27')$$

and such that

$$\lim_{t \to \infty} (k_c^{\dagger}, r^{\dagger}, \alpha^{\dagger}) = (k_c^{\dagger\dagger}, r^{\dagger\dagger}, \alpha^{\dagger\dagger}) \qquad \qquad \ldots(28)$$

no matter what the initial condition $k_c^{\dagger}$, provided it is large enough to satisfy (25') ensuring that $\alpha \leq 1$ in (26).

The proof of (i) follows directly from the indicated equation (5″). Its common-sense meaning is clear: by making r and α big enough or small enough, we generate more or less saving and for one critical level $r^{\dagger}$ and $\alpha^{\dagger}$ corresponding to the given capital ownership, we can make $\dot{K}/K$ exactly equal to n and $\dot{k} = 0$. Actually, from the first equation of (5), which gives $\dot{k}_c/k_c$ in terms of r, and from (26)'s equation for $r^{\dagger}$, we derive the following differential equation for $\dot{k}_c^{\dagger}$ in terms of $k_c^{\dagger}$ alone

$$\dot{k}_c^{\dagger} = \frac{nk^{\dagger} - s_w}{s_c - s_w} s_c - nk_c^{\dagger}. \qquad \qquad \ldots(29)$$

Equation (29) enables us to prove (ii) of the theorem. Evidently at $\dot{k}_c^{\dagger} = 0$, we get the unique stationary point, which can be labelled

$$k_c^{\dagger\dagger} = \frac{nk^{\dagger} - s_w}{s_c - s_w} \frac{s_c}{n}$$

as in (27'). Since the general solution to (29) can be written in the form

$$k_c^{\dagger}(t) = k_c^{\dagger\dagger} + (k_c^{\dagger}(0) - k_c^{\dagger\dagger})e^{-nt}$$

the fact that $n > 0$ ensures that $e^{-nt} \to 0$ and $k_c^{\dagger} \to k_c^{\dagger\dagger}$. Again the common sense of the proof is intuitive. If the division of $k^{\dagger}$ among capitalists and workers originally is lopsided in favour of the thrifty capitalists, $r^{\dagger}$ and $\alpha^{\dagger}$ will have to be initially low if excessive saving is to be avoided. But with $\alpha^{\dagger}$ so low, K_c grows at a lower rate than K_w, thereby tending to make $k_c^{\dagger}$ less lopsided than at the beginning. Thus, the correction continues until $k_c^{\dagger}$ has approached the critical $k_c^{\dagger\dagger}$ level at which $\dot{K}_c/K_c$ and $\dot{K}_w/K_w$, as well as $\dot{K}/K$, all grow at rate n.

All the above Kaldor-Pasinetti relations have a relevance, meaning, and definition only at the knife's-edge $k = k^{\dagger}$. For $k \neq k^{\dagger}$, they are vacuous. The marginal productivity theory of perfect competition is exactly the opposite: for $k \neq k^{\dagger}$, marginal productivities are well-defined—with capital redundant and $r = 0 = \alpha(k)$ if $k > k^{\dagger}$, and with labour redundant and $w = 0 = 1 - \alpha(k)$ if $k < k^{\dagger}$. But at the knife-edge $k = k^{\dagger}$ where the production function has a sharp edge or corner, marginal-productivity derivatives are undefined and the simple neoclassical theory becomes vacuous. We might therefore try to perform a marriage of complementary opposites, defining $\phi(k)$ by marginal productivity as 0 for $k > k^{\dagger}$ and as $1/k^{\dagger}$ for $k < k^{\dagger}$, but defining ϕ at $k^{\dagger}$ by the $r^{\dagger}$ formula of (26).

What makes the marriage of some interest is the fact that if $\phi(k)$ is defined away from $k^{\dagger}$ by the above marginal productivity relation, from any initial $k \neq k^{\dagger}$ the system will move to $k^{\dagger}$ in finite time regardless of how $\phi(k^{\dagger})$ itself is to be defined—a property previously lacking in the Kaldorian models. The proof is straightforward. Suppose $k > k^{\dagger}$ initially. Then $\alpha(k) = 0$ and s_w alone counts. Then always

$$\dot{K}/K = (s_w)Y/K < nk^{\dagger} \text{ Min } (1/k^{\dagger}, 1/k) = nk^{\dagger}/k < n$$

and hence $k \to k^{\dagger}$ from above. Now suppose $k < k^{\dagger}$ initially. Then $\alpha(k) = 1$ and

$$\dot{K}/K = (s_c)Y/K > (nk^{\dagger})\,\text{Min}\,(1/k^{\dagger}, 1/k) = n,$$

and hence $k \to k^{\dagger}$ from below.[1]

Once we are at $k^{\dagger}$, if $k_c^{\dagger}$ is not so small as to be incompatible with $\alpha^{\dagger} \leq 1$, and if r is put at (26)'s $r^{\dagger}$ level, our theorem guarantees an ultimate approach to the golden age of $r^{\dagger\dagger} = n/s_c$.

But we must hasten to add that whatever the value of the above model as an exercise, its economic relevance is in our view very dubious. Our scepticism applies to that portion of the path where $k \neq k^{\dagger}$ as well as to the Kaldor-Pasinetti regime. The 100 per cent share of capital that corresponds to $k < k^{\dagger}$ is as devoid of realism as is the assumption that L will continue to rise even at an imputed wage of zero. And the zero rate of return to capital associated with $k > k^{\dagger}$ poses equally formidable questions concerning the problem of maintaining adequate aggregate demand. Within the Kaldor-Pasinetti regime at $k = k^{\dagger}$, there arises in our view equally serious questions about the relevance of the model. For it is one thing to write down equations like (26) to exhibit the values of r and α for which k will remain at $k^{\dagger}$ but quite a different one *to exhibit the behavioural mechanism which will ensure that the actual distribution of income will be precisely that required by* (26). In our view none of the macroeconomic-distribution writers have thus far been able to provide a convincing formulation of the required mechanism.[2]

The perfectly competitive market gives supply and demand curves at $k = k^{\dagger}$ that are coincidental vertical lines over the range of wage share from 0 to 100 per cent of national income. If oligopoly elements are to be introduced, or national collective bargaining, a wide variety of outcomes are possible. A theory of the corporate state or of great good luck could arbitrarily posit that national bargaining results in a distribution which makes the weighted average of full-employment full-capacity thriftiness just enough to finance the widening of capital needed to match the natural rate of growth of the effective labour force. That would indeed be a theory of serendipity.[3] If one posits employers who make contracts to hire labour at fixed money wages in the short run and who earn profits as a short-run residual, one must decide what theory of price flexibility and price inflexibility is supposed to prevail in each run of time. The notion of a floating profit or interest rate r, which floats (in a fixed-coefficient model) as a result of flexible price/wage margins to produce just that distribution of income that will induce warranted-saving-growth-rates exactly equal to the system's natural rate of growth set by population and Harrod-neutral

---

[1] Will any other $\phi(k)$ function lead to $k \to k^{\dagger}$? Yes, there are many such functions that will suffice once (25) is satisfied with particular strength. But if (25) can hold with *any* strength or weakness of the inequalities, then only the competitive $\phi(k)$ can be counted on to lead *always* to $k \to k^{\dagger}$.

[2] One of us has presented a logically complete (but empirically bizarre) short-run Kaldorian full-employment model—the only logically complete model known to us that deduces full employment by a well-defined dynamic process—in R. Leckachman, *Keynes General Theory: Report of Three Decades* (Macmillan, London, 1964), final chapter by P. A. Samuelson, particularly the equations on p. 344. The present, long-run version of a Cambridge-like system was given by the latter at Berkeley in January 1964.

[3] " All this concerns the analysis of relative shares under conditions of full employment. But full employment is a postulate, not a result of the theory." (J. Robinson, *Collected Economic Papers*, Vol. II (Blackwell, Oxford, 1962), p. 157.) Historically, market economies like the U.S. and U.K. have not been uniformly at full employment. Their unemployment has oscillated, averaging out to where it has averaged out. But this is to say almost nothing. If one goes on to argue—as Marshall, Pigou and Dr Kaldor have occasionally argued—that average unemployment has been remarkably small and remarkably trendless, the question arises as to what one should mean by " small " and by " remarkable ". That hurdle somehow bypassed, how tempted is one to infer an efficacious full-employment mechanism operating within the system? And is it supposed to be classical price, money-wage, real-wage flexibility? Is it Pigou-Patinkin effects? Is it Tobin-Solow central-bank interest-rate flexibility? Is it New-Deal fiscal policy that negates or offsets fixed (s_c, s_w) coefficients? Is it God's grace? Or is it teleological shifts in the distribution of income between thrifty and thriftless that, in some run of time, assures a stylized performance of high employment with reasonable price stability? If you can believe the latter, you can—as the Duke of Wellington once said—believe anything.

technical change, cannot be left to depend on an Invisible Hand never seen on land or sea, in Timbuktu or in either Cambridge.[1]

We conclude, therefore, that the writers on macroeconomic theories of distribution have not succeeded in reconciling the relative smooth functioning of behaviour and of share imputation in observed economic systems with the properties to be expected from a fixed-coefficient model of technology. This conclusion only reinforces the scepticism generated by many other types of evidence about the adequacy of the fixed-coefficient model as a useful first approximation to modern technology. Within each process fixity of proportions may well be realistic, but there are thousands of different processes in any modern society. At worst the steps within which α is an indeterminate vertical locus are minute, being nothing like the 0 to 100 per cent of the fixed-coefficient model. In a realistic model, we suspect that relations like (27) above would only determine the higher decimal places of relative shares, a result of limited interest in view of the stochastic fluctuations of such shares anyway.[2]

XII. A NEOCLASSICAL KALDORIAN CASE

However, if one had the empirical hunch that the elasticity of substitution is *almost* zero about some critical level $k^\dagger$, we can approximate the Kaldor results by the following well-behaved neoclassical limiting sequence. Let $f(k)$ not have a corner at $k^\dagger$ but rather greater and greater $f''(k)$ curvature there, so that $f'(k)$ is well-defined but becomes very steep near $k^\dagger$. Then, for a wide range of n, the system will indeed settle down near $k^\dagger$ (as can be proved by our methods applied to well-behaved neoclassical systems) provided only that a restriction like (25) holds. If in Fig. 4 we draw the marginal curve of Fig. 2 as if it is is almost vertical near its intersection with n/s_c close to $k^\dagger$, then the long-run comparative statical properties of the system will be—to coin a phrase—almost-Kaldorian. That is $\alpha^\infty = (n/s_c)(k/y) \doteq (n/s_c)k^\dagger$. Because k/y changes little from $k^\dagger$, the elasticity of α with respect to s_c is almost -1, which is all that Kaldor's Widow's Cruse boils down to. Note also that this Kaldorian conclusion comes completely from marginal productivity relations, once (25) relations hold, there being no need for a genuine alternative theory of distribution! The stylized facts of mixed capitalism do not, alas, seem to us consonant with such violent induced changes in relative shares.

XIII. FINAL COMMENTS

We have shown that a one-sector neoclassical model with two classes of savers, a class who *forever* save a constant proportion s_c of their income that comes wholly from profits, and a class who *forever* save a constant proportion s_w of their income from wages

---

[1] Actually, in a heterogeneous capital model, where K stands for a vector of diverse capital goods and processes—alpha, beta, gamma . . . machines, inventories, etc.—there is no technically given $k^\dagger$ or aggregative capital-output ratio. Thus, in the artificial but instructive Surrogate capital model of P. A. Samuelson, " Parable and Realism in Capital Theory: The Surrogate Production Function," *Review of Economic Studies*, 29 (1962), 193-206, where an aggregative magnitude $J = K$ enters in the long-run production function $Y = F(J, L)$, there will be a different J/L that plays the role of $k^\dagger$ for each different range of long-run profit or interest rate—r or R. Except for indeterminacy in narrow ranges between the critical R levels at which one machine or another becomes optimal, the neoclassical equations stemming from (5) give a better approximation to the properties of this Neumann-Robinson-Sraffa-Dosso model than does the implicit theorizing of (26) and what follows in this present section.

In a competitive fixed-coefficient model, a relation like $f'(k^*) = n/s_c$ or $R(k^*) = n/s_c$ is lacking to permit us to solve for k^* and all the equilibrium values of the system. Formally, the missing equation $k^* = R^{-1}(n/s_c)$ is provided by setting long-run $k^* = k^\dagger$, the minimum technical capital-output (and, with our convention of setting $\lambda = 1$ in Min $(K/k^\dagger, L/\lambda)$, $k^\dagger$ is also the capital-labour ratio at full capacity).

We shall not here explore the possibility of a lagged-adjustment mechanism of α_k to its competitive $f'(k)$ level when $k = k^\dagger$ and to its $\alpha_k^\dagger$ serendipity level as defined earlier when $k = k^\dagger$. Call these norms $\alpha_k = N(k_c, k_w)$. Then $\dot{\alpha}_k = \beta[N(k_c, k_w) - \alpha_k]$ will, for proper positive time-constant β, generate together with (26) a sequence with the " Cambridge " property $\alpha(t) \to \alpha^{\dagger\dagger}$, as defined above.

[2] Refer back to footnote 1, p. 290.

and profits—will, if full-employment saving is always exactly matched by investment, approach a golden-age equilibrium state of exponential growth at n, the natural rate of population growth (augmented by Harrod-neutral technical change).[1]   We have also shown that this result can be generalized to some non-neoclassical models.   Provided the profit rate is a single-valued, declining function of the capital/labour ratio (and even if competitive imputations of marginal productivity do not define this function), there also exists a stable golden age.[2]   And we have deduced, on the basis of the special inequalities and equalities posited by Kaldorian distribution theory, the asymptotic stability of the minimum technical ratio of the value of capital to output in one particular fixed coefficient

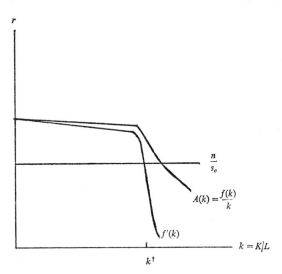

FIGURE 4

A smooth neoclassical model, with low elasticity of substitution near $k^\dagger$, yields marginal-productivity distribution of income that mimics the Cambridge behaviour equations—as e.g. that a rise in capitalists' consumption propensities soon leads to a permanent rise in their profit share.   Hence, such theories are not necessarily " alternatives " to neoclassical theories, even if their empirical presuppositions are realistic.

model.   But no one yet seems to have been able to provide a mechanism from which one can *deduce* a determinate theory of distribution at this critical configuration.   If, however, it is arbitrarily postulated that the distribution of income there will somehow become precisely such as to keep total capital growing in balance with labour, we have proved the stability of the asymptotic Pasinetti state with its unique distribution of income.

Our analysis confirms the beautiful asymptotic theorem of Dr Pasinetti for a limited range where s_w/s_c is small enough.   And it provides a completely symmetrical Dual theorem —where average-product-of-capital $= n/s_w$ replaces his net-yield-of-capital $= n/s_c$, etc.— for the (empirically quite interesting) range where s_w/s_c is greater than $\alpha(k^*)$, profits' share in national income.   We have demonstrated that the applicability of either of these regimes depends on $s_w \gtreqless \alpha^\infty s_c$ (where α^∞ is the golden-age share of profits, by whatever theory determined), a criterion that has nought [3] to do with the issue of whether smooth neo-

---

[1] The qualification concerning a Pasinetti limit cycle of Section 6 is in order here.

[2] When r does not, for some K/L, run the full gamut from infinity to zero, the Appendix shows that the only asymptotic states may involve $k \to 0$, or $r \to$ minimum r with k perhaps going to infinity.   These " pathological states " are shown to be also stable.

[3] Recall, though, last section's demonstration that the Kaldorian distribution theory does presuppose the restriction $s_w < nk^\dagger < s_c$, which *a fortiori* puts us in the Pasinetti regime $s_w < \alpha^\infty s_c \leqq s_c$.

classical or fixed-coefficient neo-neoclassical technologies are involved, or of whether imperfect competition modifies competitive marginal productivities.[1] Dr Pasinetti's results and our extensions of them have a generality that can encompass valid theories in Cambridge, Massachusetts, Cambridge, Wisconsin, or any other Cambridge. On the other hand, we have pointed out some of the real problems created if only a single fixed-coefficient technology (or narrow spectrum of technologies) is assumed.

Many realistic complications ought to be added to our analysis: the introduction of uncertainty, for example, and of heterogeneous capital-goods activities of the modern programming or Sraffa type. Some of these complications are quite easily handled by modern methods. Some offer intrinsic difficulties.

But quite aside from such modification of the model, we feel it necessary to conclude with a warning about the extremely unrealistic nature of some of our crucial assumptions. Our warning is not merely directed against oversimplifications, like exponential growth of the equivalent labour force, that are unlikely to be literally true. With a grain of salt, we cheerfully make such heroic abstractions as a first approximation—making sure to determine later whether the results depend critically upon the *exactitude* of the abstract axioms.

We are much more uneasy with the assumption of " permanent " classes of pure-profit and mixed-income receivers with given and unchanging saving propensities on which all of our theorems—Pasinetti's as well as ours—depend critically. This assumption completely disregards the life cycle and its effect on saving and working behaviour. In the first place with a large portion of saving known to occur in some phases of the life cycle in order to finance dissaving in other phases, it is unrealistic to posit values for (s_c, s_w) which are independent of n.[2] This shortcoming is probably not too serious and could be handled without changing our results drastically.

But the assumptions of *permanent* classes of income receivers raise much more serious questions. Even if we wave aside the difficulty of identifying a class whose sole source of income is income from capital, there is no reason to suppose that a person who belongs to that class at some point of his life must have always belonged to it and will continue to do so indefinitely. In a modern industrial society the capitalist's class is not a hereditary caste: its membership at any point of time is far from limited to people who were born into it by virtue of inherited wealth. This becomes especially clear when we recall that by our definition, the capitalist class would include retired households living off their capital. But even the assumption that class membership and saving propensity do not change during one person's lifetime is not enough for our purposes. Since people do not live forever, one would have to extend the asumption to one's heirs, and their heirs, and so on, until Kingdom-come—both before golden ages are reached and forever afterwards. For, the moment that one admits transfers of wealth between classes, either through living persons switching class membership or by virtue of death, *it is no longer true that $\dot{K}_c$ and $\dot{K}_w$ are equal to the rate of saving of the respective classes* and therefore differential equations of the type (3) that we and Dr Pasinetti have postulated are no longer satisfied. That being the case, simple experiments will show that results quite different from our nice theorems can result.

---

[1] Even without our $\phi(k)$ function, a necessary criterion for a Pasinetti regime is $s_w < \alpha^* s_c$ and a necessary criterion for an anti-Pasinetti regime is $s_w \geq \alpha^{**} s_c$. If $\phi(k)$ is posited, with $\phi'(k) < 0$, these are equivalent and only one regime is possible. Actually, this same conclusion would follow if r were a monotone-decreasing function of the value of capital (measured in consumption goods). If no restrictions on r are placed, one can encounter alternate Pasinetti and Dual golden ages, some of which might be locally stable.

[2] See e.g., Modigliani, " The Life Cycle Hypothesis of Saving," paper presented at the First International Meeting of the Econometric Society, Rome, Italy, September 1965 (mimeo); and " The Life Cycle Hypothesis of Saving, the Demand for Wealth and the Supply of Capital," *Social Research*, 33 (1966), 160-217; and the bibliography cited therein. Cf. also the following important contribution, which has appeared since that bibliography was completed: J. E. Meade, " Life-Cycle Savings, Inheritance, and Economic Growth," *Review of Economic Studies* 33 (1966), 61-78.

Therefore, we conclude with the caution: Beware.

Massachusetts Institute of Technology

PAUL A. SAMUELSON, FRANCO MODIGLIANI.

APPENDIX: PATHOLOGICAL CASES OF DIVERGENCE

In this Appendix we analyze certain " pathological " cases which keep coming up in the literature and seem nowhere to have been treated comprehensively. The two different pathologies refer to the cases where $k \to 0$ and where $k \to \infty$, cases which were excluded by our assumptions in footnote 3, p. 269. We now relax those assumptions.

First, consider the case of what can happen when $k = K/L \to 0$. If average product of capital $A(k)$ and marginal product $f'(k)$ both approach infinity as $k \to 0$, as is suggested by Fig. 2's curves, our general theorem needs no modifications. The horizontal lines of Fig. 2 do intersect the relevant curves and $k \to k^\infty > 0$.

But if one or both of these approach a finite level as $k \to 0$, as in the accompanying Fig. 5 redrawing of Fig. 2, then for n large enough (or both saving propensies small enough), the Pasinetti equation $f'(k^*) = n/s_c$ will have no root at all and will become an inequality. (The n/s_c horizontal now lies above the marginal curve everywhere.) If s_w is positive and $A(k) \to A(0) = \infty$, no modification of our theorems is required: for even if $n/s_c > \text{Max } r = r_m$, $A(k^{**}) = n/s_w$ can still be satisfied for $k^{**} > 0$; the n/s_w horizontal intersects the average curve in Fig. 5, and *all* the conclusions of our Dual theorem become fully applicable. (The case where $s_w = 0$ can best be handled as a footnote to the next paragraph's case.)

Suppose now that as $k \to 0$, $A(k) \to \text{Max } A = A(0) = A_m < \infty$. Then necessarily from the familiar relationship of identical finite intercepts for marginal and average curves, $r = f'(k) \to f(0) = r_m = A_m$. With n sufficiently small compared to $\text{Max } (s_c, s_w)$ no modification in our theorems are needed, since $k \to 0$ will not then occur. But when n becomes sufficiently large, neither equation $f'(k^*) = n/s_c$ or $A(k^{**}) = n/s_w$ can be satisfied; both horizontals in Fig. 5 will now be above the average and marginal curves; and then, of course, $\dot{k}$ is always negative and pushes k back to zero. The common sense reason for this is plain. If effective L now grows very fast (and/or if saving propensities are very low), the system will not be able to have enough capital formation to widen capital in balance with effective labour. The amount of capital per efficiency unit of labour steadily retrogresses, as we shall see, sometimes with dire Malthusian consequences for the hourly wage rate. Let us consider in detail the different cases.

(i) $n > \text{Max } (s_c, s_w) A_m < \infty$. Then (3) and (5) imply

$$(k_c, k_w, k, y; \ r, A, \alpha, w) = (0, 0, 0, 0; \ A_m, A_m, 1, 0)$$

$$\lim_{t \to \infty} \left\{ \left[\frac{\dot{K}_c}{K_c}, \frac{\dot{K}_w}{K_w}, \frac{\dot{K}}{K}, \frac{\dot{Y}}{Y} \right] = A_m \left[s_c, s_w, \text{Max } (s_c, s_w), \text{Max } (s_c, s_w) \right] \right.$$

$$\frac{K_c}{K} \to 1 \text{ if } s_c > s_w; \ \frac{K_w}{K} \to 1 \text{ if } s_w > s_c;$$

If $s_w = s_c$, $\left[\dfrac{K_c}{K}, \dfrac{K_w}{K} \right]$ are indeterminate, being dependent on initial conditions.

(ii) $n = \text{Max } (s_c, s_w) A_m < \infty$, and one of the horizontals intersects the curves at the A_m intercept level itself.

The same conclusions hold as above, unless $A(k) = A_m$ holds for all k in the range $0 \leq k \leq b > 0$. In that case k^∞ ends in that range rather than necessarily at zero, just where being dependent on initial conditions; if also $s_c = s_w$, the allocation of k^∞ between (k_c^∞, k_w^∞) will also depend on initial conditions. (If any $K \equiv 0$, $\dot{K}/K = 0/0$ and by harmless convention can be made to agree with all statements made.)

Since no modifications are needed when $n < \text{Max}\,(s_w, s_c)A_m$, we can complete our discussion of the pathology where $k \to 0$ with a final observation. The fact that income per efficiency unit, Y/L, goes to zero in the limit does not necessarily mean that genuine

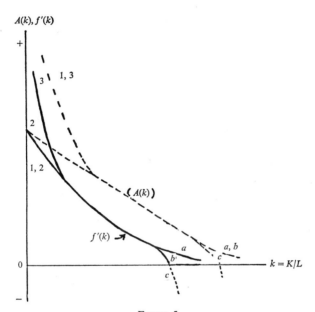

FIGURE 5

Branches 1, 2 and 3 represent variant pathologies as $k \to 0$; branches a, b, c and d (not shown) refer to the case where $k \to \infty$.

per capita income goes to zero. Capital may fail to widen relative to the enhanced supply of effective labour generated by the Harrod-neutral technical change coefficient n'', while still being capable of keeping up with the n' rate of demographic change. The condition for $K(t)$ to grow faster than the work force, $L_0 e^{n''t}$—even though $n > \text{Max}\,(s_w, s_c)A_m k \to 0$— turns out to be $s_w A_m > n' = n - n''$. If this is the case, the economy is becoming more prosperous on a true *per capita* basis even though $k \to 0$.

If capital is not growing as fast as the natural labour force, it is a foregone conclusion that the ultimately zero wage per efficiency unit must also imply an ultimately zero wage rate per natural unit of labour. But, what happens when $n' < s_w A_m$ and K does grow faster than natural L? There is then the possibility that the wage rate per natural unit of labour might rise toward infinity even though the wage rate per efficiency unit of labour goes to zero. Indeed one might at first intuition conjecture that this has to happen. But that would be a wrong guess. The stability analysis of (14) and (16) shows that $K(t)$ grows asymptotically like $e^{s_w A_m t}$, that $k(t)$ shrinks asymptotically like $e^{-(n - s_w A_m)t}$, and (surprise!) that $w(t)$ shrinks like $[k(t)]^2$ or like $e^{-2(n - s_w A_m)t}$ (this because at $k = 0$ the slope of w as a function of k turns out to be zero). Consequently the condition that the wage per natural L rise is that $w(t)e^{n''t} = e^{(n'' - 2n + 2s_w A_m)t}$ have positive exponent, giving us in the end the

217

criterion $n''/2 \gtreqless s_w A_m - n'$ for the wage per natural worker to rise, stay the same or fall. The fact that for a sufficiently high rate of Harrod neutral technical change n'', the $>$ sign would hold in the above condition, may help to make logical sense of the Marxian foreboding of a progressive immiseration of the working class due to technical change rather than due to Malthusian biology. It should be noted that, in the case under consideration, so-called Harrod *neutral* technical change is actually *labour saving* in the Hicksian sense. It is a general truth that Harrod neutral technical change is Hicksian labour saving if the elasticity of substitution is less than one, and this elasticity is assuredly less than one in the neighbourhood where the average and the marginal product of capital approach a common finite intercept. Note also that what would be needed to help cure this Marxian kind of poverty—should it ever come about—is *more* rather than less effective thrift!

The possibility that K/L goes to infinity can now be analyzed. Suppose $n = 0$ and Min $(s_w, s_c) > 0$. Then it is obvious that positive saving and investment will go on indefinitely, and that K and k will grow indefinitely. Diminishing returns implies that the interest rate will go to its minimum r_M. (The right hand of Fig. 5 shows with branches a, b and c the possible patterns of r_M.) If some positive labour is needed for positive output, the minimum interest rate cannot be positive. If capital never has a negative productivity, $r_M = 0$. However, it is easy to imagine production processes where $f'(k) = 0$ for a finite k^*; on branch c, further k produces a positive gross quasi-rent, but not one large enough to equal depreciation, and hence produces a negative $f'(k)$. In this case, income drops with further k, until finally $A(k) = 0$ has a finite root k^{**} on its c branch. So long as $s_w > 0$, the system will end up in the Dual k^{**} equilibrium, with

$$k_c^\infty / k_w^\infty = 0, \quad \dot{K}/K = \dot{K}_w/K_w \to 0, \quad \text{and} \quad r \to f'(k^{**}) < 0:$$

the workers ultimately make profit losses equal to their saving, and enjoy less consumption than they get when $s_w = 0$. For with $n = 0$, $s_c > 0 = s_w$, we end in the Pasinetti state k^*, with $r \to 0$, wages $\to 100$ per cent $y = 100$ per cent maximum Golden Rule y.

If $f'(k) > 0$ for $k < k^*$ but $f'(k) \equiv 0$ for $k > k^*$, $A(k)$ is always positive and for $n = 0 < s_w$, $k > 0$ forever. However, $\dot{K}/K = \dot{K}_w/K_w \to 0$, $r \to 0$, $K_c/K \to 0$, and $w \to$ Max w. We are in the Dual regime, but with $k^{**} = \infty$, so to speak. (If $s_w = 0 = s_c = n$, there is never anything to talk about: the system stays forever at initial (k, r, w) configuration. If $n = 0 = s_w < s_c$, we are back to the previous Pasinetti case whether or not $f'(k) < 0$ beyond k^*.)

We are left now with the case where $f'(k) > 0$ forever, and *a fortiori* $A(k) > f'(k) > 0$. If $f'(k) \to 0$ as $k \to \infty$, as on branch a, there are still two possibilities: $f(k) \to f(\infty) < \infty$, implying that $\alpha(k) \to \alpha(\infty) = 0$ (just as in the case where $f'(k^*) = 0$ for finite k^*). Again, if $s_w > 0$ at all, the Dual regime dominates with all that this implies. If $s_w = 0 < s_c$, the system approaches the infinite Pasinetti state, $k^* = \infty$, with $k_c/k \to 1$.

The second possibility is where $f(k) \to f(\infty) = \infty$. If $f'(k)/A(k) = \alpha(k)$ should approach a definite limit (and it need not), we are in the infinite Pasinetti or infinite Dual regime depending on whether $s_w \lesseqgtr \alpha(\infty) s_c$, just as in the finite case. In the Dual case, $k_c/k_w \to 0$ as usual. In the Pasinetti case, $k_c/k_w \to k_c^*/k_w^* > 0$, whose value can be computed by the happy circumstance that in the last equation of (6), the ratio k_c^*/k_w^* proves to be independent of n (except for n's influence on k^*, of course): it is given by $[s_c \alpha(k^*) - s_w]/s_w[1 - \alpha(k^*)]$, where here we take $\alpha(k^*) = \alpha(\infty)$. Paradoxically, although $(\dot{K}_c/K_c, \dot{K}_w/K_w) \to (0, 0)$, $[(\dot{K}_c/K_c)/(\dot{K}_w/K_w)] \to 0/0 = 1$! The stability of these limits follows from our differential equations: it can be checked by working out the Cobb-Douglas case, since $\alpha(k) \to \alpha(\infty)$, a definite limit, implies that the production function can be regarded as *asymptotically* Cobb-Douglas.

We are left with the v. Neumann case where zero (exogenous) labour is compatible with positive production, and where Min $r = r_M = A_M > 0$. (To keep the diagram from becoming too cluttered, we do not show this case on Fig. 5; but an example would be $f(k) = r_M k + ak$.) Now $\alpha(\infty) = 1$, and $[\dot{k}_c/k_c, \dot{k}_w/k_w, \dot{k}/k] \to r_M[s_c, s_w, \text{Max } (s_c, s_w)] > n$.

This all holds as much for small positive n as for zero n. With $\alpha(\infty) = 1$ necessarily, ratio $k_w/k_c \to 0$ whenever $s_c > s_w$, as is shown by the above formulas or by the general formula of the previous paragraph.

Whereas this v. Neumann case may be empirically uninteresting, it duplicates the complexity of the possible case of population decline, where $n < 0$. Here again $k \to \infty$, whenever algebraic $n < r_M$.

We have not given the detailed, but straightforward, stability analysis underlying the many assertions of this technical section. A pathological example that embodies the branch 1 and the v. Neumann case, is given by $F(K, L) = \bar{r}K + \bar{w}L$. Here the fate of capitalists is independent of labour, $r(t) \equiv \bar{r}$, and $K(t) \equiv K(t_0) \exp(\bar{r}s_c)t$: for $n/s_c < \bar{r}$, $k_c \to \infty$; for $n/s_c = \bar{r}$, k_c stays at its initial value. If $s_w > s_c$, $K_c/K_w \to 0$. In every case, K itself grows at the fastest of the rates $(n, s_c\bar{r}, s_w\bar{r})$, so that $k \to 0$ is impossible. If $s_w < n/\bar{r} < s_c$, $K_w/K_c \to 0$, in agreement with (6)'s last equation because then $\alpha(\infty) = 1$.

PRINTED IN GREAT BRITAIN BY OLIVER AND BOYD LTD., EDINBURGH

P. A. SAMUELSON AND F. MODIGLIANI

REPLY TO PASINETTI AND ROBINSON [1]

1. We must begin by recording our dismay that our long paper should end up appearing to Dr Pasinetti as primarily apologetics for a specific theory—the neo-classical theory of marginal productivity. We trust other readers will conclude otherwise.

It is true that we have succeeded in working out exhaustively, for the general neo-classical one-sector technology, the dynamic and statical implications of the Pasinetti hypothesis about different rates of saving out of pure-profit income and other incomes; thus, what Solow did a decade ago for the Harrod-Domar model, we have done definitively for the Pasinetti model, freeing our analysis from the earlier Cobb-Douglas assumptions of Meade and deriving stability conditions for the golden-age equilibria that are more definite than one ordinarily encounters in a model of this complexity. Just as Solow's earlier work called for subsequent extension to two-or-more-sector canonical models— by Uzawa, Solow, Inada, Findlay, Drandakis, Burmeister, and many others—so does our one-sector model of Pasinetti saving invite subsequent extensions to such technologies.

No apologies are needed then for the detail of our investigation. Furthermore, even those more critical of the degree of empirical relevance of the neoclassical notions than we are, might be expected to welcome our elucidation of just how neoclassical notions fit in with Pasinetti's earlier analysis, a task which he had only lightly touched upon (and in a set of equations blemished by a mathematical error). " Know thy enemy " is good advice for anyone, for to understand the full implications of a theory is to begin to understand its limitations.

2. None the less the major motivation for undertaking the paper was something quite different. It stemmed from our original perception that the Pasinetti golden-age equilibrium, instead of being *the general one*, had to be recognised as but one of two golden-age equilibria, being matched so-to-speak by what we called the Dual or Anti-Pasinetti equilibrium. (More neutral terminology would be Primal and Dual equilibria, a distinction that has essentially naught to do with the somewhat unfortunate earlier Meade terminology of neo-Keynesian and neo-classical.)

As is the usual case for duality relations, there is complete symmetry between the Primal and Dual equilibria. *Neither is more general than the other*. This symmetry Dr. Pasinetti once more denies. He continues to regard his golden-age equilibrium as the more general one, being in some special sense relevant independently of marginal productivity assumptions, of so-called well-behaved functional relationships between profit rates and capital-output ratios and so forth.

Let no reader misunderstand. We claim that the truth is made up of its two halves. The Dual golden-age regime is every bit as general as the Primal Pasinetti golden age: its existence has nothing to do with well-behaved marginal productivities or with one-directional functional relationships between interest rates, capital-output ratios, or other magnitudes.

Readers who have followed these discussions—read the 1962 Pasinetti article, the 1963 Meade paper and 1964 Pasinetti reply, the 1965 Meade-Hahn paper and the resulting 1966 interchange between Meade and Pasinetti, and our present paper—will, we think, sense which way the wind is blowing. But there does remain one constructive task for this reply, namely to demonstrate that the symmetry of generality between the Dual and Primal regimes does definitely hold for any *multiple-blue-print technology* of the kind that Professor Joan Robinson and MIT programmers think useful to analyze. This should

---

[1] Unfortunately, Kaldor's paper reached us too late for comment.

establish once and for all that symmetry does not depend on any simple diminishing returns assumptions of neo-classical type. The important thing is for the reader to understand the reasoning upon which the symmetry of the two regimes is based.

In providing this constructive demonstration, we shall also be able to isolate that *special* technological case, which if one believed it to be realistic, would provide considerable justification for concentrating on the Pasinetti regime to the exclusion of the Dual on the ground that the Dual regime is in the nature of a knife-edge solution. (And, dually, we shall be able to isolate that special technological case which makes the Pasinetti regime a rare and fortuitous occurrence of knife-edge type.)

Here we shall be examining only the question of *existence* of golden-age equilibrium, omitting completely all discussions of stability and instability and all consideration of the dynamic transient behaviour of the system when not in a golden age.

3. For simplicity assume a single consumption good (either simple or a composite market basket). Assume a finite number, large or small, of different blue-print pages, each corresponding to a different activity or capital process, calling different machines alpha, beta, gamma, ... in the usual Robinson fashion. As is well known, each profit or interest rate excludes many pages of the blue prints as not being competitively viable, leaving one or more sets of activities that can be viable at the given golden-age profit rate. We stress that nothing " well-behaved " is assumed about the technology other than that the factor-price frontier relating the real wage and the profit rate must be downward sloping. This frontier may have changing curvatures and along it there may be reswitching effects of the Cohen-Sraffa type, shifts toward lower capital-output ratios as the profit rate falls, and any kind of Wicksell effects. No singular equal-factor-intensity assumptions are made that might validate any surrogate capital concepts. In short, we shall demonstrate the symmetry of the two regimes where nothing faintly neo-classical is assumed about the technology.

Now assume a natural rate of growth of labour that is positive, say $n = 0 \cdot 04$ per year (for simplicity of exposition ignoring Harrod-neutral technical change). What golden-age configurations can prevail for this natural rate of growth, n, at each profit rate r? Clearly only competitively viable activities, and with a mix among the consumption and viable-machine sectors that provides for balanced growth at rate n of *all* physical inputs and stocks. Thus, for fixed n and each r, there will emerge an admissible configuration of processes and price ratios (it being understood that essential joint products like mutton and wool, which require demand conditions, are ruled out): hence, and this is what matters here, there will be for given n an admissible set of capital values and ratios of aggregate capital value to value of output, which could be plotted against the profit rates. It is slightly more convenient to work with the reciprocal of the aggregate capital-output ratio, which is the so-called average product of capital, A or $A(r; n)$: this is a percentage per annum, but is now quite divorced from any physical capital of jelly or surrogate type, being merely the ratio of value of total market stocks of capital to value of total output (both being expressed in *any* common *numeraire* unit).

4. Fig. 1 plots, for fixed positive n, all the various average products of capital (i.e. reciprocals of the capital-output ratios) that go with each rate of interest. The AZ locus thus indicates the $A(r; n)$ functional correspondence for a general blue-print technology. We have made it as " pathological " and " ill-behaved " as we could think of: for example, the locus is not single-valued, having instead vertical stretches inevitably at switch points, like RS where one finds blends of the equally-viable R and S techniques; moreover, between switch points we have not required the locus to be a rising one—as in the neo-classical parables where a lower interest rate had always to be associated with a higher capital-output ratio—but instead show the system moving to the lower capital-output ratio of R from that of S as the interest rate falls; and furthermore, on each side of the RS vertical segment, we show the curve as a falling one as a result of perfectly admissible

Wicksell effects; nor finally do we exclude any number of reswitching effects of the Cohen-*curiosum* type. (All this is in contrast with the Solow-Clark one-sector model involving neo-classical surrogate capital and smooth productivities, in which the *AZ* locus would be a simple ever-rising one.[1]) Furthermore, a change in *n* will shift the whole *AZ* locus, since the new weighting of the consumption and investment sectors would change capital-output ratios and factor shares in the absence of any special " equal factor-intensity " assumptions.

In Fig. 1 the 45° line represents points where the interest rate and average product of capital are equal, leaving no return at all for labour: thus it is the locus of capital

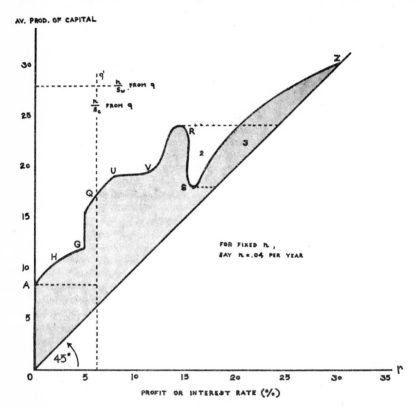

FIGURE 1

AZ is the locus of Average Products corresponding to each profit rate, where *n* has been fixed. At any point, like *Q*, the reciprocal of the slope of a ray from the origin to it measures capital's relative share, α_K: since labour's share cannot be negative, only the area above the 45° line is relevant. At *A* where $r = 0$, labour gets all; at the point of maximum interest rate *Z*, capital gets all. Vertical segments, like *RS* represent switch points; other segments where the locus slopes downward represent so-called perverse Wicksell effects and other admissible phenomena not found in one-sector well-behaved neoclassical models.

---

[1] In these neoclassical cases, $r = f'(k)$, $f'' < 0$. If the elasticity of substitution, σ, is always 1, the Cobb-Douglas case, *AZ* is a straight line through the origin with slope greater than one; for the CES function with σ a constant below unity, it is a convex curve going out from the origin and arching above the 45° line until it hits that line at the maximum *r*; if σ is a constant above unity, *AZ* begins at a point on the 45° line, accelerating above the line toward infinity like a parabola; for $\sigma = \infty$, *AZ* is a vertical curve above the 45° line; for $\sigma = 0$, *AZ* is a horizontal curve from the vertical axis to the 45° line; if $f'(k)$ is asymptotic to both axes, with σ passing through unity, *AZ* rises out from the origin but not necessarily with fixed curvature.

share equal to unity, or $\alpha_k = 1$. At any point on the locus, capital's share α_k is read off as the reciprocal of the slope of a ray out from the origin to the point on AZ, by virtue of the arithmetical relations,

$$\alpha_k = r/A = (\text{profit/capital})/(\text{output/capital}) = \text{profit/output}.$$

Since wages can never be negative, we never have use for the part of the diagram below the 45° line.[1]

Thus far all has been technology and competitive cost minimization. Fig. 2 now introduces saving behaviour of the Pasinetti type. On the horizontal axis is plotted s_c, the fraction of profit permanently saved by those who earn only profit; on the vertical axis is s_w, the fraction of income of whatever sort permanently saved by those who work *and* own capital from previous accumulation. From any point on Fig. 2, like q with its specified (s_c, s_w) values, and with n given, our task is to go back to Fig. 1 and find the corresponding golden-age equilibrium point or points. It is our contention that this can be done for a general blue-print technology; and when it is done, we find that there are two symmetrical regions, the one marked Dual and the one marked Pasinetti in Fig. 2.[2]

Let us review the requirement for golden-age equilibrium that *any* technical model must satisfy once n and (s_c, s_w) are specified. An (r, A) point on AZ of Fig. 1 can be a golden-age solution (r^∞, A^∞) if and only if it satisfies the following four conditions:

(i) It must be on the AZ locus $A(r; n)$, or $A^\infty = A(r^\infty, n)$, to be competitively viable

(ii) $r^\infty \leq n/s_c$, so that K_c does not grow faster than L

(iii) $A^\infty \leq n/s_w$, so that K_w does not grow faster than L

(iv) At least one of (ii) and (iii) must hold as an equality, or $(r^\infty - n/s_c)(A^\infty - n/s_w) = 0$, so that K grows as fast as L.

Note that (i)-(iv) hold for *any* technology.

There are two regimes satifying (i)-(iv), Pasinetti and Dual.

Pasinetti:

$$r^\infty = r^* = n/s_c$$

$$A^\infty = A(r^*; \ n) < n/s_w, \text{ or } s_w < \frac{r^x}{A^\infty} s_c = \alpha(r^*; \ n)s_c.$$

Dual:

$$A^\infty = A^{**} = n/s_w$$

$$r^\infty = r^{**} < n/s_c, \text{ or } s_w > \frac{r^\infty}{A^\infty} s_c = \alpha(r^{**}; \ n)s_c.$$

Of course, there is the borderline knife-edge where

$$r^\infty = r^* = r^{**} = n/s_c \text{ and } A^\infty = A^{**} = A^* = n/s_w$$

and we are simultaneously in both regimes, but with $(k_c/k)^\infty = 0$.

After this review, we can relate Figs. 2 and 1. To demonstrate all this, first concentrate on a point like q in Fig. 2, which represents high rentier thrift relative to worker

---

[1] The vertical axis below A is shown as part of the boundary in Fig. 1, which is debatable in that it assumes that capital goods representing excess capacity can be accumulated viably at a zero interest rate (perhaps being costlessly stored). If capital goods are subject to exponential depreciation independently of use and storage methods—say at a rate of 5 per cent per year—AZ would have to be extrapolated into the second quadrant of negative interest rates, with a vertical line down to the axis stemming from the -0.05 terminus. If money is costlessly storable and prices are not rising at a 5 per cent or greater annual rate, it might be impossible to effectuate such a negative real interest rate. When we come to discuss regions of possible " oversaving ", issues of effective demand and liquidity traps will depend upon which of the various assumptions concerning A's position is made.

[2] When the mapping is done properly, one recognises that the shaded area in Fig. 1 corresponds in a certain definite sense to the shaded Dual area in Fig. 2, and likewise for the unshaded Pasinetti regions.

thrift. In Fig. 1, Q will turn out to be the only equilibrium corresponding to q of Fig. 2, and will represent Pasinetti equilibrium. Why? Because on Fig. 1 we locate q's vertical n/s_c line and its horizontal n/s_w line: these intersect in the q' image-point on Fig. 1 corresponding to q of Fig. 2. Our equilibrium conditions above tell us we must end up either due south of the image-point q' or due west of it; and only Q on AZ, south of q', can be found to meet these conditions. Because we are on the n/s_c vertical, we are assuredly in

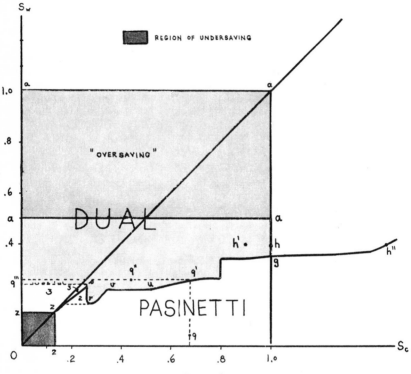

FIGURE 2

The boundary $zsrvuq'gh''$ divides the whole region of saving coefficients into the Dual equilibrium region and the Pasinetti or primal equilibrium region. This boundary provides our $s_w \gtreqless \alpha_x^* s_c$ criterion, and is given by an exact mapping of Fig. 1's AZ locus into Fig. 2's variables, after taking into account the division into n of the saving coefficients. Directions are reversed because of this reciprocation, up becoming down and left right, but vertical and horizontal segments and direction reversals correspond exactly. If saving coefficients are so low that capital cannot keep up with labour growth, we are in the undersaving region of the southwest. (If s_w becomes so large as to produce excess capacity and zero profit rate, we are in the "oversaving" region of the north with possible effective demand and liquidity-trap problems. The small regions marked with 3's and 2's represent positions of multiple equilibria, resulting from the waviness of AZ.)

Pasinetti equilibrium. The n/s_w horizontal line of our original q would intersect the AZ locus at an irrelevantly higher interest rate, and hence the dual equilibrium just cannot occur for the (s_c, s_w) values given by Fig. 2's q.

What is true for q is true for any other point on Fig. 2, on the vertical line through q, up to the boundary point q'. For all such points we are on the same vertical n/s_c going through Q, with the competing horizontal n/s_w irrelevantly higher than Q. And now we recognize why q' does indeed represent the boundary point on the border between the Primal and Dual equilibria. By definition, q' is that point which has as its image point a point on the AZ locus itself (namely Q): both its vertical n/s_c and horizontal n/s_w lines are fully relevant and hence both Dual and Pasinetti equilibrium criteria are simultaneously satisfied.

Now we can show how a Dual equilibrium point is determined. Consider in Fig. 2 the point q'', which is due west of the boundary point q'. If we plot its n/s_w horizontal, that will of course go through Q in Fig. 1 because its q'' is at q's latitude. But because its s_c is smaller than that of q', its vertical n/s_c will be east (east, not west) of Q, corresponding to a still higher interest rate. Now it is the vertical which is irrelevant, and so q'' does go over into Q — but now with a Dual equilibrium. Similarly every point due west of q' gives rise to the same Dual equilibrium at Q, as the reader should verify.[1]

It should be clear that the $zsrvuq'gh;$ boundary in Fig. 2 corresponds in precise detail to the AZ locus in Fig. 1, the only difference being that the reciprocals of the variables are taken and scale changes are made corresponding to the growth rate n. If we had plotted the capital-output ratio and the reciprocal of r (i.e. the " number of years purchase ") in Fig. 1, the diagrams would have been exactly the same except for scale factor n. If both figures had been plotted on double-log paper, one locus would simply be the upside-down reversed image of the other. The equation of Fig. 2's boundary is simply given in terms of 1's $A(r; n)$, in accordance with our general criterion:

$$s_w = \alpha_K(r; \ n)s_c = \frac{r}{A(r; n)} s_c = \alpha_K(n/s_c; \ n)s_c.$$

This last expression was called $\alpha_K^* s_c$ in our paper.

We must warn against a possible, but quite unnecessary confusion. In Fig. 2 one can be at any point whatsoever; in Fig. 1, one is at equilibrium only on the AZ locus. When you are at any point in the Pasinetti region of Fig. 1, s_w is deduced to be less than the golden-age I/Y ratio. When one is at any point in the Dual region, s_w is deduced to be equal (yes, equal) to the golden-age I/Y ratio. Dr Pasinetti has misunderstood the mathematics of our paper and of this reply if he thinks that s_w is kept from ever exceeding the golden-age I/Y ratio by some neo-classical regularity assumption on our part. Here we make no such regularity assumption, and yet s_w greater than golden-age I/Y is quite impossible. It is quite impossible from the nature of golden-age equilibrium under Pasinetti's own saving hypothesis. Remember that the workers save from two sources —from wages as well as from the same profits source that rentiers save from; and if workers saved a larger fraction than the whole community saves, that would imply the ultimate (relative) extinction of the rentier class and a self-contradiction in the form of the whole's saving more than itself saves!

There remains a need to explain the square region of undersaving $Ozzz$ in Fig. 2. For very small saving propensities, relative to the need to widen capital to keep up with labour growth, the system will be unable to come into balanced growth, instead approaching the maximum interest rate as shown at Z. This may happen with either regime dominant depending upon the relative sizes of s_c and s_w. (We have discussed such matters in our Appendix.)

Perhaps more interesting is the $aaaa$ region of " oversaving " in Fig. 2. If there is a minimum capital-output ratio beyond which capital goods become redundant, too high

---

[1] The reader can test his comprehension by examining the golden-rule golden age configuration shown at G in Fig. 1. Here the interest and growth rates are equal, $n = r$ (both being equal to 4 per cent per annum) In Fig. 2 the point g, or any point west of it or below it, will give rise to this configuration of maximum per capita consumption. But note that only in the Dual equilibrium can one attain golden ages with interest rates lower than it. This is because 100 per cent at most can be saved out of profit income and that will be insufficient to maintain capitals in a regime of still lower interest, as at H (and h or h'). If population growth is expected to fall in the distant future—or if society will want to disinvest capital in the future, perhaps to provide consumption for a transiently higher population—it may be rational for society to plan to be now at a point like H, showing that a socialist society might well often want to save much more than the income on the property it owns, preferring to use its taxing power on the labour of the people to finance greater capital formation.

saving on the part of workers can lead to a Dual equilibrium at A where the rate of interest has been bid down to zero. Needless to say it is somewhat paradoxical if people should persist in wanting to save a positive fraction of their incomes when there is no useful purpose served by further capital goods of any kind. Still, as Keynes emphasized in 1936, in a monetary economy where people might try to save or hoard against some future need, there could arise " liquidity-trap " and other effective-demand problems. It is noteworthy that the liquidity-trap-at-zero-r problem arises only in the Dual equilibrium. This is because, in the Pasinetti equilibrium, reduction of profits to zero will automatically take care of any saving out of profits. (However, if one thinks it realistic to fear " liquidity-profit traps " at higher-than-zero rates of return, because of risk aversions and other factors, then the Pasinetti regime can also run into effective demand troubles.) We put " oversaving " between inverted commas because we realize that various devices to tax money to create a negative interest rate or various assumptions excluding money or any hoardable asset might do away with some of these effective demand problems. However, this is not the place to grapple with such issues.

We relegate to a footnote the elucidation of the areas in the two figures marked with 2's and 3's, simply remarking here that reversals of direction in the $A(r)$ locus inevitably bring in the possibility of multiple Dual equilibria.[1]

In concluding this taxonomic discussion, note that in the neoclassical case with a monotonic AZ going out forever from the origin, the " oversaving " region of Fig. 2 shrinks away to nothing and the undersaving region to the point at the origin, leaving us with simple Pasinetti and Dual regions with a well-behaved boundary between them.

5. By now we think the reader will agree with us that we have shown the complete symmetry between the Primal and Dual equilibria. In general, neither is more general than the other.

There are, however, special cases in which one becomes more restricted than the other. Because Professor Meade has already touched upon elements of this in connection with his 1966 one-sector discussion, we shall be very brief.

Suppose the AZ curve is always a strict horizontal line. That is a constant capital-output ratio with a vengeance. (And it can strictly occur only if there are completely fixed coefficients in both the consumption and other sectors and if in addition there are strong " equal-intensity " or " organic composition of capital " assumptions made. Otherwise a shift in n would shift and twist the AZ locus, permitting it to be horizontal for at most one n and then only because of fortuitous and singular Wicksell effects. If AZ is to be " approximately constant ", we must be " approximately near to " the fixed coefficient case just described.)

In this special case, as Fig. 3a shows, the Dual equilibrium region is completely swallowed up by the regions of undersaving and " oversaving ". Only the Pasinetti region is free of these pathologies. So after all, detailed analysis does demonstrate what we had suspected all along—that the primacy of the Pasinetti equilibrium to the exclusion of the Dual equilibrium is not a *general* feature of these systems but rather is true only in

---

[1] Any point in the region of Fig. 2 marked with 3's has its horizontal n/s_w line intersecting AZ in three places, while at the same time its vertical n/s_c line is irrelevantly off to the east of all of them. Hence any of the three points represents Dual golden-age equilibrium. It would take us beyond our present task to discuss their local and global stabilities. (Note that horizontal segments UV and vu give rise to an infinity of alternative Dual equilibria.) Any point in the region marked with 2's has its horizontal n/s_w line with the above triplet property; but now its vertical n/s_c lies west of one of the intersections and thus invalidates it, leaving us with two valid Dual equilibria and one valid Pasinetti equilibrium due south of the point in question. These multiple Dual equilibria, with varying interest rates show that our heuristic rule that " the system tries to find the lowest interest rate " does not really represent true teleology. The system doesn't really care if it ends up at a Dual equilibrium with a higher interest rate rather than with a lower one.

Multiple equilibria for the Pasinetti case occur only on the vertical loci, RS and sr. Of course the multiplicity there does not affect the uniqueness of the profit rate, which is everywhere the same on any such vertical; but it does affect the observable capital-output ratios, which are in indifferent equilibrium along segments of such a vertical stretch.

the special case which involves a fixed capital output ratio or borders on it. Those whose studies of modern technology suggest to them that such constancy is realistic are welcome to the hypothesis. Our reading of experience and engineering points quite otherwise. But in any case our earlier discussion of the fixed-coefficient model, far from being an exercise in polemics, should be welcomed by those who believe in that model's relevance. In any case, let no one claim that from the general laws of arithmetic and logic comes any primacy of one of the equilibria as against its Dual. (Remember the Primal is Dual to the Dual, as usual.)

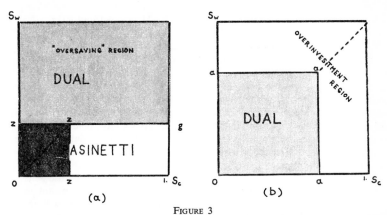

FIGURE 3

These show the complete symmetry of the singular special cases in which one of the two equilibria turns out to be more restricted than the other. In 3a we have the fixed coefficient case where the only viable Dual regime that does not involve an " oversaving " danger is along the knife-edge zg. This special case leaves the most favourable room for an alternative theory of distribution of macroeconomic type. In 3b we have the case of unlimited possibilities to use capital at a minimal interest rate, with no diminishing returns to accumulation possible. Now the only viable Pasinetti equilibrium shrinks down to the knife-edge aa; to its left there are an infinity of viable Dual equilibria, but above and to its right the saving propensities will be so great as to lead forever to investment that causes capital to grow faster than labour, permitting no finite golden age to occur.

To clinch the fact that there is symmetry even for the special cases where one equilibrium is more restricted than the other, examine Fig. 3b. This represents a technology, perhaps of robots, where the golden-age profit rate cannot be other than at one positive number. Now the Pasinetti region shrinks into the vertical razor's edge shown as aa, since only one n/s_c level will happen to match the technologically given profit rate. Any s_c below this critical level will give rise to a Dual equilibrium in which s_c is irrelevant. For any s_c (or for that matter s_w) above this critical level, the growth rate of capital goods will forever exceed that of labour, giving rise to no finite golden-age equilibrium at all. We have labelled this a region of overinvestment rather than " oversaving " since, as our Appendix had suggested, in such a case there need not be effective demand problems in virtue of the fact that interest remains positive.[1]

6. Our qualitative thesis has now been substantiated against Dr Pasinetti's objections. In general, both regimes occupy a considerable area in the crucial Fig. 2 domain. Their relative importance cannot, of course, be gauged by measuring the areas they occupy: had that been the case, the Dual regime would be given a spurious look of importance in Fig. 2. However, a look at Fig. 1 provides a corrective to such a spurious conclusion. Since reciprocation makes one area large where it had previously been small, in Fig. 1

[1] Incidentally, if AZ in Fig. 1 had begun at a point A that fell up on the 45° line itself, as in the case where σ is a constant above unity, we should already have encountered an overinvestment rather than oversaving region in the Dual domain, and might well have encountered an overinvestment region in the Pasinetti domain. However, Fig. 1 restricts itself to finite blue-print activities.

the Dual area looks smaller than that of the Primal. And if we had used double-log charts both areas would be infinite in size! Obviously the economic relevance of the two kinds of equilibrium would have to depend upon the *empirical* probability density with which it is reasonable in a modern mixed economy to expect the saving propensities in Fig. 2 to fall. To Dr Pasinetti's critical remarks on our econometric estimates of these quantities we now briefly turn. (But in doing so, we first gather some important fruit from the present qualitative exercise. We now know that the observable capital-output ratios and factor shares can be summarized completely on the AZ locus of Fig. 1; and that every such observable point can belong to a point on the boundary in Fig. 2 or to an *infinity* of points in either region which share its latitude or longitude. Hence, without *independent* measurement of at least one of s_c or s_w, one cannot in general hope to infer, even in principle, which of the equilibrium regions a given economy does truly belong to!)

7. And this leads us to comment briefly on Pasinetti's criticism of the values of α and s_c—namely 0·25 and 0·20, respectively—which we have used to illustrate why, in our judgment (s_c, s_w) is most unlikely to fall in the region of Fig. 2 which corresponds to a Pasinetti solution. We must first acknowledge that our footnote reference to the above numbers as " econometrically reasonable " was rather unfortunate since this evaluation really meant to apply only to the estimate of α. As we have made it abundantly clear in the concluding section, we do not believe that there exists an identifiable class of capitalists in Pasinetti's definition. i.e. a class of permanent pure profit receivers whose present members' forefathers and heirs derive, have derived and will derive their entire income exclusively out of capital. In view of this disbelief it would make little sense to speak of a " reasonable " estimate of their propensity to save. What we meant to convey is that, even if we set aside our qualms and just to play the game were willing to identify the capitalists with today's rentiers, we would find it hard to believe that the propensity to save of this group—a quite varied lot of hereditary aristocrats, playboys and retired households—would exceed some 20 per cent. When this figure is combined with the much more solid estimate of α it implies, that for Pasinetti's theorem to hold the saving propensity of the rest of the community, s_w should be no more than 5 per cent. This we regard as an unplausibly low figure when it is remembered that the " workers " to which s_w applies are again a quite mixed lot including labourers, professionals, self-employed entrepreneurs, civil servants, business executives of all ranks, and so on. In short, " the workers " are in fact a fairly representative cross-section of the " active population " and therefore their propensity to save should not be appreciably different from the overall average propensity—possibly a shade lower because of the exclusion of some very rich heirs, possibly a shade higher because of the exclusion of retired households and small rentiers.

Pasinetti criticizes these values of α and s_c on the ground that they " imply an investment to income ratio of 5 per cent per year . . . less than half those observed in U.S., U.K., and western Europe ". But in deriving this supposed " implication " Pasinetti is simply taking as already proven the very proposition that is under debate, to wit, that the economies from which we draw these estimates of α, n and I/Y are in fact in Pasinetti golden age equilibrium! If we are not in such a golden age equilibrium that α and s_c imply nothing about I/Y, and conversely; and if we are in (or close to) a Dual golden age, then the only implication we can draw is: $\alpha s_c < I/Y$. With I/Y of the order of 12 to 16 per cent and α of the order of 0·25, this means that s_c must be less than $\frac{1}{2}$ to $\frac{2}{3}$, perfectly consistent with our conviction that s_c is unlikely to exceed significantly some 20 per cent. In fact we submit that Pasinetti's own figures provide striking support for our contention. For, given the above values of I/Y and α, to suppose that we are in Pasinetti golden age equilibrium would imply a value of s_c of between $\frac{1}{2}$ and $\frac{2}{3}$, which, to paraphrase Pasinetti, seems to us far beyond the saving propensity of the rentier class either at present or in the foreseeable future.

8. The above discussion paves the way for a consideration of the Comment by

Professor Joan Robinson. As she says, we did put the rabbit into the hat in full view of the audience before drawing it out again. i.e. our logical theorems do follow correctly from our axiomatic conditions, a fact for self-congratulation not apology. Her further implication—that our logical proofs of stability and existence are so transparently obvious as to involve a trivial waste of time—reveals more what she considers tiresome than an objective finding. Actually, in her (incomplete) summary of our analysis there is naught for us to quarrel with or to give comfort to Dr Pasinetti's critique. What is useful in her comment is the reminder that the one-sector leets model does have special properties that must not be extrapolated to more general models. In this Reply, we have returned good for good—showing in Figs. 1 and 2 what happens to existence problems in a general blue-print technology. This same discussion throws light on the problem she once discussed under the heading of Harrod's Knife Edge.[1] Her two limiting cases

$$(s_c, s_w) = (s_c, 0) \text{ and } (s_c, s_w) = (s, s)$$

are represented in Fig. 2 by the horizontal axis and the 45° line: the Dual and Pasinetti regions of Fig. 2 show the variety of patterns to be expected (including undersaving and oversaving possibilities) and show that the Dual (or Harrod-type) equilibrium can be subject to an embarrassment of riches in the form of multiple rather than non-existent solutions.[2]

Massachusetts Institute of
    Technology

P. SAMUELSON and
F. MODIGLIANI.

[1] J. Robinson, *Collected Essays*, Vol. III, pp. 52-55.
[2] For a 2-sector model with homogeneous capital, the system satisfies equations of the form

$$k = T(k, 1; c) - nk$$
$$k_c = [s_c \partial T(k, 1; c)/\partial k - n]k_c$$
$$k = s_w[k \partial T(k, 1; c)/\partial k + \partial T(k, 1; c)/\partial L] + (s_c - s_w)[k_c \partial T(k, 1; c)/\partial k].$$

Equate the right-hand sides of the first and last relations and repeat the first two relations to get the 3-variable system of the form

$$k = f^1(k, k_c; c; n, s_c, s_w)$$
$$k_c = f^2(k, k_c; c; n, s_c, s_w)$$
$$0 = f^3(k, k_c; c; n, s_c, s_w).$$

In the neighbourhood of a golden-age stationary solution (k^∞, k_c^∞), the last equation can generally be solved for c, leading after substitution to an autonomous differential equation system

$$k = F^1(k, k_c; n, s_c, s_w)$$
$$k_c = F^2(k, k_c; n, s_c, s_w)$$

whose (k^∞, k_c^∞) point (or points) can have its stability tested by the usual methods, revealing no doubt points possibly unstable because of Wicksell effects.

PRINTED IN GREAT BRITAIN BY OLIVER AND BOYD LTD., EDINBURGH

A SUMMING UP *

PAUL A. SAMUELSON

The phenomenon of switching back at a very low interest rate to a set of techniques that had seemed viable only at a very high interest rate involves more than esoteric technicalities. It shows that the simple tale told by Jevons, Böhm-Bawerk, Wicksell, and other neoclassical writers — alleging that, as the interest rate falls in consequence of abstention from present consumption in favor of future, technology must become in some sense more "roundabout," more "mechanized," and "more productive" — cannot be universally valid.

I. THE SIMPLEST AUSTRIAN AND MORE GENERAL MODELS

Figure I shows the simple picture of Böhm-Bawerk and Hayek, in which labor is applied *uniformly* for a shorter (or longer) period of time and in consequence society gets a smaller (or larger) output

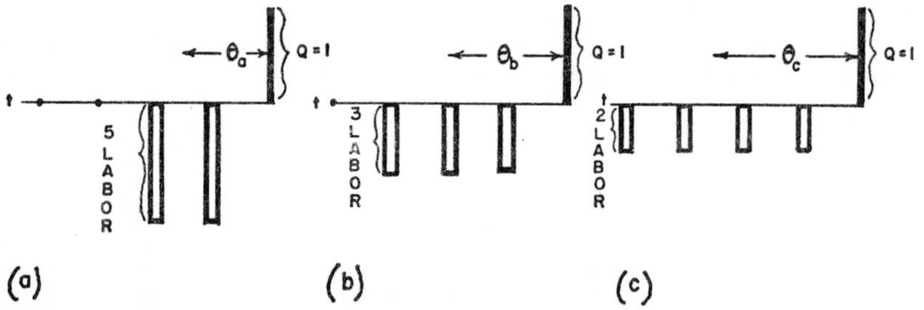

In the conventional Austrian model, labor is uniformly applied prior to production of final output. In going from Ia to Ib, the average period of production, however measured, rises and reduces the total labor needed per unit of output. Ic is still more roundabout in the Austrian sense, and lowering of interest or profit rate leads unequivocally to lengthening of the period of production and to all the conventional features of the neoclassical capital-theory parables.

FIGURE I

* My thanks go to the Carnegie Corporation for providing me with a reflective year in 1965–66 and to Felicity Skidmore for research assistance. None of the other writers in this symposium has seen this summary, which reflects my own appraisals only.

of consumption. When the structure of production is elongated, as in going from Ia's short period of production to Ib's longer period and to Ic's still longer period, each unit of consumption good is produced with successively less total labor — from $5 + 5 = 10$, down to $3 + 3 + 3 = 9$, down to $2 + 2 + 2 + 2 = 8$ units of labor. In Ia the interest rate is thought to be high in reflection of society's small stock of goods in process. By accumulating more goods in process to fill the longer-period pipeline of Ib, society ends up with one-ninth more steady-state consumption and with a lower interest rate. By building up Böhm-Bawerk's "subsistence fund" enough to get into a Ic configuration, society enjoys still another increment of steady state consumption (arriving at nine-eighths of the Ib level or ten-eighths of the Ia level) and again with a still lower interest rate.

Readers of Böhm-Bawerk's *Positive Theory* or Hayek's *Prices and Production* will not need Descartes' rule of signs to be convinced that Ic is more roundabout or mechanized than Ib or Ia, and that as the interest rate declines the competitive system can never go back to Ia (or any other Figure I state) once it has been left behind.[1]

But now look at Figure II, which tells more simply the full story of the twenty-fifth and eighth degree polynomials of the Sraffa-Pasinetti example of reswitching. Is IIa more or less round-

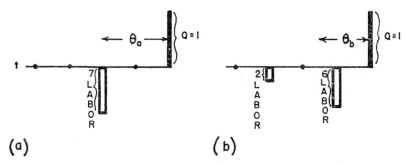

(a)   (b)

Comparing the time intensity of IIa and IIb is ambiguous: is 7 labor invested for 2 periods less or more roundabout than 2 labor for 3 periods and 6 for 1 period? At interest rate above 100 per cent per period, IIa will be used; at interest rate between 50 and 100 per cent, IIb will be used; but at interest below 50 per cent, the system reswitches back to IIa!

FIGURE II

about than IIb? Our eye looks at the time-shape of labor inputs and cannot say: are 7 units of labor invested for 2 time periods

---

1. I have not appended to Figure I the familiar triangle of goods in process, obtainable from synchronized steady-state repetitions of each of these processes. IIa's triangle would be visibly longer than IIb's. However, when labor is not applied uniformly — as in Figure II — the structures are not simple triangles and a measure of length becomes more ambiguous.

more or less roundabout than 6 units of labor invested for 1 period and 2 units invested for 3 periods of time?

There is no obvious answer. Of course, we can calculate Böhm-Bawerk's arithmetic-average-time-period of production,[2] but such a measure presupposes simple rather than compound interest and has no longer a presumptive claim on our attention. For what it is worth, IIa has a longer conventional period of production than IIb. Yet at very high interest rates, i.e., more than 100 per cent per period, IIa will win out in the competitive market over IIb. Lest you think IIb must therefore be more roundabout, be warned that when the interest rate drops below 50 per cent per period, IIa again drives out IIb and it continues to hold its own down to a zero interest rate.[3] (Admittedly, 100 per cent and 50 per cent are high

2. In Ia this weighted-mean is given by

$$\theta = \frac{5 \text{ labor} \times 2 \text{ periods} + 5 \text{ labor} \times 1 \text{ period}}{5 \text{ labor} + 5 \text{ labor}} = 1\tfrac{1}{2} \text{ periods}$$

$$= \frac{\overset{N}{\underset{1}{\Sigma} L_t \cdot t}}{\overset{N}{\underset{1}{\Sigma} L_t}} \text{ in general}$$

$$= \frac{S}{\Sigma L_t}$$ where S is the subsistence fund, consisting of total goods in process (evaluated at their *labor* costs!) and ΣL_t is total output (evaluated at labor costs).

For Ib, $\theta = \dfrac{3 \times 3 \text{ periods} + 3 \times 2 \text{ periods} + 3 \times 1 \text{ periods}}{9 \text{ labor}} = 2 \text{ periods};$

for Ic, $\theta = 2\tfrac{1}{2}$ periods.

Generally, if labor is invested *uniformly* over $(1, 2, \ldots, N)$ periods,

$$\theta = \frac{1 + 2 + \cdots + N}{N} = \frac{N+1}{2} \text{ periods}.$$

Hence, in the simple Böhm-Bawerk triangular structure of production, θ and the range N move always in the same direction (as do all higher statistical moments). Böhm-Bawerk's θ in effect neglects compound interest in favor of simple interest, ignoring interest on the interest part of the value of all intermediate goods. For IIa and IIb, we get respectively

$$\theta = \frac{2 \times 3 \text{ periods} + 0 + 6 \times 1 \text{ periods}}{8} = 1\tfrac{1}{2} \text{ periods}$$

$$\theta = \frac{0 + 7 \times 2 \text{ periods}}{7} = 2 \text{ periods}$$

3. At a zero interest rate, the process with the lowest total labor requirement, ΣL_t, the zeroth statistical moment, will win out. For two processes with tied ΣL_t, Böhm-Bawerk's measurement of mean θ, or first moment, will be decisive at low interest rates: that with lower θ will be preferred, as can be determined from simple interest calculations alone. But, as Wicksell pointed out to Böhm-Bawerk, compound interest (involving higher powers of i) means that, in general, along with the mean we must also calculate the variance, the skewness, kurtosis, and all the higher moments of the time distribution of labor invested. J. R. Hicks, *Value and Capital* (2d ed.; Oxford: Clarendon Press, 1946), Part III, Part IV, Appendix to Chap. XVII, gives a quite different definition of "the average period of production," which allegedly *always* increases as the interest rate declines. As applied to IIa and IIb, it would seem

rates, selected merely to keep the arithmetic simple. The reader can think of each period as a decade if he wants to pretend to be realistic.)

II. Why Reswitching Can Occur

To help economic intuition, suppose champagne is the end product of both IIa and IIb. In IIa, 7 units of labor make 1 unit of brandy in one period. Then 1 brandy ferments by itself into 1 unit of champagne in one more period. In IIb, 2 units of labor make 1 grapejuice in one period. In one further period 1 grapejuice ripens by itself into 1 wine. Then 6 units of labor shaking 1 unit of wine can in one more period produce 1 champagne. All champagne is interchangeable.

Now what happens at very high interests, above 100 per cent per period? Interest on interest on interest of the 2 units of labor invested for 3 periods in IIb becomes so colossal as to make the IIb way of producing champagne ridiculously dear. So, of course, IIa gets used at highest interest rates.

Now go to the other extreme. At zero interest, or negligible interest, only labor and wage cost matters. IIa takes only 7 units of labor in *all* the stages, as against IIb's 8 units in all. So again, at very low interest rates, IIa wins out competitively.

Does IIb ever give lower cost of production of champagne? Yes. For any interest rate between 50 and 100 per cent, IIb turns out to be best. Let us verify that IIa and IIb are tied at the switching point $1 + i = 1 + 1$ corresponding to 100 per cent interest per period. Suppose each unit of labor costs $W = \$1$. Then 1 brandy costs $7 wages + $7 interest = $14. And 1 champagne from IIa costs $14 brandy + $14 interest = $28. Now calculate the IIb cost. 1 grapejuice costs $2 wages + $2 interest = $4. 1 wine costs $4 grapejuice + $4 interest = $8. And 1 champagne costs ($8 wine + $6 wages) + $14 interest = $28, the same as in IIa.

The reader can verify that IIa and IIb are again tied at $1 + i$

---

to say that IIa has a longer and longer average production period as interest drops steadily from 200 per cent to 100 per cent — even though technology has not changed at all! Actually, however, the *Value and Capital* definition cannot even be applied to the comparisons of Ia, Ib, Ic or IIa, IIb. For Hicks's definition must take into account the fact that, under perfect competition with free entry and constant returns to scale, the prices of all final, intermediate, and input goods will change with the interest rate until *net* present-discounted-values are again zero. Then *his* average is found to be always infinite! Cf. P. Samuelson, *Foundations of Economic Analysis* (Cambridge, Mass.: Harvard University Press, 1947), p. 188. John Hicks, *Capital and Growth* (Oxford: Clarendon Press, 1965), Chap. XIII is in agreement with the upshot of the present symposium.

= 1 + .5, at \$15¾ each. But now try an intermediate case, $1 + i$ = 1 + .6. Then brandy costs \$7 (1.6) = \$11.2. And champagne costs \$11.2 (1.6) = \$17.920 from IIa. However, from IIb it costs only \$17.792: namely, grapejuice costs \$2(1.6) = \$3.2; wine costs \$3.2(1.6) = \$5.12; and finally, champagne from IIb costs (\$5.12 + \$6) (1.6) = \$17.792, seen to be the only economic result.[4]

Figure III summarizes the effect of interest rate changes on the relative costs of producing champagne by the two methods. At

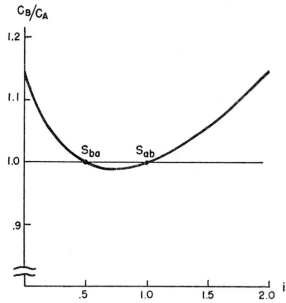

Reswitching back to IIa from IIb occurs because the plotted curve of relative costs fails to be one directional. Between switch points technique IIb is used; elsewhere IIa is used.

FIGURE III

4. The present example, like that of Pasinetti, represents a decomposable or reducible matrix. Thus, there are goods — like grapejuice or brandy — that do not require champagne as an input, directly or indirectly. Hence, the submatrixes of the two processes are also decomposable. Furthermore, brandy of one process does not need grapejuice of the other as an input. Hence, the present example does not *itself* refute the Levhari theorem, which purported to apply to indecomposable or irreducible matrixes only. However, the Levhari theorem is false, as the irreproachable counterexamples of Morishima, Sheshinski, and Garegnani show. Moreover, each of these Pasinetti-type *sub*matrixes can be made indecomposable by adding as a requirement for its first output at least a little of *its* final output. This would still leave a *total* system matrix, composed of two indecomposable submatrixes, but *itself decomposable*. This decomposability can be got rid of by the following device: Let the production of first-stage brandy and of first-stage grapejuice each require, along with labor and a little end-good champagne requirements, a little of penultimate-stage wine *and* brandy. This would convert the Pasinetti-Sraffa model into an irreproachable indecomposable matrix, and provide a legitimate counterexample to the Levhari proposition.

very high rates of i, IIb costs much more than IIa. The cost ratio, C_B/C_A, falls as i falls, reaching unity at the switchpoint S_{ab} of Figure II; it continues to fall until i is about 70 per cent per period, rising from this minimum as i falls farther. At the switch point, S_{ba}, again the cost ratio equals unity, continuing to rise to the eight-sevenths level of pure labor costs at $i = 0$.

III. RESWITCHING IN A DURABLE-MACHINE MODEL

The simplest possible example of reswitching has been demonstrated for an Austrian circulating-capital model. The same kind of arithmetic can be used to show that similar reswitching can occur in a durable-machine model.

Suppose we have two machines, each producible instantaneously by 1 unit of labor. Machine A yields 18 units of output 1 period later and 54 units of output 3 periods later. Machine B yields 63 units of output 2 periods later. Which is more durable? More capital-intensive? At a zero rate of interest, the present discount value (PDV) of A exceeds that of B (since $18 + 54 > 63$). At an interest rate of 100 per cent per period, both turn out to have equal PDV and choice will be indifferent between them. At still higher interest rate, say 200 per cent per period, machine A will turn out to have the higher PDV. At interest rates between 50 and 100 per cent per period, machine B will turn out to be more profitable. But — and this is the essence of reswitching — below 50 per cent machine A will again have the preferable PDV.[5]

In passing, I should mention that Irving Fisher's technique of calculating present discount values handles all cases, that of durable capital goods and the circulating-capital model of Böhm-Bawerk's *Positive Theory of Capital*. Moreover, Fisher's tools of general equilibrium put Böhm-Bawerk's theory of interest on a rigorous basis for the first time, showing how Böhm-Bawerk's two subjective factors of time preference interact with his third factor of technical productivity to produce an equilibrium pattern of interest. It is ironical that Böhm-Bawerk should have rejected Fisher's analysis in rather churlish terms, in part because of his propensity to differentiate his product from that of all other writers and in part be-

5. Note that the numbers (7) and (6, 2) have been modified to (18, 54) and (63) so that the switching points will again be at $i = .5$ and $i = 1.0$. For the cautious reader, I append the following table of (i: PDV_A, PDV_B), drawn up on the assumption that output sells for \$1 per unit. [0: \$72, \$63; .5: \$28, \$28; $\frac{2}{3}$: \$22.464, \$22.68; 1.0: \$15 $\frac{3}{4}$, \$15 $\frac{3}{4}$; 2.0: \$8, \$2 $\frac{1}{3}$]. A sample calculation for $i = .5$ and $1/(1+i) = \frac{2}{3}$ goes as follows:
$$\$18(\tfrac{2}{3}) + \$54(\tfrac{2}{3})^3 = \$12 + \$16 = \$28 \text{ and } \$63(\tfrac{2}{3})^2 = \$28.$$

cause of the archaic nineteenth century notion that a quasi-mathe-
matical formulation fails to come to grips with the true essence and
causality of an economic problem.

For the rest of this comment, I shall stick to circulating-capital
models merely for expositional brevity.

IV. THE WELL-BEHAVED FACTOR-PRICE FRONTIER

The fact of possible reswitching teaches us to suspect the
simplest neoclassical parables. However, we shall find that all
cases are well behaved in showing a trade-off between the real wage
and the interest or profit rate. Thus, when Marx enunciated the law
of falling rate of profit and the law of declining real wage, he was
proclaiming one law too many.

For the conventional Austrian model of Figure I, the real wage
always rises as the interest rate falls — for two reinforcing reasons.
First, even without any change in technique (i.e., when we stay in
case Ia or Ib or Ic), there gets to be less *discounting* of the wage
product at lower interest rates, a phenomenon familiar to Taussig,
Wicksell, and other neoclassical writers. Second, the changes in

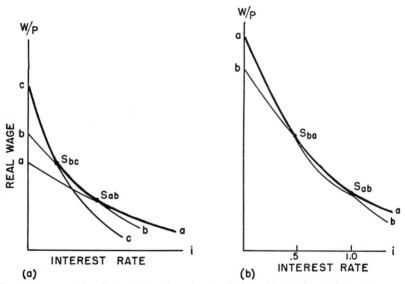

In every case, the factor-price frontier is downward sloping, with real wage
rising as interest rate drops. In the conventional Austrian case of Figure I,
there is both less discounting and an increase in prediscounting gross labor
output. In Figure II's reswitching example, only the first reason operates, being
at first partially offset by IIb's drop in prediscounting gross labor output.

FIGURE IV

technique induced in Figure I's traditional model by lower interest rates happen to be always in the direction of increasing the prediscounting total of labor product. Figure IVa gives a picture of the declining factor-price frontier, which relates the real wage, W/P, and the interest rate, i, for Böhm-Bawerk's case.

But now turn to the reswitching example of Figure II. Can we still be sure that its factor-price frontier is a declining one? Assuredly there is less discounting of wage product at lower i. But it is no longer universally true that a lower i induces a change in technique which increases the prediscounting labor product. Figure IVb shows the factor-price frontier as the outer envelope of the light frontiers appropriate to each technique. The switch points are marked S_{ba} and S_{ab}, the latter being the point at which a lowering of i shifts us from IIa's technique to IIb's. Examine S_{ba}. There a lowering of i does increase W/P for both reasons — since IIa does give greater (gross) undiscounted wage product than IIb, namely product of one-seventh rather than one-eighth. But when you examine S_{ab}, the lowering of interest rate from 101 per cent per period to 99 per cent is seen to induce a change from the IIa to IIb technique, thereby lowering prediscounting product to one-eighth from one-seventh!

Why can we be sure that in every case the envelope frontier slopes downward, which means that the improvement in real wage from less discounting always outweighs any "perverse" disimprovement in gross product? This follows geometrically from the properties of a continuous outer envelope. Economically, it follows from the workings of ruthless competition. Under perfect competition, either workers can hire capital goods or capitalists hire workers. At a lower interest rate, or cost of capital, workers can always pay themselves a higher real wage even without changing techniques; so capitalists will have to match up. And ruthless competition will ensure that, at any given i and money wage, the price of the finished product will be at its minimum — thus, ensuring the maximum W/L out on the declining envelope.

Figure IV shows the real wage in terms of the final consumption good, champagne in our case. But the same declining frontier could be drawn for the real wage expressed in terms of any intermediate product — such as grapejuice, wine, or brandy.

Both IVa and IVb show that the neoclassical parable remains valid as far as the factor-price frontier trade-off between real wage and profit rate is concerned. But that is all that remains valid regardless of reswitching.

V. Unconventional Relation of Total Product and Interest

Now let us examine the steady-state consumption levels for each different interest rate i. If population is stationary (and technology unchanging), this steady-state consumption is the same thing as real net national product per head. (If labor grows at the geometric rate of n per year, we could generalize our analysis by plotting per capita consumption against each different i rate, an easy task skipped here.)

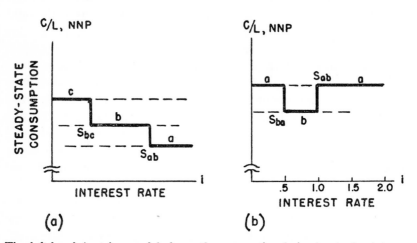

(a) (b)

The left-hand Austrian model shows the conventional rise in steady-state per capita consumption as the interest rate falls, as a result of the alleged fact that roundaboutness is productive. But the reswitching example on the right illustrates that, at first, steady-state consumption may decline at lower interest rates, only agreeing ultimately with the diminishing returns tale of the neoclassical parable.

Figure V

In the nice Austrian case of the parable, Figure Va shows that lowering interest always, if anything, raises NNP and steady-state consumption. As we move from Ia to Ib to Ic, the steps marked a, b, c in Figure IVa are shown as rising. At $i = 0$, we are in the Schumpeter-Ramsey Golden Rule state of Bliss, with maximum NNP.

But Figure Vb shows a reversal of direction of the steps as a result of Figure II's reswitching. When i drops from 101 per cent per period to 99 per cent, NNP actually falls. Of course, diminishing returns asserts itself "eventually," in that at zero interest rate we are in the Golden Rule state of Bliss. (But note that this maximum level of consumption was also reached for interest rates above

100 per cent. It is no longer literally true [6] to say, "Society moves from high interest rates to low by sacrificing current consumption goods in return for more consumption later, but with each further dose of accumulation of capital goods resulting in a lower and lower social yield of incremental product." Actually, society can go from *B* to *E* in Figure IVb without making any physical changes at all: a reduction of profit from a 200 per cent rate per period to a 5 per cent rate, merely lowers what a critic might call the "degree of exploitation of labor" prevailing. In Figure Va the apologist for capital and for thrift has a less difficult case to argue.

VI. UNCONVENTIONAL CAPITAL/OUTPUT RATIOS

Since World War II the literature on growth and development has brought the capital/output ratio into prominence. Before the war this concept was met frequently in the shape of the accelerator. And Böhm-Bawerk's average period of production, θ, was actually a primitive capital/output ratio, namely that one which would prevail if the interest rate were zero and all goods could be priced at their wage costs alone: i.e., θ can be written as the ratio of Böhm-Bawerk's subsistence fund, S, to final output, where S and NNP are both reckoned in labor terms or wage costs alone.

More accurately, we can calculate for each interest rate i, the true market cost of each intermediate and final good inclusive of interest as well as wage costs, and can calculate the aggregate value of all capital goods. This can then be divided by the true market value of all final goods, to give the capital/output ratio.

Figure VIa shows that in the simple model of Böhm-Bawerk, Hayek, and other Austrians, the capital/output ratio does rise steadily as the interest rate falls. This duplicates the behavior of the simplest J. B. Clark parable of a single homogeneous capital that, together with labor, produces aggregate output by a standard production function of Cobb-Douglas or more general neoclassical type.

6. The reversal of direction of the (i, NNP) relation was, I must confess, the single most surprising revelation from the reswitching discussion. I had thought this relation could not change its curvature if the underlying technology was convex, so that there had to be a concave, basic Fisher (intertemporal) production-possibility frontier, of the form $0 = F(K_0; C_0, C_1, \ldots, C_T; K_T)$, where K_0 is the vector of initial capital stocks, K_T the vector of terminal capital stocks, and C_t the vector of consumption goods available at any time t. I had wrongly confused concavity of F with concavity of the (i, NNP) steady-state locus. Note that reswitching *reveals* this possible curvature phenomenon, but is not necessary for it. Later I correct another misconception revealed by reswitching.

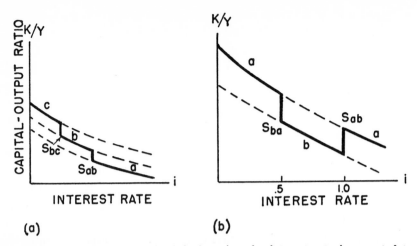

In the neoclassical case on the left, lowering the interest rate is expected to raise the capital/output ratio. However, the reswitching example of Figure II involves a fall in the capital/output ratio as *i* drops through the point S_{ab}, inducing a less rather than more capital-intensive technique.

FIGURE VI

But the reswitching model of Figure II is seen in Figure VIb to lead to a pattern of capital/output ratio that fails to move in one direction. Thus, at the switch point S_{ab}, lowering *i* a little induces a shift from IIa technique to IIb, giving rise to a significantly lower capital/output ratio.

Such an unconventional behavior of the capital/output ratio is seen to be definitely possible. It can perhaps be understood in terms of so-called Wicksell and other effects. But no explanation is needed for that which is definitely possible: it demonstrates itself. Moreover, this phenomenon can be called "perverse" only in the sense that the conventional parables did not prepare us for it.

Such perverse effects do have consequences. Thus, suppose you have a theory of life-cycle saving which, like Modigliani's, attaches significance to the wealth/income or capital/output ratio. Then the dynamic stability of some of your equilibria may be affected by the fact that the capital/output ratio drops as *i* drops. Similar stability and uniqueness problems may be raised for a Solow-Harrod growth model.

Nevertheless we must accept nature as she is. *In a general blueprint technology model of Joan Robinson and M.I.T. type, it is quite possible to encounter switch points, like S_{ab} of Figure VIb, in which lower profit rates are associated with lower steady-state capital/output ratios.*

VII. Reverse Capital Deepening and Denial of Diminishing Returns

We can use the contrasting models of Figure I and Figure II to demonstrate a startling possibility. In the conventional parable, people accumulate capital goods by sacrificing current consumption goods in return for more future consumption goods, with the interest rate depicting the trade-off or substitution ratio between such consumption goods.[7] So far so good. All this turns out to be essentially true in every case.

But, in the conventional model, successive sacrifices of consumption and accumulations of capital goods lead to lower and lower interest rates. This conventional neoclassical version of diminishing returns is spelled out at length in my *Economics*.[8] Unfortunately, until reswitching had alerted me to the complexity of the process, I had not realized that the conventional account represents only one of two possible outcomes. When we are in the Figure II technology, the story can be reversed: after sacrificing present consumption and accumulating capital goods, the new steady-state equilibrium can represent a rise in interest rate![9]

There is perhaps no need for me to describe in detail how the traditional neoclassical model of Figure I goes from the high interest rates that make short-period Ia optimal to lower interest rates that make Ib optimal. Suffice it to assert that, in going from the steady-state of Ia (where say 90 labor produce $90/(5 + 5) = 9$ units of output or consumable NNP per period) to the more roundabout steady state of Ib (where the same 90 of labor produce $90/(3 + 3 + 3) = 10$ units of NNP), there must first be a net sacrifice of consumption to below the *status quo ex ante* rate of 9 per year.

7. In all cases, $1 + i_t = - \partial C_{t+1}/\partial C_t$ along the transformation function $T = 0$ of the previous footnote; if smoothness is not present, the above equality becomes an inequality $R \leqq 1 + i_t \leqq L$, where L and R are the left-hand and right-hand derivatives $- \partial C_{t+1}/\partial C_t$, which may diverge little or much depending upon the technology.

8. (6th ed.; New York: McGraw-Hill, 1964), pp. 595–96.

9. This can happen whenever NNP rises with i, as in Figure Vb. The change in curvature of the steady-state relation $NNP/L = C/L = f(i)$, when f'' becomes greater than zero, was wrongly thought by me to be ruled out by the fact that $\partial^2 C_{t+1}/\partial C_t^2$ — or its finite-difference equivalent — can never be positive in a convex technology. The last fact is correct, and it has important implications. But it does not imply diminishing returns to the *steady-state* relations of Figure V. Teleologically speaking, the invisible hand of a competitive system cares nought what happens to net national product but only what happens to what I have called net net national product, which is that available to the primary factor labor alone, excluding the "necessitous return" to capital (which can be regarded as an intermediate product — like horses and their fodder — producible or available within the system at constant costs once the i rate is specified.)

In fact, Professor Solow has recently [1] proved what at first glance appears to be a remarkable theorem, showing that the present discounted value of all the *net* gains in future consumptions resulting from a switch from a process like Ia to a process like Ib (net in the sense that all sacrifices of consumption must be taken into account, with their proper discount, as subtractions) will balance out to exactly zero, if the interest rate used in discounting is that of the switch point S_{ab} between process Ia and Ib. In a bookkeeping sense, therefore, the Fisherian yield of product received in terms of product sacrificed is precisely measured by the market rate of interest. In this sense the market rate measures the "net productivity of capital" even in a model where there is no homogeneous capital good of the mecanno set or "leets" type, and where there are no smoothly substitutable factors in the relevant production functions.

Upon further reflection, one realizes that Solow's result is indeed as much a bookkeeping as a technical relationship. For what else can happen in a system where the rate of interest and the total of wage cost is constant in every period, except that the value of consumption plus the value of net capital formation equals the level of factor income? As we shall see, Solow's result is merely an instance of this general accounting relationship, as applied to a constant-returns-to-scale technology in which residual monopoly profit is always zero because the competitive equalities must prevail.

I rush now to show what happens in the reswitching model of Figure II when we move from high interest rate, say 101 per cent per period, down to 100 per cent, and subsequently to 99 per cent, thereby going from a steady-state equilibrium using the IIa technique to a new steady-state using the IIb technique. (Later the interested reader can perform for himself the reverse switch as we go down from 51 to 49 per cent, moving back from IIb equilibrium to IIa and this time duplicating the conventional consumption-sacrifice of the neoclassical parable.)

Table I shows us initially in equilibrium with the IIa technique. Up to time 2, all of society's labor (taken to be 56, the product of 7 and 8, to keep the arithmetic simple) is allocated to Ia, with 8 (or 56/7) output emerging 2 periods later from this stage 2 allocation. After time period 6, the system has moved to a IIb equilibrium, producing only 7, or $56/(2 + 6)$, units of output or steady-state NNP. In between society has been splashed with net consumption

1. R. M. Solow, "The Interest Rate and Transition between Techniques," a January 1966 paper to be published in a symposium.

rather than having to sacrifice consumption: thus, in the transitional periods 3 through 6, the system generates $8 + 8 + 6 + 13 = 35$ units of champagne output, which is definitely greater than $32 = 8 + 8 + 8 + 8$. Moreover, in agreement with Solow's theorem, and providing a trivial generalization of it, if we calculate the PDV of the Ib steady-state consumption stream, using the interest rate of

TABLE I

TRANSITION FROM IIa TO IIb TECHNIQUE, AND BACK AGAIN

LABOR | TIME	1	2	3	4	5	6	7	.	.	20	21	22	23	24	25	.
Stage 3	0	0	14	14	14	14	14	.	.	14	0	0	0	0	0	.
Stage 2	56	56	42	42	0	0	0	.	.	0	14	14	56	56	56	.
Stage 1	0	0	0	0	42	42	42	.	.	42	42	42	0	0	0	.
Final Output	.	.	8	8	6	6+7	7	.	.	7	7	7	2+7	2	8	.

100 per cent characterizing the switch point S_{ab} and taking into account the transitional alteration of consumption, we must get the same PDV that the system would have had if it stayed permanently in Ia.

In the Table the system is left in Ib equilibrium from period 7 to period 20. During this time we could imagine the interest rate dropping, suddenly or gradually, to 50 per cent from 100 per cent. Nothing real happens, except that the real wage goes up as a result of less discounting and also the price ratio of finished champagne rises relative to that of earlier-stage products. (Despite Ricardo and Marx, goods do not exchange in proportion to their total labor content, direct plus indirect.)

But now suppose that the system tries to accumulate capital from time 21 to 25. In going from IIb's steady-state level of 7 to IIa's steady-state level 8, the system must indeed sacrifice *consumption net*. Thus, $7 + 7 + 9 + 2 = 25$ is less than $7 + 7 + 7 + 7 = 28$.[2]

In summary, this section has shown that going to a lower interest rate may have to involve a *dis*accumulation of capital, and a surplus (rather than sacrifice) of current consumption, which is balanced by a subsequent perpetual reduction (rather than increase) of consumption as a result of the drop in interest rate. This anoma-

2. And, at either switch interest rate ($i = .5$ of S_{ba} or $i = 1.0$ of S_{ab}) there must be, at time 21, equality of PDV that would come from maintaining the old equilibrium forever after, with the PDV of the actual transition shown followed by perpetual IIa equilibrium. (Which i is then the true Solow net productivity of capital? Answer: either $i = 100$ per cent or $i = 50$ per cent will give the accountant's competitive identity of PDV, an instance of the multiplicity of Fisherian yield known ever since the 1930's.

lous behavior, which can happen even in models that do not admit of reswitching, might be called "reverse capital deepening." Whether it is empirically rare for this to happen is not an easy question to answer. My suspicion is that a modern mixed economy has so many alternative techniques that it can, so to speak, use time usefully, but will run out of new equally profitable uses and is likely to operate on a curve of "diminishing [3] returns" (at least after non-constant-returns-to-scale opportunities have been exhausted). In any case, by the time one reaches a zero interest rate (or more generally the Golden Rule state where the interest and growth rates are equal), this kind of diminishing returns must have set in.[4]

VIII. Conclusion

Pathology illuminates healthy physiology. Pasinetti, Morishima, Bruno-Burmeister-Sheshinski, Garegnani merit our gratitude for demonstrating that reswitching is a logical possibility in any technology, indecomposable or decomposable. Reswitching, whatever its empirical likelihood, does alert us to several vital possibilities:

Lower interest rates may bring lower steady-state consumption and lower capital/output ratios, and the transition to such lower interest rate can involve denial of diminishing returns and entail reverse capital deepening in which current consumption is augmented rather than sacrificed.

There often turns out to be no unambiguous way of characterizing different processes as more "capital-intensive," more "mechanized," more "roundabout," except in the *ex post* tautological sense of being adopted at a lower interest rate and involving a higher real

---

3. All my models involve constant-returns-to-scale, a fact not inconsistent with diminishing returns of consumption in terms of interest rate.

4. Suppose society maximizes a generalized Ramsey sum, $\sum_0^\infty U(C_t/L_t)/(1+\rho)^t$, where ρ begins above $i = 1.0$. Then the system will have come into steady-state equilibrium using IIa as in the first and last part of Table I. Now let ρ fall suddenly but permanently, say to $i = .55$. Then the system will ultimately come into the IIb equilibrium of the Table's middle part. But suppose the initial drop in ρ has been from, say 1.1, down to .4, skipping completely intermediate values. Will the market interest rate drop gradually from i = initial $\rho = 1.1$ to i = new $\rho = .4$? The answer is, No. The system will come *at once* into the new equilibrium, which will be identical with the old labor allocation but with higher real wage and lower profit share. There is a moral here for a system that may not show literal reswitching: as it moves from high-i equilibrium to low-i equilibrium, it may not pass at all near to the equilibrium configurations on the factor-price frontier that correspond to intermediate interest rates! Dr. Michael Bruno, visiting M.I.T. and Harvard from Israel in 1965–66, has provided valuable analysis of similar optimal dynamic programs.

wage. Such a tautological labeling is shown, in the case of reswitching, to lead to inconsistent ranking between pairs of unchanged technologies, depending upon which interest rate happens to prevail in the market.

If all this causes headaches for those nostalgic for the old time parables of neoclassical writing, we must remind ourselves that scholars are not born to live an easy existence. We must respect, and appraise, the facts of life.

MASSACHUSETTS INSTITUTE OF TECHNOLOGY

149

THE NONSWITCHING THEOREM IS FALSE

David Levhari and Paul A. Samuelson

We wish to make clear for the record that the nonswitching theorem associated with us is definitely false. We are grateful to Dr. Pasinetti for first giving examples that raise legitimate doubts about the theorem's truth, and for discussion of flaws in the purported proof of the theorem and of the bearing for general economics of the reswitching phenomenon. And we are grateful to Professor Morishima, Professor Garegnani and Mr. Sheshinski for independent counterexamples that settle this matter definitively.

Some comments on the theorem are offered to minimize misunderstanding.

1. The February 1965 paper contained two parts: a nonsubstitution theorem and an alleged nonswitching theorem. The falsity of the latter in no way affects the validity of the former.[1]

2. This paper took for granted the possibility of a decomposable system's reswitching back at a low interest rate to the technique that had been competitively viable at a much higher interest rate. Ruth Cohen, Joan Robinson, and Piero Sraffa had established this without question.

What the 1965 paper attempted to show — we now agree, wrongly — was that this could not happen in an "indecomposable"

---

1. Morishima is correct in saying that the nonsubstitution theorem is valid without regard to the "indecomposability" assumptions of the February 1965 paper. Only because it appeared in the same paper with the nonswitching theorem, which was thought to be related to indecomposability, was the exposition so worded. For early recognition of the nonsubstitution theorem, see M. Morishima, *Equilibrium, Stability and Growth* (Oxford: Clarendon Press, 1964), p. 97, Theorem 1; "A Dynamic Analysis of Structural Change in a Leontief Model," *Economica*, XXV (May 1958), 120; "Prices, Interest, and Profits in a Dynamic Leontief System," *Econometrica*, Vol. 26 (July 1958), pp. 358–80; "Some Properties of a Dynamic Leontief System with a Spectrum of Techniques," *Econometrica*, Vol. 27 (Oct. 1959), pp. 626–37. Some of the Morishima conditions on positive direct labor requirements can also be lightened. See also J. T. Schwartz, *Lectures on the Mathematical Method in Analytical Economics* (New York: Gordon and Breach, 1961). P. A. Samuelson, "A Modern Treatment of the Ricardian Economy: II," this *Journal*, LXXIII (May 1959), 228 shows that durable capital goods can give rise to a nonsubstitution theorem, as does P. A. Samuelson, "Equalization by Trade of the Interest Rate Along with the Real Wage," in Essays in Honor of Gottfried Haberler, *Trade, Growth, and the Balance of Payments* (Chicago: Rand McNally, 1965). We understand that Morishima and Murata, and Burmeister and Sheshinski, have work in process relating to extension to durable-goods models. Once one recognizes that a system with positive interest r behaves in all of its pecuniary relations just like a zero-interest system but with every input coefficient raised from a_{ij} to $a_{ij}(1 + r)$, the 1949 formulation of the earlier nonsubstitution theorem provides a convenient reference.

or "irreducible" technology (which means a situation in which *every single* output requires, directly or indirectly as input for its production, something *positive* of *every single* other output).

Morishima's example, involving two goods and labor, meets this requirement, and so do the examples in the Sheshinski-Bruno-Burmeister and Garegnani papers. The Pasinetti-Sraffa example, in which labor over eight periods makes a product or alternatively makes it over twenty-five periods, would have to be modified before it would meet the indecomposability requirement of the (false) non-reswitching theorem. Thus, call the output of labor after one period in the eight-period process *thread* and the output of labor after three periods in the twenty-five-period process *yarn*. It is clear that thread requires no yarn, directly or indirectly, in its production.

In his original 1965 Rome paper, Pasinetti went most of the way toward modifying his example to get rid of its decomposability. And now that we realize how false the nonswitching theorem is, it is clear to us that making the trifling change in coefficients sufficient to rule out decomposability can be seen, *from continuity considerations alone,* to leave us with the same reswitching possibility known to prevail in the decomposable case.

3. Once a theorem is recognized to be false, there is not much point in hashing over errors in its proof. Still, to avoid confusion in the literature, we wish to emphasize that the fundamental lemma, used in the proof of the false theorem, is itself definitely false.[2]

4. Conditions that are sufficient to make a nonswitching theorem valid — like those of Weitzman and Bruno-Burmeister-Sheshinski — are of interest to economists for their own sake. But, of course, they do not absolve from error the false nonswitching theorem.

HEBREW UNIVERSITY

MASSACHUSETTS INSTITUTE OF TECHNOLOGY

2. Professor Solow has pointed out that an arbitrary matrix can be written as the difference between two positive matrixes. Hence, we can make $a-b$ have a row of negative elements and another row of positive elements, thereby making $(a-b)x$ be, for all positive x, a vector of more than one sign — negating the lemma in a stronger way than the Pasinetti counterexample, which leaves $(a - b)x$ semidefinite. Still we agree with Pasinetti and other writers in this symposium that even if a version of the lemma could be shown to be true along the factor-price frontier, this could be of no avail in providing a proof of what is essentially a false theorem. See Bruno-Burmeister-Sheshinski for a discussion of the fact that, when an x exists such that $(a-b)x \geqq 0$ or $(b-a)x \geqq 0$ for any admissible (a,b), sufficient conditions for nonswitching are realized.

150

Indeterminacy of Development in a Heterogeneous-Capital Model with Constant Saving Propensity[1]

PAUL A. SAMUELSON

Massachusetts Institute of Technology

1. Introduction

Much attention has been paid to growth models in which saving is a constant fraction of income. Thus, Solow [12] showed that the one-sector well-behaved neoclassical version of the full-employment Harrod-Domar model would asymptotically approach a stable golden-age equilibrium.

A two-sector model, in which labor and a homogeneous capital good can make a consumption good (simple or composite) or new capital goods, has been analyzed by Uzawa, Solow, Inada, Drandakis, Findlay, Burmeister, and many others. For this "canonical model," there need not be convergence to a golden-age equilibrium of exponential growth; there can be locally unstable equilibria and limit cycles; there can even be causal indeterminacy in the sense that, for a given amount of capital and labor and prescribed propensities to save out of wage and profit incomes, there may exist a variety of different possible short-term outcomes. However, a number of alternative sufficiency conditions are known that rule out causal indeterminacy and locally unstable equilibria. (See Burmeister [1] for a review and extension of this literature, most of which appeared in the *Review of Economic Studies* since 1963.)

Recently Frank Hahn [4, 5] has investigated the considerable complications

---

[1] My thanks go to the Carnegie Corporation for granting me a reflective 1965–1966 year and to Felicity Skidmore for research assistance.

that arise for the determinacy of a model involving constant propensities to save when the assumption of a homogeneous capital good is replaced by the assumption of two or more heterogeneous capital goods. Need the system approach a golden-age equilibrium as in the simple Solow model? Is a unique short-run growth path defined and followed by the system? Hahn presents strong reasons to doubt that an affirmative answer can be given to these questions. I propose here to reinforce those doubts, elucidate the nature of the problem, and suggest some heuristic ways that the difficulties might be partially circumvented.

2. Solow Model with Homogeneous Capital

Denoting labor, homogeneous capital, consumption, and output by (L, K, C, Y), Solow's simple system is defined by

$$\dot{K} + C = Y = F(K, L) = LF(K/L, 1) = Lf(K/L) = Lf(k), \qquad f'' < 0. \quad (1)$$

The behavior equation $\dot{K}/Y = s$, a constant, leads when labor grows exponentially at rate n to the differential-equation system.

$$\frac{\dot{k}}{k} = s\frac{f(k)}{k} - n \qquad (2)$$

with stable fixed point k^{∞} by virtue of the fact that $f(k)/k$ is a declining function of k. Had saving been a constant function of profit income only, Equation 2 would be replaced by

$$\frac{\dot{k}}{k} = s_k f'(k) - n, \qquad (3)$$

which is also stable because $f'' < 0$.

The two-sector canonical model is more complicated. Now Equation 1 becomes the production-possibility frontier

$$\dot{K} = T(K, L; C) = T(K/L, 1; C/L)L = T(k, 1; c)L, \qquad (4)$$

where T is a concave function as well as being homogeneous of degree one.[2]

Using small letters for per capita magnitudes, Equation 4 becomes

$$\dot{k} = T(k, 1; c) - nk \qquad (5)$$

---

[2] Because the two sectors do not involve joint production, along with the singularity of the 3-by-3 Hessian matrix $[T_{ij}]$, where subscripts depict partial differentiation with respect to the numbered arguments $(T, L; C)$, it is known (Samuelson [10]) that the 2-by-2 principal minor must vanish:

$$\begin{vmatrix} T_{11} & T_{12} \\ T_{21} & T_{22} \end{vmatrix} \equiv 0.$$

249

with the right-hand side being concave in its (k, c) arguments by virtue of diminishing returns in each sector.

For simplicity, I stick with the Harrod-Solow case of constant saving s out of *all* income. This can be written in a variety of ways:

$$\dot{K} = s[KT_1 + LT_2]$$

$$\dot{K} = \frac{s}{1 - s} \quad \text{(value of consumption in machine } numéraire \text{ units)} \quad (6)$$

$$= \frac{s}{1 - s} C(-T_3).$$

Equating the last right-hand expression with the right-hand expression of Equation 4 and writing $s/(1 - s) = \beta$, we end up with the system

$$T(k, 1; c) + \beta c T_3(k, 1; c) = 0,$$
$$\dot{k} = T(k, 1; c) - nk. \quad (7)$$

The first part of Equation 7 can be solved for $c = c(k)$, because its Jacobian

$$T_3(1 + \beta) + \beta c T_{33}$$

is necessarily one-signed, being negative. Hence, with an equal savings rate from profit and wages, no causal indeterminacy is possible in the two-sector model, inasmuch as substitution of $c(k)$ into the last part of Equation 7 yields

$$\dot{k} = T[k, 1; c(k)] - nk, \quad (8)$$

a determinate system. A golden-age equilibrium k^∞ must satisfy

$$0 = T[k^\infty, 1; c(k^\infty)] - nk^\infty. \quad (9)$$

This will be unique if $T[k, 1; c(k)]/k$ is an ever declining function of k. Sufficient conditions for this are that the consumption-good industry be relatively capital intensive. This entails that T_{31} and $c'(k)$ be positive in sign; since $T(k, 1; c)/k$ diminishes with k when c is held constant, it will diminish still more when c grows with k. Hence, the golden-age equilibrium is unique and globally stable when the consumption industry is relatively capital intensive.

It is well known that in the case of opposite factor intensities, that is, when the consumption-good industry is relatively labor intensive (and particularly when both industries have very low elasticities of substitution σ_i), there may exist two or even an infinity of equilibria, none being globally stable and some being locally unstable.

If one considers the failure to approach a golden age somehow annoying, a radically different approach can be taken. Instead of assuming constant saving propensity $\dot{K}/Y$, one can take a programmer's approach in the spirit of Ramsey. Thus, a planned society might determine its investment $\dot{K}(t)$ and capital development $K(t)$ in order to maximize some per capita social-utility integral of the form

$$\operatorname*{Max}_{K(t)} \int_0^T e^{-\rho t} U\left(\frac{C}{L}\right) dt. \tag{10}$$

Subjecting the system to production restraints of the Solow-Ramsey type shown in Equation 2 or of the canonical type shown in Equation 5 is known to lead, for $T = \infty$, *asymptotically* to a golden-age equilibrium, with $\dot{K}$ *ultimately* ending up as a constant fraction of Y (depending on n and ρ). Thus, when $\rho = 0$, the system approaches the Swan-Phelps golden rule golden age of maximum permanent per capita consumption, with the interest rate asymptotically at $r = n$ and the proportion of income saved constant at the same fractional value as the factor share of capital.

It must be emphasized that Ramsey planners do contrive convergence to golden ages that might be unstable under *laissez faire* with constant saving propensities. How do they do this? Consider the bombing of some capital, which perturbs K and k from their golden-age paths. If the rule $\dot{K}/Y = s$ leads to instability, it should be clear that the planners—in *aiming* to maximize their integral—make sure that they depart from such a rule until they are again back on their turnpike target. A teleological purpose is definitely involved. Just as eternal vigilance is the price of liberty, eternal vigilance is the price of maintaining an optimal growth path. Each exogenous shock requires the planner to reaim his decision variables.

The role of teleology is reinforced when we recognize the *catenary* nature of the Euler differential equations.[3] These extremals surround the golden-age equilibrium point in a saddle point, not in a convergently spiraling focus or damped node. Only for one knife-edge direction of aim will the motion be convergent to equilibrium: for all other initial directions, the system ultimately fans out from the golden-age turnpikes. Indeed it is this catenary property of the motions around the turnpike that is essential for the truth of the fundamental turnpike theorem (which says you must spend most of the time indefinitely near to golden-age balanced growth even if your distant target is away from the golden-age configuration).

An analogy to the problem of stability and planning is provided by a bicycle. A bicycle is highly unstable: unless set just right (and reset just right if perturbed), it will fall cumulatively away from equilibrium. But a bicycle manned by a trained rider is stable. The biological link provides its governor.

---

[3] A catenary has the form $a \exp(\lambda t) + b \exp(-\lambda t)$, or more generally has exponentials with opposite-signed exponents, and is therefore generally unstable forward as well as backward and at best approaches "asymptotically" to the equilibrium and ultimately diverges from it. "Asymptotically" is used here in the sense of "asymptotic" rather than convergent series. The equilibrium of an upright bicycle has the catenary property. (See Samuelson [9] for catenary turnpike discussion.)

The governor, or his muscles, knows how to reaim it every instant to retain stability.

An interesting question is whether a competitive market of futures prices can provide the teleological foresight and reaimings that ideal planning is able to provide. I come back to this complex question later.

3. Heterogeneous Capital Goods

Now let us begin to grapple with models involving heterogeneous capital goods. Dynamic programming techniques, involving discrete time periods, can handle the blue-prints technology studied by Joan Robinson. However, the analogy with standard methods in the calculus of variations and with Solow's work will be closer if we make the neoclassical assumptions used earlier by Solow and Samuelson [6, 8] in generalizing the Ramsey model. Let $(K_1, \cdots, K_m)$ be a vector of different capital goods which can be used with labor to produce consumption goods $(C_1, \cdots, C_s)$ and their own net capital formations. All this can be summarized in the concave, homogeneous-of-first-degree social transformation function:

$$C_1 = F(L; K_1, \cdots, K_m; \dot{K}_1, \dot{K}_2, \cdots, \dot{K}_m; C_2, \cdots, C_s). \tag{11}$$

Just as Equations 1 and 4 could be transformed into per capita functions Equations 2 and 5, so can Equation 11 be transformed into per capita

$$c_1 = F(1; k_1, \cdots, k_m; \dot{k}_1 + nk_1, \cdots, \dot{k}_m + nk_m; c_2, \cdots, c_s), \tag{12}$$

a function concave in its arguments.

As shown in Samuelson [10], it is easy for a programmer to generalize the Ramsey problem and plan, subject to Equation 12, to maximize a per capita integral of the form

$$\max_{\left[\substack{k_j(t) \\ c_i(t)}\right]} \int_0^T e^{-\rho t} U(c_1, \cdots, c_s)\, dt, \tag{13}$$

ending up as $T \to \infty$ with an asymptotic state of golden-age equilibrium, with value of net investment a constant fraction of value of income.

But the last remarks reverse the order of our previous exposition. Suppose we ask, with Hahn, what happens when we generalize the Solow constant-saving model to heterogeneous capitals?

Recalling the definition of income as the sum of all factor payments, we write it in terms of the C_1 numéraire as

$$Y = L\frac{\partial F}{\partial L} + K_1 \frac{\partial F}{\partial K_1} + \cdots + K_m \frac{\partial F}{\partial K_m}$$

$$= LF_0(1, k_1, \cdots, k_m; \dot{k}_1 + nk_1, \cdots; c_2, \cdots, c_s)$$

$$+ \sum_{j=1}^m K_j F_j(1, k_1, \cdots, k_1 + nk_1, \cdots; c_2, \cdots, c_s), \tag{14}$$

where L is treated as the zeroth argument and F_j denotes partial derivatives.

The total value of net capital formation or investment in terms of the same C_1 *numéraire* is

$$I = -\left[\dot{K}_1 \frac{\partial F}{\partial \dot{K}_1} + \cdots + \dot{K}_m \frac{\partial F}{\partial \dot{K}_m}\right]$$

$$= -L\left[\sum_{j=1}^{m} (\dot{k}_j + nk_j)F_{n+j}(1, k_1, \cdots; \dot{k}_1 + nk_1, \cdots; c_2, \cdots)\right]. \quad (15)$$

The behavior equation $I/Y = s$ becomes, from Equations 14 and 15 in per capita terms,

$$-\sum_{j=1}^{m} (\dot{k}_j + nk_j)F_{n+j}(1, k_1, \cdots; \cdots; \cdots, c_s)$$

$$= s\left[F_0(1, k_1, \cdots; \cdots; \cdots, c_s) + \sum_{j=1}^{m} k_j F_j(1, k_1, \cdots; \cdots; \cdots, c_s)\right]. \quad (16)$$

Obviously Equations 12 and 16 are but two equations and are insufficient to determine the paths of the $m + s$ unknowns $[k_j(t); c_i(t)]$. We can easily make good the equations needed to determine the $[c_i(t)]$ by invoking consumers' sovereignty and current preference-maximizing demand functions, which allocate the funds not going to investment among the available (c_i) goods while taking account of their scarcity or market prices. Or, even simpler, we might assume fixed proportions for a composite market basket of consumption goods: with $c_i/c_1 = a_i$, we could express Equations 11 and 12 in terms of a single consumption good c_1. Or, if indifference curves are always homothetic and entail unitary income elasticities for all consumption goods, we can rigorously define a single composite consumption good (made up of changing proportions of the c_i components, depending upon relative prices). Hence, for expositional simplicity, we may often deal here with a single consumption good c_1, setting $s = 1$ and omitting the last variables to the right of the semicolon $(c_2, \cdots,)$.

With multiple capital goods $m > 1$, Equation 16 still leaves us short $m - 1$ conditions for a determinately developing system. We shall see that this is inevitable: for until we add further assumptions, such as where the system is to terminate (at some future date), how can it know precisely where to aim now?

4. Intertemporal Efficiency Conditions

But first I must digress to derive the efficiency conditions that it is known a well-running system must satisfy. (See Dorfman, Samuelson, Solow [2] and Samuelson [7].) These are also $m - 1$ in number; but, involving as they do the new variables $\ddot{K}_j$, we are left short $m - 1$ terminal conditions.

The problem of intertemporal efficiency conditions can be stated simply, omitting all mention of price or dual variables. For prescribed consumption requirements $c_i(t)$, between $t = 0$ and $t = T$, and *all but one* terminal capitals prescribed at T $(k_2{}^T, \cdots)$, and for *all* initial capitals initially prescribed $(k_1{}^0, k_2{}^0, \cdots)$, the planners (or the "Invisible Hand" under ideal laissez-faire futures-market pricing) are to select $k_j(t)$ in order to maximize the terminal stock of the one remaining capital $k_1{}^T$. Why? If this is not done, everybody can be made better off. Mathematically,

$$\underset{k_j(t)}{\text{Max }} k_1{}^T = \int_0^T k_1 \, dt \tag{17}$$

subject to given $(k_1{}^0, k_2{}^0, \cdots)$, $(k_2{}^T, \cdots)$, $[c_i(t)]$, and

$$
\begin{aligned}
c_1 &= F(1; k_1, k_2, \cdots; \dot{k}_1 + nk_1, k_2 + nk_2, \cdots; c_2(t), \cdots) \\
&= G(k_1, k_2, \cdots, k_m; \dot{k}_1, \dot{k}_2, \cdots, \dot{k}_m; t) \\
&= G(k, \dot{k}; t), \qquad \text{for short.}
\end{aligned}
$$

Replacing $\dot{k}_1$ by the Lagrangian integrand

$$\dot{k}_1 + \lambda(t)[G(k_1, k_2, \cdots; \dot{k}_1, \dot{k}_2, \cdots) - c_1],$$

we derive in the usual fashion the Euler efficiency conditions

$$\frac{d}{dt}(\lambda G_{m+j}) - \lambda G_j = 0, \qquad j = 1, \cdots, m. \tag{18}$$

We can eliminate λ from Equation 18 by substitution to get $m - 1$ efficiency conditions

$$\frac{(d/dt)G_{m+1} - G_1}{G_{m+1}} = \cdots = \frac{(d/dt)G_{m+m} - G_m}{G_{m+m}}. \tag{19}$$

A typical one of these, written out after performing the indicated time differentiation, is of the form

$$\sum_{j=1}^m A_{ij}(k, \dot{k}, t)\ddot{k}_j + B_i(k, \dot{k}, t) = \sum_{j=1}^m A_{1j}(k, \dot{k}, t) + B_1(k, \dot{k}, t), \tag{20}$$

$$i = 2, \cdots, m,$$

subject of course, from Equation 17, to

$$\dot{c}_1(t) = \frac{d}{dt} G(k, \dot{k}, t) = \sum_{j=1}^m H_j(k, \dot{k}, t)\ddot{k}_j + H_0(k, \dot{k}, t).$$

Hence, our efficiency conditions (Equation 19) introduce as many new unknowns $(\ddot{k}_j)$ as themselves. This digression on efficiency therefore shows that escape from the impasse of indeterminacy is not to be found from this direction. Yet the subject was worth elucidating for its own sake. And, what is important in linking up this discussion with that of Hahn, these efficiency conditions enable us to have the full content of his perfect-foresight price-fulfillment conditions without having to introduce any price or dual variables into the discussion.

In leaving the subject of intertemporal efficiency conditions, I stress the fact that these are quite divorced from the Ramsey problem of optimal saving. If the Ramsey integral (Integral 13) is maximized, the efficiency conditions (Equation 19) will automatically be satisfied; but not vice versa. No matter how arbitrarily consumption and total investment are determined, an ideal market system (with a complete set of futures markets) or an optimally planned program will ensure that efficiency conditions are satisfied.

5. Reduction to a von Neumann Model

The system satisfying Equations 12, 16, and 19 is seen to be indeterminate, lacking $m - 1$ terminal conditions. Nevertheless, there does exist, in general at least, one balanced-growth or golden-age equilibrium path defined by

$$k_j(t) \equiv k_j^*, \quad K_j(t) = k_j^* L(t) = k_j^* e^{nt},$$

$$c_1^* = F(1, k_1^*, \cdots; 0 + nk_1^*, \cdots; \cdots),$$

$$-\sum_{j=1}^{m} nk_j^* F_{n+j}(1, k_1^*, 111) = s\left[F_0(1, k_1^*, \cdots) + \sum_{j=1}^{m} k_j^* F_j(1, k_1^*, \cdots) \right],$$

$$r^* - n = -\frac{G_j}{G_{m+j}} = -\frac{F_j}{F_{m+j}} - n, \quad j = 1, \cdots, m. \tag{21}$$

I suspect that one might show that this stationary point $(k, \dot{k}, \ddot{k}) = (k^*, 0, 0)$ has, for fixed (c_i^*), a catenary saddle-point property. (That is, utilizing the local linear approximation to the differential equations, we determine that the characteristic roots come in opposite-signed pairs.) Rather than investigate this problem here, I shall consider an artifice that will turn our problem into a von Neumann model whose properties have already been worked out. For simplicity of exposition I work with the case of a single consumption good $c_1 = c_s$. My argument will be heuristic rather than rigorous (but at least for certain special cases, like the Cobb-Douglas technology of Hahn, I suspect it can be made rigorous).

If a constant fraction of income is being saved and a constant fraction is being consumed, we might think of the amount consumed as being a necessary input—just the way fodder for horses, or petrol for machines, is a necessary input. The surplus producible by the system, *after* subtracting off this necessary consumption, is all plowed back for growth in the familiar von Neumann manner. The effect then of a positive propensity to consume, $1 - s$, is to leave us with a von Neumann system capable of less rapid growth than our original system with $1 - s$ zero and all c zero. (This trick of creating a new pseudo-Neumann system by treating induced consumption as necessitous was used, following up an insight of Bator, in Samuelson [8], to demonstrate why $r = n$ in the golden rule state of maximum per capita consumption.)

If this heuristic trick can be made to work, successfully duplicating the constant saving case, it is just as if we have a new F function, call it f, exactly like Equation 11 but now with *all* c_s zero. This analogue to Equation 11 can be written as

$$0 = f(L, K_1, \cdots, K_m; \dot{K}_1, \cdots, \dot{K}_m; 0, \cdots), \tag{22}$$

where f is concave and homogeneous of the first degree. In per capita terms, the analogue to Equation 12 becomes

$$0 = f(1, k_1, \cdots, k_m; \dot{k}_1 + nk_1, \cdots, \dot{k}_m + nk_m; 0, \cdots)$$
$$= g(k, \dot{k}), \quad \text{for short,} \tag{23}$$

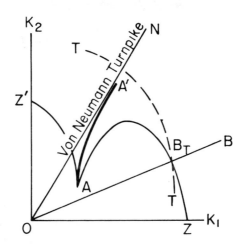

FIGURE 1. Treating the fractional amount consumed as necessitous input, we consider our system as a pseudo-Neumann model, capable of maximal balanced growth along the indicated golden-age turnpike. From any initial point, like A (which could have been on the turnpike), there streams out an infinite number of efficient paths, only one of which, namely AA', approaches the golden age (by virtue of the catenary property). For a wide class of systems, this convergent path is the only one that can be *permanently* efficient, since all others eventually hit an axis (as at Z or Z') and then, presumably, reveal themselves to be inefficient. If we supply the system with terminal-goal conditions (so-called transversality conditions), such as that at time T we be as far out as possible on the ray OB from the origin, then the path AB_T will be the determinate outcome. If $T \to \infty$, and we insist on *permanent* efficiency, the convergent heavy path will be the determinate outcome.

where $g(k, \dot{k})$ is concave in its arguments, and where we may expect (save possibly for singular cases) that $0 = g(k^*, 0)$ has a unique solution for a golden-age state or von Neumann turnpike.

Now it is fairly well known from catenary turnpike theory (cf. Samuelson [7]) that von Neumann turnpikes do have the catenary property. Still reasoning heuristically, I depict in Figure 1 the behavior to be expected of such a two-variable system that begins at any point A in the K_1, K_2 space (where $m = 2$). The diagram tells its own story: only one path from A approaches the golden-age turnpike, and (by a theorem of Furuya and Inada [3]) this is the only path through A that does not eventually hit an axis and (presumably) reveal itself subsequently to be inefficient.[4]

If one insists on permanent efficiency, a way out of the impasse of indeterminacy does seem provided—namely, by the heavy path from A which uniquely converges to the golden-age turnpike.

Alternatively, if society knows where it wants to end up at some future time T (or, what leads to the same thing, if society knows the pecuniary valuations of the K_j that will hold at terminal time T), there can be determined a unique original direction of aim—that is, a unique quantitative mix of current capital formations to reach that goal.

6. Reaiming Behavior of Speculators

My analysis, culminating in Figure 1, has confirmed Hahn's finding that merely to postulate over-all saving propensities leaves a heterogeneous system indeterminate in its development. When there was only one homogeneous good K, with $m = 1$ and $m - 1 = 0$, no similar problem of allocation of saving funds among alternative capital formations would arise.

Now how do actual economic systems resolve these indeterminacies? For a planned society of the Soviet type, the authorities presumably aim (and reaim) the system at each time period so as to achieve whatever goal they want to attain. (Of course, all this is highly idealized. Many so-called planned systems do not in fact know what they are doing at any instant of time, much less know where they are going or just why they want to end up there.)

But what about a modern mixed economy run largely by consumer sovereignty (including freedom to advertise and affect consumer demand) and by profit-seeking competitive investors? Even if we waive Chamberlinian problems of monopolistic competition, where does such a system get its guidance?

Well, for one thing we can imagine ideal futures markets. Just as there exists a price quotation today for wheat delivered in Chicago next May, we

---

[4] This exposition lacks rigor. How can I be sure it does not take an infinite time to reach Z or Z'? If Z is reached in finite time, could the motion somehow be *efficiently* extended along the axis itself?

can imagine prices quoted today for each future $[K_j(t)]$ or $[C_i(t)]$. We can imagine this, but it takes a strong imagination to indulge in such an unrealistic exercise. Very few activities are able to rely on a viable organized futures market; and even for wheat and other staples, such markets are only able to overcome the hurdle of indivisible costs for a year or two ahead (when the contingency risks are sufficiently foreseeable to motivate hedgers to pay for the transference of risks to speculators, while having to pay brokerage commissions and other costs of market maintenance).

Let us, though, indulge our imaginations and conceive of futures markets. What determines the profile of futures prices that will be self-fulfilling? Each path through A in Figure 1 calls for, and is evoked by, a different profile of futures prices (or dual variables to the primal variables of my equations). As Hahn suggests, we are left with the problem of indeterminacy of the future-price profile. Mathematically, if we knew $m - 1$ terminal price ratios $(P_{K_j}/P_{K_1})^T$, we could pick out a determinate path from the $(m - 1)$-parameter family of curves through A. Why should a laissez-faire system select that particular point in the $m - 1$ space corresponding to convergence to the golden age?

Heuristically, I feel that the fact underlying the Furuya-Inada theorem about permanent inefficiency may provide something of an answer. In the long, long future, any path but the convergent one is going to frustrate somebody's expectations and, crudely, is going to lead to bankruptcy for someone and to reaiming for the system. "Whom the Gods would destroy, they first make mad." And, I may add, "There will generally be a sharp-shooting speculator around, both to pick up the pieces after the debacle and—by foreseeing the debacle—to make money by doing some of the things that keep it from happening."

The image in my mind is that of a bicycle. The rider of the bicycle is the bulk of the market, a somewhat mystical concept to be sure—like its analogue, the well-informed speculator who gets his way in the end because his way is the correctly discerned way of the future; and those who think differently are bankrupted by their bets against (him and) the future. (It is easier to identify the well-informed speculator *ex post* than *ex ante*, and the image can easily dissolve into an empty tautology.) For a time, the less than omniscient market may chase down a false path emanating from A; but when the system is led too far from the balanced-growth configuration, some entrepreneurs begin to foresee the shoals ahead at Z, and they act to push the system back toward the turnpike. Even if there is something valid in this heuristic reasoning, one must admit that the system need not—and, generally, will not—move from its present position to the golden age in the most efficient way: it will hare after false goals, get detoured, and begin to be corrected only after it has erred. But, pragmatically, this may be the best one can hope for in an uncertain world, where changes in technology and tastes are going on continuously, making it impossible to certify *ex ante* just what is the golden-age turnpike that the system should aim for even if it possessed a greater approximation to omniscience than it actually does.

The reader may draw into Figure 1 my poetic image of a pragmatic path that streams out of *A* in the "wrong" direction but that gets repointed back toward the turnpike discontinuously by entrepreneurs sensing an opportunity for profit or for avoidance of future loss. Perhaps this would lead to a quasi-random walk that stays with considerable probability in some cone neighborhood around the golden-age path of balanced growth.

I leave this heuristic discussion with a reminder that it lacks both analytical rigor and empirical documentation.[5] And I must give warning that, in at least one economic model, there exists an *infinity* of self-fulfilling motions that are *permanently* explosive. I refer to the tulip-mania phenomenon (discussed in Samuelson [6]). If people think tulips will appreciate at 10 per cent per month, they can be motivated to act so that this will happen. Happen for how long? As far as theory can tell, forever. Even though every tulip mania and stock-market bubble have come to an end in history, economists have no good theory to explain why they last as long as they do and not twice or half as long.

One feels that the real world of tools, plant, and inventory contrasts with the purely financial dream world of indefinite group self-fulfillment. But can this feeling be given documentation and plausible explication?

References

1. Burmeister, E., "Stability and Causality in Two-Sector Models of Economic Growth," Ph.D. dissertation, Massachusetts Institute of Technology, Cambridge, Mass., 1965.
2. Dorfman, R., P. A. Samuelson, and R. M. Solow, *Linear Programming and Economic Analysis*, New York: McGraw-Hill Book Company, 1958, Chapters 11 and 12.
3. Furuya, H., and K. Inada, "Balanced Growth and Intertemporal Efficiency in Capital Accumulation," *International Economic Review*, Vol. 3 (1962), pp. 94–107.

---

[5] Empirically, the lifetime statistical studies of speculative prices by Holbrook Working suggest, for a market like wheat or onions, that the outcome is to have prices fluctuate quasi-randomly around trends that do serve to allocate goods over time so as to minimize positions of scarcity and glut and to lead to that optimal carry-over and storage that minimize fortuitous variance of price movements. Keynes was a good personal speculator; but when he described commodity markets as if they were merely gambling casinos—in which the winners guess not who really is the prettiest girl, but whom the majority will think (the majority will think . . .) is the prettiest girl—Keynes was apparently not being an accurate empirical scientist. [Since this paper was written, K. Shell and J. Stiglitz have advanced the subject, proving that *permanent* efficiency and *correct* price anticipation do rule out all indeterminacy.]

4. Hahn, F., "On the Stability of Growth Equilibrium," memorandum, Institute of Economics, University of Oslo, 1966.
5. Hahn, F., "Equilibrium Dynamics with Heterogeneous Capital Goods," *Quarterly Journal of Economics*, Vol. 80 (1966), pp. 633–646.
6. Samuelson, P. A., "Intertemporal Price Equilibrium: A Prologue to the Theory of Speculation," *Weltwirtschaftliches Archiv*, Band 79, Heft 2 (Hamburg: Hoffmann & Campe Verlag, 1957), pp. 181–219; reproduced in J. Stiglitz (ed.), *The Collected Scientific Papers of Paul A. Samuelson*, Cambridge, Mass.: The M.I.T. Press, 1966, Vol. II, pp. 946–984. Hereafter referred to as *Samuelson Papers*.
7. Samuelson, P. A., "Efficient Paths of Capital Accumulation in Terms of the Calculus of Variations," in K. J. Arrow, S. Karlin, and P. Suppes (eds.), *Mathematical Methods in the Social Sciences, 1959*, Stanford, Calif.: Stanford University Press, 1960, pp. 78–88; reproduced in *Samuelson Papers*, Vol. I, pp. 287–298.
8. Samuelson, P. A., "Comment," *Review of Economic Studies*, Vol. 29, No. 3 (1962), pp. 251–254.
9. Samuelson, P. A., "A Catenary Turnpike Theorem Involving Consumption and the Golden Rule," *American Economic Review*, Vol. 55 (1965), pp. 486–496.
10. Samuelson, P. A., "The Fundamental Singularity Theorem for Non-Joint Production," *International Economic Review*, Vol. 7 (1966), pp. 34–41.
11. Samuelson, P. A., and R. M. Solow, "A Complete Capital Model Involving Heterogeneous Capital Goods," *Quarterly Journal of Economics*, Vol. 70 (1956), pp. 537–562; reproduced in *Samuelson Papers*, Vol. I, pp. 261–286.
12. Solow, R. M., "A Contribution to the Theory of Economic Growth," *Quarterly Journal of Economics*, Vol. 70 (1956), pp. 65–94.

151

What Makes for a Beautiful Problem in Science?

... It may be logical beauty: Proof that the set of prime numbers cannot be finite—since the product of any set of finite numbers plus one gives a new prime number—is as aesthetically neat in our times as it was in Euclid's. But a problem takes on extra luster if, in addition to its logical elegance, it provides *useful* knowledge. That the shortest distance between two points on a sphere is the arc of a great circle is an agreeable curiosity; that ships on earth actually follow such paths enhances its interest.

By the above test, we must judge Professor Chakravarty's book to be fascinating. India and indeed much of the world has a desperate need to develop economically. Bringing the beautiful tools of optimal control theory to bear upon this vital problem thus cannot help but add to their luster. And Dr. Chakravarty is uniquely suited to perform this task. Along with the zeal of a patriot, his superb natural endowments have been sharpened by economic and mathematical training in Calcutta, Rotterdam, and Cambridge, Massachusetts. And here is a case of water rising above its own source: Interested as much in the dualisms of Tolstoy as in those of linear programming, Dr. Chakravarty is that rare specimen of an almost empty set—namely, the logical intersection of C. P. Snow's two cultures.

Ramsey Economics

This book can be classified as research in the economics of Frank Ramsey. Ramsey, a brilliant Cambridge philosopher and logician, died tragically young in 1930. But not before bequeathing to economics three great legacies—legacies that were for the most part mere by-products of his major interest in the foundations of mathematics and knowledge. The best known of these contributions was Ramsey's 1928 theory of saving. Essentially, this involved a strategically beautiful application of the calculus of variations to define how much an economy should invest

This Introduction is reprinted from *Capital and Development Planning* by Sukhamoy Chakravarty by permission of the M.I.T. Press, Cambridge, Mass.

rather than consume currently in order to maximize an integral of all future utility. Any glance at the journals and monographs of this last decade will show how fruitful for modern growth theory the Ramsey paper has been.

Because reviewers have called attention to various critical remarks in my *Collected Scientific Papers* concerning this Ramsey model, I should like to affirm here an admiration for his contribution. And this is an appropriate place to do so, for Professor Chakravarty has elucidated the two points that worried me about the Ramsey construction: first, I could not agree with the widespread interpretation that Ramseyism leads to a "vast amount of saving." Depending upon the form of the utility function specified, the relative and absolute level of optimal savings can be large or small—as this book demonstrates. Second, as Chakravarty elucidates, maximizing a Ramsey integral rather than some more general functional is equivalent to assuming a kind of cardinal and ordinal "independence" between the marginal utility of one time and that of another. As a young man I was impatient of "restrictive" assumptions, and insufficiently aware of the element of truth in the maxim enunciated by the Nobel biologist, Peter Medawar, that science must deal with that which can be managed, eschewing the intractable. Still, along with Sir John Hicks and Chakravarty, I was right to be concerned with the question of how much of the Ramsey result depends upon this peculiar independence assumption. Since a Foreword is above all the place to look into the future, I should like to mention here that Professor Henry Y. Wan, Jr., of Cornell University, who once honored me by studying at M.I.T., has unpublished research demonstrating that the "turnpike" properties of the Ramsey solutions can still prevail even if we weaken the postulate of strong independence.

Calculus of Variations

The present studies in the theory of development would be classified by the noneconomist as belonging to the modern theory of optimal control. This theory has a fascinating lineage: (1) What is the shortest distance between two points? A straight line. Can you prove it? (2) What about the shortest distance between two points on a curved surface? What begins as a mathematical curiosity culminates in Einstein's theory of general relativity. Indeed, much of theoretical physics can be formulated in terms of variational problems. (3) Light bends between my eye and my toe in the bathtub. How? So as to solve a variational problem; and it reflects in leaving a mirror at the same angle as that at which it has entered, again in order to solve the problem—known to the ancient Greeks and the contemporaries of Fermat—of least elapsed time of arrival. (4) To switch the example, the olive in my martini comes to rest at the bottom of the glass. To act so it need only know the simple Newton-Leibnitz calculus of a single variable, picking the coordinate at which its center of gravity is lowest. (5) What about a flexible rope or chain hanging between two pegs? To make up its mind where to recline, it must determine all the *infinite* coordinates of its snaky self so as to minimize its center of gravity. To fall into a graceful catenary requires solution of a functional problem in the calculus of variations (and modern economic growth theory can solve "consumption catenary problems" by using a lazy rope as an analogue computer!). (6) That apple in Newton's eye, how did it know when to fall? Since the time of Maupertuis, Euler, and Lagrange, Hamilton, Jacobi, and Hertz, we have known that it falls to solve the problem of least action—actually, two such problems simultaneously. (7) Mother Nature, it appears, is a great economist. Her pendulums swing in a path to *minimize* the integral of kinetic potential. But wait, the Lady is a myopic home economist: just as Nature abhors a vacuum only up to 30 inches of mercury, so Nature minimizes Hamilton's integral only over the first half-period of the pendulum. Why this myopia? Just because—just because that's the way the pendulum swings (as Chakravarty's discussion of Jacobi conjugate points can help to illuminate).

Just as some people live interesting lives, some subjects have fascinating biographies. The memoirs of the calculus of variations are especially juicy. When Queen Dido received as a dowry as much land as a bull's hide would surround, she naturally cut it into a long rope. But what shape should be the perimeter of her domain? Of all triangles, the equilateral proved the best. Of all rectangles, the perfect square. Symmetry considerations, even without the calculus, suggested a regular polygon of equal sides; and the more sides the better.[1] Eureka! A circle, the limiting form of regular polygons, was seen to be the solution to this first isoperimetric problem in the calculus of variations (where one integral is maximized subject to another integral's being constant).

The Bernoulli's were great mathematicians but rotten family men. To show up his brother James, John Bernoulli challenged the mathematicians of the world to solve an old problem of Galileo. How should we bend a wire between two points so that a bead will fall smoothly along it from one point to the other in the least time? John himself solved this brachistochrone problem by imagining that the bead was a light ray going through media of different densities so as to solve Fermat's problem of least time. James developed a general method for solving such problems, and the

---

[1] This brings to mind a related but different kind of maximum problem. What form should market areas take on a homogeneous plane if the mean trip to town is to be at a minimum? Symmetry suggests that any polygons shall be regular, but the triangle, square, and hexagon are the only regular polygons that "cover the plane." Since the hexagon is the *nearest* one to a circle (and that the circle itself will not do is known to every baker of cookies who always has dough left over from circular stampings), the hexagonal shapes of Lösch and Isard are optimal.

calculus of variations was born. (Newton,[2] no longer young, solved the problem after a long day at the Mint. When John saw his solution, he said, "I recognize the paw of the lion.") It remained only for Euler to give the general differential equation that is still associated with his name. (Euler said, in effect: As a rope, I have too many degrees of freedom to worry about in deciding how to recline; so I will pretend I am a chain with only a *finite* number of links; the simple calculus tells me how to arrange each link; letting the number of my links grow indefinitely large, I discern the differential equation that the finite-difference conditions of the discrete variables are approaching.)

All this is good enough for the brilliant eighteenth century. But by the nineteenth it was a scandal that a rigorous mathematical theory was still not known. Thanks to Jacobi, and above all to Weierstrass, the logical gaps were closed. Gauss, Riemann, Levi-Civita, and other geometers worked out the geodesics on general surfaces. In our own time, the school of Bolza and Bliss codified the classical variational theory. Like Latin, it became a dead subject.

But just at this time the sunshine of application brought the dead back to life. Richard Bellman in the United States began to tackle the general problems of dynamic programming. In Russia, the great blind mathematician, Pontryagin, initiated a whole school of investigators. Classical methods of the great Carathéodory and of Hamilton-Jacobi were disinterred and seen to have relevance. Students of Bliss-Valentine, McShane, Hestenes—independently contributed to the foundations of optimal control theory. New problems involving *inequalities* characterize this modern phase.

(1) What is the longest distance between two points? Surely, no answer is possible. (2) But consider two points a mile apart on a horizontal line in the plane. Suppose that the admissible paths cannot have an absolute slope exceeding one million. Then it is not hard to envisage that the longest distance is not a bit over a million miles. But it takes the methods of Pontryagin and not those of the classical theory to handle such

---

[2] Perhaps the first variational problem in the modern era was posed and solved by Newton—I think in the *Principia*. What shape shall a projectile take to minimize frictional air resistance? Here the master was down one for one: his solution is actually wrong, since it provides only a "weak" minimum that is dominated by a discontinuous solution. In connection with the Brachistochrone problem, the general impression among scholars was long that John's solution while more ingenious than his brother James's less elegant one, provided less profound insight. But Professor Chakravarty has unearthed for me the remarks made by the great Carathéodory at the Harvard 1936 Tercentennary, in which it is shown that John had anticipated much of the differential geometry of Gauss and Riemann. And it was the same unpleasant John who, for a tutorial stipend, sold to affluent noblemen many of the celebrated theorems in mathematics which go under their names. Which brings to mind a conversation I once had with my colleague Harold A. Freeman: "Would you," I asked, "sell your soul, Faust-like, to the Devil in return for a theorem?" "No," he replied thoughtfully, "but I would for an *inequality*."

a problem in which the control variables are constrained within a *closed* set. (3) What is the shortest distance between me and my lady love on the other side of the lake? Not being Byron, I follow a straight line until it touches the lakeshore tangentially. Then I race along that curved shore, until I encounter the tangential straight line that runs into the object of my heart's desire. Bolza and Valentine tell how to handle the inequality, "Don't go in the water," and the two tangencies are critical to an optimal solution. (4) I chase the inedible fox, but must not turn my horse in an accelerating turn that will unseat me. What now the optimum? Here the velocity variables as well as those of state are subject to inequalities, and new methods are needed. (5) In order not to neglect economics, consider the planning problem: Begin with durable hammers and robots that can make new hammers or robots with the same symmetrical input requirements for the one as for the other. Each input is subject to familiar diminishing returns; but increasing both inputs proportionally leads to constant returns to scale (e.g. the production functions are the minimum of the inputs). I begin with 10 robots and 5 hammers and must end up in minimum time with (at least) 1,000 robots and 5,000 hammers. How should I proceed? Surely, I begin by producing only hammers, since the redundant robots are subject to diminishing returns. When I reach 10 of each input, I shift gears to produce equal amounts of both, proceeding along what is known as a von Neumann—DOSSO turnpike. You might think I go along it until 1,000 of each are attained, thereafter producing only the 4,000 more hammers. And you might be right. But you might be wrong. Depending upon the exact technology, it might pay to produce more of both along the turnpike, ceasing to produce more robots only after they are somewhere between 1,000 and 5,000 in number. We end up with more than we needed of robots. Irrational, since we don't want them and they cost something? Not necessarily, since they may have been worthwhile for their help in producing the extra hammers we do want. Even though the convex technologies of Professor Chakravarty's book and this example do not permit Jacobi conjugate points to arise, here we have something like that phenomenon and again the problem of Mother Economist's possible myopia.

Cabbages, Kings, and Turnpikes

A scientific problem gains in aesthetic interest if you can explain it to your neighbor at a dinner party. That no map requires more than four colors is such a problem. Can the turnpikes of Professor Chakravarty pass this test? In a system in which everything produces everything, a critical set of proportions at which balanced growth is most rapid seems reasonable. So the general notion of the von Neumann turnpike is conveyed. But suppose we begin away from this highway, and also are to end up away from it. Still, if the journey is to be a sufficiently long one,[3] as seen we shall do well to move in the beginning toward that fast highway; catch a fast ride along it, staying so long there as to leave behind in all directions any rival who sticks to any slower path; then, toward the end of our journey, we can swing off the turnpike to our final rendezvous. The same kind of reasoning used on this production-terminal turnpike can be used for the consumption turnpike theorem. Suppose the best steady-state or golden-age level is called bliss. If we begin anywhere away from it, and are to end somewhere away from it, provided that our journey is to be long enough, surely by going to the bliss level and staying a long, long time in it, we will pile up more well-being than will some rival who stays definitely away from it during that long interval. Hence, the result: In a sufficiently long journey, stay, most of the time, indefinitely near to the turnpike.

A Foreword, like an aperitif, merely whets the appetite for the main course. To Professor Chakravarty's readers, I say, "*Bon appetit!*"

PAUL A. SAMUELSON

Massachusetts Institute of Technology

---

[3] Planning for a very long time can introduce new complexities and also new simplifications. Here is an example of the latter. As is well known, the Fisher "rate of return over cost" or Boulding "internal rate of return or yield" of an investment project may have multiple roots. Fascinating reswitching problems aside, presumably economists will reject all imaginary roots, but how shall one choose among alternative roots that are real and positive? The following asymptotic theorem has at one time or another been proved independently by Robert Solow, David Gale, and me: If one can reinvest continuously the proceeds of the investment process in similar divisible processes, then asymptotically your capital will approach a rate of growth equal to the largest positive root.

The extra complexities introduced by an infinite time horizon are much the concern of Professor Chakravarty. Ramsey had cleverly introduced satiation assumptions that made the divergence from "bliss" form a convergent infinite time integral. But if utility of consumption is unbounded, growing, say, as the square root of consumption, and if diminishing returns is absent for capital, the more saved the better without limit. The maximand is infinite for all feasible paths; but as every tot knows when pitting his infinity against his playmate's, some infinities seem better than others. Path A may, like Wonderbread, be two ways better; it gives all that Path B gives and more. This is related to the sophisticated Phelps-Koopmans concept of "permanent inefficiency." We convict a system of violating that concept if it stays permanently with more capital than in the golden rule state. But can we at any finite date, however distant, convict them of the stated crime? This is also reminiscent of an improper maximum problem, such as: What is the maximum negative real number? Mathematicians in an earlier century had overlooked these difficulties, and it was not until the time of Weierstrass and Hilbert that it was realized that there might be no minimizing solution to a Dirichlet problem in physics. Nature imitates art and savants catch up, finally, with soap bubbles.

To the paradoxes of the infinite there is no end, so I must break off without discussing competitive equilibria which fail to be Pareto optimal in an infinite-time program. Karl Shell has used in this connection Gamow's example of the fully-occupied hotel with infinite bedrooms. No applicant is ever turned away since he can be given Room 1 on condition that its occupant be given Room 2, and so forth.

PART IV

On Ricardo and Marx

152

MARXIAN ECONOMICS AS ECONOMICS

By PAUL A. SAMUELSON
Massachusetts Institute of Technology

Genius or Crank?

This coming year Marx's *Das Kapital* celebrates its hundredth anniversary. At such a birthday party, only the Good Fairies should be invited. Those who cannot find anything at all nice to say should decline the invitation. On the other hand a great scholar deserves the compliment of being judged seriously; and truth does have its claims, on holidays as well as working days.

The "contradictions of capitalism," which Karl Marx saw everywhere, are as nothing compared to the contradictions of Marx himself. Marx was a gentle father and husband; he was also a prickly, brusque, egotistical boor. (Even Engels, his ever faithful friend, found it too much when Marx greeted the news of the death of Engels' working-class mistress with the callous response that now more work could be got done.) Although Marx was a learned man, he shows all the signs of a self-taught amateur: overelaboration of trivial points, errors in logic and inference, and a megalomaniac's belief in the superiority of his own innovations. He introduced into scholarly literature manners not seen since the polemics of the renaissance. Too bad Marx could not have done systematic graduate work at Harvard under John Stuart Mill, and then been given a good chair at Columbia!

Evaluations of Marx show the same pattern of contradictions. Professor Bronfenbrenner, my colleague on today's platform, deems Karl Marx "the greatest social scientist of all times." Keynes consistently refers to the "turbid rubbish of the Red book stores" and dismisses the book we commemorate today as a "bible, above and beyond criticism, an obsolete textbook which I know to be not only scientifically erroneous but without interest or application for the modern world." This attitude Joan Robinson regards as rather a pity, saying: "Keynes could never make head or tail of Marx. . . . But starting from Marx would have saved him a lot of trouble [as it did Kalecki]." In my Presidential Address, I find Marx referred to as "from the viewpoint of pure economic theory, . . . a minor post-Ricardian . . . a not-uninteresting precursor of Leontief's input-output."

There you have a spread of opinion—from the greatest social scientist to purveyor of rubbish. To ask what view is right is like asking whether the box in an optical illusion is inside-out or outside-in. There is no test-of-truth by which bets could be settled about the correctness of one view rather than another. Let me, therefore, turn my microscope onto aspects of Marxian economics that can be fruitfully discussed. But not before mentioning a reason why, beyond his scientific merits, we find a man like Karl Marx worth discussing.

For better or worse, Marx is an important figure in the history of ideas. And much is known about him—his fugitive letters, juvenile manuscripts, I dare say even his laundry lists. When a sizable audience knows much about a man—whether he be Dr. Samuel Johnson, Sherlock Holmes, or Karl Marx—the facts about him become subject to the law of increasing marginal utility. Frederick the Great's flute compositions would not sell as well under any other name. Most of Samuel Johnson's ideas were really pedestrian; but after we have pored much over his countenance, his face becomes like that of one of the family and each wrinkle takes on an interest all its own. Many a newly published fragment by Marx would be of no interest at all if known to be the work of some 1844 John Doe; the whole becomes greater than the sum of its parts—not because the Bronfenbrenner quotation from Veblen about the organic coherence of the Marxian system is really true, and not even because each fragment contributes something to the grand symphony of his thought, but merely because of an antiquarian interest that becomes like a detective-story game. Camp is a new word for an old—and, I may add, defensible—preoccupation.

But back to my microscope.

Tableaux of Expanded Reproduction

First, we can make a deposition—as the lawyers say—that Marx did, in his posthumous Volume II, innovate two-sector models of reproduction and growth. These are useful anticipations of work done in our day by Harrod, Domar, Leontief, Solow, Robinson, Uzawa, Pasinetti, Kaldor, Findlay, and many others. I do not honestly think that modern developments were much influenced, directly or indirectly, by Marxian writings; instead they grew naturally out of a marriage of the Clark-Bickerdike accelerator and the Keynes multiplier, and out of earlier works by Von Neumann and Frank Ramsey that show no Marxian influence. But still we all might well have benefited earlier from study of the Marx tableaux.

Second, there is a point made by Leontief himself. Many of these same Marxian models stressed the role of fixed capital in a way that the Austrian School generally did not. Because Böhm-Bawerk tied himself to simple arithmetic examples, his *Positive Theory of Capital* is almost always expressed in terms of circulating-capital models of goods-in-process. For Böhm, labor alone produces goods in the earliest stage

269

of production—say wheat. Then labor and wheat produce dough. Then labor and dough produce bread. There is no explicit need for durable capital goods in this "hierarchical" structure of Austrian production. (In terms of Leontief input-output, the a_{ij} matrix is not only "triangular," permitting classification of goods into "earlier" and "later"; also, each good depends only on one earlier good, with all a's zero except, a_{i-1}, i.)

Marx on the other hand considered bread as being produced by labor and ovens; and ovens as being produced by labor and ovens. In Leontief's 1937 A.E.A. address on Marx, this is rightfully hailed as an important innovation. As Adolph Lowe and the late Frank Burchardt have stressed, the Leontief flow of circular interdependence is more Marx-like than Austrian.

Leontief refers to the "rather paradoxical situation. The dean of the bourgeois economists [Böhm] insisted on theoretical reduction of all capital goods to pure labor; he was opposed by the formidable proponent of the labor theory of value [Marx] in the role of a defender of the independent, primary function of fixed capital."

Leontief is calling attention here to a deeper paradox than that involved in the spectacle of a French Marxist advising the Indian government that labor is a redundantly free factor and capital alone is scarce—all having to be couched in terms of the concepts of the labor theory of value, a Yoga-like feat worthy of Hercules. Leontief goes on to claim superiority for the Marx model to handle the problem of high-wage-induced-substitution-of-machinery-for-labor. But is Leontief right in this contrast? In 1937 Leontief had not yet had the chance to remember the 1949 Nonsubstitution Theorem for the Leontief system. According to it, if the rate of interest or profit stays the same, that money wage increase which raises all prices proportionately in the Austrian wheat-dough-bread system will also raise all prices proportionately in the Leontief-Marx nontriangular system. Long-run substitution comes in either system only if the equilibrium interest rate changes.

Marx's model of expanded reproduction is perhaps the first example of those golden-age paths of compound interest which Cassel, D. H. Robertson, Von Neumann, Harrod, Domar, and all the rest have made so fashionable in modern economics. Before leaving it, let us note that it could lend substance to Marx's jest: "I am not a Marxian." Using it, he could say, "I'm not a post-Marxian of the Luxemburg underconsumptionist type." With historians Marx is able to have his cake and eat it too. On the one hand, he is the Ricardian critic of Malthusian underconsumptionist notions held by contemporary socialists like Rodbertus; on the other hand, he is hailed as a precursor of Keynes (and Major Douglas, Gesell, Hobson, Foster, etc.). Can a scholar have it both ways? In this respect, how can you be a precursor of Keynes without being a postcursor of Malthus? Perhaps being confused helps.

In any case, the compound interest rates of growth of the reproduction tableaux can provide the way out of some dilemmas of ultimate underconsumption that bothered Rosa Luxemburg and later Marxists. (See Paul Sweezy's valuable *Theory of Capitalist Development,* particularly Chap. X and its Appendix.) If accumulation of profits can just suffice to keep all magnitudes growing in balance with smoothly growing labor supply for a few periods, compound interest says it can continue to do so forever. Many of the demonstrations to the contrary foundered on linear rather than exponential examples. (Yet, remember that saving and accelerator coefficients must be right in the beginning if the "warranted" growth rate is to just match the "natural" growth rate of labor so that the same behavior relations can be assumed to hold indefinitely; unless, as in bourgeois economics, there is a mechanism that causes such saving-accelerator coefficients to adjust to the requirements of equilibrium, it is an improbable razor's edge case in which the Marxian tableaux can step off in equilibrium.)

The Labor Theory of Value

As every encyclopedia reader knows, Marx believed in the labor theory of value. One might expect me at this stage of the birthday party to examine its demerits. But the many economists speaking on these platforms of the American Economic Association have examined its demerits far beyond my poor powers to add or detract. Let me therefore be dogmatically terse.

Proposition 1. Adam Smith held a labor theory of value for about as long as it takes a grown man to turn two pages of his book. David Ricardo never shook himself free of this incubus, but no reader of Sraffa's edition can fail to be persuaded that only some of the simplified numerical examples in the Ricardian system need have any reliance on such a theory.

Proposition 2. From the standpoint of science, the labor theory of value breaks down even before complications of capital enter into the model. With land scarce and different goods varying in their labor-land intensity, already goods will exchange at relative prices that are not proportional to socially-necessary labor content. Ricardo nodded and thought that by going out to the external margin of no-rent land, he could "get rid of the complication" of land costing. Why should we, or the Soviet planners, nod with him? (This point is obvious and appears in the first pages of the new edition of my *Economics;* yet when I searched the literature of the labor theory of value for it years ago, I could turn up only one reference to Lionel Robbins.)

Proposition 3. If Marx had intended to use the labor theory of value to lay bare the laws of motion of capitalism and if he had been barking up the right tree, then the inadequacies of the labor theory of value as exposited in Volume I of *Capital* would not really have mattered.

Let me explain what I mean. Most of Volume I would stand up if Marx stipulated, purely for expository simplicity, that the organic composition of capital (or as we would say, labor's fractional share of value added) were the same in all industries. By fiat the contradiction between equal rates of surplus value and equal rates of profit would disappear. (And make no mistake about it, Böhm-Bawerk is perfectly right in insisting that Volume III of *Capital* never does make good the promise to reconcile the fabricated contradictions. When Paul Sweezy says that Rudolf Hilferding, in refuting Böhm's specific critiques of Marx, "gives a good account of himself and shows that even at the age of twenty-five he could stand up and trade punches with so experienced and inveterate a polemicist as Böhm-Bawerk," I have to pinch myself to remember that relative prices of goods do really change as demand changes even when their socially-necessary labor contents do not change—which is all the dispute is really about.)

In 1865, when Marx was at the height of his powers and had to boil down the message of his masterwork for a workers' audience, he introduced into the pamphlet, *Value, Price and Profit,* the simplifying notion that prices are proportionate to labor values—saying "apart from the effect of monopolies and some other modifications I now pass over." I suggest that much ink and blood would have been spared if he had done likewise in *Capital*. When a modern theorist assumes equal factor intensities in a two-sector Ramsey-Solow model, he does not defend the oversimplification: he is content to know that anything interesting turned up in it is likely to be of relevance for a more complicated model.

In summary, if labor-theory-of-value reasoning, as applied to an impeccable model of equal factor intensities, turned up new light on exploitation in an existing system or if it turned up new light on the laws of development of capitalism, it would be an invaluable tool even though not defensible as a general theory of markets.

If, and if. Let us see whether Marx was at all barking up the right tree.

Laws of Motion of Capitalism?

The usual claim for superiority of Marx's system is not that he beats the vulgar economists at their own game of describing equilibrium pricing, but that their game is not worth the playing: whereas Wicksell, Walras, and Chamberlin give a good enough description of the economic system as it is, we must turn to the Marxian system for insight into the laws of development of the capitalistic system. Its inferior statics can be forgiven considering its much superior dynamics. Such a claim, if it can be sustained, is indeed a weighty one.

Let us review the authorities. Leontief, in that same 1937 address, makes heavy weather of finding much to praise in Marx besides his anticipations of input-output. But Leontief is able to say:

> However important these technical contributions to the progress of economic theory, in the present-day appraisal of Marxian achievements they are overshadowed by his brilliant analysis of the long-run tendencies of the capitalistic system. The record is indeed impressive: increasing concentration of wealth, rapid elimination of small and medium sized enterprise, progressive limitation of competition, incessant technological progress accompanied by the ever growing importance of fixed capital, and, last but not least, the undiminishing amplitude of recurrent business cycles—an unsurpassed series of prognostications fulfilled, against which modern economic theory with all its refinements has little to show indeed.
>
> Neither his analytical accomplishments nor the purported methodological superiority can explain the Marxian record of correct prognostications. His strength lies in realistic, empirical knowledge of the capitalist system. (*A.E.R.*, Mar. sup., 1938, pp. 5, 8.)

Here Leontief is referring to the then recent work by Oskar Lange, whose death we have so recently mourned. The years 1934 to 1944 constituted Lange's wonder decade, during which he turned out brilliant articles in capital theory, welfare economics, Keynesian model building, and much else. In the 1935 *Review of Economic Studies,* Lange compares the merits of Marxian and modern economics and finds Marxian economics superior in specifying the institutional data out of which can be formed a theory of capitalistic development. Despite its outdated concepts, Marxian economics is believed by Lange to be able to explain what bourgeois economics has utterly failed to explain: "the fundamental tendencies of the development of the Capitalistic system—the constant increase of scale of production leading to the present monopolistic (or rather oligopolistic) Capitalism; the substitution of . . . 'planning' for *laissez faire; . . .* free trade to protectionism; . . . imperialist rivalry among the principal capitalist powers; increase of economic instability leading to rebellion (Socialism or Fascism)."

Here Lange is proceeding from the 1933 *Kyoto Economic Review* article by Kei Shibata, which asserted that Marxian political economy "sets forth theories which . . . enunciate systematically the organisation of present-day capitalistic society and the laws governing its development." As I understand him, Lange is agreeing with the dynamic superiority of Marxian economics and seeking its source; but, unlike Shibata, he does not concede its superiority to explain the then current economy. For Lange points out current "problems before which Marxian economics is quite powerless. What can it say about monopoly prices? . . . monetary and credit theory? . . . incidence of a tax, or of technical innovation on wages?"

You will notice that Leontief credits Marx with great prophetic powers but is noncommital as to whether Marx's economic theories helped him to arrive at these (possibly merely lucky) guesses. Lange attempts to make stronger claims for Marxian theories. He says they deduce that "the fundamental change occurs in production and that the 'necessity' of such a change can be deduced only under the institutional set-up specific to Capitalism. Thus a 'law of development' of the Capitalist system is established . . . not a mechanical extrapolation of a purely empirical trend. . . . "

So much for the claims. But is it so? Let us be honest children and ask whether the Emperor is really wearing clothes, and whether those clothes really do follow some grand theoretical pattern.

Specifically, was Marx right as a prophet of the future of Victorian capitalism? The immiserization of the working class, which he thought to deduce from the labor theory of value and his innovational concept of surplus value, simply never took place. As a prophet Marx was collosally unlucky and his system collosally useless when it comes to this key matter. This is not to deny Joan Robinson's view that such a prophecy had a certain propagandistic value. She says, "This error, like Jesus' belief that the world was shortly coming to an end, is so central to the whole doctrine that it is hard to see how it could have been put afloat without it. . . . 'You have nothing to lose but the prospect of a suburban home and a motor car' would not have been much of a slogan [for the Communist Manifesto]." With friends like this, who has need for an enemy?

Let's now move on to the growing monopolization under capitalism. For thirty years Marx seemed to have been right in this prophecy, even though for the next seventy years he does not seem to be borne out by the most careful of researches on industrial concentration. But suppose he (and numerous non-Marxian socialists) had been right in this view. Would such an extrapolation be deducible in any way from the surplus value ratios, $S/(V + C)$, of any of the volumes of *Das Kapital?* No one has yet shown how, and I have to agree with the recent book of Paul Sweezy and Paul Barran which seeks to identify as an important explanation of the stagnation of Marxian social science the fact that "the Marxian analysis of capitalism still rests in the final analysis on the assumption of a competitive economy" (*Monopoly Capital,* 1966, p. 4).

Since time is short let us rush on to consider whether it is an inevitable law of capitalist development that the business cycle should be getting worse and worse. Shibata and Lange, writing in the 1930's, might be forgiven for thinking so, just as writers in 1929 can have been expected to celebrate the demise of economic fluctuations. Who can blame someone for not having predicted in 1867 the successful development of the Mixed Economy, in view of the fact that so astute a philosopher as Joseph Schumpeter managed to miss foreseeing it as late as 1947? I throw no stone at Marx, because I have never believed in the big-picture theories of anyone—Toynbee, Spengler, Schumpeter, Veblen, Marx, or even Rostow and Galbraith. But those who have been bewitched by a belief in the timetable of history, as deduced by theoretical laws of motion of capitalism, should taste the bitter bread of disillusionment.

Had Lange been writing in 1937, after Keynes, he might have added to the 1935 sentence "Marxian economics would be a poor basis for running a central bank or anticipating the effects of a change in the rate of discount" the sentence, "and it would be a poor basis for understanding the role of fiscal policy in maintaining high employment." What admissions! This is equivalent to saying, "Marxian economics is powerless to explain the 1937-67 developments of European and American economies."

The cash value of a doctrine is in its vulgarization. To understand the pragmatic content of Marshall, you must read Fairchild, Furniss, and Buck. To prove the Marxian pudding, only read the Soviet textbooks dealing with American and Western economic systems. Aesthetics aside, their predictive powers have been unbelievably erratic and perhaps only to be understood in terms of the dictum: Marxism has been the opiate of the Marxians.

But this is a birthday party and I approach the boundaries of good taste. Let me conclude by wishing that, like Tom Sawyer attending his own funeral, Karl Marx could be present at his own centennial. When "the Moor" rose to speak, how we would all pay for our presumptuousness!

153

Understanding the Marxian Notion of Exploitation: A Summary of the So-Called Transformation Problem Between Marxian Values and Competitive Prices

By Paul A. Samuelson

Massachusetts Institute of Technology

Aid from the National Science Foundation is gratefully acknowledged.

Part One. Background Analysis

I. Introduction

IT IS WELL UNDERSTOOD that Karl Marx's model in Volume I of *Capital* (in which the "values" of goods are proportional—albeit not equal—to the labor embodied directly and indirectly in the goods) differs systematically from Marx's model in Volume III of *Capital*, in which actual competitive "prices" are relatively lowest for those goods of highest direct-labor intensity and highest for those goods of low labor intensity (or, in Marxian terminology, for those with highest "organic composition of capital"). Critics of Marxian economics have tended to regard the Volume III model as a return to conventional economic theory, and a belated, less-than-frank admission that the novel analysis of Volume I—the calculation of "equal rates of surplus value" and of "values"—was all an unnecessary and sterile muddle.[1]

Neither Marx nor Engels ever conceded this; in subsequent years it has been almost a

badge of membership to the league of Marxist theorists to subscribe to the view that the concepts of Marxian "value" are 1) philosophically fruitful, 2) sociologically and historically of interest and relevance, 3) crucial in providing insights into the nature of capitalistic *exploitation* and into the *laws of motion* of capitalist developments. In what is germane to the present survey, Marxists concerned with the technical foundations of the subject have also believed 4) that the profit rate and prices of Volume III (and hence of bourgeois economics) *must* be anchored on the total surplus deducible from Volume I's value analysis, or at least can be usefully so anchored, 5) that Marx himself showed (albeit with admittedly only approximate accuracy) how Volume I values with their microeconomic discrepancies are "transformed" into real world prices and profits, 6) that a long line of subsequent writers—including even such bourgeois economists as L. von Bortkiewicz along with Marxian analysts such as P. M. Sweezy, J. Winternitz, K. May, M. Dobb, R. Meek, *et al.*—have removed the approximations and minor inaccuracies involved in Marx's mode of transforming values into prices, so that 7) as matters now stand, Karl Marx's pioneering analysis of values and surplus-values has been finally vindicated even by

---

[1] The criticism in Böhm-Bawerk [2, 1898] is merely the longest of a great number of similar critiques. Incidentally, the view cannot be sustained that Marx, only *after* he had made his mistakes in Volume I, came to realize that he had need in Volume III to abandon or qualify his doctrines of surplus-value, for already in 1865, which was prior to the 1867 publication of Volume I, he had completed the manuscripts that formed the basis for the Volume III treatment of this issue.

the higher mathematics of modern economic analysis.

I hope to give here a long-overdue review of this famous transformation problem. With the exception of the too-little-known 1957 contribution of Francis Seton, the existing discussions have a black magic quality to them (a 1907 algebraic procedure of Bortkiewicz is employed, but its underlying significance is never made sufficiently clear). In this age of Leontief and Sraffa there is no excuse for mystery or partisan polemics in dealing with the purely logical aspects of the problem. So that the problems which are purely logical can be cleared up to the satisfaction of Marxians and non-Marxians alike, I am abstaining here from appraising the empirical fruitfulness of the exploitation hypotheses—for this or the last century, for static or dynamic insights.[2]

Part One provides the stage setting to the controversy and discusses the tools needed for its understanding. Part Two, which can be read independently of the other Parts, provides a careful statement of the issues involved in the Marxian theory of exploitation of labor; I hope it will be useful to both Marxists and their critics. Part Three reviews and elucidates the various analytical issues raised by the different contributors to the literature.

I should perhaps explain in the beginning why the words "so-called transformation problem" appear in the title. As the present survey shows, better descriptive words than "the transformation problem" would be provided by "the problem of comparing and contrasting the mutually-exclusive alternatives of 'values' and 'prices'." For when you cut through the maze of algebra and come to understand what is going on, you discover that the "transformation algorithm" is precisely of the following form: "Contemplate two alternative and discordant systems. Write down one. Now transform by taking an eraser and rubbing it out. Then fill in the other one. *Voila!* You have completed your transformation algorithm." By this technique one can "transform" from phlogiston to entropy; from Ptolemy to Copernicus; from Newton to Einstein; from Genesis to Darwin—and, from entropy to phlogiston . . . . It tells us something about the need for a systematic survey and elucidation of the transformation problem that this uncontroversial and prosaic truth is nowhere underlined in what is now a copious literature stretching over more than three-quarters of a century.[3]

II. The Labor Theory of Value

1. Begin with Adam Smith's[4] "early and rude state," where i) land is superabundant and free and ii) productive methods are of such primitive and short duration that interest and profit are somehow ignorable.[5] Then

---

[2] I provide below a more detailed list of references. In Dorfman, Samuelson, and Solow's 1958 book [10] there appears what is now the standard notation for systems like those of Leontief [13, 1941 and 14, 1966] and Sraffa [35, 1960]—namely, labor is treated as the zero[th] input, so that the amount of labor needed to produce one unit of the jth good, coal, or the amount of the ith good, iron, needed to produce that good, are written respectively as $a_{labor,\ coal} = a_{0j}$ and $a_{iron,\ coal} = a_{ij}$. These *direct* input requirements are to be distinguished from the *total* (direct plus indirect) input requirements depicted by A_{0j} and A_{ij}—as will be made clear later. Many of the footnotes will presuppose on the part of the reader familarity with modern economic analytics.

[3] For a terse algebraic demonstration of this, see my recent article [26, 1970]. Essentially the same point is discernible in the cited Bortkiewicz and Seton works, and also in the Morishima-Seton article [21, 1961] and in Johansen's 1961 note [11].

[4] In *The wealth of nations* [34, 1776], Book I, Ch. VI, we find: "In that early and rude state of society which precedes both the accumulation of stock and the appropriation of land, the proportions between the quantities of labour necessary for acquiring different objects seems to be the only circumstance which can afford any rule for exchanging them one for another."

[5] It is easier to justify ignoring land and its rent—for under primitive conditions it is easy to imagine land to be superabundant, so that it becomes a free factor and production gets carried on in a land-sated fashion. It is harder, though, to justify in a primitive community any assumption that intermediate and durable goods

certainly if it takes one hour to hunt a deer and two hours of equally simple labor to hunt a beaver, the exchange ratio must end up with deer half as dear as beaver. The net national product represented as a flow of output and as a flow of factor income could take the simple form

$$NNP = 1 \cdot \text{deer} + 2 \cdot \text{beaver}$$
$$\equiv 100 \text{ percent of wage income}$$

This result, that $P_{\text{beaver}}/P_{\text{deer}} = 2$ and $W/P_{\text{beaver}} = 1/2$ per hour, $W/P_{\text{deer}} = 1$ per hour, not only agrees with the "undiluted labor theory of value." It is also, under the postulated circumstances, the correct general equilibrium outcome according to Walras and Böhm-Bawerk! So long as deer and beaver production are both positive, the price ratio and the equilibrium ratio of marginal utilities for every consumer of the two goods will be predictable solely from the direct labor coefficients $a_{01} = 1$, $a_{02} = 2$.[6] The result also agrees both with Volume I's analysis of Marxian values and Marx's Volume III analysis of prices.

2. We can complicate the scenario a little without altering fundamentals. Suppose coats made from beaver are the relevant final good, along with fresh-eaten vension. All of the labor in the deer industry is direct labor ("live" labor). But suppose the two hours needed to hunt a beaver must be supplemented in a second period by one

further hour of sewing provided by labor that is equally simple, equally untrained, equally pleasant or unpleasant. Then a beaver coat has three hours of total labor in it: one hour of direct (live) labor and two hours of indirect ("dead") labor. With land superabundant and time ignorable, Smith, Ricardo, and any believer in a labor theory of value will agree that

$$P_{\text{beaver coat}}/P_{\text{deer}} = (2 + 1)/1 = 3$$
$$= A_{02}/A_{01} > a_{02}/a_{01}$$
$$= 2/1$$

i.e., it is total embodied labor (direct and indirect, as summarized by A_{0j}) and not merely embodied direct labor (as summarized by a_{0j}) which determines the jth good's price in the undiluted-labor-theory model.

The reader can verify that the problem is not essentially more complicated if we additionally assume that, say, four units of deer are needed as bait to hunt a unit of beaver. This merely adds further to the labor embodied indirectly in a beaver coat: now we have $A_{02} = 4+2+1 = 7$ hours in all. Most generally, if we stick with the simple Austrian "recursive" pattern, in which every final product can ultimately be decomposed into the labor at "earlier" stages, the embodied-labor ratios A_{02}/A_{01} can always be calculated by a *finite* multiplier chain.[7]

3. Leontief, and Marx before him (in Volume II's discussion of models of simple reproduction), goes beyond this recursive Austrian case to recognize that any output may also be needed as an input: to produce corn requires coal; to produce coal requires corn; to produce corn requires corn—indirectly or, as in the case of seed, directly. Recall these input-output coefficients are written as a, in contrast to a direct labor re-

---

are in such superabundant supply that time-sated productive methods are feasible. Rude economies are not low or zero interest economies; they tend to be high interest states, in which short-time methods are used precisely because of the very "scarcity of time," incident to the serious problem of living from harvest to next harvest and from random scarcity of game and crops to random abundance. As will become clear, we must therefore make some heroic abstractions to give Smith the rope he needs for his argument—*e.g.*, an assumption of instantaneous production of deer and beaver.

[6] For an elementary textbook discussion of the simple labor theory of value, see Samuelson [27], pp. 26–28, 712–26 of the 1970 (8th) edition, or pp. 27–29, 708–22 of the 1967 (7th) edition.

[7] In technical terms, the Austrian model can be written with $a_{ij} = 0$ when $i \geq j$, so that $I-a$ has all diagonal and below-diagonal elements zero, with the consequence that $[I-a]^{-1} = I+a+a^2+ \cdots +a^{n-1}$, a finite series by virtue of the fact that $a^n = 0 = a^{n+t}$, where n is the number of goods in the system.

quirement already written as a_0. (*E.g.*, $a_{\text{coal, corn}} = a_{35}$, $a_{\text{coal, coal}} = a_{33}$, $a_{\text{labor, coal}} = a_{03}$— the first subscript denoting input, the second denoting output, and labor being so to speak the zero[th] industry.)

The general notion of input-output can be quickly reviewed by positing that along with labor it takes deer itself to hunt deer (as bait, decoy, or seed). The $a_{\text{deer,deer}}$ or a coefficient must be a fraction, the (Hawkins-Simon) condition[8] for the system to be capable of producing net final deer meat. Suppose it takes $a = 3/4$ deer to produce a deer, and $a_{01} = 1$ labor also. Obviously, in the steady state, you must produce four deer gross in order to have one deer net left for consumption. So what must be embodied *total* labor hours in a deer? Obviously, $A_{01} = a_{01}4 = 4$. To get I deer net, you must produce gross $[I - 3/4]^{-1}$, or generally $[I - a]^{-1}$. (Example: if bait requires $1/2$, we need $2 = 1/(1-1/2)$; if $2/3$, we need $3 = 1/(1-2/3)$; if $1/3$, we need $1/(1-1/3) = 3/2$, which does leave one left over net.)

This total A_0 embodied labor coefficient can always be written as

(1) $$A_0 = a_0[I - a]^{-1}$$

The accuracy of this result can be verified by going back in time to add up the dead labor needed at *all* the previous stages. Thus, for $a = 3/4$, we need $a_0 \cdot 1$ for live labor to produce the 1 of final deer. How much direct labor was needed one period back to produce the $3/4$ of deer of bait? Clearly $a_0 3/4$. And two periods back, $a_0(3/4)^2$. And so forth for $a_0(3/4)^3, \cdots a_0(3/4)^n$, in a never-ending chain. In all, we find

[8] This condition, which was in fact discovered in connection with discussion of dynamic Marxian systems, is discussed in Dorfman-Samuelson-Solow [10, 1958] and boils down to the requirement that it must not take to produce one unit of any good, directly and indirectly, more than one unit of itself as input. For an indecomposable non-negative matrix a, the Hawkins-Simon condition is equivalent to the requirement that $[I-a]X = C$ has a positive solution X for some $C > 0$, or that det $[I-a] > 0$.

$$A_0 = a_0 + a_0 3/4 + a_0(3/4)^2 + a_0(3/4)^3 + \cdots$$
$$= a_0[I + 3/4 + 9/16 + 27/64 + \cdots]$$
$$= a_0 \frac{I}{I - 3/4} = a_0 4 = 4$$

We have here used the high-school algebra formula for a convergent infinite-geometric progression, $I + h + h^2 + \cdots = (I-h)^{-1}$, where h is less than one in absolute value. The numerals "I" and "1" are used interchangeably here, to prepare for the matrix case where "I" is given a special meaning as "unity."

4. To prepare for Marx and Leontief's later arithmetic, suppose a taxing government rears its head in Smith's early and rude state of the undiluted labor theory of value. It can levy a *turnover* tax of, say, $r = 10$ percent, on all transactions. Or, alternatively, a value-added tax on the labor payments of say, $s = 50$ percent. What is the "incidence" upon competitive price charged for deer, when that price is expressed in the same old wage units (*e.g.*, hours)? Now $A_0 = 4$ is definitely too small.

Let us calculate each case separately: for the turnover tax, which will correspond to Volume III's profit-price model; and for the value-added tax, which will correspond to Volume I's surplus value model. I begin with the turnover tax of $r = .10$.

In the simplest case, where two direct hours produce one beaver and one direct hour produces one deer, the price in both industries is marked up by ten percent. The new exchange ratio is clearly given by $2(1.1)/1(1.1) = a_{02}(1.1)/a_{01}(1.1)$. Exchange ratios are still the same as those given by embodied labor contents, because the tax happens to cancel out.

In the case where a beaver coat requires two units of labor to hunt the beaver and one more unit of labor of sewing, the matter is not quite so simple. The price of a coat includes the tax once on the one unit of direct sewing labor; it also includes a pyramided markup on the one unit of raw beaver input, which already has a tax in it from the two units of labor of earlier stage. Now the cost of a coat is $[2(1.1)+1](1.1) = 2(1.1)^2+1(1.1) = 3.52$, and its price ratio to simple deer price is

$$[2(1.1)^2 + 1(1.1)]/1(1.1)$$
$$= [2(1.1) + 1]/1 = 3.2/1$$
$$= A_{02}/A_{01} > a_{02}/a_{01} = [2 + 1]/1$$

Summary. Because industries are unequal in their relative-direct-labor intensities (organic compositions of capital), a turnover tax pyramids or compounds differently in the various industries, leading to exchange ratios that deviate from those given by embodied labor hours. Those with relatively most labor "dated far back" rise most in relative price.

Thus formula (1) clearly had need to be modified. A ten percent turnover tax must be paid at *every* stage and applies to non-labor costs as well as direct labor costs: its effects on prices are exactly those of supposing that *every* input requirement, a and a_0, is artificially stepped up by 1.1. So equation (1) will become in the case of a turnover tax of $1+r$,

$$(2) \quad A_0(r) = a_0(1 + r)[I - a(1 + r)]^{-1}$$
$$> A_0(0) = A_0 \text{ of (1) if } r > 0.$$

The reader can verify this by adding the pyramided tax at all the stages or turnovers, namely

$$a_0(1.1)+a_0(1.1)\{a(1.1)\}+a_0(1.1)\{a(1.1)\}^2$$
$$+ \cdots = a_0(1.1)[I+\{a(1.1)\}$$
$$+\{a(1.1)\}^2+\cdots]$$
$$= a_0(1.1)[I-a(1.1)]^{-1}$$

This demonstrates a further obvious truth: raising r, as from .1 to .2, must add to cost at every stage, and hence in toto: so $A_0(r)$ is an ever-rising function of r, with $A_0'(r) > 0$.

Indeed, r must not get too large: if it takes 3/4 deer as bait for one deer, r must stay below $33\frac{1}{3}$ percent. This is because no price could recoup a larger tax rate, since for $r = \frac{1}{3}$,

$$A_0(1/3) = a_0(1+1/3)+3/4A_0(1/3)(1+1/3)$$
$$= a_0 4/3+(3/4)(4/3)A_0(1/3)$$

showing that nothing would be left over for wages at so high a tax!

Now look at the value-added tax. This case is much simpler. The tax does not pyramid. It is paid once on direct labor at each of the many stages. If the tax is $s = .3$, then the effect is exactly as if you must pay for 1.3 hours of labor where before you paid for 1. Thus each a_0 becomes $a_0(1.3)$, but the input-output coefficients for raw materials, a, are left quite unchanged. So (1) is modified for the value-added case to read[9]

$$(3) \quad A_0(0)(1 + s) = a_0(1 + s)[I - a]^{-1}$$

Summary. A value-added tax on labor leaves all price ratios the same as embodied labor ratios, marking up *all* prices by the same percentage.

In concluding the tax arithmetic, note that one could have a "transformation" problem or a "contrast and compare" problem between the two tax regimes. For all rs, there is one spread of results; for all ss, there is a different spread of results. It is not clear how one would want to pair off a particular r^* and s^* for comparison. But, if one were a libertarian who regarded the government as a voracious octopus that takes resources away from people, one could postulate a theory of government exploitation in which, whether by a turnover tax r^* or a value-added tax s^*, taxation leaves the private worker with the same minimum-subsistence real wage. In

[9] The reader not well-versed in algebra is reminded that A_0 is short for $[A_{01}, A_{02}, \cdots]$ and that (3) is a terse way of saying: "price of any good when the rate of surplus value is positive is equal to its embodied labor content multiplied by one-plus-the-rate-of-surplus-value."

either regime the worker, so to speak, works six hours of the twelve-hour day for himself and six hours for the exploiting octopus. If the needed minimum amount of subsistence is m(say $m = 1/10$ deer per labor unit), we can solve for the alternative r^* or s^*, respectively by $W/P = m = 1/10$, thus

$$A_0(r)m = 1 \quad \text{or} \quad A_0(0)(1+s)m = 1$$

Where it takes 3/4 deer as bait and one direct hunting hour and $m = 1/10$, we find

$$(1+r)[I - 3/4(1+r)]^{-1} 1/10$$
$$= \frac{1+r}{10[1 - 3/4(1+r)]} = \frac{4(1+r)}{40 - 30(1+r)} = 1$$
$$1 + r^* = \frac{40}{34} = 1 + 6/34$$

So the turnover tax rate is 6/34 or about $17\frac{1}{2}$ percent. Alternatively

$$(1+s)[I - 3/4]^{-1} 1/10 = (1+s)(4) \, 1/10 = 1$$
$$1 + s^* = \frac{10}{4} = 1 + 1.5$$

So the value-added tax rate is one-hundred-fifty percent. Hence $(r^*, s^*) = (6/34, 1.5)$ is the relevant pairing. Naturally $s^* > r^*$, since the turnover tax, being compounded so many times, must be at a lower rate than the only-once applied value-added tax if the same real wage is to ensue.

III. Shortcomings of the Labor Theory of Value

1. Adam Smith lingered in his "early and rude state" with its undiluted labor theory for only a page. Turn the page and Eden is left behind. Now land is scarce; rent is charged for it; deer and beaver now have exchange prices that include land-rent, and except in the singular case of goods that happen to have exactly the same labor-land intensities, price ratios forever depart from embodied labor contents.

How did the Ricardians miss this elementary fact? Most of them, most of the time, thought that if Ricardo took his analysis out to the "external margin," where "no-rent land" was used, that he could "get rid of the complication of land." Out there, deer and beaver exchange at their labor requirements. But this is trivial nonsense; one doubts that clever David Ricardo could himself ever have been long fooled by it. For let society's tastes change from land-extensive deer hunting to labor-intensive beaver hunting: then Ricardo's hope to separate the important question of income distribution from the complicated problem of demand pricing is doomed. For now the external margin 'ust worth cultivating is *changed*, and the *new* embodied labor ratios have to be solved for by Walrasian conditions of the type Ricardo hoped to be able to ignore.[10]

2. There is a second limitation on the labor theory of value: people are not all alike. Ricardo and Marx hoped to evade this difficulty by redefining new units of labor power. If men are one-third as productive as women, use an hour of male labor as the lowest common denominator and then dub each female labor as being three honorary male units. In terms of the new efficiency units, $1L_1 + 3L_2 = L$, carry on with the labor theory of value.

This is fine—if it works. Remember, Marx believed that many of the differences between highly-skilled and unskilled labor rested on the differences in past training, which was produced by earlier teaching-time labor. (When one must deal with educational labor that is still bearing fruit 40 years later, Smith's postulate that time is ignorable becomes questionable. But one objection at a time; the effect of profit and interest will soon secure its attention.)

However, the efficiency-unit device will work empirically at best only as an approximation. Natural differences show a Gaussian-like spread. "A man's a man, for all of that"

---

[10] See the cited elementary discussion [27, Samuelson, 1970] or the more complete demonstration in the seventh edition, pp. 8, 28.

is a proper legal dictum. But a woman is not a man, and men are not at any age homozygous twins. Thus, let women be three times as efficient in beaver production and two times as efficient in deer production. How do we get our new quantum of "socially-necessary labor"? By $1L_1 + 3L_2$? By $1L_1 + 2L_2$? By $1L_1 + 2\frac{1}{2} L_2$? All are wrong. Given the new data about female productivities along with the original knowledge that it takes twice the male labor for a beaver as for a deer, what predictions about exchange ratios can we now obtain from the labor theory of value?

The answers are, on reflection, clear. Without the Walrasian conditions of full demand equilibrium, which Ricardo wished to avoid in dealing with income distribution, little progress is possible. The beaver/deer exchange ratio can range anywhere from 4/3 to 2/1 depending upon whether tastes are strong for deer or for beaver. Attempting to apply a simple labor theory would result in wasteful neglect of comparative advantage (in which no woman should be producing deer while any man is producing beaver, etc.). Indeed, to understand the statics and dynamics of men-women distributive shares requires use rather than neglect of the tools of bourgeois economics (*i.e.*, of simple general equilibrium pricing).

3. An exercise in overkill of the labor theory of value has little point at this date. But, of course, the most common objection to it comes from the consideration of time. Smith's early and rude state, although anthropologically rubbish, was logically irreproachable in its assumption of superabundant land and zero rent. Its notion that time can be ignored—that "capital" is superabundant and production is "time-saturated" under primitive conditions—was always suspect. So it is well that Smith, after turning the page of labor theory of value, does include interest or profit in competitive price along with labor wages and land rent.

Ricardo lingered longer over the labor theory—too long his critics thought—but from the beginning he admitted that shrimp picked up on the shore, in comparison with ancient oaks or aged wine, would *not* exchange in accordance with respective embodied labor contents. It is a sad reflection on the decadence of literary economics that so much printer's ink has been wasted on the sterile and ambiguous question of whether Ricardo had or didn't have a labor theory of value, or a 93 percent labor theory, or . . . .

In the real world, of 1776, 1817, or 1970, time was money and interest (or profit, they are the same thing when uncertainty is ignorable) rates were not zero. Interest will compound as a cost exactly like the turnover tax of my equation (2).[11] So the bourgeois economics that Marx inherited at midcentury did expect competitive price ratios to differ from embodied labor contents—just as my $A_{02}(r)/A_{01}(r)$ of (2) differs from $A_{02}/A_{01} = A_{02}(0)/A_{01}(0)$ of (1). Only by stepping up past-dated labor by the compounding factor of interest, by $a_0(1 + r)$ and $a(1 + r)$ and by

$$a_0(1 + r) + a_0(1 + r)\{a(1 + r)\} \\ + a_0(1 + r)\{a(1 + r)\}^2 \\ + \cdots \text{etc.},$$

can one calculate actual competitive costs and prices of production.

-Karl Marx, in the posthumous 1894 Volume III of *Capital*, did concur in these arithmetical facts. But his route was a more Hegelian one—of first reaction in the form of Volume I's analysis of "values" along the line of my Equation (3)'s value-added tax arithmetic, and then Volume III's later synthesis by means of the so-called "transformation process."

IV. A Pre-Marx Subsistence-Wage Model

To understand this devious path, let us now recall that the classical economists regarded labor—along with deer, or beaver,

[11] See Sraffa [35, 1960] or Samuelson [26, 1970 and 29, 1959].

or velvets—as also subject to a cost of production. The Malthus theory of population is a well known instance. Ricardo's theory is in its essentials identical with that of Malthus. With modern von Neumann[12] methods we can easily understand the logic and the biological linkages of the Malthus model. Although Marx admired Ricardo, he loathed Malthus as a reactionary and even plagiarist. To the extent that Marx insists on rejecting Malthusian models, we are left with a harder task of understanding just how *his* von Neumann linkages are envisaged to operate. My task here is not that of perhaps discovering that the Emperor wears no clothes and that perhaps Marx's hypothesis of a minimum-subsistence exploitative wage is not well determined by efficacious linkages. My task is to elucidate the logic of his model, on the basis of acceptance of its basic postulates and axioms.

1. Let us return to Smith's rude state: two units of labor produce a beaver, one unit of labor produces a deer. Suppose minimum daily sustenance requires $m = $ one deer. Then nothing is left over for luxury consumption of beaver. And nothing is left over for a possible positive profit rate or for any taxation whether of value-added or turnover type. Actually, if a tax were imposed the population would die out, just as it would if subsistence were at $m > 1$.

But suppose, perhaps because of an invention that makes vension more digestible, the minimum needed wage drops below 1. With $m < 1$, we have a contradiction: deer and labor cannot *both* be at their costs of production in terms of each other. Why not? Because the following two equations have no consistent solution:

$$
(4) \quad
\begin{aligned}
W/P_{\text{deer}} &= m < 1 = a_{01}^{-1} \\
&= 1/(P_{\text{deer}}/W) = W/P_{\text{deer}}
\end{aligned}
$$

If an obliging exploiting government came along with a tax of either $1 + s^* = 1/m$ or $1 + r^* = 1/m$, the "contradiction" would disappear. In the Marx scenario, an obliging acquisitive capitalist provides the function of appropriating the surplus, $1 - m$. He does this by commanding a positive rate of profit, $1 + r^* = 1/m > 1$, the exploitative rate of profit that leaves the real wage at the minimum subsistence level.

But actually this hypothesis is absurd in the context of Smith's early and rude state. What hold does the capitalist have there on the worker? What bargain can he strike? What that is useful can the employer withhold from the rude worker, who hunts where he pleases on superabundant acres and is free to eat his kill on the spot? Obviously, a vulgar Marxian is wrong to resolve (4)'s contradiction by positing $1 + r^* = 1/m$. And Smith himself knew better. He knew that *cost affects price only by its effect on supply.* If the real wage exceeds m of subsistence, that means population will grow. And, until Marx accepts Malthus' law of diminishing returns (to men become so numerous that land becomes crowded and no longer free), wages stay high above subsistence and population grows forever in a Neumann-Malthus golden age. Symbolically, (4) is replaced by

$$
(5) \quad \frac{1}{\text{population}} \frac{d(\text{population})}{dt}
$$

$$
= \text{a rising function of } (a_{01}^{-1} - m)
$$

$$
= k(W/P_{\text{deer}} - m) > 0, \text{ say,}
$$

where $k > 0$ and the implied solution is one of exponential growth like $e^{\lambda t}$, $\lambda > 0$.[13]

> *Summary.* In Smith's rudest state there is no tendency whatsoever for the real wage to fall to labor's minimum cost of subsistence. Instead the number of units of labor grows exponentially. At best, the Marx formula $1 + r^* = 1/m$ would

---

[12] There is a voluminous modern literature on the 1931 model of von Neumann [22, 1945].

[13] Recall my *Economics* [27, Samuelson, 1970, 8th ed., p. 713, or the 7th ed., p. 708].

give us the rate of profit that owners of *slave* power, of robots producible instantaneously out of deer, could earn on their assets. Free labor is another matter.

2. To give the crude exploitation theory of wages a better run for its money, let us alter some of Smith's strong assumptions. Now suppose subsistence consists solely of 1/3 of a new beaver coat needed each period and of nothing else. Now there is no room for deer production, for profit, or for taxation. To produce one new beaver coat, it will be recalled from our earlier example, requires two units of labor in hunting at a first stage; then in a second stage one more unit of labor in sewing—or three units of labor in all. Therefore,[14] man must again work all the twelve-hour day for his minimum subsistence: hunting and sewing in the steady state. Now the costs of production, in terms of each other—of men and beaver coats, happen to be consistent, namely

$$W/P = 1/A_0 = 1/(2 + 1) = 1/3$$
$$W/P = m = 1/3 = A_0^{-1}$$
$$= 1/(2 + 1)$$
$$= 1/(P/W)(1 + 0)$$

Now, however, *capital goods* in the form of slain beaver are seen to be needed as raw material in the steady state. If the needed final goods are to be produced, sewers must be supplied with goods-in-process to work with.

Since this is a subsistence economy with nary a surplus, it is not clear how the synchronized state ever got off the ground and got itself started. Who went without his needed m at an earlier date? No obvious answer is forthcoming. So let us now leave

[14] To relate this model more simply to Marx's image of the exploited worker as toiling so many hours of the day for himself and the remaining working hours for the exploiting employer, my earlier assumptions of *hourly* inputs has been transmuted here to *daily* inputs—for which the reader's indulgence is asked.

the subsistence economy for a surplus economy.

Imagine that an invention has reduced the minimum subsistence level, or cost-of-production level, to $m = 1/3.84 < 1/3 = 1/A_0$. Then, as back in (4), we have inconsistent costs of production for labor and wage goods in terms of each other. A sophisticated Marxist, trying to express his theory in terms a bourgeois economist (say, David Ricardo) could understand, would be tempted to write down

$$(6) \quad \begin{aligned} P_{\text{coat}} &= W2(1 + r)^2 + W1(1 + r) \\ &= WA_0(r), \text{ cost of production} \end{aligned}$$

$$W/P_{\text{coat}} = m = 1/4.08, \quad \text{labor-power cost of production}$$

$$4.08 = 2(1 + r)^2 + 1(1 + r)$$

$$\begin{aligned} 1 + r^* &= -\frac{1}{4} + \frac{\sqrt{1 + 4(2)4.08}}{4} \\ &= \frac{-1 + \sqrt{33.64}}{4} = \frac{-1 + 5.8}{4} \\ &= 1.2 \end{aligned}$$

Thus, twenty percent is the exploitation theory's equilibrium rate of profit, r^*, at which the real wage is down to the minimum of subsistence.

3. But is this a correct behavior equation? Maybe yes, maybe no. At least the theory now has a logical chance. If workers do not save—do not "abstain," do not "wait"— they will be unable to provide raw materials needed for their labor to work with. If capitalists own raw beaver, they can now strike a bargain with the workers and capture some of the producible surplus, $1/A_0 - m$ or $1/m - A_0$. But how much can capitalists get? And by what methods? Let us see.

Begin with zero profit. Immediately after the invention, if r stays zero, the workers get a wage above subsistence. In Malthus-Ricardo fashion, population grows. But now beaver-raw-material will be in short supply.

How much can capitalists capture in a competitive market? Perhaps as much as $r^* = .2$. Perhaps less. Perhaps more as workers starve and begin to die out.

What steady-state golden-age permanent equilibrium is possible? That depends on capitalists' propensity to save out of each profit level r and on how much raw-material capital is needed for the production process. I shall not, in discussing 1776 or 1867 models, write down the modern Harrod-Solow-Kalecki identities.[15] But I can summarize what has to be the proper empirical outcome:

Summary. The equilibrium profit rate will be between zero and the exploitation rate r^*, at a level just large enough to coax out the balanced capital formation (of beaver raw material) needed for the growing labor force to work with. The work force grows because the real wage exceeds the minimum cost of subsistence and of reproduction of labor power. Any increase in capitalists' propensity to save out of each profit rate will raise the real wage and the system's natural rate of growth, and will lower the equilibrium profit rate. If we superimpose continuing technological change on the system, real wages under developing capitalism can be presumed to rise—slowly or rapidly depending upon the nature of the innovations and the underlying biological and thrift propensities.

We are left with a model that could as legitimately be claimed by Nassau Senior as by Karl Marx or Joan Robinson! Thus suppose the bourgeois family lives forever. Suppose it acts as if it had a Pigouvian rate of subjective time preference for present over future utilities of exactly $\rho = 6$ percent. Then

[15] Refer to J. Robinson [24, 1956] or N. Kaldor [12, 1956].

[16] Discussion and summary of optimal control theory, as discussed by Ramsey, Uzawa, Morishima, Hicks, Shell, Cass, Samuelson and **Solow,** Arrow, Kurz, Mirrlees, and many others is given in Burmeister and Dobell [7, 1970], a convenient reference work.

the equilibrium Harrod identities will *adjust themselves*, as Ramsey[16] analysis proves, to $.06 = \rho < r^\infty < r^* = .20$.

4. Writers on the transformation problem have accepted, generally uncritically, the exploitation theory of profit and wages. So I must not supersede it here. Therefore, from now on, let us stipulate that labor reproduces itself mightily at the slightest rise in real wage and that capitalists are grudging savers, with the result that r^∞ is always up near its maximum r^* rate.

What this section has established is that the exploitation model can be couched in bourgeois terms free of the terminological innovations of Marx's Volume I. But let us note that the spirit of the model can also be attained by Marxian concepts of surplus value. Our comparison of the turnover and value-added taxes prepares us to understand this.

Thus, a turnover tax of 20 percent with the exploiting state providing steady-state reproduction of capital goods and wasting the surplus could achieve the described minimum-subsistence equilibrium. But a value-added tax on labor could also accomplish this. We now tax at the rate s the two hunting labor units and the one labor sewing unit, and solve the equivalent of (3)

$$
\begin{aligned}
1/m = 4.08 &= 2(1 + s) + 1(1 + s) \\
(7) \qquad &= 3(1 + s) = A_0(1 + s) \\
s^* &= 1.08/3 = .36
\end{aligned}
$$

The needed value-added tax is 36 percent. Or as Marx would say, the "uniform rate of surplus value or labor exploitation" (applied only to the *live* labor of each stage!) is 36 percent. Of every 12 full-hour day, under *either* the Volume III profit scenario or the Volume I surplus-value scenario, the worker works 100/136 for himself and the other 36/136 of the time for the government or for the capitalists' exaction. (What is different in the alternative regimes is the exchange ratio of directly-produced beaver and indirectly-

285

produced coats, namely 3/1 versus 3.4/1 = [2(1.2)+1]/1.)

V. Graphical Synthesis[17]

Figure 1, which uses numerical data from a table to come in Part Two (namely Table 2), can summarize the exploitation theory of wages and interest. The production-possibility frontier of net final goods, producible with fixed labor of say, 1, is given by ABZ, with slope determined by embodied labor coefficients A_{02}/A_{01}. The minimum subsistence cost-of-production level is shown by the $m'mm''$ contour, whose corner at m specifies the market basket of needed wage goods.

There are three distinct ways of getting to m: 1) by direct planning, rationing, and command; 2) by a competitive profit rate r (corresponding to a turnover tax); 3) by a postulated equal rate of surplus value s (involving a markup on direct labor costs alone, on Marx's "variable capital v_j" exclusive of his "constant capital c_j", and corresponding to a value-added tax). The first of these methods requires no further explanation.

In the second regime, charging a positive profit, $r > 0$, will push the budget-equation for the representative worker inward from ABZ, as the elements of $A_0(r)$ are marked up over $A_0(0)$. The inward shift will generally not be parallel, tending rather to steepen in recognition of the fact that the good with relatively less direct labor will have more of a markup from the compounded interest on its earlier-dated labor. These steepening lines will cover the chart and there will be a unique profit rate, r^*, that brings the worker's budget constraint down to amz, the steep line through m.

In the third regime, a positive rate of surplus value, $s > 0$, achieves the same minimum at m. But because surplus value, like a value-added tax, is charged only once on labor no matter how early is its date, the markup is

the same percentage $(1+s)$, on all goods; hence the shift of the worker's budget-equation is inward in a parallel way. And of course there will be a unique s^* that produces the indicated broken line through m parallel to ABZ. The difference between the slopes of the two lines through m depicts the "contradiction" between Volume III's bourgeois prices and Volume I's Marxian values (only the latter having ratios that still agree with the ratios of the embodied labor requirements of the undiluted labor theory of value).

Figure 2 reveals even more explicitly the determination of the unique profit and surplus-value rates. Figure 2(a) presents the "factor-price frontier"[18] relating the profit rate, r, to the real wage in terms of the first good, $W/P_1 = 1/A_{01}(r)$. Figure 2(b) relates r to the real wage in terms of the second good, $W/P_2 = 1/A_{02}(r)$. Figure 2(c) relates r to the (m_i) market basket of subsistence goods, $W/(P_1 m_1 + P_2 m_2) = 1/[A_{01}(r)m_1 + A_{02}(r)m_2]$. The exploitation equilibrium profit rate, r^*, is determined by the specified subsistence level m, as indicated at e^*.

The right-hand side of Figure 2 shows the same story, but this time told for "values." Now at the extreme right, in 2(d), the real wage of the first good is plotted against the rate of surplus value s, and is a rectangular hyperbola determined by the equation $w/p_1 = 1/A_{01}(0)(1+s)$, where values are indicated by the lower-case letters p_j. Similarly, 2(e) plots s against the real wage of the second good, expressed in the values regime. Finally, Figure 2(f) plots the real wage in terms of the market basket of subsistence wage goods, or mathematically $w/(p_1 m_1 + p_2 m_2)$ $1/[A_{01}(0)m_1 + A_{02}(0)m_2](1 + s)$. Notice that all the three right diagrams of the values regime are rectangular hyperbolae and so ratios of them all cancel out the $(1 + s)$ = common factor and do reflect embodied labor coefficients.

---

[17] This section can be skipped, or read following the reading of Part Two.

[18] For this concept, see Samuelson [32, 1962; 28, 1957; 27, 1970 and 31, 1961] or Sraffa [35, 1960].

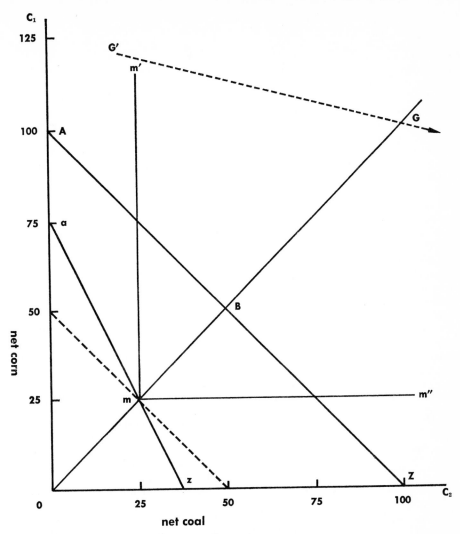

FIGURE 1

The production-possibility frontier of steady-state corn and coal, producible net by 100 labor, is given by ABZ, with slope reflecting total-embodied-labor hours, $A_{02}(0)/A_{01}(0)$. Subsistence specified as needed for reproduction of laborers is given by $m'mm''$. A planned economy might go directly to m by command. Or, in a regime of Volume I's values raising the rate of surplus value, s, would shift the workers budget constraint inward in a fashion parallel to ABZ—until at $s^* = 100$ percent we reach the broken line through m parallel to ABZ. In a regime of Volume III's prices, raising the profit rate above zero shifts the budget constraint inward, in a steepened fashion relative to ABZ—until, at $r^* = 33\ 1/3$ percent, amz is reached, with price of coal risen relative to price of corn because of the latter's relatively greater ratio of direct labor and the implied greater $A_{02}(1/3)/A_{01}(1/3)$ ratio. Because of the singular assumption of equal-internal-compositions, the gross amounts of productions are shown at G, on the same ray as Om and OB.

A natural way to pair (r^*, s^*) values is shown by the horizontal real-wage line that is common to the two regimes. As that horizontal line is raised or lowered, we generate all the (r^*, s^*) pairings that correspond to the same real wage (in terms of specified m_j proportions of subsistence). Obviously, r^* and s^* rise and fall together. Obviously, $r^* < s^*$ if any early-date labor (constant capital) is involved in producing the subsistence goods. Obviously, changing the composition of the subsistence market-basket of goods will alter the pairing relationship between (r^*, s^*).[19]

In the general case the Volume I relations on the right are simpler than those on the left. Being simple hyperbolae, they can be inverted and solved for s^* by a simple linear equation. The relations on the left involve Leontief-Sraffa compounding of profits and have to be written as ratios of a common nth degree polynomial to different nth degree polynomials for each good depending upon its time-profile of dated labor.[20]

We have now completed Part One's preparatory review and background exposition of the regimes of prices and values. We are now in a position to review the troops, interpreting what Marx proposed and what each

writer has added to the literature. In a sense these first remarks of mine have added a further contribution to the literature that can stand by itself as an elucidation of the exploitation-theory "transformation problem." The results of this investigation can be recapitulated as follows.

1. If given the direct labor coefficients, a_0 or $[a_{0j}]$, and the input-output coefficients, a or $[a_{ij}]$, and the subsistence-wage parameters, m or $[m_i]$, direct planning and command can determine the allocation of final goods and real incomes between workers and non-workers (as in Figure 1).

2. Alternatively, one can postulate a Marxian rate of exploitation or surplus value, common to every industry, and easily solve for the s^* equilibrium rate and the implied "values"—which will be seen to involve ratios still equal to embodied labor requirements of the undiluted labor theory of value.

3. If one regards such Marxian markups as completely unrealistic in comparison with equal rates of profit on *all* the cost outlays of the industry at any and every stage of production, one can make a fresh start and deduce the exploitative rate of profit and competitive prices from the (a_0, a, m) data of the problem—making no use of surplus values or of Marxian values concepts. The line amz in Figure 1 shows the resulting equilibrium.

Looking at the last two paragraphs, one realizes that "transforming from values to prices" does literally involve "abandoning the values schemata of Volume I and embracing instead the prices schemata of Volume III and of bourgeois economics"— but of course with the understanding that the bourgeois tools are applied to the non-bourgeois hypothesis that workers end up working some of the hours of the day for their bare subsistence and the remaining hours of the day for the exploiting capitalists. By symmetry, the "inverse transformation from prices to values" involves "abandoning

[19] The only exception to this is where labor intensities, a_{0j}/A_{0j} or organic compositions of capital, are the same for every good. In this singular case, *all* the factor-price frontiers are of the form $b_j(1-r/r_m)/(1+r)$—becoming straight lines in the Sraffa [35, 1960, p. 30] fashion of a standard commodity, it being understood that the wage is expressed in end-of-period postfactum rather than usual beginning-of-period terms.

[20] *I.e.*, $a_0(1+r) [I-a(1+r)]^{-1}$ has elements which are the ratios of such polynomials in r. When there are two goods, the frontiers can change curvature; with n goods, there can be more inflection points; but always the frontier must decline monotonically. And if any necessary good requires, directly or indirectly, something of itself for its production, the frontier will intersect the horizontal axis at an r_{max} intercept, which will be the same for all such necessaries and which will equal the maximum rate of growth that the system is capable of even if labor were in unlimited supply. To sum up, solving for the exploitation profit rate r^* and the corresponding real wage(s) generally involves solving an nth degree polynomial for its smallest positive root, the algebraic counterpart of finding the proper intersection of a horizontal line with a declining frontier.

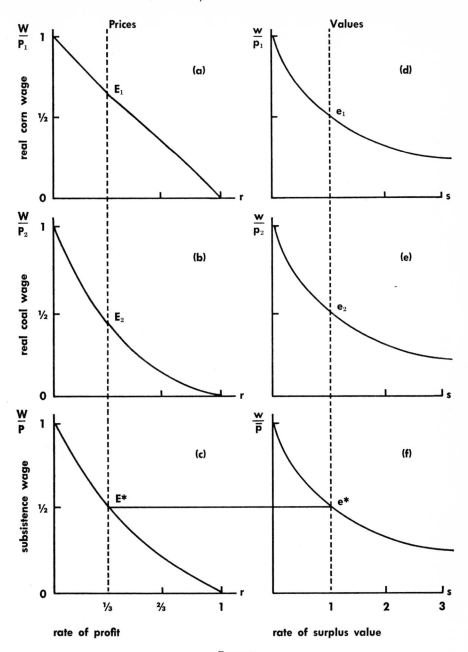

FIGURE 2

TABLE 1. MARX'S OWN TRANSFORMATION PROCEDURE

Capitals or Cost Outlays (1)	Surplus Values (2)	Values (3) = (1) + (2)	Rate of Profit (4) = (2)/(1)	Prices (5) = (1)(1+.22)	Deviations of Prices from Values (6) = (5) − (3)
I $80c_1 + 20v_1$	$20s_1$	120	20%	122	+2
II $70c_2 + 30v_2$	$30s_2$	130	30%	122	−8
III $60c_3 + 40v_3$	$40s_3$	140	40%	122	−18
IV $85c_4 + 15v_4$	$15s_4$	115	15%	122	+7
V $95c_5 + 5v_5$	$5s_5$	105	5%	122	+17
Average 100	22	122	22%	122	0

the price model in favor of working out the values directly from the (a_0, a, m) data."

Part Two. Marx's Transformation Process And The Model of Exploitation

VI. The "Transformation" Procedure of Volume III

If actual market competition causes the rate of profit to be the same in all industries, it has been established that competitive "prices" will necessarily differ from the Marxian values (save in the singular case where all industries happen to have the same "organic composition of capital," *i.e.*, the same ratio of direct wage costs to other costs). In Volume III of *Capital*, Marx faced up to the contradiction, indicating in a

⬥ At the left are shown the downward-sloping factor-price frontiers, W/P_i, for each profit rate r. In (c), the condition that 100 labor be fed 25 of corn and of coal, out of the 50 of each producible net, determines $r^* = 1/3$ at E^*. Running over to e^* in (f), we similarly determine $s^* = 1$; running up vertically to e_2 and e_1, we read off corresponding values, $w/p_i = 1/[A_{0i}(0)(1+s^*)]$. Either regime is computable without the other. If the a_0, a, m coefficients could take on more than one value, the outer envelope of such relations would be relevant, and the transformation from s^* to r^*, and vice versa, would be a more complicated problem than mere extraction of algebraic roots.

well-known table how one "transforms" values into prices.[21]

Ever since 1894 there has been a good deal of commentary on this problem and its proposed solution. None of the writers, Marx included, were satisfied with the suggested procedure, which can be illustrated by the above adaptation of the tables from Volume III.[22]

[21] As I indicate in my bibliographical Part Three, the classical reference on this is Sweezy [36, 1942, Chapter VII], where the various writings are reviewed and a full discussion of the 1907 solution of Bortkiewicz [3] is explained. See also Sweezy [37, 1949], which provides an English editing of Böhm-Bawerk's, *Karl Marx and the close of his system* and Rudolph Hilferding's, *Böhm-Bawerk's criticisms of Marx*, and, as an Appendix, an English translation of Bortkiewicz [3]. See also another 1907 paper by Bortkiewicz [4], a treatment in some ways more fundamental; also note Winternitz [40, 1948], May [18, 1948], Joan Robinson [25, 1950], and Dobb [9, 1955]. Especially valuable as well is Meek [19, 1956], to the later printing of which I shall key my references. The first landmark, since 1907, in the analytical history of the subject is provided by Seton [33, 1957]. See also Morishima and Seton [21, 1961], Johansen [11, 1961], and my paper [26, Samuelson, 1970]. For the modern reader the well-known works of Leontief [13, 1941 and 14, 1966], Sraffa [35, 1960], and Dorfman-Samuelson-Solow [10, 1958] provide relevant techniques.

[22] Table 1 is taken from the tables on pp. 183–85, Chapter IX, of the 1909 Kerr edition of *Capital*, III, except that I have corrected an obvious misprint of 150 for 105 in the first of those tables; I have also ignored Marx's complication in which all of constant capital is not used up in one period's production—so the reader can, if he wishes, subtract from the numbers in my

Marx here assumes five industries or departments. Direct wage payments (so-called variable capital) are given by 20 of v_1, 30 of v_2, . . . , etc; payments for intermediate goods (so-called constant capital) are given by 80 of c_1, 70 of c_2, ... At first he assumes a constant *rate of surplus value* (mark-up on wages) of 100 percent and derives his "values." When he relates the total of the surplus, not to the total of wage payments alone (variable capital) but to the total of all cost outlays (constant capital plus variable capital), he finds divergent rates of profit being earned in the various industries with their different labor intensities; these average out to 22 percent.[23] So in column (5) are computed the competitive prices (what we would call the Walrasian equilibrium prices). Industries like V, which are not very labor intensive, are seen to have prices high relative to their values because of the fact that their prices must carry the heavy weight of profit earned on much capital. But, for all the industries of society, Marx has *by postulate* made prices average out to equality with values.

Without exception, critics and defenders alike, have recognized that Marx was not consistent in all this. For he mistakenly kept the same constant capitals, c_j, in his price calculation as well as in his value calculations. But what are the cs? They are the items that have been produced in earlier stages of production, and the same logic that causes values to be changed into prices requires that *their* values also be converted

into prices. Thus, it is argued, Marx went only part of the way and erred in retaining some elements of values calculation in arriving at his prices.

I must agree with this. Indeed, in some of his passages Marx indicates an explicit awareness of the inconsistency;[24] all the writers since 1907 have resolved the error by some variant of the procedure recommended by Bortkiewicz. Without dissenting from this consensus, my first effort here is to point out that there is a singular case in which Marx's algorithm happens to be rigorously correct.

This singular case is worthy of explication in its own right as a *curiosum*. But much more important, by considering this case one can —in the words of the master himself— illuminate and strip bare some misconceptions concerning the sense in which one finds it necessary or useful to proceed from Volume I's analysis of interindustry *values* in order to understand the nature of exploitation actually occurring in a competitive world of prices and as possibly giving a clue to the dynamic laws of motion of exploitative capitalism. I hope to demonstrate that anyone who believes in the relevance of a minimum-subsistence wage (I myself do not, either theoretically or empirically, but that is not relevant to the present effort) will understand his own theory better if he preserves from Volume I only the spirit of the insight that there is a discrepancy between what can be produced and what constitutes

---

column's (3) and (5) the respective numbers [30, 19, 9, 45, 85] to get Marx's more complicated second table. Unfortunately for the reader in a hurry, the literature has mostly concentrated on the more complicated case, which merely slows down but does not alter the analysis. (Paging in the Kerr edition runs about 30 longer than in some other editions; citation of chapters, however, should enable one to find any quoted passages.)

[23] If Marx had not chosen all $c_j + v_j$ equal, the average profit would involve using such column (1) items as weights instead of being computed, as here, by a simple unweighted average of the separate industry profit rates.

[24] In *Capital*, III, Chapter IX, p. 194, Marx notes: "Now the price of production of a certain commodity is its cost-price for the buyer, and this price must pass into other commodities and become an element of their prices." At least one writer [19, Meek, 1956, 148ff] seems to believe that if Marx's table can ignore "mutual interdependence," no error is involved. Not so: even if the c of Department I comes from that department alone, or from an "earlier stage" of it, profit calculations will alter the c that had been appropriate for surplus-values calculations. So the same problem arises here that Meek and all the writers recognize in connection with models of simple or extended reproduction where mutual interdependencies are obvious.

the minimum wage, and he will do better to jettison as unnecessary and obfuscating to his *own* theory the letter of Volume I's analysis of inter-industry values.

VII. The Singular Case of Equal Internal Compositions

The singular case in which Marx's procedure becomes exact can now be described. It is not the well-known case where all labor intensities are equal (the case of equal organic composition of capital) for in that case the problem becomes transparent and trivial, there being no longer any "contradiction" between values and prices. If the world were like that, Marx would have had no reason to try to improve upon the bourgeois economists' analysis of prices, since relative prices and values are then identical.

Instead we may now consider what might be called the case of "equal *internal* compositions of (constant) capitals." In this case *every one of the departments happens to use the various raw materials and machine services in the same proportions that society produces them in toto.* Thus, if the five departments represent different goods (say corn, coal, . . .) then each department must have the same ratio of corn to coal in its constant capital as every other department. This technological requirement is, of course, not particularly realistic (although Leontief's input-output matrices do exhibit some curious similarities of columns) and its disparities from realism help to elucidate the objections to Marx's procedures more cogently than do many of the sometimes sterile commentaries on him. A second postulate goes along with the above technological condition; again it is not a very realistic one: we must also assume that the *minimum-subsistence budget is a market basket of goods that comes in those same relative proportions as the goods are used as inputs in production.* (This is because a subsistence-wage theory is somehow assuming that the labor supply itself is, as it were, *produced* by a

further department not all that different from other departments. Marx, it will be recalled, did not like Malthusian population arguments; but he was a classical economist who believed in a cost of production for labor power itself, even if he enunciated less clearly than von Neumann has in our day the linkages of this mechanism.) In the end it will be observed that the capitalists, who get what is left over after the specified requirements of industries and wage-subsistence have been met, will also receive goods in these same proportions. However, this is a theorem of our analysis and not a separate postulate, being already implied by our other postulates. The capitalists are free to devote these goods to luxury consumption (as in a Marxian model of "simple reproduction") or in part or whole to accumulating the increments of physical constant capitals needed to provide for balanced exponential growth (as in Marxian models of "extended reproduction," or so-called golden ages). The fact that the capitalists use goods in the same proportions as the workers is evidently at variance with those reproduction models of Marx carried over from Volume II, in which separate wage-good, luxury-good, and producer's-good departments are postulated. And this alerts us to the fact that almost all writers, though they begin with the five departments that Marx himself began with, choose somewhat gratuitously to rush on to apply the procedure of Table I to Marx's models of simple reproduction[25]—a legitimate procedure but one

[25] In the paper [3, Bortkiewicz, 1907] upon which Sweezy and later writers primarily rely, this is done. Bortkiewicz even presumes to alter some of Marx's numbers in his other 1907 paper in order to make the identification. In this he seems merely to be following in the tradition of Tugan-Baranowsky and other contemporary writers. But in his other paper, he clearly shows that he does understand how to handle the general case, indeed indicating a better understanding of the nuances of the problem than those who have essentially adopted his solution; I cannot help feel that Bortkiewicz has not been given full justice by many subsequent writers, who may have been put off by his tart defense of Ricardo against Marx's criticisms, and

that Marx himself was, as far as I can remember, too wary to attempt.

VIII. Marx Vindicated

Now let us return to Table 1 and note
how our singular case of constant-internal-
compositions-of-goods does validate Marx's
simplistic procedure. If the 80 of *c* in Department I is in fact made up of a weighted combination of column (5) prices that average
out to the same as column (3) values, and
only if this is the case, we can be sure that
80 remains the right magnitude for *both* the
price and value calculations. We prove this
by trial substitution of the asserted prices
and verification that the process is indeed
self justifying. We *also* verify something that
Marx and most pre-Seton writers other than
Bortkiewicz failed to emphasize sufficiently
—that the real wage has indeed been kept
to the same exact level in both the mode of
prices and of values. Thus, without my
postulate, Marx's procedure is open to the
further fatal objection, namely that the
market basket of subsistence will not cost
the same in the two regimes relative to an
hour's labor. (When Marx tells us that the
workers work half the day for themselves
and half the day for the exploiting capitalists,
he does not indicate in his various tables

by his tireless analysis of every detail. As is indicated
in various parts of the present paper, I cannot agree
with the mathematician May that Bortkiewicz's mathematics is overly elaborate, or dependent on overly-
strong sufficiency conditions, or that he has introduced
pseudo-mystifications, or that he has adopted normali-
zation rules for the absolute price level that are clearly
inconsistent with Marx. As May has suggested, to the
pure mathematician the algebra of eigenvalues is
trivial, as is most of physics and engineering. Still, such
eminent men as Perron, Frobenius, Markov, Fréchet,
Minkowski, and Besicovitch have devoted themselves
to his area, and it is not until the writings of Seton and
Morishima that one finds in the modern literature a full
understanding of Bortkiewicz. As Sweezy, the one
Marxian writer who does express appreciation for the
Bortkiewicz contributions, has pointed out, Bortkiewicz did glean from the Marxian analysis the essential point—that setting the real wage at a specified
subsistence does provide a determinate profit level at
which labor's full product gets "discounted."

what fraction of the goods in the different
departments make up their iron ration. If
we ourselves pick such proportions at
random, there is no reason why the properly
weighted average of the new prices should at
all come to the same level as for values even
though that is true for unweighted averages.
This would mean that Marx's 22 percent
profit rate is the wrong rate for him to use.
In the modern era, Leontief and Sraffa,
Dorfman-Samuelson-Solow, Seton, and
Morishima know how to calculate the polynomials that give the proper departure
from 22 percent; so too does Bortkiewicz
as a result of his perusal of the work of the
young Russian Dmitriev and his understanding of Walras. But the other writers, by
rushing from the five department case to
models where one industry produces all the
wage goods, hardly show an awareness that
there is a problem here. Instead they waste
much time on the unessential question of
what *absolute* level of prices should one introduce into a table whose only importance
consists in its well-determined *relative* proportions!)

But to repeat and summarize, on the basis
of my singular case of equal-internal-compositions, Marx has been preserved from all
pitfalls.

IX. The "Inverse Transformation" Problem

Table 1 now well illustrates that one
could as easily start with prices and perform
what Morishima-Seton call the "inverse
transformation" from prices to values. And
again, the simple procedure indicated by
Marx's school arithmetic will be rigorously
correct in my singular case (and only then).

Let us analyze the steps in going from
columns (1) and (5) back to columns (3) and
(2). The *total* discrepancy between the final
prices of (5) and the cost outlays of (1) is
given by $22 + 22 + 22 + 22 + 22$; these
numbers are constant only because of
Marx's penchant for simple examples that

involve hundreds, but in any case one can compute ΣS_j (reckoned in price units of course). This can be equated to Σs_j reckoned in value units.[26] Since Marx's case involves no change in the totals of values and prices, the rate of surplus value, s, is evenly computed and columns (2) and (3) can be filled in. But now, just as Marx turned Hegel on his head, we turn Marx upside down, and can say in a dozen repetitive ways that this total of *profit* is not allocated by the *value* system according to where it was "really produced" but rather "falls to the share of each aliquot part of the total social [variable] capital out of the total social profit [!]." Each time that I have inverted prices and values, rates of profit and surplus value, variable and total capital, I have introduced the bracketed interjections. To parody Marx's own words further:

Surplus value [!] is therefore that disguise of profit [!] which must be removed before the real nature of profit [!] can be discovered. In profit [!], the relation between capital and labour is laid bare [III, Chapter II, p. 62].
. . . [without Volume III's [!] analysis of profit [!], political economy would be deprived] "of every rational basis". [III, Chapter VIII, pp. 176–77]
. . . [and the average rate of surplus value [!] would be] an average of nothing (*Theories of surplus value*, p. 231, as cited by Meek [19, 1956]).

A little of this parodying goes a long way. A reader who refers to Meek's careful elucidation of what Marx seems to have intended will find many more passages open to the same mishandling. But to Marx these

were no joking matters. For we are close to the heartland of what he regarded as his theoretical innovation.[27] In a proud passage, he claims that

the actual state of things is revealed for the first time; that political economy up to the present time . . . made either forced abstractions of the distinctions between surplus-value and profit . . . or gave up the determination of value and with it all safeguards of scientific procedure, in order to cling to the obvious phenomenon of these differences—this confusion of the theoretical economists demonstrates most strikingly the utter incapacity of the capitalist, when blinded by competition, to penetrate through the outer disguise into the internal essence and the inner form of the capitalist process of production [III, Chapter IX, p. 199].

X. A Misunderstanding

One common misunderstanding of the inverse transformation problem needs to be cleared up. It is common to a critic of Marx like Böhm-Bawerk and a sympathizer like Professor Joan Robinson. In effect, both argue that only profits and prices have a reality and that Marx in beginning with values and rates of surplus value has *already* performed the inverse transformation; thus the direct transformation merely brings him back to his starting place. Mrs. Robinson put it this way:

Sweezy . . . evidently fails to realize that the transformation problem and its resolution is just a toy and that the whole argument is condemned to circularity from birth, because the *values* which have to be "transformed into prices" are arrived at in the first instance by transforming prices into values. [25, Robinson, 1950, p. 362].

This is simply incorrect. Mrs. Robinson, not knowing in 1950 the Sraffa apparatus,

---

[26] The average rate of surplus value is given by $s = \sum S_j / \sum V_j = 110/110$, or 100 percent. Now we calculate column (2) by $s_j = (1+s)V_j = (1+s)v_j$, with $\sum s_j = \sum S_j$. And finally we get the values of (3) from $c_j + v_j + s_j = c_j + v_j + sv_j$. Note two things: this simplified inverse operation is open to all the original objections against Marx's neglect of the changes in the constant capitals in going from one system to the other, and can be defended only if my singular assumption is made. Also, note that $s = \sum S_j / \sum V_j$ is not the *simple* average of the (S_j/V_j)'s, namely $\sum (S_j/V_j)/5$, but is rather the *weighted* average $\sum V_j(S_j/V_j)/\sum V_j$, where the weights are the variable capitals (expressible in either units when my singular assumption is posited).

[27] Friedrich Engels concurred with this view that the transformation problem was at the heart of Karl Marx's basic contribution to economics. In the 1885 preface to *Capital*, Volume II, Engels had already thrown out the challenge to writers to anticipate the reconciliation of prices and values that was to be forthcoming in the third volume. And in the 1894 preface to that latter work, he comments scathingly on proposals to resolve the riddle, comparing them unfavorably with the revelations in Volume III itself.

or the equivalent Leontief apparatus, has failed to realize that one can go from an un-diluted labor theory of value, in which the direct plus indirect labor-hour requirements of each good and the subsistence can be reckoned up in physical terms to Marx's tableau of values. And we do so without having to solve any high degree polynomials (for five departments, generally a fifth degree polynomial) as we should have to do to arrive at the tableau involving profits and prices.[28] Having said this, let me hasten to say that I agree with her general point of view, most particularly with the words that follow on the same page, namely that Marxian exploitation is to be conceived "in terms of the division of working time into the part necessary to procure the subsistence of the workers, and the rest, which produces surplus. *This has no meaning as applied to separate industries.*" (Italics added.)

Böhm-Bawerk, in the cited piece on the conclusion of Marx's system, and also earlier in his writings during the 1880s on the exploitation theory of interest [1, Böhm-Bawerk, 1959], has made many valid points against Marx, for which sincere Marxian scholars should be grateful rather than otherwise. But he does not do the theory of exploitation full justice on one important logical point. Repeatedly he points to the admissions by Marx and his sympathizers that equality of profit rates and the implied prices are more realistic than the equality of rates of surplus values and the implied values. He rightly regards this as a rejection of the labor theory of value in the sense that the realistic exchange ratios are not to be inferred from ratios of necessary

labor time. But it is a non-sequitur for him to think that all this has negated the labor theory of value in its undiluted, technocratic sense, namely as an algebraic procedure that tells you what can be produced with a given total of labor in the steady state when all capital goods have become adjusted.[29] As will be seen in the following, a theory of the exploitation wage can be based solely upon the analysis of profits and prices (with all the Leontief-Sraffa algebraic complications that are implied by these real-world relations). And some day Marxians will probably wish to formulate it in those terms. But this does not deny that this same level of subsistence wages *could* be arrived at in a regime which chose to organize its exchange relations on the basis of Marx's Volume I hypotheses. (Recall Figure 1 of Part One in in this regard.) One might apply Marx's theory of the materialist determination of history to arrive at the hypothesis that it was Marx's incapacity in algebra and the absence of a computer that caused him to formulate his exploitation theory in Volume I terms which are unrealistic but which happen to be simpler to handle algebraically than Volume III's Walrasian relations.

XI. Redundancy of Industry Surplus Values

By now the crucial issue is no longer whether Volume III's prices are more realis-

---

[28] I exaggerate—a little. In making up one's own arithmetic examples, one can cook the coefficients of the polynomials to produce a prescribed simple root. And one can make singular simplifications, like mine here; or can assume decomposability of the system into somewhat independent parts, etc. The point remains though: once you know total labor embodiments, values are easy for the non-mathematical to calculate, and prices are not—which is a theorem about certain matrix equations.

[29] Böhm-Bawerk correctly points out that primary factors other than labor can affect market scarcities as these work themselves out in terms of supply and demand. And with generosity we can construe him to be pointing out that, when you do not confine yourselves to steady states, the supply conditions of stocks of heterogeneous capital goods also affect scarcities as these work themselves out in supply and demand markets, so as to produce exchange relations that are at variance with simple labor-theory-of-value notions. But these cogent criticisms should not be thought to vitiate the logic of an exploitation theory based upon the discrepancy between what labor can produce in the steady state and a minimum-subsistence level at which labor power can be reproduced at will. *I.e.*, Marx's version of the von Neumann model is not illogical, despite Böhm's charges that his opponents are reneging on their own rejection of the labor theory of value

tic under competition than Volume I's values: critics and Marxians are agreed that these prices certainly are. The issue has been narrowed down to whether, as Marx and his modern defenders have claimed, the profit rate upon which Volume III's Walrasian equilibrium depends is itself crucially determined by Volume I's analysis of surplus values, $s_j = v_j s$, or crucially dependent on the *totals* of these magnitudes (in the sense that the profit rate r can only be calculated *after* these have been summed up and averaged out).

First, this section demonstrates that Marx and Engels—and, in modern times, Dobb and Meek—are simply wrong in their identification of what aspect of the labor theory of value is intrinsically involved in working out a price-profit configuration that corresponds to the minimum-wage theory of exploitation. The most clear-cut proof is mathematical.[30]

Since there is no reason to expect a scholar interested in the process of exploitation and the laws of motion of developing capitalism to be also a virtuoso in matrix algebra, the second demonstration is by means of a simplified two department numerical example. Third, graphical analysis will clinch the point that profit-price equilibrium is determinable *solely* from the production coefficient specifying the required labor embodiments of the industries and from the minimum subsistence wage-good requirements. At no stage of the argument is there

[30] As has been already indicated in Part One, from knowledge of technology alone we know the a_0 and a coefficients. After these have been supplemented by specified subsistence requirements, m, Volume III's prices stand on their own feet and are defined by $P/W = a_0(1+r)[I-a(1+r)]^{-1} = A_0(r)$, $mA_0(r) = 1$. These relations require no prior consideration of the Volume I value relations, $p/w = a_0(1+s)[I-a]^{-1} = A_0(0)$, $mA_0(0)(1+s) = 1$, and no transformation procedure in either direction. Cf. Samuelson [26, 1970], equations (3) and (2), and the demonstration in (5) that Bortkiewicz goes from values to prices by cancelling out values! In Bortkiewicz [3, 1907] equations (20) and (28) are equivalent to the above price relations, and equations (9) and (11) equivalent to the above value relations.

need for, or benefit from, utilizing the magnitudes $c_j + v_j + v_j s$ of Volume I.

Numerical Example. Let society's 100 units of labor be allocated so that 80 work in Department I (say, corn) and 20 work in Department II (say, coal). In I, 100 units of corn are produced by 80 units of labor and 10 of corn and 10 of coal. In II, 100 units of coal are produced by 20 of labor and 40 of corn and 40 of coal. Let the minimum-subsistence wage require that each labor unit consumes a market basket of 1/4 final units of corn *and* 1/4 final units of coal, so that 25 units out of each 100 of gross outputs go to workers. Since another 50 of each is seen to go for intermediate products, that leaves 25 of each for non-workers' final consumption or saving-investment.

Note that my singular assumption of equal internal compositions is realized here. Note, too, that this physical tableau can be specified completely independently of either Volume I values or Volume III prices and of profit rates or surplus-value rates. It could have been achieved by a computer-guided command economy using planning and direct rationing.

Now consider a Volume I version of this same situation. The crucial ratio of what labor produces in comparison with what it needs for subsistence has already been determined by the physical tableau *prior* to any calculation of industry surplus values or totals of these magnitudes. We can translate these 25/50 relations into Marx's rate of surplus value by setting $s = 100$ percent. As shown in Table II's second and third columns, we can calculate the exchange ratios that prevail on the bizarre empirical hypothesis that the system is organized so that it is not the rate of profit which is equalized between industries, but rather their rates of surplus value s_j/v_j.

Alternatively, could we have *first* written down the Volume III price-profit relations shown in Columns (4) and (5)? For Marx or Meek to be making a valid defense of the

TABLE 2. EQUAL-INTERNAL-ORGANIC CASE OF SIMPLE REPRODUCTION

	Capitals (1)	Surplus Values (2)	Values (3) = (1)+(2)	Profits (4) = 1/3(1)	Prices (5) = (1)+(4)	Deviations (6) = (5)−(3)
I	$(20+20)c+80v$	$80v$	200	40	160	−40
II	$(80+80)c+20v$	$20v$	200	60	240	+40

$$r = \sum s_j / \sum (c_j+v_j) = 100/300 = 1/3 \qquad 0$$

Explanation: prices and values of each of 100 units of corn, and of coal, are respectively $(P_1, P_2) = (1.6, 2.4)$ and $(p_1, p_2) = (2.0, 2.0)$. The valuations are applied to physical amounts of corn and coal used as intermediate goods; wage $= 1$ throughout. When prices are applied in (1), we get $(16+24)c+80v$ and $(64+96)c+20v$ instead of the numbers shown there, but with the same *totals*.

important role of Volume I's analysis of surplus values, the answer to this question would have to be in the negative. But, clearly, there is one and only one profit rate, namely 33 1/3 percent, which could allocate to labor the specified minimum real wages. Even one who knows no algebra can satisfy himself of this by trying all possible profit rates and working out the resulting Columns (4) and (5). For *any* $r > .33$ 1/3, the prices charged each worker would be too high to permit him to buy the specified 1/4 units of corn and 1/4 units of coal with the wages earned by a unit of his labor time. For *any* $r < .33$ 1/3, his real wages would prove to be too high. So Columns (4) and (5) are definitely computable *prior* to the calculation of any item in Columns (2) and (3)—as shown. Q.E.D.

Graphical Demonstration. The reader can now refer back to Figure 1 to see the same point clearly. The production-possibility frontier of final goods, as given by *ABZ*, is based solely on the embodied labor requirements (as determined by the numerical $[a_0, a]$ coefficients: 80/100, 10/100, 10/100; 20/100, 40/100, 40/100; and nothing else). The minimum-subsistence wage requirement, it will be recalled, is shown by the

L-shaped indifference contour, $m'mm''$ (as determined by the 100/4, 100/4 coefficients, m, and nothing else).[31] So far neither prices and profit rates nor values and surplus-values are involved.

Now, to drive home the crucial point, this time consider Volume III's case first. If the profit rate had been zero—as in Adam Smith's "early and rude state" where the undiluted labor theory of value gives all to workers and leads to exchange values not merely *proportional* to embodied labors but *equal* to those embodied labors and hence equal to bourgeois prices—the budget line for the workers would have been the *ABZ* frontier itself. Then, as profit becomes positive and r is increased, their budget line naturally shifts inward by virtue of prices being marked up relative to the wage rate. However, as Ricardo conceded, the inward shift will not be parallel with all Ps rising in the same proportion; instead, corn being

[31] The gross amount of corn and coal produced, 100 units of each, is shown back in Figure 1 at G. In my singular case of equal internal compositions, m and G happen to lie on the same OmG ray (as, hence, must B also). But if non-workers were to shift their tastes away from B, as for example toward more corn, the point G would shift upward toward the point G'. Similarly, a shift in tastes toward coal would shift G oppositely, in either case destroying the simplifications of equal internal compositions.

more labor intensive will have its price fall relative to that of coal with its larger total profit markup. So each positive r gives a line steeper than ABZ, until at $r = .33\ 1/3$ we find the unique *amz* line that goes precisely through the prescribed m point—and which is seen for our numbers to have an absolute slope of $P_2/P_1 = 240/160 = 3/2$.

For one who believes in an exploitation theory of wages (and interest), the task is done. There is no need for, or interest in, Volume I's $c_j + v_j + sv_j$ analysis. And thus there is no need for the transformation problem, either direct or inverse. I think that Marx, were he alive today, would agree with this. In any case, Marxians in the future can be expected to agree with these prosaic and uncontroversial facts of arithmetic and logic.

For completeness, and possibly out of an antiquarian interest, we can also depict in Figure 1 the redundant Volume I calculations that lead to the broken line through m parallel to ABZ. But Mrs. Robinson's 1950 assertion that this must be done by means of the inverse transformation problem, in which one must obtain that parallel line by way of first calculating the *amz* line of prices and profit, is now seen to be incorrect. Instead—and here the Volume I algebra is admittedly simpler than that of Volume III, in the same way that the incidence of a value-added tax is simpler to calculate than that of a turnover tax—we raise gradually the rate of surplus value, s, above zero. Again the worker's budget line, of what they could buy in the market place at the quoted Marxian values, is shifted inward. But this time the shift is truly a simple parallel one! (Proof: an ever-larger fraction of the workers' hours available for their own consumption can be thought of as being taken away from them and being made subject to the consumption whims of the capitalist. And 99 hours of labors' time can produce for labor only $99/100$ of *any and all* of the wage goods previously producible, etc.). Clearly,

only one parallel line will pass through m; such a shift, half way to the origin in our example, must correspond to a rate of surplus value of exactly 100 percent.[32]

➜≫≪≪

The truth has now been laid bare. Stripped of logical complication and confusion, anybody's method of solving the famous transformation problem is seen to involve returning from the unnecessary detour taken in Volume I's analysis of values. As I have cited in my mathematical paper,[33] such a "transformation" is precisely like that in which an eraser is used to rub out an earlier entry, after which we make a new start to end up with the properly calculated entry.

XII. Conclusion On What Part of Marx Is Vital

Those who believe there is merit and importance in the notion of wages as determined by a-cost-of-production-of-labor-power will not infer that my dissection of Marx has robbed him of any credit for his essential insight. Marx needs to be protected from his defenders and occasionally from himself. (After all, did he not once say, "I am not a Marxist," a proposition that does not have to be applied only to the field of ideology and tactics).

---

[32] Graphically one can read s and r off the diagram. Write the length of any line segment, such as mB, as $|mB|$. Then in Figure 1, $s = |mB| / |Om|$; and $r = |mB| / |Om + OG|$. In the general case of not-necessarily-equal internal compositions, where m, B, and G need not line up on the same ray, we measure s by passing lines parallel to ABZ and calculate the equivalent indicated distances between them. To calculate r, we use lines parallel to *amz*.

[33] The final words of Samuelson [26, 1970] read: "The present elucidation should not rob Marx of esteem in the eyes of those who believe that a subsistence wage provides valuable insights into the dynamic laws of motion of capitalism."

A conciliatory formulation that preserves honor all around would say:

> *Although* Capital's *total findings need not have been developed in dependence upon Volume I's digression into surplus values, its essential insight does depend crucially on comparison of the subsistence goods needed to produce and reproduce labor with what the undiluted labor theory of value calculates to be the amount of goods producible for all classes in view of the embodied labor requirements of the goods.*[34] *The tools of bourgeois analysis could have been used to discover and expound this notion of exploitation if only those econo-*

[34] The following quotations from various Marxian authors will show that the present conciliatory formulation is consistent with their thinking. I hope that the present paper has been persuasive that going beyond this formulation leads to unwarranted assertions. In his 1865 *Wages, price and profit*, Section VIII [17, Marx and Engels, 1968] Marx clearly noted: "Now suppose that the average amount of the daily necessaries of a labouring man require *six hours of average labour* for their production. . . . But our man is a wages labourer. He must, therefore sell his labour power to a capitalist [who will], therefore, make him work say, daily *twelve hours*. . . he will, therefore, have to work *six other hours*, which I shall call hours of *surplus labour*, which surplus labour will realize itself in a *surplus value* . . . [whose rate] will, therefore, depend on the *ratio in which the working day is prolonged*. . . ." Engels, in his 1891 introduction to Marx's 1849 *Wage, labour and capital* [17, Marx and Engels, 1968] similarly sums up the essence of Marxism: "With the present state of production, human labour power not only produces in one day a greater value than it itself possesses and costs; with every new . . . invention, this surplus of its daily product over its daily cost increases. . . ." Likewise, from Lenin in his 1913 "Three Sources and Three Component Parts of Marxism," Section II [17]: "The worker spends one part of the day covering the cost of maintaining himself and his family (wages), while the other part of the day he works without remuneration, creating for the capitalist *surplus-value*, the source of profit, the source of wealth of the capitalist class." See also the 1949 statement by Dobb [9, p. 111, n. 1] where he writes that the classical theory avers that ". . . the amount of profit (and given the stock of capital, the rate of profit) depends upon the ratio of the amount of labour time required on the average to produce a worker's subsistence . . . and the labour time worked by the worker." Having said this, Dobb would have done better to have omitted the earlier passage which asserts that ". . . exchange ratios were in the last analysis *determined* by the relative quantities of embodied labour in various commodities," a proposition clearly

mists had been motivated to use the tools for this purpose.

Leaving the realm of pure science, we may perhaps add that the path taken in Volume I, even if seen to be unnecessary in the present age, did have the advantage of being easier to expound logically. It also lent itself to a more emotive language that must have been influential in converting readers to the Marxian vision of the world. Even today, the most puristic scholar and teacher can fall back upon the Volume I terminologies with the best of conscience provided only that he prefaces his exposition with the observation that the case of equal organic compositions of capital or of labor intensities, although not particularly realistic, does provide a clear searchlight on the nature and dynamic development of a model of labor exploitation. Those who regard a subsistence wage model as a grotesque interpretation of history can also avail themselves of these harmless classroom simplifications in their critiques of the doctrine.

Part Three. Critical Review of the Literature

XIII. General Guide

A reader cannot do better than to begin with P. M. Sweezy [36, 1942], whose Chapter

denied by Figure 1's *amz*. Meek himself, in the course of an excellent 1961 review of Sraffa, *Production of commodities by means of commodities* [20, pp. 161–78], attempts to defend Marx's analysis in terms of Sraffa's "standard industry." But he does not explicitly note that Sraffa nowhere makes use of any of the Volume I $s_j = v_j s$ equivalences. Meek's own formulation of the transformation problem, as the careful reader of his long footnote 12 will discern, couched though it may be in terms of $\sum(v_j + s_j)/\sum v_j$ ratios, also has absolutely no need for these Volume I equivalences; in terms of my Figure 1, it is easy to show that the ratios that Meek does rely on are dependent only on the technical properties of ABZ and $m'mm''$ and are determinable *prior* to computation of either Marxian values or competitive prices. This remark illuminates the fact that even if one swallowed with Marx and Engels the doubtful anthropology of an earlier golden age in which an undiluted labor theory of value applied, the relevant features of that regime would be described by bourgeois prices with no need for innovations of the Volume I type.

VII gives a lucid description of the problem, of Marx's proposed solution, and of Bortkiewicz's rectification of that procedure as applied to the case of "simple reproduction." He could follow this by reading R. Meek [19, 1956] who argues the strongest possible defense of the view that Marx's Volume I concepts were not redundant and obfuscating and who cites many of the divergent writings. Finally, the reader equipped with mathematics will wish to consult the important 1957 paper by F. Seton [33], the 1961 papers by Morishima and Seton [21], that by L. Johansen [11, 1961], and, possibly, my cited 1970 paper [26, Samuelson].

On Marx's procedure itself, Part Two of this paper provides a full discussion and list of citations. From the first appearance (1867) of the first volume of *Capital*, Marx's general viewpoint and concepts of surplus value came under attack by neoclassical economists. (Mill lived for a few years after 1867 and although he had followed closely the events of the 1848 Revolution, as far as I can recall he never made a single reference to Karl Marx.) Like Böhm-Bawerk [39, Wicksteed, 1933], Pareto [23, 1966] paid Marx the compliment of "refuting" him. Although some German socialists in the 1920s rejected Marxism as an alien "English" doctrine, Shaw was probably at least half right in claiming that he was the only man in England in the 1880s who had read and understood *Capital*. Hence, the magisterial Alfred Marshall could afford for the most part to ignore Marx. Knut Wicksell on the continent was more exposed to the Marxist ideology, but with the stubborn independence that was so characteristic of him, Wicksell espoused the cause of the working poor by advocating general reform doctrines that had much in common with the Roosevelt New Deal of thirty years later.

Some twenty years ago at a conference at American University, I touched a filial nerve in John Maurice Clark when I cast some doubts about his father's belief that he, John Bates Clark, had irrefutably proved in the last decade of the last century the ethical justness of the marginal productivity mode of distribution. In his reply [41, D. M. Wright, 1951, p. 329, n. 14] J. M. Clark said that his father had been deeply conscious of the challenge offered by Marx's notions of exploitation ("under whose theory any share capital gets is outright robbery") and felt under a necessity to defend the competitive system from those charges, which if true would have admittedly constituted a grave indictment.

Marx had to be refuted by orthodox economists—if only because he was there! But to recognize this fact about ideology is not, in my view, to accept the notion that the merits of Marx's hypotheses and criticisms of them are incapable of being discussed rationally and objectively. Despite the class struggle, two and two remains four and not five; and an approximate answer to the question of whether real wages rise or stagnate over a century should be capable of being given to the satisfaction of a jury recruited in New York, Moscow, Delhi, Prague, and Peking. In any case, analysis can isolate the irreducible bones of contention.

On the narrower issues involved in the transformation problem itself, my earlier remarks have already suggested that I do not think that Böhm-Bawerk's critiques, either of 1898 [2], or in the final editions of his *Capital and interest* [1], added much; and they may, from the deepest view of the subject, have even subtracted a little. And I must agree with Joan Robinson in her evaluation of the cogency of Rudolf Hilferding's rebuttals to Böhm-Bawerk on this matter: ". . . though Hilferding scores one or two telling points against Böhm-Bawerk's own theory, he throws no light whatever . . . on the meaning of the theory that *value* determines price" [25, Robinson, 1950, p. 361].

XIV. The Bortkiewicz Contribution

As Sweezy makes clear, it was Ladislaus von Bortkiewicz who gave the transformation problem its definitive formulation. J. Winternitz errs in thinking that Bortkiewicz was an Austrian. A follower of Walras and an admirer of Ricardo, he was a rather cantankerous professor at Berlin who monitored—or better, policed—all the German literature of his day even to the point of recalculating regression coefficients to reveal their numerical inacuracies. He was a gifted mathematical statistician who did important work in demography (and also worked in connection with the Poisson[35] analysis of rare events). He was a teacher of the young Leontief. His concern with Böhm's interest theory and his knowledge of the works of the Russians [38, Tugan-Baranowsky, 1905 and 8, Dmitriev, 1968] led him to write no less than three articles on Marx in 1907; as Sweezy notes, even at the late date of 1923, eight years before his death, Bortkiewicz was still writing on this subject.

Of his two papers published in July 1907, the better known one is that in the *Jahrbücher* [3, Bortkiewicz], which Sweezy has popularized and edited. Actually, however, the other and longer paper in the *Archiv* [4, Bortkiewicz], is the deeper of the two; it shows itself capable, in principle, of handling the general case, and not simply the special model of simple reproduction. When Sweezy states the belief that it does not attempt to solve the transformation problem as Marx himself presented it, he is perhaps being misled by the fact that no tableau of Marx is worked out in numerical terms. As indicated in my footnote 33, although Bortkiewicz never quite employs the Leontief a matrix, his equations (9) and (11) are equiv-

alent to my "values" formulation and his equations (20) and (28) are equivalent to my "prices."[36]

In accordance with the usual practice of writers, let me concentrate on the treatment involving simple reproduction. In this paper Bortkiewicz follows the example of Tugan-Baranowsky [38, 1905] and contemplates a Marxian model with three departments. Department I produces goods used only as intermediate goods (say, coal). Department II produces wage goods used as minimum subsistence (say, corn). Department III produces only luxury goods for capitalists (say, velvets or wampum). Using lower-case letters for "values" and upper-case letters for "prices," he summarizes this model by the relations

$$
\begin{aligned}
(8) \quad & c_1 + v_1 + s_1 = c_1 + c_2 + c_3 \\
& c_2 + v_2 + s_2 = v_1 + v_2 + v_3 \\
& c_3 + v_3 + s_3 = s_1 + s_2 + s_3
\end{aligned}
$$

where of course $s_j = sv_j$ in every case, in accordance with the novel notions of Volume I. The left-hand sides of these relations measure the total costs (including surplus value) of the respective industries, and they are equated to the total revenues of the right-hand sides. But these right-hand sides also embody the assumption that each department has its respective role as intermediate, wage-good, and luxury industry.

The same configuration can be written in its *price* mode as

$$
\begin{aligned}
(9) \quad & C_1 + V_1 + S_1 = C_1 + C_2 + C_3 \\
& C_2 + V_2 + S_2 = V_1 + V_2 + V_3 \\
& C_3 + V_3 + S_3 = S_1 + S_2 + S_3
\end{aligned}
$$

---

[35] To him is due the well-known example of the number of Prussian soldiers killed each year by the kick of a mule, and less happily, the designation of the Poisson distribution of rare events as the "law of *small* numbers" (which is not in legitimate contrast to the "law of *large* numbers").

[36] It should be pointed out that Marx and his commentators use expressions like prices and values, not for intensive amounts *per unit* of the goods in question, namely P_j and p_j, but rather for the extensive totals of such magnitudes for the industry as a whole, namely for what we moderns would write as $P_j Q_j$ and $p_j Q_j$. As will become clear, no real confusion on this point need arise, particularly since it is often convenient to use our dimensional license and define all $Q_j \equiv 1$ along with total labor $L = 1$, in which case the distinction becomes vacuous.

where $S_j = r(C_j + V_j)$ in every case, in accordance with the Volume III and bourgeois notion of a common interest or profit rate under perfect competition.

To illustrate the "values" relations of (8) we may copy the Bortkiewicz and Tugan-Baranowsky tableau, which is reproduced as Tableau IV in Sweezy [36, 1942, p. 121]. This is based on $s = 2/3$ or 66 2/3 percent:

TABLE 3A. VALUES

	Constant Capital	Variable Capital	Surplus Value	Value
I	225	90	60	375
II	100	120	80	300
III	50	90	60	200
	375	300	200	875

To illustrate the "prior" relations of (9) I have modified Bortkiewicz's tableau, which is shown as Tableau IV in Sweezy, by the trivial change of multiplying all its entries by 15/16, so that total wages or corn are shown as the same numerical amount of needed subsistence, namely as 300 in both cases. Based on a profit rate of $r = 1/4$ or 25 percent, we have:

TABLE 3B. PRICES

I	270	90	90	450
II	120	120	60	300
III	60	90	$37\frac{1}{2}$	$187\frac{1}{2}$
	450	300	$187\frac{1}{2}$	$937\frac{1}{2}$

Since only proportions matter, how we determine scale or "normalize" the numbers is of no consequence: any two numbers in the respective tableaux could have been put in bold-face and set equal by convention. Thus, Bortkiewicz equates Department III's 200, and some Marxians equate the grand totals; some erroneously try to equate *two* numbers, or equally erroneously, to equate certain ratios of two numbers—which, singular cases aside, one cannot do, as Seton [33, 1957] has pointed out.

The equation set (9) is not written down explicitly in Bortkiewicz or Sweezy, but rather in essentially the following equivalent form

$$[(C/c)c_1 + (V/v)v_1](1 + r)$$
$$= (C/c)(c_1 + c_2 + c_3)$$
$$[(C/c)c_2 + (V/v)v_2](1 + r)$$
(10)
$$= (V/v)(v_1 + v_2 + v_3)$$
$$[(C/c)c_3 + (V/v)v_3](1 + r)$$
$$= (S/s)(s_1 + s_2 + s_3)$$

where

$$C/c = C_1/c_1 = C_2/c_2 = C_3/c_3$$
(11) $$V/v = V_1/v_1 = V_2/v_2 = V_3/v_3$$
$$S/s = (S_1 + S_2 + S_3)/(s_1 + s_2 + s_3)$$

These last three ratios, which are written as (x, y, z) by Bortkiewicz, can be identified as the respective ratios for the three industries of their unit prices to their unit values, or in my notation as being equal to $(P_1/p_1, P_2/p_2, P_3/p_3) = (y_1, y_2, y_3)$.[37] In the above numerical tables, under my normali-

[37] In Samuelson [26, 1970], values were denoted by π_j rather than p_j. Greek versus roman letters have often been used to distinguish values from prices.

When this survey was in press I received a paper dealing with a problem usually sidestepped in the literature, namely the handling of varying periods of turnover of capitals (Aleksander Bajt, "A Post Mortem Note on the 'Transformation Problem'," *Soviet Studies*, Jan. 1970, 21(3), pp. 371–374). Briefly, I shall indicate here how to handle the case that involves durable or fixed capitals in addition to circulating capital (raw materials) used up completely in each period. Assume m durable capital goods or machines ($K_1, \ldots, K_m$) are needed in amounts b_{ij} as K_i inputs to produce a unit of Q_j; let the fraction of equipment used up in such production be d_{ij}. Now add to the n industries m new industries representing gross capital formations of the equipments: thus the old a_{ij} matrix now has j going beyond n to $m+n$. And for $i > n$, the respective new augmented coefficients of a are of the form $(1+r)^{-1}(r+d_{ij})b_{ij}$. Now our augmented relations are $P/W = A_0(r) = a_0(1+r)[I - a(r)(1+r)]^{-1}$, where $a(r)$ is the above-described augmented a matrix. Values are given by $p/w = A_0(0)(1+s)$. As before A_{0j}' $(r) > 0$, and all transformation relations of this paper continue to be valid and do represent genuine improvements over Engel's editorial repairs to Marx's fragmentary manuscript of Volume III.

zation $(x, y, z) = (1.2, 1, 15/16)$ rather than $(1.28, 16/15, 1)$ as in Bortkiewicz and Sweezy. Since only the ratios of (x, y, z) are invariants, mere differences in scale are of no significance.

Why should Bortkiewicz have chosen to write C_j and V_j in the roundabout form of $(C_j/c_j)c_j$ and $(V_j/v_j)v_j$? If "values" cancel out of the price calculations, and Samuelson [25, 1970] shows that they indeed do, why introduce them in the first place? Or, at least, why not abandon them immediately and explicitly? Actually, it would have helped to avoid the misunderstandings in the literature of the significance of the transformation process if Bortkiewicz had taken a more straightforward and transparent attack in his transformation of the models of simple reproduction. But there is rhyme and reason to his procedure, as we shall see.

Although this was not brought out by Marx and his pre-1957 commentators, it is absolutely necessary to pick up from somewhere the physical and technical data of the model. Without them no formulation of equilibrium is possible and no valid comparison between the two regimes. Bortkiewicz recognized that if we happen first to have given the values totals for the industries, we can use them to calculate information about the a coefficients, after which the values are indeed abandoned in the computation of prices. Further, in what is important for the understanding of the sense in which Volume I's concepts may be necessary or fruitful for the understanding of the real world and its laws of motions, if first we are given data on the price totals, we must use these data to calculate information about the technical a coefficients, after which prices can be abandoned in the computation of values. Tugan-Baranowsky had already (a few years before 1907) performed [38, 1905] the inverse transformation from prices to values by just such an implicit calculation of the (a_0, a) data; Morishima and Seton [21, 1961] have more recently brought the

subject around full circle. What saves an expression like $(C_j/c_j)c_j$ from being a trivial tautology for c_j is (11)'s assertion that the factor C_j/c_j is the same for all industries, independently of j, in reflection of the fact that there *is* a technology underlying the tableau.

To understand how the (a_0, a) data are "identified" in their relevant aspects, let me rewrite the relations in my notation. In general, we have

$$
\begin{aligned}
&c_j + v_j(1 + s) \\
&= p_1 a_{1j} Q_j + p_2 a_{2j} Q_j + p_3 a_{3j} Q_j \\
&\qquad + w L_j(1 + s) = p_j Q_j \\
&\qquad\qquad (j = 1, 2, 3),
\end{aligned}
$$

(8')
$$
\begin{aligned}
&w(L_1 + L_2 + L_3) \\
&= w(a_{01} Q_1 + a_{02} Q_2 + a_{03} Q_3) = p_2 Q_2,
\end{aligned}
$$

where (w, p_j) represent the wage and values per unit; and

$$
\begin{aligned}
&(C_j + V_j)(1 + r) \\
&= (P_1 a_{1j} Q_j + P_2 a_{2j} Q_j + P_3 a_{3j} Q_j \\
&\qquad + W L_j)(1 + r) = P_j Q_j \\
&\qquad\qquad (j = 1, 2, 3),
\end{aligned}
$$

(9')
$$
\begin{aligned}
&W(L_1 + L_2 + L_3) \\
&= W(a_{01} Q_1 + a_{02} Q_2 + a_{03} Q_3) = P_2 Q_2,
\end{aligned}
$$

where (W, P_j) represent the wage and prices per unit.

Six (or $n\{n-1\}$) of our needed twelve (or $n\{n+1\}$) identifications are provided by the assumption that the model is one of "simple" structure, with only one good (coal) being needed as intermediate goods. This tells us that $a_{2j} = 0 = a_{3j}$, for all $j = 1, 2, 3$. Thus, once we have specified the conventional physical units in which $Q_1, Q_2, Q_3, L = \sum L_j$ are to be measured, the remaining six (or $2n$) coefficients $[a_{0j}; a_{1j}]$ can be identified from *either* tableau. Following Marx and not Tugan, let us begin with (8'), the values tableau. For brevity, I skip the general formulation and assume the convention that $Q_1=Q_2=Q_3=L=1$, or rather, to keep the arithmetic simple, I assume $Q_1=Q_2=Q_3=1$ and $L=300$. Then the wage is one, $w=1$, and all values per unit, p_j, are identical with industry total values measured in wage numeraire. Then, for Tables 3A and 3B

$$a_{11} = p_1 a_{11} Q_1 / p_1 Q_1 = c_1/(c_1 + c_2 + c_3)$$

$$= 225/375 = 9/15$$

$$a_{12} = [p_1 a_{12} Q_2 / p_2 Q_2](p_2/p_1)$$

$$= c_2/(c_1 + c_2 + c_3) = 100/375 = 4/15$$

$$a_{13} = [p_1 a_{13} Q_3 / p_3 Q_3](p_3/p_1)$$

$$= c_3/(c_1 + c_2 + c_3) = 2/15$$

$$a_{01} = [w a_{01} Q_1 / p_1 Q_1](p_1/w)$$

$$= L_1/Q_1 = (90/375)(375) = 90$$

$$a_{02} = [w a_{02} Q_2 / p_2 Q_2](p_2/w) = L_2/Q_2$$

$$= (120/300)(300) = 120$$

$$a_{03} = [w a_{03} Q_3 / p_3 Q_3](p_3/w) = L_3/Q_3$$

$$= (90/200)(200) = 90$$

For the mathematical reader, I may now quickly write down the Leontief production relations in matrix form

$$Q = aQ + \text{consumptions} = aQ + Y$$

$$= [I - a]^{-1}Y = AY$$

$$= \begin{bmatrix} 1-\left(\dfrac{9}{15}\right), & -\left(\dfrac{4}{15}\right), & -\left(\dfrac{2}{15}\right) \\ 0 & 1 & 0 \\ 0 & 0 & 1 \end{bmatrix}^{-1} \begin{bmatrix} 0 \\ 1 \\ 1 \end{bmatrix}$$

$$= \begin{bmatrix} \left(\dfrac{15}{6}\right) & \left(\dfrac{4}{6}\right) & \left(\dfrac{2}{6}\right) \\ 0 & 1 & 0 \\ 0 & 0 & 1 \end{bmatrix} \begin{bmatrix} 0 \\ 1 \\ 1 \end{bmatrix} = \begin{bmatrix} 1 \\ 1 \\ 1 \end{bmatrix}$$

$$L = a_0 Q = [90 \quad 120 \quad 90] \begin{bmatrix} 1 \\ 1 \\ 1 \end{bmatrix} = 300$$

$$= a_0 [I - a]^{-1} Y$$

$$= [90 \quad 120 \quad 90] \begin{bmatrix} \left(\dfrac{15}{6}\right) & \left(\dfrac{4}{6}\right) & \left(\dfrac{2}{6}\right) \\ 0 & 1 & 0 \\ 0 & 0 & 1 \end{bmatrix} \begin{bmatrix} 0 \\ 1 \\ 1 \end{bmatrix}$$

$$= A_0(0) Y = [225 \quad 180 \quad 120] \begin{bmatrix} 0 \\ 1 \\ 1 \end{bmatrix} = 300$$

Since only 180 labor units are needed to produce the total subsistence for laborers, i.e., to produce $Q_2=1$, and since we have 300 labor units available, the rate of surplus value is defined by $1+s^*=300/180=1+2/3$.

Our value relations then become, in matrix terms,

$$p = w a_0(1 + s^*) + pa$$

$$= w a_0 (1 + s^*)[I - a]^{-1} = a_0(1 + s^*)A,$$

$$\text{for } w = 1$$

$$= [90(5/3) \quad 120(5/3) \quad 90(5/3)]A$$

$$= [150 \quad 200 \quad 150] \begin{bmatrix} \left(\dfrac{15}{6}\right) & \left(\dfrac{4}{6}\right) & \left(\dfrac{2}{6}\right) \\ 0 & 1 & 0 \\ 0 & 0 & 1 \end{bmatrix}$$

$$= [375 \quad 300 \quad 200]$$

which checks with the last column of Table 3A above.

To derive the price relations in matrix form, we must find that unique rate of profit, r^*, which will raise the price of subsistence corn from 180 units to 300, so that the workers will have just enough wage income to buy the $Q_2=1=Y_2$ of subsistence. Prices are defined by

$$P = W a_0(1 + r) + Pa(1 + r)$$

$$= W a_0(1 + r)[I - a(1 + r)]^{-1}$$

$$= a_0(1 + r)[I - a(1 + r)]^{-1}, \quad \text{for } W = 1$$

$$= A_0(r)$$

Rather than solve $A_{02}(r)=300$ for its relevant root, which involves solving a quadratic, we can easily verify that, for r^*

$=1/4$, $P_2/W = A_{02}(1/4) = 300$, namely

$$\frac{P}{W} = \begin{bmatrix} 90(5/4) & 120(5/4) & 90(5/4) \end{bmatrix} \begin{bmatrix} 1 - \left(\dfrac{9}{15}\right)\left(\dfrac{5}{9}\right), & -\left(\dfrac{4}{15}\right)\left(\dfrac{5}{4}\right), & -\left(\dfrac{2}{15}\right)\left(\dfrac{5}{4}\right) \\ 0 & 1 & 0 \\ 0 & 0 & 1 \end{bmatrix}^{-1}$$

$$= \begin{bmatrix} 450/4 & 600/4 & 450/4 \end{bmatrix} \begin{bmatrix} 4 & \left(\dfrac{20}{15}\right) & \left(\dfrac{10}{15}\right) \\ 0 & 1 & 0 \\ 0 & 0 & 1 \end{bmatrix}$$

$$= \begin{bmatrix} 450 & 300 & 187\tfrac{1}{2} \end{bmatrix}$$

which checks with the last column of Table 3B.

The analysis of Seton [33, 1957] may be briefly related to that here. Instead of specifying the vector of wage-subsistence $[m_i]$, he adds to the production requirements $[a_{ij}]$ further input requirements needed to feed the workers, $[k_{ij}]$. Thus if every worker consumes $[m_i]$ independently of the industry he works in, Seton's k_{ij} would take the special form $m_i a_{0j}$, and the results given here would be reached by him but by a different path of exposition. The only possible disadvantage of his exposition in that case would be the fact that, every time any m_i changed, he would have to rework the whole of his $I - (a + k)(1 + r)$ matrix calculations; the present conventional Leontief-Walras approach takes advantage of the decomposability of the subsistence requirements from the rest of the relationships. On the other hand, the Seton hypothesis is a genuinely broader empirical one and can handle cases not admissible to the present formulation. A necessary price to pay for this greater generality is that it robs Volume I's surplus-value analysis of its greater algebraic simplicities; instead of the basic relations being linear in $1+s$, one must in Seton's general case solve an eigenvalue polynomial $|I - a - k(1 + s)| = 0$ that is of as high algebraic degree as is $|I - (a + k) \cdot (1 + r)| = 0$. Morishima and Seton [21,

1961], and Johansen [11, 1961], develop this 1957 model further.

Since my text has already registered its agreements and disagreements with such writers of the 1940s and 1950s as Joan Robinson [25, 1950] and Meek [19, 1956] only a few comments are needed here.[38] Winternitz [40, 1948] correctly points out that any luxury goods, such as Department III, which contribute neither directly nor indirectly to the production of subsistence goods, can be ignored in determining the exploitation rate of profit; K. May [18, 1948], for unclear reasons, seems to deny this, but no subsequent writer follows him in this

[38] Since the writing of this paper, my old classmate from Chicago days, Professor Martin Bronfenbrenner of Carnegie-Mellon University, has inquired as to the connection between the solution proposed here and the solution to the transformation problem that he had suggested [5, 1965 and 6, 1967]. I pointed out that his 1965 and 1967 formulas, if taken literally, are subject to a defect that goes beyond the defect of the Marx 1894 formulation—namely that the newly proposed competitive prices do not each equal the sum of their costs of production including stipulated profits. Professor Bronfenbrenner writes that in 1971 he would prefer to have his formulas (expressed in *his* notation of p. 210 of the first reference and p. 634 of the second)

$$P' = p_i W_i / (C_i + V_i) \quad \text{replaced by}$$
$$P' = [S_i + (p_i - 1)W_i]/(C_i + V_i)$$

with appropriate modifications being made in his later formulas. Simple manipulation of the new formulas will show that the modified Bronfenbrenner solution is precisely that of Marx's 1894 Volume III, with all the defects of false evaluation of intermediate-good costs referred to by other writers and by my text.

respect. As I have already indicated, writers err in thinking that this decomposability of luxuries is a correction or simplification of Bortkiewicz; I should also add that writers err in believing that such a decomposability property adds to, or subtracts from, the empirical validity of an exploitation model (contrary to vague suggestions among modern commentators on Ricardian constructions).

In a useful survey M. Dobb [9, 1955] points out that he had earlier erred in thinking that the transformation from values to prices would involve a substantive change in resource allocations. Indeed so long as technological coefficients and subsistence-quanta are frozen constants no such change takes place. But Dobb's original instinct was a good one. All classical writers, particularly when discussing inventions, show an awareness that the blueprints of life contain more than one page. As soon as $[a_{0j}, a_{ij}, m_i]$ cease to be uniquely-given constants, but instead have to be selected from two or more options in terms of cost minimization, the discussions reviewed here become overly simple. As one goes from r^* to s^*, and vice versa, the $[a_0, a, m]$ regime may change and the indicated correspondences between them will no longer hold. Now the price regime can no longer be defined by purely algebraic procedures of root extraction; instead, competitive cost minimizations may involve switchings (and reswitchings). Such substitutions cannot happen if cost minimization takes place in terms of values, since relative values, p_i/p_j, are independent of s, as was indicated in the parallel shiftings in Figure 1 and as is clear from the proportionality between values and labor costs. One would expect this to be registered as a defect of the Volume I values scheme, since for planning purposes it requires the richest and poorest societies to use the same production methods. It is difficult, however, to compare the efficiencies of the two regimes until the problem is better posed. Efficiency in terms of what? And for

whom? This much can be said in favor of price-profit as against value-surplus configurations: the former could, and the latter generally could not, serve as the efficient golden-age asymptote of a rationally planned solution to an optimal-control problem of generalized Ramsey and von Neumann type.[39] Thus, as soon as goods have some substitutability for each other for workers and non-workers, generally *everybody* can be made better off by a judicious transformation from values to prices. This is an important fact in weighing the merits of the Volume I innovations.

In closing I wish to emphasize that, except inadvertently, I have not discussed any evidence bearing on the empirical usefulness (for the last century or this one) of the exploitation model as throwing light on the laws of motion of the system. In the present paper I have tried only to clarify the logic of that model—in the hope that any evaluation of how it has worked out over time can benefit from an understanding of how it works in every instant of time.

[39] While this article was in press C. C. von Weizsäcker and P. A. Samuelson in "A New Labor Theory of Value for Rational Planning Through Use of the Bourgeois Profit Rate" (*Proceedings of the National Academy of Sciences*, June 1971, *68*) proved the following theorem: if labor grows at exponential rate $1+g$, and goods are to be priced at their "synchronized labor costs," then the bourgeois pricing formula $A_0(g) = a_0(1+g)[I - a(1+g)]^{-1}$ must be charged by rational planners. More generally, if in addition to population growth at $(1+g)$, invention causes direct labor requirements to decrease like $(1+h)^{-t}$, then pricing goods so that all which does not go to wages goes for "widening" of capital goods will require ratios P_i/P_j to equal $A_{0i}(G)/A_{0j}(G)$, where the profit rate satisfies $1+G = (1+g)(1+h)$.

REFERENCES

1. BÖHM-BAWERK, E. VON. *Capital and interest*. 3 vols. South Holland, Illinois: Libertarian Press, 1959.

2. ———, *Karl Marx and the close of his system* (1898), in Sweezy, P., ed. *Karl Marx and the close of his system by Eugen von Böhm-Bawerk and Böhm-Bawerk's criticism of Marx by Rudolf Hilferding*

with an appendix by L. von Bortkiewicz. New York: Augustus M. Kelley, 1949.

3. BORTKIEWICZ, L. VON. "On the Correction of Marx's Fundamental Theoretical Construction in the Third Volume of *Capital*," *Jahr. Nationalökonomie Statistik*, 1907, *34*(3), pp. 370–85; reprinted in English in SWEEZY, P., ed. *Karl Marx and the close of his system*. . . (see reference 2 above).

4. ——, "Value and Price in the Marxian System," *Archiv für Sozialwissenschaft und Sozialpolitik*, 1906, *23* (1), pp. 1–50; 1907, *25*(1), pp. 10–51; 1907, *25*(2), pp. 445–88; reprinted in English in *International Economic Papers*, 1952, *2*, pp. 5–60.

5. BRONFENBRENNER, M. "*Das Kapital* for the Modern Man" reprinted from *Science and Society*, Autumn 1965; also in HOROWITZ, D., ed. *Marx and modern economics*. New York: Modern Reader Paperbacks, 1968, pp. 205–26.

6. ——, "Marxian Influences in 'Bourgeois' Economics" in "*Das Kapital:* A Centenary Appreciation," *Amer. Econ. Rev.*, *Papers and Proceedings*, May 1967, *57*(2), pp. 624–35 (especially see the Appendix, pp. 633–35).

7. BURMEISTER, E. AND DOBELL, A. *Mathematical theories of economic growth*. New York: Macmillan, 1970.

8. DMITRIEV, V. *Essais economiques esquisse de synthèse organique de la théorie de la valeur-travail et de la théorie de l'utilité marginale.* Paris: Editions du Centre National de la Recherche Scientifique, 1968.

9. DOBB, M. "A Note on the Transformation Problem" in *On economic theory and socialism*. London: Routledge and Paul, 1955, Ch. 17, pp. 273–81.

10. DORFMAN, R.; SAMUELSON, P. AND SOLOW, R. *Linear programming and economic analysis*. New York: McGraw-Hill, 1958.

11. JOHANSEN, L. "A Note on 'Aggregation in Leontief Matrices and the Labour Theory of Value'," *Econometrica*, April 1961, *29*, pp. 221–22.

12. KALDOR, N. "Alternative Theories of Distribution," *Rev. Econ. Stud.*, 1956, *23*(2), pp. 83–100.

13. LEONTIEF, W. *The structure of the American economy, 1919–1929; An empirical application of equilibrium analysis.* Cambridge, Massachusetts: Harvard University Press, 1941.

14. ——, *Input-output economics.* New York: Oxford University Press, 1966.

15. MARX, K. *Capital.* Volume I (1867); Volume II (1885); Volume III (1894).

16. ——, *Theories of surplus value, Capital.* Volume IV. Moscow: Foreign Languages Publishing House, 1963.

17. —— AND ENGELS, F. *Selected works.* New York: International Publishers, 1968.

18. MAY, K. "Value and Price of Production: A Note on Winternitz's Solution," *Econ. J.*, Dec. 1948, *58*, pp. 596–99.

19. MEEK, R. "Some Notes on the Transformation Problem," *Econ. J.*, March 1956, *66*, pp. 94–107; reprinted in MEEK, R. *Economics and ideology and other essays; Studies in the development of economic thought.* London: Chapman and Hall, 1967, pp. 143–57.

20. ——, "Mr. Sraffa's Rehabilitation of Classical Economics," *Scottish J. Polit. Econ.*, June 1961, *8*, pp. 119–36; reprinted in MEEK, R. *Economics and ideology and other essays.* . . (see reference 19 above).

21. MORISHIMA, M. AND SETON, F. "Aggregation in Leontief Matrices and the Labour Theory of Value," *Econometrica*, April 1961, *29*, pp. 203–20.

22. VON NEUMANN, J. "A Model of General Equilibrium," *Rev. Econ. Stud.*, 1945, *13*, pp. 1–9.

23. PARETO, V. *Marxisme et economie pure*, Tome 9, *Oeuvres complètes.* Genève: Droz, 1966.

24. ROBINSON, J. *The accumulation of capital.* London: Macmillan, 1956.

25. ———, "Review of SWEEZY, P., *Karl Marx and the close of his system . . . ,*" *Economic Journal,* June, 1950, *60,* pp. 358–363 (see reference 37 below).

26. SAMUELSON, P. "The 'Transformation' from Marxian 'Values' to Competitive 'Prices': A Process of Rejection and Replacement," *Proceedings of the National Academy of Sciences,* Sept. 1970, *67*(1), pp. 423–25.

27. ———, *Economics.* 8th. edition. New York: McGraw-Hill, 1970.

28. ———, "Wages and Interest: A Modern Dissection of Marxian Economic Models," *Amer. Econ. Rev.,* Dec. 1957, *47,* pp. 884–912; reprinted in SAMUELSON, P., *Collected scientific papers,* edited by J. STIGLITZ. 2 vols. Cambridge, Massachusetts: M.I.T. Press, 1965, Ch. 29, pp. 341–69.

29. ———, "A Modern Treatment of the Ricardian Economy" in two articles, *Quart. J. Econ.,* Feb. 1959, *73,* pp. 1–35; May 1959, *73*(2), pp. 217–31; reprinted in SAMUELSON, P. *Collected scientific papers.* (See reference 27 above.) Chs. 31, 32, pp. 373–442.

30. ———, "Marxian Economics as Economics," *Amer. Econ. Rev.,* May 1967, *57*(2), pp. 616–23.

31. ———, "A New Theorem on Non-Substitution" in *Money, growth, and methodology and other essays in economics in honor of Johan Akerman,* edited by HUGO HEGELAND. Lund, Sweden: CWK Gleerup, 1961, pp. 407–23; reprinted in

SAMUELSON, P. *Collected scientific papers.* Ch. 29, pp. 520–36.

32. ———, "Parable and Realism in Capital Theory: The Surrogate Production Function," *Rev. Econ. Stud.,* June 1962, *29,* pp. 193–206.

33. SETON, F. "The 'Transformation Problem'," *Rev. Econ. Stud.,* June 1957, *25,* pp. 149–60.

34. SMITH, A. *The wealth of nations.* Cannan Edition. New York: Modern Library, [1776] 1937, Book I, Ch. VII.

35. SRAFFA, P. *Production of commodities by means of commodities.* Cambridge: Cambridge University Press, 1960.

36. SWEEZY, P. M. *The theory of capitalist development.* Oxford: Oxford University Press, 1942.

37. ———, ed. *Karl Marx and the close of his system by Eugen von Böhm-Bawerk and Böhm-Bawerk's criticism of Marx by Rudolf Hilferding with an appendix by L. von Bortkiewicz.* New York: Augustus M. Kelley, 1949.

38. TUGAN-BARANOWSKY, M. *Theoritische Grundlagen des Marxismus.* Leipzig: Duncker and Humboldt, 1905.

39. WICKSTEED, P. *The common sense of political economy, and selected papers and reviews on economic theory.* 2 Vols. London: G. Routledge and Sons, 1933.

40. WINTERNITZ, J. "Values and Prices: A Solution of the So-Called Transformation Problem," *Econ. J.,* June 1948, *58,* pp. 276–80.

41. WRIGHT, D. *The impact of the union.* New York: Harcourt Brace, 1951.

Reprinted from
THE JOURNAL OF ECONOMIC LITERATURE
Volume IX, Number 2, June 1971

154

The "Transformation" from Marxian "Values" to Competitive "Prices": A Process of Rejection and Replacement

Paul A. Samuelson

DEPARTMENT OF ECONOMICS, MASSACHUSETTS INSTITUTE OF TECHNOLOGY, CAMBRIDGE, MASSACHUSETTS 02139

Communicated May 25, 1970

Abstract. The well-known transformation procedure for transforming from Marxian values to competitive prices is shown to be logically of the form: "Anything" equals "anything else" multiplied by "anything/anything else."

Alternative Systems of Values and Prices. Let $a_0 = [a_{0j}]$ be the row vector of direct labor inputs needed to produce the outputs of n industries; $a = [a_{ij}]$ be the Leontief square matrix whose elements denote the input of the ith good needed to produce the output of the jth industry; $m = [m_i]$ be the column vector of minimum-subsistence goods needed as real wage to cover the cost of production and reproduction of labor. Karl Marx in Volume I of *Capital* assumes that every industry adds to cost outlays on labor and raw materials a constant percentage of the wage payments alone, namely s the "rate of surplus value or labor exploitation."[1] If W is the wage rate, the row vector of Marxian "values," $\pi = [\pi_j]$, is defined by[2]

$$\begin{aligned} \pi &= Wa_0 + \pi a + sWa_0 = Wa_0[I - a]^{-1}(1 + s) \\ &= WA_0(0)(1 + s) \\ \pi m &= W \end{aligned} \tag{1}$$

An alternative—and incompatible system unless a_{0j}/A_{0j} happen to be identical for all industries—is that provided by the competitive "prices" of bourgeois economics (so-called Walrasian equilibrium) and of Marx's posthumous Volume III. Here the row vector of prices, $P = [P_j]$, is determined by adding to cost outlays a constant percentage rate of profit or interest, r, reckoned on *all* cost outlays (wage payments plus raw material outlays), and is defined by

$$\begin{aligned} P &= [Wa_0 + Pa](1 + r) = Wa_0(1 + r)[I - a(1 + r)]^{-1} \\ &= WA_0(r) \\ Pm &= W \end{aligned} \tag{2}$$

Generally the solution of (2) involves solving an nth degree polynomial for the appropriate positive root r^*, whereas (1) involves solving only a linear equation for s^*.

The Transformation Process. Generally, also, when confronted with a tableau of values in which the aggregates $\pi a = [\Sigma_i \pi_i a_{ij}]$ are not broken down into their components, it is impossible to "identify" the underlying technical a coefficients and to infer unambiguously the equilibrium prices of (2). However, since 1907, Bortkiewicz and a long line of writers have proposed a "transformation" algorithm applicable to the special 3-industry model, in which industry 1 provides only intermediate goods (e.g. coal), industry 2 provides only subsistence wage goods for labor (e.g. corn), and industry 3 provides only luxury goods for non-labor (e.g. velvets). In this canonical model of "simple reproduction," we may as a convention define the observed industry outputs to be unity, $Q_j \equiv 1$, and total labor as unity. With this choice of units the system has the property

$$
\begin{bmatrix} a_0 \\ \overline{a} \end{bmatrix} = \begin{bmatrix} a_{01} & a_{02} & a_{03} = 1 - a_{01} - a_{02} \\ a_{11} & a_{12} & a_{13} \\ 0 & 0 & 0 \\ 0 & 0 & 0 \end{bmatrix}
$$

and the equations of (1) can be rewritten in terms of the Marxian categories of constant capital (c_j), variable capital (v_j), and surplus values $(s_j = sv_j)$:

$$
\begin{aligned}
\pi_j &= \pi_1 a_{1j} + W a_{0j} + s W a_{0j} \equiv c_j + v_j + s_j \quad (j = 1,2,3) \\
c_1 + v_1 + s_1 &= c_1 + c_2 + c_3 \\
c_2 + v_2 + s_2 &= v_1 + v_2 + v_3 = W \\
c_3 + v_3 + s_3 &= s_1 + s_2 + s_3 = sW
\end{aligned}
\tag{3}
$$

A celebrated example of such a values tableau is the following

$$
\begin{aligned}
225 + 90 + 60 &= 375 \\
100 + 120 + 80 &= 300 = W, \qquad s^* = {}^2/_3 \\
50 + 90 + 60 &= 200
\end{aligned}
$$

To "transform" this into a price tableau, Bortkiewicz defined transformation coefficients between prices and values in the form of the row vector $y = [y_j]$, defined by the relations

$$
\begin{aligned}
(y_1 c_1 + y_2 v_1)(1 + r) &= y_1(c_1 + c_2 + c_3) \\
(y_1 c_2 + y_2 v_2)(1 + r) &= y_2(v_1 + v_2 + v_3) \\
(y_1 c_3 + y_2 v_3)(1 + r) &= y_3(s_1 + s_2 + s_3)
\end{aligned}
\tag{4}
$$

In order for these three homogeneous linear equations to have a nonzero solution, it is necessary that the first two of them have such a solution, which obviously requires the following determinantal quadratic to vanish:

$$
0 = \begin{vmatrix} c_1/\Sigma c_j - (1 + r)^{-1} & v_1/\Sigma c_j \\ c_2/\Sigma v_j & v_2/\Sigma v_j - (1 + r)^{-1} \end{vmatrix} = (1 + r)^{-2} - b_1(1 + r)^{-1} + b_2 = 0
$$

This can be solved for the relevant positive root, $1 + r^*$. For the above numerical tableau, it can be shown that $r^* = {}^1/_4$ and $y_1/y_3 = {}^{32}/_{25}$, $y_2/y_3 = {}^{16}/_{15}$, so that the price tableau must be *proportional* to

$$
\begin{aligned}
288 + 96 + 96 &= 480 \\
128 + 128 + 64 &= 320 = W \\
64 + 96 + 40 &= 200
\end{aligned}
$$

How one scales or normalizes W and these numbers is an unessential issue even though it has given rise to some acrimonious and sterile debate among scholars.

Explication of the Transformation's Meaning. This completes the traditional transformation problem, which has frequently been regarded as a vindication of Marx's Volume I analysis. However, direct and simple substitution of (3) into (4) shows that the latter's Bortkiewicz algorithm is equivalent to solving

$$y_j\pi_j = [Wa_{0j} + \sum_{i=1}^{n} y_i\pi_i a_{ij}](1 + r), \qquad (j = 1,\ldots,n)$$

$$\sum_{j=1}^{n} y_j\pi_j m_j = W$$

(5)

But (5) is seen to be precisely that of (2), with

$$P_i = y_i\pi_i, \, y_i = P_i/\pi_i \qquad (i = 1, 2,\ldots,n)$$

Hence when value magnitudes such as $\pi_i a_{ij}$ are multiplied by y_i, *all that is being done is to cancel out the π_i values from the problem*—as in $y_i\pi_i a_{ij} = (P_i/\pi_i)\pi_i a_{ij} = P_i a_{ij}$!

In summary, "transforming" from values to prices can be described logically as the following procedure: "(1) Write down the value relations; (2) take an eraser and rub them out; (3) finally write down the price relations—thus completing the so-called transformation process." The present elucidation should not rob Marx of esteem in the eyes of those who believe a subsistence wage provides valuable insights into the dynamic laws of motion of capitalism.

* Aid from the National Science Foundation is gratefully acknowledged.

[1] Sweezy, P. M., *Theory of Capitalist Development* (New York: Oxford University Press, 1942), Ch. 7.

[2] Dorfman, R., and P. Samuelson, and R. Solow, *Linear Programming and Economic Analysis* New York: McGraw-Hill, 1958), Ch. 10; Seton, F., *Review of Economic Studies*, **24**, 149 (1957); Samuelson, P., forthcoming in the *Journal of Economic Literature*, **8** (1970).

155

A New Labor Theory of Value for Rational Planning Through Use of the Bourgeois Profit Rate

(golden-rule state/Marxian values/technical progress)

C. C. VON WEIZSÄCKER AND PAUL A. SAMUELSON*

Heidelberg University, Heidelberg, Germany; and * Massachusetts Institute of Technology, Cambridge, Mass. 02139

Communicated March 31, 1971

ABSTRACT To maximize steady-state per capita consumptions, goods should be valued at their "synchronized labor requirement costs", which are shown to deviate from Marx's schemata of "values" but to coincide with bourgeois prices calculated at dated labor requirements, marked-up by compound interest, at a profit or interest rate equal to the system's rate of exponential growth. With capitalists saving all their incomes for future profits, workers all there is to get. Departures from such an exogenous, or endogenous, golden-rule state are the rule in history rather than the exception. In the case of exponential labor-augmenting change, it is shown that competitive prices will equal historically embodied labor content.

MARKET RELATIONS

In an economic system where all goods are ultimately producible by labor, i.e., in which any one good is produced with direct labor and one or more of the goods in the system (including possibly itself), if the rate of profit or interest were always zero, the equilibrium competitive prices would be exactly *equal* to the *total* embodied labor required for each good. This accords with the views of Karl Marx, both in Volume I of Capital [1] and Volume III, and with the views of bourgeois economists such as Adam Smith, David Ricardo, Leon Walras, and Wassily Leontief.

If, however, there is a positive interest or profit rate, labor will not receive a real wage large enough to buy all the consumption goods producible by labor in the stationary synchronized equilibrium. Bourgeois economists, and Marx in the posthumous Volume III, demonstrate that with positive interest the prices will no longer be proportional to the respective total embodied labor contents. Thus, if the same historic labor total, say 1 labor, is needed for either a liter of grape juice or for a liter of wine, but for wine the labor is needed 2 time-units earlier rather than only 1 time-unit earlier as for grape juice, the ratio of wine price to grape juice price will not be $P_2/P_1 = 1/1$, but will instead vary with the profit rate per period r, being $P_2/P_1 = 1(1 + r)^2/1(1 + r) = 1 + r$. In terms of the familiar Leontief notation [2], in which $a = [a_{ij}]$ denotes input needed of good i to produce a unit of good j and $a_0 = [a_{0j}]$ denotes the corresponding amount of direct labor input, we have in matrix terms for bourgeois prices

$$[P_1, \ldots, P_n] = a_0(1 + r)[I - a(1 + r)]^{-1}$$

$$= [A_{01}(r), \ldots, A_{0n}(r)], A_{0i}'(r) > 0. \quad (1)$$

In volume I, Marx hoped to break new ground by insisting that all "profit" or "surplus" be reckoned at each stage of production as a mark-up on direct labor alone. Hence, Marx's "values" systematically "contradict" bourgeois "prices" and do remain proportional to embodied labor—but no longer equal to such labor contents because of the mark-ups. In matrix terms, values $[\pi_i]$ are defined by

$$[\pi_1, \ldots, \pi_n] = a_0[I - a]^{-1}(1 + s)$$
$$= [A_{0j}(0)(1 + s)] \quad (2)$$

where s is the "rate of surplus value" or mark-up. Note that for *all* s, we get π_i/π_j equal to the P_i/P_j calculated for $r = 0$ and representing total embodied labor requirements.

Clearly $P_i/P_j \neq \pi_i/\pi_j$ since, in general,

$$A_{0i}(r)/A_{0j}(r) \neq A_{0i}(0)/A_{0j}(0).$$

Thus, grape juice and wine have equal "values" since they both involve unit labor inputs; but their bourgeois "prices" differ from the Marxian values because the former calculate labor requirements, *dated* by when they occur and carried forward at nefarious compound interest.

OPTIMAL PLANNING RELATIONS

Suppose a technocratic computer allocates resources in a population growing exponentially, so that total labor supply is given by

$$L(t) = L^0(1 + g)^t, \quad g \geq 0 \quad (3)$$

Suppose any one good, say Q_j, is alone to be produced for consumption, presumably by workers. The maximum amount of this good available for steady-state per capita consumption can be easily demonstrated also to grow at the exponential rate $(1 + g)$ or by

$$C_j(t) = C_j^0(1 + g)^t \quad (4)$$

Let us define $L(t)/C_j(t)$ as the "synchronized needed labor cost" of good j, $\lambda_j(g)$, or

$$\lambda_j(g) = L(t)/C_j(t) = L^0/C^0 \quad (5)$$

Then surely in a rational planned society, where class exploitation is abolished, all goods should be "valued" or "priced" (the terms may now be used interchangeably) at their true "synchronized needed labor costs". Thus, along and in contrast with bourgeois prices of (1) and Marxian values of (2), we have "rational values or prices"

$$[P_1^*, \ldots, P_n^*] = [\lambda_1(g), \ldots, \lambda_n(g)]. \quad (6)$$

IDENTITY OF RATIONAL VALUES AND BOURGEOIS-CALCULATED PRICES

We now state a fundamental theorem [3] that in a sense brings into discount the worthwhileness for planning of Marx's innovations in Volume I of *Capital*.

THEOREM. *Rational values for optimal planning in synchronized exponential growth, namely "synchronized labor requirements costs" of each good, are identically equal to bourgeois costs of production calculated by marking up dated labor with a golden-rule profit or interest rate equal to the system's rate of exponential growth* g.

I.e., $[\lambda_1(g), \ldots, \lambda_n(g)] \equiv [A_{01}(g), \ldots, A_{0n}(g)]$

$$\neq [\pi_1, \ldots, \pi_n] = [A_{0j}(0)(1 + s)].$$

To prove this basic theorem, we have only to calculate explicitly the respective synchronized labor requirement costs for producing the respective goods.

Thus, consider the grape juice–wine example. Only 1 unit of direct labor is needed, but for wine it is needed two periods earlier, when we have only $L(t)/(1 + g)^2$ available. In contrast, for grape juice the required labor is needed only one period ago, when we have $L(t)/(1 + g)$ available. It is obvious, then, that the ratio of steady-state wine consumable to grape juice consumable is $1/(1 + g)$, so that wine is "rationally dearer" than grape juice by the factor $1 + g$. Thus, g, the rate of growth, does act like a fictitious profit rate that *must* be applied for all rational planning.

To prove the theorem in the general case, we write down the allocations of total labor and total *gross* productions of all goods—which will generally all be positive even though only a specified good j is to be consumed net by final consumers, because intermediate inputs of all goods will generally be needed somewhere along the line to produce net C_j:

$$L(t) = L_1(t) + \ldots + L_n(t)$$
$$= a_{01}Q_1(t + 1) + \ldots + a_{0n}Q_n(t) \qquad (7)$$
$$Q_i(t) = Q_{i1}(t) + \ldots + Q_{in}(t) + \delta_{ij}C_j(t)$$
$$= a_{i1}Q_1(t + 1) + \ldots + a_{in}Q_n(t + 1) + \delta_{ij}C_j(t),$$

where $\delta_{ij} = 1$ when $i = j$ and zero otherwise. Note that inputs at time t produce outputs at one period later, $t + 1$. Now verify that all totals, $Q_i(t)$, grow at the exponential rate $(1 + g)$, according to

$$Q_i(t) = {}_jQ_i^0(1 + g)^t = Q_i(t + 1)/(1 + g), \qquad (8)$$

where this newly-defined coefficient, ${}_jQ_i^0$, depends on g, on which good is chosen for consumption (as shown by the prefix j), and on the $[a_{0j}, a_{ij}]$ technology of the system. These constants must satisfy (7), or

$$L^0 = \sum_{k=1}^{n} a_{0k}(1 + g)_jQ_k^0$$

$${}_jQ_i^0 = \sum_{k=1}^{n} a_{ik}(1 + g)_jQ_k^0 + \delta_{ij}L_0/\lambda_j(g) \qquad (9)$$

Note that use has been made here of the definition in (5) of $\lambda_j(g)$. Solving in matrix terms, we have

$[{}_jQ_i^0] = L_0/\lambda_j(g)$ times jth column of $[I - a(1 + g)]^{-1}$

$L_0 = L_0/\lambda_j(g)$ times $a_0(1 + g)$ times jth $\qquad (10)$

column of $[I - a(1 + g)]^{-1}$

Hence,

$$[\lambda_j(g)] = a_0(1 + g) [I - a(1 + g)]^{-1}$$

column for column $\quad (11)$

$$\equiv A_0(g) = [A_{0j}(g)]$$

by the definition of (1) provided the profit rate there, r, is set equal to the system's growth rate, g. Q.e.d.

Synchronized labor costs, as defined here, are seen to be interpretable as the ordinary embodied labor requirements for a fictitious system in which every $[a_{0j}, a_{ij}]$ coefficient of the actual system is pretended to be blown up by the growth factor $(1 + g)$. The common sense of this blow-up rests in recognition of the fact that, for a rapidly growing system, the actual labor is required at an earlier date; hence, when we relate the C_j producible to the current *higher* labor, we do find enhanced Labor/Consumption (L/C) ratios.

LABOR-AUGMENTING INVENTION

A second case in which the bourgeois price relations of (1) and (2) will hold is provided by an economy in which the direct labor requirements are subject to a result of technological change, i.e., in which $[a_{0j}(t)] = [a_{0j}(1 + \gamma)^{-t}]$. If the planners in such a dynamic economy insist upon costing goods out so that there is no surplus over and above wage and raw material outlays—and if they wish to be in the highest growth path with price ratios expressing the relative availability of goods, they must so price—then equilibrium prices are proportional to Marxian values. Prices reflect the amount of labor time "necessary to produce the goods" (in the sense of past labor actually historically "embodied" in the current goods). The equilibrium price relations become, in matrix terms,

$$P(t) = [W(t - 1)a_0(1 + \gamma)^{-t} + P(t - 1)a] (1 + 0) \quad (12)$$

Setting

$$W(t) \equiv 1, \qquad P(t - 1) = [p_j(1 + \gamma)^{-t}] = (1 + \gamma)^{-1}P(t)$$

defines the equilibrium row vector $(1 + \gamma)^t P(t - 1)/W(t) = p$,

$$p = a_0(1 + \gamma) [I - a(1 + \gamma)]^{-1} \qquad (13)$$
$$= A_0(\gamma) = [A_{01}(\gamma), \ldots, A_{0n}(\gamma)]$$

This proves a second dynamic theorem already enunciated by one of us [4].

THEOREM. *A system subject to labor-augmenting technical change at percentage rate* γ *will have its zero mark-up cost ratios, and hence values in the orthodox Marxian sense, that are proportional to bourgeois prices calculated at a profit rate precisely equal to the rate of technical change.*

The two theorems come together in the case where the natural rate of growth of labor, g, is compounded with labor-augmenting growth, γ, so that total labor in "efficiency units" grows like $1 + G = (1 + g)(1 + \gamma)$. Then, rationally-planned price ratios will be formed from ratios of the $A_0(G)$ elements, whose G must be the rate of profit used in all price-ratio calculations. Charging these prices will give the highest possible consumption to labor consistent with financing the widening of capital or net investment needed to keep every intermediate good growing at the system's exponential rate G. That highest possible consumption involves growth of the real wage at the rate of labor-productivity growth, γ.

In connection with the second dynamic theorem, one is warned that with rising real wages the proportions in which goods are consumed will presumably change, away from necessities and toward luxuries. When proportions change, golden-age states of steady-state equilibrium lose relevance, and relations like (1), (6), or (13) have to reckon with capital-gains effects as determined in optimal-control models.

If, along with the reductions in the a_{0j} direct-labor requirements, the a_{ij} intermediate coefficients are also lowered by technical progress, approaching asymptotically, as $t \to \infty$, limiting values, a_{ij}^*, then (13) will hold asymptotically in terms of a^*. If the a_{ij} were exponentially declining without limit, relative prices would ultimately approach those of direct-labor requirements alone.

CONCLUSION

The truth of these basic theorems will come as no surprise to those familiar with the golden-rule theories [5]. However, a succinct statement and demonstration of the *technocratic* interpretation of "labor costs" in such a state should be useful. Of course the present g is not necessarily an exogenous parameter, but might depend on the excess of real-wages over some specifiable subsistence notion. If capitalists always accumulate all—Marx's "Law of Moses and the Prophets"—g^* will get positivistically determined (i.e., by laissez-faire interactions, without planning) at that rate which, when it is applied as a positive profit that reduces the real wage from all that labor can truly produce, just evokes a rate of population increase equal to itself.

Such a theory, which is a generalization of Marx's exploitation theory, need in principle encounter no eventual breakdown or realization crisis [6]. It has refutable or verifiable consequences, such as that technical improvements will raise (a) the rate of profit, (b) the rate of growth of the system, and (c) the real wage. (The same consequences follow even if capitalists and workers each save any constant proportions of their respective incomes, but then the interest rate may well exceed the growth rate.) But to accord with the facts of recent centuries, we must modify the view that (i) population growth is a simple, rising function of the real-wage level, that (ii) capitalists save all with workers saving nothing, and (perhaps) modify the view that (iii) nothing can be hypothesized about the character of technical change in terms of its probable effects on wages and profits. Limitations of nonproducible natural resources should also be recognized.

* We acknowledge aid from the Ford Foundation permitting a (1971) period of collaboration at M.I.T., financial aid from the National Science Foundation, and editorial assistance from Mrs. Jillian Pappas.

1. Marx, K., *Capital*, Vol. 1 (1867), Vol. III (1894).
2. Samuelson, P., *Proc. Nat. Acad. Sci. USA*, **67**, 423–425 (1970), gives notations and references.
3. (See) von Weizsäcker, C. C., forthcoming lecture notes on capital theory (Springer Verlag, Heidelberg, 1971), and Samuelson, P., "The Marxian Notion of Exploitation: the So-called Transformation Problem", to be published in the *Journal of Economic Literature*, 1971.
4. von Weizsäcker, C. C., "Bemerkungen zu einem Symposium über Wachstums—theorie und Produktions funktionen," *Kyklos*, **16**, 438–457 (1963).
5. (See) Phelps, E., *Golden Rules of Economic Growth: Studies of Efficient and Optimal Investment* (Norton, New York, 1967), for references.
6. (See) Sweezy, P., *Theory of Capitalist Development* (Oxford University Press, New York, 1942), for references to Marx, Rosa Luxemburg, *et al.*

BOOK TWO

Topics in Mathematical Economics

PART VIII

Mathematical Investigations

156

A NEGATIVE REPORT ON HERTZ'S PROGRAM
FOR REFORMULATING MECHANICS

Classical conservative mechanics, as developed by Newton, D'Alembert, Euler, Lagrange, Hamilton, Jacobi, and Helmholtz made use of a potential energy function. In his 1893 philosophical exposition of mechanics Hertz wished to avoid use of a potential energy function, replacing it by the assumption of kinetic motions of hidden masses in the background and by rigid connections. Taking advantage of the recent work by Routh, Thomson and Helmholtz on « ignorable » or « cyclic » or « kinesthenic » coordinates, Hertz hoped to reduce mechanics to the study of geodesics on a Riemann surface. The present paper tackles the longneglected task of seeing whether the Hertz program successfully duplicates the classical motions. In even the simplest case of a falling apple it is shown that the method of ignorable coordinates leads to a cumbersome formulation that has to be redefined in each range of the variables. This negative verdict on the Hertz program does not deny the fruitfulness of the quite different geometrization of mechanics provided by Gauss, Appell, Einstein and others.

INTRODUCTION

1. - *Heinrich Hertz's Principles of Mechanics* [1] has been much admired and discussed in the last 70 years, but apparently little read in depth. Duhem correctly called Hertz's formulation less a doctrine than a program, and one would have thought that by this late date some investigators would have pushed on with the program to settle whether the Hertzian reformulation had been worth while. Here I propose to move one tiny step along that program. Such conclusions as I arrive at seem, in their small way, to be adverse to the Hertz formulations.

First, how to account for the benevolent press Hertz's book has received? Axiomatics, after all, are not usually caviar to the general. Most practitioners of science regard such discussion as belonging to dead science. However, the important discovery by Hertz of electromagnetic radiation confirmed his reputation as a brilliant experimenter. Added to this was his theoretical eminence as the leading disciple of von Helmholtz, giving a total reputation that is properly greater than the sum of its independent parts. Moreover, Heinrich Hertz died young, stricken down by a malignancy at 34 when at the height of his powers with the best ahead, and dead at 37. As Helmholtz said, it was as if he had fallen victim to the envy of the gods. *Principles of Mechanics* was written in those last years, perhaps as an anodyne for pain and a substitute for experimentation. The book was never quite finished and had to be given a first editing by the faithful Lenard. In a sense, therefore, the book has received the benefit of the doubt because of the author's demonstrated eminence in other matters, because philosophers are rarely physicists and physicists rarely philosophers, because of the melancholy romanticism surrounding its origin, and because it is an incomplete, posthumous work.

[1] - H. Hertz, *The Principles of Mechanics: Presented in a New Form* (Dover, N. Y. edition 1956), translated from the 1893 German edition, with an Introduction by R. S. Cohen and a Preface by H. von Helmholtz.

2. - On its merits Hertz's goal — to reduce all classical mechanics to differential geometry of Riemann surfaces — seems to have had some intrinsic appeal to physicists and philosophers. In effect, Hertz approved of formulations involving the concept of « kinetic energy », $\dfrac{1}{2}$ mv² or more general quadratic forms of velocities. But the concept of « potential energy », for some reason, bothered him; and he wished to eliminate it by reducing it down to the observed effect of the kinetic motions of certain « hidden masses ». Relatively recent work (from 1877 to 1895) by Routh, J. J. Thomson, and Helmholtz himself on « ignorable » (or « cyclic » or « kinosthenic ») coordinates had given Hertz the hope that such a reduction would be feasible.

3. - It is not an impertinent question to ask, « Why would one want to do this ? » Certainly Hertz's own teacher, Helmholtz, in the last two paragraphs of his Introduction to the *Principles*, demonstrated that he was unable to muster up much enthusiasm for the endeavor. For himself, Helmholtz was content with the terse and comprehensive differential equations of classical mechanics (which do involve potential energies), and the best that he can say for the effort is that if three such great physicists as Maxwell, Kelvin, and Hertz « derived a fuller satisfaction from such explorations (involving tangible models) than from the simple representation of physical facts in the most general form, as given in systems of differential equations ... I have no essential objection to raise against a method which has been adopted by three physicists of such eminence ».

This is not so much an argument as an appeal to authority. And actually the search by Kelvin for a model of vortex atoms and the search by Maxwell for cells with rotating contents to give a mechanical explanation of electromagnetic processes are quite different from Hertz's search for the motions of hidden masses connected by rigid connections; they can be properly lumped together with the Hertz program only in that each represents a dissatisfaction with a surface description and an attempt to find a deeper explanation or interpretation under the surface. It is particularly surprising that Hertz should have felt the same temptations as Kelvin and Maxwell, not because one agrees with Duhem's chauvinistic denunciation of English as against Continental physicists as having an alleged weakness for concrete models, but because it was Hertz who had earlier written the beautiful passage:

« To the question, 'What is Maxwell's Theory?' I know of no shorter or more definite answer than the following: Maxwell's Theory is Maxwell's system of equations. Every theory which leads to the same system of equations, and therefore comprises the same possible phenomena, I would consider as being a form or special case of Maxwell's Theory; every theory which leads to different equations, and therefore different possible phenomena is a different theory ». (Quoted in R. S. Cohen's introduction to the 1956 Dover edition of Hertz's *Principles* from Hertz's earlier book, *Electrical Waves*, German edition, p. 23).

Occam's razor was never wielded more skillfully, and Helmholtz himself or even Mach could have been proud to have penned these lines.

Actually, as will be discussed, Hertz has a bag of quite different motives, different not only from that mentioned by Helmholtz but differing among themselves. For example, he is dissatisfied with the circularities involved in the use of the « force » concept which, as he well knows, has nothing to do with his doubts about the admissibility of the «potential energy» concept. Indeed, he admits that the latter formulation had been shown to render the former unnecessary. Or, again, Hertz points out that Hamilton's Principle, the pillar of orthodox mechanics of his day, cannot properly handle the case of an ideal ball that rolls without slipping upon an ideal surface.[1]

Heuristically, a critic interested in the validity and logic of a proposed system should be warned when he finds it defended by unrelated arguments. But a psychologist, concerned with the motivations for the proposals, finds multiplicity of unrelated arguments both fascinating and informative.

4. - To practitioners of a developing, and yet imperfect, science, « extraneous explanations » seem not to appear extraneous. Even Helmholtz, in his Preface to Hertz's *Principles*, admits that he and Hertz preferred Maxwell's theory of electromagnetics to the traditional one of W. Weber because the notion of « action at a distance » was as repugnant to them as it had first been to Newton (even though Newton had in the end learned to live contentedly with it in formulating the illustrious law of gravitation). But in the end it was not this aesthetic preference, so much as the experimental confirmation of the Maxwell theory where its predictions differed from the older theory, that carried the day. It turned out to make a difference to reject « action at a distance » in the field of electromagnetism.

What difference does it make to believe in Hertz's reformulation? This is the question one would have expected Hertz's posterity to have investigated and settled. At least three outcomes might have been imagined: (i) that Hertzian hidden masses would successfully duplicate the observed phenomena of classical mechanics; (ii) that Hertzian theory would overlap with the classical theory in explaining many facts, but differ with it on some new facts; (iii) that Hertzian theory would be inconsistent with the brute facts of classical mechanics.

The last outcome would represent a signal defeat for the Hertz program. The first would represent some kind of an intellectual victory — possibly an empty victory from the standpoint of advancing our knowledge of reality, or even a Pyrrhic victory in the sense of replacing a simple straightforward second-order differential equation by a complex redundant higher-

---

[1]. - This is admittedly true: when so-called non-holonomic contraints in the form of non-exact differential equations are put on a mechanical system, the simplest variational theory has to be modified. This had already been done by Gauss in connection with his « principle of least constraint »; and Hertz, in developing these principles of least curvature along the lines of contemporaneous differential geometry by Darboux and others, made a genuine contribution to analytical dynamics, helping pave the way for the 1900 formulation (seven years later) of Appell's equations. But no one should think that Appell or Gauss had any commitment to the radical Hertz notion of introducing the kinetic motions of concealed rigidly-connected masses to replace the concept of potential energy — and it is this latter basic Hertz program that I am appraising here.

For an attempt to provide a new local minimum formulation of mechanics going beyond that of Gauss, see P. A. Samuelson, « Some Notions of Causality and Teleology in Economics », in D. Lerner (ed.), *Cause and Effect*, Free Press of Glencoe, 1965.

order system. The second outcome would be the most exciting of all, particularly if the Hertzian prediction about new phenomena proved more accurate than those of the classical theory. (Perhaps it is this that Helmholtz is hinting at, not, I sense, with much conviction, in his Preface's final sentence: « In the future this book may prove of great heuristic value as a guide to the discovery of new and general characteristics of natural forces »).

As far as I can tell from a search through the literature, the second happy outcome [1] has not yet materialized. After 70 years, no one seems to have come up with a *single* new prediction that differs in any way — for better or worse — from the standard Newton-Lagrange-Hamilton-Helmholtz-Appell formulations! I hope I am wrong in saying this and will be grateful for specification of exceptions to this sweeping statement.

Most writers seem to have the impression that outcome (i) has materialized, and that the Hertzian program has at least *duplicated* the standard analysis. If so, the conclusion may bring less excitement for physical science, but the effort must still rank as an intellectual (and perhaps) aesthetic adventure. People do not climb the Matterhorn to get to the other side; but once its being there has been noticed, it is nice to have settled the issue that one could use that route of transport.

Outcome (iii), that simple Hertzian methods are inconsistent with classical mechanics, is incompatible with (i). Yet is is, in a sense, this conclusion to which the following tentative researches seem to lead.

ANALYSIS

5. - Consider some elementary examples. Consider a particle of unit mass that is subject to no gravitational or other force in the direction of north y and east x. Since it lacks acceleration, its behavior is described completely by:

(1) $\qquad \ddot{x} = 0, \quad \ddot{y} = 0; \quad x(t) = \dot{x}_0 t, \quad y(t) = \dot{y}_0 t; \quad t > 0$

where $\dot{x} = dx/dt$, $\ddot{x} = d^2x/dt^2$, etc. and where $\dot{x}_0$ and $\dot{y}_0$ are initial velocities at time zero. These simple Newtonian facts would be described by Hamilton and Helmholtz by the minimum formulation in the calculus of variations:

(2) $\qquad \underset{\{x(t),\ y(t)\}}{\text{Min}} \quad \int_0^1 \left[\frac{1}{2}\dot{x}^2 + \frac{1}{2}\dot{y}^2 - 0 \right] dt = \int_0^1 L(q, \dot{q})\, dt$

$$\begin{array}{ll} x(0) = 0 & y(0) = 0 \\ x(1) = \dot{x}_0 & y(1) = \dot{y}_0 \end{array} \qquad = \int_0^1 \left[T(q, \dot{q}) - V(q) \right]$$

The Euler-Lagrange conditions for a minimum for this standard problem are known to be:

(3) $\qquad \dfrac{d}{dt}\dfrac{\partial L}{\partial \dot{x}} - \dfrac{\partial L}{\partial x} \equiv 0 \ , \qquad \dfrac{d}{dt}\dfrac{\partial L}{\partial \dot{y}} - \dfrac{\partial L}{\partial y} \equiv 0 \qquad$ or

$$\dfrac{d}{dt}\dot{x} - 0 = \ddot{x} \equiv 0 \ , \qquad \dfrac{d}{dt}\dot{y} - 0 = \ddot{y} \equiv 0$$

Hence, the received theory fully accounts for the facts.

[1]. - I include in traditional mechanics the non-holonomic conditions of Appell and others.

Moreover, Hertz would have approved fully of this formulation. For the Lagrangian expression $L(q, \dot{q})$ involves only kinetic energy, a positive-definite quadratic form in the $(\dot{x}, \dot{y})$ velocities, with the potential energy $V(q)$ function vanishing entirely from the scene. And obviously the straight-line paths are geodesics on a Euclidean-plane surface, describable by all of Hertz's notations of Riemannian differential geometry.

But now consider movement of the particle in the vertical downward direction z. It, like any apple, will accelerate toward the earth; and we must add to (1) the Galileo-Newton behavior equation:

$$(4) \qquad \ddot{z} = +g \ , \qquad z = \frac{1}{2}gt^2 + \dot{z}_0 t \ , \qquad t > 0$$

Helmholtz would economically deduce these results from:

$$(5) \qquad \begin{array}{c} \text{Min} \\ \{x(t), \ y(t), \ z(t)\} \end{array} \int_0^1 \left[(\frac{1}{2}\dot{x}^2 + \frac{1}{2}\dot{y}^2 + \frac{1}{2}\dot{z}^2) - (-gz) \right]$$

$$= \int_0^1 \left[T(q, \dot{q}) - V(q) \quad dt \right]$$

where $0 \neq V(q) = -gz$.

6. - The Hertz program proposes to get rid of this potential energy term by employing the device of Routh, Thomson, and Helmholtz for handling so-called ignorable coordinates. These men had shown that when $L(q_1, q_2, \ldots, \dot{q}_1, \dot{q}_2, \ldots)$ happened not to involve q_1 directly, so that $\partial L/\partial q_1 \equiv 0$ and $L(q_1, q_2, \ldots, \dot{q}_1, \dot{q}_2) = f(q_2, \ldots, \dot{q}_1, \dot{q}_2)$, the problem could be converted into a new problem with a new $\bar{L}, (q_2, \ldots, \dot{q}_2, \ldots)$ that did not involve even $\dot{q}_1$ *and which would have* new potential energy components $V(q_2, \ldots)$ even if previously $V(q_1, q_2, \ldots)$ had not existed

So let us pursue the Hertz program of trying to utilize ignorable coordinates. Can a new concealed mass be found to do the trick? Mathematically, we seek a new variable *w* and a new function:

$$2T(q, \dot{q}) = a_{11}\dot{w}^2 + a_{12}\dot{w}\dot{x} + a_{13}\dot{w}\dot{z}$$
$$+ a_{21}\dot{x}\dot{w} + a_{22}\dot{x}^2 + a_{23}\dot{x}\dot{z}$$
$$+ a_{31}\dot{z}\dot{w} + a_{32}\dot{z}\dot{x} + a_{33}\dot{z}^2$$

where the a_{ij} are functions of x, z but not of w, namely $a_{ij}(x, z)$, which form a symmetric positive definite matrix. (For simplicity, I can ignore y completely, working in one vertical plane).

If we minimize the integral of $L(q, \dot{q}) = T(q, \dot{q}) - 0$, we get the following Euler conditions for $q_1 = w$, $q_2 = x$, $q_3 = z$:

$$(7) \qquad \frac{d}{dt}\frac{\partial L}{\partial \dot{q}_i} - \frac{\partial L}{\partial q_i} = 0 \qquad (i = 2,3)$$

$$\frac{d}{dt}\frac{\partial L}{\partial \dot{q}_1} - 0 = 0, \qquad \text{or} \quad \frac{\partial L(q, \dot{q})}{\partial \dot{w}} = c, \text{ a constant}$$

$$a_{11}\dot{w} + a_{12}\dot{x} + a_{13}\dot{z} = c$$

We substitute this last expression into L to get a function of $(x, z, \dot{x}, \dot{z})$ alone. Patently the term c will introduce linear terms in the $(\dot{x}, \dot{z})$ velocities in the new $\overline{L}$, of the form $a_{ij}\, \dot{x}c/a_{11}$. Since we do not want to end up with such gyroscopic terms for our simple falling-body problem, we choose at the beginning to set $a_{12} = 0 = a_{13}$. Then we find:

$$(8) \qquad \overline{L} = \frac{1}{2}\left(a_{22}\,\dot{x}^2 + 2a_{23}\,\dot{x}\dot{z} + a_{33}\,\dot{z}^2 + \frac{c^2}{a_{11}}\right)$$

$$= \overline{T}\,(x, z, \dot{x}, \dot{z}) - \overline{V}\,(x, z)$$

$$(9) \qquad \text{where } \overline{V}\,(x, z) = -\frac{c^2}{2a_{11}} \quad \text{or} \quad a_{11} = -\frac{c^2}{2V\,(x, z)}$$

All the above is standard practice from any text on dynamics (as e.g. E. Whittaker, *Analytical Dynamics*, 1937, p. 57 or C. Lanczos, *Variational Principles of Mechanics*, 1949, p. 126).

Now Hertz would like the new $\overline{L}$ to be identical with the integrand of the Hamilton-Helmholtz formulation in (5). This we can achieve if we set:

$$a_{22} = \frac{1}{2} = a_{33},\ a_{23} = 0 \,,$$

$$a_{11} = \frac{c^2}{2gz}$$

Theorem: The three-variable Hertzian integrand without potential energy:

$$L\,(q_1, q_2, q_3, \dot{q}_1, \dot{q}_2, \dot{q}_3) = \frac{1}{2}\dot{x}^2 + \frac{1}{2}\dot{z}^2 + \left(\frac{c^2}{2gz}\right)\frac{w^2}{2}$$

gives rise to variational equations for x and z identical to those arising from the two-variable Helmholtz integrand:

$$\overline{L}\,(q_2, q_3, \dot{q}_2, \dot{q}_3) = \frac{1}{2}\dot{x}^2 + \frac{1}{2}\dot{z}^2 - (-gz)$$

7. - This elementary derivation seems to have justified the Hertzian program, at least for the simplest case. But note certain difficulties of a practical and aesthetic nature. It is important for Hertz that a_{11} be positive to correspond to a true local minimum of least curvature, and to agree with the physicists notion of kinetic energy. From (9) we ask can:

$$a_{11}\,(z) = \frac{c^2}{2gz}$$

be everywhere positive? Presumably c can be made non-zero. But when z passes through zero, the radical ceases to give a real number. Admittedly, only *differences* in potential energy matters: $V\,(q) + A$ will lead to the same results as will $V\,(q)$ since $\int_0^1 A dt$ is independent of path when A is a constant. What is the same thing, we can always select our arbitrary origin for altitude z in such a way as to make the new gz of whatever sign we like at any range of altitudes. But everytime we consider a path that falls out of that range, we would have to change in advance our origin for z, a procedure both practically messy and aesthetically repugnant. Or, as a Hertzian would put is, this construction would seem to lack « appropriateness ».

CONCLUSION

8. - This completes my brief testing of the Hertzian program. In the simplest case of all, the falling apple of Newton and Galileo, it seems to lead at best to an inappropriate model. Moreover, the phenomenon discussed here is general: V (q) will for many natural problems want to run through a gamut of values from $-\infty$ to $+\infty$, leading to the same messy requirement that we add new arbitrary constants to V in each different range. Why take a local train involving many transfers when an express train rides right through?

9. - There is another possible difficulty. The parameter c depends on the initial conditions of the hidden masses. Yet we want the *same* value of c and a_{11} everytime, in order ot give us the time invariance of V that is actually observed. Suppose Hertz has an Assistant who actually builds a hidden *w* mass in a black box. His Assistant is supposed to be able to duplicate our observed experiments, which we run off by calling out arbitrary (x, z, $\dot{x}$, $\dot{z}$) initial conditions. How exactly will the Assistant do the trick? He must ensure that the hidden mass gets set off at the critical rate $\partial L/\partial \dot{q}_1 = a$ *fixed* c. So to speak, he must wind up the hidden mass each time; or, he must have a « governor » on it that keeps it in the motion for which $\partial L/\partial \dot{q}_1 = c$ and not $= d$ or a or b. Must we worry ourselves about the equations of the governor? Or does Maxwell's Demon have a brother, Hertz's Demon, who polices the hidden motions? If Duhem disliked Kelvin's otiose vortex's, what would he say of this (admittedly non-English) rigamarole?

Lest too much be made of the present point, let me admit that an exactly similar problem rises when the physicist turns from Hamilton's Principle to the older Maupertuis-Euler principle of least action. In the latter formulation the total energy of the system is held constant (but not the time of the motion). Going from the former principle to the latter is mathematically just like eliminating an ignorable coordinate. A physicist who is content with the latter principle cannot conscientiously make too much of the argument I have given in the last paragraph.

10. - Finally, a warning is in order. Hertz has not here been given all the rope that is his due. Would two hidden masses, u as well as w, do better?

My desultory researches suggest not. Others should settle the matter. Will an infinite number of masses do better? This needs careful investigation. But suppose the answers were affirmative. How happy should we be to be able to handle a straight-forward problem with a few degrees of freedom only, by an *infinite*-variable formulation? [1]

11. - My primary purpose is not to present these negative findings about the Hertz program, for these researches are at best tentative and fragmentary. But rather, I hope to show by example that after 70 years there ought to be less talk about the abstract philosophy of Hertz's system and more prosaic study of its concrete mathematical and physical content.

Massachusetts, Institute of Technology.

P. A. SAMUELSON

---

[1] - Will rigid connections of the form g (u, w, x, t) = 0 help? This needs study What about a non-holonomic condition of the form $\dot{w}^2 = - V (q)$. Aside from involving the same problem of algebraic sign, what is the point of ousting potential energy functions V (q) from the integrand only to readmit them unaltered through the back door of side conditions?

I am not competent to judge whether the admittedly important geodesic formulations of general relativity confirm the Hertzian program and enable it to be defended against various of the objections developed in this paper. This problem seems worth investigating.

157

RECIPROCAL CHARACTERISTIC ROOT PROPERTY OF DISCRETE-TIME MAXIMA

PAUL A. SAMUELSON*

MASSACHUSETTS INSTITUTE OF TECHNOLOGY

1. Being able to express a mathematical system as an extremum problem is known to have advantages (easy existence proofs of a solution, convenient transformation of coordinates, implied invariants, etc.). In particular, a classical theorem of Poincaré[1] asserts that the characteristic roots associated with Lagrange-Hamilton differential equations in the neighborhood of a stationary-equilibrium point, a limit cycle, or general periodic solution must always come in opposite-signed pairs. The present paper shows that the characteristic roots associated with the stationary-equilibrium points of a discrete-time dynamic programming model must always come in reciprocal pairs. Since damped stability of such a system requires that no characteristic root exceed unity in absolute value, the present theorem rules out all possibility of damped stability in such models.

2. Avoiding Hamilton's canonical formulation, we review a direct proof of Poincaré's result for differential equations. Let the Euler-Lagrange extremal equations of a time-free variational problem

$$
(1) \quad \frac{d}{dt} \frac{\partial L(x^1, \ldots, x^n, \dot{x}^1, \ldots, \dot{x}^n)}{\partial \dot{x}_i} - \frac{\partial L(x^1, \ldots, x^n, \dot{x}^1, \ldots, \dot{x}^n)}{\partial x_i} = 0
$$

$$
(i = 1, 2, \ldots, n)
$$

have a stationary solution $x^i(t) \equiv x^i$. Then neglecting quadratic and higher-power terms in $y^i = (x^i - \bar{x}^i)$ and their derivatives, we associate with the equilibrium point the linear differential-equation system

$$
0 = \frac{d}{dt} \left[\sum_j \frac{\partial^2 L}{\partial x_i \partial \dot{x}_j} \dot{y}_j + \sum_j \frac{\partial^2 L}{\partial \dot{x}_i \partial x_j} y_j \right] - \sum_j \frac{\partial^2 L}{\partial \dot{x}_i \partial x_j} \dot{y}_j - \sum_j \frac{\partial^2 L}{\partial x_i \partial x_j} y_j
$$

$$
= \sum_j \frac{\partial^2 L}{\partial \dot{x}_i \partial \dot{x}_j} \ddot{y}_j + \sum_j \left[\frac{\partial^2 L}{\partial x_i \partial \dot{x}_j} - \frac{\partial^2 L}{\partial \dot{x}_i \partial x_j} \right] \dot{y}_j - \sum_j \frac{\partial^2 L}{\partial x_i \partial x_j} y_j
$$

where the partial derivatives of L are evaluated at $(\bar{x}^i)$ and are constants.

*Financial aid from the National Science Foundation is gratefully acknowledged. While the present paper was in the press, I learned that I had overlooked a basic 1963 paper of Lionel W. McKenzie which essentially etablishes the reciprocal root property. *Mea culpa.*

[1] H. Poincaré, *Les Méthodes nouvelles de la Mécanique céleste* (1892), Vol. 1, Chap. 4; G. D. Birkhoff, *Dynamical Systems* (1927), Chap. 3; E. Whittaker, *Analytical Dynamics* (1937), 4th ed., Chap. 15.

In matrix terms, this system can be written

(2) $$0 = A_{11}\ddot{y} + (A_{12} - A_{21})\dot{y} - A_{22}y,$$

(3) $$A_{11} = A'_{11}, \quad A_{22} = A'_{22}, \quad (A_{12} - A_{21})' = -(A_{12} - A_{21}),$$

where A' is the transpose of A.

The solution of the linear system consists of linear superposition of terms involving $exp\lambda_k t$ where (λ_k) are roots of the determinantal polynomial

(4)
$$0 = D(\lambda) = det[A_{11}\lambda^2 + (A_{12} - A_{21})\lambda - A_{22}] = c(\lambda - \lambda_1) \ldots (\lambda - \lambda_{2n})$$
$$= c(\lambda - \lambda_1)(\lambda + \lambda_1) \ldots (\lambda - \lambda_n)(\lambda + \lambda_n)$$

This follows from the symmetry properties of the A_{ij} matrices, since by transposition

$$det\,[A_{11}'(-\lambda)^2 + (A_{12} - A_{21})'(-\lambda) - A_{22}'] = det\,[A_{11}\lambda^2 + (A_{12} - A_{21})\lambda - A_{22}]'$$
$$= D(\lambda) = D(-\lambda)$$

3. For discrete time, instead of maximizing an integral we maximize a sum

$$S_T = f(x_0,x_1) + f(x_1,x_2) + \ldots + f(x_T,x_{T+1})$$
$$= \sum_{t=0}^{T} f(x_t,x_{t+1})$$

subject to prescribed terminal conditions (x_0,x_{T+1}). Here each x_t can be considered a vector of variables $(x_t^1, x_t^2, \ldots, x_t^n)$, but first I exposit the case where $n = 1$.

The "extremal" conditions for a regular interior maximum solution are

(5) $$\frac{\partial S_T}{\partial x_t} = 0 = \frac{\partial f(x_t,x_{t+1})}{\partial x_t} + \frac{\partial f(x_{t-1},x_t)}{\partial x_t}, \qquad (t = 1, \ldots, T)$$

Suppose that these non-linear difference equations have a solution $x_t \equiv \bar{x}$ and we rewrite them in terms of $y_t = x_t - \bar{x}$. Then, neglecting quadratic and higher powers of y_t, we have the associated linear difference-equation system

(6) $$A_{12}y_{t+2} + (A_{11} + A_{22})y_{t+1} + A_{21}y_t = 0$$

where

$$A_{11} = \frac{\partial^2 f(\bar{x},\bar{x})}{\partial x_t^2}, \quad A_{12} = \frac{\partial^2 f(\bar{x},\bar{x})}{\partial x_t \partial x_{t+1}}$$

$$A_{21} = \frac{\partial^2 f(\bar{x},\bar{x})}{\partial x_{t+1} \partial x_t}, \quad A_{22} = \frac{\partial^2 f(\bar{x},\bar{x})}{\partial x_{t+1}^2}$$

This linear system has solutions that are superpositions of λ_1^t and λ_2^t where the λ's are roots of the characteristic polynomial

(7) $$0 = A_{12}\lambda^2 + (A_{11} + A_{22})\lambda + A_{21}$$

Since $A_{12} = A_{21}$, and in all non-trivial cases do not vanish, clearly

$$\lambda_1 = b + \sqrt{b^2 - 1},$$

$$\lambda_2 = b - \sqrt{b^2 - 1},$$

$$\lambda_1 \lambda_2 = 1$$

where $b = - (A_{11} + A_{22})/2A_{12}$.

Thus, characteristic roots do come in reciprocal pairs for a one-variable discrete-time maximum system. Q.E.D.

4. To prove the theorem for the general case

$$S_T = \sum_{t=0}^{T} f(x_t, x_{t+1}) = \sum_{t=0}^{T} f(x_t^1, \ldots, x_t^n, x_{t+1}^1, \ldots, x_{t+1}^n),$$

let (5) stand as the vector short-hand for

$$0 = \frac{\partial f(x_t^1, \ldots, x_{t+1}^n)}{\partial x_t^i} + \frac{\partial f(x_{t-1}^1, \ldots, x_t^n)}{\partial x_t^i}, \qquad (i = 1, 2, \ldots, n)$$

In (6) interpret the A's as the following $n \times n$ matrixes:

$$\begin{bmatrix} A_{11} & A_{12} \\ A_{21} & A_{22} \end{bmatrix} = \begin{bmatrix} \partial^2 f/\partial x_t^i \partial x_t^j & \partial^2 f/\partial x_t^i \partial x_{t+1}^j \\ \partial^2 f/\partial x_{t+1}^i \partial x_t^j & \partial^2 f/\partial x_{t+1}^i \partial x_{t+1}^j \end{bmatrix}$$

where these partial derivatives are evaluated at

$$(x_t, x_{t+1}) = (\bar{x}^1, \ldots, \bar{x}^n, \bar{x}^1, \ldots, \bar{x}^n).$$

Now, instead of the quadratic (7), we have the characteristic polynomial in determinantal form

$$0 = \Delta(\lambda) = det [A_{12}\lambda^2 + (A_{11}+A_{22})\lambda+A_{21}] = C(\lambda - \lambda_1) \ldots (\lambda - \lambda_{2n})$$

$$= C(\lambda - \lambda_1) (\lambda - \frac{1}{\lambda_1}) \ldots (\lambda - \lambda_n) (\lambda - \frac{1}{\lambda_n})$$

To prove that the roots come in such reciprocal pairs, we use the symmetry properties of the A_{ij} matrixes, noting that

$$\Delta(\lambda^{-1}) = det \left[A_{12}(\lambda^{-1})^2 + (A_{11} + A_{22})\lambda^{-1} + A_{21} \right]$$

$$= \frac{1}{\lambda^{2n}} \, det \left[A_{12} + (A_{11} + A_{22}) \, \lambda + A_{21}\lambda^2 \right]$$

$$= \frac{1}{\lambda^{2n}} \, det \left[A'_{12} + (A'_{11} + A'_{22})\lambda + A'_{21}\lambda^2 \right]$$

$$= \frac{1}{\lambda^{2n}} \, det \left[A_{12}\lambda^2 + (A_{11} + A_{22})\lambda + A_{21} \right] = \frac{1}{\lambda^{2n}} \, \Delta(\lambda)$$

Hence, barring the singular case where $\lambda_i = 0$ is a root, we have λ_i^{-1} a root wherever λ_i is a root.[2]

In the singular case, A_{12} itself will be a singular matrix and (6) will not be a well-determined causal system. Such pathologies will occur when the maximal stationary path is not locally unique, implying existence of constant solutions to the associated linear system. They may also occur in borderline cases where the stability properties of the motion depend upon examination of the higher-power terms in y_t.

In the case where $\lambda_1 = \pm 1$ is a root, there necessarily must be a repeated root $\lambda_1^{-1} = \pm 1$. One might then fear that "resonance" terms of the form $t\lambda_1{}^t$ would enter into the solutions. But as Weierstrass showed in correction of one of Lagrange's rare errors, the symmetry of the A_{ij} matrixes, which is itself a basic property of an extremum formulation, permits the system to be "diagonalized" into independent components, and such resonance cannot appear.

5. How the general Poincaré theorem applying to the characteristic exponents of periodic motions can be generalized to discrete-time system will be discussed in a forthcoming paper.

[2] See L. W. McKenzie, "The Dorfman-Samuelson-Solow Turnpike Theorem," *Internat. Econ. Rev.*, Jan. 1963, 4, 29-43, which proves in Lemma 4, p. 38, precisely this property.

158

CLASSICAL ORBITAL STABILITY DEDUCED FOR DISCRETE-TIME MAXIMUM SYSTEMS

PAUL A. SAMUELSON[*]

Massachusetts Institute of Technology

1. Poincaré established the celebrated theorem that the characteristic exponents associated with the periodic motion of a maximum system in the calculus of variations appear in opposite-signed pairs. A special case of this theorem on orbital stability is that of steady-state equilibrium, a degenerate periodic motion, whose characteristic exponents (or roots) must appear in opposite-signed pairs.

In an earlier paper,[1] I proved the counterpart of the Poincaré theorem for the steady-state equilibrium of discrete-time variational problems, namely that the associated characteristic roots appear in reciprocal pairs, thereby ruling out damped stability either forward or backward in time. Here I shall prove the more difficult theorem concerning the orbital stability of periodic solutions of a discrete-time system. Two different methods of proof will be sketched.

2. Consider the maximum problem:

$$\text{Max } S = \sum_{t_0}^{t_1} f(x_t^1, \ldots, x_t^n; x_{t+1}^1, \ldots, x_{t+1}^n) = \sum_{t_0}^{t_1} f(x_t; x_{t+1}) \text{ for short.}$$

This is the discrete-time analogue of the calculus of variations problems of classical mechanics.

$$\text{Max } I = \int_{t_0}^{t_1} f(x; \dot{x}) dt$$

Note that time does not enter explicitly into the integrand or summand.

For an interior smooth maximum, we derive the variational equations for an extremal:

(1)
$$\frac{\partial S}{\partial x_t^i} = 0 = \frac{\partial f(x_t; x_{t+1})}{\partial x_t^i} + \frac{\partial f(x_{t-1}; x_t)}{\partial x_t^i} \qquad (i = 1, \ldots, n)$$

*Aid from the National Science Foundation is acknowledged. I thank Robert Merton for valuable assistance.

1. P. A. Samuelson, "Reciprocal Characteristic Root Property of Discrete-Time Maxima," *Western Econ. Jour.*, March 1968, 6, 90-93, which gives references to the classic works of H. Poincaré, G. D. Birkhoff, and E. Whittaker; M. Kurz, "The General Instability of a Class of Competitive Growth Processes," *Rev. Econ. Stud.*, Apr. 1968, 35, 155-74, which applies and generalizes the Poincaré theorem; N. Liviatan and P. A. Samuelson, "Notes on Turnpikes: Stable and Unstable," *Jour. Econ. Theory*, Dec. 1969, 1, 454-75.

These difference equations correspond to the usual Euler differential equations for extremals.

3. Now suppose our equations (1) have a periodic solution:

$$(2) \qquad\qquad x_t^i = X_t^i \equiv X_{t+N}^i \qquad\qquad (i = 1, \ldots, n)$$

and consider the following linear variational equation associated with the small divergence $x_t^i - X_t^i$ from this periodic motion:

$$(3) \qquad\qquad f_t^{12} y_{t+1} + (f_t^{11} + f_{t-1}^{22}) y_t + f_{t-1}^{21} y_{t-1} = 0$$

where in matrix notation:

$$(4) \qquad\qquad y_t = [x_t^i - X_t^i]$$

$$f_t^{11} = \left[\frac{\partial^2 f(X_t; X_{t+1})}{\partial x_t^i \, \partial x_t^j} \right]$$

$$f_t^{22} = \left[\frac{\partial^2 f(X_t; X_{t+1})}{\partial x_{t+1}^i \, \partial x_{t+1}^j} \right]$$

$$f_t^{12} = \left[\frac{\partial^2 f(X_t; X_{t+1})}{\partial x_t^i \, \partial x_{t+1}^j} \right]$$

$$f_t^{21} = (f_t^{12})', \text{ the transpose of } f_t^{12}$$

$$(f_t^{11})' = f_t^{11} ; \ (f_t^{22})' = f_t^{22}$$

As is usual, (3) represents a Taylor's expansion of (1) around the solution (2), with the remainder that depends on squares or higher products of the divergence set equal to zero. Rigorously, (3) is an exact linear equation satisfied by partial derivatives of (1)'s exact solutions, taken with respect to changes in initial conditions. It is well-known that the stability of the non-linear set (1) depends in certain ways upon the stability of the more tractable linear set (3).

Because of (2)'s periodic property, the coefficients of the linear equations are strictly periodic:

$$f_{t+N}^{ij} \equiv f_t^{ij} \qquad\qquad (i, j = 1, 2)$$

these being evaluated in (4) along the periodic motion.

4. If f_t^{12} is always nonsingular, the second-order difference equations (1) or (3) can always be regarded as a causal system, forward and backward: i.e., knowledge of two adjacent states, (x_t, x_{t+1}), permits explicit

calculation of x_{t+2} and x_{t-1}, and hence of all other states on the optimizing trajectories. I posit this non-singularity property throughout.

Premultiplying (3) by $(f_t^{12})^{-1} = (B_t)'$, we have:

(5) $$y_{t+2} + C_t y_{t+1} + (B_t)'(B_{t-1})^{-1} y_t = 0$$

where

$$C_t = (f_t^{12})^{-1} [f_t^{11} + f_{t-1}^{22}]$$

$$(B_{t-1})^{-1} = (f_{t-1}^{12})' = f_{t-1}^{21} \text{ from (4)}$$

By defining vectors of new variables:

$$Y_t^1 = y_t = [y_t^i]$$

$$Y_t^2 = y_{t+1} = [y_{t+1}^i]$$

we can convert the n second-order difference equations of (5) into $2n$ first-order difference equations in normal form:

(6) $$Y_{t+1} = \begin{bmatrix} Y_{t+1}^1 \\ \vdots \\ Y_{t+1}^2 \end{bmatrix} = \begin{bmatrix} 0 \cdots\cdots 0 & 1 \cdots\cdots 0 \\ \vdots & & \\ 0 \cdots\cdots 0 & 0 \cdots\cdots 1 \\ -(B_t)'(B_{t-1})^{-1} & -C_t \end{bmatrix} \begin{bmatrix} Y_t^1 \\ Y_t^2 \end{bmatrix} = A_t Y_t$$

Clearly, A_t is a periodic matrix:

(2') $$A_{t+N} \equiv A_t$$

by virtue of the periodic relation of (2).

5. By iteration and use of the periodic property:

(7) $$Y_{t+2} = A_{t+1} Y_{t+1} = A_{t+1} A_t Y_t$$

$$\cdots\cdots\cdots\cdots$$

$$Y_{t+N} = (A_{t+N-1} A_{t+N-2} \cdots A_{t+1} A_t) Y_t \equiv J_t Y_t$$

$$Y_{t+2N} = (J_t)^2 Y_t$$

$$Y_{t+mN} = (J_t)^m Y_t$$

Freezing the initial t at an arbitrary τ (which might as well be on the interval $0, 1, \ldots, N-1$), and defining $Z_m = Y_{\tau+mN}$, we end up with a simple timeless difference equation:

(8) $$Z_{m+1} = J_\tau Z_m$$

where, from (2),

(9) $$J_\tau = (A_{\tau+N-1} \ldots A_\tau) \equiv J_{\tau+N}$$

The asymptotic properties of y_t or Y_t evidently depend only upon the characteristic roots of the J_τ matrix, and must certainly be the same for any τ since J_τ and $J_{\tau+i}$ are similar matrices, as can be seen inductively from the relation:

(4a) $$J_{\tau+1} = A_{\tau+N} A_{\tau+N-1} \ldots A_{\tau+1}$$

$$= A_{\tau+N} (A_{\tau+N-1} \ldots A_{\tau+1} A_\tau) A_\tau^{-1}$$

$$= A_\tau J_\tau A_\tau^{-1} \qquad\qquad \text{from (2')}$$

The characteristic roots are defined by the polynomial:

$$\det [\lambda I - J_\tau] = \lambda^{2n} + \ldots + (\det J_\tau) = 0 = (\lambda - \lambda_1) \ldots (\lambda - \lambda_{2n})$$

If these roots occur in reciprocal pairs, it is necessary that $\det J_\tau = 1$. And, for $n = 1$, this condition is also sufficient.

But,

(10) $$\det J_\tau = \prod_{i=0}^{N-1} \det A_{\tau+i}$$

$$= \prod_{i=0}^{N-1} (-\det I)(-\det (B_{\tau+i})'/\det B_{\tau+i-1}), \qquad \text{from (6)}$$

$$= 1, \text{ by periodicity of } B_\tau$$

Hence, we have proved our theorem for $n = 1$. To prove the theorem in general by this line of attack does not seem promising.

6. Exactly parallel to the theory of linear differential equations with periodic coefficients can be developed the theory of linear difference equations with (6)'s periodic property. I follow the exposition of E. A. Coddington and N. Levinson, *Theory of Ordinary Differential Equations* (1955), Chapter 3, hereafter referred to as C-L. We consider the general linear-homogeneous system:

(11) $$Z_{t+1} = A_t Z_t$$

where A_t is initially *any* never-singular $n \times n$ matrix. Then also

$$Z_{t-1} = (A_t^{-1}) Z_t$$

so that the system is reversible.

By induction we easily establish the existence of a unique solution for all $t \gtreqless t_0$:

$$Z_{t+1} = A_t Z_t, \; Z_\tau = \xi$$

written as

$$Z_t = \phi_t (\xi).$$

Now let (ξ_{ij}) be n linearly independent column vectors of complex numbers, with det $(\xi_{ij}) \neq 0$.

Then

$$\Phi_t = [\phi_t(\xi_1), \; \phi_t(\xi_2), \; \ldots, \; \phi_t(\xi_n)]$$

is a square matrix whose columns satisfy the matrix difference equation system:

(12) $$\Phi_{t+1} = A_t \Phi_t; \; \Phi_\tau = [\xi_{ij}]$$

It is evident that Φ_t is never singular, since:

(13) $$\det \Phi_t = (\det A_{t-1})(\det A_{t-2}) \ldots (\det A_{t-t+\tau}) \det \Phi_\tau,$$

$t > \tau$ and likewise for $t < \tau$.

Hence Φ_t constitutes what may be defined as a *fundamental matrix solution* for (11), (C-L, p. 69), namely a matrix whose n columns satisfy the linear-homogeneous equation and which are linearly independent for all t. It is easy to prove for linear difference equations the exact analogue of well-known theorems on linear differential equations, namely:

1. *The set of all solutions of our linear-homogeneous-difference-equation system for all* t *form a* n-*dimensional vector space over the complex field.* (THEOREM 2.1 of C-L);

2. *A necessary and sufficient condition that a solution matrix* Φ *of (12) form a "fundamental matrix" is that det* $\Phi_t \neq 0$ *for (some, and then all)* t. (THEOREM 2.2 of C-L);

3. *Any two fundamental matrices,* Φ_t *and* Ψ_t, *must be related by* $\Psi_t = \Phi C_t$, *where C is a complex non-singular constant matrix.* (THEOREM 2.3 of C-L).

Because the proofs are straightforward and parallel to the differential-equation case, I omit them here.

7. Now we consider A_t in (11) that is periodic,

(14) $$Z_{t+1} = A_t Z_t; \; A_t \equiv A_{t+N}$$

For the moment, no other restrictions are placed on A_t.

Then exactly analogous to the differential-equations case, we have:

THEOREM: If Φ_t is a fundamental matrix for (14), then so is Ψ_t, where

$$(15) \qquad\qquad \Psi_t = \Phi_{t+N}$$

Corresponding to every such Φ_t, there exists a periodic nonsingular matrix P_t with period N, and a constant matrix $C^{1/N}$ such that:

$$(16) \qquad\qquad \Phi_t = P_t \, C^{1/N}$$

To prove this counterpart of C-L THEOREM 5.1, note that

$$\Psi_{t+1} = \Phi_{t+N+1} = A_{t+N}\Phi_{t+N} = A_t\Phi_{t+N} = A_t\Psi_t$$

Thus Ψ_t is a solution matrix and it is a fundamental matrix since $\det \Psi_t = \det \Psi_t = \det \Phi_{t+N} \neq 0$.

Therefore there exists a constant nonsingular matrix C such that $\Phi_{t+N} = \Phi_t C$. Now define P_t by:

$$(17) \qquad\qquad P_t = \Phi_t (C^{1/N})^{-t}$$

where $C^{1/N}$ is a (non-unique) solution of the matrix equation:

$$(18) \qquad\qquad X^N = C$$

For C real, this need not have a real solution for N odd. But a nonsingular solution does always exist (see C-L, pp. 79-80) in the complex field.

We now verify that P_t is periodic, since

$$P_{t+N} = \Phi_{t+N} C^{-(t+N)/N} = \Phi_t C C^{-1} C^{-t/N} = \Phi_t C^{-t/N} = P_t,$$

which completes the proof.

Remark: If N is even and A_t real, a real P_t will exist. Since a function with period N also is of period $2N$, for stability purposes we can always employ a real P_t if we want to.

To prove the orbital stability property of this paper, it is necessary and sufficient to show that the specialization of A_t given in (6), resulting from the maximum character of the problem, implies that C (and hence $C^{1/N}$) has characteristic roots that appear in reciprocal pairs. To show this in the $n>1$ case appears to be difficult, and so for the rest of this paper I sketch out a second, quite different, method of attack.

8. Revert to our original maximum problem, and note that it can be rewritten as:

$$(19) \qquad \operatorname{Max} S = f(x_0; x_1) + \operatorname*{Max}_{\{x_2, \ldots, x_{T-1}\}} \sum_1^{T-1} f(x_t; x_{t+1}) + f(x_T; x_{T+1})$$

$$= f(x_0; x_1) + S(x_1; x_T) + f(x_T; x_{T+1})$$

Any optimal solutions $(x_0, x_1, x_2, \ldots, x_{T-1}, x_T, x_{T+1})$ to the original problem must correspond to optimal solutions (x_0, x_1, x_T, x_{T+1}) of our new problem.

On the other hand, since for causal systems (x_0, x_1) determine all subsequent x_t and hence the pair (x_T, x_{T+1}), we must get the same causal relationship from our new problem as from our old. Let us therefore deduce the extremal equations for the new problem, namely:

$$(20) \qquad \frac{\partial S}{\partial x_1{}^i} = 0 = \frac{\partial f(x_0; x_1)}{\partial x_1{}^i} + \frac{\partial S(x_1; x_T)}{\partial x_1{}^i} \qquad (i = 1, \ldots, n)$$

$$\frac{\partial S}{\partial x_T{}^i} = 0 = \frac{\partial S(x_1; x_T)}{\partial x_T{}^i} + \frac{\partial f(x_T; x_{T+1})}{\partial x_T{}^i}$$

Our basic assumption of causality, that $\left[\dfrac{\partial^2 f(x_t; x_{t+1})}{\partial x_t{}^i \, \partial x_{t+1}{}^j} \right]$

is nonsingular guarantees that the Jacobian of these implicit equations, taken with respect to $(X_T; X_{T+1})$ is non-zero, so that we can solve them explicitly for:

$$(21) \qquad x_T = F^1(x_0, x_1); x_{T+1} = F^2(x_0, x_1).$$

If our original problem had a periodic solution $X_t{}^i \equiv X_{t+N}{}^i$, then for $T = N$, equations (20) must have a fixed point, as e.g.:

$$(22) \qquad X_0 = F^1(X_0, X_1); X_1 = F^2(X_0, X_1)$$

Now it is easy to study the stability of this non-linear-difference-equation system and show that the associated linear system, whose coefficients are now constants and not periodic functions of time, have characteristic roots that appear in reciprocal pairs.

Sticking with (20) and defining divergence from equilibrium and matrices like those of (4), we define:

(23)
$$Y_t^1 = [x_0{}^i - X_0{}^i]$$

$$Y_t^2 = [x_1{}^i - X_1{}^i]$$

$$Y_{t+1}^1 = [x_N{}^i - X_N{}^i], \quad Y_{t+1}^2 = [x_{N+1}{}^i - X_{N+1}{}^i]$$

$$f^{11} = \left[\frac{\partial^2 f(X_0; X_1)}{\partial x_0{}^i \, \partial x_0{}^j} \right] = (f^{11})'$$

$$f^{22} = \left[\frac{\partial^2 f(X_0; X_1)}{\partial x_1{}^i \, \partial x_1{}^j} \right] = (f^{22})'$$

$$f^{12} = \left[\frac{\partial^2 f(X_0; X_1)}{\partial x_0{}^i \, \partial x_1{}^j} \right] = (f^{21})'$$

$$S^{11} = \left[\frac{\partial^2 S(X_1; X_0)}{\partial x_1{}^i \, \partial x_1{}^j} \right] = (S^{11})'$$

$$S^{22} = \left[\frac{\partial^2 S(X_1; X_0)}{\partial x_0{}^i \, \partial x_0{}^j} \right] = (S^{22})'$$

$$S^{12} = \left[\frac{\partial^2 S(X_1; X_0)}{\partial x_1{}^i \, \partial x_0{}^j} \right] = (S^{21})'$$

Then associated with the non-linear difference equation (20), we have after neglecting higher powers of $(x^i - X^i)$ in its Taylor's expansion around the periodic motion, the linear-homogeneous equations:

(24)
$$f^{21} Y_t^1 + (f^{22} + S^{11}) Y_t^2 + S^{12} Y_{t+1}^1 + 0 = 0$$

$$0 + S^{21} Y_t^2 + (S^{22} + f^{11}) Y_{t+1}^1 + f^{12} Y_{t+1}^2 = 0$$

Since the general solution of these second-order difference equations can be built up from terms containing $(\lambda_i)^t$, we find by substitution that the characteristic roots, λ_i, must satisfy the determinantal polynomial:

$$(25) \quad \Delta(\lambda) = \begin{vmatrix} f^{21} + \lambda S^{12} & f^{22} + S^{11} \\ (S^{22} + f^{11})\lambda & S^{21} + \lambda f^{12} \end{vmatrix} = 0$$

$$= \lambda^n D(\lambda) = \lambda^n \begin{vmatrix} f^{21} + \lambda S^{12} & f^{22} + S^{11} \\ S^{22} + f^{11} & \lambda^{-1} S^{21} + f^{12} \end{vmatrix}$$

$$= \lambda^n \begin{vmatrix} f^{12} + \lambda S^{21} & S^{22} + f^{11} \\ f^{22} + S^{11} & f^{21} + \lambda^{-1} S^{12} \end{vmatrix} \text{, by transposition}$$

$$= \lambda^n \begin{vmatrix} f^{21} + \lambda^{-1} S^{12} & f^{22} + S^{11} \\ S^{22} + f^{11} & f^{21} + \lambda S^{21} \end{vmatrix} \text{, by interchange of rows and of columns}$$

$$= \lambda^n D(\lambda^{-1}).$$

Since $D(\lambda)$ and $D(\lambda^{-1})$ vanish together, so do $\Delta(\lambda)$ and $\Delta(\lambda^{-1})$ and our theorem concerning pairs of reciprocal characteristic roots is proved.

Remark: This proof for periodic motions contains as a special case my earlier-proved theorem about stability of equilibrium. Setting $N = 1$ covers that simpler case.

9. As an example, consider the small vibrations of a pendulum. These undergo simple harmonic motion, obeying Hamilton's principle:

$$(26) \qquad \delta \int_0^T [(\tfrac{1}{2})\dot{x}^2 - (\tfrac{1}{2})x^2] \, dt = 0$$

$$\ddot{x} + x = 0$$

$$x = x_0 \cos t + x_0{}' \sin t$$

$$\tfrac{1}{2}\dot{x}^2 + \tfrac{1}{2}x^2 = \text{Kinetic energy} + \text{Potential energy} = \text{constant}$$

Suppose that our observations come only at equally-spaced time intervals $t = \pm 0, \pm 1, \ldots$. A Galileo might by empirical measurement observe the law of behavior:

$$(27) \qquad \Delta^2 x_t = x_{t+2} - 2x_{t+1} + x_t = -a^2 x_{t+1}$$

where a^2 is a constant dependent upon the time interval (and, of course, the length of the pendulum, which has not been shown in (26) by virtue of dimensionless units).

And we might observe that this prescribes the optimal trajectories to the minimum problem:

(28) $$\text{Min } S = (\tfrac{1}{2})(x_{t+1} - x_t)^2 - (\tfrac{1}{2})a^2 x_t^2$$

where

(29) $$\frac{\partial S}{\partial x_{t+1}} = 0 = x_{t+1} - x_t + x_{t+1} - x_{t+2} - a^2 x_{t+1}$$

$$= -(x_{t+2} - 2x_{t+1} + x_t) - a^2 x_{t+1}$$

which is identical with the observed law (27).

If in (28) we replace x_t^2 by $x_t^4/2$, the new (29) becomes nonlinear and an associated linear system has periodic coefficients, calling into play all the methods of this paper.

For $a^2 = 1$, the optimality equations become, respectively for the quadratic and fourth degree case

$$x_{t+2} = x_{t+1} - x_t \text{ and } x_{t+2} = 2x_{t+1} - x_{t+1}^3 - x_t$$

The first has an infinity of periodic solutions of the form $(0, b, b, 0, -b, -b, 0, b, \ldots)$. The linear equation associated with each of these has the same constant coefficients as the equation itself. The second has a periodic solution of the form $(0, 1, 1, 0, -1, -1, 0, 1, \ldots)$. Its associated linear equation has periodic coefficients

$$y_{t+2} = c(t)y_{t+1} - y_t$$

where $[c(i)] = [2, -1, -1, 2, 5, 5, 2, \ldots] = [c(i + 6)]$ and this will be subject to the present generalization of the Poincaré conditions.

159

CONSTRUCTING AN UNBIASED RANDOM SEQUENCE*

PAUL A. SAMUELSON

Massachusetts Institute of Technology

Independent tosses of a biased coin are known to be convertible, by a device due to von Neumann, into a sequence of unbiased independent tosses. If the independence presupposed by the von Newmann method is lacking, because of simple Markov dependence of each toss upon the outcome of the previous toss, it is here shown that independence can be achieved by the simple device of working with conditional probabilities, namely, concentrating only on tosses that follow a common outcome.

E VEN though one cannot be sure that a given coin will have exactly the same probability of coming up heads as tails after each toss, von Neumann[1] suggested a way of using the sequence of its independent tosses to produce a sequence that does represent equal probabilities. We simply consider successive pairs of outcomes, concentrating only upon those pairs which differ in outcome: then writing h for (H, T) and t for (T, H), we now have a sequence of hs and ts with respective probabilities $P(h) = P(t) = \frac{1}{2}$.

The von Neumann trick presupposes, of course, independence in the repeated tossings of the coin. This cannot always be guaranteed, since picking up a coin that shows heads may affect the initial conditions of the next toss so as to make the probabilities of (H, T) different from those of (T, H). Specifically, alter the above axiom to $P[X_i = H \mid X_{i-1} = H] = p_H \neq p_T = P[X_i = H \mid X_{i-1} = T]$; but suppose that the process is a simple Markov process with matrix

$$M = \begin{bmatrix} p_H & 1 - p_H \\ p_T & 1 - p_T \end{bmatrix}$$

This does still involve a definite limitation on nature, but does take into account the effect on initial conditions of the position of the coin after the last throw.

By what simple trick can we find a new sequence that is both unbiased and independent (i.e. itself subject to a 2-by-2 Markov matrix with identical rows and elements all equal)? Here the use of certain conditional probabilities is proposed to give one obvious solution to the problem.

Before stating the new rule, however, we might notice that the problem would be effectively solved to a high degree of approximation by the von Neumann method itself, if only we agree to pair up, not adjacent items, but those say 10 items apart. Thus, from our original series we select items 1, 11, 21, · · · etc., and apply the pairing techniques to this new series; but now, instead of having the matrix M, we have the matrix M^{10}. Because of the ergodic theorem applied to Markov matrices,[2] we know that high powers of M will have almost identical rows, even when there are significant differences in the original p_H

---

* Aid from the National Science Foundation is gratefully acknowledged.

[1] J. von Neumann, "Various Techniques Used in Connection with Random Digits," in *Monte Carlo Method, Applied Mathematics Series, No. 12* (U. S. National Bureau of Standards, Washington, 1951), pp. 36–8.

[2] W. Feller, *Probability Theory and its Applications* (John Wiley and Sons, Inc., New York, 1950), v. 1, chap. XV.

and p_T. Thus, to a high degree of approximation, effective independence can be secured by wasting some of the observations.

Avoiding approximation, we can secure perfect independence regardless of the size of $p_H - p_T$ by the following procedure:

Consider in the original sequence of heads and tails successive triples of observations, concentrating only on those which begin with a heads and whose final two items are of opposite type. Effectively we will have observations only of the form $[H, H, T]$ and $[H, T, H]$, which we may label respectively h and t. Then this new sequence has a Markov matrix, m, with identical rows; and the von Neumann procedure applied to it gives us the desired result of an unbiased independent sequence.

To prove this, merely note the first-order Markov property $\mathrm{Prob}[X_{i+1}, X_{i+2}| X_i$ and $X_{i-j}]$ is independent of X_{i-j} for all j.

Certain simple extensions of this technique are obvious in case the probabilities of a head now depend upon the last two, three, or finite-n outcomes. However, in still more general stationary time-series models, wasting observations and relying on the ergodic theorem may have to suffice.[3]

---

[3] Many alternatives to the present method are fairly easily found. Thus, John W. Pratt has mentioned to me that it would be enough to look only at pairs of the form HH and HT interpreting them as h and t and simply applying to them the v. Neumann procedure. As with the method I described, this breaks off any simple Markov dependence by employing the conditional probabilities following a common element (in this case H). Alternatives to the v. Neumann method, itself, also suggest themselves. Thus, Dean R. L. Bishop of MIT suggested to me that calling every other side that comes up by its genuine name, but reversing the designation for the sides that come up on the even tosses, will convert a biased sequence into an unbiased one, i.e., we replace $HHTHT \ldots$ by $htttt. \ldots$ But in order to get rid of the asymmetry from the initial conditions, one would want to consider only pairs of the form hh or tt, and this version of the Bishop method turns out to be identical with the v. Neumann concentration on pairs of the form HT and TH.

160

HOW DEVIANT CAN YOU BE?

Paul A. Samuelson

Massachusetts Institute of Technology

For a finite universe of N items, it is proved no one can lie more than $\sqrt{N-1}$ standard deviations away from the mean. This is an improvement over the result given by Tchebycheff's inequality: and a similar improvement is possible when speaking of how far from the mean any odd-number r out of N observations can lie. However, the relative inefficiency of Tchebycheff's inequality as applied to a finite universe does go to zero as N goes to infinity.

1. To assert that a man is a million standard deviations above the mean is to assert a falsehood (there being less than 4 billion men extant). Where does error leave off and truth begin?

Let the number of men be finite, $N < \infty$. Intuitively one realizes that the greatest relative deviant will occur when all men but one are bunched together. (Proof: putting 2 measurements at their common mean reduces the standard deviation while leaving the mean invariant; so continue doing so.) For $(X_1, X_2, \cdots, X_n) = (a, b, \cdots, b)$, it is a harmless convention to set $(a, b) = (1, 0)$ by proper choice of arbitrary scale and origin constants: hence,

$$m = E[X] = \frac{1}{N}, \qquad \sigma^2 = \overset{n}{\underset{1}{E}}\,[(X - m)^2] = \frac{N - 1}{N^2}.$$

The distance of X_1 from the mean in units of standard deviations is

$$\frac{X_1 - m}{\sigma} = \frac{\left(1 - \dfrac{1}{N}\right)N}{\sqrt{N - 1}} = \sqrt{N - 1}.$$

Theorem. If there are N items in the universe (say $36 \times 10^8 + 1$ men), no one can be more than $\sqrt{N-1}(= 60{,}000)$ standard deviations away from the mean in any measured attribute.

Rigorous proof of the theorem requires demonstration of the following inequality:

$$\phi(x_1, \cdots, x_n) =$$
$$\underset{(X_i)}{\mathrm{Max}}\Big\{\,|\,X_i - \textstyle\sum X_j/N\,| - (N - 1)^{\frac{1}{2}}\big(\sum [X_k - \sum X_j/N]^2/N\big)^{\frac{1}{2}}\Big\} \leq 0 \quad (1)$$

To maximize ϕ is a problem in (non-smooth) concave programming, which by a variety of artifices can be converted into a problem in the standard calculus with maximum solution $\phi(a, b, \cdots, b) = 0$.

The above constructive solution shows that the inequality cannot, in general, be improved upon. However, with special restrictions, sharper inequalities can be found. Thus, if the probability distribution is known to be symmetric, the greatest relevant deviant will be found where all but two of the observations are clustered half way between the remaining two. Thus, for $(-1, 0, \cdots, 0, +1)$, $m=0$, $\sigma^2 = 2/N$, and for symmetric distribution the above theorem can have $\sqrt{N-1}$ replaced by $\sqrt{N/2}$, a definite improvement whenever $N > 2$.

2. By use of Tchebycheff's inequality (T.I.), we can derive a result almost as good. That inequality states that, for all $t > 0$,

$$P\left\{ \left| \frac{X-m}{\sigma} \right| \geq t \right\} \leq \frac{1}{t^2} \tag{2}$$

Applied to a universe of N items, $1/t^2$ is equated to $1/N$ to give

$$P\left\{ \left| \frac{X-m}{\sigma} \right| \geq \sqrt{N} \right\} \leq \frac{1}{N} \tag{3}$$

This says literally that at most 1 observation can lie as much as $\sqrt{N}$ standard deviations from the mean. For $\sqrt{N-1} = 60,000$, $\sqrt{N} = 60,000.000017$, not much of a difference. However, for $N = 2$, T.I. merely says "not more than 1 observation can lie more than 1.4 ... standard deviations away from the mean," whereas the present inequality yields the sharpest statement possible, namely that no observation can lie more than 1 standard deviation away from the mean.

Knowledge that a probability distribution is symmetric adds nothing to the sharpness of Tchebycheff's inequality. To see this, from any cumulative distribution $P\{X \leq x\} = F[x-m]$ construct a symmetric distribution $\frac{1}{2}\{F[x-m] +1-F[(m-x)-0]\}$, with identical mean m, identical standard deviation σ *and* identical $P\{|X-m|/\sigma \geq t\} = p(t)$ function.

3. The literal interpretation of T. I.'s (3) can be improved on, if we consider a valid variant form for (2)'s Techebycheff's inequality, namely

$$P\left\{ \left| \frac{x-m}{\sigma} \right| > t \right\} < \frac{1}{t^2} \tag{4}$$

This differs from the ordinary* T.I. in the omission of *both* equalities from (2). Since any observation from a finite universe must have probability at least equal to $1/N$, we can now replace (3)'s literal rendering "At most 1 item can be $\sqrt{N}\sigma$'s from the mean" by (4)'s implication "No item can be more than $\sqrt{N}\sigma$'s from the mean". This follows from

$$P\left\{ \left| \frac{x-m}{\sigma} \right| > \sqrt{N} \right\} < \frac{1}{N} . \tag{5}$$

4. A generalization of the present problem involves answering the question: What is the minimum function $F_r(N)$ for which it is valid to say, "Of N observations, no r can be more than $F_r(N)\sigma$'s away from the mean?".

---

* I am grateful to a referee for pointing out that (4) is a well-known result, both for Tchebycheff's inequality and the more general Markoff inequality. A first casual sampling of introductory and intermediate texts failed to turn it up; but an elapse of time improved my luck and now I find it with about the same frequency that I encounter the spelling Chebychev. (Empirical rule: the newer and more advanced the book, the more likely that it is a translation from the Russian, then the more likely that the name is spelled with an initial "c".) Neither form of T.I. is stronger than the other; neither logically implies the other directly; both are true. The whole subject seems worth pursuing elsewhere, particularly to show that the alleged greater generality of the Markoff over the Tchebycheff inequality is not valid: i.e., from T. I. we can deduce M.I., and not just vice versa.

The solution is fairly intuitive. For r even, say $2R$, the Tchebycheff inequality cannot be improved upon since the probability distribution $Nf(1) = Nf(-1) = R$, $Nf(0) = N - 2R$ will achieve its equality. Hence $F_{2R}(N) = \sqrt{N/2R}$. For r odd, say $2R+1$, we can approximate the even-r case by concentrating r of our observations as equally as possible far away from the mean. This suggests—what can be proved by quadratic programming or other methods—that the most stringent case to consider is where

$Nf(-1) = R$, $Nf(1) = R + 1$, $Nf(0) = N - r$. This yields

$$m = \frac{1}{N}, \quad \sigma^2 = \frac{2R + 1}{N} - \left(\frac{1}{N}\right)^2 = \frac{r}{N} - \frac{1}{N^2}$$

$$F_r(N) = \frac{1 - m}{\sigma} = \frac{1 - \dfrac{1}{N}}{\sqrt{\dfrac{Nr - 1}{N^2}}} = \frac{N - 1}{\sqrt{Nr - 1}}$$

For $r/N = x$ and N large, the T.I. result is asymptotically relatively "efficient." The T.I. result is at its relative worst for N even and $r = N - 1$. We have already seen the case $r = 1$, $N = 2$. The next worst case is $r = 3$, $N = 4$. Here T.I. gives $\sqrt{4/3} = 1.16$, while $F_3(4) = 3/\sqrt{11} = .90$.

We may summarize as follows.

Theorem. Of N observations, no r can be more than $F_r(N)$ standard deviations away from the mean where

$$F_r(N) = \sqrt{\frac{N}{r}} \qquad \text{for } r \text{ an even number}$$

$$= \frac{N - 1}{\sqrt{Nr - 1}} \qquad \text{for } r \text{ an odd number}$$

and

$$\lim_{N \to \infty} F_{xN}(N) = \sqrt{\frac{1}{x}}, \quad 0 < x < 1.$$

6. It is natural to reverse the question and ask: By how many σ's from the mean must we encounter at least 1 observation? At least 2? . . . At least r? Some answers are trivial. By 1 σ you must meet at least one observation (and may meet them all). For $N = 2$, you must have met all observations by $\sigma = 1$. For any N, if you have met an observation before $\sigma = 1$, you cannot have met them all by $\sigma = 1$.

7. Instead of using mean and σ, one can use median and mean-absolute-deviation, or still other measures. Replacing our first theorem would then be the following:

Theorem. No one of N observations can be more than N mean-absolute-deviations away from the median.

Since the case $(1, 0, \cdots, 0)$ leads to one deviation exactly N m.a.d.'s from the median, this inequality cannot be improved upon. That it is true follows from the consideration that moving 2 discordant observations to the median lowers the m.a.d. while leaving the median unchanged: hence, $(1, 0, \cdots, 0)$ is indeed optimal.

Further generalization will occur to the reader.

8. *Summary.* Although Tchebycheff's inequality cannot, in general, be improved upon, for universes (or samples) known to consist of a finite number of items N, an improvement on Tchebycheff's inequality is possible when dealing with r of N items, r being odd, but with the relative amount of improvement $\rightarrow 0$ as $N \rightarrow \infty$.

BOOK THREE

Trade, Welfare, and Fiscal Policy

PART IX

Trade

161

SUMMARY ON FACTOR-PRICE EQUALIZATION*

BY PAUL A. SAMUELSON

1. THE TWO-GOOD TWO-FACTOR CASE

1. *Graphics.* Since 1949 the facts about neoclassical international factor prices have been beyond dispute in the 2-good 2-factor case. Figure 1, which shows the food-clothing production-possibility frontier for a fixed amount of land and varying amounts of labor, summarizes the situation as follows:

If food were always labor intensive and clothing always land intensive (as in Figure 1 *below EE'*), two economies that end up producing and trading both goods freely would end up with equalized factor prices. (For example, at any two countries on the lower *BD* branch, there will have to be equal factor prices.)

The theory is also a theory of non-equalized factor prices in situations where the goods change their relative factor intensities. Thus, along *EE'* the goods are shown to have identical intensities; above *EE'*, food has become labor intensive and clothing land intensive. Hence, above *EE'* and along the locus *FH* where countries are producing and trading both goods, factor prices are also being equalized. But comparing two countries which lie on the two different branches, one on *BD* and one on *FH*, we find factor prices necessarily unequal: the labor-abundant branch has lower real wages and higher land rents than does the labor-scarce branch.

Finally, between any two distinct branches of equalized returns, there is a watershed of specialization provided by a singular straight line like *EE'* (along which equilibrium can never be unique) and the connecting locus of specialization, *DEF*.[1]

2. *Analytical formulation.* Let us relate these 2-good 2-factor facts to the analytic equations

$$(1) \qquad P_j = \sum_{i=1}^{n} W_i a_{ij} = A^j(W_1, W_2, \cdots, W_n), \qquad (j = 1, 2, \cdots, n)$$

where a_{ij} are the non-negative coefficients of production

$$a_{ij} = \frac{V_{ij}}{X_j},$$

where X_j is the output of good j and V_{ij} is the i-th input used to produce X_j, and where the a_{ij} coefficients are connected by the neoclassical production functions.

$$X_j = 1 = X^j(a_{1j}, \cdots, a_{nj}), \qquad (j = 1, 2, \cdots, n)$$

---

* Manuscript received June 21, 1967, revised July 28, 1967.

[1] All this follows from the graph in [**9**, (188, note 1)]. The fact that the *BD* isocline locus rises to the northwest as shown is sometimes known as Rybczynski's Theorem.

the latter being concave, homogeneous-of-first degree, non-negative production functions monotone non-decreasing in their arguments. The A^j are minimized non-negative costs of production, definable for (and only for) non-negative factor prices (W_i).[2]

It is well-known [10] that $\partial A^j/\partial W_i = a_{ij}$ wherever A^j is differentiable; and even at the set of measure zero where derivatives are not defined $\sum_i W_i a_{ij}$ provides a supporting plane for the A^j function.

Now consider $n = 2$. Along EE', the locus of equal factor intensities, $\Delta(W_1, W_2) = |A| = \det[a_{ij}] = 0$. Elsewhere[3] in Figure 1, $|A| \neq 0$.

Hence, for $n = 2$, if $\Delta(W_1, W_2)$ never vanishes and two countries produce two goods in common at equalized commodity prices, equalized factor prices are assured.

3. *A general theorem.* Before turning to the $n > 2$ case to see whether the $\Delta(W_1, \cdots, W_n)$ non-vanishing is *sufficient* for factor price equalization, let me note that the determinant of factor inputs

$$\delta = \det[V_{ij}] = \det[a_{ij}X_j] = X_1 \cdots X_n \Delta(W_1, \cdots, W_n)$$

must vanish somewhere between two economies that fall on different branches with unequal factor prices.

Thus, consider two countries with different factor endowments, $(V_1^A, \cdots, V_n^A)$ and $(V_1^B, \cdots, V_n^B)$ and let us move continuously from (V_i^A) to (V_i^B) by some smooth continuous arc $[V_i(S)]$ holding (P_j) constant and observing changing equilibrium values for (W_i, X_j) as a function of S.

THEOREM. *If and only if*

$$\delta(S) = X_1(S) \cdots X_n(S)\Delta(W_1(S), \cdots, W_n(S))$$

vanishes for some $[V_i(S)]$ *on the interval between the two different economies, can they differ in factor prices.*

In Figure 1, from C to any point before D, $\delta(S) \neq 0$. At the first point of specialization D, one X_j vanishes; hence so must δ.

This theorem, which is visibly true for $n = 2$, is also valid for any n, as will be shown. It is essentially contained in McKenzie's classic 1955 paper [4].

4. *Miscellaneous remarks.* For $n = 2$, the global univalence of non-nega-

---

[2] If any W_i were negative, the monotone character of X^j will make $A^j = -\infty$ and be undefined.

[3] Along a straight line like AZ, where one of the factors is redundant and free, $W_1 W_2 \Delta(W_1, W_2) = 0$; hence, all straight lines correspond to the vanishing of this expression. If both goods have isoquants with corners (as in a linear programming model), the p-p frontier can be concave, lying above the line connecting its intercepts; but it may have straight-line segments along which it is not strictly concave. These correspond to cases where the isoquants are themselves locally straight lines (joining their corners) and where the a_{ij}'s are not single-valued functions of (W_1, W_2), instead assuming indifferently any values in an interval. If the usual strong factor intensity assumptions are made, $\det[a_{ij}]$ will not vanish for any admissible choice of a's.

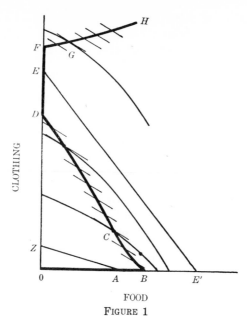

FOOD

FIGURE 1

PRODUCTION FRONTIERS AS LABOR GROWS

Adding labor to a fixed unit of land gives a family of production-possibility frontiers. If, as below EE', clothing is relatively labor intensive, the heavy BD locus of equal-slopes (or international goods prices) is negatively sloped as shown. At EE' factor intensities are the same, and international specialization is mandatory except at EE''s critical slope. Above EE' the goods have reversed their factor intensities, clothing now being land intensive. Any two economies that come into free trade equilibrium along BD necessarily have equalized factor prices; same holds for two countries on FH; but comparing economies that fall on *different* branches, we necessarily have *unequal* factor prices, with the labor-abundant upper branch having definitely lower real wages and higher land rents. But between two such branches there must in the two-good two-factor case be at EE' a vanishing $|a_{ij}|$ and specialization along DF.

tive solutions to (1) can follow from the Gale-Nikaidô theorem of [1], since along with non-vanishing $\varDelta$ we can always find positive elements a_{ij} that can be numbered so as to be principal minors. Simpler still, the fact that

$$\frac{d(P_2/P_1)}{d(W_2/W_1)} = \varDelta \times (\text{a positive variable})$$

rules out multiplicity of solutions when $\varDelta \neq 0$.

Diagonal dominance, which McKenzie rightly defends against the Pearce view of being a property of each equation by itself, cannot necessarily be evoked in the general $n = 2$ case. Nor can the 1966 corrected version [11] of my 1953 false theorem—that

$$\det\left[\frac{\partial \log P_j}{\partial \log W_i}\right] = \det\left[\frac{W_i a_{ij}}{P_j}\right] = \frac{W_1 W_2}{P_1 P_2} \varDelta(W_1, W_2) > m_2 > 0$$

$$\frac{\partial \log P_1}{\partial \log W_1} = \frac{W_1 a_{11}}{P_1} > m_1 > 0$$

always be applied to prove that in the whole Euclidean space, E^2, of $(\log W_1,$ $\log W_2)$ (1) can have but a single solution. Later, for $n > 2$ examples will be shown that these corrected conditions can be useful in some cases where Gale-Nikaidô and diagonal-dominance conditions are not applicable.

2. THE MULTI-FACTOR MULTI-GOOD CASE

5. *Non-singular intensity matrix and strict concavity.* Now suppose $n > 2$, say $n = 3$. The production-possibility frontier of Figure 1 now becomes a surface in three dimensions, somewhat like a segment of a sphere or the face of an umbrella. Normalizing on one factor, say labor, and then adding all possible amounts of the other 2 factors—say sandy land and clay land—we can no longer expect a single family of non-intersecting surfaces.

But freezing factor supplies at one prescribed vector, (V_i), we can verify that the p-p frontier will be strongly concave at any point where

$$|A| = \det [a_{ij}] = \begin{vmatrix} a_{11} & a_{12} & a_{13} \\ a_{21} & a_{22} & a_{23} \\ a_{31} & a_{32} & a_{33} \end{vmatrix} = \Delta(W_1, \cdots, W_n) ,$$

is well-defined and non-zero. Why? If this matrix were singular, we could find a way of contracting in balance *all* inputs of one good and allocating them in exact proportions among the remaining two goods so that each of them could expand in balance; with the result, that the p-p surface would have a straight line on it and *not* have the strict concavity that guarantees unique production determination at the prescribed international prices. All this follows from the fact that for $\Delta = 0$, and suitable renumbering of goods, there exist non-negative non-trivial constants such that

$$\begin{bmatrix} a_{11} \\ a_{21} \\ a_{31} \end{bmatrix} 1 = \begin{bmatrix} a_{12} \\ a_{22} \\ a_{32} \end{bmatrix} C_2 + \begin{bmatrix} a_{13} \\ a_{23} \\ a_{33} \end{bmatrix} C_3 .$$

It is these C's which provide the weights needed for the simultaneous balanced-scale expansions and contractions of industries (and without such balanced movements strict concavity is seen to be intuitively mandatory).

As a simple example, suppose all three goods have the same production functions. Or, suppose that two goods have the same. Or suppose that, at an observed (W_1, W_2, W_3) situation, one industry uses all factors in amounts exactly half way between those used by the other two industries.

6. *Multiple solutions with non-singular intensities.* Now we see the economic intuitive meaning of the $|A| \neq 0$ condition. Given that $n > 2$ and $\Delta(W_1, \cdots, W_n)$ never vanishes for non-negative W's, can we infer that (1) has a unique universe? My 1949 paper does not quite say that; but, dissatisfied with my own wording, I explicitly asked Meade [3] to add to his 1950 paper a disclaiming footnote on the matter. And in 1951 Pearce [6] gave a similar denial of the sufficiency of $\Delta \neq 0$ for univalence. Imagine then my surprise,

and that of all of the experts known to me, when Pearce [7] in 1959 enunciated the conjecture that $\varDelta \neq 0$ is after all a sufficient condition in the $n > 2$ case.

Pearce is correct that the discussion of his paper is like an iceberg, nine-tenths submerged in personal correspondence. The logic of the 1959 Appendix was not apparent to the experts; and widespread knowledge of the existence of McKenzie's counterexample, in which $\varDelta(W_1, \cdots, W_n) \neq 0$ in the positive orthant coexisted with multiple factor prices, settled the issue in the minds of most of us.

The topological propositions brought forward in Pearce's present paper [8], like McKenzie's theorem [5] of Favard, will be welcomed by all economists. Like Pirandello's play, "Six Characters in Search of an Author," these mathematical tools will find a use in modern economics. But in no sense meaningful for the traditional factor-price equalization model do they, in my opinion, vindicate the 1959 Appendix or sidestep the McKenzie counter-example. For, to extend the definition of the A^j functions beyond the non-negative orthant of the factor prices is impossible for the traditional case of monotone non-decreasing neoclassical production functions. If Professor Kaldor were to persuade Her Majesty's government to give a subsidy large enough to make a factor have a negative price, one would hire an indefinitely large amount of that factor and eventually bankrupt that government. If, as is the case in most such subsidies, there is a limit put upon the amount of the factor that can be eligible for the subsidy, we are out of the field of competitive price taking and into the area of rationing. No international trade theorist known to me has hitherto considered the problem of factor price equalization to be interesting in such a context.

7. *Factor endowment determining equilibrium.* Returning to the neoclassical case, suppose that for (V_1^A, V_2^A, V_3^A) and (V_1^B, V_2^B, V_3^B) we find two economies coming into equilibrium at the same internationally-set commodity prices and producing positive amounts of all three goods. And suppose that there is a well-defined observed $|A| \neq 0$. Then the observed quantities produced, (X_j^A), are uniquely determined by tangency of the strictly concave p-p frontier and the planes of equal value, $\sum P_j X_j$. And the observed factor prices, (W_i^A), are also uniquely determined. This theorem on global univalence follows from the maximum character of the problem and the strict concavity implied by $|A| \neq 0$. Curiously, it is easier to speak of univalance of the $2n$-by-$2n$ system

$$(1) \qquad P_j = \sum_{i=1}^{n} W_i a_{ij} = A^j(W_1, W_2, \cdots, W_n) \qquad (j = 1, 2, \cdots, n)$$

$$(2) \qquad V_i = \sum_{j=1}^{n} a_{ij}(W_1, \cdots, W_n) X_j, \qquad (i = 1, \cdots, n)$$

than of (1) alone! McKenzie's example shows that (1) may not have a unique solution by itself, even though in the presence of (2) the solution for $(W_1, \cdots, W_n)$ is unique.

Mathematically, the Gale-Nikaidô conditions need not be satisfied by the

Jacobian matrix of (1)—(2)

$$J = \begin{bmatrix} a_{ji} & 0 \\ b_{ik} & a_{ij} \end{bmatrix} ,$$

where

$$b_{ik} = \sum_{j=1}^{n} \frac{\partial a_{ij}}{\partial W_k} X_j$$

$$\sum_{i=1}^{n} W_i b_{ik} = \sum_{i=1}^{n} \sum_{j=1}^{n} W_i \frac{\partial a_{ij}}{\partial W_k} X_j = \sum_{j=1}^{n} [0] X_j = 0 , \qquad \text{(by homogeneity).}$$

8. *Conversion to a maximum problem.* But sufficiency comes from the strong concavity assumption applied to the maximum problem

$$\max_{\{V_{ij}\}} \quad \sum_{j=1}^{n} P_j X^j(V_{1j}, \cdots, V_{nj})$$

subject to

$$\sum_{j=1}^{n} V_{ij} = V_i , \qquad\qquad (i = 1, \cdots, n) .$$

Using the Lagrangian expression

$$L(V_{ij}; W_i) \equiv \sum_{j=1}^{n} P_j X^j(V_{1j}, \cdots, V_{nj}) + \sum_{i=1}^{n} W_i(V_i - \sum_{j=1}^{n} V_{ij})$$

the maximum is assured by the solution to

(3)
$$\frac{\partial L}{\partial V_{ij}} = P_j \frac{\partial X^j}{\partial V_{ij}} - W_i = 0 , \qquad (i, j = 1, \cdots, n)$$

$$\frac{\partial L}{\partial W_i} = V_i - \sum_{j=1}^{n} V_{ij} = 0 \qquad (i = 1, \cdots, n) .$$

The Jacobian of this system is the symmetric Hessian matrix of the second partial derivatives of L. It does not satisfy the Gale-Nikaidô conditions on *all* principal minors, as can be seen from the constrained nature of the maximum. But the fact that its principal minors formed from crossing out any $r < n^2$ of the first n^2 rows and columns are of the sign needed for the maximum suffices, I believe, to assure univalence of the equation set (3).

9. *Uniqueness of factor prices for fixed endowments.* Paradoxically, the combined equations (1)—(2) have generally a unique solution for $[W_i]$ even when $\Delta = 0$ (or Δ changes sign) and the $[X_j]$ are not uniquely determinable. This follows from the fact that the determinateness of (W_i) in (3) is independent of the non-vanishing of Δ and the determinateness of $[V_{ij}]$ and $[X_j]$. To demonstrate this, we need not even assume that the number of factors, m, equals the number of goods, n. Indeed in the general case, we set up the concave programming problem

(4)
$$\max_{\{V_{ij}\}} \quad \sum_{j=1}^{n} P_j X^j(V_{1j}, \cdots, V_{mj})$$

subject to

$$V_i - \sum_{j=1}^{n} V_{ij} \geqq 0 \qquad\qquad (i = 1, \cdots, m)$$

$$V_{ij} \geqq 0, \quad P_j \geq 0, \quad V_i > 0, \qquad\qquad n \gtreqless m.$$

Provided X^j is single-valued and continuous, this maximum is assuredly attained on the simplex defined by feasible $[V_{ij}]$. Call the maximum $N(P_1, \cdots, P_n; V_1, \cdots, V_m)$. Under the regularity condition that X^j is strictly quasi-concave with $\partial X^j/\partial V_{ij} > 0$ for all $V_{ij} > 0$ and $\partial X^j/\partial V_{ij} = \infty$ for $V_{ij} = 0$, $W_i = \partial N/\partial V_i$ is well-defined and, for some j, $= P_j \partial X^j/\partial V_{ij}$.

Of course, if we drop smoothness assumptions, as for example when we write

$$X_j = \min \left[\frac{V_{1j}}{a_{1j}}, \cdots, \frac{V_{mj}}{a_{mj}} \right], \quad a_{ij} \text{ positive constants,}$$

we can find exceptions to the conclusion of the above theorem on determinate factor prices. Thus, set $n = 1$, $m = 2$ and $V_1/V_2 = a_{11}/a_{21}$. Then $N(P_1; V_1, V_2) = P_1 N(1; V_1, V_2)$ has a "corner" for such a critical ratio of factors, and the W_1/W_2 ratio can be anything from 0 to ∞.

Postulating strict quasi-concavity for *both* the $X^j(V_{1j}, \cdots, V_{mj})$ production functions and their dual unit-cost functions $A^j(W_1, \cdots, W_m)$ will ensure the postulated smoothness. Where, as in activity analysis, such smoothness is not supposed, it will suffice to assure determinate (W_i) and $(\partial N/\partial V_i)$ partial derivatives that the rectangular matrix of observed optimal V_{ij}, $[V_{ij}^*]$, should have rank m. This implies that the number of goods actually positively producible should be at least as great as the number of factors. Where this sufficiency condition is realized, there will necessarily exist an $m \times m$ non-singular $[a_{ij}] = [V_{ij}^*/X_j^*]$ matrix.

To show that postulating smoothness of all the production functions emancipates the theorem on determinateness of $[W_i]$, once $[P_j, V_i]$ is given, from any $n \geq m$ condition, set $n = 1$, $m > 1$ and note that

$$\frac{\partial N}{\partial V_i} = \frac{\partial X^1(V_1, \cdots, V_m)}{\partial V_i} = W_i$$

are by hypothesis determinate. Or, along EE' in Figure 1,

$$\frac{\partial N}{\partial V_i} = \frac{\partial X^1(V_{11}, V_{21})}{\partial V_{i1}} = \frac{\partial X^2(V_{12}, V_{22})}{\partial V_{i2}} = W_i, \qquad (i = 1, 2).$$

10. *The general case.* The fully general maximum problem of (4) leads to the equalities of (1)−(2) or of (2) only in "regular" cases. More generally, these become the Kuhn-Tucker[4] inequalities for $(i = 1, 2, \cdots, m; j = 1, 2 \cdots, n \gtreqless m)$

----

[4] In [2] Kuhn gives a set of conditions on A^j sufficient for univalence which resemble the Weak Axiom of revealed preference. He also gives an intensity condition sufficient to prove existence of equilibrium factor prices in (3′) or (1′)−(2′). However, I do not see that I had need for such a condition in 1953 since economic intuition assured the existence of the maximizing solution to (4) and its equivalence with competitive equilibrium.

$$(1') \qquad \Pi_j = A^j(W_1, \cdots, W_m) - P_j \geqq 0 = \Pi_j X_j = \Phi_j(W_1, \cdots, W_m, X_1, \cdots, X_n) \,,$$

$$(2') \qquad \varepsilon_i = V_i - \sum_{j=1}^{n} a_{ij}(W_1, \cdots, W_m) X_j \geqq 0 = \varepsilon_i W_i$$

$$= \Phi_{n+1}(W_1, \cdots, W_m, X_1, \cdots, X_n) \,,$$

$$(3') \qquad \Pi_{ij} = W_i - P_j \frac{\partial X_j}{\partial V_{ij}} \geqq 0 = \Pi_i V_{ij} = \Psi_{ij}(V_{11}, \cdots, V_{mn})$$

$$\varepsilon_i = V_i - \sum_{j=1}^{u} V_{ij} \geqq 0 = \varepsilon_i W_i = \Psi_i(V_{11}, \cdots, V_{mn}) \,.$$

Whether useful univalence conditions like those of Gale-Nikaidô can be found on the Jacobians of the $[\Phi_k]$ or $[\Psi_{ij}, \Psi_i]$ functions is an open question.

11. *Graphical summary for $n = 3$.* For each fixed set of factor endowments, like (V_1^A, V_2^A, V_3^A), we can in the non-singular case, $\varDelta \neq 0$, picture a strictly-concave p-p frontier surface. For every other endowment, say (V_1^B, V_2^B, V_3^B) there is another strictly-concave frontier if $\varDelta$ alway remains of one sign. Thus if we hold one factor constant, say $V_1^A = V_1^B$, and increase both of the other factors, we will have $V_2^B > V_2^A$ and $V_3^B > V_3^A$, and the new frontier will lie outside of the old one.

Now imagine that we move continuously from (V_i^A) to (V_i^B) along the smooth arc $[V_i(S)]$ with $[V_i(0)] = [V_i^A]$ and $[V_i(1)] = [V_i^B]$. Then we pass continuously through a family of intermediate frontiers that can be made to be successively further out if $V_2(S)$ and $V_3(S)$ are properly monotone in S.

If everywhere $\varDelta(W_1, \cdots, W_n)$ is non-vanishing, say $\varDelta > 0$, all these frontiers will be strictly concave. For unchanging positive prices (P_j) at which all goods are produced in (V_i^A), there will go through the observed point (X_1^A, X_2^A, X_3^A) an iso-cline locus just like CB in Figure 1. Similarly if (X_i^B) are all positive, there will go through it such a locus; and as the parameter S goes from 0 to 1, taking us from (V_i^A) to (V_i^B), we begin on the locus through (V_i^A) and end on the locus through (V_i^B).

Now there are two possibilities. First, the locus between the points may never have left the positive orthant (X_1, X_2, X_3). This will necessarily be the case if (V_i^B) is sufficiently near to (V_i^A). In this first case, we can be sure that the two countries are on the same branch—just like two countries falling on the BCD branch of Figure 1; and then we must have complete factor-price equalization.

The other possibility is that specialization intervenes between (V_i^A) and (V_i^B). This is shown by the fixed-price locus's hitting, at an intermedia S, one of the boundaries of the positive orthant with one or more (X_j) becoming zero. When this happens the factor matrix

$$\delta(S) = X_1 X_2 X_3 \varDelta = |X_{ij}(S)|$$

necessarily vanishes (and the a_{ij} matrix becomes undefined since the a's are not defined at the *origin point* of a production function, even though the $A^j(W_1, \cdots, W_n)$ is itself capable of being defined—irrelevantly defined in view of the non-production of the good in question). The proof of this assertion about vanishing of $\delta(S)$ follows from embedding (1) into the (1)—(2) system and noting that the latter's univalence implies staying on the same local branch of (1).

What the McKenzie counter-example shows is this: in the three-dimensional case there need not necessarily be a singular frontier in between two points that are separated by a region of specialization. And, on reflection, there is nothing surprising about this despite Pearce's 1959 remarks.

12. *Final footnote.* There remains the task of showing the independence of my corrected-version sufficiency condition from that of Gale-Nikaidô or of diagonal dominance.

Consider a case where all production functions are Cobb-Douglas, so that

$$\log P_j = \sum_{i=1}^{n} \log W_i E_{ij} , \qquad \text{where } E_{ij} = \frac{\partial \log A^j}{\partial \log W_i} , \qquad (j = 1, 2, \cdots, n) ,$$

are a set of strictly linear equations for [log W_i]. In this special case, Pearce is right that $\varDelta \neq 0$ suffices for factor price equalization. And he would be right to point out that $\varDelta \neq 0$ is a much weaker condition than those of Gale-Nikaidô or *a fortiori* McKenzie which specify something about numerous principal minors.

But let us now perturb our Cobb-Douglas case so that one or more of the production functions is a sum of two different Cobb-Douglas functions, as for example

$$X_j = b_j V_{1j}^{\alpha_1} V_{2j}^{\alpha_2} V_{3j}^{\alpha_3} + b'_j V_{1j}^{\alpha'_1} V_{2j}^{\alpha'_2} V_{3j}^{\alpha'_3} .$$

Now consider the case where either $\sum_i |\alpha_i - \alpha'_i|$ is sufficiently small or else b'_j is sufficiently small. If previously the $[a_{ij}]$ matrix was non-singular, with $[E_{ij}] = [\partial \log A^j/\partial \log W_i]$ non-singular, this will continue to be the case inasmuch as the new $[E_{ij}]$ matrix, which is no longer a constant, is a weighted average between two non-singular constant matrices that are nearly the same.

In producing this example, I would never consider it worth saying that my sufficient conditions are weaker than some others. In some respects they are not. But even if they were, we must be grateful to have "overly-strong" sufficiency conditions that are applicable when "weaker" ones are irrelevant.

It is rarely the case in any mathematics problem that we can successfully find the *weakest* sufficiency conditions which are of any interest, and Pearce's 1959 conjecture appears to me to have set back the cause of understanding.[5]

Massachusetts Institute of Technology, U.S.A.

---

[5] To keep an overlong discussion from lengthening further, I confine my reactions to Professor Pearce's "Rejoinder to Professor Samuelson's Summary" to this terminal footnote. (i) Pearce's post-1959 concrete results seem to come to this: a counter-example like McKenzie's cannot be extended to certain wider domains of Pearce's discussion without somewhere having its crucial determinant vanish. How constructive is this result? Could one, in a particular case, where the Jacobian does not vanish in the positive orthant, actually determine whether it is or is not a counter-example of McKenzie type? And easily do so? (ii) My "corrected version" of the 1953 condition

(*Continued on next page*)

REFERENCES

[1] GALE, D., and H. Nikaidô, "The Jacobian Matrix and Global Univalence of Mappings," *Mathematische Annalen*, Bd. 159, Heft 2 (1965), 81–93.

[2] KUHN, HAROLD W., "Factor Endowments and Factor Prices: Mathematical Appendix [to an A. H. Land article]," *Economica*, XXVI (May, 1959), 142–44.

[3] MEADE, J. E., "The Equalisation of Factor Prices: The Two-Country Two-Factor Three Product Case," *Metroeconomica*, II (December, 1950), 129–33. This footnote is referred to in my 1951 comment on Pearce, [11, (chapter 69, 887)].

[4] McKENZIE, L. W., "Equality of Factor Prices in World Trade," *Econometrica*, XXIII (July, 1955), 239–57.

[5] ———, "Theorem and Counter-example," *International Economic Review*, this issue.

[6] PEARCE, I. F., and S. F. JAMES, "The Factor Prices Equalisation Myth," *Review of Economic Studies*, XIX(2) (1951–52), 111–20.

[7] ———, "A Further Note on Factor-Commodity Price Relationships," *Economic Journal*, LXIX (December, 1959), 725–32.

[8] ———, "More About Factor Price Equalization," *International Economic Review*, this issue.

[9] SAMUELSON, P. A., "International Factor-Price Equalisation Once Again," *Economic Journal*, LIX (June, 1949), 181–97. This is reproduced in [11] as chapter 68; chapter 67 reproduces my 1948 *Economic Journal* paper.

[10] ———, "Prices of Factors and Goods in General Equilibrium," *Review of Economic Studies*, XXI(1) (1953–54), 1–20, particularly page 5. This is chapter 70 in [11].

[11] ———, *Collected Scientific Papers*, Vol. 2 (Cambridge, Mass.: MIT Press, 1966), 908.

is not of much interest economically. Still it is useful for Pearce to now show that boundedness away from zero need only be specified for the Jacobian $|\partial \log A^j / \partial \log W_i|$, and I applaud results from the new topological methods. But I must warn that it is necessary to keep purely mathematical and specific economic conditions distinct. For *general mathematical* equations, we must definitely correct the 1953 results by specifying bounds on certain minors as well as on the Jacobian itself, even if in the case of economic matrices with special non-negative properties there may happen to be weaker sufficiency conditions that will serve. None of this is meant to imply disagreement with any deductive statement by Pearce.

162

AN EXACT HUME–RICARDO–MARSHALL MODEL
OF INTERNATIONAL TRADE *

Paul A. SAMUELSON

Massachusetts Institute of Technology, Cambridge, Mass.

1. Introduction

The textbooks and learned journals rebound with expositions that involve bits and pieces of Ricardian comparative advantage, Cournot–Marshall partial-equilibrium schedules of supply and demand, incomplete and self-contradictory explanations of the Hume gold-flow mechanism for exchange rate equilibrium. These are generally not integrated with the general equilibrium models of trade associated with work on reciprocal demands and factor-price determination by Mill, Marshall, and Edgeworth; or, in our day, by Ohlin, Viner, Haberler, Lerner, Leontief, Meade, Stolper–Samuelson, McKenzie, and many others. Recently, in connection with the transfer problem, I bridged this gap between partial and general equilibrium. [1]

The present paper will provide needed mathematical foundations for the rigorous partial-equilibrium handling of general equilibrium and will also adjoin to it a much needed explication of the Hume financial mechanism.

Fortunately, neo-classical models of international trade are better than their usual expositions. Thus, when we read about the Hume gold-flow equalisation process, we are likely to read: 'The deficit country loses gold and the surplus country gains it. By the Quantity Theory, this lifts the "general price level" of the receiver and lowers the "price level" of the loser: with the deficit country's prices now relatively lower and the surplus country's prices now higher, the imports of the gainer swell and the imports of the loser fall, thus eventually wiping out the initial deficit and leading to a new equilibrium without gold drain'.

* I owe thanks to the National Science Foundation.
[1] In the forthcoming Kindleberger *Festschrift*.

In the quoted passage, a pedantical student might be forgiven for thinking that we are denying that the same good must (transport costs aside) always sell for a common competitive price everywhere in the world (when prices are expressed in comparable foreign-exchange units). And even such a profound scholar as Jacob Viner, after correcting the impression that the Hume adjustment process must rely on price differentials for the same good in different markets, wrongly asserts that it must rely on 'relative variations in the prices of different commodities in the same market, and primarily [on] ... variations in prices as between export and import commodities'. Since stable equilibrium may result from induced changes in factor prices that change all prices in any market the same way, the re-formulation is not correct. [2] In any case, it is a scandal that by this date none of the texts or treatises seem to have set out a mathematically complete explication of the process.

2. Graphical depiction

Fig. 1 presents for a 2-country case, America and England, the partial equilibrium version of international equilibrium. It combines the essence of the Cournot back-to-back diagrams with the Bickerdike version of exchange rate equilibrium, and also provides a classical monetary determination of absolute price levels. [3]

The graph can be simply explained. The vertical scales are logarithmic and are aligned so that American prices on the left and British prices on the right are in competitive arbitrage equilibrium along the

---

[2] J.Viner, 1937, p. 319 contains the quoted words. Related quotations can be found on pp. 292, 293, 305, 318, and elsewhere. That Viner senses the correct doctrine, which involves changes in factor prices, induced by money flows, and having in turn differential effects on costs in the different countries and therefore in their effective sharing of the markets, is shown by the following: 'It is the relative changes in the *supply* prices [i.e., in the supply schedules] of identical commodities or between different potential sources of supply ... [which] exercises a significant role in the mechanism of adjustment of international balances'. But he nowhere spells out a complete model, and his p. 332 criticism of Yntema for assuming that a balanced money change has effects as much on supply functions as demand functions raises doubt as to whether he had ever worked out a consistent Hume model. He was in good company, as one can verify by reading the treatises of Ohlin and Haberler or the standard critiques of the purchasing-power-parity doctrine with their failure to identify clearly its essential grain of truth.

[3] My cited *Festschrift* paper gives references and elucidation of the model, which combines elements from Hume (1749), Cournot (1838), Bickerdike (1920), and which has been much discussed by Joan Robinson, Haberler, Yntema, and a host of modern writers.

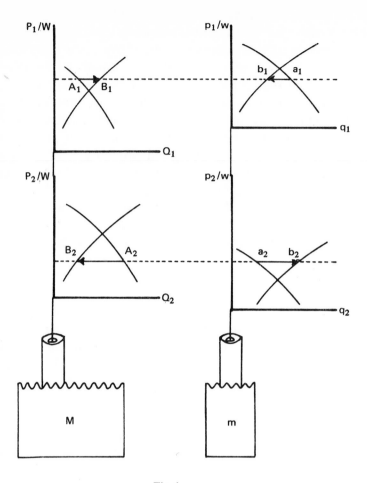

Fig. 1.

same horizontal lines (with the ratio of American to British prices exactly equalling the exchange rate). America is shown exporting in equilibrium the first good and importing the second good from Europe, as shown by the matching but opposing export arrows A_iB_i and a_ib_i. Because the scales are logarithmic, no simple rectangular areas under A_iB_i and a_ib_i can show the equivalence in equilibrium of value of exports to value of imports, but that is definitely assumed to be realized in the graph. Finally, it will be noted that the axes do not measure price alone but rather price divided by the wage rate. This is for two reasons: first, as will be shown, the curves have an invariance only with respect to such normalized, 'real' prices; second, an increase in the money wage in any country can be shown as a parallel upward shift of all the curves of that country, just as if the vertical axis were made of wire with all the curves soldered to it. Such a differential change in one country's wage relative to the others will thus, the exchange rate being unchanged, definitely shift the schedules compared to each other and lead to a new equilibrium in each market (and of course will upset the posited balance of payments equilibrium). Finally, a shift in the exchange rate, with money wage rates unchanged in each country, will likewise shift one country's curves in a parallel fashion relative to the other country's curves. Thus a depreciation of the dollar relative to the pound would lower *all* the American curves by the same number of inches in comparison with unchanged British curves.

At the bottom of the graph the stock of money of a country is shown as a volume of water upon which the vertical axis and related curves float. This is merely a rendition of Hume's Quantity Theory of Money, which postulates that a doubling of the gold or money supply will ultimately double the wage rate and all prices: with twice the water, the floating axis and curves are shifted upward (reflecting now doubled wage rate in the P/W variables).

We can now simply describe the comparative statics of gold or money changes. Suppose world gold doubles. In equilibrium it will be divided between countries in the same proportions as before. Both tanks of water ultimately have their level raised by the same doubled amount. All curves get shifted upward by the same amount. *The real equilibrium is thus completely unchanged:* all export arrows and amounts are as before, and so are all amounts consumed and produced; all price ratios, P_i/W and p_i/w are as before since both numerators and denominators have doubled with the world doubling of every price and wage; terms of trade, as measured by $P_2/P_1 = p_2/p_1$, are also unchanged. (The fact that total world gold gets redivided among the countries in the same determinate proportions as before constitutes the only meaning to Hume's metaphor that money and water find the same equality of level in all countries. What the determinative proportions of gold between countries are will depend, as Hume knew, on the reserve ratios followed by different countries, their relative sizes, spending habits, and all the other factors that moderns throw into the catch-all of V and Q in the $MV = PQ$ equation of exchange.)

One must realize that the graph depicts only long-run equilibria, not transitional states. Thus, suppose the doubling of world gold first enters Britain from the Indies. Hume would expect this to raise cost levels in Britain, as shown by the upward floating of all her schedules when the water level rises on the right. This will transiently disturb balance of trade equilibrium, Britain's deficit being covered by loss of gold to (North) America. The process comes to an end only when enough water has moved from right to left to lead to proportional wage and price rises all over the world. Either at no instant of time, or for no more than the instants needed for corrective good flows to be initiated, will there be a deviation from equality of prices for the same goods in the different markets. And, as readers of Joan Robinson and Haberler now realize, there is no necessity for the terms of trade to change even during the transition phase between stable equilibria, since it is easy to specify elasticities of the curves which dictate that P_1/P_2 and p_1/p_2 ratios stay the same throughout the relative shifting of the vertical scales and curves!

We may now drop the assumption of a universal gold standard with unchanged exchange rate. Instead imagine that each government sets its own money supply by fiat. Thus, let Britain double her money supply. Such an act would have the same consequences already portrayed for the case where Britain got gold from the Indies provided pounds were readily acceptable in America. But under inconvertibility, where the American authorities set the American money supply in terms of dollars, the initial rise in British money wages and upward shift of her cost and schedules will, in a stable system, cause her to run trade deficits. If these cannot be financed by exporting of pounds (or IOUs), the exchange rate must fall. How far must the pound depreciate when the only permanent change has been a doubling of the English money supply? Obviously the pound must depreciate to exactly half its previous value. For the only way that a doubling of British wages will be compatible with unchanged American wages and with trade equilibrium will be for the upward shift of the right-hand vertical axis and curves to be offset completely by having the vertical axis sink down into the float-cylinder by an equivalent amount: that is the meaning of an exchange rate change in the diagram, and the only way to restore the real equilibrium with all the arrows intact is for the exchange rate to halve when the British fiat money doubles.

This portrays the unshakable nucleus of truth in the purchasing-power-parity doctrine. I have called this obvious. But however obvious it may have been to Hume, Ricardo, Cassel, and Yntema, the doctrine has been bitterly criticized by most writers. And they were right to criticize many of the feeble arguments given for it by Cassel, who rendered his mathematical models poorly into prose. Moreover, this geographical version of the neutral-money model was early confused by Keynes with a trivial doctrine of equality of price for identical goods in zero-transport-cost markets, with which it has no intrinsic connection. [4]

[4] To see this, imagine that substantial transport costs rupture all approximate price equality relations for the same goods in different markets. Thus, let half of all goods melt in the export process. Then we must replace the horizontal lines connection A_iB_i and a_ib_i with the following kinked lines, $\underline{\Gamma}$ for American exports and $\underline{\mathsf{L}}$ for British exports, the size of the bend representing logarithmically the halving of delivered goods and its effect on arbitraged prices; likewise each country's import arrows will no longer match the length of the other country's export arrows, but instead have to be only half as long. Now let us double money in one country: it is as easy to demonstrate in this case as in the no-trade-impediment case that the result must still be a halving of the exchange rate of the depreciating country. Of course, the same argument applies also to tariff impediments. If it is said that changes in tariffs will destroy the p–p–p argument, the answer is: 'It certainly will. The only thing about purchasing power parity that is valid is its application to situations that closely approximate *pure* money changes with no concomitant real changes. Except in connection with certain dramatic inflations, the *application* of the doctrine is properly subject to criticism'. This is to say that in all but the most singular applications neither the absolute nor comparative version of the p–p–p doctrine can be expected to be valid. Except in the trivial sense of being applicable to freely-transportable competitive goods, the absolute version is never valid (and even where it is valid it is *trivially* valid as a theory of exchange rate equilibrium). In the singular case of balanced monetary changes, the comparative version is valid since *every* price and wage ultimately shows relative movements over time equal to the relative movements in the exchange rate: this means our index number comparisons can involve (i) any single good, (ii) any fixed batch of goods (domestic or international, export or import), (iii) any input rather than output prices, and indeed the p–p–p identity will be realized if you compare (iv) an index number of British beer with an index number of American sawdust – for when all things move together one can select incommensurate items by lot and get the same result! For similar points, see P.A.Samuelson, 1964. (In reviewing typical mishandling of purchasing power parity, I have come across a new interpretation in L.B.Yaeger's valuable *International Monetary Relations* (Harper & Row, New York, 1966) p. 170 ff., where it is gratuitously argued that the essence of the doctrine is denial of the realism of elasticity pessimisms, a notion that would have surprised Cassel, Keynes, Ricardo, and Hume, to say nothing of the dozens of modern writers I have recently reviewed.

3. Mathematical summary

We can summarize the present model by the following behavior equations:

$$P_i = Rp_i \quad (i = 1, 2, ..., n) \quad \text{[competitive arbitrage]}$$

$$[D_i(P_i/W) - S_i(P_i/W)] + [d_i(p_i/w) - s_i(p_i/w)] = 0$$

$$\text{[industry market clearing]}$$

$$\sum_1^n (p_j/W)[D_j(P_j/W) - S_j(P_j/W)] = 0 \quad \text{[balance-of-trade equilibrium]}$$

$$W/M = A, \quad w/m = a \quad \text{[quantity theory]}$$

Either $M + m = \overline{G}$ and $R = \overline{R}$,

or $M = \overline{M}$ and $m = \overline{m}$ [exogenous money supply].   (1)

Here upper-case letters denote American variables, P_i being prices and W the dollar wage rate, D_i and S_i demand and supply functions with the usual 'stable' intersections $D_i' - S_i' < 0$, R the dollar price of the pound, and M the American money supply (or gold).

Similar interpretations apply to Britain's lower-case variables, but $r = 1/R$ and Britain's balance-of-trade equality are skipped as redundant.

The first set of equations is shown on the graph in the chosen alignment of the vertical axes. [5] The second set of relations is shown by the equality and opposition of the matching trade arrows at the indicated equivalent latitude levels. The third set of relations is not shown because of the logarithmic scales, but would be depicted on the related back-to-back diagrams of conventional trade theory by the equivalence of the rectangular areas of either country's exports with those of its imports.

The fourth set of relations constitutes each country's adherence to a homogeneity property underlying all long-run Quantity Theory reasoning. [6] It is to be stressed that the expressions A and a are not constants

[5] This will perhaps be seen more clearly if we rewrite the arbitrage relations as $(P_i/W) = (Rw/W)(p_i/w)$, where $\Lambda = Rw/W$ is the 'real' exchange rate — the ratio between the British wage expressed in dollars to the American wage (as e.g. $0.5 \times \$2.40/\$4.00 = 1.2/4 = 0.3$).

[6] Avoiding the self-contradictory assumptions of timelessness, perfect certainty, and frictionless transactions, I have spelled out elsewhere the form of such a neo-classical monetary system. See P.A.Samuelson, 1968. In this model both the money supply and the public debt must double together if the change is to be neutral to interest rates and all real magnitudes and price ratios. So, with Hume, I ignore modern public debts in what follows.

as in various versions of the $MV = PQ$ identity, which gratuitously postulate constancy of V independently of interest rates and everything else and which take full employment for granted. Here A will typically depend upon all the price *ratios* P_i/W, upon interest rates, and the other endogenous *real* variables, and will be a different function depending upon the size of the country and its various institutions and behavior patterns. All that needs emphasizing is that in longest-run equilibrium the A function is homogeneous of first degree in all values, so that balanced changes in all prices and wages do not affect it.

In the final relations, Hume would have taken exchange rates as frozen and total world gold, $M + m$, as exogenously given. But in modern times, one often takes each M and m as exogenously given.

A count of our equations, plus the usual assumptions about elasticities, will show that they suffice to establish one (or sometimes more) equilibrium solution for all the variables, including the exchange rate.[7] It was Hume's triumph to demonstrate that one-way gold drains that go on forever are impossible.[8]

The present model permits, in the two-country case, ranking of commodities to determine which each country will export at high and low exchange rates, just as in the familiar constant-cost case analyzed by Mangoldt, Edgeworth, and Taussig.[9] It will be recalled that if, in that

---

[7] A useful procedure for solving the equations might be the following: substitute the first relations into the second, thereby eliminating the P's and enabling the second set to be solved for $p_i/w = f_i[\Lambda]$ and $S_i - D_i = E_i[\Lambda]$ with $f_i' < 0$ and $E_i' > 0$, where $\Lambda = Rw/W$, the 'real' exchange rate. Substituting these functions into the trade balance gives

$$-\Lambda \sum f_j[\Lambda] \, E_j[\Lambda] = B[\Lambda] = 0 \,,$$

a single equation that must have at least one root Λ^* for the equilibrium real exchange rate. If $B'[\Lambda^*] < 0$, the normal case for Marshall–Lerner elasticities, the equilibrium will be locally stable. Corresponding to Λ^*, all the P_i/W, p_i/w, and other real magnitudes that enter into A and a will be determinate, giving us the absolute wage and price levels and R^* from $W = A^*\bar{M}$, $w = a^*\bar{m}$, $R^* = (\Lambda^*a^*/A^*)\bar{M}/\bar{m}$ – the p–p–p doctrine! If total world gold, $M + m$, is prescribed at G, we solve for $\bar{M}/G = [1 + (\Lambda^*a^*/A^*)]^{-1}$, ending up with R^* and all real magnitudes or price ratios independent of G, but with all absolute prices and wages proportional to world gold supply – Hume's global quantity theory.

[8] Ironically, Hume himself proved all that any rational mercantilist could want: namely, that if all countries but one play the rules of the free-trade gold-standard game, that one country by increasing indefinitely its gold reserve ratio (to more than 100 per cent) can hope to accumulate an arbitrarily large fraction of the world's gold, for use in future war emergencies or royal adventures!

[9] P.A.Samuelson, 1964, analyzes n-good comparative advantage.

case, $(A_1, ..., A_n)$ and $(a_1, ..., a_n)$ represent the unit labor requirements for the different commodities in America and Britain respectively, we may suppose the numbering to have been done in order of American comparative costs, so that

$$A_1/a_1 \leq A_2/a_2 \leq ... \leq A_n/a_n . \tag{2}$$

Then if America produces and exports any goods at all, good 1 will certainly be among them. I.e., as the real exchange rate Rw/W gets ever lower, more and more of the American goods will be priced out of the market and good 1 will be the last good to be competitively viable. Similarly, good n will certainly be in any set of British goods that are internationally competitive. It will depend upon the exchange rate relative to money wage levels, i.e., on $\Lambda = Rw/W$, just where the line will be drawn between our exports and imports; and as Graham used to emphasize, there is some probability of a limbo situation for some intermediate good, $1 < j < n$, for which a trivial purchasing-power-parity relation holds exactly, $(A_j/W)(a_j/w) = Rw/W$.

In this constant-cost case, $S_i(P_i/W)$ and $s_i(p_i/w)$ are not strictly speaking well-defined single-valued functions: the second equations of my (1) above should then be replaced by

$$P_i = \min(WA_i, Rwa_i) \qquad (i = 1, ..., n)$$

$$Q_i + q_i = Y_i + y_i ,$$

$$Y_i = 0 \quad \text{if} \quad P_i < WA_i \quad \text{and} \quad y_i = 0 \quad \text{if} \quad p_i < wa_i , \tag{3}$$

where Y_i and y_i represent the amounts produced in the respective countries and Q_i and q_i the amounts consumed.

Now what can be said about the order of exporting and importing in the non-constant-cost case? Surprisingly, we can still give a prior ordering that depends only on wage and exchange rates independently of the compositions of demands and forms of the cost functions. Instead of computing simple A_i/a_i ratios, we must now make a prior computation of all autarky price ratios. I.e., we find the roots of $D_i(p_i/W) = S_i(P_i/W)$ and $d_i(p_i/w) = s_i(p_i/w)$ to define $(P_i/W)_{au}$ and $(p_i/w)_{au}$. Then we imagine the goods numbered to make

$$(P_1/W)_{au}/(p_1/w)_{au} \leq ... \leq (P_n/W)_{au}/(p_n/w)_{au} . \tag{4}$$

Then much as before we can state that as the dollar appreciates and so to speak becomes progressively overvalued, the higher-numbered goods will become non-competitive and good 1 will become the last American good to be internationally competitive. Likewise Britain's last viable good will be good n. These statements about the qualitative nature of trade should not blind us to the fact that, depending upon the elasticities and shapes of the schedules, it would be possible for the depreciation of an exchange to induce greater quantitative changes in goods that are either high or low in order among those eligible for export.

Needless to say the trick of Marshallian bales, which just happens to work in the constant-cost case, is of no avail here. There is no substitute for the full conditions of equilibrium as embodied in all my equations and not just in the second set of them. And no special significance attaches to the trivial purchasing-power-parity equivalence that may now hold in a marginal-cost sense for all goods produced in both countries. This point was already made in my cited 1964 comment on certain Houthakker notions about purchasing-power-parity.

When more than two countries are involved, no simple orderings are possible. The determining equations for N countries become

$$P_i^\alpha = R^\alpha P_i^1 , \quad (\alpha = 2, ..., N; \ i = 1, ..., n)$$

$$\sum_{\alpha=1}^{N} D_i^\alpha(P_i^\alpha/W^\alpha) = \sum_{\alpha=1}^{N} S_i^\alpha(P_i^\alpha/W^\alpha) , \quad (i = 1, ..., n)$$

$$\sum_{j=1}^{n} (P_j^\alpha/W^\alpha)[D_j^\alpha(P_j^\alpha/W^\alpha) - S_j^\alpha(P_j^\alpha/W^\alpha)] = 0 , \quad (\alpha = 2, ..., N)$$

$$W^\alpha/M^\alpha = A^\alpha \quad (\alpha = 1, ..., N)$$

Either all M^α prescribed, or

$$\sum_{\alpha=1}^{N} M^\alpha \text{ and } (R^2, ..., R^N) \text{ prescribed.} \tag{5}$$

Here $W^\alpha = (W^1, W^2, ..., W^\alpha, ..., W^N)$ are the respective countries' wage rates; $[P_i^\alpha]$ their prices; $R^\alpha = [1, R^2, ..., R^N]$ their exchange rates relative to the numeraire country 1; A^α the quantity-theory functions homogeneous of 0th degree in each country's prices and wage; M^α the respective money supplies; and D_i^α and S_i^α being functions whose superscripts denote respective countries. These equations, except for their rigorous justification and expression in terms of P/W variables, are essentially the same as those of Yntema, and his elegant theorems show how prescribed transfer payments from country α to β (or other disturbances) can be analyzed for comparative statics. [10]

The comparative statics of the system are much as in the two-country case. The first three sets of equations can be solved for all $(P_i^\alpha/W^\alpha, Q_i^\alpha, Y_i^\alpha, R^\alpha W^1/W^\alpha)$ independently of the M's. With these solutions substituted into the $W^\alpha/M^\alpha = A^\alpha$ relations, all $(P_i^\alpha/M^\alpha, W^\alpha/M^\alpha)$ are determined in quantity-theory fashion. Combining these solutions with the first set of arbitrage relations completes the purchasing-power-parity relations, according to which all ratios of the form $[M^\alpha/R^\alpha M^1, (M^\alpha/R^\alpha)/M^\beta/R^\beta]$ are determinate independently of the values of $(M^1, ..., M^\alpha, ..., M^N)$.

No mention has been made of domestic goods, but there can be as many of them as we wish without affecting this model. We merely adjoin to the second set of eqs. (5), autarky equations for every domestic good, of the form

$$S_{n+k}^\alpha(P_{n+k}^\alpha/W^\alpha) = D_{n+k}^\alpha(P_{n+k}^\alpha/W^\alpha)$$

$$(\alpha = 1, ..., N; \quad k = 1, 2, ...) \qquad (6)$$

4. The transfer problem

The traditional transfer problem, in which America permanently pays a reparation payment to Britain, can be handled in this model merely by adding to the balance-of-trade equation a permanent unilateral payment. The incidence of this transfer will be to depreciate the exchange rate of the paying country, with all that is thereby implied, as I showed in the Kindleberger *Festschrift*. In the Ricardian constant-cost case of horizontal supply curves, there will necessarily be a secondary burden

---

[10] T.O.Yntema, 1932. For $N > 2$, only the two-good case can be handled graphically.

on the payer in the form of worsened terms of trade (save in the limiting case where both countries produce something of a borderline good and no change in exchange rate is needed). But in general one cannot be sure that there is a secondary burden in the form of deterioration of the payer's net terms of trade (as measured by a necessary fall in $P_1/P_2 = p_1/p_2$). [11]

5. Rigorous foundations of partial equilibrium

Partial equilibrium is not general equilibrium: when you must deal with each industry in turn by holding other things constant, you cannot come to grips with mutual interdependence and simultaneous determination. But, as Marshallians and their critics have occasionally realized, there is one singular case in which the mutual interdependences are strictly absent and in which partial-equilibrium schedules provide an exact general-equilibrium model.

The singular case needed if the separate Cournot—Marshall demand functions are to have an independent, invariant existence must assume (a) all goods have independent, additive utilities $\Sigma\, U_j[Q_j]$; (b) one good or service — labor and its counterpart, leisure — has strictly constant marginal (dis)utility. Thus, if we pick units of utility so that one unit of labor has always one unit of disutility, any consumer maximizes an expression of the form $\Sigma\, U_j[Q_j] - L$.

To give the rising (or horizontal) supply functions an independent, invariant existence, we must make the Ricardo—Viner assumption that each good is produced by transferable labor working on lands that are, respectively, completely-specific to the industry in question. The labor needed to produce output Y_i of the ith industry can then be written as the convex (from below) function $L_i[Y_i]$, whose slope or marginal-cost function $L_i'[Y_i]$ is a rising function with $L_i'' \geq 0$ because of the well-known law of diminishing returns. The $L_i'[Y_i]$ of *marginal cost* (expressed in labor units) is the reciprocal of labor's *marginal productivity* and hence will, in competitive equilibrium, be equal to P_i/W. The rent return to the specific land will be 'price-determined' rather than 'price-

---

[11] There is though, generally, an induced secondary burden on the payer in the following sense: if America must pay Britain a given reparation expressed initially in a market basket of American export goods, she will generally be worse off than she would be in the singular situation where Britain — by reason of vast size or peculiarities of tastes and technology — would face America with almost infinitely elastic schedules. Thus, in the present model, the Ohlin criticisms of the orthodox view on the transfer problem are not vindicated.

determining' and will be competitively set as a function of output Y_i – and hence ultimately as a function of P_i/W – namely by

$$\{P_iY_i - W_iL_i[Y_i]\}/W = H_i[Y_i] = H_i(P_i/W) , \quad H_i' \geq 0 .$$

In the last expression, the supply relation connecting Y_i and P_i/W, namely $Y_i = S_i(P_i/W)$, has been used to eliminate Y_i. Finally, note that aggregation over all the separate, and possible heterogeneous acres within an industry, can be assumed without loss of precision to have already been done in the background through the familiar process of horizontal summation of curves. [12]

Just as the supply function has been related to the marginal cost function, we can relate the demand function to the marginal utility function. Again, this can be done for a single person, for a large number of 'representative', *identical* persons, or by prior horizontal summation of 'diverse persons' marginal utility curves to form a rigorously-valid nation demand curve. The demand response is given by the solution of the following maximum problem:

$$\max_{Q_i, L} [\sum_1^n U_j(Q_j) - L] \quad \text{subject to the budget equation}$$

$$\sum P_j Q_j = \text{income}$$

$$= WL + \text{rents} = WL + W \sum_1^n H_j(P_j/W) . \tag{7}$$

Provided both labor and leisure end up positive, the following Gossen conditions for a maximum are assumed to hold

$$U'(Q_i) = P_i/W , \quad U'' < 0 . \tag{8}$$

[12] One can admit capital goods in this model in the Von Neumann–Leontief fashion provided all intermediate goods used in any industry are producible from labor and the specific lands of those industries. (Of course, one must also specify the interest rate in each country or the equations determining it.) Then, in what is a simple generalization of the non-substitution theorem, as discussed in *Collected Scientific Papers*, Vols. I and II, Chs. 36 (1949), 37 (1961), 70 (1965), the requisite marginal-costs will be monotone functions of the form:

$$Q_j^\alpha = S_j^\alpha(P_j^\alpha/W^\alpha) \leftrightarrow P_j^\alpha/W^\alpha = C_j^\alpha[Q_j^\alpha] ,$$

where the latter is the 'generalized' derivative of a convex 'net' input–requirement function. The capital goods are there, but they can be kept in the background!

In short, our original demand and supply functions are rigorously identified as marginal utility and marginal cost functions invariant for each industry taken by itself. Thus

$$U_i'(Q_i) = P_i/W \longleftrightarrow Q_i = D_i(P_i/W) \,,$$

$$L_i'(Y_i) = P_i/W \longleftrightarrow Y_i = S_i(P_i/W) \,,$$

(9)

where the D_i and S_i functions are those met already in (1).

Everything written down here for America in upper-case letters has its exact counterpart in Britain's lower-case letters: the reader may supply such equations. Fig. 2 summarizes the American relations. Now the scales are not logarithmic, so that the ratio of the shaded rent areas $S_i C_i N_i$ (so-called 'producer's surplus', but here rigorously defined) to the wage areas $0 M_i C_i S_i$ will depict factor shares by industry, and, when aggregated, for the economy as a whole.

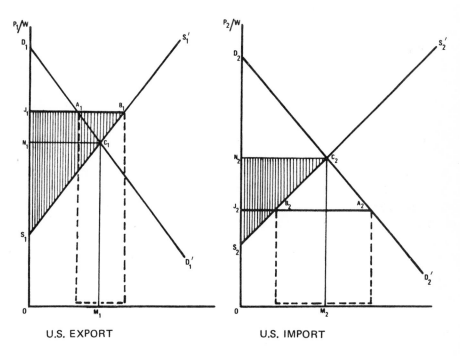

U.S. EXPORT   U.S. IMPORT

Fig. 2.

If autarky prevails, equilibrium is defined at the intersections C_1 and C_2, where

$$U_i'[Q_i] = P_i/W = L_i'[Q_i] , \quad Q_i = Y_i \quad (i = 1, ..., n)$$

$$L = \sum_1^n (P_j/W)Q_j - \sum_1^n H_j[Q_j]$$

$$= \sum_1^n L_j[Q_j] . \tag{10}$$

The last equivalence holds by virtue of the residual definition of rents, and states that the final total demand for labor by all employing industries equals the amount of labor supplied by maximizing consumers. The equality between value of total product and total incomes earned is also asserted. [13]

Fig. 2 also can show a post-trade situation, in which America is exporting good 1 to Britain, and importing good 2 from Britain. A careful measurement of the value rectangles under A_1B_1 and A_2B_2 will show them to be equivalent in areas, assuring balance-of-trade equilibrium. This also assures that American total labor supplied equals total labor our industries demand.

Note: suppose we ran a balance-of-trade deficit, as for example if our B_2A_2 imports on the right were accompanied by our staying at C_1 on the left. That would destroy the equivalence between the value of what we produce and what we consume; and it would destroy the equivalence between the value of what we consume and what our wage and rent incomes amount to. If we insisted on supplying labor so as to keep our consumptions equal in value to our incomes, our labor supplied as consumers, L, would exceed $\Sigma L_j[Q_j + E_j]$, the amount of labor demanded by American producers. [14] Thus, we seem near the situation feared by

---

[13] A lump-sum tax would have all its effects on extra labor supplied, there being zero income effects on all goods. If the government uses the tax receipts to buy goods $(G_1, ..., G_n)$, the extra labor will be exactly what is needed to produce those goods and realize the conditions: $U_i'(Q_i) = P_i/W = W_i(Q_i + G_i)$.

[14] Arithmetically, the deficit $(P_1/W)0 - (P_2/W)|E_2|$ would exactly equal in absolute amount the shortfall of employment, $L - \Sigma L_j[Q_j + E_j]$.

mercantilists and neo-mercantilists, in which an 'overvalued' currency produces involuntary unemployment.

But we have not said how the trade deficit is financed. Suppose it is financed by our sending gold abroad, each of us without the intermediary of governments. Then presumably our excess of consumption is to be financed by voluntary dissaving, rather than by our wanting to work more. So full-employment equilibrium can be envisaged as being preserved through the transition by a trade deficit financed by dissaving. [15]

There remains the final task of going behind the $W/M = A$ relationship of Hume. Without spelling out the cited 1968 version of neoclassical monetary theory, let me give a minimal justification for Hume's quantity theory. Suppose systematic subjective time preference of, say five per cent, sets equilibrium interest rates at $i = 0.05$ in the long run. Suppose to utility of goods $\Sigma\, U_j[Q_j]$ we prefix independent utility of cash balance, $U_0[M, P_i, ..., P_n, W]$, where U_0 is homogeneous of degree one in reflection of the fact that money has no intrinsic utility but is only wanted for the sake of the goods it can buy. The form of U_0 might well depend on, among many other things, the amounts and values of the earning assets, lands. The opportunity cost of increasing your M balance permanently is the interest foregone on the extra land that you might put your wealth in. Thus we generalize (7) to solve

---

[15] I shall not spell out here a Ramsey optimal-control model in which it is shown how maximizing an integral of possibly-discounted utility over infinite time, and in which the utility includes the 'utility of gold holding', will determine the rate at which we gladly give up gold when tempted by a pattern of relatively-lower prices from abroad. The extra leisure induced in this classical process should not be confused with involuntary unemployment. (Outside puritannical mercantilists might object though to this induced reduction in working.)

It should be pointed out that a permanent transfer of reparations payments from Britain to America would finance a permanent trade deficit here and trade surplus there. A lump-sum tax on Britons causes them to work more; the proceeds are sent to our government either in kind or in terms of either currency; our government gives these receipts to American citizens who are thereby motivated to work less by exactly the amount needed to match our deficit, our shortfall of production over consumption. It is worth mentioning that the transfer process here described is Pareto–optimal, in the sense that American $U = \Sigma\, U_j[Q_j] - L$ is at a maximum for each attained level of British $u = \Sigma u_j[q_j] - l$, as can be noted from the equivalences

$$U_1'/u_1' = U_2'/u_2' = ... = U_n'/u_n' = Rw/W = \Lambda.$$

Aside from welfare implications, this truth enables us to use a Meade trade-indifference diagram to show the transfer, tracing along its contract curve any induced change in the terms of trade.

$$\max_{M,Q_i,L} \; U_0[M, P_1, ..., P_n, W] + \sum_1^n U_j[Q_j] - L \,, \tag{11}$$

subject to

$$\sum_1^n P_j Q_j = WL + 0.05 \text{ (capitalized value of lands)} \tag{12}$$

or

$$0.05M + \sum_1^n P_j Q_j = WL + 0.05 \text{ (total wealth)}$$

$$= WL + 0.05 \text{ landvalue} + 0.05\,\bar{M}.$$

Note M on the left is money demanded and $\bar{M}$ on the right the fixed supply of money that is owned and must end up voluntarily held.

The generalized Gossen maximizing conditions are

$$\frac{1}{W} = \frac{\partial U_0/\partial M}{0.05} = \frac{U_i'}{P_i} \quad (i = 1, ..., n)\,. \tag{13}$$

Solving these, we get the reduced-form demand relations

$$Q_i = D_i(P_i/W) \quad (i = 1, ..., n)$$

$$M = D_0[W; P_1, ..., P_n; \bar{M}]$$

$$= \bar{M}\, D_0[W/\bar{M}; (P_1/W)(W/\bar{M}), ..., (P_n/W)(W/\bar{M}; 1] \tag{14}$$

$$L = \sum_1^n (P_j/W) D_j(P_j/W) - 0.05 \text{ landvalue} - 0.05\,(M - \bar{M})\,.$$

If, in equilibrium, we can set $\bar{M} = M = D_0$, the last term on the right will vanish. And we can set

$$D_0[W/\bar{M}; (P_1/W)(W/\bar{M}), ..., (P_n/W)(W/\bar{M}); 1] = 1 \,. \tag{15}$$

Since this function is monotone increasing in $W/\overline{M}$, we can solve for

$$W/\overline{M} = A(P_1/W, ..., P_n/W) .\qquad(16)$$

A similar derivation for Britain of $w/m = a(p_1/w, ...)$ completes the justification of the final Hume quantity-theory relations at the end of eqs. (1) above.

6. Conclusion

A rigorous model has been presented here. No attempt has been made to lighten the strong assumptions needed (as for example in the usual Marshallian rigmarole of postulating some 'approximate' constancy of marginal utility). Although all the strong assumptions made here are needed if the partial-equilibrium diagrams are to be valid, many of the properties of the classical models — e.g. the Hume price-level adjustments — will be valid in much more general models that dispense with simple graphs and are definable by simultaneous equations.

References

Bickerdike, C.F., 1920, The instability of foreign exchange, Economic Journal 30, 118–22.

Cournot, A.A., 1838, Mathematical principles of the theory of wealth, transl. by Nathaniel T. Bacon, 1927 (Macmillan & Co., New York) Ch. X.

Haberler, G., 1949, The market for foreign exchange and the stability of the balance of payments: A theoretical analysis, Kyklos 3, 193–218. Reprinted in: R.N.Cooper, ed., 1969, International finance (Penguin Books, Ltd., Harmondsworth, England) pp. 107–134.

Haberler, G., 1952, Currency depreciation and the terms of trade, in: E.Lagler and J.Messner, eds., Wirtschaftliche Entwicklung und soziale Ordnung (Verlag Herold, Vienna) pp. 149–158.

Robinson, J., 1937, Essays in the theory of employment (Macmillan & Co., London and New York) pp. 183–228.

Samuelson, P.A., 1964, Theoretical notes on trade problems, Review of Economics and Statistics 46, 145–154, reproduced in *Collected Scientific Papers,* Vol. 2, Ch. 65, pp. 821–830.

Samuelson, P.A., 1968, What neo-classical monetary theory really was, Canadian Journal of Economics 1, 1–15.

Viner, J., 1937, Studies in the theory of international trade (Harper & brothers, New York) p. 319.

Yaeger, L.B., 1966, International monetary relations (Harper & Row, New York) p. 170 ff.

Yntema, O., 1932, A mathematical reformulation of the general theory of international trade (The University of Chicago Press, Chicago, Illinois).

163

ON THE TRAIL OF CONVENTIONAL BELIEFS
ABOUT THE TRANSFER PROBLEM

Paul A.SAMUELSON*

15.1. Introduction

When Germany was made to pay war reparations at Versailles, economists fell into dispute on the question of whether a unilateral transfer will, aside from the primary burden of the payment itself, also cause a secondary burden as a result of a presumed induced deterioration of the terms of trade of the paying country. In this famous transfer problem debate, Keynes, Pigou, Taussig, Robertson, and many others upheld this orthodox view of presumed secondary deterioration. Ohlin, pointing out that income effects had been neglected, asserted that no such clear-cut presumption was possible; and Viner demonstrated that the classical writers were by no means unanimous in holding to the orthodox position[1]

Analytically, the discussion remained confused, because models involving effective demand and financial considerations were rarely carefully separated from those involving pure barter. (In connection with barter models, even the

* Grateful acknowledgment is made to the National Science Foundation for research support and to Karen H.Johnson for assistance in the preparation of this paper.

[1] See for example the debate and rejoinders of J.M.Keynes and B.Ohlin, *Economic Journal*, Vol. XXXIX (1929) pp. 1-7, 172-182, 400-408. The principal article of each man is reproduced in H.S.Ellis and L.A.Metzler, eds. for the American Economic Association, *Readings in the Theory of International Trade* (Philadelphia: Blakiston Company, 1950) pp. 161-178. For a broad review see J.Viner, *Studies in the Theory of International Trade* (New York: Harper & Brothers, 1937) pp. 326-360. In the Taussig festschrift, "Note on the Pure Theory of Capital Transfer", Chapter 8, in: *Explorations in Economics, Notes and Essays Contributed in Honor of F.W.Taussig* (New York: McGraw-Hill Book Co. Inc., 1937) pp. 84-91. W.W.Leontief provided an alleged possible example in which the secondary burden was on the receiver, and so strongly as to make the payer better off in consequence of its paying a transfer.

great Marshall erred by shifting the paying country's offer curve while leaving that of the receiving country intact.) Empirically, the situation also remained confused, because it was not even clear whether Germany's reparations equalled the unilateral investments made to her from abroad.

Not until the 1930s did Pigou[2] clarify the barter aspects by appeal to an exact Jevons model of exchange. This enabled one to see how much the orthodox result depended upon particular assumptions made about transport costs and impediments in international trade. In two rather exhaustive articles[3], I concluded that, in the absence of transport costs or impediments, the orthodox presumption lacked basis (thus, in a sense, awarding the palm to Ohlin as against the pre-*General Theory* Keynes). With transport costs and tariff impediments, the outcome was shown to be very complex indeed, because once we isolated the crucial income-propensities upon which the result depended, clear-cut presumptions became difficult.

There the matter stood until recently Professor Ronald Jones[4] provided a beautifully simple argument that demonstrates an anti-orthodox (and, hence, partially anti-Ohlin) presumption even in the purest model involving zero transport costs and tariffs. Jones shows that random differences in tastes, which are independent of random differences in comparative advantage, result in countries' tending to import goods that are peculiarly taste-appreciated by them. (If I am a drunkard and you are a fop, I am more likely to export cloth and import rye than vice versa.) In consequence of Jones's hypothesis, my test criteria deduce that the receiving country is likely to have a *deterioration* of its terms of trade, giving to the paying country a secondary blessing rather than the secondary burden of the orthodox school or the zero burden of the Ohlin school.

[2] A.C.Pigou, "The Effects of Reparations on the Ratio of International Exchange", *Economic Journal*, Vol. XLII (1932) pp. 532-542. This is summarized in A.C.Pigou, *A Study in Public Finance*, 3rd ed. (London: Macmillan & Co. Ltd., 1947), Chapter XIX.

[3] P.A.Samuelson, "The Transfer Problem and Transport Costs: The Terms of Trade When Impediments are Absent", *Economic Journal*, Vol. LXII (June 1952) pp. 278-304, and P.A.Samuelson, "The Transfer Problem and Transport Costs, II: Analysis of Effects of Trade Impediments", *Economic Journal*, Vol. LXIV (June 1954) pp. 264-289. Both articles are reproduced in *The Collected Scientific Papers of Paul A.Samuelson*, Joseph E.Stiglitz, ed. (Cambridge, Massachusetts: The M.I.T. Press, 1966) pp. 985-1037. In abridged form these are reproduced in R.E.Caves and H.G.Johnson, eds. for American Economic Association, *Readings in International Economics* (Homewood, Ill.: Richard D.Irwin, Inc., 1968) pp. 115-147.

[4] R.Jones, "The Transfer Problem Reconsidered", *Economica*, Vol. XXXVII (1970) p. 178 ff.

I applaud the Jones result. Yet, even though I know better, I often find myself falling into the orthodox presumption. Why is this? Is it forgetfulness? Is it stupidity? Or is it perhaps that I, along with Keynes and Taussig, have implicitly in mind a tempting model in which the orthodox result is legitimately implied? The present paper explores the affirmative answer to the last question and hopes to throw light on the reasons that earlier writers fell into the orthodox view.

15.2. Partial Equilibrium Models

Implicitly, economists tend to use partial equilibrium models and to combine financial analysis with real. Less systematically, they tend to use simple Ricardian constant costs. Put all this together and you will not be surprised at the orthodox thesis. Moreover, by some sophisticated specifications, these top-of-the-mind notions can be made part of an *exact* general equilibrium model that combines Marshall, Ricardo, and, for that matter, Hume. However, I confine myself here to the transfer problem, leaving for publication elsewhere[5] the rigorous general equilibrium model.

Begin with fig. 15.1 which provides an interesting variant on the familiar back-to-back diagrams of Cournot, Barone, Bickerdike, Joan Robinson, Haberler and many others[6]. In fig. 15.1a one has the usual supply and demand curves for wheat in America expressed in dollars. In fig. 15.1c one has similar curves for wheat but expressed for England in terms of the pound. In fig. 15.1b the foreign exchange rate R, giving the dollar costs of £1 (e.g., \$3/£1) is denoted by the slope of the OR ray. (The exchange rate giving the pound cost of \$1, $r = 1/R$, is denoted by the slope of the ray referred to the vertical axis, thus preserving symmetry between countries.)

At each exchange rate R, there is determined an equilibrium dollar wheat price P_1, also a pound wheat price p_1, and, finally, the physical (algebraic) export of wheat from America to England. We can write the algebraic export functions as the difference between supply and demand in the respective countries, namely, $E_1(P_1) = S_1(P_1) - D_1(P_1)$ and $e_1(p_1) = s_1(p_1) - d_1(p_1)$ with E_1' and e_1' posited to be positive as a condition of stability. (This says the supply schedule, if negative, must be more vertical than the demand curve, in the usual Walrasian manner ?

---

[5] P.A.Samuelson, "An Exact Hume-Ricardo-Marshall Model of International Trade", *Jour. Int. Econ.,* Vol. I (February, 1971) pp. 1-18.

[6] For footnote, see page 331.

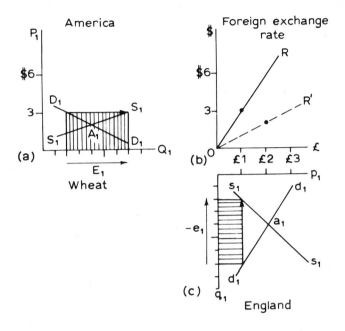

Fig. 15.1. The OR ray in (b) translates each dollar P into its equivalent pound p. Wheat market equilibrium occurs where America's export arrow is just matched by England's import arrow. If wheat were the only good, America at OR would enjoy an export surplus measured in dollars by the rectangle in (a) or in pounds by the rectangle in (c). For one-good balance of payments equilibrium, OR would have to depreciate to OR' so that both rectangles vanish. Any such clockwise move of the ray increases America's exports algebraically and reduces England's algebraic exports. Lowering R lowers all £p's and raises all P's. Thus, in a one-good case, an indemnity from America to England moves OR' counterclockwise to OR and induces a necessary depreciation of the payer's currency.

Competitive arbitrage requires that prices in two markets be equal when expressed in common currency units. Hence,

$$P_1 = Rp_1 \, . \tag{15.1}$$

Finally, equilibrium is determined by the equality of export of wheat from one country with import of wheat in the other; namely, by solving

$$-e_1(p_1) = E_1(RP_1) \tag{15.2}$$

377

in order to get p_1 as a declining function of R. I.e., appreciating the pound will lower the price of wheat in London. By symmetry, depreciating the dollar relative to the pound (i.e., raising R) will tend to raise the dollar price of

[6] As applied to single commodities in international trade, the familiar back-to-back diagram or its equivalent goes back to A.A.Cournot, *Mathematical Principles of the Theory of Wealth* (1938) tr. by Nathaniel T.Bacon (New York: The Macmillan Co., 1927) Chapter X; J.Viner, *Studies in the Theory of International Trade*, pp. 589-591 gives references to Cunyngham (1904), Barone (1908), Pigou (1904) and H.Schultz (1935); also see C.F.Bickerdike, *Economic Journal* XVII (1907) p. 98 for simple Cournot-like formulas; for a nongraphic literary exposition see F.W.Taussig, *Some Aspects of the Tariff Question* (Cambridge, Mass.: Harvard University Press, 1915 and 1931) Chapter I; see also G.Haberler, *The Theory of International Trade* (London: William Hodge & Co., Ltd., 1936) Chapter 15, pp. 227-236, and also the reference there to R.Schuller (1905). Or see P.A.Samuelson, *Economics*, 8th ed. (New York: McGraw-Hill Book Company, Inc., 1970) Chapter 34, pp. 651-653, whose fig. 34-2 has identical functions to those of fig. 15.1 here. The 1967, 1964, and 1958 editions also contain similar diagrams in Part Five.

The Cournot problem has been generalized to any number of commodities and given a solution by S.Enke in "Equilibrium Among Spatially Separated Markets: Solution by Electric Analogue", *Econometrica*, Vol. XIX (January 1951) pp. 40-47; see also P.A. Samuelson, "Spatial Price Equilibrium and Linear Programming", *American Economic Review,* Vol. XLII, No. 3 (June 1952) pp. 283-303, and P.A.Samuelson, "International Price Equilibrium: A Prologue to the Theory of Speculation", *Weltwirtschaftliches Archiv*, Band 79, Weft 2 (Hamburg: Hoffmann & Campe Verlag, December 1957) pp. 181-219; both these articles are reproduced in *The Collected Scientific Papers of P.A. Samuelson*, op. cit., Vol. II, pp. 925-984. Karl Fox and also G.C.Judge and T.Takayama have generalized the problem to multiple commodities.

As applied to exchange rate equilibrium, the earliest exact reference seems to be C.F.Bickerdike, "The Instability of Foreign Exchange", *Economic Journal*, Vol. XXX (1920) pp. 118-122 (which in a sense predates Pigou's 1932 rigor); J.Robinson, *Essays in the Theory of Employment* (London and New York: The Macmillan Co., 1937) pp. 183-228 further advances the subject. For graphical formulation and advance see G. Haberler, "The Market for Foreign Exchange and the Stability of the Balance of Payments: A Theoretical Analysis", *Kyklos*, Vol. III (1949) pp. 193-218 which is reproduced in *International Finance, Selected Readings*, R.N.Cooper, ed. (Harmondsworth, England: Peguin Books Ltd., 1969) pp. 107-134; also G.Haberler, "Currency Depreciation and the Terms of Trade", in: *Wirtschaftliche Entwicklung und soziale Ordnung,* Ernst Lagler and Johannes Messner, eds. (Vienna: Verlag Herold, 1952) pp. 149-158. In the modern literature innumerable writers have worked out elasticity expressions for so-called Marshall-Lerner stability conditions based upon such models. Similar matters are ingeniously formulated in John Burr Williams, *International Trade Under Flexible Exchange Rates* (Amsterdam: North-Holland Publishing Co., 1954). See also T.O. Yntema, *A Mathematical Reformulation of the General Theory of International Trade* (Chicago, Ill.: The University of Chicago Press, 1932), a beautiful work that has never been appreciated at its true worth.

wheat, making the American dollar P_1 an increasing function of the foreign exchange rate.

Fig. 15.1 shows all this. As the pound depreciates, OR pivots clockwise. As it does so, American wheat exports decline. When the exchange ray shifts to OR' in fig. 15.1b, all trade ceases.

Now suppose that wheat were the only good. Balance-of-payments equilibrium requires an equivalence of aggregate value of exports to aggregate value of imports. If wheat is the only good, this can be realized only when R depreciates to the OR' level of zero wheat export. This equilibrium R^* is given by the solution of

$$E_i(RP_i) = -e_i(p_i) \qquad\qquad i = 1 \qquad\qquad\qquad (15.3)$$

$$\sum_{i=1}^{1} p_i e_i(p_i) = p_1 e_1(p_1) = 0 \, .$$

We thus have, in addition to the balance-of-payments equation, an export equation for every good, namely in our case of the single good wheat, eq. (15.2). Hence, we always do have $n + 1$ equations to determine the np's and the equilibrium R^*. From p, we get P by eq. (15.1).

15.3. Exchange Depreciation For The Paying Country

What is the moral? What implication is there for the transfer problem? Suppose America is now to make a unilateral payment to England. How will the previous one-good autarky equilibrium at OR' be disturbed? Obviously, OR' must pivot upward (counterclockwise) toward OR. For such a depreciation of the dollar is the only way[7] that an American trade surplus can be generated.

Thus, the Keynes intuition that the *paying country's exchange rate depreciates* is vindicated in this primitive model. But this tells us nothing about any secondary movement induced in the terms of trade. Indeed, with wheat the only good, there is no price ratio P_1/P_2 for America to compute as a measure of the (so-called *Taussigian net*) terms of trade.

---

[7] The usual perverse violation of Marshall-Lerner stability conditions is *not* possible at a one-good autarky point.

15.4. Constancy of Some Marginal Utility

Before introducing a second good, we must notice that when America produces more wheat than she consumes, this must be financed. Since there is no investment or disinvestment in our model, how can the value of net national product fall short of the value of net national income received from wheat production? Evidently this value of the export surplus is financed by American government taxation of earned income to pay for the reparations. (In England, the reverse problem is easily resolved. English product consumed exceeds income earned domestically by the amount of government subsidy. But how does the English government finance this subsidy? From its "reparation" receipts.)

The reparation is, in effect, paid in wheat. One might even have the American tax and the English subsidy paid in terms of wheat. Everything would then seem to be in terms of wheat, the only good named. If wheat were truly the only economic good, what is the meaning of supply and demand curves? What is the American dollar supply and demand for P_1 in terms of?. What is English pound supply and demand for p_1 in terms of?. On reflection, we realize that "money" must in a rigorous model be a Marshallian euphemism for some domestic good or a host of such goods and factors.

Let us postulate that wheat is producible in each country by labor applied to fixed wheat land. The law of diminishing returns shows up as the rising supply functions. More precisely, suppose we use labor hours as our *numeraire*, so that wage rates, W in America and w in England, are each set equal to unity. Then our functions $S_1(\cdot), D_1(\cdot), E_1(\cdot)$, are really functions of P_1/W. Likewise, we write $s_1(p_1/w), d_1(p_1/w), e_1(p_1/w)$.

But there is still a snag. When governments tax us or subsidize us, particularly if these fiscal variables were payable in wheat rather than in wage units of income, that tax or subsidy can usually be expected to distort and alter the Marshallian demand functions. How does a conscientious Marshallian get rid of this distortion and complication? He can do so if he stipulates that labor has strictly constant marginal disutility (or that leisure, regarded as "money", has strictly constant marginal utility). In this singular model, all consumer-surplus and producer-surplus concepts are valid. And, what is important to an Ohlin skeptic, *all* income effects are exhausted on labor (or leisure), which unlike wheat and other traded goods, are purely domestic goods.

One last caveat if my Marshallian model is to be rigorous: as one moves up the supply curve, the absolute level of rent rises. Property's relative share is given by the ratio of two areas: the producer-surplus "triangle" between the supply curve and the rectangle formed by each supply point all divided by the rectangle's whole area. However, we need not worry if landlords have different wheat-leisure preferences than workers or worry about intraclass taste differences. Provided everybody values leisure at constant marginal utility and is not satiated with it, each person's independent demands for wheat, or cloth, or steel will be simply added to form nonshifting aggregate demand functions $D_i(P_i/W)$ and $d_i(p_i/w)$. In order that the supply functions for the different goods be independent, I postulate the Ricardo-Viner case where *labor is the only transferable input between industries*, all wheatlands and woollands being specialized to single industries and earning simple Ricardian residual rents. This can justify the independence and invariance of the $S_i(P_i/W)$ and $s_i(p_i/w)$ functions.

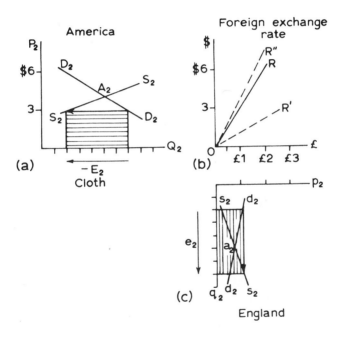

Fig. 15.2. At each exchange rate, cloth equilibrium is found where arrows match as in fig. 15.1. To find two-good balance of payments equilibrium, pivot ray until in either country export rectangle(s) cancel out import rectangle(s), as at *OR*. If now America pays transfer to England, *OR* must shift up to *OR''* and currency of the payer depreciates. Because of Robinson curiosum, such a rise in *R* could perversely improve payer's terms of trade $P_1/P_2 = p_1/p_2$; but in Ricardian case where *SS* curves are horizontal and exchange market stable, payer's terms of trade *must* depreciate.

15.5. Many Goods

Now in fig. 15.2 a second good along with wheat is added, say wool or cloth. Now at an exchange rate such as OR, each country has an export advantage in one of the goods, America in wheat and England in cloth. Before reparations the common OR ray in figs. 15.1b and 15.2b provides equilibrium $R*$ because the export and import rectangles in each country cancel out to zero or balance-of-payments equilibrium.

If we try a higher R, England runs a deficit. If we try a lower R, the dollar (and r) appreciates, and America runs a trade deficit.. The $R*$ equilibrium is unique and stable[8].

Mathematically, our equilibrium is defined by

$$E_i(RP_i) + e_i(p_i) = 0 \qquad i = 1, 2, ..., n \qquad (15.4)$$

defining

$$p_i = p_i[R] \qquad p_i' < 0$$

$$P_i = P_i[R] \qquad P_i' > 0$$

and

$$b[R] = \sum_1^n p_i e_i(p_i) = \sum_1^n p_i e_i(p_i[R]) = \sum_1^n p_i e_i[R] = 0, \qquad (15.5)$$

where $e_i'[R] < 0$.

All the ink spilled over so-called Marshall-Lerner stability (for which see Haberler's 1949 *Kyklos* citation of works of Hirschman, A.C.Brown, L.A. Metzler, and others beyond those I had already cited) conditions merely produces breakdowns of the terms involved in $b'[R]$. It suffices to note that $b' < 0$ is not inevitable even though probable in many specifications.

Now return to the transfer problem. If America now pays an indemnity

---

[8] It is well known that great inelasticity of the functions could negate the Marshall-Lerner conditions for such stability. Provided the curves have the usual shapes, there will exist at least one finite equilibrium $R*$ at which trade balances. Our drawing satisfies stability conditions. And generally the Ricardo constant-cost case, which we shall discuss later, makes for high elasticity and a tendency toward stability.

to England, how must the two-good OR ray of equilibrium rotate to produce an American export surplus? Clearly the dollar must depreciate and OR must move counterclockwise (as to OR'' in fig. 15.2), thereby increasing our wheat export and diminishing our cloth imports. In symbols, if America pays Europe a unilateral transfer of £t, we replace eq. (15.5)'s balance-of-payment condition by -t rather than zero on the right-hand side, namely,

$$b[R] = -t \qquad\qquad (15.6)$$

and, provided $b' < 0$, the stable case, we confirm for any number of goods the earlier theorem, namely

Theorem: The exchange rate of the paying country is depreciated by a unilateral transfer.

15.6. Deteriorating Gross-Barter Terms of Trade

Because currency depreciation increases *every* physical export algebraically (i.e., cuts down on any physical import), the paying country is "hurt" by the transfer. This shows that, regardless of what happens secondarily to the (Taussigian net) terms of trade, the 1935 Leontief phenomenon — of an alleged possibility that a transfer can have secondary effects so much opposed to the primary burden as to lead to a utility gain to the payer — definitely cannot happen in our model.

For a two-good model Taussig's "gross barter terms of trade", the ratio of the paying country's physical imports to its physical exports, $e_2[R]/-e_1[R]$ in the wheat-cloth case, must definitely deteriorate. This is because the numerator declines with R and the denominator grows with R. Of course there is nothing very surprising about this result, since one does expect there to be a primary burden.

When we face more than one export and more than one import, and when goods can pass from one category into the other, an index number problem arises for any definition of the terms of trade, gross or net. Our two-good result concerning the deterioration of gross-barter terms of trade can, however, be generalized as follows.

In view of the fact that *every* algebraic export from England is reduced by the transfer receipt, if we can divide the n goods into m American imports $e_i[R]$ and n-m American exports $-e_j[R]$, then for any *fixed* positive weights $(k_1, k_2, ..., k_m, k_{m+1}, ..., k_n)$, the following definition of the gross-barter terms of trade, $\Sigma_1^m k_i e_i [R] / \Sigma_{m+1}^n (-k_j e_j [R])$), will definitely fall, just as in the case of the two-goods example.

15.7. Likely, But Not Inevitable, Secondary Burden

To explain impressionistic views of the past, we have come far enough. In the present partial-equilibrium model (which elsewhere I call the B-R-H model because Bickerdike, Joan Robinson, and Haberler have perhaps written most about it), the transfer *does depreciate* the currency of the paying country[9]. And for the majority of economists, a deterioration of the exchange rate is practically identified with a deterioration of the terms of trade. Indeed some economists even go so far in their thinking as to believe that it is the lowering of the terms of trade that brings about the correction in the trade balance incident to a currency depreciation. This too-facile identification of the terms of trade with the foreign exchange rate has many roots. For one thing, as already mentioned, there is the common confusing together of barter and financial models. Thus an expression such as the Marshall-Lerner elasticity criterion for stability is used interchangeably for (1) a barter model like that involved in Marshall's 1879 *Pure Theory of Foreign and Domestic Commerce* or the Appendix to his 1923 *Money, Credit and Commerce* where reciprocal offer curves cross and (2) a money model such as the B-R-H one now under discussion. (Of course, this model is itself not really a financial model but is also a special kind of barter model, as my version of it makes clear for perhaps the first time.) In the typical two-good barter model of J.S.Mill, Marshall (1879), Edgeworth, and others, stability is restored only by changes in the price ratio of the traded goods or the (net) terms of trade. But such reasoning is not really valid for the model here under discussion.

[9] This result does *not* have to be qualified even for an unstable equilibrium as I shall demonstrate in fig. 15.3. If fixed parities are imposed by the gold standard, the Hume mechanism accomplishes the equivalent result by ultimately lowering the W in the P_i/W expressions and raising the w in the p_i/w expressions so that w/W appreciates by *exactly* the same percentage as does the exchange rate R in my exposition. Part of Keynes's skepticism concerning the feasibility of transfer had nought to do with the change in the terms of trade as much as with his skepticism concerning the ease with which the conventional gold standard mechanism made adjustments under a regime of fixed parities. Perhaps he would have been less skeptical if he had been contemplating a regime of floating exchange rates. In the companion paper already referred to, I prove the illogic of those who oppose floating exchange rates on the grounds of elasticity-pessimism demonstrating that if the econometric conclusions of these critics is correct, then the fixed-parity equilibrium under the Hume mechanism is *also* unstable!

For many years after 1920 when Bickerdike first published such a model, economists took it for granted that exchange depreciation causes a nation's export prices to fall relative to its import prices. Even in the gold-standard case, equilibrium is loosely said to be restored as prices of the deficit country fall relative to prices of the surplus country. (In the referred to companion paper to this one, I analyze the flaw involved in such wording.) Actually, however, as we have seen, and as our diagrams will confirm, when R rises in virtue of depreciation of the dollar, prices of both export *and* import goods fall in dollar terms; and prices of both British imports *and* exports rise in pound terms. Therefore, it is gratuitous to jump to the conclusion that the prices of exports of the depreciating country drop relative to those of its imports.

Yet it was not until the late 1930s that Joan Robinson[10] pointed this out in the literature — much to the surprise of specialists in international trade theory. When they first became aware of the Robinson curiosum, they thought that perhaps her effect was brought about only in cases where the equilibrium was unstable by virtue of reversal of the Marshall-Lerner stability criterion. But it was easy to provide examples of perfectly stable equilibria where the terms of trade actually turned in favor of the depreciating country, and yet depreciation did restore the disturbed equilibrium.

We can state then that it is quite possible for the secondary effects of the transfer payment to go either way: the net terms of trade of the paying country could improve or they could deteriorate as a result of the transfer.

To see this, consider a two-good case of say wheat and cloth. It is easy to construct along Robinson lines an example of a stable system and in which P_1/P_2 *rises* as a result of the transfer rather than falls as the orthodox view would hold. Where economists went wrong in denying this possibility was in comparing prices *across* countries — comparing a P with a p, as for example P_1 with p_1. It is true that the price of cloth has risen in dollars and fallen in pounds. But, since such a ratio is nothing but the exchange rate in a free market, what else could it do when R changes? Such a ratio has nothing to do with a properly computed measure of the terms of trade, which should involve a comparison of export prices with import prices in the same market, whether it be the dollar or pound market. Thus, whatever P_1/P_2 does, so must p_1/p_2 do, since they are the same thing. (I.e., cancelling out R from numerator and denominator of the former will give you the latter, no matter what is the new exchange rate R.) When index numbers of prices become involved, and also certain impediments and costs of trade, one can become

[10] J.Robinson, *Essays in the Theory of Employment,* pp. 218-221, particularly p. 219, *n.* 1.

confused on these fundamentals. Such confusions are common in connection with historic discussions of purchasing-power parity, as I have discussed elsewhere[11]; and I fear that sometimes Keynes added to the confusion on this matter.

Although the Robinson curiosum shows that no unambiguous answer is possible concerning the secondary burden of a transfer, economists have tended to think that this phenomenon is abnormal in the sense of being unusual. Because we are discussing what is after all a rather idealized model, I am not sure that sense can be made of a statement that one result is "empirically more realistic" than another. But in any case, economists have often supplied conditions that they hoped were sufficient to rule out the Robinson curiosum. Broadly speaking, they sought such conditions in extreme elasticity of postulated supply. In my present concern to try to explain why older economists fell naturally into the orthodox view, I shall now present a rather extreme case of elastic supply — namely, the classical model of Ricardian constant costs. For, within that model, we shall see that the Marshallian partial-equilibrium approach does lead to deterioration of the terms of trade along the lines of the orthodox presumption.

15.8. Combining Marshallian Curves and Ricardian Comparative Advantage

Because my companion paper elaborates upon the present subject and because my 1962 paper, just cited, presented a complete account of the production side of the many-good Ricardian model, I shall be brief here and omit diagrams.

Now labor is assumed to be the only factor, A_1, A_2, A_3, ... units of American labor being required to produce a unit of goods 1, 2, 3, ... To produce a unit of those same goods in England requires a_1, a_2, a_3, ... units of English labor. Recall that W is the dollar wage rate for American labor and that w is the pound wage rate for English labor. In good classical fashion, we rule out migration between countries. As before, the exchange rate giving the cost of one pound in terms of dollars is R, with $r = 1/R$ being the number of pounds per dollar.

How is supply affected in figs. 15.1 and 15.2? Supply is affected by having the supply curves all become horizontal, in consequence of the Ricardian

[11] P.A.Samuelson, "Theoretical Notes on Trade Problems", *Review of Economics and Statistics*, Vol. XLVI, No. 2 (May 1964) pp. 145-154, reproduced in *The Collected Scientific Papers of Paul A.Samuelson*, Vol. II, pp. 821-830.

assumption of constant costs. For example, with labor the only factor and lands ignorable, diminishing returns has no scope. Elsewhere I spell out the minor variations needed in the B-R-H model when it is made Ricardian. (This involves merely introducing some inequalities into eqs. (15.4) earlier.) However, we can dispense with that examination here, because on reflection we notice that the way relative prices change is *completely predictable* from the movement of the exchange rate alone.

For it is an easy theorem in the constant-cost case that depreciating the dollar must reduce all prices of the goods America exports in comparison with those she imports; and it will leave intact the price ratios of all goods that a country continues to produce.

Where are these price ratios to be measured? In England or in America? It does not matter; in a perfect market, the price ratios in one country are identical with those in another, regardless of the production origin of the goods in question.

Specifically, for any two goods that America continues to produce, the price ratio is given by A_i/A_j. For any two goods that England continues to produce, the price ratio anywhere in the world is given by a_i/a_j. The only interesting case then is the comparison, in any one place, of the price ratio of an American export to a European export as R rises. Let us consider the net terms of trade as England sees them between cloth and wheat as measured by p_2/p_1 or P_2/P_1. Using the latter dollar version, one calculates it as the European labor cost of cloth a_2 translated from pounds into dollars by the exchange rate R, all divided by American labor cost (in dollars) of wheat. Hence, so long as each country's cost for its indicated export is the lowest cost anywhere in the world, the expression for England's terms of trade becomes

$$P_2/P_1 = a_2 w R / A_1 W .$$

This is seen to be linear in the exchange rate and hence grows whenever R grows (up to the point where England is priced out of the market and America's A_2/A_1 takes over or down to the point where America is priced out of the market and a_2/a_1 prevails). Of course a change in the exchange rate might be offset by a wage rise in the depreciating country and a wage fall in the appreciating country. But the real transfer will not be possible unless the wR/W factor in the above expression does in fact rise and that is all we need for the argument. Incidentally, as remarked before in a footnote, although my discussion is couched primarily in terms of flexible exchange rates, it applies fully to the gold standard case of fixed parities: in that case, R stays constant, but, as a result of specie flows or managed money, the called-for percentage changes all take place in the wage ratio w/W.

Let us take stock to see what the Ricardian case has added to the intuitive expectations of literary economists concerning the transfer problem. What constant cost has done is to rule out the Robinson curiosum.

Now any exchange depreciation induced by a unilateral payment must (save in the limiting and frequent case, beloved by Frank Graham, of "limbo" where one country is both producing and importing a good in proportions determined by reciprocal demand and where secondary burdens are nil) create a secondary burden on the paying country in the form of a deterioration of its export prices relative to its import prices. Q.E.D.

My task is completed. I have shown that any economist who reasoned in the back of his mind in terms of simplified partial-equilibrium industries, foreign exchange equilibrium, and comparative cost, could be forgiven from falling into the orthodox presumption in connection with the transfer problem. For that presumption is a valid theorem in terms of the B-R-H model, or at least in my B-R-H-S version of it.

15.9. Comparative-Static Stability in the Large

He who reads and runs can now run. But there are a couple of loose threads that I would like to tie up. First, as mentioned before, there is the possibility of a locally unstable equilibrium. (I must stress that the Ricardian horizontal supply does not, for all its infinite elasticity, rule that out — even if it perhaps makes instability less likely and does negate the Robinson curiosum.) As far as both dynamics and comparative statics are both concerned, such local instability does not — repeat, *not* — change the conclusion that a transfer will end up deteriorating the exchange rate of the payer. This strong conclusion, which might be dignified as being an extension of the "correspondence principle"[12], seems to have been overlooked and misunderstood in the literature. Second, there remains the minor problem of relating this defense of the orthodox position to my earlier 1952 and 1954 exhaustive examination and near rejection of that position.

Fig. 15.3 illustrates a case of multiple equilibrium. Between the two stable equilibria A and C, there is the unstable equilibrium B. Now along comes an indemnity of t paid to Britain (say, in pounds). This shifts my plot of $-b[R]$ to the right. Or what is the same thing, find the new equilibrium in fig. 15.3

---

[12] For footnote, see next page.

by looking for the intersection of the curve, not as before with the vertical axis, but with the vertical line t distance to the left of the axis. And again one has three equilibria, stable a and c and unstable b.

This accords with the usual discussions. Writers say, "See how the stable A has shifted upward, to a, as the receiving country's currency appreciates. And see how the stable C shifts upward to c. All this is as one should expect: according to the simplest correspondence principle, when an equilibrium is dynamically stable, its comparative statics behaves normally. But see how the unstable B shifts *perversely* to b. This too is in accordance with the correspondence principle that relates perverse dynamics to perverse comparative statics. Now we have room for paradox: if the world begins at the unstable B, America could better her terms of trade by forcing a reparation payment on England!"

Some of this argument is correct. But some is simply wrong. It is true that

---

[12] For the heuristic "correspondence principle", see P.A.Samuelson, *Foundations of Economic Analysis* (Cambridge, Mass.: Harvard University Press, 1947, and in paperback, Atheneum Publishers, New York, N.Y., 1965). Chapters IX, X and Appendixes A, B. As applied to a linear system or to the linear approximation near equilibrium of a nonlinear system – say to $\Delta y_i = A[y_i] + [b_i]$, or to $d/dt[y_i] = A[y_i] + [b_i]$ – its comparative statics will depend on the nonsingularity of its Jacobian matrix A, while its dynamic properties will depend on the latent roots of A defined by det $[A-(1+x)I] = 0$, or by det $[A-xI] = 0$. When a root x_1 becomes or passes through zero, the qualitative dynamic behavior reverses (as from stability to instability) and so too will the comparative static behavior (as from normality to perverseness). As an example, when $k = 1 + x$ in the multiplier expression $1 + k + k^2 + ...$ passes through unity and above, dynamic instability occurs; at the same point, the comparative static multiplier expression, $1/(1-k)$ perversely turns negative. But, as will be argued in connection with fig. 15.3 below, $1/(1-k)$ is not really a true comparative static observed phenomenon.

Since 1947, a number of economists have questioned the generality and unambiguity of the correspondence principle; let me make some disclaimers here. When x_1 is complex rather than real and has its real part change sign as x_1 passes through a pure imaginary number or has $|1+x|$ pass through unity, the argument needs modification because only the dynamic behavior is reversed. Furthermore, the heuristic principle works best when A is a definite matrix as in connection with an extremum problem; for then real roots are assured, and not only do we have knowledge about A but also about its principal minors. Similarly if A is a Leontief-Metzler-Frobenius matrix, in which all off-diagonal elements are of one sign and A possesses diagonal dominance, then similar sweeping conclusions are possible about principal minors and the reality of the relevant root; and indeed, as I pointed out in the 1960 Frisch *Festschrift*, my version of the LeChatelier principle holds for such structures. See P.A.Samuelson, "An Extension of the LeChatelier Principle", *Econometrica* 28 (1960) 368-379 (reproduced, with the first paragraph misprint "inelastic" corrected to read "elastic", in: *Collected Scientific Papers I*, pp. 626-637).

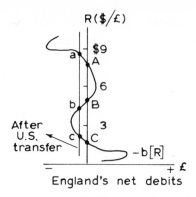

Fig. 15.3. Here is a typical case where elasticity-pessimism does create unstable equilibrium *B* between stable equilibria *A* and *C*. Payment of transfer by America to England of *t* pounds is like shift of vertical axis leftward by amount *t*. New intersections give effect of transfer on exchange rate (and in constant cost case, equivalent deterioration of terms of trade). That stable equilibria shift upward to *a* and *c* is obvious. But conclusion that unstable *B* shifts to new unstable *b*, thereby perversely improving terms of trade of payer is quite false. In the short run, transfer produces positive excess demand at *B*; with such excess demand *R* is dynamically bid up; final equilibrium ends up at *c*. Thus, both comparatively statically as well as dynamically, payment depresses currency of paper – even though the unstable branch has opposite slope. The correspondence principal in the large is thus established for this one-dimensional case.

a system that starts at either stable equilibrium will move upward to the indicated new equilibrium – with all the effects indicated in the present paper. But it is simply not true that starting the system at the unstable *B* equilibrium, and then disturbing it by a payment to England, will cause *R* to fall – either in the end or at any time during the transitional process.

Let us see what must actually happen. The instant the payment begins England runs a surplus in the foreign exchange markets (i.e., in the first instant we move due west of *B*). In the second instant, this bids up the price of the pound *R*. (This is in accord with the dynamic adjustment equation that says that *dR/d*(time) has the algebraic sign of "excess demand" for pounds.) So in the transition *R rises* just as in the stable cases. In those stable cases, however, the transition ends when *R* has risen into the new, nearby, stable equilibrium. What happens in this unstable case? There is no new, nearby, stable equilibrium, so the transition process just goes on and on. The *R* continues to rise. Continues to rise forever? No, it cannot rise above the highest stable equilibrium *c*. And so it rises until that equilibrium is reached. In short, one always has a comparative-static rise in *R* with or without instability! So one can say that "in the large", as contrasted to local un-stable and irrelevant branches of the $b[R] + t = 0$ relation, the final observed dR/d(transfer) movements have the same positive sign as in the stable case. No matter how many stable and unstable equilibria, *every* initial equilibrium is displaced into a higher stable equilibrium. Q.E.D.

How this sweeping correspondence result must be modified when the prob-lem is more than two dimensional must remain an open question. However, our result does have some policy implications: if momentarily trapped in an unstable equilibrium, and it becomes a nice question as to how *that* could have come about, a country can benefit by using its monopoly power and restricting goods in international trade so as to force the world into a stable equilibrium more agreeable to the country in question. But it cannot do so by throwing its bread on the waters in the form of gifts and transfers. (Also one shudders at the prospect of two von Neumann countries jockeying for position between stable equilibria more agreeable to one than to the other — an indeterminate problem in bilateral monopoly.)

Fig. 15.3 brings out another facet of the policy problem. From Versailles on, Keynes warned that Germany might not have the capacity to pay the imposed reparations. (Some have dismissed this as Francophobia; and in the Weimar republic, Schumpeter made himself rather unpopular by saying that of course Germany *could* pay the reparations if she set her will to it.) Whether Keynes was right in his impressionistic econometrics back in 1919, fig. 15.3 shows that if the vertical line is moved too far westward, there might be *no* possible equilibrium. Making Germany pay so large an indemnity would result merely in an endless depreciation of the mark and galloping inflation inside the country. (Whether the 1920-1923 German hyperinflation had much to do with reparations is not at all clear.)

Finally, there remains the task of reconciling the present strong affirmation of the orthodox position with the earlier skepticism concerning it.

15.10. Reconciliation with 1952-1954 Results

Of my two cited *Economic Journal* articles on the transfer problem, it was the first 1952 one that largely assumed no transport costs and no domestic goods. And it was that article which (the new Jones result aside) demonstrated that Ohlin agnosticism was warranted in criticism of the orthodox presump-tion of a secondary burden, the terms-of-trade charges were shown to depend upon *relative income propensities* for the two goods in the two countries; and with transport costs ignorable and demand not at all localized, the principle of insufficient reason suggested that *any* result was equally likely. How does the present model fit in?

Both wheat and cloth are certainly freely transportable. However, leisure in America and leisure in England are not internationally transferable items. They are domestic goods par excellence, with so to speak infinite transport costs as the result of the usual Ricardian assumptions that factors are immobile in international trade. Recall that leisure and labor are different names, or different aspects, of the same thing. Therefore at first blush, one is inclined to say that the present paper takes one out of the agnosticism of my first paper and into the morass of my second 1954 paper, with its many possible patterns of transport costs[13]. But that would seem too sweeping a conclusion. What use would my first 1952 model be if the existence of any immobile factors were considered to render it inapplicable? It, after all, did allow explicitly for transformation trade-offs between the two goods, with labor and land thus being understood to be in the background; and nothing could be less mobile than land. Therefore, it cannot be the mere presence of localized labor that frees the present inquiry from the conclusions of my first paper.

At a slightly deeper level, it might be argued that "leisure" never entered into my 1952 paper at all. Labor did, but the supply of labor as with the supply of every factor was implicitly taken there as fixed. There was no need, explicitly or implicitly, to consider leisure. In other words, it is the *variability* of the supply of labor or of some domestic good that seems to be involved here. This suggests that the present model falls into the category of what was described on p. 302 of the 1952 article (p. 1099 of my *Collected Scientific Papers*, Vol. II) as follows:

"...To my knowledge the only logically air-tight successful defense of the orthodox view is that given by Viner [*Studies*, p. 348-349], in which he explicitly introduces into the problem transport costs great enough to make international trade prohibitive for some 'domestic commodities'. Naturally a high percentage of our income is spent on such commodities."

Hence it does become likely that my test criterion involving income propensities on food and cloth of payer and receiver, suitably generalized for induced production effects, will indicate the orthodox presumption. As is said in a footnote on the next page of the 1952 article: "Viner's successful vindication of the orthodox presumption was possible because of his (quite realistic) introduction of an element of asymmetry into the problem: his

---

[13] See P.A.Samuelson, *Economic Journal*, 1954, op. cit. The only definite conclusion reached there was that the orthodox presumption had much to be said for it; but where the impediment involved real, exhaustive cost, Ohlin agnosticism seemed justified.

domestic good is made (infinitely) substitutable for the region's export good production and not at all substitutable for the import good production."

Simple mathematical analysis can show that the Ricardian case analyzed here is indeed of this general class involving asymmetric relations between a country's exports and its domestic goods or factors in variable supply.

To show this I shall make use of an Edgeworthian device pioneered by James Meade, the trade-indifference contours. (In the cited Caves-Johnson American Economic Association's reproduction of my 1952-1954 article, I added a 1966 postscript suggesting that my case of variable production could be reduced to "box-diagram" format by the use of the now-familiar Meade device. But for the present purpose, I have to go beyond the usual form of the Meade device and optimize also with respect to labor supply in the background. For example, for prescribed levels of $-E_1$ and $-E_2$, I maximize America's utility from wheat consumed, cloth consumed, and leisure enjoyed, subject of course to the Ricardian labor-cost contraints. This gives me in the end "contours of trade indifference". Fig. 15.4 illustrates these for America and Europe. The European contours are shown as broken lines and are to read from right to left and upside down in the usual box-diagram fashion.

Actually, and this will come as no surprise to students of Kuhn-Tucker nonlinear programming or of Edgeworthian trade theory, these contours will now be parallel straight lines in a large part of the field (i.e., where a country is producing something of both goods), with slope equal to A_2/A_1 or a_2/a_1 as the case may be. Beyond the boundaries of this field, the differences in comparative cost will introduce discernible asymmetries in fig. 15.4's income propensities or Engel's curves. Thus, suppose we begin at a prereparation point where each country is specializing on the good in which it has a comparative advantage. Also, let us evaluate the crucial income propensities there, to see if we do find that they differ in a systematic fashion predictable from comparative-cost theory alone. The answer is, yes. An international income change (because of reparation or anything else) alters the amount exchanged of a country's *export* good alone. In that case, transferring abstract purchasing power from America to England will cause the price of England's export good, cloth, to be bid up (by her) and will cause the price of America's export good, wheat, to be bid down (by the drop in America's income). Thus the orthodox presumption is indeed triumphantly established. Q.E.D.[14]

---

[14] Of course the present theorem is a restatement, from a different point of view, namely the 1952-1954 viewpoint, of what has already been established in this paper.

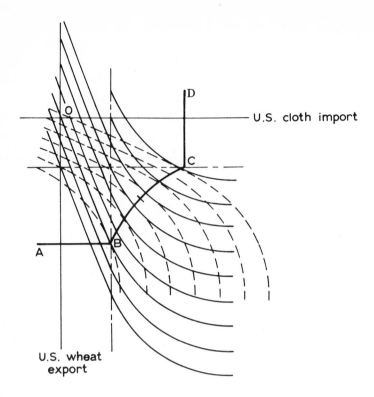

U.S. cloth import

U.S. wheat
export

Fig. 15.4. Reading upward and in the usual left-to-right fashion, one sees the American trade-indifference contours. Reading upside down and from right-to-left, one sees the English trade-indifference contours. Directly below the origin, both sets of contours are straightlines determined by comparative cost ratios. In case where America exports wheat and imports cloth, transfer moves equilibrium on the contract curve *CB* toward *B*, necessarily depreciating wheat/cloth price ratio.

A last word. One of the triumphs of the 1952 paper was the demonstration that, for stable systems, no matter what the complexity of conditions in the background, the simple food-cloth income propensities were determinative. What then do *they* tell us about the present case? Because of the assumption that leisure-labor has constant marginal utility, all consumption-income effects for cloth and wheat are zero in both countries. As a result, my 1952 criterion becomes 0/0, an indeterminate number that tells us nothing but which is consistent with orthodox deterioration proved by other methods.

Mathematically, I shall reduce the behavior equations of the problem to the solution of a certain maximum problem for each country. We have seen that the independent demand curves of the different citizens can be horizontally added to get the market demand curves. These individual demand curves are, by virtue of our assumption of constant marginal utility of leisure-labor, identical to marginal utilities for each citizen. When summed horizontally, these marginal utilities provide an aggregate marginal utility function in the sense of being the derivative of its own integral. The integral[15] for each good can be written as the concave function $U_i(Q_i)$ and $u_i(q_i)$, which serve as the Gossen-like utilities for America and England, respectively. Lest anyone raise an eyebrow that I work with a collective concept such as total utility of a country, let me hasten to point out that this is completely rigorous because of my assumption that each person has labor-leisure of constant marginal utility. So long as workers never run out of leisure and provided that they have run into work, all is completely rigorous.

I shall leave to the reader the parallel case of England and shall concentrate on America. Our programming problem is to find the quantities that America is to produce of wheat and cloth, Y_1 and Y_2, so as to maximize national utility. If one selects utility units in such a way that one unit of labor corresponds to one util, and if one eliminates labor by substituting the production-possibility frontier of Ricardo, $L = A_1Y_1 + A_2Y_2$, the simple Kuhn-Tucker concave-programming problem results:

---

[15] Except for the algebraic sign of the import variable, these are what I introduced as "social-payoff" functions in the cited articles on spatial and intertemporal price equilibrium: P.A.Samuelson, *American Economic Review*, 1952, op. cit., pp. 283-303 and *Weltwirtschaftliches Arkiv*, 1957, op. cit., pp. 181-219. It may be asked, how are collective indifference curves possible in view of my earlier proof that they exist only when the indifference curves are homothetic and identical between citizens? The present case does not quite fall into that category. But, as has been discussed elsewhere, there is a wider class in which collective indifference contours hold within a range, namely the Gorman-Theil case where all Engel's curves are straight lines with slopes (at each price ratio) common to all the citizens. Now actually the only lines that can stay straight lines through the nonnegative orthant are lines through the origin — my homothetic case. In the present example, where the Engel's curves are lines parallel to the leisure axis, when the individual stops buying leisure, because he cannot afford any, or when he buys 24 hours of leisure because it does not pay him to work at all, we lose the simplifications that constancy of marginal utility does for us in providing solid underpinning for partial equilibrium. So, as in all Gorman-Theil deviations from my narrower conditions, the collective indifference curves will break down as a concept in the large. (Actually, for indemnity large enough, some Englishmen will quit working and some American will find himself working every possible hour. And then partial equilibrium cannot be used.) However, for the purpose of the present exercise, within a range of indemnities, the trick does work even though it cannot work unconditionally.

$$\max_{Y_i} U_1(Y_1-E_1) + U_2(Y_2) - A_1 Y_1 - A_2 Y_2 = U^*(-E_1,-E_2) \quad Y_i \geqslant 0$$

where the levels of goods imported or exchanged $-E_i$ are taken as given.

The well-known necessary and sufficient conditions for an optimal solution are given by

$$U_i'(Y_i-E_i) - A_i \leqslant 0 \,,$$

with the inequality holding only when $Y_i = 0$. This gives us as many conditions as there are goods. After we have substituted these optimal decisions into the maximand, we get the desired U^* function that provides our generalized-Meade, trade-indifference contours. The slopes of these U^* contours are given by the ratios of the partial derivatives of the U function. It is now evident that these slopes are the constant A_2/A_1 where both goods are being produced. Where America is producing wheat alone, our interesting case, the slope is given by $U_2'(-E_2)/A_1$ and the contour is strongly convex. The convex field joins up with the parallel-straightline field at a critical value of $-E_2^*$, and hence the boundary is the vertical line through the point market B in fig. 15.4. To the right of that vertical boundary, the Engel's curves are also vertical lines for America.

By similar mathematical reasoning, the reader will establish that Europe's critical boundary, at which her production of wheat ceases, is the horizontal line through the point C; and her Engel's curves in the interesting region below that boundary all have Engel's curves that are horizontal. And so, utilizing the income propensities of my 1952 paper, we have the asymmetry needed to justify the orthodox position. Q.E.D.

Any reader who wishes to skip this mathematical argument is invited to compare the "contract locus" $ABCD$ of fig. 15.4 with the CC contract locus of figs. 1 and 2 of my 1952 paper. The techniques developed there, when applied to fig. 15.4 will indeed vindicate the orthodox Keynes-Taussig presumption.

As my colleague Professor Bhagwati has suggested to me after reading a first draft of the present paper, there is an easy heuristic way to understand why the present model results in the orthodox deterioration of the payer's terms of trade: First, assume all prices unchanged. Since income effects go entirely on to the domestic good leisure, there is no change in the amounts consumed of wheat and cloth in either country. So far, then, no presumed change in terms of trade. But recall that the payers are all forced to work more and thereby to produce more of something: under complete specialization, that something can be only the exportable good of the paying country. Similarly, the receivers all work less and produce less of their exportable good. With consumptions otherwise unchanged, an increase in America's wheat production and a decrease in England's cloth production can only result in a deterioration of the terms of trade between wheat and cloth if markets are to be cleared. Q.E.D. I may add: the moral is that, when productions are variable, the criteria of my earlier papers based on consumption propensities, $\partial C_i/\partial I$, have to be modified by income-induced production and cross-effects.

15.11. Conclusion

We have come a long way. The orthodox way of thinking has been in a sense traced down to its possible intuitive origins. But this has been done in a rigorous way only in the context of a very strong model in which the conditions for partial-equilibrium analysis are rigidly met.

I hold no brief for orthodoxy. Actually my own vested interests have been on the other side. But rereading my 1952-54 papers in the light of the present analysis convinces me that these papers underestimate the strength of the orthodox presumption. This is because these papers concentrated on the criterion of income-induced changes in the consumptions of the traded goods. An exception was noted in the Viner airtight successful defence of the orthodox view (1952, p.302 and 1954, p.289) but this was illegitimately treated as an esoteric case. So let me redress the balance here.

In all trade models there are "domestic (i.e., non-traded) factor inputs" in the background and their supplies may well be variable, being subject to income propensities triggered off by transfers. And in most realistic models there do exist transport impediments which create a regime of purely-domestic commodities in each country. These too are subject to income propensities. Finally, although an increased consumption of a domestic or a reduced supply of an input triggered by receipt of a transfer could squeeze the production of *any* good traded internationally, there is perhaps a definite presumption that the competitive squeezing of supply will be greatest for the good which the receiving country is actually exporting — because in some sense it is for that country "relatively important"; and for the paying country, where resources are released by the reparation, the prime effects would seem to be on increasing the supply of the international goods which the payer exports. If this is so, the orthodox or anti-Ohlin presumption is upheld.

Note that no reliance is made here on constancy of marginal utilities or of costs or on the independence assumptions typical of partial equilibrium. The Bhagwati argument paraphrased in the last section could be applied to the general case of a concave production possibility frontier involving two or more traded goods, one or more domestic good in each country, and one or more labor or other input that has normal income effects. I should warn though that the orthodox presumption is not, so to speak, ironclad. This for the reason that we cannot always presume that an indirect income effect impinges relatively most on the good a country exports[16]. A beautiful counterexample is provided by a case involving classical factor-price-equalization. Let every person in both countries have identical tastes for wheat, cloth, and a domestic good bricks at every income level. (I.e., tastes are homothetic and income elasticities unitary.) Land and labor totals are frozen. Production functions are identical geographically. America, being land rich, exports wheat; England exports cloth. Specialization though is incomplete, all goods being produced in positive amounts in both countries. Obviously, the conditions for the factor-price equalization theorem are realized both before and after transfer.

Now America pays a transfer to England. What is the effect on the terms-of-trade of wheat and cloth? Surprisingly, we can assert that all price ratios will remain unchanged, in accordance with Ohlin's anti-orthodox view. To prove this realize that the world is, before and after the transfer, on its pro-duction-possibility frontier producing unchanged totals of the three goods. Totals are preserved because the income effects are so nicely balanced. Given three goods and two factors, there is an indeterminacy of where the total of bricks is to be produced geographically. Without disturbing the equilibrium goods-factor price ratios, if localized demand decrees that more of bricks is to be produced after the transfer in the receiving country and less in the paying country, that can take place. Hence, the only effect of the transfer is to cause the paying country to produce and consume less of its domestic good, and hence produce more of the traded goods; but with its consumption of those goods down, it is now financing the transfer by exporting more than before; in the receiving country, opposite effects take place. But note that this all meshes at unchanged price ratios. Q.E.D.

---

[16] In my 1954 paper, p.289, this point was already made in answer to a query from Professor Haberler.

PART X

Welfare Economics

164

Principles of Efficiency—Discussion

PAUL A. SAMUELSON: I agree with Koopmans' remark that Harberger builds an upper floor in a house that needs established foundation. But I defend him against the quaint view of Jorgenson that the (allegedly recent!) discovery of how we can treat corn in Chicago as a different good from corn in Denver or from corn in Chicago tomorrow represents a point against Harberger's theoretical system. If Harberger's $\Sigma\Delta P\Delta Q$ measures were theoretically valid at a point now, economists have long known they would be theoretically valid in a Fisher world involving future goods. (Of course, workshopmen would find it harder to stuff those "empty boxes.")

Simple consumer's surplus is known to be exact only in the empirically bizarre case of parallel indifference curves (where it happens to be superfluous). The ancient theory of its approximate validity remains a modern mess; but the generalized theory of revealed preference tells precisely what inferences about individual and group preferences can be derived from various (P,Q) observations. In the end, the economist can hope only to make certain statements about (1) whether an individual is ordinally better off in situation A than B, (2) whether a specified Bergson social welfare function is better there, or (3) whether certain feasible production-possibility and ordinal-utility-possibility frontiers have shifted outward locally or globally. Waiving technical flaws, I believe that the proposed dollar efficiency measurements are likely to end up merely telling us whether the Hicks-Kaldor criterion is satisfied. This much-debunked criterion, which favors the *status quo* and a Panglossian theory of property, is properly open to the Scitovsky objection (and my later generalization of it).

But even if that were overcome, the whole procedure may remain misleadingly pretentious. I am reminded of the case where a jury must determine which of two stones is heavier. The first stone can allegedly be weighed to a high degree of numerical accuracy (dollar efficiency measures). The second cannot in principle be so weighed (value-judgment decisions). What is the point in measuring the first stone if in the end we must put that exact weight in the balance with the second—particularly if, as is the true case, the two stones have no independent existence and weights? Harberger's valid defense would be to admit he is really trying to make estimates of possibility-frontier shifts. To answer, as he did to Vickrey, that since economists are no good at weighing the second stone they should concentrate on weighing the first is to fall prey to the pathetic fallacy that the universe was created to keep economists busy at something or other.

There is a technical flaw in using the device of holding the percentage distribution of money incomes constant (whatever that is supposed to mean in a world where people differ in their disutility attitudes towards work and risk). With people's tastes different, it is simply not true that the $f(D,G,T)$ functions represent well-behaved demand functions with the Slutsky symmetry properties that Harberger invokes and that preference theory needs. This flaw could be circumvented by using the device suggested in my 1955 *Q.J.E.* paper on "Social Indifference Curves." (Let ideal lump-sum redistributions of income take place in the background to ensure there is maximized a Bergson welfare function that requires all men's welfare to rise and fall together along some arbitrarily specified pattern. Of course, this would involve the same partial self-contradiction as does Harberger's case, which tried to tackle the problem of imperfect feasible taxation while assuming in the background that ideal lump-sum taxes were available to keep percentage income distribution constant.) If shares of linear product are kept constant, the S-H integrability conditions will be locally approximated for such an "undercompensated change."

This permits me to end on a constructive note with an exact theory of approximation (no contradiction). Consider an optimal laissez faire situation that maximizes a social welfare function with zero government expenditure and taxes. Now introduce government services as a (vector) function of a small or large parameter y, $G(y)$. Suppose excise taxes (on goods or services) to be alone feasible, and introduce a (vector) pattern of excises $T(y)$ sufficient to provide resources for the G. What is the optimal $T(y)$ pattern to maximize the welfare function $W(y) = W(T,G)$? This is the problem set by Pigou to Frank Ramsey in the 1920's. Approximate answers were given by Ramsey, Boiteux (and in unpublished form by Hotelling and Hicks). In a pearl cast before the U. S. Treasury in 1950, I gave an exact solution for large and small programs; namely, that the optimal pattern is the one at which the response of all goods and factors to a further compensated-Slutsky price distortion would result in equal percentage (virtual) reductions.

My literary wording is loose, but there is no need for approximative consumer's surplus at all. However, under the stated artificial conditions, some exact statements can be made about small programs (actually about derivatives not finite differences). Expand $W(y)$ in a Taylor's expansion involving a quadratic plus an exact remainder. If distribution had not been correct to begin with, all consumer surplus terms would be of the second order and negligible in comparison with redistributional effects. (Robin Hood knew that. Does Harberger's reader?) But with ethical optimality realized, the first-power term in y becomes independent of the tax pattern. The coefficient of the second power of y, aside from involving one-signed cardinal factors of utility, will be found to involve a factor that looks like a consumer's surplus triangle $\frac{1}{2}\Delta Q\Delta T$; namely, $\frac{1}{2}\Sigma[dT_i(O)/dy]\ [dQ_i(O)/dy]$. This measure of "deadweight loss," which is as exactly defined as Koopmans might want, can be minimized by choice of tax pattern $[dT_i(O)/dy]$ subject to the constraint that resources are raised for G. The exact Boiteux solution for this small tax case corrected Ramsey's neglect of income effects; and Harberger's consumer-surplus measures could legitimately arrive at this same result. (He has built well on the upper floor!)

Applying stochastic theory to the "pure theory of public goods," one can derive, by appropriate assumption, conclusions that disagree or agree with Professor Hirshleifer's tentative dictum that government should use the same high interest rates that industry does. The most plausible assumptions do not point his way. I agree with Vickrey that many risks are unavoidable to the private investor and corporation which simply do not exist for We, Inc. The 1923 German inflation wiped out every *rentier;* it left the real economy and taxing power virtually intact. A private investor faces depression risk in every venture. It would be a blessing if the government incurred dollar losses at such times. Only those huge decisions that bring on serious results to all citizens—atomic bomb treaties, and not regional dams—need strong discounting for risk dispersion. (The many projects our large government does may give Koopmans the near-normality needed if Markowitz (μ,σ) efficiency is to be valid necesssary condition. Quadratic utility is an empirically weak reed for the (μ,σ) theory to rest on. It is a fallacy to think that 2-parameter probability distributions removed from normality provide a valid defense. Even if we forget atomic bombs, and waive cases like the Cauchy distribution where variances are not finite, being on the Markowitz frontier need not be a necessary condition for utility maximization: an average of two independent variates may have lower expected utility than each separately—even when they each belong to well-behaved 2-parameter families and utility is regularly concave.)

One can look at much of government as primarily a device for mutual reinsurance. General Motors can borrow at a lower rate than American Motors because it is a pooler of more independent risks. It would be absurd for G.M. to apply the same high risk-interest-discount factor to a particular venture that A.M. must apply. The same holds for We, Inc., which is a better pooler of risks than even G.M. (If I thought that bureaucrats made rotten estimates of future benefits, I'd adjust their benefit estimates since it would be accidental in principle if I could achieve the optimal correction by stepping up the time-discount factor. An erratic branch manager of G.M. merits the same readjustment procedure; indeed, raising the interest rate on optimistic fools hampers them little, since they promise you pie in the sky tomorrow!)

If G.M. adds more and more risky investment, that should affect its credit standing. Thus, a risky project may raise the bond yield it must pay from 4.0 percent to 4.0001 percent. The "marginal cost" of the project is not the last low number, but rather that number plus the increase that has to be paid on all the "previous" borrowings. There is also the incremental risk on equity owners due to leverage. The G.M. president will take all such facts into account as will the U.S.A. President.

Obviously, stochastic elements make for bigness and "collectivism." Collectivism need not be governmental; it can also mean monopolies and mutual funds. Often, government is one of the "cheapest" ways of providing insurance against important risks. Why are there no mutual funds that enable me to invest in 15 percent risks (and that could enable society to bring down the cost of risky projects)? If such institutions were efficiently possible and existed, that could drive government out of some activities just as civilian job opportunities drive me out of the peacetime army! If Hirshleifer were right for America with a properly valued dollar, he would become wrong in a situation where there was no feasible way to revalue it. If he were right after a burst of capital-using inventions, he could become wrong in an era where deepening of capital brought down all yields of each degree of riskiness and (by Keynesian reasoning) called for greater collectivism, private and public. The problem is one of costs: What costs in freedom are involved in risk reduction by government? Value judgments and interests are involved. Since unanimity will never be possible, coercion in the sense of acquiescence by dissenters can never be absent; nor can its minimum quantity be defined independently of discordant value judgments.

165

A FALLACY IN THE INTERPRETATION OF PARETO'S LAW OF ALLEGED CONSTANCY OF INCOME DISTRIBUTION

by

PAUL A. SAMUELSON

Massachusetts Institute of Technology

Seventy years ago Pareto's Law was enunciated ([1]). In a vulgarized form it may be stated

> In all places and all times, the distribution of income remains the same. Neither institutional change nor égalitarian taxation can alter this fundamental constant of the social sciences.

Actually, what Pareto had noticed was that the cumulative frequency of persons with incomes above each stated level formed almost a straight line when plotted on double-log paper against the size of income. And the slope of this line tended to be remarkably similar for different places and times. The conservative conclusion he drew from this was turned upside-down by critics of capitalism, who argued that amelioration of inequality by the welfare state was not possible short of a thoroughgoing communist revolution.

Pareto's Law has gone through many cycles of popularity. Other measures of « inequality », such as the Lorenz curve and its implicit Gini concentration coefficient of standardized mean-absolute-difference-of-income have been used to show that the mixed economies of the modern world — such as Sweden, Greece, the U. K., U. S. and the Netherlands — have

---

[1] V. PARETO, *Cours d'économie politique* (1897). F. MACAULAY, *Pareto's Laws and the General Problem of Mathematically Describing the Frequency Distribution of Income,* in « Income in the United States, Its Amount and Distribution, 1909-1919 », Vol. II (New York : National Bureau of Economic Research, 1922), chap. xxiii.

less inequality than do underdeveloped nations such as Ceylon or the Western nations at earlier stages of their historical development. The apparent divergence between the evidence adduced from Pareto coefficients and from Lorenz-Gini coefficients has sometimes been attributed to the alleged fact that Pareto is merely describing the extreme tail of high incomes.

There is reason to think that so-called Pareto-Lévy distributions ([2]) are about to make a comeback in modern economics. Thanks primarily to the work of Dr. Benoit Mandelbrot of Paris, I.B.M., Harvard, and M.I.T., these fundamental distributions have been shown to characterize many economic processes : income distributions, speculative price changes, and so forth. Pareto-Lévy distributions keep appearing because they share with the familiar Normal Distribution of deMoivre-Laplace-Gauss the important problem of *stability* : If the sums of independent variates are to have the same distribution as each separately, they must belong to the « stable family of Pareto-Lévy »; and this means the limit laws that sums of many variables obey must also belong to this same family.

The members of the Pareto-Lévy stable family have « Pareto coefficients », usually written as α, which range from $\alpha = 2$ of the Normal Distribution to $\alpha = 1$ of the notorious Cauchy distribution (which has infinite moments of all order, including the mean), to $\alpha = \dfrac{1}{2}$ of the arc-sine distribution relevant to the limiting behavior of cumulative differences of heads versus tails in long sequences of coin tossing, down to the limiting value of $\alpha = 0$. Income and price data usually yield values of α nearer to 2 than 1 but definitely below the Gaussian 2.

Historically, there has been much confusion over whether a rise in the Pareto coefficient meant greater or less « inequality » of income. Even expert opinion has been divided on the question. And with good reason. For, *within the Pareto-Lévy family, the coefficient α is not really a measure of inequality in the usual sense of the word.* To illustrate this, I state the following trivial theorem.

---

(2) B. MANDELBROT, *The Pareto-Lévy Law and the Distribution of Income,* in « International Economic Review », I (1960), pp. 79-106; *New Methods in Statistical Economics,* « Journal of Political Economy », LXXI (1963), pp. 421-440; Paul LÉVY, *Calcul des probabilités* (1925), and *Théorie de l'addition des variables aléatoires* (1937, 1954). See M. KENDALL, *Advanced Theory of Statistics,* Vol. 1 (1943, 1958), Ch. 2, for discussion of Gini's coefficient and references there. See W. FELLER, *An Introduction to Probability Theory and its Applications* (John Wiley & Sons, 1957), Vol. 1, Second Edition, Chapter 3 for arc-sine law.

Theorem 1 : If every income recipient in a Pareto-Lévy distribution is moved half way (or λ-way, where $\lambda \lessgtr 1$) toward the mean income, the resulting Pareto coefficient α remains *exactly* the same as it was previously.

To prove this, I write the 4-parameter Pareto-Lévy family in the following form ([3]) :

$$\text{Prob.} \left\{ \text{Income} \leq x \right\} = F\left(\frac{x - \mu}{\lambda}; \beta, \alpha \right)$$

where x is income; μ is an origin constant of « central tendency »; λ is a scale constant of « dispersion around the measure of central tendency »; β is a measure of skewness, equal to zero if there is left-right symmetry around the median; and Pareto's α is a measure of « kurtosis » or degree to which large *and* small deviants from the median (or mean when $\alpha > 1$) are numerous relative to inbetween deviants. After the égalitarian change, the same F, but with $\lambda/2$ replacing λ, will describe the data. Note that α stays constant.

Pareto, along with his disciples and opponents, in effect confused α and λ. From the alleged stability of α, they wrongly inferred the invariance of average dispersion of incomes. They did not realize that successful égalitarian taxation, which halved the dispersion parameter λ and changed nothing else, would truly halve the Lorenz-Gini coefficient of inequality but leave the α Pareto coefficient unaltered. Indeed, if the median income and skewness are left unchanged, the only change that can leave α unchanged is such a balanced égalitarian (or reverse) change in λ. (See Figures 1-3).

Thus, there would be no conflict between the testimony of Lorenz curves that generally show mixed capitalism to be developing less inequality and the testimony of relatively invariant Pareto coefficients.

Policy Implications

Of course, it may be asked whether a so-called égalitarian program that leaves Pareto's α unchanged has really, for good or evil, accomplished anything. And the definite answer can be given in the form of the following theorem.

---

(3) Except for the three mentioned cases, where $\alpha = \frac{1}{2}$, 1, 2, these functions have not yet been tabulated explicitly. Usually mathematicians work with their characteristic function, whose form is well known.

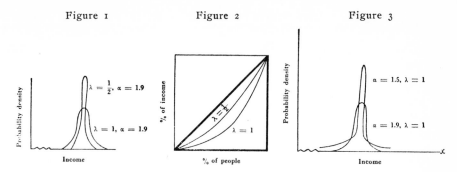

Figure 1   Figure 2   Figure 3

Figure 1 depicts a reduction in dispersion around the mean with no change in Pareto's coefficient. The Lorenz curve of concentration in Figure 2 correctly shows a move toward equality. Figure 3 shows a genuine change in Pareto's α, which does not affect total dispersion but rather increases frequency of very small *and* very large deviations relative to middling deviations (i.e. low α means « fat tails » and « peaked middle », with compensating « hollow inbetween »).

Theorem 2. If social welfare is deemed in Bentham fashion to be a symmetric sum of the (strictly-concave à la Gossen or Bernoulli) cardinal utilities of different individuals, then a successful lowering of λ will always increase social welfare, even though Pareto's α stays constant in the range between 1 and 2. (If diminishing marginal utility is replaced by a postulate of increasing marginal utility, the theorem holds true in reverse).

The proof of Theorem 2, which is a bit more complicated than that for Theorem 1, follows from its mathematical statement as

For $\alpha > 1, \displaystyle\int_{-\infty}^{\infty} t \, d P \, (t; \beta, \alpha) = 0$, and $U''(x) < 0$,

$$W(\lambda) = \int_{-\infty}^{\infty} U(x) \, d P\left(\frac{x - \mu}{\lambda}; \beta, \alpha\right)$$

$$= \int_{-\infty}^{\infty} U(\lambda t + \mu) \, d P(t; \beta, \alpha)$$

$$W'(\lambda) = \int_{-\infty}^{\infty} U'(\lambda t + \mu) \, t \, d P(t; \beta, \alpha), \text{ with exact Taylor's expansion}$$

$$= U'(\mu)\int_{-\infty}^{\infty} t \, d P(t; \beta, \alpha) + \int_{-\infty}^{\infty} U''(\Theta\lambda t + \mu) t^2 \, d P(t; \beta, \alpha),$$
$$0 < \Theta < 1$$

$= O +$ negative number   Q. E. D.

A final disclaimer is in order. The error described here is so obvious because I have slightly overstated the case. Pareto wrote before Paul Lévy did his brilliant work in the mid-1920's on « infinitely-divisible » distribution functions. So, strictly speaking, Pareto and his original commentators worked only with the truncated tail of the income distribution and not with the full Pareto-Lévy distribution ([4]). This left enough ambiguity in the problem and its relevant definitions to make it possible for scholars to remain confused.

Summary

Pareto's coefficient has been shown to be a measure not of inequality around the mean income, but rather of the degree of « peakedness » (or kurtosis) or of « frequency of both large and small deviations from the middle in comparison with deviation of inbetween size from the middle ». An alleged constancy of this coefficient — I write alleged because careful research shows that Pareto and his disciples overdid their claims for its empirical invariance — tells us nothing about the ability of society to alter its inequality of wealth or income, and merely reflects the overlooked fact that Pareto's coefficient is an insensitive measure of true changes in inequality.

([4]) Thus, for the full Pareto-Lévy distribution, $\alpha \leq 2$. But the asymptotic absolute slope on double-log paper of the tail of a distribution, which is Pareto's coefficient in the original sense, can certainly exceed 2. In one sense, the modern Pareto-Lévy formulation represents a retreat from reality : negative income may make no economic sense in many realistic contexts, but the Pareto-Lévy distribution will give them some small finite weight. When we calculate expected values of U over the $(-\infty, \infty)$ range, this can give rise to awkward problems and even to divergent integrals. Incidentally, if we write $W(\lambda, \beta, \alpha)$, it is not clear that $\delta W / \delta \alpha$ is of any definite sign : this means that it depends on higher derivatives of $U(x)$ whether increasing the relative frequency of large and small deviants from the mean $| \alpha - \mu |$ will contribute to Benthamist social utility or subtract from it. Even $\delta W / \delta \beta$ at $\beta = 0$ is ambiguous in sign : « skewness » sounds like a bad thing and symmetry a good thing; but is this really always so?

166

FOREWORD

If somebody asks me what modern welfare economics is about, I always recommend to them Graaff's *Theoretical Welfare Economics*. Less than 200 pages in length, the book has become a classic in our own time. And one test of its classical stature is the fact that one sees often, in contemporary books and journals, rediscoveries of results already contained in the book.

The welfare economics treated here is the culmination of a great tradition. By 1930 the ethical hedonism of Bentham, Sidgwick, Edgeworth, and Marshall had come under heavy attack by Gunnar Myrdal and Lionel (now Lord) Robbins as involving a-scientific interpersonal comparison of utility. Professor Abram Bergson of Harvard, while still a young graduate student, founded in a too-little known article in the 1938 *Quarterly Journal of Economics*, the modern theory of welfare economics. Introducing from outside of positive economics a social welfare function appropriate to a given set of ethical norms, Bergson was able to show what its maximization implied for observable economic variables. Bergson was thus able to avoid (or, alternatively, to include) the hedonistic summation of cardinal utilities, and at the same time to value at their true (limited) worth the Pareto-optimality necessary conditions that are themselves expressible independently of a social welfare function. So to speak, this put the narrow 'new welfare economics' of Pareto, Hotelling, A. P. Lerner, Kaldor, and Hicks in its proper place. The late Oskar Lange, of Poland and Chicago, I, and Graaff developed the Bergson foundations.

When I say that this kind of welfare economics has today swept the field, I wish to make clear that it is not true, as many used to believe, that Professor Kenneth Arrow of Stanford has proved 'the impossibility of a social welfare function'. What Arrow has proved in his pathbreaking 1951, *Social Choice and Individual Values*, is the impossibility of what I prefer to call 'a political constitution function', which would be able to resolve *any* interpersonal differences brought to it while at the same time satisfying certain reasonable and desirable axioms. This Arrow result is a basic theorem of what might be called ' mathematical politics ' and throws new light on age-old conundrums of democracy. But it does not detract, I believe, from the Bergson formulations nor from the lasting value of the present work.

PAUL A. SAMUELSON
Institute Professor
Massachusetts Institute of Technology

May 1967

167

Arrow's Mathematical Politics

PAUL SAMUELSON

Massachusetts Institute of Technology

I. INTRODUCTION

PROFESSOR ARROW'S PAPER is essentially a summarizing description of the fundamental work he has done in connection with Welfare Economics. I am not able to judge how easy or difficult it is for a noneconomist—say, a philosopher—to apprehend the nuances of such a description. But I very much hope that philosophers, sociologists, and political scientists will become familiar with Arrow's analysis.

I say this because I believe that Kenneth Arrow has made a first-rate contribution to man's body of knowledge. In the middle of the twentieth century there are not to be found many new milestones in the history of ideas. *The Theory of Games* by Von Neumann does represent an imperishable advance upon a problem that intelligent men have brooded over since the beginning of intelligence. The analysis of personal, subjective probability, in its relationship to decision-making, is another intellectual breakthrough that should bring lasting fame to Ramsey, Savage, and Marschak. If the Muse of history has its wits about it and succeeds in doing justice—two hypotheses of a somewhat romantic nature—I believe that Kenneth Arrow's name will be long remembered for a new and important insight into the permanent problem of the nature of democracy.

My sense of justice requires me to bestow this high praise. In addition I must admit that my vanity as an economist is gratified that one of the soldiers in our regiment should have made a contribution of universal interest. Indeed, I shall argue again here the thesis that the Arrow result is much more a contribution to the infant discipline of mathematical politics than to the traditional mathematical theory of welfare economics. I export Arrow from economics to politics because I do not believe that he has proved the impossibility of the traditional Bergson welfare function of economics, even though many of his less expert readers seem inevitably drawn into thinking so.

II. A WELL-BEHAVED (INDIVIDUAL) ORDERING

Some re–exposition will, I think, be helpful. Consider three alternative states of the world: A or B or C. Suppose that you, Man i, have an ordering of them: you like A better than B or C, you like B better than C. Write this ordering as $(A, B, C)^1$. This is a shorthand description of several choices that you would make, namely: (A over B); (A over C); (B over C). Alternatively, suppose that some of the states of the world were "tied" for your affections: A indifferent to B; either better than C. Deliberately omitting commas in order to show indifference, write this as $(AB,C)^1$. The meaning of $(ABC)^1$ will now be clear, where of course the order of the letters *between* commas is immaterial.

How many different complete orderings could you have? Omitting your identifying superscript for brevity, we can list only thirteen alternative patterns that your tastes or values might take:

(A,B,C); (A,C,B); (B,A,C); (B,C,A); (C,A,B); (C,B,A); (AB,C); (AC,B); (A,BC); (BC,A); (B,AC); (C,AB); (ABC).

Although this may seem a great variety of possibilities, it is actually less than half the number of patterns that would be possible if we did not insist that all orderings be *transitive*. To see this, list a matrix of all possible pairs:

$$
\begin{array}{c}
\quad\quad\;\; \mathbf{A} \quad\;\; \mathbf{B} \quad\;\; \mathbf{C} \\
\begin{array}{c} \mathbf{A} \\[20pt] \mathbf{B} \\[30pt] \mathbf{C} \end{array}
\left[
\begin{array}{ccc}
\cdot & \cdot & \cdot \\
\begin{array}{c} +1 \\ 0 \\ -1 \end{array} & \cdot & \cdot \\
\begin{array}{c} +1 \\ 0 \\ -1 \end{array} & \begin{array}{c} +1 \\ 0 \\ -1 \end{array} & \cdot
\end{array}
\right]
\end{array}
= [a_{AB}, \ldots]
$$

Only the cells below the diagonal line need be considered. If B is preferred to A, select in the first cell $+1$; if they are indifferent, select 0; if A is preferred to B, select -1. In each of these 3 cells, there are 3 independent possibilities. Hence, in all there are $3^3 = 27$ different binary matrices possible. But only 13 of them are consistent with the transitivity requirement: if A is at least as good as B, and B is at least as good as C, then it must already be predictable that A is at least as good as C. Thus, of the following matrices, only the first is admissible in a "well-behaved" (transitive) ordering:

$$
\begin{bmatrix} \cdot & \cdot & \cdot \\ -1 & \cdot & \cdot \\ -1 & -1 & \cdot \end{bmatrix} ;\quad
\begin{bmatrix} \cdot & \cdot & \cdot \\ -1 & \cdot & \cdot \\ 0 & -1 & \cdot \end{bmatrix} ;\quad
\begin{bmatrix} \cdot & \cdot & \cdot \\ -1 & \cdot & \cdot \\ +1 & 0 & \cdot \end{bmatrix} ;\quad
\begin{bmatrix} \cdot & \cdot & \cdot \\ 0 & \cdot & \cdot \\ +1 & 0 & \cdot \end{bmatrix}
$$

If we go from 3 to 4 states of the world, the admissible orderings will be evident. E.g., (A,B,C,D); ... (D,C,B,A); (AB,C,D); ... ; (ABCD). There will be much less than the $3^6 = 729$ matrix possibilities; and generally for N states of the world, only a small subset of the $3^{N(N-1)/2}$ possible matrices will correspond to a well-behaved transitive ordering.

One final observation. If the ordering is transitive, it *automatically* satisfies the condition called "independence of irrelevant alternatives." Thus, omitting C from any of the 13 patterns for A or B or C, leaves us with the *same* $+1$, 0, or -1 matrix element in the cell for B's row and A/s colu-n as we had when C was included. Likewise for leaving out any other one of the 3 states. Likewise for leaving out any N—2 of N states of the world.

Now consider the case of 3 different men. Each can have 13 possible orderings for A and B and C. There are thus $13 \times 13 \times 13 = 2,197$ possible situations that could confront us for ajudication. Given R persons, there are 13^R different contingencies that could arise. Clearly for many persons and many alternative states the total number of possibilities that could arise is vast in number (but computable as a finite integer).

Professor Brandt is within his rights in questioning whether what has here been called a well-behaved ordering should be dignified with the name "a rational preference-ordering." There is no need to do so. And if he wishes to discern "intrinsic values," let him. Furthermore, suppose I always choose to forego fish on Friday even though I love fish, in order to live up to some code of obligation; or suppose I would always enter a burning house to rescue my baby even at the cost of my own life; or would sacrifice future pleasures of living in order to fall on a bomb that threatens my companions-at-arms. So long as my acts fit in with a well-behaved ordering, there is no particular need to take note of the distinctions that Brandt may himself want to take note of. By all means, let him consider what we ignore.

III. A WELL-BEHAVED SOCIAL ORDERING

Now I shall consider a (Bergson) Social Welfare Function, contrasting it with a (Arrow) Constitutional Function. Conventionally, either of these somehow defines, in addition to the 3 persons' individual ordering, a new fourth ordering. [Or, if there are R persons, there is an $(R+1)$th "social" ordering to be considered.] Note that it, *if it is well-behaved*, can take on only 1 of our 13 possibilities.

Now it is a "natural" requirement in a culture obsessed by "individualism" to require that the social ordering be somehow defined in terms of the specified individual's orderings. E.g., if we are given $[(A,B,C)^1; (A,B,C)^2; (A,B,C)^3]$, representing unanimous agreement of all individuals, the social ordering might be required to be $(A,B,C)^0$, where the "o" superscript refers to the social ordering. Where unanimity is lacking—as in the case $(A,B,C)^1$, $(C,B,A)^2$, $(ABC)^3$—it is not so easy to find the "natural" corresponding social ordering. But from the artificial symmetry of the example, perhaps $(ABC)^0$ might be the tempting choice as the corresponding social ordering.

What needs stressing is that Arrow, and Bergson for that matter, specify that only the *order* relations of individuals determine the social ordering.

Suppose we learn that, although Man 1 "slightly" prefers A to B and B to C, and Man 3 is quite indifferent among all three, Man 2 "strongly" prefers C to B and B to A. Many ethical observers might in this case be willing to have $(ABC)^0$ be replaced by $(C,B,A)^0$.

But this appeal to cardinality—to quantitative intensity of preference that underlies the qualitative ordering—is not consistent with Arrow's first and basic Axiom. A number of people, confronted with Arrow's Impossibility Theorem and their natural feeling that cardinal intensity of preference ought to count (at least to break "ties"), have contemplated replacing mere ordinality by a cardinality formulation, thereby rejecting Arrow's very first Axiom.

Thus, Brandt refers to utilitarianism or hedonism and to "intensity of joy, etc." Even Arrow, in his final section, seems to be ready to explore use of cardinality, if some interpersonal comparisons can somehow be made. Professor A. K. Sen, of the Delhi School of Economics, at the 1966 Biarritz Meeting of the International Economic Association, has raised the question whether an escape from the Impossibility Theorem may be found through cardinalism. As I remarked at Biarritz, I think that cardinality will not so much provide an escape from the Impossibility Theorem as a plunge into a new Impossibility Theorem of cardinal type.

IV. ARROW'S CONSTITUTIONAL FUNCTION

What Arrow seeks is a way of going from *any* possible pattern of well-behaved individuals' orderings—all 2,197 of them when N=3 and 3 persons are involved—to a well-behaved social ordering. A Constitution Function is a way of mapping *any one* of the 2,179 points in individuals' space into 1 (and 1 only) of the 13 points of the social space.

What "reasonable" restrictions on the Constitution Function are we tempted to stipulate? Arrow lists them in 4 Axioms. I present the same content in 3 Axioms.

Axiom 1. The well-behaved social ordering matrix $[a_{AB}, \ldots]^0$ is to be, element for element, a unique function of the *corresponding* elements of the individuals' $[a_{AB}, \ldots]^1$, $[a_{AB}, \ldots]^2$, . . . matrices *for each and all admissible patterns of those matrices.*

This merely restates the definition of an individualistic well-behaved cardinality-free social ordering. But note that my Axiom 1 *already* implies the full content of Arrow's Axiom on Independence of Irrelevant Alternatives. This is because each binary cell, such as a_{AB}^0, depends only on the corresponding cells a_{AB}^1, a_{AB}^2, . . . and not at all on other cells such as a_{BC}^1, plus the stipulation that the resulting social $[a_{AB}, \ldots]^0$ matrix belong to the class of 13 *"well-behaved"* "transitive" matrices.

Already Axiom 1 makes almost impossible the task of finding a well-behaved Constitution Function. If you try most rules of mapping the 2,179 points on to the 13, you will find the result is *not* a transitive ordering. However, there are some trivial exceptions. Try the rule: "Disregard all choices but Man 1's, and use his ordering." That will certainly meet the test of Axiom 1. But that is Dictatorship, and neither appealing nor logically nontrivial. Hence, the following is stipulated:

Axiom 2. (Non-Dictatorship) The Social Constitution is not to be dictatorial, merely reflecting one chosen man's ordering.

Does this rule out all remaining Constitution Functions? Not quite. Suppose we make the social ordering $[a_{AB}, \ldots]^0$ reflect no individuals' choices, being imposed by some outsider's ordering. That gives us 13 admissible Constitutions. But such an imposed matrix is hardly compatible with the individualistic notion that people's tastes and values are to be respected provided they don't interfere with other people's. Hence, the final requirement.

Axiom 3 (Non-imposition and Pareto-optimality or unanimity). Any a_{AB}^0 element is to be a non-decreasing function of each and every corresponding individual a_{AB}^1 element, so that if *all* men prefer A to B, so will the social ordering.

This says that if A moves from being worse than B to being as good or better for some people, while staying as before for the rest of the people, then the social ordering must *not* now demote A and make it worse in comparison with B than it was before.

All three Axioms seem reasonable. Arrow's great feat was to prove that no Constitution Function can satisfy them all.[1] The problems that have vaguely plagued us in connection with democracy—voting paradoxes, etc.—are apparently permanent ones. Which Axiom should we reject? It is like asking which triplet one should put up for adoption.

Many people think that the Independence of Irrelevant Alternatives is the one that must go. I cannot agree. My formulation builds it *from the beginning* into Axiom 1. Give up Axiom 1—a well-behaved ordering with transitivity—and the whole problem vanishes into thin air. It is not solved; it is evaded. In a moment I shall comment on the suggestion that cardinal intensities of preference be brought in, to make the impossible possible; little comfort will, I fear, be found from this approach. A third avenue of escape from the Impossibility Theorem is to retreat to the Possible, by narrowing down the domain of possible individuals' preferences from the full 2,197 possibilities to some more limited set.

V. THE BERGSON SOCIAL WELFARE FUNCTION

The Social Welfare Function of conventional economics, although named and analyzed by A. Bergson in the classic 1938 article cited by Arrow, was used in special form by writers since the time of Jeremy Bentham and before. I deem it a misfortune that Arrow chose to call what I have here dubbed a Constitution Function by the same name as Bergson's Social Welfare Function. In consequence, many readers can be forgiven for thinking that Arrow has proved the impossibility of a Bergson Social Welfare Function, thereby dealing a death blow to the magnificent edifice of modern welfare economics.

Orally and in writing, many authors (including me and I. M. D. Little) have criticized this usage of Arrow's as unfortunate and confusing. In his 1963 new chapter (pp. 104–105) Arrow stands his ground, asserting in effect that if Bergson did not have in mind the same concept, he should have. After rereading a dozen times the 1963 words, I fail to find in them arguments that I can accept.

Now it is fruitless to argue about word usage. (How do we know Uranus is "really" Uranus? Should America be called a Republic or a Democracy? Etc.) But it is important to be able to recognize when different things are indeed different. My previous exposition of the relation between a well-behaved social ordering $[a_{AB}, \ldots]^0$ and individuals' orderings $[a_{AB}, \ldots]^1$, $[a_{AB}, \ldots]^2$, $\ldots$ is well designed to bring out the difference between a Bergson Social Welfare Function and an Arrow Constitutional Function (or so-called "social welfare function").

For Bergson, one and only one of the 2,197 possible patterns of individuals' orderings is needed. It could be *any* one, but it is *only* one. From *it* (not from each of them all) comes a social ordering. Thus, a Bergson ethical observer need only know how to map 1 particular of the 2,197 points in individuals' space into 1 of the 13 points in social space. The only Axiom restricting a Bergson Social Welfare Function (of individualistic type) is a "tree" property of Pareto-optimality type.

Axiom A. The social ordering over the states of the world, $[a_{AB}, \ldots]^0$ must put A over B, i.e., $a_{AB}^0 = -1$, if every individual ordering does so, $a^1_{AB} = -1$ for all i; more generally, if no $a^1_{AB} = +1$, $a^0_{AB} \leqq 0$, the strong inequality being required if, with no $a^1_{AB} = +1$, $\Sigma_i a^1_{AB} < 0$.

This looks like the conjunction of Arrow's Axioms 1 and 3. But it is not. Thus, the point out of the 2,197 possibilities specified for the Bergson problem will—in all likelihood—not be subjected to any restriction by this Pareto Axiom A. Example: let the specified point be $[(A,B,C)^1; (B,C,A)^2; (C,A,B)^3]$. No state can be excluded by the Pareto-optimality principle of optimality. Any of the 13 outcomes are possible for $(\quad)^0$. Where Pareto-optimality acquires content in Bergsonian welfare economics is in cases, hardly mentioned in Arrow's paper for this conference, where each individual's tastes depend on variables of consumption that are all *his* alone, without altruism or envy being involved. In such cases, two different states—say C and D—are indifferent to all but Man 1, and his choice among them becomes decisive for the social ordering. Example: Consider $[A,B,C,D]^1$, $[B,CD,A]^2$, $[CD,A,B]^3$. Whatever else is decided, Axiom A tells us that $a_{CD}^0 = -1$ and socially C is preferred to D—because Man 1 ranks them that way and *all* other men are indifferent.

It is the "decomposability," or "tree," or (to use Arrow's happy phrase) "factorability" property of individualistic consumption that makes possible efficient use of a market-price system. The miracle is not that a pricing system works, but that the strong conditions for it to work are approximately present in nature. It was for this reason that I, in the discussion of Milton Friedman's discussion of Kenneth Boulding's paper, referred to Friedman's analogy between free pricing and free speech as poetry not prose. Not merely is such poetry not good poetry; not merely is it not persuasive; worst of all is the fact that such analogy denigrates, to the knowing ear, the genuine beauty and efficiency of market pricing in those situations where special "decomposability" properties are present.

VI. THE IMPOSSIBILITY OF CARDINALITY

Since space is short, let me jot down my conjecture that a full-fledged formulation of the Constitutional Function in terms of cardinal intensity will lead again to an Impossibility Theorem.

Replace the 13 patterns of A or B or C by all possible triplets of numbers (U_A, U_B, U_C) where

$$(A,B) \leftrightarrow U_A > U_B$$
$$(AB) \leftrightarrow U_A = U_B$$

The origin and scaling of the U numbers is unimportant, so long as the ratio $(U_A-U_B)/(U_B-U_C)$ is kept invariant. This will be the case only if we confine ourselves to linear transformations of the U's. For simplicity, assume that these $(U_A-U_B)/(U_B-U_C)$ intensity-differences are definable operationally by stochastic betting experiments: thus, $U_A-U_B = U_B-U_C$ if B with certainty is deemed indifferent to an even chance of A or C.

Now we can always add a fourth or Nth state to the sequence and find its new U number. Also, we can drop as many states as we like.

Let each man's cardinal ordering be identified by his triplet of numbers $(U_A, U_B, U_C)^1$. The problem now is to define a social cardinal ordering $(U_A, U_B, U_C)^0$, whose intensity-difference ratio $(U_A{}^0 - U_B{}^0)/(U_B{}^0 - U_0{}^0)$ is determinate as a function of the point in 3×3, or generally $N \times R$, dimensional space of the individuals' U's.

Let us place 3 or 4 reasonable Axioms on the functional relations

$$U_A{}^0 = f_A(U_A{}^1, \ldots)$$
$$U_B{}^0 = f_B(U_A{}^1, \ldots)$$

Thus $(f_A - f_B)/(f_B - f_C)$ must be a determinant function. It must not be dictatorial or imposed. It must have the Pareto-optimality property, etc.

Do there exist any $(f_A, f_B, \ldots)$ functions satisfying these restrictions? My conjecture is, No. An Impossibility Theorem can be proved for such cardinal cases just as in the ordinality case.

NOTES

1. See K. Arrow, *Social Choice and Individual Values* (New York: Wiley, 1951 and 1963), pp. 75–77, 80 for discussion of Duncan Black's case of "single-peaked" preferences. A trivial case would be where we consider only cases where "all (wise!) men think alike" and $[a_{AB}, \ldots]^i \equiv [a_{AB}, \ldots]^j$ for all i and j. Then an Arrow function is possible and Axiom 3 tells us it is $[a_{AB}, \ldots]^0 = [a_{AB}, \ldots]^1$.

168

CONTRAST BETWEEN WELFARE CONDITIONS FOR JOINT SUPPLY AND FOR PUBLIC GOODS

Paul A. Samuelson *

1. THE theory of public goods [1] is sometimes confused with the theory of joint production. This is in the nature of a pun, or a play on words: for, as I have insisted elsewhere, as we increase the number of persons on both sides of the market in the case of mutton and wool, we converge in the usual fashion to the conditions of perfect competition. But when we increase the number of persons in the case of a typical public good, we make the problem *more indeterminate* rather than less.

To elucidate the difference, I shall fill in what appears to be a minor gap in the literature, namely a needed statement in terms of modern welfare economics of the various optimality conditions as they appear in the case of joint products. The analysis is straightforward; and after it is before us, we can clearly see the difference between it and the well-known optimality conditions for the case of public goods.

2. I begin with an examination question given recently at the Massachusetts Institute of Technology:

"Corn is produced by land and labor; and so are wool-bearing mutton-bearing sheep. Assume the totals of available land and labor to be fixed. Write down the various welfare optimality conditions in the case where all people happen always to consume wool and mutton in the same proportions that sheep bear these products. And then, by contrast, write down the conditions that would have to prevail if

* Aid from the National Science Foundation is gratefully acknowledged.

[1] My *Review of Economics and Statistics* papers on this subject of 1954, 1955, 1958 are reproduced in P. A. Samuelson, *Collected Scientific Papers* (Cambridge, Mass.: M.I.T. Press, 1966, J. E. Stiglitz, editor), vol. II, chapters 92, 93, 94. See also R. A. Musgrave, *The Theory of Public Finance* (New York: McGraw-Hill, 1959); L. Johansen, *Public Economics* (Chicago: Rand McNally, 1965); J. M. Buchanan, *Public Finance in Democratic Process* (Chapel Hill: University of North Carolina Press, 1967, pp. 221–222), where the typical joint-supply interpretation is given in the form, "With public or collective goods; jointness in supply is the essential characteristic." I make reference later to my as yet unpublished 1966 Biarritz paper at the International Economic Association conference on public expenditure.

individuals' indifference contours for wool, mutton, and corn involve the usual variability of proportions."

This proved a difficult question for first-year graduate students in economic theory. Still many perceived that in the first case they could essentially work with two rather than three goods, substituting sheep as a kind of composite good for wool and mutton, and thereby ending up with the standard welfare conditions for two ordinary (private) goods, corn and sheep.

Literary Discussion

3. An adequate answer for this first part might go as follows:

"I assume in the first part that we can replace mutton and wool by sheep and consider a two-good problem in which many men choose between corn and sheep, in the presence of an ethical observer who prescribes a social welfare function that ordinally relates interpersonal deservingnesses.

"Condition 1. *Production-optimality*. To be on society's 'efficient' production-possibility frontier, Lerner's Rule must hold: the ratio between labor's marginal productivity in corn to its marginal productivity in sheep must equal the ratio of land's marginal productivity in corn to its marginal productivity in sheep, the common ratio being the marginal rate of substitution of sheep for corn (or marginal opportunity cost) along the production-possibility frontier. (This gives us the 'most goods' for the 'least bads.')

"Condition 2. *Interpersonal consumption 'efficiency'*. As with ordinary private goods, there must be a common *subjective* marginal rate of substitution for all men between sheep and corn, this common ratio equalling the earlier-mentioned sheep-to-corn *technical* marginal rate of substitution.

"Condition 3. *Interpersonal Deservingness*. Finally, in order that the social welfare function be at a maximum, the previous Pareto-optimality necessary conditions must have adjoined to them the requirement that the marginal social significance of any one good (corn alone will suffice) must be equal for all men. (*All* of the above conditions could be deduced from the formulation that every resource must be allocated to make its marginal social contribution equal in every use.)"

4. Now for the second, harder half of the question.

"If mutton and wool are not necessarily consumed in the same fixed proportions that they are produced by each sheep, we can still leave conditions 1 and 3 intact. But condition 2 now becomes more complicated and has to be reworded as follows:

"*Condition 2'. Interpersonal Efficiency Conditions*. Between any pair of the *three* goods, mutton, wool, and corn, we must have for all men a common marginal rate of *subjective* substitution. But now for each and every man the *sum* of his mutton-to-corn MRS and his wool-to-corn MRS must — when we use units of the by-products so that 1 sheep produces 1 of mutton and 1 of corn — equal the sheep-to-corn *technical* MRS of Condition 1."

Such an answer cannot be faulted, although of course in limited examination time it does not go into such complications as "total" conditions or "sufficient" as well as "necessary" conditions.

5. For the purpose of distinguishing between public goods and jointly-supplied goods, let us now ask:

Second quiz question: "If instead of private goods, corn and sheep, we specify a private good, corn, and a public good, hours of free television time, how will the optimality conditions be modified?"

An adequate answer might go as follows:

"Assuming both new goods are made with labor and land, the previous Conditions 1 and 3 need no modification. But the previous Condition 2 must now be modified to read:

"*Condition 2". Interpersonal Efficiency Conditions*. The (vertical) sum of the subjective MRS between the public and private good must be totaled and set equal to the technological MRS of the public-to-private good as determined in Condition 1." [2]

[2] See P. Samuelson, "The Pure Theory of Public Expenditure," this REVIEW, XXXVI, pp. 387–389 (reprinted

Now if one rereads Conditions 2' and 2", their difference will be apparent. They have an entirely different meaning.

Geometric Discussion

6. While a literary answer is adequate, it does inevitably involve some measure of brevity and omission of explicit theorizing; so let us consider a graphical answer to the alternative questions of joint supply and public goods.

Unless some simplifying assumptions are made, no manageable diagrammatic answer is possible. Hence, the candidate might write:

"To make simple diagrams possible, I simplify and assume that each man acts as if corn has to him *strictly constant* marginal utility. Mutton and wool are in the second half of the problem assumed to be each subject to diminishing marginal utility that is unaffected by changes in any of the other two goods; but in the first half of the question I can assume that mutton and wool are consumed in fixed proportions, constituting a composite commodity that I can call sheep; and sheep involve to each man diminishing marginal utility that is independent of corn. To make partial-equilibrium concepts of cost simple and chartable, let me assume that corn and sheep are of the same labor-land factor intensities, so that the optimality conditions 1 yield a constant-cost production-possibility line whose technical (or marginal) cost is C_2 units of corn per sheep.

"To prepare for graphs in the public-good case, I make the similar simplifying assumption that the constant cost of the public good in terms of the private good is C_2 corn units per hour of television. And television to each man is subject to diminishing marginal utility that is independent of corn, the only other good in this base; corn still is assumed subject to constant marginal utility as in all the cases.

"*Case of Simple Private Goods*. Figure 1 now shows the standard equilibrium for two simple private goods, corn and sheep. Note that all of the different men's demand curves are added *horizontally*, and the total demand, *dd*, intersects the constant cost supply, *ss*, to

as chapter 92 of *Collected Scientific Papers*, volume II [Massachusetts Institute of Technology Press, 1966] pp. 1223–1225]. The set of equations (1), (2), and (3) there corresponds to the present set of Conditions 1, 2", and 3.

determine the final sheep equilibrium at E. After we have E, we go back to show individual's equilibrium at E^1, E^2, . . . (All the ethical allocations of income among persons is done in the background in terms of corn, but this process creates no income-effect shifts on our curves because of the assumed constancy

FIGURE 1. — STANDARD GOODS (HORIZONTALLY-SUMMED DEMANDS)

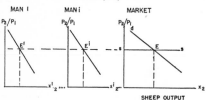

of marginal utility of corn. No price breakdown of the sheep price among its wool and mutton components is needed here because their joint demand just matches their joint supply, by hypothesis.)

"Case of Jointly-supplied Goods. Figure 2 plots the separate demand curves for wool and mutton for each man. Again we sum *horizontally* for each good to get total market demands for wool and mutton. After we have them, these

FIGURE 2. — JOINT PRODUCTS (BOTH HORIZONTAL AND VERTICAL SUMMING OF DEMANDS)

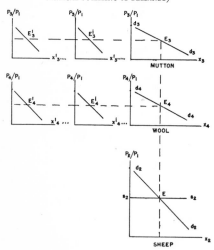

total demands for the wool and mutton markets, we sum such market curves *vertically* to get total sheep demand, ending up at final equilibrium E. (Again, equity is achieved in the background through reallocations of corn alone. Again, the positivistic equilibrium has been brought about by the same invisible hand that ensures Pareto-optimality along with the full Bergson optimality that is achieved by lump-sum transfers in the background.)

Although a little cryptic, this completes the graphical answer to both parts of our original question. The two E equilibria correctly depict realization of our literary Conditions 2 and 2′.

7. Let us now go on to contemplate the graphical answer to the public good question.

"Case of Private and Public Good. Figure 3 shows the separate marginal utility (or

FIGURE 3. — PUBLIC GOOD CASE (VERTICAL SUMMATION OVER ALL PEOPLE)

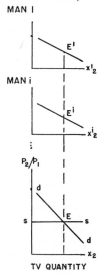

"pseudo-demand")[3] curves for the public good for each man, but now they are *vertically* aligned. Now we have to add their demand curves *vertically* to get total demand. (Note

[3] In my 1966 Biarritz paper on public goods, still to be published by the International Economic Association, I presented graphs like these and explained that they are pseudo-price-tax relations in the sense that no individual would ever be motivated to reveal and act along them.

that we now add over *people* and not over *products* as in figure 2's vertical addition!) Final equilibrium is shown at E. (Again, because of our simplifying assumptions, all interpersonal equity redistributions of income are done in the background in terms of corn and are ignorable here.)"

8. There remains the simple task of pointing out the logical difference between figures 2 and 3. Just because a process of vertical addition is involved in both cases does not make them logically the same. To bring this home, let us compound the problem by having a public good that itself involves joint products: instead of television consider the Tennessee Valley Authority (TVA) with its national-security and flood-control public benefits. (I ignore its power production because that power can be allocated like private goods and, except for its decreasing-cost aspects, adds nothing new to the problem.) The welfare equilibrium conditions can now be indicated, but I shall leave it to the reader to draw in the indicated figure 4.

"*Case of Private Good and Joint-supply Public Goods.* Figure 4 shows for *each* man *two* vertically-aligned marginal utility curves of defense and flood-control. Now we get the total ("pseudo") demand by adding vertically across *both* people *and* goods, and again find the equilibrium at E. Note the contrast between figures 4 and 2."

Mathematical Discussion

9. This ends the discussion. But these days a perfect examination question supplements words and graphs with symbols. To pin down definitely the general optimality conditions for joint supply, we can append the following:

"*Mathematical Optimality Conditions.*" Using the 1954 notation for goods, write corn as x_1; sheep as x_2; mutton as x_3; wool as x_4. For men $1, 2, \ldots, i, \ldots s$, let superscripts denote the man. Then the corn consumed by man i is x^i_1, and, similarly for the mutton consumed by him. As in the cited 1954 paper, we have a social welfare function. $U = U[u^1, \ldots, u^i, \ldots, u^s]$, and for each man ordinal utility functions of the form $u^i(x^i_1, \ldots)$. After the optimality conditions of 1 are realized, we have a production-possibility frontier defined by $F(x_1, x_2, \ldots) = 0$. As in the 1954 paper, let sub-

scripts to functions denote partial derivatives with respect to the indicated numerical argument: e.g.

$$U_i = \partial U / \partial u^i, u^i_j = \partial u^i / \partial x^i_j, F_j = \partial F / \partial x_j, \text{etc.}$$

Then in the case of ordinary private non-jointly supplied goods, such as corn, sheep, ..., Conditions 1 and 2 are summarized by the 1954 (1), and to which can be adjoined Conditions 3 in the 1954 form of (3). In all, we have, as in my 1954 paper

$$\frac{u^1_j}{u^i_1} = \ldots = \frac{u^i_j}{u^i_1} = \frac{F_j}{F_1},$$
$$(i = 2, \ldots, s; j = 2, \ldots, n). \quad (1)$$

where by Lerner's Rule on marginal productivities

$$\frac{\partial x_1 / \partial \text{ labor}}{\partial x_j / \partial \text{ labor}} = \frac{\partial x_1 / \partial \text{ land}}{\partial x_j / \partial \text{ land}} = \frac{F_j}{F_1}.$$

$$1 = \frac{U_i u^i_1}{U_1 u^1_2}, \quad (i = 2, \ldots, s) \quad (3)$$

where,

of course, $x^1_j + \ldots + x^i_j + \ldots + x^s_j = x_j$ for each private good. If we now add to the n private goods m new public goods:

$$x_{n+k} = x^1_{n+k} = \ldots = x^i_{n+k} = \ldots$$
$$= x^s_{n+k}, \quad (k = 1, \ldots, m)$$

we adjoin to 1954's (1) and (3) 1954's

$$\sum_{i=1}^{s} \frac{u^i_{n+k}}{u^i_1} = \frac{F_{n+k}}{F_1}, \quad (k = 1, \ldots, m) \quad (2)$$

By contrast, along with adding public goods, suppose we *also* adjoin one set of r jointly-produced private goods (mutton, wool, ...), produced in equal amounts, and allocated component by component among the different individuals $x_{n+m+1} = \ldots = \ldots = x_{n+m+r}$

$$\sum_{i=1}^{s} x^i_{n+m+1} = \ldots = \sum_{i=1}^{s} x^i_{n+m+r}.$$

Now we need equations of the Condition 2' type to place alongside equations (1) and (2). These are private-good relations akin to (1), and hence call them (1*):

$$\frac{u^i_{n+m+1}}{u^i_1} = \frac{P_{n+m+1}}{P_1}, \ldots, \frac{u^i_{n+m+r}}{u^i_1}$$
$$= \frac{P_{n+m+r}}{P_1}, \quad (i = 1, \ldots, s) \quad (1*)$$

$$\frac{P_{n+m+1}}{P_1} + \frac{P_{n+m+2}}{P_1} + \ldots \frac{P_{n+m+r}}{P_1}$$
$$= \frac{F_{n+m+1}}{F_1},$$

425

where F is written as $F(x_1, \ldots, x_n; x_{n+1}, \ldots,$ $x_{n+r}; x_{n+r+1})$, or F(corn; television; mutton).

10. Suppose we had relaxed the assumption of joint production in strictly fixed proportions, and replaced it by an assumption that sheep can be bred to produce more mutton and less wool, or vice-versa, along a smooth trade-off frontier. Then we could classify such goods as mutton and wool in and along with ordinary goods such as corn in the F function, enlarging the number n of such goods and dispensing with the category of goods beyond $n + m$; of course we can then dispense with the (1*) conditions supplementary to (1).[4]

---

[4] An example is the case where (mutton^2 + wool^2)$^{1/2}$ = sheep, with sheep being produced from labor and land by the usual production function. Then $0 = f$[corn, sheep] $\equiv f$[corn, (mutton^2 + wool^2)$^{1/2}$] $= f$(corn, mutton, wool) as in the standard private-goods case. Note that in (1*), wool and mutton are included in the $r = 2$ case but we do not double count by *also* including sheep. It should be mentioned that in (1*), we could omit all pecuniary vari-

Conclusion

The "externality" involved in the production of wool along with mutton creates no new problems for laissez-faire pricing. If the corn and sheep production functions satisfy the strict returns conditions conducive to perfect competition, we can leave to the invisible hand of the market place the determination of optimal resource allocation (it being understood that lump sum redistributions of income take place in the background to ensure ethical equality of the marginal dollar to every person). There is nothing "pseudo" about the demand functions involved in standard joint products, an intrinsic contrast to the public good case. In this sense I find it misleading to characterize the public good case as a case of joint supply.

ables P_{n+m+j}/P_1; alternatively in (1) and (2) more explicit mention could be made of price pecuniary variables and of market algorithms.

PART XI

Dynamics and Statics of Income Determination

169

Some Notions on Causality and Teleology in Economics

PAUL A. SAMUELSON

WHEN I started to prepare this paper, I decided it would be wise to read the transcript of my predecessors in this series. In reading the words of a distinguished sociologist, a distinguished political scientist, a distinguished philosopher, and a distinguished expert in the mathematics of communication, I gained many bits of knowledge. But the most reassuring lesson I learned was that it would not be absolutely necessary to stick closely to the assigned subject. Causation apparently is one of those scaffoldings inside which you can build a sermon of almost any type.

I propose to discuss various problems of causality that arise in day-to-day economic research. There are numerous semantic problems connected with causality and I must confess they are not my major interest. And for the most part I shall be discussing causality with a small c, not cosmic causality with a large C. Thus, I shall be shamelessly begging all the deep epistemological questions connected with the subject, offering only as my feeble defense that most scientists and practical workers in the field find that if they beg fundamental questions there seem to be very few penalties for doing so.

WHO KILLED COCK ROBIN?

A typical semantic question arises whenever we have a whole chain of events that precede or lead up to an event. If *any* element of the chain were different or lacking, then a last event would not have happened the way it did happen. It is rather like electric switches arranged in series. Open but one switch and of course the current will not flow. So in economics, people used to debate seriously—I am afraid they still do—questions like the following: Does M, the amount of money, cause an increase in business activity and price levels? Or is it the change in the interest rate (or the structure of interest rates and degree of credit rationing) that is to be invariably associated with those changes in prices and activity? Lauchlin Currie wrote a book, *The Supply and Control of Money in the United States,* back in the early 1930s when I was a student. The ink was hardly dry before he had repudiated all its contents, but nobody told me that; and when I received the book with the dried ink, I had to wrestle with the question of whether after all it was not M that had really caused the change, since allegedly without the change in M there would not have been the change in interest rates to produce the final effect. A similar issue arose about a decade ago when Professor Milton Friedman of the University of Chicago and I found ourselves on the same panel testifying on money and banking before a Congressional Committee. I spelled out in great detail what I considered to be the mechanisms and sequences involved in attempts to affect the level of national income through use of federal reserve monetary policy. From the oral confrontation I could not tell whether there was agreement with this analysis; so when I got back to the office, I wrote a letter to Professor Friedman specifically asking whether there were any points at which our views were in variance. Being busy, he wrote back briefly that while he had no quarrel with my analysis, he considered it redundant. So long as a change in M can be counted upon to achieve the desired effect in the end, why bother to elucidate the intermediate steps involving the interest cost of loans and availability of credit? Friedman likened the discussion to a quarrel over whether it is the loss of blood, the bullet of the murder weapon, the gun itself, the finger that pulled the trigger, or the gunman who kills the victim.[1] So long as we can be sure that death

[1] In some traditions a responsible and free human agent has to be regarded as the "cause" of anything. When Professor Jacob Viner and I served on the advisory board to the Commission on Money and Credit, I was interested to hear him remark that there was good precedent in the fields of jurisprudence and torts to lay any possible blame for postwar inflation upon the Federal Reserve Board rather than on such factors as the backlog of demand or level of public debt, since "they" were the responsible agents whose duty it was to prevent the evil.

will "follow" the "initial" act, why quibble about the details? And the same goes for monetary policy: so long as an engineered change in M can be counted on not to induce an offsetting opposite change in the "velocity of circulation of money," Friedman prefers to skip the intervening stages.

I am not much interested in the semantic problem of isolating one or more "causes" in a complex of causes, and at this late hour I don't suppose you are either. If there is agreement on the facts, that we do face something like a sequence of switches in series and that any one open switch will break the circuit, there is nothing left to argue about. And actually some of the reasons debates continue are not methodological at all, even though they may appear to be. Thus, I probably do not have Friedman's confidence that the gun will invariably kill the victim. More specifically, what is usually defined as an increase in M, if it is brought about by open-market operations, which in deep depression give people more cash and take away from them infinitesimal-yielding treasury bills that are close money substitutes, I should not expect to have anything like the appreciable effect on employment, total spending, and production that a massive gold find would have during a boom year. Similarly, some economists might think Currie right to have emphasized M and not interest rates, if they hold the theory that it is wealth-effects which are important for total spending and not interest rates.

LIGHTNING CAUSES THUNDER?

In considering complications introduced by multiple causes, the above discussion runs ahead of the story. The simplest sense in which an economist or anyone else would understand causation lies in the motto: *post hoc, ergo propter hoc.* I call this a motto but of course it is usually dubbed a fallacy. Yet no one would have had occasion to label it a fallacy if it did not already suggest some germ of truth. Leave out the word *ergo* and you are left with the unsophisticated notion that whenever A happens, B always (sometimes, or usually) happens soon afterward. A is the cause of the B that happens soon after it. Indeed in the previous section of my talk my tongue could hardly avoid the question-begging word "antecedent." This asymmetry of time is thus often regarded as the key test for causation. My bullet penetrates the heart (or his heart sucks in my bullet, it does not matter) and *then* mine enemy bleeds. Two elastic billiard balls collide and then they rebound from each other.

This time sequence of events seems to be reduced down to an irreducible unit, which must be accepted. True, we can put a fast camera on the happenings and play back the record in slow motion. But no matter how fast our cameras, all we can do ultimately is record the happenings as they play themselves out—the first contact of the balls, the bending of the surfaces, their subsequent snapping back, and so forth. Only in the fairy tales of elementary physics books do rebounds take place instantaneously. All we can say is that a detailed set of pictures will reveal the billiard balls going through their appointed waltz. We can hope to describe the process in greater or less detail. But in no ultimate sense can we "explain" the process. Nor, as David Hume showed long ago, can we ever "prove" its logical necessity or empirical inevitability.

I have been using loose language in saying that the effect takes place some time after the cause. How much time later? The process is continuous and no matter how small we make the time interval, it can, in principle, be made smaller still. There appear to be no irreducible instants involved in the notion of causality. (This has led some economic theorists to insist upon taking the limit and replacing a difference-equation formulation by a differential-equation formulation, a topic which will be touched on later.) True we can give more interesting descriptions that will cover many cases other than that of colliding billiard balls. And we may be able to correlate the description of how the ball bounces with a description of what happens under a microscope to various molecular interactions. But, like Margaret Fuller, or Newton looking at a falling apple, in the last analysis we must merely accept the universe.

It is not always easy to identify the true cause of an effect. Is it witchcraft or arsenic that kills the rats? Is it the tobacco or the paper which increases the probability of lung cancer? Because economists cannot employ controlled experiments, our problems of identification are difficult ones. Occasionally, we can hope to observe a cause so dramatic that it stands out like a physicist's controlled-experiment causes: a massive tax cut or dominating war incident may provide a worthy case for intensive study and follow-up. But such opportunities are exceptional. I am sure that I am not alone among social scientists (and meteorologists and cosmogonists) who confess to a certain *Schadenfreude* over the plight of medical scientists in trying to decide whether smoking as such is harmful to health and longevity. "Mere statistical association can prove nothing about cause and effect," the purists aver. "Instead of X causing Y, they may both be the effect of some common Z." True enough, but remember, nothing can prove anything about an empirical regularity. All one can ever hope to do about an empirical invariance is recognize it and describe it. To say: "X is not the 'genuine cause' of Y but Z is" is merely to say: "Z and Y are more invariantly correlated empirically than are X and Y." I know that some will find the above sentence a startling one, but it is time they learn to face the facts of life.

Difficult problems of timing are often involved. When we see lightning before hearing thunder, we may falsely infer that the first caused the second. But more careful examination will reveal that sound travels sufficiently slower than light to account for both being the simultaneous accompaniment of an electric discharge. Particularly in case of business cycle oscillations, it is often hard to know whether one time series is turning down before the crowd or is belatedly following the crowd's previous cyclical downturn. Of this, an example is provided by money M and national output Y. Historically, M has lagged behind Y at turning points. Crude cause and effect would then lead to the inference that Y is cause and M effect. But those who want to reverse the direction of causation can always take foolish comfort in the fact that the *rate of growth* of M, dM/dt, will for a quasi-sinusoidal fluctuation turn down one-quarter cycle before M itself—and thus the causal sequence $dM/dt \rightarrow Y$ may help save the appearances.

Molière's listeners laugh at the notion that morphine puts one to sleep because of its "soporific" quality. But whom is the joke on? Strike out the word "because" as I have suggested you strike out the word "*ergo*" in the *post hoc* phrase and you are left with the important recognition of a regularity. For, never forget that morphine does put one to sleep and coffee does not. And the chemist working to produce a new drug does seek a compound with the sleep-inducing quality of morphine but without its "addicting" quality.

DIFFERENCE EQUATIONS

To a mathematical economist, the crudest notion of cause and effect involves a time lag and could be depicted by a simple difference equation, such as

$$(1) \qquad Y(t+1) = f[X(t)] \qquad \text{or} \qquad X(t+1) = F[X(t)]$$

In the first case we have some functional relation that tells us what is the effect on Y at time $t + 1$ when one period *earlier* X took place at t. This first case still leaves us with two unknowns and only one relation; so the answer is indeterminate. Until we are somehow given knowledge of the arbitrary function $X(t)$, we cannot solve to know $Y(t+1)$. Of course in the simplest chain, we might have $X(t)$ depending causally in turn on some third, still prior variable $Z(t-1)$. This, as in the search for a first cause or in the proof of God's existence, can lead to an infinite regress. All our yesterdays had a yesterday.

The second form of the causal relation closes the circle. The behavior of the system now depends upon its own immediate past. Now the system is almost determinate, the number of our functional equations being equal to the number of our unknown time-sequence variables. What we need to get a determinate system is arbitrary knowledge of the initial condition of X at some arbitrary beginning of time: given $X(t^*)$, repeated use of the F function will give us $X(t)$ for all subsequent time periods, $t > t^*$.

Particularly in the field of business cycles, such autonomous and timeless difference-equation models have been frequently employed these last thirty years. A typical example is the case of the cobweb fluctuations of a farm price, as farmers produce this period a high crop if last period's price was high, thereby giving rise to a series of oscillations in output and price that may or may not damp down to equilibrium. Such names as Tinbergen, Frisch, Kahn, Clark, Lundberg, Robertson, Samuelson, Domar, Metzler, and Hicks have been associated with such model sequences. I shall give only some trivial examples here.

Logistic population

Malthus thought population would, if unchecked, grow biologically at a constant percentage rate per period. In effect he stipulated the hypothetical linear causal system

$$X(t+1) = a\,X(t)$$

where a can be set about equal to 2 if a generation of about a quarter of a century is used as the time period. But Malthus also believed in the law of diminishing returns: we can represent this by saying that the percentage increase in population on a fixed acreage of land declines as the size and density of the population increases. If the law of decline is linear in X, we get the finite-difference form of the Verhulst-Pearl logistic model of population

$$(2) \quad \frac{X(t+1) - X(t)}{X(t)} = b - c\,X(t) \qquad b>0, c>0, X(t) \geqq 0$$

While the exact solution to this cannot be expressed in terms of tabulated elementary functions, the system is determined in its behavior once we know an initial non-negative value for $X(t^*)$. And it is easy to show that there are two equilibrium levels for the system: the zero level, where it never changes at all, but which is unstable once any positive population leads to a Malthusian explosion away from zero; and the asymptotic level $X = b/c$, where returns have been diminished so much that the net balance of births over deaths is zero. This upper equilibrium is locally stable, and can be shown to be returned to from initial disturbances above or below it.[2]

If a single variable depends causally upon its own state just a single period earlier, it cannot display a very rich variety of behavior. Even if the law of dependence is nonlinear, the system must either approach an equilibrium or diverge to infinity; a first-order system cannot, by its nature, oscillate (except in a simple, every-other-period way). However, if we reinterpret the symbol $X(t)$ to be a whole vector of different variables, and $F[X(t)]$ to be a whole set of functional dependences—one for each variable, giving its present level in determinate dependence upon *all* the other variables at the previous period—we get a simple causal system which can show richer variety of behavior. (And we also automatically cover the case where a variable depends upon its values at several earlier periods.)

Oscillations in the struggle for existence

Thus, let $X(t)$ stand for $[y_1(t), y_2(t)]$, where y_1 stands for the population of edible deer and y_2 the population of predatory humans. Adapting the simple fables of Lotka and Volterra[3] on the struggle for existence between two species, let us postulate that deer, y_1, would follow a Malthus-logistic law if vile man were at the level $y_2 = 0$. But suppose that each increment of hunters y_2 reduces deer's percentage growth rate by a constant amount, d. And now let us postulate that the percentages rate of increase of man increases by a constant amount for each increment of

[2] P. A. Samuelson, *Foundations of Economic Analysis*, (Cambridge: Harvard University Press, 1947), disscusses these matters in Part II and Mathematical Appendix B. For b and c small enough, as when we use short periods in (2), the stability assertions hold.

[3] A. J. Lotka, *Elements of Mathematical Biology*, (Baltimore: Williams and Wilkins, 1925; New York: Dover, 1956,), 89; V. Volterra, *Leçons sur la theorie mathématique de la lutte pour la vie*, (Paris: Gauthier-Villers, 1931). In addition to this summary of Volterra's post-1926 work, see for a summary of his post-1936 results relevant to the calculus of variations, "Principes de biologie mathématique," *Acta Biotheoretica*, V. III (1937), reproduced in Volterra, *Opere Matematiche*, V, 414-47.

deer per capita: i.e., plentiful enough venison means human population growth. Our system can now be written as

$$\frac{y_1(t+1) - y_1(t)}{y_1(t)} = b - cy_1(t) - dy_2(t)$$

(3)

$$\frac{y_2(t+1) - y_2(t)}{y_2(t)} = -e + g\frac{y_1(t)}{y_2(t)}$$

While this system is so simple that it could be thought up and
written down in a matter of seconds, no mathematician can write
down its explicit solution in terms of known elementary functions. Still, mathematics assures us of its unique solution, which
for any initial conditions can be rapidly computed. Also, mathematical analysis and common sense enable us to assert many of
its simple properties:

1. If both species begin at zero, they stay at zero.
2. If man begins at zero but deer are positive, deer will grow
   alone in the Malthus-logistic fashion.
3. If man begins without deer for food, he will move toward
   extinction (in accordance with the negative-signed coefficient e).
4. If both are positive but man is scarce, deer will multiply.
   Before they reach their saturation level, man will multiply
   and almost certainly (for c sufficiently small) there will be
   an overshoot of human population, which will subsequently
   kill off many deer, leading in turn to a great decimation
   of men. This goes on until men are again scarce compared
   to deer, and we are off qualitatively on another cycle.
5. There is a critical density of deer and men around which
   the system will oscillate, derived by setting the left-hand
   sides of (3) equal to zero and solving the resulting linear
   equation for the equilibrium level of (y_1, y_2) that will be
   self-perpetuating.

Cause and Effect

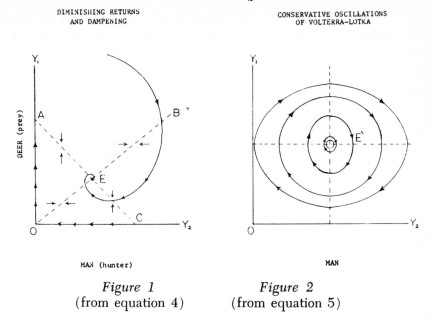

Figure 1
(from equation 4)

Figure 2
(from equation 5)

Figure 1 shows the equilibrium point E at which the system could settle down. Why must there be such a point? From the second equation for human growth, we know that human population will be stationary along some line of balanced per capita food, namely OEB. Above that line, deer are so abundant that men will increase (as shown by the fact that all arrows above the line point westward). Below the line all arrows point eastward as men die out from shortage of food.

On the other hand, it must be obvious that deer cannot grow indefinitely to ever higher levels, for two reasons. The first involves the law of diminishing returns, as indicated by the depressing c coefficient in the first equation. The second involves the fact that numerous hunters will kill off deer. The curve of balance, where deer growth turns into decay, is shown by the curve AEC: above it deer decline as shown by the southward-pointing arrow; below it, deer increase back toward it. If deer are stationary on AEC, and men are stationary on OEB, then, at their intersection point E both are stationary and we have an equilibrium point.

Actually, the equilibrium point eventually will be attained by the system from any point that starts out with both species. The equilibrium point is thus "stable," with all swings around it being ultimately damped down and spiraling into the stationary state *E*.

I shall not give rigorous mathematical proof of these assertions (which are valid for a rather wide choice of positive constants). But let me now consider some alternative formulations of the problem. Suppose we let the time period be cut in half from 1 to ½; then to be cut in half again, each time writing out some idealized difference equations purporting to show the laws of population development. In the limit, as the time period shrinks to zero, if we let terms like $[y_1(t + \triangle t) - y_1(t)]/\triangle t$ go the limit as $\triangle t$ goes to zero, we replace our finite time differences by derivatives, which we may write as $dy_1(t)/dt$ or $\dot{y}_1$. The adapted Lotka-Volterra system (3) then might become the differential equation system

(4)
$$\frac{\dot{y}_1}{y_1} = B - Cy_1 - Dy_2$$

$$\frac{\dot{y}_2}{y_2} = -E + G\frac{y_2}{y_1}$$

If these new coefficients are related properly to the old, Figure 1 will still give a picture of the resulting motions. In fact, the continuous trajectories of the figure are really more appropriate for this differential-equation formulation than for the difference-equation formulation. Actually to depict (3) accurately in Figure 1, I should have used a set of discrete dots, or used straight-line segments or arrows in showing the move from one period's position to the next period's.

To tie this discussion up with the usual Lotka-Volterra model and pave the way for the later issue of time reversibility, I should mention that most such writers do not take account of diminishing returns or the problem of density of food to hunter. Their simplest equations take the form

(5)
$$\frac{\dot{y}_1}{y_1} = a_1 - a_{12}\, y_2$$

$$\frac{\dot{y}_2}{y_2} = -a_2 + a_{21}\, y_1$$

Cause and Effect

It is not hard to show that these give rise to Figure 2's closed oscillations, corresponding to a *perpetuum mobile* around the equilibrium level E'. These "conservative oscillations," which neither damp down nor build up amplitude in anti-damped fashion, resemble the swings of frictionless pendulums so beloved of classical mechanics. (Later I shall show important differences for teleology between the conservative and dissipative cases.)

DERIVATIVES OR DIFFERENCES?

Does reality dictate that true causal analysis should be thrown into the form of "cause now creating effect later," requiring us to use a difference-equation formulation like that of (1) or (3)? Or, since time intervals can be cut down as much as we like, does reality call for a differential-equation formulation like that of (4) or (5)? Some economists and scientists have acted as if such a question has a unique answer. In economics, I believe Richard M. Goodwin has argued that events take place in finite time and our observations come in discrete intervals, and that therefore in principle a difference-equation formulation is optimal. Against this, economists such as R. F. Harrod have asserted the equally one-sided view that derivative flows are somehow more fundamental than lagged differences. Most of modern physics involves use of Newtonian derivatives and partial derivatives. At least one physicist, perhaps influenced by the conceptual importance of the quantum theory, has proposed that all physics be recast in terms of finite differences; and my old teacher, E. B. Wilson, the last student of Willard Gibbs and himself a distinguished mathematical physicist and statistician, once told me that Gibbs mentioned, in his last years, an attempt to express as much as possible in terms of finite differences.

In a sense, the quarrel is an empty one, involving unimportant semantic distinctions. In a sense, the answer can be arbitrary, depending upon the convenience of the investigator. In a sense, both of the suggested optimal solutions are wrong. Let me explain.

If we deal with analytic functions possessing Taylor's expansions, a difference equation could be written as an infinite series of differential equations. Conversely, in finding the actual solutions of differential equations, as in exterior ballistics, the usual methods of numerical approximation involve using difference equations to achieve any desired degree of accuracy. So it would seem that there is not much to choose between the two devices. Either or both will often do. And, as will be seen, each is but a special case of the more general use of "functionals," in which the position of a system now and forever depends upon all its past behavior.

"Hysteresis" phenomena

For, if we really go back to a detailed picturing of the colliding billiard balls, we realize that at best all we can observe is that the present position of the system is in a determinate relationship to *all* of its past behavior. When we come to divide time most meticulously, we usually do not conclude with a simple, low-order differential equation. When we come to abandon our difference equations for a more exact description, we seem to end up with some causal law that has to be written as a functional of past behavior. We must now go back and rewrite the difference equations of (1) not as a simple differential equation but rather as the following functionals

$$(1)' \qquad Y(t) = f \left| t : x(s) \begin{matrix} s=t \\ \\ s=-\infty \end{matrix} \right| \qquad \text{or} \qquad X(t) = F \left| t : X(s) \begin{matrix} s=t \\ \\ s=-\infty \end{matrix} \right|$$

The first says that the *behavior of an effect* Y *at time* t *depends upon the whole shape of behavior at all previous times of its cause* X. The second example is one of a closed or complete causal system in which the present of a system is uniquely determined by *all* of its past. The struggle for existence was a good example to use since Volterra has set down a simple model of "hysteresis type" (which remembers and depends upon its detailed past), of which the following is a simple instance

Cause and Effect

$$\dot{y}_1 = y_1(a_1 + a_{12}y_2 + \int_0^t F_{12}(t-s)y_2(s)ds)$$

(5)′

$$\dot{y}_2 = y_2(a_2 + a_{21}y_1 + \int_0^t F_{21}(t-s)y_1(s)ds)$$

The last integrals are among the simplest functionals that take account of "hereditary" influences of all the past. If the $F_{ij}(x)$ functions are certain simple sums of polynomial-exponential terms, of the form $t^k e^{\lambda j^t}$, the system may be capable of being written as an ordinary differential equation of high order. If the F_{ij} memory functions are all damped down toward zero, the system will behave rather like a causal system and unlike the actual stream of history, of which the Bible says, "We pass this way only once." When the equilibrium of a system depends on (and is dictated) by its path toward equilibrium, the scientist has an uncomfortable feeling.

Examples of differences and derivatives

I do not want to gloss over the difference between differential- and difference-equation systems. Galileo's studies of falling bodies paved the way for Newtonian dynamics; but for his problem Galileo did not really need the concepts of the infinitesimal calculus. For slow motions of a falling ball on a smooth inclined plane, Galileo could record the distance the ball traveled in t periods after it started from rest, in the accompanying table.

Observations on Falling Body (Galileo)

Time	t	0	1	2	3	4	... n ...	
Distance	$S = f(t)$	0	1	4	9	16	... n^2 ...	
Average speed	$\dfrac{f(t+1)-f(t)}{1}$		1	3	5	7	9 ...	... $2n+1$
Instantaneous speed	$\dot{S} = \dfrac{df(t)}{dt}$	0	2	4	6	8	... $2n$	

In this hypothetical table, since the unit of time and the unit of distance is at my disposal, I have arbitrarily assumed that Galileo uses as his unit of distance for the experiment the distance covered in the first arbitrary time period. He discovered that this distance would, of course, differ with the angle of the inclined plane but (in contradiction to Aristotle) would not depend upon the "heaviness" of the ball. Since we still have the time unit at our disposal, we can assume it selected so that the ball (which is to anyone's eye obviously speeding up) travels exactly twice as far in the second period as in the first. However, after the first three entries in the second row of the table are filled in, there is nothing to do but complete the rest according to nature's testimony.

The remarkable fact emerges that nature's entries follow a very simple law or formula, and will be the same for any size ball and (in terms of these adjusted units) for any angle of inclination. Galileo knew the basic rule that the distance is proportional to the square of the time. This pattern is a logical implication of the fact that "the distance traversed in *each* time period grows as the odd numbers grow," like 1, 3, 5, 7, . . . as shown in the third row of the table. Or, what is the same thing, if we call the distance covered in each single time period its average speed, "the average speed is proportional to the time, growing from one time period to the next by a constant amount," which we know is proportional to the fundamental constant of gravity. (I have not yet called it an acceleration constant because I still want to avoid Newtonian calculus.) Symbolically, Galileo's law for a falling body can be summarized by

$$(6) \quad \left\{ \frac{[S(t+1)-S(t)]}{1} - \frac{[S(t)-S(t-1)]}{1} \right\} = \triangle^2 S = +c$$

The fourth row of the table introduces the Newtonian notion of instaneous speed, which is the limiting average speed as the

Cause and Effect

time interval shrinks to zero without limit. It too is proportional to t, a fact about which both Galileo and Descartes were confused simply because of logical errors on their part. (They thought it proportional to distance $s(t)$ rather than to $\sqrt{s(t)}$.)

Using the concept of first and second derivatives for instantaneous speed and acceleration, we can express Galileo's law in alternative differential equation form

$$(7) \qquad \qquad \frac{d^2 S(t)}{dt^2} = +C$$

where C and c are closely related but not quite identical. And only with the concept of instantaneous speed could Galileo have formulated the later law of conservation of energy: kinetic energy plus potential energy always equals a constant, or

$$(8) \qquad \qquad (ds/dt)^2 + (-2S) \equiv 0$$

When Newton saw the apple fall, he was not led merely to rediscover Galileo's rule. The point of this not completely apocryphal incident is that Newton realized that the moon and Kepler's planets behaved *like* the falling apple in terms of the laws of gravity. However, even in the simplest case of the earth going around the sun in an elliptical Keplerian orbit, as if its acceleration is inversely proportional to the square of the distance between it and the sun, we need differential equations like

$$(9) \qquad \frac{d^2 x_1}{dt^2} = \frac{m_1 m_2}{\sqrt{x_1^2 + x_2^2}} \quad , \quad \frac{d^2 x_2}{dt^2} = \frac{m_1 m_2}{\sqrt{x_1^2 + x_2^2}}$$

and cannot summarize this behavior in any simple difference equation system

$$(10) \qquad x_i(t+1) = F^i[x_1(t), x_2(t), \ldots] \qquad (i=1,2, \ldots)$$

Only after we have named two instantaneous magnitudes of the Newtonian type, $x_3 = dx_1/dt$ and $x_4 = dx_2/dt$ can equations (10) be put in the vector form $dX/dt = F(X)$ and solved to give $X(t) = G[t;X(t_0)]$ and, eventually, in what appears to be the difference-equation form $X(t+1) = G[1;X(t)]$. Without being able to define the final two instantaneous velocities, we could attribute no meaning to these last difference equations.

FROM LAPLACE'S WORLD EQUATION TO MARKOV'S PROBABILITY MATRIX

Newtonian mechanics led Laplace to believe that the whole universe could be described by a world equation of the (vector) form $dX/dt = F(X)$. He boasted that given these laws of causality and the initial conditions of the universe at any instant of time, he could, in principle, predict the whole future in all of its details. When Napolean asked Laplace, "What is the role of God in your system?", the illustrious writer of *Celestial Mechanics* replied, "Sire, I have no need for that hypothesis." (On hearing of this, Lagrange, who has been called the Shakespeare of mathematics, is supposed to have said, "Yes, but what a beautiful hypothesis it is.")

Note that the Laplacean causal system is in differential-equation form and makes no use of any time interval between antecedent cause and subsequent effect. How paradoxical that this most ideal case of a causal system has no asymmetry of time connected with it at all!

The position of the universe determines its own motions at the instant, and thus forever. As far as the mathematics is concerned, there are no time lags involved. And the same existence theorems that guarantee the uniqueness of a determinate solution forward in time also guarantees its existence backward in time. Just as we can know where the earth will be five minutes or millennia from now, we can know where it must have been five minutes or millennia ago.

What has just been said is true of *any* set of differential equations. Thus, it is just as true of my damped struggle-for-existence system (4) as it is for the standard Lotka-Volterra system (5).

We can run the motion picture backward in Figures 1 and 2, reversing the direction of the arrows. However, the undamped L-V system of Figure 2 shows conservative oscillations that look essentially the same backward as forward, the only difference being the inessential one that a clockwise motion is converted into a counterclockwise one. This can be seen from the structure of (5). Making the substitution $t = -T$ gives essentially the same differential equations in terms of the new, reversed time variable T, except that the human hunter now acts as if he were the prey, and the deer now appears to be the predator.

In conservative mechanics we have the same true time reversibility. Thus, if we consider the case of a truly frictionless pendulum, which is undergoing swings so limited as to be considered simple harmonic motion, we get for its dynamics the differential equation

(11)
$$\frac{d^2y}{dt^2} + my = 0$$

On the other hand, if we introduce a little viscous friction, the pendulum follows the more realistic equation.

(12)
$$\frac{d^2y}{dt^2} + a\frac{dy}{dt} + my = 0$$

where $a > 0$ depicts the dampening effect of the deceleration from the friction attributable to velocity. This last formulation departs from the conservation of energy condition of classical mechanics, as the forces of friction lead to the creation of heat. No longer is it true that the sum of kinetic energy and potential energy remains constant. In order to save the law of conservation of energy, the physicists must introduce the new entity of thermal energy. This is not, however, merely a case of juggling the books, creating a fictitious balancing item in order to save appearances. The First Law of Thermodynamics, discovered by Joule and Mayer in the first half of the nineteenth century, does note a strong regularity of cause and effect, namely that the same amount of mechanical energy always gets converted into the same amount of thermal energy.

IS TIME REALLY REVERSIBLE?

Here we encounter a paradox of time reversibility that is very relevant to the problem of effect following cause. Early writers such as Count Rumford felt that heat must reflect the kinetic energies of molecules in motion at a level that the eye cannot observe. Clausius, Maxwell, Boltzmann, and finally Willard Gibbs tried to develop a kinetic theory related to statistical mechanics. The same formal laws of Newtonian-Lagrangean-Hamiltonian mechanics were now to be applied to a vast assemblage of molecules. It turned out, after such writers as G. D. Birkhoff, B. O. Koopman, J. von Neumann, N. Wiener, and E. Hopf had, by means of the "ergodic theorem," cleared up some of the diffculties of logical analysis, that the classical mechanics of this extended assemblage of molecules still had the intrinsic time reversibility properties of the frictionless pendulum. While none of this caused any great problems for the First Law of Thermodynamics relating to the law of conservation of energy, it did pose serious problems for the Second Law of Thermodynamics. Clausius and Kelvin had formulated this law as requiring that a magnitude called "entropy" should increase asymmetrically in time. My Figure 1 case, in which things settle down rather than oscillate conservatively, is the more indicated image.

At this point, classical thermodynamics became less convenient than kinetic theory and statistical mechanics. Boltzmann interpreted entropy in terms of probability, much as is done today in information theory. Instead of saying that my cream is certain to mix with my coffee, cooling it and being heated by it until they are in temperature equilibrium, probability says that it is very likely indeed that this will happen but that by chance alone the two substances *might* separate out again and display diverging temperatures.

The paradox connected with time irreversibility did not disappear completely with the introduction of probability. True, if our cards are well shuffled I shall I shall be surprised to see thirteen spades come in my next hand of bridge. But I should be just as surprised to have the same mixed hand come up next time as came up last time. Curiously enough, one of the most interesting reconciliations of these difficulties connected with time reversibility of cause and effect in a mechanical system comes from abandoning tight causality in favor of a probability model. The most celebrated one was given half a century ago by P. and T. Ehrenfest, and is described in M. Kac, *Probability and Related Topics in Physical Sciences* (N. Y., Interscience, 1959), Chapter 3.

Number 100 balls from 1 to 100. Divide them into two boxes. Now pick by some symmetric random device any number from 1 to 100. Suppose the number that comes up is 17; then move the ball 17 to the other box. Continue this process, always moving the ball whose number has come up. What happens to the number of balls in each box? It should be intuitively obvious that there is a tendency for the numbers to become equal at 50 each. Why? Because the box which at any time has the greater number of balls is more likely to have one of its numbers picked by the sampling device and hence is more likely to lose a ball. From him who hath shall (more likely!) be taken away, which, as every Bible reader knows, results in a "tendency" toward equality.

This Ehrenfest model is an example of what has come to be known as a Markov transitional probability matrix. In the mid-1930s such concepts were not fashionable in American statistics courses, although now, thanks to W. Feller's classic text, *An Introduction to Probability Theory and Its Applications*, New York, Wiley, 1950), they are popular. While thinking about F. W. Taussig's data showing that the sons of businessmen were much more likely to become businessmen than were the sons of farmers or laborers, I was led as a young student to rediscover the concept of a transitional probability matrix. It was with wonderment that I inferred the theorem that the transition probabilities for grandsons of businessmen and other social classes followed the simple rules of matrix multiplication or squaring, and likewise for still later generations.[4]

Probability matrices have become very popular in modern econometrics. Just as Laplace had the rather grandiose notion of a causal world equation, bold scholars like Guy Orcutt of the University of Wisconsin have dreamt of determining empirically for the economic system a grand stochastic probability matrix, which would give information like the following: The chance of a bachelor's becoming a married father is q per cent, and the chance of his buying a car is p per cent. The future of the world would not be exactly determinate, but its probability laws would

[4] See P. A. Samuelson, *Economics* (New York: McGraw-Hill, 1964, 6th ed.) 125, n. 1, for the following brief description: "The arithmetic of 'transition probabilities' can be made to yield the following results. Divide society into two classes, so that I am either a U in the Upper class or a *non*-U in the Lower. If a child's chance to move out of his parents' class is as great as to stay in, then ½ the children, grandchildren, great-grandchildren, and descendants generally of a U parent will be U's. But if there is social stratification so that a child has only ¼ chance of moving into a class different from his parents, ¾ (= ½ + ¼) of the children of U's will be U's. However, it can be deduced that only ⅝ (= ½ + ⅛) of grandchildren of U's will be U's; and only 9/16 (= ½ + 1/16) of their greatgrandchildren. Evidently, the chance of remote descendants of U's being also U's goes ultimately down to ½ [the ergodic state], with 50 per cent of the excess above the ½ equality level wiped out at each new generation."

This quotation explains in words the following matrix identity, where the probability ¾ is written as $1/2 + s/2$, with $s = 1/2$

$$
\begin{bmatrix} \dfrac{1}{2} + \dfrac{s}{2} & \dfrac{1}{2} - \dfrac{s}{2} \\[2ex] \dfrac{1}{2} - \dfrac{s}{2} & \dfrac{1}{2} + \dfrac{s}{2} \end{bmatrix}^{n} = \begin{bmatrix} \dfrac{1}{2} + \dfrac{s^{n}}{2} & \dfrac{1}{2} - \dfrac{s^{n}}{2} \\[2ex] \dfrac{1}{2} - \dfrac{s^{n}}{2} & \dfrac{1}{2} + \dfrac{s^{n}}{2} \end{bmatrix}
$$

As $n \to \infty$, all probabilities $\to 1/2$, the ergodic state for this doubly-stochastic matrix.

be exactly determinate in such a model. I know some readers will wince when I use the words "exact" and "probability" in the same sentence. But I see no contradiction: there are many models in which the probability laws are specified with exactitude, with only the sample outcome being left to chance. Often, in these models, as the size of the sample becomes large, certain probabilities approach unity in value, which is an exact statement even though it does not purport to express a "certainty" of actual outcome.

DETERMINISM VERSUS FREE WILL?

The notion of a causally determinate world was depressing to many nineteenth century students of science. The materialism of physics seemed to grind out any role for the free exercise of the human spirit. Along with Percy Bridgman and many exponents of logical positivism, I have not been able to find much conceptually refutable meaning to this debate: what difference does it make if one believes in one side or the other? All facts fit in equally well or equally badly. (If I claim to have chosen not to fly on the plane that crashed yesterday, my opponent can claim that this choice was preordained.)

Yet many physicists and laymen thought that the discovery of radioactivity and of quantum mechanics broke the spell of mere causality and reopened the way for free will. This view seems rather odd. It is true that many of the models of quantum mechanics do involve magnitudes called probabilities, but what has that to do with the question of whether that murderer in the dock was free to have led an upright rather than dissolute life? Note, too, that many of the theories are mathematically exact in their determination of probability laws. Finally, and this seems to be enormously important and yet commonly overlooked, *quantum mechanics has introduced some of the strongest regularities into physics that have ever been discovered.* Just as earlier physics stated the strong laws that one cannot build a perpetual motion machine of the first or of the second type, quantum theory says one cannot ever determine simultaneously with complete accuracy the position and velocity of a certain particle. The strongest laws of nature, which limit what one can expect to observe, are just such impossibility laws. And far from lessening their number, it seems to me that quantum mechanics has increased it.

CONSERVATION OF ENERGY IN ECONOMICS?

Why should a person interested in economics for its own sake spend time considering conservative oscillations of mechanics? Experience suggests that our dynamic problems in economics have something in common with those of the physical or biological *sciences*. But, as I long ago indicated,[5] it is not useful to get "bogged down in the research for economic concepts corresponding to mass, energy, momentum, force, and space." And I may add that the sign of a crank or half-baked speculator in the social sciences is his search for something in the social system that corresponds to the physicist's notion of "entropy."

The ecological system of Figure 2 appears to satisfy a law like the conservation of energy equation of (8). But this is true mainly because Lotka and Volterra set up an overly simple razor's-edge case. If we were to add to the first equation of (5) a tiny term $-hy_1$, to reflect diminishing returns (or $+hy_1$ for increasing returns), Figure 2 would begin to look like Figure 1 and show damped (or explosive) oscillations that run into (or out of) the equilibrium point. But it would be quite uninformative to explain this by a physics concept of friction or to try to save the appearance of a conservation-of-energy law by creating a fictitious form of dissipated thermal energy.

Of course, if Lotka or Volterra were alive, they might defend their razor's-edge conservative oscillations by an appeal to experience. The jungle and the sea do both display a *perpetuum mobile*, in which prey and predator fluctuate in numbers over the years.

---

[5] See P. A. Samuelson, *Foundations of Economic Analysis* (Cambridge: Harvard University Press, 1947), Chapter XI, 311, where reference is made to the 1943 article in the *Review of Economic Statistics Festschrift* issue for Joseph A. Schumpeter (1943), 58-61.

Cause and Effect

One year deer abound; another year they are decimated. Attempts have even been made to do for ecology what econometricians do for economics, namely evaluate by statistical methods the parameters of the model. And Lotka and Volterra might argue, as M. Kalecki [6] has done, that the fact of *nondying-out and non-exploding oscillations* calls for a specification of a model which, like (5) and unlike (4) is neither damped nor antidamped and which does obey a conservation law. I believe such a defense is misguided for the following reasons.

As Malthus well knew, the struggle for existence does lead to fluctuations around the bare subsistence level. But the system is not an isolated and stationary one. It is the exogenous fluctuation in the weather—in rain and sun and flood and lightning—that causes fluctuations in crops and in numbers. In the false glow of an unusual harvest, species multiply; and they pay the price when chance brings the weather back to normal or below.

Just as Ehrenfest and other physicists had to add probability to the causal systems of physics to get around the time-reversibility feature of classical mechanics that was so inconsistent with the time asymmetry of the Second Law of Thermodynamics, so we must, in the interests of realism, add stochastic or probability disturbances to our economic and biological causal systems. Thus, systems (4) or (5) now take the general form

(13)
$$\dot{y}_1 = f_1(y_1, y_2) + u_1(t)$$
$$\dot{y}_2 = f_2(y_1, y_2) + u_2(t)$$

where the $u_i(t)$ are exogenous stochastic disturbances subject to whatever probability laws are appropriate to the weather or to technical innovations and political events.

[6] See *Foundations, op. cit.*, 337 for my critique of the Kalecki insistence upon conservative oscillations.

Causality and Teleology in Economics

It can be shown that superimposing such random fluctuations on a conservative system of the Lotka-Volterra or frictionless-pendulum type will not lead to the factually correct observations of fluctuation that show *no historical trend in amplitude.* On the contrary, a conservative system "remembers" forever, so to speak, each shock it has ever received; and as time passes, it has more and more shocks to remember. In consequence of this, we have to predict that its future position will wander further from any equilibrium point.

So what the facts of a "stationary time series" call for is precisely the reverse of the Lotka-Volterra-Kalecki case. My damped pattern of (4) and Figure 1 has the property that each past shock is, so to speak, gradually forgotten. Thus, as time passes and more exogenous shocks are experienced, we reach an "ergodic state," where the new shocks are just enough to balance out the forgetting of old shocks. This has the following meaning: If I begin by knowing where the system is in Figure 1, I can then specify tight probability limits on where it will be a little later, because only a few $u_i(t)$ shocks can be registered in that interval. If I try to predict for a longer time T ahead, my probability guesses widen. But, and this is the point, they do not widen indefinitely; instead, they approach a limiting distribution (which is quite independent of where I started). We can imagine a hill of probability piled up somewhere around the E equilibrium point, since any extreme departure from E tends to be pulled back by the internal dampening of the system toward E again.[7]

---

[7] The system $f_i(y_1,y_2)$ will be antidamped if we add a little *temporary* increasing returns to the first equation of (5), in the form say of $+h(y_1-r)^2$. Then we should have to draw Figure 3 showing spirals oscillating *out of* E and approaching a crucial "limit cycle." Now adding a little stochastic disturbance $u_i(t)$ will lead to an ergodic distribution which has its probability spread like a doughnut around the limit cycle.

Cause and Effect

FREE WILL AND DETERMINISM AGAIN

The contrast between a system which gradually (forgets and) becomes independent of its past (and forgets it) and one which is changed greatly and forever by the slightest disturbance to it has been likened by some philosophers to the contrast between causality and free will. Clerk Maxwell asserted that a belief in free will was like a belief that the universe reacts in a sensitive and even explosive way to minute changes in its initial conditions, while a belief in determinism is like the belief that the development of the system is insensitive (at once or eventually) to transitory changes in initial conditions. From this standpoint, the causal system of Figure 1 and (4) is to be contrasted with the causal system of Figure 2 and (5) and with an exponentially evolving causal system that could be shown in still another figure.

This same distinction can illuminate the difference between probabalistic chance and deterministic causality. The stochastic disturbances $u_i(t)$ might depict the results of coin or dice tossing. The weather seems to be the outcome of a dice game of the gods. But if our knowledge were better, weather might be describable by a causal process. In the same way, if I could toss a nickel carefully in a windless room, controlling precisely the coin's initial position and torques, I might be able to predict whether heads or tails would come up. (Some schoolboys can control card and coin tosses with uncanny precision.) However, as Poincaré and others have pointed out, what makes a roulette wheel a good chance device is a situation where *the most minute change in initial conditions will have discontinuous effects on the outcome.* A fast turn of the wheel of chance is harder to predetermine and predict than a slow one.

We have here, of course, a hierarchy of knowledge and ignorance. What appears to be inexplicable probability and chance at one level may appear as predictable cause and effect at another. Whether there exists in economics and social sciences, as there does in the quantum mechanics of Heisenberg's uncertainty principle, an *irreducible* level of probability ignorance can only be a subject for idle speculation. With better statistical surveys, I expect economists will learn to predict the volume of next year's investment better. With better study of businessmen's psychology, we might further improve our prediction batting average. But whether we can hope to reduce our imprecision gradually to zero is an issue upon which I confess to some skepticism. But my mind is open to new experience.

TELEOLOGY

There is not space left to do justice to my second topic, teleology. Whereas cause and effect seems to run from earlier time to later time, teleology and purpose seem to reverse the direction of time: where my target will be later determines how I must position myself now. Brute Cause and Lady Purpose seem to be quite distinct, and even opposites. But appearances can be deceiving. And often, just as the behavior of light shows both corpuscular and wave properties, so does the waltz of a pendulum show teleology as well as causality.

Let us watch a ball roll down an inclined plane. Newton describes this causally: at each point and velocity, its rates of change of position and velocity are uniquely determined, as by equation (7). We saw that Galileo could describe this behavior by difference equations (6) alone. But Hamilton (and before him, Fermat, Maupertuis, Euler, and Lagrange) can describe the ball's motion thus: It moves with that special velocity which minimizes a certain integral of action, in comparison with any other behavior-pattern which starts and ends at the same points in the same time! Mathematically, the Newton-Galileo causal law

$$\ddot{S} = C, \; S(t) = \tfrac{1}{2} Ct^2$$

is the necessary and sufficient condition for minimizing Hamilton's integral

$$I = \int_{t_0}^{T} (\tfrac{1}{2}\, \dot{S}^2 + CS) \, dt = \int_{t_0}^{T} L(S,\dot{S}) \, dt$$

(14)
$$= \int_{t_0}^{T} (\text{Kinetic energy} - \text{potential energy}) \, dt,$$

$$S(t_0) = 0, \quad S(T) = \tfrac{1}{2}\, CT^2$$

I.e.,

$$\int_{t_0}^{T} [\tfrac{1}{2}\,(Ct)^2 + C\tfrac{1}{2}Ct^2] \, dt < \int_{t_0}^{T} [\tfrac{1}{2}\, \dot{S}(t)^2 + CS(t)] \, dt$$

for any $S(t)$ path different from Nature's actual path but starting and ending at the same times and places as the actual ball's motion.

Hamilton's Principle is applicable to all conservative mechanical systems and not merely to falling bodies. According to it, Nature is a great Economist, or economizer. Nature acts *as if* she has purpose and aims.

A NEW BIOLOGICAL PRINCIPLE OF "LEAST ACTION"

I should like to point out that the conservative oscillations of Lotka-Volterra's Figure 2, even though they seem to describe the causal struggle for existence, can, in fact, be shown to accomplish the maximization or minimization of a certain integral.[8] This

[8] Volterra has given a quite different minimum formulation of his problem, involving the cumulative number of each species since the beginning of time, $X(t) = \int_0^t N(s)\,ds$ $\dot{X}=N$; and instead of an integrand of the form $L(N_1,\dot{N}_1)$, his is of the form $L(X_1,X_2,N_1,N_2)$. As far as I know the present formulation is new, but it would not be surprising if its contents have probably been glimpsed by earlier writers.

integral has no physical-energy connotations and can be written in the form

$$I = \int_{t_0}^{T} L(Y_1, \dot{Y}_1) \, dt, \qquad Y_1(t_0) = Y_1^{0}, \quad Y_1(T) = Y_1^{T}$$

$$Y_1(t) = \log y_1(t), \quad y_1(t) = e^{Y_1\,(t)}$$

(15)

$$L(Y_1, \dot{Y}_1) = \left\{ (a_1 - \dot{Y}_1) \log (a_1 - \dot{Y}_1) - (a_1 - \dot{Y}_1) \right\}$$
$$- \left\{ + a_2 Y_1 - a_{21} e^{Y_1} \right\}$$
$$= T(\dot{Y}_1) - V(Y_1)$$

The conditions sufficient for a minimum of $I, T - t_0$ being not too large, are known to be

$$0 = \frac{d}{dt}\frac{\partial L}{\partial \dot{Y}_1} - \frac{\partial L}{\partial Y_1} \quad, \quad 0 < \frac{\partial^2 L}{\partial \dot{Y}_1^{2}} = T''(\dot{Y}_1)$$

(16)
$$= \frac{-d}{dt} \log (a_1 - \dot{Y}_1) + a_2 - a_{21} e^{Y_1}$$

$$= \frac{\ddot{Y}_1}{a_1 - \dot{Y}_1} + a_2 - a_{21} e^{Y_1}$$

or

(16)′
$$\ddot{Y}_1 = (a_1 - \dot{Y}_1)(-a_2 + a_{21} e^{Y_1})$$

But it is easy to convert (5) into this equivalent form. Differentiate the first equation of (5), and then substitute for $\dot{Y}_2$ the expression given for $\dot{Y}_2$ from the second equation, to get

$$\frac{d}{dt}\frac{\dot{y}_1}{y_1} = \ddot{Y}_1 = \frac{d}{dt}(a_1 - a_{21}e^{Y_2}) = - a_{21}e^{Y_2}\dot{Y}_2$$

$$= (a_1 - \dot{Y}_1)\dot{Y}_2 = (a_1 - \dot{Y}_1)(-a_2 + a_{21}e^{Y_1})$$

This shows the equivalence of (16)′ to the Lotka-Volterra causal system (5). Finally, note that $T''(\dot{Y}_1) = -1/(a_1 - \dot{Y}_1) = 1/a_{21}e^{Y_2} > 0$, which is the Legendre condition sufficient for a minimum when $T - t_0$ is sufficiently limited.

MOTHER NATURE'S MYOPIA

One marvels that the causal motion of a pendulum (or deer-man system) actually solves a minimum problem, producing a lower value to Hamilton's integral than any other motion that begins and ends at the same places and at the same times. But closer examination shows that this minimizing holds *only if the time of the motion is shorter than a half-cycle of the pendulum.* (In mathematical terms, there will be a Jacobi "conjugate point" that violates the minimum when the time duration becomes too long.)

Men used to marvel that "Nature abhors a vacuum," until experience with air pressure required the prosaic codicil, "Nature abhors a vacuum only up to 30 inches of mercury." At the least, Mother Nature acts as if she were careless or shortsighted in her mechanics. It is as if I am trying to go from New York to Chicago, and I carefully work out the great-circle route that goes through them. But instead of heading directly west and truly minimizing the distance of travel, I permit myself to head east. Along this round-about path I am forever minimizing the distance between every pair of *nearby* points, but my grand purpose of minimizing distance between New York and Chicago has been thwarted. (Actually, I could have taken any great-circle route going through New York and its antipodal point, and then finished by the unique, direct great-circle route from that antipodal point to Chicago; any of these routes would do as well, or badly, as the unique, indirect great-circle route.

Nature thus seems to favor the motto, "It is better to travel than to arrive." But that is an understatement, for she does travel efficiently for short times. She seems to be a myopic economizer.[9]

This consideration can serve to debunk the mystical notion of teleology introduced by Maupertuis and other eighteenth-century philosophers of nature and deism.

Furthermore, the minute we introduce an iota of friction into the pendulum model, we completely lose the minimum characterization. Adding the viscous-friction term $a\dot{y}$ (or $-a\dot{y}$) to the $\ddot{y} + my = 0$ of (ii) destroys the Euler-Lagrange-Hamilton minimizing.

Similarly, introducing diminishing returns into the Lotka-Volterra system (5) gives us Figure 1's damped notion. And to this causal system, there is no simple teleological counterpart.

---

[9] How short is a short time? In some problems one adds more and more oscillators along a line. In the limit as the number of particles becomes indefinitely large and the intervals between them indefinitely small, we approach the mechanics of a continuous rope or membrane. However, it can be shown that adding each new particle may reduce (even halve) the time before the critical conjugate point comes to destroy the minimum. So when we go to the infinite limit, we are left with no finite time within which the minimum takes place. This explains the paradox that the partial differential equation of the rope or membrane may represent a vanishing of the first variation of a generalized Hamilton integral, but *not* provide any kind of a minimum. Physicists rarely seem to care whether their vanishing first variations represent a true extremum; indeed, one gathers in wave mechanics that the mere presence of a stationary value will lead to observable reinforcements of waves and probabilities. (I do not know whether my suggested instaneous minimum principle will survive through the limit process involved in approaching the continuous rope or membrane.)

Cause and Effect

A NEW INSTANTANEOUS MINIMUM PRINCIPLE

Some minds boggle at the thought of "action at a distance." Why rely on Nature's having even short-sighted prevision and purpose? Is there not some way of preserving the causality format of the behavior equation—in which the pendulum's acceleration $\ddot{y}$ is related instantaneously to its current position y and velocity $\dot{y}$—while saying that Nature chooses out of all possible accelerations $\ddot{y}$ precisely that critical observed $\ddot{y}^*$ that minimizes some definable magnitude?

I propose to sketch here an affirmative answer to these questions, introducing a limit process into the suggestive Caratheodory method of steepest descent.

This formulation may have some parallel with Gauss's principle of least constraint, which is also an instantaneous minimum principle. But there is no dependence here upon Newtonian laws in Euclidean space, concepts which have no relevance to biological systems (like that of Lotka-Volterra) or to economic systems.[10]

Write the standard integral as a function of its right-hand end point and as a functional of $x(t)$ in the interval

$$(17) \quad I \begin{bmatrix} t = T \\ T,X: & x(t) \\ t = t_0 \end{bmatrix} = \int_{t_0}^{T} L\left[t, x(t), \dot{x}(t)\right] dt \qquad \begin{array}{l} x(t_0) = x_0 \\[1em] x(t) = X \end{array}$$

[10] The proposed principle has nothing to do with the trivial device by which any law $\ddot{y} = E(y, \dot{y}, t)$ is given the minimum formulation $(\ddot{y} - E)^2$ to be a minimum.

Suppose $\partial^2 L/\partial \dot{x}^2 > 0$ everywhere so that I is truly minimized for $T - t_0$ sufficiently small.

Let $x(t) = x(t)^*$ be the minimizing extremal satisfying the Euler condition

$$\frac{d}{dt}\frac{\partial L}{\partial \dot{x}} - \frac{\partial L}{\partial x} = 0, \quad \text{or} \quad \ddot{x}^* = E(t,x,\dot{x})$$

Denote by V

$$V(T,X) = I[T,X : x(t)^*] \begin{array}{c} t=T \\ \\ t=t_0 \end{array}$$

and let $U\ (T,X)$ be the value of I along *any* other path $x(t)$. Now in U and V let the end point X be subject to this same arbitrary path $X(T) = x(T)$, giving

$$U(T,X(T)) = U(T), V(T,X(T)) = V(T)$$

These are parametric equations which define a unique relation, for T-t_0 small and the integrand arranged so that $U'(0) \neq 0$, between U and V, namely

(19) $\qquad U = f(V) = a_0 + a_1 V + a_2 V^2 + a_3 V^3 + R_4$

where the remainder term R_4 involves terms of the fourth degree and higher.

Of course, if the arbitrary path $X(T) = x(T)$ happened to be picked as the extremal path $x(T)^*$, then $f(V) \equiv V$. By virtue of the Legendre minimum condition, we know that

(20)
$$f(V) > V \quad \text{for } V > 0$$
$$\text{and } x(T) \neq x(T)^*$$
$$f(V) < V \quad \text{for } V < 0$$

Cause and Effect

This last condition follows from the fact that setting $T < 0$ leads to changing the sign of the integrand in I and to a maximum rather than minimum problem.

Routine (but tedious) calculation shows that

$$a_0 = 0, \ a_1 = 1, \ a_2 = 0, \ a_3 = A[t_0, x(t_0), \dot{x}(t_0), \ddot{x}(t_0)]$$

Indeed, from (20) alone, we could deduce $a_2 = 0$. Furthermore, from the minimum properties of (17) and (20), we can deduce that Nature's choice of $\ddot{x}_0 = E(t_0, x_0, \dot{x}_0)$ does indeed minimize a_3, actually, at zero. Thus, we are led to the following basic theorem

Theorem: If $\ddot{x}^* = E\ (t, x, \dot{x})$ provides the minimizing solution to

$$I = \int_{t_0}^{T} L(t, x, \dot{x}) dt \ , \qquad \frac{\partial^2 L}{\partial \dot{x}^2} > 0$$

$$x(T) = X, \quad x(t_0) = x_0$$

then it also provides the minimum solution to the scalar problem

(21)
$$\underset{\{\ddot{x}\}}{\text{Min}} \ A(t, x, \dot{x}, \ddot{x}) = A(t, x, \dot{x}, E(t, x, \dot{x})) = A^* = 0$$

The same holds if x is a vector of functions and whatever the side-conditions on the minimum problem.

To complete the proof of this theorem one need only note that unless $a_3 > 0$, the inequalities of (20) would be violated. And of course $a_3 = 0$ is the condition for the optimizing motion.

RUNNING TIME BACKWARD

If teleology differs from causality by a reversal of time effects, economics can provide numerous interesting examples of the difference, alone with some amusing false examples.

1. One false example would be the fallacy connected with "regression toward the mean." Sir Francis Galton pointed out that the children of very tall (or short) parents tend to be less tall (or short) on the average. From this some inferred wrongly that the race was becoming more homogeneous in height. But actually, in a stationary time series, the parents of very tall children will tend to be less tall—in a perfectly symmetric way, just by virtue of the fact that an imperfect correlation coefficient must be less than 1 in absolute value.

2. In connection with simple Yule-Wold autoregressive schemes, of the type

$$(21) \qquad y(t+1) = ay(t) + u(t) \qquad , \qquad |a| < 1$$

where $u(t)$ is a random shock, we shall observe the serial correlation coefficient $r(y_t, y_{t+1}) < 1$ and with the sign of a. But from the sample of observations alone, can we ever *know* that the system was not generated *teleologically* by

$$(22) \qquad y(t-1) = ay(t) + u(t)$$

If so, is a belief in cause and effect a dogma or convention rather than an empirical inference?

3. If a set of observations, such as data on social classes of fathers, sons, grandsons, . . . is generated by a simple Markov chain, as discussed in an earlier section, no one can stop us from working out for the sample in question the "conditional frequencies" of previous generations. Thus, given that a man is in the upper classes, what fractions of the parents or grandparents of

such a typical man were also *U* rather than non-*U*? Interestingly, the resulting two-way conditional frequency would have the Markov-chain property. I.e., knowing what that man's son status was will add no information to help narrow down our prediction as to what status his father had, and so on indefinitely.[11]

4. A simple Keynes multiplier model traces expenditure today to incomes received yesterday, as in

$$Y(t+1) = A\,Y(t) + G(t)$$

where *A* represents the "marginal propensity to consume" (in simple or in matrix form). For a single impulse of autonomous investment or government expenditure *G*, or for a repeated plateau, we end up with the convergent multiplier formula

$$(23) \qquad Y = (I + A + A^2 \ldots .)\,G = (I - A)^{-1}\,G = MG$$

But exactly the same mathematics of positive *A* matrixes is

---

[11] A special case is the Ehrenfest win model mentioned earlier. If urn *A* now has N_t of the 100 balls, the probability that it will next period have $(1 + N_t)$ is $(100 - N_t)/100$ and that it will have $(N_t - 1)$ is $N_t/100$. In a long sample, what is the empirical frequency ratio that it had $(1 + N_t)$ and $(N_t - 1)$ respectively at the *previous* time $t - 1$? The exact result will depend on the *initial* number of balls in urn *A*, N_0. Or we might stipulate an initial probability for each value of N_0, perhaps giving each N_0 the probability it would have in the ergodic state, which is its average frequency in a very long sample. However, in a long sample of size *N*, as *N* goes to infinity, we expect the required empirical frequency ratio to become more and more insensitive to the initial condition; and in many such special cases, the backward or inverse probability matrix will have the same numbers as the original Markov matrix. Thus, if *A* has no balls now, it must have one ball next period with $P = 1$. But if it has none now, it must, with $P = 1$, have lost one last period. The Ehrenfest schemata to dissolve the paradox of time's asymmetry and increasing entropy seems itself to have the paradox of a time reversibility pattern in its "inverse" Markov matrix. Indeed, it is the stochastic version of Figure 1, with its probability ergodic state created by its dampening, that seems to possess the property of Ehrenfest's interpretation of the Second Law of Thermodynamics. "Increasing entropy" becomes merely "regression toward the mean" in a stationary (not evolving) time series.

involved in a Leontief input-output model. But now inputs are required before outputs, and we write

(24)
$$X(t - 1) = A X(t) + G(t)$$

$$X = (I + A + A^2 + \dots) G = MG$$

where now G represents autonomous consumption, and where each of the rounds take place backward in time: one period before G, we need AG; the period before that, to produce AG, we need $A(AG) = A^2G$; and so the multiplier chain goes backward forever in the teleological scenario of preparation for *Der Tag*.

5. In dynamic capital models of the Dorfman-Samuelson-Solow [12] or von Neumann type, often there is a dualism of prices and quantities. If the quantity relations are well behaved backward in time, as in the previous Leontief example, the prices may be well behaved running forward in time; or vice versa.

6. In connection with ideal futures market pricing, the analysis becomes so forward looking as to reek of teleology. As in the famous 1928 Frank Ramsey model of saving, one must know how things work out until the end of time. The problem bristles with paradoxes and divergent integrals; only in certain special cases, can use of "bliss" and "discounting" devices lead to determinate results.

Of course, most paradoxes come from considering idealized models that involve infinity somewhere. Thus, the Ruml Plan introduced during the Second World War, which forgave us one year of taxes permanently but required us to be taxed currently, ends up in an ever-growing economy giving the government more, rather than less money. "To him who forgives, shall be given" is unsound for each closed cycle; but if you pile on more and more incomplete cycles, the absurd becomes sound. I can

[12] R. Dorfman, P. A. Samuelson, R. M. Solow, *Linear Programming and Economic Analysis* (New York: McGraw-Hill, 1958), especially Chapters 9-12. M. Morishima, *Equilibrium Stability and Growth* (Oxford: Oxford University Press, 1964) p. 99 deals with dynamic price behavior, and gives references to 1959 work of Solow.

Cause and Effect

refer the reader to P. A. Samuelson, "An Exact Consumption-Loan Model of Interest," *Journal of Political Economy*, Vol. 16, No. 6 (1958), pp. 467-82 for more paradoxes created by never-ending exponential growth. Also, "Intertemporal Price Equilibrium," *Weltwirtschaftliches Archiv.*, Vol. 79 (1957), pp. 181-22, for a mixed teleological-causal, speculative-price model which depends, in principle, upon all the harvests that are ever to come. See p. 217, where H_t represents the sequence of harvests; Q_t the sequence of stocks of grain; $C_t = H_t + Q_t - Q_{t+1}$ the sequence of consumptions; $F(C_t) = P_t$, the sequence of market prices; and $T(Q_{t+1}) = P_{t+1} - P_t$, the sequence of Working equilibrium price differences corresponding to each level of stocks that must be carried. This yields the infinite sequence of equations

$$(25) \quad F(H_{t+1} + Q_{t+1} - Q_{t+2}) - F(H_t + Q_t - Q_{t+1}) - T(Q_{t+1}) = 0$$

If we start out with known $(H_0, H_1, \ldots, H_n; Q_0, Q_{n+1}, P_{n+1} = F)$, and write the above equation for $t = 0, 1, \ldots, n-1$, we get a determinate solution for $Q_1, \ldots, Q_n$. The fact that our boundary conditions are two-sided shows that the system is neither time-phased backward in the causal sense nor forward in the teleological sense, but, rather, is time-reversible like the classical pendulum case. Around an equilibrium harvest plateau $H_t \equiv H$, a small transient disturbance can be analyzed by the linear approximation

$$(26) \quad (Q_{t+1} - 2Q_t + Q_{t+1}) + \lambda Q_t = 0$$

where $\lambda = T'(Q^*)/F'(C^*) < 0$. The result is indefinite propagation of the disturbance backward and forward throughout all time. This implies that the linear approximation has to be abandoned and suggests to me that generalized limit cycles of the cobweb type may be involved.

7. I am not sure but that the last phenomenon of indefinite propagation of a disturbance is linked up to the oldest problem

of business-cycle theory. In 1929 we saw a repetition of what has happened often in the last several hundred years: for whatever reason, people begin to think that common stocks or tulips will rise in price; so they buy and hold them, ensuring the rise in $P(t)$ they had expected. If the percentage rise in price, measured by $\dot{P}/P$ or by $[P(t + 1) - P(t)]/P(t)$, stays constant, the process could, in principle, go on indefinitely. The rising putative terminal value at some future date justifies present actions.

Now obviously, if in a finite time we have to go through a complete cycle, the stupendous rise in P will be seen to have been mistaken. After the Dutch "Tulip mania" of the seventeenth century was over, people realized that one bulb should not be worth one horse and carriage. But if the time involved were infinite, the absurd exponential solution could formally go on forever!

The important thing for economics is not that market booms will go on forever. The important thing is that economists do not have any good theory of *how long they are likely to go on.* This oldest problem of empirical business cycles may be one of the last we shall be able to give a scientifically valid solution to.

8. Consider the following stochastic process:

$$
(27) \qquad \begin{bmatrix} a_{11} & a_{12} \\ a_{21} & a_{22} \end{bmatrix} \begin{bmatrix} Ey_1 \\ Ey_2 \end{bmatrix} = \begin{bmatrix} b_{11} & b_{12} \\ b_{21} & b_{22} \end{bmatrix} \begin{bmatrix} y_1 \\ y_2 \end{bmatrix} + \begin{bmatrix} u_1 \\ u_2 \end{bmatrix}
$$

where $Ey_i(t)$ is short for $y_i(t + 1)$ *and* $E^{-1}y_i(t) = y_i(t - 1)$, and the u_i are stochastic disturbances. It can be written in brief matrix terms as

$$
(27) \qquad\qquad AEy = By + U
$$

Cause and Effect

In modern econometrics, we would speak of a case of simple causality if the off-diagonal terms in A were zero: then, with A a "diagonal matrix," each y_i is a simple function of the past variables and the stochastic u_i. We would speak of a "recursive system" if A could be made "triangular," with all the off-diagonal elements above (or below) the diagonal being 0. Finally, we have a "simultaneous" system, if the A matrix (which I assume to be nonsingular, with an existent inverse A^{-1}) cannot be put into triangular form.

But (27) can easily be converted into diagonal-causal form, thus

$$A^{-1}\, AEy = A^{-1}\, By + A^{-1}\, U$$
$$Ey = \tilde{B}y + \tilde{U}$$

where $\tilde{B}$ is the new matrix $A^{-1}B$, and so on. Indeed, if A is non-singular, we can, in a variety of ways, convert it into triangular form: i.e., there exists a nonsingular matrix S, such that $A^*Ey = B^*y + U^*$, where the triangular matrix $A^* = SA$, and $B^* = SB$ is a new B matrix.

Without the disturbance terms U, these reformulations would be indistinguishable. With the disturbances, they differ in the specified stochastic properties of the U, $\tilde{U}$, U^* disturbances. Thus, suppose an original A is not diagonal or triangular, and the original U are serially uncorrelated random variables independent of any $y_i(t)$. If we convert the system into $(\tilde{A}, \tilde{B}, \tilde{U})$ or (A^*, B^*, U^*) the new U variables will be correlated with each other and with some of the y_i variables. And so, of course, the usual conditions for unbiased least-squares estimation are *not* met.

Now some investigators believe in the dogma that, *if* we could reorganize the right variables, reality is really diagonal-causal with the U disturbances "well-behaved." Others believe that ultimate reality is "really" triangular-recursive with the U disturbances well behaved. Still others, perhaps those connected with the Frisch-Haavelmo Oslo group and the Cowles Foundation, believe the general case is admissible.

Causality and Teleology in Economics

I am not sure how a deep issue like this could, in principle, be resolved. Personally, if I had to believe in a dogma, it would be one so general as to degenerate into a convention. I suppose the vector $[y_i(t), u_i(t)]$ would be a nonlinear functional, as is (1)′, of the past time-profiles of all variables. Since the stochastic variables are themselves determinately "explained" at their own level, there is nothing involved in putting the system into diagonal-causal form. Indeed, as in physics, we may always work with generalized coordinates, which are related by nonsingular, not necessarily linear transformations to (y_i, u_i). What a miracle that the coordinate we happen to use or observe should be truly in triangular or diagonal form!

As soon as we recognize that all systems like (27) are idealizations, we are at liberty to assume the most general form for A, raising all the difficult problems of simultaneous-equation estimation. As a familiar illustration of this, let me mention a theorem that I stumbled on years ago.

Suppose A is truly diagonal (or triangular), with well-behaved independent U's. But suppose, instead of observing each $y_i(t)$, we observe the nonoverlapping totals $y_i(t + 1) + y_i(t + 2) + \ldots + y_i(t + N) = Z_i(T)$ where $Z_i(T)$ is defined only for $T = Nt$ integral values. Then, in a stationary time series as N becomes large, Z_i becomes more and more a constant. To avoid disappearance of variance, let us change each u_i to $f(N)u_i$, where $f(N)$ is an appropriate increasing function of N.

Now let us put the $Z_i(T)$ observed variables into the form

$$(28) \qquad A_N Z(T+N) = B_N Z(T) + U_N(T)$$

The theorem says that the best choice of A_N will almost certainly *not* be diagonal or triangular but will require simultaneous-equation estimation procedures.

The implications are far-reaching and not particularly favorable to ordinary least-squares. If true causality takes place at the microsecond level, but our observations involve months or years (and they must involve such long periods if uninteresting "error" is to be cancelled out), then we cannot expect triangular-recursive least-squares methods to be useful very often. (One way of looking at "controlled experimentation" is that it may give truly diagonal-causal estimation models.)

PSEUDO-TELEOLOGY

I shall conclude with some examples in economics and other sciences that are couched in terms of teleology and purpose but which can be found to be essentially free of true teleology. Or, to put the matter in a different way, important aspects of what we ordinarily call teleology can be related to certain aspects of causality.

1. Economists deal with maximum systems, and these behave in definite ways. After you have dealt with such systems for a long time, you may fall into the natural anthropomorphic habit of imputing "will" and "volition" to them. This is perhaps only a figure of speech; but often it is a useful one, for the maximum systems do react to certain disturbances *as if* they were reasoning beings.

For example, a rope will hang in the shape of a catenary if suspended freely between two points that are closer together than its length. Why? Because a catenary is the shape that leads to the lowest center of gravity of the rope. And just as an olive, subject to a little friction, will run down the cocktail glass to its bottom, where the olive's center of gravity is at a minimum, so the rope "tries" to achieve the lowest center of gravity. (Both olive and rope are subject to purely causal laws of swing; but friction slows them down according to causal laws and they can come to rest only where the center of gravity is at a minimum.) Suppose I nail down a midpoint of the rope to an arbitrary point: now the rope will readjust and hang in catenaries for each of the segments, acting as if it knows it has a rendezvous to minimize (subject to the new constraint) its center of gravity.

We need not stick to ropes, olives, and soap bubbles. If farmers are maximizing profits, they will react to the reduction in the price of fertilizer by using more of it. What is surprising about that? As profit maximizers they are teleologists. But consider all the independent farmers in a county or region. Add their fertilizer purchases together and study how this total reacts to a lowering of the price of fertilizer. It acts qualitatively the same as any one farm's purchase does. And yet there is no trade association for the whole county, which has a mind and which uses that mind to maximize the profits of the group. Still, and this is the point, the observing economist can set up the fictional hypothesis that there is such a maximizing mind, and often he can make fruitful predictions from it.

When we come to certain other aspects, like the LeChatelier Principle (which is treated in my cited *Foundations*, Chapter 3), it is even more uncanny how detailed will be the predicted reactions of a maximum system, just as if it were exercising intelligence.

2. Thus far, I have been describing positive facts about economic behavior. Now turn to the problem of *welfare economics* —how a system ought normatively to behave. Adam Smith was one of the first, but certainly not the last, to speak as if within the impersonal market place of perfect competition there was a magical "invisible hand" leading the system to a certain kind of optimum—even though each individual is merely pursuing his own selfish well-being. Smith could not state the principle correctly, nor could anyone before this century. But modern economists know that there is a germ of truth (along with a virus of falsehood) in this theorem. Of course, there is no invisible hand. But it is true that the conditions of perfect competition lead to equations—just as the dying out of rope swings lead to catenary equations—which have certain *efficiency* properties. As a result, in my technical work in mathematical economics, I often reduce my equations down to those of such a maximum system and then reason correctly from the obvious properties of a maximizer. The point is that this normative approach leads to correct positive descriptions about the resulting observable equations.

3. Biology provides even better examples of teleology or pseudo-teleology. We say that the function of the kidney is to purify the

blood—as if some watchmaker had designed it, or as if the kidney were an alert sentry knowing its job. Actually, there are only cause and effect relations of osmotic pressure going on in the kidney. But the biologist has learned heuristically that he can often shortcircuit his description by speaking in the parable language of teleology.

4. Even without any original far-sighted designer, a world that involves struggle for survival may evolve in such a way as to appear to have certain maximizing properties. In economics, Armen Alchian of UCLA[13] has pioneered in pointing out how mere survival of competitors may lead to persistence of those units which act as if they were maximizing, whether or not everybody or anybody is really maximizing. But earlier, such biologists as L. J. Henderson, the ancient Greeks, and many Darwinians already had an inkling that "stable forms tend to persist." Henderson even wrote a seminal book entitled *The Fitness of the Environment*, in which he pointed out how unusual were the conditions on this planet and how appropriate they were to support life as we know it. Had he lived on another kind of planet, he would have had to write another kind of a book, and on lifeless planets no books get written.

I suppose the most striking version of this kind of teleology in biology is to be found in the classic writing by Walter Cannon on *The Wisdom of the Body*. Although the usual laws of physics, and particularly of negative feedback circuits, are all that are involved in most physiological processes, one gets a shorthand description of actual behavior by using the image and terminology of purpose and teleology. Only after one realizes that this is merely a figure of speech should one be permitted to use the figure of speech—just as we should only permit those people to continue to smoke who are able to break themselves of the habit.

5. There are numerous examples in economics of the negative feedback concept which is so dear to the hearts of modern electrical and systems engineers. Thus, suppose people spend ⅔ of their incomes on consumption and save or invest the remaining

[13] Armen A. Alchian, "Uncertainty, Evolution, and Economic Theory," *Journal of Political Economy*, LVIII (June, 1950), 211-21.

⅓. Then if new investment spending of a billion dollars comes along, economists say loosely, "National income must go up by 3 times the increment of investment, because no other multiplier would cause income to grow enough to create the new saving needed to finance the investment." Actually, that is precisely what will happen in simple models but it does not happen because the system or anybody in it knows that it has a rendezvous with this new equilibrium level. It happens because the sum of the billion dollar investment spending plus ⅔ of that amount plus ⅔ of ⅔ of that amount . . . leads ultimately to a total of 3 times that amount, by virtue of the algebraic identity]

$$[1 + \tfrac{2}{3} + (\tfrac{2}{3})^2 + \cdots + (\tfrac{2}{3})^n + \cdots] = 1/(1 - \tfrac{2}{3}) = 3.$$

I do not think that this interplay between ideas in economics and in biology is accidental. I would remind you that not only was Charles Darwin led (as he has told us) to his theory of evolution by thinking about the economic population theories of Malthus but also Alfred Wallace, the independent discoverer of evolution, was led (as he has told us) to the theory by thinking about the work of Malthus.

6. Even in physics, if one takes the prosaic view of Mach, one may be able to reduce the statement that light travels between two points in a straight line to the Darwin-Huygens formulation that, although light raylets travel in every direction at every point, the fastest arrivers are those survivors who have drunkenly straggled in the straight-line path and not been cancelled out by interference patterns. This adds a new duality to my earlier duality of causality and teleology, namely a duality of wave and particle in nonquantum mechanics phenomena.

Let me conclude with the remark that my resolution to stick primarily to economics got violated as I became carried away by my subject. I would have stuck to this subject that many people unaccountably think dull, but, like Dr. Samuel Johnson's schoolmate who had hoped to become a philosopher, I was thrown off my purpose as cheerfulness kept randomly breaking in.

170

A UNIVERSAL CYCLE?

Paul A. Samuelson
Massachusetts Institute of Technology

I

The business cycle, as we have known it for the last century and a half, has been a creature of mixed capitalist enterprise. Had the organization of banking and industry been different — if that is imaginable — the pattern of business fluctuations might have been different, or absent. Is it possible to find, on the spur of the moment, so to speak, a fundamental cyclical mechanism which could operate almost independently of the institutional environment? As the one-hundredth anniversary of *Das Kapital* approaches, one can parody the master by setting this problem for solution.

Here, I give an affirmative answer. If one posits two permament features of economic life — exploitation and increasing returns — one can deduce a permanent business cycle (and, moreover, one with a unique *amplitude* of fluctuation as well as period).

II

I take my clue from biology. A.J. LOTKA and V. VOLTERRA some forty years ago wrote down simple equations for "the struggle for existence"[1]. They postulate two species, an exploiting or hunting species N_2 and an exploited or hunted species N_1. Call them tigers and rabbits; bacteria and men; or capitalists and proletariat. In the absence of predatory exploiters, the number of N_1 will grow exponentially. (Although this view would shock Malthus, it would not faze Marx, who for reasons I cannot fathom regarded Malthus as a "libel in the human race".) But each new increment of N_2 hunters will slow down the net reproductive rate of N_1 prey. Mathematically,

1) A.J. LOTKA, *Elements of Mathematical Biology*, (1925, Williams and Wilkins; 1956, Dover), p. 89; V. VOLTERRA, *Lecons sur la théorie mathématique de la lutte pour la vie*, (1951, Gauthier-Villers).

(1)
$$\frac{1}{N_1}\frac{dN_1}{dt} = a_1 - a_{12}N_2, \qquad a_1, a_{12} > 0.$$

LOTKA and VOLTERRA assume that the hunters are parasites who would die out without their prey. But each increment of the exploited add to the net reproductive rate of the N_2 exploiters. Mathematically,

(2)
$$\frac{1}{N_2}\frac{dN_2}{dt} = -a_2 + a_{21}N_1, \qquad a_2, a_{21} > 0.$$

Equations (1) and (2) together define a determinate causal system, whose behavior has been completely analyzed. Figure 1 shows that a *perpetuum mobile* ensues: starting from positive amounts of both species, there are recurrent swings around the equilibrium level (which by proper choice of units can be set at the level of unity for each species). The fact that these swings never die out follows from the fact that the right-hand sides of (1) and (2) involve a different variable from the left-hand sides[2].

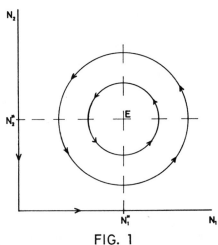

FIG. 1

2) Elsewhere I have shown that the *perpetuum mobile* is preserved even when the linear expressions on the right are replaced by general monotone functions which cross the zero axis once in the indicated direction; and the denominators on the left are replaced by arbitrary positive, increasing functions that represent arbitrary stretchings of the N_i variables. The only feature of the linear $L-V$ model that is lost by this generalization is the property that "the mean value of N_i around any complete cycle exactly equals the equilibrium value $N*$". But such a property is in any case singular and gratuitous, and not to be expected for the general case where
$$\dot{N}_1 = -G_1(N_1)\,G_{12}(N_2), \quad \dot{N}_2 = +G_2(N_2)\,G_{21}(N_1), \quad G'_{ij}, G'_i > 0,\ G_i > 0, G_{ij}(N_j^*) = 0.$$

Incidentally, the fact that $N_1(t)$ turns down and turns up *before* $N_2(t)$ should not be construed to mean that it is more causal than the other, since mutual causation is alone involved here, which should serve as a warning to careless business cycle analysts.

III

No economist could have devised the LOTKA-VOLTERRA model, which ignores diminishing returns and the ratios of the species to fixed land. A classical economist, like RICARDO, MALTHUS, or WICKSELL, would be tempted to write down the alternative equations,

$$\frac{dN_0}{dt} \equiv 0$$

(3)
$$\frac{dN_1}{dt} = F^1(N_0, N_1, N_2)$$

$$\frac{dN_2}{dt} = F^2(N_0, N_1, N_2)$$

where N_0 represents fixed land (the "original, inexhaustible, gift of nature"). The function $F^i(N_0, N_1, N_2)$ would, for classical and neoclassical economists be homogeneous functions of the first degree, exhibiting constant returns to scale. This enables us to work with normalized per-acre variables or densities, $(x_1, x_2) = (N_1/N_0, N_2/N_0)$, for which (3) becomes

$$\frac{d(N_i/N_0)}{dt} = F^i\left(1, \frac{N_1}{N_0}, \frac{N_2}{N_0}\right) = f^i\left(\frac{N_1}{N_0}, \frac{N_2}{N_0}\right) \qquad (i = 1, 2)$$

(4) $$\frac{dx_1}{dt} = f^1(x_1, x_2)$$

$$\frac{dx_2}{dt} = f^2(x_1, x_2)$$

Neglecting the limitation of space N_0 is legitimate in the one case where the homogeneous $F^i(N_0, N_1, N_2)$ functions of (3) are truly independent of N_0, i.e., where $\partial F^i/\partial N_0 \equiv 0$. In this case

(5)
$$F^1(N_0, N_1, N_2) = F^1(N_1, N_2) = N_1 F^1(1, N_2/N_1)$$

$$F^2(N_0, N_1, N_2) = F^2(N_1, N_2) = N_2 F^2(N_1/N_2, 1)$$

Since it does no harm to divide N_i by N_0 and work with densities (5) makes (4) now become

$$\frac{1}{x_1} \frac{dx_1}{dt} = - f_1\left(\frac{x_2}{x_1}\right) \qquad\qquad - f_1(u) = F^1(1, u), f_1' > 0$$

(6)   where

$$\frac{1}{x_2} \frac{dx_2}{dt} = + f_2\left(\frac{x_1}{x_2}\right) \qquad\qquad f_2(u) = F^2(u, 1), f_2' > 0$$

This scale-free system *cannot* have a unique equilibrium. For if (x_1^*, x_2^*) were an equilibrium, so too would be $(\lambda x_1^*, \lambda x_2^*)$ where λ is any arbitrary scale constant. Indeed the probability is indefinitely great that there will not be any equilibrium at all. Only if, by odd chance, the same value of $(x_2/x_1)^*$ happened to cause f_1 and f_2 to vanish simultaneously, could there be an equilibrium proportion or ray in the Figure 2 diagram. This would require a common root $(x_1/x_2)^* = y^*$ to

(7) $$f_1\left(\frac{1}{y^*}\right) = 0 = f_2(y^*)$$

Since the f_i functions are monotone, there could be, at most, but one such coincidental equilibrium. To test whether such an equilibrium were stable, we subtract the second equation of (5) from the first to get an equation for the $x_1/x_2 = y$ ratio above

$$\frac{1}{x_1} \frac{dx_1}{dt} - \frac{1}{x_2} \frac{dx_2}{dt} = \frac{1}{(x_1/x_2)} \frac{d(x_1/x_2)}{dt} = - f_1\left(\frac{x_2}{x_1}\right) - f_2\left(\frac{x_1}{x_2}\right)$$

(8) $$\frac{1}{y} \frac{dy}{dt} = - f_1\left(\frac{1}{y}\right) - f_2(y) = \psi(y)$$

The point y^* is a stable equilibrium point of this first-order differential equation if

(9) $$\psi'(y^*) = + \frac{1}{y^{*2}} f'\left(\frac{1}{y^*}\right) - f_2'(y^*) < 0$$

If this sign is reversed, the equilibrium is unstable and will be departed from after any transient disturbance. If $\psi'(y^*) = 0$ and the first non-vanishing derivative is odd, the system will be stable or unstable depending upon whether that coefficient is negative or positive. If the first non-vanishing term is even, the equilibrium ray will be stable on its one side and unstable on its other side.

Now turn to the usual case where the coincidental conditions of (7) are not satisfied. Then there will be no equilibrium other than zero for both species. Since equation (8) still holds, there will be equilibrium proportions $(x_1/x_2)^*$; but along such a ray the system will either expand or contract in a balanced way. At an equilibrium where $\psi(y^*) = 0$ in (8), $f_1(1/y^*)$ and $f_2(y^*)$ will have the same algebraic sign. If both are positive, the species will grow indefinitely in number and density; if both are negative, both species will become extinct along the $(x_1/x_2)^*$ ray. As before, the stability of the equilibrium ray depends on the sign of $\psi'(y^*)$ there.

Figure 2 shows all six of the principal kinds of rays: 2a, 2b, and 2c are all stable; 2d, 2e, and 2f unstable. Ray OA in 2a is a stable ray at which the species can remain in equilibrium. By coincidence their f_i functions are so geared to each other that any scale along OA can persist. Moreover, this proportion is asymptotically stable, as indicated by the arrow converging to OA. OA is a singular razor's-edge case and hence rather unconvincing. The equilibrium along OA is a neutral one: we can, so to speak, raise or lower the system by pulling on its moustache. Clearly, the slightest change in the environment will change the f_i enough to upset (6) and change OA to a non-stationary ray like OB or OC in 2b and 2c.

In 2b and 2c we have stable rays OB and OC, as shown by the converging arrows; whereas the species explode along OB, they become extinct along OC.

Figures 2d, 2e, and 2f show the corresponding cases of unstable rays. Finally, 2g shows an OG ray that is unstable on one side and stable on the other. It also indicates that a system can have multiple equilibria of rays, alternately stable *(OG')* and unstable (like OG*)*.

When the number of species is greater than 2, ignoring space limitations and the law of diminishing returns leads to the same indeterminacy of equilibrium and scale. We have

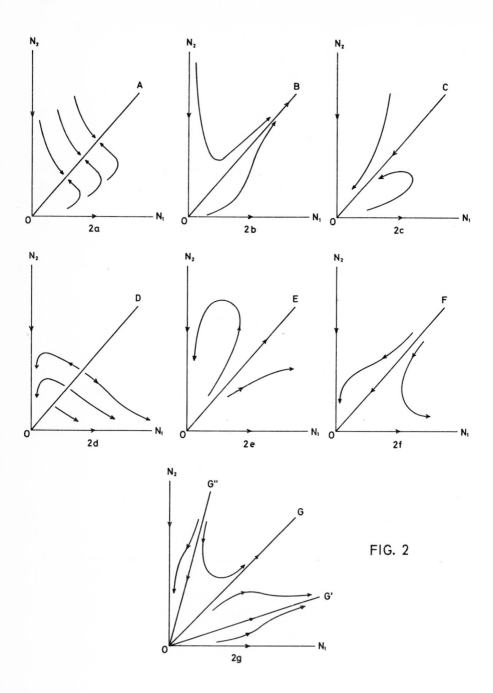

FIG. 2

(10) $\dot{N}_0 \equiv 0$, $\dot{N}_i \equiv F^i(N_0, N_1, \ldots, N_n)$ $\qquad$ $(i = 1, \ldots, n)$

where the F^i are homogeneous of the first degree. If $\partial F^i/\partial N_0 \equiv 0$, we get for $N_i/N_0 = x_i$,

$$(11) \quad \dot{x}_i = F^i(1, x_1, \ldots, x_n) = x_i F^i\left(1, \frac{x_1}{x_i}, \ldots, \frac{x_n}{x_i}\right)$$

$$= x_1 F^i\left(1, 1, \frac{x_2}{x_1}, \ldots, \frac{x_n}{x_1}\right) \quad \text{if } \partial F^i/\partial N_0 \equiv 0$$

$$= x_1 f^i\left(\frac{x_2}{x_1}, \ldots, \frac{x_n}{x_1}\right)$$

Now calculate $x_i/x_1 = y_i$, $(\dot{x}_i/x_i) - (\dot{x}_1/x_1) = \dot{y}_i/y_i$,

by subtracting the first of these equations from the rest to get the system

$$(12) \quad \frac{1}{y_i}\dot{y}_i = g^i(y_2, \ldots, y_n) = \frac{f^i}{y_i} - f^1 \qquad (i = 2, \ldots, n)$$

$$\frac{1}{x_1}\dot{x}_1 = f^1(y_2, \ldots, y_n)$$

In this form, we see that an equilibrium set of proportions

$$(y_1^*, \ldots, y_n^*) = [x_2/x_1, \ldots, x_n/x_1]^* = [N_2/N_0)/(N_1/N_0), \ldots]^*$$

is defined by

$$(13) \quad g^i(y_2^*, \ldots, y_n^*) = 0 \qquad (i = 2, 3, \ldots, n)$$

But unless $f^1(y_2^*, \ldots, y_n^*) = 0$ by coincidence, the system will expand or contract along the y^* ray according as $f^1 \gtrless 0$. If the Jacobian matrix $[\partial g^i/\partial y_j]$ has characteristic roots at y^* that are all negative in their real parts, the Routh conditions for local stability of the equilibrium ratios will be assured.

Law of Diminishing Returns

Species that die out are hardly worth talking about. Stationary, neutral equilibrium, we have seen, is too singular a case to be relevant. An exponentially expanding system, as MALTHUS pointed out, must *ultimately* run into space limitations as diminishing returns sets in. Actually, LOTKA, VOLTERRA, and other mathematical speculators about biology recognized this in their discussions of the VERHULST-PEARL logistic law of population growth. Suppose we set $N_0 = 1$ and consider the growth of the N_1 prey in the absence of the N_2 exploiter. With $N_2 = 0$, we examine $F^1(1, N_1/N_0, 0) = F_1(x_1)$. Instead of making this the constant a_1, as in the L-V system (1), Raymond PEARL assumed it to be a decreasing function of species density. Fruitflies in a bottle, when very rare, do at first grow exponentially at the rate $F_1(0) > 0$; but with $F_1'(x_1) < 0$, the net rate NRR ultimately becomes zero, at $F_1(u_1) = 0$, and negative for $x_1 > u_1$. Thus u_1 is the upper-asymptote for the isolated x_1 proportion.

PEARL and VERHULST assumed the simplest decreasing function, making F_1 linear (as in certain models of chemical interactions) to get the logistic law

$$\dot{x}_1 = x_1(a_1 - a_{11}x_1) \qquad\qquad a_1, a_{11} > 0$$

$$(14) \quad x_1(t) = \frac{a_1}{a_{11} + Ce^{-a_1 t}} \qquad\qquad C = \frac{a_1 - a_{11}x_1(0)}{x_1(0)}$$

$$\lim_{t\to\infty} x_1(t) = \frac{a_1}{a_{11}} = u_1 \quad \text{for all} \quad x_1(0) > 0$$

Suppose now we add to the standard LOTKA-VOLTERRA system of (1) the diminishing-return-term $-a_{11}x_1$. And while we are at it, we might as well recognize that crowding many hunters on the same acres will, for fixed supply of N_1 food, cause the hunters to get in each other's way and lower their own rate of growth. Thus, a diminishing-returns term $-a_{22}N_2$ might as well be added to (2) also. (If we wanted *"increasing returns"* rather than diminishing, the algebraic sign of a_{ii} would have to be reversed.)

With $N_0 \equiv 1$, our resulting system can be expressed in terms of the x_i densities of N_i numbers to get

$$(15) \quad \frac{\dot{N}_1}{N_1} = a_1 - a_{11}N_1 - a_{12}N_2$$

$$\frac{\dot{N}_2}{N_2} = -a_2 + a_{21}N_1 - a_{22}N_2 \qquad\qquad a_i, a_{ij} > 0$$

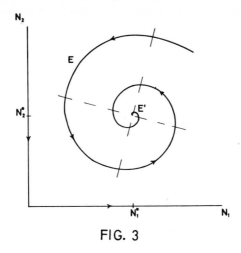

FIG. 3

Figure 3 shows the effects of the new diminishing-returns terms (a_{11}, a_{22}). Its equilibrium point has been displaced to E′ from E, and the closed-trajectories corresponding to conservative oscillation have now become damped spirals. The stationary equilibrium corresponds to $(N_1, N_2; \dot{N}_1, \dot{N}_2) = (N_1^*, N_2^*; 0, 0)$, where N* comes from solving the linear equations

$$a_{11}N_1 + a_{12}N_2 = a_1$$

(16) $$-a_{21}N_1 + a_{22}N_2 = -a_2$$

$$N_1^* = \frac{a_1 a_{22} + a_2 a_{12}}{a_{11}a_{22} + a_{12}a_{21}}$$

$$N_2^* = \frac{-a_{11}a_2 + a_{21}a_1}{a_{11}a_{22} + a_{12}a_{21}}$$

Diminishing returns has caused N_2^* to fall, which is not surprising. But it has caused N_1^* to *rise*, which may seem paradoxical. We may summarize the effects of the a_{11} and a_{22} terms as follows:

1. If the hunted alone experience diminishing returns, their number is unaffected and only the number of N_2 hunters is diminished. If the hunters alone experience diminishing-returns, their number is unaffected and the number of N_1 hunted actually increases. (Note that we cannot dissolve the paradox by saying that it is a reduction in hunters which permits the hunted to grow.)

2. If both species experience weak diminishing-returns, the number of hunters falls and of hunted rises.

3. If both species experience very strong diminishing returns, the equilibrium numbers of both diminish. Indeed, if the prey encounter strong enough diminishing-returns as measured by a_{11}, the numerator of N_2^* in (16) will fall to zero. It makes no sense to solve for a negative N^* corresponding to still larger a_{11}. For what happens, when a_{11} reaches or exceeds the critical level $a_{21} a_1 / a_2$ is that the hunting species gradually becomes extinct and the prey approaches the asymptote of (14's) autonomous logistic growth, facts which cannot be inferred from the linear algebra of (16).

To show that the N^* equilibrium of (16) is dynamically stable, we replace (15) by its approximating local linear system derived from retaining only first-degree terms in the Taylor's expansion of

$$\dot{N}_1 = N_1(a_1 - a_{11}N_1 - a_{12}N_2) = f^1(N_1, N_2) = f^1(N_1^* + n_1, N_2^* + n_2)$$
$$\dot{N}_2 = N_2(-a_2 + a_{21}N_1 - a_{22}N_2) = f^2(N_1, N_2) = f^2(N_1^* + n_1, N_2^* + n_2)$$

$$
(17) \quad
\begin{bmatrix} \dot{n}_1 \\ \dot{n}_2 \end{bmatrix} =
\begin{bmatrix} \dfrac{\partial f^i(N_1^*, N_2^*)}{\partial N_j} \end{bmatrix}
\begin{bmatrix} n_1 \\ n_2 \end{bmatrix}
$$

$$
=
\begin{bmatrix} -a_{11}N_1^* & -a_{12}N_1^* \\ +a_{21}N_2^* & -a_{22}N_2^* \end{bmatrix}
\begin{bmatrix} n_1 \\ n_2 \end{bmatrix}
= Jn
$$

The characteristic roots of the above matrix are those of its characteristic polynomial

$$0 = \det[J - \lambda I] = \lambda^2 + (a_{11}N_1^* + a_{22}N_2^*)\lambda + N_1^* N_2^*(a_{11}a_{22} + a_{12}a_{21})$$

Since both coefficients of the polynomial are positive, the real parts of both its roots are negative, ensuring local stability of equilibrium.

Moreover, for a_{11} and a_{22} sufficiently small the discriminant of the quadratic must be negative, yielding conjugate complex roots that correspond to damped sinusoidal motion like the stable spiral focus of Figure 3. As one or both of (a_{11}, a_{22}) become large, the roots stay stable but become real and give rise to a stable node at E.

Increasing Returns [3]

Suppose that increasing numbers leads to economies of scale, to increasing rather than diminishing returns. As economists have emphasized since Adam SMITH, a more elaborate division of labor may be feasible only on a larger scale; there may be an initial indivisibility that has to be overcome. In nature, changes in size give rise to qualitatively different effects: an atomic pile goes critical when its mass and volume reach a size big enough to reduce its loss of neutrons at the surface; species or gametes encounter each other more often if their density is not too dilute. Where increasing returns prevails, a few firms begin to grow, thereby reaping further advantages of growth, until perfect competition has been replaced by some kind of monopoly or oligopoly.

In terms of the present exploiter-exploited model, we can introduce increasing returns by reversing the algebraic signs of a_{11} and a_{22} in (15). It will be simplest to rewrite (15), using A_{ij} instead of a_{ij} and treating A_{11} and A_{22} as algebraic numbers to get

$$(18) \quad \frac{\dot{N}_1}{N_1} = A_1 + A_{11} N_1 - A_{12} N_2$$

$$\frac{\dot{N}_2}{N_2} = -A_2 + A_{21} N_1 + A_{22} N_2$$

$$N_1^* = -\frac{-A_1 A_{22} + A_2 A_{12}}{A_{11} A_{22} + A_{12} A_{21}} \geq 0$$

$$N_2^* = \frac{A_{11} A_2 + A_2 A_1}{A_{11} A_{22} + A_{12} A_{21}} \geq 0 ,,$$

---

3. The great Russian mathematician A. KOLMOGOROFF, has generalized the Volterra model along lines somewhat similar to my discussion here. (A. Kolmogoroff, "Sulla Teoria Di Volterra Della Lotta Per L'Esistenza", *Giornalle dell Istituto Italiano degli Attuari*, Volume 7, 1936, pp. 74−80.) He writes $\dot{N}_i = N_i K_i (N_1, N_2)$, $(i = 1, 2)$ and postulates $\partial K_i / \partial N_2 < 0$, $N_1 (\partial K_1 / N_1) + N_2 (\partial K_1 / \partial N_2 < 0$, $N_1 (\partial K_2 / \partial N_1) + N_2 (\partial K_2 / \partial N_2) > 0$, $K_1 (0, 0) > 0$, $K_1 (0, A) = 0$ for some $A > 0$, $K_1 (B, 0) = 0$ for some $B > 0$, $K_2 (C, 0) = 0$ for some $B > C > 0$. The motivation for the third inequality is obscure to me. He seems to deduce from his postulates, but without proof, that almost any behavior around the (N^*) equilibrium point is possible, including numerous limit cycles. Perhaps he is asserting that $N_i (\infty) \to \infty$ or 0 is impossible..

The characteristic polynomial of stability now becomes

(19) $\quad \lambda^2 - (A_{11} N_1^* + A_{22} N_2^*) \lambda + N_1^* N_2^* (A_{11} A_{22} + A_{12} A_{21}) = 0,$

which, for $A_{ii} > 0$, always has a root with positive real part. As before, when A_{ii} are sufficiently small, the roots are complex and give rise to anti-damped sinusoidal motions; as one or both get large, the unstable focus turns into an anstable node.

A Unique Cycle

At last we are in a position to combine the analysis of diminishing and increasing returns to produce a cycle of determinate amplitude. It is unthinkable that explosive densities of species can be viable on a fixed amount of land. Assuming A_{ii} positive and constant would lead ultimately to absurd growth of population, without even standing room being provided. Eventually then the forces of decreasing return must be postulated to prevail over the forces in increasing returns. In short, we must abandon the linearity assumption, replacing $A_{ii} N_i$ by concave functions $\lambda R_i (N_i)$ with the following properties

$$R_i' (N_i) > 0 \qquad \text{for } N_i < \overline{N}_i > N_i^*$$
(20) $\quad R_i (N_i) < 0 \qquad \qquad N_i > \overline{N}_i \qquad \qquad (i = 1, 2)$
$$R_i (\infty) = -\infty$$

Now (15) and (15)′ become

$$(15)'' \frac{\dot{N}_1}{N_1} = A_1 + \lambda R_1 (N_1) - A_{12} N_2$$

$$\frac{\dot{N}_2}{N_2} = -A_2 + A_{21} N_1 + \lambda R_2 (N_2) \qquad A_i, A_{ij} > 0$$

For $\lambda = 0$, we have the closed trajectories of the LOTKA-VOLTERRA system. For small positive values of λ, the equilibrium point is an unstable focus. But clearly the outward spiral cannot continue to indefinitely great amplitudes, by virtue of our assuming that the $R_i (N_i)$ functions ultimately encounter strong diminishing returns. We must then have a stable limit cycle, like that of Figure 4. For all positive (N_1, N_2) except (N_1^*, N_2^*), the system will approach in the limit the indicated closed contour $QQQQ$.

The final model of $(15)'$ is merely illustrative of an auto-relaxation mechanism that produces limit cycles. It can be varied in many ways: provided one of the species has strong increasing return, assuming conventional diminishing returns for the other species will not alter the qualitative position. Indeed consider the more general model

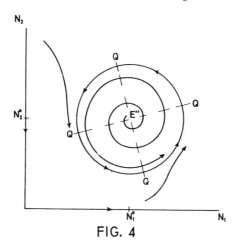

FIG. 4

$$\frac{N_i}{N_i} = F^i(1, N_1, N_2) \ , \ N_0 \equiv 1, \qquad (i = 1, 2)$$

$$0 = F^i(1, N_1^*, N_2^*) = 0$$

$$\frac{\partial F^i(1, N_1^*, N_2^*)}{\partial N_j} = \begin{bmatrix} + & - \\ + & + \end{bmatrix}$$

$$\frac{\partial F^i(1, \infty, \infty)}{\partial N_j} = \begin{bmatrix} -\infty & -\infty \\ + & -\infty \end{bmatrix}$$

Intuitively one can see that one (or more) limit cycles are necessarily implied.

Conclusion

From the basic postulates of increasing returns and exploitation, a cycle with characteristic period and amplitude has been deduced. Whether or not the result is of any interest is an empirical question that cannot be decided by logical manipulation of a priori constructs, definitions, and slogans about the class struggle. The fact that the derivation is of some aesthetic interest and links up with modern techniques of non-linear mechanics lends no genuine significance to the model. The line between a scientific parable and parody is a fine line.

Prof. Dr. Paul A. Samuelson,
Department of Economics,
Massachusetts Institute of Technology,
Cambridge, Massachusetts 02139.

171

Generalized Predator–Prey Oscillations in Ecological and Economic Equilibrium

PAUL A. SAMUELSON

Department of Economics, Massachusetts Institute of Technology, Cambridge, Mass. 02139

Communicated March 2, 1971

ABSTRACT The standard predator–prey model is generalized beyond the Volterra linear-log form. Conservative oscillations are deduced and also conversion to a variational Hamiltonian form. Generalization to more than two species is also castable into Hamiltonian form, with small vibrations around equilibrium being of undamped sinusoidal type by virtue of associated characteristic exponents all being pure imaginaries. However, introduction into ecological equilibrium of a recognition of limited space and inorganic matter destroys the autonomous periodicity of the motions and makes inapplicable the elegant formalisms of classical statistical mechanics. Introduction of simple diminishing returns leads to damped motions that are kept cyclically alive by shocks of the weather and other exogenous stochastic elements. Introduction of increasing returns solely in an interval near equilibrium leads to autonomous self-exciting oscillations near a stable limit cycle; under stochastic forcing functions, a long-run ergodic state becomes predictable.

TWO-SPECIES MODELS

Conservative periodic motions are a characteristic feature of the well-known predator–prey model of Lotka (ref. 1) and Volterra (ref. 2)

$$\dot{X}_1 = X_1(a_1 - a_{12}X_2)$$
$$\dot{X}_2 = -X_2(a_2 - a_{21}X_1), \qquad (1)$$

where X_2 is the predator species (tigers, foxes, capitalists), X_1 the prey species (deer, rabbits, laborers), and $\dot{X}_1$ denotes dX_1/dt. The numbers of "interactions" that give rise to a decrease in prey and increase in predator are assumed proportional to the products X_1X_2.

This is the special case of the more general model

$$\dot{Y}_1 = F_{12}(Y_2), \qquad F_{ij}(Y_j{}^*) = 0$$
$$\dot{Y}_2 = -F_{21}(Y_1), \qquad F_{ij}' < 0 \qquad (2)$$

got by letting $Y_i = \log X_i$, $F_{ij}(Y_j) = a_i - a_{ij} \exp Y_j$. System (2) is a special case of the trivially more general model

$$\dot{Z}_1 = g_1(Z_1)f_{12}(Z_2)$$
$$\dot{Z}_2 = -g_2(Z_2)f_{21}(Z_1) \qquad (3)$$

where $Y_i = \int_{C_i}^{Z_i} g_i(u)^{-1}du$ a monotone increasing and reversible function of Z_i, implying $Z_i = G_i[Y_i]$, $F_{ij}(Y_j) = f_{ij}(G_i[Y_i])$.

It is usually convenient to reduce (3) to standard form (2), but occasionally there are advantages to the

alternative form

$$\dot{W}_1 = W_2$$
$$\dot{W}_2 = -g_2(W_2)F_{21}(W_1), \qquad (4)$$

where $W_2 = F_{12}(Y_2)$, $Y_2 = F_{12}{}^{-1}(W_2) = \psi(W_2)$, $g_2(W_2)^{-1} = \psi'(W_2)$.

Under various regularity conditions, differentiating the first equation with respect to time and utilizing its original form to eliminate all dependence on Y_2 will lead to a second-order differential equation in a single variable

$$\ddot{Y}_1 = -f_1(\dot{Y}_1)F_{21}(Y_1) \qquad (5)$$

where $f_1(\dot{Y}_1) = F_{12}'(F_{12}{}^{-1}[\dot{Y}_1]) < 0$. In (5), one cannot necessarily be free to select $\dot{Y}_1$ arbitrarily in the interval $(-\infty, \infty)$, as can be seen from a case like that in which $F_{12}(Y_2) = \arctan Y_2$, and $\dot{Y}_1$ is confined to the range $(-\pi, \pi)$. (Of course (4) is essentially a variant of (5), but with $Y_2 = W_2$ being the autonomous variable instead of Y_1.)

Eqs. (1)–(5) are all seen to be qualitatively unchanged if time is reversed, as in the transformations $T = -t$, $dX_i/dT = -\dot{X}_i$, provided the roles of the species are reversed. That is, if you run a movie film of the struggle backwards in time, it will appear, so to speak, that rabbits are the predators feasting on the tigers. This time reversibility is consistent with the first law of thermodynamics, as applied to frictionless mechanical systems, but is quite inconsistent with a macroscopic second law of thermodynamics in which some entropy steadily increases as time's arrow flows irreversibly forward. As will be seen in the final two sections, introducing limited land and inorganic environmental elements, with the implied action of diminishing returns (or in the final section, varying returns), will give the system a one-directional asymmetry in time that is incompatible with conservative periodicity.

CONSERVATIVE OSCILLATIONS

Integrals of motion for the L–V model of (1) can be derived by elementary integration. But even for the general model (2), where no solution in terms of elementary functions can be found, simple quadratures yield integrals of motions that are closed, periodic orbits around the unique stationary state $Y^* = (Y_1^*, Y_2^*)$, defined as the root of the simultaneous equations

$$F_{12}(Y_2^*) = 0, \qquad F_{21}(Y_1^*) = 0.$$

To derive integrals of motions, multiply the first equation by $F_{21}(Y_1)$, the second by $F_{12}(Y_2)$, and add, to get

$$F_{21}(Y_1)\dot{Y}_1 + F_{12}(Y_2)\dot{Y}_2 = 0 = \frac{d}{dt}\{H_1(Y_1) + H_2(Y_2)\},$$
$$(6)$$

where $H(Y) = \sum H_j(Y_j)$ is a concave Hamiltonian function with $H_i'(Y_i) = F_{ji}(Y_i)$, and which reaches its minimum at $H(Y^*)$, where $H_i'(Y_i^*) = 0$, $H_i''(Y_i^*) = F_{ij}'(Y_i^*) < 0$.

Let θ be the period of a complete cycle of $[Y_i(t)]$. Since $Y_i(t + \theta) = Y_i(t)$,

$$0 = \frac{1}{\theta}\int_t^{t+\theta} \dot{Y}_i(u)du = \frac{1}{\theta}\int_t^{t+\theta} F_{ij}(u)du$$

$$\lim_{T \to \infty} \frac{1}{T}\int_t^{t+T} F_{ij}(u)du = 0. \qquad (7)$$

When, as in the case of (1), F_{ij} is proportional to the linear expression $X_i^* - X_i$, this yields immediately Volterra's *law of conservation of the means* of species. Such an interpretation will not hold for the general case, although for small-enough vibrations we will have

$$\lim_{T \to \infty} \frac{1}{T}\int_t^{t+T} Y_i(u)du = Y_i^*(1 + \epsilon),$$

where ϵ will go to zero as the initial distance from equilibrium

$$\sum |Y_i(0) - Y_i^*| \to 0.$$

CONVERSION TO A MINIMUM PROBLEM

Eqs. (2) can now be rewritten in Hamilton's canonical form

$$\dot{Y}_1 = \partial H/\partial Y_2 = H_2'(Y_2)$$
$$\dot{Y}_2 = -\partial H/\partial Y_1 = -H_1'(Y_1). \qquad (2')$$

Even if Andronow and Chaikin (ref. 3) had not shown that Eq. (1)'s motions possess a Poincaré integral invariant of the form $\iint (dX_1/X_1)(dX_2/X_2)$, the canonical form of $(2')$ would alert one to the possibility of relating these struggle-for-life equations to a minimizing variation problem, as I have already shown (ref. 4).

We have merely to invert the first equation of $(2')$ to get

$$Y_2 = T'(\dot{Y}_1), \ T'' = (H_2')^{-1} < 0,$$

where $T(Y_1)$ is kind of a kinetic-energy function, in terms of which Y_2 can be defined as a Newton–Hamilton momentum.

In terms of these transformed variables, $(2')$ becomes

$$d/dt\ T'(\dot{Y}_1) + H_1'(Y_1) = 0, \qquad (8)$$

which is essentially of form (5), and can be seen to be the Euler extremal condition for the maximization of

$$I = \int_{t_0}^{t_1} [T(\dot{Y}_1) - H_1(Y_1)]dt,$$

$$\delta \int_{t_0}^{t_1} [T(\dot{Y}_1) - H_1(Y_1)]dt = 0. \qquad (8')$$

That the solution represents a true minimum of I and not merely a stationary value is assured by the fact that the strict convexity of $T(\dot{Y}_1)$ implies strong Legendre and Weierstrass conditions that suffice for a strong minimum provided that $|t_1 - t_0|$ is sufficiently small. However, when the time interval becomes larger than a half period of oscillation, the existence of a Jacobi conjugate point will destroy the minimum character of the struggle-for-life motion.

A classic theorem of Poincaré requires that the characteristic roots associated with a stationary point of Hamiltonian variational system come in opposite-signed pairs. For the present case of closed contours of motion, those roots must be pure imaginaries, so that small vibrations around the equilibrium state will perform the sinusoidal oscillations of simple harmonic motion.

MULTI-SPECIES PREDATOR-PREY MODEL

The case of $n > 2$ predators $(Y_1, \ldots, Y_n)$ interacting with preys $(y_1, \ldots, y_n)$ to produce conservative fluctuations around an equilibrium (y^*, Y^*) can be analyzed by exact analogy to the previous general procedures. We consider

$$\dot{y}_i = \partial H_I(Y_1, \ldots, Y_n)/\partial Y_i =$$
$$\partial[H_I(Y) + H_{II}(y)]/\partial Y_i$$
$$\dot{Y}_i = -\partial H_{II}(y_1, \ldots, y_n)/\partial y_i =$$
$$-\partial[H_I(Y) + H_{II}(y)]/\partial y_i \qquad (i = 1, 2, \ldots, n),$$
$$(9)$$

with the immediate integral of motion

$$\sum_{j=1}^n [\partial H_{II}(y_1, \ldots, y_n)/\partial y_j]\dot{y}_j +$$

$$\sum_{j=1}^n [\partial H_I(Y_1, \ldots, Y_n)/\partial Y_j]\dot{Y}_j =$$

$$\sum_{j=1}^n [\partial H_{II}/\partial y_j][\partial H_I/\partial Y_j] - \sum_j [\partial H_I/\partial Y_j][\partial H_{II}/\partial y_j] =$$

$$0 = \frac{d}{dt}[H_I(Y_1, \ldots, Y_n) + H_{II}(y_1, \ldots, y_n)]. \qquad (10)$$

If $H = H_I + H_{II}$ is a strongly convex function, the first set of equations of (9) can be uniquely inverted to

488

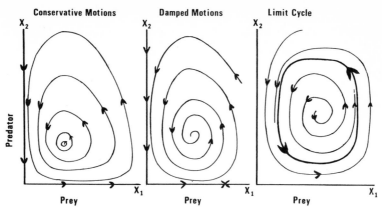

Figs. 1, 2, and 3 show, respectively, the contours of motion for the conservative razor's-edge case, the case recognizing simple diminishing returns, and the case where returns are increasing at intermediate scales near the equilibrium.

give

$$Y_i = \partial T(\dot{y}_1, \ldots, \dot{y}_n)/\partial \dot{y}_i \qquad (i = 1, \ldots, n). \quad (11)$$

where T is a convex "kinetic energy function" and Y_i are "generalized momenta".

The motions of (10) can now be recognized as the Euler variational condition for minimization of the integral

$$I = \int_{t_0}^{t_1} [T(\dot{y}_1, \ldots, \dot{y}_n) + H_{II}(y_1, \ldots, y_n)]dt$$

$$\delta \int_{t_0}^{t_1} [T - H_{II}]dt = 0$$

$$\frac{d}{dt}\partial T(\dot{y}_1, \ldots, \dot{y}_n)/\partial \dot{y}_i - \partial H_{II}(y_1, \ldots, y_n)/\partial y_i = 0. \quad (12)$$

From classical mechanics, it is straightforward to deduce that the conservative motions approach, in the neighborhood of the equilibrium point $(y^*, \dot{y}^*) = (y^*, 0)$, defined by the saddlepoint of $T - H_{II}$,

$$T(0) - H_{II}(y), \leqslant T(0) - H_{II}(y^*) \leqslant T(\dot{y}) - H_{II}(y^*)$$

superimposed sinusoidal motions of the form

$$y_i - y_i^* \cong \sum_1^n C_{ij} \sin(\omega_j t + \gamma_j).$$

Eqs. (9) are both more and less general than Volterra's many-species case

$$\dot{N}_i/N_i = a_i + \sum_{j=1}^m a_{ij}N_j \qquad (i = 1, \ldots, m)$$

$$a_{ij} = -a_{ji}$$

For $m = 2n$ and $a_{ij} \equiv 0$, when both i and j are greater than n or are less than $n + 1$, Volterra's system becomes a special case of (9), but not otherwise. On the other hand, Volterra's system generally lacks the independence of H_I of y_i, and the independence of H_{II} of Y_i. A formulation that includes all cases is

$$\dot{y}_i = +\partial H/\partial Y_i$$
$$\dot{Y}_i = -\partial H/\partial y_i, \qquad (i = 1, \ldots, n)$$

where $H(Y_1, \ldots, Y_n, y_1, \ldots, y_n)$ is strictly convex, say, with a positive definite Hessian matrix of second partial derivatives, so that $H(Y^*, y^*)$ is a true minimum, with closed contours on which the motions around equilibrium must lie. If H has a minimum, the Lagrangian $L(\dot{y}_1, \ldots, \dot{y}_n, y_1, \ldots, y_n) = L(\dot{y}, y)$ enjoys a saddlepoint, $L(0, y) \leqslant L(0, y^*) \leqslant L(\dot{y}, y^*)$, and the characteristic exponents of the extremal motions must be pure imaginaries as in the $H_I + H_{II}$ sinusoidal case.

DISSIPATIVE DIMINISHING RETURNS

The pretty formalisms above should not blind us to the fact that the Lotka-Volterra struggle for existence has forgotten all about the limitation of land and inorganic elements in the environment. Ecological equilibrium without the law of diminishing returns is like Hamlet without the Prince. Conservative motions are always a razor's-edge state: if the first law of thermodynamics, the law of conservation of energy, were not a brute fact of nature, one would have to consider its invention infinitely improbable. Although the molecules and rabbits satisfy energy laws, the macrocosmic variables denoting population numbers do not.

Thus, as I have shown (ref. 5), adding into the right-hand-side parenthesis of (1)'s first equation a small perturbing term $-\epsilon X_1$, to reflect the fact that the prey would ultimately encounter diminishing returns, will destroy the periodicity of the motions in phase space

(X_1, X_2), causing them instead to spiral inward toward a stable focus. This is exactly analogous to the effect of introducing the slightest amount of viscous friction into a simple pendulum system, causing dissipative energy loss and a damping of the swings. Basically, the X_i variables are now to be regarded not as *extensive* variables but as intensive densities, the ratios of extensive magnitudes x_i/x_0, where x_0 is a scalar denoting available square meters of homogeneous land or of other inorganic elements in the environment.

In (1), we may use our freedom to define X_1, X_2 and time units to make $a_2 = 1 = a_{12} = a_{21}$. Then, with diminishing returns recognized, (1) takes the form

$$\dot{X}_1 = X_1(a_1 - \epsilon X_1 - X_2)$$
$$\dot{X}_2 = -X_2(1 - X_1), \tag{13}$$

with equilibrium for ϵ small being approximately $(X_1^*, X_2^*) = (1, a_1 - \epsilon)$, and with deviations from equilibrium approximating

$$X_i - X_i^* \cong C_i[\exp - (\epsilon/2)t] \sin(2\sqrt{a}\,t - \gamma), \tag{14}$$

and thus being slightly damped.

To account for persistence of ecological fluctuations in the face of dissipative diminishing returns, we invoke the influence of exogenous stochastic disturbances from weather and other forces. If these exogenous forcing functions themselves follow a stationary stochastic process, the dissipative damping is exactly what is needed to assure an ergodic state for

$$\lim_{T \to \infty} \text{Prob}\{X_1(t + T), X_2(t + T)|X_1(t), X_2(t)\} =$$
$$P[X_1(t + T), X_2(t + T)] \tag{15}$$

independently of $[X_i(t)]$. The conservative L-V system of (1), if it has exogenous forcing functions to perturb it, will have expected variance that grows progressively with T, presumably like $\sqrt{T}$, leading to the absurd inference that there are no natural limits to the densities of different species.

STABLE LIMIT CYCLE

If autonomous periodicity in the struggle for existence is insisted upon, I found it more plausible to introduce into the parentheses of (1) a nonlinear term $\epsilon f(X_1)$, with the property that f is increasing in the neighborhood of the X^* equilibrium point but reverses its direction at small and large scales for X_1. This will imply an auto-relaxation limit cycle of the Rayleigh-van der Pol type (refs. 3–5). Such a stable periodic motion will be of unique amplitude, independently of initial conditions. Moreover, a small change in any of the coefficients of the system will not destroy the periodicity as it would for a vulnerable, razor's-edge conservative system.

Figs. 1, 2, and 3 show, respectively, the contours of motion for the conservative razor's-edge case, the case recognizing simple diminishing returns, and the case where returns are increasing at intermediate scales near the equilibrium. Only in the first case will the elegant methods of classical statistical mechanics apply.

Financial aid from the National Science Foundation is gratefully acknowledged, as is editorial assistance from Mrs. Jillian Pappas.

1. Lotka, A. J., *Elements of Mathematical Biology* (Williams & Wilkins, Baltimore, Md., 1925; Dover, New York, N.Y., 1956), p. 89.
2. Volterra, V., *Leçons sur la théoric mathématique de la lutte pour la vie* (Gauthier-Villers, Paris, 1931); *Acta biothéoretica*, III (1937), reproduced in Volterra, V., *Opera Matemicha*, V, 414, gives an alternative variational principle to that given here.
3. Andronow, A., and S. Chaiken, *Theory of Oscillations* (Princeton University Press, Princeton, N.J., 1949), p. 100.
4. Samuelson, P. A., "Causality and Teleology in Economics," in *Cause and Effect*, ed. D. Lerner (The Free Press, New York, N.Y., 1965), p. 126; Kerner, E. H., *Bulletin of Mathematical Biophysics*, **19**, 121–146 (1957); **21**, 217–255 (1959); Goodwin, B., *Temporal Organization in Cells* (Academic Press, London, 1963).
5. Samuelson, P. A., "A Universal Cycle?" *Operations Research-verfahren* (1967), Vol. 3, p. 307.

BOOK FOUR

Economics and Public Policy

PART XII

Pure Theory of Public Expenditure

172

Pure Theory of Public Expenditure and Taxation [1]

P. A. Samuelson

1 INTRODUCTION

About a decade ago, I set out in three brief papers [2] a unifying theory of optimal resource allocation to public or social goods and optimal distribution of tax burdens. This theory proved to be, although I did not know as much about its history as I should have, a culmination of a century of writing on public expenditure, by such authors as Pantaleoni (1883), Sax (1883), Mazzola (1890), Wicksell (1896), and above all Lindahl (1919).[3] On the problem of optimal taxation, I had behind me the writings of all the great neo-classical writers: Walras, Marshall, Pareto, Edgeworth, Wicksell and Pigou, culminating in the classic 1938 synthesis of modern welfare economics by Abram Bergson.

The time was ripe for a grand theoretical synthesis of 'benefit' and 'optimal burden' theories of taxation. The building blocks were all there, and what only was needed was for a chimpanzee to come along with the motivation to put them together. My motivation came from dim remembrance of the basic Lindahl diagram in a pre-war article by Richard Musgrave. I perceived it was not quite right for the general case, and when a challenge came, in another connection, to show the worth of mathematics in economics, I used the pure theory of public expenditure as an instance to show how fruitful symbolic methods could be.

In one way, this was fortunate. From the beginning the theory was formulated in definitive general terms: three pages provided the nucleus

[1] I am grateful to Felicity Skidmore for research assistance and to the Carnegie Corporation for a reflective 1965–6 year.

[2] P. A. Samuelson, 'The Pure Theory of Public Expenditure', *Review of Economics and Statistics*, XXXVI (1954) 387–9; ibid. XXXVII (1955), 'Diagramatic Exposition of a Theory of Public Expenditure', 350–6; ibid. XL (1958), 'Aspects of Public Expenditure Theories', 332–8. These are reproduced in P. A. Samuelson, *Collected Scientific Papers*, vol. II, ch. 92, pp. 1223–5; ch. 93, pp. 1226–32; ch. 94, pp. 1233–9. Special acknowledgements are made there to the contemporaneous researches of Richard A. Musgrave and Howard R. Bowen, and to criticisms by S. Enke, J. Margolis and G. Colm.

[3] R. A. Musgrave and A. T. Peacock (eds.), *Classics in the Theory of Public Finance* (London, Macmillan for International Economic Association, 1958) give valuable English translations, and also related works by Adolph Wagner, Barone and many others.

from which all the corollaries could be drawn. In another way, the mathematical garb was unfortunate. Only a few people interested in public finance handle mathematical economics easily, and a number of the theory's essential points have, I think, been misunderstood by writers in the field.[1] A subsequent diagrammatic and literary exposition apparently did not suffice to elucidate sufficiently the theory's essential properties, perhaps not a surprising fact in view of the intrinsic complexities of the subject and the historical misconceptions that have become fossilised in the literature.

I propose here to give a brief review of the analysis, both in its expenditure and tax sides, trying to relate it to modern economic theory and to previous public finance writings. In the alloted space, probably more can be accomplished in trying to clear up misunderstandings than in making new applications.[2] Although the model is primarily concerned with normative, optimality conditions, some attention will be paid to actual behaviour patterns and to the deviations from optimality to be expected from various proposed mechanisms.

2 HISTORICAL DICHOTOMIES

Public finance treatises tended to separate the discussion of expenditure from that of taxation. Most words were devoted to taxes: expenditure somehow got decided and had to be paid for. Two main theories of who should bear the taxes were distinguished: those with greater ability to pay – somehow defined and measured – should pay more; those who received greater 'benefit' from the expenditure should pay more. Eclectric writers, like Smith, hoped that both arguments could be used to reinforce the notion that people with more wealth or income (or 'faculty') should pay more taxes.

By and large, conservative writers liked to stress benefit theories, as a way of holding down the role of government;[3] radical writers liked to

[1] Leif Johansen, *Public Economics* (Amsterdam, North Holland, 1965) ch. 6, is a notable exception. Except with respect to two issues that will be later mentioned, his work and mine run parallel.

[2] Because Musgrave's *The Principles of Public Finance* (New York, McGraw-Hill, 1958) has displaced Pigou's treatise as the classical work on the subject, I devote some attention to its exposition of these matters. Many of my criticisms are met by the reformulations of Musgrave in his paper for this conference; and from neighbourly conversations I know that we are in basic agreement on most issues. Nevertheless, the 1958 text does reflect, and shape, views of many other scholars and therefore does deserve notice.

[3] Wicksell was a partial exception: though not a conservative, he was almost an anarchist in his fear of unresponsive government.

stress ability-to-pay, as a wedge toward reducing inequality of incomes and property.

Legalistic modes of thought dominated. Had governmentless men once come together in a social compact which kept limits on the coercive power government might use against free men?[1] Such views conduced to a benefit point of view, culminating in the Wicksell–Lindahl voluntary-exchange theory of public finance. Did not men have a property right to their property, and therefore was government free to implement ability-to-pay notions by significantly redistributing incomes among the citizenry? Proudhon's saying, 'all property is theft', was a *tu quoque riposte* to the view, 'all interference with property is theft'.

It is silly in 1966 to brood over legality notions of earlier centuries (but folly to read earlier writers without realising that this is germane to understanding their words). Yet disputes over legalisms do give some reflections of the hazy value judgements and sketchy social welfare functions that various people have below the surface.

At least from the time of Bentham, a new notion gained in prominence. Would this public expenditure programme coupled with that tax structure lead to a greater sum total of human happiness than some other one? Which pattern is socially optimal? Even if we strip this utilitarian formulation of its crude and materialistic calculus of hedonism, replacing it by some ordinal notion of a modern social welfare function, it tends to subvert the older notions of 'legitimacy' – that things are done as they are because they have always been so done; that people have a contractual right to no changes; that it is 'unjust' to do certain things to people, even under the purpose of maximising the social welfare.

Bentham and his successors were individualists. At least, individuals provided the parts out of which they formed the whole. But it was the whole on which they concentrated – the maximisation of social welfare. Two quite different notions of 'justice' or 'equity' have lived on in unpeaceful coexistence within western men these last two centuries: a thinker like Stuart Mill was quite torn between them.

On the one hand, a just or equitable society is one in which incomes are properly allocated to produce the greatest bliss for the whole universe

[1] If one assumes that a man has no alternative on this or any other planet to being a citizen, or that the loss of consumers' surplus he would experience if he opted to 'quit civilisation' were great, then society by an all-or-none offer could 'coax' him into acquiescence to almost any tax burden. So even if one accepted the dubious premises of a social compact theory, little would follow therefrom. If one allows any group of citizens to form a coalition and opt out, more interesting consequences follow but we end up in the morass of indeterminate *n*-person game theory.

– even if that means sacrificing something of one man's well-being in the good cause of adding more to the rest of mankind's well-being. Against this is the notion that each man, by virtue of being a man, has an inviolable core of rights that cannot be infringed even to secure some net increment to the social good,[1] or at least cannot be infringed in his case unless all others (who are somehow comparable!) are being similarly treated.

This second notion of justice, an analytic philosopher would notice, is somehow tied up with a 'symmetry principle', in which other traits than being a man are posited to be irrelevant. Whether women, minor children, lunatics, neurotics, drunks, chimpanzees, ants, amoebae, carrots, and DNA molecules are to be excluded or included in the universe of discourse becomes a nice question. Furthermore, men may be alike in being men but unlike in other respects: how do you dole out equal treatment to unequals? In the twentieth century, this second notion of justice is appealed to, not very successfully, to exercise veto power in extension of activities of government.[2]

I suspect that a persevering scholar could work up a social welfare function that incorporated into itself *both* notions of justice. I shall not assay such an ambitious task here, but shall concentrate on the ordinary case of a social welfare function – pleading as possible justification that, if we address ourselves to the problem of optimal public finance for a society *far* in the future, there will be plenty of time to make changes without thwarting people's expectations or trampling on their legal rights

[1] Wicksell illustrates the confusion. His just theory of taxation is designed to protect each man from injustice in the second sense; but his famous sentences underlying application of his theory, 'It is clear that justice in taxation tacitly presupposes justice in the existing distribution of property and income' (Musgrave and Peacock, op. cit. p. 108), points in the Bentham-welfare direction – as does Lindahl's quotation from him 'it would obviously be nonsense to speak of "a just proportion of an unjust whole"' (Musgrave and Peacock, op. cit. p. 227). Neither Wicksell nor Lindahl – nor for that matter a host of discredited worshippers of Pareto-optimality – face up to the consequences of non-tacit failure of the presupposition about optimal interpersonal distribution of dollars. Moreover, a failure of Pareto-optimality could be identified as a regrettable and pitiable inefficiency, without implying an identifiable unjustly treated party.

[2] Not surprisingly, its spokesmen like to appeal to unanimity – or, to use an Irish Bull – to near-unanimity in social decision making. However, a unanimity requirement can, and usually does, lead to no way of deciding between two alternatives (and leads, at best, to a non-transitive ordering); and they hope either that this will be resolved by favouring the *status quo*, putting the burden of proof upon *all* change, or – and this will become an increasingly important strain in libertarian thinking, the farther away recedes the laissez faire conditions of Victorian capitalism – putting the burden of proof upon any departure from their defined condition of inviolable natural rights and individual liberties (inclusive of property rights).

(human and property). Furthermore, as part of optimal feasibility theory, if we wish we can embody some of these second notions of justice as side-constraints on the maximum social welfare problem.

3 PSEUDO-DEMAND ALGORITHM TO COMPUTE EQUILIBRIUM

Although my analysis is in the tradition of the voluntary-exchange tax theories of Wicksell and Lindahl, one of my main findings has been the falsity of that theory's relying upon voluntarism.[1] Another has been the impossibility of truly separating benefit-allocation and redistribution-equity considerations, since these intrinsically overlap and must be simultaneously resolved. Neither of these views seem to have been embraced by public finance experts with complete joy. A third source of criticism of my analysis concerns itself with the alleged assumption in my model of 'equal consumption' by all.

This last confusion can be simply disposed of. A public good – call it x or x_2 or x_{n+m} – is simply one with the property of involving a 'consumption externality', in the sense of entering into two or more persons' preference functions simultaneously. Thus, public good x_2 might be liked by Man 1, disliked by Man 2, and be quite indifferent to all other men; or it might be 'much' liked by Man 1 and 'little' liked by Man 2, and be disregarded by all others. This was made clear to any careful reader of my papers: when I equated $x_2^1 = x_2^2 = \ldots = x_2^s = x_2$, that did not imply any equality in the relevant marginal rate of substitutions $(\partial u^i/\partial x_2)/\partial u^i/\partial x_1^i$, or even that they have the same sign.

I shall now present [2] a pseduo-demand analysis that would provide an *omniscient* planner with one method of solving the optimality equations of the original model:

$$\text{I} \quad F\left(\sum_{i=1}^{s} x_1^i, \ldots, \sum_{i=1}^{s} x_n^i, x_{n+1}, \ldots, x_{n+m} \right) = 0$$

---

[1] R. A. Musgrave, op. cit. p. 86 n. gives the opposite impression, failing to mention that more than one-third of my original exposition was given to the game-theoretic reasons why people will not reveal their preferences for public goods as they do in the case of private goods.

[2] This mathematical version can be skipped by those content to read the special case of the Graphical Appendix. The Johansen interpretation of Lindahl, which Musgrave's current paper develops, can be generalised to the pseudo-demand model. I received Robert Dorfman's paper for the conference, 'General Equilibrium with Public Goods', too late to relate it to this discussion.

$$\text{II} \quad \frac{u_j^i}{u_1^i} = -\frac{F_j}{F_1}, \qquad (j=2,\ldots,n;\ i=1,\ldots,s)$$

$$\text{III} \quad \sum_{i=1}^{s} \frac{u_{n+k}^i}{u_1^i} = -\frac{F_{n+k}}{F_1}, \qquad (k=1,\ldots,m)$$

$$\text{IV} \quad \frac{U_i u_1^i}{U_1 u_1^1} = 1 \qquad (i=2,\ldots,s)$$

where $F[\,.\,]$ is the social production-possibility frontier relating public and private goods (including private factors of production as negative goods); where $u^i(x_1^i,\ldots, x_n^i, x_{n+1},\ldots, x_{n+m})$ is the ith man's ordinal preference function for public and private goods; where $U(u^1,\ldots, u^s)$ is the (individualistic) social welfare function of Bergson type that provides an ethical evaluation of the well-beings of different persons; and where numerical subscripts to a function denote such partial derivatives as $\partial F/\partial x_r$, $\partial u^i/\partial x_r$, $\partial U/\partial u_r$.

If there were only private goods, we could rely on each man to calculate and present his demand functions once we gave him his budget income and market prices at which he could trade freely. *With public goods, he has every reason not to provide us with revelatory demand functions.* So I imagine a referee, who is appointed by the planning authority and who somehow knows man i's indifference function u^i. This referee calculates for him what I call his pseudo-demand functions, for both private and public goods, on the assumption that his utility is maximised subject to a budget equation involving a fixed lump-sum algebraic net income L^i, provided for him by the State (and aside from his incomes from owned factors, which are already included in some of the private variables $-x_j^i$); and subject to fixed (uniform) prices, $(P_1,\ldots, P_n)$, at which he can freely buy (or sell) private goods; and subject to fixed (non-uniform between people) *pseudo*-tax-prices $(P_{n+1}^i,\ldots, P_{n+m}^i)$ at which the referee *pretends* the man can buy as much or as little of the public goods as he pleases. (What kinds of exclusion devices would be needed to make this pretence less bizarre, I shall not go into since this is all merely a computing algorithm, which an electronic computer could use, dispensing with the dramatic device of a referee and market terminology.)

The referee solves for each man the maximum problem

$$\max_{(x_j^i,\, x_{n+k})} u^i(x_1^i,\ldots, x_n^i;\ x_{n+1},\ldots, x_{n+m})$$

subject to the pseudo-budget equation

$$(P_1 x_1^i + \ldots + P_n x_n^i) + (P_{n+1}^i x_{n+1} + \ldots + P_{n+m}^i x_{n+m}) = L^i \gtrless 0,$$

to get the pseudo-demand functions:

$$x_j^i = D_j^i(P_1, \ldots, P_n; \ P_{n+1}^i, \ldots, P_{n+m}^i; \ L^i), \qquad (j=1,\ldots,n)$$
$$x_{n+k} = D_{n+k}^i(P_1, \ldots, P_n; \ P_{n+1}^i, \ldots, P_{n+m}^i; \ L^i), \qquad (k=1,\ldots,m)$$

The co-ordinator of all the referees now solves the pseudo-general-equilibrium problem in which all markets are cleared in terms of supply and demand, but taking into account the necessary equality of all public good variables, $D_{n+k}^1 = D_{n+k}^2 = \ldots = D_{n+k}^s$.[1] The full conditions of pseudo-market equilibrium are:

(a) $F\left(\ldots, \ \sum\limits_{i=1}^{s} x_j^i, \ldots, \ \ldots, x_{n+k}, \ldots\right) = 0$

(b) $\dfrac{P_j}{P_1} = -\dfrac{F_j}{F_1} \qquad (j=2,\ldots,n)$

(c) $\sum\limits_{i=1}^{s} \dfrac{P_{n+k}^i}{P_1} = -\dfrac{F_{n+k}}{F_1} \qquad (k=1,\ldots,m)$

(d) $x_j^i = D_j^i(\ldots, P_j, \ldots; \ \ldots, P_{n+k}^i, \ldots; \ L^i) \qquad (i=1,\ldots,s; \ j=1,\ldots,n)$

(e) $x_{n+k} = D_{n+k}^i(\ldots, P_j, \ldots; \ \ldots, P_{n+k}^i, \ldots; \ L^i) \quad (i=1,\ldots,s)$

(f) $\dfrac{U_i u_1^i}{U_1 u_1^1} = 1 \qquad (i=2,\ldots,s)$

Careful examination of (a)–(f) shows we can eliminate from them the pecuniary variables $(P_1, \ldots, P_m; \ \ldots, P_{n+1}^i, \ldots, P_{n+m}^i, \ldots; \ L^1, \ldots, L^s)$ and be left with the solution to I–IV above. So we do have a possible (but not necessarily practical or most-efficient, and certainly not a spontaneous) computing algorithm for achieving the desired optimum.

Similar careful examination of (a)–(e) will show that by manipulating the pattern of lump-sum (L^i), we can trace out *all* the Pareto-optimal solutions to I–III: i.e. by giving Man 1 relatively much L^1 at the expense of Man 2's L^2, we can increase the ordinal utility u^1 at the expense of u^2 along society's utility-possibility frontier.[2]

[1] This has no implications of equal satisfaction from the public good. Moreover, if Man i hates a good, x_{n+k}, its pseudo-price to him may have to be negative, namely $P_{n+k}^i < 0$.

[2] This is Chart 4 in my second paper; it is also Fig. 4–6 of Musgrave, op. cit. p. 83, despite the author's belief that only two of his points are on it. The author is confused in thinking that he can validly derive a different utility frontier from mine by 'a difference in the treatment of income distribution' (p. 81). When he subjects his men to

Finally, let us consider a pseudo *laissez-faire* solution of the equations in which all lump-sum redistributions are set equal to zero. With $L^i \equiv 0$, and returns conditions suitable for viable competitive *laissez-faire*, one particular solution will be found for (a)–(e), but, of course, with (f) not honoured. It is a theorem that pseudo *laissez-faire* does lead to Pareto-optimality,[1] but generally not to ethically-optimal maximum welfare.

---

different benefit-tax payments, he washes out his own assumption of predetermined income distribution (or effectively offsets it). This may be a convenient place to note, for the interested reader, the few places where a close reading of Musgrave leads to disagreement between us. The possibility or impossibility to apply an 'exclusion principle' is less crucial than consumption externality, since often exclusion would be wrong where possible (8–9). 'Joint consumption' is not an apt name for consumption externality (10 n. 1). The Benefit vs. Ability-To-Pay Dichotomy of the whole book needs careful qualification along with the Allocation vs. Distribution Dichotomy. The partial equilibrium analysis of Lindahl and Bowen (74–80) is not something different from my general equilibrium analysis (81–86); as the present Appendix makes clear it can be rigorously treated as a special case of my analysis. The p. 86 footnote and relevant text discussion does not do justice to my game-theoretic objections to the voluntary-exchange theory, and the income distribution assumptions underlying Fig. 4 come to the same theory as mine if the Fig. 4–6 frontier is validly derived. On p. 84, paragraph 2, the author seems to be saying that Pareto-optimality is unique for private goods but not for public: in fact, neither is unique and the same distributional problem arises.

An important final point should be recognised. Suppose we ignore Musgrave's Stabilisation Branch, as we ought to be able to do in a timeless Say's Law world. Should his Allocation Budget 'balance', and his Distribution Budget balance out algebraically to zero? Only if constant-returns-to-scale holds for the production functon $F(\cdot)$ can there be a balance of $\Sigma_k \Sigma_i P^i_{n+k} X_k$ pseudo-receipts and cost to government of public goods. Under increasing returns ΣL^i must be negative to subsidise losses from MC pricing. Even if ΣL^i can be zero under constant returns, it need not: lump-sum divergences from P^i_{n+m} can be offset by divergences from the (L^i) solution of (a)–(e) or (a)–(f) *without harming the optimal solution*!

[1] Leif Johansen, op. cit., has proved this theorem for his version of the Lindahl mechanism, pp. 134–5. In his following pages, particularly at pp. 136–8, Johansen misses perceiving the theorem of my previous paragraph – that with *proper* choice of (L^i), the Lindahl pseudo-market algorithm will provide a maximum to a specified social welfare function – and he is therefore too hard on the mechanism in the sense of criticising it for the wrong reason. Musgrave's paper at this current I.E.A. September 1966 Meeting, in his paragraph 21 commenting on Lindahl and Johansen does seem to perceive the essential theorem, recognising tacitly that the proper reallocation of income is not *prior* to public good determination but must be done *simultaneously* with it. (This is also the case in a Good Society involving only private goods and optimal income distribution.) But in the following paragraphs, Musgrave is too easy on the Pseudo-Demand mechanism; in his desire to be 'parochial', attributable perhaps to an underlying desire to be 'practical', he overlooks the *necessarily* 'pseudo' character of the pseudo-demand analysis of (a)–(e). Moreover, he tacitly lapses into the cardinal sin of the narrow 'new welfare' economists: 'If you can't get (or even define!) the maximum of a social welfare function, settle for Pareto-optimality', as if *that* were second-best or even 99th best.

I believe that those conservative economists who have been most doubtful about or antagonistic toward ability-to-pay redistributional theories of taxation have been groping toward some notion like that of my pseudo *laissez-faire* equilibrium. Another group, less conservative, have been groping toward the notion of my pseudo general-equilibrium with whatever degree of redistribution (of the lumpsum L^i, or more feasible progressive taxation involving some dead-weight losses) is considered currently optimal or feasible. Within this pseduo analysis, the partial separation of Benefit-Allocation and Equity-Redistribution elements can be given some analytical meaning.

4 AFFIRMATION OF DOUBTS

Whatever the relevance of the pseudo-equilibrium algorithm to a computer omniscient with respect to the F, u^i and U functions, we must not forget that it has *no* relevance to motivated market behaviour. Moreover, it is striking how Wicksell and Lindahl, and even Musgrave and Johansen (and now Dorfman's name can perhaps be added), after getting a glimpse of pseudo-equilibrium descend to the swampland of mathematical politics, ending up with inconclusive behaviour patterns by legislatures, factions and parties, running inevitably afoul of Arrow's Impossibility Theorem. Game theory, except in trivial cases, propounds paradoxes rather than solves problems.

It is possible that Professors Harsanyi or Bishop could apply advanced game theory – Nash threat points, etc. – to the problem of how two or more consumers of public goods will actually interact; even if one has doubts about the axioms of such models, the fruit of such an exercise might be of some interest. But I am not aware that those fascinated by the benefit notion have done much in this area. I find naive the belief of Wicksell that simultaneous voting on expenditure and taxes will promote an optimum. His requirement for 'unanimity', which pitifully degenerates into a requirement for 'approximate (!) unanimity', comes as an anti-climax. (What does a three-quarters majority have that a four-quarter doesn't have? Less unlikelihood. By that criterion, we edge back toward a simple majority, with its paradoxes.)

A corrosive nihilism seems needed to puncture the bubble of vague and wishful thinking in these matters. Let me select an example from one of the most acute of the modern writers, Leif Johansen. He seems to believe that Pareto optimality will be arrived at by voting [perhaps by unanimity?] concluding, 'If all questions which in one way or another are interrelated are dealt with simultaneously, one should in principle arrive at Pareto-optimality' (op. cit. p. 52). I find no warrant in game theory for this. 'Simultaneity' is a red herring. If there were only one Pareto-optimal configuration, a valid theorem might be demonstrated that it would be selected by unanimous vote. In that Utopia no problems would arise, and *every* social welfare function, $U(u^1, u^2, \ldots)$, would lead to the same outcome. But in the economic cases under consideration, why should one man not refuse to go to a particular Pareto-optimal point in the hope of being able to better himself by refusing to make the vote unanimous? The Prisoner's Dilemma – in which it is Pareto-optimal for neither of two accomplices to confess secretly, but in which it is safer for either to confess if the other might – is merely the philosopher's reminder, of what economists studying break-down of cartel behaviour have always known, that Pareto-optimality is a definition not an inevitable destination.

My doubts do not assert that passably good organisation of the public household is impossible or unlikely,[1] but merely that theorists have not yet provided us with much analysis of these matters that has validity or plausibility. If I stimulate someone to resolve my doubts, that will make two people happy.[2]

5 SEMANTICS OF SOCIAL OR PUBLIC GOODS

I should like to close with a final regret. In my papers I often spoke of 'polar' cases: e.g. the polar case of a 'pure private good', like $x_1 = x_1^1 + x_1^2 + \ldots$, whose x_1^i 'entered' in a single person's utility function. At

[1] If someone did demonstrate such an assertion, its corollary would not necessarily be 'Spend less on government' or 'Spend more on government'.

[2] After reading my first draft, Professor James Buchanan of the University of Virginia wrote me that in my earlier papers I had been almost too easy on Wicksell, but in this paper I am very hard on him. I agree. Since 1954, I have had a chance to read him in English and not just German. Professor Kolm has also expressed the view that I am too critical of Wicksell. Since Knut Wicksell is my scientific hero, I should explicate. I agree that Wicksell should not be confused with Lindahl, even though his mathematical help to Lindahl made precise what Lindahl meant; and Wicksell deserves credit for exposing the nonsense of voluntarism in pseudo-tax and other formulations. In this sense Wicksell is a devastating critic of Lindahl. But where I must fault Wicksell, and here my opinion differs from that of Kolm and Johansen, is in connection with his unsubstantiated faith that somehow within Parliament or political democracy an efficacious unanimous move to Pareto-optimality (and the ethically right point of this set) can be found. Professor Kolm seems to share Wicksell's belief that n men in a room or a universe will end up on the Pareto frontier. I do not. If they were right, there would be never any practical problem of welfare efficiency. Society would spontaneously get itself efficiently organised always.

the other pole was what I called a 'pure public good', which 'entered' into everybody's utility: thus, with $x_2 = x_2^1 = x_2^2 = \ldots$, we have $u^i(x_1^i, x_2)$ in each case. I did not demur when critics claimed that most of reality fell between these extreme poles or stools, but instead suggested that these realistic cases could probably be analysed fruitfully as a 'blend' of the two polar cases.

I now wonder whether this was optimal semantics. Since, as I have already pointed out and insisted upon, a public good may have zero or negative influence on some person(s), most of the cases brought forward as allegedly not involving either pole can in fact be regarded formally as belonging to the public-good pole rather than having to be regarded as a blend between the two poles.

Thus, consider what I have given in this paper as the definition of a public good, and what I might better have insisted upon as a definition in my first and subsequent papers: 'A public good is one that enters two or more persons' utility.'[1] What are we left with? Two poles and a continuum in between? No. With a knife-edge pole of the private-good case, and with *all* the rest of the world in the public-good domain by virtue of involving some 'consumption externality'.[2]

---

[1] Perhaps the word 'enters' should be replaced by 'enters irreducibly' to take account of a subtle semantic difficulty. Whether the same good appears in two utility functions can be affected by the definitions and symbolisms used to represent variables. Thus, we may have fireworks in your function and mine; but, without changing the substance of the case, suppose we redefine as distinct variables, fireworks exploded in the sky, y; fireworks observed (or observable) by you, z; fireworks observed by me, v. Then it might be misleadingly said that there are no variables entering literally into more than one utility function and we have here 'purely private' goods. However, by such a change in symbolism all public good phenomena could be defined out of existence. This shows the need for some such word as 'irreducibly' in any formal definition. In the last analysis, we can diagnose the existence of the private good phenomena which can be optimally handled by the market only by a simultaneous scrutiny of the variables and of how they enter in both the utility functions and the technological side constraints. This warning is all the more necessary in the case where there could conceivably be found an 'exclusion' device that would enable the joint-supply nature of the problem to be dramatised; the point is that we need the theory of public goods to decide just when such devices ought to be used. Later in the Appendix I work with various dummy variables that give point to these remarks.

For the $(n+1)$th time, let me repeat the warning that a *public good* should not *necessarily* be run by public rather than private enterprise.

[2] Consider the last half of the current Musgrave paper, which is supposed to be concerned with non-polar cases of social goods. In particular, consider the taxonomic table in paragraph 30. The most general case there can be written in my terminology as

$$u^1(\ldots, x_2, x_3, \ldots) = f^1(\ldots, \lambda^1 x_2 + \gamma^1 x_3, \ldots)$$
$$u^2(\ldots, x_2, x_3, \ldots) = f^2(\ldots, \lambda^2 x_2 + \gamma^2 x_3, \ldots)$$

instead of as $U_A(Y_A + \beta Y_B)$ and $U_B(Y_B + \gamma Y_A)$. But please note the vital point: formally the above u^i fit *perfectly* into my original analysis and if it be called a polar

It is like the problem of pure competition and monopoly. Once people thought of these as two poles: pure (or perfect?) competition vs. pure (or perfect) monopoly, with real-world phenomena mostly an inbetween blend called 'imperfect' or 'monopolistic' competition. After decades of debate, it is now pretty much agreed, I think, that it is more fruitful to abandon the pole of 'perfect monopoly', and consider the real world as being a good or bad approximation to the pure competition role, with various new phenomena coming in as we depart in different directions from pure competition.

So I now think the useful terminology in this field should be: pure private goods in which the market mechanism works optimally, and possibly close approximations to them, versus the whole field of consumption-externalities or public goods.

This does, however, lead to an uncomfortable situation. If the experts remain nihilistic about algorithms to allocate public goods, and if all but a knife-edge of reality falls in that domain,[1] nihilism about most of economics, rather than merely public finance, seems to be implied.

What is the reply to this grave query? I am not sure. But here are some considerations I believe to be relevant.

First, if worst came to worst and there were found to be no way out of

---

case *then the second half of Musgrave's paper is formally as much concerned with the polar case as is the first.*

[1] Those who build social norms out of individual norms, so that social $U = U(u^1, u^2, \ldots)$ rather than belonging to some external group mind, must note that little is left of the 'tree property' of private goods in U, if people through altruism or envy have in their u^i the bread consumption of other people, namely x_1^2 in u^2. Against critics who believe in an organic theory of the state or in a patriotic code of good conduct, individualists win a hollow victory if *every* good now becomes a public good. Formally, my equations (II'–III') now become

$$\frac{\Sigma_i U_i u^i_{n+k}}{\Sigma_i U_i u^i_{n+1}} = -\frac{F_{n+k}}{F_{n+1}}, \qquad (n=0; \ k=2, \ldots, m).$$

These $m - 1$ conditions can be split up into a Pareto-optimality set II' and an interpersonal-equity set III' in the regular case where $s < m - 1$ and the rank of $[u^i_{0+j}]$ is always s. We can then, by renumbering of goods if necessary, write down the $m - s$ and the $s - 1$ conditions

II' $\qquad\qquad\qquad (u^j_{0+i}, f_i)$ is to be of rank s

III' $\qquad\qquad \dfrac{\Sigma_i U_i u^i_{0+k}}{\Sigma_i U_i u^i_{0+1}} = -\dfrac{F_{0+k}}{F_{0+1}}, \qquad (k=2, \ldots, s).$

Now the pseduo-market equilibrium conditions (a)–(e) become completely pseudo. To the degree that a near-tree property prevails for some variables, it may pay to keep a $U(u^1, u^2, \ldots)$ formulation rather than work directly with a general $U(x_{0+1}, x_{0+2}, \ldots)$. I wish to thank Professor S. Kolm for pointing out an error in my first-draft formulation.

the indictment, we should have to face up to the disappointing truth. It would be ostrich-like to do otherwise.

Second, much of reality may be found *near* to the pole of private goods, and to this degree the problem becomes less acute.

Third, and this is much the most constructive and comforting point, nihilism or doubt about the solution for the general case of any public good might be out of order in connection with many particular forms of public goods. It is here that many of my critics will turn out to have a valid point (but not, I hope in the end, a point against me or my analysis).

Let me illustrate by some possible examples. Consider cinemas in a large town. Because of deviations from constant-returns-to-scale ('indivisibilities', if you like), my well-being depends on your being willing to watch movies and in fact I might get a greater thrill out of a film if I watch it in the same room with hundreds of other people. Doubtless, film watching will enter more than one u^i function as a public good variable x_{n+k}. But, if the town is populous and distances are small, free enterprise might well result in optimal replication of cinema theatres, each operating at capacity audiences, with fares set competitively at short and long-run marginal and average costs. This is a case where an exclusion principle can, and should, operate.[1]

What is much needed, I believe, are serious analytical studies of cases where public good situations can be solved by algorithms immune to bilateral-monopoly or game-theoretic objections.

Until such cogent analyses are forthcoming, an attitude of sympathetic scepticism seems justified. For the theory of public goods is not simply an extension of Mangoldt–Marshall joint supply or of joint demand. In general, they involve 'consumption externality'[2] with a game-theoretic or bi-lateral monopoly element of indeterminacy of the sort that may not be removable by use of an 'exclusion' device or that cannot *optimally* be handled by such a device.[3]

The Appendix, which is not less important than the paper, relates my general equilibrium analysis to traditional analyses of partial equilibrium.

---

[1] I believe that Herbert Mohring has adduced cases of public road financing where replication provides optimal solutions. See my paper 'The Monopolistic Competition Revolution', in R. E. Kuenne (ed.), *Monopolistic Competition Theory: Essays in Honor of Edward H. Chamberlain* (Wiley, New York, 1967) pp. 105–38, particularly pp. 128–37 where replication and 'asymptotic homogeneity' is rigorously analysed.

[2] In his current paper Musgrave uses the somewhat doubtful term 'non-rivalness in consumption' for what I call 'consumption externality'.

[3] At the end of my Graphical Appendix I illustrate with examples of electricity and roads some of the varieties of experience that enter into the case of public goods.

APPENDIX: PSEUDO MARKET EQUILIBRIUM

(A) THE LINDAHL–JOHANSEN CASE

Since the 1880s it has been known that partial equilibrium is a rigorously legitimately special case of general equilibrium if the marginal utility of money is *strictly constant* for each person, and it is in this case that the concepts of consumers' surplus become unambiguously simple. Wicksell (pp. 101–3 of Musgrave and Peacock), Lindahl (pp. 171–2 and 223–4 of Musgrave and Peacock), and Johansen (pp. 163–75 of *Public Economics*), and Dorfman (I believe, implicitly, in using his numerical measure of benefit) have considered this strong case. If we couple with constancy of the marginal utility of money, the assumption of constant opportunity cost, an assumption much more special than that of constant returns to scale, the pseudo equilibrium of my text becomes identical to the equilibrium of the famous Lindahl diagram (Musgrave and Peacock, p. 170 and Musgrave, Fig. 4-2).

Specifically, for $(i = 1, 2)$, let

$$u^i(x_1^i, x_2) = 1 \cdot x_1^i + f_i(x_2), f_i'' < 0$$
$$F(x_1^1 + x_1^2, x_2) = 1 \cdot (x_1^1 + x_1^2) + Mx_2 - \overline{V}^1 - \overline{V}^2 = 0$$

where $\overline{V}^i$ represents the fixed labour supply of Man i that will always be employed and without disutility.

Set $P_1 = 1$ as numeraire, and face each man with respective pseudo tax-prices P_2^1 and P_2^2. Each man's referee will maximise his u^i by setting

$$f_i'(x_2) = P_2^i \qquad (i = 1, 2); \tag{1}$$

adding all P_2^i vertically and equating to marginal cost, M, we have the equilibrium condition

$$f_1'(x_2) + f_2'(x_2) = M, \tag{2}$$

which can be solved for the optimum level of public good, x_2^*.

Because of the independence of utility of the good and constancy of marginal utility of the private good (which serves as numeraire or money), there is only *one* pseudo-demand curve for each man (independently of considerable variations in income and taxes).

To convert the pseudo-demand analysis into the Lindahl–Johansen diagram, as can be done without reinterpretations only in the constant-cost case, call $P_2^1/M = h = x$, the percentage of cost of the public good charged to Man 1. The condition

$$\frac{P_2^1}{M} + \frac{P_2^2}{M} = 1 \tag{3}$$

becomes their $h+(1-h)=1$. So we can plot $h=f_1'(x_2)/M$ against x_2 and $1-h=f_2'(x_2)/M$ against x_2, to get the Lindahl diagram.

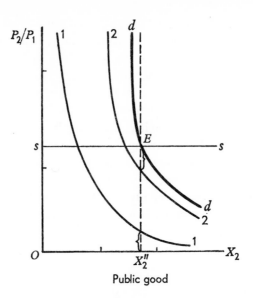

FIG. 1

In this Bowen form of the Lindahl diagram, 11 represents pseudo-demand for Man 1; 22 that for Man 2; their vertical sum, *dd*, intersects the *ss* supply curve to give pseudo-tax equilibrium

We can superimpose on this diagram the contours of equal

$$u^1(x_1^1, x_2) = u^1(\overline{V}^1+L^1-P_2^1x_2, x_2) = 1\cdot(\overline{V}^1+L^1-hMx_2)+f_1(x_2)$$
$$u^2(x_1^2, x_2) = u^2(\overline{V}^2+L^2-P_2^2x_2, x_2) = 1\,(\overline{V}^2+L^2-(1-h)\,Mx_2)+f_2(x_2). \quad (4)$$

The generalised contract curve of mutually tangent u^i contours is seen to be vertical in this case of constant marginal utility of the private good, going through E and confirming the Pareto-optimality of the Lindahl case of pseudo equilibrium. The Bowen and Lindahl curves, and their intersections, are in this case unchanged by a redistribution of income.

It also happens to be true, what should not have impressed Lindahl as being important, that the total of *money* utilities summed over people,

$$\{\overline{V}^1+L^1-P_2^1x_2+f_1(x_2)\} + \{\overline{V}^2+L^2-P_2^2x_2+f_2(x_2)\}$$
$$= \sum_i \overline{V}^i + \sum_i L^i - Mx_2 + \sum_i f_i(x_2) \quad (5)$$

is in this case at a maximum at the pseudo equilibrium of Lindahl x_2^*. But who thinks social welfare can be measured in terms of money independently of the distribution of incomes? Thus, the social welfare function might be

$$U = W_1(u^1) + W_2(u^2), \quad W_i'' < 0 \qquad (6)$$

and only at one particular $(x_1^{1*}, x_1^{2*}, x_2^*)$ configuration will true U be at a maximum. Yet at all possible $(x_1^{1*} + A, x_1^{2*} - A, x_2^*)$ will Lindahl's E equilibrium be found to maximise the sum of *money* utilities.

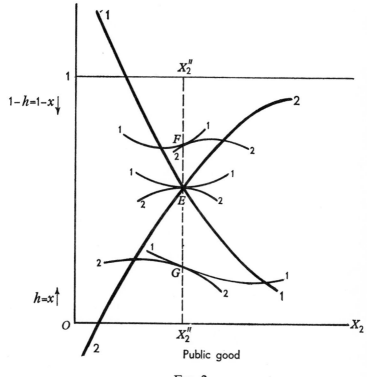

FIG. 2

Here Man 2's pseudo-demand is turned upside down and measured downward from the cost level shown earlier as *ss*. The pseudo-demands intersect at E level, that point of mutual *horizontal* tangency of the men's indifference contours. The special assumption of constant marginal utility of the private good is what makes the contract curve of mutual tangencies, *FEG*, happen to be vertical so that redistributions of income will not affect the optimum X_2^* – an unrealistic result

How can the maximum U of (6) be achieved? It can be achieved by charging each man the P_2^{i*} (i.e. $h^* = x^*$) that can be read off the diagrams, and by giving men the proper $(L^{1*}, L^{2*}) = (B^*, -B^*)$ lump-sum transfers, This should delight Musgrave or anyone who wishes to keep separate the benefit Allocation and ability-to-pay Distribution components.

However, the primacy of such a taxing pattern is negated once we see that there are an *infinity* of other tax patterns that lead to exactly the same thing. Thus, set x^* as above but with

$$P_2^1 = P_2^{1*} + C$$
$$P_2^2 = P_2^{2*} - C$$
$$L^1 = B^* - Cx_2^*$$
$$L^2 = -B^* + Cx_2^*. \tag{7}$$

Then for *any* C, not only $C = 0$ as the Lindahl theory formally requires, we end up with Pareto-optimal configuration that maximises true social welfare U!

It may be argued that setting tax-prices at $P_2^{i*} \pm C$ will produce false pseudo-prices and lead to the wrong determination of x_2. But remember these are *pseudo* tax prices, not *actual* ones at which people are non-excluded from using the public good. The referee for Man i is a fiction, used for exposition of the computation. Once x_2^* is optimally determined, it is there regardless of stated tax-prices. All anyone cares about in the end is his total (algebraic) tax, $P_2^i x_2 - L^i$, and not how Musgrave or anyone else cares to compartmentalise it.

Suppose by a clever 'excluder device', one could make *pseudo-tax* prices genuine prices. Thus, set x_2 so large that after one uses the excluder on Man i, his x_2 – now called x_2^i – can agree with his no-longer-pseudo demand function, $D_2^i(P_1; P_2^i; L^i)$. (Such an experiment involves social waste, but never mind: charge it as a temporary cost of learning enough to achieve optimal organisation.) Will an actual citizen, man in the street i and not an imaginary omniscient referee, act out his demand function $D_2^i(\ldots)$? Certainly he will not. If all but one man is foolish enough to act as the Lindahl theory requires, it pays that last man to dissemble and hide his true liking for x_2.[1]

---

[1] I agree with Johansen's characterisation of the problem as one of indeterminate bilateral-monopoly. Marshallian joint supply is *not* a true analogy. Suppose wool, Y_1, and mutton, Y_2, are produced by sheep, Y_3, in equal amounts, with $Y_1 = Y_2 = Y_3 = Y$ by choice of units and $P_3 = S(Y_3)$ is the supply curve of sheep, while $P_1 = D_1(Y_1)$ and $P_2 = D_2(Y_2)$ are the demand curves for wool and mutton. Then equilibrium can be written as

$$P_1 + P_2 = P_3, \qquad P_1(Y) + P_2(Y) = S(Y),$$

which looks like the Bowen demand diagram. But note that the Bowen curves are pseudo and not genuinely motivated observable relations. Increasing the number of men, s, only makes things worse; by contrast, in ordinary private markets, increasing the number of sellers and numbers of buyers increases the relevance of the supply-demand relations. The true analogy is with joint supply of sheep, where each of mutton, wool and other products are in the hands of *separate* complete *monopolists*!

Hence, as Wicksell sensed when he threw the problem out of the market-place and into the legislature, it pays no one to behave according to the voluntary-exchange theory. So they will not. All of Lindahl's prattling about 'equality of bargaining power' as leading to his solution, with the implication that unbalanced power situations will spread around his solution the way errors spread around a mean value, is gratuitous assertion. Who believes it? Why should anyone?

In point of fact, Wicksell (and I suppose Lindahl himself), Musgrave and Johansen (and Dorfman) all throw the matter into the game-theoretic wilderness of Parliament. Does Wicksell's discussion of voting lead anywhere? And if the chapters of Musgrave and Johansen dealing with mathematical politics do lead anywhere, what possible connections do such chapters have with their Lindahl sections? I ask to be informed, not to criticise.

Take for example the Galbraith view that the public sector is too small compared to the private sector. It may be true that x_2 (or x_{n+k}) is too small and x_1^i (or x_j^i) too large. But how convincing is Johansen's attempt to deduce this bias from the Lindahl apparatus? Actually, other economists have argued that public good x_{n+k} tend to be too large because each legislator thinks he might as well get public works for his region, since others are getting some for theirs and since the cost of his region's projects will tend to get spread over all – and yet, these economists argue, if all legislators together could act by agreement, they would all admit the nation would be better off with a sizeable cut in public expenditures. This is a possibility but, to me, just as inconclusive a generalisation as an alleged game-theoretic corroboration of the Galbraith thesis.

I hope this Appendix shows that whatever are the demerits of my general equilibrium formulations, they are shared by the special Lindahl version of them.

(B) THE DEFINITIONAL PROBLEM

A warning should be registered in connection with my present jettisoning of the concept of a polar public good. Even if, semantically, a variable can be put into more than one individual utility function, we shall not have a *standard* public good case unless it enters in the production-possibility frontier and industry production functions in the standard way (as an earlier footnote mentioned). Moreover, the variable in question may not have the returns and other properties of an ordinary good, private or public.

Here are some examples. Suppose two (or more) families have summer homes out on a peninsula. The cost of bringing electricity to them has a separable-cost and joint-cost aspect. Thus, each can properly be charged the separate marginal cost of the electricity that he draws from outside the system. But the common cost of the line is a public good. Suppose x_1^1 and x_1^2 are the respective powers drawn. Suppose x_2 is the (annual) common-cost variable, arranged to take on only the two values: zero if the line is not useable, one if it has been made useable. The utility to Man i of the power *consumed* can be written as the formal product $x_2 x_1^i$; and, with x_0^i an ordinary private good, the maximum problem can be written with proper choice of units

$$\max \ U\{u^1(x_0^1, x_2 x_1^1), u^2(x_0^2, x_2 x_1^2)\} \tag{8}$$

subject to

$$x_0^1 + x_0^2 + (x_1^1 + x_1^2) + M x_2 = 0$$

and x_2 restricted to 0 or 1.

Because the dummy variable x_2 has the discrete (0, 1) property, the tangency conditions of my equations have no applicability and must be replaced by finite-difference maximum conditions. Even if x_2 could be regarded as a continuous real-variable function, the resulting tangency conditions might be boundary inequalities of the type familiar in modern non-linear programming. Even here, because the product $x_2 x_1^i$ is involved, one would not have the quasi-concavity conditions on the u^i functions that make necessary and sufficient conditions identical and rule out multiple local maxima. As is well known in non-concave programming, the resulting 'search' problem can be a formidable combinatorial task. Moreover, turning that task over to a hypothetical perfectly discriminating monopolist, who is supposed to find out people's tastes by a great variety of all-or-none offers is simply to fob off the computational problem on a middleman; to make things worse, the perfect discriminator would face the game-theoretic problem of bilateral monopoly, a fact that the ordinary theoretical discussion conveniently and blissfully forgets.

(C) ROAD USE AS PUBLIC GOODS

The use of dummy variables, like x_2 with the (0, 1) property, is a convenient way of handling some problems where exclusion is possible (albeit not always socially desirable). Another example that illustrates the all-pervasiveness of the consumption externality property of public goods is provided by optimal car road or rail road pricing and allocation. Suppose marginal cost of using a road by car or truck is zero (being the negligible amount of induced wear and tear). Let there be an annual cost of building (and replacing) the road of A. If the road is uncrowded, once built, it should charge no use tolls. If we call x_2, a zero-one variable that indicates absence or presence of the road, our maximum problem is

$$\max\ U[u^1(x_1^1, x_2), u^2(x_1^2, x_2)] \text{ subject to } x_1^1 + x_2^2 = C - Ax_2, \tag{9}$$

with Pareto-optimality defined by

$$\max\ u^1(x_1^1, x_2) \text{ subject to above constraint and } u^2(x_1^2, x_2) \geq \bar{u}^2 \tag{10}$$

Benefit theorists attracted to the Lindahl approach would be tempted to raise the cost A as the sum of two pseudo tax-prices $P_2^1 + P_2^2$, which would also have to pass the test

$$u^1(\bar{V}^1 + L^1 - P_2^1, 1) \geq u^1(\bar{V}^1 + L^1, 0)$$
$$u^2(\bar{V}^2 + L^2 - P_2^2, 1) \geq u^2(\bar{V}^2 + L^2, 0). \tag{11}$$

There is absolutely no reason why the $[L^i]$ expressions should be assignable prior to the decision whether or not to build the roads. Indeed, it is quite possible that the above inequalities would be met for one set of $[L^i]$, at the same time that another set of $[L^i]$ satisfy the opposite criteria for *not* building the road:

$$u^i(\bar{V}^i + L^i - P_2^i, 1) < u^i(\bar{V}^i + L^i, 0). \tag{12}$$

This means, 'Along one part of the Pareto-optimality frontier, the road should not be built; but along another part, it should be built.' There is nothing paradoxical about this: hospitals for the poor are good things with one income-distribution goal and bad things with another. Given a $U(u^1, u^2, \ldots)$ social welfare function, the proper place on the Pareto frontier is selected, along with its implied public-good decisions.

Again, there is no need to use pseudo-tax-pricing with $A = P_2^1 + P_2^2$. I cannot agree with Musgrave that 'Each tub should stand on *its* own bottom'. The purpose of benefit-pricing is not to secure justice for each man, but rather to ensure that we do not end up (i) with everybody worse off, (ii) and where 'society' doesn't want to be. The true problem is to determine 'how big the bottoms shall be' *and* 'what shall be over them'.

Specifically, as a perfectly-good alternative to Lindahl-Musgrave pricing:

(i) Decide to produce the road (if they so decide).
(ii) Set benefit pseudo-tax prices at zero: $P_2^1 = 0 = P_2^2$.
(iii) Allocate remaining private income by optimal (L^1, L^2) lump-sum items that add up to a negative (rather than a zero) total.

Moral: If you know enough to use the Lindahl pseudo prices, you don't have to use them.

Finally, here is a further example of consumption externalities of the public good – or rather, 'public bad', type.

Let the road get crowded. Now Man i's pleasure in using it depends on how many others are using it. As before, let x_1^i be an ordinary private good such as bread, x_2 be a $(0, 1)$ variable depending on whether the road is there or not. Let x_{2+i} be the amount of riding on the road than Man i does. Now we write

$$u^i = u^i(x_1^i, x_2 x_{2+i}, x_2 \sum_{q \neq i} x_{2+q}), \quad u_1^i > 0, \quad u_2^i > 0, \quad u_3^i < 0. \tag{13}$$

Our production-budget constraint for society is

$$1(\sum_i x_1^i) + Ax_2 = C \tag{14}$$

since increasing x_{2+i} use adds nothing to *physical* resource cost.

If we decide to build the road, and set $x_2^* = 1$ the proper programme involves the equation (III')

(III') $$\frac{u_2^i}{u_1^i} = 0 - \sum_{q \neq i} \frac{u_3^q}{u_1^q} = \sum_{q \neq i} \left|\frac{u_3^q}{u_1^q}\right| = \mu_i > 0.$$

Clearly there should be a toll or tax price that is *not* a pseudo price. It *should exclude* us from using a bit more of x_{2+i} if we cannot meet the 'psychological marginal cost', μ_i. If all people are 'alike', with all u_3^q/u_1^q alike, we would get *uniform* toll tax prices, $\mu \equiv \mu_i$. Their purpose is to hold down use in order to benefit us all. The revenues they collect have nought to do with A, unless the road can be replicated with each new road costing A. Then it can be shown – and I suppose this is what Mohring's result involves – as the number of people $\to \infty$, there is an optimal density of traffic for each road, an optimal number of roads (asymptotically proportional to s), and for which use-tolls u^* exactly cover long-run costs A. But it is this large-number replicability that has taken us out of government enterprise and back to private-good market optimality. (Note: the private good is then the single road with all *its* joint users, x_{2+q}.)[1]

(D) DECREASING COSTS PHENOMENA AS PUBLIC GOODS

Where marginal cost pricing will not cover full costs, we encounter a version of the public-good problem. There is a popular but fallacious notion that this calls for uniform percentage markups over MC, a result

[1] See my cited essay on the Chamberlin monopolistic competition revolution for statement and proof of a theorem that replicability of indivisible units leads asymptotically to the constant-returns-to-scale homogeneity relations of viable perfect competition. R. E. Kuenne (ed.), op. cit.

that happens to be true when such a pattern is equivalent to putting a tax on a factor inelastic in supply. In the general case, if a subsidy financed by ideal lump-sum taxes is not feasible, the feasible optimum involves greater P/MC discrepancies where demand is inelastic. Suppose the government operates a network of uncrowded roads. Let the demands for roads $1, 2, \ldots, k, \ldots, K$ be given by independent functions $B_k(q_k)$, where $B_k(q_k)$ can be taken because of optimal lump-sum L_i redistribution to represent the social money value of total utility from the indicated amount of road use. Let the total cost of road k, measured in money of constant social marginal utility, be $C_k(q_k)$. Then the social magnitude to be maximised is of the consumer-producer surplus form

$$\max_{q_k} \sum_1^K \{B_k(q_k) - C_k(q_k)\}. \tag{15}$$

This leads to $P = MC$ conditions of the form

$$B_k'(q_k) = P_k = C_k'(q_k), \qquad (k = 1, \ldots, K) \tag{16}$$

with solution $(q_1^*, \ldots, q_K^*)$. If average costs are falling, the government will run the roads at an algebraic loss given by

$$\sum_1^K \{C_k(q_k^*) - q_k^* B_k'(q_k^*)\}. \tag{17}$$

This loss should ideally be made up out of lump-sum taxes (L^i) optimally distributed among the populace. (If the loss is a gain it should be optimally distributed as a negative tax.)

The above conditions (16) are only local marginal conditions and must be supplemented by the 'total' or 'global' test-conditions

$$B_k(q_k^*) - C_k(q_k^*) \geq B_k(0) - C_k(0), \qquad (k = 1, \ldots, K). \tag{18}$$

The case of interdependent utilities and costs provide an example of the formidable problem of total or global conditions associated with public goods, a problem in principle like the Chamberlinian one of finding the optimal regime of differentiated products. When one compares a situation with one or more q_k zero rather than positive q_k^*, any 'prior' rectification of the social marginal utility of money will become upset. So, generally, a consumer-surplus money magnitude cannot be found as a surrogate or social utility (or for Pareto-optimum problems). None the less, as an illustration of the formidable difficulties involved in getting any usefulness out of total conditions, consider the case where we are to maximise such a consumer-producer money surplus sum

$$B(q_1, \ldots, q_k, \ldots) - C(q_1, \ldots, q_k, \ldots)$$
$$= N(Q) \text{ for short}$$

The number, K, of potential goods can be indefinitely large, many being alternatives and only a small subset being optimally positive at any one time. Even though it is more realistic to consider discontinuities (due to 'indivisibilities') at the origin, where a $q_k = 0$, let us for simplicity assume B and C have smooth partial derivatives. Then, according to modern Kuhn–Tucker non-linear programming

$$\max_{q_k} N(q_1, q_2, \ldots)$$

requires

$$\frac{\partial N}{\partial q_k} = 0 \qquad \text{if } q_k > 0$$

$$\frac{\partial N}{\partial q_k} \leq 0 \qquad \text{if } q_k = 0$$

Consider all the points that satisfy these conditions. They could be infinite in number. They could even be a non-denumerable infinity. But suppose they are finite in number, being $Q^1, Q^2, \ldots, Q^M$, where M can easily be in the millions. Then to *find* this set and verify that the *optimum optimorum*, which may be denoted by Q^1, does satisfy the 'total' tests

$$N(Q^1) \geq N(Q^j) \qquad (j = 2, \ldots, M)$$

might well involve trillions of hours of computing-machine time. No practical market algorithm for solving such a search problem has ever been found.

(E) THE OPTIMAL MARKUP THEOREM

Now let us consider the 'feasibility' problem. Given that some specified (algebraic) subsidy, S, is available to help meet the loss, we solve the problem

$$\max_{q_k} \sum_1^K \{B_k(q_k) - C_k(q_k)\} \text{ subject to}$$

$$\sum_1^K \{q_k B_k'(q_k) - C_k(q_k)\} = -S$$

By Lagrangean multiplier technique, we set up

$$L(q_1, \ldots, q_K; \ \lambda) = \sum_1^K \{B_k(q_k) - C_k(q_k)\} + \lambda \left[\sum_1^K \{q_k B_k'(q_k) - C_k(q_k)\} + S \right]$$

and require for a maximum that L be at a stationary point defined by

$$\frac{\partial L}{\partial q_k} = 0 = \{B_k'(q_k) - C_k'(q_k)\}(1 + \lambda) + \lambda q_k B_k''(q_k) \tag{20}$$

$$\frac{\partial L}{\partial \lambda} = 0 = \sum_1^K \{q_k B_k'(q_k) - C_k'(q_k)\} + S$$

The first K equations can be rearranged to become

$$\frac{B_k' - C_k'}{B_k'} = \frac{P_k - MC_k}{P_k} = \frac{+\lambda}{1 + \lambda} \frac{1}{E_k} \qquad (k = 1, \ldots, K) \tag{21}$$

where E_k is the usual absolute Marshallian elasticity of demand

$$E_k = -\frac{dq_k}{dP_k} \frac{P_k}{q_k} = -\frac{B'(q_k)}{q_k B''(q_k)} \tag{22}$$

Calling $(1 + \lambda)/\lambda = 1 + \beta$, which will normally be greater than one, we end up with the discriminating-welfare markup rule

$$\frac{P_k - MC_k}{P_k} = \frac{1}{(1 + \beta)E_k}. \tag{23}$$

This rule, which is a straightforward extension of the feasibility analysis of Frank Ramsey and M. Boiteux, and which has also been independently derived by J. Drèze, has the following interpretation:

> To maximise feasible welfare, do not use a uniform markup rule. Instead act like a discriminating monopolist (not a 'perfectly discriminating one' but one who can charge different prices in the K independent markets, in the Yntema–Robinson fashion) – but, blow up the true elasticity of demand, E_k, of every market by the same proportion, pretending that it is $(1 + \beta)E_k$, where the coefficient $1 + \beta$ depends on the plentitude of S, the available subsidy.

Thus, if S is fully plentiful, $\beta = 0$ and we have ideal $P = MC$ pricing. Should S be so small that a discriminating monopolist could only break even, β would become 0. (This shows that, although all monopoly is a bad or non-optimal thing, in a sense discriminating monopoly pricing is 'better' than uniform pricing.) Even if an Yntema–Robinson discriminator could not break even by any pricing, which means *a fortiori* that a simple monopolist could not, it may still pay in terms of consumer-producer surplus to operate the roads. The total conditions, for each feasible S, involves testing each road's right to exist and that of every possible subset. If the decision is between the whole road network or none, the total condition is

$$\sum_1^K \{B_k(q_k^*) - C_k(q_k^*)\} - S \geq \sum_1^K B_k(0) - C_k(0) \tag{24}$$

where the right-hand side may have a different interpretation in the short run than in the long.

All of the above analysis applies with small modification if costs or demands are not independent. Thus, if we replace additive costs, $\Sigma C_k(q_k)$, by $C(q_1, \ldots, q_K)$, we merely have to replace marginal costs, $C_k'(q_k)$, by the partial derivative, $\partial C(q_1, \ldots, q_k)/\partial C_k$; and similarly for non-independent utilities. In particular, the usual Yntema–Robinson discussion of discriminating monopoly replaces $\Sigma C_k(q_k)$ by $C(\Sigma q_k)$, it being assumed that the products sold to different markets are exactly alike physically.

This has an important application to our road problem. Two separate demands, say $B_1'(q_1)$ and $B_2'(q_2)$, could be for rides on the same road but by different users. The theory says, 'Don't charge different men the same price for the same service, charge the one with more inelastic demand the higher price – and this in the interest of minimising the deadweight loss due to unfeasibility of financing social losses by ideal lump-sum tax.' Is this not 'unjust', in the second sense described earlier? (Does it not violate the Churchmen notion of 'commutative justice'?) One can answer: 'It does maximise the total of social utility expressed in money (and presumably reflecting the fact that in the background proper redistributions and compensations are being made to keep social $U(u^1, u^2, \ldots)$ at its feasible maximum).' But one should also note that there is a partial self-inconsistency in the problem. If you have to rely on $P - MC$ markups, that must be because ideal lump-sum L^i are not feasible. Then how can they be counted on to be operating in the background to keep incomes distributed equitably and ensure equality of social marginal utility of every person's dollar? As mentioned in my third paper, the proper optimum under these feasibility conditions involves pricing that favours people with dollars of greater ethical weight and involves a compromise between deadweight-loss-minimisation and interpersonal 'Robin-Hood' pricings.

(F) RAMSEY'S FEASIBILITY OR SECOND-BEST OPTIMALITY

Not only is the above a theory of subsidy, it is also a theory of optimal goods-and-services taxing of the Ramsey–Pigou type. Suppose $C_k(q_k)$ represents integrated marginal costs of a competitive industry. And suppose that S is now a negative subsidy, namely the amount of revenue that has to be raised from *ad valorem* or *specific* taxes on $(q_1, \ldots, q_K)$. (This can include taxes on factors of the income-tax type if we vary our convention and let some q_k represent inputs with algebraic signs changed; but this extension I ignore here.)

Then the optimality conditions of (20) define for us the ideal Ramsey–Pigou pattern of (differentiated!) excises.

If (percentage) tax rates are defined by

$$t_k = \frac{P_k - MC_k}{P_k} \tag{25}$$

then conditions (20) and (21) give us directly the optimally-differentiated pattern

t_k inversely proportional to elasticity of demand, E_k, or

$$t_k = \frac{1}{(1 + \beta)E_k} \tag{26}$$

where β depends on the size of the revenue to be raised, $-S$. This accords with the modern notion: Taxes on things in inelastic demand tend to do the least harm.[1]

It is easy to show that, for *small* $|S|$, we get the Ramsey rule: 'Select $P_k - MC_k$ tax discrepancies so as to change every q_k in the same proportion away from the ideal $P_k = MC_k$ configuration.' So long as R'_k and C'_k remain strictly linear, such a rule is exact for large, finite changes.

---

[1] Note: my assumption of constancy of the marginal utility of money banishes the income effects that separate ordinary price elasticities of demand and the more relevant Slutsky–Hicks compensated-elasticities-of-demand.

173

PUBLIC GOODS AND SUBSCRIPTION TV: CORRECTION OF THE RECORD

PAUL A. SAMUELSON
Massachusetts Institute of Technology

"The Heart has reasons that Reason will never know." Pascal
"So do the viscera." Freud

Having been extended the courtesy of commenting on the interpretation[1] of my writing[2] on the theory of public goods and subscription television, I shall be candid and terse. My remarks have been scandalously misinterpreted. However, my job here is not to pontificate on the mores of scholarship but to try to correct the record.

The reader of this paper could be pardoned for thinking that I have opposed subscription television. Upon reading my paper, he will be surprised to learn that I expressed no opinion on the merits of commercial television versus subscription television. What I did do was point out that the essence of the public-good phenomenon was not intrinsically tied up with the inability to "exclude" consumers from some common service; that even if a subscription TV service could find a descrambler that would enable such exclusion to take place technically, we should still be faced with an instance of intrinsic increasing returns and that in all such cases there is an element of the public-good dilemma. Specifically, I pointed out that departing from the consumption pattern consistent with price equals marginal cost—in this case, essentially zero price—could be proved to lead to a non-Pareto-optimal state of the world. This means that there will necessarily exist (but not necessarily be "socially feasible") an infinity of other configurations that make *everybody* better off; and this means that such a configuration cannot represent a maximum of a Bergson social welfare function.

A competent student of modern welfare economics must know how to use

[1] Minasian, Television Pricing and the Theory of Public Goods, 7 J. Law & Econ. 71 (1964).

[2] Samuelson, Aspects of Public Expenditure Theories, 40 Rev. Econ. & Stat. 332 (1958). Earlier papers were The Pure Theory of Public Expenditure, 36 Rev. Econ. & Stat. 387 (1954) and Diagrammatic Exposition of a Theory of Public Expenditure, 37 Rev. Econ. & Stat. 350 (1955). This is in the tradition of earlier writings by Wicksell, Lindahl, Howard R. Bowen, and various continental writers. *Cf.* Musgrave, The Theory of Public Finance (1959) for discussion and references.

logic. He must be able to make boring distinctions between a necessary condition, several necessary conditions, a set of sufficient conditions, another such set, and a set of necessary and sufficient conditions. I stated that a necessary condition for Pareto-optimality would be violated under subscription TV, which is in contrast to what would happen under *laissez faire* in a private-good world subject to constant-returns-to-scale, absence of uncertainty, institutional monopoly, etc. Since *laissez faire* does not provide, outside of these last situations, an algorithm for achieving the efficient allocation of resources, I made a plea that economists study the merits of various new and old algorithms.

Only one who confuses a necessary condition with a set of sufficient conditions could read into my argument the absurd pattern: Since subscription TV violates $P = MC$ and commercial TV [allegedly] does not, the former should be prohibited.

Only one who confuses one necessary condition with a set of necessary conditions could attribute to me the absurd pattern: If $P =$ short-run MC, there is no need for long-run considerations concerning the amount of indivisible resources to be allocated to an activity to take into account the opportunity cost of those resources in alternative uses. Why did not the commentator quote and understand my paragraph

There is a related significant point that needs stressing. It is not enough in the decreasing cost case to come closer to marginal cost pricing in the Lerner-Lange manner, making up the deficits by general taxation. As soon as decreasing cost and diversity of product appear, we have the difficult non-local "total conditions" to determine what finite mix of product is optimal. This involves a terrible social computation problem: we must scan the almost infinite number of possible products and select the best configuration; we cannot feel our way to the optimum but must make judgment at a distance to determine the *optimum optimorum*.[3]

Only one who misunderstands the relevance of Pareto-optimality when important feasibility conditions make it impossible to achieve ideal lump-sum redistributioned taxes and impossible to achieve the various other stringent conditions could attribute to me the pattern of illogic: *The* (!) Pareto-optimal situation is better than any non-Pareto-optimal situation. Why did not the commentator quote and understand my paragraph

Having called attention to the nature of the difficulty, I do not wish to be too pessimistic. After all, the world's work does somehow get done. And to say that market mechanisms are non-optimal, and that there are difficulties with most political decision processes, does not imply that we can never find new mechanisms of a better sort.[4]

[3] Aspects of Public Expenditure Theories, 40 Rev. Econ. & Stat. 336 (1958).
[4] *Id*. at 334.

There are dozens of specific passages one might comment on, but the point has been made. What is especially regretful is that some of the arguments the author appears to be making are deducible from the general theory of public goods and modern welfare economics; but the good and the bad have been all jumbled together.

The final question is, Why all this? Is it because, despite all denials, Chicago is not so much a place as a state of mind? Is it because of the fear that finding an element of the public-good problem in an area is prone to deliver it over to the totalitarian state and take it away from the free market? The line between conviction and paranoia is a fine line.

Let the record be clear. The merits or demerits of subscription TV cannot be settled by an appeal to abstract reasoning or principles. Imperfections of one arrangement must be weighed against imperfections of another. Value judgments must enter into the final resolution: one category of citizens stand probably to gain, and one to lose; there is no feasible mechanism by which the gainers can efficiently compensate the losers; nor is there a presumption that they ought to compensate if they could, or ought not to either. In decreasing-cost situations, and areas generally that have in them a significant element of the public-good problem, there is no valid theorem that restrictions on entry are *necessarily* bad (although there is such a valid theorem in certain constant-returns-to-scale models of private goods). So, pragmatically all such cases have to be studied and resolved on their complicated and controversial merits and demerits. One cannot avoid the difficult problem of deciding whether a particular man is a murderer by posing the problem, "Does he carry the (unique) name of the man who did commit the murder?" No more can one decide what market or social mechanisms should be used for an activity by *first* deciding whether it is a private or is a public good. Instead, in terms of how important are its various features (externalities or lack of same, etc.), society decides what degree of market autonomy or public decision-making shall be applied to it. Only a bigoted devotee of *laissez faire* will find the theory of public goods, properly understood, subversive.

Indeterminacy of Governmental Role in Public-Good Theory

The pure theory of public expenditure that I presented in the 1950's in the <u>Review of Economics and Statistics</u> (reproduced in my <u>Collected Scientific Papers</u>, Vol. 2, pp. 1223-1239) often uses the term "public good" but cannot properly be interpreted to imply that private goods should be produced by private enterprise and public goods should be produced by government directly. Indeed in my first paper on public expenditure I used the term collective good, in contrast to a private good that enters directly into but one person's utility function. And in the last few editions of my textbook <u>Economics</u> I often use the expressions social goods and social wants. Where the consumption externalities intrinsic to a non-private good occur, all that I would insist on is that laissez faire cannot be counted on to lead to an optimum. There is a <u>prima facie</u> case, so to speak, for social concern and scrutiny of the outcome; but that does not necessarily imply outright state ownership or in every case public regulation. The exact form in which the social concern ought to manifest itself depends on a host of considerations that have to be added to the model.

But I cannot agree with the assertion: "What actually the Samuelsonian pure theory of public expenditure gives is not a theory of public goods but only a theory of public transfers..." The equations of my model specify the conditions that must be satisfied by Pareto-optimality and by maximization of a prescribed individualistic Bergson social welfare function. They do not pronounce on what institutional set of rules and behavior will approximate to these conditions, although they do specify how self-interest will cause game-theoretic deviations from the optimum. The most difficult part of the calculations, from many viewpoints, is the determination of what the optimal magnitudes of the non-private goods should be; this problem goes well beyond the mere task of determining what <u>transfer</u> payments shall be made among individuals and organizations to achieve the optimum.

Paul A. Samuelson

PITFALLS IN THE ANALYSIS OF PUBLIC GOODS*

PAUL A. SAMUELSON
Massachusetts Institute of Technology

1. Professor Buchanan hopes to illuminate the problem of public good provision by a simplified, idealized example of a TV relay on an island. I cannot agree that this "ideal-type situation, or one closely resembling it" captures what "Samuelson initially had in mind in his reference to TV signals as an application of his theory of public goods" because Buchanan's con-stantcost postulate assumes away the initial-indivisibility, increasing-returns aspects that I consider intrinsically involved in TV and related public utility problems.

Nevertheless, Buchanan's example is a special case that my papers have repeatedly analyzed. By commenting on his analysis, I can hope to bring out the complexities of the problem.

2. Given the constant average cost (in an opportunity as well as dollar sense) of his TV programming, and having simplified his example further by assuming that every man has constant marginal utility of his private good, we can summarize all the information of Buchanan's example by the shapes of the marginal-utility curve of the public good to each man.[1] Each man knows this function for himself. But only God knows them for all men. Buchanan does not; I do not; the government does not; monopolists and competitors do not.

* This is an invited comment on Buchanan, Public Goods in Theory and Practice: A Note on the Minasian-Samuelson Discussion, 10 J. Law & Econ. 193 (1967). Aid from the National Science Foundation is gratefully acknowledged.

[1] My 1954, 1955, and 1958 Review of Economics and Statistics papers are reproduced, with original pagination, in 2 The Collected Scientific Papers of Paul A. Samuelson 1223-1239 (1966). In their notation, let Buchanan's TV time be $X_2 = X_2{}^1 = \ldots = X_2{}^s$; let $X_1{}^1$ represent the amount consumed by the ith man of a private good (or composite market-basket of all private goods, which could for simplicity be measured as dollars' worth of private goods), with $X_1 = \Sigma_1{}^s X_1{}^i$, the total of private goods. Then each man's tastes are summarized by ordinal $u^i(X_1{}^i, X_2{}^i)$. On the simplifying assumption of constant costs of X_2 in terms of X_1, society's production-possibility frontier, F, can be written $1 \cdot \Sigma_1{}^s X_1{}^i + C X_2 =$ constant. In Chart 3 of my 1955 paper, the AB frontier becomes a straight line by Buchanan's constant-cost postulate. To softpedal redistributional demand effects, add the strong postulate of constant marginal utility of the private good to each man, letting us write

$$u^i(X_1{}^i, X_2) = 1 \cdot X_1{}^i + f_i(X_2)$$

where f^i is the ith man's concave Gossen utility for the public good (measured in utils of foregone private good).

If the unknown marginal-utility functions appertained to *private* goods, this lack of knowledge would not matter. *Laissez faire* would introduce and police perfect competion. It would be to each man's interest to act along his MU function as an observable demand function. The "organizers" of this society could rely on the anonymous market to (1) reach equilibrium, (2) achieve Pareto-optimality, and (3), by means of optimal lump-sum transfers of the private good, attain the maximum of a prescribed social welfare function.

Summary: For ideal private goods, people are motivated to "reveal" their tastes.

3. Buchanan starts out by playing God, examining the results of "an ideally-operating tax-financed, collective facility." He provides an amount of the public good, X_2^*, representing a certain optimal number of minutes of TV programming; he levies selective taxes on each man, in terms of dollars or foregone private goods, X_1^1, such that in total the resource cost of TV is covered; moreover, acting as a Gladstone-like Victorian God, he gauges the separate taxes of each man at that level where, if he actually could buy a minute more or less of TV time at his stipulated average-tax-rate per minute, he would choose to stay at exactly the provided level of TV time.

This result satisfies my equations of Pareto-optimality (1954, Equations (1) and (2); 1955 tangencies of page 351 and vertically-summed intersections of page 354). How did God get there? Buchanan does not tell us; but since he says people "cannot, under this arrangement, purchase divisible units of service," presumably no excluder devices were yet introduced. In short, the use of Lindahl-Johansen-Samuelson pseudo-tax-pricing[2] was not used to find and maintain this equilibrium. Intuition with a capital "I" was enough.

4. What hath God wrought? Pareto-optimality. But Buchanan has not noted that there are an infinity of other Pareto-optimal points, all consistent in this simplified example with the same X_2^* level of the public good.[3] Thus, charge Man 17 more in tax and charge Man 99 less, while keeping the same tax total and public good expenditure level. If Buchanan's solution is written as $(\ldots ; X_1^{17} = X_1^{17*}, X_2^{17} = X_2^*, \ldots ; X_1^{99} = X_1^{99*}, X_2 = X_2^*)$, this new solution is written as $(\ldots ; X_1^{17} = X_1^{17*} - A, X_2^{17} = X_2^*, \ldots ; X_1^{99} = X_1^{99*} + A, X_2^{99} = X_2^*)$, and is also Pareto-optimal. And it will be

---

[2] This pseudo-tax pricing is defined in my forthcoming paper on public goods given at the International Economic Association Biarritz meeting of 1966, which Buchanan refers to. My paper cites Johansen, Public Economics 125-140 (1965), and Lindahl's papers appearing in Classics in Public Finance (Musgrave & Peacock eds. 1958). The word "pseudo" is emphasized by me because each man is motivated in the public good case *not* to reveal his demand function, $f_i(X_2)$; so pseudo-pricing is a mental exercise not a practical device.

[3] See my Biarritz paper for discussion of this.

even more "equitable" for a social welfare function that imputes higher marginal social utility for Man 99 than for Man 17.

Of course, someone like Musgrave can argue that interpersonal equity could have been as well achieved by prior lump-sum transfers of private goods among people; this would achieve my social-welfare optimal conditions (1955, Equations (3); 1954, chart 4 tangency). It could have been done, but needn't have been: *changes in public-good so-called benefit tax rates can achieve exactly the same purpose so long as we don't apply them with excluder devices to distort efficient use.* We should note, however, the following:

Theorem: In the strong case of constant returns, a utopian pseudo-tax-pricing equilibrium that just balances the budget and collects use taxes equal to individual relative marginal utilities can—with appropriate lump-sum transfers—achieve *all* possible Pareto-optimal positions and hence can achieve the optimum point of a prescribed social welfare function, $U[u^1(X_1^1, X_2), \ldots, u^s(X_1^s, X_2)]$.

This theorem tells us nothing as yet about the real world of socialism, public utility regulation, or *laissez faire*.

5. I now skip over Buchanan's second case (of a franchised monopolist charging uniform prices for TV use) to consider his God-like case of a "perfectly discriminating monopolist." Although that fellow gets referred to in textbooks, he does not exist on land or sea and never will. He is just another name for God. How does he "find out" each man's marginal-utility function? Only by playing a zero-sum game with him. Each man has every incentive not to reveal to his Opponent his marginal utility. Only by fiat of the textbook writer, does the Opponent always win the game's maximum stakes. For Him to look into the hearts of 200 million, or 20 thousand, or 2 consumers, and guess right requires miracles.[4]

Let the miracle take place. Then again a similar Pareto-optimal equilibrium is attainable. (More precisely, unless we tax away the perfect discriminator's monopoly profits and, God-like, rebate them to each man in exact amount of his foregone consumer's surplus, we must allow for redistributional effects upon demands and on the optimal level of X_2^*. In any case, by suitable lump-sum transfers and taxes on the perfect discriminator, God could achieve *any* Pareto-optimal configuration and achieve maximum equity à la some prescribed social welfare function.)

I think it is somewhat dangerous for Buchanan to call his first God-like case "the ideal collective solution" and to call the perfectly-discriminating monopoly case "the ideal 'private' solution." The latter is just as "collective"

---

[4] Abstractions like frictionless pendulums and perfect competition are quite different from the abstraction of a perfectly-discriminating-monopolist. In real life, these former conditions are approximated by limiting cases. On the other hand, the latter is like the concept in physics of Maxwell's Demon, an entity that can "see" each atom and discriminate among them. Such concepts exist to create illuminating paradoxes.

and just as far removed from competitive wheat markets as the former. Removing the crown from the stationery of an organization and renaming it the East India Company changes nothing if that company has all the exclusive privileges of the State itself. A Canadian Pacific with exclusive franchise in some regions may have all the properties of a Canadian National even though only the latter is nominally government owned.[5]

Buchanan's first case of free usage financed by benefit tax-prices is only one special case—and that very much a business-oriented case—of the general solutions to my Pareto-optimality Equations. Indeed let me add for consideration one more variant. The optimal level of TV public good, X_2^*, is set at the same God-determined level, but the resources are paid for out of general tax revenues (ideally lump-sum to preserve Pareto-optimality). Although nobody is excluded from using TV services (each being charged only the zero marginal cost of having an extra person tune in on an existing program), readers of Minasian's earlier article should realize that his dictum—that "the optimal principle dictates the use of costs, the value of foregone alternative uses of scarce resources"[6]—has not at all been neglected in this X_2^* solution. The public-good level is optimally determined in every run of time precisely because the sum of all marginal benefits exactly matches the *ex ante* and *ex post* marginal cost of providing the TV program for anyone to tune in on.

6. Now let me leave celestial for more mundane realms. Let us go back to consider Buchanan's second case where a private enterprise is given a franchise to charge uniform (monopoly) price to all users. An excluder device would be the most natural way to police this; and do I have to regard as "far-fetched" Buchanan's device where "the community gives the entrepreneur property rights in the signals and allows him to sue for damages all those who use his property without proper compensation," for the courts would have to have God-like powers to determine the $f_i(X_2)$ utilities of different users. But waiving such niceties, we can assume that the consumer acts in the expectation that, if he does use the TV signal at all, he will be subject to the same uniform price as if he avails himself fully of the provided $X_2^i = X_2^*$ public-good service.

At any uniform price that the monopolist charges, some users will opt out

---

[5] Further, it is misleading to regard the "theory of public goods" as one particular extension of the Marshallian theory of joint supply as Buchanan suggests. Competitive Mangoldt-Marshall equilibrium of wool and mutton involves no game-theoretic elements. Increasing the number of separate parts of a sheep, each demanded by a separate monopsonist, is the true analogy to the public-good case. As the number of men grows, the problem becomes *more* game-theoretically indeterminate, quite unlike the case of increasing the number of Marshallian sheep farmers. Hence, public goods are a contrasting case to conventional joint supply.

[6] Minasian, Television Pricing and the Theory of Public Goods, 7 J. Law & Econ. 71, 75 (1964).

even though they could have got positive marginal-utility from the service. As Buchanan says, the private-enterprise result cannot be Pareto-optimal even if the simple monopolist is regulated so as to equate his price rather than his marginal revenue to his marginal cost, leaving him with no profit. In the most favorable circumstance, the most we can say is this: if at some uniform price the TV service can break even, positive X_2 is better than zero X_2. Moreover, outside of the present trivial constant-cost case, this break-even condition is misleading. Even if no firm or bureau can break even, the total consumer surplus may justify positive X_2 and a subsidy. It is immaterial whether the government socialistically provides the service or subsidizes private enterprise; and certainly *laissez faire* with uniform pricing will involve certain inefficiencies.

Buchanan's case of simple monopoly can have added to it the case of discriminating, but not "perfectly discriminating," monopoly. Suppose the discriminator can charge each ith man a different price for use of any and all of $X_2^1 = X_2^*$. Then there will exist a pattern of such prices which will exactly duplicate Buchanan's first case of free usage with benefit tax prices. Without regulation, the monopolist will not be motivated to achieve this; and without God-like powers of ascertaining information, he will not be able to determine this.

7. Let us now examine some of the costs of getting information through use of excluder devices and use prices. In the case of truly private goods, there are no such costs; since, in the case of public goods, there do exist such costs, one cannot apply the analogy of private good pricing to deduce cogently the advisability of use prices for public goods. Here it may become a case of digging up the plants to see whether their roots are healthy, a destructive test. Doctors do not examine the appendix to make sure it is normal. As in the Heisenberg uncertainty principle, where observing an atom disturbs it, excluding consumption by use of any price in excess of true social marginal cost involves deadweight loss. Whether such inefficiency involves benefits in knowledge so great that pricing brings more *net* benefits than can be obtained from feasible alternative methods is a question quite incapable of being answered on a priori or general grounds. Depending upon institutions and cases, I can recognize no presumption one way or another. Therefore, I cannot agree with Buchanan that "Minasian's point is well taken when he suggests that ordinary profitability criterion, whether applied by a private or a public monopolist would be a more instructive guide than opinions of a governmental authority." In the case of unexhausted increasing returns, which I have argued in the *Chamberlin Festschrift*[7] is the essential case where

[7] Samuelson, The Monopolistic Competition Revolution, in Monopolistic Competition Theory: Studies in Impact 105 (Kuenne ed. 1967). In increasing returns situations there cannot even be a presumption in favor of freer entry, as is illustrated by the following

optimal differentiation of product must be determined, there is no warrant for the view that profit seeking *laissez faire* will, in Buchanan's words "most closely satisfied consumer demand."

8. Only when Buchanan considers the possibility of choice between mutually-exclusive retransmittable TV signals does he stumble on to the "total conditions" of Pareto-optimality. They were there in the single signal case but rendered redundant by his constant returns postulate. When we now drop this gratuitous postulate, that same God-like omniscience which found the solution to my local Pareto-optimality conditions can find the solution to the total optimality conditions involved in my complete theory of public goods.[8] Again I must warn against the danger of putting off on to that *deus ex machina*, the perfectly discriminating monopolist, the exercise of God-like powers; and of favoring any private enterprise solution of the public good problem by relating it in any way to the case of the perfect discriminator.

9. In conclusion, the theory of public goods emphasizes the subtlety of policy problems rather than their simple solution.

footnote remark in Samuelson, "Personal Freedoms and Economic Freedoms in the Mixed Economy," in The Business Establishment 216 n.16 (E. Cheit ed. 1964):

"There appears to me to be technical flaw in the view of Friedman and A. P. Lerner that regulated or publicly owned monopolies should always (as a matter of principle as well as pragmatic expediency) be permitted to have competition from free entrants. The mathematics of the increasing-returns situation admits of no such theorem; it is simply false game theory and bilateral monopoly theory, which asserts that letting one more viable person in the game must lead to a "better" result in any of the conventional senses of better. To make the Scottish Airlines keep up unprofitable schedules and at the same time permit a free enterpriser to make a profit partially at the regulated lines' expense can easily result in dead-weight loss to society under the usual feasibility conditions. The crime of legally abolishing the Pony Express because it competed with the Post Office would have to be examined on all its complicated demerits."

[8] My Biarritz paper explicitly presents certain non-local Pareto-optimality conditions; in the earlier papers, my simplifying convexity postulates rendered these "total conditions" redundant.

PART XIII

Principles of Fiscal and Monetary Policy

176

WHAT CLASSICAL AND NEOCLASSICAL MONETARY THEORY REALLY WAS*

PAUL A. SAMUELSON   *Massachusetts Institute of Technology*

Qu'était au juste la théorie monétaire classique et néo-classique ? L'article présente le point de vue d'un de ceux qui ont contribué à la théorie monétaire classique et néo-classique. Comme l'auteur à cru pendant les années 1932 à 1937, cette théorie (jamais formulée d'une façon formelle sous forme d'un système d'équations) supposait, sans en contester le bien-fondé, qu'en longue période le volume monétaire n'avait aucune importance une fois que l'économie considérée était devenu une économie monétaire. Toutefois, la théorie n'allait pas jusqu'à prétendre qu'une économie monétaire et une économie de troc fussent identiques même si l'on supposait des goûts, des connaissances techniques et des quantités de facteurs de production identiques.

Certains tenants ont aussi postulé que ces facteurs réels affectaient les prix et les niveaux de production relatifs, alors que le volume monétaire affectait le niveau absolu des prix. Il y avait ainsi deux dichotomies au lieu d'une, mais la seconde dichotomie n'a jamais été prise tellement au sérieux par qui que ce soit. Elle constituait plûtot une simplification provisoire. L'essentiel de la formulation présente est d'inclure la monnaie dans la fonction d'utilité, puis de considérer la fonction comme jouissant de la propriété d'homogénéité suivant laquelle un doublement de tous les prix et de la monnaie n'avantage personne. Par conséquent, lorsque chacun pèse la commodité de détenir de la monnaie en comparaison de son coût en intérêt, sa fonction de demande pour les biens est indépendante du niveau absolu des prix, mais sa demande pour la monnaie est proportionnelle aux augmentations balancées de tous les prix.

Quoi qu'il en soit, les deux dichotomies sont légitimes pourvu que les modèles sousjacents soient définis en conséquence. L'auteur présente ensuite un modèle qui démontre le bien-fondé d'une dichotomie entre « les éléments réels » et « l'élément monétaire qui ne détermine que le niveau absolu des prix ». L'auteur prétend que les meilleurs auteurs néo-classiques avaient intuitivement ce modèle en tête, même s'ils ne l'ont jamais explicité ou publié. L'auteur termine son article par une discussion des contributions de Lange, Patinkin, et Archibald et Lipsey.

To know your own country you must have travelled abroad. To understand modern economics it is good to have lived long enough to have escaped competent instruction in its mysteries. When Archibald and Lipsey try to draw for Patinkin a picture of what a "classical" monetary theorist believed in, they are pretty much in the position of a man who, looking for a jackass, must say to himself, "If I were a jackass, where would I go?"

Mine is the great advantage of having once been a jackass. From 2 January 1932 until an indeterminate date in 1937, I was a classical monetary theorist. I do not have to look for the tracks of the jackass embalmed in old journals and monographs. I merely have to lie down on the couch and recall in tranquillity, upon that inward eye which is the bliss of solitude, what it was that I believed between the ages of 17 and 22. This puts me in the same advantageous position that Pio Nono enjoyed at the time when the infallibility of the Pope was being enunciated. He could say, incontrovertibly, "Before I was Pope, I believed he was infallible. Now that I am Pope, I can *feel* it."

Essentially, we believed that in the longest run and in ideal models the

*I owe thanks to the National Science Foundation.

Canadian Journal of Economics/Revue canadienne d'Economique, I, no. 1
February/février 1968

amount of money did not matter. Money could be "neutral" and in many conditions the hypothesis that it was could provide a good first or last approximation to the facts. To be sure, Hume, Fisher, and Hawtrey had taught us that, under dynamic conditions, an increase in money might lead to "money illusion" and might cause substantive changes—e.g., a shift to debtor-entrepreneurs and away from creditor-rentiers, a forced-saving shift to investment and away from consumption, a lessening of unemployment, a rise in wholesale prices relative to sticky retail prices and wage rates, *et cetera*.

But all this was at a second level of approximation, representing relatively transient aberrations. Moreover, this tended to be taught in applied courses on business cycles, money and finance, and economic history rather than in courses on pure theory. In a real sense there *was* a dichotomy in our minds; we were schizophrenics. From 9 to 9:50 a.m. we presented a simple quantity theory of neutral money. There were then barely ten minutes to clear our palates for the 10 to 10:50 discussion of how an engineered increase in M would help the economy. In mid-America in the mid-1930s, we neoclassical economists tended to be mild inflationists, jackasses crying in the wilderness and resting our case essentially on sticky prices and costs, and on expectations.

Returning to the 9 o'clock hour, we thought that *real* outputs and inputs and price ratios depended essentially in the longest run on real factors, such as tastes, technology, and endowments. The stock of money we called M (or, to take account of chequable bank deposits, we worked in effect with a velocity-weighted average of M and M'; however, a banking system with fixed reserve and other ratios would yield M' proportional to M, so M alone would usually suffice). An increase in M—usually we called it a doubling on the ground that after God created unity he created the second integer—would cause a proportional increase in *all* prices (tea, salt, female labour, land rent, share or bond prices) and values (expenditure on tea or land, share dividends, interest income, taxes). You will hardly believe it, but few economists in those days tried to write down formal equations for what they were thinking. Had we been asked to choose which kinds of equation system epitomized our thinking, I believe at first blush we would have specified:

A. Write down a system of real equations involving *real* outputs and inputs, and *ratios* of prices (values), and depending essentially on real tastes, technologies, market structures, and endowments. Its properties are invariant to change in the stock of money M.

B. Then append a fixed-supply-of-M equation that pins down (or up) the absolute price level, determining the scale factor that was essentially indeterminate in set A. This could be a quantity equation of exchange—$MV = PQ$— or some other non-homogeneous equation. More accurately, while A involves homogeneity of degree zero in *all Ps*, B involves homogeneity of degree 1 of Ps in terms of M.

I have purposely left the above paragraphs vague. For I doubt that the typical good classical monetary theorist had more definite notions about the *mathematics* of his system.

Moreover, I must leave room for an essential strand in our thinking. Our expositions always began with barter and worked out fundamental pricing in barter models. But then we, sensibly, pointed out the *real* inconvenience of barter and the real convenience of an abstract unit of money. Here we made explicit and tacit reference to the real facts of brokerage or transaction charges, of uncertainties of income and outgo, and so on. In short, we did have a primitive inventory theory of money holding, but we were careful to note that true money—unlike pearls, paintings, wine, and coffee—is held only for the *ultimate exchange* work it can do, which depends upon the scale of *all Ps* in a special homogeneous way.

So there was another dichotomy in our minds, a very legitimate one. We had, so to speak, *qualitative* and *quantitative* theories of money. According to our qualitative theory, money was not neutral; it made a big difference. Pity the country that was still dependent upon barter, for it would have an inefficient economic system. But once this qualitative advantage had been realized by the adoption of market structures using M, the *quantitative* level of M was of no particular significance (except for indicated transient states and uninteresting resource problems involved in gold mining or mint printing). We liked the image of John Stuart Mill that money is the *lubricant* of industry and commerce. As even women drivers know, lubrication is important. But M is quantitatively a special lubricant: a drop will do as well as a poolful. So an even better image was the post-Mill one: money is like a catalyst in a chemical reaction, which makes the reaction go faster and better, but which, like the oil in the widow's cruse, is never used up. To push the analogy beyond endurance, only an iota of catalyst is needed for the process.

What I have just said makes it unmistakably clear that a classical monetary theorist would not go the stake for the belief that the real set of equations A are independent of M, depending essentially only on price ratios as in barter. If time were short on a quiz, I might carelessly write down such an approximation. But if asked specifically the question "Is Set A really independent of M?" I and my classmates would certainly answer "No" and we would cite the qualitative aspects mentioned earlier.

In a moment we shall see that this considered qualitative view requires that *M enter quantitatively in Set A in certain specified homogeneous ways.* But first let us investigate how those of us who were mathematically inclined would have handled the Set A and Set B problem. The economists interested in mathematics tended to be specialists in value theory. They had a big job just to describe the real relations of A, whether under barter or otherwise. They wanted to simplify their expositions, to sidestep extraneous complication. Hence, many would have followed the practice (which I seem to connect with Cassel's name, at least) of writing Set A purely in barter terms, and essentially giving enough equations to determine real quantities and price ratios—as follows:

$$A' \quad f_i(Q_1, \ldots, Q_n, P_1, \ldots, P_n) = 0 \ (i = 1, 2, \ldots, 2n)$$

where there are n inputs or outputs, with n prices. However, the f_i functions are made to be homogeneous of degree zero in all the Ps, and, luckily, the $2n$ functions f_i are required to involve one of them as being dependent on the other, thus avoiding an overdetermination of the $2n$ functions. This homogeneity and dependence postulate enables us to write A′ in the equivalent form:

$$A' \quad f_i(Q_1, \ldots, Q_n, \lambda P_1, \ldots, \lambda P_n)_\lambda \equiv 0 \ (i = 1, 2, \ldots, 2n).$$

This formulation does not contain price ratios explicitly. But since λ is arbitrary, it can be set equal to $1/P_1$ to give us price ratios, P_i/P_1. Or if you have an interest in some kind of average of prices, say $\pi(P_1, \ldots, P_n) = \pi(P)$, where π is a homogeneous function of degree one, you can rewrite A' in terms of ratios $P_i/\pi(P)$ alone, by suitable choice of λ. Hence, Set A' involves $2n-1$ independent functions which hopefully determine a unique (or multiple) solution to the $2n - 1$ real variables $(Q_1, \ldots, Q_n, P_2/P_1, \ldots, P_n/P_1)$. With the special structure of A', we are now free to add any non-homogeneous B' we like, of the following types:

$P_1 = 1$, good 1 being taken as numéraire, or
B' $P_1 + P_2 = 3.1416$, or
$P_1 + P_2 + \ldots + P_n = 1$, or
$P_1[(Q_1{}^* + (P_2{}^*/P_1)Q_2{}^* + \ldots + (P_n{}^*/P_1)Q_n{}^*] = \overline{M} \times$ Fisher's Constant,
where $Q_i{}^*$, $(P_i/P_1)^*$ are solutions of A'.

Of course, the last of these looks like the Fisher-Marshall formulation of the "quantity equation of exchange." But, since some Q_i are inputs, my way of writing it recognizes the realistic fact that money is needed to pay factors as well as to move goods.[1]

I do not defend this special A', B' formulation. I am sure it was often used. And even today, if I am behind in my lectures, I resort to it in courses on pure theory. But we should admit that it is imperfect. And we should insist that the classical writers, when they did full justice to their own views, did not believe that this formulation was more than a provisional simplification.

What is a minimal formulation of (A, B) that does do full justice? I am sure that I personally, from 1937 on at least, had a correct vision of the proper version. It is as if to understand Gary, Indiana, I had to travel to Paris. I began to understand neoclassical economics only after Keynes' *General Theory* shook me up. But I am sure that I was only learning to articulate what was intuitively felt by such ancients as Ricardo, Mill, Marshall, Wicksell, and Cannan. I regret that I did not then write down a formal set of equations. I did discuss the present issue at the Econometric Society meetings of 1940, of which only an incomplete abstract appeared, and also at its 1949 meetings, where W. B. Hickman, Leontief and others spoke; and there are fragmentary similar remarks in half a dozen of my writings of twenty years ago. The nub of the matter is contained in my 1947 specification[2] that the utility function contain in it, along with physical quantities of good consumed, the stock of M and all money Ps, being homogeneous of degree zero in $(M, P_1, \ldots, P_n)$ in recognition of money's peculiar "neutral" quantitative properties.

Frankly, I was repelled by the abstract level at which Oskar Lange, Hicks, and others carried on their discussion of Say's Law, staying at the level of equation counting and homogeneity reckoning, without entering into the

---

[1]An equation like the last one could be split into two equations without altering the meaning:
B'$_1$ $(1/FC)\Sigma^n{}_{j=1} (P_j/M)Q_j{}^* = 1$
B'$_2$ $M = \overline{M}$, a prescribed total. The important thing to note is that B'$_1$, even if it looks a little like some A' equations, is completely decomposable from the set A'.
[2]P. A. Samuelson, *Foundations of Economic Analysis* (Cambridge, Mass., 1947), 119.

concrete character of the models. And this was one of the few continuing controversies of economics from which I steadfastly abstained.

For the rest of this discussion, what I propose to do is to get off the couch and go to the blackboard and write down an organized picture of what we jackasses implicitly believed back in the bad old days.

The way things are

I abstract heroically. We are all exactly alike. We live forever, We are perfect competitors and all-but-perfect soothsayers. Our inelastic labour supply is fully employed, working with inelastically supplied Ricardian land and (possibly heterogeneous) capital goods. We have built-in Pigou-Böhm rates of subjective time preference, discounting each next-year's independent utility by the constant factor $1/(1 + \rho)$, $\rho > 0$. We are in long-run equilibrium without technical change or population growth: the stock of capital goods has been depressed to the point where all own-interest-rates yielded by production are equal to r, the market rate of interest; in turn, r is equal to the subjective interest rate ρ, this being the condition for our propensity to consume being 100 per cent of income, with zero net capital formation.

We equally own land, and such capital goods as machinery and material stocks. We own, but legally cannot sell, our future stream of labour earnings. We hold cash balances, because we are *not* perfect soothsayers when it comes to the uncertainty of the timing of our in-and-out-payments, which can be assumed to follow certain probability laws in the background; this lack of synchronization of payments plus the indivisible costs of transactions (brokerage charges, need for journal entries, spread between bid and ask when earning assets are converted into or out of cash, etc.) requires us to hold money. To keep down inessential complications, while not omitting Hamlet from the scenario, I am neglecting the need for cash balances for corporations; it is as if consumer families alone need cash balances for their final consumption purchases, whereas in real life cash is needed at every vertical stage of the production process. Later we can allow our holdings of earning assets—titles to land and machines—to economize on our need for M balances, just as does the prospect of getting wage increases.

Our system is assumed to come into long-run equilibrium. This equilibrium can be deduced to be unique if we add to our extreme symmetry assumptions the conventional strong convexity assumptions of neoclassical theorizing—constant returns to scale with smooth diminishing returns to proportions, quasi-concave ordinal utility functions that guarantee diminishing marginal rates of substitution, and so on.

We should be able to *prove rigorously* what is probably intuitively obvious— doubling all M will exactly double *all* long-run prices and values, and this change in the absolute price level will have absolutely no effect on real output-inputs, on price ratios or terms of trade, on interest rate and factor shares generally.

For this system, it is not merely the case that tautological quantity equations of exchange can be written down. Less trivially, a simple "quantity theory of prices and money" holds exactly for the long-run equilibrium model. Although Patinkin has doubts about the propriety of the concept, I think our meaning was unambiguous—and unobjectionable—when we used to say that the "demand curve for money" (traced out by shifts in the vertical supply curve of M) plotted in a diagram containing, on the x axis, M and, on the y axis, the "value of money," (as measured by the reciprocal of *any* absolute money price $1/P_i$ or any average price level) would be a rectangular hyperbola with a geometrical Marshallian elasticity of exactly minus one.

To prove this I write down the simplest possible set of equations. These do split up into two parts, showing that there is a legitimate "dichotomy" between "real elements" and "monetary elements which determine only the absolute level of prices." Call these two parts A and B. Now this legitimate dichotomy will not be identical with the over-simple dichotomy of A' and B' mentioned earlier. If Patinkin insists upon the difference, I am in complete agreement with him. If he should prefer not to call the (A, B) split a dichotomy, that semantic issue is not worth arguing about so long as enough words are used to describe exactly what the (A, B) split is, and how it differs from the (A', B') split. If Patinkin insists on saying that my A equations do have in them a "real balance effect," I see no harm in that—even though, as will be seen, my formulation of A need involve no use of an average price index, and hence no need to work with a "deflated M" that might be called a real balance. Peculiarly in the abstract neoclassical model with its long-run strong homogeneity properties, all Ps move together in strict proportion when M alone changes and hence no index-number approximations are needed. By the same token, they do absolutely no harm: Patinkin is entitled to use any number of average price concepts and real-balance concepts he wishes. If Patinkin wishes to say that the principal neoclassical writers (other than Walras) had failed to *publish* a clear and unambiguous account of the (A, B) equation such as I am doing here, I would agree, and would adduce the worth and novelty of Patinkin's own book and contributions. On the other hand, the present report on my recollections claims that the best neoclassical writers did *perceive* at the intuitive level the intrinsic content of the (A, B) dichotomy which I am about to present. All the more we should regret that no one fully set down these intuitions thirty years ago!

Now what about Archibald and Lipsey?[3] I want to avoid semantic questions as to what is meant by real-balance effects being operative. If they claim that the (A', B') dichotomy does justice to the tacit neoclassical models of 1930, I think they are wrong. If they think an (A', B') dichotomy does justice to a reasonably realistic long-run model of a monetary economy, I think they are also wrong. Whether, as a *tour de force*, some special, flukey (A', B') model might be found to give a representation of some monetary economy is a possibility that I should hate to deny in the abstract; but I should be surprised if this issue turned out to be an interesting one to linger on or to

---

[3]Don Patinkin, in his *Money, Interest, and Prices* (New York, 1966), summarizes his path-breaking writings on money over the last twenty years. For a critique of aspects of its first (1954) edition, see Archibald and Lipsey (*Review of Economic Studies*, XX) and articles in subsequent numbers of that journal.

debate. For what a casual opinion is worth, it is my impression that Patinkin's general position—which I interpret to be essentially identical to my (A, B) dichotomy *and* to the tacit neoclassical theory of my youth—is left impregnable to recent attacks on it. There is one, and only one, legitimate dichotomy in neoclassical monetary theory.

Abjuring further doctrinal discussion, I proceed now to the equations of my simplest system.

Structure of the model

1. PRODUCTION RELATIONS

To keep down inessentials, let land, T, real capital, K (assumed homogeneous merely as a preliminary to letting K stand for a vector of heterogeneous capital goods), and labour, L, produce real output which, because of similarity of production factors in all sectors, can be split up into the linear sum of different physical consumption goods $\pi_1 q_1 + \ldots + \pi_n q_n$ and net capital formation $\dot{K}(= dK/dt)$, namely: $\dot{K} + \pi_1 q_1 + \pi_2 q_2 + \ldots + \pi_m q_m = f(K, \bar{L}, \bar{T})$ where F is a production function of the Ramsey-Solow type, homogeneous of first degree, and where the π_i are constants, representing marginal costs of the ith goods relative to machines. From this function, we can deduce all factor prices and commodity prices relative to the price of the capital good P_K, namely:

$$\text{A}_{\text{I},1} \quad \frac{P_i}{P_K} = \pi_i \qquad (i = 1, 2, \ldots, n)$$

$$\text{A}_{\text{I},2} \quad \frac{W}{P_K} = \frac{\partial F(K, \bar{L}, \bar{T})}{\partial L}, \quad \text{the marginal productivity wage,}$$

$$\frac{R}{P_K} = \frac{\partial F(K, \bar{L}, \bar{T})}{\partial T}, \quad \text{the marginal productivity rent,}$$

$$r = \frac{\partial F(K, \bar{L}, \bar{T})}{\partial K}, \quad \text{the marginal productivity interest rate.}$$

Bars are put over L and T because their supplies are assumed to be fixed. To determine the unknown stock of capital K we need:

$r = \rho$, the subjective time preference parameter;[4]

$\text{A}_{\text{II}} \quad \dot{K} = 0$, the implied steady-state long-run equilibrium condition;

$r = R/P_T$, the implicit capitalization equation for the price of land.

Hence, $\rho = \partial F(\bar{K}, \bar{L}, T)/\partial K$ henceforth gives us our fixed $\bar{K}$.

The above relationships determine for the representative man the wage and interest income (inclusive of land rentals expressed as interest on land values) which he can spend on the $(q_1, q_2, \ldots, q_n)$ goods and on holding of M cash balances which bear no interest and thus cost their opportunity costs in terms of interest forgone (or, to a net borrower, the interest on borrowings). What

---

[4]In unpublished memos and lectures, using a Ramsey maximum analysis I have shown how the long-run steady-state condition where $r = \rho$ is approached so that $\dot{K}$ (or $K^{t+1} - K^t$) is zero. The steady-state analysis of U (q: M, . . .) here is shorthand for the perpetual stream $\Sigma_0^\infty U$ (q^t; $M^{t+1}, \ldots)/(1 + \rho)^t$, etc. My colleague, Professor Miguel Sidrauski, has independently arrived at such dynamic formulations.

motive is there for holding any M? As I pointed out in *Foundations*, one can put M into the utility function, along with other things, as a real convenience in a world of stochastic uncertainty and indivisible transaction charges.[5]

If, however, one does put M directly into U, one must remember the crucial fact that M differs from every other good (such as tea) in that it is not really wanted for its own sake but only for the ultimate exchanges it will make possible. So along with M, we must always put all Ps into U, so that U is homogeneous of degree zero in the set of monetary variables ($M, P_1, \ldots, P_m$), with the result that ($\lambda M, \lambda P_1, \ldots, \lambda P_m$) leads to the same U for all λ.

In *Foundations*, I wrote such a U function:

$$U(q_1, q_2, \ldots, q_n; M, P_1, P_2, \ldots, P_n)_\lambda \equiv U(q_1, \ldots, q_m; \lambda M, \lambda P_1, \ldots, \lambda P_n),$$

where Ps are prices in terms of money. Here I want merely to add a little further cheap generality. The convenience of a given M depends not only on Ps, but also upon the earning assets you hold and on your wage prospects. It is not that we will add to M the earning-asset total EA, which equals $P_T \bar{T} + P_K \bar{K}$. Nor shall we add EA after giving the latter some fractional weight to take account of brokerage and other costs of liquidating assets into cash in an uncertain world. Rather, we include such new variables in U to the right of the semicolon to get:

$$U(q_1, \ldots, q_n; M, EA, W\bar{L}, P_1, \ldots, P_n) = U(q; x) = U(q; \lambda x).$$

That is, increasing all Ps, including those of each acre of land and machine and of hourly work along with M, will not make one better off. Thus U ends up homogeneous of degree zero in M and *all* prices ($M, P_K, P_T, W, P_1, \ldots P_n$) by postulate.

Now, subject to the long-run budget equation indicated below, the representative man maximizes his utility:

$$\underset{\{q_1, \ldots, q_n, M\}}{\text{Max}} \quad U(q_1, \ldots, q_n; M, P_K \bar{K} + P_T \bar{T}, W\bar{L}, P_1, \ldots, P_n)$$

subject to

$$P_1 q_1 + \ldots + P_n q_n = W\bar{L} + r \,(\text{Total Wealth} - M)$$

or

$$P_1 q_1 + \ldots + P_n q_n + rM = W\bar{L} + r \,(\text{TW}) = W\bar{L} + r \,(P_K \bar{K} + P_T \bar{T} + M^*),$$

where each representative man has Total Wealth defined as:

$$\text{Total Wealth (in money value)} = EA + \text{Money Endowment}$$
$$= P_K \bar{K} + P_T \bar{T} + M^*,$$

where M^* is the money created in the past by gold mining or by government.

---

[5]This is not the only way of introducing the real convenience of cash balances. An even better way would be to let U depend only on the time stream of qs, and then to show that holding an inventory of M does contribute to a more stable and greatly preferable stream of consumptions. The present oversimplified version suffices to give the correct general picture.

The maximizing optimality conditions give the demand for all q_i and for M in terms of the variables prescribed for the individual, namely:

$$(P_1, \ldots, P_n, W, P_K, P_T; r, \bar{K}, \bar{L}, \bar{T}, M^*).$$

The optimality equations can be cast in the form:

$$\frac{\partial U / \partial q_1}{P_1} = \cdots = \frac{\partial U / \partial q_n}{P_n} = \frac{\partial U / \partial M}{r}$$

or

$$(\text{A}_{\text{III},1}) \quad \frac{\partial U / \partial M}{\displaystyle\sum_1^n q_j \frac{\partial U}{\partial q_i} + M \frac{\partial U}{\partial M}} = \frac{r}{W\bar{L} + r(P_K \bar{K} + P_T \bar{T} + M^*)}$$

$$(\text{A}_{\text{III},2}) \quad \frac{\partial U / \partial q_i}{\displaystyle\sum_1^n q_j \frac{\partial U}{\partial q_j} + M \frac{\partial U}{\partial M}} = \frac{P_i}{W\bar{L} + r(P_K \bar{K} + P_T \bar{T} + M^*)}$$

$$(i = 1, 2, \ldots, n).$$

But for society as a whole (and hence for the representative man who, even if he does not know it, represents 1/Nth of the total in our symmetrical situation) total money demanded, M, must end up equalling total money endowment, M^*:

$$(\text{A}_{\text{III},3}) \quad M = M^*.$$

An important comment is in order.[6] Although $\text{A}_{\text{III},3}$ holds for society as a whole, being essentially a definition of demand-for-money equilibrium, each representative man (one of thousands of such men) can*not* act in the belief that his budget equation has the form:

$$P_1 q_1 + \ldots + P_n q_n + rM = W\bar{L} + r(P_K \bar{K} + P_T \bar{T} + M)$$

even though substituting $\text{A}_{\text{III},3}$ into the earlier budget equation would yield this result. What is true for all is not true for each. Each man thinks of his cash balance as costing him forgone interest and as buying himself convenience. But for the community as a whole, the total M^* is there and is quite costless to use. Forgetting gold mining and the historical expenditure of resources for the creating of M^*, the existing M^* is, so to speak, a free good from society's viewpoint. Moreover, its *effective* amount can, from the community's viewpoint, be indefinitely augmented by the simple device of having a lower absolute level of *all* money prices. To see this in still another way, with fixed labour L and land T and capital K big enough to give the interest rates equal to the psychological rate ρ, the community can consume on the production possibility equation:

$$P_1 q_1 + \ldots P_n q_n = F(\bar{K}, \bar{L}, \bar{T}) = W\bar{L} + r(P_K \bar{K} + P_T \bar{T})$$

and to *each* side of this could be added rM of any size without affecting this true physical menu.

[6]The next few paragraphs can be skipped without harm.

Evidently we have here an instance of a lack of optimality of laissez-faire: there is a kind of fictitious internal diseconomy from holding more cash balances, as things look to the individual. Yet if all were made to hold larger cash balances, which they turned over more slowly, the resulting lowering of absolute price would end up making everybody better off. Better off in what sense? In the sense of having a higher U, which comes from having to make fewer trips to the bank, fewer trips to the brokers, smaller printing and other costs of transactions whose only purpose is to provide cash when you have been holding too little cash.

From society's viewpoint, the optimum occurs when people are satiated with cash and have:

$\partial U/\partial M = 0$ instead of $r \times$ (positive constant) > 0.

But this will not come about under laissez-faire, with stable prices.[7]

Now let us return from this digression on social cost to our equations of equilibrium. Set A consists of the A_I equations relating to production and implied pricing relations, and of the A_{II} equations relating to long-run equilibrium of zero saving and investment, where technological and subjective interest rates are equal and provide capitalized values for land and other assets. Finally, A_{III} are the demand conditions for the consumer, but generalized beyond the barter world to include explicitly the qualitative convenience of money *and to take into account the peculiar homogeneity properties of money resulting from the fact that its usefulness is in proportion to the scale of prices.* Though the exact form of A_{III} is novel, its logic is that implied by intuitive classical theories of money.

All of equations A have been cast in the form of involving ratios of prices, values, and M^* only (to put A_{III} in this form, multiply M into the numerators on each side). That means they are homogeneous functions of degree zero in all Ps, and M^* or M, being capable of being written in the general form:

A $\qquad G_i\left(q_1, \ldots, q_n, K, \bar{L}, \bar{T}, r; \dfrac{P_K}{M}, \dfrac{W}{M}, \dfrac{R}{M}, \dfrac{P_1}{M}, \ldots, \dfrac{P_n}{M}, \dfrac{\mathrm{TW}}{M}\right) = 0$

where all the magnitudes to the left of the semicolon are "real" and all those to the right are *ratios* of a price or a value to the quantity of money. If a price ratio like P_i/P_j appears in an equation and no M, we can rewrite the ratio as $(P_i/M)/(P_j/M)$.

To the set A, we now append a decomposable single equation to fix the supply of money:

B $\qquad M$ or $M^* = \bar{M}$, an exogenous supply.

This single equation is not homogeneous of degree zero in Ps and M and therefore it does pin down the absolute scale of all Ps and values in direct proportion to the quantity of M^*. Why? Because Set A consists of as many indepen-

---

[7]See P. Samuelson, "D. H. Robertson, "*Quarterly Journal of Economics*, LXXVII, 4 (Nov. 1963), 517–36, esp. 535 where reference is made to earlier discussions by E. Phelps, H. G. Johnson, and R. A. Mundell. This article is reproduced in Joseph E. Stiglitz, ed., *The Collected Scientific Papers of Paul A. Samuelson* (Cambridge, Mass., 1966).

dent equations as there are unknown real quantities and ratios. Let us check this. Omitting fixed $(\overline{L},\overline{T})$, we count $n + 2 + n + 5$ unknowns in G_i when we ignore both $\dot{K}$ and the $\dot{K} = 0$ equation. We count $n + 3$ equations in A_I, 2 equations in A_{II}, and $n + 2$ *equations in* A_{III}. Thus $2n + 7 = 2n + 7$. Another way of looking at the matter is this: A_I and A_{II} determine all Ps as proportional to P_K. Then for fixed P_K and M^*, A_{III} determines all qs and M, the latter doubling when P_K and M^* double.

Summarizing, Set A determines all real quantities and all prices and values in ratio to the stock of M^*. Then equation B determines $M^* = \overline{M}$ and hence the absolute level of all prices in proportion to $\overline{M}$.

Where in A or B is the quantity theory's "equation of exchange" to be found? Certainly not in B. If anywhere, an $MV = PQ$ equation must be found in A. Where? Certainly not in A_I or A_{II}. In A_{III}, equation $A_{III,1}$ deals with the relative marginal utility of the cash balance. By itself, it is not an $M = PQ/V$ equation. Only after all the A_{III} equations are solved, can we express M in a function that is proportional to any (and all) P_i:

$$M = P_i \psi_i (\ldots)$$

where the ψ functions depend on a great variety of real magnitudes.

This suggests to me that the late Arthur Marget was wrong in considering it a fault of Walras that, after the second edition of his *Elements*, he dropped a simple $MV = PQ$ equation. Classical and neoclassical monetary theory is much better than a crude quantity theory, although it can report similar results from special ideal experiments. In particular, correct neoclassical theory does not lead to the narrow anti-Keynesian view of those Chicago economists who allege that velocity of circulation is not a function of interest rates.

How M gets allocated

Symmetry plays an important role in the model given here. With every man exactly alike, it does not matter where or how we introduce new money into the system; for it gets divided among people in exactly the same proportions as previous M. We classical writers were aware that the strict (A,B) dichotomy held only when every unit's M (say M^1, M^2, ...) stayed proportional to total $\overline{M} = \Sigma M^k$. But being careless fellows, we often forgot to warn that this was only a first approximation to more complicated incidents of gold inflations and business cycle expansions.

Can this rock-bottom simplicity be retained if we relax this extreme symmetry assumption (which renders the problem almost a Robinson Crusoe one)? Providing all income elasticities, including that for M, are (near) unity, it never matters (much) how things are divided among people. Collective indifference curves of the Robinson Crusoe type then work for all society. The simple structure of A_{III} is preserved and the uniqueness of equilibrium is assured. Again, it matters not how the new M is introduced into the system.

Finally, there was an even more interesting third assumption implicit and explicit in the classical mind. It was a belief in unique long-run equilibrium independent of initial conditions. I shall call it the "ergodic hypothesis" by analogy to the use of this term in statistical mechanics. Remember that the classical economists were fatalists (a synonym for "believers in equilibrium"!). Harriet Martineau, who made fairy tales out of economics (unlike modern economists who make economics out of fairy tales), believed that if the state redivided income each morning, by night the rich would again be sleeping in their comfortable beds and the poor under the bridges. (I think she thought this a cogent argument against egalitarian taxes.)

Now, Paul Samuelson, aged 20 a hundred years later, was not Harriet Martineau or even David Ricardo; but as an equilibrium theorist he naturally tended to think of models in which things settle down to a unique position independently of initial conditions. Technically speaking, we theorists hoped not to introduce *hysteresis* phenomena into our model, as the Bible does when it says "We pass this way only once" and, in so saying, takes the subject out of the realm of science into the realm of genuine history. Specifically, we did not build into the Walrasian system the Christian names of particular individuals, because we thought that the general distribution of income between social classes, not being critically sensitive to initial conditions, would emerge in a determinate way from our equilibrium analysis.

Like Martineau, we envisaged an oversimplified model with the following ergodic property: no matter how we start the distribution of money among persons—M^1, M^2, . . .—after a sufficiently long time it will become distributed among them in a unique ergodic state (rich men presumably having more and poor men less). I shall not spell out here a realistic dynamic model but content myself with a simple example.

Half the people are men, half women. Each has a probability propensity to spend three-quarters of its today's money on its own products and one-quarter on the other sex's. We thus have a Markov transitional probability matrix of the form

$$
A = \begin{bmatrix} \dfrac{3}{4} & \dfrac{1}{4} \\ \dfrac{1}{4} & \dfrac{3}{4} \end{bmatrix} = \begin{bmatrix} \dfrac{1}{2}+\dfrac{a}{2} & \dfrac{1}{2}-\dfrac{a}{2} \\ \dfrac{1}{2}-\dfrac{a}{2} & \dfrac{1}{2}+\dfrac{a}{2} \end{bmatrix}
$$

with $a = \frac{1}{2}$ and

$$
A^t = \begin{bmatrix} \dfrac{1}{2}+\dfrac{a^t}{2} & \dfrac{1}{2}-\dfrac{a^t}{2} \\ \dfrac{1}{2}-\dfrac{a^t}{2} & \dfrac{1}{2}+\dfrac{a^t}{2} \end{bmatrix}
$$

$$
\lim_{t \to \infty} A^t = \begin{bmatrix} \dfrac{1}{2} & \dfrac{1}{2} \\ \dfrac{1}{2} & \dfrac{1}{2} \end{bmatrix}, \text{ the ergodic state.}
$$

Suppose we start out with men and women each having M of ($100, $100). Now introduce a new $100 to women only. Our transitional sequence in dollars will then be ($200, $100), ($175, $125), ($162½, $137½), ($156¼, $143¾),

540

($151\%_{16}$, $148\%_{16}$), . . . with the obvious limiting ergodic state $150, $150) since the divergence from this state is being halved at each step. Such an ergodic system will have the special homogeneity properties needed for the (A,B) dichotomy.[8]

None of this denies the fact that the leading neoclassical economists often recognized cases and models in which it does make a difference, both in the short and the long run, how the new money is introduced and distributed throughout the system. One of the weaknesses of a crude quantity theory is that it treats M created by open-market purchases by the central bank as if this were the same as M left over from last century's (or last minute's) mining. A change in M, accompanied by an opposite change in a near-M substitute like government short-term bonds, is *not* shown in my Set A.

Indeed, when all men are alike and live for ever, we have too simple a model to take account of the interesting effect upon the system of permanent interest-bearing public debt which we as taxpayers know we will not have to pay off or service beyond our lifetimes.[9]

Epilogue

With the positive content of traditional monetary theory now written down concretely for us to see, kick, and kick at, a few comments on some controversies of the last twenty years may be in order.

Oskar Lange began one line of reasoning on price flexibility in 1939 which culminated in his 1944 Cowles book, *Price Flexibility and Employment.*[10] Hicks' *Value and Capital*,[11] with its attempt to treat bonds and money just as some extra $n + 1$ and $n + 2$ goods along with n goods like tea and salt, had, I fear, a bad influence on Lange. It led to his suppressing possible differences between stocks and flows, to attempts to identify or contrast Say's Law with various formalisms of Walrasian analysis (such as the budget equation), and to discussion in the abstract of functions of many variables possessing or not

---

[8]Let me warn that this discussion in terms of a Markov probability matrix is meant to be only indicative. The temporal sequence of decisions to exchange money for goods and services and goods for money, with all that is implied for the distribution among units of the stock of M at any time, is more complicated than this. In our most idealized models, we assumed that, whatever the complexity of the process, after enough time had elapsed the M would get distributed in a unique ergodic way. This does not beg the question, since there are models in which this is a theorem. In our more realistic moods, we tacitly used models involving *hysteresis*: Spain would never be the same after Columbus; Scarlett O'Hara would be permanently affected by the Confederate inflation, just as Hugo Stinnes was by the 1920–23 German inflation. Obviously, in such models all real variables do not end up unchanged as a result of certain unbalanced introductions of new M into the system. In that sense realistic equations do not seem to have the homogeneity properties in ($M, P, \ldots$) of my Set A; but if we were to write in A the variables ($M^1, M^2, \ldots$) and not merely their sum ΣM^k, it is still possible that homogeneity properties would hold—so that doubling *all* M^k together would be consistent with doubling all Ps. But this is too delicate a question to attempt in brief compass here.

[9]My *Economics* (6th ed., New York, 1964), 342, shows that (M, public debt) and (λM, λ public debt) play the role in more complicated systems that (M) and (λM) play in the simple classical system given here. Crude quantity theorists should take note of this distinction, which Franco Modigliani has also insisted on.

[10](New York, 1944).

[11](Oxford, 1939).

possessing certain abstract homogeneity properties. There are many interesting points raised in Lange's book, and several analytical contributions to non-monetary economic theory. But only about a dozen pages grapple with the key problem of money (e.g., pp. 5–19), and these stay at a formalistic level that never deals with the peculiar properties and problems of cash balances. I do not say that this approach of Lange's cannot be used to arrive at valid results, but in fact it remained rather sterile for twenty years.

I had thought that Don Patinkin's work from 1947 on, culminating in his classic *Money, Interest, and Prices* was much influenced by the Lange approach, and I thought this a pity. But, on rereading the book, I am not sure. What Patinkin and Lange have in common is a considerable dependence upon the *Value and Capital* device of lumping money in as an extra good. This approach has not kept Patinkin from arriving at a synthesis consistent with what I believe was the best of neoclassical theory, or from going beyond anything previously appearing in the literature. But it may help to account for his attributing error to earlier thinkers when a more sympathetic reading might absolve them from error. When we become accustomed to approaching a problem in a certain way and using a certain nomenclature, we must not confuse the failure to use this same language and approach with substantive error. Still, beyond that, Patinkin scores many legitimate points: monetary economists had better intuitions than they were able to articulate. Thus I suspect that my (A,B) dichotomy is really very similar to what Cassel had in mind, but the only form in which he could render it mathematically was (A', B'), which is inadequate (as Patinkin insists, though perhaps not for all the reasons he insists on). In what sense can one say that a man believes one thing when he says something else? In this non-operational sense: if one could subpoena Cassel, show him the two systems and the defects in one, and then ask him which fits in best with his over-all intuitions. I believe he would pick (A,B) and not his own (A', B').[12] I might add that Cassel is not Walras; and it seems to me that Walras comes off better on Patinkin's own account than he is given credit for.

Some will interpret Archibald and Lipsey as defending an (A', B') dichotomy against Patinkin's rejection of that dichotomy. If that is their primary intention —and I am not sure that it is—I fear I must side with Patinkin. Logically, one can set up (A', B'), as I did here and as Cassel did. But I think it is bad economics to believe in such a model. *All* its good features are in the (A,B) dichotomy and none of its bad ones.

On the other hand, there is certainly much more in Archibald and Lipsey than a defence of (A', B') and this important part of their paper seems to me to be quite within the spirit of Patinkin's analysis and my own. Here, however, I shall comment on the two different dichotomies.

I begin with (A', B').

[12]Needless to say, the test is not whether Aristotle, apprised of Newton's improvements over Aristotle, would afterwards acquiesce in them; the test is whether in Aristotle's writings there are non-integrated Newtonian elements. If so, we credit him only with non-integrated intuitions.

A′ $\quad F_i(q, P) \underset{\lambda}{\equiv} F_i(q, \lambda P)$ $\qquad\qquad (i = 2, \ldots 2n)$

B′ $\quad P_1 = 1$ or $\sum_{j=1}^{n} q_j\, P_j = \bar{V}M,\ M = \bar{M}.$

Suppose that we can solve n of the A′ equation to eliminate the qs, ending up with the independent homogeneous functions

A′ $\quad f_i(P) \underset{\lambda}{\equiv} f_i(\lambda P) \equiv f_i(1, P_2/P_1, \ldots, P_2/P_1)$ $\qquad (i = 2, \ldots, n - 1)$

B′ $\quad \sum q_j^*(P_j/M) = \bar{V},\ M = \bar{M}.$

Although f_i involve actually money Ps, it is not logically or empirically mandatory to interpret them as "excess-demand" functions which drive up (or down) the *money* Ps. Some students of Hicks, Lange, and Patinkin fall into this presupposition. Logically, there *could* be dynamic adjustments of price ratios— as e.g. P_i/P_1 or P_i/P_j, either of which could be written as $(P_i/M)/(P_j/M)$—of the type

a′ $\quad [d\,(P_i/P_1)]/dt = k_i f_i(1, P_2/P_1, \ldots, P_n/P_1)\ (i = 2, \ldots, n)$

b′ $\quad [d\,(P_1/M)]/dt = k_M[\bar{M} - \sum(P_j/P_1)(P_1/M)\,q_j^*(1/V)], k_j, k_m > 0,$

where the ks are positive speed constants of adjustment and where the q^* and V may be functions of relative Ms. Such a system could dynamically determine *relative* prices within a decomposable real set A′ and then determine the absolute price level in Set B. Note that no version of Walras' Law relates B′ to A′ or b′ to a′. Walras' Law in the form that merely reflects the Budget Equation of each consumer is expressed in the functional dependence of the $f_1(1, P_2/P_1, \ldots)$ function (which we can ignore) on the rest—namely

$$f_1(1, P_2/P_1, \ldots) \equiv -\sum_2^n (P_j/P_1) f_j(1, P_2/P_1, \ldots).$$

If (a′,b′) is dynamically stable, $P_i/M \rightarrow$ constant is in agreement with the long-run quantity theory.[13]

---

[13]A short-run quantity theory need not hold. Doubling M this minute or this week need not double this week's prices. But there is a sense in which homogeneity holds in *every* run. Suppose as a *fait accompli* we are all made to wake up with every dollar of M *exactly* doubled and every P (present *and* future) exactly doubled. If nought else has changed, we recognize this to be indeed a new equilibrium. And if the time-profile of equilibrium is unique, how can we have any other time-profile of prices? At the root of this paradox is the assumption of perfectly balanced changes in M, perfect foresight, and the postulate of uniqueness of equilibrium. All this is a far cry from interpreting the stream of contemporary history.

177

NONOPTIMALITY OF MONEY HOLDING UNDER *LAISSEZ FAIRE**

PAUL A. SAMUELSON   *Massachusetts Institute of Technology*

My paper, "What Classical and Neoclassical Monetary Theory Really Was,"[1] had for its major purpose the clarification of the special homogeneity properties that any money stuff has when it is wanted only for the work that it can perform in facilitating present or future transactions. These homogeneity properties provide a basis for the only version of the quantity theory of money that is economically valid, and my formulation aimed to clarify this centuries-old matter. One way of describing the properties of the resulting theoretical structure is to speak of a fundamental dichotomy between the relations that determine all *relative* prices and *real* magnitudes and the set which determines the *absolute* price level or *scale* factor in the vector of all prices. (That is, I showed how the whole set of relations decomposes into two subsets with the above properties.)

Professor Clower[2] apparently accepts this fundamental conclusion. But he objects to another aspect of my paper – namely my demonstration (as a digression!) that the size of real balances under *laissez faire* is non-optimal. I think it is perhaps an unfortunate use of language for him to characterize this other aspect as a "second dichotomy," since the word dichotomy has a special meaning that perhaps should not be cheapened by using the word in a more general sense. Yet it is a legitimate question as to whether I have made a fundamental mistake in connection with this second aspect. I do not think I have, but *if* I have, that should not confuse one into rejecting necessarily the basic properties of the neoclassical system that my paper has deduced. Reading of my paper will confirm what Professor Clower has not brought into question, that this second aspect has to do primarily with recent thinking on the subject and does not (like my basic dichotomy) purport to have been closely in the minds of anyone a generation ago.[3]

Professor Clower finds my result incredible – that society could get something for nothing – and rejects it as quite untrue. Indeed he goes so far as to set up a counter-assertion: that, in a general equilibrium system with the idealized properties I have assumed, *laissez-faire* will *optimize* the level of real balances! I am not aware that anywhere in his remarks he has sketched a proof of this remarkable assertion, but at least we can examine the properties of my system to see whether such a theorem is valid. Actually, though, Professor Clower seems to be an Indian giver. After seeming to acknowledge that my system and its

*I owe thanks to the National Science Foundation for financial support.
[1]This JOURNAL, I, 1 (Feb. 1968), 1–15.
[2]R. W. Clower, "What Traditional Monetary Theory Really Wasn't," this JOURNAL, 299.
[3]Cf. Martin J. Bailey, "The Welfare Cost of Inflationary Inflation," *Journal of Political Economy*, LXIV (April, 1956), 43–110 for an early statement of this second effect. Older writers, such as Hume, Cannan, Bresciani-Turroni had often commented on the changes in real balances produced by different rates of price inflation or deflation. But they were not always clear on the differences between unanticipated and exponential-balanced inflation; and I do not recall their commenting on the special benefit of higher real balances under balanced deflation. Besides Bailey, also Phelps, Johnson, Mundell, Friedman, and Marty have held the position that Clower claims to be nonsense.

Canadian Journal of Economics/Revue canadienne d'Economique, II, no. 2
May/mai 1969. Printed in Canada/Imprimé au Canada.

first dichotomy are valid and relevant, he argues toward the end that my production possibility frontier is "curiously empty" and makes other remarks[4] to the effect that my equation system is defective in comparison with the enlarged system suggested by my verbal remarks. It could be therefore that it will be a thankless task for me to demonstrate the falsity of Clowers' critique of the logical implications of my equation system, since he may then come to reject it. But that risk I cannot avoid.

Before getting down to business, let me try to answer some of Professor Clower's criticisms. First, there is a minor aberration in which he attributes to my position the view that the larger the real cash balance the better, *and without end*. Let me state emphatically that there is no reason why utility as a function of the real balance should not reach its maximum at a *finite* level, and all that is needed for my argument is that this optimum level be different from that which is the root of my *laissez-faire* equations.

But second, suppose it were the case that U never reverses direction as a function of M. I still cannot agree with Clower's attempted *reductio ad absurdum*, which reads: "That something is amiss with Samuelson's argument may be seen intuitively by noting that the only vector of money prices that can be counted on to 'satiate people' with real cash balances is the zero vector . . . But what sense could be made in this case of the budget equations of representative men . . . which would entail a postponement of all trade to the millenium . . ." (p. 300).

I choose to consider steady states only: and it would be a finding of the first importance if it could be shown that each finite plateau of real balances greater than that of *laissez-faire* produced a superior plateau of welfare. So we come back to the basic logical query of Clower. Is the *laissez-faire* root of my equations also the normative root of a social welfare maximum problem?

My critic seems methodologically confused on how to examine this problem. He tries to quote my 1947 *Foundations* against me on this. Let me say facetiously that after twenty years the Statute of Limitations protects me against such blows even were they valid: reversing the usual Preface acknowledgment to an author's helpers, the years enable me now to claim all that is good in the book and reject all that is defective as the work of an inexperienced youngster. But the critic has not read his text closely enough. Here it is not a case of accepting – like a Presbyterian – a comparative statical equilibrium system as being fatalistically determined (by its own equations, and subject only to changes in an exogenous parameter). Rather here is a case of considering a *virtual change* in which we suspend the laws of market competition to examine all the *technically feasible* states of the world in order to compare them with the root that *laissez-faire*

[4]Readers should refer to my fifth footnote, Samuelson, "Classical and Neo-Classical Monetary Theory," 8, in which I explicitly state that putting money directly into a steady-state utility function is a second-best surrogate for the alternative more-complicated approach of putting money into the production and trading relations so that its *derived* utility comes from the more copious and more steady time profiles of consumption goods that it enables us to enjoy in our utility function defined over useful goods only. I quite agree with Modigliani, Ando, Patinkin, and no doubt Clower in this. But I deny that the fuller treatment leads to reversal of my contention against the optimality of *laissez-faire*. The present discussion hopes to suggest why this is so.

determines. Quite aside from the area of money, the methodology that I am describing is a commonplace of modern economics. To say that Smith's invisible hand of competition is Pareto optimal is not to say that the competitive solution is what it is – both the best and worst state of the world because it is the *only* state of the world compatible with its own axioms. That is worse than a tautology: it is a fatuity. Rather we set up two alternative systems – that of market competition under *laissez-faire*, and a "technocratic" system, *in natura*, in which we specify that subset of feasible points which maximizes the specified utility function of all the identical representative men; or some specified social welfare function; or, for Pareto optimality, the utility of any residual man after the levels of wellbeing of all others have been specified. Then, as was clarified only in the last 30 years, it is indeed a valid normative theorem for a *moneyless* economy, that perfect competition of Walrasian equilibrium is led, as if by an Invisible Hand, to achieve Pareto optimality.

To see this concretely, imagine a statical system without M in it. Suppose all men have identical utility functions in terms of goods alone, $u(q_1, ..., q_n)$; and suppose these goods can be produced by a constant-cost production frontier like that of my article (Samuelson, 7), namely

$$\pi_1 q_1 + ... + \pi_n q_n = F(\bar{K}, \bar{L}, \bar{T})$$

where the supplies of capital, labour, and land in the neoclassical production function are fixed and are identically distributed among all men so that $\bar{F}$ is output of the representative man.

Then the technocratic best state of the world, $(q_1^{**}, ..., q_n^{**})$ is described by the root of the equations

$$\frac{\partial U / \partial q_1}{\pi_1} = ... = \frac{\partial U / \partial q_n}{\pi_n} = \frac{\sum_1^n q_j \partial U / \partial q_j}{\bar{F}}$$

Now, for comparison, write down the full equations of *laissez-faire* equilibrium. I shall not bother to write down these supply and demand equations; but they are contained in my paper's equations if we ignore all terms in U involving M and P_j. It can be shown that the root to this *laissez-faire* system, which we may write as $(q_1^*, ..., q_n^*, P_1/P_F^*, ..., P_n/P_F^*)$, is identical in its non-pecuniary (q_j^*) components with the technocratic normative root (q_j^{**}) from above. QED

To prove me wrong for my system with money, all Professor Clower would have had to do would have been to repeat this procedure of comparing (i) the technocratic system freed of market clearing supply-and-demand conditions and searched out for its optimum – and all this in the presence of a need for real money balances, as indicated by the presence of M and Ps in my U function – with (ii) my actual *laissez-faire* root, ending up with the triumphant demonstration of exact equivalence between the resulting q^* and q^{**} vectors. But this he cannot do, I now reassert. For I claim there are an infinite number of feasible solutions to my non-market equations *in natura* that do make every identical man better off.

And there is no mystery about it. No something-for-nothing elixir is involved; we simply reduce the deadweight inefficiency that is entailed under *laissez-faire* by everyone's thinking myopically that more money truly costs society more resources *as measured by the interest rate.*[5]

I can be more specific and talk in terms of real transaction costs that Professor Clower would like to emphasize. Let me posit that the good that M does in the U function comes from the fact that with twice the average real cash balance I have to use up only half the shoe leather in walking from my home to the bank during the week between getting paid.[6]

Now suppose that we caused everybody to make a mistake and to hold more M at each level of prices than he would want to when achieving the equivalence between the marginal usefulness of cash and its alleged true marginal cost in terms of foregone interest – alleged, because the homogeneity properties of my functions shows that there is a fallacy of composition in thinking that what seems to cost each separate individual more does actually cost more to all of them regarded as a society. In the moneyless case where Adam Smith's Invisible Hand does lead to a *laissez-faire* optimum, it is easy to show that causing people to make a mistake in their marginal calculations ends them up all worse off. But in this money model, all do end up better. How better? Each man is spared the need to do as much after-hours cobbling because now he has lowered the wear on his shoe leather by virtue of less trips when (M/P_j) increases.

Who is worse off? There is as much land and capital as before, as much coffee and tea as before, the same allocation of rents and wages among the factors of production. (Of course, building banks half way between existing banks would

[5]I readily agree with a point made to me by Professor Franco Modigliani of MIT, and independently by Professor Frank Hahn of the LSE, that in most models of saving a larger real balance may well reduce the level of real capital formation or stock of capital. Hence, in such models where real money is not neutral, $r = 0$ may provide an underestimate of the true social cost of more real cash balances, and $\partial U/\partial M$ should then be positive rather than zero for optimality. But even in such models, the proper marginal cost of more real balances will generally not equal the interest rate on real capital, as Clower alleges. And in the long-run model of my neo-classical paper, where K^* is determined by time preference, ρ, independently of real balances, the Modigliani-Hahn consideration does not apply.

[6]To keep the analysis simple, suppose that all of my cobbling is done at home out of my leisure hours and involves independent disutility. Suppose further, in order that the optimal cash balance be a finite one, that guarding more money at home involves similar disutility. Let $u(q_1, ..., q_n)$ be my independent utility from goods consumption alone on the supposition that shoe leather and money-guarding at home are free goods (i.e., u is my wellbeing if miraculously all "transaction or real balance costs" that use up resources were zero). My final total utility, U, must now have subtracted from it the disutility function that comes from shoe-leather labour used up in more frequent trips to the office as modified by guarding labour needed to protect a given level of real balances. Thus we have

$$U \equiv u(q_1 ..., q_n) - D(M, P_1, ..., P_n),$$

where D is a disutility function that remains the same when both M and all Ps have changed in the same proportion (because then the real trips, shoe leather etc., are all constant) and which, for fixed Ps reaches a minimum for some finite M. Thus, I have given a concrete explication of the equations of my model that does satisfy Professor Clower's legitimate preoccupation with the true social costs of carrying different real balances. Yet logic deduces a result opposite to his allegation of optimality of *laissez-faire*. Only if I put $r = 0$ into the myopic budget equation of the representative individual can one achieve the genuine optimum. Of course, $r = \rho$ is needed to keep capital at its optimal long-run level.

also save shoe leather; but presumably the optimal returns of scale make the present network of bank locations optimal and building so many branches would involve a true extra cost in terms of carpentry, hammers, and land sites. Such a marginal cost would not be fictitious.)

To illustrate dramatically the falseness of Clower's assertion that *laissez-faire* is optimal, consider the special case where the production function lacks smooth substitutability so that the marginal-efficiency demand schedule for capital is vertically inelastic. Then, for factor supplies given, both low and high interest rates can be equilibrium rates, and without affecting anything real (since identical men don't care how much of their unchanged income product is imputed to their capital rather than to their land and labour. Thus, let the system change from psychological time preference ρ_1 to a lower ρ_2 then, under *laissez-faire*, the system will move from $r^* = \rho_1$ to $r^* = \rho_2 < \rho_1$. And now that the interest rate is lower, we must all under *laissez-faire* end up with larger real cash balances. But nothing has really changed! Production and consumption are exactly the same as before. If, before, the system was at Clower's optimum real balance, it can no longer be. (Warning: there is no reason to suppose that there is a genuine zone of indifference here as to optimal cash balance; for, why should the mere fact of an inelastic $F(K,L,T)$ function make for indifferent choices about shoe leather and the general transaction elements that Clower rightly stresses? Conclusion: the *laissez-faire* interest rate is a false guide to optimality of real balances and of their true costs. *QED*

Having denied that my equations *need* to be parameterized in the manner that Clower has thought to infer from the *Foundations*, I can now chivalrously oblige by doing so. In particular, suppose we put a subsidy, s, on holding of cash balances big enough to counterbalance interest costs, making sure that these subsidies are financed by lump sum taxes that do no distortion. Now we have a parameter s. And when we differentiate the final level of utility achieved by the identical men with respect to this subsidy, we find that U^* rises as the subsidy rises positively from its zero *laissez-faire* level. Again my position is vindicated.

An even better way of linking my analysis with the literature on balanced inflation and deflation is to replace my plateau of M with an exponential trend e^{mt}, where m is a negative parameter in the case of deflation and positive in the case of inflation. Then after some manipulation of my equations, we find the real rate of interest (expressed in any q_j^* own rates) the same as before. The money rate of interest, which was r^* in my previous notation, is now equal to the old $r^* + m$. It is this combined magnitude which represents to the small individual the apparent cost of holding a larger cash balance. With m negative we have given him what Clower calls "cheap money." And lo and behold, we have splashed him with welfare in the form of more leisure from the task of cobbling shoes to replace shoe leather. I.e. U^* grows as m declines and pushes the system away from its constant-price-level steady-state of *laissez-faire*.

I conclude therefore that my position has been vindicated against the objections made to it. One of the advantages of having set out a complete system of neoclassical equations is that it enables us to go beyond the ancient history of what used to be thought to shed new light on modern concern with the non-optimality of real balances under *laissez-faire*.[7]

[7]This is a good place to list some typographical errors appearing in my original paper, "What Classical and Neo-Classical Monetary Theory Really Was."

1   P. 2, line 2 from the bottom: "our" should be "out".
2   P. 4, line 2: "$P_i/_1$" should be "P_i/P_1".
3   P. 4, line 13: "Q_n0" should be "Q_n*", and "$\overline{\text{M}}$, Fisher's Constant," should be "$\overline{\text{M}}$ $\times$ Fisher's Constant,".
4   P. 4, note 1, line 2: "$1/FC$" should be "$(1/FC)$".
5   P. 4, note 1, line 3: "$B_2'M = M$" should be "$B_2'M = \dot{\overline{M}}$".
6   P. 5, line 12: "$(l + \rho)$" should be "$(1 + \rho)$".
7   P. 6, line 5: "Y" should be "y".
8   P. 7, note 4, line 2: "K" should be "$\dot{K}$".
9   P. 7, note 4, line 4: "$(1 + p)^{t}$" should be "$(1 + \rho)^{t}$", and "Sidrouski" should be "Sidrauski".
10 P. 8, line 29: "Max $\{q_1, ..., q_n, M\}$" should be shifted up two lines to line 27 before $U(q_1, ..., q_n; M, ...)$.
11 P. 8, note 5, line 2: "may" should be "way".
12 p. 9, line 1: "q_1" should be "q_i".
13 P. 9, line 3: "$(P_1, ..., P_n, W, P_K, P_T; r, \bar{K}, \bar{L}, \bar{T})$" should be "$(P_1, ..., P_n, W, P_K, P_T; r, \bar{K}, \bar{L}, \bar{T}, M*)$."
14 P. 9, line 18: "$(P_K\bar{K}_tP_T\bar{T} + M)$" should be "$(P_K\bar{K} + P_T\bar{T} + M)$".
15 P. 9, line 3 from the bottom: "T" should be "$\bar{T}$", and "K" should be "$\bar{K}$".
16 P. 10, line 1 from the bottom: "M" should be "$M*$".
17 P. 11, line 6: delete the sentence beginning with "Then for fixed" and ending with "M* double" and insert in its place the following sentence: "Then A_{III} determines all qs and P_K/M at values independent of $M*$, and also determines M (and hence P_K and all Ps) as proportional to $M*$."
18 P. 11, line 9: "M" should be "$\bar{M}$".
19 P. 12, line 2 from the bottom: "sequent" should be "sequence".
20 P. 15, line 1: "$F_i(q, P)_\lambda \equiv$" should be "$F_i(q, P) \underset{\lambda}{\equiv}$".
21 P. 15, line 2: "$q_j{}^k$" should be "q_j".
22 P. 15, line 5: "$f_i(P)_\lambda \equiv$" should be "$f_i(P) \underset{\lambda}{\equiv}$".
23 P. 15, line 14: "Q_j*" should be "q_j*", and "$]k_j, k_m$" should be "$], k_j, k_m$".

178

⎰ NOTE: The following summary was presented by the author ⎱
⎱ at the meeting. The full text appears after the summary. ⎰

MONEY, INTEREST RATES AND ECONOMIC ACTIVITY: THEIR INTERRELATIONSHIP IN A MARKET ECONOMY

PAUL A. SAMUELSON

MR. SAMUELSON: I understand that my paper is considered to be heavy going. My excuse is that of every writer of letters—"Excuse the length of this letter, I was too busy to make it shorter."

Gabe Hauge is a very hard taskmaster. He has given me instructions to be brief and also to be clear. That is like the problem of a colleague of mine who went to the MIT Health Service and was told to quit smoking and lose 20 pounds. He said, "Doctor, I can do one or the other, but I can't do both." Well, I have 15 minutes at my disposal. Let me proceed.

I want to call your attention to what Professor Howard Ellis called "the rediscovery of money" around 1950. To illustrate that money had been lost and needed to be rediscovered, let me tell a story that went around in Washington during World War II.

The rumor was spread that the Federal Reserve was going to lose its air conditioner to the Social Security building where important people like Mr. Nathan were sweltering from running the War Production Board. I don't know whether there was any basis to that rumor, but it was believed in Washington.

Money seemed to be very unimportant at that time. A member of the Federal Reserve Board told me that he felt like a slacker in wartime. But he consoled himself by the thought that he was releasing for active duty a spot welder or soldier for the Army.

Well, times have changed. Money is now very important. I would even say that an excessive amount of importance is being attached to it by some economists.

How did money get lost? Why did it once begin to seem unimportant? To understand that is to begin to understand how money affects economic activity.

One of the advantages of being old is that you can construct history from memory—like the farmer who lost his jackass and said to himself, "If I were a jackass, where would I go?" He went there and found the animal.

I know how money was lost because I was once a jackass who didn't believe in it, and I have only to lie on the couch and reconstruct in tranquility what I believed around 1939, and why I believed it.

In 1939 Oxford questionnaires were sent to businessmen and investors generally asking whether interest rates were of any importance to them and whether availability of credit was of any importance to them. To a man they all answered: "No, no importance whatsoever." So, this is coffin nail No. 1 on the importance of money.

At the Harvard business school, the late Professor Ebersole did case studies on finance, and what do you think they all showed, every one of them? They showed that money and finance were of no importance.

If that doesn't convince you, let's turn to econometrics. Professor Tinbergen of Rotterdam did the first econometric studies—giant computer models for an economy. He tried regression coefficients, and no matter how he regressed investment on the interest rate, he always got a zero coefficient.

Finally, if more is necessary, economic theory came to the rescue of this view and people like Sir John Hicks said that as far as short-term investment is concerned, interest is of no consequence as a cost; and as far as long-term investment is concerned, uncertainty is so great that it completely swamps interest, which leaves you with only a miniscule of intermediate investment that is interest elastic.

Well, that was the 1939 view. Unfortunately, some people get frozen into what they learned in their youth, and those views still prevail in some circles. Still, those fellows are dying out in this country.

The Radcliffe Committee in England held extensive investigations and the majority view pretty much came out, I would say, with the conclusion that money doesn't matter.

Now, if this were my classroom I would go to the blackboard and I would write three sentences. I will ask you to imagine them there.

Proposition No. 1—Money does not matter.

Proposition No. 2—Money does matter.

Proposition No. 3—Money alone matters.

I am plagiarizing some remarks made by Professor Tobin at the A.B.A. Conference of University Professors at Princeton. Professor Tobin was quoted to me as having said that some of the monetary fanatics disprove the first proposition that money does not matter, and think they have then established the third proposition that money alone matters; whereas, in fact, by the use of ordinary logic, all that you have established is a second proposition.

I want to call your attention to the similar fallacy, the converse fallacy, made by the Radcliffe Committee. They had witness after witness testify before them, witnesses who were rather badgered if they said that money mattered. The Radcliffe Committee shot down the thesis that money *alone* matters; and they proceeded to the non sequitur, money does not matter.

Well, that is not the sound doctrine as expounded in the American universities of today. In the American universities of today money does matter. Money does not alone matter, and the debate goes on as to whether in some sense money matters most or doesn't.

Now, I will very briefly summarize my view on this subject. The late C. O. Hardy said, "Fiscal policy really has no independent importance. It is just a complicated way of getting the banking system to create some extra money. It is like burning the house in order to roast a pig." Or let me use a more vulgar example: There is the fellow who is playing the xylophone with great skill in the foreground, and the crowd is going wild clapping; and all the time in the background there is a girl stripping. The music player thinks that *he* is accomplishing all that is taking place.

Well, the view of the late C. O. Hardy was that the girl in the background, where the action really was, is monetary policy, and fiscal policy is just the window dressing that goes on. So, to add to my mixed metaphors, why not skip the middle man?

I think that this view is profoundly wrong. I think, for example, that by remaking history we could imagine a crucial experiment to test that view. Let's suppose that in 1961 to get the country moving again we had embraced an austere fiscal policy, balanced the budget at a low level, and tried to accomplish the recovery by monetary policy alone. According to the view of Hardy, which I am caricaturing, but only very slightly—it is hard to caricature what is already a caricature—the effects would have been the same as those which took place in 1961–1967. In my judgement they would have been entirely different.

By the Hardy-Friedman route, you would have had to depress interest rates enormously. A balance-of-payments crisis would have been upon us from the very beginning. I think that the mixture of fiscal policy and monetary policy we actually used was absolutely crucial in this and other regards, Hardy notwithstanding.

Now, how does money affect things? Once, around 1950, I asked a man who is here today why he was so keen for tighter money, how did he think it worked?

I said, "Do you think, for example, that it will affect the level of consumption spending?" He said, "No, not at all."

I said, "Do you think it will affect the level of investment spending?" He said, "No, not at all."

I said, "Why then are you for it?" He said, "I cannot help but think that it would be a good thing."

Well, how does it actually work, this good thing? I shall consider primarily one weapon of the Federal Reserve—open-market purchases or open-market sales.

There are other weapons of the Federal Reserve—for example, discount rate. Parenthetically, when I was sent off by a delegation from Boston, knowing that I was coming here to represent that fair city, they told me that the money market now needs a signal—that it needs a discount-rate cut as a signal of the intentions of the Federal Reserve to continue credit ease.*

Well, that is the kind of thing I am not going to talk about here today because much the same effects could be created by means of open-market operations, and I will concentrate upon them.

An open-market operation is like buying or selling a used car. It is a dealing in secondhand assets. The Federal Reserve spits out money and takes in a money substitute—not a perfect money substitute to be sure, and, of course, it depends upon whether it is operating in Treasury Bill markets only, and it depends also upon the times.

In 1939, when part of my mind froze, open-market operations could not be expected, in my judgement, to have today's potency because, as I mentioned in my paper, the Treasury Bill rate at times was $3/8$ of $3/8$ of 1 per cent. Under those circumstances, a Treasury Bill was almost a perfect substitute for circulating medium.

That is not the case today. Now the first effect of an open-market purchase is to bid up the price of some securities, bid down the yield. This translates itself, in gradually increasing amount, into the lowering of effective yield rates that mortgage payers who want to build buildings must pay, of rates on commercial loans, and so forth.

Although President Conn was glad to be absolved as a banker from affecting interest rates, even conduits have their effects upon the system; depending upon how the banking industry administers the changed credit situation, you can get different effects.

Several years ago I argued—I now have less conviction about that than I did then—that "the credit rationing effect" is important only in the short run, and that the longer the tightness prevails, the more

---

* Added later: Apparently, so great was my eloquence that the cut came the afternoon of my speech!

it will get translated into actual interest costs as against mere availability.

I don't know how correct that view is. I refer you to my paper in which I discuss the pros and cons of it. But in either case, we do have a reinforcing effect upon durable goods spending when money is tight—particularly at the business level, and in some degree at the consumer level.

And that is how, and not by any mystical way, monetary policy has its effects.

The big dispute within academic circles, I think I can summarize most briefly thus: One view holds that if there is an excess of money, it just burns a hole in the pocket of somebody and gets spent on some goods market. Whereas the view which I have been expounding suggests that if the increase in money was the kind of money engendered by central bank action, it impinges, in the first instance, *on the financial markets,* and if there is an excess of money forced upon the system it shows itself in a bidding up of security prices and a bidding down of interest rates, and through that mechanism affects business activity.

Now, I am just about finished and will conclude with the issue: What is it that the central banker ought to watch?

We have a professor at Harvard named Talcott Parsons, a very profound man. He is so profound that almost nobody understands him; he is a sociologist.

I once asked another sociologist, "Can you explain to me why he is such a great man?" He said, "I will give you an example. Parsons wrote an article recently, and in it he asked this question: 'How is it we all have two parents, a father and a mother, and only one psychoanalyst?'"

You really have to think about that to realize how profound it is. Well now, the Good Lord gave us two eyes. He didn't give us one eye. He might have given us one eye in the middle of our forehead, but He gave us two eyes.

In the debate, what should a central banker watch—should he watch the money stock or should he watch the interest rate structure?—this is relevant. I think when the Good Lord gave us two eyes, He had a purpose in that. He didn't want us to watch just one thing, He wanted us to watch both of those things.

But, of course, it takes a brain behind the eyes to get the proper mixture of what it is that you perceive and what you see when you look at both of those things.

MONEY, INTEREST RATES AND ECONOMIC ACTIVITY: THEIR INTERRELATIONSHIP IN A MARKET ECONOMY

PAUL A. SAMUELSON

REAL AND MONETARY DETERMINANTS OF THE INTEREST RATE STRUCTURE

Classical Real Theory: Statics

Although interest appears superficially as a percentage yield on money values, to the classical economist it represents at the deeper level the real productivity of roundabout, time-consuming production embodied in machines, industrial plants, and unfinished goods in process. Capital goods are limited in amount, and their scarcity can be relieved only by sacrificing current consumption—transferring resources from them to enhanced capital formation. More roundabout processes may be more productive, but it takes *waiting* by consumers to get them going. The disutility of labor was thought to keep labor scarce and its productive wage high, and thus the wage can in a sense be called the reward for sweat. In the same way, the disutility of *abstaining* from current consumption and of engaging in further waiting is what keeps capital instruments scarce and productive. Thus, interest can be regarded as the reward for abstinence or waiting, the price needed to overcome this natural human impatience to consume now and not in the future.

The classical view regards interest as determined by demand and supply—the productivity of capital goods providing the main elements of demand (albeit reinforced by consumer-loans demand on the part of especially needy and impatient borrowers), and the supply of capital being limited by the reluctance to abstain from current consumption and do more saving, resulting in cumulative capital formation.

What follows from this classical model of interest as being determined solely by real factors? Here are some consequences.

1. Though interest is paid in money terms on money loans and assets, *the level of interest has nought to do with the level of money and with the price level.* If metal coins form the currency, and if their supply is much augmented by, say, past mining discoveries of precious metals, the only effect is to raise the level of *all* prices proportionately. Thus, if money M doubles, so will be doubled the prices of tea, cloth, lumber, machinery, and land. The dividends of stocks and the coupons of bonds will, in the new equilibrium, be exactly doubled, but so too will the principal values of these assets be exactly doubled—with the result that the percentage ratio of money yield to money principal will work out to exactly the same interest rate. (David Ricardo and Knut Wicksell were nineteenth-century writers who clearly insisted on this classical fact.)

2. Commercial banks are mere *conduits* for the more efficient channelling of savings into the best investment outlets. Except for transitional states in which the system moves from one long-run equilibrium to another, the banks do not affect the level of interest rates.

3. Suppose banks can issue currency in the form of bank notes or checkable bank deposits which the people treat as the equivalent to holding currency. Then laissez faire in banking can *not* be counted on to lead to equilibrium with stable price levels. In particular, a basic notion underlying the founding of the Federal Reserve System in 1913 is quite false; providing for an "elastic" total supply of money and credit by enabling banks to create new money whenever they can lend

to manufacturers, merchants, and farmers on genuine productive assets (to finance inventories, permit production maintenance and expansion, et cetera), will *not* be conducive to stability of the price level and of general business activity.

At what levels of interest are the "legitimate" demands of production and trade to be met? If market interest rates prevail below the real equilibrium levels set by the classical quasi-barter model, the total money supply will grow, thus creating demand-pull inflation. Lending against real goods (the so-called real-bills doctrine) is *not* guaranteed to produce an enhanced supply of goods that will quench (at unchanged prices) the manufactured increase of new M (and the resulting increased flow of its MV spending).

Although the level of the money supply and prices cannot affect the interest rate in the crudest classical system, classical writers are correct to insist that there must be some limitation on the total supply of money set by the Government if the price level is to be determinate. And if there can be expected to be a steady growth of population and productivity, leading to a steady growth of real output—and if there can be expected to emerge a generally constant level of interest rates, as the result of cancelling out innovations of a capital-saving- and labor-saving-type in comparison with any capital accumulation relative to labor supply—then a desire for a generally stable level of prices can only be achieved if the Government contrives that there be a rise in the supply of money commensurate with the changes in real output.

Dynamic Modifications of the Crude Classical System

The above real system abstracts from innumerable factors known to be of importance in any economy that actually exists, whether it be the Victorian model of England in the nineteenth century or the mixed economies of the present. Thus, its postulates leave no room for a Great Depression with mass unemployment on a lasting basis; its postulates throw no light on the fluctuations of business conditions as they have been studied by the National Bureau of Economic Research for this country and for the major industrial nations. The classical model that I have caricatured above operates upon the premise of quixotic flexibility of prices. The 25 per cent rate of unemployment that prevailed both in the United States and in Germany in the 1930s could not have happened if downward flexibility of prices and wages existed. So, at a low enough wage level all the unemployed could find willing employers (whose effective demand had not, because of the "Pigou effect," been undetermined by the hyperdeflation itself). On the inflationary side, the classical model has no room within its postulates for cost-push inflation, such as many observers claim to have observed in many mixed economies of the post-World War II generation.

However, within the classical system itself, we can discern some systematic theorizing about dynamic transitional states between states of stable equilibrium. Since the time of David Hume, two centuries ago, classicists noted that unforeseen inflation could be expected to favor debtors at the expense of creditors, to favor entrepreneurial profit-seekers at the expense of *rentiers* and contractual wage earners, and to favor vigorous high-employment conditions at the expense of more stagnant conditions.

After the 1890s Wicksell, the great Swedish neoclassical economist, kept insisting that practical men were right to think that lowering the market interest rate in the short run, by having the banks create and lend out money, would indeed raise prices and expand business activity. Wicksell insisted, however, that once the system was at full employment such expansion of money would lead only to an increase in price tags; and each impulse of new-money creation by the banks would be followed by a tendency for all prices to rise, including those of the rents from capital goods and the market values of those goods—so, ultimately, the interest rate would tend to move back to its real classical level. Indeed, once the market rate of interest was set by the central bank back at that classical real level, there would cease to be an increase in the money supply and in the price level. But, if the central bank persisted in keeping the market rate of interest below the true real rate, it would thereby give rise to a more or less permanent rate of money creation and price inflation (adding to the real interest rate a percentage price-increase allowance).

We may summarize thus: *The independence of the interest rate from the behavior of money and banks that is posited in the statical classical theory disappears in considerable part once dynamic assumptions are made about the creation of money growth as a result of mines, banks, or governments.*

By the early 1930s there had grown up the so-called neo-Wicksellian view [1] that the real supply-and-demand curves determining interest rates should have added to them a component of the supply of saving which is associated with the creation of new money, or M. According to this view banks have a great deal to do in the short run with increasing the flow of capital formation and reducing the market rates of interest. If banks are able to create new M, which they lend out to would-be investors in new construction, inventory, and equipment, they change the mix of gross national product toward capital formation and away from current consumption; and they are able to "force" this money on the system only by lowering the explicit interest rate, or diminishing the effective stringency of rationing, and thereby implicitly lowering the interest costs of borrowing. The rest of the community, even if it wants to save the same fraction of its incomes as before, undergoes "forced saving" in consequence of the fact that the banks have created inflation of the price level; and by the time the community comes to spend its incomes, it buys less in the way of real goods.

Moreover, in our day when the Government is committed to following a militant fiscal policy of its own, involving budget surpluses and deficits at different levels of total taxation and spending, we recognize that fiscal policy interacts with monetary policy in shaping the behavior of interest rates, capital supplies, price levels, and intensity of unemployment.

For example, if fiscal policy is chronically expansionary—in the sense of involving high levels of public expenditure with low levels of tax receipts so that large budget deficits continuously take place—and if monetary policy is chronically tight—so that interest rates are kept high enough and the rate of growth of M slow enough to hold down investment and consumer-durable spending to a level low enough to wipe out demand-pull inflationary gaps—then the community will evolve with less capital formation than would otherwise have taken place. It will evolve with higher short-term and higher long-term interest rates than would otherwise be the case.

The last two cases involved maintenance of full employment and assumed no cost-push inflation problem. If we consider mixed economies that are character-

---

[1] See Gottfried Von Haberler, *Prosperity and Depression; A Theoretical Analysis of Cyclical Movements* (originally published by the League of Nations in 1937; later postwar editions available), Chapter 3, for an exposition of the writings of F. Hayek and other similar writers.

ized by price-wage inflexibilities and which display chronically different degrees of unemployment and underemployment, different policies by the Fed can lead to different levels of achieved employment and production. Expansionary monetary policies that keep investment spending higher than would otherwise be the case lead initially to lower money rates of interest and ultimately to lower real-productivity yields on the enhanced stock of physical capital equipment. But they achieve this not at all at the expense of current consumption, for consumption too is higher than would otherwise be the case. Both capital formation and consumption can be increased by utilizing resources that would otherwise be dissipated in mass unemployment and industrial excess capacity.

The Extreme Keynesian Case

A few years after J. M. Keynes wrote his 1936 *General Theory of Employment, Interest and Money*, there grew up the strong notion that the interest rate is purely a monetary phenomenon. Passages can be found in the *General Theory* claiming that interest is merely the difference between the yield on safe money and risk-involving securities, and therefore interest is merely the price for giving up the liquidity of holding money. Statements like these can be harmless if nothing is read into them. They can be misleading if we read into them the view that the real productivity of capital has nought to do with the short- or long-run levels of interest, or infer that current thrift has nought to do with interest rates, or that shifts in the marginal efficiency of capital cannot affect the rate of interest as it can in the classical system. And if we look critically at the actual properties of the system of relations in the *General Theory*, we find they are usually in agreement with the results previously mentioned.

For example, if banks are given extra reserves and use them to bid down the yields of loans and bonds, that increase in M leads, in the Keynesian system, to lower interest rates, more investment, and greater total dollar spending. If employment was not previously full and still falls short of full employment, there is no reason why the increase in M should cause a proportional increase in prices generally.

If businessmen discover new investment opportunities, that will, with total M fixed, raise interest rates and the level of dollar GNP. If people save less out of current incomes, that will depress money GNP and interest rates. In short, if one reads the *General Theory* rigorously, one ends up with conclusions not too different from those of an eclectic neoclassical monetary theorist.

Nevertheless, in times like those which prevailed in, say, 1938 when most disciples were just mastering the *General Theory,* banks held considerable excess reserves and short-term interest rates on Treasury Bills were often down to ⅜ of ⅜ of 1 per cent.[2] Hence, massive changes in M have little effect even on short-term interest rates, and, a fortiori, little changes in employment, production, or capital formation. Moreover, in times of deep depression, such as in 1932 when existing plants were operating at losses and idle capacity was everywhere, even if one could contrive by monetary policy a substantial change in short- and long-term interest rates, little new investment could be coaxed out by such monetary policies. And, since we are discussing conventional central bank operations

---

[2] On occasions the yield was zero or even negative, a fact to be accounted for presumably in terms of personal property tax exemptions and subscription rights. Often, Treasury Bills were not cashed in at maturity. When I then asked a Government official why, he said to me, "Do you know a better way to hold a million dollars?"

which merely involve buying existing assets with M (old bonds and Treasury Bills), there is no significant change in the *net worth* of the public generally. Investors have no incentive to spend more on capital formation, and consumers have no new incentive to spend more on consumption. In consequence, Federal Reserve operations of N billion dollars then involve less than their normal potency.[3]

The Neoclassical Synthesis

As I have insisted upon in the recent editions of my ECONOMICS, once we introduce systematically into a post-Keynesian system treatment of stocks of assets, monetary and real, and take into account fluctuating levels of real unemployment, there remain no inconsistencies between the classical system and the Keynesian system. The synthesis of common content emerges with an eclectic position on the interplay of real and monetary factors in determining the structure and levels of interest rates.

In the short run, changes in the money supply contrived by conventional Federal Reserve open-market operations produce opposite effects upon the level of interest rates. Within limits, changes in the composition of Fed purchases as between short bills and long bonds can slightly influence the shape of the yield differentials between long- and short-term assets. But apparently only within narrow limits unless massive "twists" are indulged in.

In the longer run, if expanded credit achieves a restoration of full employment and beyond, there tends to be a permanent bidding up of all prices, and there reemerges a strong tendency for interest rates to revert to their real level. This is the continuing kernel of truth in the classical crude "quantity theory."

Fiscal policy changes can produce substantial changes in total GNP or MV magnitudes. If M is not changed concommitantly, this can be expected to produce changes in the interest rate (and opposing changes in V).[4]

HOW MONETARY POLICY AFFECTS THE LEVEL OF ECONOMIC ACTIVITY

Scope of Monetary Policy

By monetary policy we mean primarily Federal Reserve actions designed to affect the tightness and easiness of credit conditions, and the behavior of the total

---

[3] In this model we have one of those rare cases in which a contrived increase in M can be predictably expected to induce an opposing change in velocity of circulation V, with the product MV little increased.

[4] The valid core of the "quantity theory" that is implied by neoclassical reasoning does not require constancy of the velocity of circulation, V. It requires only that a balanced change in *all* prices should itself have no effect on V. Moreover, it is only a quirk of law that keeps banks from paying interest on demand deposits. In eras when the market would determine a high, short-term interest rate, free competition would permit us to use as our circulating medium interest-bearing bank deposits. When fiats prevent banks from paying interest on checkable accounts, nature ordains that competitive substitutes will flourish, time deposits will in fact require no notice, they will pay daily interest, they will become negotiable, and institutional arrangements will be made so that they can serve as a close money substitute for most exchange purposes. As soon as the liquid assets that we use to perform the function of money begin to pay interest, an entirely new pattern of velocity is to be expected from a rational man. That is why I should not expect V to be constant in the future, even if it had been more constant in the past than it actually has been.

Furthermore, along with the noninterest-bearing public debt that we call money, there is the interest-bearing public debt. This too acts like an "outside asset" making the community feel richer than it really is. As soon as we realize this, we see not that there is substantive difference between an increase in M resulting from *past* gold mining or greenback financed war expenditure and an equal increase in M resulting from an open-market purchase. The gold and greenbacks result in a permanent increase in the net worth as envisaged by the typical person. The M created by open-market purchase takes from people some of their net worth embodied in bonds, and in return gives them some net worth in the form of M.

supply of money and money substitutes (that is, the supply of currency, checkable bank deposits, various categories of time deposits, and other liquid instruments).

The chief weapon of the Federal Reserve in doing all this is its *open-market purchases and sales of Government securities*. But intermittently, as last month, changes in the *legal reserve requirement ratios* that must be held against various categories of demand and time deposits have effects like those of open-market operations. Furthermore, *raising or lowering the discount rate* at which banks can borrow from the Federal Reserve can reinforce or offset the the effects of open-market operations. And aside from the quoted rate at which discount borrowing is permitted to take place, *the manner in which access to the discount window is administered* can have powerful effects upon the actual volume of such borrowing and hence on the reserves of the banking system.

Moral suasion, by which I mean the whole atmosphere in which banking is carried on—including letters to the banks like that of last year which urged them to go easy in making loans, and including voluntary programs of foreign lending by the banks—is constantly being pooh-poohed by many economists as a factor of any quantitative importance for monetary policy. But in my judgement, it is often a significant variable and, as in so many countries abroad, it will become an increasingly important variable in the future.

Although I have mentioned these five weapons of the Federal Reserve, the first is by all odds the most important. And in principle, by more vigorous use of open-market operations alone in both the downward and upward direction, we could achieve most of the same goals that can be achieved by all five weapons. (This is only approximately true and is not meant as a recommendation for a monistic reform.)

I am purposely defining monetary policy broadly to include attention to credit conditions as well as to the supply of money. I am thus explicitly rejecting the view that it should be concerned only with achieving some desired pattern of behavior in some defined magnitude of "money," such as currency plus demand deposits or the latter plus certain categories of time deposits. Like fiscal and other macroeconomic policies, monetary policy is concerned with achieving the desired total of gross national product spending; and if one writes GNP as the product of some defined M and its implicitly defined V, then the neoclassical position which I have already expounded militates against considering the factor M independently of the V in MV. Moreover, one cannot stipulate in advance that a modern mixed economy will be indifferent to the composition of the GNP, as for example between residential construction and other forms of investment. And hence the central bank, as an important and indispensable arm of the modern state, has a responsibility in conducting overall macroeconomic activities to take into account alternative effects upon sectors. Ours is a pluralistic society, and properly so. In a pluralistic society it makes no sense to set up institutions with a monistic function and then have to set up new superagencies to coordinate them.

Hence, although it is the principal function of the Federal Reserve to deal with overall credit conditions, it must also perform many selective functions. The Board and the System are not now so overworked that this will negate accomplishment of their principal function, and if the System were to shrink back from these duties, that would only create a political vacuum into which other agencies would rush. I do not think it would be a good thing to have competing central banks in this country, one dealing primarily with residential real estate, one with farm problems, and so forth.

From the broad way in which I have defined monetary policy, it will be evident that the Federal Reserve is merely the chief instrument of such policies, not the exclusive instrument. In particular, the United States Treasury, in connection with the way that it floats and refunds debt—using at one time long-term and at other times short-term instruments, selling at one time to its Trust Funds and at another to the open market—is also powerfully affecting monetary and credit conditions. And within the sector of finance, commercial banks which are outside of the Federal Reserve are of some importance in just the way that mutual savings and savings and loan institutions are important in affecting the overall pattern of monetary conditions and GNP aggregates. Because financial intermediaries both initiate and reinforce changes in credit conditions, they too come within the province of my broad definition of monetary policy.[5]

How Federal Reserve Policy Affects GNP

We may concentrate upon the open-market purchases and sales of the Federal Reserve. If the Fed were to print bank notes or write checks in order to provide free current services for the people (weather forecasting, national defense, research and development) or to give people transfer incomes every month (Social Security payments, relief, et cetera), that would be quite another thing from what it actually does. Instead, it buys and sells existing assets—not used cars or factories, but Government securities of all durations. Like any bidder or seller of Government bonds, it has a direct effect on the market price of those bonds and an opposite effect upon the bonds' yields. Indeed, only by bidding up or down the yields of existing bonds can the Fed persuade people and banks to let it consummate its open-market operations. It has no powers of eminent domain or fiat.

Direct effects on interest rates and credit availability. Whenever anybody bids up or down the yields on Government bonds, that automatically has an effect upon the supply-and-demand bids that determine the pattern of yields on corporate bonds and other securities that are alternatives to Government bonds. There is, thus, a direct effect upon the structure of interest rates from open-market purchases by the Fed. Such purchases directly lower the yields on the issues bought and (with attenuation) tend to lower the yields on Governments of other maturities and the yield of corporate bonds. Since bonds are substitutes, albeit not terribly close ones, for other forms of investment such as mortgage loans, the lowering of bond yield tends to channel funds into mortgages and to lower their yield, at the same time making mortgage loans somewhat more available, and more available with lower down payments and longer amortization periods.

Indirect effects on interest and credit conditions. What has been already described would be the whole story if ours was not a fractional reserve banking

---

[5] Fiscal policy questions, such as whether there should be an increase in personal income tax rates, affect directly the flow of income and would be distinguishable from monetary policy actions. But policies that call for earlier payments of accruing tax obligations are definitely akin to monetary policies. Some authorities would even try to draw the line between monetary and fiscal policy actions by means of the functional criterion: Does the policy act primarily upon a *stock* (the stock of money, of outstanding bonds, of liquid money substitutes, of less-liquid housing assets, et cetera); or does it act primarily upon a *flow* (as in the case of a reduced tax rate on current incomes or increased expenditure on current public services)?

system. Because the Fed's puchase has increased the cash of someone in the system, and because that someone is likely to hold most of that cash in some bank, there is now an increase in the investable reserves of the banking system. These will generally not be left in the form of excess reserves, but instead will encourage the banks to make new loans or acquire other securities. We thus have a repetition and reinforcement of the bidding down of the yields of the whole spectrum of assets in the community, and concomitantly this increases the availability of loans to borrowers at the same time that costs of borrowing are being bid down. There is nothing mechanical about the process; it takes place at each stage of the game in terms of people being motivated to make new supply-and-demand bids. It rests on the multilateral willingness of people to leave their money in banks, of banks to make loans or buy bonds, and of the rest of the community to borrow money and to issue new securities or give up old ones in favor of holding demand or time deposits. Although not mechanical, the process is in normal times highly predictable. A certain fraction of the Fed's created reserves will go into currency holdings, a certain fraction into repayment of discounts, a certain fraction into holding of deposits, a certain (normally very small) fraction into extra excess reserves; and in consequence we can predict that there has been created somewhere in the system several times as much of new bank deposits for each dollar of open-market purchase.[6]

Direct and indirect effects on net worths. When Federal Reserve open-market purchases achieve some lowering of interest yields, they produce some increase in the capitalized value of assets people own. My 20-year bonds now sell for $103 instead of $100, and I may somewhat increase my consumption spending on food, travel, TV sets. My home may sell for a bit more, and it may be regarded by me as more easily sellable and hence a bit more liquid. This may increase my consumption and depress my current saving rate. The same is true of business enterprises—their balance-sheet assets may be bid up in price and be of increased liquidity, and this could be one of the determinants of their spending more on new investments.

In sum, open-market purchase creation of M has some upward effects on total community net worth, and therefore some direct effects upon increasing current consumption and investment spending. But this is not a strong effect by itself. The new M is not burning a hole in someone's pocket and aching to be spent at the old velocity of circulation. On the contrary, we have got hold of this new M in exchange for selling liquid securities; if they were not burning a hole in our pockets, neither will the new M, particularly since our securities have been bid up just enough by this process to make us content to forego them and instead hold cash as an asset.

I do not wish to be misunderstood. In a moment I shall trace through how the direct and indirect lowering of interest rates coaxes out more spending on investment goods and creates an increased flow of current income and employment. That has a powerful effect on total spending. But it is the much smaller effects on saving through the channel of increased net worths that I am now trying to evaluate.

---

[6] In deep depression when short-term yields had already been bid down to a fraction of a per cent, and when everybody was pessimistic about the marginal profitability of additions to inventory, plant, and equipment, the predictable results would be quite different from that in normal times. Conceivably, the only effect would be to exchange near-M for M and to bid up slightly the existing value of long-term securities. Existing excess reserves would be added to in such times.

To make my point, imagine an unrealistic experiment. Suppose rationing on capital formation kept the Fed's open-market purchase from inducing any increased inventory spending or plant and equipment spending. Suppose that consumers' durable finance was already copiously available at rates that could be brought down very little, even if the Treasury Bill rate were negligible. Then where would a substantial increase in the current flow of spending come from? The M itself does not represent any increase in net worth for the banks and public; it is only the rise in securities prices that it created in coming into existence (that is, in coming out of the Fed in exchange for bonds that go into the Fed) that raises net worth. Undoubtedly, under my bizarre rationing of investment, the resulting drop in interest rate from the open-market purchase would be all the larger; prices for existing bonds would be bid up a lot before people would be content to hold the zero-earning new M. Only if you have what I regard as an unrealistic theory for the functional relationship between velocity and interest rates will you conclude that net worths in the community will be bid up to whatever gigantic levels are needed to get all the new-M spending on comsumption at the old rate of turnover.[7]

In any case when we trace through realistically the *modus operandi* of an expansion of credit, we find that it works only slightly through direct increases in net worth; instead it works primarily through inducing new investment spending (including in the term "investment spending," spending on consumers' durables in excess of their being used up). It is to this vital link that I now turn.

Increase in investment spending induced by lower-cost and more available credit. Now comes the most important step in the process by which monetary policy works to affect business activity. When banks and lenders generally have more funds to lend, and when the interest yields of investments have been bid down, the result will tend to be an increase in lending and borrowing activity. It does not matter in the first instance whether the increase in business spending on inventory, plant, or equipment comes from a lowered interest cost of finance which makes projects pay that previously did not pay; or whether the increased investment spending comes because the investor is able to arrange for financing that was previously just not available to him. In either case, there follows an increase in investment spending which gives jobs to someone and which directly increases production in the form of capital formation or investment. The incomes received in these new lines of activity are spent by their recipients in considerable measure by the familiar propensity-to-consume mechanisms. Hence, the primary expansion in investment, induced by credit-easing, results in a secondary chain of consumption respending in accordance with familiar multiplier sequence.

Nor is this all. With production higher, the profitability of existing capital goods is enhanced; there is both an extra desire for additions to capacity and also an extra cash and income flow available to would-be investors to finance such activity. So, along with secondary consumption respending, the multiplier chain sets off a tertiary flow of acceleration-principle investment spending. This in turn begins another multiplier-accelerator chain. I do not imply that the process leads to perpetual expansion. Far from it; in most circumstances any particular once-and-for-all open-market purchase leads to a subsequent increment

---

[7] See the equation on page 55.

of spending that is finite in total amount, and which reaches a maximum effect within a finite time (perhaps one or two quarters) and then tails off to insignificance.

It should be understood that this induced investment leads to the creation of real capital and adds to the lasting net worths of people and businesses. While it is generating the higher flow of incomes, it also leads to a desire for the holding of more cash for transaction purposes, and thus transiently to a higher velocity of circulation than would be the case without the income increase; and it thus leads transiently to less of a fall in the interest rate than will ultimately take place after the induced expansion production subsides.

All the above is premised upon the postulate that the open-market purchase impinged upon a sytem which was at underemployment and which was capable of increase in production and employment. If industry is already operating at capacity, and if the labor market is already so tight as to be nonexpandable, the induced increase in investment demand will serve merely to produce an inflationary gap. At preexisting prices, there will be a demand-pull gap and there will tend to result a bidding up of commodity prices generally, and through derived demand, a bidding up of wages. Although money wages will be observed to be growing faster than the growth in physical productivity, there is no need to conclude that any cost-push inflation is going on. It could be—and as I am describing it, would be—all demand-pull inflation. As long as this is going on, there is being generated an enhanced need for cash balances for purely transactional purposes.

If the price level ultimately rises by as great a percentage as the increase in the M created by the open-market purchase, there can emerge a new equilibrium with the interest rate back to where it was in the beginning. In this particular case, the effect of the open-market purchase has been to raise prices and nothing else. Only in the transitional stages have there been real effects. Here we have a case, often envisaged by economists like Marshall, where an initial decrease in the interest rate leads ultimately to a restoration of the old interest rate at a higher price level. And indeed if we envisage a dynamic system with some momentum in it which generates psychological and other self-reinforcing mechanisms, we should not be surprised to meet a model in which an initial lowering of interest rates by open-market M creation leads penultimately to raising the interest rates above the *ex ante* level. If the system is ultimately stable, this penultimate state would, in its turn, subside.

For the specialist, symbolism may clarify. Let *net worth* equal the sum of *money* plus *Government bonds* (mostly short-term) plus *value of capital goods*.

$$NW = M + B + K$$
$$= M + \pi\ (i)\ (b+k)$$
$$= NW\ (a_1 + a_2 + a_3)$$

where $\pi\ (i)$ represents the capitalization factor that depicts a bidding up of prices of existing machines or face-value bonds when the interest rate drops; and where (a_i) represents the respective fractions of NW represented by the three kinds of assets. An open-market purchase represents an increase in M matched by a decrease in b; except that this would involve a lowering of i and a (slight) increase in $\pi\ (i)$, the drop in b would equal the rise in M. Writing Y for money income and assuming for expositional simplicity that the price level of consumption, C, and investment goods, I, remains constant until full employment is reached, our simplest system becomes—

(1) $\quad Py = P\,C\left(\dfrac{Y}{P},\ \dfrac{NW}{P}\ ;\ a_2,\ a_3\right) + P\,I\left(i, \dfrac{Y}{P},\ k\right)$

(2) $\quad \dfrac{M}{Y} = L\left(i, \dfrac{\pi\,(i)\,b + \pi\,(i)\,k}{P},\ \dfrac{Y}{P}\right),$

with the usual properties—

$$\dfrac{\partial C}{\partial y} > 0,\ \dfrac{\partial C}{\partial\,(NW/P)} > 0,\ \dfrac{\partial I}{\partial i} < 0,\ \dfrac{\partial I}{\partial y} > 0,\ \dfrac{\partial I}{\partial k} < 0$$

$$\dfrac{\partial L}{\partial i} < 0,\ \dfrac{\partial L}{\partial\,(\pi\,b)} > 0,\ \dfrac{\partial L}{\partial y} > 0$$

The first row above is noncontroversial. The second row relations would be challenged by those who believe that L is a constant, a view that I respect but differ with. Particularly at a low i, such constancy seems doubtful to me. In (1), an increase in a_2 and a_3, at the expense of M's share of net worth, I judge to be, at most, a mild depressant on C; that is, $\partial\,C/\partial a_i < 0$, but small in magnitude.

For this model, an increase in M through an open-market operation that lowers b will slightly decrease i, slightly raise NW, significantly raise I, and thereby Y and C. After full employment is reached (and assuming no cost-push Phillips-curve problem), increases in M will tend to result ultimately in rises in P with small ultimate further changes in i or y. If k/y is increased in the transition by the positive M, k and y will be permanently higher and i lower.

AVAILABILITY OF CREDIT AS A FACTOR DIFFERENT FROM THE COST OF CREDIT

My argument thus far can be briefly summarized: Central bank open-market operations produce their primary effects on the economic system *by lowering or raising the spectrum of interest rates*, thereby increasing or decreasing the flow of investment and durable-goods spending, which leads in turn to expansion or contraction in the aggregate of GNP flow. How the change in dollar spending is divided into real output or price-level changes depends upon the amount of slack in the system and upon the institutional factors that make for price-wage inflexibility or for cost-push rises in prices and wages.

In using the expression "spectrum of interest rates," I wish to make room explicitly for various intensities of rationing of credit. Loans are not auctioned off in perfect markets so that the scarcity of funds can be accurately measured by a quoted market rate of interest. Loans and securities are negotiated in a great variety of retail and wholesale markets. Often interest rates are like administered prices—the rates quoted are changed, but infrequently. However, the unavailability of funds at these rates changes markedly and in sympathy with the movement of market interest rates.

Thus, when the Treasury Bill rate is rising from 4 to 5 per cent, when the long-term bond yields on corporate and Government securities are rising from 5 to 5½ per cent, and when the discounts are growing on mortgages quoted in the secondary markets, you will find your friendly banker less friendly. No longer will he press funds on you. If you ask for a $50,000 loan for six months, he may agree only to $30,000 for four months. And although he may stick by the 6 per cent rate he has long been charging you, there may now be an insistence that you maintain at least 30 per cent in the form of compensating balances instead of the usual 10 per cent (a shift which already raises 6 per cent effectively to almost 8 per cent). Moreover, many people who have been relying on such 6 per cent bank loans will now be turned down and will have to go to a finance company and pay 7 per cent or more. Hence, even though each posted interest rate may seem to change little, the effective interest rates at which people really borrow will have gone up much by virtue of the concomitant changes in the severity of rationing of credit.

How important is this factor of rationing? And (since it seems to operate in the same direction as changes in market interest rates) does the subject matter? I think that practical men exaggerate the importance of the rationing factor, and academic men underestimate its short-run effectiveness. Aside from those who deny that rationing plays any important role, there exist two schools. Both agree it is important, but one insists that this is a dreadful phenomenon which is in fact responsible for giving bankers such a bad name and which leads to serious distortions and inequities as between small and large business, new and old businesses, and different sectors of the economy. The other school congratulates monetary policy on its potency and effectiveness that stems from the alleged importance of induced credit availability conditions.

Lending and borrowing and evaluation of securities must from their nature involve uncertainties and different degrees of imperfection of knowledge and information. From its nature, therefore, we must expect the banking and investment business to be peculiarly vulnerable to Chamberlinian imperfections of competition. In such markets we expect to encounter somewhat inflexible administered prices with hidden or open departures from those quoted rates. And even in a steady state where there are no changes in overall money supply or market rates of interest, the lenders must always be forming judgements about creditworthiness so that a decision process involving rationing of credit is inevitable. Nevertheless, the longer changed credit conditions prevail, the more will differences in degree of rationing tend to be replaced by differences in stated rates. If funds are scarce, the efficient way of allocating them is to change their market prices; and it is increasingly to the self-interest of parties on both sides of the market to push in that direction. Why should the banks throw a gift in the direction of those firms lucky enough to qualify for loans in terms of credit stringency? And why penalize the refused firms? Moreover, what good are low rates to a firm that can not get a loan? The excluded firms will, one way or another, try to bribe the providers of funds into meeting their needs; that is, meeting them at a price.

Some might say that we live in the best of all possible worlds. It is precisely in the short run that economists would expect the demands for investable funds to be inelastic, thereby reducing the dollar-for-dollar potency of central bank operations. And it is in this short run that highly effective (if inequitable and distorting) elements of rationing prevail. Then in the longer run, just when rationing is dissipating its effects and spreading into differences in the cost rather than mere availability of credit, we can expect lowering of interest rates to coax out new long-term projects, and raising of interest rates to discourage such projects.

Before leaving the subject of credit rationing, I ought to mention some transitional frictions that also help to increase the short-run potency of Federal Reserve credit policy.

New-issue bottlenecks. When interest rates are hardening, new securities issues often go to a discount in the period when the underwriters are bringing them out. Since underwriters are subject to the tremendous risks involved in their extreme leveraging, one or two debacles of this type can discourage them from bidding and can dry up the effective supplying of any new issues.[8]

Bottlenecks from inherited notions of normal rates. If long-term interest rates have been at one level for some time, and if the Federal Reserve engineers a tightening of them, many localities and states will drop out of the new-issue market completely. By law or custom they may be restricted from borrowing at the higher rate. By psychological belief that they can do better if they wait until rates are not so high, they may desist from borrowing. Often such phenomena have been observed. Of course, in the longer run, should the high-rate trend continue, many borrowers will be forced to come into the market willy-nilly later on, paying a penalty for their mistaken delay. And, to the degree that some canny borrowers correctly appraise the beginning of a rising trend of interest rates, they may overborrow in the early stages of a period of credit contraction. This can lead to a frictional weakening, rather than enhancing, of the short-term potency of monetary policy.[9]

EFFECTS OF MAXIMUM-RATE REGULATIONS ON INTEREST

The Bible, Aristotle, and the medieval Schoolmen have generally mirrored the everpresent disapproval of interest and usury. After the Reformation, antipathy toward interest diminished, but we still have laws and regulations that put limits on interest rates. Indeed, in many countries and in some states ceilings on interest rates did no harm only because market rates happened to fall well below the ceilings. But the recent rise in interest rates has resulted in collisions with such ceilings and created important economic problems. I shall here discuss only those most important for recent American monetary policy.

Government-insured mortgages by FHA and VA played an important role in the postwar period. Ceilings on their rates could be circumvented only by devices that involved some inconvenience. In consequence, whenever interest rates tended to harden above the ceiling rates, mortgage money for these sources tended to dry up completely. Contrariwise, when the Fed wished to ease credit, there resulted a powerful stimulus to residential construction from the coming back to life of these guaranteed mortgages.

Thus, almost by inadvertence, ceiling interest rates on insured mortgages worked out to be powerful stabilizers in the first postwar decades when such

---

[8] Analytically, a high level of i discourages new investment, but so does a transitional large negative value of di/dt.

[9] When the Federal Reserve is trying to ease credit conditions, correct anticipation by speculators can speed up and amplify the decline in market interest rates; although di/dt is negative, juicy capital gains are to be earned from buying bonds (but, unfortunately, this could lead to a high level of yield inclusive of capital gains and thus temporarily raise the attractiveness of alternative to real investment in new brick and cogs).

mortgages were quantitatively important. Upward shifts in demand were kept from evoking a higher supply response to higher yields; control of maximum rates automatically tended to lead to self-control of supply by suppliers. By the 1960s insured mortgages became of much less importance.

More important for recent monetary policy have been interest ceilings on deposits. As already mentioned, prohibiting interest on demand deposits is bound, in a time of high and safe short-term interest rates, to lead to a shrinkage of those deposits in favor of time deposits, and is bound to lead to all kinds of subterfuges and substitutes for the paying and receiving of interest on checkable balances. The negotiable certificate of deposit, if it had not been invented in the last decade by the First National City Bank, would have had to be invented by somebody else.

Regulation Q, which puts ceilings on time deposit interest rates, created the same difficulties once Treasury Bill rates began to exceed these ceilings. It was for this reason that ceiling rates had been repeatedly raised in the 1960s. Although raising Regulation Q ceilings improved the competitive position of the commercial banks, by the same token it undermined the competitive advantage that the savings and loan associations had previously been enjoying. They began to run into informal ceilings imposed by their regulatory authorities and by prudence as to what their actual earnings from mortgages could stand.

This not only depressed the flow of funds available for housing, thereby depressing starts, but in addition it began to impair the liquidity and solvency of the savings and loans. Something of a crisis was thus precipitated by tight money; actually what the crisis did was to unveil a situation already existing that has within it certain disturbing properties.

Time deposits are nominally liquid within 30 days of some similar brief period, but S&Ls invest such funds in mortgages that have a duration which runs into decades. Moreover, the interest rate payable on such mortgages is set at the beginning of the period at a frozen level. Consequently, even with Government insurance of such time deposits, it is easy for the whole system to become technically insolvent, having short-term liabilities that require a higher interest rate to hold them than can be earned on long-term assets. For short periods of time, there is no reason why the S&Ls should not pay quite high rates to hold deposits; yet such a solution could not meet the long-term problem if it should persist.

The importance of all this for monetary policy is twofold: (1) Disorderly markets inhibit the authorities from using monetary policy strongly (this same point holds for disorderly security markets, a phenomenon whose importance is, in my view, often exaggerated) ; and (2) relaxing of Regulation Q tends to make the impact of tight money particularly harsh on residential construction and on the smaller banks outside the great urban centers.

Last year's reimposition of Regulation Q ceilings gave us but temporary relief from this long-term structural problem. By accident, the fact that the need for tight money ended in the fall of 1966 put off the longer-run consequences of these stopgap measures.

Without further research I am not able to make an unequivocal diagnosis as to whether the potency of monetary policy is helped or hindered by Government regulation of interest rates. There are crosscurrents in each direction; numerical estimation is needed to appraise the final effect.

My earlier discussion touched upon the issues raised by the mix of stabilization and growth policy as between monetary and fiscal measures. Because this paper is already long, and because so much has been written about the international balance of payments, I shall merely state that our international deficit severely limits the scope of independent domestic monetary policy. Only within limits, and only by concomitant use of selective controls on the capital accounts, can we contrive monetary ease at home in order to offset deflation and to promote capital formation. Conventional central banking measures would have to be supplemented (as, for example, by increased investment tax credits for domestic investment) if domestic credit ease were to be relied on in the face of international deficits.

Let me conclude by stating the view that the position taken here is a modern middle-of-the-road position. It reflects what some people would contemptuously, and others admiringly, call the "conventional wisdom." It differs in degree and in kind from the following various viewpoints.

1. Some economists (such as J. K. Galbraith) are against the use of restrictive monetary policy. They believe the only good interest rate is a low one, and rates should be kept low. Some of this persuasion think monetary policy has little or no potency; others think it has too much potency and will have bad social effects. This school of thought is important in populist politics, but of decreasing importance among American academic economists.

2. Some economists (for example, Milton Friedman) think that control of the supply of money is the important goal of monetary policy. They believe that steady trends in the supply of M should be contrived by the Federal Reserve and that preoccupation with interest rates or net free reserves will only serve to distract the Fed from its legitimate goals. Variants of this school abound. Some think that tracing the impact as I have done through effects on interest rates and credit availability, as these impinge on investment and durable-goods spending, is unnecessary; and some think it is wrong.*

3. Associated with one-time New York Federal Reserve economists such as John H. Williams, Robert Sproul, and Robert Roosa, is the view that monetary policy has very great potency indeed because of the importance of credit rationing, the contriving of uncertainty by the monetary authorities, and the dominance of lenders' supply attitudes over borrowers' demand elasticities. In the last dozen years the market quotation in the bourse of academic opinion has perhaps gone down, just as that of the supply-of-M school has perhaps gone up.

Personally, I prefer to stick to the middle-road of good, strong value.

COMMENTARY

In my oral remarks I suggested that the central bank watch both money supply and interest rates. Although the Lord gave us only two eyes, the Fed should watch many more variables such as level and change in unemployment, shifts in velocity, productivity accelerations and decelerations, degree of cost-push, and degree to which these should be resisted or accommodated. In short, the Fed should use its intelligence in leaning against the wind, taking into account the goals of domestic employment and price behavior and international constraints,

---

* See commentary added by Professor Samuelson.

and taking into account the lags in the response of the system to its own acts. This will involve making the best guesses possible concerning probabilities of future events, with appreciation of the variance and uncertainties of such estimates.

To jettison the monistic goal of controlling the money supply, only to put on the throne the controlling of the interest structure, is nonsense and prescribed by no one. As Milton Friedman said in his oral remarks (page 101), the response of interest rates to contrived changes in M (and, I may add, to other factors) is complicated—indeed more complicated than his three-stage sequence in which new M first lowers i, then restores it to its previous level, and then causes it to be higher still. If one were trying to stabilize interest rates, this complexity would be a difficulty; but no one prescribes such a target. Indeed, only those who advocate a steady growth in the M supply, come what may, are in search of simple formulas for behavior. There are many simple formulas that are worse than that, but the point is not to look for simple formulas that are better than that one (itself perhaps not an impossible task). The point is that no simple formula can be expected to work well, or anywhere near as well, as intelligent action by the Federal Reserve in pursuit of a high-employment, optimal growth, and properly effective demand program.

I want to associate myself with Henry Wallich's statement (page 62) that stabilizing the rate of growth of M can be expected to be accompanied by a drifting away from feasible social targets of other economic variables. I go beyond him and stress that this would be the case even if there were no balance-of-payments problems (or if those problems were handled by floating exchange rates). Pursuing fiscal policies that are desired for their own sake and encountering, say, a period in which the marginal efficiency of capital has been shifted to a low level by past capital formation, we might well find that good policy required a speeding up of the growth of M in order to offset interest-induced declines in V. Or in another epoch, when cost-push was deemed great enough to require full-employment GNP to grow at 7 per cent per year, being stuck with a fixed 3 or 4 per cent formula for M growth could result in a period of stagnating employment.

No scientist interested in landing a satellite on the moon would be so foolish as to try to *prescribe in advance* an exact flight plan—which is the logical equivalent of the frozen rate of M growth. Because he knows that unpredictable meteorites will impinge on the rocket, and that the gravitational forces it is subject to will drift in an unpredictable way, the control engineer merely provides for an intelligent reaiming of the missile based upon accumulating information. Similarly, fiscal and monetary authorities will be constantly reaiming their policies to meet the new information patterns that are forever emerging.

179

TAX DEDUCTIBILITY OF ECONOMIC DEPRECIATION TO INSURE INVARIANT VALUATIONS

PAUL A. SAMUELSON

Massachusetts Institute of Technology

THERE seems to be no published formulation and solution to the problem: How must "income" be defined if present discounted valuations of all assets, and therefore all optimization decisions, are to be independent of the tax rate each person is subject to?

The following general theorem is established here:

Fundamental theorem of tax-rate invariance.— If, and only if, true loss of economic value is permitted as a tax-deductible depreciation expense will the present discounted value of a cash-receipt stream be independent of the rate of tax.

To prove this, consider the general Fisher formula[1] for valuation of an algebraic cash-receipts stream

$$V(t) = \int_t^n R(t) R(x)^{-1} N(x) dx, \quad (1)$$

where $N(t)$ is the net cash receipts as a function of time in the finite interval $(0, n)$; $R'(t)/R(t) = r(t)$, the instantaneous force of interest at which each person can borrow or lend in unlimited amounts at time t, with

$$R(t) = \exp \int_o^t r(w) dw, \qquad = e^{rt}$$

in case $r(t) \equiv r$, a constant.

The fundamental equation of yield was derived in my 1937 paper by differentiating equation (1) with respect to t explicitly, to get

$$\frac{V'(t)}{V(t)} + \frac{N(t)}{V(t)} \equiv r(t), \quad V(n) = 0. \quad (1')$$

[1] Irving Fisher, *The Theory of Interest* (New York: Macmillan Co., 1930); P. A. Samuelson, *Quarterly Journal of Economics*, LI (1936–37), 469–96.

Equation (1') is the full equivalent to equation (1), and vice versa.

Now if a man is subject to a uniform tax rate of $1-T = T'$, his after-tax borrowing and lending rate is $Tr(t) < r(t)$, and his after-tax cash receipt would be $TN(t) < N(t)$. One might be tempted to substitute these new expressions in equation (1), but it is easy to show that the result will generally vary with the tax rate, making distorting optimization decisions and tax deals inevitable. For this reason alone, but also to promote equity among individuals and to avoid converting a so-called income tax into a tax on principal, the law will want to allow subtractions from $N(t)$ of some kind of depreciation allowance, $D(t)$, before reckoning the income tax. Hence equation (1) now becomes

$$V(t) \equiv \int_t^n R(t) \, {}^T R(x)^{-T} \{ N(x) \\ - (1-T)[N(x) - D(x)] \} dx, \quad (2)$$

and we require that both sides of this identity be independent of the tax rate. Our basic theorem can now be succinctly stated in terms of mathematics.

Theorem: The functional identity (2) has the unique solution

$$D(t) = -V'(t) = \\ -\frac{d}{dt} \int_t^n R(t) R(x)^{-1} N(x) dx \\ = N(t) - r(t) V(t) \\ V(t) = \int_t^n R(t) R(x)^{-1} N(x) dx.$$

To prove this, rewrite equation (2) in the form of the most general expression involving the tax rate in the permitted depreciation formula to get

$$V(t, T) = \int_t^n R(t) \, ^T R(x)^{-T} [TN(x) \qquad (3)$$
$$+ (1 - T) D(x, T)] \, dx \, .$$

Just as a differentiation with respect to time converted equation (1) to (1'), it converts equation (3) to the identity in T

$$\frac{\partial V(t, T)}{\partial t} - Tr(t) V(t, T) \qquad (3')$$
$$+ TN(t) \equiv -(1 - T) D(t, T) \, .$$

If this, by hypothesis, is to have a solution independent of T, we can set $V(t, T) \equiv V(t, 0) \equiv V(t)$; since $V(t)$ satisfies equation (1'), we can combine equation (1') with equation (3') to get

$$V' - TrV - T(V' - rV) \equiv (1 - T)V'(t)$$
$$\equiv (1 - T)D(t, T) \, .$$

Hence

$$D(t, T) \equiv -V'(t)$$

is indeed the correct, and unique, solution of our problem. Note that it has the nice property of making the permitted depreciation charges the same for high- and low-bracket taxpayers, a boon to teachers of accounting.

While this analysis is couched in terms of continuous functions and integration, the results are applicable to the discount formulas for discrete time periods: summation can be expressed by a Stieltjes integral where $dM(x)$ replaces $N(x)dx$ and a finite difference can replace the derivative. Thus, the fundamental formula for after-tax income must always be

$$Ti_t V_t = N_t \qquad (4)$$
$$- (1 - T)[N_t - (V_t - V_{t+1})] \, ,$$

where the translation of equation (1) into the following discrete form

$$V_t = \sum_{j=t}^n \frac{N_j}{(1 + i_t)(1 + i_{t+1}) \dots (1 + i_j)}$$

defines all the new variables.

The power of the theorem can be illustrated by its clear implication that a rational businessman will not borrow more just because the government in effect pays part of the tax-deductible interest cost. It also provides the important insight that a uniform income tax has, in a perfect capital market, no effect on the saving-consuming habits of a rational person other than what a different (and lower) interest rate will have: for he maximizes the functional of his consumption stream subject to the budget equation

$$\int_{t_0}^\infty R(t) \, ^T R(x)^{-T} dC(x) = V(t_0),$$

a tax invariant.

All of this analysis presupposes a tax rate that is uniform over time for each person. Obviously, if a man is to be subject to different rates, with T being a function of time, his optimal decision will be distorted by this fact. A proper system of carry-forwards and carry-backs, which makes T average out to a constant and which takes account of just when a man pays the tax accruing to him, will avoid such distortions; it is noteworthy that many such reforms have been introduced in recent years.

Some far-reaching conclusions follow from this theorem. I shall sketch only a few.

1. Distinguished economists keep repeating the nonsense that tax deductibility of interest "weakens" monetary policy because it causes high-bracket men to have greater, and less elastic, loan demand. Except for optical illusion and for legislative loophole deviations from my formula, this is wrong. If the fruits of the loan are taxed at the same rate as the interest deduction, everyone's present discounted value is maximized by the *same* loan decisions quite independently of the tax rate T. (I speak here of personal taxation, not corporate taxation with its discrimination against equity financing.)

2. My formula for depreciation is algebraic. When $V'(t)$ is positive instead of negative, the deduction for depreciation becomes

an inclusion of so-called capital appreciation. Many, if not most, things called capital gains should be taxed at full-income rates. Thus, when interest rates have risen, rich men buy bonds at a discount from poor men so that part of the bond's true interest will appear as a so-called capital gain that is lightly taxed. Such a tax swap involves the purchase by the rich of the low tax base of the poor, at the expense of the government. By my formula, this would be impossible. All this illustrates how odd it was for certain British economists to try to exclude discussion of capital-gains taxation from the deliberations of the postwar United Kingdom Royal Tax Commission. Old-fashioned tax administrators perpetuate the myth that a capital-gains tax leads to administrative headaches. American Treasury and legal experience is just the opposite: It is *hard* to administer an income-tax system if you do not tax capital gains or if you tax them lightly, because then devices multiply to convert ordinary income into the semblance of capital gains.

3. More subtle insights are provided by the theorem. It enables one to perceive the drawbacks of proposals, like the recent suggestion that property be permitted over-rapid depreciation but with the proviso that "the depreciated base go with the property" and that any subsequent buyer be denied full depreciation of *his* cost basis. That will encourage sales to the poor and to low-bracket charitable foundations, leading both to dead-weight distortions and to Treasury revenue losses.

4. Finally, this discussion reminds lawyers and accountants that the only sensible definition of depreciation relevant to measurement of *true money income* is putative decline in economic value. Fast-depreciation gimmicks in the Swedish, Japanese, German, British, and American tax codes are *not* a return to just recognition of economic obsolescence—as any dealer in used machines will privately tell you. They are competitive bribes and giveaways, designed to undertax *money* income (and perhaps obviate the bias against capital formation inherent in taxing income rather than consumption or wealth), in order to attract investment from other countries and to stimulate the total of domestic investment growth. If we call spades spades, let's call bribes bribes.

180

AN ANALYTIC EVALUATION OF INTEREST RATE CEILINGS
With the assistance of Felicity Skidmore

INTRODUCTION

In the American economy, prices are generally determined by market forces.[1] The interest rates payable on bank and savings association accounts are a partial but significant exception to this generalization. Demand deposits of commercial banks, upon which checks can be drawn at will, have for more than a third of a century been prohibited by law from earning explicit interest. Under Regulation Q, the Board of Governors of the Federal Reserve has long set maximum ceilings on the interest rates payable on the various categories of time deposits. De jure and de facto, savings and loan associations, mutual savings banks, and various other financial institutions have limits placed upon their ability to compete for funds. They do not, in other words, have complete freedom to set whatever interest or dividend rates they please.

What are the merits and demerits of this network of regulations? Should they be abolished altogether? If so, should they be dissolved gradually or at once? Should interest ceilings be extended to other areas, thereby providing more even-handed treatment of commercial banks and other financial institutions?

These are the questions I propose to examine in the present survey.

HISTORICAL BACKGROUND

Feelings against interest go deep. The Old Testament spoke out against usury; Aristotle and the classical philosophers formulated arguments against interest; the early Christians and the medieval schoolmen deplored the taking of it. When lawgivers were obsessed with a concept of the "just price," the only "just" level for the interest rate was deemed to be zero.

Nor were these mere philosophical positions. The ancient Jews were forbidden by law to charge any interest except to Gentiles. Classical civilizations not only formulated arguments, they also legislated against interest.[2] The Church, through the centuries increased the severity of its penalties against all interest. As the synthesis of the Middle Ages waned, within both canon and civil law circumlocutions and contrivances developed to get around the interest prohibitions. Thus, although I could not legally charge you 5 percent interest

---

[1] I am indebted to Irwin Friend, Jack Guttentag, and Harry Schwartz, for their constructive comments on an earlier draft.

[2] The current Pakistani constitution even states that the charging of interest will be prohibited as soon as it is practicable to do so.

per year, I could sell you land capable of producing a perpetual net harvest at "20 years purchase." Or, we could arrange in advance that you be fined a penalty for late repayment, it being tacitly understood between us that you would conveniently be late. Casuistical arguments were developed by which foregone alternatives were used as an excuse for the sanctioning of interest. Although money itself was sterile and could not properly command a positive yield, the fact that the moneylender was thereby deprived of an alternative opportunity (of buying land, say, that would yield a net harvest and still be salable at the end of the period for what he paid for it) made an interest charge perfectly acceptable.

One of the economic aspects of the Reformation consisted of a revolt against usury and interest prohibitions. John Calvin provided logical and ideological justifications for treating interest like other prices. A simple theory of the economic determination of history might say that the nascent commercial and industrial revolutions were providing new times in which the impediments imposed by interest restrictions had to go; and ideology could be counted upon to provide the rationalization called for by emerging technology. It is certainly no accident that the Netherlands and Britain forged ahead of Catholic Spain in this period. However literally and devoutly one accepts Max Weber's thesis of the Protestant Ethic as an important factor in economic development, it is clear that many traditionally Catholic countries, in Latin America and elsewhere, have been hobbled in their development by the simple vestiges of restrictions against interest.

By the time Adam Smith wrote The Wealth of Nations, many of these hobbles had been de facto removed in the countries of Northern Europe. Yet even Smith, uncharacteristically, failed to apply to interest regulations the scornful and persuasive strictures that he brought to bear against mercantilistic interferences with free market pricing. It is not surprising that the young Jeremy Bentham, who never spared the traditional ways of doing things from ruthless examination, should have written to Smith, chiding him for backsliding on this. And it is characteristic of the good and sensible Adam Smith that he should cheerfully admit Bentham had a point.

Although modern economic systems have largely become emancipated from interest restrictions in the past, there do remain many traces of that inheritance. Many of our States still have maximum interest rates applicable to mortgages and general loans. (These are quite aside from regulations of interest charges on small loans, about which more will be said later.) And countries like Canada have, until quite recently, labored under interest ceilings on the rates that banks can charge (not pay out!). These atavisms did no harm in the decades when market rates were comfortably below the statute ceilings. But in the last decade, when interest rates all over the world have climbed

to levels not seen for 40 years, such fiats have at worst created inefficiency and distortion and at best had to be circumvented under one
pretext or another. (For example, if a mortgage cannot pay more than
x percent, issuing it at a nominal rate of x percent but deducting points
from the principal actually conveyed to the borrower, can increase
its effective yield.)

Looking to the future, we have every reason to expect interest rates
to vary over a wide range. We have therefore no right to conclude that
the fortuitously low level of past rates—that rendered restrictions
innocuous because they were inoperative—can be expected to prevail
all or even much of the time.

ATTITUDES TOWARD INTEREST

We cannot accept these historical attitudes toward interest and usury
as simple fact. What are the reasons underlying them?

First, it is clear from Biblical and subsequent writings that loans
were conceived of as loans between consumers. Once loans are primarily
related to productive activity—toward the provision of working capital or plant and equipment—many of the ethical concerns become less
relevant.

Second, even within the province of pure consumption, loans have
been primarily conceived of as taking place between the rich and the
poor—the poor being of course the borrowers, and the rich the lenders.
Alongside the ethic that people deserve to enjoy differentials in income
and wealth based upon their different productive contributions and
their legitimate ownership of property, there also runs the ethic that
income and wealth should be more equally distributed—that every
person has a right to a minimum level of subsistence and even comfort. From this viewpoint it is bad enough for the lender to insist upon
the return of his principal. The injustice is only compounded if in
addition he insists upon an extra pound of flesh in the form of interest.

Third, there is the concern that the poor, being so near the verge
of starvation and destitution, will be inevitably led by the temptation
of available credit to mortgage their own futures. That desperate men
will sell themselves into slavery is a familiar fact of history. That
men should not do so—that they should be freed from this temptation,
and that would-be lenders should be enjoined from taking advantage
of their necessity—is a recurrent theme in jurisprudence.

Fourth, the loan bargain—whether it be in the Bible, in ancient
writings, or in the case reports of modern social welfare workers—is
often conceived of as taking place in a situation where the lender
enjoys monopoly power. The borrower cannot know all the alternative opportunities open to him, and indeed there may be no such relevant alternatives. He is in a "take it or leave it situation" and he per-

force must take it. The impatient borrower may be willing to promise anything, and to sign anything. Or he may not understand what it is that he is signing. Moreover, when the time comes for repayment, he may find that difficult. Or he may find repayment impossible; and in this case the penalties begin to mount, and the effective rates of usury become even more usurious. Even in our own day there exists, alongside the legitimate and legal business of consumer lending, the loan sharks' jungle in which the lender hopes not to be promptly repaid, and in which illegal force is used to police loan agreements.

What are we to make of all this? It is evident that if every transaction between two persons is to be conducted primarily in terms of charity and need, then the kind of marketing system—based upon price—that most societies have relied upon over a millenium simply cannot be allowed to operate. Perhaps the Schoolmen's distinction between "commutative justice" and "distributive justice" reflects the gradual realization of this incompatibility. Even though I as a butcher am more affluent than you as a consumer—provided I deliver over to you meat seen to be (a) fresh, (b) in accordance with our mutual understanding, and (c) at a price arrived at through arm's-length bargaining and in a nondiscriminatory fashion—then the requirements of commutative justice have been met. This, of course, does not free me from the responsibility of performing charitable acts toward those less affluent and/or subject to special needs.

As these notions gradually began to be applied to interest-loan transactions as well as other transactions, there began to be emphasized the distinction between interest proper and usury—the latter connoting interest rates that are "too high" by some standard. Modern doctrines of diverse religious institutions seem now to accept positive interest, but still to proscribe usury—whatever that may mean. (It is usually a requirement in any diocese, for instance, that careful husbandry be made of all surplus funds, insuring that they be invested at whatever prudent yields of interest prevail. The Church of England even has a large equity position in diversified common stocks.)

Indeed, according to a recent treatise by an eminent Jesuit [3] on this subject, interest rates set by the interplay of supply and demand in markets that an economist would call "perfectly competitive," would be ethically acceptable. If so, in view of the inevitable tendency for supply and demand schedules to shift, and to shift in such a fashion as to have intersections that move over wide ranges depending upon the balance of diverse market forces, even high interest rates—so long as they are arrived at in broad markets where knowledge is not

---

[3] Thomas F. Divine, *Interest, An Historical and Analytical Study in Economics and Modern Ethics,* Marquette Press, 1959.

seriously imperfect—would be tolerable and indeed, from the efficiency point of view, desirable.[4]

In this analysis I shall, for the most part, ignore legislation designed to protect the small consumer against exploitation, taking for granted such recent legislation as "truth in lending" acts at the State and Federal levels, and the long-established State limitations on maximum interest charges applicable to small loans.[5]

PRESENT STATUS

We can conclude from this survey that there exists a presumption, in a modern mixed economy, that any explicit Government interference in market pricing needs to be scrutinized with a skeptical eye and needs to be defended by cogent arguments demonstrating just why the public interest requires such fiats. This is in fact the general practice in our society. Most of the items in the gross national product are produced in response to market forces alone. Where there is a prima facie case that effective competition is impossible, as in the case of public utilities and railroads, specific responsibilities of review and execution are taken over by the Government.[6] The analysis that follows accepts this presumption that specific Government regulations on prices and interest rates need to be scrutinized for justification, and the burden of proof placed on them.

PROHIBITION OF INTEREST ON DEMAND DEPOSITS

Prior to the great depression, commercial banks were free to pay whatever interest rates they pleased on all classes of deposits. In the 1920's, when interest rates were generally high on securities of all durations—one could earn, for example, 5 or 6 percent by putting money into the 1-day call market in New York—banks were moved by the

---

[4] Only the fourth of the historical objections to interest listed above is in fact met by this formulation of the acceptability of perfectly competitive interest rate determination. Actually, in our basic system of jurisprudence, there exist many explicit safeguards against men selling themselves into slavery and overborrowing. These include such features as non-garnisheeing of wages, noncollectability of certain contracts and bargains, and various forms of limited liability.

[5] To the uninitiated, maximum rates like 3 percent per month seem outrageously high. But experience has shown that legitimate business incurs substantial administration and default costs from small loans—so that setting maximum rates that seem "reasonable" to the uninformed in fact hurt the poor rather than help them because the supply of legitimate funds dries up, sending the consumer from the pawn shop and commercial credit organizations into the clutches of loan sharks.

[6] For 40 years the Federal Government has taken an active role in modifying the workings of agricultural markets. These interferences, like those involved in protective tariffs and quotas, cannot be defended on the basis of imperfections of the competitive market mechanism, and hence it is no coincidence that polling of professional economists shows overwhelming opposition to such devices. The professional economist as such does not deny society the right to transfer resources from the urban to the rural community, but he does insist that such transfers involve less deadweight loss to society if they take the form of outright subsidies; and he also believes that if farm programs are meant to ameliorate poverty in the countryside, that end can be better accomplished by subsidies explicitly designed for the relevant recipients.

competitive situation to offer interest payments on demand deposits. Thus, early in the 1920's a Boston bank might pay 5 percent on the demand deposit of one of its customers. He could draw checks against his balance with the bank and any standing balance not drawn upon would earn him a substantial yield. The alternative custom also grew up in the 1920's whereby many banks permitted the holders of time or savings deposits to draw checks upon their savings deposits. In this case too the depositor could, so to speak, have his cake and eat it too—receiving an interest yield on the very funds against which he could draw checks.

Actually, so long as demand deposits could pay interest, and so long as time deposits were in fact both withdrawable upon demand without notice and even capable of being checked against, the distinction between demand and time deposits became extremely difficult to make. There was no place to draw the line, and no need to do so. The same situation still prevails in many foreign countries, where banks pay an elaborate schedule of different interest rates depending on the degree of liquidity of the account in question.

But then came the Great Depression. Many banks failed and money markets were in chaos. This occasioned considerable new legislation designed to reform and regulate both the banking and securities industries. One of the major reforms from the present point of view was the strict requirement prohibiting commercial banks from paying explicit interest on any deposits subject to checking. The motivations for this particular measure are lost in the darkness of history.[7] Certainly there was the then-popular belief, whether correct or not, that one of the major causes of the bank failures had been "over-banking" and overstrenuous competition by weak banks. These weak banks tried to grow through offering overly generous interest rates, which in turn forced them to undertake high-yield investments involving more genuine risk than could be deemed healthy, so the argument went, for a commercial bank.

But there was another, completely different motivation for the legislation, coming from what might be called the cartel self-interest of the banking community itself. These, after all, were the days of the National Industrial Relations Act, when both radicals and conservatives alike fell prey to the illusion that the capitalistic system could be saved only by introducing industry self-regulation. Much of this legislation suffered subsequently at the hands of the courts, and the arguments behind such syndicalist devices for the succor or reform of an enterprise system have suffered even more at the hands of the economic

---

[7] I am indebted to Professor Guttentag of the University of Pennsylvania for the reminder that much of the steam for interest-rate ceilings has come, for more than a century in our history, from the fear, on the part of rural banks and financial interests generally, that the large-city money markets will drain them in time of shortage of their funds. This sentiment has not disappeared and traces of it can still be found throughout the land.

experts. There is now a general presumption among economists against cartel pricing.

For many years after the early 1930's, market rates of interest on gilt-edge bonds remained so low, and investment opportunities for the banks to make profitable loans remained so limited, that the law forbidding interest on demand deposits had little effect for good or evil. Even without the law, commercial banks were not eager to add to their demand deposits since they had so little to do with them in a profitable way. The force of competition was operating, if anything, to reduce the yield of active demand deposits to below zero, by introducing substantial transaction charges for checks written and for other services.

However, with the ending of World War II and the subsequent upward trend in yields on short-term governments, and with the revival of strong demands for loans by customers of the commercial banks, the prohibition against interest payments on demand deposits did begin to interfere with the natural competitive forces of the market. The proportion of time to demand deposits began to rise; and there was a strong incentive for rational depositors to keep down to their minimum transaction needs the amount of money they kept in the form of demand deposits. Competition now began to force the banks to look for subterfuges to compensate depositors, in effect, for their demand deposits: They would give credit against clearing charges for minimum balances held; they would absorb various clearing fees; they would provide auxiliary services in the form of computers and investment advice at less than true marginal costs; finally, they would reduce and even abolish transaction charges on checks drawn.

When law tries to hold back the tide of competitive forces, there is the usual scramble to avoid or evade it. Some of the larger banks began to rue their earlier espousal of the fiat prohibiting interest on demand deposits. But of course the smaller country banks, faced as they were with a more inelastic supply of demand deposits, for guild-cartel reasons still wished to keep the prohibition against interest payments on demand deposits. In consequence, demand deposits continued to shrink in relative importance. Fortunate it is that the growth of various categories of time deposits was able to provide a kind of safety valve or loophole to soften the distorting effect of the interest prohibition. Otherwise we should have witnessed earlier, and with a vengeance, the process which came in the 1960's to be called disintermediation.

Corporate treasurers and controllers, and the public itself—when faced with what in effect was a daily rate of return of 4, 5, or 6 percent per annum—would increasingly have had to become their own bankers and hold short-term securities directly to get around the effects of the interest ban. Early in this decade, indeed, the device of the C.D.'s or negotiable time deposits—which could be transferred to someone else at any time and could thus provide a safe and liquid instantaneous return—was invented at least partly to head off the disintermediation process. It should be stressed here that such a process is the simple result of the artificial fiat against interest, and does not reflect any true comparative advantage of corporations and the public in becoming little banks on their own.

I have dwelt at some length on the baleful effects of the fiat against interest on demand deposits for several reasons. For one thing, it illustrates well the same principles we shall see involved in regulation Q ceilings on interest rates payable on time deposits generally. For another, the problem is still with us and is not likely to go away; indeed it may well get worse in the future.

Still another cause for concern arises: Many unofficial and official groups (for example, the Commission on Money and Credit and a committee advisory to Controller of the Currency Saxon) have advocated that legal reserve be required only against demand deposits and not against time deposits—this on the ground, among other things, that only demand deposits are truly money, and that only money needs to be controlled by the device of legal reserve requirements. I was against this view at the time, and nothing has happened since to make me more sanguine. There is a real danger that the quantity of money, narrowly defined as demand deposits, may shrink away into relative insignificance; and what those groups have dismissed as near moneys or as mere money substitutes will in fact come to rule the roost. What then will become of the community's effective control over the money supply if time deposits are freed completely from legal reserve requirements? The total of time deposits will not go to infinity because the banks will wish, for internal reasons of prudence, to hold some cash reserves against them. But such reserve ratios might well be far below those of current legally required ratios, and they might also fluctuate widely, leading to instability of total time deposits.

Indeed, there may be cause for serious concern in the strong differential that now prevails between reserve requirements on time and on demand deposits. It is to the self-interest of the banks to collude with their depositors to shift compensatory and other deposits over into the category of time rather than demand deposits to minimize reserve requirements and maximize assets that earn. And there is an ever-present temptation to blur the lines between demand and time deposits, by setting up various overdraft privileges and for quickly replenishing demand deposits from the customer's time deposits, thus enabling the banker to do what competitive forces motivate both him and his customer to do—namely, let deposits that are the virtual equivalent of checkable demand deposits earn interest. The banks themselves in connivance with their customers even institutionalize the process.[8]

---

[8] See Richard G. David and Jack M. Guttentag, "Balance Requirements and Deposit Competition," *Journal of Political Economy*, December 1963, in which there is discussion of how businesses buy services from banks and pay for them by holding demand balances.

All this creates thorny and even hopeless problems for the authorities trying to prevent interest from arising by hook or crook.

There is a final objection to the prohibition of interest payments on demand deposits that many economists have brought forward. Because of this regulation—and we shall later see that the same is true of time deposits because of the differential impact of regulation Q on them—the task of the observing economist, in appraising the causal laws of money behavior to provide a diagnosis and forecast of the emerging state of the economy, is sometimes made extremely tricky. Certain monetary economists (such as Allan Meltzer of Carnegie-Mellon University and Karl Brunner of Ohio State University) prefer to use the narrow definition of the money supply, so-called M_1—which includes currency outside the banks and demand deposits of the banks—in order to explain the development of the money gross national product and the state of inflationary demand. But other monetary economists, such as Milton Friedman of the University of Chicago, feel forced to use a broader definition of the money supply, so-called M_2—which adds certain components of time deposits to the narrower definition. In some degree this preference for M_2 stems from its better historical success in predicting GNP by means of simple regression equations; but in part it stems from the belief that the fiat against interest is distorting the true measure of M_1 and distorting our ability to discern the true behavior equations relating it to the economy. Similar complaints can be made against regulation Q for its distorting effects on the behavior of time deposits (and M_2) in relation to the macromagnitudes that the economist wishes to predict and control.

Although I recognize the difficulty that may be created for the economic observer by interest ceilings, and although I do not welcome such difficulties for their own sake, I cannot agree with the view that the world owes the analytical economist an easy life. We are to serve the economy, not it us. If there were substantive merits to interest ceilings in their own right, one of the prices that the economist would have to pay—cheerfully or otherwise—would be the complications that they entail for his analytical model building and inference.

I turn therefore from the topic of interest prohibitions on demand deposits to an analysis of the effects of regulation Q ceilings on time deposits.

Interest and Dividend Ceilings on Time Deposits

The discussion of the zero interest rate ceiling on demand deposits paves the way for consideration of our major concern here; namely, the economic effects of regulation Q ceilings on interest rates payable on time deposits at commercial banks. Much the same analysis will be found applicable to interest ceilings on mutual savings banks; and much will be applicable to the broader question of whether non-commercial-bank intermediaries (such as savings and loan institutions) should not also be subject to interest rate ceilings, either as desirable things in their own right, or to give them the same disadvantages as the commercial banks now enjoy, as a matter of competitive equity.

The original motivations for regulation Q are, once again, shrouded in historical obscurity. The Federal Reserve, in its reply to the questionnaire of the Commission on Money and Credit, seems to attribute the original rationale for interest rate ceilings to the alleged positive correlation between: (a) The insolvency of particular banks in the 1930's, and (b) the excessively high interest rates paid by them, before the depression, on their deposits. Such allegations are easy to make, but hard to buttress. Thus, when a bank is already in trouble, it may well put off the evil days of insolvency by raising its interest rates in a desperate attempt to attract and hold deposits. Yet such a positive association of high interest rates and insolvency may mean simply that the former are effects rather than causes of the latter.

In any case, as long as the economy remained depressed, and money market yields remained vanishingly low, the regulation Q ceilings were pretty well a dead letter. Being above the competitive rates the banks wanted to pay, the ceilings did no good and no harm.

Nonetheless, even in the 1930's and the war years, there began a trend toward faster growth of savings and loan associations in comparison with the growth of mutual savings banks and commercial banks. The full force of economic law is not felt immediately, but in the longer run small differentials in the rate of return may cumulate to produce vast gaps in the levels of achieved growth.

When market yields began to harden, the effects of regulation Q began clearly to manifest themselves. Now the savings and loan associations began to enjoy a great competitive advantage—not due to superior efficiency on their part nor to more vital social performance, but due in large part to the fiat of the Federal Reserve, which estopped the member banks from offering attractive enough yields to be competitive.

Figure 1a presents a self-contained story of the economic impact of interest ceilings. At C'C', a ceiling level far above the competitive equilibrium, E, regulation Q is having no effect at all. But at CC, a ceiling level definitely below that of competitive equilibrium, regulation Q is biting in. It is creating a distortion between supply and demand as measured by the horizontal arrow, FF. This distance reflects nonprice rationing in the capital markets. Although a simple Marshallian diagram cannot depict fully the gray-market adjustments to the Government-imposed distortions, the vertical arrow, FG, measures the discrepancy between what demanding banks deem the deposits worth and what regulation Q permits them to pay legally to the supplying depositors. This surplus tends to be frittered away in various arbitrary fashions: promotional premia and selling costs; ostentatious buildings; excessive numbers of branch banks; provision of supplementary services at below full cost or even at no cost; and so forth.

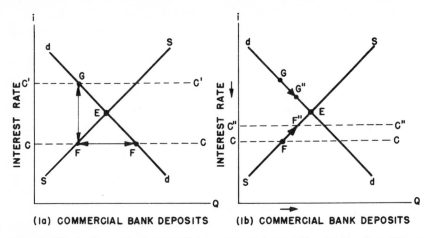

Figure 1.—Without ceilings on interest rates, equilibrium would be at 1a's E intersection. A higher ceiling at C'C' would be ineffective. Too low a ceiling at CC would lead to a FF gap that must be bridged by nonprice rationing. The FG gap could be frittered away in wasteful promotion costs, graft, or favoritism. Paradoxically, raising the ceiling from CC to C''C'' will lower effective interest costs and raise total of deposits available to borrowers. In 1b, we move from F to F'' as shown by the arrow on the supply curve; effective scarcity cost to borrowers drops from G to G'' as shown by the arrow on the demand curve.

The analysis so far applies only to a closed capital market, where depositors have no escape alternatives such as sending their money to a savings and loan association not subject (before 1966) to an interest ceiling like that of regulation Q. Before leaving this closed-market case, let us illustrate in figure 1b the paradox that raising interest rate ceilings can actually make money easier rather than tighter! In figure 1b the effective ceiling, CC, is raised to C''C''. When such a policy was advocated in the Kennedy administration by Under Secretary of the Treasury Robert V. Roosa, and Council of Economic Advisers member, James Tobin, it was vigorously opposed by easy-money Congressmen and even by the then head of the FHLBB, Joseph P. MacMurray, Jr. The critics thought that raising interest rates— that is, raising interest rate ceilings—would mean higher cost and lower availability of credit; and as practical men they castigated the economic theorists who proposed such sadistic policies in a time of too high unemployment and too low residential construction. The theorists, however, knew whereof they spoke. They predicted (and correctly as appears to be the case from hindsight) that the shift from CC to C''C'' would cause a northeast movement as shown by figure 1b's FF'' arrow. Such a climb along the upward-rising supply curve would in fact increase the available amount of credit. Although the nominal interest rates are rising from F to F'', the actual scarcity return of money to the credit demanders is in fact falling from G to G''.

But now we must go from a single closed capital market to a system of interconnected markets. Figure 2a duplicates figure 1a in depicting the commercial banks' single market. Figure 2b depicts the related market belonging to savings and loan associations. Because of the postwar need for housing, particularly in the Far West and South, the equilibrium intersection is drawn to be higher in 2b's market than in 1a. If there were no connection between the markets and no ceiling distortions, equilibrium would take place at E and e, respectively. Suppose now that the markets become interconnected, again with the absence of ceiling distortions. Then by the Barone-Cournot techniques familiar in international trade theory, we can find the common equilibrium interest-rate level at BB and bb, where the desired export of funds from the North and East is just matched by the desired import of funds (as shown by the equal and opposite arrows) in the West and South.

Economic analysis shows that such an equilibrium represents pretty much of an ideal in terms of capital market efficiency. True, rates are higher in the East at B than they would have been under self-sufficiency at E. But savers in the East are reaping the benefit; and, as can be seen from the diagram, they are essentially more numerous than the eastern credit demanders who are now forced to pay higher interest rates. In the West, interest costs at b are lower than they would have been at self-sufficiency—that is at e. Western savers are receiving less than they could hope to get under the artificial scarcity of a protected market; but this is more than matched by the reductions in interest cost to the western demanders of credit, who are seen in the diagram to be more numerous than the western savers. From the national viewpoint there is a presumption that these capital flows optimize [9] the Nation's level of capital formation, in terms of geographical urgency and against the background of the country's total saving propensities.

What is the effect of imposing upon figure 2a's commercial bank market a strong interest ceiling of the regulation Q type? Such an effect is shown by the CC ceiling in 2a. Actually this speeds up the outflow of funds from the commercial banks to the savings and loans. Since there has been a vast postwar housing need, and since it was the intention of Congress in setting up the FHLBB system to stimulate housebuilding, one might think that regulation Q's acceleration of the relative growth of savings and loans represented a good thing. Modern welfare analysis, however, shows that it may be [10] too much of a good

---

[9] Interferences with free market determination of rates definitely affects allocational efficiency. One cannot assert so definitely that the total of capital formation is necessarily lessened by such interferences : Models can be specified in which the total might actually increase ; but perhaps there is a presumption that what interferes with allocational efficiency will also reduce the incentive to invest for the future.

[10] One must say "may be" rather than "will be" because the free market might not have been operating optimally even in the absence of interferences. Why should mortgage rates have been so high in the immediate postwar years compared to bonds and other securities? The market may have exaggerated irrationally the risks inherent in housing : certainly in the subsequent decades bond yields climbed substantially relative to mortgage rates. Sometimes two wrongs almost make a right, and this is perhaps a case where a Government distortion may have undone, at least in part, a preexistent, private-market distortion.

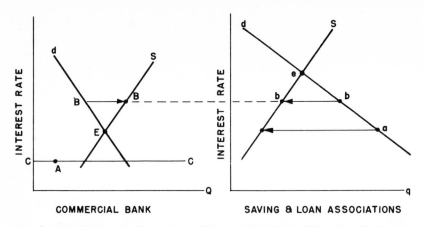

Figure 2.—Standard foreign-trade diagrams show equilibrium would be at E and e if the bank and S. & L. markets were completely sealed off from each other. If there were no impediments to deposits seeking the highest yields, competitive equilibrium would be at BB and bb common level, where funds shipped from eastern banks could just be absorbed by western S. & L.'s. But now suppose that the low ceiling of CC is imposed on commercial banks alone. Now it pays for funds to flee from that market to higher yielding S. & L. market. Final equilibrium might be at A and a, with an inadequate supply at A and with western interest rates depressed at a to a level below the competitive equilibrium.

thing. Now nonresidential investment activity is stymied by the ceilings, and residential housebuilding is being stimulated beyond its true merits. The process is not only inefficient, but also unfair. It is as if one said to two brothers: "You, Henry, are to be hobbled in bidding for what you want. As a result you, Dick, are presented with an inequitable advantage in bidding for scarce resources." Just as the British Empire was formed in a fit of absentmindedness, we can be sure that there was no conscious policy in the mind of the authorities, during the decades since the 1930's, to use regulation Q for the purpose of favoring the savings and loans and the housing industry. But nevertheless the British Empire was formed, and regulation Q did work in this way.

Those not interested in the details of diagrammatical analysis can skip the next few paragraphs, contenting themselves with the following summary of the results:

(1) Tight ceilings on interest rates payable by the commercial banks increase the outflow of funds to the savings and loan associations. Such ceilings reduce, rather than increase, the true cost of credit to those who ordinarily borrow from the commercial banks. And, other things equal, any lowering of the ceiling relative to market rates—or what is the same thing, any rise in natural market rates relative to unchanged ceilings—will intensify the outflow of funds away from those whom the ceilings might be supposed to help.

(2) This outflow of funds induced by the ceilings may be to the savings and loans who are not hampered by equally tight ceilings, or it may be to the direct market for Treasury bills. Thus, too-tight ceilings encourage the process called disintermediation, in which the

586

banks that are boggled by those ceilings are simply bypassed by savers entirely. Even though savers are not particularly efficient in investing their funds directly into the market, they will be forced into these inefficient acts when the ceilings become sufficiently distortive.

(3) If the savings and loans are also placed under ceilings, similar effects now follow. Ceilings on the savings and loans will tend to lessen the inflow of funds into them. Lowering ceilings on savings and loans dividend rates, at the same time that ceilings under regulation Q are unchanged, will reduce rather than increase the flow of funds to the residential industry.

(4) In short, by differential movements in the ceilings placed on commercial banks and on other saving institutions, society does have a new instrument to hand which will enable it to affect in either direction the division of saving funds between nonresidential and residential activity.

To spell out and justify these assertions, let us return to figure 2. Putting the ceiling, CC, on the commercial banks ends us up at a point like A, which is on the ceiling but with a smaller amount of savings available for borrowers of the commercial bank. Meantime the savings and loans end up as a result of the CC ceiling at a point like *a*, which depicts definitely cheaper and more plentiful credit than had prevailed without the ceiling.

Figure 3 shows that raising the ceiling on the commercial bank does reduce the flow of funds outward to the savings and loans, making credit actually more plentiful to customers of the banks and less plentiful for the builders who depend on the savings and loans.

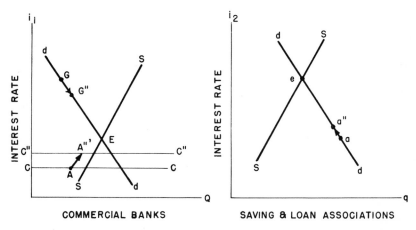

Figure 3.—Raising the CC ceiling to C″C″ would tend to bring funds back to commercial banks, lowering the scarcity cost of credit from G to G″ and increasing bank deposits from A to A″. Contrariwise, loss of S. & L. deposits will raise interest costs from a to a″.

Figure 4 shows the effects of introducing, along with the ceiling on commercial banks, higher ceilings on dividends payable by the savings and loans. Usually the ceilings on savings and loans will be higher than those on commercial banks; and the effect of the savings and loan ceilings is to lower their share of the total supply of savings.

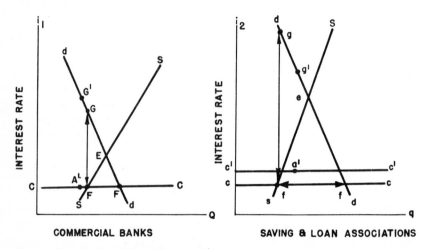

COMMERCIAL BANKS   SAVING & LOAN ASSOCIATIONS

Figure 4.—To see the effects of the cc ceiling for S. & L.'s at about the same level as for banks, figure 4 shows both markets with gaps rationed by nonprice methods, of FF and ff, respectively; and FG and fg gaps show a discrepancy between the scarcity cost to borrowers and interest received by savers, a discrepancy that encourages bribes, favoritism, and promotional expense. Distortion is the greatest in the S. & L. market because the ceiling is more below the competitive market equilibrium. Hence, suppose the S. & L.'s are allowed a higher ceiling, at c'c' above CC. Now we end at A' and a', which are intermediate between the points where only banks have a ceiling and the points where equal-level ceilings are imposed. Generally, raising cc or lowering CC will raise the share of the S. & L.'s relative to the commercial banks (moving a to the right and g' downward, and moving A' to the left and G' upward).

Summary of Effects of Ceilings

We can now summarize the results of the self-contained diagrammatical analysis of the effects of interest ceilings:

(1) Interest rate ceilings, set below the competitive level that would prevail in a single, self-contained market, create a shortfall of the supply of savings in comparison with the borrowers' demands for those savings. This shortfall has to be bridged by wasteful and inequitable nonprice rationing methods (advertising promotion, premia, rendering of auxiliary services, favoritism); now the scarcity cost of funds to those who wish to borrow for building and other capital-formation purposes lies above the interest rate received by the savers. The result is both inefficient and inequitable: Inefficient, in that there is deadweight loss because everyone may suffer; inequitable, in that one group of savers do not receive what the market thinks is the worth of their thriftiness, and inequitable in that identical people may receive different rewards depending on the caprice of nonprice rationing. In particular, the banks as a whole may earn something of a monopoly profit on the difference between what the law permits them

to pay and what the scarce funds can be auctioned off for among eager borrowers. If entry into banking is free, this monopoly profit may be frittered away in proliferation of banks and branches and chamberlainian nonprice competition.

(2) If there are two interconnected markets—as for example the markets for commercial bank deposits and those for saving and loan associations—under free competition funds will flow to the place of highest yield, lowering interest rates there and raising them elsewhere. This funnels funds into the areas of greatest urgency—e.g., the growing West and South, where the construction industry is burgeoning as demographic factors call for more homebuilding. The result is both efficient and equitable.

However, if a ceiling is imposed on one of the markets, the flow of funds will speed to the market that has no ceilings. Although this forced flow may be to regions and purposes of greatest economic need, the amount of the flow may be quite haphazard, depending upon the happenstance of the ceiling levels in comparison with shifting supply and demand equilibria.

(3) Paradoxically, raising an interest ceiling may lower actual effective interest costs by coaxing out a larger effective supply of savings. If the ceiling on commercial banks is raised, while no change is made in the savings and loan area (either because there never were ceilings or because any existing ceilings have been left intact), then a reverse flow of funds will take place back toward the market which is no longer so hamstrung by ceilings. While this may be a move toward a more efficient and more equitable position in the longrun, in the shortrun the vested interests that have grown up under the umbrella of the previous ceilings will certainly be hurt. And innocent third parties [11]—namely, those in the building industries who have had reason to think that they could turn to the savings and loans for credit accommodation—can be harmed along with the stockholders in privately owned savings and loans. Even where the customers of the savings and loan own the organization, there can easily be a risk of technical insolvency when the market interest rates that have to be paid to bad deposits rise above the contractual mortgage rates that can be earned on past loan commitments.

In the long run these short-term problems may come out in the wash. But the long run may seem very far away when a vast industry is in serious short-run difficulties. Moreover, governmental agencies have a stake in this matter. It is partly because of the various government insurance guarantees that funds have been flowing so freely into the home construction industry these past 20 years. Suppose all the West Coast savings and loans became simultaneously technically

---

[11] Because accounts in savings and loans are insured, the worst harm that can come to depositors is that they might have to wait temporarily for their money.

insolvent, not because of any particularly bad management but rather because they will be forced for a long time to borrow on short term from their depositors at high market rates of interest at the same time that their assets are frozen into lower-yielding long-term mortgages. If this happens, the Government insurance agency that guarantees their deposits could conceivably itself become technically bankrupt or at the least be forced to turn to the general purse for help. Needless to say, any breakdown of a large segment of our financial institutions is a matter of concern to the whole Nation and therefore to every part of the Government (including the independent Federal Reserve itself), and not just a matter of concern to the FHLBB and the agencies concerned with residential building and with thrift institutions.

Policy Recommendations

In view of the strong case that has been put forward for letting competitive markets operate without legal interferences in order to achieve efficient and equitable allocation of capital markets, why should an economist not simply recommend that regulation Q be repealed forthwith, along with similar interest rate ceilings on mutual savings banks and savings and loan associations? Certainly there is a temptation to make such a recommendation and many economists have succumbed to it. But first let me put the case for the defense of a more gradual modification of the existing network of interest-rate ceilings.

It is a tautology in modern economics that optimal performance requires that there be as many distinct weapons of policy as there are distinct goals or objectives.

Illustration: In principle, full employment with reasonable price stability could be attained by an appropriate fiscal policy. Thus prevention of demand-pull inflation might require a budgetary surplus with higher tax rates and lower public expenditures. But alternatively, one could rely on monetary policy to achieve the desired level of aggregate demand, having the Federal Reserve fight demand-pull inflation by slowing down the rate of growth of the money supply and raising the cost and availability of credit. Or with two policy weapons available to achieve one prescribed goal, we can employ an arbitrary mix of fiscal and monetary policy.

Suppose, though, that we add a second goal to our social agenda. Alongside a desired level for aggregate demand, suppose we wish to achieve an optimal division of full-employment product between capital formation and current consumption. Now that we have two goals, it is indeed fortunate that we have the two separate weapons of fiscal and monetary policy. For, in general, there will be but one definite mix of fiscal and monetary policy capable of achieving the desired mix of capital formation and consumption. Specifically, if an increase in the percentage of resources devoted to investment is desired, society will want to tighten up on fiscal policy by raising taxes and cutting expenditures; but instead of letting this result in unemployment, society will simultaneously wish to ease up on monetary policy, inducing higher investment and deepening of capital by means of lowered interest rates.

Let us appraise the case for interest ceilings in terms of the need to have policy weapons as numerous as our social goals. Society does want full employment. Society also wants a proper growth program involving a proper mix of investment and consumption. But along with wanting the proper aggregate of investment, society also often has a keen interest in keeping the total of residential construction within certain broad limits. Thus one of the things which seems most wrong in retrospect about the "money crunch" of 1966 was the fact that it produced a drastic decline in total housing starts.

With escalation in Vietnam creating an inflation problem, the public authorities would perhaps have welcomed a decline in starts from a level of 1½ million to something above 1 million. But to have the full effect of the temporary money crunch fall upon the construction industry, almost halving the number of starts, was deemed much too much of a good thing. I need only sketch here the considerations involved, not trying at all to justify or evaluate them. First, in the last part of the 1960's the age structure of the population was foreseeably moving in the direction of requiring a larger stock of the Nation's housing. Second, purely temporary cutbacks in an industry that would result in dispersion of its work teams could involve an inordinate long-run economic cost.

Suppose then that we face three economic goals. Where are we to find the third weapon that will enable society to control, in a discriminating and selective way, the level of construction activity? It will be recalled from our previous graphical analysis that, inadvertently so to speak, interest-rate ceilings do definitely provide a selective control which might be mobilized to serve social goals.[12] Therefore, even though interest rate ceilings are not perhaps the ideal weapon to control the mix of investment going into housing, and even though their use can involve some cost in terms of efficiency and equity, a society should think twice before turning its back on this control device by abolishing all ceilings. To illustrate the point further, had Congress in 1966 not followed a course diametrically opposed by libertarians enamored of the workings of free markets, there would

[12] Of course, alternative new weapons could be envisaged. Congress could instruct the Federal Reserve Board to support in a selective manner the housing industry during periods of overall monetary constraint. Such recommendations do not sit well with economists who believe that the Federal Reserve should exercise only general controls over the supply of money, and should never be distracted from that central purpose. However, such counsel fails to accept the brute fact that society (i.e., the electorate through its legislators and selected officials) does specify limits on the level of housing as a legitimate goal.

no doubt have been even greater disruption of the housing industry and of capital markets generally. If Congress had forestalled such an outcome as unthinkable, say coercing the independent Federal Reserve into selective supporting of residential construction, the libertarian critics would in any case still have been unappeased.[13]

In pointing out that interest rate ceilings do provide a possible new weapon for selective control of residential constructive activity as against other capital formation, I do not mean to imply that this is a decisive argument for keeping such ceilings or reinstating them. But it is a germane consideration in any objective appraisal of the case for or against such ceilings.

The final defense of interest rate ceilings is not the least important: Over a period of decades these ceilings, even though interest rates may not have been high enough to bring them into effect, have provided a sheltered environment in which a system of financial intermediaries has sprung up. And the continued solvency and liquidity—particularly in periods of stress—depends on such ceilings. It will not do to say that these institutions should not have been allowed to develop along the lines that they have. Such arguments, with whatever validity they have, are beside the point. We are confronted with a vast savings and loan complex, which has evolved over a period of many decades and at least in part as a result of definite social policy. One cannot, even if one wanted to, turn one's back on these institutions. If it were true that interest and dividend ceilings could save these institutions from bankruptcy and ruin, and that only ceilings could perform this function, then despite some of the costs in terms of equity and efficiency involved in ceilings, many men of goodwill would accept ceilings as the lesser of evils. Or, even if other devices could perform this salvaging function, ceilings might still be advocated as involving the least compromise with evil. In other words, we may be faced here, at least in the short run, with a "feasibility" problem in which national policy is forced to look for a "second best" policy, no completely optimal one being possible.

To appraise this important argument in defense of ceilings, let us review the basic dilemma created by savings and loans as an institution. Some years ago at a conference on this industry attended by economists in Chicago, I pointed out an odd feature of our modern world. "If a man from Mars were to come down to Earth," I suggested, "surely he would be astonished to be told that the highest yield that you can earn on essentially liquid savings is through putting those funds into long-lived residential structures of some 30 to 50 years of

---

[13] It is well known that in the 1950's the existence of maximum interest rates on VA and FHA mortgages similarly, and with the same inadvertence, performed a stabilizing function. In boom times FHA and VA mortgage money dried up; in slack times such money became rapidly more available. To have achieved the same anticyclical stabilization without this ratchet effect might well have required much greater amplitude of fluctuation of monetary policy, with all the various destabilizing effects on capital markets implied thereby.

duration." For, at that time you could have earned 4 or 5 percent by sending your money to a coast savings and loan, while your yield on Government or corporate bonds would have been a good deal less than that. Moreover, you could not be sure that these bonds would not fluctuate in value. To be sure, you might in principle have to give 30 days notice in cashing in a savings and loan account, but you would have been very surprised if anyone had insisted on that notice.

As I tried to analyze the reason for this anomalous discrepancy between liquidity of the liabilities of the savings and loans and the illiquidity of their assets, I decided that it was *the insurance of accounts by Government* that made all the difference. The Government, as a matter of deliberate policy, wished to stimulate and favor homebuilding and construction generally. So with its magic wand, it guaranteed that savers would get high yield from putting their funds in that industry, and without taking any risk of loss or even having to give up shortrun liquidity.

This is all very well if in fact the housing industry can—as a whole and not with respect to each housing venture—turn out to create a return which is higher than that of any other industry. But there seems no good reason to expect that this would be the case in the longrun. As a result, the Government would have to make up the extra yield that savers are to get by means of outright subsidies. But of course there has been no such program for transferring money from the public purse to each savings and loan and its customers; and no such program has ever been seriously contemplated. The only other alternative would be for savings and loans to be encouraged to go on paying out more than they earn, until finally they become bankrupt; and at this point, the Government makes good, out of its own purse and out of general tax revenues, its insurance guarantee. It should be understood that I am not speaking here of bankruptcy on the part of ill-run organizations, but rather of chronic, staggered, designed bankruptcy on the part of each organization in the industry. Obviously, this is a chaotic way of getting a continuing Government subsidy to an industry; and no matter how vital the industry, few would actually recommend that this be the selected form of subsidy.

Instead, what has happened is what could have been expected to happen. As the regulation Q hobbles that had been put on the competitors to the savings and loans were relaxed, and as the yields on Government and corporate bonds competitive to savings and loan accounts began to rise on a long-term basis, the savings and loans discovered that they had to raise the dividend rates that they pay on their accounts in order to compete. If there existed a large volume of housing activity that could produce yields as big or bigger than those of the competition, then the existing size of the savings and loan industry might have been retained intact. But there is no reason why there should exist such a large volume of superyielding housing activity. Hence under the perpetual shiftings of supply and demand in a free market the natural course of evolution would have been for the savings and loan industry to shrink in size, along with the shrinking in relative importance of the construction industry as it loses preeminence in the competition for capital funds.

Even if such a transition to a smaller scale could have been done smoothly and without friction, the question arises as to why society should want to dismantle the work teams and capacity that had been built up in this industry. Instead of having funds go to build up new institutions while the old ones are decaying, why would it not be more efficient to have the funds stay in the old institutions but to have those same institutions funnel the funds into new and dynamic uses— say into consumer loans, into commercial loans to business, or even into term loans to finance durable producers' equipment? This after all is how the commercial banks tend to behave in performing their function as conduits between savers and the changing mix of capital formation.

At this point we run into a familiar institutional difficulty. Remember that the savings and loans were originally conceived of as an aid to the housebuilding industries. In exchange for the various privileges and subsidies tendered them, they were put under an obligation to refrain from diversifying their investments into areas and purposes outside that of residential real estate. Hence, they lack the resilience to adjust to hard-money times. And yet they de facto are expected to provide complete liquidity to their customers!

It is in recognition of this fundamental inflexibility of any credit organization tied rigidly to the construction area that many have been putting forward in recent years a new reform: Change the system so that savings and loans can have more diversified investments, in much the same way that commercial banks can. Naturally the commercial banks might be expected to resent the creation of a new competing industry performing many of their functions. But they already resent many of the functions of the savings and loan industry; and we are in any case not taking a trade association view of the problem, concentrating instead on the grand issues of national economic policy.

There is much to be said for basic reform of the savings and loan industry to permit it wider diversification of investments. Such a reform would undoubtedly go part of the way in improving its ability to avoid illiquidity and insolvency at times of money scarcity. But it should be realized that this gain in solvency and liquidity would be partially at the expense of another goal that has been put forward as a matter of national policy. Letting the savings and loans diversify their investments would improve their balance sheet solvency in hard-money times at the expense of an even more drastic impact of hard money on the homebuilding industry. You cannot have it both ways; namely, *both* using the savings and loans as a special source of funds for housing, *and* letting them preserve liquidity and solvency by avoiding that industry. Already we know that insurance companies and commercial banks tend to turn their backs on the mortgage market in times of money stress; what little strength remains for that market may have been due precisely to the monopoly that the mortgage market has over savings and loan investments; so that freeing the savings and loans from the monopoly fetters of providing exclusively real estate loans could mean, in another era like 1966, even more of a decline in housing starts.

This raises the important question as to why savings and loan institutions face a special problem of illiquidity and insolvency which stems from the simple fact that they are forced to hold most of their assets in the form of long-term mortgages. I spoke earlier of the high liquid return promised to their depositors at the same time that their assets are long-lived durable housing structures. But that does not quite do justice to the situation. The assets of the savings and loans are not literally houses, they are only tied up in houses. Their direct assets are the mortgage obligations of those who build and buy houses by means of the funds they borrow from the savings and loans. If capital gains accrue on real estate, the savings and loan does not derive benefit nor do its depositors, even indirectly. It is primarily the owner, and not the savings and loan, which has the equity interest, that experiences any capital gain-loss. Only when the drop in house value is so unexpectedly large that the savings and loan must take over the property and sell it off at a loss does the savings and loan have a capital loss.

It is not, however, the threat to solvency of the savings and loan industry stemming from wholesale drops in values of real estate to below their mortgaged values that concerns me here. If a time like 1929–33 were to return, that could indeed become a problem on a national scale; but I cannot think the odds are appreciable that such a time is likely soon, or perhaps ever, to threaten us again. What concerns analysts who study this industry is the peculiar long-term yield that is built into the conventional mortgage contract.

The fundamental defect of the savings and loan industry is that it borrows short from its depositors and then freezes those funds into very long-term assets whose yield is also frozen for a long period of time.

Only think of many mortgages that were written at the low interest rates of a dozen years ago and are still outstanding. In 1956, a mortgage yield that earned 5 percent looked to be a good thing in that one had to pay 4 percent or less to depositors. But now in 1969 one must pay something like 5½ percent to depositors, and after one figures the expense of administration, any 5 percent mortgage involves the lender in a chronic out-of-pocket loss. To put the matter in the language of the theoretical economist: If we calculate the present discounted value of the association's or bank's near-term liabilities and calculate the present discounted value of the bank's long-term frozen mortgage, using the current high rates of interest that prevail in the marketplace for both short- and long-term securities, we find that the banks net asset position is negative. And it may even be more negative than its capital and surplus (if it is a stock company), or than its various contingency reserves for losses (if it is a mutual enterprise).

This means that the Federal agency guaranteeing its deposits, if we calculate correctly its present discounted value, has a large explicit loss position. Of course, there is usually no need for these present discounted values to be insisted upon by the marketplace, so a condition of technical bankruptcy can go on for a long time unnoticed. But it cannot go on forever. What has saved this industry so far is the fact that the periods of very hard money have tended to be short in duration. Let us make no mistake about it: If the economy were to move into a new era in which rates of return like 8 percent persisted permanently, then most of our financial intermediaries whose assets consist of mortgages frozen into returns of 4, 5, 6, and 7 percent would be technically insolvent. If the institution had to pay 8 percent to hold its deposits, it would run large annual deficits that would have to be financed out of principal. In the end, someone would be left holding the bag: Either the depositors or the Government agency which had insured those deposits. And the calls upon the insurance fund would not be at random, and would not be moderate and self-canceling. They would all bunch up at one time and be pervasive throughout the industry. No actuarial payments could ever build up a fund large enough to honor such commitments. Inevitably the general Federal Government, with or without help from its tool, the Federal Reserve, would have to step in to avert default on the insurance obligation and to avert the financial panic that could well ensue.

Why have none of these dire things yet happened? Of course, on a small scale they have happened, but primarily to savings and loans whose mismanagement and overextension have been brought to public notice by the intervention of hard-money periods. Secondly, the shifts toward higher interest rates have been gradual and erratic, often being followed by a return to lower rates. Fortunately for the institutions committed largely to housing investment, the average length of life of a mortgage written for 25 years is in fact more like half that. For one thing, it is always in the process of being amortized, so that at any time some part of its principal has been repaid. For another thing, even in a steady state, the average life-to-go would be less than half the total life in a growing population. But even more important, we are a mobile people. Long before a house wears out, it changes ownership. In a

25-year period a house may have several occupants. And although some of these may take over mortgages from their predecessors, many do not; and some who do are forced to refinance at higher rates.

As far as short-term periods of money stringency are concerned, a savings and loan could be technically insolvent and still be able to work its way out of its difficulties if it is permitted to borrow at the high rates which are temporary. Critics say, "Why should a group who has already made the mistake of paying interest that is too high compared to what it can prudently earn, be permitted to try to bail itself out of an emergency by paying even higher interest rates?" This argument in favor of tight dividend ceilings during periods of hard-money stringency confuses the long-term problem of discouraging over-venturesomeness and risktaking by banks, with the short-term problem of being able to continue in business. If the new money requires only temporarily high rates and yet can be advantageously invested in high-yielding mortgages that will continue to pay this high interest long after the tight money period is over, then the solvency of the organization is definitely helped by letting it compete for funds by paying rates higher than it can earn on the average on its old portfolio.[14] (Of course, if the high rates are permanent and the organization cannot find even-higher assets to put funds into, then letting it bid high for funds becomes simply the old Ponzi game in which lenders are fleeced of their funds by the offer of high returns, with those returns being financed out of depletion of principal. Only so long as Ponzi can find a geometric progression of new suckers can he avoid the inevitable day of final reckoning and disaster. Since no Government-insured Ponzi, he was not subject to the same vigilance of bank examination that should be standard for any organization that does get the benefit of Government insurance. Many of the problems that people try to handle by control of ceilings—namely avoidance of overbanking and risktaking—should be kept within the province of responsible bank examinationship.)

Rather than use the inefficient device of manipulating differential ceiling rates between savings and loans and the commercial banks, many would argue that one should go to the heart of the problem of savings and loan solvency by a more basic reform. According to this view long-term mortgages should never be made at frozen interest rates. Instead, the interest rate payable should be flexibly related to changing money-market conditions. Thus, at yearly or perhaps 2-year intervals the contractual rates of interest payable should be some specified excess above the average prime rate, or discount rate, or free market mortgage rate that has prevailed in the past. It is argued that this is a more equitable arrangement, and also a more viable one.

---

[14] To the degree that high current rates require raising interest payable on old accounts, tight money periods, of course, threaten the solvency of the S. & L.'s.

Of course the reduction of uncertainty on the part of the lender has been at the expense of an increase in the uncertainty shifted to the borrower. Now the borrower may wake up to find that the interest costs on his home have gone up. To make this more palatable to the typical houseowner, it has been suggested that his monthly payments need never be altered. These monthly payments are divided between interest costs and amortization of the mortgage principal. Under the proposed reform, when interest rates fall, the same monthly payment would represent a more rapid reduction of principal. Hence, a 25-year mortgage might in fact be paid off in 20 years. Likewise, when interest rates rise, the same monthly payment represents a larger fraction going to interest costs, with the principal inevitably being reduced at a slower rate. Thus, in a time of generally rising interest rates, 25-year mortgages would be automatically extended and might have an effective life of 30 or 35 years.

The effect of this reform would be far reaching indeed. Automatically it would enable the lending institutions to refinance their assets so as to adjust quickly to changing money-market conditions, rather than adjusting slowly as under present conditions, when one must wait for the natural rollover out of old and into new mortgages, in the meantime running the risk both of illiquidity and insolvency.

This major reform, I fear, will not be deemed practical. Apparently something like it has long prevailed in the money markets of England, which are more cartelized. On a modest and limited scale, varying interest rates have occasionally been introduced into American mortgage contracts. One gathers, though, that the borrowers have not read the fine print carefully; and on that sad day when increases in interest costs were sprung upon them, they have reacted with articulate resentment and violence.

I am always ready to bow in the end to arguments based upon practical feasibility if they are indeed correctly so based. But if a fundamental reform makes good sense for all the parties involved, I am loath to back away from it merely because of the first reaction to it which takes the form that it is not practical. Specifically, I think it would be a pity if we were forced to keep on a permanent basis the inefficient and inequitable device of interest and dividend ceilings, thereby papering over the need for more fundamental reform. However, I have been able to find very few informed people who seriously hold out much hope for a widespread abandonment of frozen interest mortgage contracts in favor of sliding-scale interest costs that fluctuate with intermediate swings in money-market conditions, even though this would be the most valuable single reform that could be introduced.

In concluding my analytical survey, I should mention still another argument that can be made for interest ceilings. Irwin Friend has put it this way:

One other possible risk associated with the removal of interest rate ceilings should be mentioned. Many economists believe that the level of interest rates at any time is substantially influenced by expectations which are highly volatile. It is at least conceivable that in a period of credit squeeze, rapidly rising interest rates in the absence of ceilings might, with expectational interactions between deposit and loan markets, result in a self-feeding spiral and a credit panic. Serious damage might be done before even immediate monetary measures to reverse the process were effective. As a consequence, it is not certain that the efficiency of monetary control would be enhanced by the removal of interest ceilings. The Commission on Money and Credit recommendation for standby authority would be one possible way of cutting down on this type of risk as well as the default risk, though there are obvious problems associated with the implementation of such authority.[15]

I quite agree that all markets are subject to oscillations of destabilizing expectations. When the cocoa harvest is short, speculative enthusiasms may cause prices to overshoot beyond the new equilibrium. The capital markets are far from being an exception. History is replete with stock-market crashes and money-market panics. But the proper action to prevent or ameliorate such phenomena is, I believe, given by modern theories of monetary and fiscal policy; and we no longer run the danger of the gross errors in overall monetary and fiscal policy characteristic of old-time capitalism.

Still, even if we succeed in the future much better than we have performed in the past, it is only realistic to suppose that there will remain some irreducible degree of overall instability. Recessions may be less frequent than in the past and less virulent, but some probability of recession and slowdown must still be reckoned with. And the problems associated with inflation are, of course, far from having been solved. Agreeing that actual capital markets when left to themselves may be subject to psychological oscillations that are not socially optimal, I would question whether retaining interest rate ceilings is likely to make those markets perform better. Over the long run, a world of ceilings might have about the same degree of market-generated instability and inefficiency. But there might be particular times when the retention of ceilings or their reintroduction could serve to moderate the intensity of free market movements. Since our weapons capable of discrimination are so few, one should not lightly renounce standby authority to reinstate any one of these weapons.

A related reason for favoring retention of ceilings comes from those who are apprehensive concerning "over banking." They point to the universal temptation for certain institutions to offer ever higher inter-

---

[15] See discussion entitled, "Interest Rates and Their Economic Implications," in U.S. Savings and Loan League Conference on Savings and Residential Construction, *Proceedings,* 1966, p. 66.

est rates in order to attract or retain funds. Then in order to be able to pay out such rates, they tend to be attracted toward ever riskier investments. Competitive market forces could be counted upon to prevent and police such situations only in a world of perfect certainty. In the world as we know it, there is an irreducible amount of uncertainty. Lenders would not place their funds in high interest accounts were they aware of the risk; before the facts of default and bankruptcy occur, borrowers are either genuinely optimistic or manage to persuade themselves that their operations are sound. Interest ceilings, it is suggested, can protect lenders from disappointment and protect borrowers from themselves.

I must agree that there is a problem here. But it seems to me that this provides a powerful argument for qualitative regulation of saving institutions. It is a justification for rigid auditing and bank examination by the requisite authorities. In the long run the consumer will be better served by such qualitative regulation than by ceilings as such.

Final Conclusions

1. *After reviewing all the pros and cons, I cannot think it responsible advice to urge immediate abolition of all interest and dividend ceilings.* I do believe it to be the main thrust of economic analysis that we evolve away from dependence upon these inefficient and inequitable devices. One way to achieve this evolution toward freedom would be to raise gradually the levels of the ceilings relative to free market interest rates. If a ceiling comes high enough, it ceases to be any limit at all.

In the process of evolution, it would be quite dangerous to have ceilings rise in an uncoordinated way. Thus, if the Federal Reserve were to raise regulation Q ceilings on the interest that commercial banks can pay—and to do this in a rapid fashion—while at the same time the agencies responsible for the savings and loan associations were to keep a tight lid on the ceilings governing their dividends, one could precipitate a crisis outflow of funds from these last institutions. Better that we should float into freedom by a coordinated elevation of ceilings.

Or this might be brought about if future market interest rates were to decline appreciably from present levels. Then, just as a ship is floated off a sandbar by the incoming tide, freedom of competitive markets could be restored simply by not having either ceiling follow the market down from present levels.

A period of tight money, such as the current one, does not provide a very propitious time for beginning a smooth evolution toward the abolition of ceilings. In times like these many funds would not be where they are were it not for the dykes provided by such ceilings; at the least, if such dykes are precipitously removed, the authorities had better be prepared with resources to offset the flooding that might follow.

2. Even if we were to move toward a time when ceilings become in effect inoperative, *a strong pragmatic case can be made for maintaining the power to reinstate ceilings on a standby basis*. Everybody says that, however lucky we were in 1966 to be able to manipulate ceilings to help handle the "money crunch," we shall have no need for such luck again inasmuch as a recurrence of that tight money episode is highly unlikely. But how do those who say this know? How can one be sure that in the future, perhaps even within the next year, we may not once again witness a difficult period of disintermediation? As we approach the end of the 1960's a precipitous reduction in residential housing construction, brought about by the caprice of a money-market emergency, would be even more tragic and costly to the Nation than during the middle 1960's when demographic forces did not put such heavy demands upon housing. In time of emergency, it is easier to take a weapon off the shelf than to forge a new one. Therefore, standby powers to reimpose ceilings do make good sense.

3. It should be emphasized that recommending evolutionary departure from ceilings and retention of standby powers to reimpose them should not be interpreted as excuse for retaining such ceilings permanently or as an excuse for a rear-guard action to delay their elimination.

4. Finally, I should add the warning that our analysis here has not been reassuring with respect to the good health and robustness of our present institutional division of labor between commercial banks and other lending agencies on the one hand, and on the other hand between society's interest in residential construction as opposed to other forms of capital formation. To the degree that we remove gradually the crutch of interest and dividend ceilings, we may force upon ourselves confrontation of the continuing basic flaws in our present arrangements. We may precipitate greater calls upon the Government insurance funds designed to protect depositors. We may hurry the day when savings and loan associations will be given greater freedom to invest in areas outside real estate. We might even increase the chances of a conversion to mortgage contracts that involve sliding-scale interest rates which are more appropriately related to changing money-market conditions. And, it is only fair to say after we have voluntarily denied ourselves the weapon of interest ceilings, we might even in a future emergency period bring down upon ourselves the threat of financial crisis.

But just as Sigmund Freud has shown that adults are better for meeting their problems head-on rather than suppressing them from attention, so I believe a healthy democratic society should be the better for facing up to the problems that are really there.

PART XIV

The Individual and the State

181

Personal Freedoms and Economic Freedoms in the Mixed Economy

Paul A. Samuelson

I

Although businessmen do not constitute a completely homogeneous group, it can be documented that generally they share a particular set of political and economic beliefs. These beliefs overlap in some degree with those of other groupings in the community; but in some degree they differ, and the differences can become quite sharp. That is, the typical view among academic economists and other social scientists on topics such as the proper role of government expenditure and regulation has become increasingly different from that of the typical view among businessmen.

How can we account for business ideology? Much of this discussion will be devoted to this question and to previous attempts to answer it. Since it takes two to make a difference, the business ideology of intellectuals will also be studied.

The second part of the essay attempts to analyze various interrelations among economic and personal freedoms. Agreeing that governments everywhere take a more active role in the conscious direction and regulation of economic life, we may speak loosely of "a decline in business freedoms." At least some people will want to distinguish between the concept of the freedom of a seller to market his product as he wishes and the freedom of a family man to go to the church of his choice; to think and utter the thoughts of his fancy; and to read his evening paper within the four walls of his castle, with the secure feeling that the moat separating it from the outside will not be breached by bailiffs without due process of law. They will be willing to fight to the death to defend these personal freedoms but will not care to risk more than a few scratches and bruises in the cause of business or economic freedoms.

Yet it can be argued—and, hence, has been so argued—that freedom is one and indivisible: that it is as grave a sin to condemn a man's property and take it over (at court-determined cost) for an urban renewal project as it is to whisk his wife into the county jail on arbitrary charges or on no charges at all. Or (and this is by no means the same argument) that the empirical nature of the political process is such that infringement of business freedoms must lead inevitably to infringement of personal freedoms. Beliefs about the relationships between personal freedoms and economic freedoms represent one of the most important tenets in business ideology. Before beginning to analyze these specific beliefs, I will attempt to account for business ideology in general.

The Business Creed as Delusion

Although this discussion purports to be objective, by its very nature it begins with certain preconceptions. When a social scientist speaks of the puzzle of business ideology, he has already committed himself to the view that these beliefs cannot be explained in terms of their self-evident objective merits. But this is not because he has prejudged the issue from the beginning of time, having known already before his ninth-grade civics course that the pretended merits of laissez-faire are all bunk. Rather, the historian of ideas has built upon numerous earlier studies in the field of economics and politics, which suggest strongly that the conservative business ideology overstates the objective merits of its own case.

When most academic discussions of the business creed begin with this viewpoint as an explicit or implicit axiom, they unavoidably irritate the businessman that they are talking about. There is no real harm in that, any more than there is in the case where radicals become irritated when psychologists attempt to explain their behavior on the picket line in terms of jealous resentment over their mother's love for her husband. The danger is all the other way. When Western anthropologists go to live with South Sea islanders, they end up too often with an exaggerated fondness for the quaintness of the sex rituals there, in just the way that an economist working for an aid program in Pakistan finds himself arguing with the Washington office on behalf of his constituency, using the same arguments that he had himself been previously rebutting. What one must hold against a generation of anthropologists is that they were so taken in by the phenomena they were objectively studying that they made bad empirical predictions about the hardness of the cake of custom and its resistance to material change. I need not point out the danger implied in the proverb, "To know all, is to forgive all."

But an opposite warning is also necessary. Most of the literature that I have seen on this subject starts out too blithely with the postulate that the views of the conservative businessman are palpable delusions, which must, therefore, be approached with the tools appropriate to the analysis of odd beliefs. I exaggerate a little, but copious quotation could show that I do so in a good cause.

Let me illustrate with a recent book on American intellectual history edited by Arthur M. Schlesinger, Jr., and Morton D. White.[1] This excellent work represents the joint contributions of able scholars in the diverse areas of history, literature, philosophy, sociology, and economics. Several essays touch upon the development of conservative business thought in the last century. None of them—my own included—can be fairly termed a panegyric to the views under contemplation. Indeed, the following passage by Max Lerner [2] is more typical:

> One of the paradoxes of American social and intellectual history is that laissez-faire reached its height as a system of economic thought and judicial decision at the very time that its doom as a system of economic organization was already clear.

[1] A. M. Schlesinger, Jr., and Morton White: *Paths of American Thought,* Houghton Mifflin, Boston, 1963.

[2] *Ibid.,* p. 147. This is the opening sentence in Max Lerner's essay, The Triumph of Laissez-Faire.

Lerner is referring here to conservative ideology at the turn of the century. Many other writers have pointed out the apparent paradox of the Jacksonian era, when the Jeffersonian idyll of the prosperous and self-sufficient farmer was being replaced by the growth of industrialism and urbanization. Yet, just as the reality was turning to interdependence and away from independence, Emerson and Tocqueville were articulating the great American belief in individualism. How explain the discrepancy between fact and word? Hallucination? Self-deception? Mendacity?

It is a widespread view among academics that conservative sermons about laissez-faire and individualism represent a simple denial of the reality of society. Maybe this is so. Maybe it is patently so, and no danger can come from prejudging the case in advance. But it is certainly a matter of some moment that what is taken for granted not be wrong. I am here stressing, without guile, *the crucial importance of a scientific assessment of the merits of an ideology as a preliminary to understanding its nonrationalistic content and function.* In handling an upset person who claims to have seen a ghost, it is of some moment to know whether he *has* seen a ghost. It is one thing to be told by an individual in a sanitarium near New York City that he is Napoleon Bonaparte and quite another to be told the same thing by a short, swarthy individual who inhabits the island of St. Helena in 1817.

The way that you calibrate the respondent's verbal behavior and the explanation appropriate to account for it is much altered in the two cases. And the way I calibrate *your* rejection of his claiming to be Napoleon is equally affected by the circumstances. What are we to think of A, who knows that B is crazy to claim he is Napoleon for the sufficient reason that all sane men should know that A is the true Napoleon?

At last I have revealed my hand; I intend to play a double game. I shall try not only to understand businessmen's beliefs about economics and business, but also intellectuals' beliefs on these matters as refracted by *their* reactions to business ideology. The mind reels at this prospect of wheels within wheels. But it is all good, clean fun. At bottom I am an intellectual myself, as ready as the next boy to throw a snowball at the top hat of a nearby tycoon (or at the mortarboard of some dear, departing colleague).

The Economist as Go-between

Actually, this is in a genuine sense no frivolous exercise. The economist is in the unique position of being able to assist the historian of thought and social movements. Just as a pathologist can help a psychiatrist appraise the meaning of a patient's assertion that he has a brain tumor, the economist can—alas, imperfectly—help certify what the reasonable facts are, the necessary benchmark against which to measure delusion and rationalization.[3]

Although the thought would spoil digestions at a downtown eating club, the economist has always played the role of interpreter to the academic community of the businessman and of material activity generally. Fifty years ago, conservative advocates would perhaps invoke the authority of the local Ph.D. in political economy; today they are more likely to regard him as an impractical enemy and send for their lawyer to find that needle in the haystack of economists that a sensible man can rely on. But their view of the economist does not refute my point that we are go-betweens.

Historians and political scientists will go on taking seriously the economic doctrines of Henry George or Bernard Shaw long after any quorum of economists will deem them significant. A sociologist well-trained in what is politely called intellectual history will laugh to hear a businessman claiming that *his* investment will benefit the working man in the future. The sociologist knows that this "filter-down" theory was killed off when John Stuart Mill accepted Thornton's refutation of the classical

[3] An example is provided by the apparent incompatibility of individualism and a post-Jeffersonian interdependent economy. The historian needs to be told by the economist that a system of ideal pricing in perfectly competitive markets *can* coordinate the activities of quite egotistic individualist atoms through the impersonal market mechanism. (I discuss this in greater detail later.) Hence, the paradox of post-Jacksonian ideological individualism evaporates as a logical self-contradiction. The Lerner problem remains: Is it oligopolists who will be most fervent in the praise of competition and laissez-faire?

wage-fund theory a hundred years ago. What the sociologist does not realize is that, in another form, most modern economists place some credence in that murdered notion while, perhaps, sopping their social consciences by suggesting that workers be given both the increased wages stemming from the new capital *and* the fruit of the capital itself, if it is *their* present sacrifices that are to be involved.

As the general economist is to the other social scientists and the historians, often the business economist is to the general economist. Business school economists will, I think, agree with my observation that in past decades professors in commerce departments voted more conservatively than their colleagues in economics departments. Times have changed a little. Where only two out of the hundreds of professors at the Harvard Business School chose Franklin Roosevelt over Wendell Willkie in 1940, a majority chose Kennedy over Nixon in 1960. The more things change, the less they are the same, as a Frenchman might say. Yet, it is still the case, I believe, that the majority for Kennedy was greater in the Harvard economics department (and liberal arts faculty) than in the Business School. And it is still fairly typical of colleges everywhere that business school professors are more sympathetic toward business than are members of the other faculties (with the possible exception of the engineers).

I am not saying that management school faculty members are "kept" men, apologists for business. In part, their difference in attitude may be traceable to their more detailed research into the complexities of business life; in part, to the evident attitudes of men who have chosen as their lifework the training of accountants, marketing experts, and other business practitioners. Economists who are known to be radical are less likely to be courted by business school deans and are less likely to succumb to available suitors. This may be just as well. The man who adores business is likely to lose objectivity. And the man who hates business is also handicapped in being objective. Neither Casanovas nor misogynists are apt to make cracker-jack obstetricians.

Here, I think my role as an economist can be a useful one. If you "know," as many social scientists know, that the praise of laissez-faire is beside the point, your analysis has to run along different lines than would be the case if, like Professors Frank Knight and Milton Friedman of the University of Chicago or Professors Gottfried Haberler of Harvard and William Fellner of Yale, you "know" there is much objective merit in the viewpoint. To be sure, a rabid business spokesman like Mr. Edgar M. Queeny of the Monsanto Chemical Company [4] does not state with any meticulousness the scientific findings of economists who belong to the secret lodges of the *Mont Pelerin* Society; but, then, neither did Franklin Roosevelt catch correctly the nuances of doctrine of his brain trust in the week in question; and few of the New Frontiersmen who have returned from Washington to their ivory towers would give top grades to their intermediate students for the utterances that they admire in high officials. Samuel Johnson's dictum on walking dogs and preaching women must be invoked here.

Business Ideology on the Defensive?

Before we try to account for business ideology, it may be well to examine its importance. Certainly, one cannot take for granted that its dominance in our society can be measured by its decibel count. Happy is the nation that has no history. And most secure may be the laissez-faire economy that no one bothers to talk about. In the 1920's, when Calvin Coolidge was Chairman of the Board, the business of America was business. As a boy entrepreneur I used to sample my own wares and read in the *Saturday Evening Post* (and in the now-defunct *American Magazine*) the success stories of American businessmen. Although they appeared in the nonfiction columns, they read like fiction. (Only after 1929 did I learn that they actually were part fiction!)

Nevertheless, despite the considerable volume of such panegyrics, there seemed to be less ideological defense of private enterprise in the 1920's than appeared in the mid-1930's, when Roosevelt's New Deal was at the apex of its power and when the rearguard actions of the Liberty League served the function of self-expression more than that of persuasive social propaganda.

[4] Edgar M. Queeny, *The Spirit of Enterprise,* Scribner, New York, 1943.

The felt need for articulation of business creed and *apologia* may itself be a sign of inner uncertainty on the part of the business community and conservative leaders. In the vigor of manly growth the motto is "Ask me no questions, and I'll tell you no lies." As the bachelor balds, and perhaps begins to pall, come the better rationalizations for the lively life. Eulogy and obituary are not accidentally related words.

Implicitly, I have been raising the suspicion that the business ideology may no longer have the importance for good or evil that it once had. How can this be reconciled with the common observation that radical reform has become a dead movement in American life? Communism has no following. Socialism has lost even the small appeal it once had. No utopias fire the imaginations of Americans and provide an alternative to the philosophy of business enterprise. In short, business is allegedly now in the saddle.

Now, this is not quite the way I hear it down at the Union League Club. There, they would be astonished to learn that they are in the saddle. The active businessman has not these many years been fearful of utopian socialists; nor of card-carrying communists, as such. He has regarded it as an over-nice distinction to worry about whether an intellectual is a fellow traveler or a lodge member. Since Karl Marx advocated a progressive income tax in the *Communist Manifesto* of 1848, why bother to distinguish between Marxians and progressives who hold such uncomfortable views? I believe it was the retired President Herbert Hoover who introduced into the vocabulary of American political life the compound word Marx-and-Keynes.

To say that people are now merely New Dealers or New Frontiersmen is not even to provide cold comfort to business ideologies. Franklin Roosevelt was the enemy, not Earl Browder or Norman Thomas. The thing to fear is not the full-fledged alternative social system, so much as the hard-to-differentiate "mixed economy." For one thing, Eugene Debs, the I.W.W., and earlier radical movements (including Populism) have, I suggest, an importance in the minds and writings of historians, social scientists, and conservative alarmists out of proportion to their actual historical importance. And although Norman Thomas can claim with some factual accuracy that many of the programs in his platform were adopted by Franklin Roosevelt, it would be politically naive to suppose that the socialist party was the spearhead and wedge for these social changes. The dawn does not pull up the sun, any more than the rear guard pushes the army in front of it.

The Mixed Economy

I question whether business has climbed back into the saddle. The story is much more complicated; history does not consist of one-way trends. History oscillates, backtracks, and spirals. Admittedly, in the twenty years after 1929 the trend seemed to be toward limitations on business, but during the last dozen years of that period, the strength of strong radical dissent was also on the ebb. One forgets how desperate the populace was in 1932. Half of the small-town editors, for example—a group usually about as conservative and reactionary as any that can be found—then favored nationalization of the banks. The success of Roosevelt's New Deal in stemming the tide of collapse acted as a lightning rod in dissipating the forces of fascism and drastic reform.

Since 1950, both in America and the West generally, there has been some comeback of private enterprise and an increasing reliance on markets rather than government controls. But even this movement has been a spotty one; thus, Germany, Japan, France, and Italy—to say nothing of The Netherlands and Great Britain—have, by planning, interfered extensively with laissez-faire. In the United States, the Eisenhower Administration retained most of the post–1933 economic institutions. Although the Kennedy-Johnson Administration has paid less lip service to the business cause and has been regarded by businessmen as a hostile adversary, its performance has been mixed. Labor unions these days regard themselves as being in the descendancy, both in terms of public opinion and government support. It is ironical that the first major step in gutting America's egalitarian structure of taxation should have been taken by a Democratic rather than a

Republican administration. And still, it is this same administration that pushes medical care for the aged, regulation of drugs and security markets, and other programs distasteful to business.

Perhaps the one discernible trend is toward less polarization of ideology; less of laissez-faire versus socialism; of freedom versus totalitarianism. This does not mean that the conflict is over, but rather that it is taking place along other battlelines. It is in this sense that I contend that the "mixed economy" is the enemy and the ever-present effective challenge of the business ideology.

The mixed economy is not a very definite concept. I have purposely left it vague, in part because that is its intrinsic nature and in part because increased precision should come at the end rather than at the beginning of extensive research.

Search for New Goals

The vagueness of the opposing ideology naturally begets a responding vagueness in the business creed itself. The old clear-cut bastions become too vulnerable. Yet, once they are left behind, the new ground to be defended becomes hard to define. This leads to a certain frustration and an urge to find a new formulation of the business creed. Professor Jesse W. Markham of Princeton University in his editor's introduction to R. Joseph Monsen, Jr., *Modern American Capitalism: Ideologies and Issues* [5] asks why capitalism, despite its demonstrated performance in producing highest real incomes, should be seriously challenged in the new uncommitted nations and at home. Markham concludes:

In this book Professor Monsen provides some meaningful and thoughtful answers to this question, the most plausible of which is the absence of a clearly articulated ideology of private capitalism.

Monsen himself puts the matter bluntly:

Americans will never be able to persuade other countries to follow an anti-communist route to development if they cannot explain and understand what they themselves are for—and why. [6]

[5] R. Joseph Monsen, Jr., *Modern American Capitalism: Ideologies and Issues*, Houghton Mifflin, Boston, 1963, p. vi.
  [6] *Ibid.*, p. ix.

I regard the Monsen study as valuable in demonstrating the differences and the nuances in capitalist ideology. It is debatable that the best defense of a system comes from a thorough understanding of its nature and a self-conscious articulation of its merits and demerits; and, therefore, I should be less sad than Monsen if it turned out that a would-be missionary, starting out to sell the American way of life to the Hottentots, Laotians, and Yankees, were to find his eloquence paralyzed by learning from Monsen that there are at least five versions of capitalistic ideology:

1. Classical Capitalist Ideology (of the N.A.M. and the Chicago economics department).
2. Managerial Ideology of Capitalism (of the C.E.D. and *Fortune* magazine).
3. Countervailing Power Ideology (of J. Kenneth Galbraith, and of whom else?).
4. People's Capitalism (of the New York Stock Exchange's Keith Funston and the American Advertising Council).
5. Enterprise Democracy (associated with the Eisenhower Administration, and particularly with its "semi-official ideologist" Arthur Larson).

Since it is not clear that the best preparation for the soap salesman is a thorough briefing in the scientific laboratory that produces soap, one cannot be sure that Monsen's contribution towards a sixth ideology will restore the aplomb of the American missionary:

> It is suggested that the U.S.I.A.'s currently exported American Capitalist Ideology be reoriented toward these basic elements of the American system, particularly pragmatism and compromise, elements not at present included in Enterprise Democracy.[7]

A New Capitalism?

The five versions of capitalism cited from Monsen can be boiled down to two categories: old-fashioned profit maximizing markets that are perfectly or imperfectly competitive; and the

---

[7] *Ibid.,* p. 128.

newer notion of "managerial capitalism"—that the corporation (and its officials) are responsive to the interests of *all* parties it deals with—employees, customers, shareowners, the public, the federal government. I fancy that most of the big business guinea pigs dissected by Robert Heilbroner lean toward this last view. And so do the well-known writings of A. A. Berle on the separation of ownership and control of the modern corporation and on new roles of property and of corporate bureaucrats.

Many economists have been skeptical about this new capitalism. Edward S. Mason, a judicious scholar of industrial organization, has gently debunked it. A more cavalier rejection is provided by Jack Hirshleifer:

> There are several interesting things about this defense of capitalism —that capitalists are really not selfish after all. The first is that, as a defense, it is a hopeless failure. There are many reasons why this argument must fail, but perhaps the most conspicuous reason is that it is untrue. . . . What does all this prove? Simply that all the world is largely governed by self-interest, and all the world knows it. . . .[8]

Of course, every schoolboy knows that "what everybody knows" is true only about half the time. Although I agree that there is exaggeration in the new view, the matter cannot be carried far by *a priori* reasoning.

My colleague, Morris A. Adelman, in a too-little known essay, "Some Aspects of Corporate Enterprise," [9] has emphasized some of the limits of corporate political power. He has also emphasized that in these days the political power of many small businesses is more potent than that of giant corporations. Congressmen know that. Often a large firm will try to get an association of small firms linked to its cause; and an outsider is amused to see an international oil firm frightened of its domestic subsidiary, when the latter has powerful allies among the small, but numerous, local producers. General Motors would be foolish to risk

---

[8] Jack Hirshleifer, Capitalist Ethics—Tough or Soft?, *Journal of Law and Business*, II (October 1959), p. 116. E. S. Mason, The Apologetics of "Managerialism," *The Journal of Business*, XXXI (January 1958), pp. 1–11.

[9] In R. E. Freeman, ed., *Postwar Economic Trends in the United States*, Harper, New York, 1960, pp. 291–307, particularly pp. 299–302.

the wrath of Congress by pushing its dealers around, and many a giant has been blackmailed by its numerous pygmies. Although one group may have a controlling vote in a corporation, in politics it is still one vote for one head. (The coefficients of reactionariness and of bigness are certainly *not* correlated in any simple, positive fashion.)

Adelman also has some trenchant remarks on the corporation as a profit maximizer, and I think Earl Cheit and he would form a heroic minority of dissenters against the fashionable interpretation of the Berle–Means thesis concerning dispersed ownership of corporations and its separation from management control. By and large, what is good for General Motors *is* good for Charles E. Wilson, GM president. This does not ignore the existence of some conflicts of interest between ethical and unethical inside officers. Degree of concentration of ownership among different corporations turns out on sober examination to have few predictive consequences for corporate behavior. Standard Oil of New Jersey has employee board members. Some oil companies have family control. What differences in behavior are traceable to this difference? More research would be needed to give a significant answer to this question—a fact that you might not guess from reading the vast literature on this subject.

As Adelman has indicated, simple profit maximizing for owners and exercising trusteeship for pluralistic claimants do not lead to very significant differences in behavior. To be significantly different, a change must make a difference. When it is damnably difficult to make an operationally meaningful experiment (even in principle) in order to detect a difference, why care much? For example, some economist friends work for one of the largest companies in the world. In privacy, they have tried to get top management to admit that it "really acts so as to maximize long-run profits." They have never been able to squeeze out such an admission. Is this surprising? The men at the top are *not* completely free wills. But they have spent most of their 40 years of adulthood with the company; the crises in their lives—the "hard times"—have no more been associated with stockholder pressure than with pressure from government and labor. But suppose that such an admission had been wrung out of them?

What difference would it have made? Really none at all, since this company acts much like its rivals, which are organized differently. Economists are like pedants (a redundancy!) in wanting to save the face of their principles even when naught is at stake.

If it is wrong to think that separation of ownership and control makes a great deal of difference, that does not mean that corporations can be regarded as simple conduits for funneling earnings into the hands of owners and for funneling decisions of owners into corporate acts. Large corporate oligopolies have considerable degrees of freedom in the short run (and to a degree even in the long run), which atomistic competitors lack. The folkways and mores that these authorities follow are, therefore, somewhat indeterminate and tend to be self-determining by the group.

Corporations act *as if* they were independent entities; ask any fund raiser, and he will tell you that. Corporations have behavior patterns, personalities, and styles. It is witchcraft to impute these persistent patterns of behavior back to something antecedent to the corporation called "owners," and Occam's razor can kill off these antecedent spirits. Corporations have attitudes toward Negroes and Jews, toward wage rates and work conditions, toward research and charity. To say that the vast differences in behavior between U. S. Gypsum and National Gypsum are merely reflections of the personal tastes of a man called Avery and a man called Baker is either to be saying nothing or to be saying something wrong. When Sewell Avery died, U. S. Gypsum did not change *its* spots.

Just as we call a spade a spade, we must call a corporation an actor in the scenario of economic life—no different from the rest of us puppets. This is quite distinct from the normative question whether it would be a bad thing for corporations to exercise independent choices in the pursuit of goals other than simple profit maximization. Professors Hirshleifer and other writers of the Chicago school have expressed disapproval of any such actions. There is little that is compelling in such opinions. Contrary to allegation, economic theory does not tell us that a farmer should first maximize his profits and then satisfy his personal utilities and tastes. There is no such inherent separation of functions, either in fact or in ideal theory. Similarly, in a diverse corporation there is no basis in economic theory for the assertion that decisions *should* be taken so as to maximize that single thing called "profit." Although it is possible that observing economists could more simply predict the behavior of entities that maximize a simple magnitude called "dollar profit," there is no reason why the world should accommodate itself to our desire for a lazy life.

If it comes to ethical issues of value judgment, I, for one, can as easily imagine a good society in which corporations freely act according to certain patterns as one in which private individuals are given the ostensible power to make decisions about fair employment and other practices. Indeed, one of the few positive arguments for bigness in corporations is that such entities are less able to break the law and resist the social pressures of democracy. The family farmer can and will cheat where the vast corporate farmer will not. Altruism is a scarce good, and corporations may help society economize on its use.

Explaining the Business Creed

By far the most important attempt to describe and explain the business ideology is that of Francis X. Sutton, Seymour E. Harris, Carl Kaysen, and James Tobin in the *American Business Creed*.[10] Although they are friends, I think no one will think me partial when I call them the cream of the elite of American scholarship. Here a leading sociologist, disciple of Talcott Parsons and Ford Foundation administrator, teamed up with three economists of the highest distinction. Without disrespect to my profession, one must admit that here is a case where the three economists seem pretty much won over to the view of the sociologist. (This must be qualified by the recognition that economists have never been happy about the fashionable economic interpretation of history or of events; those who knew little of technical economics have been the ardent boosters of the doctrine that economic interests are dominant in life.)

[10] Harvard University Press, Cambridge, Mass., 1956, and Schocken Paperback, New York, 1962, hereafter referred to as Sutton et al.

Their book has received a fair measure of attention but, except among connoisseurs, not nearly the attention it deserves. Its value is great, even though—as will become evident—I think it has essentially failed in its attempt to explain business ideology in terms of a theory of "strain" in the business role. This failure, I cannot help but think, throws some light on the weakness of our present-day best sociology. In the brief space at my disposal and in view of my amateur status in these realms, I make no pretence to giving a convincing proof of the view that I have just expressed. Certainly I shall not pretend to put up a better theory than the one I criticize; but I do not think that criticism is beside the point, if it is not able to be constructive and to provide a superior alternative to what is being criticized. They also serve who merely point out that the emperor has no clothes or that the clothes he does not have fit badly.

It will be economical of space if I first quote at some length from these authors. (In every case, the emphasis is mine.)

Our aim in this study is to answer the questions: Why does the business ideology say what it does? On what theory can the themes, symbols, arguments, which form the business ideology be explained? . . . To reach the answer to our ultimate question, we first seek to define the general role of ideologies in social life. We find our answer, broadly speaking, in the strains and conflicts inherent in every institutional position in a complex society, whether the position be that of businessman, or university professor, or labor leader. These conflicts are of several kinds: conflicts between the demands of the particular position and the broader values of society; gaps between the demands of social positions and the capabilities of the human beings who hold them to fulfill these demands; inherently conflicting demands built into the social definition of certain positions. This general proposition is applied to an investigation of the particular strains inherent in the business role in the United States, and the major themes of business ideology are shown as verbal and symbolic resolutions of these conflicts. This is our central proposition . . . (page vii).

We have rejected the "interest" theory, that ideologies simply reflect the economic self-interest, narrowly conceived, of their adherents. Ideology, in this view, is merely an attempt to manipulate symbols and marshal arguments which will persuade others to take actions from which the ideologist stands to profit financially. The ideologist may or may not believe the things he says. If he does happen to believe them, it is maintained, it is only because he has succeeded by wishful thinking in convincing himself that truth and self-interest coincide.

The "interest theory" contains important elements of truth. It is easy to understand why the ideology of the domestic watch industry, both management and labor, features support of tariff protection and includes all the venerable arguments and symbols which might persuade the Tariff Commission, the Congress, and the public of the protectionist case. Were this the model for all ideology, there would indeed be little problem of explanation and little need for our book. Actually the relationship between specific ideologies and economic interest is seldom so clear. A more typical example is provided by the passionate support a businessman gives to the principle of a *balanced federal budget.* We surely cannot conclude that he has reached this position by sober calculation of his profit prospects *under balanced and unbalanced budgets.* Assessing the ultimate effects of alternative budgetary policies on the profits of a specific business firm is a formidable econometric problem. Yet businessmen speak on the subject with such confidence, emotion, and unanimity that, in the "interest theory" of ideology, we would be forced to conclude that they have no trouble knowing on which side of the issue their economic interests lie, and that varying effects on different groups of businessmen are never to be anticipated.

It is true that with sufficient ingenuity one can construct a chain which reconciles practically any ideological position to the economic interest of its holder. Or one can make the task easier by attributing to the ideologist a mistaken or unduly certain conception of his own interest. One can make the task still easier by widening the notion of self-interest to encompass psychological satisfactions other than economic returns. But these expedients are really the end of the theory they are designed to salvage. They reduce it to a tautology: "Men act in their own interests" becomes "Men act as they are motivated to act" (pages 12–13).

. . . Why do businessmen so fiercely oppose *deficit financing* on the part of the government? Such opposition cannot be the result of a rational calculation of their tangible interests. In the short run many businesses (for example, construction firms) stand to gain from this policy. It is possible that in the long run, business interests may be injured by *deficit financing,* but it is certainly not inevitable. In any particular instance it is exceedingly difficult if not impossible to assess the remote consequences of *deficit financing.* And so there is **no** rational basis for the simplicity and certainty of business opposition.

If we stick to a theory of rational self-interest we can only dismiss examples such as this as evidence of ignorance or error. But this is obviously unsatisfactory. . . .

The clearest way to give the theory a definite character is to equate interests with objective, private economic advantage. Formulated in this way, the interest theory, *as our deficit financing example shows,* simply cannot account for a considerable part of the business ideology (pages 303–304).

A Trial Balance

Where do such explanations get us? The simple notion of strain as nervous collapse, in which the businessman says gibberish because he is in a state, is, of course, not what is intended. This is a pity, in that the vulgarization of a theory usually contains its operationally meaningful content in the sense of logical positivism and Peirce-James pragmatism.

I do not think that vulgar or sophisticated self-interest theories have been given a fair shake by the authors. The space spent on refuting what they point out is the single most popular and natural theory is, by my count, amazingly small and amazingly repetitive. You cannot get very far in proving that Americans are very tall by telling anecdotes about how many tall men you know. And this is particularly the case, if you keep repeating the one name of John Kenneth Galbraith. Yet, as my repeated italicizing of words in the quotations from the Sutton book will show, about the only case they cite in which businessmen *seem* to be acting against self-interest is the case of opposition to deficit spending (and we might add to expansionary monetary policy). Where are the hundreds of other examples? I believe I could find half a dozen, and no doubt they could triple this number. But I suspect that the end product will not be terribly impressive. Personal views, in fact, rarely contradict personal interest. Read the papers for a month and count the score.

I agree that it is a terribly interesting question why business generally has been antiexpansionary in the area of aggregate demand. I wish the authors had addressed themselves more specifically to it. Indeed, they cite, but do not really linger on, the attempt made by Sidney S. Alexander [11] to tackle this very problem. I must report that there is more wisdom *on this specific matter* in the short essay by Alexander than in their whole book (and yet Alexander would be the first to admit that he has not said the last word on the puzzle).[12]

In my limited space I can say but little on this specific subject. Let me stress that macroeconomics is not an easy problem for a businessman or any lay person to understand. Moreover, I am not sure that businessmen are *in the concrete* opposed to expansionary policies. They have trouble in rationalizing their frequent longing for such policies, which seems to me to be natural. But when it counts, the defense producers are eager for increased expenditures. We have had much recent experience that business, if it can save face and get *its* kind of tax cut, is willing to let deficits soar in a good cause. General Motors has repeatedly criticized tight money, when it hurt sales of cars on credit. Bankers, who benefit from tight money, are its most vocal exponents.

To make the point that businessmen believe in what they say publicly, the authors quote a public opinion poll showing that the business ideology on budget balancing is that "of the population at large; a variety of polls indicates that the people as a whole are 'budget balancers,' and it seems safe to infer that the polled sentiments of businessmen would show the same pattern" (page 324). If true—and in a degree this is true—what has become of their one case where a strain theory proves to be the superior one? There is apparently no peculiar business view here that has to be explained by peculiar business-role strain!

[11] S. S. Alexander, Opposition to Deficit Spending for the Prevention of Unemployment, in Alvin H. Hansen et al., eds., *Income, Employment and Public Policy*, Norton, New York, 1948.

[12] Alexander classified business opposition to deficit financing under four headings: misunderstanding of the validity of the mechanism; desire to have slack labor markets to keep worker performance high relative to wages; class antagonism, which associates deficit spending with other liberal programs that are against business; fear of increasing power of the state and of groups other than the business elite. Interestingly, he omits opposition to inflation, even though he wrote during the 1947–48 postwar inflation.

I suspect that the Sutton group somewhat exaggerates the element of unpleasant strain involved in business, perhaps because of the natural tendency of any academic person to suppose that others experience the discomfort that *he* would experience if placed in business life. The great Cambridge physicist, J. J. Thomson (discoverer of the electron), was once asked how he felt about the fact that any broker in the City made three times the income he did as a professor. "But just think of the work they have to do," he replied. Like most academics, he used his preferences to project into the business role strains and unpleasantnesses that businessmen may not feel. Brokers like being brokers, hard as that is for professors of botany to believe. Business is a great game to many people. It is a relatively well-paid game, as every prospective father-in-law knows. A second-class violinist in the family is a tragedy; a third-class businessman is someone you can lean on in your old age.

In every country the party of business is the more conservative party. In every case, when it comes to marginal decisions that bear on business interests, the party of business acts friendlier to those interests. Why then deny or overlook the obvious? Admittedly, no *explanation* has been provided by this recognition. But that is no reason to reject the fact. We laugh when a Molière character speaks of the power of opium to induce sleep *because* of its "soporific" quality; however, that should never make us overlook the fact that opium does induce sleep.

Rich and (what is not necessarily the same thing) acquisitive men do labor under the strain of being natural objects of dislike and envy. The Bible tells us that and so does a theory of self-interest. It is hard for people to believe that the road to heaven is paved with selfish intentions, even when it is true. That much I grant to the business-strain theory.

In its wider sense, a strain theory that finds associated with each occupation a characteristic strain explaining its ideology comes full circle to a materialistic interpretation of ideology of the Marxian type. To see this, repeat the word "strain" over and over again. It is like repeating "ice-cream cone" over and over again; the words begin to lose meaning. But in the last case, the mind's eye can keep looking at the dripping cone.

However, since strain does not mean anything so concrete as biting one's nails or experiencing facial tics and the shakes,[13] one can replace "strain" by x. A farmer believes in this or that because of the x of the farmer trade; the money lender believes what he believes because of his job's x. Why not cancel out the x and stick to the bare facts of differential ideologies, pending the time when fewer x factors than occupations can be found to provide a mnemonic pattern. On the whole, I am left with the impression that an interests-cum-prestige theory provides more of a simplifying pattern than any proposed alternative.

I could go on giving criticisms; they are not intended to be captious but are merely copied from the margin of my copy of their book. But I have said enough to demonstrate my disappointment with the strain theory of business ideology. Let me repeat that the Sutton group has been led to observe things about business strains that are interesting for their own sake, even where they fail to explain the business creed.[14]

Up to now I have largely discussed the problem of explaining business ideology without giving my evaluation of its intrinsic content. My remaining task is to appraise the specific part of it that relates to freedom and coordination.

II

As a prelude to discussing the empirical and analytical relations between business and personal freedoms (which is roughly the distinction between economic and political freedoms), I might usefully give some reflections on the nature of individualism, liberty, freedom, coercion, and the marketplace.[15]

---

[13] Apparently actuarial statistics do not show relatively more heart attacks and ulcers among business decision makers than among routine workers.

[14] One can derive a superficial explanation of intellectuals' behavior from a retaliating use by a businessman of the Sutton-Parsons strain theory of academic life.

[15] Some of the following thoughts appeared in two recent lectures. Since I do not believe in elegant variations, some of the words that follow will be in the same sequence as is published elsewhere. I own to no sense of self-plagiarism since, as indicated there, many of those words were stolen from the present research investigation.

How Divine the Natural Order?

Adam Smith, our patron saint, was critical of state interference of the prenineteenth-century type. And make no mistake about it; Smith was right. Most of the interventions into economic life by the state were then harmful both to prosperity and freedom. What Smith said needed to be said. In fact, much of what Smith said still needs to be said; good intentions by government are not enough; acts have consequences that must be taken into account, if good is to follow.

One hundred per cent individualists concentrate on the purple passage in Adam Smith, where he discerns an Invisible Hand that leads each selfish individual to contribute to the best public good. Smith had a point; but he could not have earned a passing mark in a Ph.D. oral examination by explaining just what that point was. Until this century, his followers—such as Bastiat—thought that the doctrine of the Invisible Hand meant (1) that it produced maximum feasible total satisfaction, somehow defined; or (2) that it showed that anything resulting from the voluntary agreements of uncoerced individuals must make them better (or best) off in some important sense.

Both of these interpretations, which are still held by many modern libertarians, are wrong. They neglect the axiom concerning the ethical merits of the preexisting distribution of land, property, and genetic and acquired utilities. This is not the place for a technical discussion of economic principles, so I shall be very brief and cryptic in showing this.

First, suppose that some ethical observer, such as Jesus, Buddha, or for that matter, John Dewey or Aldous Huxley, were to examine whether the total of social utility (as that ethical observer scores the deservingness of the poor and rich, saintly and sinning individuals) was actually maximized by 1860 or 1964 laissez-faire. He might decide that a tax placed upon yachts whose proceeds go to cheapen the price of insulin to the needy

---

George J. Stigler and P. A. Samuelson, *A Dialogue on the Proper Economic Role of the State,* Graduate School of Business Selected Papers No. 7, 1963; P. A. Samuelson, Modern Economic Realities and Individualism, *The Texas Quarterly* (Summer 1963).

increased the total of utility. Could Adam Smith prove him wrong? Could Bastiat? I think not.

Of course, they might say that there is no point in trying to compare different individuals' utilities, because they are incommensurable and can no more be added together than can apples and oranges. But if recourse is made to this argument, then the doctrine that the Invisible Hand maximizes total utility of the universe has already been discarded. If they admit that the Invisible Hand will truly maximize total social utility *provided the state intervenes so as to make the initial distribution of dollar votes ethically proper,* then they have abandoned the libertarian's position that individuals are not to be coerced, even by taxation.

In connection with the second interpretation that anything resulting from voluntary agreements is in some sense, *ipso facto,* optimal, we can reply by pointing out that when I make a purchase from a monopolistic octopus, that is a voluntary act; I can always go without Alka Seltzer or aluminum or nylon or whatever product you think is produced by a monopolist. Mere voluntarism, therefore, is not the root merit of the doctrine of the Invisible Hand; [16] what is important about it is the system of

[16] Milton Friedman, *Capitalism and Freedom,* University of Chicago Press, Chicago, 1962, Chapters 1 and 2 seem grossly defective in these matters. In the first chapter, he regards market behavior as optimal merely because it is voluntary, save for the single passage: ". . . perhaps the most difficult problems arise from monopoly—which inhibits effective freedom by denying individuals alternatives to the particular exchange" and promises to discuss this matter in more detail in the next chapter. It turns out there that "Exchange is truly voluntary only when nearly equivalent alternatives exist." Why this new element of alternatives? Because, as I point out, *perfect* competition is efficient in the Pareto-optimality sense, and it is this property that modern economists have *proved* optimal (and interesting) about such competition.

Libertarians, like Hayek and von Mises, would be annoyed to learn that their case stands or falls on its nearness to "perfect competition." Unlike George J. Stigler and Milton Friedman, neither of these two men has remotely the same views on perfect competition as do modern economists generally. What libertarians have in common is the hope that departures from perfect competition are not too extreme in our society; Friedman, himself, has apparently come full circle to the view that public regulation of "monopoly" and state regulation of "monopoly" are greater evils than letting well enough alone. I do not feel competent to report on the algebraic degree

checks and balances that prevails under perfect competition, and its measure of validity is at the technocratic level of efficiency, not at the ethical level of freedom and individualism. That this is so can be seen from the fact that such socialists as Oskar Lange and A. P. Lerner have advocated channeling the Invisible Hand to the task of organizing a socialistic society efficiently.

The Cash Nexus

Just as there is a sociology of family life and of politics, there is also a sociology of individualistic competition. It need not be a rich one. Ask not your neighbor's name; enquire only for his numerical schedules of supply and demand. Under perfect competition, no buyer need face a seller. Haggling in a Levantine bazaar is a sign of less-than-perfect competition.

These economic contacts between atomistic individuals may seem a little chilly or, to use the language of wine tasting, "dry." This impersonality has its good side. Negroes in the South learned long ago that their money was welcome in local department stores. Money can be liberating. It corrodes the cake of custom. It does talk. In the West Indies there is a saying, "Money whitens." Sociologists know that replacing the rule of status by the rule of contract loses something in warmth; it also gets rid of some of the bad fire of olden times.

Impersonality of market relations has another advantage, as was brought home to many "liberals" in the McCarthy era of

---

of his agreement with Stigler and others who put considerable emphasis on antitrust action. [There appears to me to be a technical flaw in the view of Friedman and A. P. Lerner that regulated or publicly owned monopolies should always (as a matter of principle as well as pragmatic expediency) be permitted to have competition from free entrants. The mathematics of the increasing-returns situation admits of no such theorem; it is simply false game theory and bilateral monopoly theory, which asserts that letting one more viable person in the game must lead to a "better" result in any of the conventional senses of better. To make the Scottish Airlines keep up unprofitable schedules and at the same time permit a free enterpriser to make a profit partially at the regulated lines' expense can easily result in dead-weight loss to society under the usual feasibility conditions. The crime of legally abolishing the Pony Express because it competed with the Post Office would have to be examined on all its complicated demerits.]

American political life. Suppose it were efficient for the government to be the one big employer. Then if, for good or bad, a person becomes in bad odor with government, he is dropped from employment and is put on a black list. He really has no place to go then. The thought of such a dire fate must in the course of time discourage that freedom of expression of opinion that individualists most favor.[17]

Many of the people who were unjustly dropped by the federal government in that era were able to land jobs in small-scale private industry. I say small-scale industry, because large corporations are likely to be chary of hiring names that appear on anybody's black list. What about people who were justly dropped as security risks or as members of political organizations now deemed to be criminally subversive? Many of them also found jobs in the anonymity of industry.

Many conservative people, who think that such men should not remain in sensitive government work or in public employ at all, will still feel that they should not be hounded into starvation. Few want for this country the equivalent of Czarist Russia's

[17] F. A. Hayek, *The Road to Serfdom*, University of Chicago Press, Chicago, 1944, p. 119, aptly presents the following quotations from Lenin (1917) and Trotsky (1937):

The whole of society will have become a single office and a single factory with equality of work and equality of pay.

In a country where the sole employer is the State, opposition means death by slow starvation. The old principle: who does not work shall not eat, has been replaced by a new one: who does not obey shall not eat.

M. A. Adelman in Freeman, *op. cit.*, p. 295, says:
. . . It has probably become clearer in the last ten years that the chief objection to socialism is not strictly economics but lies rather in its startling resemblance to the oldfashioned mining town where the one employer was also the landlord, the government, the school, etc., with the vital difference that there was a world outside the town which afforded means of escape for a few and, in time, of release for all.

See also the valuable words on this matter in Friedman, *op. cit.*, pp. 20–21.
David McCord Wright, *Democracy and Progress*, Macmillan, New York, 1948, p. 41, has observed: "Main Street creates the very diffusion of authority which protected them [the intellectuals] from Main Street."

Siberia or Stalin Russia's Siberia either. It is hard to tell on the Chicago Board of Trade the difference between the wheat produced by Republican or Democratic farmers, by teetotalers or drunkards, Theosophists or Logical Positivists. I must confess that this is a feature of a competitive system that I find attractive.

Still, I must not overstress this point. A mixed economy in a society where people are by custom *tolerant* of differences in opinion may provide greater personal freedom and security of expression than does a purer price economy where people are less tolerant. Thus, in Scandinavia and Great Britain civil servants have, in fact, not lost their jobs when parties with a new philosophy come into power. In 1953, the Eisenhower Administration "cleaned house" in many government departments for reasons unconnected with McCarthyism. In 1951, when the Tories came to power, they deliberately recruited Fabian socialists to the civil service! Business freedoms may be fewer in those countries, but an excommunist probably meets with more tolerance from employers there.

This raises a larger question. Why should there be a perverse empirical relation between the degree to which public opinion is, in fact, tolerant and the degree to which it relies on free markets? In our history, the days of most rugged individualism —the Gilded Age and the 1920's—seem to have been the ages least tolerant of dissenting opinion.[18]

Fallacy of Freedom Algebra

I must raise some questions about the notion that absence of government means increase in "freedom." Is freedom simply a

[18] Years ago someone asked me, "Why is it that economists who are most libertarian in economic philosophy tend to be personally more intolerant than the average and less concerned with civil liberties and such matters?" I replied, "Is this true?" He said, "Look at the monolithic character of the three most libertarian departments of economics." I said, "The three departments most radical or anything else can hardly be expected to show average tolerance of differences." Our conversation broke off. However, in the last dozen years I have been alert to observe the attitudes and actions of economic libertarians in connection with nonmarket issues—teachers' oaths, passport squabbles, and the like. I am sorry to have to report that my friend

quantifiable magnitude, as much libertarian discussion seems to presume? Traffic lights coerce me and limit my freedom. Yet in the midst of a traffic jam on the unopen road, was I really "free" before there were lights? And has the algebraic total of freedom, for me or the representative motorist or the group as a whole, been increased or decreased by the introduction of well-engineered stop lights? Stop lights, you know, are also go lights.

Whatever may have been true on Turner's frontier, the modern city is crowded. Individualism and anarchy will lead to friction. We now have to coordinate and cooperate. Where cooperation is not fully forthcoming, we must introduce upon ourselves coercion. When we introduce the traffic light, we have, although the arch individualist may not like the new order, by cooperation and coercion created for ourselves greater freedom.

The principle of unbridled freedom has been abandoned; it is now just a question of haggling about the terms. On the one hand, few will deny that it is a bad thing for one man, or a few men, to impose their wills on the vast majority of mankind, particularly when that involves terrible cruelty and terrible inefficiency. Yet where does one draw the line? At a 51 per cent majority vote? Or, should there be no action taken that cannot command unanimous agreement—a position toward which such modern exponents of libertarian liberalism as Professor Milton Friedman are slowly evolving. Unanimous agreement? Well, virtually unanimous agreement, whatever that will come to mean.

The principle of unanimity is, of course, completely impractical. Aside from its practical inapplicability, the principle of unanimity is theoretically faulty. It leads to contradictory and intransitive decisions. By itself, it argues that just as society should not move from laissez-faire to planning because there will always be at least one objector, so society should never move from planning to freedom because there will always be at least one objector. Like standing friction, it sticks you where you are. It favors the status quo. And the status quo is certainly

had a point (although there are one or two persons who are residuals from his regression).

not to the liking of arch individualists. When you have painted yourself into a corner, what can you do? You can redefine the situation, and I predicted some years ago that there would come to be defined a privileged status quo, a set of natural rights involving individual freedoms, which alone requires unanimity before it can be departed from.[19]

At this point the logical game is up. The case for "complete freedom" has been begged, not deduced. So long as full disclosure is made, it is no crime to assume your ethical case. But will your product sell? Can you persuade others to accept your axiom, when it is in conflict with certain other desirable axioms?

Property and Human Rights

Closely related to ethical evaluation of business activity for its own sake are ethical attitudes towards the rights of property. Today, demagogues never tire of emphasizing the primacy of human over property rights; this is not an accident but rather a recognition that such sentiments evoke an increasingly resonant response from modern public opinion.

Today when we defend the rights of property, we often do so in the name of the *individual* rights of those who own property or hope one day to do so. The tides of modern politics pay little regard to the older view that property in all its prerequisites is a natural right and that whenever the democratic action of even $99\frac{44}{100}$ per cent of the electorate limits property rights

[19] A friend of mine is a justly famous expert on law. He has participated in world conferences, here and behind the Iron Curtain, dealing with such weighty concepts as "the Rule of Law." Apparently, the Russians do not view the matter in quite his way. I am not sure I do. After listening to his view, an eminent judge asked him, "Was slavery in Virginia in 1859 contrary to your 'Rule of Law'?" My friend squirmed. Finally, he replied, "Yes, really. Because the law permitting slavery was essentially a *bad* law." I congratulated my friend on his good luck: how fortunate that he had happened to be born in just those few years of the globe's history when *the* Rule of Law (about equivalent to that approved by a conservative New-Deal type) happened to be in bloom. Libertarians like Hayek are on the same boat, but they want it to stop at a different port; Gladstone's age turns out to have been the nearest approach to *the* (I mean Hayek's) Rule of Law. F. A. Hayek, *op. cit.,* Chapter 6.

in any degree, then an act of theft has taken place. Instead, the effective defense of property rights consists largely of specifying the inefficiencies that will result at the level of means and mechanisms from their impairment—the paralysis of risk taking, the effects upon saving, efforts and incentives; the certain or uncertain ruin that must follow wherever taxation exceeds 10 (or 90) per cent of national income.

All this may be true enough. But for some people it does not go far enough. It is a little like the saying: "Honesty is the best policy." Or, "The golden rule is good business." Beyond the level of expediency, there can be thought to be human property rights at the ethical level in the sense that the individual's property is to be taxed or affected by state action only in an orderly manner, within the framework of constitutional procedures and with "due process" being legally observed.

As a bulwark to historical property rights, this is not saying very much. To say that the electorate cannot arbitrarily do something to one millionaire without doing the same thing to another (essentially similar) millionaire provides little protection to the class of all millionaires, some of whom may even have amassed their millions at a time when it seemed reasonable *not* to anticipate policies of heavy income or capital taxation. Whether we approve or disapprove, we should face squarely the fact that neoclassical economic-welfare policies—which hold that after the ethically desirable distribution of income has been properly determined by democratic decision, a pricing system is to organize and allocate production in response to individuals' purchases—provide little protection to ancient property rights.

Personal Liberties and Rights

This makes it all the more important to study the question of the relation of property rights and market institutions to essential individual freedoms and liberties. These were enumerated by Lord Beveridge in his *Full Employment in a Free Society* as

. . . freedom of worship, speech, writing, study and teaching; freedom of assembly and association for political and other purposes, including the bringing about of a peaceful change of the governing authority;

freedom of a choice of occupation; and freedom in the management of a personal income . . . including freedom to decide to spend now and save so as to have the power of spending later . . . it being recognized that none of these freedoms can be exercised irresponsibly. . . .

The list of essential liberties given above does not include liberty of a private citizen to own means of production and to employ other citizens in operating them at a wage. Whether private ownership of means of production to be operated by others is a good economic device or not, it must be judged *as a device.* (The italics are mine.) [20]

To Americans this British view is interesting, because the distinction is made clear-cut between (1) human individual civil liberties or freedoms and (2) ethical evaluations of property rights and of business activity for their own sakes. So-called diehard conservatives will not alone be shocked by the distinction. At the extreme left, violent exception will also be taken to the view that "political democracy" can exist in the absence of what is called "economic or industrial democracy." Both extremes seem to argue that the essential human freedoms are inseparable from the institutional framework under which production is carried on. But, of course, they believe this in diametrically opposite senses; the extreme conservatives at the ethical level link human freedoms with relatively unhampered free enterprise, whereas the extreme radicals proclaim that human freedoms are empty and meaningless in the absence of "industrial democracy" (in one or another of the many senses in which the last two words are used).

From the standpoint of pure logic, I believe that the two concepts are conceptually distinct at the purely ethical level of ends. Moreover, whatever its pragmatic wisdom, there appears to be nothing inherently illogical (whatever its wisdom) in the ethical belief that individual human liberties have an ethical primacy over the freedoms associated with property and commercial activity.

However, this brings us to a quite different, but possibly important, question: "Granted that human rights are to be accorded ethical primacy over property rights, is it not true that human rights can only flourish and be preserved in a society that organ-

[20] Norton, New York, 1945, pp. 21–23.

izes its economic activity on the basis of relatively free private enterprise?" Many economic libertarians strongly proclaim an affirmative answer to this question. Friedrich Hayek's *The Road to Serfdom* (1944) is an eloquent attempt to read this same empirical law in the tea leaves of history. Frank Knight and Milton Friedman have enunciated interesting views along the same line. It is ironical, but not incriminating, that this is a conservative's variant of the strong Marxian doctrine that economic relationships allegedly determine political relationships.

As stated, this is not at all a philosophical question. Nor is it very much a question of economics. It is primarily a political, sociological, and anthropological question. Basically, it is an empirical question of inductive extrapolation or forecasting rather than one of consistent logical deduction from universally true *a priori* premises. And unfortunately, the patterns of history have not been optimally designed to perform the controlled experiments that would enable us to make either certainty or probability inferences on the hypothesis in question.

It will be plain that I have little confidence in emphatic generalizations concerning the empirical linkage of human political rights with any one economic system. Evidence—as I understand this term—is not at hand to validate strong inferences; and such evidence as may exist has not, to my knowledge, been carefully brought together anywhere and sifted to bring out the degree of our knowledge and lack of knowledge. In a world where economists cannot even accurately predict national income one year ahead or identify the demand elasticity for a single commodity, I find it somewhat *simpliste* to think that economists can arrive at confident answers to an infinitely more complex and important question, resting primarily on noneconomic data. Certainly the degree of confidence and emphasis with which judgments on this matter are proclaimed seems to weaken rather than strengthen one's trust in their validity. I may add as a digression that I greatly resent the prevailing tendency to regard the broad questions of social development as being too important to be left to mere judicious scholarly investigation and to handle them instead by the transcendental poetic talents of a Toynbee or Spengler.

The Limited Nature of Individual Political Liberties

The above discussion has left civil liberties almost completely emasculated of intrinsic economic content. The doctrine "a man's home is his castle" is to apply to rented as well as self-owned homes. But some of the methods and tools used to analyze theoretical economic concepts do have an application in this field of political theory.

For one thing, basic civil rights of the individual are shot through with "external effects." The ideal frontier community never existed in which freedom for the individual meant that he could live on his acre of land exactly as he wished, leaving others to live as they chose on theirs. Certainly today, the right of one man to speak what he wishes conditions the rights of another man to listen to what he wishes. The right of one man to "fair" consideration for a job has implications for the right of another man to "discriminate" as to whom he shall hire. The right of one group to preach nondemocratic principles has effects on the future existence of democracy itself. In the pursuit of happiness, we all interact.

Once we have recognized these external aspects of individual rights, we must recognize that precious little is being said in the familiar qualification that people are free so long as they do not inhibit the freedom of others. Any degree of limitation on freedoms can be rationalized by this formula.

Dogmatic absolutes being thus ruled out, democratic society is left in the position of pragmatically attempting to choose among partial evils so as to preserve as much as possible of human liberties and freedoms. Nor is it only in time of war and siege that it may become necessary to sacrifice some aspects of democratic freedoms in order to prevent losing more important aspects. Those who abandon the unproved faith that democratic individualism *is by its nature viable under all conditions* must compromise with evil at every turn. And it is not at all unlikely that they will end up killing, in the name of its salvation, much of what they wish to save, perhaps in these "scorched earth" operations killing even more than realistically had to be sacrificed.

Final Questions

Consider the little that is known concerning the interrelations between human rights and the organization of economic activity in the U.S.A. (1870, 1920, 1964) and the U.K.; the German Empire, the Weimar Republic, and the Third Reich; Norway, Sweden, Denmark, Australia, and New Zealand; pre– and post–1917 Russia; Italy, Czechoslovakia, and the Balkans—to say nothing of China, Arabia, Fiji, and non-Western cultures. Then ask ourselves what simple truths can be confidently inferred.

For a quite different appraisal of these same matters consider, in the cited Friedman book, the first chapter, "The Relation Between Economic Freedom and Political Freedom." A few quotations cannot do him justice but can give the flavor of the divergence of his view from mine.

The citizen of Great Britain, who after World War II was not permitted to spend his vacation in the United States because of exchange control, was being deprived of an *essential* freedom no less than the citizen of the United States, who was denied the opportunity to spend his vacation in Russia because of his political views. . . .

The citizen of the United States who is compelled by law to devote something like 10 per cent of *his* income to the purchase of a particular kind of retirement contract, administered by the government, is being deprived of a corresponding part of his personal freedom (page 8). (My italics.)

So is the man who would like to exchange some of his goods with, say, a Swiss for a watch but is prevented from doing so by a quota. . . .

Historical evidence speaks with a single voice on the relation between political freedom and a free market. I know of no example in time or place of a society that has been marked by a large measure of political freedom, and that has not also used something comparable to a free market to organize the bulk of economic activity (page 9).

Economists love diagrams. Figures 1 and 2 plot economic freedom (as if it were measurable as a scalar) on the horizontal axes, and political freedom (as if that too were separately measurable as a scalar) on the vertical axes. What I regard as the grossly oversimplified views are shown in Figure 1. Social reform (moving "west") inevitably plunges society ("southward") into serfdom. Hayek does not tell us what his predicted delay period is, but since he formulated his thesis as early as 1938 (and using the simplifying assumption that we are not unknowingly now in serfdom), the mechanism must involve lags of more than a quarter of a century. Friedman also believes in strong positive correlation between Y and X but indicates that economic freedom is a necessary but not a sufficient condition for political freedom. (Sidney and Beatrice Webb, particularly in their final honeymoon stage of infatuation with Stalin's Russia, would relabel the axes as X = Economic Democracy—whatever that means—and Y = Political Democracy. The U.K. and U.S.A. they would place up in the northwest and, except *in extremis* of infatuation, would put Russia in the southeast. As Fabians, they would maneuver the U.K. eastward.)

Figure 2 represents the more relevant question. Will a little more of the welfare state push the U.S.A. westward and necessarily southward? For years libertarians have been challenged to explain what appears to most observers to be the greater political freedoms and tolerances that prevail in Scandinavia than in America. In Norway, a professor may be a communist; a communist may sit by right on the Board of the Central Bank

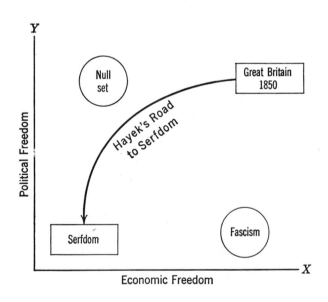

Figure 1

Personal Freedoms and Economic Freedoms

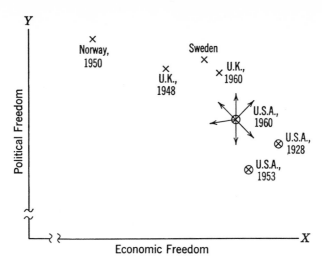

Figure 2

or as an Alternate Board member. The B.B.C. and Scandinavian airwaves seem, if anything, more catholic in their welcome to speakers of divergent views than was true in McCarthy America or is true now. In 1939, I was told that none of this would last; active government economic policy had to result in loss of civil liberties and personal freedoms. One still waits. Figure 2 does not represent my informed evaluation of the facts but merely poses the problem provocatively.

These are subjects that need serious empirical study, not strong *a priori* utterances or casual travelers' anecdotes.

BOOK FIVE

Economics — Past and Present

PART XVI

Essays in the History of Economics

182

REPLY

PAUL A. SAMUELSON

I undertook an obituary article on Dennis Robertson because I did not like the prospect that so major a writer would be permitted to slip into the sea without a suitable salvo. In preparing the essay, I reread all the published writings of Sir Dennis, an arduous but rewarding operation. I must confess that pressure of other work did not allow me to reread at the same time the collected works of my old friend from graduate school days at Harvard, Professor David McCord Wright.

Wright's assertion that my paper contained much that is controversial is true for at least three reasons: first, a logician will have noticed that his is by its nature a self-confirming proposition; second, Robertson often dealt with controversial matters; third, I deliberately chose unsettled topics, eschewing much that is important but securely established. Here are my brief reactions to the points raised concerning two longish paragraphs of my paper. I deal first with my complete paragraph on page 526, and then with the complete paragraph on page 523.

1. Will a permanent increase in the propensity to save — by itself, unaided by Pigou effects, price-*level* flexibility, or a decline in total income — lead to a lower level of interest rates? That is the problem that puzzles me in Robertson's discussions. And I may now add the further question suggested by Professor Wright's note. Will its *ceteris paribus* effect on the level of unemployment be presumably zero?

This is a question both about what would factually happen in a mixed system and about what complete equilibrium system Robertson had at least vaguely in the back of his mind. Personally, I should think that such a rise in thrift *might* lead to some permanent drop in the price and cost level, thereby (at least in some degree) preventing the drop in total money income from reflecting a drop in real income, real production, and employment. But that process and its concomitant lowered level of interest rates would involve the Pigou-Keynes effects which on my reading of Robertson (quite possibly incorrect) were not to be required. Still sticking to the probable factual outcome, I should not expect in our mixed society that there would emerge sufficient price-level flexibility to offset anywhere-nearly-completely the incipient "deflationary gap" engendered by the shift in the propensity-to-consume-and-to-save schedules. And in saying this, I wish to make clear that I am *not* thinking of deep-depression cases where there may be (i) liquidity traps of infinitely-elastic liquidity-preference schedules, or (ii) perfectly inelastic marginal-efficiency-of-investment schedules, or (iii) rigid fixed-proportions accelerator assumptions relating capital stock and consumption sales or consumption-plus-investment sales. In other words, mere *relative*-price flexibility between the bread and investment industries does not appear to me to be a realistic mechanism to rely on for any version of Say's Law that is to operate without dependence on Pigou-Keynes effects involving price-level changes.[1]

If Wright thinks otherwise I must, with respect, disagree.

2. I have studied my page 523 paragraph in the light of Wright's criticism, and I must confess that I still like it very much. Just now rereading the patient discussion in Professor Haberler's classic[2] on "The Over-Investment Theories" brought back to me the old feelings of puzzlement connected with the capital-shortage theories of Hayek and Spiethoff, a school with which Haberler properly associates some aspects of Robertson's writings. Furthermore, there is nothing in my paragraph at variance with staple notions like the following.

"Too much capital formation can lead to an inflationary gap, to an unmaintainable rate of expansion as high-employment and capacity ceilings are reached, and to a bounce-back into recession as profit hopes and expectations are changed. In modern and underdeveloped countries, restraints on over-all demand certainly may be desirable in order to achieve reasonable price stability, stretch out expansions, and accelerate sustainable growth rates." It is not the general notion that "too much investment (and total demand) *now* can lead to too little investment (and demand) *later*" which I find mystical. What I have always found puzzling was the version of capital-shortage theory which (from the pens of Hayek, Robbins, and others) asserted that expanding consumption spending in time

---

1. The logical, in contrast to factual, question is whether one can specify a rigorous system which, without price-*level* changes, has for its condition of settling down to a new equilibrium the restoration of full employment. If it can be found, it will provide a new version of Say's Law. Let me point out that, by adding saving directly into the liquidity preference equation $r = L$ $[M, Y, s(Y)]$, page 526, I did indicate one way sense might be made of the position tentatively assigned to Robertson. So it is not a question of logical impossibility that I was arguing about. Alas, in economics just about anything is a logical possibility.

2. G. von Haberler, *Prosperity and Depression* (Geneva: League of Nations, 1939), Chap. 3.

of slump would make that slump worse off by reinforcing the "shortage of capital" then. And I was happy to point out that Robertson concurred in this doubt.

3. I leave to a footnote [3] discussion of Wright's useful final footnote. May I conclude by asserting firmly: My mind — brilliant or not, influential or not — has not been "proved" guilty of coming "perilously close to nonsense." And, on a happier note, may I record the impression that Wright is in greater disagreement with me than I am with him?

3. My discussion of Robertson's crucial fractions and the "real bill doctrine" — that meeting the legitimate needs of trade and industry will lead to optimal M and price stability — does need amplification. My example of a gratuitous doubling of M and the price level was designed merely to show that Robertson's fractional identities might be maintained but that *this* would be no guarantee against money mismanagement; and the example was germane to the contention (of economists generally) that there is no longest-run determinate level of *absolute* prices unless some restriction is placed on some *numéraire*, or money, or money-and-public-debt magnitude. But I should have added, and am grateful to Wright for raising the point, that Robertson performed a valuable function in pointing out that certain special empirical equivalences among M velocity, capital-output ratios, and bank finance would be required if "free" banking were not to initiate strong fluctuations in prices. In such harmonious cases, the guiding hand of society's controller of money and liquidity would still be needed, but perhaps its scale of operations could be much reduced.

I should like to mention here that David Meiselman, A. L. Marty, and other correspondents have called to my attention earlier references that could be added to my final footnote.

With the editor's indulgence, this is a convenient place to put into the record a disagreement with the criticism, contained in E. J. Mishan, "Say's Law and Walras' Law Once More," which appeared in the same issue as my Robertson piece. Dr. Mishan, pp. 621–23, alleges that Dorfman, Samuelson, and Solow, *Linear Programming and Economic Analysis* (New York: McGraw-Hill, 1958) perpetrated an error in stating an identity between total factor costs and total value of output in a conventional Walras-Cassel general-equilibrium system. Whether or not it was appropriate for Professor Oskar Lange to have analyzed realistic time-phased macrosystems in terms of the equations of Walras-Cassel, I do not believe it is appropriate to attach blame to them or to regard as erroneous the elucidation of functional identities in a nonlinear programming system. If a programmer were to state the fundamental duality theorem, "Max PX subject to $a > 0 \leqq ax \leqq L > 0$ is equal to Min WL subject to $Wa \geqq P > 0$," it would be ridiculous to criticize *him* for not having discussed hoarding, borrowing, saving, and investment. It would be equally ridiculous to reject every supply and demand intersection in Marshall's *Principles*. I leave it to the informed reader to decide whether Mishan's point is better taken.

MASSACHUSETTS INSTITUTE OF TECHNOLOGY

183

The Editorial Committee of the Review of Economic Studies decided to celebrate the sixtieth birthday of Professor A. P. Lerner by inviting Professor P. A. Samuelson to write an article in his honour in view of Professor Lerner's early association with the Review of Economic Studies. The initial initiative in this matter came from Professor Thomas Mayer.

A. P. Lerner at Sixty

1. *Skoal.* Abba Lerner has been a great theoretical economist in a vintage epoch for theorists. This last third of a century he has poured out one brilliant paper after another —in micro theory and macro, in pure thought and in the realms of policy. At every public gathering of the fold, it is his dynamic wit that brings up the house, and at any age he is still the glorious *wunderkind* of our guild. He was one of the young founders of the *Review of Economic Studies*. His contributions as much as anyone's made its first volumes so exciting. When the editors asked me to sing of the man and his work, I was delighted. For like Tom Sawyer, who enjoyed his own funeral, I believe the best wakes to be those in which the guest of honour is present in the full vigour of his powers. If you can't take it with you, why not get it long before you go?

2. *Portrait of the artist as a young blade.* I believe it was Wassily Leontief who once said you can gauge the quality of a scientist by his first paper. If Keynes and Walras are exceptions, Lerner certainly is high on the Leontief regression curve. His great 1932 paper, " The Diagrammatical Representation of Cost Conditions in International Trade "[1] was written after he had studied economics part-time for scarcely two years! Indeed in the 10 years after first beginning economics, Lerner had written top papers on (1) pure inter-national trade, (2) welfare economics, (3) elasticity of demand and substitution, (4) index numbers, and (5) Keynesian theory.

It tempts one to advise students in Economics A to quit college, fail in business, marry and raise a family, and resist being overpaid. Girl swimmers reach their peak at 15—something to do with metabolism perhaps. Lerner's virtuosity from the beginning disproves the notion that the years 17 to 21 are the crucial ones for prodigies. If we are to believe that he is now 60, he was 26 when John Hicks discovered his quality in an *LSE* class and called him to the attention of Lionel Robbins and he was 28 when his first paper appeared. Lerner's case, like that of Wicksell, reconfirms my suspicion that it may be the number of years after you *enter* economics that counts and not the number of years after birth. (Try the experiment of giving your uncle *and* your nephew a copy of Marshall next Christmas.)

Undoubtedly Lerner popped up at the right time in the right place. At *LSE* Lionel Robbins was the youthful professor, mentor, and friend of a group that included such names as R. G. D. Allen, Victor Edelberg, J. R. Hicks, Nicholas Kaldor, Paul Rosenstein-Rodan, Ursula Webb (Hicks), and others. What a collection!

Some twenty years ago I read a speech by Pigou, in which he reminisced about the good old days when the *Economic Journal* was founded. Giants walked the earth in those early Nineties. Poppycock, I thought. J. Shield Nicholson a giant? The economists of the 1930's could match the crew of any earlier age in quality, and overwhelm them in numbers. And of course I was right. If you don't believe me, ask any old-timer of my vintage.

---

[1] Unless otherwise indicated, cited articles appear in *Essays in Economic Analysis* (Macmillan, London, 1953), a collection of Lerner's papers.

3. *Words and pictures.* At first Lerner was known as a diagram man. In those days graphs did represent the frontier of our science. (When Ingram wrote a famous nineteenth century blast against mathematical economics, it was Marshallian supply-and-demand charts he was fulminating against! Each generation must carve out its own enemies.) A typical Lerner paper was brief, tightly packed with results, but straightforward and clear. From the beginning Lerner wrote ideal scientific prose—a lively and unpretentious style that the reader never noticed. What happened to the notion that good prose can be written only by those who have heard the King James version of the Bible from their mother's lips and who have turned Horace's faltering Latin into limpid English? The excellence of Abba Lerner's writing does not bear it out.

The brief 1933 articles on arc elasticity of demand and the elasticity of substitution might be termed finger exercises. But, like the practice scales of Bach, they reveal power. The ordinary formula for arc elasticity of demand that Hugh Dalton and other post-Marshallians used was $E_1 = -(\Delta Q/\Delta P)(P/Q)$. Applied to (100, \$100) and (101, \$99), this was often computed as $(1/1)(100/100) = 1$, even though total revenue declines by \$1 from the price cut. If we want $E \gtreqless 1$ according as total revenue rises, stays the same, or falls with a price cut, such a computation is defective. (However, the *other* Dalton measure $(1/1)(99/101) < 1$ *does* warn us that the isoelastic curve going through these two points is indeed inelastic.)

Lerner recalled Marshall's demonstration that the *point* elasticity on a straight-line DD curve equals the ratio of the line's length above the point to its length below the point. This rule holds for any curve, as we see when we recall that elasticity of a curve at a point equals elasticity computed for its tangent-straight-line at the point. Lerner proceeded then to generalize: between 2 separate points, draw a straight line from axis to axis; compute arc elasticity E_2 as the ratio of the line's length above the *upper* point to its length below the *lower* point. (A dual E_3 comes from interchanging upper and lower in the above sentence.) He pointed out that E_2, unlike Dalton's E_1, does provide a correct indicator of total revenue behavior.

This goes about as far as simple graphics can go. But why not provide a *direct* test of total revenue in the form: $E_4 = (P_L Q_U)/(P_U Q_L) = (99 \times 101)/(100)(100) = 9999/10,000 < 1$? (I inherited this formula at MIT in 1940, I suspect from Professor Emeritus Donald S. Tucker.) While E_4 satisfies the total revenue criterion, Lerner would clearly reject it on the ground that it depends on the *size* of the arc and approaches unity for *all* demand curves in the limit as the arc becomes small. However, if we add the new criterion that a measure of arc elasticity is to approximate as closely as possible to point elasticity—either asymptotically, or more strongly—then obviously the log formula $E_5 = -\Delta \log Q/\Delta \log P$ becomes defined as the only ideal one. (Had Lerner used log-log paper, his pencil and ruler would still have found employment.) Without intuition, graphics alone could not easily show that $E_6 = -(\Delta Q/\Delta P)(P_m/Q_m)$, where m stands for any symmetric mean (geometric, arithmetic, harmonic, etc.) would approach point elasticity with an error that becomes vanishingly small in comparison with the errors of either of Lerner's E_2 and E_3; however, any symmetric mean of *them* will agree to the same powers of $(\Delta P)^k$ in the Taylor's expansion of " error."

In the first and third editions of my ECONOMICS, I followed Lerner's E_2. But in the second and in later editions I used Stigler's $E_6 = -(\Delta Q/\Delta P)(\frac{1}{2}P_1 + \frac{1}{2}P_2)/(\frac{1}{2}Q_1 + \frac{1}{2}Q_2)$ because I got tired of receiving letters from students (and teachers!) thinking that I had made a slip in reasoning.

There is much more in early Lerner graphics worthy of extended comment. Need to keep this tribute down to finite length forces me merely to sample: but I must mention the quality of his definitive 1935 paper on the economic theory of index numbers, which well illustrates his ability to summarize the work of people like Könus, Staehle, Frisch, and Leontief—and to carry it forward.

4. *International trade.* The maiden 1932 *Economica* paper " The Diagrammatical Representation of Cost Conditions in International Trade ", was the first to combine Haberler's 1930 opportunity-cost or production-possibility frontier concept with collective indifference curves to show a two-country equilibrium of international trade. Much this same ground was covered by Leontief's celebrated 1934 *Quarterly Journal* article, " The Use of Indifference Curves in International Trade," and not until James Meade introduced the ingenious device of trade-indifference-curves (in *Geometry of International Trade,* 1952) was this staple analysis improved upon. There is no sign that Lerner had been particularly influenced by the earlier solutions of the simpler exchange problem by such writers as Jevons (1871), Walras (1874), Edgeworth (1881 and later), Pareto (1897 and later), or Bowley (1924); the time was ripe for adaptation of Haberler's P-P curve to the problem, and aside from Leontief, Viner had also developed this analysis in lectures given here and abroad. No one, however, equalled Lerner in the virtuosity with which he showed how P-P curves are to be optimally " added," matching equal slopes and generalizing inequalities in a modern manner. Already this paper lays the basis for production-optimality conditions in modern welfare economics, complementing the earlier Italian work of Barone (1905).

The only thing better than a Lerner paper is its sequel. The 1934 paper " The Diagrammatical Representation of Demand Conditions in International Trade " shows how to dispense with the incubus of collective indifference curves. We should let great men be their own improvers. Oddly enough, this paper starts out with a somewhat flimsy defense of collective indifference curves: First, he argues that the parts of a single man's mind—his desire for food as against fuel—are no more divided than that of a community in which some men are made better and some worse; hence, if indifference curves work for one man, they will work for two—a faulty argument. Second, he introduces the red herring that a single man's tastes for goods may depend on the work he does, as if this were a difficulty for an analyst not wedded to 2-dimensional graphs and as if this makes collective indifference contours no more vulnerable (to the contamination of tastes by production) than one-man contours. Third, the realistic fact of myopia, so that a man does not know his tastes well for distant situations, is somehow supposed to make collective indifference contours no-less-defensible than one-man contours. But his heart is not really in his work, and he notes explicitly that the " system may be considered as changing in shape as one moves along the path;" and he seems to realize that the concepts which can be used to depict certain aspects of the equilibrium after it is attained cannot be relied on to get you to the equilibrium.[1]

Fortunately, and this is the point of the 1934 paper, he realizes he can throw away the (inadmissible) community indifference curves and merely add up the net market demands of all persons in whatever country to find the equilibrium prices which clear all markets. In short the analysis has caught up with Walras (1874), Marshall (1879), Wicksell (1893); except for the generalization to n-goods and determination of its properties, the equilibrium model of Hicks *Value and Capital* (1939), Part II, is isomorphic with this paper (and both differ in production assumptions from a constant-returns-to-scale Clark-Walras world). Papers like these of Lerner's are so packed with results that few readers have ever gleaned all their fruits. (For example, on pp. 120-1 of *Essays*, there is foreshadowed an important *envelope* that I and others had to develop " independently " years later.)

---

[1] Even at this date one often meets the odd belief that Scitovsky or other collective indifference curves can provide as many equations as are needed to determine equilibrium. Except (1) where all men are identically identical (so each stands for any and all), (2) where indifference contours are homothetic so that every dollar has the same tastes, or (3) where lump-sum payments are made in the background to ensure maximization of a social welfare function, price ratios *cannot* be expressed as invariant functions of goods totals as collective indifference contours presuppose. But 25 years of scolding has made small dent on writers.

5. *Factor-price equalisation.* Between the dates of his classic 1932 and 1934 papers dealing with international cost and demand Lerner wrote, but did not publish, a brilliant proof of the conditions under which free trade in goods equalises international factor prices even when factors are immobile. The rediscovery of Lerner's paper is worth recounting again. After I had enunciated the same result in 1948, Lord Robbins mentioned to me that he thought he had a seminar paper in his files by Lerner of a similar type. His memory was better, apparently, than Lerner's. He exhumed this gem, which appeared 17 years later in the 1950 *Economica*. While one expects there to be but one logic, the parallelism of our researches is remarkable.

There is a further amazing parallel. When my 1948 *Economic Journal* paper appeared, Joan Robinson wrote to point out that if both goods have identical production functions, there will generally not be equalisation. This is a just observation, which points up the crucial need for factor-intensity assumptions. Now recall that everyone had forgotten the very existence of the 1933 Lerner paper, including Joan Robinson and its author. So you can imagine my surprise when, after Robbins sent me a copy of the paper, I found the footnote (p. 73 of *Essays*) where Lerner acknowledges this suggestion " by Mrs. J. Robinson of Cambridge." The French must have a saying for this sort of thing.

6. *Welfare economics.* If forced to choose among Lerner's many contributions, I suppose I should have to pick his work on welfare optimality, as exemplified in his masterly 1934 *RES* paper, " The Concept of Monopoly and the Measurement of Monopoly Power," his numerous writings on the economics of socialism, and culminating in his great *Economics of Control*. Although the writings of Pareto were known to economists at the *L.S.E.* of 30 years ago, the concept of Pareto-optimality had to be rediscovered individually by such people as Lerner, Kaldor, Hicks, and others. This is in part because Pareto is himself obscure and a bit confused; because the issue is a deep one; and because that is the way gifted scientists operate. The following 1934 passage shows how clear-sighted Lerner was in formulating the Edgeworth-Pareto contract-curve utility-frontier notion (all pages referring to *Essays*):

> The social optimum relative to any distribution of resources (or income) between different individuals (and we cannot here go into the problems connected with optimum distribution) will . . . show itself in *the impossibility of any individual being put in a preferred position without putting another individual in a worse position.* (p. 13).

Note that avoiding the excesses of the " new welfare economics," which tended to confuse ethical necessary with ethical sufficiency conditions, Lerner goes on[1] to identify the $P=MC$ optimality condition.

> From this analysis we see that the optimum is reached when the price reflects the alternatives given up at the margin, whether this alternative is considered in physical terms of some other commodity or whether we go direct to the satis-factions that the physical alternatives represent. The loss involved in monopoly can be seen in the divergence between price and this marginal cost. (pp. 18-19). Immediately this leads him to a measure of " degree of monopoly ".

> . . what we want in the measure of monopoly is not the amount of tribute

[1] Lerner's acknowledgment to V. Edelberg, p. 15 n. 1, for his crucial tangency diagram, stands as a worthy testament to that brilliant scholar. The graph has since become a staple; and those who are not reproducing it, are rediscovering it.

individuals can obtain for themselves from the rest of the community, by being in an advantageous monopolistic position, but the divergence of the system from the social optimum that is reached in perfect competition . . . [Here is the] formula that I wish to put forward as the measure of monopoly power. If P = price and C = marginal cost, then the index of the degree of monopoly power is $\frac{P-C}{P}$. (pp. 25-26).

Today this may seem simple, but I can testify that no one at Chicago or Harvard could tell me in 1935 exactly why $P=MC$ was a good thing, and I was a persistent Diogenes.

In rereading this paper for the present occasion, I find in it a clear recognition that Marshall's dictum, that one should tax increasing cost industries to subsidize decreasing (or constant!) cost industries, simply represents an error, being based upon Marshall's having forgotten to include the area of producers surplus in with his area of consumers surplus. (Lerner treats this as a well-known error!) The doctrine of pyramided harm in all layers of production resulting from P-MC discrepancies, which I have generally associated with the brilliant postwar works of McKenzie and Scitovsky, is also in this paper.

Along with so many flowers and fruits, an occasional weed is almost endearing. But weeds belong in footnotes [1] and, as usual, Lerner's later *Economics of Control* provides the most pungent refutation of the half-truth that proportionality of prices to marginal costs suffices for " optimum distribution of services between different commodities."

In the next section I shall comment on but one small part of the *Economics of Control*. So let me say here that it is a *tour de force* of non-mathematical exposition. Lerner concentrates on the optimum, never stooping to feasibility or second-best analysis. While he regards the book as a useful blue-print for social organization, I regard it primarily as an unequalled tone poem of necessary marginal efficiency conditions. It is didatic, polemical, and creative. One could thumb its pages and turn up interesting projects for further theoretical research.

7. *Equality and ignorance.* Like Benthamite utilitarians, Lerner evidently believes in cardinal utility for each man, which is subject to the Gossen-Bernoulli law of diminishing marginal utility. These individual concave (from below) utilities can be made commensurable and be added together to form total social utility, which is to be maximized. If people are all alike, or potentially all alike in the longer runs as environmentalists like Bentham and Mill believed, total U is maximized by an equal distribution of income (achieved by ideal lump-sum redistributions that have no distorting substitution effects). If people differ in pleasure capacities, maximum U requires an income distribution which equalizes (social) marginal utilities everywhere. All this is standard doctrine, known since Edgeworth and Carver of the 1890's; and except for probability considerations, it will perhaps appear to non-hedonists as rather naive ethics.

Robbins, in his 1932 *Essay on the Nature and Significance of Economics*, had pointed out that stating that Jones and Smith have unequal, or equal, marginal (social) utilities is not like stating the empirical fact that each has a nose or that they differ in height and in

---

[1] On p. 32, Lerner almost seems to be saying that equal degree of monopoly everywhere (including leisure!) is as good as zero degree, and that only the standard deviation of the degree of monopoly and not its mean value matters. Whether or not he momentarily became obscure, his later insistence on distortions of effort if $P \neq MC$ is the correct one.

demand elasticities for caviar; nor is it like stating that $2+2=4$, that *pauvreté* means poverty, or that raising output lowers total revenue when demand is inelastic. In short, as Bergson made clear in his classical 1938 *Q.J.E.* article on welfare economics, ethical postulates have to be postulated, not inferred from positive facts or deduced by logic. In *Economics of Control*, Lerner believes that we can never know, even approximately, that man 1's marginal utility is greater than or equal to man 2's; and this even though he is willing to insist on the postulate " that different people enjoy similar satisfactions." Yet he claims to state a remarkable theorem.

> " . . . If it is impossible, on any division of income, to discover which of any two individuals has a higher marginal utility of income, the probable value of total satisfactions is maximized by dividing income *evenly*." (p. 29).

While some reviewers, such as Meade (*E.J.*, 1948), have considered this an elegant demonstration, other economists have been puzzled by it. Call the *status quo A*, and equal incomes *B*. Suppose I cannot know whether *U* is higher in *B* than in *A*, but God or Plato can. Then the probability is either one or zero that an improvement has been made, depending upon whether $U(A) \gtreqless U(B)$. But if not even God can know after-the-fact whether $U(A) \lesseqgtr U(B)$, most people will think the whole exercise is pointless. So let us assume that God does know, but that we do not. We are still left with the query of how probability and repeated events come into the problem. There is only one *status quo*, and only one movement to equality, and only one answer possible as to whether *U* goes up or down—if only we knew it.

In many respects, however, the problem resembles that which arises in any life situation involving uncertainty. You toss a coin and hide the result from me. The probability of a heads, against a tails, is one or zero depending upon which (*you* see) has come up. But my degree of belief that it has come up heads is a personal probability; and if a jury observes with me that the coin has seemed always to exhibit symmetry properties, it will think me reasonable not to offer heavy odds that it will have come up one rather than the other. If this game is repeated again and again, I shall be deemed wise by the jury to act on the above strategy; but, wherever I am able to observe some asymmetry in the coin or its tossing, I shall likewise be wise to modify my rule accordingly.

In the case of the coin, symmetry suspicions represent a kind of assumption of " equal ignorance." What is Lerner's tacit assumption of equal ignorance? If asked whether there were more men or typewriters on the moon, perhaps he would guess them equal; if the question involved blond men, non-blond men and typewriters, perhaps he would guess them to be all equal. It will certainly spoil the fun at the beginning if he asserts that " from ignorance can come only ignorance."

Lerner's assumption of equal ignorance seems to be the following: at *A* let Man 1 be richer than Man 2; at *B* they are equally rich. Not knowing whether the *MU* schedule of Man 1, MU_1, is (uniformly) higher than MU_2, Lerner evidently thinks there are 3 possibilities: MU_1 schedule like MU_2; MU_1 higher than MU_2; MU_1 lower than MU_2. In the first of these 3 cases, equal distribution is obviously an improvement. Provided Lerner can postulate that the last two cases are equally likely, going from *A* to *B* will with equal probability make things worse or better. But the mean or expected value of the algebraic change in utility, taken over these equally-weighted cases, will be positive, as can be shown by simple calculus applied to concave functions (which says that a point half-way between two points *on* a concave curve will lie below the curve). Thus, for any two concave functions, $F_1(X)$, $F_2(X)$, with $F_i''(X) < 0$.

$$F_1(Y) + F_2(Y) < \tfrac{1}{2}[F_1(Y+h) + F_2(Y-h)] + \tfrac{1}{2}[F_1(Y-h) + F_2(Y+h)]$$

$$= \sum_1^2 \left\{ \tfrac{1}{2}F_i(Y+h) + \tfrac{1}{2}F_i(Y-h) \right\}$$

where each expression in the brackets is, for positive h, less than the corresponding $F_i(Y)$ value on the left-hand side. The above result holds for any number of summed concave F_i functions.

Well, what are we to think of Lerner's argument as spelled out here? Milton Friedman (in his 1947 *Journal of Political Economy* review article, which is reproduced in his *Essays in Positive Economics*) thought its assumptions and proof could be, and needed to be, restated in order to make it rigorous. The notion of " equal ignorance " stuck in Friedman's throat.[1] In place of " equal ignorance " Friedman gives (p. 308) the postulate " if individuals were classified by capacity to enjoy income, the probability distribution of income would be the same for all such classes." Let us apply this to a 2-man (or billion-man) universe. Does this mean that God will declare that, if the 2 men have different utility capacities, they must (already) have equal incomes? If so, rigor has produced a mouse, and not Lerner's mouse. If not, we are left with the problem. This, however, is not Friedman's birthday party and I must simply content myself with the observation that Friedman's discussion (pp. 308-9) does not appear to be a rigorous restatement of *my* interpretation of Lerner. Two footnotes further on I return to Friedman's analysis.

I should like now to propose a rather different formulation of the problem, one that is spiritually akin to Lerner's but which will not even require that different individuals' utilities be commensurable or addable. I shall show that, if the crucial equal-ignorance assumption were really acceptable to every reasonable observer, then each and every person (subject to the postulated concave utility that renders him a risk averter) would vote for a regime of equal-distribution of income, and this constitutional feature would be instituted by *unanimous* vote. It will suffice to state the following obvious theorem on (each) concave function:

> Let total social income be divided up into n non-negative magnitudes $(y_1, y_2, \ldots, y_n)$ with $\Sigma y_j = Y$ and let each y_i be written on a separate card. Now let the deck of cards be shuffled and be dealt out at random to each of us n individuals, so that every permutation is equally likely and each of us can expect with equal probability to receive each (y_i). Then you (and I) will prefer that all the y's be equal to $Y/n = \Sigma y_j/n$ rather than anything else (including the historical distribution of incomes under mixed capitalism). Thus, even if it makes no sense to sum different $F_i(y_i)$, the fact that each $F_i'' < 0$ implies

Each $\displaystyle\sum_{j=1}^{n} \frac{1}{n} F_i(y_j)$ is at a maximum subject to $\displaystyle\sum_1^n y_j = Y$

for $y_1 = y_2 = \ldots = y_n = Y/n$ where $F_i'(y_1) = \ldots = F_i'(y_n)$.

[1] Remember, he was writing in 1947, before Bayesian probability returned to fashion, and while readers of R. A. Fisher thought that the Master had successfully banished " inverse probability " from statistical inference, he not having yet made clear to them (and perhaps himself) that his somewhat mysterious notion of " fiducial probability " rested at bottom on some kind of balanced *ignorance*.

The problem has been reduced to one of prudent personal insurance. If inequality means a random dispersion around the equal-share value, all risk averters will vote égalitarian whether they be exquisite or coarse pleasure machines.[1]

Note that we have excluded God and Plato from the problem. And now each man will be in a position to critize the particular version of equal ignorance assumed by Lerner and us. If I have a beautiful singing voice, a pretty face, a high I.Q., an inherited title, or the gift of salesmanship, I shall be stupid to think that the égalitarian state is the safest hedged state *for me*. I don't expect the inégalitarian state to deal me a random selection of the cards. *My* ignorance is balanced around a favourable deal, and I shall certainly not make the vote unanimous even if I have concave utility. That is why the class struggle is a reality, even though it gets attenuated by the recognition emphasized here that the welfare state does provide certain elements of mutual insurance.[2]

Anyone with an ounce of philosophical leaning will be grateful to Abba Lerner for posing an intriguing problem, even if remaining doubtful that you can reap ethical results without planting ethical postulates (in the form of Bergson social welfare functions.)

8. *Macroeconomics.* In connection with this Review, Lerner contributed articles primarily in microtheory and this is the side I am now stressing. But, of course, he was one of the able converts to Keynes' *General Theory*. (When Newman went over to Rome, there were plenty to claim the credit. Credit, unlike cash, adds up to more than 100 per cent. Joan Robinson has told me that a certain weekend meeting on neutral ground of Cambridge, Oxford, and London economists was crucial in changing the Hayekian Saul into the Keynesian Paul; be that as it may, Lerner himself felt that the term he spent at Cambridge in the mid-1930's provided the basic stimulus.) Along with Kalecki, Robinson, Kaldor, and other stalwarts, Lerner helped spread the new Gospels. Young students who reread those writings may wonder today what all the shooting was about; may wonder whether the debaters on either side of the question, Does saving equal investment? stated the issues optimally; and may wonder, with hindsight, whether it was nec-

---

[1]One risk lover with convex (from below) utility will be a lonely soul with no one to gamble against. He will keep the vote from being unanimous since the insured position is a minimum for him. Two or more risk lovers will gamble together; the remainder of the populace will voluntarily mutually insure. If risk averters outnumber risk lovers, under democracy they will tend to coerce *all* into égalitarian legislation. The same self-interest which economists rely on to make people display predictable demand curves will make voters use the state to redistribute incomes. Since redistribution in real life can never be of the distortionless type, égalitarianism will not (and should not) be carried all the way. But, since it is a theorem that dead-weight distortion grows only with the squares of the amounts redistributed, the optimal compromise between " equity " and " efficiency " will always involve some sacrifice of the latter to the former (and vice versa).

[2]These considerations seem to cut also against the relevance of Lerner's equal ignorance postulate. Concretely, consider the issue of voting for *laissez faire*, A, or for equal shares, B. Certain groups will stand to benefit *systematically* under the former; Malthus knew that. Unless Plato can assure Lerner, or Lerner can assure himself, that there is the same *ex ante* probability distribution of pleasure capacity in that group as in the rest, what can Lerner *scientifically* advise? Superficially, this may appear to be what Friedman was postulating in the earlier paragraph; still, the conditional probability distribution of incomes for fixed pleasure capacity is quite different from the conditional probability distribution of pleasure capacities for fixed income prospects. I.e., for a bivariate distribution $P(X, Y), P(X/Y)$ must not be confused with $P(Y/X)$. However, if X and Y are *independent*, $P(X, Y) = F(X)G(Y)$; and $P(X/Y)$ will be independent of Y if and only if $P(Y/X)$ is independent of X. It is legitimate to worry about the distributions of pleasure capacity in the privileged and the remaining groups; but the needed postulate is not, I think, so much a substitute for an equal-ignorance assumption as itself a particular kind of Bayesian equal-ignorance assumption. The probability distributions in question seem *not* to be the *ex post* frequency distribution of pleasure capacities as Plato would record them in the case of a 2-person or n-person universe, and which I hope Friedman did not have in mind; but rather the *ex ante* distributions which Lerner and any jury of ethical observers might reasonably be expected to hold subjectively (whatever that means). Since Lerner has cut himself off *in principle* from ever knowing how to gauge two men's pleasure capacity, one is left with doubts as to what the exercise has accomplished. To say more would be merely to repeat.

essary for some Keynesians to insist that cuts in money wages, could in principle, have no substantive effect in reducing involuntary unemployment. Still even for today's reader, there is much to learn from Lerner's macro papers of the late 1930's.

And certainly no economist can be the same after reading Lerner's *Functional Finance*. (I once asked him why he didn't call it Lernerism. He answered, rather seriously, that some of his students at Kansas City had urged this, but he feared it might limit the popularity of the doctrines.) How revealing (even if overly simple) is the notion that we tax only to prevent inflation. Those who don't read Lerner will still enjoy the freedom from the fetters of fiscal orthodoxy that he helped secure.

Of Lerner's many accomplishments in macroeconomics, let me mention only his happy naming of " sellers' inflation." In demand-pull inflation, spenders would try to

acquire at steady prices more than 100 per cent of the available and producible national product, leading to a self-perpetuating inflationary gap. In " How To Pay For the War," Keynes in 1939 made an important contribution to this analysis of demand-pull inflation. In the postwar, Lerner improved upon the analysis of " cost-push " inflation. In his model, sellers of labour and of products—units with market power to keep their named prices or wage rates steady (or to raise them) even when they cannot sell all they want to at their named prices—may as a group insist on trying to get more than 100 per cent of the available product; as a result, even in the presence of unemployed men and plants, they may raise prices. The process may involve profit-push as well as wage-push, and need not depend on unilateral trade-union wage pressure or on wicked attitudes of union leaders.

This diagnosis has predisposed Lerner toward advocating an " income policy," in which the largest firms and economic units must justify certain increases in administered prices or wages. This is just one of his many pivotal discussions.

9. *Shalom*. Abba Lerner, the scholar, inhabits the same skin as Abba Lerner, the artist, and Abba Lerner the social reformer. He began with an interest in socialism. If legend can be believed, when Abba Lerner visited Leon Trotsky in Mexico before the War, he tried to sell Trotsky the virtues of parametric pricing and decentralized organization of production and consumption by Lerner-Lange-Taylor pricing. (Was it M. Allais who hoped the French radical left could be sold market pricing and Pareto optimality after the War?) Certainly Lerner was no ordinary socialist. His critique of Marx and Marxists could win an A in a Hayek seminar both for downrightness and content.

His *Functional Finance* aims to provide the economic system with, to use a favourite Lerner image, a " steering wheel." Not for Lerner are crude considerations of feasibility: he has always believed matters can be put so simply that people will understand them and be converted. Thus, in World War II, Lerner seriously proposed that Generals Eisenhower and MacArthur each be given abstract purchasing power, to be funnelled down to lower officers, so that the war effort could be directed by auctioning off resources in a Pareto optimal way. I believe he has never ceased to regret that his friend Oskar Lange (to protect Lerner's reputation!) persuaded him not to publish his book on the subject. Nor has he confined his suggestions to pure economics. I believe he once organized a rump session at the Christmas AEA meetings to deal with the atomic bomb, proposing in the days when we had a monopoly that we threaten totalitarian states with bombing if they did not instantly introduce free speech, free thought, free press, and perhaps, free parametric pricing. (In 1948 at the *L.S.E.*, two of his old teachers asked me how Lerner was doing. I replied, " Fine, but he certainly has some audacious notions." When I illustrated with the auction-market war organization, one teacher said, "What's the matter with that? I've proposed as much myself." After I had shifted the topic to the atom bomb proposals, the other teacher said, "What's the matter with that? I've proposed the same thing." I decided that I must be a very unaudacious citizen.)

Always Abba Lerner has been on the side of the angels. It is customary, people say, for economists to become more conservative as they grow older. If this is a common pattern, Lerner seems to be an exception. He has not sold out to the interests nor, as often happens, bought in to romantic idiocies. Like Knut Wicksell, he stands up to speak for the public interest as his scholarly findings interpret that interest, letting those who will charm college Deans.

The drum beat Abba Lerner answers to is that of science, and when he plays his pipe we economists of all ages become like the little children of Hamlin.

Paul A. Samuelson

Massachusetts Institute of Technology

184

Irving Fisher and the Theory of Capital

PAUL A. SAMUELSON

The calendar of American saints in economics is not a very long one. A history of economic thought written prior to the modern age would certainly include John Bates Clark as a leading theorist. And it inevitably would include, along with Benjamin Franklin and Alexander Hamilton, the names of Henry Carey, Henry George, Francis Walker, and Thorstein Veblen. But that would have been about it. You would have to go to a more specialized monograph to come upon the further names of Frank Taussig, Thomas Nixon Carver, and Irving Fisher.[1]

But each generation must rewrite its history books. Starting out today, we would not find ourselves studying the history of *doctrines* and giving equal weight to a Robert Owen and a David Ricardo. Instead, in the spirit of Schumpeter's classic *History of Economic Analysis*, we would give greatest weight to *analytical* contributions. And from this standpoint, Irving Fisher would emerge as perhaps the greatest single name in the history of American economics.

As an example, the terms of trade between Clark and Fisher have, over the years, turned in Fisher's favor. Clark had two claims to fame: as an independent discoverer of the theory of marginal utility and as the first discoverer of the marginal productivity theory of

---

[1] Ely, Fetter, Dunbar, and Davenport continue to be remembered. A case can be made for including List as an American rather than German economist, since his ideas were much shaped by his sojourn here but then we might have to give up John Rae. The generation born after the 1860s would include the names of Wesley Mitchell, Allyn Young, H. L. Moore, Frank Knight, Jacob Viner, H. G. Brown, and Henry Schultz.

distribution. Posterity can honor only the last claim. To learn *for yourself* a new theory of marginal utility ten years or more after it has been widely published is to invite from the jury an indictment for negligence rather than an award for brilliance. Without discounting Clark's claim for originality, we must recognize that Wicksell, Wicksteed, Barone, and Walras rediscovered very soon after Clark his marginal productivity notions. And the modern world has gone well beyond them.

Of Fisher, it might be said that the world has just been catching up to his best theories. When Robert Solow gave the 1964 De Vries lectures in Rotterdam on the theory of capital, he was able to sidestep the major pitfalls involved in the controversial subject of defining a real capital magnitude by adhering to Fisher's 1907 concept of the terms of trade between todays and tomorrow's consumption as the objective counterpart of the rate of interest.

And to illustrate the singular merits of Fisher's 1930 book, *The Theory of Interest*, let me tell a story that has, I believe, the irrelevant merit of being largely true. Soon after the liberation of Paris, John and Ursula Hicks were the first academic economists to visit the city. As Ursula tells the story, all was still confusion. But upon learning that the Hicks's were economists, their hosts whisked them up to an attic where an enthusiastic lecturer was speaking. Perhaps I am improving upon her tale, but I seem to recall that the room was found to be full of workers and miners, the latter with their miner lamps still on their heads. As the Hicks's ears gradually became accustomed to the rapid French of the animated speaker, imagine their surprise to learn what it was he was discussing so excitedly. It was the question, "Would the rate of interest be zero in the stationary state?" Perhaps you will have guessed that the speaker was Maurice Allais. According to legend, Allais, an engineering graduate without much training in economics, had, during the war, worked out for himself most of the findings of modern economic analysis working only with a copy of Fisher's *Theory of Interest*. Now we come to the point of my story: it is hard to imagine a better book to take with you to a desert island than this 1930 classic. In it you would have not only the fundamentals of interest theory but also the basic theory of general equilibrium of exchange and production, the essential equivalent to the microeconomic part of the 1939

Value and Capital treatise of Hicks and to the post-1931 Lerner-Leontief-Meade model of international trade.[2]

The Yale Connection

On this occasion and in the present company, perhaps I may be permitted to speak of the connection between Fisher and Yale. Yale has had many great scholars, of whom the following are relevant to Irving Fisher's career: President Arthur Hadley, an able applied economist in the decades before World War I; William Graham Sumner, a forgotten man whose advocacy of hard-boiled *laissez faire* needs to be read in order to be believed—and, withal, a fearless enemy of American imperialism at the time of the Spanish-American War; most important of all, the great physicist Willard Gibbs. A tradition has grown up that Yale never adequately appreciated Gibbs, because Gibbs was too far ahead of his contemporaries and was of a diffident personality. My old teacher E. B. Wilson, himself Gibbs's last student, always denied the truth of this romantic notion. But it is a fact that Yale came to make Gibbs a professor at a salary of a few thousand dollars a year, only after President Gilman of Hopkins tried to woo him away. And the story is told that the bachelor Gibbs used to drive his sister around in a buggy to do her shopping because her husband, the librarian at Yale, was too important a man for such activity. Yet, as Wilson always insisted, Gibbs was admired by his peers, Clerk Maxwell and the great physicists of Europe, and felt repaid in the only currency that *he* deemed of value.

Fisher was Gibbs's student, and we can see the mark of Gibbs in the 1892 thesis. (For example, the vector analysis of Gibbs is used to portray indifference contours in multidimensions, and the important problem of "integrability conditions" is already recognized by Fisher.) A grateful Fisher in later years gave intellectual and financial support to the republication of Gibbs's collected works. Perhaps the statute of limitations has run out and it will not be taken amiss if I raise the question of whether Yale properly appreciated the genius of Fisher. Twenty years ago when I visited New Haven I had the

---

[2] The general equilibrium model of Walras, in which constant-returns-to-scale industries get organized under competition by firms of indeterminate size, differs somewhat from the Fisher-Hicks model.

definite impression that some local residents took the view, "If he was so smart, how come he got caught in the 1929 crash? And besides, isn't it a bit silly to be concerned with eugenics, world peace, fresh air and diet to prolong longevity, alcoholism and cigarette addiction, and stable money?"[3]

It is a fact that Fisher trained remarkably few students and disciples in his half century at Yale. This is particularly surprising in that he was such a master of the art of written exposition: writing plain prose with homely illustrations; carefully organizing chapters, summaries, and detailed tables of contents; making skillful use of geometry; and, for the most part, boxing his mathematical equations in the ghettos of appendixes, along with patient explication of their meanings. Perhaps this paucity of students is due to the fact that Fisher was ahead of his time. Perhaps it was because his independent means and reforming zeal permitted him to spend only part time in teaching and to take many leaves of absence. Perhaps it was because he preferred to spend his time in advancing his researches. (This itself requires, however, an explanation: Why wasn't graduate teaching an activity ideally suited to advance his research interests? Could it be that the Yale of the first third of the century was too much a college and too little a university?)

In one way Fisher did have a major impact on American education.

---

[3] For many of the facts about Irving Fisher I am indebted to the valuable biography by his son, Irving Norton Fisher, *My Father Irving Fisher* (Comet Press, New York, 1956). Through the courtesy of Martin Beckman, I have had a chance to read Irving Fisher's best-selling book on health, I. Fisher and E. L. Fisk, *How To Live* (Funk and Wagnalls, New York, 1915, 1921). From .the standpoint of hindsight it is a naive and faddish book, but it is interesting to appraise it from a modern viewpoint. Fisher correctly attributes impaired longevity to overweight. He takes a similar view with respect to tobacco, but because of circulatory effects rather than lung cancer. Whether because of a predilection for vegetarianism or not, he correctly identifies high protein diets as bad for longevity. He favors exercise in the modern Paul Dudley White manner, even though cholesterol as such is not mentioned; and, for whatever such advice is worth, he advocates mental serenity. On the other hand, he exaggerates the importance of good posture, shoe fit, thorough mastication, and fresh circulation of air. And he states as findings of science deleterious effects of alcohol that cannot today be substantiated. Where his predilections are concerned, he is sometimes credulous in evaluating "scientific" evidence. And, of course, modern drugs (sulpha, penicillin, antibiotics, reserpine) have done more to prolong life expectancies than any of the self-help methods advocated by Fisher. Still, in 1921, if you could have lived up to the book, it would have made you a better insurance risk. And Fisher's pioneering work in promoting regular health examinations of a clinical type was profoundly important.

I have a copy of what must be a rare item, Fisher's introductory textbook of 1911, entitled *Elementary Principles of Economics*. In many ways it is an unusual and original book. Copious use is made of diagrams, perhaps making it the first Marshallian text in America. Plentiful reference is made to Fisher's own advanced researches—the rate of interest, the theory of capital and income, the nature of marginal utility and demand. Coming out as it did about the same time as Taussig's two-volume *Principles of Economics*, its sales are hard for me to estimate. Certainly it was used for many years at Yale. And one discerns in the Fairchild-Furniss-and-Buck text a strong Fisher influence. If I am not overstretching the point, we can say that through this best-seller of the between-the-wars period, Irving Fisher exercised a definite influence on the economic education of American youths.

When I came to know Harvard's Sumner Slichter better, toward the end of his life, I developed an admiration for him as a man and as a political economist. Slichter was much sought after as a speaker to business groups; but when I was a graduate student many of us felt that this was because he was always telling them things they liked to hear—such as, there should be a tax rebate for this purpose or that. Slichter later told me that whenever he gave a speech and told the audience things that they like to hear, he tried to be sure to add something that they *ought* to hear even if it came as unpleasant news to them. All this is an elaborate preamble to my performing the ungracious duty of telling the host something not necessarily pleasant. In reviewing for this occasion Irving Fisher's life and Yale connections, I could not help but be struck by the fact that the old-time Yale was a highly inbred group. With few exceptions, the faculty of Fisher's time seemed to consist of Yale-trained men. Now it is asking much of a place that it alone should have produced the best scholars in the nation; and if I use "the other place" as a control sample, I have to report that only half of the Harvard faculty of those generations came from Harvard itself—and by no means the better half. I should not dare say this if, looking around me, I did not see in the new Yale department men from outside of Connecticut.

Highlights of Fisher's Scientific Achievements

Before turning to Fisher's theory of capital and interest, let me touch the bases of his many original contributions.

1. Pure Theory. First, there is his 1892 *Mathematical Investigations in the Theory of Value and Prices*, which I once hailed as the greatest Ph.D. dissertation ever written in economics. When writing it, Fisher knew only Jevons and Auspitz and Lieben; he did not know Edgeworth or Walras. Much of the book consists of a derivation of the conditions of general equilibrium for the case of independent cardinal utilities. Speaking for myself, I find the hydraulic tanks that serve as analogue computers less exciting than did the author and many of his readers. (And this reminds me of another true story. As Irving Fisher's seventieth birthday approached, my colleague Harold Freeman and his young assistant, Louis Young, thought it would be nice to present Fisher with a replica of the model that had long since rusted away. But Young found it would be rather an expensive present, and therefore drew up plans for a mechanical equivalent. When he made the pilgrimage from Cambridge to New Haven, Professor Fisher apparently became very frosty at the thought that what should be hydraulic was to be made mechanical; and, as Professor Freeman tells the story, only the good offices of Mrs. Fisher kept Young from being shown the door.) But let me return to the 1892 contribution. Just before receiving a copy of Edgeworth's *Mathematical Psychics*, Fisher had gone beyond the case of independent utilities to the case where utility is written as a general function $U = F(Q_1, Q_2, \ldots, Q_n)$ with cross-partial-derivatives that could be positive in the case of complementary goods and negative in the case of rival goods. Moreover, he had also sensed, prior to Pareto, that the whole theory could be based upon the noncardinal invariants of the indifference contours. This represented a definite advance in the modern direction.

Although Fisher was one of the first to realize that only ordinal utility was needed for demand theory, he had a lifelong interest in computing cardinal utility. Perhaps this stemmed from his hope to learn how taxation could be used to maximize the total of social utility or, more likely, to achieve some specified goal of "equisacrifice." This theoretical and empirical interest of his culminated in his 1927 contribution to the *Festschrift* for J. B. Clark, in which he showed how empirical observations could be used to determine a unique cardinal measure of utility on the basis of the axiom that some good had definitely independently additive utility.[4] This line of reasoning much stimulated Ragnar Frisch and gained for Fisher Schumpeter's great admiration. I have to confess that I do not fully share their enthusiasms for such measurements; and to show my good faith, let me say that my penchant for ordinalism has not kept me from succumbing to the method of identifying a privileged scale of cardinal utility on the basis of the probabilistic models of Bernoulli, Ramsey, von Neumann, Marschak, and Savage.

Aside from its intrinsic merits, the 1892 thesis proved invaluable for the 1907–1930 masterpiece on interest.

2. *Monetary Theory.* Fisher's early work on bimetallism is of minor interest. But his correct depiction of the accounting relations between a time profile of cash payments and its present-discounted-value as a market asset represented a major achievement and culminated in his 1906 book on *The Nature of Capital and Income*. Interesting, but less earthshaking, is his demonstration that changing prices and price levels cause a divergence between various real (own) rates of interest and the nominal money rate of interest. This was a notion known to Henry Thorton around 1800, to Stuart Mill, to Marshall, to Wicksell and in our time to Sraffa and Keynes. But Fisher did most to give it econometric substance, developing along the way the important statistical tool of distributed lags.

Skipping the 1907 *Rate of Interest* for later discussion I note the 1911 *Purchasing Power of Money*. In its day this was considered Fisher's greatest work. But in later years, interest in the Quantity Theory of Money abated; moreover, the independent derivation of the demand for money equations by the Cambridge School—consisting of Marshall, Pigou, and the early Keynes—detracted somewhat from the world's appreciation of Fisher's contribution. Fisher's stock, however, is rising on the bourse of expert opinion. Thus my colleague Franco Modigliani claims that the trend is now

---

[4] Mathematically, Fisher shows how knowledge of two income-expansion paths, such as might come from budget studies in two different price situations, enables one to approximate the additively independent utility function that generated the data. In order to have a well-posed problem in partial differential equations, the two situations must be infinitely close together; the further apart they are, the coarser the final approximation. With knowledge of three or more income-consumption paths, we could perform the task always shunned by economists—testing the independence assumption.

toward a Neo-Fisher demand for money, stressing his analysis of the institutional and technical factors relating to the stochastic non-synchronization of inpayments and outpayments; this inventory theory of money holding largely for transactions purposes, Modigliani thinks, is closer to the Fisher view than to the Cambridge view, which stresses the portfolio-distribution-of-wealth aspects of the demand for money. Only in deep depression, when there comes to be absent in the marketplace a safe interest-bearing asset payable on demand, which therefore dominates in the Markowitz sense the holding of money for portfolio purposes, will there be a significant nontransaction motive behind the demand for money.

3. Index Numbers. By 1911, when Fisher was 44, he had accomplished enough for any lifetime. Yet he was to continue for another 36 years. Aside from his masterly revised exposition in 1930 of his works on capital and interest, Fisher made contributions to the econometrics of index numbers. His 1922 *Making of Index Numbers* represented a culmination of the kind of statistical work associated with the names of Edgeworth, Bowley, Warren Persons and Allyn Young. It was a subject much taught in my youth but not one which in retrospect seems very exciting. When I read Fisher, Persons, and Frickey on the subject of whether the arithmetic mean had an upward bias in comparison with the harmonic or even the geometric mean, I never could understand how one defined *the par from which algebraic bias was to be measured.* Moreover, none of these statistical investigations had anything to do with the more fruitful economic theory of index numbers associated with the names of Pigou, Könus, Keynes, Staehle, Leontief, Frisch, Lerner, R. G. D. Allen, Wald, and my own theories of revealed preference.

The *reductio ad absurdum* to the Fisher program came when in 1931 Frisch proved that *no* index *could ever exist* which *simultaneously* satisfied the many axioms that Fisher felt to be reasonable. Examples of these axioms are the following: when all prices rise in the same proportion, so should the index, $\bar{P}$, which is to be a function of the respective price relatives. If we shift the index numbers of two or more years from one base to any other base, the results shall differ only by a scale factor; when we apply the same axioms to a quantity index, $\bar{Q}$, the movement of the product $\bar{P}\bar{Q}$ should agree with the movement of total values $\sum_{1}^{n} p_j{}^t q_j{}^t$.

It is like the case of Kenneth Arrow's celebrated Impossibility Theorem, on the nonexistence of a Constitutional-Welfare function satisfying the several plausible axioms for a democracy. Something[5] has to give—or rather be given up; and I presume that those of us least interested in the equation of exchange, $MV = \bar{P}\bar{Q}$, will give up the so-called "factor reversal test" involving $\bar{P}\bar{Q}$.

4. Managed Money and Cycle Stabilization. Although Fisher spent much of the last third-century as an advocate of Stable Money, little time need be spent here on that subject. Repenting of his opposition to bimetallism in the 1890s, he long advocated a "compensated dollar" in which the gold content of the dollar would rise and fall in weight with the rise and fall in general prices. How this scheme would work out today in practice might make a good take-home quiz question for honors students. Suffice it to say that Fisher only favored this scheme on the grounds of expediency, thinking it might sell. He personally ended up in favor of managed money, and no doubt would approve today of Federal Reserve and fiscal policy.

Fisher's theories of the business cycle—as primarily a "dance of the dollar"—and his debt-deflation theory of financial crisis had perhaps more relevance to the 1929–1933 slump than to earlier minor cycles or today's milder fluctuations. Still, if anyone is enamored with the use of hyperdeflation to produce recovery by means of the "Pigou effect," let him read Fisher's compelling analysis of the process of debt-deflation in a *laissez-faire* economy.

5. Constructive Income Taxation. There is an amazing unity to Fisher's thought stretching over the years from the 1890s to the 1940s. By 1897 his scientific researches persuaded him that income

---

[5] Since the Frisch article has given rise to some obscurities and controversy, I would state the matter thus. Mathematically, assume (I): $P_{21} = f(p_2, q_2; p_1, q_1)$ where p_t, q_t represent vectors of n prices and quantities, namely, $p_t = (p_t^1, \ldots, p_t^n)$, etc. Similarly, assume the same form for the quantity index, (I'): $Q_{21} = f(q_2, p_2; q_1, p_1)$. And to handle the case where all prices change proportionally, assume (II): $f(mp, q_2; p, q_1) = m$. And assume the time reversal test, (III): $P_{21}P_{12} = 1$, or the more general circular reversal test, (IV): $P_{21}P_{13}P_{32} = 1$. From (IV) and a few regularity assumptions on f (differentiability, etc.), we deduce $f(p_2, q_2; p_1, q_1) = f(p_2, q_2)/f(p_1, q_1)$. But (II) requires $f(mp, q_2)/f(p, q_1) = m$ or $f(p, q) = f(p) = (p^1)^{k_1}(p^2)^{k_2} \cdots (p^n)^{k_n}$, $\Sigma_j k_j = 1$. This leads to a weighted geometric mean $(p_2^1/p_1^1)^{k_1} \cdots (p_2^n/p_1^n)^{k_n} = P_{21}$ with weights independent of any periods' quantities. If, finally, we impose the factor reversal test, (V): $P_{21}Q_{21} = \Sigma_i p_2^i q_2^i / \Sigma_j p_1^j q_1^j$ we are led (for $n > 1$) to a contradiction. Even (IV) by itself seems overstrong.

should be defined as "that which gets summed to constitute (present-discounted) value of wealth." Thus income for a nation is what it *consumes* during a year, not what it *earns*. Marshall (and German writers before him, as well as Haig after him) would add to Fisher's magnitude net saving in order to arrive at the more common definition of income as "that which *could* be permanently consumed (without depleting the tree of capital that bears the fruit of consumption)."

Which is the right definition of income? That must depend on one's purpose. (I have gone into the welfare aspects of the problem in the Corfu volume of the I.E.A.[6] and arrived at the rather unexpected conclusion that neither is as good as a third magnitude, which is more akin to Fisher's wealth concept.) In any case, Fisher proposed that the "income tax" be converted into an "expenditure tax"; or, as he would prefer to say, that the income tax be levied on income, not on earnings. To this, Henry C. Simons gave the classic reply, "Let Fisher call whatever he likes income; but why should we tax what Fisher chooses to call income?" Irving Fisher had noted with some derision that Aristotle had been misled by the accident that "interest" in Greek means "offspring" into ruling that interest was inadmissible in view of the fact that "money (unlike the rabbit) is barren." Hence Fisher was in fact prepared to argue on its merits the case that an expenditure tax is better than an earnings tax in that it avoids the dead-weight loss inherent in so-called double taxation of saving. (Of course, the difficulties of achieving desired progression must be weighted against the dead-weight burden, leading in the end perhaps to a wealth tax.)

The Theory of Interest

This brings me finally to the *pièce de résistance* of Irving Fisher's scientific contribution, his masterly theory of interest. I could never forgive myself if I spent all my limited space on the aperitif and hors d'oeuvre and left none for the main course.

To understand Fisher's signal contribution, you must realize that Böhm-Bawerk, who at the turn of the century was perhaps the leading economist in the world, dominated the theory of capital and interest with his *Positive Theory of Capital* (1889) and correlative writings. It was no accident that Knut Wicksell, coming on the scene of economics after Böhm-Bawerk's writings on capital, should have tried to meld the mathematics of Walras and the dynamic models of

---

[6] F. A. Lutz and D. C. Hague, eds., *The Theory of Capital* (Macmillan, London, 1961). Chapter 3, "The Evaluation of 'Social Income': Capital Formation and Wealth," pp. 32–57.

Böhm-Bawerk. Similarly, Fisher was writing against the backdrop of the Böhm-Bawerkian influence.

Böhm-Bawerk was a forceful writer, an untiring polemicist, and, it must be confessed, a tedious hairsplitter. He first set down to review the interest theories of all his predecessors, producing in 1884 *Capital and Interest: A History and Critique of Interest Theories.* In this book he reviews all his predecessors and finds them lacking. If Senior attributes interest to abstinence, then Senior errs. If Turgot attributes interest to land's permanent net product, then Turgot argues in a circle. If Marx regards interest as exploitation, then Marx errs. If Say believes in a "naive-productivity theory of interest"—that is, just because a machine is productive its gross rents must therefore exceed its replacement costs—then Say is naive. If Thünen sophisticatedly points to the existence of a positive net yield in a machine, over and above its replacements, then Thünen is begging the issue and assuming what needs to be proved: the existence of positive interest. So it goes, down a long and patient roll call of imperfect predecessors.

This, of course, clears the deck for Böhm-Bawerk's own 1889 *Positive Theory of Capital*, which rushes in to fill the vacuum that nature has faced him with. The explanation of positive interest, as given in the *Positive Theory*, is anything but easy to follow. The book abounds with numerical examples, casuistical distinctions, categorical definitions, and an insistence that everything be stated in exactly the way that the author prefers to state matters. Although Böhm-Bawerk gave more than 30 years of his life to the subject, and painstakingly answered every criticism made of this work (incidentally, finding *all* of them in the end wrong), he never took the time to set down in an orderly and understandable fashion exactly what his own theory was.[7]

---

[7] Therefore it comes as something of an anticlimax to learn from Wicksell's last article that when, in 1911, he met Böhm-Bawerk and commented on what seemed to him a lack of unity in the *Positive Theory*, Böhm-Bawerk "said quite simply, that because of external circumstances he had to hurry so in the publication of the first edition of his book, that the first half of the manuscript already found itself at the printing office before he had completed the writing of the second half. In this latter section he had in fact been confronted by difficulties of a theoretical nature in the last hours of its writing...." Wicksell's 1928 paper is cited and quoted in G. J. Stigler, *Production and Distribution Theories* (Macmillan, New York, 1941), p. 194, n.2. Since Böhm-Bawerk entered the finance ministry in 1889, I suspect it was this that hurried him. Those same public duties perhaps explain why he never revised much in the second edition, contenting himself with fragmentary polemical *excursi* to deal with his critics.

In many ways, Irving Fisher can be said to have written what Böhm-Bawerk should have intended to be his proper theory. Perhaps Böhm-Bawerk sensed this, because in his later review of his critics,[8] Böhm-Bawerk devotes a hundred pages to quibbling about Fisher's theory. He classified Fisher into the category of those not so much trying to disprove his theory as to improve upon it. And it is not clear which he would deem the more dastardly crime.[9]

Böhm-Bawerk follows the old-fashioned methodological procedure (which was still lingering in my graduate-school days) that first he must establish the *essence* of interest—why there should (have to) be a positive rate of interest. After this qualitative question is settled, then one can investigate the quantitative question of the level and trends in the interest rate. He ended up with what he called an "agio" theory, in which present goods enjoy a systematic premium over future goods. This systematic undervaluation of future goods by the marketplace—which is just another way of asserting the existence of a positive interest rate—Böhm-Bawerk traced to *psychological* or *subjective* facts (indifference-curve phenomena as Fisher taught us to see) and to asserted technological facts about the possible trade offs nature offers us between present and future goods (opportunity-cost or production-possibility frontiers to post-Fisher writers).

In particular, Böhm-Bawerk ends up with his famous three causes for (positive) interest:

1. Because people can expect to be richer in the future, they will gladly pay a premium to transfer some of tomorrow's chocolates into today's chocolates. ("Difference in want.")

2. Making decisions today about today's and tomorrow's consumptions, men—either for "rational" reasons such as the uncertainty of life's duration or "irrational" reasons such as plain weakness of the imagination—are supposed to display systematic time preference for

---

[8] These are now gathered in a 1959 English translation as Eugen von Böhm-Bawerk, *Capital and Interest*, Vol. III, *Further Essays on Capital and Interest* (Libertarian Press, South Holland, Ill., 1959). Just before the war, Hugh Gaitskell was working on a new translation to replace the classic 1890 and 1891 Smart translations of Böhm-Bawerk; but again the requirements of public service were at the expense of economic scholarship.

[9] Böhm-Bawerk shows similar ambivalence concerning the long-lost 1834 classic, John Rae, *The Sociological Theory of Capital*, which Fisher believed anticipated the essence of the correct theory. Had Böhm-Bawerk known of this work in 1884 and agreed in this judgment, it would have been a cruel blow to his psychological pride.

consuming present chocolates over future chocolates. That is, {5 chocolates today, 4 chocolates tomorrow} will always be preferred to {4 chocolates today, 5 chocolates tomorrow}. ("Systematic subjective time preference or discount.")

3. Capital goods tend to have a "net productivity," consisting of the alleged technical fact that Nature's "roundabout methods are more productive," giving us more than 1 chocolate tomorrow for 1 chocolate sacrificed today. ("Technological superiority of present over future goods.")[10]

Fisher, misleadingly, in 1907 called his own theory an "impatience" theory. This suggested to everybody in the world but him that he was neglecting the third technological factor of Böhm-Bawerk. He was criticized for this by Böhm-Bawerk, H. G. Brown, H. R. Seager, and many others. In my view he laid himself open to such criticisms by virtue of many of his lines of exposition. And I find it unrewarding to review his arguments with his critics and predecessors.

There is a moral here. When someone tells you that modern mathematical economics is decadent, often splitting hairs about whether a particular axiom requires continuity alone or differentiability as well, he may or may not be right. But don't believe that the previous period of literary economics was a golden age. The Böhm-Bawerkian pattern of logical exegesis and casuistry was most certainly decadent, and Fisher was sucked into such modes of scholarship.

Fisher realized this (at times) and when he came to revise the 1907 *Rate of Interest*, he emphasized the productivity aspect of his own theory in the symmetric subtitle: *The Theory of Interest: As Determined by Impatience to Spend Income and Opportunity to Invest It.* Indeed, the jest is that Fisher always insisted that his own originality had not been in the subjective sphere of impatience, but rather in his invention of the *opportunity frontier* (and the correct discounting relations between future cash receipts and present-discounted value) to handle the productivity notion of early writers and of Böhm-Bawerk's third factor of more productive roundaboutness.

---

[10] As Wicksell pointed out, Böhm-Bawerk must himself in the end assume this as a blunt fact (if it is a fact!), even though he had criticized Thünen and earlier productivity writers for having argued in a circle by assuming what they are required to deduce.

Figure 2 will show how the Fisher theory serves as a brilliant synthesis and exposition of what should be Böhm-Bawerk's theory. But first I want to point out that the greatest contribution in Fisher's 1907 classic is its presentation of a definitive model of general equilibrium determination of interest rates. As indicated earlier, this *completely* anticipates in its formal structure the post-1930 models of international trade that Haberler, Viner, Lerner, Leontief, Meade and others developed; and the 1907 Fisher system, which antedates the work of Slutsky (1915) or W. E. Johnson's classic exposition of indifference curves (*Economic Journal*, 1913), is completely isomorphic to the microeconomic model of general equilibrium in J. R. Hicks, *Value and Capital* (1939).

Fisher gives us a supply-and-demand determination of interest rates. Despite Böhm-Bawerk's desire to get at the essence of the matter (and despite his fear of circular reasoning in "assuming an interest rate in order to deduce one"), this is all one needs or can ever get here on earth. But, as Fisher would insist, it is not a superficial description of supply and demand but rather a formulation that analyzes these to their ultimate source in taste and technology.

Fisher's exposition (like that of Jevons and Hicks) begins with a first approximation in which production endowments are given; and then follows the general equilibrium of exchange. If all men were alike and endowed by Nature with outputs at Q in Figure 1 (which is reproduced from the *Rate of Interest*, p. 409, but with axes labeled), equilibrium would be determined by the absolute slope or marginal rate of substitution at Q, with $(1 +$ interest rate) equal to that slope. If men differ—say, for graphical simplicity, fitting into two categories of a million identical men and a million identical women—the same equilibrium would be shown on the familiar Edgeworth box diagram, where the offer curves (generated by the tangency of each party's indifference contour to the trade vector going from a fixed endowment point like P to the post-trade point Q) intersect.

But, as Fisher's figure shows in his second approximation, people can trade with nature along the production-possibility or opportunity frontier ZPW. Now each man must first act to maximize his present discounted value, taking the interest rate as given, and ending up at P's tangency to the frontier. Then he trades along PQ with others in

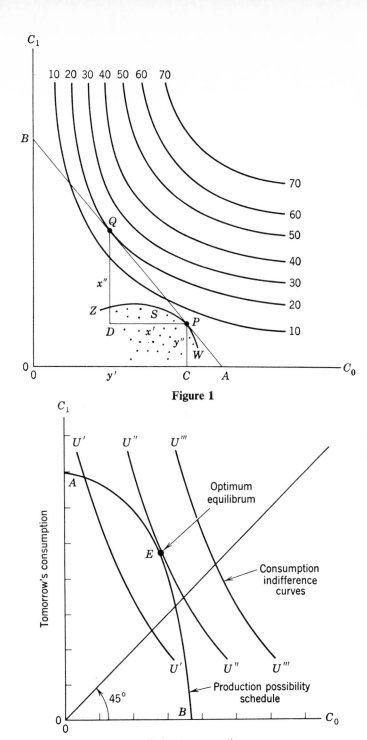

Figure 1

Figure 2

the market. And only when all others have a QP that cancels out his PQ with the market will final equilibrium be reached.[11]

To show how Fisher's model of general equilibrium illuminates Böhm-Bawerk's theory of interest, Figure 2 is reproduced from the last few editions of my *Economics*. Böhm-Bawerk's second basic cause for (positive) interest, systematic subjective discount of future utilities and preference for present utilities, is shown by the fact that the indifference contours $U'U'$ have a "vertical bias": instead of being symmetric around the 45° line of equal consumptions in time, all their absolute slopes are shown steeper than unity above or on the 45° line. Böhm-Bawerk's third basic cause of interest, the technological superiority of roundaboutness or of present goods over future goods, is shown by the vertical bias of the opportunity frontier AB, which is not symmetric around the 45° line but instead shows a slope steeper than unity on the 45° line. Böhm-Bawerk's first cause for interest, the expectation of having more income in the future, is

---

[11] To handle graphically the case where production is variable, we replace the box diagram by a now-familiar Meade diagram involving trade-indifference contours. From each man's indifference contours we "subtract" his opportunity frontier (pairing points with equal slopes to show maximum achievable welfare for each amount algebraically traded). Reversing the directions of the amounts traded by one of the parties, in the usual box-diagram fashion, and proceeding from a common origin, we now treat the problem exactly as if it were a box diagram, achieving determinate equilibrium where offer curves intersect and reading off the equilibrium interest rate from the slope of the resulting trade vector.

Incidently, although Fisher is known for his concept of "rate of return over cost" and "marginal rate of return over cost," the former is not really needed for his mathematical exposition of the complete theory. *Maximization of present discounted value* is the key concept; and in the general case of several periods, all with different equilibrium interest rates, the rate of return over cost is not a useful concept. When Keynes introduced the marginal efficiency of capital into his *General Theory*, someone (I seem to recall it was Redvers Opie) pointed out to him that Fisher had beat him to the concept; so Keynes acknowledged Fisher's priority. A. A. Alchian in a 1955 *American Economic Review* paper chides Keynes for his "carelessness" in identifying his marginal efficiency (or "internal rate of return") with Fisher's rate of return over cost. Alchian is correct that Fisher (in 1907 as well as 1930) always reckoned his concept as the rate of discount which equalizes *two* alternative investment options. But it is also the case that, after computing a single option's internal rate, we can set up as a reference second option *any* receipts stream that just earns that rate of interest and reduce the concepts to formal identity. Actually, the practice of listing society's alternative projects in order of their internal rates of return goes back a century to John Rae and is referred to approvingly by Fisher, Böhm-Bawerk, and others.

akin to his third factor in reflecting the vertical bias of the opportunity frontier.[12]

In the case where all people are identical in tastes and opportunity, Figure 2 depicts equilibrium by tangency of the frontier with an indifference contour. To demonstrate positive interest, first deny all three of Böhm-Bawerk's causes. This implies tangency on the 45° line of a time-symmetric frontier and time-symmetric indifference contour, yielding an equilibrium absolute slope of unity and hence a zero interest rate. (This depicts Schumpeter's famous theory and shows it to be free from *logical* error.)

Now affirm any one of Böhm-Bawerk's three causes or any set of them simultaneously. In every case this increases the slope at tangency. (Examples: (1) Affirming the third by steepening the frontier leads, on the line of equal consumptions, to an excess of technological interest above subjective, coaxing out saving and postponed consumption at the resulting positive interest rate. (2) Biased indifference contours similarly can be tangential to an unbiased frontier only at a positive interest rate, with dissaving produced by the excess of subjective discount over technological that would prevail at equal consumptions. (3) Shifting an unbiased frontier upward, in accordance with Böhm-Bawerk's first cause, is like example (1) just mentioned. (4) Finally, give the frontier and the contours a vertical bias and we have to end with a positive-interest tangency because the frontier's slope is less than one only above the 45° line whereas the contours' slopes are less than one only below that line, precluding a common tangency with $1 + i < 1$.)

---

[12] If endowments were fixed, as in Fisher's first approximation where the frontier becomes a box, the third cause would be irrelevant; but the first cause would show up in the fact that the box's corner would fall *above* the 45° line. The diagram can illuminate a quarrel between Fisher and Böhm-Bawerk over the third cause. Often Böhm-Bawerk seems to be arguing as if "technical superiority of present over future goods" means that the opportunity frontier must *everywhere* have an absolute slope in excess of unity. Fisher was right to insist that this need not be the case, and he gives quite proper examples (decaying figs or storable hardtack) where the technological interest rate could be negative or zero. Böhm-Bawerk's elaborate numerical examples of roundabout production show confusion; at times he seems almost to be arguing from the asymmetry of time itself, from the fact that 1888 goods have the superiority over 1889 in coming first (and perhaps being tacitly assumed to be storable and hence at least as good as those of 1889—which, as in the case of "money," rules out *negative* own rates of interest).

The Fisher diagram can go beyond Böhm-Bawerk. Since mankind typically faces retirement years of low incomes, I have argued (*Journal of Political Economy*, 1958) that Böhm-Bawerk's first cause probably is the reverse of the truth for each mortal man: we can each expect to be poorer in the future; our frontiers have thus a reverse-bias component, and negative real interest (as Fisher had recognized) would prevail if Nature did not provide us with opportunities for technological trade-offs.

Fisher never faced up to an infinite-period equilibrium model. For the case of identical men, Frank Ramsey was the first to handle such a case in his classic 1928 paper; and I believe it was not until 30 years later that the general case was tackled (as in my previously cited *J.P.E.* paper). Here I shall briefly sketch a rigorous but simple case.

First, summarize the consumption-saving tastes of the community by

$$U = u(C_0) + \frac{u(C_1)}{1 + R} + \frac{u(C_2)}{(1 + R)^2} + \cdots = \sum_0^\infty \frac{u(C_t)}{(1 + R)^t}$$

and the technology by a one-sector exponential-depreciation model

$$C_{t+1} + K_{t+1} - K_t = F(K_t) - dK_t = f(K_t)$$

where f and F are concave neoclassical production functions, K_t is the stock of capital and $0 \le C_t \le F(K_t)$, gross product. Then for K_0 given, and on the assumption that $K_2 = K_0$ (a putative long-run equilibrium), the frontier is given by

$$C_1 = f[K_0 + f(K_0) - C_0] + f(K_0) - C_0$$

with tangency at

$$\frac{U'(C_0)}{U'(C_1)} (1 + R) = 1 + f'(K_1)$$

Only if subjective discount R equals technological discount f' will $C_0 = C_1$ be an equilibrium solution that justifies the $K_{t+1} \equiv K_t$ assumption that we have tacitly made in reducing an infinite-period problem to Fisher's 2-dimensional graph. Thus the generalized catenary turnpike defined by $R = f'(K^*)$ is the only possible long-run solution, with $C^* = f(K^*)$.

If initially $K_0 < K^*$, we can only indicate on the diagram the system's evolution. We perceive that $K_{t+1} < K_t$ and $\lim_{t \to \infty} K_t = K^*$. In every case, short-term tangency gives

$$\frac{U'(C_t)}{U'(C_{t+1})}(1 + R) = 1 + f'(K_{t+1}) > 1 + R$$

In successive periods, the frontier shifts outward, but with less vertical bias because of diminishing returns—until asymptotically the frontier's slope is $1 + R$ on the $45°$ line of long-run equilibrium.

I must resist temptation to explore the Fisher ideas further—to show how probabilistic uncertainty can bias saving in either direction or to discuss multiple roots and reswitching phenomena.[13] Enough has been said to show how modern is Irving Fisher's theory of interest. In a science's complacent phase, the highest compliment to pay an earlier author is to call him modern.

Finale

In conclusion, let me speak of Irving Fisher the man and of the American scene that was his stage. At the beginning of Sir Roy Harrod's *Life of John Maynard Keynes*, the author speaks of the Cambridge environment and of Keynes's roots in 6 Harvey Road. The writing is fine, even precious, and I quote:

> If I achieve my purpose, the life-work of Keynes will be seen, in part as an expression of this Cambridge civilization, both in its stability and self-confidence and in its progressiveness.

But Harrod goes on to make a contrast:

> The American civilization is nicely different from that of Harvey Road .... Intellectual Cambridge may have had its counterpart in the

---

[13] When we introduce heterogeneous capital goods by making K_t a vector, the transformation frontier becomes $T(K_t; C_t, C_{t+1}; K_{t+2}) = 0$. For long-run equilibrium, which can easily be generalized to handle exponentially growing labor and golden-age states, $T(K; C, C; K) = 0$ and $1 + R = -(\partial T/\partial C_t)/(\partial T/\partial C_{t+1})$. Reswitching cannot occur if T is smooth with all partial derivatives defined everywhere; but it alerts us to what *can* happen even without reswitching: R and C need *not* always move in the opposite direction as in the simpler parables of neoclassical capital theory. One final remark: Fisher treats C_t as a dollar magnitude, a practice which Sraffa and Joan Robinson might criticize as circular; we can avoid all circles by letting C_t be chocolates, or a market basket of consumer goods, or best of all a vector of heterogeneous capital goods (whose "own rates," $-\partial C_{t+1}/\partial C_t$, all equal the same $1 + R$ in equilibrium).

United States; but it cannot be deemed to have resembled the more usual pattern. Keynes was not predisposed to admire the American way of life.

When I first read these passages, I noted resentment rising in my breast, some protesting chauvinism no doubt. And I scribbled in the margin of my book something to the effect that William James's children in the Harvard of a century ago must have been experiencing a life very similar to that of Harvey Road in the other Cambridge.

But then later by chance I came to read the autobiography of Thomas Nixon Carver, who taught at Harvard through much of the period Fisher taught at Yale. And I had to admit there was a rawness reflected in it that would be hard to match in Britain, or for that matter in Europe. It was not merely that Carver was born in a sod hut on the prairie; that was true also of Alvin Johnson (who still survives) and who has yet always appeared to be a more cosmopolitan personality than someone like Carver, or even, one dares to guess, than Irving Fisher. There was a quality of earnestness about Protestant America of the last century which seems to have been characteristically ours. "New England Congregational evangelicism," Paul Douglas called it, after Irving Fisher died; and Douglas, who came from Salem and Maine, should know whereof he speaks. And it says something for the openness of American society that someone like Irving Fisher, it would appear almost to his own surprise, should have been tapped for Skull and Bones, an act that the Harvard Porcellian Club cannot be imagined capable of. Furthermore, those who have read Henry Seidel Canby's charming memoir, *Alma Mater*, which tells of Yale and New Haven in the Edwardian era, will understand the charm of the serene life at 460 Prospect Street. Only in America, as the man says, can the children of a Carver move into Harvey Road in one generation.

If there is truly a difference between the America of Irving Fisher and the England of Maynard Keynes, then I say *Vive la différence*. Our Lord's house has many mansions and not all of them need be occupied by the Bloomsbury Set.

We are gathered here to celebrate the Centennial of a great economist's birth. And I am privileged to be here. The more so since I was able to be present at the little celebration that Joseph Schumpeter and the Harvard Economics Department gave in honor of Irving Fisher's seventy-fifth birthday. I recall it as a charming occasion.

The food at the Hotel Commander was better than could have been expected. If memory serves, our guest of honor was indulgent and the cocktails were delicious. (Lest I be accused of a credibility gap, let me hasten to add that the guest was indulgent, not indulging: it was *our* cocktails that were delicious; I cannot speak for Fisher's tomato juice!) The speeches were good; E. B. Wilson was in the chair; Schumpeter was at his flowery best; the guest of honor was visibly touched to receive honors richly merited, if long overdue.

There is an expression coined outside of Harvey Road or Brattle Street: "Next year in Jerusalem!" In concluding this Centennial appreciation for Irving Fisher, I know you will join me in the toast:

"Twenty five years from now, again in New Haven!"

By that time the contribution of Irving Fisher will be appraised at its true worth, and Schumpeter's prophecy will have come true that Irving Fisher's "name will stand in history . . . as the name of this country's greatest scientific economist."

PAUL A. SAMUELSON

ON

JOSEPH SCHUMPETER

Just as there is a stock exchange on which stocks and bonds are quoted, so too there is the bourse of intellectual opinion on which literary and scientific reputations are evaluated.

For a long time Henry James was quoted at a severe discount. Canny investors could have taken a flyer in him for fabulous capital gains. But beware! Even T.S. Eliot could not revive Rudyard Kipling, and the long-awaited George Meredith comeback never got off the ground.

Just because prices fluctuate, do not think the process is a random walk, lacking all rhyme and reason and subject only to dart-board strategy. For one thing, after a writer dies he tends for a time to go into a decline. If not at once, after a few old scores can be risklessly paid off.

It is just twenty years since Joseph Schumpeter died. Although it is not my practice to tout profitable speculations, today I'd like to suggest that Schumpeter's diagnosis of the probable decay of capitalism deserves a new reading in our own time. The general reader cannot do better than begin with his 1942 "Capitalism, Socialism, and Democracy."

SOUR SMELL OF SUCCESS

Nothing that has happened in recent years at Berkeley or Harvard would come as a surprise to those who have absorbed this work. And if there are good clubs in the great beyond, one can picture Schumpeter—a spry 87-year-old by this time, Martini glass in hand—reading The New York Review of Books and chuckling with clinical amusement. Only his Viennese veneer keeps him from saying, "I told you so. The successes and rationalism of bourgeois capitalism will breed a swarm of discontented intellectuals— to fan the flames of hostility toward an efficient but unlovable system with no mystique to protect it."

George Bernard Shaw wisecracked, "He who can, does. He who cannot, teaches." Schumpeter, also something of a believer in the superman thesis, gave this canard an extra twist, asserting in effect: And he who cannot teach, agitates.

For all his tone of objectivity, Schumpeter was a reactionary. But as Holmes said of Spengler, he is the kind of rascal who gives you a run for your money. His pages are larded with insights, as for example:

■ Monopoly pricing and restrictions on output "are often unavoidable incidents of a long-term process of [innovational] expansion, which they protect rather than impede. There is no more of paradox in this than there is in saying that motorcars are traveling faster than they otherwise would *because* they are provided with brakes."

■ "... Precisely because of the fundamental stability of the social structure ... the intellectuals were driven into a desperate radicalism and ... criminal violence. Theirs was the kind of radicalism whose intensity is in inverse proportion to its practical possibilities, the radicalism of impotence."

Schumpeter is referring here, not to Weathermen or black militants, but to life under the Russian czars. This cool conservative goes on to say: "Marx's glowing phrases and chiliastic prophecy were exactly what they needed to get out of the dreary desert of nihilism."

MIND SHRINKERS

I was reminded of all this on a recent trip to England. All the Sunday papers there carried favorable reviews of a new series of Fontana paperbacks, each devoted to a "master" who had "made" the modern mind.

What a crew the first five were! No one begrudges a pivotal role to Camus. But surely it is a libel on any age to claim Marcuse, Fanon, Lévi-Strauss, and Guevara for its gurus.

Herbert Marcuse: now there's a great short sale for you. And as for Guevara: nobody could be as spoiled, incompetent, and mindless as his admiring biographer makes him out to be. Obviously, here is a case where the CIA has commissioned a *reductio ad absurdum*. But it will never work. We do not remember Robin Hood for his efficiency, and Guevara, like Roland, will live forever precisely *by virtue of* his incompetence.

Fanon, like de Sade, radiates to a wave length in the human soul—not to be confounded with *mind*. The few weeks that Lévi-Strauss spent in the bush were quite enough for his prepared Cartesian mind. Since Stephen Leacock died, I have encountered nothing so ... so rare as his new algebra of cookery. One doubts his vogue will outlast the midi.

But there I go. A disgruntled intellectual, with tongue out of joint because no economist was included in the series. No Keynes. No Schumpeter. No, not even a Galbraith.

PRESIDENTIAL ADDRESS

THE WAY OF AN ECONOMIST

Paul A. Samuelson

Introduction

The general theme of this Third World Congress of the International
Economic Association is 'The Future of International Trade'. My
purpose this afternoon is to talk about its *past*. When the young son of
Harlow Shapley, the eminent astrophysicist, was asked on the phone
whether Doctor Shapley was there, he replied, 'He's not the useful kind.'
Many of the distinguished papers at this Congress are of the useful kind,
but I warn you that mine is not. This is an honorific occasion, and mine
is an honorific function.

But I must not overdifferentiate my product. All of our major speakers,
despite their preoccupation with the future, also aim their telescopes at the
past. Where else can a man aim? What's past is indeed prologue – if
anything is. When the weatherman has to give the betting odds on
tomorrow's weather, he must in effect say, 'I recall a sky like this one, and
it was followed by rain.' The experienced physician makes his diagnoses
by analogy with cases encountered or read about. I realise this Baconian
account of scientific induction will infuriate historians and philosophers
of science, so let me restate the point in a more elegant, Newtonian,
manner. 'Because observations of the past were capable of being organised
and understood by some deductive model or theory – quantum mechanics,
atmosphere heat flow, electromagnetic or kinetic theory, double helixes,
interactions of accelerators and multipliers . . . – we predict the results of
unperformed experiments and of the future by means of that past-based
theory.'

Before I read the useful papers of this Congress, I made a prediction
(based of course on past experience), namely that they would indeed be
pre-occupied with the hopefully-relevant past. It was not a hard bet to
win. If anything, one is struck by how *far* back into the past our authors
go in order to illuminate the future.

Still I must not underdifferentiate my product. Let us grant that the
scientist is kind of an historian. That does not make all historians
scientists. I would be prepared to argue – but, thankfully, not here – that
most of the best history is essentially a pursuit of the scientific method
applied to a terrain of necessarily sparse observations. But there is a
branch of history which is pure antiquarianism. It spins a tale, not to

point a moral; nor to suggest a generalisation; but to describe a happening merely because it happened, or as the poet says 'to tell it like it was'. When we pore over our own family album, we are not looking for what is typical of the general culture in our time. For that purpose we could as well look at the picture album of a random neighbour, and what is more dull than to look at someone else's snapshots? We value our own pictures for their *uniqueness* as a sample, not for their likeness to some general universe. While it is a doubtful truth that no man is a hero to his valet, it is a sure-thing bet that no man is a bore to himself.

It is in this spirit that I am ranging today over the development of international trade doctrine. This is a family gathering and I am recounting the annals of our family. There has been an abundance of excellent histories of the *substance* of international trade theory: for example, Jacob Viner's *Studies in the Theory of International Trade* (1937) and Richard Caves' *Trade and Economic Structure* (1960). And I need only refer you to the comprehensive recent technical surveys by Gottfried Haberler, Jagdish Bhagwati, and John Chipman. These are primarily histories of thought in the spirit of Joseph Schumpeter's monumental *History of Economic Analysis*. A Friedrich List gets less attention in them than a Wassily Leontief because List's insights were not primarily analytical. Such analytical surveys need to be supplemented by histories of international policies and ideas that are more in the spirit of the old text by Gide and Rist. But provision of such a supplement is certainly no part of my present purpose here. Rather I am interested in the process of intellectual activity itself: the subjects of my account are not the subjects of international economics; instead they are our sweating predecessors, struggling for a breakthrough in scientific knowledge.

THE RESEARCHER OBSERVED

In literature, the New Critics insisted upon the difference between describing the life and times of an author and analysing the structure and meaning of his poem. In science there is no need to labour such a distinction. Indeed it is the fashion among scientists to embalm their results in a form that disguises the process of actual discovery. When Isaac Newton came to write up his *Principia Mathematica*, you would never guess from its text that the differential calculus had been a useful prerequisite for the subject: good old geometry was sufficient to demonstrate Newton's majestic and eternal verities. Not only is there no mention of falling apples: there is not even an indication that publication had been held up for twenty years because of the difficulty in showing that a spherical object like the moon can be regarded as a single mass-point located at the moon's centre of gravity, or because of discrepancies between the model and facts due to the faulty estimate of the earth's circumference that Newton was first given. (Can you imagine a modern econometrician holding up publication a month for such a reason?) And certainly nothing is said of the role that Newton's jealousy of Hooke played in accelerating and decelerating the publication of Newton's masterpiece.

Science and the History of Science are then two quite separate things. In his heart of hearts the pukka scientist paraphrases Shaw: Those who can do: those who can't – become philosophical historians of science. When G. H. Hardy came to write his charming *A Mathematician's Apology* he felt it necessary to apologise, beginning the book with the words:

> It is a melancholy experience for a professional mathematician to find himself writing about mathematics. The function of a mathematician is to do something, to prove new theorems, to add to mathematics, and not to talk about what he or other mathematicians have done. . . .

With all respect, this is nonsense. Hardy did not have to wait until he was past sixty and lacked the freshness of mind for proper mathematics in order to talk about the role of the mathematician. At no time of life did he begrudge the time spent on tennis or on talking about cricket. Because martinis are not appropriate for breakfast, it is not necessary for you to be a teetotaller. When I was an undergraduate at the University of Chicago, I was told that you could see the eminent mathematician Dickson at the Quadrangles Club playing bridge every afternoon all afternoon. When reproached for his idleness, Dickson (who was a prolific writer) is supposed to have replied: 'If you worked as hard at mathematics as I do from 8 to 12, you too could play bridge in the afternoon.'

Let me not be misunderstood. Of course I would rather have Newton's *Principia* than his diary or laundry list. But would not the world rather have Poincaré's marvellous account of how the idea came to him for Fuchsian functions as he was stepping on a bus during military service than have the theory of Fuchsian functions itself? Economists know that value depends upon scarcity. There is no rarity of the products of normal science. Yet few indeed are the genuine accounts of the creative process by which new knowledge came into existence. We value the journals of Boswell, not so much because his reveries were outstandingly different from anyone else's, but because his peculiar exhibitionism for once reveals – nonsense and all – what he thinks; and there is not one of us, who, conscious of our own wandering reveries, does not recognise the genuineness of Boswell's testimony.

Virgil began: *Arma virumque cano.* But it is not of man as man that I sing here. It is with *economist man.* And mark this well: 'economist man' is not the same thing as that textbook stereotype 'economic man' ... *Homo economicus.* They are quite different. When somebody says to me, 'How come you are such a learned economist and yet you spend your money so foolishly?' I draw myself up to my full seven feet of height and reply haughtily, 'I am not a home economist.'

FAMILIAR FACES

As Schumpeter would say, let us now turn to review the troops. What a goodly company it is, those who have contributed to the field of international economics. Almost every great name in the field of economics turns out to be represented in the international field as well.

Let me go back three centuries and begin with David Hume, who wrote in years that have to be labelled B.A.S. – Before Adam Smith. Hume of course made an imperishable contribution to our subject in the form of his specie-flow quantity theory equilibration of the balance of payments. This first appeared in his 1849 letter to Montesquieu, and we can only agree with the latter's notation on the letter, that 'It is full of insight and good sense.'

Adam Smith himself made no great theoretical advance on Hume's self-adjusting mechanism in the field of international finance. But assured of the existence of such a mechanism, Smith could extol the role of *laissez-faire* in this and other matters, and bitterly criticise the doctrine of mercantilism. I should add that Smith's emphasis upon the advantages of the division of labour is itself a primitive theory of international trade; and, stretching matters a bit, I might include him as a precursor of Bertil Ohlin's emphasis upon increasing returns to scale as a cause of inter-regional and international trade. To quote the words of the dying Hume in writing to Smith to congratulate him on *The Wealth of Nations*, Smith's work 'has Depth and Solidity and Acuteness, and is so much illustrated by curious Facts . . .'.

We think of Ricardo as following Smith. But actually there was a gap of more than forty years before David Ricardo chanced upon his four magic numbers that constitute the core of the doctrine of comparative advantage theory. I say Ricardo's numbers, but it may well be that Colonel Torrens has equal or even better claims to priority on comparative cost than Ricardo. As so often happens in the history of thought, the greater name drives out the lesser one. Ricardo's claims to the doctrines of rent and diminishing returns seem no better than those of Malthus or Sir Edward West, and yet we tend to speak of Ricardian rent. (Actually, Hume in his dying letter to Smith had anticipated all of them, saying to Smith, 'If you were here at my Fireside, I should dispute some of your Principles. I cannot think that Rent of Farms makes any part of the Price of the Produce. . . .') I shall say more later about Ricardian comparative advantage. Let me only note here an amusing fact: when Ricardo wishes to contrast a country that is more productive in every industry than another, he uses for his example the names of Portugal and

England and chooses for his two goods the classic case of wine and cloth. (Mill later switched to linen and cloth, England and Germany. Much later Frank Graham used wheat and watches, countries A and B. Taussig used wheat and linen, the United States and Germany. Tiring of the whimsy of countries with names like Ruritania and of trivial commodities, I earned undying fame by introducing food and clothing, Europe and America – but with the difficulty that in the field of finance the dollar had to stand for America and the pound for Europe, even though the pound has had little in common with the currencies of the important European nations.) Writing in the heyday of England's industrial revolution, which country do you think Ricardo made out to be the most productive? Obviously I should not have raised the question if Ricardo had not selected Portugal as the superior of England in every respect, having a real per capita G.N.P. in Colin Clark units that is somewhere between one-ninth and one-half greater depending upon whether you are a drunkard or a dandy. Why this odd economic geography? Was it *noblesse oblige*, to give the other fellow the advantage? I doubt it: probably, Ricardo regarded his reader as one who was tempted by the protectionist arguments of the mercantilists, and in need of being reassured that another country could not undersell him in everything even if it were *more* productive in everything. Coming as I do from a country that is top dog – like Ricardo's Portugal – I have to persuade students that low-wage (low-productivity!) nations cannot undersell us in everything.

Cournot's great 1838 book appeared between the time of Ricardo's 1817 *Principles* and publication of Mill's 1844 *Essays* and 1848 *Principles*. Although Cournot is marvellously modern and fruitful, his analysis of tariff protection appears to be ambiguous and of doubtful validity. I should like, however, to call attention to his analysis of interspatial price equilibrium, which in 1838 treated rigorously the partial equilibrium relations that modern texts handle by the familiar back-to-back diagrams. This analysis was constantly being rediscovered, as for example around the turn of the century by Cunynghame, Pigou, Schüller, and Barone; and again within the next couple of decades by Taussig and Henry Schultz. To show the continuity in the theory of international trade, note that in the 1950s Stephen Enke showed how an electric network could handle the case of any number of regions, leading me to give a solution to the problem in terms of linear and non-linear programming theory. Fox, Judge, and other agricultural economists have worked out empirical applications to many regions and more than one commodity, utilising quadratic and other programming methods. Moreover, this same Cournot kind of partial equilibrium analysis, but now made logarithmic in order to handle exchange rate changes rather than unit tariff duties and transport costs, has been used by a long line of writers to analyse the effects of currency depreciation. I shall mention only the names of Bickerdike,

Joan Robinson, and Haberler and the intricate equations of elasticities that serve as Marshall-Lerner stability conditions and as criteria for deteriorations of the terms of trade. That something new under the sun is always possible is shown by Joan Robinson's observation in the present age that a depreciation of the home currency raises prices of both exports and imports in the home market and lowers them both in the foreign market, making it quite impossible to deduce that in general there is to be expected a deterioration of the terms of trade of the depreciating country. This conclusion was at first greeted with surprise; but, as usually happens, later treated as fairly obvious.

John Stuart Mill is my candidate for most underrated economist. The reasons are simple: he was too modest; he was too eclectic; he was too clear; and he had the misfortune of appearing to Karl Marx as a rival needing to be put down as a vulgar bourgeois economist. Nowhere is Mill's originality greater than in the field of international values. And actually in this area he was led to put down the first instance of a rigorous general equilibrium model. How ironic that Jevons, who gained undying fame because he was the first one to produce a rigorous equilibrium model of exchange, thereby anticipating Walras's general equilibrium by a few years, nursed a great hatred towards Mill as an Establishment figure standing in the way of progress. If Mill had used graphs or equations and had applied his international tools to domestic values, Jevons could not have been so original. It took Marshall, who was a trained mathematician and who was born in the age after Jevons, to recognise the general equilibrium implicit in Mill. The only elegantly exciting economic theory that Marshall ever produced was his 1879 privately published *Theory of Domestic and Foreign Values*, later reproduced as Appendix in his *Money, Credit and Commerce*. This work is directly inspired by John Stuart Mill.

Now I must begin to move fast, skipping such names as Cairnes, and in Schumpeter's grand manner barely mentioning such names as Pareto and Bastable. An international flavour is introduced into the discourse when important improvements on the Ricardo-Mill constant-cost case were discovered by Edgeworth in the writings of the German Mangoldt. In Mangoldt we have an underrated economist; and indeed because of the brilliance of the Anglo-Saxon tradition a century ago and the local dominance of the Historical School, German contributions to economic analysis of that time have tended to be underestimated. Mangoldt's case was not helped by the kind friend who brought out a posthumous edition of his textbook, omitting the mathematical parts as being unappetising and unimportant. Actually, most of what we remember Mangoldt for today comes from these omitted parts. (If scientific activity constitutes a zero-sum game, when someone is getting too little credit, someone else must be getting too much. My candidate for the most overvalued currency in economics is Alfred Marshall. When you subtract from his accomplishment what he acknowledgedly got from Cournot, Mangoldt, and Dupuit, he loses the position of primacy that he enjoyed when I began the study of economics. I never dreamed that Walras and Wicksell would come to enjoy their present, quite-deserved dominance in modern thought over Böhm-Bawerk and Marshall, the big guns of my undergraduate days.)

Edgeworth has made Mangoldt's treatment of many goods and countries a standard item in the international trade textbooks. This analysis has been carried forward by Taussig, Viner, Haberler, above all by Frank Graham – and in our times by Metzler, Elliott, McKenzie, and Ronald Jones. As recently as 1962 I found that it still could bring new understanding to such a problem as the possible overvaluation of the American dollar.

HEROIC TIMES

Unlike Tristram Shandy who could take a year to write up the first few weeks of his life, if I am to finish I must quicken my pace. The World War I years added primarily to our understanding of Cassel's purchasing-power-parity doctrines and to a posing by Keynes of the 'transfer problem'. Then just about forty years ago, international trade theory began its third heroic age. The great names are our contemporaries and teachers: Bertil Ohlin, Haberler – who broke away from one-factor Ricardian costs by the brilliant introduction of the production-possibility frontier – Viner, Lerner, and Leontief. My own work, and that of my contemporaries, stems from this seminal outburst. And to show once again that there is always something new under the sun, as recently as 1950 James Meade was able to innovate – in the form of his trade-indifference envelope contours – a fundamentally useful new gadget in the tool box of economics. The 1937 book of Viner more or less concludes an era; I may refer you to Richard Caves' book for the chronicles of what followed.

I must confine myself to only a few of the major topics of international economics in the last third of a century: macro-economic multiplier analysis of the post-Keynes type; to welfare economics; and to the factor-price equalisation discussions.

After Keynes, Kahn, and J. M. Clark had developed the domestic multiplier, around 1936 Harrod, Paish, Colin Clark, Robertson, Machlup, and Metzler created a multi-sector multiplier analysis. At this point the mathematicians took over, joining the multiplier matrixes with those of (i) Leontief input-output, (ii) Mosak-Hicks cross-substitutes, (iii) Markov-Frêchet transition probabilities. Just to drop a few names, here are Frobenius, Minkowski, and *our* old friends Metzler, Chipman, Goodwin, Solow, Johnson, and Morishima. The convergence of formal structure of diverse problems of economics is indeed remarkable.

These income effects were combined with terms-of-trade price effects by

Metzler-Laursen, Harberger, Meade, Johnson, Alexander, and perhaps by most of the people in this room.

At the micro-economic level, the scientific tariff problem was re-discovered from Mill, Bickerdike, and Edgeworth in our own era: I, with Kaldor, Scitovsky, and a host of other writers, connected up international trade discussion with the developing 'new welfare economics', in the broad version of Bergson and the narrower, now somewhat outmoded compensation economics of Pareto and Hicks.

Also at the micro-economic level, Stolper and I initiated in 1940 a vast post-Ohlin discussion on factor proportion and trade. I cannot here summarise that literature, but merely drop the names of Lerner (that man again!), Tinbergen, Meade, Pearce, McKenzie, and many others. At the two-factor level, the matter was early resolved; and Leontief's Paradox gave the debate an empirical relevance. At the many-factor level, mathematical innovations were made by Gale and Nikaido, and I defer to the later discussion by Murray Kemp for reference for further work by Rochester, Japanese, and Australian economists.

The importance of the factor-price equalisation analyses is not solely, or perhaps primarily, for the understanding of regional trade patterns. Rather, the development of analysis of the box-diagram relation between factor intensities and opportunity costs was long overdue. Except for fragmentary early work by Benham and Harrod, in 1940 most of the work still remained to be done. And I need only remind you that modern two-sector growth theory, which has nothing to do with international relations, leans heavily on these post-1940 innovations. (Rybczinski's Theorem is just one instance.)

PERCEPTIONS

Well, what have we learned from our review of the troops? Almost all the great names are there. Let me recapitulate them. Hume, Smith, Ricardo, Mill, Marshall, Edgeworth, Taussig, Viner, Haberler, Ohlin, and Keynes. And still others are there in the background. Thus, Pigou and Robertson were able to contribute to a solution of the Keynes-Ohlin controversy over the transfer problem by using essentially the barter model of Jevons. The Lerner–Leontief–Viner indifference curve analysis of trade is essentially isomorphic with the general equilibrium of Hicks' *Value and Capital*. And Hicks' *Value and Capital* is identical in its general equilibrium structure with Irving Fisher's 1907 *Rate of Interest*. Decades before Haberler's 1930 use of the transformation frontier, Fisher had used it to resolve once and for all, and for essentially the first time, what I may dare to call the positive theory of interest.

A living science is indeed an in decomposable web of interrelationships.

Having reviewed the troopers, let us say a word about their manoeuvres. Travel is broadening in the sense that it gives one a deeper understanding of one's own country. Similarly, even if one wanted to be an economist dealing purely with the problems of a closed economy, he would be well advised to study international economic analysis. So to speak, our subject puts its best foot forward when it speaks out on international trade. This was brought home to me years ago when I was in the Society of Fellows at Harvard along with the mathematician Stanislaw Ulam. Ulam, who was to become an originator of the Monte Carlo method and co-discoverer of the hydrogen bomb, was already at a tender age a world famous topologist. And he was a delightful conversationalist, wandering lazily over all domains of knowledge. He used to tease me by saying, 'Name me one proposition in all of the social sciences which is both true and non-trivial.' This was a test that I always failed. But now, some thirty years later, on the staircase so to speak, an appropriate answer occurs to me: The Ricardian theory of comparative advantage; the demonstration that trade is mutually profitable even when one country is absolutely more – or less – productive in terms of every commodity. That it is logically true need not be argued before a mathematician; that it is not trivial is attested by the thousands of important and intelligent men who have never been able to grasp the doctrine for themselves or to believe it after it was explained to them. (Just to give one instance: 'Boss' Kettering was a famous inventor of the recent epoch, having developed the self-starting auto and many other important devices. Yet this founder of General Motors and pioneer in cancer research never could understand why it might pay to send American cotton to Japan to be spun into cloth and then sent back to the United States.)

World I never made

And now if I may presume to close on a more personal note. It is not so much to my credit as to my good fortune that I have been able to participate in the development of our economic science. How do the lines of A. E. Housman go? ... here I am, ... 'lonely and afraid, in a world I never made'. I certainly came into a world of scholarship that I never made. But lonely it has not been. And if I may borrow a technical term, my scholarly life has been splashed with consumer's surplus. In the great days of the University of Chicago – of Frank Knight and Jacob Viner and Henry Schultz, and of Oskar Lange just around the corner – I happened to be there as an undergraduate. Then when the action moved to the golden age of the Harvard Yard, your humble servant happened to be there. Joseph Schumpeter, Alvin Hansen, Wassily Leontief, and Edwin Bidwell Wilson were my masters. These men could give nothing to each other. But they gave much to me. Though I never migrated far from the

Harvard Yard, when I became a grown-up in my own house I found at MIT worthy shipmates. At the end of his life G. H. Hardy could say with pride, 'I collaborated with Littlewood.' Well, I can claim to have made beautiful music together with Robert Solow. And I have even survived collaboration with Franco Modigliani.

Particularly in the field of the subject of this Congress on international trade have I been a lucky man. Both Viner and Haberler were my teachers. (Indeed, if I may lapse into geneology, my blood lines would do credit to a Daughter of the American Revolution. Being the son of Schumpeter, I am the grandson of Böhm-Bawerk and Menger. Being the son of Leontief, I am the grandson of Bortkiewicz and am the great-grandson of Walras. Being the son of E. B. Wilson, I am one of those rare grand-children of Yale's great physicist, Willard Gibbs. Since Alvin Hansen rose full-blown from the forehead of Jove, I am, to mix the metaphor, a son of Adam.) Abram Bergson and Lloyd Metzler have been my companions at arms. And to speak plainly, I have served my turn at stud. Ronald Jones, Mundell, Bhagwati, Wan, Romney Robinson, Fei, Lefeber, Findlay, Ichimura, Sohmen, Vanek, and more international trade theorists than I can remember here to enumerate have been my pupils. If the greatest thing in the universe is to have a Ph.D. in economics at Harvard, I can even claim to have contributed that last final bit of Böhm-Bawerkian value-added to Harry Johnson when he, already a distinguished scholar, deigned to take his Special Examinations at Harvard.

J. J. Thomson was a great physicist who won a Nobel Prize for his discovery of the electron and achieved what some would consider to be an equivalent honour in being made the Master of Trinity College, Cambridge. In his autobiography Thomson has said something like the following: Mine has been a happy life as a scholar. I have had good teachers and good students. I have been paid to do what I like to do, and can take some satisfaction in the good work of my hands.

Amen to that can say I. When I think of Wicksell, who was almost my present age before he received his first professorial chair; when I think of the lonely figure of Stanley Jevons, walking on the Australian shore and vowing to make his scholarly mark; when I think of Karl Marx sitting painfully in the British Museum; and when I think of Leon Walras writing all over the globe for some pitiful sign of professional recognition. When I think of all these things, I know how to measure out the consumer's surplus which I have enjoyed.

But it would not be like me to end up on too humble a note. As Schumpeter said about the innovator, half the battle is to know how to take advantage of your opportunities. And sometimes I say facetiously to my classroom students that I had advantages in the good old days now denied to them. All of my teachers had the blessed property of being imperfect. No problem seemed solved; everything seemed left to do.

Being a student of someone like Robert Solow obviously has its marvellous advantages. But still, may there not be a price for a youth of twenty to pay in terms of self-confidence and zest?

For better or worse, the picture album whose pages I have been turning is that of the main stream of international economics. Many of its advances lie in what the historian of science Thomas Kuhn would call 'normal' rather than 'revolutionary' science. It is hard to imagine having had *too* good an education and *too* good a research environment. And yet as we grapple with the ever-changing problems of the modern world that are arising in the deliberations of this World Congress, we know we must put aside the pictures and souvenirs of the past, and we must turn a youthful eye out to meet the emerging universe.

FOREWORD TO THE JAPANESE TRANSLATION OF FOUNDATIONS OF ECONOMIC ANALYSIS

Some sage has said, perhaps it was I, "The only thing better than an economic classic is its Japanese translation." Reversing the usual corruption of text that goes with transcription and translation, Japanese scholars purge from a treatise those Poisson-distributed random errors that authors blame on the printer. In his little book on the mathematics of quantum theory, Harvard's distinguished George Mackey has a line in his preface that goes something like this: If at one place or another the reader is tempted to put a minus sign into a formula, he is probably right to do so. Similar counsel will certainly not apply to this excellent translation of my *Foundations*, whose appearance I hail with pleasure and pride.

A scholar's books are like his children. They come to lead a life of their own but he tends to remember how they were at the beginning. Much of this book was written in the glorious prewar days. As Talleyrand might have said, only those who have known the *ancien régime* can savor its sweetness. Being a Junior Fellow at Harvard from 1937 to 1940 was the perfect environment for creative work: no duties, adequate pay; reams of blank paper, sharpened pencils; and best of all, most of what needed doing in economic theory not yet done.

As I turn the pages of the book, I can recall that certain of its theorems were developed in walks along the Charles river; and some while sitting in the front seat of a car, being driven westward at 70 miles an hour by my wife. In those days thinking about economics filled my every hour. I did not say wakeful hour because often I dreamed of theorems in my sleep — some of them true. Indeed the latest researches on the nature of sleep have corroborated my own heretical notions: I could never believe in the fashionable hypothesis that all our dreams take place in the few instants of awakening, even though, in common with everyone else, I have had the experience of being awakened by a bell and being left with the illusion that all of my dreaming had taken place subsequent to its ringing. But I had also often the experience of going through involved syllogistic reasoning in dreams, in about the same sequence of steps as when awake; and I would find it incredible to believe that in sleep one could prove the Pythagorean Theorem instantaneously, while being unable to do it in less than five minutes when in full possession of one's faculties.

In describing Isaac Newton's genius, Keynes spoke of his enormous powers of concentration. Concentration, if you can manage it, is indeed a powerful asset for the creative scholar. It is like a hidden asset working for you silently all the time. And you need hardly be aware of it. Newton himself has spoken disparagingly of his own accomplishments, saying that to himself he appeared merely like a boy playing with pretty pebbles on the beach. Similarly Gauss, whom anyone would have to reckon as one of the mathematical geniuses of all time, dismissed his abilities in the statement, "If anyone had thought as hard on these mathematical matters as I have done, they too would have made similar discoveries." One is entitled to doubt the correctness of these self-appraisals.

Yet there is something genuine in them. Abilities being equal, the harder worker will produce the greater and more valuable scientific output. Moreover, even if abilities were *initially* equal, they will not stay so. Each new theorem, each new insight, is like money in the bank, waiting to be drawn upon in some quite unexpected connection. But this much is true. Suppose a Gauss gets ahead of the pack. And suppose, as is not really quite the case, that Gauss can run no faster than the rest of the pack. Yet, if once he is ahead, he need only run at their speed and still he will always be ahead; any new theorem they discover, he will already have reached in his private notebooks. It is a little like the case of my despairing children, who realized at five years of age that they could never, never quite catch up with their six-year-old brother. But, as Marx would ask, How do you get that initial head-start? How do you contrive that act of primitive accumulation? This is the point at which talent and genius must be involved.

In those days someone once asked me which economic journals I read. I had to reply that I read them all; and that meant essentially all of each journal, an article on labor relations being as much grist for my mill as one on the pure theory of nonintegrable indifference. It is not a procedure that I can widely recommend. Some people are so constituted that they can only be original if they do not read the works of others. To be sure, this is often a deceptive originality — what Schumpter used to call ironically "subjective originality" and part of what Myrdal once referred to as "that quite unnecessary Anglo-Saxon originality." For myself, it was a matter of pride to try to do justice to the literature. Not only did equity require this, but also the efficiency of building up the edifice of scientific knowledge called for integrating new findings with old. He who goes out each morning to invent the wheel, furthers his vanity more than his locomotion. And the consumers of scholarly output are ill served when important ideas get lost and keep being reenunciated in new forms. But most of all I think it is pride that makes one accept the much, much harder challenge of trying only to produce value-added rather than gross contributions to the body of scientific knowledge. (I may say that the problem was easier in the good old days when the number of interested and competent scholars was less. The mere replication of numbers in any area of research necessarily lowers the uniqueness of the contributions of any one person, leading inevitably to psychological problems. One escape, of course, is into fragmentation and specialization of interest — so that the same number of people who used to be studying universal gravitation are now studying the constant-elasticity-of-substitution production function.)

I have brought up the problem of originality and priority of scientific discovery, which some will think is bad taste in polite conversation. But that is only a convention. One might as well try to banish from society discussion of sex. As Robert Merton has pointed out in his important researches on the sociology of science, one should not be surprised that there is great sensitivity among scientists concerning the issues of priority, issues which must inevitably arise because of the great probability of nearly simultaneous discovery. For, as Merton points out, reputation for originality is the only coin that the scholar can work for: who robs me of my theorem steals not trash but all that there is to steal. Nor have the greatest scientists been immune to this (even though they are in the favored position of being able to create a new theorem if one is snatched from them). Thus take the case of Newton himself. He discovered the theory of the world during the year of the great plague when he was still in his early twenties. But he did not publish his *Principia* for a score of years. Why? Some time was perhaps needed to embalm his calculus relations in the amber of classical geometry; and Newton did have to struggle with a problem that any MIT freshman would today find easy — to show that assuming all of a body's mass to lie at its center of gravity involves no distortion.

But the usual reason given for Newton's delay is that he had an incorrect radius of the earth and held up publication until his calculations came into agreement with the actual behavior of the moon in falling toward the earth. (Can one imagine a modern econometrician holding up publication for two months for such a reason!) All of these are nice hypotheses. But it is just as probable that Newton was held back from publication by his stubborn unwillingness to concede, as he was asked to do, that Hooke had also contemplated attraction according to the inverse square of the distance. An anal type like Newton would rather never publish than have to make any such reference!

To go back to the gestation of this book, World War II held up its final revision; and, like a prospective mother who becomes weary of her condition and longs for delivery, I must confess that at one time I became rather estranged from my brainchild. In the backwash of the Keynesian macroeconomic revolution and at a time when war created special economic problems, the niceties of pure economics seemed somewhat decadent. However, the book was a great success from the time of its 1947 appearance. It is sweet revenge upon a departed head of the Harvard economics department, who had to be forced into printing a thousand copies and who had the type immediately destroyed despite the expense of mathematical typesetting, that the book still continues to sell as many in each year as he had wanted to print in all. Since books, like children, do lead a life of their own, I have never brought out a second edition, being content to correct the various errors — most of them, fortunately, minor — that were pointed out to me. By good fortune the emphasis in the *Foundations* on inequalities, which emerged from my earliest works on revealed preference, turned out to be the wave of the future in economic theory. And within a year of the book's appearance, and after the first edition of my elementary *Economics* had appeared, George Stigler was able to say in a witty introduction, "Professor Samuelson, having achieved fame, now seeks fortune."

It is true that both have come to me in good measure. And I am grateful. All the more so to see the *Foundations* now taking on a new career in the Japanese language.

PAUL A. SAMUELSON

Cambridge, Mass.
July, 1967

188

FOREWORD TO THE CHINESE TRANSLATION OF FOUNDATIONS OF ECONOMIC ANALYSIS

Occasionally I have toyed with the notion of bringing out a revised edition of this book, or even following it up with a second volume that would bring up to date the treatment of its subjects. But it is more fun to do new research than polish up old. And besides once a work has achieved a certain place in the literature of a scholarly subject, it takes on an existence of its own. Who am I in my mid-fifties to tamper with the creation of the young scholar who wrote this book in his twenties?

What one can do with a child, even a brain-child, is to wish it happy birthdays and reminisce about its earlier life. Or one can look into its future. Or, as the passage of time begins to lend some semblance of objectivity, one can assay an appraisal of its character and place in the history of the subject — in this case, analytical economics. So a few random reflections may not be out of place on the occasion of this Chinese translation of *Foundations*.

First, I was lucky in my general choice of subject matter. The first half of *Foundations* was essentially concerned with the inequalities implied by the process of maximization. I had no way of knowing, before the days of linear programming and of von Neumann game theory, that inequalities would come to play so central a role in economic theory as has turned out to be the case since 1947. A reader of this work was in a good position to appreciate the new formulations of a George Dantzig (linear programming), a von Neumann (game theory and growth models), and a Koopmans or Arrow or McKenzie or Debreu (convex-set theory, topology, probability). Indeed, in a sense my *Foundations* approach was more general than many of the modern formulations that posit more convexity than I was assuming: thus, consider a person with indifference-contours that are nonquasi-concave; it is hard to fit him into a modern proof of the existence of a competitive equilibrium because of the discontinuities in his demand function, and yet all the basic global conditions of revealed preference still do apply to him.

Second, I was lucky that I did not too-consistently stick to my program of deriving operationally meaningful theorems, for otherwise topics like welfare economics and economic dynamics might have been excluded. Though the accelerator-multiplier interactions cannot usefully be analyzed in terms of any maximum problem, it would be a shame to leave such models out of an economic discussion. On the other hand, were the book being written today with knowledge of the revival of interest in Ramsey growth models, I would certainly have added a chapter on optimal-control theory and similar dynamic maximization matters. And then instead of being preoccupied with the problem of damped stability of dynamic motions, I would have been interested as well in stationary points which are saddlepoints, surrounded by dynamic motions of the catenary type that we associate with modern turnpike theory. (Although I was aware of the catenary property of a Ramsey system when this book was written, it was not until a 1949 sojourn at Rand in California that I formulated a version of what is today known as turnpike theory, more specifically production-turnpike theory.)

But what is the point at a twenty-fourth birthday party in mentioning that one had not done by the time of birth itself all that there was to do? To say that everything in science might have come earlier is to assert an empty truism, and carries the perverse implication that everything was to be known at the beginning. The fun in scientific research, as in life itself, is in the dynamics and not the statics of the problem.

M.I.T., May, 1971   PAUL A. SAMUELSON

189

MONEY AND HISTORY
by Paul A. Samuelson

I

To know our country we must have travelled abroad. To know our times we must know something of the past. Unlike the chemist or physicist, who can create history in his laboratory, we in the social sciences are alms seekers who must take gratefully the scraps that happen to get thrown our way. Clio, the Muse of History, is a most capricious philanthropist, absent-mindedly giving us an occasional glimpse of her petticoat, teasing us as much with what she withholds as reveals. Like the astronomer and geologist, we must treasure ever scrap of experience, scrutinizing it in the hope that it will be the Rosetta Stone to a wider understanding.

Documents and statutes are the hardware of history. Antiquarians become archaeologists through no choice of their own. It has been said that history is written by survivors. More accurately, I assert that history is written *about* survivors. What else is there to write about? All else is science fiction, a contradiction in terms. In using the documents of an earlier age, we can guard against the fatal contamination of the past by the present, a felony which by comparison makes introducing the common cold or syphilis to the moon a misdemeanor.

But archaeology has, of course, its own distortions. Man does not live by arrowheads alone. What survives is only a sampling of what there was, and by no means an unbiased sample. Once, in Nara, Japan, I visited the oldest *wooden* building in the world. To a son of the Middle Border, born on the frontier—I mean in Gary, Indiana, which had sprung full-blown from the temple of United States Steel within the decade of my birth— who had never seen a structure a century old until going East as an adult, I found this an impressive sight. But an Egyptian would have laughed at pretensions that cannot span even a millenium, and a Roman could have been forgiven a chuckle. Yet most people since the beginning of time, or more accurately the beginning of recordable history, have lived in wooden

From *Documentary History of Banking and Currency in the United States,* edited by Herman K. Krooss. (1969) Published by Chelsea House in association with McGraw-Hill Book Company.

structures, every one of which was destined to end in flame. Or consider the importance for the past of the *public* as against the *private* sector of the economy. Cathedrals, castles, monuments, and forums are more resistant to time's abrasions than thatched roofs and hovels: a perverted view of past inequality in the distribution of wealth is drawn if one naively infers that the red and white balls drawn from Clio's urn are an unbiased sample of the urn's true universe.

What to do about it? Stop digging for vases and axes? Neglecting the pot in hand will not bring back half an ounce of evaporated stew. One does what one can with what one has. There is, though, a special obligation to separate, as the magazine says, fact from opinion—inference from data. There is an obligation to report the findings of history in such a way that each consumer can make his own inferences. In this regard, I have always found a story* about Harvard University President Charles W. Eliot more instructive than all five feet of his edited classics.

Once, according to what I must admit may be legend, President Eliot was to lecture at the Harvard Club of New York. When he left his hat with the attendant, he was given no hat check, a fact which bothered him throughout the dinner and even during his speech. However, all ended well, for at the door he was handed his hat by the Negro attendant. A seeker of truth, Eliot did not leave well enough alone. The following dialogue ensued:

Eliot: Since you gave me no check, how do you know it is my hat?
Attendant: I don't.
Eliot: Then why did you give it to me?
Attendant: Because *you* gave it to me.

This is sticking to the evidence, the next thing for a scientist or historian to do after he has garnered it.

The documents that Professor Krooss has skillfully selected to illuminate money in American history speak for themselves. It would be absurd for me to read Benjamin Franklin's 1729 essay, "A Modest Enquiry into the Nature and Necessity of a Paper Currency" and conclude that I am a better economist. Of course I am. But only in the sense that any M.I.T. freshman is a better physicist than Isaac Newton. When T. S. Eliot was told that we know more than the ancients, he countered, "Yes, and it is the ancients that we know." Sir Isaac Newton, the greatest genius of any

---

*Since history requires footnotes, here is one. I heard the story from Harvard President A. Lawrence Lowell on some Monday evening during the years 1937–40, in (if you please) Eliot House at Harvard.

age, said he saw further than his predecessors because he stood upon the shoulders of giants. What a privilege, to be able to give a foothold to a Newton—it makes one a giant!

To read Franklin on money is a delight, partly because it is a delight to read him on any subject. The man was incapable of being boring. Or unoriginal. Even if Franklin had not written it, the essay would be worth reading for its content, its foreshadowing, so to speak, of the *Weltanschauung* that we associate with the name of Keynes—departure from financial orthodoxy in order to promote vigorous employment and growth. Being the authentic work of Franklin, the essay takes on a special significance as a corrective to certain false notions about him that pass as true history. Those of us brought up on the copybook aphorisms of *Poor Richard's Almanac* may think of Benjamin Franklin as a homespun and rather boring Polonius, a figure of the Protestant Ethic who appears more attractive seen in the telescope from the safe distance of Germany than from down the block. Professor Krooss has shown us there was another Franklin, one quite unknown to George Babbitt.

When someone asks me what is the significance of economic study, if I am in a defensive mood I can always answer: "Advanced economics is the needed antidote for incorrect primitive economics." The same defense can be made for history. Knowledge of the truths of history is needed to guard against its untruths. In what I think were his only memorable words, Henry Ford once said: "History is bunk." These are true words but not in the way that the sage of Dearborn intended them. History is not bunk because the past is not worth knowing. Men will always want to hear about it for the simple reason that it was there. Much of what passes for history is indeed bunk by virtue of being untrue. According to Napoleon, "History is a fable agreed upon." As some wit has said, Napoleon should have known better, and so should have Voltaire before him. Where history is concerned the jury is always out. When that plain man down at the Club says, "I don't know much about history or science, but. . ." stop him there and take him at his word.

The know-nothings who run the world may claim to be innocent of theories about the past, but that means merely that they are implicit believers in the legends and notions that we all acquire before we have reached the age of consent. Statutory rape takes place all the time quite outside the realm of biology. Since few have been in Alexander the Great's enviable position of having Aristotle as a Nanny, unlearning is as much the task of life as learning.

I have been speaking as if history could be an exact science. Of course that is not possible. It is one thing to guard against forged documents, to recognize the typical as against the atypical fossil. An arrowhead may be an arrowhead may be an arrowhead. But the minute you put two of them together in a showcase, that is a 1969 act of selection. Just as a kaleidoscope makes new designs from the same materials, each generation must arrange into new patterns its threads of history. We call it Whig history when a Macaulay interprets the past as a gestation period to produce a Thomas Babington Macaulay. Yet to a degree, there can be no other kind of history.

Moreover, the consumer of history—the gentle reader—is an active agent in the scenario. The Silver Acts of 1918, 1934, and 1938 take on a new significance to me in light of the recent Silver Act of 1965, and the imminent demise of silver as an element in America's monetary system. Outside of Montana, silver's departure will not be mourned; but in the manner of its going something may perhaps be learned about the vicissitudes that gold is likely to go through in the next decade or two. Thus, history is both a jolly good yarn, a tale told by an idiot signifying nothing, and at the same time a cautionary tale, pointing the moral—"there but for the grace. . ." Precisely in its dualistic quality—half-mortal, half-godlike—lies history's special fascination.

Significance as well as beauty is in the ears of the listener. Those who did not live through the Great Depression cannot possibly comprehend the impact of President Roosevelt's Fireside Chat of March 12, 1933 in that first post-Inaugural week when all the banks had shut down and the economy was at a standstill. The document of this speech, like Edward R. Murrow's recording (*I Can Hear It Now*) which contains it, does what can be done to convey the flavor of history.

When Orson Welles played *Julius Caesar* in the modern garb of a blackshirt Nazi, the script had a vitality for Alfred North Whitehead it had not possessed in the days of his youth when Victoria's in-laws peopled the thrones of Europe and dictators were bogeymen invented by nurses to titillate the fears of gullible children. Not until the dark days of World War II could I appreciate Shakespeare's lines of *Henry V* at Agincourt:

> We few, we happy few, we band of brothers
>
> . . . .
>
> That fought with us upon Saint Crispin's Day

II

In all of economic history there is no subject more fascinating than money. It and love are supposed to be the things for which we will do almost anything—a two-thirds truth at best, since you can't take it with you, and books on health are also on the bestseller list. My publisher once said to me: "You can't buy good health with money. Or happiness. You can't buy love with money. . . Of course, I mean Confederate money."

He had a better point than he realized. Until recently the affluent had a life expectancy much superior to that of the poor: for documents to prove this, examine the rates that used to be charged on ordinary life insurance and on the so-called industrial policies sold in small denominations to the poor. Money enabled you to purchase extra years of life—and at the end where they are shortest in supply! Physical health counts for little if you are neurotic and mentally unwell. It appears not to be the case that the moody Hamlets are to be found on Park Avenue while Main Street teems with happy children of nature. The Federal Commission on Mental Illness and Health made a survey in 1960 which found that college graduates reported greater happiness and less mental illness; in contrast to the poor, when they worried, their worries tended to be over genuine rather than imagined troubles.

"Marry the boss's daughter, not his secretary," advised an erstwhile M.I.T. professor in a much-quoted 1929 speech. (Anthony Trollope had said it earlier: "Don't marry for money. But marry where money is.") Youth does not have to be told its business: nuptiality tables show there are relatively fewer spinsters among the class of heiresses than among the populace at large. Sir Ronald Fisher, the greatest statistician of our age, actually had a theory of the decay of civilizations based upon the proclivity of heiresses, by definition the offspring of sterile strains, to fasten upon and sterilize the ablest elements of any mobile society. Alas, for the glory that was Greece, the grandeur that was Rome—done in by the almighty drachma. When the noted anthropologist Melville Herskovits made a survey of marriage among American Negroes, he found that men marry for glamour, women for security; hence, in those days before a resurgence of race pride, men tended to marry women lighter in color than themselves. (*Porgy and Bess* put this well: ". . . yo'r Pappy's rich, and yo'r Mammy's good lookin'. . .") Sir Francis Galton, an eminent Victorian who studied hereditary genius (and had himself as a relevant target for investigation), once tried to find out where in Britain the women were the prettiest. As he walked down the street of any town, he would punch a pin into a piece of paper in his right or left pocket depending upon whether the female he passed was comely or plain. The prettiest women turned out to be in London; the plainest in Aberdeen. Again the correlation between affluence and beauty is unmistakable. Even innocent children are not immune from the contaminating effect of money. Kindergarten children were asked to rate each other in terms of prettiness, handsomeness, and ugliness. (A panel of adult strangers made a separate rating for control purposes.) It turned out that wealthier children are deemed prettier by their classmates than they really are, a truly depressing find. After marriage, do the wealthier live happily ever after? It is commonplace that destitute families in the Ozarks have more children than do the professional classes with high incomes. Like so many commonplaces, the observation is misleading: when we control for factors other than family income, as for example in studying the alumni of Princeton who share the same education and general ethnic background, we find that just as the purchase of autos, vacations, and the other good things of life goes up with increases in money income, so too does the pleasure of having a larger family. In Stockholm, where birth control has long since permeated to every part of the populace, fertility is low in all classes but less among the wealthy than among the poor. Whether or not a pattern in which the birth rate is positively correlated with money is optimal from a eugenics standpoint, it is a form of spreading the wealth and reducing the concentration of incomes.

It is an American saying that money talks. To an acute and fastidious observer, such as de Tocqueville, in the fluid American society it seemed to shout. A century ago if an Englishman made a fortune in the China trade, *he* could not hope to break into the upper class. Only after going to Eton could his son pass into County society. Not so here. A century ago in San Francisco two tycoons would meet on the waterfront and start tossing gold coins into the ocean. The one who turned chicken first fell behind in the pecking order. On the effete East Coast, upward mobility was only a little harder to contrive. Mrs. Vanderbilt could buy her way into Manhattan society and in her own lifetime lead the cotillion. A civilization in which money counts for much is subject to a more rapid circulation of the elite than one based upon ancient lineage. One can get rich overnight; to become wellborn takes longer. A system based on caste is immutable, or mutable only over a long period of time. The pace quickens where money is concerned. In the West Indies there used to be a saying, "Money whitens." Long ago Negroes in the South learned how welcome their money was in local department stores. Like a gun in the

Old West, money is a great equalizer: it makes a David or a Billy Rose into a great Goliath, and the power it conveys can be nicely calculated down to the last penny.

This emphasis on money has its good side. It is better to throw a coin into the ocean than your neighbor. Or, as John Maynard Keynes put it, "It is better for a man to tyrannize over his pocketbook than over his neighbor." Yet money does convey power over other people, a fact we must not forget when considering Keynes's approval of man's tyrannizing over his pocketbook: in doing so, he may at the same time be tyrannizing over his employee or local legislator. To a Bob Cratchit, the penuriousness of an Ebenezer Scrooge can hardly be deemed an amiable and *private* weakness.

Above all, the chief property of money is its vulgarity, as is illustrated by many an aphorism of folk wisdom. "You can see what the Almighty thinks of money when you look at the people he gave it to." "Money has no pride and no shame, it's not particular whom it goes to." A Southerner once put it to me: "You don't have to be smart to make money. But you do have to know how to make money." Like IQ, which has been defined as a certain low cunning in passing exams, the ability to make money is a trait only loosely correlated with braininess, animal vigor, or aesthetic sensibility. Not for nothing is the capitalist caricatured as a fat man with a sly penchant for arithmetic. When J. J. Thomson, the Nobel Laureate who discovered the electron, was told that any broker in the City made three times his salary as professor at Cambridge, he proudly replied: "Yes, but look at the work they have to do." Everyone, even the village idiot, can feel superior to the *nouveau riche*. To be sure, there is often a strong flavor of sour grapes in this. As W. Somerset Maugham said about a simple Mondrian painting, "It looks easy, as though you had only to take a ruler, a tube of black paint and a tube of red, and you could do the thing yourself. Try." Twenty-five hundred years ago, Thales of Miletus, weary no doubt of the taunt, "If you are so smart, why aren't you rich?" tried to prove that philosophers could make money if only they wanted to. But who can take seriously Aristotle's account in which Thales used his science to predict an eclipse, enabling him to foresee a bumper olive crop and to profit by buying up all the olive presses. This is excellent astronomy, ridiculous meteorology and agronomy, and only passable economics. When you base a speculation on a syllogism, it is not enough to have one of your premises right! Newton, Shakespeare, Ricardo, Willard Gibbs, and Keynes all did well as private investors. But many of their contemporaries did better; and the list of Einsteins who died wise but impecunious men could be a long one.

There are two times when one can despise money: when, as in the *postbellum* South, one doesn't have it; or, as now in Western cultures, when one is possessed of affluence. After Baron Rothschild tipped his hansom driver 10 gulden he met the reproach, "Your son tips me 100 gulden." Rothschild replied dryly, "But, of course, *he* has a rich father." The graduates of Yale and Princeton can today look down their noses at corporate recruiters and choose to do graduate work in Sanskrit, in part because earlier generations of Americans believed in Calvin Coolidge's dictum, "The business of America is Business." It is well said of the Harvard Law School: "The top third of the class provide the nation with its professors of law. The middle third with its judges. And the bottom third support the rest." And why not? It used to be the case in America, and it is still the case in the underdeveloped world, that it takes nine on the farm to feed every ten in the population. Today one man on the farm can feed thirty Americans well. That is why population has left the countryside. Rats leaving a sinking ship? Yes, and damned sensible of rats to do so. As productivity continues to rise it will cease to be the case that men live by taking in each other's washing. Increasingly, we shall live by teaching each other. The question "Am I my brother's psychoanalyst?" will be answered by the Census, "Yes, in considerable probability."

History debunks the present. In this sense it robs the future of its terrors.

III

Up until now I have been using money as a surrogate for all economic well-being. Many of my observations could be germane to a documentary history of any aspect of past economic development. There is ample precedent for this usage. We say of a firm that it is worth billions of dollars, but of course that does not imply that we expect its balance sheet to have billions of dollars, or even millions, in the form of cash. If someone takes too literally the identification of money with economic wealth, we deem him mad. This was the mistake of King Midas, whose fetish for money as such entitles him to a role in the catalogue of Krafft-Ebing. This was the cardinal error of the mercantilistic predecessors of Adam Smith, who were preoccupied with a desire for their country to export more than its imports in order to accumulate gold bullion from abroad.

In the present volumes Professor Krooss has gathered documents that bear on money as such. Although money is not the end-all of economic activity, it does have a crucial importance in its own right, and of all the subjects in economics it is certainly one of the most fascinating. The King Midas tale lives on because, while we pity him, we understand from our own feelings how he might have fallen into that excess. What Chairman Martin of the Federal Reserve Board recently called the barbaric custom of retaining gold as the basis of international trade evidently has some deep Freudian roots in modern man. As far back as 1919, Ernest Jones, Freud's official biographer, prophesied that the world would atavistically return to gold at *antebellum* levels: under the blundering hand of Chancellor-of-the-Exchequer Winston Churchill this came to pass in 1925, and England still shows the scars from that unhappy choice.

Money is not only uncommonly fascinating. It is also uncommonly important. Lenin is supposed to have recognized this when he said, "We shall debauch the capitalistic system by forcing it to mismanage its currency." I cannot be sure of the accuracy of the quotation because nobody has ever been able to find it in the voluminous Lenin writings; documentary research traces its attribution to the writings of Lord Keynes, a not completely reliable source. Still the aphorism is well told, and like all folk wisdom sometimes too well told, as for example when it leads to the absurd views of ex-President Herbert Hoover, who pronounced in the midst of the Cold War, "Inflation is worse than Stalin." By the same reasoning one could deduce: "Hitler is less harmful than an excess-profits tax." Or "The Lisbon Earthquake was no worse than the OPA."

Like the thyroid, money receives little attention so long as it is not performing badly. But often in our history it has behaved very badly indeed. Each of our wars has included among its casualties the stability of the price index. And between our greatest wars there have intervened long periods of deflationary times, with effects that have reached out beyond the economic system to the point of threatening the stability of our democratic institutions.

American history is peculiarly well-suited to throw light on the nature and development of money. For one thing, America from the beginning has tended to depend upon formal contracts and charters, a trait as useful for the compiler of a documentary history as a propensity to keep a diary and write letters is useful to the student of intellectual history and biography. From the Mayflower Compact on, we have tried to get it down in black and white.

Related to this propensity is the very newness of American society. The origins of European institutions and customs are shrouded in antiquity. The towns around Milan were always there. No act of creation or of will can be found, only the slow processes of evolution, which like the hands of a clock move—but in so continuous a fashion as never to be seen changing position. Newcomers to America found here no going concern. They had to forge new traditions: self-consciously, they had to decide what words to write down on the clean slate. Like the Japanese who awoke into the modern world after a long sleep in isolated feudalism, Americans have had to plunder the Old World for patterns to imitate. Should the new lands grow Asian rice, European barley, American maize, or some of each? Should the new country have a system of pounds and pence or of dollars and cents? (Thank Providence that Jefferson's wish for the decimal system prevailed. Would that the Revolutionary reverence for France had extended to imitating the metric system, saving American school-children two centuries of unnecessary drudgery!) The Bank of England was founded in the seventeenth century more or less as the British Empire had been founded—in a fit of absent–mindedness. In 1790 the United States had the chance to set up once and for all a proper central bank. As these volumes help explain, it was not until 1913 that the Federal Reserve System was finally established. (Whether we have yet achieved a *proper* central bank must be left to the open jury of experts.)

One cannot interpret evolution as an optimal march toward progress. While it is not the random walk of a drunken sailor, it does involve considerable meandering and some backtracking. Along with the sin of knowing too little history there can go the less common crime of knowing too much. If Alexander Hamilton had not so successfully honored the debts inherited by the new Republic, England might not have made the mistake after the Napoleonic Wars of returning to the *antebellum* parities. She paid for that mistake by years of deflation and stagnation. It might have been better had even greater disaster followed. For then the United States might have been less tempted by the folly of financial orthodoxy, which led after the Civil War to an attempt to roll back the inflation created by that war. We might then have been spared what pre-1929 historians called "the Great Depression," those decades a century ago that culminated in periods of falling prices and rising populism. Along with being spared the economic ills of what economists call Kondratieff and Kuznets cycles, history might even have been spared William Jennings Bryan, the boy orator of the Platte, whose opposition to the crucifixion of mankind on a cross of gold drove out—according to a process foretold long ago by Sir Thomas Gresham—more effectual opposition to the conventional wisdom of Mark Hanna and William McKinley. Nor did the story end there. In history one thing leads to another, and another. The Churchill folly of restoration of the pound to its 1913 level is traceable in part to remembered decisions from the times of Napoleon. On the other hand, history is not *merely* a matter of more of the same. By

1945 that kind of financial orthodoxy which had passed for wisdom in 1790, 1816, 1866, and 1925 was selling at a deep discount in the market of ideas. The historian took up his pen to record new kinds of follies, but not a postwar attempt to roll back wartime inflation.

Documents are like pictures in the family album. They bear dates, and being dated they are obsolescing from the moment of their birth. There were many proud fathers of the 1913 Federal Reserve, more than enough to go around. The grandchildren of Carter Glass can boast that their sire drew a good longbow at Hastings. So can the progeny of Winthrop Aldrich. Of Paul Warburg. Of H. Parker Willis. Of Woodrow Wilson. But why go on: credit, unlike cash, need not add up to a mere 100 percent. The good work of these founders is embodied in the Act creating and reforming the Federal Reserve. They had certain evils of the previous national banking system firmly in mind and were determined to eradicate them. Yet how many of the features that the founders were most proud to claim are still operative today? And which of those relics that still prevail would receive the approbation of present-day experts?

Consider, for example, the view that the major need was for an "elastic" money supply, freed from the "inelasticity" of the past. And consider the related view that rediscounting of promissory notes, representing loans by Main Street's commercial banks to legitimate farmers, merchants, and traders, would permit the money supply to expand automatically along with the "needs of trade" and thereby to achieve lasting prosperity. This root notion of 1913 is diametrically opposed to *all* the fashionable views of monetary experts today: all now agree, "Money will not manage itself." All agree that it is destabilizing and antisocial if fluctuations in the supply of money are permitted to reinforce the fluctuations in the demand for money: that way booms get boomier and inflations cumulative; that way recessions are allowed to turn into chronic slumps. And along with the departure of philosophy and practice from the wisdom of the founders, as embalmed in statutes and documents, goes the institutional change in which all banks now do their discounting on the basis of securities of the federal government and not on the basis of rediscounting of Main Street's commercial paper. Open market operations, the principal weapon of the modern Federal Reserve, were invented by accident during Governor Strong's pre-1929 rule. Only years after they had been *invented* were they *discovered* by economists and central bankers! No christening papers mark their birth.

The documents of history preserve the wise acts of the past. They also preserve the fossils of earlier folly. Because many critics believed in 1932 that the Great Depression was caused by the payment of interest on checking deposits, we are stuck to this day with an edict against that practice. In the opinion of many modern experts, this has harmful consequences and more baleful effects are still to come. Similarly, how many experts today would be sure that the separation of investment banking and commercial banking by the reform laws of the New Deal constitutes a net improvement for the capital markets?

In any case we find in the annals of the past the materials for dialogues of the present. Here are the documents—warts, ink blots, and all. They do not tell their own story. We must read them, and read into them. But they do provide us the stage props for the continuing drama of economic life.

ECONOMIC GROWTH

The decades following World War II have been years of extraordinary economic growth. The growth of real output has surpassed the growth in population, and average standards of living have improved in such diverse countries as the United States and Japan, Sweden and Switzerland, Soviet Russia and Thailand, Taiwan and France. Art imitates nature. Economic theory in the modern era, stimulated by the progress taking place in the real world, has increasingly become preoccupied with problems of growth and development.

In a sense this reorientation of emphasis is a return to the older tradition of Adam Smith and his predecessors. Smith's 1776 *The Wealth of Nations*, which is rightly regarded as progenitor of economics as a science, can be read as a bible of economic development. Like his mercantilistic predecessors, Smith believed in the importance of rising productivity and living standards. But unlike them, he had little faith in manipulation of governmental policy to further this goal, preferring instead the efficiencies of individual enterprise under the checks and balances of market competition. When Adam Smith extolls the virtues of honesty and thrift, his goal is the promotion of future prosperity.

The classical followers of Adam Smith, notably David Ricardo and Malthus, represented a retreat from preoccupation with dynamic progress, retreat to a gloomy concentration upon the law of diminishing returns and stationary equilibrium at a subsistence standard of living. Once optimistic hopes of progressive growth were abandoned, it was natural for political economists like Ricardo to concentrate upon the distribution of the fixed national product among competing classes — wage-earning labor, profit-seeking capitalists, and rent-collecting landlords.

Karl Marx, following Ricardo but diverging from the neoclassical successors of Ricardo, retained the emphasis upon distribution of product as against preoccupation with its growth. Regarding labor as entitled to the whole of the product, Marx viewed the classical equilibrium as a process of bourgeois exploitation. Combining his theory of the economic or materialist interpretation of history with his theory of the class struggle as the key to all development, Marx attempted to enunciate the laws of motion of capitalist development, according to which, just as bourgeois capitalism had evolved out of feudalism, so inevitably would capitalism sow the seeds of its own decay and evolve into emerging socialism.

Marx and Engels fully appreciated the technological dynamism of capitalism, as glowing passages in the 1848 Communist Manifesto testify to. But just as a flower inevitably goes beyond its bloom, so, Marx believed, was it inevitable that under capitalism the frantic urge to accumulate capital would result in a declining rate of profit. Irresistible technological innovation would displace laborers, throwing men into the reserve army of the unemployed, and leaving inevitably to the immiseration of the working classes. According to Marx, despite the frantic attempts of capitalists to undertake ever larger-scale production and to form monopolies for the purpose of holding up the rate of profit, the ultimate capitalistic disaster — chronic depression and collapse — could not possibly be averted. The rising working class, the protelariat, would take over monopoly capitalism, just as the over-ripe fruit of the tree is there to be picked up by any out-thrust hand. Presumably the site of the first socialist revolution would be in the most advanced industrial country, England — or perhaps from the vantage of hindsight a good Marxian at the turn of the century might have expected the revolution to break out first in the United States.

We have, then, among the descendants of Adam Smith and David Ricardo two diametrically opposing theories of economic growth. On the one hand the predictions of Marx and Engels that the system's accumulating poisons would bring it to stagnation, decay, and extinction. On the other hand, the neoclassical writers — from John Stuart Mill to Alfred Marshall in Britain, from Knut Wicksell in Scandinavia to Gunnar Myrdal, from Keynes to Galbraith in modern times — all these looked forward to continued real progress, rather widely shared among the various income classes, the rich and the poor. These neoclassical economists expected that scientific discoveries could more than offset the scarcity of natural resources, and could thereby banish the

Malthusian specter of over-population and famine. They believed that the democratic state could intervene to ameliorate the inequities and cruelties resulting from the Darwinian jungle of ruthless economic competition. And, ever since the age of John Maynard Keynes, Western economists came to believe that undiluted capitalism was evolving, not into socialistic ownership of the means of production and totalitarian bureaucratic control, but rather into the "welfare state," the modern "mixed economy."

In the mixed economy many of the decision processes determining how society is to use its material resources are to be performed by the mechanism of markets and prices. But government is to set the rules of the game and to have a vital function in providing for the ever-more-important collective needs of an interdependent populace. By use of scientific macroeconomic policies — fiscal policy in the form of budgetary deficits and surpluses, monetary policy in the form of control over the supply of money, purchasing power, and credit — the mixed economy was believed to be capable of ending for all time mass unemployment and chronic depressions. Keynesian policies to stimulate total spending could banish once and for all the fear of under-consumption that was ever present in a laissez-faire world made up of the thrifty rich and the eager-to-spend poor. Thus, one no longer had to be fearful that automation and labor-displacing technological invention would cause total unemployment to grow, even though particular skills might be made obsolescent in the same way that the introduction of machines killed off the earning power of traditional craftsmen. Most important of all, according to the neoclassicists of the mixed economy who synthesized the doctrines of Keynes and such microeconomists as Alfred Marshall and Leon Walras, the new ability to control the supply of domestic purchasing power at will has made obsolete the neo-Marxian view, associated sixty years ago with the names of Rosa Luxemburg and Lenin, that prosperity and full employment in a Marxist system is absolutely impossible without exploitation of colonial peoples and recourse to foreign investments in outside markets in a desperate struggle to maintain purchasing power and prevent a precipitous decline in the domestic rate of profit.

Men make prophecies about the future. History decides which of the forecasts turned out to be correct. Have real wages declined since 1867 when Marx published the first volume of his *Das Kapital*? Has the relative share of wages in the vastly growing national product steadily declined? Have the poor become poorer as the rich became richer? Has there been a long-term downward trend in the rate of profit in the predicted Marxian fashion? Has the business cycle worsened as each slump became more virulent than its predecessor, culminating ultimately in a grand collapse of the system? Has it been impossible for trade-union organization and democratic intervention by government to ameliorate the most glaring evils of historic capitalism within the framework of peaceful evolution and constitutional government?

The historical facts are not in dispute. In the last century real wages in the advanced countries of the "West" — North America, Europe, Japan, Australasia — have steadily risen. The share of wages and salaries in national income has, if anything, more than held its own. The rise of life expectancies among the urban and rural poor has been dramatic testimony to the material progress made. Within this century the average rate of interest and of profit has oscillated, but with definitely no manifest downward trend. The world depression of the 1930s did appear at the time to be confirmatory of Marx's most gloomy expectations. But the evolution of the individualistic capitalistic system into the post-Keynesian mixed economy has pulverized into separate regional fluctuations what used to be a common international pattern of the business cycle. In the twenty-five years since the end of World War II, there has been intermittent creeping inflation, punctuated by periods of economic retardation. But no mixed economy has suffered any lasting depression or even what would have been considered a serious recession back in the days of unbridled capitalism. Countries like West Germany and Japan, relieved of the need to maintain military forces and left devoid of colonies, far from being thrown thereby into economic stagnation as would be predicted by a follower of the Luxemburg-Lenin theory of imperialism, have instead displayed sustained growth of an almost miraculous character.

False though Karl Marx's basic projections of scientific socialism were, still he was correct in his insistence that Victorian *laissez faire* would not persist. But neither he nor his followers correctly foresaw the evolution into the mixed economy, even though they did correctly envisage the growth of large-scale corporations. The new industrial state of Galbraith is a far cry from the atomistic competition of Adam Smith's world. It is also a far cry from one great capitalistic monopoly. Experts in the realm of industrial organization recognized the burgeoning of monopolies and trusts at the turn of the century. They recognized at the middle of the century a probable higher level of competitiveness and lower level of unilateral market power than had prevailed at the century's beginning. Not enough time has elapsed since mid-century for the experts to delineate with scientific confidence any significant trend toward great or lesser trends of monopoly power. The Galbraithian giants grew bigger, but each industrial market is subject to the rivalry of giant against giant. The common complaint against the vast national and international corporation is not its decadence but rather its ruthless efficiency and dynamic expansion.

If Marx was wrong about the theory of growth in the advanced nations, any optimistic neoclassical economist who predicted a century ago that the poor and backward regions of the world would progress in step with the leaders would have also been woefully wrong. Modern experts in economic growth, such as Simon Kuznets of Harvard, have found that where countries are concerned, it is indeed the sad truth that the rich get richer and the poor get — *relatively* — poorer. India and Southeast Asia, Latin America, the new nations of Africa find the gap between their per capita incomes and those of the advanced nations growing even larger. When science introduces medical improvements that increase life expectancies in the developing nations, birth rates drop only after a lag, with the result that rapidly growing population again brings into play the classical law of diminishing returns. Among the developing nations economics remains what Carlyle called "the dismal science."

Little wonder then that it was in the most backward country of Europe that the 1917 Communist revolution took place. Little wonder that the most populous country in the world, China, should have skipped the stage of the mixed economy in favor of a collectivist push for more rapid development.

On the theory of economic growth there is no shortage of treatises: Sir Arthur Lewis, *The Theory of Economic Growth* (George Allen & Unwin, London, 1955); Simon Kuznets, *Six Lectures on Economic Growth* (Free Press, New York, 1959); C. P. Kindleberger, *Economic Development* (McGraw-Hill, New York, 2nd edition, 1965); Paul Baran, *The Political Economy of Backwardness* (Monthly Review Press, New York, 1957); Joseph A. Schumpeter, *Theory of Economic Development* (First German edition 1912, English translation, Harvard University Press, Cambridge, Mass., 1934). The interested reader will also wish to consult the many writings of Jan Tinbergen, Paul Rosenstein-Rodan, Albert Hirschman, Hollis Chenery, Benjamin Higgins, Peter Bauer, Gunnar Myrdal, Everett Hagen, and others.

These writings demonstrate that the process of economic growth is to be understood in terms of the basic four factors — natural resources endowment, the quantity of population and the skills and energies that it possesses, accumulation of capital as the result of private thrift or public fiscal and planning programs, technological invention and entrepreneurial innovation (including a rapid or slow imitation of technical methods used elsewhere). For test cases reference may be made to the quite different economies of Japan and the Soviet Union. As Angus Maddison has explained, the fact that the Japanese economy has grown faster in the 1950s and 1960s than any other economy is associated with the fact that her industrial working population has grown so greatly in both numbers and skills, and that she has had a more rapid rate of capital accumulation than any other advanced economy

(Japan's ratio of plant and equipment investment to her Gross National Product being 22½ percent, in contrast to an American ratio of but 12⅓ percent). In addition Japan has had the zeal to imitate the already available technology of the more advanced nations, thereby narrowing her gap with them.

Although the Soviet Union has been run along entirely different political lines, it appears that much of the decline in her rates of industrial growth in the 1960s, which were considerably below those of the early 1950s, can be explained by the slowing down in the rate of growth of Soviet manpower, a trend that has been paralleled by a slowing down in the rate of her accumulation of capital. Although the Soviet Union is in a stage of economic development at which one might expect her to benefit much from imitation to close her technological gap, econometric studies are unable to identify a strong trend in the productivity of her capital and labor inputs. The accuracy of these interpretations of Japanese and Soviet growth patterns is not so important as is the suggestion that there can be no substitute for an economic theory of growth based upon the determinants of production.

No discussion of the theory of economic growth should be complete without mention of the fact that growth in the gross national product is only one aspect of modern economic goals. If higher GNP means more pollution and deterioration of the environment, and if the fruits are distributed inequitably among the few or squandered in militaristic ventures, then it can become an evil and not a good. And yet, those who are seriously concerned for the quality of life and for the environment will realize, upon reflection, that only through more skillful use of the benefits of science can a nation afford to clean up its rivers and streams, purify its atmosphere, and distribute to all a decent minimum standard of life and economic opportunity. Growth is no end by itself, but without growth modern problems are unlikely to get solved.

191

PAUL A. SAMUELSON

ON

MEMORIES

When Diaghilev revived his ballet company he had the original Bakst sets redone in even more vivid colors, explaining, "so that they would be as brilliant as people remember them." Recent events on college campuses have recalled to my inward eye one of the great happenings in my own lifetime.

It took place at Harvard back in the days when giants walked the earth and Harvard Yard. Joseph Schumpeter, Harvard's brilliant economist and social prophet, was to debate Paul Sweezy on "The Future of Capitalism." Wassily Leontief was in the chair as moderator and the Littauer Auditorium could not accommodate the packed house.

Let me set the stage. Schumpeter was a scion of the aristocracy of Franz Josef's Austria. It was Schumpeter who had confessed to three wishes in life: to be the greatest lover in Vienna, the best horseman in Europe, and the greatest economist in the world. "But, unfortunately," as he used to say modestly, "the seat I inherited was never of the topmost caliber."

Half mountebank, half sage, Schumpeter had been the *enfant terrible* of the Austrian school of economists. Steward to an Egyptian princess, owner of a stable of race horses, onetime Finance Minister of Austria, Schumpeter could look at the prospects for bourgeois society with the objectivity of one whose feudal world had come to an end in 1914. His message and vision can be read in his classical work of a quarter century ago, "Capitalism, Socialism, and Democracy."

WHOM THE GODS ENVY

Opposed to the foxy Merlin was young Sir Galahad. Son of an executive of J.P. Morgan's bank, Paul Sweezy was the best that Exeter and Harvard can produce. Tiring of the "gentlemen's C" and of the good life at Locke-Ober's with Lucius Beebe, Sweezy had early established himself as among the most promising of the economists of his generation. But tiring of the conventional wisdom of his age, and spurred on by the events of the Great Depression, Sweezy became one of America's few Marxists. (As he used to say, you could count the noses of American academic economists who were Marxists on the thumbs of your two hands: the late Paul Baran of Stanford; and, in an occasional summer school of

unwonted tolerance, Paul Sweezy.)

Unfairly, the gods had given Paul Sweezy, along with a brilliant mind, a beautiful face and wit. With what William Buckley would desperately wish to see in his mirror, Sweezy faced the world. If lightning had struck him that night, people would truly have said that he had incurred the envy of the gods.

So much for the cast. I would have to be a William Hazlitt to recall for you the interchange of wit, the neat parrying and thrust, and all made the more pleasurable by the obvious affection that the two men had for each other despite the polar opposition of their views.

MEETING OF OPPOSITES

Great debaters deserve great moderators, and that night Leontief was in fine form. At the end he fairly summarized the viewpoints expressed.

"The patient is capitalism. What is to be his fate? Our speakers are in fact agreed that the patient is inevitably dying. But the bases of their diagnoses could not be more different.

"On the one hand there is Sweezy, who utilizes the analysis of Marx and of Lenin to deduce that the patient is dying of a malignant cancer. Absolutely no operation can help. The end is foreordained.

"On the other hand, there is Schumpeter. He, too, and rather cheerfully, admits that the patient is dying. (His sweetheart already died in 1914 and his bank of tears has long since run dry.) But to Schumpeter, the patient is dying of a psychosomatic ailment. Not cancer but neurosis is his complaint. Filled with self-hate, he has lost the will to live.

"In this view capitalism is an unlovable system, and what is unlovable will not be loved. Paul Sweezy himself is a talisman and omen of that alienation which will seal the system's doom."

All this I had long forgotten. And a few years ago when I reread Schumpeter's book, I graded him down for his gloomy views on the progress that would be made by the mixed economy—capitalism in an oxygen tent, as Schumpeter put it. His failure to predict the miraculous progress of the postwar years earned Schumpeter a C in my eyes.

However, university happenings reveal an alienation of privileged youth entitling Schumpeter to a recount.

PART XVII

Lectures and Essays on Modern Economics

192

Problems of the American Economy—Hard and Easy*

WITH SOME TREPIDATION I undertook to prepare a
Franklin Lecture on certain new-fashioned principles of
modern economics, being acutely aware that much of what
I say will sound opposed to old-fangled principles of economics we associate with Benjamin Franklin's *Poor Richard's Almanac*. I found it heartening therefore to learn
that Dr. Leo M. Franklin was himself a pioneer in social
and humanitarian movements. And upon reflection, I realized that it is a libel on the memory of that versatile
scientist to think that Benjamin Franklin was a staid dog-
matist on economic matters: For it was Franklin who
espoused a regime of paper money in the Pennsylvania
colony; not, as skeptics think, because he was a printer but
rather because the actual experience of Pennsylvania
showed that it enjoyed one of the longest periods of prosperity under such a regime of money management to be
found in the early American annals.

Not long ago I was invited to give a public lecture in
England, and sat down to write out some of the things
American economists worry about. You may be sure the
list was not a short one. Ours may in some sense be an affluent society, but the day in which all economic problems
wither away is still far off in the future. There is nothing

---

* Although this was delivered before President Kennedy's death, subsequent events and the Kennedy-Johnson 1964 tax cut seem to corroborate
its general viewpoint.

surprising in what I have said yet. But the order of importance which I will attach to the different economic problems might seem very surprising to a non-economist. For
example, if you go to a good businessman's club or if you
listen to heated political debates on radio and television,
you might be forgiven for thinking that one of the most
important economic problems facing America today is that
of the outstanding public debt and the rate at which it is
growing as a result of deficit fiscal policies. Now I would be
among the first to recognize that there are some geniune
economic problems connected with the level of our outstanding public debt; yet in all candor I must admit that
the debt would not appear in the first half dozen problems
that most concern an expert in political economy today.
How we deploy our economic resources to enhance the security of America and the free world in these cold war
days is a tremendously more important problem than that
of the debt. Our international balance of payments is a
much more important problem. Our past and future
growth rate is more important. Unemployment is more
important. So, I think, is the problem of urban blight and
regional development.

I could go on listing problems indefinitely. Still one
thing that we economists are supposed to believe in is the
division of labor, and perhaps not everyone should worry
about everything. This was brought home to me some considerable years ago when I gave a luncheon address to the
austere Boston Finance Club. In the course of my talk some
reference was made to the problem of gold, which I could
see was beginning to rear its ugly head again. After thanking me prettily for my speech, the master of ceremonies
said: "I was specially struck by your remarks about gold,

particularly when I realized that I haven't heard the subject mentioned since way back in the 1930's. At that time everybody seemed to talk about nothing else. How I used to worry about the problem! Until finally one morning I pulled myself together and made a firm resolution. 'I have too many things to worry about already. From now on I'm going to let somebody else worry about gold.' And you know I've been a happy man ever since." Well, since 1957 gold has become more of a problem and there are fewer happy men these days.

Of course the good Lord did not create the world so as to make economists happy. It would be irresponsible of me, just in order to attain extra peace of mind, to stick my head in the ground and ignore a problem. I am afraid, though, some ivory tower economists are a bit like that. For example, last academic year we had one of America's most brilliant theorists as a visiting professor at Massachusetts Institute of Technology. You may recall that late in October at the height of the 1960 Presidential campaign there was something of a gold crisis in the London market. Speculators were so avid to hoard gold that they bid the price from its normal level of about $35 an ounce up to $40 an ounce or more. Some of us economists were sitting around the lunch table discussing the matter. When I expressed my concern, our brilliant visiting professor said: "Stop worrying about the gold problem." Most of us were amazed to hear our guest telling us he was not particularly worried about the gold drain. Finally our chairman had the wit to ask: "Adam Smith,"—I must confess that I disguise the name to protect the guilty—"what is it that you do worry about?" The answer was informative: "Why should I worry about gold? I don't worry about anything!"

That may be an admissible attitude for someone in the ivory tower to take; but any economist who sticks his neck out of the ivory tower must pursue another strategy. As President Truman once said: "If you can't stand the heat, stay out of the kitchen." In my youth there used to be in gift shops something called a *worry bird.* You bought this little wooden artifact for a few dollars and then turned all your worries over to it. I am afraid that we economists who address ourselves to policy problems have to be on the firing line; we cannot buy draftees to keep us out of the army. It is our job to be the worry birds for the nation; that's what we get paid for. When my descendants gather about my knee and say, "Grandpa, what did you do to add to the gross national product?" my reply will have to be, "I worried."

Hard Problems

Let me now list a few economic problems, roughly in order of their importance, first giving the intrinsically hard ones and second those that are in a certain sense easy.

1. *The problem of excessive unemployment.* The percentage of people unable to find work has grown at each business cycle peak during the last decade. Although the first year and a half of the Kennedy recovery reduced unemployment from 7 per cent of the civilian labor force to 5½ per cent, we never came near the 2½ per cent level of a decade ago. And even the minimal 4 per cent proximate goal never came clearly in sight. Few countries in the Western world have had so poor a record as ours, and I say this even after making the necessary adjustments for the lack of comparability between our statistical measuring rods and theirs.

2. *The problem of creeping cost-push inflation.* For most of this century the cost of living has shown a persistent upward trend. What has become most disquieting is the apparent recent tendency for prices and wages to rise even when America is still intolerably far from reasonably full employment and capacity production.

3. *The problem of our chronic international balance-of-payments deficit.* At first in the postwar years, there was a tendency for us to sell more abroad than foreigners could pay for by sending us their goods. All this changed in the last decade; and our private exports of goods and services no longer exceed private imports by an amount sufficient to enable us to carry on (1) our public, military, and civilian aid programs and (2) our private long-term investments abroad. The result has been a steady drain of our gold supply, a steady piling up of short-term IOU's to the rest of the world, and a shakier confidence in the stability of the dollar.

4. *The problem of growth in our full-employment potential to produce.* West Germany, Japan, France, Italy, and the Netherlands—to say nothing of the collectivistic Soviet Union—have been demonstrating postwar growth rates far above our postwar average. How can a mixed economy, dominated by private initiative but subject to public control and stimulus, raise its average rate of growth from, say, $3\frac{1}{2}$ per cent to $4\frac{1}{2}$ or 5 per cent?

All these are hard economic problems, and important ones.

"Easy" Economic Problems

1. *The problem of federal deficits and rising public debt.* The 1950's and early 1960's look to be years of al-

most continuous unbalance in the budget (the so-called Administrative Budget).

2. *The problem of automation.* It is widely believed that we have now moved into a second industrial revolution, in which computers, servo-mechanisms, and robots will make man technologically obsolete, causing mass unemployment and necessitating a drastic shortening of the work week.

3. *The problem of disarmament's economic impact.* Were peace to "break out," would mass unemployment and chronic slump like that of the 1930's be the inevitable fate of the American economy, showing that our vaunted postwar prosperity depends necessarily on armament expenditure?

4. *The problem of our inability to forecast the future.* If we cannot decide what conditions will be later, how can we now initiate the proper economic programs?

"These are easy problems?" you will ask. "If automation and sudden end of the cold war are easy, then heaven defend us from the hard ones."

In reply, let me clarify the sense in which such problems can be classified as easy. Provided that we learn how to solve the hard problems in the first list, the secondary problems can have a straight-forward solution. It is in this sense that they may be called easy.

Ideology as a Debit [1]

A problem like that of the public debt becomes major because of its psychological rather than economic nature, as the following will show.

Back in January, 1961, my task force made a report to

President-elect Kennedy on the American economy (January 4, 1961). The general pattern envisaged in it turned out, by some sad miracle, to have been right:

(i) the thing to fear was not the persistence of the 1960 recession itself, but rather the danger that the next recovery would be a disappointing one like that of 1959–60;

(ii) unemployment looked to remain a problem well into the new recovery;

(iii) the American economy appeared to need nothing so much as a *stimulus in its over-all demand spending,* such as a vigorously expansionary monetary policy and *a planned* ("prudent") *deficit* could alone give it.

In pointedly opposing the Eisenhower philosophy of contained government expenditures and "sound" budget balance (like that appropriate to any civilian or army family), I was merely reflecting the considered opinions of the bulk of economists who have been analyzing the facts about national income determination and American growth. While these are the views that scholars all over the free world are almost unanimous in holding, they have never been the views of the man in the street. And in Congress itself the Eisenhower philosophy, as interpreted by Secretary George Humphrey (in opposition to the then Economic Advisor Arthur F. Burns) and by Secretary Anderson (in opposition to no heard voice in the last Eisenhower administration), had led to a *reversion* of economic understanding even among the moderate leadership of the Democrats—as exemplified by such men as Vice-President Johnson and the late Congressman Rayburn. Needless to say the Byrds and Goldwaters in Congress required no Eisenhower influence to make them revert to a position they had never left.

I linger on this irrational question of ideology because it must have made the job of the new Administration a hard one. Had President Kennedy come out boldly for the sizable deficit which objective economic analysis called for, he would have run into severe opposition in the divided Congress; and, by becoming tarred with the asinine label of an "irresponsible spender," the President might have put all his new programs in jeopardy. Here then was one of those reminders that politics is the art of the feasible: while it is always easy for expert advisers to urge that the head of state exercise his "leadership," he must ever deliberate on how best to spend and conserve his limited bank-balance of leadership.

Though the outgoing Administration bequeathed a budget document purporting to show a budget in balance, it was readily apparent to any intelligent observer that it was bequeathing an economy which was already running a deficit and which could not possibly end up the fiscal year without a still bigger one. The fact that the deficit could be blamed on the previous Administration eased the ideological task; and in the early messages, President Kennedy described his own program as one of "balancing the Eisenhower Budget," in the sense of recommending programs that would not of themselves unbalance the budget if it had been true that the Eisenhower Budget had been itself in balance—which, because of the decline in tax revenues due to the recession, it clearly was not. (If the above sentence is an involved one, no blame attaches to me as a writer but must instead be attributed to the subtlety of its content.)

Bluntly, the straight economics of the 1961 situation required a sizable deficit. How might this best come about?

There were a number of new Kennedy programs that could be justified on their intrinsic merits, independently of any anti-recession need. A temporary tax cut, with or without some relinquishing by Congress of discretionary authority, was a possibility. Structural improvements in our unemployment compensation system and in other transfer programs naturally recommended themselves. On the other hand, the outlook for defense expenditures at the beginning of 1961 was cloudy, and expert opinion could be found suggesting that these would not have to rise in any appreciable amount.

Whatever the economic merits of a tax cut, this was then politically out of the question. The President had run on a platform that asked sacrifices of the American people. How then could he begin by giving them what many would regard as a "handout?" Also, how could one be sure that the new civilian and defense programs might not require maintenance of the tax base? And what about the possibility of raising our growth rate by changing our full-employment composition of demand away from consumption and toward net capital formation by means of maintaining tax rates and offsetting the ultimate implied full-employment budget surplus by a militant policy of credit expansion?

In the first years of this recovery there has not seemed to be much steam behind the American economy. Car sales and residential contracts have been the only bright spots. Business investment in equipment and stocks has simply not been buoyant. The verdict seems to be increasingly evident that this recovery has been one primarily dependent upon government stimulus. If it were somehow possible to divide up the total forces making for expansion into the mutually exclusive categories of private and public, I suspect that the contribution of the private sector would compare unfavorably with that of most historical recoveries.

I state this as a fact, not as an accusation. I do not think it is really anybody's fault. With the war seventeen years behind us and in the face of the comfortable levels of capacity relative to effective dollar demand, I would find it rather rational were I a businessman to be behaving about as they have generally been doing. A corollary of this view, that capitalists cannot be charged with being on a deliberate sit-down strike, is this: the undoubted friction which has grown up between President Kennedy and the business community cannot validly be given much blame for the lack of steam in the American economy.

Since 1956 economists have become increasingly suspicious that we are in an intermediate period where the only thing that can bring the American economy close to a full employment growth rate is an unusually expansionary fiscal and monetary policy. With the international balance of payments putting a constraint upon militant use of stimulating credit policy, the burden cannot help but be put upon fiscal policy. This means, let us face it, a sizable deficit in what is called the Administrative Budget.

As one of our leading economists said privately, "It may be that the optimal deficit of the United States in the next few years is about equal to our so-called largest peacetime deficit, the unplanned $12 billion of President Eisenhower in fiscal 1959." Should this diagnosis turn out to be at all near the mark, the prospect would not be too cheerful. For there is little evidence as yet that many of our congressmen and voters have been able to overcome their ideological opposition to large government deficits.

A Basic Cost-Push Problem?

After these preliminaries, let me state bluntly what it is that I do worry about. I am fearful that *the institutions of our American economy are such that any time we approach reasonably close to full employment, we thereby face the threat of an inflationary price creep.* Such an inflationary price increase has repercussions on the distribution of income between old and young, between creditors and debtors. It has repercussions on the deterioration of our international balance of payments. It jeopardizes the successful attainment of high levels of employment and the banishment of unemployment. It increases the political pressures for restrictive tariff barriers and for other costly devices (such as lowering the length of the working week to far below what workers would really want if given the choice of steady employment). And, of course, as a result of all this, it threatens to hamper seriously our rate of growth —in comparison with that of the Soviet Union or other parts of the world.

The problem I speak of is by no means peculiar to the United States. If you read English books and newspapers, you will note much concern there over the possibility of a cost-price spiral. The same seems to be true of Sweden and the other Scandinavian countries. I wish I knew the underlying reasons why West Germany, and perhaps Japan, do not seem to be susceptible to this modern ailment in so great a degree as is the United States. (The Soviet Union and the totalitarian economies on the other side of the Iron Curtain are not immune from all economic problems. Russia in the past had terrible famines and Mainland

China may right now be suffering from similar catastrophes. A change in the pace of industrialization for military expenditure must cause massive reallocations of labor even in planned economies. The USSR has had to rely for years on heavy turnover taxes to keep down the excess of consumer purchasing power. But so long as a centralized governmental authority can put controls on wages and prices by direct fiat, the problem is a different one from that I am describing for the Western democracies.)

I do not wish to sound dogmatic. My diagnosis may be a false one and I may be a doctor in search of a disease that isn't there. It would delight me immensely if I turned out to be wrong and there proved not to be in the American economy any basic tendency toward "cost-push" or "sellers' inflation." I cheerfully admit that a minority of modern economists, including some very good ones, believe that cost-push inflation is a mirage and an illusion.

The Perfectly-Competitive Artificial Model

How can we best understand the mechanism of cost-push inflation? I think it will be useful to start out by mentioning a quite artificial economic model in which all wages and prices are determined in *perfectly*-competitive markets. Just imagine that all consumers goods were to be auctioned off for what they would bring, in the way that wheat is auctioned off on the floor of the Board of Trade in Chicago. Since we know that in the real world goods are predominantly sold by manufacturers and retailers who name a price and then wait for the consumer to decide how much he will buy at that price, this notion of an auctioneer's market requires some stretch of the imagination.

But I must ask you to stretch your imaginations still further. Imagine that labor too is auctioned off. I don't have in mind the slavery markets of Charleston and Savannah; but I do picture a model in which each day or each month we all throw our labor services on the market to fetch whatever wage rate will be determined by spirited supply and demand offerings and biddings. Unless I am an utterly useless person, possessing ten thumbs and being a trouble-maker to boot, I need never in such a world be unemployed. All I have to do is offer to undercut the wage of those now holding jobs, and at the right wage rate I will find employment of some kind. That doesn't mean I can be sure of getting a job with the New York Yankees, or that I can become the Archbishop of Canterbury just by offering to take the job for less. But it does mean that somebody may be able to bump me from my chair of political economy at M.I.T., if he can deliver equally good lectures and is willing to work for less.

Can such an artificial economy as I have described ever experience inflation? Of course it can. Let the Federal Reserve System or the Treasury start printing $100 bills in unlimited amount, spending them on elaborate post offices and battleships, or mailing them to all beyond the retirement age as weekly pensions. There will soon result the classical case of "too much money-spending chasing too few goods." To be sure, if the economy had earlier been experiencing a good deal of unemployment for some unexplained reason, the printing of the new money might *at the very first* cause an expansion of total production. So long as extra employment makes possible a production of new physical goods apace with the creation of money, there would be no need for the price level to rise. But we all realize that there is a limit to total employment and capacity; and after this limit had been reached, further putting out of money from the printing presses would cease to have what the textbooks describe as its "real multiplier effects" and will begin to have "purely price tag multiplier effects."

You will recognize that what I have been talking about is not complete fantasy. Plenty of times in the past, galloping inflations have taken place just along the lines of the model I have been describing. Our own Revolutionary War was an instance and gave rise to the expression "not worth a continental," the latter being the name then given to the printed currency. The same thing happened in the Confederate South during our Civil War. After World War I, the galloping German inflation resulted from unbounded issue of German marks. There are many other examples; and even though our model is an artificial one, it is a pretty good bet that the same thing would happen in modern America if an unlimited amount of money were to be issued by our central bank or Treasury.

What I have been describing would go under the name of "demand-pull" inflation. The image is this: the vast increase of dollar spending pulls up prices. No doubt wages and other costs will rise too, but they would be rising from the indirect pull on prices.[2]

Up until now all my examples of my demand-pull inflation for our ideally competitive economic model have had to do with the creation of currency. Of course, you will realize that operations that are designed to increase the amount of checkable demand deposits can also be construed as effective measures for changing the amount of total money and thereby having repercussions upon price levels. Nor is that all. Governmental fiscal policy can also, in such a model, create changes in the general level of prices. For example, if the government spends much more than it is taxing and finances the difference by means of bond sales to the public, that process too can create an inflationary gap and cause the general price level to rise. If, on the other hand, the government is running a budgetary surplus rather than deficit, the current rate of such a surplus can have a depressing effect upon the price level even prior to any changes in the supply of money or in the long-run level of public debt outstanding.

These various matters can be described in more than one way. Older economists who are fond of terminology like that of the quantity theory of money will say that changes in the velocity of circulation of money can have effects upon total spending and prices just as changes in the total amount of money itself. Economists who like to use the terminology of modern income determination will put the same matter something like this: Changes in government fiscal policy, like changes in central bank policy or in the rate at which mines are turning out gold, will shift the point of intersection of the saving and investment schedules (or of the $C + I + G$ and 45°-line schedules); this can lead to an opening up of the inflationary gap and a resulting demand-pull inflation.

If demand-pull inflation were all we had to fear, life would be simple. It would then be merely a problem of the proper dosage of fiscal and monetary measures: not too much so as to cause inflation; not too little so as to cause excessive unemployment. Thus, when automation had created temporary unemployment, that could be offset by expansionary demand policies; when automation had created over-full-employment, the reverse dosage would be called for. But with wage and other cost inflexibilities, this problem—and others, such as the balance of international payments—may become very hard.

Armaments and Prosperity

"Does America's prosperity depend upon military expenditures? If there were a relaxation of cold war tension and a massive reduction in governmental security expenditures, would the effect on the American economy be a profound crisis, followed by a sustained slump like that of the post-1929 Great Depression?"

When I lecture abroad in Japan or Europe, somebody always eagerly asks these questions. Curiously, American audiences seem less concerned with such issues. Psychoanalysts of businessmen's wives report that their patients' spouses worry about many things, but not over the breaking out of peace.

While the layman in Europe still registers concern that disarmament might cause a capitalistic collapse, there seems to be a new look in Soviet opinion on this matter. The Soviet economic journals, I am told, increasingly take the line that the American economy could weather (and benefit from) extensive demilitarization. Just the year-before-last a group of eminent Soviet economists visited this country to meet with American academicians for an informal and scientific exchange of viewpoints. When they met in Cambridge, Massachusetts, with some of my colleagues at M.I.T. and Harvard University, I was interested to hear that they were prepared to stipulate in advance of the discussion that cessation of the cold war would not engender colossal unemployment and crisis in the United States. Since this was billed as a scientific discussion and not a political free-for-all, I was prepared to believe that their detailed analyses of postwar economic developments in America had led them to reverse the usual Marxian analysis of our problems. I must confess, though, that I did not hear there the scientific reasons for this revisionist attitude.

I am not a Marxian economist. Some years ago Paul Sweezy claimed you could count the Marxian economists in American universities on one nose—his; and it may be significant that he no longer holds a regular university post and the nose is now worn by Stanford's Paul Baran. I am inclined to agree with the recent statement of Peter Wiles, formerly of Oxford and now of Brandeis University, that, although one can detect some influence of bourgeois economics on Soviet practice in the realm of linear programming and input-output, there appears to be no detectable reverse influence of Marxian economics on present-day Anglo-Saxon economics, as she is taught in our institutions of higher learning and as practiced by economic specialists in business and government.

My own preoccupation is with the understanding of behavior in mixed-economies of the American and Western European type. If it is necessary to learn mathematics to help explain them, I steel myself to this task. If it were necessary to learn Sanskrit, I would grudgingly do so. If to predict the pattern of future events an economist had to spend his middle years hanging by his heels from the ceiling, I would perforce make the sacrifice. And if my reading of Marxian economists generated fruitful hypotheses concerning realistic economic behavior, I would unhesitatingly put in the effort. My only sticking point would come if Dr. Faust's devil required my immortal soul in exchange for understanding of political economy; and even here, so great is my zeal for scientific objectivity, I would certainly feel tempted.

An uncommitted student will, I fear, find little to help him in his understanding of the postwar American economy from trying to master the dialectic and language of Marxist economists. In a way I regret this, for our knowledge is not so perfect as to permit us the luxury of spurning help from any source. In other moods when my scientific spirit flickers and the winds of chauvinism sweep through my drowsy thoughts, I find myself enjoying a secret satisfaction that our rivals in the struggle for coexistence should be so weak in their analysis of our system. I suppose this is merely a natural weakness of the flesh and an atavistic survival of the caveman's feeling that for someone to know his name and understand him represents a vague threat to his well-being. Seriously, were I the all-powerful head of a Communist state, I would follow the practice of the ruthless Nazis who created the rank of "honorary" Aryan for those individuals whose scientific or other talents were deemed useful for the Fatherland. That is, I would set up in the Kremlin a secret economic unit, forbidden to hamper itself by the use of Marxian categories, and required to use the most up-to-date of modern economics to analyze Western reality. (I reject as frivolous the view that the best Soviet economists, after they have applied the most powerful M.I.T. methods to analyzing America, then interline their reports with harmless and irrelevant Leninist slogans as a cover.) If, as some wit has said, Marxism is the opiate of the Marxists, there is no reason why the Soviet struggle for dominance should be sacrificed to this luxury activity. I wish to add that my remarks about the sterility of Marxism apply to the understanding of economic trends. Some wiser men than I claim to find benefit from Marxian hypotheses in understanding *political* developments.

A Dollar Is a Dollar Is a Dollar

So much then for Marxian economics in the present context. Nonetheless the questions about the effect of defense expenditures upon the American economy are valid. And they are important. They deserve objective examination and require from us the most careful analysis modern economics can bring to them.

Present-day analysis of income determination makes it quite evident that the additional military expenditures resulting from the Berlin crisis are one of the causes for our vigorous post-recession expansion.

Chairman Heller and his associates on the Council of Economic Advisers were rightly impressed with the size of the gap between our recent performance and our economic potential. They rightly were concerned with the prospect that unemployment would recede slowly; the new facts becoming available are beginning to confirm the Heller view that *the intensification of our unemployment* cannot be attributed primarily to an increase in structural or hard-core unemployment among the aged, young, regionally stranded, and technologically obsolete workers.

From public utterances and published gossip, one infers that the Council of Economic Advisers—taking full account of our international balance of payments position and the risks with respect to creeping inflation of the cost-push type—believed that our economy was in need of more expansionary fiscal monetary policy than appeared politically in the cards a few months ago. It appears to me that the Berlin crisis has fortuitously brought the economy the extra expenditures we needed for a more vigorous recovery. While it reflects a naïve misunderstanding of purchasing-power mechanics to think that military dollars have some extra potency in reviving a capitalistic system and to think that ordinary civilian expenditures and tax cuts could not provide an efficacious substitute, there is no reason to blink the fact that these extra expenditures will be a stimulus in the quarters ahead.

This has a bearing on recent American debates. In April, 1961, Arthur F. Burns, Eisenhower's first Economic Adviser, stated the view that full employment (as defined, for example, by a 4 per cent unemployment rate) would be reached in about the third quarter of 1962. In the August, 1961, *Morgan Guaranty Survey*, Dr. Burns pushed the date for our having come close to full employment to nearer the end of 1962. If Burns was then more nearly correct in his view than the less optimistic Council predictions of the same dates, the addition of the substantial post-Berlin and other new expenditure programs would, one supposes, push the date of 4 per cent unemployment toward the middle of 1962 (or in terms of some of the quantitative expenditure estimates, even earlier still). Now, I find the odds to be against this possibility and to be closer to the Council position when that position is adjusted for the additional programs. But Burns has often been right in the past and may well be vindicated by events. In any case, a person who thinks the Kennedy programs excessive might, even in the face of disappointing unemployment percentages in 1962, shift over to the quite different argument that the very failure of the economy to get down to 4 per cent unemployment would itself suggest that 4 per cent is too "activistic" a definition of present-day full employment. At least this is a view of a colleague, who disagrees with Burns's prediction, but has subscribed all along to the view that *whatever* the Kennedy administration has planned in the way of expenditure expansion has always been too great.

The last four years of the Eisenhower administration did, as I hinted earlier, serve to set back public and congressional understanding concerning rational fiscal policy. That being the case there may well be something to the following argument:

> Proper civilian fiscal and monetary policy are capable of generating enough dollar demand to banish slackness in our economy. True. Yet such may be the state of economic understanding and political ideology as to make it much easier for the American governmental system to do, *in the form of defense and security programs,* the things necessary for high employment.

This hypothesis has nothing to do with the peculiar terminology and models of Marxism, but to the degree that it represents a one-half truth or a three-quarters truth we should recognize it on its own merits.

Before World War II Harvard's Alvin Hansen promulgated the hypothesis of "secular stagnation." By this he meant the natural forces of consumption and investment spending were unlikely to be strong enough to keep us in high employment. He rested his theory on many factors that need not be discussed here.

Postwar employment has been generally high and therefore some would construe this to be a refutation of the Hansen theory. (I imagine that Professor Hansen would today admit that such a reversal of his non-economic expectation as the postwar surge in population has indeed altered his envisaged economic pattern. But certainly he can offer the defense that the population revolution gave no foreshadowing of itself in the prewar vital statistics, and that his critics at the time did not base their case so much on an hypothetical upsurge in population as on the allegation that population trends were not important causal factors in determining the sufficiency of total effective demand.) Hansen can very well argue, and I believe he may somewhere have done so, that it is precisely the increased role of government expenditure that staved off the slackness he feared; and that far from being the boy who cried wolf when there was no wolf, he was the boy who scared off the wolf by crying wolf.

Although Hansen was my revered teacher and is my good friend, I have no vested interest in the stagnationist hypothesis. What I merely want to emphasize here is that the increase in government expenditure, even if balanced by higher tax rates, could achieve whatever favorable effects it was capable of just as much if spent on useful public goods as on useful or useless *arms* programs.

A corollary of the above facts and reasonings appears to me to be this:

A sharp reduction of military expenditures, unlikely as that must seem to a dispassionate observer of world events, would have as its *short-term* consequences a considerable unsettling of production and occupation.

Such transitional difficulties would be minor were one assured that a new configuration of high employment lay just ahead. And, if a sizable reduction in military expenditure were to be followed by considerable tax reduction and by some compensating increase in useful civilian public programs, that would go a long way to offset the deflationary impact of total disarmament.

Nonetheless, in estimating the new configuration of fiscal and monetary policy that would restore high employment, an objective modern economist would have to admit the possibility (1) *that a vigorously expansionary monetary policy would be in order and* (2) *that a prudent budgetary* DEFICIT *would be called for.*

What is the political feasibility that the American people would cheerfully legislate the required budgetary deficit?

This is a question that takes me outside the sphere of my professional economic accomplishments. Still I am willing to venture a tentative guess.

The political pressures in our democracy would, I suspect, become strong to produce whatever deficits are needed to keep unemployment from rising much above say 8 per cent in any brief period. There is no guarantee, though, that those pressures would be efficacious to create whatever deficit is needed to keep unemployment at the 4 per cent level. Moreover, without the dynamic leadership of somebody with the personal magnetism of John F. Kennedy, there would be a significant possibility that our percentage of unemployment could slowly rise and level off at what most of us would regard as a socially undesirable rate.

I do not wish to end upon a pessimistic note. I am quite confident that the American electorate will rise to the future challenges put on it. My reason for discussing the matter is to illustrate the need for an economist who professes to be a scientist to follow his objective analysis wherever it leads him. It is a final bit of irony that Marxists, hypnotized by terminology that may have lacked relevance in its own day and certainly is misleading in the middle of the twentieth century, should still be obsessed by the specter of dramatic capitalistic crisis like that of the 1929 stock market crash rather than appreciating the more realistic Achilles heel of a contemporary mixed economy.

193

STABILIZATION POLICIES

IN THE CONTEMPORARY

U.S. ECONOMY

Paul A. Samuelson

I. CHASTENING REMEMBRANCES

In connection with stabilization policies for the contemporary American economy, we economists are at the moment riding very high. If there are malicious spirits running around [in] the universe, you might even say we are riding for a fall.

As we look up from our charts and computer print-outs, why is it that every prospect pleases? For one thing we are now in the fifth year of the post-1961 economic expansion. As the American annals go, that is a ripe old age. If you want to equate the age of a dog with the age of a man, I believe you multiply by seven. To bring phases of our business cycle up to a comparable basis, you have to multiply the number of years of expansion by a factor of more like 20. By this reckoning the Kennedy-Johnson expansion is just past 90, and, according to the only prediction I shall be unguarded enough to make tonight, I confidently expect it to go beyond the century mark. If the powerful magic of the modern generation of economic medicine men continues to operate, we may not soon see the euthanasia of poverty, but there might well ensue the euthanasia of the National Bureau of Economic Research—or at least an atrophying of its vital organs. To appreciate the euphoria of present day avant-garde economists that makes such joking possible, you must understand that I do not attribute the nation's recent good performance to anything as prosaic as sheer luck. Rather it is a case of the right thing being done for the right reason—and most miraculously being followed by the right results.

What really makes the cup of the econometrician overflow is the remarkable success of the 1964 massive tax cut. Economists flew in the face of all orthodoxy to recommend this measure. They used all their arts of persuasion to beat down ideological resistance. They predicted quantitatively the pattern of benefits to be obtained from the new tax measures. And, for once, all the universe conspired to bring the tale to a happy conclusion.

So perfect is the picture that it reminds me of another occasion of high spirits in our profession. Almost exactly 20 years ago this night, the best brains in our profession were gathered together in Washington. A great war had just come to an end. In the course of that war economists had conducted themselves with great distinction, worthy at least of the Victoria Cross.

For example, in 1941 President Roosevelt was told by practical men that gross national product was capable of but little expansion. Economists in the OPA and elsewhere took out their little slide rules—I will remind the younger men in this audience that electronic computers were not available to our gallant forefathers—and on the basis of economic calculation they reckoned that output still had a long way to grow. As events turned out, the economists were right.

I shall not go on to enumerate other triumphs of our profession in wartime, but—as I can say with good grace since I was then involved in other kinds of work—the triumphs were many and solid.

Little wonder, then, that the assembled experts of government felt considerable confidence in the rather gloomy forecast of heavy postwar unemployment that the cream of the various government agencies all arrived at. (I wish that my own guilt in this faulty diagnosis could be Freudianly forgotten.)

The rest is history. As a minority of economists *had* predicted, after an initial reconversion dip, there followed a period of strong aggregate demand. The honor roll of this minority included such diverse names as Sumner Slichter, Alvin Hansen, and William Fellner—who proved to be right for pretty much of the right reasons, namely [that] cumulative wartime backlogs of demand and need [existed], coupled with cumulative wartime accretions of purchasing power. (I shall omit reading the names of some of our distinguished brethren who were able to say "I told you so," but only on the basis of an ideological presumption that the good old American system can always be counted on to weather all storms.)

Very germane to the subject of my discussion, and indeed to the subject matter of this whole conference, is still another period of complacency within what Maynard Keynes called "our most agreeable branch of the moral sciences." I refer to what is said to have been a widespread feeling at the end of the 1920s—that Governor Strong in New York and the Federal Reserve Board in Washington—with only occasional help from cousin Montagu Norman on Threadneedle Street—had learned to utilize monetary policy to banish forever the instability of capitalistic enterprise. When you read in your modern textbooks about the "rediscovery of money," you can be sure that this rediscovery will include rediscovery of all the grandiose claims for control of the money supply as a panacea for eternal stability.

By now you may be thinking that the burden of my sermon tonight is that there is nothing new under the sun. It is true that I have been raking up the scandals of the past to warn the present generation, myself included, against overconfidence. But let the record also show that I do believe we have made genuine progress in learning how to reduce instability and promote real growth in the modern mixed economy. Furthermore, the development of economics as a science has, in my judgment, played an important role in this improved performance. And—what is, alas, not the same thing—an increased understanding of economic fundamentals on the part of the electorate and men of affairs has also helped. As far as the banishing of deep depression is concerned, the much talked-about contemporary "decline of moral fiber" has even had a constructive role to play. (I hasten to add, parenthetically, that the same complacency is not justified when it is a matter of long-term stability of the price index.)

II. FISCAL AND (RATHER THAN FISCAL OR) MONETARY POLICY

Let me now get down to business. Our chief instruments for macro-economic control are obviously fiscal policy and monetary policy. In the days of Governor Strong, fiscal policy was given a very limited role in the stabilization drama. This is not because there is truth in the old wives' tale that the employment-creating effects of public works were unknown before the days of Richard Kahn and of J. M. Keynes. Actually, you will often find, going back into remote history, recourse by practical men to such devices in time of depression. (I was shocked to read Cecil B. Woodham-Smith's *Great Hunger,* which tells the unbelievable story of how laissez-faire England tried to cope with the terrible Irish potato famine of the last century. Then starving people were actually made to work on the roads in order to qualify for meager allotments of imported grain. This tragic misidentification of what was needed in the way of social policy is mentioned here only to emphasize the point that income maintenance by means of emergency public works was already so customary as to have become clothed in a spurious legitimacy.)

In 1929 American fiscal policy was of limited scope, not because the intricacies of the multiplier doctrine had yet to be developed, but rather because the federal government was still limited in its scope of operation and the state governments and localities had neither the will nor the financial leeway to do much in this respect.

Had people of that day the imagination to insist that extreme anticyclical federal fiscal policy be started late in 1929, I am convinced the debacle of the 1930s could have been much averted; and, in case anyone thinks this an unimportant consideration, we would probably have ended up by the late 1930s with a smaller federal debt than was actually the historical case.

The late Charles O. Hardy regarded fiscal deficits as at best an indirect and roundabout way of creating an expansionary money supply. Why burn houses to roast pig? And why list fiscal policy as a supplement to monetary policy, since—according to this extreme view of Hardy and of of some recent money enthusiasts—it is merely an unnecessary and round-about way of getting the Federal Reserve to do what it ought to be doing anyway, namely, determining the supply of M (somehow de-fined) in the pattern best suited to overall stability and healthy growth.

I personally go along with the Irishman who said: "If whiskey is good and gin is good, how glorious must be whiskey and gin." I do not regard fiscal policy as the olive that wags the dry martini. I must confess that this was the view I held before I read the valuable *A Monetary History of the United States*, by Mrs. Schwartz and that other fellow. And I have to report that, while I ended up a better man for having read that work, I was left with no belief that the velocity of circulation of money remains unaffected by the level and financing of public budgets.

It is fortunate that fiscal policy does have a separate potency. For in this era of balance-of-payments deficits, militant use of credit expansion to restore full employment has not been politically feasible.

To be specific, consideration of domestic employment and growth would have called for the "Fed" to expand bank reserves enough after 1960 to bring the short-term bill rate down as much below 2 percent or 1½ percent as would be needed to promote an intensive deepening of capital in the United States. That would undoubtedly have sent dollars and gold abroad in great amounts under existing currency parities. In-stead, unemployment was brought in the 1960s from a 7 percent level down to its recent 4½ percent level by determined recourse to expansion-ary fiscal policy.[1]

Since the money supply did rise substantially in the years 1961-65, I do not want to attribute the expansion to fiscal policy alone. It was a case of active fiscal policy which was coupled with or financed by a sup-porting monetary policy. I suppose a modern-day Hardy who believes "the change in money income—attributable to a change in federal spend-ing or in taxing or in their budgetary difference—is negligible, provided the total of the money supply is held constant" might be tempted to dis-miss the constructive role of fiscal policy in this period. I cannot agree. The macroeconomic models I consider realistic do not display a velocity

---

[1] The next two paragraphs have been added to the original manuscript to take account of the oral discussion that followed the paper.

of circulation of money that is invariant under substantial changes in fiscal policy. Instead, had we kept the Eisenhower spending and taxing programs while the Fed tried to make M (the money supply) grow as it actually did grow in 1961-65, I am confident short-term interest rates would have been strongly depressed. Cool money would have left our shores in considerable volume. At a much lower structure of interest rates, people could have been content to hold larger cash balances relative to their earning assets and income streams. So unemployment would not have fallen in the quantitative degree that it did; nor would production have shown its historical growth; and similarly for profits and other indicators of sustained growth.

In historical fact we used expansionary fiscal policy and expansionary monetary policy together. We wisely ignored the advice of those European and American financiers who said we should reduce taxes only if we [could] make sure that the resulting deficit be financed out of "genuine savings" rather than by money creation. As an academic question one might ask, "Suppose the latter-day Hardy view quoted above were correct? Couldn't the government still use budget deficits as the excuse to print new money, offsetting any tendencies for interest rates to fall by specific open-market sales in the money market?" I am inclined to answer in the affirmative to this leading question[2] as a possibility; but I think this would require a more complicated model than the limiting one in which the liquidity-preference demand for money is interest inelastic.

Let me say in what must be a brief aside, that abandonment of the "bills only" doctrine and embracement of "operation twist" did enable monetary policy to make a small deliberate contribution to economic expansion. Probably more important still was the raising of the ceilings on deposit interest set by Regulation Q. These adjustments were in any case long overdue but were precipitated by the desire to keep our large banks competitive with foreign branches here and to forestall direct investment in Treasury bills by large official and unofficial foreign agencies.

Here again was a case where economic law and knowledge of it triumphed over lay opinion. "If you let some banks pay higher interest rates on deposits," so it was said by easy money fanatics, "then all banks will have to pay the higher rate. The only way they'll be able to afford to do that will be by raising the interest rates they charge on mortgages and loans to borrowers." Trained economists like Undersecretary Robert Roosa and Economic Adviser James Tobin, drew the opposite conclusion. They agreed: "If interest on deposits is allowed to rise to the competitive equilibrium level, that will make *more* funds available for mortgage and commercial lending. More funds imply both cheaper interest rates and greater availability." It was a dramatic fact that the

---

[2] Of Paul Wonnacott.

long-term interest rate remained low unprecedentedly long in the current expansion. I think this indicates that the expert economists were thus proved right. But I don't honestly know whether any of them predicted what seems to have also occurred—namely, a willingness of all the banks together to reach out for riskier long-term investments in order to be able to offer high competitive interest rates on the new certificates of deposit. In a sense, one device we have used to stabilize domestic employment in the face of an international deficit has been a contrived deterioration of the quality of credit on a mild scale. It is a paradox that this may be sound social policy and one of its certain consequences is an implicit new responsibility thrust upon government—by which I mean the Federal Reserve and the federal government—to help bail out the banking system if widespread problems of insolvency should ever develop.

This reminds me of our shocking failure to avert the collapse of all the banks in the 1930s. Future historians will consider it fantastic that we did not print whatever money would have been necessary to have staved-off runs on the banks. You can be sure that present-day stabilization programs would include such super-duper Reconstruction Finance Corporation salvage operations where the nation's banking system is concerned.

In this sense I agree with Milton Friedman that economic policy from 1930 to 1933 constituted a tragedy of errors. With present attitudes and institutions of government I am convinced the worst of the Great Depression could have been averted. But I have to emphasize that the measures to protect a multiunit banking system from internal drains and disaster involve much more than mere conventional open market operations by the Fed. The errors of omission that must never again be repeated are not definable simply in terms of permitting the statistical total of the money supply to decline.

If important institutions that have nothing to do with money narrowly defined—life insurance companies, mutual funds, even the stock market itself—were to be plunged into a vicious downward spiral of liquidation and bankruptcy, economists and politicians would today take it for granted that government had an overriding obligation to stem the tide. And make no mistake about it—armed with the constitutional powers of money creation, taxation, and borrowing—a great country like the United States would have power to spare in avoiding such a disaster.

III. HOW TO SYNTHESIZE A STABILIZING SERVOMECHANISM

Suppose we agree that fiscal policy and monetary policy are complementary mechanisms to promote growth and stability. What rules, procedures, and policies ought we to choose to follow?

Notice my wording of the last sentence. What rules should we choose? This will seem almost self-contradictory to those who pose the debate in terms of polar opposites: government by rules and laws rather than government by the discretion and intelligence of men. I won't rehash the arguments and counterarguments here. Let me merely summarize by saying that it takes discretion to institute a system of rules; and it takes discretion to desist from interfering with those rules. There is no true philosophical difference between the competing approaches: discretionary policy by men in government can be venal or disinterested; can be intelligent or stupid; can be arbitrary and capricious; or consistent and equitable.

Purely on the level of tactics one can ask the question [of] whether a simple policy of using open market operations to keep some definition of the money supply growing at some-such rate as 3 percent per annum is the best servomechanism that present-day economics can devise for a mixed economy like that of the United States.

Even if we had the floating exchange rates that we do not have and the perfect flexibility of wages and prices that we do not have, wouldn't it be something of a miracle if this turned out to be the optimum rule of all rules? Indeed, until you have a specific notion of the statistical properties of the load that is to be put upon a servomechanism, you cannot know in advance what is the best combination of resistances, capacitances, and inductances needed to synthesize the optimal stabilizing circuit. If the American economy in the decades ahead is to be subject to Kuznetslike intermediate waves, attributable to such exogenous factors as construction, population, and cold wars, an intelligent jury would expect that destabilizing fluctuations in the velocity of circulation of money would be discernible in our statistical data. The Federal Reserve Board would not have to consist of saints and wizards to be able to make at least a modest contribution toward minimizing unemployment and accelerating maintainable growth. Why sacrifice this feasible improvement of the system to that almost paranoid distrust of government which some zealots inherited from the nineteenth century?

I go further. While admitting that there are hazards in anticipating turns of the business cycle, I think it lamentable that the footprints of the Federal Reserve were so often in the past to be found among the lagging indicators. Why always bring up the rear? Let us find such financial series as the money supply and interest rates more often among the current indicators or even among the leaders. Naturally this would involve some errors of the false alarm variety. But what is the vaunted flexibility of monetary policy for . . . its alleged ability to reverse its ground like a Big-Ten football quarterback?

Both fiscal policy and monetary policy are on an equal footing in this regard. Each [of them] involve time-lags of many months before they achieve their final effects. Such time-lags make it all the more important to use some measure of forecasting and anticipatory action. And what I am saying in this respect will become less controversial if, as many think, the important problem ahead is not that of a choppy 30-month National Bureau inventory cycle but rather that of longer undulations in the rate of growth of our economy. If it is the-case that the servomechanism is to bear such a load, then many of the old clichés will go out of the window.

I refer to such bits of unconventional wisdom as the following: "Don't employ public works for stabilization purposes. By the time they get the money out you'll already be in the next boom." And yet, when President Kennedy came into office in January, 1961, his economic advisers could predict with some confidence that there would continue to be an unemployment gap for some considerable time.

I don't want to give away any secrets—and fortunately I don't happen to know any—but isn't it quite possible that some shrewd economic historian of the future will characterize the fiscal policy of the Kennedy and Johnson administration in the following provocative way:

With much ingenuity and untiring zeal, the New Frontiersmen of the Great Society contrived to emasculate the automatic stabilization built-in on the upside by our progressive tax system. Brick by brick they hauled down the implicit budgetary surplus which would have prevailed at full employment if the Eisenhower levels of expenditure had been preserved with unchanged Eisenhower rates of taxation.

I don't say anybody planned it in quite that way, but perhaps I am underrating the perspicacity of our political economists. In any case the whole nation has been the beneficiary. And I can think of no better contrast to bring this out than a comparison of the anemic and short-lived business expansion from 1958 to 1960 with the current post-1961 cyclical expansion. I will remind you that unemployment stayed above the 5 percent level during the last years of the 1950s; yet the Federal Reserve—in its fanatical determination to root out any trace of inflation—engineered a tighter pattern of interest rates than can be found in the annals of the National Bureau for almost a century. At the same time the federal budget was permitted to go within a year from the largest peacetime deficit ever experienced to a whopping surplus. All this involved stabilization with a vengeance; but it was, if not stabilization of *rigor mortis,* something like the stabilization of hibernation.

I am a dutiful speaker—and when I am given the assignment to talk on stabilization I try to live up to it—but I am also a devious person with a Machiavellian cunning. If it is to be stabilization, it must be stabilization on my definition.

The pattern of stability that should interest people today cannot be one of sluggishness or stagnation. Nor does the problem pose itself as that of perpetuating an average level of unemployment midway between such extremes as 7 and 4 percent. Good economic performance means infrequent and only transient departures from high-employment production along a growth trend of some 4 percent per annum.

In part because of the new Viet Nam spending, I think we are beginning to approach our goal. I refuse to believe our public is so economically retarded as to have to rely on cold-war emergencies to back into full employment growth. I think that we have learned something since 1953 (when we lacked the imagination to offset the end of the Korean War with a massive cut in taxes). I even venture to think that the phobia against noninflationary deficits is beginning slowly to disappear.

So I stand before you tonight as something of a "cockeyed optimist." Most of us here are not bankers. But we have absorbed enough of the banker's neutrality to know that one ought to be wary in lending money or credence to optimistic idealists. In order then to restore my credit and standing as a man of prudence and sobriety, I must end my sermon with a warning of problems still unsolved.

Can a mixed economy like ours enjoy continued full employment without having wages and other costs push up the wholesale price index beyond a tolerable rate? Or, to use technical jargon, can we contrive stabilization devices to ensure a healthy Phillips curve for the American economy?

I don't know the answer. Few mixed economies have met with success in engineering an "incomes policy." Certainly our English brethren are no less intelligent than we in cooking up beautiful economic theorems and models and today London is swarming with civil servants recruited from the universities. Yet, even the most sympathetic observer must wonder whether the British are getting anywhere in the field of income-policy stabilization; and despite the many miracles we have been able to observe in Japan and the Common Market, conspicuously absent has been the miracle of full employment with free markets and reasonable price stability.

The first speaker at a conference ought to set a good example. Money, besides being the root of all evil, is the source of much bad temper among economists. If I have stepped on someone's doctrinal toes, I apologize and beg his pardon. Only the late hour can extenuate such gauche behavior. I hope you will agree that much can be forgiven a speaker who uses up only 45 minutes of his 50-minute hour.

194

Reflections on Recent Federal Reserve Policy
by Paul A. Samuelson

I. Introduction: Monetarists' Indictment

LET ME BEGIN by stating flatly an unpopular view. I believe that Federal Reserve policy in the decade of the 1960's has been very good. It has not been perfect. But when I consider the situation within which the decision makers have had to operate, I suspect that we are not likely in a future decade to do as well. And certainly Federal Reserve policy in the 1960's has been superior to that of the 1950's, both in terms of technical proficiency and the social-welfare goals that the central bank has pursued.

In view of this generally approving evaluation of recent money and credit policies, how can one account for the more frequently heard view that since 1965 the Federal Reserve has behaved remarkably badly—that it has committed gross errors in one direction and then *compounded* them by gross errors in the opposite direction, with the result that it is the Federal Reserve system itself which must be convicted for the crime of having originated and amplified the inflation and instability which has plagued the U.S. economy in the last five years?

Others in this Symposium who are critical of the Federal Reserve will provide their own answer to this question. I suspect the answer they will give can be summarized as follows: If one believes that the proper norm against which to appraise Central Bank policy is whether it has tried to and has succeeded in stabilizing one or another measure of the aggregate money supply within a narrow range around (say) 4 or 5 per cent per annum, then the Federal Reserve Bank can be adjudged guilty of having failed to do this.

Money, narrowly or broadly defined, has not since 1945 actually grown at a steady rate. Nor has it done so in the decade of the 1960's. In particular, the rate of growth of money increased after the mid-1965 escalation of the Vietnam War; then in 1966 the increase dipped below a prescribed trend rate, and even turned negative in the "money crunch" months of mid-1966; after mid-1967, the Fed permitted the rate of increase to overshoot above the trend average.

PAUL SAMUELSON *is Institute Professor at Massachusetts Institute of Technology.*

Reprinted from the *Journal of Money, Credit, and Banking*, Vol. II, No. 1 (February, 1970), pp. 33–40.

And even more specifically, following the assured passage of the mid-1968 tax surcharge, the monetary authorities are impeached for having made especially ludicrous vacillations of judgment: Being misled by overconfidence in the restrictive potency of fiscal contraction, they made M grow too fast in the last half of 1968, and then from the spring of 1969 to the present moment (October–November, 1969) have throttled the money supply to the point of no growth at all. Finally, to complete the charge, this woeful departure from gradualism has made a serious recession inevitable in 1970.

If one accepts this norm of steady money growth, the case is an open and shut one. There is no need for a symposium, and nought for the Fed to do but plead guilty. The Federal Reserve has been caught *in flagrante*, and one has only to take out the chart book, measure the discrepancies above and below the trend line, square them, and tote up the damages that are to be assessed against the culprit.

To accept this criterion in advance is to beg the issue and prejudge the case. At the least, extended analytical discussion of all the pros and cons is needed. My own final resolution of the conflicting considerations, as must be obvious, leads to rejection of the monistic norm provided by a steady trend of the money supply.

II. BROADENING AND REFOCUSING CRITERIA OF GOOD MONETARY BEHAVIOR

However, for the sake of the argument let me for the moment accept stability in the growth rate of money as the norm. Does it follow that we can grade the report card of the Federal Reserve in each epoch by the smallness of the average squared deviation from a proper trend rate? Not necessarily in my view. When it comes to scoring behavior, we do not censure a starving man who steals a loaf of bread as severely as an affluent one who faces less stress and fewer temptations. As every electrical engineer concerned with synthesis of an optimal-control mechanism knows, two network filters that have imposed on them quite different exogenous stochastic variations might display the same mean-square-error of performance; yet it is unfair to deem them equal, since one has a ridiculously easy task and the other a task fraught with irreducible complications.

War Finance

So it is with economic history and the challenge to the Central Bank. I have before me a chart plotting the rate of change of the money supply from 1919 to the present.[1] As I look at it, probably the worst single period of performance

[1] See Michael W. Keran, "Monetary and Fiscal Influences on Economic Activity—the Historical Evidence," Federal Reserve Bank of St. Louis *Review* (November, 1969), Chart III, pages 16 and 17. While this paper was in the press, I received a different chart of rate of

as measured by the stability of trend of M is that of the war years itself. In 1942 the money supply grew at annual rates of more than 30 per cent per annum, and the chart records ups and downs in 1941 and 1942 and in 1943 and 1944. There is no great interest here in discussing whether it was optimal to have the wartime pattern of rationing, price and wage controls, deliberate deficit financing, and accommodating monetary policy anchored to a pegged interest-rate structure. I dare say God in His heaven, particularly with the benefit of hindsight, could have done somewhat better. So let me simply enter into the record the finding of one who lived through that period and is able to look back on it with the advantage of hindsight—if history could be rerun again and again in independent experiments, we should find ourselves extremely *lucky* whenever the sample turns up as successful a pattern of wartime re-source allocation as was actually contrived in World War II.

The Stable 1920's

Turning back to the chart of $\dot{M}/M$, to the naked eye the Fed seems to have done distinctly better since World War II than in the period between the two wars as far as stability, in the standard deviation sense, is concerned. For the 1919–69 period, two epochs of stability particularly stand out, that of 1926–29 and perhaps the Eisenhower years in their entirety, 1953–60. Certainly in comparison with the standard deviations of the depression years, these loom up as oases of stability. To be sure, in the last half of the 1920's, the average around which the growth rate was centered was much nearer to zero than to the popular 4 to 5 per cent recently fashionable among monetarists. But have we not been reassured repeatedly that the important thing is stability around *some* level, whose exact amount is really not very important? Indeed after selling various academics and Congressmen on the 4 or 5 per cent range, Professor Friedman has jolted some of them by his more recent determinatioı that a much lower level consistent with a contrived decline in the price level, would be truly optimal.[2] If you are not a fixed-rule-for-ever-and-a-day man—and even for the sake of the argument and in the role of the Devil's advocate, I am not willing to be such—you can rationally say, "The institutional structure of the labor market is different in the 1960's and 1970's from in the 1920's; and hence

change of the money supply prepared by Dr. Beryl W. Sprinkel of the Harris Trust and Savings Bank for presentation at the Fourth Annual Business Forecasting Luncheon, University of Rochester College of Business Administration, Rochester, New York, December 10, 1969.

To my astonishment $\dot{M}/M$ looked quite different on the Sprinkel chart for the period of the 1920s, which produced some consternation in me, but nothing to what would have been the case were I a monetarist. In consultation with Mrs. Karen Johnson, one of my graduate students and co-workers at M.I.T., I have decided that the difference is probably due to the fact that the St. Louis Bank data have been taken from Friedman and Schwartz but with different smoothing of monthly data and "centering." I presume that each monetarist will have to decide for himself which treatment of the data he considers optimal: my comments here apply to the St. Louis chart.

[2] Milton Friedman, *The Optimum Quantity of Money and Other Essays* (Chicago: Aldine Publishing Co., 1969).

with less forces of cost-push to be encountered in the earlier period, it was expedient then to aim for a lower growth rate in the money supply. As times change, so do optimal prescriptions change, and thus there is no real inconsistency in trying today for a 4.5 per cent rate, in comparison with trying in 1926 for a 1 or 0 per cent growth of $\dot{M}/M$."

Depression Lunacy

The boom years of the 1920's are reinterpreted to look better now than they were perceived to be in the disastrous decade that followed. So one finds it today less far-fetched that analysts in the 1920's should have proclaimed that the Federal Reserve had once-and-for-all conquered the business cycle. Perhaps sufficient unto the day is the good thereof; but in any case we know that the good monetary performance *in* the 1920's was not a sufficient condition to avert the dreadful slump of the 1930's. My point is not that we should debit the Federal Reserve regime prior to Governor Strong's death in 1929 all that happened *subsequent* to that epoch. And my point is certainly not that the Fed was powerless to act better in the 1930–33 years. My point is this. In terms of awarding credit and blame, one must recognize that it would have been intrinsically much harder to have attained a prescribed goal under the unsettled conditions of stress in the post-1929 period than in most earlier and later periods.

Put it this way. Suppose you believe the Fed can and should have any money supply pattern it desires. Suppose you believe that money is all-important, dwarfing in significance fluctuations in fiscal policy, technological innovations, over-all private investment opportunities and exuberances. And then suppose you witness fluctuations in business which by your hypothesis could not have occurred had they not originated in the criminal caprices of the monetary authorities. Then what theory of the business cycle are you left with? You are left with a sporadic-lunacy theory of the cycle. For some unaccountable reason a group of men, the Open Market Committee of the Fed and its subsidiary apparatus, suddenly all go beserk together and contrive a massive destruction of the money supply.

This is a great theory of history. It not only explains depressions, but also explains inflations! For at still other times, witches enter the bodies of the Reserve Authorities and cause them to go beserk in the other direction, causing them to contrive explosive increases in $\dot{M}/M$.

Demand as Well as Supply

Do I exaggerate? It is really hard to vulgarize the doctrines of the monetarists when they wax eloquent. I have even seen the inflation after World War I and the subsequent deflation explained away in terms of the caprices of the Treasury and Federal Reserve. Now, in their less eloquent moments, monetarists know better. They would fail students in the classroom who appraise price-stabilization programs for wheat or corn in terms of only *one* of the schedules of supply and demand. You can quote numerous passages in leading monetarists in which it is recognized that there are fluctuations in the demand side for money. Indeed you can catch them out talking sense during the ongoing stream of history—as in 1967 when some of them argued persuasively that in the aftermath of the 1966 crunch, there was an enhanced desire on the part of corporations and the banks for liquidity,—a discernible shift in the demand for money and perhaps in part a shift back toward a more normal, long-run schedule.

A good analogy is provided by the problem of statistical identification. We know from the work of Elmer Working, Frisch, Schultz, Haavelmo, and others, that if it is supply alone which is shifting, the *ex post* scatter of prices and quantities will trace out a demand curve. We know that in the absence of a determination that demand has not shifted, there is a recognizable bias in treating the *ex post* scatter as a demand curve.

Even from the writings of monetarists—and I use the word "even" because they themselves underplay in actuality the importance of the formal point—it is naïve to use *ex post* mean-square-deviation-around-target-trend-average as a proper score card for Federal Reserve performance. Lest I be thought to be setting up a straw man, and be rebutted by the assertion that few have calculated such explicit scorecards, it should be recognized that this is what is implicitly involved in critiques which penalize the Federal Reserve twice in years like 1966–67: once for below average $\dot{M}/M$, and again for above average $\dot{M}/M$, with the two errors *added* rather than cancelled out.

Improving on Mean-Square Error of Deviations from Trend

Let me explicate my criticisms of using stability of money growth as itself the proper target for *ex ante* policy and as a scorecard for *ex post* performance evaluation.

The average trend value around which the deviations are reckoned does, as already mentioned, make a big difference. I believe that any number agreed upon for an M_1 or M_2 target in 1946 would have worked out disastrously. It is easy to see retrospectively, and perhaps not hard to suspect at the time, that the War left us with a swollen money supply and a slow velocity that was sure to accelerate. Under a fixed rule, we should have enjoyed in the years 1945 to 1960 a quite unnecessary price inflation, and the more naïve one is as a zealot for monetarism the more confidently can one make this assertion.

If one for the moment drops a target prescribed in advance for the mean growth rate of M, the case for a stability-around-trend criterion still remains vulnerable. I mentioned that M growth had been relatively stable in two epochs. The case of the 1920's has already been discussed. Consider now the other case, that of the Eisenhower years. That was also a period of rather steady growth at a low average rate. Indeed if one is a monetarist, the lion's share of the blame for the lamentable stagnation of that epoch—real growth from early 1953 to late 1960 barely exceeded 2 per cent on the average!—must go to the lowness of the average M growth rate.

I realize that those living through this epoch found plenty to complain about the lack of stability in the supply of money, and I remember vividly criticizing the Federal Reserve for aiming at such a tight credit market in 1959 as led to no growth at all in the total of currency and demand deposits. But with a chart before me of the money supply covering the last forty years, I still have to regard this as a period of relative stability. It is my point that what seems most objectionable about the 1950's was the average rate of monetary tightness, not the dispersion around that average.

III. Leaning against the Wind

It is a vulgar error to couple together a belief in monetarism in (1) the sense of a belief that the supply of money is the overwhelmingly important determinant of the state of effective demand, and a belief in monetarism in the sense of (2) a belief in adherence to a rule of an invariable trend rate of growth in M. That this is an error is recognized, occasionally, by monetarists themselve (viz. Milton Friedman and Allan Meltzer). If I were more of a monetarist than I am, I could imagine subscribing to (1) above while forcefully rejecting (2), being led instead to advocate a compensatory or counter-cyclical monetary target. Whatever the agreements of the monetarists may be on the distinction that I am drawing, it seems to me they tend to lose sight of it or underplay the distinction when it comes to divvying up the scorecard of Federal Reserve felonies and misdemeanors.

The years 1965, 1966, and 1967 are a case in point. If one is a monetarist who believes in leaning against the wind, then as an offset to the demerits awarded the Fed in the fall of 1965 for not leaning hard enough against the wind of inflation, one should award some merits and brownie points for their having atoned in 1966. And suppose one thinks that the Fed overacted in 1966. (I must stress that this is not at all a decided conclusion except to those who beg the case by reference to a stable trend criterion. As I am writing we all realize that it is crucially a question of value judgments as to how severe the retardation sought for 1970 in order to moderate inflation ought to be. Just so, from mid-1966 to mid-1967 it was a matter of value judgment as to how strong the macroeconomic restraint aimed at by the authorities should have then been.) But suppose we agree that between July and November of 1966 monetary tightness was overdone. Then a monetarist who believes in a leaning-against-the-wind policy will award some merit points to Federal Reserve policy in the first half of 1967 as an offset to the demerits he is awarding for over-tight, late-1966 policy.

Political Pundits

What I am saying is so obvious as to constitute almost a truism or banality. Why then is the picture so often painted in a contrary fashion? After examining a number of the usual argumentations by monetarists, I think I have isolated the difference of view in the implicit or explicit intrusion of certain alleged "political" uniformities. Suddenly the economist doffs his sorcerer's cap of wisdom and puts on the cap of the political sage. Written out explicitly, I think the argument goes something like the following: "If you overdo 1966 tightness, then you will inevitably induce so great a populist reaction as to make it equally inevitable that you will be forced into overdoing looseness in the later months of 1967, but this in turn leads to inflation and backlash against inflation, with the result that we have an *anti-damped oscillatory* model based on political uniformities of creation."

Let me first make the general point that I do not believe that there exist such simple, regular, plausible political uniformities upon which to base a solid case for an invariable M-rule. And I certainly am skeptical that economists have the training or skills to discern with any confidence such political regularities as may be valid.

But I do not rest my case on the *a priori* plausibility of this contention. I lived through the 1967 period; I advised in an informal way Administration policymakers, and I testified before Congress. I can testify against the thesis that there was an overwhelming political outcry from the voters in any month of 1967. The biggest outcry that was to be heard during that whole year came in its *first* months, and from monetarists who were predicting a recession that turned out to be no recession at all (or, as some of them say in the attempt to preserve face, that proved to be a "mini-recession"). As late as June, 1967 I personally was still concerned lest the economy move into a period of too-sluggish growth. But after the middle of the year official government economists, like Gardner Ackley and Arthur Okun, had recovered their nerve and concern over inflation and were again urging on Congress fiscal restraint.

Meantime, what was happening back at the Federal Reserve? For the political model of anti-damped explosion to be valid, the Fed should have been, *after* mid-year, under intense pressure from Wright Patman, from a Texan President, from Senator Proxmire, and from the flow of mail from Main Street —in order to explain the Fed's permitting what monetarists regard as too fast a rate of growth of the money supply. But I believe research will show this to be largely a figment of the imagination. Wright Patman the Fed has always with it, but any shrewd scholar in the realm of politics will know that his influence on the Fed was very much greater in the months *of the money crunch of 1966* than in 1967.

The Post-1965 Vietnam Inflation

I do believe that, except possibly for a few months in early 1967, the American economy has been subject to too much demand-pull inflationary pressure. That is why as early as December, 1965 I counseled President Johnson, both publicly and privately, to ask for an increase in tax rates. (It is now a matter of *public* record that the Ackley Council of Economic Advisors privately recommended to President Johnson in early 1966 that he ask for a tax increase, a request which he refused. This Presidential decision was quietly accepted by those advisors.)

Since my researches lead to the eclectic view that both fiscal policy and monetary policy are potent to affect aggregate demand, these same empirical inferences led me to the recommendation that, in the absence of fiscal constraint, the Fed would have to all the more exercise monetary restraint; but, of course, my calibration of how monetary restraint is to be measured was in terms of a *vector* of indicators—including the behavior of the structure of interest rates—and not simply in terms of the rate of charge of the money supply alone. Thus, one would want to allow something for the shift in liquidity preference, i.e. in the demand for money, which was to be discerned in the year following the 1966 crunch. And, more subtly, one had to be prepared for a *subsequent* reactivation of those extra liquidity holdings. I.e., it is seen to be optimal, for business cycle stabilization, to plan for an overshoot in money growth in the period following the crunch and to be prepared to engineer a later overshoot in the opposite direction. I leave to the reader the diagraming of this interpretation in terms of time-phased shifts in both the demand for money and its supply, but wish to emphasize that it is not "fine tuning" that I am advocating but rather modest, reasonable actions in the light of most probable conditions in the year ahead.

IV. Interpreting the Last Few Years

But suppose in retrospect we agree that there was excessive aggregate demand for the most part after 1965 and have allocated some of the blame for this to President Johnson, Congress, and the electorate at large. What is the residual error and blame that one must attach to the Fed?

1. Did the Fed fail to forecast correctly what was happening?
2. Did the Fed fail to recognize quickly what had been happening?
3. Was there a long lag between perceiving what was happening, what was about to happen, and what ought to be done about it, before action was taken?

The Post-Surcharge Miscalculation

I cannot give a single answer to these questions for the whole period. My answers for the last half of 1968 would be quite different from my answers for the period I have just been discussing, the year from mid-1967 to mid-1968.

I think a good case can be made that in mid-1968 the Federal Reserve authorities were misled by what turned out to be a bad forecast. I don't think there is much disagreement on this matter, either among Board Governors, monetarists, or post-Keynesian eclectics.[3] When Congress passed the mid-1968 10 per cent tax surcharge (partially retroactive) the Fed expected a considerable slowdown in growth for the last half of 1968. They were willing to cushion this a little. So to speak, they were willing to reward Congress for its courageous fiscal policy by showing that this enabled monetary policy to be thereby a bit easier; and perhaps they wanted to drive home the lesson that all in authority were showing a proper concern against "overkill." (Yes, Virginia, many of those who opposed a tax increase in early 1968 did warn darkly against *weakness* ahead for the economy.)

Having been misled by the common forecast for 1968–69, the Fed may perhaps be faulted for delaying so long in undertaking an agonizing reappraisal. And I am prepared to believe that part of their slowness to change course may be traceable to the technical fact that the Reserve authorities pay a great deal of attention to interest rate conditions along with changes in the money supply itself. This part of a monetarist's indictment seems to me to be worthy of consideration and further investigation.[4]

The Fed may have insufficiently realized that the inflation itself was one of the reasons for the high and rising trend of interest rates. This is a point that monetarists do well to emphasize, but speaking as a non-monetarist I wish to

[3] The simon-pure monetarist identifies the forecasting error as attributable to a mistaken belief in fiscal policy's potency to affect aggregate demand. Over this identification dispute is possible. I myself believe that much of the unexpected strength in the economy since mid-1968 must be attributed to the cumulative effect of the inflation itself, which for the first time became an important variable in the behavior functions determining spending propensities. Indeed the monetarists' forecasts that I have been collecting periodically since mid-1968 have also shown an average downward bias, although not necessarily to the same degree as GNP models of the Wharton School type.

[4] I believe that the Fed will soon be changing over in its operation of the Open Market Committee toward more explicit use of the behavior of monetary aggregates as the proximate targets and goals of action. Some of the credit for this salutary change must go to the chidings of monetarists. But it is interesting that the minority spearhead within the Fed in favor of this shift toward aggregates is composed of such "Keynesians" as Governors Maisel and Mitchell and Boston Federal Reserve President Frank Morris. Is this paradoxical? I think not. Practical banking types tend to be the ones who put greatest emphasis on moderating changes in interest rates, and a post-Keynesian who has never been tempted in the slightest degree by recent versions of monetarism has long tended to be critical of interest rate stabilization for the *General Theory* teaches that a sine-like wave of autonomously destabilizing investment ought to be countered by a change in the stock of money in the opposite direction so that higher interest rates can cut back investment *along* the shifted-out marginal efficiency schedule. Also, and this is a somewhat independent point, when the Fed incurred my wrath for causing the money supply to shrink in 1959, I think it was led into this misdemeanor not really by an excessive concern with interest rates as such, but more importantly because they desired a "tone of *business* tightness" much like what they got.

make clear that the view that the money rate of interest is derivable from the real rate of interest plus an allowance for anticipated inflation is also a notion Keynesians wish to emphasize. This idea has an ancient geneology, being found in Henry Thornton before Waterloo, occurring in the nineteenth century writings of Marshall and Wicksell, and in this century in the writing of Irving Fisher, Keynes, Seaffa, and many others.

The Reason Why

But let me return to the period of mid-1967 to mid-1968, the period when the Vietnam inflation resumed. If the Federal Reserve was too expansive in that period, I suggest it was not because of bad forecasting, not because of faulty recognition of what was currently happening, and not because of technical lag in making up one's mind as to what was to be done and then doing it. Rather, I think it was because of the value judgments that guided a majority on the Federal Reserve Board. The quest for full employment was a serious one in their eyes. The definition of what constituted full employment was gradually in their minds becoming more perfectionist. Since for more than a decade the country was deemed to have suffered more from excessive unemployment and product-gap than from undue inflation, faced with the trade-off between unemployment and inflation, the Federal Reserve authorities opted for a policy stance which gave greatest weight to real growth rather than price stability.

In the two and one-half years that have since elapsed, the country has been aching from cumulative and stubborn inflation. Now that we are enjoying our Monday morning hangover, we look back with a different perspective on our weekend motivation to lead a gay life. It is not my intention here to condone any mistake of this kind, but rather to make sure that we correctly identify the nature of the mistake that was made.

IV. CONCLUSION

My general viewpoint will be clear. Independently of the merits of monistic monetarism, I find little appeal in appraisals of monetary policy based upon the criterion stability-around-target-trends.

I do not believe in mechanical or numerical cardinal criteria. But if forced to construct one, I would use as its components something like squared deviations from full-employment combined in some kind of a weighted average with squared divergence from tolerable price stability. In consequence, successful use of intelligence that led to a speed-up of M growth in recession times and to a slowdown or even reversal of M growth when demand-pull threatens would lead to enlarged "mean square error of deviation from M target trend" in comparison with strict adherence to the Rule, and although I do not relish monetary instability for its own sake, I would enthusiastically accept this kind of instability.

It is not fine tuning that I am after. Minor short-term movement will not bulk large in my welfare indicator, and I dare say that much of such Brownian movements are irreducible. But often, I believe, the prudent man or prudent committee can look ahead six months to a year and with some confidence predict that the economy will be in other than an average or "ergodic" state. Unless this ascertion of mine can be demolished, the case for a fixed growth rate for M, or for confining M to narrow channels around such a rate, melts away.

These general presumptions arise out of what we know about plausible models of economics and about the findings of historical experience. I believe they are reinforced by contemporary economic happenings.

By the second month of this year monetarists were sharply criticizing the Fed for over-restraint. I could not agree, and I found it reassuring that my colleague Franco Modigliani was also of my view. As the winter advanced, week after week, I heard the cry from monetarists that the Federal Reserve should increase $\dot{M}/M$ by two or three per cent *more than* they were doing.[5]

I must confess then that it appeared somewhat comical when we discovered that the Federal Reserve had been miscalculating the true rate of growth of M by an improper treatment of the Eurodollar borrowings. During those precise weeks and months of fulmination against the perfidious Fed, it now appears $\dot{M}/M$ was almost precisely on target as called for by the Rule.

I believe there is a lesson to be learned from this quasi-comical incident. My gravest objection to garden-variety monetarism is that it is a "black box" theory. Its alleged empirical *post hoc* regularities stand on their own merits. Its reduced-form multiple-correlation regressions, in which the dependent variable ΔGNP is to be predicted from lagged values of ΔM, are to be judged by the size of their calculated R^2. In the last fifteen years I have again and again been chided by monetarists for insisting upon tracing out all the channels of credit and fiscal operations (e.g., studying how an open market sale involves an exchange of interest-bearing government liability for non-interest-bearing money; how in the first instance interest rates are bid up and how this affects the capitalized value of non-money wealth; how an increase of the structure of interest rates in varying degrees affects the cost and availability of credit to

---

[5] I shall not stop here to consider at any length the peculiar form that "gradualism" took among Republican task forces set up to advise President-elect Nixon. So sensitized against fine tuning were they that, if their advice had been followed to the letter, we should in the first year after 1968 have experienced a drop of $\dot{M}/M$ from eight per cent or more to six per cent, and then by 1970 we would ease our way down to the four-to-five target level. One shudders to think where the price level would be by now; but as I have written several times, one hesitates to condemn gradualism over-loudly since it may be the good Lord's way of giving to the Republican party a more humane compromise along the trade-off between unemployment and inflation.

different kinds of investors and to consumers of new durable goods).[6] Instead I have been urged to believe in the philosophy of "as if", accepting the fact that changes in M are as inevitably followed by changes in GNP as death follows the shooting of a gun. Out of considerable experience, I have learned that it is inexpedient to trust in mechanical empirical regularities not spelled out by plausible economic theory.

Therefore, when I learned that I had been wrong in my beliefs about how fast M was growing from December, 1968 to April, 1969, this news was just one of twenty interesting items that had come to my knowledge that week. And it only slightly increased my forecast for the strength of aggregate demand at the present time. That was because my forecasts, so to speak, do not involve "action at a distance" but are loose Markov processes in which a broad vector of current variables specify the "phase space" out of which tomorrow's vector develops. (In short, I knowingly commit that most atrocious of sins in the penal code of the monetarists—I pay a great deal of attention to all the dimensions of "credit conditions" rather than keeping my eye on the solely important variable $\dot{M}/M$.)

But if you are stuck with a black box model, whose primary input is money, think how agonizing must be your predicament to learn that you have been using the wrong numbers. One anguished monetarist was stung by the incident to protest that "letting the wicked Fed keep the official tally on the money supply was as bad as turning over to the Mafia the auditing of Internal Revenue tax receipts." Truly the responsibility on the St. Louis District of the Federal Reserve is a weighty one.

As I now write—November, 1969—I learn from prominent monetarists that they expect 1970 to be a year of serious recession even if the Fed from this day forward made M grow at two to three rather than zero per cent. I learn that some of the giant computer GNP concur in this drastic forecast. It is my view that such an expectation is not yet warranted by the evidence available. I do not join in the criticism that a virtually level supply of money from May to November, 1969 was decidedly suboptimal, but I do think that enough evidence has now appeared to justify some easing up by the Federal Reserve, as measured by preventing short-term interest rates from rising any further and by whatever concomitant positive growth in the money supply this entails. But if I am wrong in this, as for example should the economy show more strength after New Year's than I expect it to, I shall not judge myself too harshly, for my philosophy does not pre-suppose that correct policy must be set in one direction and adhered to for a considerable period of time. I believe in reversals and over-shoots and tentative heading on a new tack according to the accumulating pattern of information and evidence.

[6] For a typical exercise in this vein see my article in the American Bankers Association, *Proceedings of A Symposium on Money, Interest Rates and Economic Activity* entitled, "Money, Interest Rates and Economic Activity: Their Interrelationship in a Market Economy."

PART XVIII

Comments on Methodology

195

Professor Samuelson on Theory and Realism

In a discussion of "Problems of Methodology" at an AEA meeting [4], Paul Samuelson embarks on a critique of theories which employ unrealistic assumptions. He concludes with this strong indictment of "unrealistic, abstract models": "If the abstract models contain empirical falsities, we must jettison the models, not gloss over their inadequacies" [4, p. 236].

Let us first indicate how Samuelson reaches this judgment. He defines a theory "as a set of axioms, postulates, or hypotheses that stipulate something about observable reality [4, p. 233]. Denoting the theory as B, the "consequences" derived from it as C, and the "assumptions" antecedent to it as A, he argues that A, B, and C must actually be identical in meaning, mutually implying one another. Thus, he holds, if the assumptions are empirically false, and the theory therefore unrealistic, the deduced consequences cannot possibly be empirically valid. In other words, an unrealistic theory cannot yield realistic consequences.

Samuelson also considers the possibility that the assumptions are *wider* than the theory, and that the theory is *wider* than the consequence, so that there is a subset $C-$ of C, while A is a subset of $A+$. In this case $A+$ may imply B, without B implying $A+$; and C may imply $C-$, without $C-$ implying C. If $C-$ happens to be empirically valid, does this "validate" the wider theory B, or the even wider set of assumptions, $A+$? Samuelson explicitly rejects this. He regards as "nonsense" the claim that the validity of $C-$ justifies holding an unrealistic theory B, let alone the completely unwarranted set of assumptions $A+$.

What Samuelson does here is to reject *all theory*. A theory, by definition, is much wider than any of the consequences deduced. If the consequences were to imply the "theory" just as the theory implies the consequences, that theory would be nothing but another form of the empirical evidence (named "consequence") and could never "explain" the observed, empirical facts.

In addition, Samuelson errs in another way. We never deduce a consequence from a theory alone. We always combine the postulated relationships (which constitute the theory) with an assumption of some change or event and then we deduce the consequence of the *conjunction* of the theoretical relationships and the assumed occurrence. Thus, we do not infer C or $C-$ from B, but rather from the conjunction of B and some occurrence O. If $C-$ can be deduced from B *cum* O; and if both O and $C-$ are found to *correspond* to data of observaton which can be regarded as the empirical counterparts (referents, proxies) of the theoretical O and $C-$; then we rule that the theory B has sustained the test. This test does not prove that B is "true," but we have no reason to "jettison" B—unless we have a better theory B'.

Let us now leave aside the argument by which Samuelson reached his decision against "unrealistic, abstract models" and theories; let us, instead, confront Samuelson's judgment with Samuelson's pattern of theorizing when he discusses, not methodology, but substantive propositions of economics. Let us choose the brilliant performance with which he demonstrated an important proposition in the theory of international trade.

In his ingenious papers on international factor-price equalization [2] [3], Samuelson shows "that free commodity trade will under certain specified conditions, *inevitably* lead to *complete* factor-price equalisation" [2, p. 181]. He admits that "it would be folly to come to any startling conclusions on the basis of so simplified a model and such abstract reasoning," but he submits—very rightly, in my opinion—that "strong simple cases often point the way to an element of truth present in a complex situation" [2, p. 181].

What are his assumptions, hypotheses, conditions? Here is the list:

1. There are but two countries, America and Europe.
2. They produce but two commodities, food and clothing.
3. Each commodity is produced with two factors of production, land and labour. The production functions of each commodity show "constant returns to scale". . . .
4. The law of diminishing marginal productivity holds. . . .
5. The commodities differ in their "labour and land intensities". . . .
6. Land and labour are assumed to be qualitatively identical inputs in the two countries and the technological production functions are assumed to be the same in the two countries.
7. All commodities move perfectly freely in international trade, without tariffs or transport costs, and with competition effectively equalizing the market price-ratio of food and clothing. No factors of production can move between the countries.
8. Something is being produced in both countries of both commodities with both factors of production. . . .

From this he concludes: "Under these conditions, real factor prices must be exactly the same in both countries (and indeed the proportion of inputs used in food production in America must equal that in Europe, and similarly for clothing production)" [2, p. 182].

In his "intuitive proof" he goes so far as to state this: "I have *established unequivocally* the following facts:

> Within any country: (a) a high ratio of wages to rents will cause a definite decrease in the proportion of labour to land in both industries; (b) to each determinate state of factor proportion in the two industries there will correspond one, and only one, commodity price ratio and a unique configuration of wages and rent; and finally, (c) that the change in factor proportions incident to an increase in wages/rents must be followed by a one-directional increase in clothing prices relative to food prices" [clothing being the more labor-using commodity, food the more land-using commodity] [2, p. 187].

It may be fair to state that Samuelson had characterized the problem as "a purely logical one" [2, p. 182]. But he sometimes uses language of empirical operations, for example, when he speaks of "observing the behaviour of a representative firm." It should be clear, however, that what he "observes" is merely the logical consequence of a set of assumptions; that the "behaviour" is purely fictitious; and that his representative firm is only an ideal type, a theoretical construct. Let me quote the sentence: ". . . if we *observe* the *behaviour* of a *representative firm* in one country it will be exactly the same in all essentials as a representative firm taken from some other country —regardless of the difference in total factor amounts and relative industrial concentration—provided only that factor-price ratios are really the same in the two markets" [2, pp. 187-88, emphasis supplied].

At the end of his discussion Samuelson evaluates some important qualifications which he finds help to "reconcile results of abstract analysis with the obvious facts of life concerning the extreme diversity of productivity and factor prices in different regions of the world" [2, p. 196]. These "qualifications" to the theorem furnish Samuelson with the "causes" of the factor-price diversities. In other words, he does not hesitate, quite rightly in my view, to explain the observed facts of life—factor-price differentials—by the divergences of real conditions from the ideal ones which form the basis of the factor-price equalization theorem.

Would the Samuelson of the *A-B-C* argument against unrealistic, abstract models approve of the Samuelson of the intuitive proof of the factor-price equalization theorem? Frankly, I do not know. Perhaps both Samuelsons make a distinction between a theorem and a theory, meaning by the former a proposition deduced from counterfactual assumptions and postulates, and by the latter a proposition stipulating something about observable reality. But the Samuelson of the *Foundations of Economic Analysis*, who preceded both other Samuelsons, did pledge allegiance to a program emphasizing "the derivation of *operationally meaningful* theorems" [1, p. 3].

Since, according to Samuelson, a theorem deduced from counterfactual hypotheses cannot yield empirically true consequences, and does not contain operationally defined terms, it is not immediately clear just what an "operationally meaningful theorem" is supposed to be. If it is supposed to be a "strong simple case" pointing the way to "an element of truth present in a complex situation" [2, p. 181], then we have no quarrel. For, I submit, this is what the bulk of economic theory does. It is based on counterfactual assumptions, contains only theoretical constructs and no operational concepts, and yields results which, we hope, point to elements of truth present in complex situations. To call such theorems "operationally meaningful" is to confer on them a designation which is slightly deceptive; but in any case it gives them the recognition which Samuelson, as critic of the Friedman position, or "the F-twist," wants to deny.

I conclude that Samuelson, one of the most brilliant theorists in present-day economics, produces his best work when he deduces from unrealistic assumptions general theoretical propositions which help us interpret some of the empirical observations of the complex situations with which economic life confronts us.

Fritz Machlup*

* The author is professor of economics and international finance at Princeton University.

References

1. PAUL SAMUELSON, *Foundations of Economic Analysis.* Cambridge, Mass. 1947.
2. ———, "International Factor-Price Equalisation Once Again," *Econ. Jour.*, June 1949, *59*, 181-97.
3. ———, "International Trade and the Equalisation of Factor Prices," *Econ. Jour.*, June 1948, *58*, 163-84.
4. ———, "Problems of Methodology—Discussion," *Am. Econ. Rev., Proc.*, May 1963, *53*, 231-36.

Theory and Realism: A Reply

1. The art of jujitsu is to direct your opponent's strength against himself. As I read Fritz Machlup's attempt to use my earlier writings on international factor-price equalization and on operationally meaningful theorems to annihilate my recent contention that the contrafactual content of a theory is its shame and not its glory, I am all admiration for his pretty footwork. Indeed I feel like the friend of Abraham Lincoln, who said he could have foregone the pleasure of being run out of town on a rail if it weren't for the honor of it.

But the issue is a serious one, and I must record the impression that, after examining Machlup's argument, I see no reason to change my view or to acknowledge any inconsistency between my precept and my practice.

2. Let the issue be clear. No one expects that anything be *perfect*, much less a simplified theory. All scientists settle for some degree of approximation; and, by gad, they had better! However, the whole force of my attack on the F-twist (which I believe is not well rendered by the first sentence that got quoted from my paper) is that the doughnut of empirical correctness in a theory constitutes its worth, while its hole of untruth constitutes its weakness. I regard it as a monstrous perversion of science to claim that a theory is *all the better for its shortcomings;* and I notice that in the luckier exact sciences, no one dreams of making such a claim.

In connection with slavery, Thomas Jefferson said that, when he considered that there is a just God in Heaven, he trembled for his country. Well, in connection with the exaggerated claims that used to be made in economics for the power of deduction and a priori reasoning—by classical writers, by Carl Menger, by the 1932 Lionel Robbins (first edition of *The Nature and Significance of Economic Science*), by disciples of Frank Knight, by Ludwig von Mises—I tremble for the reputation of my subject. Fortunately, we have left that behind us. Still there is no reason to encourage tolerance of falsification of empirical reality, much less glorify such falsification.

3. My position is so innocuous as to be platitudinous. Yet from it, Machlup believes, must follow a rejection by me of all theory. (In my copy the last two words are double-underlined!) He says: "A theory, by definition, is much wider than any of the consequences deduced." By whose definition? Machlup's? God's? Webster's? Well, not by mine—as those who read my earlier note will have seen. And I have to confess to an even sharper disagreement with Dr. Machlup on this issue.

Scientists never "explain" any behavior, by theory or by any other hook. Every description that is superseded by a "deeper explanation" turns out upon careful examination to have been replaced by still another description, albeit possibly a more useful description that covers and illuminates a wider area. I can illustrate by what everyone will agree is the single most successful "theory" of all time. I refer to Newton's theory of universal gravitation.

Kepler's ellipses gave better descriptions of the planets than did the epicycles of the Greeks. Newton showed that second-order differential equations relating the accelerations of bodies to the inverse square of their distances from neighboring bodies could still better *describe* astronomical observations. After Newton had described "how," he did not waste his time on the fruitless quest of "why?" but went on to run the Mint and write about religion. Nor has anyone since Newton provided "the explanation."

The second greatest achievement of scientific theory was Maxwell's formulation of electromagnetism. Heinrich Hertz, the great discoverer of radio waves, made my methodological point in the strongest terms when he said, "All of Maxwell's theory boils down to the simple question of whether the observable measurements on light and waves do or do not satisfy Maxwell's partial differential equations."

My third and final example illustrates how a stubborn fact can kill a pretty theory. Mercury's orbit never quite agreed with Newtonian gravitation. An F-twister would have said: "So much the worse for the fact. The theory is even the better for its inadequacy." That, of course, is rot. One would not jettison Newton's theory until a better one was found to replace it, for the very good reason that Newton did describe many facts *correctly*. But any specialist on the perihelion of Mercury would prefer to use mechanical extrapolations to reliance on the false theory. Then along came Albert Einstein. His special theory of relativity described well (but did not "explain") a host of facts, including the perihelion of Mercury. For velocities small compared to the speed of light, Newton's theory came close to duplicating Einstein's. But when the factual chips were down, the simpler Newtonian equations had to be replaced by the Einstein-Lorenz equations *because the facts called for this*.

4. About my 1948 factor-price equalization analysis I can be brief. From certain empirical hypotheses taken as postulates, by cogent logic I *deduced* as theorems certain other empirical properties. After the demonstration, the implications were obvious. When one looks at the complicated real world, one finds it obvious that the hypotheses of the syllogism are far from valid; and, also, the consequences are far from valid. This is indeed a matter for regret and full disclosure of inaccuracy should be made. Nevertheless, and here I imagine Dr. Machlup and I for once will agree, a strong polar case like this one can often shed useful light on factual reality.

Thus, writing before the Marshall Plan and at a time when many were despairing of Europe's future, I was led by my factor-price model to make the diffident suggestion that moving goods by trade might be able to do nearly as much for living standards as moving Europeans to Australia and elsewhere. Any validity to such a lucky insight would have to be attributed to the degree of realism of the model, and I can only pray for my brain children that they be ever more realistic.

5. Since the emphasis of my *Foundations of Economic Analysis* on "operationally meaningful theorems" has been brought up, it gives me the opportunity to use my strength against my friendly critic. The doctrines of revealed preference provide the most literal example of a theory that has been stripped down to its bare implications for empirical realism: Occam's Razor has cut away every zipper, collar, shift, and fig leaf. In 1938 I had shown that the regular theory of utility maximization implied, for the two-good case, no more and no less than that "no two-observed points on the demand functions should ever reveal the following contradiction of the Weak Axiom":

$$P_1^a Q_1^a + P_2^a Q_2^a > P_1^a Q_1^b + P_2^a Q_2^b$$
$$P_1^b Q_1^b + P_2^b Q_2^b > P_1^b Q_1^a + P_2^b Q_2^a$$

In *Foundations*, I showed that the complete theory of regular utility for *any* number of goods could be exhausted by the empirical hypothesis that the following Slutsky-Hicks matrix of compensated-substitution terms be singular, symmetric, and nonpositive definite of rank $n-1$. *I.e.*, the demand functions $Q_i = Q_i(P_1, \cdots, P_n, I)$ satisfy

$$S = [S_{ij}] = \left[\frac{\partial Q_i}{\partial P_j} + Q_j \frac{\partial Q_i}{\partial I} \right] = [S_{ji}]$$

$$\sum_{j=1}^{n} S_{ij} P_j \equiv 0$$

$$\sum_{1}^{n} \sum_{1}^{n} S_{ij} P_i P_j x_i x_j < 0 \qquad \text{for } x_i \neq \lambda P_i, \quad \lambda \neq 0$$

In 1950, Professor H. S. Houthakker, in a brilliant maiden work, strengthened the Weak Axiom to show that the whole conventional theory, for any number of goods, boils down (aside from obvious regularity conditions of continuity and smoothness) to the testable requirement that one never observe the following contradiction of the Strong Axiom:

$$\sum P^a Q^a > \sum P^a Q^b, \quad \sum P^b Q^b > \sum P^b Q^c, \cdots, \sum P^z Q^z > \sum P^z Q^a.$$

I beg that Dr. Machlup take me literally and seriously when I assert that the conventional theory has *no* wider implications than these prosaic factual implications. Once the two formulations had been rigorously proved to imply each other mutually, that issue was settled.

6. The F-twist, in the crude form set up and massacred by me, represents an unlamented lost cause. Let me conclude by mentioning some genuinely puzzling methodological problems that Dr. Machlup and I might continue to argue about fruitfully.

a. Quine, Polanyi, Kuhn, Hanson,[1] and other students of science have

---

[1] W. V. O. Quine, *From a Logical Point of View* (New York, 1961), Ch. 2, "Two Dogmas of Empiricism"; M. Polanyi, "Tacit Knowing," *Reviews of Modern Physics*, Oct. 1962, *34*, 601-16; T. Kuhn, *The Structure of Scientific Revolutions* (Chicago 1962); N. R. Hanson, *Patterns of Discovery* (Cambridge, U.K. 1961).

been propounding variants of the view that what is a fact (and what is a truism!) is a very subjective thing. While I should guess that much of this discussion involves a confusion between the psychological problem of forming scientific notions and the valid findings of science, undoubtedly there are deep problems here that need further study.

b. Scientists constantly utilize parables, paradigms, strong polar models to help understand more complicated reality. The degree to which these do more good than harm is always an open question, more like an art than a science.

c. Finally, in some areas at least, Nature seems to show an inexplicable simplicity. This is a brute fact, more or less of a bonus, which if it had not existed could not have been expected. As a result, the working scientist learns as a matter of routine experience that he should have faith that the more beautiful and more simple of two equally (inaccurate) theories will end up being a more accurate describer of wider experience.

This bit of luck vouchsafed the theorist should not be pushed too far, for the gods punish the greedy.

PAUL A. SAMUELSON*

* The author is professor of economics at the Massachusetts Institute of Technology.

196

Professor Samuelson on Theory and Realism: Reply[1]

When first seduced to discuss methodology, I warned that it is a field in which Gresham's Law holds in the form, "Hot air drives out cold." I should also have predicted that it is an activity where the law of diminishing returns holds in the most virulent form. And yet it is a field where, as Editor Gurley has learned the hard way, every economist feels his ideas are as good as anyone else's. Though many call themselves, few are chosen: the papers of Garb, Lerner, and Massey are but the visible peak of the iceberg of submitted comments.

The discussion has progressed, I think, away from the issue of an F-twist that considers unrealism of a theory as a virtue, to controversy over the role and nature of "theory" and over the meaning of "explanation" as against "description." A Gallup poll count of the mail would seem to show that there is a widespread will to disbelieve in my rather hard-boiled insistence upon "theory" as (strategically simplified) description of observable and refutable empirical regularities, and a widespread hankering for a more exalted Machlup role of theoretical explanation. To stand one's ground against the majority merely in order to be provocative I regard as contemptible in a scientist. But candor requires me to state that the arguments of my critics are suspiciously diverse and unrelated: since what they have in common is primarily their dissatisfaction with me, they really do not provide a common alternative credo to which I could subscribe even were their arguments tempting.

I.

Alphabetically, Garb comes first. His discussion reminded me that there are worse movements than the zero movements of a deadlock—namely, movements backward in understanding and in isolating differences of opinion. Example: his long third paragraph simply misinterprets what I wrote. My approving of Hertz's assertion that Maxwell's theory *is* his equations represented

[1] I am grateful to the Carnegie Corporation for a reflective year, and to F. Skidmore for research aid.

no backsliding on my part: instead it emphasized the view that a description (equational or otherwise) that works to describe well a wide range of observable reality is all the "explanation" we can ever get (or need desire) here on earth. Careful reading of my words will show that I only insisted that the validity of the *full* consequences of a theory implies the validity of the theory and so of its *minimal* assumptions. Had Garb added the words "full" and "minimal," the alleged disagreement with Machlup would have disappeared. Example: when Garb says "an explanation does not have to be 'ultimate,' " I think he is resaying what I said, not controverting it. *An explanation, as used legitimately in science, is a better kind of description and not something that goes ultimately beyond description.* Example: the final beautiful quotation from Einstein is an irrelevancy. It has to do with the technical issue of whether in quantum mechanics probability statements can be replaced by causality statements like those of classical mechanics. It has nothing to do with methodological differences as to the role of theory itself. So much for Garb.

II.

Lerner's paper shows that many a false word has been said in jest. He in effect says that Samuelson and Machlup both do good work, acting alike in their practical work during the six days of the week. Therefore on Sunday they can't be in genuine disagreement on methodology. By this reasoning, a thousand philosophers err in thinking that Ernst Mach and Arthur Eddington differ diametrically on the methodology of physics: since both men contributed mightily to the Gross National Product of physical knowledge, why pay attention to the detail that Eddington thought he could deduce from the laws of thought (!) the number of electrons in the universe, while Mach claimed the scientist merely discerns mnemonic devices for describing brute facts. I remind Lerner that the aphorism, "All wise men believe in the same true religion," is an atheist's joke not a pithy truism.

If Lerner had read with sympathetic care my writings, he would have seen at the beginning what it was I denied—namely, that "a theory is much wider than any [in the sense of 'any and all'] of the consequences deduced." Precisely because of the ambiguity of words like "any," I used the unambiguous logical symbols of set theory (p. 234 of my original article [8]); by attentive reading of this passage, he could have been spared the labor of "Saving my logic," particularly since I have to reject his charitable rescue. It is nonsense, and not *my* nonsense, "to include all the conceivable assumed changes and events that can be combined with the postulated relationships as well as. . . ." Moreover, Machlup and I are one in objecting to the requirement that a usefully realistic theory must be completely accurate. Who seriously thinks otherwise? Lerner regards it as Sunday nodding on my part to think that anyone could be so stupid as to believe that a theory "is even better for its inadequacy." He does not disagree that such an assertion is stupid. Having been at pains to state the matter so plainly, I am glad to learn the conclusion is *now* obvious. Lerner's final conclusion represents what the logicians call a *non sequitur:*

if in the end it turns out there is no real difference between Samuelson and Machlup, this will follow from considerations not discernible in Lerner's note.

III.

I turn now to the *pièce de résistance*, Massey's valuable paper. I have no quarrel[2] with Massey's Part I, which provides a masterly summary of the semantics of scientific analysis that will be useful to all economists and novel to most. In Part II, the impractical philosopher shames the practical economic scientist and puts his finger on the one critical issue in the present controversy—the relationships between observable reality and the various assertions made by the scientific theorist. Part II makes, I think, a definite contribution to the discussion;[3] but I must confess that, in reading it, I was overtaken with aspirations of grandeur, and came to wish that I were Massey and could re-write Part II. For as it now stands, it could be misinterpreted by the casual economist reader to exalt "indirectly observable" empirical regularities over "directly observable" empirical regularities. Concretely, the reader might mislead himself into believing that the special theory of relativity, which is founded on directly observable empirical regularities, is intrinsically less noble or less something than the kinetic theory of gases, which is based upon allegedly nondirectly observable tiny molecules; and indeed that this kinetic theory is better than the classical theory of thermodynamics *merely because* the first and second laws of classical thermodynamics are so beautifully capable of direct empirical confirmation in every steam engine or housewife's kitchen. So let me restate the issues.

Hempel [3, p. 23] denies the following assertion: "Any term in the vocabulary of empirical science is definable by means of observation terms." A reader like Massey might be forgiven for thinking that I differ from Hempel on this point and therein lies my heresy. So let me make the following clear: when I read the grounds on which Hempel denies this doctrine (which he calls the *narrower thesis of empiricism* [Hempel 3, p. 24]), I find no reason to differ on this point with Hempel or Machlup or anyone else. For what are Hempel's difficulties with such an assertion? They are of the following type. Point (i): Scientists say an object is "magnetic" and mean by this that, if a small iron object is put near it, that object will be attracted by it. But what if

[2] Almost none. I doubt that "consistency" provides the problem for any science like economics or physics that it provides for the mathematical logician concerned, say, with the consistency of Hilbert's axioms for arithmetic. The status of the special theory of relativity or of consumer demand was the same after Gödel as before. To say that we take consistency of a scientific theory for granted because it is so devilishly hard to prove this fact is like saying we assume a woman virtuous unless proved otherwise because it is so hard to prove any woman lacking in virtue. That is surely not so: Bayesian probabilities, that most women are virtuous in our culture and that few scientists have won undying fame for themselves in finding flaws of consistency in important scientific theories, suffice to explain why we take for granted what we do.

[3] To help my understanding of these issues, Professor Massey kindly provided me with minimal references to related writings that should be of interest to economists, namely the Hempel and Nagel references of my bibliography. I benefited from this course of study, which I believe deepened my understanding of my own position.

no iron object is found near it? Is it an empirical statement that it is (still) magnetic? Point (ii): Scientists use metrical terms like "the length of this stick can be any real positive number" or "the apple had an instantaneous velocity of so much at noon and an acceleration of this definite magnitude."

Well? Narrow empiricism is supposed not to be able to handle these two difficulties, whereas a *"liberalized thesis of empiricism"* [Hempel 3, p. 31] can. O.K., then I am a liberal empiricist. The concept of limits—in which one does not have to go *to* the limit—enables us to go from integral- to real-number systems and from average velocities to instantaneous derivatives; hence, point (ii) offers no room for controversy here. And, while I am prepared to believe that point (i) has presented a problem to the philosopher trying to represent scientific procedures, I find it hard to imagine any two modern physicists or economists ever having a substantive dispute about such a matter.

I elaborated on the above because the reader of Hempel might easily be tempted to think that the demonstrated difference between narrow and liberal empiricism has something basic to do with Hempel's repeated contrast between (a) description and (b) prediction and explanation. I was amused in reading these authors through a magnifying glass to see how Freudianly guiltily they (with the exception of Braithwaite) shy away from validly distinguishing description from explanation. A *description* of an empirical *regularity* provides the basis of *prediction,* which will be as accurate or inaccurate as is the regularity being described. Because prediction is good and a case is being made for "explanation" as something beyond "mere" description, prediction is again and again coupled with explanation and gratuitously demarcated from description. In this too-brief discussion I hope to have cast doubt on Hempel's Points (i) and (ii) as a proper basis for *this* distinction.

When we move on to Nagel and to Massey, we find the alleged basic distinction in the difference between "directly observable" empirical regularities (or descriptions) and "indirectly observable" regularities. In Nagel the tone is rather tentative; in Massey, an imperialistic vocabulary is introduced in which all directly observable empirical regularities are squeezed out of "theory" completely (being called "basic sentences"); and indirectly observable regularities are alone called "theoretical sentences." That this is a perversion of usage can be demonstrated by the following examples. And if one agrees with the point these examples are designed to make, one suddenly finds Samuelson innocent of such grave charges as "rejecting *all* theory."

Consider four of the most important physical theories of all time, by any physicist's admission. (1) Galileo's analysis of a falling body; (2) Newton's theory of universal gravitation as applied to the n-body problem; (3) Einstein's special theory of relativity; and (4) classical thermodynamics of Carnot, Clausius, Kelvin, and pre-1900 Gibbs. Later add a fifth theory, (5) the kinetic theory of gases (and various models of statistical mechanics).

I have checked with several physicists and find they agree with me that the first four of these historic theories are expressible completely in terms of Massey's "basic sentences" alone.

Example: if S_t represents the position of a rolling ball on an inclined plane at time t, Galileo's law of gravity can be expressed in the directly observable hypothesis,

$$(S_{t+h} - S_t) - (S_t - S_{t-h}) = 0 = \Delta^2 S_t = d^2 S_t / dt^2.$$

Example: if the coordinates of the 2-body problem are depicted by the usual notation, Newton's behavioral equations become

$$m\ddot{x} = - GMmx/r^3, \qquad m\ddot{y} = - GMmy/r^3, \qquad r = (x^2 + y^2)^{1/2}$$

and can be verified directly by acceleration measurements, without indirect checking of elliptical orbits and Kepler's Law. Indeed for $n > 2$, the differential equations are not integrable in terms of elementary functions but the differential equations can be directly tested.

Example: Einstein built the axioms of special relativity on the precise direct observations of the Michelson-Morley experiment, extrapolated to every observer of light no matter what his uniform velocity with respect to any other observer. (Incidentally, Professor Royall Brandis of Illinois pointed out to me that the observations of the perihelion of Mercury provided an indirect test of the *general* theory of relativity and not, as I erroneously said, the *special* theory.)

Final example. The most high-fallutin' theoretical formulation of classical (nonstatistical) thermodynamics is certainly that of Carathéodory of 1909. If *it* is not a theory, the word theory is surely being redefined in a way strange to all usage. Yet, in terms of Massey's new definition of "theoretical sentences" ["which, though tied semantically to experience, do not enjoy the same direct relation that characterizes the basic sentences" (such as "Fido has 4 legs" or "the velocity of this ball increased proportionally with time since it was relesased")], Carathéodory turns out to be "eschewing all theory." For Carathéodory's symphony begins with the proud words, "One of the more notable results of the investigations made in thermodynamics during the last century is the realization that this science may be developed without any hypotheses which cannot be empirically verified." He goes on to squeeze out even the concept "heat," as superfluous, and builds directly on the empirical observations of Joule and Clausius. (It is true he uses ideal concepts of "insulating walls" and the like, but properly refers to "thermos bottles" that approach the realization of such concepts. My own position never rejected approximating concepts.)

Since Hempel, Nagel, Massey, Machlup, and all sensible men argue from empirical observation of what celebrated scientific theories have been like in the past, I consider it fair game to give these examples in order to reject as tragically misleading Massey's key conclusion at the end of his Part II, of which I requote only two sentences.

> If, e.g., there is any methodological moral to be drawn from the century-and-a-half-long successful life of the atomic theory of matter, it would seem to be that an empirical science comes to maturity only after it effects a clean break with basic sentences, only after it boldly postulates theoretical statements that ultimately are anchored, though not sub-

merged, in experience by means of semantic ties to basic sentences. Thus I myself would proclaim the contrary of Samuelson's Razor, viz. all economic theories that can be explained to your wife are *theoretically* worthless.

* *

Never, never make a joke. My remarks about Samuelson's Razor, and my experience that only the simple theories that can be explained so as to make sense to an intelligent outsider (one's wife) turn out to hold up in economics, was intended as a humorous *obiter dictum* as far as the controversy over the role of theory was concerned. My remark referred to theories of stock market prediction like the famous Gridiron Law: "In every year that Harvard beats Yale and there is confirmation by Penn beating Cornell, the Dow Jones averages will rise." Jobbing *backwards*, we find this fits the facts of 1920-40: but what scientist was surprised when it failed in the postwar? It represents a bad description in terms of width of empirical coverage, in contrast to the following: "When Kennedy's fiscal policies send up GNP, that's good for profits and makes me think we ought to invest in common stocks that do not already have a high price-earnings ratio and which stand to share in the general prosperity." You can call the latter an "explanation" of equity price trends, but that does not deny me the right to formulate it as a description of regular concomitance of fiscal policy variables, GNP changes, profit changes, and equity price changes.

What about case 5 of the kinetic theory of gases, which I agree differs from the first four cases and involves the indirectly observable hypotheses that Kempel, Nagel, and Massey talk about? Here we do need some less imperialistic name than Massey's "theoretical sentences." Let me henceforth refer to them as "indirectly observable" sentences or Sentences$_2$ in contrast with Sentences$_1$ = Basic Sentences. I gladly welcome both kinds of sentences and wish that the philosophers of science had probed more deeply into their nature. Thus, Kepler's 3 laws might legitimately be considered as indirect ways of verifying Newton's inverse square law of acceleration. If we call them Sentences$_2$, we should realize (Cf. Born, [1, p. 2]) that it can be easily demonstrated that the three Kepler Laws *together* (elliptical orbits in one plane, radius sweeping equal areas in equal time, period of revolution of any planet around the sun proportional to the 3/2 power of its distance from the moon) are necessary and sufficient conditions for the truth of Newton's 2-body acceleration laws, which are Sentences$_1$. So such indirectly observable sentences do differ from the following kinetic-theory ones.

Suppose I tell my wife that the air in that transparent balloon consists of small molecules averaging 600 miles per hour—about the speed of a bullet. Why should she believe me? If only macroscopic data about balloon pressures and volumes are observed, she needn't. "But," she says, "I read in a book there are 4.5×10^9 molecules in each c.c. of the air in the balloon." I reply, "Suppose there are. Without a microscope you couldn't possibly detect that fact, and separate it from the fact that there are 4.6×10^9 or 45×10^9. But you can be sure that there are certainly not as few as 4.5×10 heavy molecules; for if there were, you would see the balloon pulsing not to mention lots of other things." Being a sensible woman, she would reply, "So long as there are no observable consequences to me of there being 4.5×10^9 or 45×10^9 molecules, I am completely indifferent to your assuming or not assuming the existence of that many. And how did you get that odd idea?" My reply, "By reading Greek poetry of Democritus and Lucretius. By thinking that endless paddling of water warms it up, which suggests (to me and Count Rumford) hotness must somehow be related to motion rather than being a substance. By finding that postulating a sufficiently large number of hard, small balls gives me (and Maxwell) a model whose directly observable *average* energy of collisions on the wall of the balloon agrees numerically with the directly observable pressure on the walls of the balloon. By finding that mixing balls twice as heavy with the original balls gives me *average* energy of collisions on the wall agreeing with the surprising observable fact that mixing together a balloon of light gas with one of heavy gas gives me a predictable pressure of the mixture satisfying the so-called Dalton Law of Partial Pressures. It is an agreeable fiction, if you please, that there are 4.5×10^9 molecules *or more*. And this fiction usefully prepares me for what happens when I crush the balloon. Now the balls get closer together; now I can't neglect their Newtonian attractions; and now the model predicts that halving the balloon's observable volume will *less* than double the observable pressure. And this agrees with directly observable descriptions, such as the gas in the balloon becoming liquid."

Up to this point, say 1897 when Planck first wrote up his treatise on *Thermodynamics,* one could regard the Sentence$_2$, "This gas has a given number of molecules," as merely a convention. Mach, Stallo, and Ostwald too stubbornly held to such a view—too stubbornly, I think, but not without excuse. Thus, Stallo said, why explain an elastic gas that you can see directly in terms of hypothetical elastic balls you can't see? One answer is, "Why not? To do so is harmless and it does help me remember by Newtonian calculation, if I should happen to forget, how observed gases behave." Mach, who insisted on the mnemonic nature of all scientific statements, should not have objected to this in principle. He should merely have said, "Don't forget that your results at the macroscopic level are quite independent of the number 4.5 $\times 10^9$. And actually Planck [7, p. 26] said, "This, of course, need not be a whole number. . . ."

But now move into this century. Give my wife a microscope and show her Brownian motion. Have her look at a radium-dialed watch with an ordinary magnifying glass. Listen to a Geiger counter. Observe a Wilson Cloud chamber. Literally see a single atom with a field emission microscope trained on a tungsten point. Count molecules emitted from a radioactive substance. Observe photoelectric effects as chemical reactions on an exposed film. Now, though I do not insist on the point, she does observe and describe molecules in almost the same literal sense that anyone counts the 4 legs of a dog. Avogadro's Number now takes on a more concrete meaning: after Einstein and Perrin calculated it from Brownian movements, Mach and Ostwald properly threw in the towel. If they are to be criticized, it is in being too impatient

771

with Boltzmann's (at worst, harmless) calculations in the pre-Einstein era.

The philosophers of science should bring their most fashionable example of indirectly observable theoretical concepts up to date. In terms of modern techniques of measurement, atoms are no longer a-empirical concepts; neither in 1965 are genes and chromosomes in the theory of particulate genetics.

IV.

Let me summarize. There has been no successful demolition of my view that science consists of descriptions of empirical regularities; nor of my insistence that what is called an explanation in science can always be regarded as a description at a different level—usually a superior description in that it successfully fits a wide range of empirical regularities. This, in my view, is the proper basis for the Braithwaite-Ramsey distinction [in Braithwaite] between a superior description that can be given the honorific title of "explanation" and an ordinary description. My detailed analysis of the molecular theory of gases permits me now to amplify the logical symbolism of my original paper. Let the full assumptions of the molecular kinetic theory be called B. Let its full consequences be C, which can be broken down into its macroscopic consequences C_1 (pressure, volume, etc.) and into its microscopic consequences C_2 (standard deviation of Brownian movement, etc.). If the observed facts confirm both C_1 and C_2 (as after 1910, it became known that they do), no one will quarrel with the theory B. Suppose, as before 1900, the known facts confirm only C_1? What then? So long as the theory's C_2 implications are not known to contradict empirical data, the kinetic theory B is no worse (except perhaps aesthetically) than some rival theory β, whose *full* implications are also the confirmed C_1. Occam's Razor suggests, "Choose β rather than B, other things being equal." But Occam's Razor, as Einstein almost said, like elegance is for tailors. Other things may not be equal, as for example the superior ability of B to be "remembered" by virtue of its "simplicity" or deducibility from theories applicable to other areas of empirical reality (e.g. Newton's laws applied to colliding elastic particles).

A harder problem is one where C_1 of B is confirmed but C_2 of B is refuted by the facts. How big must the discrepancy of C_2 from the facts be to make us want to drop B? That always depends on the "importance" attached to discrepancy and agreement. I can imagine cases where scientists would say, "B has C_2 implications that are unmistakably refuted by the facts at the microscopic level. But who cares about such discrepancies, which do no harm and are unimportant. Because B predicts the important truth C_1, we stick with it as a theory." I cannot quarrel with this if (i) scientists are truly agreed that C_2 discrepancies are unimportant and (ii) there is no readily available truncated theory, B-, which can be distilled from B by lopping off its C_2 aspects and which can provide pretty much the same mnemonic patterning of the facts that B does. My original quarrel with the F-twist was a reminder of the importance of (i) above. This should not be controversial.

Where I must be careful not to overstate my case is in connection with the following: After a theory's implications C_1 are well confirmed by the facts, and even prior to our testing its C_2 implications, we increase our Bayes-probability belief in the likelihood that its C_2 implications will be confirmed.

This heuristic principle seems to be well founded by past experience and reflects, I suppose, a bonus in the form of an underlying simplicity of Nature which—if it had not existed—could not be legitimately invented.

PAUL A. SAMUELSON*

*The author is professor of economics at the Massachusetts Institute of Technology.

REFERENCES

1. MAX BORN, *Natural Philosophy of Cause and Chance.* Oxford 1951.
2. R. B. BRAITHWAITE, *Scientific Explanation.* Cambridge, England 1953.
3. C. G. HEMPEL, *Fundamentals of Concept Formation in Empirical Science,* monograph of the *International Encyclopedia of Unified Science,* Vol. 2, No. 7, Chicago 1952 [Cf. especially pp. 34-39].
4. ———, "The Theoretician's Dilemma," in H. Feigl, M. Scriven, and G. Maxwell, eds., *Minnesota Studies in the Philosophy of Science,* Vol. 2, Minneapolis 1958 [Cf. especially Sections II, IV, and VIII].
5. GERALD J. MASSEY, "Professor Samuelson on Theory and Realism: Comment," *Am. Econ. Rev.,* Dec. 1965, 55, 1155-64.
6. ERNEST NAGEL, *The Structure of Science,* New York 1961 [Cf. especially pp. 79-90].
7. MAX PLANCK, *Treatise on Thermodynamics.* New York 1945.
8. P. A. SAMUELSON, "Discussion of Methodology," *Am. Econ. Rev., Proc.,* May 1963, *53,* 231-36.
9. ———, "Theory and Realism: A Reply," *Am. Econ. Rev.,* Sept. 1964, *54,* 736-39.

197

How to Guess, or Outguess, the Future

ECONOMIC FORECASTING AND SCIENCE

By Paul A. Samuelson

IF PREDICTION is the ultimate aim of all science, then we forecasters ought to award ourselves the palm for accomplishment, bravery, or rashness. We are the end-product of Darwinian evolution and the payoff for all scientific study of economics. Around the country, students are grinding out doctoral theses by the use of history, statistics, and theory—merely to enable us to reduce the error in our next year's forecast of GNP from $10 billion down to $9 billion.[1]

Just as ancient kings had their soothsayers and astrologists, modern tycoons and prime ministers have their economic forecasters. Eastern sorcerers wore that peaked hat which in modern times we regard as a dunce's cap; and I suppose if the head fits, we can put it in.

Actually, though, I am not sure that the ultimate end of science is prediction—at least in the sense of unconditional prediction about what is likely to happen at a specified future date. Students are always asking of professors, "If you are so smart, how come you ain't rich?" Some of our best economic scientists seem to be fairly poor forecasters of the future. One of our very best economists, in fact, couldn't even correctly foresee the results of the last election. Is it legitimate to ask of a scholar: "If you are so

MR. SAMUELSON (B.A., Chicago, '35; M.A., Ph.D., Harvard, '36, '41), Past President of the American Economic Association and of the Econometric Society, author and co-author of many books, widely honored in this country and abroad, is Professor of Economics at M.I.T. This essay is his Dinner Address at the Twelfth Annual Conference on the Economic Outlook at The University of Michigan last year.
[1] Grateful acknowledgment is made to Mrs. Felicity Skidmore for valuable research assistance in preparing this paper.

scientific and learned, how come you are so stupid at predicting next year's GNP?"

I think not, and for several different reasons. In the first place, a man might be a brilliant mathematician in devising methods for the use of physicists and still be a very poor physicist. Or he might be a genius in devising statistical methods while still being rather poor at conducting statistical investigations. Let us grant then at the beginning, that a person might be poor himself at *any* predictions within a field, and still be a useful citizen. Only we would then call him a mathematician—rather than simply a physicist, statistician, or economist.

The late Sir Ronald Fisher, for instance, was a genius, as we all gladly acknowledge. And perhaps he did good empirical work in the field of agronomy and applied fertilizer. But I must say that his work on genetics—in which he blithely infers the decline of Roman and of all civilizations from the dastardly habit infertile heiresses have of snatching off the ablest young men for mates, thereby making them infertile—seems awfully casual statistical inference to me. And I can't think Fisher covered himself with immortal glory at the end of his life when he doubted that cigarette smoking and inhaling has anything to do with reducing longevity.

Yet even a good economist or physicist may be a bad predictor—if we want simply an ability to forecast the future. My old teacher, Joseph Schumpeter, was by anyone's admission a pretty good economist. But I would certainly not have trusted him to predict next year's income or tomorrow's stock market. His vision was focussed to a different distance. He could tell you what was going to happen to capitalism in the next fifty years, even though he often had to ask his wife twice for the time of day. Of course, the *in*ability to predict well does not thereby make a man a better economist. Schumpeter would not have been soiled if he had been able to make shrewd guesses about the near future.

A good scientist should be good at *some* kind of prediction. But it need not be flat prediction about future events. Thus, a physicist may be bad at telling you what the radioactivity count in the air will be next year, but be very good at predicting for you what will be the likely effects on air pollution of a given controlled experiment involving fissionable materials. If he is a master scientist, his hunches about experiments never yet performed may be very good ones.

Similarly, a good economist has good judgment about economic reality. To have good judgment means you are able to make good judgments—good predictions about what will happen under *certain specified conditions*. This is different from having a model that is pretty good at doing mechanical extrapolation of this year's trends of GNP to arrive at respectable guesses of next year's GNP. Time and again your naïve model may win bets from me in office pools on next year's outcome. But neither of us would ever dream of using such a naïve model to answer the question, "What will happen to GNP, compared to what it would otherwise have been, when the Kennedy-Johnson massive tax cut is put into effect?" The mechanical, naïve model does not have in it, explicitly, the parameter tax rates. And if we insist upon differentiating the result with respect to such a parameter, we will end up with a zero partial derivative and with the dubious conclusion that massive tax cuts cannot have any effect on GNP. The model that I use, which is perhaps very non-mechanical and perhaps even non-naïve, may be bad at predicting unconditionally next year's GNP, and still be very good at answering the other-things-equal question of the effect of a change in tax rates or in some other structural parameter of the system.

What I have been saying here can be put in technical language: to make good year-to-year predictions, you need not necessarily have accomplished good "identification" of the various structural relations of a model. And conversely, to be a scientist skilled in making predictions about various hypothetical structural changes in a system, you do need to have what Haavelmo, Koopmans, and others call "identification," of the type that is by no means necessarily contained in models that perform well in ordinary predictions.

Is it possible to have everything good?— to be able to make good annual predictions as well as good predictions of identified structural relationships? The best economists I have known, in the best years of their lives, were pretty good at making just such predictions. And that is what I call good judgment in economics.

Obviously, they have to be men of much experience. In the last analysis, empirical predictions can be made only on the basis of empirical evidence. But it is an equal empirical truth that the facts do not tell their own story to scientists or historical observers, and that the men who develop topnotch judgment have an analytical framework within which they try to fit the facts. I should say that such men are constantly using the evidence of economic time series; the evidence of cross-sectional data; the evidence of case studies and anecdotes, but with some kind of judgment concerning the frequency and importance of the cases and instances. And they are even using conjectures of the form, "What if I were no smarter than these businessmen and unionists? What would I be likely to do?"

We all know the great statistical problems involved in the small samples economic statisticians must work with. We have few years of data relevant to the problem at hand. Maybe the data can be found by months or by quarters; but since there is much serial correlation between adjacent monthly data, we can by no means blithely assume that we have increased our degrees of freedom twelve-fold or more by using monthly data. Nature has simply not performed the controlled experiments that enable us to predict as we should wish.

This means that the master economist must piece together, from all the experience he has ever had, hunches relevant to the question at hand. In short, we begin to accumulate "degrees of freedom" from the first moment we draw breath and begin to take in observations of the world around us. Indeed, we could perhaps begin the integral of experience even before birth. Are we born with a *tabula rasa*? I used to laugh at Jung's notion of inherited experience, and still do. But I have been impressed by the experiments of Nikolaas Tinbergen and others—which suggest that evolution has built into us certain programmed capacities for action and decision. I feel energetic when the sun shines, perhaps because the mutations that produced this took place in my ancestors and helped them and me to survive. It may be that I take an eclectic judgment in making forecasts because that has proved to be a "profitable" thing to do both in *my* lifetime and that of my forefathers.

At any rate, just as there is a time for remembering, there is a time for forgetting. Economics is not a stationary time-series. Getting a year's extra data for 1864 is not worth nearly so much as getting extra data for 1964. We must learn both to regard experience and to disregard it. I've known men who paid dearly for every thousand dollars of profits they made from selling short in 1929-1932. They never recovered from being bears—even in 1946-1955!

But if economics does not deal with a stationary time-series, neither is ignorance bliss in our profession. There are thousands of ways for the really uninformed man to be wrong in the field of forecasting. Today will not simply repeat yesterday. But to think that the laws of the universe were born anew this morning when you opened your eyes is pitiful nonsense. The essence of science is mastering the art of filtering out the obsolete patterns of the past and filtering in the patterns of persistence.

If science becomes a private art, it loses its characteristic of reproducibility. Here is an example. Sumner Slichter, from 1930 to his death in the late 1950's, was a good forecaster. Dr. Robert Adams of Standard Oil (New Jersey), comparing different methods of forecasting, found that "being Sumner Slichter" was then about the best. But how did Slichter do it? I could never make this out. And neither, I believe, could he. One year he talked about Federal Reserve policy, another year about technical innovation. Somehow the whole came out better than the sum of its parts. Now what I should like to emphasize is that the private art of Sumner Slichter died with him. No less-gifted research assistant could have had transferred to him even a fraction of the Master's skill. And thus one of the principal aims of science was not achieved—namely, reproducibility by any patient person of modest ability of the empirical regularities discerned by luck or by the transcendental efforts of eminent scholars.

The models of Klein, Goldberger, Tinbergen, and Suits have at least this property. Take away Frankenstein and you still have a mechanical monster that will function for awhile. But unlike the solar system, which had to be wound up by Divine Providence only once, any economic model will soon run down if the breath of intelligent life is not pumped into it. When you see a 7094 perform well in a good year, never forget that it is only a Charlie McCarthy; without an Edgar Bergen in the background it is only a thing of paint and wood, of inert transistors and obsolescing matrices.

How well can economists forecast? The question is an indefinite one, and reminds us of the man who was asked what he thought about his wife, and had to reply, "Compared to what?"

Most of us battle-scarred veterans would make only modest claims to clairvoyance in economic affairs. This is a special kind of modesty, however, like that illustrated by what I believe is a true story. A few years ago, someone at Princeton asked the eminent Japanese mathematician Kakutani, "Are you a great mathematician?". "Me a great mathematician?", was the reply. "Oh no, I am a mere nothing." "Well in that case," went on the interrogator, "name me a greater mathematician." According to the legend, Kakutani thought and thought, and finally in desperation said, "John von Neumann," which makes it a very funny story to those who know the reverence in which the late von Neumann was held.

When I say that as an economist I am not very good at making economic forecasts, that sounds like modesty. But actually, it represents the height of arrogance. For I know that bad as we economists are, we are better than anything else in heaven and earth at forecasting aggregate business trends—better than gypsy tea-leaf readers, Wall Street soothsayers and chartist technicians, hunch-playing heads of mail order chains, or all-powerful heads of state. This is a statement based on empirical experience. Over the years I have tried to keep track of various methods of forecasting, writing down in my little black book what people seemed to be saying before the event, and then comparing their prediction with what happened. The result has been a vindication of the hypothesis that there is no efficacious substitute for economic analysis in business forecasting. Some maverick may hit a home run on occasion; but over the long season, batting averages tend to settle down to a sorry level when the more esoteric methods of soothsaying are relied upon.

What constitutes a good batting average? That depends on the contest. In baseball these days, .300, or 300-out-of-1,000, is very good. In economic forecasting of the direction of change, we ought to be able to do at least .500 just by tossing a coin. And taking advantage of the undoubted upward trend in all modern economies, we can bat .750 or better just by parrot-like repeating, "Up, Up." The difference between the men and the boys, then, comes between an .850 performance and an .800 performance. Put in other terms, the good forecaster, who must in November make a point-estimate of GNP for the calendar year ahead, will, over a decade, have an average error of perhaps one per cent, being in a range of $12 billion dollars, with reality being $6 billion on either side of the estimate. And a rather poor forecaster may, over the same period, average an error of 1½ per cent. When we average the yearly results for a decade, it may be found that in the worst year the error was over 2 per cent, compensated by rather small errors in many of the years not expected to represent turning points.

In a sense this is a modest claim. But again I must insist on the arrogance underlying these appraisals. For I doubt that it is possible, on the basis of the evidence now knowable a year in advance, to do much better than this. An expert owns up to the limits of his accuracy, but goes on arrogantly to insist that the result cannot be bettered. His range of ignorance is, so to speak, based on experience. It is ignorance based on knowledge, not ignorance based on ignorance. It reminds one a little bit of Heisenberg's Uncertainty Principle in quantum mechanics. According to it, an observer cannot simultaneously determine both the position and the velocity of a particle: if he arranges his observational experiment so as to get an accurate fix on position, his recording instruments will make the velocity indeterminate with a range; and if he rearranges the observational instruments so as to get an accurate fix on velocity, the cost he must pay is giving up knowledge of position. Something like the Heisenberg Uncertainty Principle seems to operate in economics—if we do not insist on a close analytical analogy. Animal spirits do play a part in human affairs. It is as if Nature does not even begin to toss the dice upon which next year's fate will depend by November of this year. There is then nothing that the clever analyst can peek at to improve his batting average beyond some critical level.

I do not mean to imply that this critical level is fixed for all time. Once our profession got new surveys of businessmen's intentions to invest, of their decisions as to capital appropriations, and of consumers responses to random polling, the critical level of imprecision was reduced. In all likelihood, the critical level of uncertainty is a secularly declining one. But is its asymptote (for forecasting a year ahead, remember) literally zero? I do not know how to answer this question. Although it may seem pessimistic to give a negative answer, I am tempted to do so. For remember, you cannot find what is in a person's mind by interrogation, before there is anything in his mind. That is why preliminary surveys of the McGraw-Hill type, taken in October before many corporations have made their capital-budgeting decisions, are necessarily of limited accuracy —which does not deny that they are of some value to us.

The imprecision inherent in forecasting raises some questions about the propriety of making simple point-estimates. If you twist my arm, you can make me give a single number as a guess about next year's GNP. But you will have to twist hard. My scientific conscience would feel more comfortable giving you my subjective probability distribution for all the values of GNP.[2] Thus, I might reckon the rough probability to be one-half that GNP will be at most $655 billion in 1965; one-quarter that it will be at most $650 billion; and three-quarters that it will be at most $662 billion. Actually, it is a pain in the neck to have to work out the whole probability distribution rather than to give a single point-estimate. But satisfying one's scientific conscience is never a very easy task. And there is some payoff for the extra work involved.

For one thing, just what does a point-estimate purport to mean? That is often not clear even to the man issuing it. Do I give the number at which I should just be indifferent to make a bet *on either side,* is forced to risk a large sum of money on a bet whose side can be determined by an opponent or by a referee using chance devices? If that is what I mean in issuing a point-estimate, I am really revealing the *median* of my subjective probability distribution. Other times estimators have in the back of their mind that over the years they will be judged by their mean-square-error, and hence it is best for them to reveal the *arithmetic mean* of their subjective distribution.

I have known still others who aimed, consciously or unconsciously, at the mode of their distribution—sometimes perhaps using the modal value of forecasts among all their friends and acquaintances as the way of arriving at their own mode. Warning: the dis-

[2] Six months after I made this speech (i.e., in April, 1965), new evidence caused me to raise all the GNP numbers by 5 billion, itself an interesting fact.

tribution of all point-estimates issued from a hundred different banks, insurance companies, corporations, government agencies, and academic experts is usually more bunched than the defensible *ex ante* subjective probability distribution any one of them should use in November. This is illustrated by a story I heard Roy Blough once tell at a Treasury Meeting. He said: "Economic forecasters are like six eskimos in one bed; the only thing you can be sure of is that they are all going to turn over together." Blough is right. In a few weeks time one often sees all the forecasts revised together upward or downward.

The difference between median, mean, and mode is not very significant if our expected distributions are reasonably symmetrical. But often they are not: often it will be easier to be off by $15 billion through being too pessimistic rather than too optimistic. Making your soothsayer provide you with a probability range may seem to be asking him to be more pretentiously accurate than he can be. But that is not my interpretation: using the language of arithmetical probability is my way of introducing and emphasizing the degree of uncertainty in the procedure, not its degree of finicky accuracy. There is a further advantage of using probability spreads rather than single point-estimates. One of the whizziest of the Whiz Kids in the Pentagon told me that they get better point estimates from Generals and Admirals if they make them always give high and low estimates. Before, you could never be sure whether some conservative bias or discount was not already being applied to data. Henri Theil of Rotterdam has studied how well forecasters perform and has found a similar tendency toward conservative bias in economic forecasters.

Suppose we think that GNP is likely to rise, say by $30 billion. If we issue the forecast of a rise of $20 billion, we shall certainly have been in the right direction. And we shall be in the ball park with respect to general magnitude. Why be hoggish and try for better? Particularly since GNP might go down, and then you would be standing all alone out there in right field, more than $30 billion off the mark. "Better be wrong in good company, than run the risk of being wrong all alone" is a slogan that every Trustee knows to represent wisdom for his actions.

But here I am talking about science, not about gamesmanship for the forecaster. Gamesmanship introduces a whole new set of considerations. Many forecasters, particularly amateurs, don't really care whether they turn out to be wrong or by how much they turn out to be wrong. They want to tell a good story. They want to back the long-shot of possible success when their wild forecasts that depart from that of the fashionable mob might just possibly happen to be right. Then their prescience will be noted and remembered, whereas if they turn out to be woefully wrong, who is going to be there to remind people of that? If that is how you want to play the game, then naturally you should do what the rational entrant in an office pool on the election does. He does not place his bet at 61 per cent of the popular vote for Johnson, even if that is his best belief. Why not? Because there are people who are picking numbers all around that. Instead, he looks for the open spaces—measured of course in his probability metric—where few entrants in the pool have selected their estimates. Why is this rational? Because to amateurs it usually does not matter by how much you are wrong. The only prize is to be at the top. In science and in real economic life, it is terribly important not to be wrong by much. To be second-best year after year in a stock-portfolio competition would be marvelous for a mutual fund manager, and especially where the first-place winners are a shifting group of crap-shooters who stake all on one whim or another.

As an economic scientist, I take economic forecasting with deadly seriousness. I hate to be far wrong. Every residual is a wound on my body. And I'd rather make two small errors, than be right once at the cost of being wrong a second time by the sum of the two errors. The reason is not vanity—because forecasting serves a purpose: each dollar of error costs something in terms of corporate or national policy; and if the "loss function" or "social welfare function" is a smooth one in the neighborhood of its optimum, it will be the square of the error of forecast that gives a rough measure of local error.

If we use means-square-error as our criterion of fit, I think it will be found that forecasters have another persistent bias, namely a tendency to be too pessimistic. This is different from the conservatism that makes forecasters shade both their upward and downward forecasts below the true magnitude. Why is there this downward bias? First, because it is never easy to know where next year's dollar is going to come from, and many forecasters try to build up their total by adding up the elements that they can see. There is a second, perhaps more defensible, reason for erring on the downward or pessimistic side in making a forecast. The social consequences of unemployment and underproduction may be deemed more serious than those of over-full-employment and (mild) demand inflation. I once shocked the late John Maurice Clark at a meeting in Washington by saying, "Although the chance of a recession next year is only one-third, for policy purposes we should treat it as if it were two-thirds." He thought that a contradiction in terms. But in terms of his colleague Wald's loss-function concept, I could make sense of my statement by postulating that each dollar of deflationary gap had social consequences more serious than each dollar of inflationary gap.

Often a forecaster is forced to give a single point-estimate because his boss or consumers cannot handle a more complicated concept. Then he must figure out for himself which point-estimate will do them the most good, or the least harm. Years ago one of the publishing companies used to have every staff member make a prediction of the sales each textbook would enjoy. If people tried to play safe and guess low figures, the President of the company would penalize them for having too little faith in the company's sales staff and authors. (Incidentally, the sales manager used to come up with the least inaccurate predictions, odd as that may sound.)

A good speech should tell the audience

something that it already knows to be true. Then having gained their good approval for soundness, it should tell them something they didn't previously know to be true. I don't know whether I have been able to complete the second part of this recipe, but I want to add a third requirement for a good speech. It should call attention to some problem whose true answer is not yet known. Let me conclude, therefore, by raising an unanswered question.

Naïve models based upon persistence, momentum, or positive serial correlation do rather well in economics as judged by least-square-error of predictions. An extreme case is one which merely projects the current level or the current direction of change. Yet such models do badly in "calling turning points." Indeed, as described above, such naïve models are like the Dow System of predicting stockmarket prices, which never even tries to call a turning point in advance and is content to learn, not too long after the fact, that one has actually taken place.

Forecasters regard models which merely say, "Up and up," or "more of the same," as rather dull affairs. When I once explained to editors of a financial magazine that one disregarded this continuity only at one's risk, they said: "Professor, that may be good economic science, but it's darn dull journalism." But are we forecasters here to have a good time? Dullness may be part of the price we must pay for good performance. More than that? Are we here to cater to our own vanity? One hates to be wrong; but if one's average error could be reduced at the cost of being more often wrong in direction, is that not a fair bargain?

I don't pretend to know the answer to these questions. But they do have a bearing on the following issue. Often an economist presents a model which he admits does worse than some more naïve model, but which he justifies for its better fit at the turning points. Is this emphasis legitimate? That question I leave open.

Is policy action most important at the turning points? Is policy action most potent at the turning points? Is a correct guess about turning points likely to lead to correct guesses for the next several quarters? And if so, why doesn't this importance of accuracy of the turning points already get duly registered in the minimum-squared-error criterion? The whole notion of a turning point would be changed in its timing if we shifted, as many dynamic economies in Europe have to do, to changes in direction of trend-deviations rather than changes in absolute direction as insisted on by the National Bureau. Does this lack of invariance cast doubt on the significance of turning points?

Finally, is it possible that public preoccupation with economics is greatest at the turning point and that we are essentially catering to our own vanity and desire for publicity when we stress accuracy at such times?

I promised to end up with a question, and I find by count that I have ended up with seven. I guess that is what practical men must expect when they invite an academic theorist to give a lecture.

But for all that, to the scientific forecaster I say, "Always study your residuals." Charles Darwin, who lived before the age of Freud, made it a habit to write down immediately any arguments *against* his theory of evolution, for he found that he invariably tended to forget those arguments. When I have steeled myself to look back over my past economic forecasts in the London *Financial Times,* they have appeared to be a little less prescient than I had remembered them to be. Janus-like, we must look at the past to learn how to look into the future.

After I had made some innocent remarks like this in my 1961 Stamp Memorial Lecture at the University of London, I ran into Professor Frank Paish, himself one of England's best economic forecasters.

"Great mistake ever to look back," he quipped, "you'll lose your nerve."

This is almost precisely what the great Satchel Paige of baseball said. "Never look backward. Somebody may be gaining on you."

Like Sir Winston, I bring you blood, sweat, and tears. The way of the scientific forecaster is hard. Let Lot's wife, who did look back, be your mascot and guide. What Satch Paige didn't mention is that "they may be gaining on you anyway." Know the truth —and while it may not make you free—it will help rid you of your amateur standing.

PART XIX

Portfolio Selection, Warrant Pricing,
and the Theory of Speculative Markets

198

Proof That Properly Anticipated Prices Fluctuate Randomly

Paul A. Samuelson
Massachusetts Institute
of Technology

The Enigma Posed

"In competitive markets there is a buyer for every seller. If one could be sure that a price will rise, it would have already risen." Arguments like this are used to deduce that competitive prices must display price changes over time, $X_{t+1} - X_t$, that perform a random walk with no predictable bias.

Is this a correct fact about well-organized wheat or other commodity markets? About stock exchange prices for equity shares? About futures markets for wheat or other commodities, as contrasted to the movement of actual "spot prices" for the concrete commodity.

Or is it merely an interesting (refutable) hypothesis about actual markets that can somehow be put to empirical testing?

Or is it a valid deduction (like the Pythagorean Theorem applicable to Euclidean triangles) whose truth is as immutable as $2 + 2 = 4$? Does its truth follow from the very definition of "free, competitive markets?" (If so, can there fail to exist in New York and London actual stock and commodity markets with those properties; and must any failures of the "truism" that turn up be attributable to "manipulation," "thinness of markets," or other market imperfections?)

The more one thinks about the problem, the more one wonders what it is that could be established by such abstract argumentation. Is the fact that American stocks have shown an average annual rise of more than 5 per cent over many decades compatible with the alleged "fair game" (or martingale property) of an unbiased random walk? Is it an exception that spot wheat prices generally rise (presumably because of storage costs) from the July harvest time to the following spring and drop during June? Is the fact that the price of next July's future shows much less strong seasonal patterns a confirmation of the alleged truism? If so, what about the alleged Keynes-Hicks-Houthakker-Cootner pattern of "normal backwardation," in which next July's wheat future could be expected to rise in price a little from July harvest to, say, the following March (as a result of need of holders of the crop to coax out, at a cost, risk-disliking speculators with whom to make short-hedging transactions); and what about the Cootner pattern in which, once wheat stocks become low in March, processors wishing to be sure of having a minimum of wheat to process, seek short-selling speculators with whom to make long-hedging transactions, even at the cost of having the July quotation dropping a little in price in months like April and May?

Consideration of such prosaic and mundane facts raises doubt that there is anything much in celestial a priori reasoning from the axiom that what can be perceived about the future must already be "discounted" in current price quotations. Indeed, suppose that all the participants in actual markets are necessarily boobs when it comes to foreseeing the unforeseeable future. Why should "after-the-fact" price changes show any systematic pattern, such as non-bias? Are the very mathematical notions of probability of any relevance to actual market quotations? If so, how could we decide that this is indeed so?

PROOF THAT PROPERLY

Whatever the answers to these questions, I think we can suspect that there is no *a priori* necessity for actual Board of Trade grain prices to act in accordance with specific probability models. Perhaps it is a lucky accident, a boon from Mother Nature so to speak, that so many actual price time series do behave like uncorrelated or quasi-random walks. Thus, Maurice Kendall[1] almost proves too much when he finds negligible serial correlation in spot grain prices. For reasons that I shall discuss, we would not be too surprised to find this property in futures price changes. But surely spot prices ought to vary with shifts in such supply and demand factors as weather, crop yields, and crop plantings; or population, income, and taste changes. Who says that the weather must itself display no serial correlation? A dry month does tend to be followed by a dryer-than-average month because of persistence of pressure patterns, etc. Perhaps it is true that prices depend on a summation of so many small and somewhat independent sources of variation that the result is like a random walk. But there is no necessity for this. And the fact, if it is one, is not particularly related to perfect competition or market anticipations. For consider a monopolist who sells (or buys) at fixed price. If the demand (or supply) curve he faces is the resultant of numerous independent, additive sources of variation each of which is limited or small, his resulting quantity $\{q_t\}$ may well behave like a random walk, showing variations like the normal curve of error.

At this point, the reader may feel inclined to doubt that the arguments of my first paragraph have even a germ of interest for the economist. But I hope to show that such a rejection goes too far.

By positing a rather general stochastic model of price change, I shall deduce a fairly sweeping theorem in which next-period's price differences are shown to be uncorrelated with (if not completely independent of) previous period's price differences. This martingale property of zero expected capital gain will then be replaced by the slightly more general case of a constant mean percentage gain per unit time.

[1] See ref. [1].

You never get something for nothing. From a nonempirical base of axioms you never get empirical results. Deductive analysis cannot determine whether the empirical properties of the stochastic model I posit come at all close to resembling the empirical determinants of today's real-world markets. That question I shall not here investigate. I shall be content if I can, for once, find definite and unambiguous content to the arguments of the opening paragraph—arguments which have long haunted economists' discussions of competitive markets.

A General Stochastic Model of Price

Let $\{\ldots, X_{t-1}, X_t, X_{t+1}, \ldots, X_{t+T}, \ldots\}$ represent the time sequence of prices—as for example the price of spot #2 wheat in Chicago (or it could be a vector of prices or even quantities of several different goods). Given knowledge of today's price and of past prices $[X_t, X_{t-1}, \ldots]$, suppose we cannot know with certainty tomorrow's price X_{t+1}, or any future price X_{t+T}. Suppose there is at best a probability distribution for any future price, whose form depends solely on the number of periods ahead over which we are trying to forecast prices, given by

$$(1) \quad \text{Prob}\{X_{t+T} \leqq X | X_t = x_0, X_{t-1} = x_1, \ldots\} = P(X, x_0, x_1, \ldots; T)$$

These P's are assumed not to depend on, or change with, historical calendar time. In that sense, I posit a "stationary" process (but one consistent with, say, chronic inflation).

From the fundamental logic of probability, we can relate these probabilities relevant to different future forecast spans: $T = 1, 2, \ldots$. All are ultimately deducible from the basic one-period $P(X, x_0, x_1, \ldots; 1)$. Thus, always

$$P(X, x_0, x_1, \ldots; 2)$$
$$= \int_{-\infty}^{\infty} P(X, y, x_0, x_1, \ldots; 1)$$
$$dP(y, x_0, x_1, \ldots; 1)$$

$$(2) \quad \cdots \cdots \cdots \cdots \cdots \cdots \cdots$$

$$P(X, x_0, x_1, \ldots; T)$$
$$= \int_{-\infty}^{\infty} P(X, y, x_0, x_1, \ldots; T-1)$$
$$dP(y, x_0, x_1, \ldots; 1).$$

SAMUELSON

These general Stieltjes integrals include summation of finite (or countably-infinite) probabilities and ordinary integrals of probability densities; no real ambiguity concerning the variable over which dP is being integrated will usually arise.

In words, (2) merely says that the probability of an event's happening is the sum of the probabilities of the different mutually-exclusive ways by which it could happen. If $P(X, x_0, x_1, \ldots; 1)$ had the Markov property of being quite independent of $(x_1, x_2, \ldots)$, (2) would be the so-called Chapman-Kolmogorov equation. But I do not assume any special Markov property. The generality of (1) and (2) must be emphasized. Nothing necessarily Gaussian or normal is assumed about any $P(X, x_0, x_1, \ldots; T)$. It is possible, but not necessarily assumed, that an ergodic state for P will emerge in the limit as T goes to infinity. Thus,

(3) $\quad \lim_{T \to \infty} P(X, x_0, x_1, \ldots; T) = P(X)$

independently of $(x_0, x_1, \ldots)$

would involve such an ergodic property.

Here are some examples of possible processes that define the P's. Suppose $\{X_t\}$ satisfies a Yule-Wold autoregressive linear equation of the type

(4) $\quad X_{t+1} = aX_t + \{u_t\} \ , \ |a| < 1,$

with $\{u_t\}$ independent drawings from the same table of random digits or of Gaussian variates.

Or suppose the X_t price can take on only the finite discrete values $[Q_1, Q_2, \ldots, Q_n]$; and let a_{ij}, the nonnegative coefficients of a Markov transitional-probability matrix, represent the probability that a price now observed to be Q_i will one period later be observed to be Q_j, where $\Sigma_j a_{ij} = 1$ for all i. If $[a_{ij}] = A$, the reader can verify that A^2 defines $P(X, x_0; 2)$ and A^T defines $P(X, x_0; T)$. If all $a_{ij} > 0$, A^∞ is a well-defined ergodic state, composed of the matrix $[\mathfrak{e}_j]$ with identical rows and hence independent of the initial observed Q_i value.

As a third possible model let $\{X_t\}$ take a random walk in the sense of doubling in the next period with probability 1/3 and halving with probability 2/3. This defines $P(X, x_0; 1)$, and the reader can verify that (2) gives for $P(X, x_0; 2)$ the property that

X_{t+2}/X_t will be (4, 1, 1/4) with respective probabilities (1/9, 4/9, 4/9), and so on with the usual binomial distribution for each T and with the central-limit theorem showing that a normal distribution is approached for $\log(X_{t+T}/X_t)$ as $T \to \infty$. This is an instance of a multiplicative Brownian motion applied to prices. Unlike the absolute or additive Brownian motion, it has the grace to avoid negative prices.

Specification of a Model Defining Behavior of a Futures Price

Now consider today's "futures price quotation" for the actual spot price that will prevail T periods from now—i.e., the price quoted today at t for a contract requiring delivery of actual physical goods at time t + T. If the present time is t, with present spot price X_t, the relevant spot price that is to prevail later is given by X_{t+T}. The newly defined futures price, quoted today, for that future X_{t+T}, we might denote by $Y(T, t)$. When another period passes, we shall know $(X_{t+1}, X_t, X_{t-1}, \ldots)$ instead of merely $(X_t, X_{t-1}, \ldots)$; and the new quotation for the same futures price we have been talking about will be written as $Y(T - 1, t + 1)$. It in turn will be succeeded by the sequence $[Y(T - 2, T + 2), \ldots, Y(t - n, t + n), \ldots, Y(1, t + T - 1), Y(0, t + T)]$. After $t + T$, there is no problem of pricing this particular futures contract. Thus, the July, 1964, Chicago Wheat Contract for delivery of wheat became closed, ancient history after July, 1964; but for more than twelve months prior to that date, its quotation oscillated from period to period and could be read in the newspaper.

What relationship shall we posit between the sequence $\{Y(T - n, t + n)\}$ and the sequence $\{X_{t+1}\}$? When the due date for the futures contract arrives, arbitrage will ensure that

(5) $\quad Y(0, t + T) = X_{t+T}$, commissions aside.

A period earlier no one can know what X_{t+T} will turn out to be. If interest and risk-aversion can be ignored, it is tempting to assume that people in the market place make as full use as they can of the posited probability distribution $P(X_{t+T}, X_{t+T-1}, X_{t+T-2}, \ldots; 1)$ of next-period's price and bid by supply and demand $Y(1, t + T - 1)$

to the mean or mathematically-expected level of tomorrow's price. That way neither short-sellers nor long-buyers stand to make a positive gain or loss. This constitutes the rationale of my first model of futures price, which is based on the following.

Axiom of Mathematically Expected Price Formation. If spot prices $\{X_t\}$ are subject to the probability distribution of (1), a futures price is to be set by competitive bidding at the now-expected level of the terminal spot price. That is,

$$(6) \quad Y(T, t + T) = E[X_{t+T}|X_t, X_{t-1}, \ldots],$$
$$(T = 1, 2, \ldots)$$
$$= \int_{-x}^{x} X \, dP(X, X_t, X_{t-1}, \ldots; T).$$

The Basic Theorem

Equations (1) and (6) completely determine the properties of the model. I can now derive from them the basic theorem at which I hinted in the usual vague arguments expressed in the opening paragraph. Let us observe numerous sequences of futures prices generated by this model, up until their terminal data. They will turn out, *on the average,* to have no upward or downward drift anywhere! (This will be true, regardless of the systematic seasonal patterns in X_t. This would be true, under our axiom, even in time of severe inflation or deflation of X_t itself—only remember, please, that the neglect of interest underlying our axiom would seem unwarranted in time of confidently-anticipated extreme inflation.)

Theorem of Fair-Game Futures Pricing. If spot prices $\{X_t\}$ are subject to the probability laws of (1) and (2), and the futures price sequence $\{Y(T, t + T), \ Y(T - 1, t + T - 1), \ldots, Y(1, t + T - 1), Y(0, t + T)\}$ is subject to the axiom of expected price as formulated in (5) and (6), then the latter sequence is a fair game (or martingale) in the sense of having unbiased price changes, or

$$(7) \quad E[Y(T - 1, t + T - 1)|X_t, X_{t-1}, \ldots] \equiv Y(T, t), \quad \text{or}$$

writing

$$Y(T - 1, t + T - 1) - Y(T, t) = \Delta Y(T, t),$$
$$(8) \quad E[\Delta Y(T, t)] \equiv 0;$$

from which it follows inductively that

$$(9) \quad E[\Delta^n Y(T, t)] \equiv 0 \quad (n = 1, 2, \ldots T).$$

This means that there is no way of making an expected profit by extrapolating past changes in the futures price, by chart or any other esoteric devices of magic or mathematics. The market quotation $Y(T, t)$ already contains in itself all that can be known about the future and in that sense has discounted future contingencies as much as is humanly possible (or inhumanly possible within the axiom of the model).

The theorem does not imply that the sequence of Y's perform a Brownian motion. It does not imply that $\Delta Y(T, t)$ is statistically *independent* of $\Delta Y(T + 1, t - 1)$; it implies only that given knowledge of $Y(T, t)$ the Pearsonian correlation coefficient between the above two Δ's will be zero. It is a source of comfort to the economist, rather than otherwise, that wheat prices should not perform a Brownian random walk. A Brownian walk, like the walk of a drunken sailor, wanders indefinitely far, listing with the wind.

Surely, economic law tells us that the price of wheat—whether it be spot $\{X_t\}$ or futures $\{Y(T, t)\}$—cannot drift sky-high or ground-low. It does have a rendez-vous with its destiny of supply and demand, albeit our knowledge of future supply and demand trends becomes dimmer as the envisaged date recedes farther into the future. We would expect people in the market place, in pursuit of avid and intelligent self-interest, to take account of those elements of future events that in a probability sense may be discerned to be casting their shadows before them. (Because past events cast *their* shadows after them, future events can be said to cast their shadows before them.)

Although the sequence $\{\Delta Y(T - n, t + n)\}$ has a zero first moment at all time periods $T - n$, there is no reason to suppose that the riskiness of holding a futures —in the sense of the second movement or variance, as measured by $E[\{\Delta Y(T - n, t + n)\}^2]$—should be the same when T is large and the terminal date far away as when $T - n$ is small and the futures contract about to expire. It is a well-known rule of thumb that nearness to expiration date involves greater variability or riskiness per hour or per day or per month than does farness. Partly this is due, I think, to factors not encompassed in the present model —for example, the real-life complications that make arbitrage equality shown in (5) hold only approximately. However, the present theory can contribute an elegant explanation of why we should expect far-distant futures to move more sluggishly than near ones. Its explanation does not lean at all on the undoubted fact that, during certain pre-harvest periods when stocks are normally low, changes in spot prices $\{\Delta X_t\}$ can themselves be expected to experience great volatility and second moment. Instead, it uses the contrary minor premise of posited *uniformity* through time of the distribution of $\{\Delta X_t\}$—so that it constitutes a stationary time series—to deduce the law of increasing volatility of a maturing futures contract. Before deriving the result, I present a proof of the martingale theorem.

By definition

$$Y(T,t) = \int_{-\infty}^{\infty} X dP(X, X_t, X_{t-1}, \ldots; T) \ ,$$

axiom of (6)

$$Y(T-1, t+1)$$

$$= \int_{-\infty}^{\infty} X dP(X, X_{t+1}, X_t, X_{t-1}, \ldots; T-1) \ ,$$

axiom of (6)

$$= f(X_{t+1}, X_t, X_{t-1}, \ldots.)$$

$$E[Y(T-1, t+1)|X_t, X_{t-1}, \ldots]$$

$$= \int_{-\infty}^{\infty} f(Z, X_t, X_{t-1}, \ldots) dP(Z, X_t, X_{t-1}, \ldots; 1)$$

$$= \int_{-\infty}^{\infty} \left[\int_{-\infty}^{\infty} X dP(X, Z, X_t, \ldots; T-1) \right]$$

$$dP(Z, X_t, \ldots; 1)$$

$$(10) = \int_{-\infty}^{\infty} X d \left[\int_{-\infty}^{\infty} P(X, Z, X_t, \ldots; T-1) \right]$$

$$dP(Z, X_t, \ldots; 1) \right]$$

$$= \int_{-\infty}^{\infty} X dP(X, X_t, \ldots; T) \ , \text{ by } (2)$$

$$= Y(T,t) \quad \text{Q.E.D.}$$

In thus proving (7), I have made permissable interchanges in the order of integration of the double Stieltjes integrals.

The content of this general theorem can be illustrated by some specific stochastic processes.

(a) Thus, suppose $\{X_t\}$ represents a simple Brownian motion without bias. Then $Y(T,t)$ becomes nothing but X_t it-

self. Since $\{X_t\}$ is a fair-game with $E[\Delta X] = 0$, then so must $E[\Delta Y] = 0$.

(b) Going beyond this simple case, suppose $\{X_t\}$ is a random walk with biased drift so that $E[\Delta X] = \mu \neq 0$. Then $Y(T,t) = X_t + \mu T$ and $E[\Delta Y] = E[\Delta X] + \mu(T - 1 - T) = \mu - \mu = 0$, as the theorem requires.

(c) Now let $\{X_t\}$ satisfy an autoregressive stochastic relation

$$X_{t+1} = aX_t + \{u_t\} \ , \ E(u_t) = \mu,$$

where $\{u_t\}$ is an unserially correlated random variable with distribution $P(U)$. Then

$$Y(T,t) = a^T X_t + \mu T$$

$$E[\Delta Y] = \int_{-\infty}^{\infty} a^{T-1}(aX_t + U_t) dP(U_t)$$

$$+ \mu(T - 1) - a^T X_t - \mu T$$

$$= 0 + \mu - \mu = 0.$$

(d) Finally, let $A = [a(i,j)]$ be a finite Markov transition-probability matrix giving

$$\text{Prob}\{X_{t+1} = Q_i | X_t = Q_j\}.$$

Write $A^T = [a_{ij}^T]$, and

$$Y(T,t) = [Q_1, \ldots, Q_n] \text{ times the } j^{th} \text{ column of } A^T, \text{ by Axiom}$$

$$= \sum_i Q_i a_{ij}^T, \text{ denoted by}$$

$$Y(T|Q_j).$$

Then

$$E[Y(T-1, t+1)|X_t = Q_j]$$

$$= \sum_k Y(T-1)|Q_k) a_{kj},$$

by definition

$$= \sum Q_i a_{ij}^{T-1} a_{kj}$$

$$= \sum Q_i a_{ij}^T, \text{ since } A^{T-1}A = A^T$$

$$= Y(T,t) \quad \text{Q.E.D.}$$

The theorem is so general that I must confess to having oscillated over the years in my own mind between regarding it as trivially obvious (and almost trivially vacuous) and regarding it as remarkably sweeping. Such perhaps is characteristic of basic results. And actually the empirical question of the applicability of the model to economic reality must be kept distinct from the logical problem of what is the model's implied content.

Figure 1 should help to explain the theorem. It supposes $\{X_t\}$ is generated by

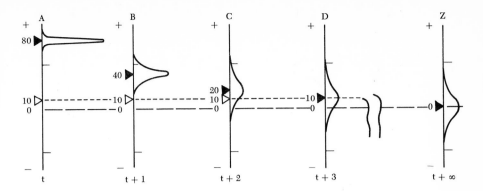

Figure 1A.
At time t, we know $X_t = 80$ with certainty. We can expect, from (4) with a $= 1/2$ and $\{u_t\}$ approximately normally distributed, that X_{t+1} be distributed as shown, with $E[X_{t+1}|X_t = 80] = 40$; for X_{t+2}, X_{t+3} the distributions are becoming slightly more dispersed, with means drifting downward like $80(2^{-2})$, $80(2^{-3})$; because a $= 1/2 < 1$, there is a limiting ergodic state for t $+ \infty$, much as shown, with $E[X_{t+z}|X_t] = 0$ independently of X_t. At time t, the futures price X_{t+3} is evaluated at 10, as shown by the white arrow at A, which merely reflects what can now be known about the distribution and mean of the spot price three periods from now. Now ask

yourself the question, What do I think at this time t will be the likely distribution of this futures price $Y(3, t)$ at the next period when it will have become $Y(2, t + 1)$? It will be distributed around 1/4 of next period's spot price X_{t+1} in exactly the same way that C shows X_{t+2} distributed around 1/4 of the period's spot price X_t. You do not today know where tomorrow's X_{t+1} will fall; but B does give you its probability distribution. Combining these bits of information, Figure 1B below plots (with enlarged vertical scale) what you *now* are entitled to regard as the probability distribution for $Y(3, t)$, $Y(2, t + 1)$, $Y(1, t + 2)$, $Y(0, t + 3) = X_{t+3}$.

(4)'s autoregressive model with a $= 1/2$. Random shocks $\{u_t\}$ aside, if price is once perturbed above (or below) its normal value (set at zero by convention), in each period it will return one-half way back to zero.

Generalizing the Theorem

If money has to be tied up in holding the $Y(T,t)$ contract and if there is a positive safe rate of interest, the process—being a fair game—does not stand to earn even the opportunity-cost of foregone safe interest. If, in addition, people have risk aversion (so that the utility whose expected value they seek to maximize is a strictly concave function of money wealth or income), the contract will probably have to promise a positive percentage yield per unit time, R, where $1 + R = \lambda > 1 +$ safe interest.

Therefore, we replace the simple axiom of mean expected value by a slightly more general axiom.

Axiom of Present-Discounted Expected Value: At each point of time t for a future price, we posit

$$Y(T, t) = \lambda^{-T} E[X_{t+T}|X_t, X_{t-1}, \ldots] ;$$

or, slightly more generally, since the variability of Y may be slightly different for each value of T, we may expect a different $(\lambda_1, \lambda_2, \ldots, \lambda_T)$ yield for which people hold out if they are to hold for the next period a futures contract with T years to go. The present-discounted expectation becomes

$$Y(T, t) = \lambda_1^{-1}\lambda_2^{-1}\ldots\lambda_T^{-1} \ E[X_{t+T}|X_t, X_{t-1}, \ldots] .$$

Just as the simple axiom of expected gain led to the theorem of unbiased price change, the new general axiom leads to the theorem on "normal backwardation".

Theorem of Mean Percentage Price Drift. If spot prices $\{X_t\}$ are determined by the stipulated general stochastic process $P(X_{t+T}, X_t, X_{t-1}, \ldots; T)$ and we define the sequence

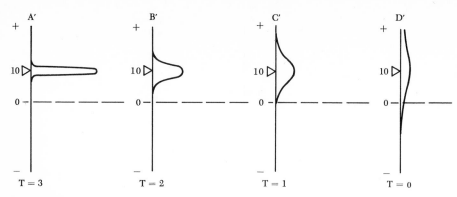

A'	B'	C'	D'
+	+	+	+
10 ▷	10 ▷	10 ▷	10 ▷
0 –	0 –	0 –	0 –
–	–	–	–
T = 3	T = 2	T = 1	T = 0

Figure 1B.

A', B', C', and D' give the probability distributions you are entitled to envisage on the basis of today's certain knowledge of $[X_t, X_{t+1}, \ldots$ and $Y(3, t)]$ for next periods' $[Y(2, t + 1), Y(1, t + 2), Y(0, t + 3) = X_{t+3}]$. Note that all have the same mean of 10 but that your cone of uncertainty widens as the time in which new unknown, independent disturbances $\{u_{t+i}\}$ can intervene. Note that after one period passes, both diagrams will have to be redrawn: A and A' will be irrelevant; a particular point on B and B' will become the new present, and the new (C, C') and (D, D') will bear the same relation to (B, B') that now (C, C') and (B, B') bear respectively to (A, A'). If the stochastic variables u_{t+1}, u_{t+2}, and u_{t+3} were identically zero, the futures price would show no variability, staying always at 10. $Y(3,t)$ and $Y(2, t + 1)$ are likely to be more alike with a less volatile difference ΔY than can $Y(2, t + 1)$ and $Y(1, t + 2)$. (For equation (4), the variance of $\Delta Y(t - n, t + n)$ is proportional to a^{T-n}, diminishing as $T - n$ becomes large.) Why? Because the first pair stand to have (u_{t+2}, u_{t+3}) in common and differ only in that the first of the pair also has u_t as a source of variation.

The fact that this pair has two out of three elements of variation in common is stabilizing on their difference ΔY in comparison with the second pair which have only u_{t+3} out of the possible (u_{t+2}, u_{t+3}) in common. A far-distant future will not change much in the next month since so few of the disturbances upon which its fate depends will change in this month; it stays close to the general level given by the so-called law of averages. At the other extreme, $Y(1, t + 2)$ and $Y(0, t + 3) = X_{t+3}$ will differ because of the single unknowable u_{t+3}, and this sudden-death kind of situation will subject their difference to great variance without any cushioning from the law of large numbers. A striking way of seeing this is to disregard the varying means and to think of the passage of one period as leaving us at the left of the diagram subtracting the last (rather than the first, as when we shift the present from A to B) of the vertical axes. Precisely because D approaches an ergodic state, C and D differ less than do A and B in Figure 1A. So losing the last axis, which is like making C become the new D, gives less of a change than would shifting B to A.

$\{Y(T,t), Y(T-1, t+1), \ldots, Y(1, t+T-1), Y(0, t+T)\}$ by

$$Y(T, t) = \lambda_T^{-1} \ldots \lambda_1^{-1} E[X_{t+T}|X_t, X_{t-1}, \ldots].$$

$$= \lambda_T^{-1} \ldots \lambda_1^{-1} \int_{-\infty}^{\infty} X dP(X, X_t, X_{t-1}, \ldots; T),$$

it follows that

$$E[Y(T-n, t+n)|X_t, X_{t-1}, \ldots] = \lambda_T \ldots \lambda_{T-n+1} Y(T, t)$$
$$= \lambda^n Y(T, t) \text{ if } \lambda_i \equiv \lambda.$$

In words, this says that the futures price will rise in each period by the percentage

$\lambda - 1$ (or $\lambda_T - 1$, where presumably $\lambda_1 > \lambda_2 > \ldots > \lambda_T$ if people abhor the extra riskiness inherent in a futures contract as it matures). This theorem provides rational account of the Keynes-Houthakker-Cootner[2] doctrine of "normal backwardation". It says that, within the defined model, all chart methods attempting to read out of the past sequence of known prices $[X_t, X_{t-1}, \ldots, Y(T,t), Y(T + 1, t - 1), \ldots]$ any profitable pattern of prediction is doomed to failure. So to speak, the market has already,

[2] See refs. [2], [3], [4], [5], and [6].

PROOF THAT PROPERLY

788

by our axiom, discounted all knowable future information so that the present-discounted variable $(\lambda_T \ldots \lambda_1)^{-1} \, Y$ sequence is itself a fair-game martingale.

Re-examining the proof of the simple theorem, we see that the same interchange of order of integration in the relevant double integral gives an immediate proof of the theorem.

Finally, examining the proof shows that a still more general theorem is valid. Wherever we have had X_{t+T} in $E[X_{t+T}|X_t, X_{t-1}, \ldots]$ or X in the double integral, we could have put in any function of X, say $g(X)$ or $g(X_{t+T})$ and still preserved the martingale properties. This is important because, as mentioned, we may want to interpret X_t as a vector—as e.g. with components (soft wheat price, hard wheat price, corn price, midwest rainfall, national income, etc.). Then the scalar $g(X_{t+T})$ might be the selection of soft wheat price, the deliverable goods for the futures contract in question. Only a deluded chartist would think that extraneous variables, such as rainfall, can be excluded from an optimal *probability* description of future soft wheat prices; and yet it is true that, after speculators have taken such variables into account in implementing the axiom of expected gain, the resulting Y sequence tells its own (simple!) story.

Still one more bargain in cheap generality can be garnered. As far as the theorem's proof is concerned, $g(X_{t+T})$ could just as well be a function also of all present known data and be written as $g(X_{t+T}, X_t, X_{t-1}, \ldots)$, without affecting its general martingale property. It would even be possible to put now-known values of $Y(T+k, \, t-k)$ as variables in g, but there would seem to be no need to do this since ultimately all known Y's should be reducible to functions of the X_{t-k} inputs. Still there is no harm in so including the Y's, and in some cases the form of the function might be much simplified by including such Y's (and even the Y's of other terminal date). To illustrate how one might want X_t in $g(X_{t+T}, X_t, \ldots)$, suppose that either number 1 or number 2 grades of soft wheat are deliverable on the July, 1965, contract. Let the vector X_t contain as elements price data on both grades; and suppose that if one of these is now known to be much cheaper than the other, one can be pretty sure that this cheaper grade will be the grade actually delivered on the contract at the terminal date; and hence for certain value of the elements of the vector X_t, $g(\ldots)$ will be the expected price of one grade rather than of the other.

Conclusion

A result of some generality has now been established. Anyone who thinks it obvious should reflect on the following fact: if instead of taking an expected value or mean value for X_{t+T}, we set $Y(T,t)$ at, say, its median value, then it will not necessarily be true that expected value of ΔY is zero. Nor is it true that the median of ΔY so defined is zero. For example, let $P(X_{t+1}, X_t, 1) = P(X_{t+1}/X_t)$ with $P(1) > 1/2 = P(m)$, $0 < m < 1$. Then $Y(T,t) = mX_t$, $Y(T+1, \, t+1) = mX_{t+1}$. For median $\Delta Y = 0$, we require

$$\text{Prob}\{Y_{t+1} \leq Y_t\} = \text{Prob}\{mX_{t+1} \leq mX_t\}$$

$$= \text{Prob}\{X_{t+1} - X_t\} = \frac{1}{2}.$$

But actually,

$$\text{Prob}\{X_{t+1} \leq X_t\} = \text{Prob}\left\{\frac{X_{t+1}}{X_t} \leq 1\right\} = P(1) > \frac{1}{2}.$$

Hence, ΔY is more likely to be negative than positive—even if $P(X/x)$ defines a fair game with $E(X/x) = x$.

One should not read too much into the established theorem. It does not prove that actual competitive markets work well. It does not say that speculation is a good thing or that randomness of price changes would be a good thing. It does not prove that anyone who makes money in speculation is *ipso facto* deserving of the gain or even that he has accomplished something good for society or for anyone but himself. All or none of these may be true, but that would require a different investigation.

I have not here discussed where the basic probability distributions are supposed to come from. In whose minds are they *ex ante*? Is there any *ex post* validation of them? Are they supposed to belong to the market as a whole? And what does that mean? Are they supposed to belong to the "representative individual," and who is he? Are they some defensible or necessitous compromise of divergent expectation patterns? Do price quotations somehow produce a Pareto-optimal configuration of *ex ante* subjective probabilities? This paper has not attempted to pronounce on these interesting questions.

References

1 Kendall, Maurice G., "The Analysis of Economic Time-Series—Part I: Prices," *Journal of the Royal Statistical Society* 96, Part I (1953), pp. 11-25; also pp. 85-99 in Cootner, Paul H. (editor), *The Random Character of Stock Market Prices*. Cambridge: The M.I.T. Press, 1964.

2 Keynes, J. M., *A Treatise on Money*, Vol. II: *The Applied Theory of Money*. London: Macmillan & Company, 1930.

3 Houthakker, H., "The Scope and Limits of Futures Trading," pp. 134-159 in Abramovitz, Moses (editor), *Allocation of Economic Resources*.

4 Houthakker, H., "Systematic and Random Elements in Short-Term Price Movements," *American Economic Review* 51 (1961), pp. 164-172.

5 Cootner, Paul H., "Returns to Speculators: Telser vs. Keynes," *Journal of Political Economy* 68 (1960), pp. 396-404.

6 Cootner, Paul H., "Rejoinder," *Journal of Political Economy* 68 (1960), pp. 415-418.

PROOF THAT PROPERLY

199

Rational Theory of Warrant Pricing

Paul A. Samuelson
Massachusetts Institute
of Technology

Introduction

This is a compact report on desultory researches stretching over more than a decade.

In connection with stock market fluctuations, L. Bachelier[1], a French mathematician, discovered the mathematical theory of Brownian motion five years before Einstein's classic 1905 paper. Bachelier gave the same formula for the value of a warrant (or "call" or put) based upon this "absolute" or "arithmetic" process that Dr. R. Kruizenga[2] developed years later in a thesis under my direction. Under this formula, the value of a warrant grows proportionally with the square-root of the time to go before elapsing; this is a good approximation to actual pricing of short-lived warrants, but it leads to the anomalous result that a long-lived warrant will increase in price indefinitely, coming even to exceed the price of the common stock itself—even though ownership of the stock is equivalent to a perpetual warrant exercisable at zero price!

The anomaly apparently came because Bachelier had forgotten that stocks possess limited liability and thus cannot become negative, as is implied by the arithmetic Brownian process. To correct this, I introduced the "geometric" or "economic Brownian motion," with the property that every dollar of market value is subject to the same multiplicational or percentage fluctuations per unit time regardless of the ab-

solute price of the stock. This led to the log-normal process for which the value of a call or warrant has these two desired properties: for short times, the $\sqrt{t}$ law holds with good approximation; and for $t \rightarrow \infty$, the value of the call approaches the value of the common stock. (All the above assumes that stock-price changes represent a "fair-game" or martingale—or certain trivial generalizations thereof to allow for a fair return. In an unpublished paper and lecture, I made explicit the derivation of this property from the consideration that, if everyone could "know" that a stock would rise in price, it would *already* be bid up in price to make that impossible. (See my companion paper appearing in this same issue, entitled "Proof That Properly Anticipated Prices Fluctuate Randomly.")

The above results, which have been presented in lectures since 1953 at M.I.T., Yale, Carnegie, the American Philosophical Society, and elsewhere have also been presented by such writers as Osborne,[3] Sprenkle,[4] Boness,[5] Alexander,[6] and no doubt others.

However, the theory is incomplete and unsatisfactory in the following respects:
1. It assumes, explicitly or implicitly, that the mean rate of return on the warrant is no more than on the common stock itself, despite the fact that the common stock may be paying a dividend and that the warrant may have a different riskiness from the common stock.

° Acknowledgment is made to the Carnegie Corporation for research aid, but sole responsibility for the results is mine.

[1]Ref. [1].
[2]Ref. [2].

[3]Ref. [3].
[4]Ref. [4].
[5]Ref. [5].
[6]Refs. [6], [7].

2. In consequence of the above, the theory implies that warrants (or calls) will never be converted prior to their elapsing date. Necessarily, therefore, no proper theory is provided for the conditions under which warrants will cease to be outstanding.

3. The existing theory, in effect, assumes that the privilege of converting the warrant at any time in the interval (rather than at the end of the period) is worth literally nothing at all.

4. Finally, the theory leads to the mentioned result, that the price of a perpetual warrant should be literally equal to the stock itself—a paradoxical result, and one that does not agree with the observed facts of life (for example, the fact that perpetual Tri-Continental Warrants sell for less than their equivalent amount of common stock, and are in fact being continuously converted into stock in some positive volume).

The present paper publishes, I believe for the first time, the more difficult theory of rationally evaluating a warrant, taking account of the extra worth of the right to convert *at any time in the interval* and deducing the value of the common stock above which it will pay to exercise the warrant. I am glad to acknowledge the valuable contribution of Professor Henry P. McKean, Jr. of the M.I.T. Department of Mathematics, in effecting certain exact solutions and in proving the properties of the general solutions. His analysis appears as a self-contained mathematical appendix. It will be clear that there still remain many unsolved problems. (For example, *exact* explicit solutions are now known in the case of perpetual warrants only for three cases: the log-normal, the log-Poisson, and the case where the only two possibilities are those of instantaneous complete loss or of a gain growing exponentially in time. Only for this last case is an exact explicit solution known for the finite-time warrant. These exact solutions, which are all due to McKean, correspond to various intuitive conjectures and empirical patterns and can be approximated by the solutions to the simpler problem of discrete, albeit small, time periods.)

The Postulated Model

Let the price of a particular common stock be defined for all time and be denoted by X_t. If we stand at the time t, we know with certainty X_t (and all of its past values $X_{t-\tau}$). Its future price $X_{t+\tau}$ is knowable only in some probability sense, its probability distribution being in the most general case a function of the whole past profile of $X_{t-\tau}$. A special simplification involves postulating a Markov property to the process, so that future $X_{t+\tau}$ has a distribution depending only on present X_t—namely

$$(1) \quad \text{Prob}\{X_{t+\tau} \leq X \mid X_t = x\} = P(X,x;T).$$

Obviously, (1) involves the critical assumption of a "stationary time series."

I further posit that each dollar of present value must be expected to have some mean gain per unit time, α, where α may perhaps be zero or more likely will be a positive quantity whose magnitude depends on the dispersion riskiness of X_t and the typical investor's utility aversion to risk. (A deeper theory would posit concave utility and deduce the value of α for each category of stocks.) This expected-returns axiom says

$$(2) \quad E[X_{t+\tau} \mid X_t] = \int_0^\infty X dP(X,X_t;T)$$
$$= X_t e^{\alpha t}, \alpha \geq 0$$

(Since money bears the safe return of zero, α cannot be less than zero for risk averters; indeed, it cannot be less than the safe return or pure interest on funds, if such exists. If utility were convex rather than concave, people might be willing to pay for riskiness, and α might be permitted to be negative—but not here.)

The integral in (2) is the usual Stieltjes integral: if the probability distribution $P(X,X_t;T)$ has a regular probability density $\partial P(X,X_t;T)/\partial X = p(X,X_t;T)$, we have the usual Riemann integral $\int_0^\infty Xp(X,X_t;T)dX$; if only discrete probabilities are involved, at $X = X_i$ with probabilities $P_i(X_t;T)$, the integral of (2) becomes the sum $\Sigma X_i P_i(X_t;T)$, which may involve a finite or countably-infinite number of terms. The reader can use the modern notation $\int_0^\infty XP(dX,X_t;T)$ rather than that of (2) if he prefers.

In (2) the limit of integration is given as 0 rather than $-\infty$, because of the important phenomenon of limited liability. A man cannot lose more than his original investment: General Motors stock can drop to zero, but not below.

SAMUELSON

If the probability of a future price X_{t+T} depends solely on knowledge of X_t alone, having the Markov property of being independent of further knowledge of past prices such as X_{t-A}, then

(3) $P(X_{t+T}|X_t,X_{t-A}) \equiv P(X_{t+T}|X_t)$

and (1) will satisfy the so-called Chapman-Kolmogorov equation

(4) $P(X_{t+T},X_t;T) \underset{s}{\equiv}$

$\int_0^\infty P(X_{t+T},x; T-S)dP(x,X_t;S), O \leq S \leq T.$

Remarks about Alternative Axioms

To see the meaning of this, suppose t takes on only discrete integral values. Then, without the Markov property (3), (1) would have the general form

(5) $\text{Prob}\{X_{t+k} \leq X|X_t,X_{t-1}, \ldots\}$

$= P(X,X_t,X_{t-1}, \ldots;k)$

with

(2)' $E[X_{t+1}|X_t,X_{t-1}, \ldots] =$

$\int_0^\infty XdP(X,X_t,X_{t-1}, \ldots;1) = e^\alpha X_t.$

Instead of (4), we would have

(4)' $P(X_{t+2},X_t,X_{t-1}, \ldots;2) =$

$\int_0^\infty P(X_{t+2},X_{t+1},X_t, \ldots;1)$

$dP(X_{t+1},X_t,X_{t-1}, \ldots;1)$

where the integration is over X_{t+1} and where X_t is seen to enter in the first factor of the integrand. Even without the Markov axiom of (3), from (2)' applied to the next period's gains, we could deduce the truth of (2) for two periods' gains as well and, by induction, for all-periods' gains—namely

$E[X_{t+2}|X_t,X_{t-1}, \ldots]$

$= \int_0^\infty XdP(X,X_t,X_{t-1}, \ldots;2)$

$= \int_0^\infty Xd \int_0^\infty P(X,x,X_t,X_{t-1}, \ldots;1)$

$dP(x,X_t,X_{t-1}, \ldots;1)$

(6)

$= \int_0^\infty e^\alpha xdP(x,X_t,X_{t-1}, \ldots;1)$

$= e^{2\alpha}X_t.$

Then, by induction, (2) or

$E[X_{t+k}|X_t,X_{t-1}, \ldots] = e^{k\alpha}X_t$

follows from the weak assumption of (5) and (2)' alone even when the Markov property (3) and Chapman-Kolmogorov property (4) do not necessarily hold.

However, I shall assume (3), and a fortiori (4), in order that the rational price of a warrant be a function of current common stock price X_t alone and not be (at this level of approximation) a functional of all past values X_{t-T}. A more elaborate theory would introduce such past values, if only to take account of the fact that the numerical value of α will presumably depend upon the estimate from past data that risk averters make of the riskiness they are getting into when holding the stock.

I might finally note that Bachelier assumed implicitly or explicitly

(7) $P(X,x;T) \equiv P(X-x;T), \quad \alpha = 0$

so that an absolute Brownian motion or random walk was involved. He thought that he could deduce from these assumptions alone the familiar Gaussian distribution—or, as we would say since 1923, a Wiener process—but his lack of rigor prevented him from seeing that his form of (4):

(8) $P(X-x;T) \underset{s}{\equiv}$

$\int_{-\infty}^\infty P(X-x-y;T-S)dP(y;S), 0 \leq S \leq T$

does have for solutions, along with the Gaussian distribution, all the other members of the Lévy-Khintchin family of infinitely-divisible distributions[7], including the stable distribution of Lévy-Pareto, the Poisson distribution, and various combinations of Poisson distributions.

The "Geometric or Relative Economic Brownian Motion"

As mentioned, Bachelier's absolute Brownian motion of (7) leads to negative values for X_{t+T} with strong probabilities. Hence, a better hypothesis for an economic model than $P(X,x;T) = P(X-x;T)$ is the following

(9) $P(X,x;T) \equiv P\left(\dfrac{X}{x};T\right), \quad x > 0$

$P(X,0;T) \equiv 1$ for all $X > 0.$

[7]Refs. [8], [9].

By working with ratios instead of algebraic differences, we consider logarithmic or percentage changes to be subject to uniform probabilities. This means that the first differences of the logarithms of prices are distributed in the usual absolute Brownian way. Since the arithmetic mean of logs is the geometric mean of actual prices, this modified random walk can be called the geometric Brownian motion in contrast to the absolute or arithmetic Brownian motion.

The log-normal distribution bears to the geometric Brownian motion the same relation that the normal distribution does to the ordinary Brownian motion. As the writings of Mandelbrot[8] and Fama[9] remind us, there are non-log-normal stable Pareto-Lévy distributions (of logs) satisfying the following form of (4):

$$(10) \quad P\left(\frac{X}{x};T\right) \equiv$$

$$\int_0^\infty P\left(\frac{X}{y};T\text{-}S\right) dP\left(\frac{y}{x},S\right).$$

Some of our general results require only that (1), (2), and (4) hold. But most of our explicit solutions are for multiplicative processes, in which (9), (10) and the following hold:

$$(11) \quad E[X_{t+T}|X_t] = \int_0^\infty X dP\left(\frac{X}{X_t};T\right)$$

$$= X_t e^{aT}, \quad \alpha \geq 0.$$

Actually, (9) and (10) alone require that the family $P(X;T)$ is determined once a single admissible function $P(X;T_1) = P(X)$ is given, as for $T_1 = 1$. Then if α is defined by

$$(12) \quad e^{aT_1} = E[X_{t+T_1}/X_t] = \int_0^\infty X dP(X),$$

(11) is provable as a theorem and need not be posited as an axiom. McKean's appendix assumes the truth of (9) and (10) throughout. It is known from the theory of infinitely-divisible processes that $P(X)$ above cannot be an arbitrary distribution but must have the characteristic function for its log, $Y = \log X$, of the Lévy-Khintchin form:

[8]Ref. [10].
[9]Ref. [11].

$$(13) \quad E[e^{i\lambda Y}] = \int_{-\infty}^\infty e^{i\lambda Y} dP(e^Y) = e^{g(\lambda)}$$

$$g(\lambda) = \mu i\lambda +$$

$$\int\left(e^{i\lambda z} - 1 - \frac{i\lambda z}{1+z^2}\right)\frac{1+z^2}{z^2} d\psi(z),$$

where $\psi(z)$ is itself a distribution function. In the special cases of the log-normal distribution, the log-Poisson distribution, and the log-Lévy distribution, we have respectively

$$g(\lambda) = \mu i\lambda - \frac{\sigma^2}{2}\lambda^2$$

$$(14) \quad g(\lambda) = e^{i\lambda\mu} - 1$$

$$g(\lambda) = \mu i\lambda - \gamma|\lambda|^{\alpha^\circ}[1 +$$

$$i\beta(\lambda/|\lambda|)\tan(\alpha^\circ\pi/2)], 0 \leq \alpha^\circ \leq 2.$$

All of (14) is on the assumption that

$$\lim_{X\to 0} P(X) = P(0) = 0.$$

If $P(0) > 0$, there is a finite probability of complete ruin in any time interval, and as the interval approaches infinity that probability approaches 1. An example (the only one for which *exact* formulas for rational warrant pricing of all durations are known) is given by

$$\text{Prob}\{X_{t+T} = X_t e^{aT}\} = e^{-bT} \quad a, b > 0$$

$$(15)$$

$$\text{Prob}\{X_{t+T} = 0\} = 1 - e^{-bT}$$

where $\alpha = a - b \geq 0$.

Letting $w(X;T)$ be an infinitely-divisible (multiplicative) function satisfying (13), the most general pattern would be one where

$$P(0,T) = 1 - e^{-bT} \qquad b > 0$$

$$(16) \quad P(X,T) = e^{-bT} w(X,t) + P(0,T)$$

with $P(\infty,T) = e^{-bT} 1 + 1 - e^{-bT} = 1.$

One final remark. Osborne, by an obscure argument that appeals to Weber-Fechner and to clearing-of-free-markets reasoning, purports to deduce, or make plausible, the axiom that the geometric mean of the distribution $P(X/x;T)$ is to be unity or that the expected value of the logarithmic difference is to be a random walk without mean bias or drift. Actually,

SAMUELSON

794

if $\alpha = 0$ in (2), so that absolute price is an unbiased martingale, the logarithmic difference must have a negative drift. For α sufficiently positive, and depending on the dispersion of the log-normal process, the logarithmic difference can have any algebraic sign for its mean bias. Only if one could be sure that $P(X/X;T) = P(1;T) \equiv \dfrac{1}{2}$, so that the chance of a rise in price could be known to be always the same as the chance of a fall in price, would the gratuitous Osborne condition turn out to be true.

If $P(X, x; T)$ corresponds to a martingale or "fair game," with $\alpha = 0$ as in the Bachelier case, the arithmetic mean of the ratio X/x is always exactly 1 and the geometric mean, being less than the arithmetic mean if P has any dispersion at all, is less than 1. Its logarithm, the mean or expected value of $\log X_{t+T}/X_t$ is then negative, and the whole drift of probability for $P(X,x;T)$ shifts leftward or downward through time. In long enough time, the probability approaches certainty that the investor will be left with less than 1 cent of net worth— i.e., $P(0+,x;\infty) = 1$. This virtual certainty of almost-complete ruin bothers many writers. They forget, or are not consoled by, the fact that the gains of those (increasingly few) people who are not ruined grow prodigiously large—in order to balance the complete ruin of the many losers. Therefore, many writers are tempted by Osborne's condition, which makes the expected median of price X_{t+T} neither grow above nor decline below X_t.

However, in terms of present discounted value of future price, $X_{t+T}e^{-\alpha T}$, where the mean yield α is used as the discount factor, most people's net worth does go to zero, and this occurs *in every case of* $\alpha \geq 0$. Relative to the expected growth of X_{t+T}— i.e., relative to $X_t e^{\alpha T}$, X_{t+T} does become negligible with great probability. I call this condition "relative ruin," with the warning that a man may be comfortably off and still be ruined in this sense. And I now state the following general theorem:

Theorem of virtual certainty of (relative) ruin: Let $P(X,x;T)$ have non-zero dispersion, satisfying

$$\int_0^\infty X \, dP(X,x;T) \equiv e^{\alpha T},$$

$$P(X,x;T) =$$
$$\int_0^\infty P(X,y; T-S)\,dP(y,x;S), \quad \alpha \geq 0$$

as in (2) and (4). Then

$$\lim_{T\to\infty} P(X e^{-\alpha T}, x; T) = 1$$

for all $(X,x) > 0$

In the multiplicative-process case, $P(X, x; T) = P(X/x; T)$ and the theorem follows almost directly from the fact that the geometric mean is less than the arithmetic mean.

In words, the theorem says that, with the passage of ever longer time, it becomes more and more certain that the stock will be at a level whose present discounted value (discounted at the expected yield α of the stock) will be less than 1 cent, or one-trillionth of a cent.

As is discussed on page 30, we can replace relative ruin by absolute ruin whenever the dispersion of the log-normal process becomes sufficiently large. Thus, even if $\alpha > 0$ in accordance with positive expected yield, whenever the parameter of dispersion $\sigma^2 > 2\alpha$, there is virtual certainty of absolute ruin. Indeed, for the log-normal case we can sharpen the theorem to read

$$\lim_{T\to\infty} P(0+, x; T) = 1, \quad \sigma^2 > 2\alpha$$

Summary of Probability Model

The X_{t+T} price of the common stock is assumed to follow a probability distribution dependent in Markov fashion on its X_t price alone and on the elapsed time:

(1) $\text{Prob}\{X_{t+T} \leq X | X_t\} = P(X, X_t; T)$

(4) $P(X_{t+T}, X_t; T) \equiv$
$$\int_0^\infty P(X_{t+T}, x; T\text{-}S)\,dP(x, X_t; S), \ 0 \leq S \leq T$$

with the expected value of price assumed to have a constant mean percentage growth per unit time of α, or

(2) $E[X_{t+T}|X_t] = X_t e^{\alpha T} =$
$$\int_0^\infty X \, dP(X, X_t; T), \quad \alpha \geq 0.$$

In many cases $P(X,x;T)$ will be assumed to be a multiplicative process, with the ratio X_{t+T}/X_t independent of all X_{t-w}. Then we can write

$$P(X,x;T) \equiv P\left(\frac{X}{x};T\right),$$

where $P(u;T)$ belongs to the special family of infinitely-divisible (multiplicative) distributions of which the log-normal, log-Poisson, and log-Lévy functions are special cases. (If the Lévy coefficient α° in (14), which must not be confused with α of (2), were not 2 as in the log-normal case, we can show that α in (2) will be infinite. Ruling out that case will rule out the Lévy-Pareto-Mandelbrot distributions.)

Arbitrage Conditions on Warrant Prices

A warrant is a contract that permits one to buy one share of a given common stock at some stipulated exercise price X° (here assumed to be unchangeable through time, unlike certain real-life changing-terms contracts) at any time during the warrant's remaining length of life of T time periods. Thus, a warrant to buy Kelly, Douglas stock at $4.75 per share until November, 1965, has $X^{\circ} = \$4.75$ and (in March, 1965) has $T = 7/12$ years. A perpetual warrant to buy Allegheny Corporation at $3.75 per share has $X^{\circ} = \$3.75$ and $T = \infty$.

When a warrant is about to expire and its $T = 0$, its value is only its actual conversion value. If the stock now has $X_t = X^{\circ}$, with the common selling at the exercise price to anyone whether or not he has a warrant, the warrant is of no value. If $X_t < X^{\circ}$, *a fortiori* it is worth nothing to have the privilege of buying the stock at *more* than current market price, and the warrant is again worthless. Only if $X_t > X^{\circ}$ is the expiring warrant of any value, and—brokerage charges being always ignored—it is then worth the positive difference $X_t - X^{\circ}$.

In short, arbitrage alone gives the rational price of an expiring warrant with $T = 0$, as the following function of the common price known to be $X_t = X$, $F(X,T) = F(X,0)$, where

$F(X,0) = \text{Max}[0, X - X^{\circ}]$.

A warrant good for $T_1 > 0$ periods is worth at least as much as one good only for $T_2 < T_1$ periods and generally is worth

more. Hence, arbitrage will ensure that the rational price for a warrant with T_1 time to go, denoted by $F(X,T_1)$, will satisfy

$$F(X,T_1) \geqq F(X,T_2) \quad \text{if} \quad T_1 \geqq T_2.$$

A perpetual warrant is one for which $T = \infty$. But recall that outright ownership of the common stock, aside from giving the owner any dividends the stock declares, is equivalent to having a perpetual warrant to buy the stock (from himself!) at a zero exercise price. Hence, a perpetual warrant cannot now sell for more than the current price of the common stock Or, in general, arbitrage requires that

$$(17) \quad X \geqq F(X,\infty) \geqq F(X,T_1) \geqq$$
$$F(X,T_2) \geqq F(X,0) = \text{Max}[0, X-X^{\circ}]$$

where

$$\infty \geqq T_1 \geqq T_2 \geqq 0.$$

In all that follows we shall, by an admissible choice of conventional units, be able to assume that the exercise price is $X^{\circ} = 1$. Thus, instead of working with the price of one actual Kelly, Douglas warrant, which gives the right to buy one share of Kelly, Douglas common stock at $4.75, we work with the standardized variable $X/X^{\circ} = X/4.75$—the number of shares purchasable at $1, which is of course $1/4.75$ actual shares; correspondingly, the warrant price Y_t we work with is not the actual Y_t but the standardized variable Y_t/X°, which represents the price of a warrant that enables the holder to buy $1/4.75$ actual shares at the exercise price of $1. We are able to do this by the following homogeneity property of competitive arbitrage:

$$(18) \quad \frac{F(X,X^{\circ};T)}{X^{\circ}} \equiv F\left(\frac{X}{X^{\circ}},1;T\right),$$

a property that says no more than that two shares always cost just twice one share. Wherever we write $F(X;T)$, we shall really be meaning (18). (Note that Tri-Continental perpetual warrants involve the right to buy 1.27 shares at $17.76 per share. In calculating $X/X^{\circ} = X/17.76$, we use for X the price of 1.27 shares, not of one share.)

Our conventions with respect to units ought to be adopted by advisory services dealing with warrants, to spare the reader

SAMUELSON

the need to calculate X/X° and Y/Y°. All this being understood, we can rewrite the fundamental inequalities of arbitrage shown in (17) as follows:

$$(19) \quad X \geqq F(X,\infty) \geqq F(X,T_1)$$
$$\geqq F(X,T_2) \geqq F(X,0)$$
$$= \text{Max}(0,X\text{-}1), \infty \geqq T_1 \geqq T_2 \geqq 0.$$

In Figures 1a and 1b, the outer limits are shown in heavy black: OAB is the familiar function $\text{Max}(0,X\text{-}1)$. (In McKean's appendix, this is written in the notation $(X\text{-}1)^+$.) The 45° line OZ represents the locus whose warrant price equals X, the price of the common stock itself.

Axiom of Expected Warrant Gain

Mere arbitrage can take us no further than (19). The rest must be experience—the recorded facts of life. Figure 1a shows one possible pattern of warrant pricing. The expiring warrant, with $T = 0$, must be on the locus given by OAB. If positive length of life remains, $T > 0$, Figure 1a shows the warrant always to be worth more than its exercise price: thus, OCD lies above OAB for all positive X; because OEF has four times the length of life of OCD, its value at $X = 1$ is about twice as great—in accordance with the rule-of-thumb $\sqrt{T}$ approximation; because T is assumed small, and $P(X/x;T)$ approximately symmetrical around $X/x = 1$, the slope at C is about ½—in accordance with the rule-of-thumb approximation that if two warrants differ only in their exercise price X°, the owner should pay \$1/2 for each \$1 reduction in X°, this being justifiable by the reasoning that there is only a half-chance that he will end up exercising at all and benefitting by the X° reduction. Note that all the curves in the figures are convex (from below) and all but the OAB and OZ limits are drawn to be strictly convex (as would be the case if $P(u;1)$ were log-normal or a distribution with continuous probability density). Our task is to demonstrate rigorously that the functions shown in the figures are indeed the only possible rational pricing patterns.

The pricing of a warrant becomes definite once we know the probability distribution of its common stock $P(X,x;T)$ if we pin down buyers' reactions to the implied probability distribution for the warrant's price $Y_t(T_t)$, in the form of the following axiom:

Axiom of mean expectation. Whereas the common stock is priced so that its mean expected percentage growth rate per unit time is a nonnegative constant α, the warrant is priced so that it, too, will have a constant mean expected percentage growth rate per unit time for as long as it pays to hold it, the value of the constant being at least as great as that for the stock—or $\beta \geqq \alpha$. Mathematically

$$(20) \quad E[Y_{t+T}(T_t - T) | Y_t(T_t)] = e^{\beta T}Y(T_t)$$

for all times T it pays to hold the warrant, where

$$(21) \quad \beta \geqq \alpha = \log_e \int_0^\infty XdP(X, x; 1) \geqq 0.$$

The reader should be warned that the expected value for the warrant in (20) is more complicated than the expected value of the stock in (2). The latter holds for any prescribed time period; but in (20), the time period T must be one in which it pays to have the warrant held rather than converted. (In the appendix, McKean's corresponding expectation is given in 2.8 and in 4.8.) It is precisely when the warrant has risen so high in price (above C_T in Figure 1b) that it can no longer earn a stipulated positive excess β-α over the stock that it *has* to be converted. Actually if β is stipulated to equal α, we are in Figure 1a rather than Figure 1b: there is never a need to convert before the end of life, and hence all points like $C_1, \ldots C_T$ are at infinity; as we shall see, the conventional linear integral equations enable us easily to compute the resulting functions in Figure 1a.

Warrants, unlike calls, are not protected against the payment of dividends by the common stock. Hence, for any stock that pays a positive dividend, say at the instantaneous rate of δ times its market value, the warrant will have to have a $\beta > \alpha$ if it is to represent as good a buy as the stock itself. Taxes and peculiar subjective reactions to the riskiness patterns of the two securities aside, at the least $\beta = \alpha + \delta > \alpha$. However, even if $\delta = 0$ and there is no dividend, buyers may feel that the volatility pattern of warrants is such that owners must be paid a greater mean return to hold warrants than to hold stocks. I do not pretend to give a theory from which one

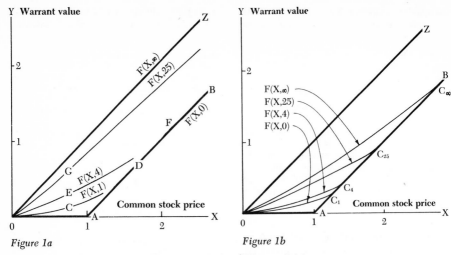

Figure 1a   Figure 1b

Figure 1   Rational Warrant Pricing

These graphs show the general pattern of warrant pricing as a function of the common stock price (where units have been standardized to make the exercise price unity). The longer the warrant's life T, the higher is $F(X,T)$. For fixed T, $F(X,T)$ is a convex function of X. In Figure 1a, the perpetual warrant's price is equal to that of the stock, with $F(X,\infty)$ falling on OZ; it never pays to exercise such a warrant. In Figure 1b,

the points C_1, C_1, C_{25}, and C_x on AB are the points at which it pays to convert a warrant with $T = 1$, 4, 25 and ∞ years to run. Note that $F(X,\infty)$ is much less than X in this case. The pattern of Figure 1b will later be shown to result from the hypothesis that a warrant must have a mean yield β greater than the stock's mean yield α.

---

can deduce the relative values of β and α. Here, I merely postulate that they are constants (independent, incidentally, of T, the life span of the warrant).

My whole theory rests on the axiomatic hypotheses:
1. The stock price is a definite probability distribution, $P(X,x;T)$, with constant mean expected growth per unit time $\alpha \geq 0$.
2. The warrant's price, derivable from the stock price, must earn a constant mean expected growth per unit time, $\beta \geq \alpha \geq 0$.

Once these axioms, the numbers α, β, and the form of $P(X,x;T)$ are given, it becomes a determinate mathematical problem to work out the rational warrant price functions $Y_t(T_t) = F(X_t, T_t)$ for all non-negative T_t, including the perpetual warrant $F(X_t, \infty)$.

Some Intuitive Demonstrations

Before giving the mathematical solutions, I shall indicate how one can deduce the

paradoxical result that a perpetual warrant must have the same price as the common stock if they both have to earn the same mean yield. The reader may want to think of the fair-game case where $\beta = \alpha = 0$, a case which has a disproportionate fascination for economists because they wrongly think that if prices were known to be biased toward rising in the future, that fact would already be "discounted" and the price would already have risen to the point where α can be expected to be zero. (What is forgotten here by Bachelier and others—but not by Keynes, Houthakker, Cootner[10], and other exponents of "normal backwardation"—is that time may involve money, opportunity cost, and risk aversion.)

A warrant is said to involve "leverage" in comparison with the common stock, and in the real world where brokerage charges

---

[10]Refs. [12], [13], [14], [15], [16]. See my cited companion paper in this issue.

SAMUELSON

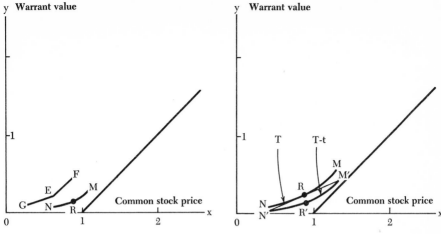

Figure 2   Warrant Pricing—The Perpetual Case

and imperfect capital rationing are involved, leverage can make a difference. The exact meaning of leverage is not always clear, and writers use the term in two distinct senses. The usual sense is merely one of *percentage* volatility. Suppose a stock is equally likely to go from $10 to $11 or to $9. Suppose its warrant is equally likely to go from $5 to $6 or to $4. Both are subject to a $1 swing in either direction; but $1 on $5 is twice the percentage swing of $1 on $10, as will be seen if equal dollars were invested in each security. In this sense, the warrant would be said to have twice the leverage of the stock. Leverage in the sense of mere enhanced percentage variability is a two-edged sword: as much as it works for you on the upside, it works against you on the downside. It is perfectly compatible with $\alpha = \beta = 0$. (However, if there were a two-thirds chance of each security's going up $1 and a one-third chance of its going down $1, the warrant's β would be definitely greater than stock's α, since a mean expected return of $+33\ 1/3$¢ on $5 is twice that of $+33\ 1/3$¢ on $10; and this impinges on the second sense of leverage.)

The second sense of the term leverage is merely enhanced expected yield from the warrant in comparison with the common stock. Here is an example from the R.H.M. Warrant and Stock Survey of February 25, 1965: Newconex Holdings Warrant, To-

ronto Exchange, "would rise about 2.25 times as fast as the common stock on the upside and decline no faster than the common on the downside." To one who believes this, the warrant offers very good value or "leverage" in this second sense of the term. Indeed, by selling one common short and buying one warrant, one could presumably break even if the stock went down in price and make money if the stock rises—a sure-thing hedge that cannot lose if one believes the stated probability judgment.

Figure 2 shows for a hypothetical perpetual warrant a convex corner at the existing price E, with EF steeper for a rise than EG for a fall. Obviously, GEF could not persist if the warrant's β gain were to be no bigger than the stock's α gain. Similarly, the strongly convex NRM could not persist with $\beta = \alpha$. What pattern for a perpetual warrant could persist? Only a straight-line pattern, since for any convexity at all the mean of points along a curve must lie above the curve itself.

What straight line can be fitted in between OZ and OAB of Figure 1? Obviously, only the line OZ itself—proving that the only rational price for a perpetual warrant must be that of the common stock itself when $\alpha = \beta$. (Any straight line not parallel to OZ and AB will intersect one or both of them; any intermediate line parallel to OZ and AB will hit the zero axis at positive X

RATIONAL THEORY

and then develop a corner there. So OZ alone remains as the formula for $F(X,\infty) \equiv X$.)

The curve of $F(X,T)$ for finite T can and will be convex. But as time passes, one does not move up and down the curve itself—say from R to M if X rises or from R to N if X falls. Instead, as time passes T diminishes, and one moves from R to a point below M or N on the new $F(X,T-t)$ curve; and if the two convex curves have been sketched correctly and placed in the proper shift relationship to each other, it will be found that the mean expectation of gain from the warrant is precisely that from the stock.

The moral of this is not that surveys are wrong when they recommend a bargain. It is rather that one recognizes correct or rational pricing and the absence of bargains when the warrants are priced in a certain way relative to the common stock. It is only as people act to take advantage of transient bargain opportunities that the bargains disappear. When I speak of rational or correct pricing, I imply no normative approval of any particular pattern but merely describe that pattern which (if it were to come into existence and were known to prevail) would continue to reproduce itself while fulfilling the postulated mean expectations in the form of α in (2) and β in (20). It would be a valuable empirical exercise to measure the α for different stocks at different times and deduce the value of β that the warrants earn *ex post* and that can rationalize the observed scatter of warrant and stock prices.

Intuition can carry us a bit further and throw light on the case where $\beta > \alpha$. With the warrant having to produce a better gain than the common, the curve for a perpetual warrant becomes strictly convex—as in Figure 1b and in contrast to Figure 1a. Furthermore, when the common price becomes very high compared to the exercise price—i.e., when X/1 is very large—the conversion value of the warrant becomes negligibly less than the common—i.e., $(X-1)/X = 1$. If in the period ahead the warrant can rise at most $1 more in price than the common rises, the warrant's gain will approach indefinitely close to the common's α. But that contradicts the assumption that $\beta > \alpha$. So for X high enough, $X > C_\infty < \infty$, it will never pay to hold

the warrant in the expectation of getting $\beta > \alpha$; above this C_x cut-off point, the warrant must be converted. What has been demonstrated here for perpetual warrants holds *a fortiori* for finite warrants with finite T. Even sooner, at $C_T < C_x$, it will pay to convert since with the clock running on and running out, there will be even less advantage in holding the warrant for an additional period when the stock and it have become very large.

Linear Analysis where $\beta = \alpha \geq 0$

If the expected yields of common and warrant are to be the same in (2) and (20), there is never any advantage in converting the warrant before the end of its life. That is

$$(22)\quad F(X,T) > F(X,0) = \text{Max}(0,X\text{-}1),$$

$$T > 0; \quad \beta = \alpha \geq 0.$$

Equation (20), postulating that the warrant have an expected gain per unit time of β, can therefore be written, for all times S,

$$(23)\quad E[Y_{t+s}(T\text{-}S) = F(X_{t+s},T\text{-}S)$$

$$|Y_t(T) = F(X_t,T)]$$

$$= e^{\beta S}F(X_t,T) = \int_0^\infty F(X,T\text{-}S)\,dP(X,X_t;S)$$

or

$$(24)\quad F(x,T) \equiv e^{-\beta S}\int_0^\infty F(X,T\text{-}S)\,dP(X,x;S)$$

$$= e^{-\beta T}\int_0^\infty F(X,0)\,dP(X,x;T)$$

$$= e^{-\beta T}\int_1^\infty (X\text{-}1)\,dP(X,x;T).$$

This last integral equation provides, by a quadrature, the solution of our problem. From the fact that $P(X,x;0) = 1, X > x$ and $= 0, X < x$, it is evident that

$$\lim_{T\to 0} F(x,T) = F(x,0) = \text{Max}(0,x\text{-}1).$$

We can now prove that

$$(25)\quad \lim_{T\to\infty} F(x,T) = x = F(x,\infty), \quad \beta = \alpha \geq 0.$$

Substitute $F(x,\infty) = F(x)$ into both sides of (24) to get a self-determining integral equation for $F(x)$,

$$(26)\quad F(x) = e^{-\beta S}\int_0^\infty F(X)\,dP(X,x;S).$$

The substitution $F(x) = x$ does satisfy

SAMUELSON

800

(26), since by (2)

$$x = e^{-\beta S} \int_0^\infty X dP(X,x;S)$$

(27)
$$= e^{-\beta S} e^{\alpha S} x = e^{(\alpha-\beta)S} x = x, \quad \beta = \alpha.$$

Any kx would also satisfy (26), but only for $k = 1$ do we satisfy

$$x \geq F(x) = kx \geq Max(0,x-1).$$

To prove that the stationary solution of (26) does in fact fulfill the limit of (25), rewrite (24)

$$F(x,T) = e^{-\beta T} \int_1^\infty (X-1) dP(X,x;T)$$

$$= e^{-\beta T} \int_0^\infty (X-1) dP(X,x;T) +$$

$$e^{-\beta T} \frac{\int_0^1 (1-X) dP(X,x;T)}{\int_0^1 dP(X,x;T)} \int_0^1 dP(X,x;T)$$

(28)
$$= e^{-\beta T} e^{\alpha T} x - e^{-\beta T}$$

$$+ e^{-\beta T} \theta_1(x,T) \theta_2(x,T),$$

where $|\theta_i| \leq 1$.

Obviously, if $\beta = \alpha > 0$, $F(x,\infty) = x + 0$, as was to be proved. For $\alpha = 0$

$$\lim_{\alpha \to \infty} \theta_2(x,T) =$$

$$\int_0^1 dP(X,x;\infty) = 1, \text{ since } P(0+, x; \infty) \equiv 1$$

(29)
$$\lim_{t \to \infty} \theta_1(x,T) =$$

$$\frac{\int_0^1 (1-X) dP(X,x;\infty)}{\int_0^1 dP(X,x;\infty)} = 1,$$

$$\text{since } P(0+, x; \infty) \equiv 1$$

Hence, for $\alpha = 0 = \beta$, $F(x,\infty) = x-1+1 = x$, as required.

Now that (24) gives the explicit solution in the case $\alpha = \beta$, we can put in for $P(X,x;T)$ any specialization, such as

$$P(X,x;T) = P(X/x;T) \text{ log-normal with}$$

(30)
$$P(x;T) = N(\log x; \mu t, \sigma\sqrt{t}) \text{ where}$$

$$N(y;0,1) = N(y) = \frac{1}{\sqrt{2\pi}} \int_{-\infty}^y e^{-u^2/2} du;$$

or

$$\text{Prob}\left\{ \frac{X}{x} = e^{at} \right\} = e^{-bt}$$

(31)

$$\text{Prob}\left\{ \frac{X}{x} = 0 \right\} = 1 - e^{-bt}$$

$$a - b = \alpha = \beta; \ a,b > 0.$$

For this last case, (24) calculates out to

(32) $$F(x,T) = Max(0,x - e^{-aT}).$$

Note that the $\sqrt{T}$ law does not hold true here for small T, but rather, at $x = 1$

(33) $$F(x,T) = F(1,T) = 1 - e^{-at} =$$

$$1 - 1 + aT + \text{remainder } (T^2) \doteq aT.$$

Hence, a warrant for twice the duration of a short-lived warrant should be worth about twice as much when (31) holds—even though the ratios X_{t+T}/X_t are strictly independent.

Valuation of End-of-Period Warrants

The exact solution of (24) holds only for the case $\beta = \alpha \geq 0$. It will be shown that new formulas must handle the case of $\beta > \alpha$. However, the simple integral (24) does give a solution under all cases to the simpler case of a warrant that can be exercised *only* at the end of the period T. We might call this a "European warrant" by analogy with the "European call," which, unlike the American call that is exercisable at any time from now to T, is exercisable only at a specified terminal date.

Obviously, the additional American option of early conversion can do the owner no harm, and it may help him. Denote the rational price of a European warrant by $f(x,T)$, in contrast to $F(x,T)$ of the American type warrant. Then

(34) $$f(x,T) \leq F(x,T), \ 0 \leq T$$

and our axiom of expected gain (20) is now applicable in the form that gives the last version of (24), namely

(35)

$$f(x,T) = e^{-\beta T} \int_0^\infty Max(0,X-1) dP(X,x;T)$$

$$= e^{-\beta T} \int_1^\infty (X-1) dP(X,x;T), \ \beta \geq \alpha \geq 0.$$

Since this is the same formula as held in (24) for $F(x,T)$ when $\beta = \alpha$, we note that in such a case the American warrant's early conversion options are actually of no market value; or

(36) $f(x,T) \equiv F(x,T)$ if $\beta = \alpha$.

When $\beta > \alpha$, (35) still holds. But now

(37) $f(x,T) < F(x,T)$

for all or some positive (x,T). In the log-normal case, the strong inequality must always hold.

There seems to be a misapprehension concerning this inequality. Thus some people argue that the owner of a European call or warrant can in effect exercise it early by selling the stock short, thereby putting himself in the position of the owner of an American warrant. If this view were valid there would be no penalty to be subtracted from $F(x,T)$ to get true $f(x,T)$. Such a vew is simply wrong—as wrong as the naive view that giving your broker a stop-loss order gives you the same protection as buying a put. (The fallacy here has naught to do with the realistic fact that in a bad market break your broker will not be able to execute your stop-loss order at the stipulated price; waive that point. Suppose I buy a stock at $100 and protect it by buying (say for $10) a six-month put on it at exercise price of $100. You buy the stock and merely give your broker a stop-loss sell order at just below $100. If the stock drops below $100 at some intermediate time during the next six months, you are sold out without loss; but you do as well as I do only if the stock never subsequently rises to above $100; and the $10 cost of the put is precisely the market value of my opportunity to make a differential profit over you in case the stock does end up at more than $100, after at least once dipping below $100.) By the vector calculus that Kruizenga and I worked out for various options, after one sells a stock short and still holds a European call or warrant on it, he is not for the remainder of the time T in the position of a man who has sold out his American warrant; instead he is in the net position of holding a put on the stock. (If $(1,0)$ and $(0,1)$ represent holding a call and put respectively, the owner of an American warrant goes through

the cycle $(+1,0)$ and—in midstream— $(-1,0)$, ending up with $(0,0)$. The holder of the European warrant goes through the cycle $(+1,0)$ and—in midstream— $(-1,+1)$, leaving him for the remainder of the period with $(0,+1)$.)

To see that (37) does hold when $\beta > \alpha$, recall that $F(x,T)$ cannot decrease with T. But applying to (35) the version of (24) given in (28), we can see that a long-lived European warrant does ultimately approach zero in value as $T \to \infty$. Thus, by (28) applied to $f(x,T)$,

(38)
$$f(x,T) = e^{-\beta T} \int_1^\infty (X\text{-}1)\,dP(X,x;T)$$
$$= e^{-\beta T}e^{\alpha T}x - e^{-\beta T} + e^{-\beta T}\,\theta_1\theta_2,$$
$$|\theta_1| < 1$$
$$\lim_{T \to \infty} f(x,T) = f(x,\infty) = f(x) =$$
$$e^{-(\beta-\alpha)\infty}x = 0,\ \beta > \alpha \geqq 0.$$

General Formula for $\beta > \alpha \geqq 0$

The last section's demonstration that $f(x,T) < F(x,T)$ when $\beta > \alpha$ provides a rigorous proof that the linear integral equation of (24) cannot apply to the proper $F(x,T)$ for this case. Hence $\beta > \alpha$ does imply that a warrant cannot possibly be worth holding at very high prices. I.e., the inequality

(39) $F(x,T) \geqq x - 1,\quad x \geqq 1$

must for sufficiently high x become the equality

(40) $F(x,T) = x - 1,$
$$x > C_\alpha(T;\beta,\alpha) < \infty,\ \beta > \alpha$$

where $\partial C_x/\partial T \geqq 0$, $\partial C_x/\partial \alpha \geqq 0$, $\partial C_x/\partial \beta \leqq 0$. (McKean's appendix also proves this fact, in 2.8 and 4.7.)

In place of the integral equation (24), we have the following basic inequality to define $F(x,T)$ where $\beta > \alpha$:

(41) $x \geqq F(x,T) \geqq \mathrm{Max}[0, x\text{-}1,$
$$e^{-\beta S}\int_0^\infty F(X,T\text{-}S)\,dP(X,x;S)\,]$$

McKean's appendix terms any solution of this relation an "excessive function," and he seeks as the solution to the problem the *minimum* function that belongs to this class. Rather than arbitrarily postulate that it is the minimum function which constitutes the desired solution, I deduce from my axiom of expected gain (20) the only solution which satisfies it and which satisfies the basic inequality. It follows as a provable theorem that this does indeed give the minimum of the excessive functions. That is, any excessive function which is not the minimum will fail to earn β per unit time whenever it is being held.

How shall we find the simultaneous solution to (20) and (41)? I begin from the intuitive consideration that splitting up continuous time into small enough finite intervals will approach (from below) the correct solution for the continuous case. If a warrant can be converted only every hour, its value will be a bit less than one that can be converted at any time—less because an extra privilege is presumably worth something, only a little less because not much of a price change is to be expected in a time period so short as an hour. The approximation will be even better if we split time up into discrete minutes and still better if we use seconds. In the limit, we get the exact solution.

Let $\Delta T = h$ and define recursively in (41) for fixed h and integral n

(42)

$$F_{n+1}(x;h) =$$

$$\text{Max}[\,(0, x-1, e^{-\beta h} \int_0^\infty F_n(X;h) dP(X,x;h)\,]$$

$$F_0(x;h) = \text{Max}\,(0, x-1).$$

Then

(43)
$$\lim_{\substack{h = \frac{T}{n} \to 0}} F_n(x;h) = F(x,T),$$

the desired exact solution to our problem as formulated by (20) and (41). In principle, by enough integrations, the degree of approximation can be made as close as we like.

The general properties of the solution can also be established by this procedure. Thus, if $P(X,x;1) = P(X/x;1)$ is a multiplicative process—or even if some weaker conditions are put on the way that P shrinks with an increase in x—we begin with a convex function $F_0(x;h)$ and end at each stage with a convex expectation function. Hence, by induction $F(x,T)$ and $F(x) = F(x,\infty)$ must be convex. ($F(x,T)$ will be strictly convex if $P(X/x;1)$ is log-normal

or similarly smooth.) Where the slope $\partial F_n(x;h) \partial x$ exists it can be shown inductively that its value must lie in the closed interval [0,1], a property which must hold for $F(x,T)$. At the critical conversion point C_T, where $C_T - 1 = F(C_T,T)$, one expects the slopes of the two equal branches to be equal.

It will be instructive to work through an example in which time itself is divided into small, discrete intervals $t = 0, 1, 2, \ldots$, etc. And suppose that $P(X,x;1)$ corresponds to a simple, multiplicative random walk of martingale type, where

$$\text{Prob}\left\{\frac{X_{t+1}}{X_t} = \lambda > 1\right\} = p > 0,$$

$$\text{Prob}\left\{\frac{X_{t+1}}{X_t} = \lambda^{-1}\right\} = 1 - p = q > 0.$$

The gain per unit time is now given by

$$e^\alpha = p\lambda + q\lambda^{-1} = 1, \quad \text{where } \lambda = \frac{1-p}{p}.$$

It will help to keep some simple numbers in mind: e.g. $p = 1/3$, $q = 2/3$, $\lambda = 2$, making $\alpha = 0$ and the $[X_t]$ sequence a "fair game" or martingale, with zero net expected yield.

If β is also set equal to zero, so that it never pays to exercise the warrant, (41) reduces to the simple form (35), and we are left with the familiar partial-difference equation of the classical random walk (but in terms of $\log_\lambda X_t$, not X_t itself). Specifically, $\log_\lambda X_t/X_0$ will take on only integral values for $t > 0$; if later we make λ nearer and nearer to 1, the fineness of the grid of integral values will increase; and it will cause little loss of generality to suppose that initially $X_0 = \lambda^k$, where k is a positive or negative integer. This being assured, a two-way $F(X,m) = F(\lambda^n,m)$ can always be written as a two-way sequence F_{nm}, where m denotes non-negative integers and n integers that can be positive, negative, or zero. Corresponding to (35), we now have:

$$F_{n0} = \text{Max}(0, \lambda^n - 1)$$

$$F_{n1} = pF_{n+1,0} + q\,F_{n-1,0}, p + q = 1$$

$$\cdots \cdots \cdots \cdots \cdots \cdots$$

$$F_{n,m+1} = pF_{n+1,m} + qF_{n-1,m}$$

$$\cdots \cdots \cdots \cdots \cdots \cdots$$

$$F_{n\infty} = F_n = pF_{n+1} + qF_{n-1}.$$

The last of these is an ordinary second-order difference equation with constant coefficients, whose characteristic polynomial is seen to be

$$p\sigma^2 - \sigma + (1-p) = p(\sigma-1)(\sigma-\sigma_2),$$

$$\text{where } \sigma_2 = \frac{1-p}{p} = \lambda > 1.$$

Write the general solution for F_n as

$$F_n = c_1(1)^n + c_2\sigma_2^n$$

Since $F_n \to 0$ as $n \to -\infty$, we must have $c_1 = 0$. Since

$$\text{Max}(0, X-1) = \text{Max}(0, \lambda^n - 1)$$

$$\leq F(X) = c_2\lambda^n \leq \lambda^n = X,$$

we must have

$$c_2 = 1, \quad F_n = \lambda^n, \quad F(X) = X$$

verifying the general derivation of (25).

Now drop the assumption that $\alpha = 0$, but still keep $\beta = \alpha$. The above partial-difference equations are unchanged except that now (p,q) are replaced by (Bp, Bq) where

$$B^{-1} = e^a = p\lambda + q\lambda^{-1} > 1.$$

Again it can be shown that $\sigma_2 = \lambda$ is a root of the characteristic polynomial, and that only if $(c_1, c_2) = (0, 1)$ can the boundary condition be satisfied. Again we confirm (35)'s $F(X) = X$ solution for $\alpha = \beta$.

Now let $B^{-1} = e^\beta > e^a = p\lambda + q\lambda^{-1} = \Phi(\lambda) \geq 1$.

For $m \leq \infty$, there will exist critical integral constants n_m, equal (except for the coarseness of the integral grid) to $\log_\lambda C_m$, above which warrant conversion is mandatory. The partial-difference equations derivable from (41) now become

$$F_{n,m} = \lambda^n - 1, \quad n \geq n_m > 0$$

$$F_{n,m} = BpF_{n+1,m-1} + BqF_{n-1,m-1}$$

$$\leq \lambda^n - 1, n < n_m, \quad (m = 1, 2, \ldots)$$

$$F_{n,\infty} = F_n = BpF_{n+1} + BqF_{n-1}, \quad n < n_\infty$$

$$= \lambda^n - 1, \quad n \geq n_\infty.$$

These relations define the sequence (n_m) recursively—e.g., n_1 is the lowest integer for which

$$\lambda^{n_1} - 1 \geq Bp(\lambda^{n_1}\lambda - 1) + Bq(\lambda^{n_1}\lambda^{-1} - 1).$$

With n_1 known, we have initial conditions to the right to determine $F_{n,1}$ for $n \leq n_1$. The difference equation for $F_{n,1}$, which can be written symbolically in terms of the operators E and E^{-1} defined by $E\,F_{n,m} = F_{n+1,m}$, $E^{-1}F_{nm} = F_{n-1,m}$ as $\Phi(E)F_{n,1} = 0$ then determines F_{n1}. With this known we determine n_2 as the smallest integer for which

$$\lambda^{n_2} - 1 \geq B\Phi(E)F_{n,1};$$

then determine $F_{n,2}$ by $\Phi(E)F_{n,2} = 0$, etc.

The constant n_x can be determined along with $F_{n,x}$ by the following relations

$$\Phi(E)F_n = 0; \quad F_n = c_1\sigma_1^n + c_2\sigma_2^n,$$

where the characteristic polynomial can be shown to be

$$\sigma\Phi(\sigma) - \sigma = Bp(\sigma-\sigma_1)(\sigma-\sigma_2),$$

where

$$0 < \sigma_1 < 1 < \lambda < \sigma_2 = \lambda^\gamma, \quad \gamma > 1.$$

If $F_n \to 0$ as $n \to -\infty$, $c_1 = 0$; to determine c_2 and $n_x = a$ for short, we set

$$c_2\lambda^{\gamma a}\lambda^\gamma = \lambda^a\lambda - 1, \quad c_2\lambda^{\gamma a} = \lambda^a - 1, \text{ or}$$

$$(\lambda^a - 1)\lambda^\gamma = \lambda^a\lambda - 1, \ (\lambda^\gamma - \lambda)\lambda^a = \gamma - 1$$

$$a = \log_\lambda(\gamma - 1) - \log_\lambda(\lambda^\gamma - \lambda),$$

$$c_2 = (\lambda^a - 1)\lambda^{-\gamma a},$$

where of course γ is a function of α and β through its dependence on the coefficients Bp and λ. $F_n = \lambda^{\gamma n}$ means in terms of X, the antilog of n, that $F(X) = cX^\gamma$, $\gamma \geq 1$ as our first general answer.

We can always convert one-period partial difference equations into N-period equations. When we do this (p,q) are replaced by $(p^2, 2pq, q^2)$, $\ldots$ and by $(p^N, {}_NC_1 p^{N-1}q, \ldots, q^N)$ where ${}_NC_i$ are the familiar binomial coefficients. By the usual central limit theorem, these approach the normal distribution. But since these coefficients apply to the $F_{n,m}$, which refer to the logarithms of X, we arrive at the log-normal distribution. Hence, if we can prove that the partial-difference equation, not merely for $\Phi(E)F_n = (BpE + BqE^{-1})F_n$ but for any general set of probabilities

$$\Phi(E)F_n = B \sum_{-k}^{+r} p_j E^j F_n = F_n, \ \sum_{-k}^{+r} p_j = 1,$$

SAMUELSON

satisfies the $F(X) = cX^\gamma$ power law, we have strong heuristic evidence that this will be the exact case for the log-normal case—as McKean has rigorously proved in the Appendix. The characteristic polynomial of this last becomes

$$-1 + \sigma^k \Phi(\sigma) = (\sigma - \sigma_1)(\sigma - \lambda^\gamma)\, \Phi_2(\sigma),$$

where, as before

$$0 < \sigma_1 < \lambda \leq \lambda^\gamma, \quad \gamma \geq 1$$

and $\Phi_2(\sigma)$ is a polynomial with no roots greater than 1 in absolute value. Hence, in the general solution

$$F_n = \Sigma c_j \sigma_j{}^n = c_2 \lambda^\gamma + \text{Remainder},$$

all the c's except c_2 must vanish if $F_{-x} \to 0$. The value of c_2 and the critical conversion point n_x is determined just as in the simple (p, q) case. If the grid is very fine because $\lambda \to 1$, $\lambda^{n_x} = c_x = \gamma/(\gamma - 1)$ to an increasingly good approximation.

As a preview to McKean's exact result for the continuous-time case, I shall sketch the usual Bachelier-Einstein derivation of the partial differential equations of probability diffusion—of so-called Fokker-Planck type—by applying a limit process to the discrete partial difference equations. From now on consider $n = \log x$ as if it were a continuous rather than integral variable. Bachelier wrote in 1900

$$p_{n,t} = \frac{1}{2} p_{n+1,\, t-1} + \frac{1}{2} p_{n-1,\, t-1},$$

or

$$p_{n,\, t+\Delta t} = \frac{1}{2} p_{n+\Delta n,\, t} + \frac{1}{2} p_{n\Delta n,\, t}$$

$$\frac{\Delta t}{(\Delta n)^2} \frac{p_{n,t+\Delta t} - p_{n,t}}{\Delta t} =$$

$$\frac{1}{2} \frac{(p_{n+\Delta n,\, t} - p_{n,t})}{(\Delta n)^2} +$$

$$\frac{1}{2} \frac{(p_{n-\Delta n,\, t} - p_{n,t})}{(\Delta n)^2}$$

Now if $\Delta t \to 0$, with $\Delta t/(\Delta n)^2 \to 2c^2$, we get the Fourier parabolic equation

$$c^2 \frac{\partial p(n,t)}{\partial t} = \frac{\partial^2 p(n,t)}{\partial n^2}$$

Bachelier assumed a fair game with probabilities of unit steps in either direction

equal to $1/2$. If we replace $(1/2, 1/2)$ by (p, q) so that the random walk has a biassed drift of α as its expected instantaneous rate of growth, we find $p(n - \alpha t, t)$ satisfying the above equation and hence the requisite distribution $r(n, t) \equiv p(n - \alpha t, t)$ satisfies

$$\frac{\partial^2 r(n,t)}{\partial n^2} = c^2 \frac{\partial r(n,t)}{\partial t} + c^2 \alpha \frac{\partial r(n,t)}{\partial n}$$

Bachelier and Einstein were talking about the diffusion of probabilities. But we have seen that the warrant prices $F_{n,t}$, now written as $F(e^n, t) = \psi(n,t)$, satisfy similar partial-difference equations, the only difference being i) that the coefficients add up to less than 1 when $\beta > \alpha$; and ii) the boundary conditions for c_t become rather complicated. Just as we had a simple second-order (partial) difference equation $E\Phi(E)F_{n,t} = EF_{n,t}$, we derive in the limit —as McKean shows in 3, and 5, drawing on the work of E. B. Dynkin—a simple (partial) second-order differential equation for $\psi(n,t)$, which in terms of $\log_e x = n$ becomes,

$$\frac{\sigma^2}{2} \frac{\partial^2 \Psi(n,t)}{\partial n^2} + \delta \frac{\partial \Psi(n,t)}{\partial n} - \frac{\partial \Psi(n,t)}{\partial t} -$$

$$\beta\Psi(n,t) \equiv 0, \quad \delta = \alpha - \frac{\sigma^2}{2}$$

$$\Psi(n,0) = \text{Max}(0, e^n - 1)$$

$$\Psi(\log c_t, t) = c_t - 1$$

It is understood that the equation holds for (n,t) to the left of $n = \log c_t$ and that $\Psi(-\infty, t) \equiv 0$. However, it is a difficult task to compute the c_t function, even using the high contact property $\partial F(c_t, t)/\partial x = 1$.

The perpetual warrant is much simpler, since then $\Psi(n, \infty) = \Psi(n)$ with $\partial \Psi(n, \infty)/\partial t = 0$, giving the *ordinary* differential equation

$$\frac{\sigma^2}{2} \Psi''(n) + \delta \Psi'(n) - \beta \Psi(n) = 0,$$

$$n < \log c_\infty$$

$$\Psi(-\infty) = 0, \quad \Psi(\log c_\infty) = c_\infty - 1,$$

$$\Psi'(\log c_\infty) = c_\infty$$

The general solution can be written as a sum of two exponentials, in terms of the roots of the characteristic polynomial

$$\frac{\sigma^2}{2}\rho^2 + \delta\rho - \beta = \frac{\sigma^2}{2}$$

$$(\rho - \rho_1)(\rho - \rho_2), \quad \rho_1 = \gamma > 1 > \rho_2$$

If the boundary conditions are to be realized, the ρ_2 root must be suppressed and we are left with

$$\Psi(n) = (c_x - 1)\frac{e^{n\gamma}}{c_x}, \text{ or}$$

$$F(x) = (c_x - 1)\left(\frac{x}{c_x}\right)^\gamma$$

$$\gamma = \frac{c_x}{c_x - 1}$$

Intuitive Proofs from Arbitrage

Equation (18), which related the rational price of a warrant with any exercise price X° to the formula for a warrant with $X^\circ \geq 1$, can be used directly to deduce restrictions on the way $F(x,T;X^\circ)$ varies with X°. Because $F(x,T)$ has been shown to be convex with numerical slope on the closed interval $[0,1]$, (18) can deduce that the numerical slope of $F(x,T;X^\circ)$ with respect to X° must be on the closed interval $[-1,0]$—i.e.,

$$-1 \leq$$
$$\frac{F(x,T;X^\circ + \Delta X^\circ) - F(x,T;X^\circ)}{\Delta X^\circ} \leq .0, \quad \text{or}$$

$$(44) \qquad -1 \leq \frac{\partial F(x,T;X^\circ)}{\partial X^\circ} \leq 0,$$

where the last partial derivatives, if they do not exist at certain corners, can be interpreted as either left-hand or right-hand derivatives.

One proves (44) directly by differentiating (18) with respect to X°, to get

$$(45) \qquad \frac{\partial F(x,T;X^\circ)}{\partial X^\circ} =$$

$$\frac{\partial}{\partial X^\circ}\left\{ X^\circ F\left(\frac{x}{X^\circ}, T\right)\right\} =$$

$$F\left(\frac{x}{X^\circ}, T\right) - \frac{x}{X^\circ}\frac{\partial F\left(\frac{x}{X^\circ}, T\right)}{\partial(x/X^\circ)}$$

That the right-hand expression in (45) is non-positive follows directly from the definition of convexity of $F(x,T)$ when $F(0,T) \equiv 0$. That it is not algebraically less than -1 follows from the fact that $F(x,T) \geq \text{Max}(0, x-1)$.

Intuitive economic arguments provide an alternative demonstration that

$$(46) \qquad -1 \leq \frac{\partial F(x,T;X^\circ)}{\partial X^\circ} \leq 0$$

An increase in the exercise price X° must, if anything, lower the value of the warrant since it then entails a higher future payment. But a fall of \$1 in X° can never be worth more than \$1, since stapling a \$1 bill to a warrant with X° exercise price is a possible way of making it the full equivalent of a warrant exercisable at $X^\circ - \$1$. Hence, we have established (46).

The condition for high contact at a conversion point C_T, namely $\partial F(x,T)/\partial x \to 1$ as $x \to C_T$, seems intuitively related to realization of left-hand equality in (46) as $x \to C_T/X^\circ$, which in turn seems intuitively related to the probability that, when x is already near C_T, x will be reaching C_t in a sufficiently short future time. For the log-normal Brownian motion of (30) and the special case of (31), these conditions for high contact will be realized. But for any solution of the Chapman-Kolmogorov equation (4) of log-Poisson type, like that discussed by McKean and involving jumps, high contact will definitely fail. If we rule out combinations of Poisson jumps, only (30) and (31) and combinations of them like that shown in (16) would seem to be relevant. For them high contact is indeed ensured. And for both of these types an exact power-of-x solution for the perpetual warrant has been shown by McKean to hold.

Final Exact Formula for Perpetual Warrant in Log-Normal Case

McKean has proved in (3.0) the following exact smooth formula for $F(x,\infty) = F(x)$, for the log-normal case

$$(47) \quad F(x) = \frac{(\gamma-1)^{\gamma-1}}{\gamma^\gamma}x^\gamma =$$

$$(c-1)\left(\frac{x}{c}\right)^\gamma, \quad x \leq c = \frac{\gamma}{\gamma-1} > 1$$

SAMUELSON

x	0	.25	.50	.75	1.0	1.25	1.50	1.75	2.0	2.5	3.0	3.5	4.0	4.5	5.0
$\frac{1}{4}x^2$	0	.016	.062	.141	.250	.391	.562	.766	1.0°	1.5°	2.0°	2.5°	3.0°	3.5°	4.0°
$2\left(\frac{x}{3}\right)^{3/2}$	0	.048	.136	.250	.385	.538	.707	.891	1.088	1.521	2.0°	2.5°	3.0°	3.5°	4.0°
$3\left(\frac{x}{4}\right)^{4/3}$	0	.074	.188	.322	.472	.636	.811	.996	1.190	1.603	2.044	2.511	3.0°	3.5°	4.0°
$4\left(\frac{x}{5}\right)^{5/4}$	0	.094	.225	.373	.535	.707	.888	1.078	1.572	1.682	2.112	2.561	3.026	3.506	4.0°

Figure 3   Rational Price for Perpetual Warrant in Log-Normal Model

[Explanation: $x = X/X°$, the common stock price ÷ exercise price. $y = Y/Y°$, warrant price ÷ exercise price is given by $y = (c - 1)(x/c)^\gamma$ where $\gamma = c/(c - 1)$; value of γ depends on α/σ^2 and β/σ^2 as given in Equation (48).]

° Warrant at conversion value, $x - 1$.

$$= x - 1, \quad x \gtrless c, \quad \gamma = \frac{c}{c - 1} > 1.$$

This has the nice property of high contact, with $F'(c) = 1$ from either direction. Examples of (47) for different values of γ would be

$$F(x) = 3 \left(\frac{x}{4}\right)^{4/3}, \quad \gamma = 4/3, \ c = 4$$

$$F(x) = 2 \left(\frac{x}{3}\right)^{3/2}, \quad \gamma = 3/2, \ c = 3$$

$$F(x) = \frac{1}{4}x^2 \quad , \quad \gamma = 2, \ c = 2$$

The last of these formulas has been proposed, in different notation, on a purely *ad hoc* empirical basis by Giguère.[11]

I append a brief *table of values* (Figure 3) of $F(x)$ for what would seem to be empirically relevant values of γ.° Figure 4 plots as straight lines on double-log paper $F(x)$ for various values of γ.

To relate γ to α, β, and the dispersion parameter σ^2 in the log-normal distribution,

I rewrite McKean's formula for γ (in the Appendix) as

$$(48) \quad \gamma = \left(\frac{1}{2} - \frac{\alpha}{\sigma^2}\right) + \sqrt{\left[\frac{1}{2} + \frac{\alpha}{\sigma^2}\right]^2 + 2\left[\frac{\beta}{\sigma^2} - \frac{\alpha}{\sigma^2}\right]}.$$

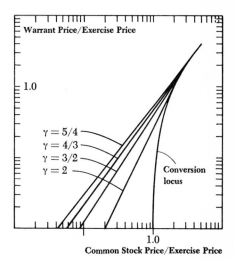

Warrant Price/Exercise Price

$\gamma = 5/4$
$\gamma = 4/3$
$\gamma = 3/2$
$\gamma = 2$

1.0

Conversion locus

1.0

Common Stock Price/Exercise Price

Figure 4   Rational Price for Perpetual Warrant in Log-Normal Model

[11]Ref. [17]. The notation there, of course, needs to be related to my notation involving $\dfrac{X}{X°}$ and $\dfrac{Y}{Y°}$, as in Figure 3.

°Acknowledgment is made to F. Skidmore for these computations.

That γ is a function of $(\alpha/\sigma^2, \beta/\sigma^2)$ follows from the invariance of the problem under transformations of the unit used to measure time. Similar ratios of parameters occur in the log-Poisson process and the multiplicative-translation-with-absorption process of (15).

It is instructive to hold (α,β) fixed in (48), and examine how γ varies with the dispersion parameter σ^2 of the log-normal process for the stock. When $\sigma^2 \to \infty$, the difference $(\beta - \alpha)/\sigma^2 \to 0$ and $\gamma \to 1$, the case where the warrant never gets prematurely converted. Such a large value for the dispersion parameter σ^2 would create a very large α if the drift of log X_t were not strongly negative. Any such negative drift implies that it is "almost certain" that the holder of the stock will be "eventually" ("almost completely") ruined—even though the stock does have a positive mean capital gain. Note the tricky statement involving a triple limit, as in the earlier theorem on (virtually) certain (relative) ruin.

We'll see in (50) that $\gamma = \sqrt{\beta/\alpha}$ when $\sigma^2 = 2\alpha$ and there is no drift at all to log X_t and hence to X_t. In this knife-edge case of Osborne, where the geometric mean of future X_{t+T} just equals X_t, the probability of a future capital loss (or gain) is exactly one half. At the other limit, where the dispersion $\sigma^2 \to 0$, we put $(\alpha/\sigma^2, \beta/\sigma^2) = (\infty,\infty)$ in (48) and find $\gamma \to \beta/\alpha$. This can be verified by substituting into $y = (c - 1)(X/c)^\gamma$ the now-*certain* path $X(t) = X_0 e^{\alpha T}$ and deducing $Y(t) = Y_0 e^{\beta t} = Y_0 e^{\gamma \alpha T}$, with $\gamma = \beta/\alpha$.

To estimate γ empirically, one might regress log warrant price against log common price, γ being the regression coefficient. Then α might be estimated statically by calculating the mean percentage gain per unit time of the common, or by computing $E[X_{t+1}]/X_t = e^\alpha$. Then β will be determined by the formula (48) for γ once one has an estimate of σ^2. Since σ is the standard deviation of $\log(X_{t+1}/X_t)$, it can be estimated from the sample variance of this last variate. The consistency of the model with the facts could then be checked by calculating β separately as the mean value of the warrant's gain, or by

$$E[Y_{t+T}]/Y_T = e^{\beta T}$$

where T is always less than the time after t

when it pays to convert the warrant. A further check on the log-normality model comes from the fact that, when the "instantaneous variance per unit of time" of X_t is σ^2, the instantaneous variance for unit time of Y_t should work out to be $\gamma^2 \sigma^2$, greater than σ^2 by the factor $\gamma^2 > 1$.

I am not presenting any empirical results here. But I shall draw upon some findings of others by way of illustrating the theory. (Incidentally, they suggest remarkably high β/α, giving the warrants a suspiciously favorable return.)

Osborne[12] finds some empirical warrant for his theoretically dubious axiom that log X_t takes an unbiased random walk, with neither upward nor downward drift. If μt represents the net drift of log X_t, we have

$$(49) \qquad \mu = \alpha - \frac{\sigma^2}{2} = 0, \qquad \frac{\alpha}{\sigma^2} = \frac{1}{2}.$$

Substituting these values into (48) gives

$$(50) \qquad \gamma = \sqrt{\frac{\beta}{\alpha}}, \qquad \text{when } \frac{\alpha}{\sigma^2} = \frac{1}{2}.$$

Osborne and many investigators report average capital gains on a stock of three to five per cent per year. So set $\alpha = .04$. Finally Giguère in the cited paper[13] infers $\gamma = 2$ from empirical scatters of perpetual warrant prices against their common stock prices. (My casual econometric measurements suggest $\gamma = 2$ is much too high: these days one can rarely buy a long-lived warrant for only one-fourth of the common when the common is selling near its exercise price. But accept $\gamma = 2$ for the sake of the demonstration.) Combining $\mu = 0$, $\alpha = .04$, $\gamma = 2$, we get for the mean return per year for holding the warrant no less than 16 per cent!—i.e., $\beta = \gamma^2 \alpha = 4(.04) = .16$.

This does seem to be a handsome return, and one would expect it to be whittled away over time—unless people are exceptionally averse to extra risk. The high β return would be whittled away as people bid up the prices of perpetual warrants until they approached the value of the common stock itself—at which point $\beta =$

[12]Ref. [3], p. 108.
[13]Ref. [17].

SAMUELSON

α, $\gamma = 1$, and $c = \infty$. There is no other way. Yet this does not seem to happen. Why not? One obvious explanation is that whenever a stock pays a regular dividend of δ per period, β will, taxes aside, naturally come to exceed α by at least that much. But there are stocks that pay no dividend which still sell much above their perpetual warrants. Perhaps a departure from our assumption of a stationary time series, in the form of a supposition that there will later be a regular dividend, can help explain away the paradox. Coming events do cast their shadow before them.

I should like now to sketch a theory to explain why $\beta - \alpha$ cannot become too large. If $\beta > \alpha$ so that $\gamma > 1$, hedging will stand to yield a sure-thing positive net capital gain (commission and interest charges on capital aside!). This follows from the concept of leverage as curvature in Figure 2. Let the stock be initially at X_0 with the warrant at $F(X_0) = Y_0$. Then buying \$1 long of the warrant and selling \$1 short of the common gives the new hedged variate $Z = Y/Y_0 - X/X_0$. Whether X goes up or down, Z is sure to end up greater than 1, with a positive gain. Indeed, its expected gain per unit time is $\beta - \alpha$. But there will be a variance per unit time around this mean value that works out to $(\gamma - 1)^2 \sigma^2$. This variance will be quite small when γ is near to 1, but with $\gamma \doteq 1$ it is likely that the difference $\beta - \alpha$ will also be small.

In the example worked out earlier from the data of Osborne and Giguère, a hedger would have the same variance as would a buyer of the common stock; but instead of earning 4 per cent a year, he would earn 12 per cent a year. And, commissions aside, he would have no risk of a positive loss. This would seem like almost too much of a good thing. Under the stock exchange rules, I believe he would have to put up about the same amount of money as margin to engage in the hedged transaction as to buy a dollar's worth of the warrant or stock outright; he would not need margin money for each side of the hedged transaction. So he would have to reckon in the opportunity cost of the safe interest rate per unit time of money itself, ρ. Presumably though, the buyer of the common stock has already felt that its $\alpha = .04$ return was adjusted to compensate for that ρ.

(If the stock pays a percentage dividend, δ, the excess $\beta - \alpha$ includes compensation for δ, ρ and for extra riskiness. Actually, if the excess of β over α comes only from the fact of the dividend δ, there is no advantage to be gained from the hedge; this is because the man who sells the common short must make good the dividend, and that will reduce the apparent profit of the hedge to zero. Hence in what follows, I deal only with the excess of β over α that is unrelated to dividends, and I ignore all dividends.)

If hedging arbitrage *alone* is counted on to keep $\beta - \alpha$ small, under present margin requirements we should expect $\beta - \alpha = \rho$ if riskiness were not a consideration. Since there is some aversion to dispersion around the mean gain from the hedge, we should not expect from hedging arbitrage *alone* that $\beta - \alpha < \rho$. On the other hand, if people are risk averters and $\gamma < 2$, as seems realistic, it is hard to see how one could get $\beta - \alpha > \alpha$, since people would shift from holding X outright to holding a hedged position Z if the latter had the greater return, less variance, and no chance of loss. One could, in principle, learn from stock exchange records how much hedging is in fact being done, since a rational hedger will minimize margins by dealing with one firm on both sides of his hedge. It is my impression that not much warrant hedging is in fact done, although in convertible bonds there does seem to be a greater volume of hedging. Still if γ and $\beta - \alpha$ threatened to become too large, potential hedgers would become actual hedgers. Hence, the limits derived above do have some relevance, particularly

$$(51) \qquad \beta - \alpha < \alpha.$$

Conclusion

The methods outlined here can be extended by the reader to cases of calls and puts, where the dividend receives special treatment different from the case of warrants, and to the case of convertible bonds.

References

1 Bachelier, L., *Theory of Speculation* (translation of 1900 French edition), pp. 17-78 in Cootner, P.H., editor, *The Random Character of Stock Market Prices*. Cambridge, The M.I.T. Press, 1964.

2 Kruizenga, R. J., "Put and Call Options: A Theoretical and Market Analysis," unpublished Ph.D. thesis, Massachusetts Institute of Technology, 1956. Also "Introduction to the Option Contract," pp. 277-391 in Cootner (see reference 1); and "Profit Returns from Purchasing Puts and Calls," pp. 392-411 in Cootner (see reference 1).

3 Osborne, M. F. M., "Brownian Motion in the Stock Market," *Operations Research* 7, pp. 145-173, 1959. Also pp. 100-128 in Cootner (see reference 1).

4 Sprenkle, C. M., "Warrant Prices as Indicators of Expectations and Preferences," *Yale Economic Essays* 1, pp. 178-231, 1961. Also pp. 412-474 in Cootner (see reference 1).

5 Boness, A. J., "Some Evidence on the Profitability of Trading in Put and Call Options," pp. 475-496 in Cootner (see reference 1).

6 Alexander, S. S., "Price Movements in Speculative Markets: Trends or Random Walks," *Industrial Management Review* 2, Spring, 1961, pp. 7-26; also pp. 199-218 in Cootner (see reference 1). Also "Price Movements in Speculative Markets: Trends or Random Walks, No. 2," pp. 338-375 in Cootner (see reference 1).

7 Kendall, M. G., "The Analysis of Economic Time Series—Part I: Price," *Journal of the Royal Statistical Society* 96 (Part I), pp. 11-25; also pp. 85-99 in Cootner (see reference 1).

8 Lévy, Paul, *Calcul des probabilités.* Paris: Libraires du Bureau des Longitudes de l'Ecole Polytechnique, 1925.

9 Gnedenko, B. V., and Kolmogorov, A. N., *Limit Distributions for Sums of Independent Random Variables.* Cambridge: Addison-Wesley Publishing Company, Inc., 1954.

10 Mandelbrot, B., "The Variation of Certain Speculative Prices," *Journal of Business* 36, October, 1963, pp. 394-419; also pp. 307-332 in Cootner (see reference 1).

11 Fama, E. F., "Mandelbrot and the Stable Paretian Hypothesis," *Journal of Business* 36, October, 1963, pp. 420-429; also pp. 297-306 in Cootner (see reference 1).

12 Keynes, J. M., *A Treatise on Money—II:* *The Applied Theory of Money*, pp. 142-147. London: Macmillan and Company, 1930.

13 Houthakker, H., "The Scope and Limits of Futures Trading," pp. 134-159 in Abramovitz, M., editor, *Allocation of Economic Resources,* 1959.

14 Houthakker, H., "Systematic and Random Elements in Short-Term Price Movements," *American Economic Review* 51, pp. 164-172, 1961.

15 Cootner, P. H., "Returns to Speculators: Telser vs. Keynes," *Journal of Political Economy* 68, pp. 396-404, 1960.

16 Cootner, P. H., "Rejoinder," *Journal of Political Economy* 68, pp. 415-418, 1960.

17 Giguère, G., "Warrants: A Mathematical Method of Evaluation," *Analysts Journal* 14, pp. 17-25 (1958).

Paul A. Samuelson, Ph.D., *Professor of Economics, Massachusetts Institute of Technology.* Formerly consultant to the Natural Resources Planning Board (1945) and the U. S. Treasury (1945-52). Guggenheim Fellow, 1948-49, Ford Faculty Research Fellow, 1958-59. Social Science Research Council Predoctoral Fellow, 1935-37. Society of Fellows, Harvard University, 1937-40. Member of the American Academy of Arts and Sciences, the American Philosophical Society, and National Commission on Money and Credit Advisory Board (1958-60); President's National Goals Commission Adviser (1960). Honorary Degrees from the University of Chicago, Oberlin College, Ripon College, and Boston College. President of the American Economic Association (1961) and of the Econometric Society (1951). Author of *Foundations of Economic Analysis,* 1947; *Economics, An Introductory Analysis,* 1948; *Readings in Economics,* 1955; *Linear Programming and Economic Analysis,* 1958.

Appendix: A Free Boundary Problem for the Heat Equation Arising from a Problem of Mathematical Economics*

Henry P. McKean, Jr., M.I.T.

1 Introduction

Paul A. Samuelson has developed in the preceding paper a model of warrant pricing from the economic standpoint; the purpose of the present article is to add some mathematical complements.

Samuelson supposes that the motion of the price x of the common stock is a (multiplicative) differential process; this means that for each $s \geq 0$, the (scaled) future motion $x(t + s)/x(s) : t \geq 0$ is independent of the past $x(t) : t \leq s$ and has the same statistics as $x(t)/x(0) : t \geq 0$. Define $P_1(B)$ [$E_1(f)$] to be the chance of the event B [expectation of the function f] for prices starting at $x(0) = 1$ and impose the

*The partial support of the Office of Naval Research and of the National Science Foundation, NSF G-19684, is gratefully acknowledged.

MCKEAN

810

condition $E_1(x) < \infty$. $E_1(x) = e^{at}$ follows and it is assumed that $\alpha \geq 0$.

Define $h = h(t, \xi)^\circ$ to be the "correct" price of a warrant to purchase the common stock at unit price, as a function of the time of purchase $t \geq 0$ and of the current price $\xi \geq 0$, subject to the additional condition that the warrant appreciate at the rate $\beta \geq \alpha$ up to such time as it becomes unprofitable still to hold it. The problem of computing h has the following mathematical expression: *find the smallest solution* $f = h$ *of*

$$f(t, \xi) \geq e^{-\beta s} E_1[f(t - s, \xi x(s))]$$
$$(s \leq t, \xi \geq 0)$$

that lies above $(\xi - 1)^+ \equiv$ *the greater of* $\xi - 1$ *and* 0; the simpler problem of finding the "correct" price $h(\infty, .)$ of the perpetual warrant can be expressed in the same language as follows: *find the smallest solution* $f = h$ *of*

$$f(\xi) \geq e^{-\beta t} E_1[f(\xi x(t))]) \qquad (t \geq 0, \xi \geq 0)$$

that lies above $(\xi - 1)^+$.

The existence of h is proved and its simplest properties discussed in sections 2 and 4 below: if $\beta > \alpha$, h turns out to be an increasing convex function of ξ up to a point $\xi = c(t) > 1$ [the corner], to the right of which it coincides with $\xi - 1$; c and h increase with time to $c(\infty) < \infty$ and $h(\infty, \xi) < \xi$. $h(\infty, .)$ is computed in section 3 for a (multiplicative) Brownian motion of prices $[h = (c-1)(\xi/c)^\gamma, c = \gamma/(\gamma-1)]$, and also for a (multiplicative) Poisson process of prices $[h = $ a broken line]; and in section 5, h is computed for $t \leq \infty$ and a (multiplicative) translation of prices with possible absorbtion at 0. A partial solution of the problem for $t < \infty$ and a (multiplicative) Brownian motion of prices is described in section 6: it leads to a free boundary problem for the heat equation, the free boundary being a solution of an unfortunately intractible integral equation due to I. I. Kolodner [4].

An unsolved problem is to find a nice condition on the prices that will make $h^-(c) = 1$. $h^-(c)$ is the left slope at the corner. $h^-(c) \leq 1$ is automatic. Samuelson has conjectured that this will be the case if $Q = P_1[x(t) \leq 1, t \downarrow 0] = 0$ [the alternative is $Q = 1$], but I could not prove it. Another inviting unsolved problem is to discuss the integral equation for the free boundary of section 6.

I must not end without thanking Professor Samuelson for posing me this problem and for several helpful conversations about it.

2 Perpetual Warrants

Consider a (multiplicative) differential process with sample paths $t \to x(t) = x(t+) \geq 0$,

probabilities $P_1(B)$, and expectations $E_1(f)$, starting at $x(0) = 1$, *i.e.*, let $P_1[x(0) = 1] = 1$ and, conditional on $x(t_1) > 0$, let $x(t_2)/x(t_1)$ be independent of $x(s) : s \leq t_1$ and identical in law to $x(t_2 - t_1)$ for each choice of $t_2 \geq t_1 \geq 0$. $P_a(B)$ and $E_a(f)$ denote probabilities and expectations for the motion starting at $x(0) = a \geq 0$; this motion is identical in law to $[ax, P_1]$; *esp.*, $P_0[x(t) = 0, t \geq 0] = 1$ and $P_a[x(t) < b] = P_1[x(t) < b/a]$ for a, b > 0. $[x, P.]$ *begins afresh at stopping times. A stopping time is* a non-negative function $t \leq \infty$ of the sample path, such as $t = 1$ or the exit time $t = \inf(t : x > 1)$, such that for each $t \geq 0$ the event $(t < t)$ depends upon $x(s) : s \leq t$ alone. *Beginning afresh means that if* $\mathbf{B}_{t+}$ is the field of events B such that $B \cap (t < t)$ is measurable over $x(s) : s \leq t$, then *conditional on the present* $a = x(t)$ *and on the event* $t < \infty$, *the future* $x(t + t) : t \geq 0$ *is independent of the past* $\mathbf{B}_{t+}$ *and identical in law to* $[x, P_a]$:

$$P.[x(t + t)\epsilon db|\mathbf{B}_{t+}] = P_a[x(t)\epsilon db] \quad if \ t < \infty;$$

see G. Hunt[1] for a complete explanation of stopping times for (additive) differential processes. WARNING: The reader is cautioned that the italic letter t [stopping time] must be carefully distinguished from the roman letter t [a constant time]; italic x [stopping point $x(t)$] must likewise be distinguished from roman x [sample path].

$E_1(x) = f(t)$ is a solution of $f(t - s)f(s) = f(t)$ $(s \leq t)$ and $0 < f \leq \infty$, so $E_1(x) = e^{at}$ for some $-\infty < \alpha \leq \infty$. $P_1[x = 1, t \geq 0] = 0$ or 1 because $P_1[x(s) = 1, s \leq t] = f(t)$ is a solution of $f(t - s)f(s) = f(t)$ $(s \leq t)$ and $0 \leq f \leq 1$, so that $f = e^{-\gamma t}$ for some $0 \leq \gamma \leq \infty$ and $f(\infty) = 0$ or 1 according as $\gamma > 0$ or not. $P_1[x = 1, t \geq 0] = 0$ *is assumed below*.

A non-negative function $f \not\equiv \infty$ defined on $[0, \infty)$ is $(\beta-)$ excessive if $e^{-\beta t} E_1[f(x)] \uparrow f$ as $t \downarrow 0$; in this language *the problem of the perpetual warrant is to find the smallest excessive function* $h \geq (\xi - 1)^+$ *in case* $\infty > \beta \geq \alpha \geq 0$. h is constructed and its simplest properties derived in a series of brief articles.

1. *Define* $h^0 = (\xi - 1)^+$ *and* $h^n = \displaystyle\sup_{t \geq 0} e^{-\beta t}$ $E.[h^{n-1}(x)]$ *for* $n \geq 1$; *then* $(\xi - 1)^+ \leq h^n \uparrow$ $h \leq \xi$ *as* $n \uparrow \infty$.

PROOF: $h^{n-1}(\xi) \leq h^n(\xi) = \displaystyle\sup_{t \geq 0} e^{-\beta t} E_\xi[h^{n-1}(x)]$

$\leq \displaystyle\sup_{t \geq 0} e^{-\beta t} E_\xi(x) = \displaystyle\sup_{t \geq 0} e^{-\beta t} e^{at}\xi = \xi$

if $h^{n-1} \leq \xi$, and the obvious induction completes the proof.

[1]See ref. [3].

APPENDIX

2. h *is increasing, convex (and so continuous), and its slope is* ≤ 1.

PROOF: $h^n(\xi) = \sup_{t \geq 0} e^{-\beta t} E_1[h^{n-1}(\xi x)]$ inherits all the desired properties from h^{n-1}; now use induction and let $n \uparrow \infty$.

3. h *is the smallest excessive function* $\geq (\xi - 1)^+$.

PROOF: $e^{-\beta t} E_.[h(x)] \leq h$ is obvious from 1, and since $h \epsilon C[0, \infty)$ (2), an application of Fatou's lemma implies $\lim_{t \downarrow 0} e^{-\beta t} E_.[h(x)] \geq$ $E_.[\lim \inf h(x)] = h$, completing the proof that h is excessive. Also, $h \geq (\xi - 1)^+$, and if j is another such excessive function, then the obvious induction supplies us with the underestimate $j \geq h^n \uparrow h(n \uparrow \infty)$.

4. $h = (\xi - 1)^+$ *to the right of some point* $1 < c \leq \infty$. $h > (\xi - 1)^+$ *to the left*.

PROOF: Given $s \leq t$ and a, b > 0,

$P_1[x(t) \geq ab] \geq P_1[x(s) \geq a, x(t)/$
$x(s) \geq b] = P_1[x(s) \geq a]P_1[x(t-s) \geq b]$

so that $P_1[x(nt) \geq d^n] \geq P_1[x(t) \geq d]^n$, and either $P_1[x \leq 1] \equiv 1$ ($t \geq 0$) (use $E_1(x) \geq 1$) or $P_1[x(nt) \geq d^n] > 0$ for some t > 0, d > 1, and each $n \geq 1$. But in the second case, $h \geq e^{-\beta nt} E_.[(x(nt) - 1)^+] > 0$ for $n \uparrow \infty$, and the statement follows from 2.

5. $h \equiv \xi$ *if* $\beta = \alpha \geq 0$.

PROOF: $\xi \geq h \geq e^{-\beta t} E_\xi[x - 1] = \xi(1 - e^{-\beta t})$ $\uparrow \xi$ as $t \uparrow \infty$ if $\beta = \alpha > 0$, while if $\beta = \alpha = 0$, then $E_\xi[(x - 1)^+] \geq (\xi - 1)^+$ so that $h = \lim_{t \uparrow \infty} E_.[(x - 1)^+] = E_.[h(x)]$. Because h is convex (2), its 1-sided slope h^+ is an increasing function,

$$h(\xi) = h(1) + (\xi - 1)h^+(1) + \int_1^\xi [h^+(\eta) - h^+(1)]d\eta,$$

and putting $\xi = x$ and taking expectations (E_1) on both sides, it follows that $h^+ \equiv h^+(1)$ between $0 < a < 1$ and $b > 1$ if $0 < P_1[x \leq a]$ $P_1[x \geq b]$ for some t > 0. But $P_1[x(nt) \geq d^n]$ > 0 for some t > 0, d > 1, and each $n \geq 1$ as in 4, and using the same method, it is also possible to make $P_1[x(nt) \leq d^{-n}] > 0$ for the same t > 0, some (perhaps smaller) d > 1, and each $n \geq 1$ (use $E_1(x) = 1$). $h^+ \equiv h^+(1)$ is immediate and $h \equiv \xi$ follows from the bounds $\xi - 1$ $\leq h \leq \xi$ and the fact that $h(0+) = 0$.

WARNING: $\beta > \alpha \geq 0$ *until the end of the next section.*

6. *Given a closed interval* $0 < a \leq \xi \leq b < \infty$ *with exit time* $t = t_{ab} \equiv \inf(t : x < a \text{ or } x > b)$ *and exit place* $x = x(t)$, $P_.[t < \infty] \equiv 1$ *and* $j = j_{ab} \equiv E_.[e^{-\beta t}h(x)]$ *lies under* h.

PROOF adapted from E. B. Dynkin[2]: $P_.[t < \infty] \equiv 1$ since in the opposite case, $0 < p(\xi) =$ $P_\xi[a \leq x \leq b, t \geq 0]$ for some $a \leq \xi \leq b$, and putting $p_{ab} = \sup_{ab} p(\xi)$, the bound $p(\xi) =$ $E_\xi[p[x(n)], a \leq x \leq b, t \leq n] \leq p_{ab}P_\xi[a \leq x \leq b, t \leq n]$ decreases to $p_{ab}p(\xi)$ as $n \uparrow \infty$, proving $p_{ab} = 1$. But $p_{ab} = \sup_{ab} P_1[a/\xi \leq x \leq$ $b/\xi, t \geq 0] \leq P_1[a/b \leq x \leq b/a, t \geq 0]$, and this cannot be 1 without violating the estimate $P_1[x(nt) \geq d^n] > 0$ of 4. Define $G_\gamma f =$ $E_.\left[\int_0^\infty e^{-\gamma t}f(x)dt\right]$ for non-negative f and $\gamma \geq 0$. $G_\gamma h \equiv u < \infty$ if $\gamma \geq \beta$ and $G_\gamma = G_\beta[1 + (\beta - \gamma)G_\gamma]$, so that if $\gamma \geq \beta$ and $v = h + (\beta - \gamma)u$, then $u = G_\beta v = E_.\left[\int_0^\infty e^{-\beta t}v(x)dt\right]$.

Because of $v \geq h + (\beta - \gamma)\int_0^\infty e^{-\gamma t}dt \, e^{\beta t}h = 0$, it follows that

$u \geq E_.\left[\int_t^\infty e^{-\beta t}v(x)dt\right] =$
$E_.\left[e^{-\beta t}\int_0^\infty e^{-\beta t}v[x(t + t)]dt\right]$,

and since x begins afresh at the stopping time t while t itself is measurable over $\mathbf{B}_{t+}$,

$$u \geq E_.[e^{-\beta t}G_\beta v(x)] \doteq E_.[e^{-\beta t}u(x)]$$

with $x = x(t)$. Now use the fact that $(\gamma - \beta)$ $u \uparrow h$ as $\gamma \uparrow \infty$.

7. j *is excessive.*

PROOF: Because x begins afresh at time $t \geq 0$,

$$e^{-\beta t}E_.[j(x)] = E_.[e^{-\beta t \circ}h(x^\circ)] \equiv j^\circ$$

with t° defined as the next exit time from $a \leq \xi \leq b$ after time t and $x^\circ = x(t^\circ)$. Using the notation and method of proof of 6,

$E_.[e^{-\beta t \circ}u(x^\circ)] =$
$E_.\left[\int_{t^\circ}^\infty e^{-\beta t}v(x)dt\right] \leq E_.\left[\int_t^\infty e^{-\beta t}v(x)dt\right] =$
$E_.[e^{-\beta t}u(x)]$,

and since $(\gamma - \beta)u \uparrow h$ as $\gamma \uparrow \infty$, it follows that $j^\circ \leq j$. But also $t^\circ \downarrow t$ as $t \downarrow 0$ and $x(t+) = x(t)$, so Fatou's lemma implies

---

[2]See ref. [2].

MCKEAN

$$\lim_{t \downarrow 0} j^\circ \geqq E.[\lim \inf e^{-\beta t}h(x^\circ)] = j,$$

completing the proof.

8. $c < \infty$ and $E.[e^{-\beta t}h(x)] \equiv h$ with $t = \min(t : x \geqq c)$, $x = x(t)$, and $e^{-\beta t}h \equiv 0$ if $t = \infty$, in case $P_1[t_{ab} \downarrow 0$ as $a \uparrow 1$ and $b \downarrow 1] = 1$.

PROOF: Define for the moment $t = t_{ab}$ and $x = x(t_{ab})$. Because x is differential and $h > (\xi - 1)^+$ near $\xi = 1$, it is possible to choose a $< 1 < b$ so as to make $\min_{ab} E_\xi[e^{-t-|x-1|}]$ so large that $j_{ab} \geqq (\xi - 1)^+$. But $j_{ab} \leqq h$ is excessive while h is the smallest excessive function $\geqq (\xi - 1)^+$, so $j_{ab} \equiv h$ for this choice of $a < 1 < b$. Given 2 overlapping closed intervals $a_1 \leqq \xi \leqq b_1$ and $a_2 \leqq \xi \leqq b_2$ with $0 < a = a_1 < a_2 < b_1 < b_2 \equiv b < \infty$ and corresponding functions $j \equiv h$, it is to be proved that $j_{ab} \equiv h$ also. Consider for the proof paths starting at $a_1 \leqq x(0) = \xi \leqq b_1$ and define stopping times

$$t_1 = \text{the exit time from } a_1b_1,$$

$t_2 = t_1$ or the next exit time from a_2b_2 according as $t_1 = t_{ab}$ or not,

$t_3 = t_2$ or the next exit time from a_1b_1 according as $t_2 = t_{ab}$ or not,

etc.

$t_1 \leqq t_2 \leqq$ etc. $\leqq t_n$ is constant $(= t_x = t_{ab})$ from some smallest $n = m$ on, and putting $x_n = x(t_n)$ $(n \leqq \infty)$, a simple induction justifies

$$h(\xi) = E_\xi[e^{-\beta t_n}h(x_n)] =$$
$$E_\xi[e^{-\beta t_x}h(x_x), n \geqq m] +$$
$$E_\xi[e^{-\beta t_n}h(x_n), n < m].$$

As $n \uparrow \infty$, this tends to j_{ab} since $P_\xi[m < \infty] = 1$ while $h(x_n) \leqq b < \infty$ on $(n < m)$. $j_{ab} \equiv h$ follows at once. Now choose $0 < a < 1 < b < c$ so that $j_{ab} \equiv h$. Repeating the first part of the proof, it is clear that the function j associated with a small neighborhood of b is identical to h, and using the second part, it follows that $j_{ab} \equiv h$ for a little bigger b. Because a can be diminished for the same reason, it is clear that if $0 < b < c$ (or if $b = c$ in case $c < \infty$), then it is possible to find closed intervals $0 < a_n \leqq \xi \leqq b_n < b$ increasing to $0 < \xi < b$ with $j_n \equiv h$. But for paths starting at $0 \leqq x(0) = \xi \leqq b$ and $n \uparrow \infty$, the exit times t_n from $a_n \leqq \xi \leqq b_n$ increase to the exit time $t_x = \min(t : x = 0$ or $x \geqq b)$ while $x_n = x(t_n)$ tends to $x_x = x(t_x)$,[*] so

$$h(\xi) = \lim_{n \uparrow \infty} j_n(\xi) = \lim_{n \uparrow \infty}$$
$$E_\xi[e^{-\beta t_n}h(x_n)] = E_\xi[e^{-\beta t_x}h(x_x)]$$

---

[*] G. Hunt [3].

because of the bound

$$e^{-\beta t_n}h(x_n) = e^{-\beta t_x}h(x_x) \qquad \text{if } x_n \geqq b$$
$$< b \qquad \text{if } x_n < b,$$

and to complete the proof, it suffices to replace t_x by $t = \min(t : x \geqq b)$ and to prove $c < \infty$. As to t_x, since $h(0) = 0$, $h = E.[e^{-\beta t_x}h(x_x)$, $x_x \geqq b] = E.[e^{-\beta t}h(x)]$ with $x = x(t)$ and the convention $e^{-\beta t}h \equiv 0$ if $t = \infty$. As to the proof that $c < \infty$, if $c = \infty$, then $h = E.[e^{-\beta t_n}h(x_n)]$ with $t_n = \inf(t : x > n)$ and $x_n = x(t_n)$. Because

$$\xi - 1 \leqq h(\xi) \leqq E_\xi[e^{-\beta t_n}x(t_n)] =$$
$$E_\xi[e^{-\beta t_{n/\xi}}\xi x(t_{n/\xi})]$$

for $n > \xi$, $1 \leqq E_1[e^{-\beta t_2}x(t_2)]$ as follows on putting $n/\xi = 2$ and letting $n \uparrow \infty$. Because $\beta > \alpha$, $E_1[e^{-\beta t_2}x(t_2)] < E_1[e^{-\alpha t_2}x(t_2)]$, and adapting the proof of 6 to the $(\alpha-)$ excessive function $f \equiv \xi$, one finds $E_\xi[e^{-\alpha t_2}x(t_2)] \leqq \xi$. But this leads to a contradiction: $1 < E_1[e^{-\alpha t_2}x(t_2)] \leqq 1$.

9. $c < \infty$ and $E.[e^{-\beta t}h(x)] \equiv h$ with $t = \min(t : x \geqq c)$ and $x = x(t)$ in general.

PROOF: 8 covers the case $P_1[t_{ab} \downarrow 0$ as $a \uparrow 1$ and $b \downarrow 1] = 1$; otherwise, $P_1 \begin{bmatrix} \lim \\ a \uparrow 1 \ t_{ab} > 0 \\ b \downarrow 1 \end{bmatrix} = 1$

according to Kolmogorov's 01 law, so the particle moves by *jumps* with exponential holding times between. Consider the modified motion $x^\circ = e^{\epsilon t}x$ with so small a positive ϵ that $\beta > \alpha^\circ = \alpha + \epsilon$ and let h° and c° be the analogues of h and c. Because $e^{-\beta t}E.[h^\circ(x)] \leqq e^{-\beta t}E.[h^\circ(x^\circ)] \leqq h^\circ$, it is clear that $h^\circ \geqq h$ and $c^\circ \geqq c$. As $\epsilon \downarrow 0$, $h^\circ \downarrow j \geqq h$ and $c^\circ \downarrow b \geqq c$. Because x° satisfies the conditions of 8, $c^\circ < \infty$ (*esp.*, $c \leqq b < \infty$) and $h^\circ = E.[e^{-\beta t^\circ}h^\circ(x^\circ)]$ with $t^\circ = \min(t : x^\circ \geqq b)$ and $x^\circ = x^\circ(t^\circ)$. Now an unmodified path starting at $x(0) = \xi < b$ jumps out of $[0, b)$ landing at $x \geqq b$; this means that $t^\circ = t$ and $x^\circ = e^{\epsilon t}x$ for $\epsilon \leqq 1/n$ for some n depending upon the path, so $e^{-\beta t^\circ}h^\circ(x^\circ) \downarrow e^{-\beta t}j(x)$ as $\epsilon \downarrow 0$ for a class of paths with as large a probability as desired, while on the complement of this class $e^{-\beta t^\circ}h^\circ(x^\circ) \leqq e^{-\beta t}e^{\epsilon t}b \leqq b$. Because $h = j = \xi - 1$ $(\xi \geqq b)$ and $x \geqq b$, it follows

$$j(\xi) = \lim_{\epsilon \downarrow 0} E_\xi[e^{-\beta t^\circ}h^\circ(x^\circ)] =$$
$$E_\xi[e^{-\beta t}j(x)] = E_\xi[e^{-\beta t}h(x)] \leqq h$$

for $\xi < b$, *i.e.*, $j \equiv h$, and since $b \geqq c$, the result follows after a moment's reflection.

SUMMING UP: if $\beta = \alpha \geqq 0$, then $h \equiv \xi$, while if $\beta > \alpha \geqq 0$, then h is convex with slope $0 \leqq h^+ \leqq 1$, $h > (\xi - 1)^+$ to the left of some point

APPENDIX

$1 < c < \infty$, $h \equiv \xi - 1$ *to the right of* c, *and* $h = E.[e^{-\beta t}h(x)]$ *with* $t = \min(t: x \geq c)$, $x = x(t)$, *and* $e^{-\beta t}h \equiv 0$ *if* $t = \infty$.

3 Two Examples

Consider the multiplicative Brownian motion with drift $x = \exp[\sigma b + \delta t]$ with $\sigma > 0$, $b = b(t)$ a standard (additive) Brownian motion, and $-\infty < \delta < \infty$. $E_1(x) = \exp[\sigma^2/2 + \delta t]$ so $\alpha = \sigma^2/2 + \delta$. Because $h = E.[e^{-\beta t}h(x)]$ with $t = \min(t : x \geq c)$, it follows from a formula of E. B. Dynkin[3] that if G is the generator of $[x, P.]$:

$$Gf(\xi) = (\sigma^2/2)\xi^2 f''(\xi) + (\sigma^2/2 + \delta)\xi f'(\xi),$$

then $Gh = \beta h$ to the left of c. Now solve for $h = (c-1)(\xi/c)^\gamma$ with an adjustable γ and find $(\sigma^2/2)\gamma^2 + \delta\gamma - \beta = 0$, or, what is the same,

$$\gamma = -\delta/\sigma^2 + \sqrt{2\beta/\sigma^2 + \delta^2/\sigma^4} > 1$$

(the negative radical is excluded). γ is actually a function of α/σ^2 and β/σ^2 alone. Besides the above formula for h, the solution requires us to locate the corner c. Consider for this purpose G expressed in terms of the new scale $d\overset{\circ}{\xi} = \xi^{1+2\delta/\sigma^2}d\xi$ and the so-called speed measure $e(d\xi) = 2\sigma^{-2}\xi^{-1+2\delta/\sigma^2}d\xi$:

$$Gf(\xi) = \frac{f^\oplus(d\xi)}{e(d\xi)} = \lim_{\substack{a\uparrow\xi \\ b\downarrow\xi}} \frac{f^\oplus(b) - f^\oplus(a)}{e(a,b)}$$

$$\text{with } f^\oplus(a) \equiv \lim_{b\downarrow a} \frac{f(b) - f(a)}{\overset{\circ}{\xi}(b) - \overset{\circ}{\xi}(a)};$$

in this language, the fact that h is excessive is expressed as $h^\oplus(d\xi) - \beta h e(d\xi) \leq 0$, and computing the mass that this distribution attributes to a small neighborhood of $\xi = c$, one finds $h^\oplus(c) - h^\ominus(c) = c^{-1-2\delta/\sigma^2} [h^+(c) - h^-(c)] \leq 0$. But $h^+(c) = 1$, while $h^-(c) \leq 1$ since h is convex, so $1 = h^-(c) = (c-1)\gamma/c$, and solving for c gives $c = \gamma/(\gamma - 1)$.
The reader can easily compute all desired probabilities for this Brownian model with the help of the formulas:

$$P_\xi[x(t)\epsilon\, d\eta] = (2\pi\sigma^2 t)^{-1/2}e^{-(\lg \eta/\xi - \delta t)^2/2\sigma^2 t}d\eta/\eta,$$

$$P_\xi[t\,\epsilon\, dt] = (2\pi\sigma^6 t^3)^{-1/2}(\xi/c)^{-\delta/\sigma^2} e^{-\delta^2 t/2\sigma^2}$$

$$\lg(\xi/c)\, e^{-(\lg \xi/c)^2/2\sigma^2 t}\sigma^2 dt,$$

and

---

[3]See ref. [11].

$P_\xi[x(t)\epsilon\, d\eta, t < t] = P_\xi[x(t)\epsilon\, d\eta]$

$$-(\eta/\xi)^{\delta/\sigma^2} e^{-\delta^2 t/2\sigma^2} (2\pi\sigma^2 t)^{-1/2}$$

$$e^{-(\lg \eta\xi/c^2)^2/2\sigma^2 t}d\eta/\eta;$$

in the first formula t, ξ, $\eta > 0$, while in the second and third, $t > 0$, $0 < \xi, \eta < c$.

Consider as a second example, the (multiplicative) Poisson process $x = \exp[p(\sigma t)]$; p is a standard (additive) Poisson process with jump size 1 and unit rate, i.e., $P.[p(t) - p(0) = n] = t^n e^{-t}/n!$. $E_1(x) = \exp[\sigma(e-1)t]$ so $\alpha = \sigma(e-1)$. Given $\xi < c$ with exit time $t = \inf(t : x \neq \xi)$ and exit place $x = x(t)$,
$h(\xi) = E_\xi[e^{-\beta t}h(x)] =$

$$\int_0^\infty \sigma e^{-\sigma t}dt\, e^{-\beta t}h(e\xi) = \frac{h(e\xi)}{1 - \beta/\sigma},$$

esp., $h(\xi) = (e\xi - 1)(1 - \beta/\sigma)^{-1}$ for $c/e \leq \xi < c$, and letting $\xi \uparrow c$ and solving for c, one finds $c = (1 - \alpha/\beta)^{-1}$. h itself is a broken line with corners at $2^{-n}c$ ($n \geq 0$), *esp.*, $h^+(c) = 1 > h^-(c) = (\sigma + \alpha)(\sigma + \beta)^{-1}$.

4 General Warrants

Now the problem is to find *the smallest excessive function* $h \geq (\xi - 1)^+$ *for the stopped space-time motion*

$$z(s) = [t - s, x(s)] \qquad (s \leq t)$$
$$= [0, x(t)] \qquad (s > t),$$

i.e., the smallest function $h(t, \xi) \geq (\xi - 1)^+$ such that $e^{-\beta s}E_\xi[h(t - s, x(s))] \uparrow h(t, \xi)$ as $s \downarrow 0$ for each $(t, \xi)\epsilon[0, \infty) \times [0, \infty)$.

1. *Define* $h^0 = (\xi - 1)^+$ *and* $h^n = \sup_{s\leq t}$ $e^{-\beta s}E.[h^{n-1}(t - s, x(s))]$ *for* $n \geq 1$; *then* $(\xi - 1)^+ \leq h^n \uparrow h \leq \xi$ *as* $n \uparrow \infty$.

PROOF as before.

2. *h is a convex function of* $\xi \geq 0$ *with slope* $0 \leq h^+ \leq 1$.

PROOF as before.

3. *h is an increasing function of* $t \geq 0$.
PROOF: h^0 is independent of $t \geq 0$, and

$$h^n(t_2, \xi) = \sup_{s \leq t_2} e^{-\beta s}E_\xi[h^{n-1}(t_2 - s, x(s))]$$

$$\geq \sup_{s \leq t_1} e^{-\beta s}E_\xi[h^{n-1}(t_1 - s, x(s))]$$
$$= h^n(t_1, \xi)$$

if h^{n-1} is an increasing function of $t \geq 0$; now use induction and let $n \uparrow \infty$.

4. *h is the smallest (space-time) excessive function* $\geq (\xi - 1)^+$; *it is continuous from below as function of* $t > 0$.

PROOF: $h \geq e^{-\beta s}E.[h(t - s, x(s))] \; (s \leq t)$ is obvious. Now

$$\lim_{s \downarrow 0} \; e^{-\beta s}E_\xi[h(t - s, x(s))] \geq$$
$$h(t-, \xi) \geq (\xi - 1)^+$$

for $t > 0$, and since

$$j = (\xi - 1)^+ \qquad (t = 0)$$
$$= h(t-, \xi) \qquad (t > 0)$$

is a (space-time) excessive function $\geq (\xi - 1)^+$, it is enough to prove that h is the smallest solution $\geq (\xi - 1)^+$ of $j \geq e^{-\beta s}E.[j(t - s, x(s))]$. But this is obvious.

5. $h(0 +, \xi) \equiv \lim_{t \downarrow 0} h(t, \xi) = (\xi - 1)^+$.

PROOF: $k(t, \xi) = E_\xi[(x(t) - 1)^+] \geq (\xi - 1)^+$, and since $k = E.[k(t - s, x(s))]$, $e^{-\beta s}E.[k(t - s, x(s))]$ increases to k as $s \downarrow 0$, proving $k \geq h$. Now as $t \downarrow 0$,

$$k = e^{\alpha t}\xi - 1 + E_\xi[1 - x(t), x(t) < 1]$$

tends to $\xi - 1$ if $\xi > 1$. But $0 \leq k(0+, \xi) = \lim_{t \downarrow 0} E_1[(\xi x - 1)^+]$ is increasing, so the proof is complete.

6. $h(\infty, \xi) = \lim_{t \uparrow \infty} h(t, \xi)$ *coincides with the perpetual warrant.*

PROOF: $h(\infty, \xi)$ is continuous (its slope falls between 0 and 1), so $e^{-\beta s}E_\xi[h(\infty, x(s))] \leq h(\infty, \xi)$ increases to $h(\infty, \xi)$ as $s \downarrow 0$, i.e., $h(\infty, \xi)$ is excessive; that it is the smallest excessive function $\geq (\xi - 1)^+$ is obvious.

7. $h \equiv \xi - 1$ *to the right of some point $1 < c = c(t) < \infty$ for $0 \leq t \leq \infty$. c is increasing, $c(t-) = c$, and $c(\infty) < \infty$. $h > (\xi - 1)^+$ between c and $d = d(t)$. d is decreasing, $d(t-) = d$, and $d(\infty) = 0$. $h \equiv 0$ to the left of d. $d = e^{-t} > 0$ if $x = e^t$. $d \equiv 0$ if x is a multiplicative Brownian motion.*

PROOF: use the information above and $c(\infty) < \infty$ (2.9).

8. $h(t, \xi) = E_\xi[e^{-\beta t}h(t - t, x)]$ *if t is the (space-time) exit time from the region*

$$R: 0 < s \leq t, 0 < \xi < c(s)$$

and $x = x(t)$ is the exit place (see Figure 1 for R and t).

PROOF: as before with some (mild) technical complications.

5 General Warrant for a Multiplicative Translation with Absorbtion

Consider the motion of translation $x = \xi$

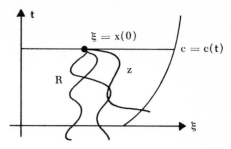

Figure 1

$\exp[(\alpha + \delta)t]$ with absorbtion at a rate $\delta \geq 0$, *i.e.,* let

$$P_1[x = \xi e^{(\alpha+\delta)t}] = e^{-\delta t} = 1 - P_1[x = 0],$$

and let us prove that

$$h(t, \xi) = e^{-(\beta+\delta)t}[\xi e^{(\alpha+\delta)t} - 1]^+ \quad \xi \leq c e^{-(\alpha+\delta)t}$$
$$= (\xi/c)^\gamma(c - 1) \qquad c e^{-(\alpha+\delta)t} \leq \xi \leq c$$

with $\gamma = (\beta + \delta)(\alpha + \delta)^{-1}$ and $c \equiv c(\infty) = \gamma(\gamma - 1)^{-1}$.

2.9 implies that the perpetual warrant is a solution of

$$e^{-(\beta+\delta)t}h[\xi e^{(\alpha+\delta)t}] = e^{-\beta t}E_\xi[h(x)] = h(\xi)$$

for $t \geq 0$ and $\xi \exp[(\alpha + \delta)t] \leq c$, or, and this is the same, a solution of

$$Gh(\xi) = \xi(\alpha + \delta)h'(\xi) - \delta h(\xi) = \beta h(\xi)$$
$$(\xi < c).$$

Now solve and find $h(\xi) = (\xi/c)^\gamma(c - 1)$ with $\gamma = (\beta + \delta)(\alpha + \delta)^{-1}$ and an unknown corner $c \geq 1$. Because $h^-(c) \leq 1$, $(\gamma/c)(c - 1) \leq 1$, while from the fact that h is excessive, it follows that

$$e^{-(\beta+\delta)t}[\xi e^{(\alpha+\delta)t} - 1] =$$
$$e^{-\beta t}E_\xi[h(x)] \leq h(\xi) = \xi - 1 \qquad (\xi \geq c),$$

and this cannot hold for $\xi = c$ and $t \downarrow 0$ unless $(\gamma/c)(c - 1) \geq 1$, i.e., unless $c = \gamma(\gamma - 1)^{-1} = (\beta + \delta)(\beta - \alpha)^{-1}$.

As to the general warrant, if $\xi \geq c(t)$, then

$$e^{-(\beta+\delta)s}[\xi e^{(\alpha+\delta)s} - 1] =$$
$$e^{-\beta s}E_\xi[h(t - s, x(s))] \leq h(t, \xi) = \xi - 1,$$

and solving for $\xi = c(t)$, one finds $c(t) \geq \gamma(\gamma - 1)^{-1} = c = c(\infty) \geq c(t)$, i.e., $c(t) \equiv c(\infty)$. Now if $c \exp[-(\alpha + \delta)t] \leq \xi \leq c$ and if $s \leq t$ is chosen so that $\xi \exp[(\alpha + \delta)s] = c$, then $h(\infty, \xi) \geq h(t, \xi) \geq e^{-\beta s}E_\xi[h(t - s, x(s))]$

$$= e^{-(\beta+\delta)s}h[t - s, e^{(\alpha+\delta)s}] =$$
$$e^{-(\beta+\delta)s}(c - 1) = (\xi/c)^\gamma(c - 1),$$

so that $h(t, \xi) = (\xi/c)^\gamma (c - 1)$, while if $\xi \leq c \exp[-(\alpha + \delta)t]$, then in view of 4.8,

$$h(t, \xi) = e^{-\beta s} E_\xi[h(t + s, x(s))] =$$
$$e^{-(\beta+\delta)t}h(t - s, \xi\, e^{(\alpha+\delta)s})$$
$$= e^{-(\beta+\delta)t}h(0+, \xi\, e^{(\alpha+\delta)t}) \qquad (s = t-)$$
$$= e^{-(\beta+\delta)t}[\xi\, e^{(\alpha+\delta)t} - 1]^+,$$

as stated. Note that $h^+(t, \xi)$ jumps at $\xi \exp[(\alpha + \delta)t] = 1$ and c but not at $\xi = c$.

6 General Warrant for a Multiplicative Brownian Motion with Drift

Now let us compute as far as possible the general warrant for the multiplicative Brownian motion $x = \exp[\sigma b + \delta t]$ of 3, granting that c and the left slope $h^-(t, c)$ are continuous, that $c(0+) = 1$, and that c has a continuous slope $c^\bullet$ for $t > 0$. Consider

$$Gf(\xi) = (\sigma^2/2)\xi^2 f''(\xi) +$$
$$(\sigma^2/2 + \delta)\xi f'(\xi) = f^\oplus(d\xi)/e(d\xi)$$

as in 3 and let us prove that h is a solution of the *free boundary problem*:

$$(G - \partial/\partial t)h = \beta h \text{ on the region}$$
$$R: t > 0, 0 < \xi < c(t)$$
$$h(t, 0+) = 0 \qquad (t > 0)$$
$$h(0+, \xi) = 0 \qquad (\xi \leq 1)$$
$$h(t, c-) = c - 1 \qquad (t > 0)$$
$$h^-(t, c) = 1 \qquad (t > 0).$$

R (or, what is the same, the free boundary c) is unknown, and it is the extra (flux) condition $h^- = 1$ that makes it possible to solve for *both* R and h. 4.8 implies the partial differential equation, and the evaluations of h on the 3 sides of ∂R follow from 4.1, 4.5, and 4.7. As to the flux condition $h^-(t, c) = 1$,

$$\int_{[t_1, t_2] \times [a, b]} dt[h^\oplus(t, d\xi) - \beta h e(d\xi)] \leq$$
$$\int_a^b [h(t_2, \xi) - h(t_1, \xi)] e(d\xi)$$

is an expression of the fact that h is (space-time) excessive, and adding up the masses that these distributions attribute to the non-overlapping boxes:

$$\frac{k-1}{n} \leq t \leq \frac{k}{n}, c\left(\frac{k-1}{n}\right) \leq \xi \leq c\left(\frac{k}{n}\right)$$

for $k \leq m$, one finds

$$\Sigma_{k \leq m} \int_{\frac{k-1}{n}}^{\frac{k}{n}} dt\left[h^\oplus\left(t, c\left(\frac{k}{n}\right)\right) - h^\oplus\left(t, c\left(\frac{k-1}{n}\right)\right)\right]$$

$$\leq \Sigma_{k \leq m} \int_{c\left(\frac{k-1}{n}\right)}^{c\left(\frac{k}{n}\right)} \left[h\left(\frac{k}{n}, \xi\right) - h\left(\frac{k-1}{n}, \xi\right) + \beta \int_{\frac{k-1}{n}}^{\frac{k}{n}} h\, dt\right] e(d\xi)$$

$$\leq \Sigma_{k \leq m} \left[c\left(\frac{k}{n}\right) - c\left(\frac{k-1}{n}\right) + \frac{\beta}{n} c\left(\frac{m}{n}\right)\right] \int_{c\left(\frac{k-1}{n}\right)}^{c\left(\frac{k}{n}\right)} e(d\xi).$$

Because c is continuous, it follows on letting $n \uparrow \infty$ that

$$\int_0^\infty dt\, c^{-1-2\delta/\sigma^2}[1 - h^-(t, c)] = 0,$$

and since $h^-(t, c) \leq 1$ is also continuous, the flux condition $h^- = 1$ is proved.

Now transform the free boundary problem by the substitution $h = e^{-\beta t}w(t, \sigma^{-1}[\lg \xi + \delta t])$:

$$\frac{\partial w}{\partial t} = \frac{1}{2}\frac{\partial^2 w}{\partial \xi^2} \text{ on the region:}$$
$$t > 0, -\infty < \xi < b \equiv \sigma^{-1}[\lg c + \delta t]$$

$$w(t, -\infty) = 0 \qquad (t > 0)$$
$$w(0+, \xi) = 0 \qquad (\xi \leq 0)$$
$$w(t, b-) = e^{\beta t}(c - 1) \qquad (t > 0)$$
$$w^-(t, b) = e^{\beta t}c \qquad (t > 0).$$

Because

$$w(t, \xi) \leq e^{\beta t}h(\infty, e^{\sigma\xi - \delta t}) =$$
$$e^{\beta t}[c(\infty) - 1]c(\infty)^{-\gamma} e^{\gamma[\sigma\xi - \delta t]}$$

to the left of $\xi = b$, it is legitimate to take a Fourier transform $\hat{w}(t, \eta) = \int_{-\infty}^b e^{i\xi\eta}w(t, \xi)d\xi$.

$c(0+) = 1$ implies $\hat{w}(0+, .) \equiv 0$; this leads at once to

$$\hat{w}(t, \eta) = \int_0^t e^{-\eta(t-s)/2}e^{\beta s}$$
$$e^{i\eta b}\left[\frac{c}{2} + \left(b^\bullet - \frac{i\eta}{2}\right)(c - 1)\right]ds,$$

or, what is the same,

$$\int_0^t \frac{e^{-[\xi + b(t) - b(s)]^2/2(t-s)}}{\sqrt{2\pi(t - s)}} e^{\beta s}$$
$$\left[\frac{c}{2} + \left[b^\bullet - \frac{\xi + b(t) - b(s)}{2(t-s)}\right](c - 1)\right]ds$$
$$= w(t, \xi + b) \quad (\xi < 0)$$
$$= 0 \qquad\qquad (\xi > 0),$$

MCKEAN

and from this it is possible to deduce an infinite series of integral equations for the free boundary c by a) evaluation at $\xi = 0+$, b) evaluation of the slope at $\xi = 0+$, etc.:

a)
$$\frac{c-1}{2} = \int_0^t \frac{e^{-[b(t)-b(s)]^2/2(t-s)}}{\sqrt{2\pi(t-s)}} \, e^{-\beta(t-s)} \left[\frac{c}{2} + \left[b^{\bullet} - \frac{b(t)-b(s)}{2(t-s)}\right](c-1)\right] ds,$$

b)
$$\frac{c}{2} = \int_0^t \frac{e^{-[b(t)-b(s)]^2/2(t-s)}}{\sqrt{2\pi(t-s)}} \, e^{-\beta(t-s)} \left[b^{\bullet} + \beta(c-1) - \frac{b(t)-b(s)}{2(t-s)} c\right] ds,$$

etc.

I. I. Kolodner[4] treated such free boundary problems and derived a) and b) by a more complicated method. Unfortunately, it is not possible to obtain explicit solutions, though machine computation should be feasible; as a matter of fact, even the existence and uniqueness of solutions is still unproved.

---

[4]See Ref. [4].

References
1 Dynkin, E. B., "Infinitesimal Operators of Markov Processes," Teoriya Veroyatnost. i ee Primenen. 1, pp. 38-60 (1956).
2 Dynkin, E. B., "Natural Topology and Excessive Functions Connected with a Markov Process," Doklady Akad. Nauk S.S.S.R. 127, pp. 17-19 (1959).
3 Hunt, G., "Some Theorems Concerning Brownian Motion, Transactions of the American Mathematical Society 81, pp. 294-319 (1956).
4 Kolodner, I. I., "Free Boundary Problem for the Heat Equation with Applications to Problems of Change of Phase," Communications in Pure and Applied Mathematics 9, pp. 1-31 (1956).

Henry P. McKean, Jr., Ph.D., Professor of Mathematics, Massachusetts Institute of Technology. Author of "Diffusion Processes and Their Sample Paths" (with K. Itô), Grundlehren der Math. Wiss. 125, Berlin, 1965; and other papers.

APPENDIX

817

200

A Complete Model of Warrant Pricing
that Maximizes Utility*

Paul Samuelson, Massachusetts Institute of Technology
Robert C. Merton, Massachusetts Institute of Technology

This paper presents a realistic theory of warrant prices which overcomes some deficiencies or oversimplifications of an earlier model developed by Paul A. Samuelson and published in the Spring 1965 issue of the IMR. The analysis here is very complex, and can be extended beyond warrant pricing to other types of securities. Further elaboration of the theory and its application is supplied in two appendices which follow the article. Good luck. *Ed.*

Introduction[†]

In a paper written in 1965, one of us developed a theory of rational warrant pricing.[1] Although the model is quite complex mathematically, it is open to the charge of over-simplification on the grounds that it is only a "first-moment" theory.[2] We now propose to sketch a simple model that overcomes such deficiencies. In addition to its relevance to warrant pricing, the indicated general theory is of interest for the analysis of other securities since it constitutes a full supply-and-demand determination of the outstanding amounts of securities.

Cash-Stock Portfolio Analysis

Consider a common stock whose current price X_t will give rise n periods later to a finite-variance, multiplicative probability distribution of subsequent prices, X_{t+n}, of the form:

$$\text{Prob} \left\{ X_{t+n} \leq X \mid X_t = Y \right\} = P(X, Y; n) \equiv P(X/Y; n) \tag{1}$$

where the price ratios, $X_{t+n}/X_t = Z = Z_1 Z_2 \ldots Z_n$, are assumed to be products of uniformly and independently distributed distributions, of the form

Prob $\left\{ Z_l \leq Z \right\} = P(Z; 1)$, and where, for all integral n and m, the Chapman-Kolmogorov relation $P(Z; n+m) = \int_0^\infty P(Z/z; n) dP(z; m)$ is satisfied. This is the "geometric Brownian motion," which at least asymptotically approached the familiar log-normal. Ignoring for simplicity any dividends, we know that a risk averter, one with concave utility and diminishing marginal utility, will hold such a security in preference to zero-yielding safe cash only if the stock has an expected positive gain:

$$0 < E[Z] - 1 = \int_0^\infty Z dP(Z; n) - 1 = e^{\alpha n} - 1, \text{ that is, } \alpha > 0 \tag{2}$$

where the integral is the usual Stieltjes integral that handles discrete probabilities and densities, and α is the mean expected rate of return on the stock per unit time. (We have ensured that α is constant, independent of n.)

---

*Aid from the National Science Foundation is gratefully acknowledged.
†Footnotes for this article appear at the end of the article.

A special case would be, for n=1, the following discrete distribution, where $\lambda > 1$:

$X_{t+1} = \lambda X_t$, with probability $p \geq 0$
$X_{t+1} = \lambda^{-1} X_t$, with probability $1 - p \geq 0$ (3)

This simple geometric Brownian motion leads asymptotically to the log-normal distribution. Condition (2) becomes, in this special case, $0 < E[Z] - 1 = p\lambda + (1-p)\lambda^{-1} - 1$. If, for example, $\lambda = 1.1$ and $p = 1 - p = 0.5$, then $E[Z] - 1 = 1/2(1.1 + 10/11) = .004545$. If our time units are measured in months, this represents a mean gain of almost one-half a per cent per month, or about 5½ per cent per year, a fair approximation to the recent performance of a typical common stock.

To deduce what proportion cash holding will bear to the holding of such a stock, we must make some definite assumption about risk aversion. A fairly realistic postulate is that everyone acts now to maximize his expected utility at the end of n periods and that his utility function is strictly concave. Then by portfolio analysis[3] in the spirit of the classical papers of Domar-Musgrave and Markowitz (but free of their approximations), the expected utility is maximized when $w = w^*$, where w is the fraction of wealth in the stock:

$$\text{Max}_w \, \overline{U}(w) = \text{Max}_w \int_0^\infty U[(1 - w) + wZ]dP(Z; n)$$ (4)

where $w = w^*$ is the root of the regular condition for an interior maximum

$$0 = \overline{U}'(w^*) = \int_0^\infty \{ZU'[(1 - w^*) + w^*Z] - U'[(1 - w^*) + w^*Z]\} \, dP(Z;n)$$ (5)

or

$$1 = \frac{\int_0^\infty ZU'[(1 - w^*) + w^*Z]dP(Z;n)}{\int_0^\infty U'[(1 - w^*) + w^*Z]dP(Z;n)}$$

Since U is a concave function, U'' is everywhere negative, and the critical point does correspond to a definite maximum of expected utility. (Warning: Equations like (4) posit that no portfolio changes can be made before the n periods are up, an assumption modified later.)

If zero-yielding cash were dominated by a safe asset yielding an instantaneous force of interest r, and hence e^{rn} in n periods, terms like (1-w) would be multiplied by e^{rn} and (5) would become

$$e^{rn} = \frac{\int_0^\infty ZU'[(1-w^*)e^{rn} + w^*Z]dP(Z;n)}{\int_0^\infty U'[(1-w^*)e^{rn} + w^*Z]dP(Z;n)} < e^{\alpha n}, \text{ if } w^* > 0$$ (5a)

This relationship might well be called the Fundamental Equation of Optimizing Portfolio theory. Its content is worth commenting on. But first we can free it from any dependence on the existence of a perfectly safe asset. Re-writing (4) to involve any number m of alternative investment outlets, subject to any joint probability distribution, gives the multiple integral:

$$\text{Max}_{\{w_j\}} \, \overline{U}[w_1, \ldots, w_m] = \text{Max}_{\{w_j\}} \int_0^\infty U\left[\sum_{j=1}^m w_j Z_j\right] dP(Z_1, \ldots, Z_m; n)$$ (4a)

Introducing the constraint, $\sum_{j=1}^{m} w_j = 1$, into the Lagrangian expression, $L = \overline{U} + \gamma[1 - \sum_{j=1}^{m} w_j]$, we derive as necessary conditions for a regular interior maximum:[4]

$$\frac{\partial L}{\partial w_k} = 0 = \int_0^\infty Z_k U'[\sum_{j=1}^{m} w_j Z_j] dP(Z_1, \ldots, Z_m; n) - \gamma, \quad \text{for } k = 1, \ldots, m$$

Dividing through by a normalizing factor, we get the fundamental equation:

$$\int_0^\infty Z_1 dQ(Z_1, \ldots, Z_m; n) = \int_0^\infty Z_2 dQ(Z_1, \ldots, Z_m; n) = \ldots = \int_0^\infty Z_m dQ(Z_1, \ldots, Z_m; n) \tag{5b}$$

where

$$dQ(Z_1, \ldots, Z_m; n) = \frac{U'[\sum_{j=1}^{m} w_j^* Z_j] dP(Z_1, \ldots, Z_m; n)}{\int_0^\infty U'[\sum_{j=1}^{m} w_j^* Z_j] dP(Z_1, \ldots, Z_m; n)}$$

The probability-cum-utility function $Q(Z; n)$ has all the properties of a probability distribution, but it weights the probability of each outcome so to speak by the marginal utility of wealth in that outcome.

Figure 1 illustrates the probability density of good and bad outcomes; Figure 2 shows the diminishing marginal utility of money; and Figure 3 plots the "effective-probability" density whose integral $\int_0^z dQ(z; n)$ defines Q.[5] Conditions (5), (5a), and (5b) say, in words, that the "effective-probability" mean of every asset must be equal in every use, and, of course, be equal to the yield of a safe asset if such an asset is held.   Note that $\overline{U}'(O) = E[Z] - e^{rn} = e^{\alpha n} - e^{rn}$, and this must be positive if w^* is to be positive.   Also $\overline{U}'(1) = \int_0^\infty Z dQ(Z; n) - e^{rn}$, and this cannot be positive if the safe asset is to be held in positive amount.   By Kuhn-Tucker methods, interior conditions of (5) could be generalized to the inequalities needed if borrowing or short-selling are ruled out.

For the special probability process in (3) with $p = \frac{1}{2}$ and Bernoulli logarithmic utility, we can show that expected utility turns out to be maximized when wealth is always divided equally between cash and the stock, i.e. $w^* = \frac{1}{2}$ for all λ:

$$\text{Max } \overline{U}(w) = \text{Max } \{\tfrac{1}{2}\log(1 - w + w\lambda) + \tfrac{1}{2}\log(1 - w + w\lambda^{-1})\}$$

$$= \tfrac{1}{2}\log(\tfrac{1}{2} + \tfrac{1}{2}\lambda) + \tfrac{1}{2}\log(\tfrac{1}{2} + \tfrac{1}{2}\lambda^{-1}), \text{ for all } \lambda. \tag{6}$$

The maximum condition corresponding to (5) is

$$0 = \overline{U}'(w^*) = \frac{\frac{1}{2}}{\frac{1}{2} + \frac{1}{2}\lambda}(-1 + \lambda) + \frac{\frac{1}{2}}{\frac{1}{2} + \frac{1}{2}\lambda^{-1}}(-1 + \lambda^{-1}), \text{ and} \tag{7}$$

$w^* \equiv \frac{1}{2}$ for all λ.   Q.E.D.

(The portfolio division is here so definitely simple because we have postulated the special case of an "unbiased" logarithmic price change coinciding with a Bernoulli logarithmic utility function; otherwise changing the probability distribution and the typical person's wealth level would generally change the portfolio proportions.)

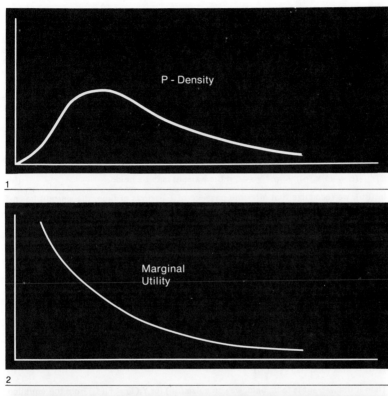

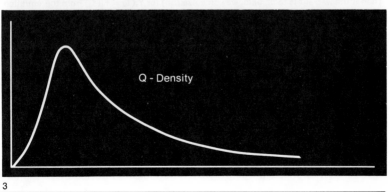

Recapitulation of the 1965 Model

Under what conditions will everyone be willing to hold a warrant (giving the right to buy a share of the common stock for an exercise price of $1 per share at any time in the next n periods), and at the same time be willing to hold the stock and cash? Since the warrant's price will certainly move with the common rather than provide an opposing hedge against its price movements, if its expected rate of return were not in excess of the safe asset's yield, the warrant would not get held. In the 1965 paper, it was arbitrarily postulated that the warrant must have a specified gain per dollar which was as great or greater than the expected return per dollar invested in the common stock. Thus, if we write $Y_t(n)$ for the price at time t of a warrant with n periods still to run, the 1965 paper assumed for stock and warrant,

$$E[X_{t+T}/X_t] = e^{\alpha T} \geq e^{rT} \tag{8a}$$

$$E[Y_{t+T}(n-T)/Y_t(n)] = e^{\beta T} \geq e^{\alpha T}, \text{ if the warrant is to be held.} \tag{8b}$$

In (8b), we recognize that after the passage of T periods of time, the warrant has n-T rather than n periods left to run until its exercise privilege expires. It should be stressed that the warrant can be exercised *any* time (being of "American" rather than "European" option type) and hence in (8b) the warrant prices can never fall below their arbitrage exercise value, which in appropriate units (i.e., defining the units of common so that the exercise price of the warrant is unity) is given by Max $(0, X_t - 1)$.   Thus, we can always convert the warrant into the common stock and sell off the stock (commissions are here neglected).

In the 1965 model, the expected percentage gain β of a warrant and the expected percentage gain α of a common were arbitrarily postulated as exogeneously given data, instead of being deduced from knowledge of the risk aversion properties of U. Postulating a priori knowledge of α and β, the model was derived by beginning with the known arbitrage value of a warrant about to expire, namely:

$$Y_t(0) = \text{Max}(0, X_t - 1) = F_0(X_t) \tag{9}$$

Then if the warrant is to be held, we can solve (8b) for $Y_t(1) = F_1(X_t)$ from the equation:

$$e^\beta = E[F_0(XZ)/F_1(X)|X]$$

$$= \frac{\int_0^\infty F_0(XZ)dP(Z;1)}{F_1(X)} \tag{10}$$

In this integral and elsewhere we can write X for X_t. If (10) is not achievable, the warrant will be converted, and will now be priced at its $F_0(X)$ value. Hence, in every case:

$$F_1(X) = e^{-\beta}\int_0^\infty F_0(XZ)dP(Z;1), \text{ if held}$$

$$= X - 1 \geq e^{-\beta}\int_0^\infty F_0(XZ)dP(Z;1), \text{ if now converted}$$

$$= \text{Max}[0, X-1, e^{-\beta}\int_0^\infty F_0(XZ)dP(Z;1)], \text{ in all cases.} \tag{10a}$$

Successively putting in these expressions F_2 and F_1 for F_1 and $F_0, \ldots, F_{n+1}$ and F_n for F_1 and F_0, the 1965 model deduced rational warrant price formulas, $F_n(X) = F_n(X_t) = Y_t(n)$, for any length of life; and the important perpetual warrant case, $F_\infty(X) = F(X)$, can be deduced by letting $n \to \infty$:

$$F(X) = e^{-\beta} \int_0^\infty F(XZ)dP(Z;1), \text{ if } X \leq C\ (\alpha, \beta)$$
$$= X - 1 \geq e^{-\beta} \int_0^\infty F(XZ)dP(Z;1), \text{ if } X \geq C\ (\alpha, \beta) \tag{11}$$

where $C(\alpha, \beta)$ is the critical level at which the warrant will be worth more dead than alive. This critical level will be defined by the above relations and will be finite if $\beta > \alpha$.[6]

The special case of the 1965 theory in which $\alpha = \beta$ is particularly simple, and its mathematics turns out to be relevant to the new utility theory presented here. In this case, where conversion is never profitable (for reasons which will be spelled out even more clearly in the present paper), the value of the warrants of any duration can be evaluated by mere quadrature, as the following linear integrals show:

$$F_n(X) = e^{-\alpha T} \int_0^\infty F_{n-T}(XZ)dP(Z;T)$$
$$= e^{-\alpha n} \int_0^\infty F_0(XZ)dP(Z;n)$$
$$= e^{-\alpha n} \int_{1/X}^\infty (XZ - 1)dP(Z;n) \tag{12}$$

In concluding this recapitulation, let us note that the use of short, discrete periods here gives a good approximation to the mathematically difficult, limiting case of continuous time in the 1965 paper and its appendix.

Determining Average Stock Yield

To see how we can deduce rather than postulate in the 1965 manner the mean return that a security must provide, let us first assume away the existence of a warrant and try to deduce the mean return of a common stock. The answer must depend on supply and demand: supply as dependent upon risk-averter's willingness to part with safe cash, and demand as determined by the opportunities nature affords to invest in real, risky processes along a schedule of diminishing returns.

To be specific, suppose one can invest today's stock of real output (chocolates or dollars when chocolate always sell for $1 each) either (a) in a safe (storage-type) process — *cash*, so to speak — that yields in the next period exactly one chocolate; or (b) in a *common stock*, which in the special case (3) gives for each chocolate "invested" today λ chocolates tomorrow with probability p, or λ^{-1} chocolates with probability $1-p$. If we allocate today's stock of chocolates so as to maximize the expected utility, we shall shun the risk process unless its expected yield exceeds unity. For the special case,[7] $p = 1-p = \frac{1}{2}$, this will certainly be realized, and as seen in the earlier discussion of (7), for all λ, a Bernoulli-utility maximizer will choose to invest half of present resources in the safe (cash) process and half in the risky (common-stock) process.

Now suppose that the risky process — say growing chocolate on the shady side of hills where the crop has a .5 chance of being large or small — is subject to diminishing returns. With the supply of hill land scarce, the larger the number of chocolates planted, rather than merely stored, the lower the mean return per chocolate (net of any competitive land rents for which the limited supply of such land will be bid to at each level of total investment in risk chocolates). Although it is admittedly a special-case assumption, suppose that λ in (3) drops toward unity as the absolute number of chocolates invested in the risky process rises but that $p = 1-p = \frac{1}{2}$ throughout. Then the expected yield, $a = e^{\alpha} - 1$, drops toward zero as λ drops toward one.

Given the initial supply of chocolates available for safe or risk allocations, the expected yield of the common stock, a, will be determined at the equilibrium intersection of total supply and demand — in our simple case at the level determined by the λ and a yields on the diminishing returns curve where exactly half of the available chocolates go into the risk process.[8]

Determining Warrant Holdings and Prices

Using the general method outlined above, we can now deduce what warrants must yield if a prescribed amount of them is to be held alongside of cash and the common stock by a maximizer of expected utility.

Specifically, assume that cash in an insured bank account, or a safe process, has a sure yield of e^r-1 per unit time. Assume that each dollar invested in the common stock has a mean ex-ante yield $\{\int_0^{\infty} ZdP(Z;1)-1 = e^{\alpha} - 1\}$ per period. It will be desirable now to specialize slightly our assumption of concave total utility so that the behavior of a group of investors can be treated as if it resulted from the deliberation of a single mind. In order that asset totals should behave in proportions independent of the detailed allocations of wealth among individuals, we shall assume that every person has a constant elasticity of marginal utility at every level of wealth and that the value of this constant is the same for all individuals.[9] Just as assuming uniform homothetic indifference curves frees demand curve analysis in non-stochastic situations from problems of disaggregation, a similar trick comes in handy here.

Finally, we must specify how many of the warrants are to be outstanding and in need of being voluntarily held. There is a presumption that to induce people to hold a larger quantity of warrants, their relative yields will have to be sweetened. Let the amounts of total wealth, W, to be invested in cash, common stock, and warrants be respectively w_1, w_2, and w_3. As already seen, there is no loss of generality in setting $W = 1$. Then subject to the constraint,[10] $w_1 + w_2 + w_3 = W = 1$, we consider the following special case of (4a) and generalization of (4):

$$\text{Max } \bar{U}[w_1, w_2, w_3] = \text{Max} \int_0^{\infty} U [w_1 e^{rT} + w_2 Z + w_3 \frac{F_n(XZ)}{F_{n+T}(X)}]dP (Z;T) \qquad (13)$$
$$\{w_j\} \qquad\qquad \{w_j\}$$

where, as before, we assume that the decision is made for a period of length T. (Setting $T = 1$, a small period, would be typical.) To explain (13), note that e^{rt} is the sure return to a dollar invested in the common stock. Since we can with \$1 buy $1/F_{n+T}(X)$ units of a warrant with $n+T$ periods to go, and since these turn out after T periods to have the random-variable price $F_n(XZ)$, clearly w_3 is to be multiplied by the per-dollar return $F_n(XZ)/F_{n+T}(X)$ as indicated.[11] As in (4a), we seek a critical point for the Lagrangian expression $L = \bar{U} + \gamma[1 - \sum_{j=1}^{3} w_j]$ to get the counterpart of (5b), namely:

$$\frac{\partial L}{\partial w_1} = 0 = -\gamma + = \int_0^\infty e^{rT} U' [w_1 e^{rT} + w_2 Z + w_3 \frac{F_n(XZ)}{F_{n+T}(X)}] dP(Z;T)$$

$$\frac{\partial L}{\partial w_2} = 0 = -\gamma + \int_0^\infty ZU' [w_1 e^{rT} + w_2 Z + w_3 \frac{F_n(XZ)}{F_{n+T}(X)}] dP(Z;T)$$

$$\frac{\partial L}{\partial w_3} = 0 = -\gamma + \int_0^\infty \frac{F_n(XZ)}{F_{n+T}(X)} U' [w_1 e^{rT} + w_2 Z + w_3 \frac{F_n(XZ)}{F_{n+T}(X)}] dP(Z;T)$$

$$\frac{\partial L}{\partial \gamma} = 0 = 1 - w_1 - w_2 - w_3 \tag{14}$$

Eliminating γ, we end up with special cases of (5b), namely:

$$e^{rT} = \frac{\int_0^\infty ZU' [(1 - w_2^* - w_3^*) e^{rT} + w_2^* Z + w_3^* \frac{F_n(XZ)}{F_{n+T}(X)}] dP(Z;T)}{C} \tag{15}$$

$$e^{rT} = \frac{\int_0^\infty \frac{F_n(XZ)}{F_{n+T}(X)} U' [(1 - w_2^* - w_3^*) e^{rT} + w_2^* Z + w_3^* \frac{F_n(XZ)}{F_{n+T}(X)}] dP(Z;T)}{C} \tag{16}$$

where we have the normalizing factor

$$C = \int_0^\infty U' [(1 - w_2^* - w_3^*) e^{rT} + w_2^* Z + w_3^* \frac{F_n(XZ)}{F_{n+1}(X)}] dP(Z;T),$$

so that, as in (5b),

$$dQ(Z;T) = \frac{U' [(1 - w_2^* - w_3^*) e^{rT} + w_2^* Z + w_3^* \frac{F_n(XZ)}{F_{n+1}(X)}] dP(Z;T)}{C}$$

If the w_j^* were prescribed — e.g. as the solution to a simultaneous-equation supply and demand process that auctions off the exogeneously given supplies of common stock and warrants at the prices that will just get them held voluntarily[12] — then, for $T = 1$, (16) would become an implicit equation enabling us to solve for the unknown function $F_{n+1}(X)$ recursively in terms of the assumed known function $F_n(X)$. Since $F_0(X)$ is known from arbitrage-conversion considerations, (16) does provide an alternative theory to the 1965 first-moment theory.

Let us now call attention to the fact that the implicit equation in (16) for $F_{n+T}(X)$ can be enormously simplified in the special case where the number of warrants held is "small". Thus, for $w_3^* = 0$, or nearly so, the dependence of $U' [\cdot]$ on $F_{n+T}(X)$ becomes zero, or negligible; and (16) becomes a simple, *linear* relationship for determining $F_{n+T}(\cdot)$ recursively from $F_n(\cdot)$. If $w_3^* = 0$, (15) and (16) become:

$$e^{rT} = \int_0^\infty \frac{ZU' [(1 - w_2^*) e^{rT} + w_2^* Z] dP(Z;T)}{C} \tag{15a}$$

$$e^{rT} = \frac{\int_0^\infty \frac{F_n(XZ)}{F_{n+T}(X)} U' [(1 - w_2{}^*)e^{rT} + w_2{}^*Z]dP(Z;T)}{C} \tag{16a}$$

Our task will thus be simplified when we specify that the number of warrants to be held is "small"; that is, warrant pricing is to be determined at the critical level just necessary to induce an incipient amount of them to be voluntarily held. This is an interesting case because it is also the critical level at which hedging transactions, involving buying the common and selling a bit of the warrant short, just become desirable.[13] Most of our paper will be concerned with this interesting "incipient-warrant" case based on (15a) and (16a), but we will first digress briefly to show how one might deduce the quantitative level of all $w_i{}^*$ in terms of given supplies of the various securities.

Digression: General Equilibrium Pricing

To illustrate how warrants would have to be priced if their exogenously given supply is to be absorbed voluntarily by utility maximizers, it suffices to consider the simplest case of one-period warrants that are available in a fixed amount V. And let us assume for expositional simplicity that diminishing returns (e.g., in connection with the choco-late-growing hillsides above) operate so slowly that we can take the probability distri-bution of common-stock price changes as exogenously given, with $P(Z;1)$ given and the common stock's expected yield a known parameter e^α. Assume that the present common stock price is known to be at the level $\overline{X} = x$. Also let the amount of the safe asset ("money" or "near-money") be prescribed at the level $\overline{M}$, and with a prescribed safe yield e^r being a parameter of the problem.

We can now deduce, for utility maximizers, the equilibrium values for the unknown number of shares of common stock held, S, and the unknown equilibrium pattern of warrant prices $F_1(x)$. Our equations are the balance sheet identities, definitions, and supply conditions:

$$W = \overline{M} \cdot 1 + Sx + \overline{V} F_1(x)$$

$$= \overline{M}(1 + \frac{w_2}{w_1} + \frac{1 - w_1 - w_2}{w_1}) \tag{17}$$

$$S = \frac{w_2}{w_1} \frac{\overline{M}}{x} \tag{18}$$

$$\overline{V}F_1(x) = \frac{1 - w_1 - w_2}{w_1} \overline{M} \tag{19}$$

and also our earlier equations (15) and (16) with $T = 1$ and $n = 0$:

$$e^r = \frac{\int_0^\infty ZU' [w_1e^r + w_2Z + (1 - w_1 - w_2)\frac{F_0(xZ)}{F_1(x)}]dP(Z;1)}{C} \tag{15b}$$

$$e^r = \frac{\int_0^\infty \frac{F_0(xZ)}{F_1(x)} U' [w_1e^r + w_2Z + (1 - w_1 - w_2)\frac{F_0(xZ)}{F_1(x)}]dP(Z;1)}{C} \tag{16b}$$

Equations (19), (15b), and (16b) are independent equations for the three unknowns w_1^*, w_2^*, and $F_1(x)$. Hence we do have a determinate system.[14] When $V \to 0$, we have the simpler theory of the rest of this paper.

Utility-Maximizing Warrant Pricing: The Important "Incipient" Case

After our digression, we go back to equation (16a), rearranging its factors to get, for $T = 1$,

$$F_{n+1}(X) = e^{-r} \int_0^\infty F_n(XZ)dQ(Z;1) \quad \text{where } dQ(Z;1) \text{ is short for:} \tag{20}$$

$$dQ(Z;1;r,w_2^*) = \frac{U'\,[(1 - w_2^*)e^r + w_2^*Z]\,dP(Z;1)}{\int_0^\infty U'\,[(1 - w_2^*)e^r + w_2^*Z]\,dP(Z;1)}$$

Here w_2^* is a parameter already determined from solving (15a), and indeed is precisely the same as the w^* determined earlier from solving equation (5a). It will be recalled that $Q(Z;1)$ is a kind of util-prob distribution. Precisely because of (15a), we know that the expected value of Z calculated, not in terms of the true objective probability distribution $dP(Z;1)$, but rather in terms of the util-prob distribution $dQ(Z;1)$, has a "yield" per unit time exactly equal to that of the safe asset. Rearranging (14a), we have:

$$\int_0^\infty ZdQ(Z;1) = e^r < e^\alpha = \int_0^\infty ZdP(Z;1). \tag{21}$$

Taken together with the initial condition from (9): $F_0(X) = \text{Max}(0, X-1)$, equations (20) and (21) give us *linear* recursion relationships to solve our problems completely, provided we can be sure that they always yield $F_n(X)$ values that definitely exceed the conversion value of $F_0(X)$. Because of (21), we are here in a mathematical situation similar to the 1965 special case in which $\alpha = \beta$, and indeed no premature conversion is ever possible. But of course there is this significant difference: in the 1965 case, dP rather than dQ is used to compute α and β, and to emphasize this, we write $\alpha = \alpha_P = \beta_P$ for that case; in the present case, where dQ is used in the computation, we write α_Q and β_Q, recognizing from (21) that $\alpha_Q = r$ and from (20) that $\beta_Q = r = \alpha_Q < \alpha_P = \alpha$. The α_Q and β_Q "yields" are purely "hypothetical" or subjective; they should not be identified with the higher "objective" α_P and β_P yields computed with actual probability dP. These are the true ex ante expected percentage yields calculated from actual dollar gains and losses; they are objective in the sense that Monte Carlo experiments replicated a large number of times will, within this probability model characterized by $P(Z;1)$, actually average out ex post with mean yields of α_P and β_P on the common stock and warrants respectively.[15]

The mathematics does not care about this dP and dQ distinction. The same kind of step-by-step algorithm is yielded whatever the interpretation of the probability distribution used. But this new approach does raise an awkward question. In the 1965 paper, it could be taken as almost self-evident that conversion can never be mandatory if both warrant and stock have the same ex ante yield. In this case, where the yields calculated with $dQ(Z;1)$ are of a hypothetical kind, it is desirable to provide a rigorous proof that our new theory of warrant pricing never impinges on the inequalities set by arbitrage as discussed above and in the 1965 paper.

If we are assured of non-conversion, the value of a perpetual warrant can be determined from the linear integral equation (20). For n so large that it and $n+1$ are indistinguishable, we can write:

$$F_n(X) = F_{n+1}(X) = F_\infty(X) = F(X),$$

and (20) becomes:

$$F(X) = e^{-r} \int_0^\infty F(XZ)dQ(Z;1) \qquad (22)$$

Substituting $F(X) \equiv X$ into (22) does turn out to provide a solution. So too would cX, but only for $c = 1$ can we satisfy the two-sided arbitrage conditions $X > F(X) > X - 1$.

Actually, the homogeneous integral equation (22) has other solutions of the form cX^m, where substitution entails

$$cX^m = e^{-r}cX^m \int_0^\infty Z^m dQ(Z;1)$$

$$1 = e^{-r} \int_0^\infty Z^m dQ(Z;1) = \phi(m). \qquad (23)$$

This last equation will usually be a transcendental equation for m, with an infinite number of complex roots of which only $m = 1$ is relevant in view of our boundary conditions.[16]

That our new theory leads to the perpetual warrant being priced equal to the common stock may seem paradoxical, just as in the 1965 special case where $\alpha_P = \beta_P$. We shall return to this later.

Explicit Solutions

In a sense, our new theory is completed by the step-by-step solution of (20). In the 1965 theory, however, it was possible to display explicit formulas for non-converted warrants by quadrature or direct integration over the original $F_0(X)$ function. The same procedure is possible here by introducing some further generalizations of our util-prob distribution $Q(Z;1)$.

There are some by-no-means obvious complications in our new theory. Given the quadrature formula:

$$F_1(X) = e^{-r} \int_0^\infty F_0(XZ)dQ(Z;1) \qquad (24)$$

one is temped at first to write, as would be possible in the 1965 case, where dP replaced dQ:

$$F_2(X) = e^{-2r} \int_0^\infty F_0(XZ)dQ(Z;2)$$

$$. \quad . \quad . \quad . \quad . \quad . \quad . \quad . \quad . \quad . \qquad (25)$$

$$. \quad . \quad . \quad . \quad . \quad . \quad . \quad . \quad . \quad .$$

or, in general:

$$F_n(X) = e^{-nr} \int_0^\infty F_0(XZ)dQ(Z;n) \qquad (26)$$

where, as in (5b), we define

$$dQ(Z;n) = \frac{U'[w_1*e^{rn} + w_2*Z]dP(Z;n)}{\int_0^\infty U'[w_1*e^{rn} + w_2*Z]dP(Z;n)}$$

But these relations are *not* valid. They would be valid only if, say in the case n = 2, we locked ourselves in at the beginning to a choice of portfolio that is frozen for both periods, regardless of the fact that after one period has elapsed, we have learned the outcomes of X_{t+1} and by (20) would want to act anew to create the proper w_i* proportions for the final period. (For example, suppose as in (7), we have U = logW and there is an equal chance of the stock's doubling or halving, with $\lambda = 2, p = \frac{1}{2} = 1-p$. Suppose we put half our wealth into cash at the beginning and freeze our portfolio for two periods. Then we are violating the step-by-step solution of (20) if, after we have learned that the stock has doubled, we do not sell-out half our gain and put it into cash for the second period.)[17] In summary, (25) is not consistent with (24) and

$$F_2(X) = e^{-r}\int_0^\infty F_1(XZ)dQ(Z;1). \tag{27}$$

If direct quadrature with Q(Z;n) is not valid, what is? What we need are new iterated integrals, $Q_2(Z), \ldots, Q_n(Z)$, which reflect the compound probabilities for 2, ..., n periods ahead when the proper non-frozen portfolio changes have been made. Rather than derive these by tortuous economic intuition, let us give the mathematics its head and merely make successive substitutions. Thus, from (20) applied twice, we get:

$$F_{n+2}(X) = e^{-r}\int_0^\infty F_{n+1}(XZ)dQ(Z;1)$$

$$= e^{-r}\int_0^\infty [e^{-r}\int_0^\infty F_n(XZV)dQ(V;1)]dQ(Z;1)$$

$$= e^{-2r}\int_0^\infty F_n[X(ZV)]d\int_0^\infty Q[\frac{(ZV)}{Z};1]dQ(Z;1)$$

$$= e^{-2r}\int_0^\infty F_n(XR)dQ_2(R) \tag{28}$$

where

$$Q_2(R) = \int_0^\infty Q(\frac{R}{Z};1)dQ(Z;1)$$

and where the indicated interchange in the order of integration of the double integral can be straightforwardly justified.

This suggests defining the iterated integrals[18] by a process which becomes quite like that of convolution when we replace our variables by their logarithms, namely, relations like those of Chapman-Komolgorov:

$Q_1(Z) \equiv Q(Z;1)$, by definition

$$Q_2(Z) = \int_0^\infty Q_1(\frac{Z}{V}) dQ_1(V) \neq Q(Z;2)$$

. . . .

. . . .

$$Q_{n+1}(Z) = \int_0^\infty Q_n(\frac{Z}{V})dQ_1(V) \tag{29}$$

Then, by repeated use of (28)'s substitutions, the results of the step-by-step solution of (20) can be written in terms of mere quadratures, namely,

$$F_1(X) = e^{-r} \int_0^\infty F_0(XZ)dQ_1(Z)$$

$$F_2(X) = e^{-2r} \int_0^\infty F_0(XZ)dQ_2(Z)$$

. . . .

. . . .

$$F_n(X) = e^{-nr} \int_0^\infty F_0(XZ)dQ_n(Z) \tag{30}$$

Fortunately, the "subjective yields," α_Q and β_Q, calculated for the new generalized util-prob functions $Q_t(Z)$, do all equal r per unit time. That is, we can prove by induction:

$$\int_0^\infty ZdQ_1(Z) = e^r < e^\alpha$$

$$\int_0^\infty ZdQ_2(Z) = e^{2r}$$

. . . .

. . . . . .

$$\int_0^\infty ZdQ_n(Z) = e^{nr} \tag{31}$$

This is an important fact, needed to ensure that the solutions to our new theory never fall below the arbitrage levels at which conversion would be mandatory.

Warrants Never to be Converted

It was shown in the 1965 paper that for $\beta > \alpha$ and β, a constant, the warrants would always be converted at a finite stock price level. We will show that in the present model with its explicit assumption of no dividends, the warrants are never converted (i.e., $F_n(X) > F_0(X)$).[19]

Theorem: If $\int_0^\infty ZdQ_n(Z) = e^{rn}$ and $F_n(X) = e^{-rn} \int_0^\infty F_0(XZ)dQ_n(Z)$,

then $F_n(X) \geq F_0(X) = \text{Max}(0, X - 1)$

and we are in the case where the warrants need never be converted prior to expiration.

Since $F_0(X) \geq X - 1$, it is sufficient to show that

$$X - 1 \leq e^{-rn} \int_0^\infty F_0(XZ)dQ_n(Z) \equiv \phi_n(X;r) \tag{32}$$

holds for all $r > 0$, $n > 0$, and $X > 0$. We show this as follows:

$\phi_n(X;r) \geq e^{-rn} \int_0^\infty (XZ - 1)dQ_n(Z)$ because $F_0(XZ) \geq XZ - 1$ and $dQ_n(Z) \geq 0$

$\qquad \geq Xe^{-rn} \int_0^\infty ZdQ_n(Z) - e^{-rn}$

$\qquad \geq X - e^{-rn} \geq X - 1$ from (31) for all $r \geq 0$, $n > 0$, and $X \geq 0$.

Therefore, (32) holds and the theorem is proved.

Thus, we have validated the step-by-step relations of (20) or the one-step quadrature formula of (30).

As an easy corollary of this theorem, we do verify that longer life of a warrant can at most enhance its value, i.e., $F_{n+1}(X) \geq F_n(X)$.

For, from the theorem itself $F_1(X) \geq F_0(X)$, and hence

$$F_2(X) = e^{-r} \int_0^\infty F_1(XZ)dQ(Z;1) \geq e^{-r} \int_0^\infty F_0(XZ)dQ(Z;1) = F_1(X).$$

And, inductively, if $F_t(X) \geq F_{t-1}(X)$ for all $t \leq n$, it follows that

$$F_{n+1}(X) = e^{-r} \int_0^\infty F_n(XZ)dQ(Z;1) \geq e^{-r} \int_0^\infty F_{n-1}(XZ)dQ(Z;1) = F_n(X).$$

If $Q(Z;1) > 0$ for all $Z > 0$ and $Q(Z;1) < 1$ for all $Z < \infty$, we can write strong inequalities $F_{n+1}(X) > F_n(X) > F_{n-1}(X) > \ldots > F_1(X) > F_0(X)$.

The log-normal case belongs to this class. If, however, as in example (3), $Q(Z;1) = 0$ for $Z < \lambda^{-1} < 1$ and for $Z > \lambda > 1$, $F_1(X)$ will vanish for some of the same X values where $F_0(X)$ vanishes; $F_1(X)$ will equal $(X - 1) = F_0(X)$ for large enough X values.

Hence, our weak inequalities are needed in general. However, for n large enough and X fixed, we can still write the strong inequality, namely, $F_{n+1}(X) > F_n(X)$, for $n > n^*(X)$.

The crucial test is this: If for a given X, one can in T steps end up both above or below the conversion price of 1, then $F_T(X) > F_0(X)$ and $F_{n+T}(X) > F_n(X)$. Also, if $F_n(X) > F_0(X)$ for a particular X, $F_{n+T}(X) > F_n(X)$ for that X.

Exact Solution to the Perpetual Warrant Case

We now shall show that the stationary solution to (30), $F(X) \equiv X$,[20] is indeed the limit of the finite-duration warrant prices as $n \to \infty$.
From (30),

$$F_n(X) = e^{-rn} \int_0^\infty F_0(XZ)dQ_n(Z)$$

$$= e^{-rn} \int_{\frac{1}{x}}^\infty (XZ - 1)dQ_n(Z)$$

$$= e^{-rn} \int_0^\infty (XZ - 1)dQ_n(Z) - e^{-rn} \left[\frac{\int_0^{1/x} (1 - XZ)dQ_n(Z)}{\int_0^{1/x} dQ_n(Z)} \right] \cdot \int_0^{\frac{1}{x}} dQ_n(Z) \qquad (33)$$

$$= X - e^{-rn} + e^{-rn} \theta_1(X;n) \theta_2(X;n), \text{ from (31)}$$

But $|\theta_i(X;n)| \leq 1$ for $i = 1,2$. So as $n \to \infty$, $r > 0$,

$$F(X) = \lim_{n \to \infty} F_n(X) = X.$$

Thus, the result is shown for $r > 0$. For $r = 0$, the proof is similar and follows closely the proof on page 23 of the 1965 paper. For $r = 0$, (30) becomes:

$$F_n(X) = \int_{1/x}^{\infty} (XZ - 1)dQ_n(Z)$$

$$= X - 1 + \theta_1(X;n)\,\theta_2(X;n) \quad \text{as before}$$

$$\theta_1(X;n) = \frac{\int_0^{1/x} (1 - XZ)dQ_n(Z)}{\int_0^{1/x} dQ(Z)} = 1 - \frac{X \int_0^{1/x} ZdQ_n(Z)}{\int_0^{1/x} dQ_n(Z)}$$

$$\lim_{n \to \infty} \theta_1(X;n) = 1 - \frac{X \int_0^{1/x} ZdQ_\infty(Z)}{\int_0^{1/x} dQ_\infty(Z)}$$

$$= 1 - 0 \quad \text{because } Q_\infty(0^+,X) = 1 \tag{34}$$

for precisely the same reasons that $P(0^+,X;\infty) = 1.$[21] Similarly,

$$\lim_{n \to \infty} \theta_2(X;n) = \int_0^{1/x} dQ_\infty(Z) = 1 \quad \text{because } Q_\infty(0^+,X) = 1.$$

Therefore,

$$\lim_{n \to \infty} F_n(X) = X - 1 + \lim_{n \to \infty} \theta_1(X;n)\,\theta_2(X;n)$$

$$= X - 1 + 1 = X$$

So the result is shown for $r = 0$.

Admittedly, our new theory has arrived at the same paradoxical result as the special case of the 1965 theory, namely that a perpetual warrant should sell for as much as the common stock itself. Such a result would seem empirically bizarre. In real life, perpetual warrants generally do sell for less, and since the common stock is equivalent to a perpetual right to itself at zero exercise price, one would have thought it would dominate a perpetual warrant exercisible at $1. Indeed, one of the purposes of the general 1965 theory was to construct a model that would keep perpetual warrants down to a price below the common.

What is there to do about the paradox? First, one can recognize that the common stock may be paying dividends now or can be expected to pay dividends at some time in the future. Therefore, the analysis presented in Appendix B may be deemed appropriate, and this will serve to dispel the paradox. Second, one might have thought that dropping the $w_j^* = 0$ incipient case would dispel the paradox. But such a guess would seem to be erroneous, since $w_3^* > 0$ is compatible with having a warrant price, like $F_\infty(X) = X$, because the variance of a perpetual warrant and the common stock are the same. Finally, we may dispel the paradox by accepting it as prosaic. If a stock's mean gain is almost certain to rise indefinitely above the exercise price in the distant future, and that is what $\alpha > 0$ implies, why should not the $1 exercise price be deemed of negligible percentage importance relative to the future value of the common? (Recall too that the $1 is not paid now, but only after an infinite time.) Hence, why should not the perpetual warrant sell for essentially the same price as the common? And, if people believe this will be the case, it will be a self-fulfilling belief. (If most people doubt this, the person who believes in it will average a greater gain by buying warrants.)

Illustrative Example

Now that the general theory is complete, it is of interest to give a complete solution in the easy case of the binomial process with Bernoulli utility as was described in (3); where $\lambda > 1$:

$X_{t+1} = \lambda X$, with probability $p = \frac{1}{2}$.

$X_{t+1} = \lambda^{-1}X$, with probability $1 - p = \frac{1}{2}$ (3a)

and the Bernoulli logarithmic total utility function, $U(W) = \log W$. We further assume the yield on cash is zero (i.e., $r = 0$), and the mean yield of the common stock, $1+a$, is:

$1 + a = \frac{1}{2}(\lambda + \lambda^{-1})$.   (35)

The utility maximum equation corresponding to (13), for $T = 1$, is:

$$\underset{\{w_j\}}{\text{Max }} \overline{U} = \underset{\{w_j\}}{\text{Max}} \left\{ \frac{1}{2}\log[w_1 + w_2\lambda + w_3 \frac{F_n(X\lambda)}{F_{n+1}(X)}] + \frac{1}{2}\log[w_1 + w_2\lambda^{-1} + w_3 \frac{F_n(X\lambda^{-1})}{F_{n+1}(X)}] \right\}$$ (36)

Since we already know that $w_1{}^* = w_2{}^* = \frac{1}{2}$ is optimal for $w_3{}^*$ imposed at zero from the previous analysis of (6) and (7), the first-order conditions corresponding to equations (14) reduce to a single equation:

$$0 = \frac{\frac{1}{2} + \frac{1}{2}\lambda - \dfrac{F_n(X\lambda)}{F_{n+1}(X)}}{\frac{1}{2} + \frac{1}{2}\lambda} + \frac{\frac{1}{2} + \frac{1}{2}\lambda^{-1} - \dfrac{F_n(X\lambda^{-1})}{F_{n+1}(X)}}{\frac{1}{2} + \frac{1}{2}\lambda^{-1}}$$ (37)

Solving for the warrant prices corresponding to (20), we have:

$F_{n+1}(X) = (1 + \lambda)^{-1}F_n(X\lambda) + (1 + \lambda^{-1})^{-1}F_n(X\lambda^{-1})$.   (38)

We have previously shown that the arbitrage conditions imposing premature conversion are not binding. Therefore, (38) and the initial condition

$F_0(X) = \text{Max } [0, X - 1]$ (39)

are sufficient to determine the warrant prices.

The coefficients in (38) can easily be interpreted by our new notion of the util-prob function. They are dQ's discrete probabilities (q_1, q_{-1}) corresponding to the original dP discrete probabilities $(P_1, P_{-1}) = (\frac{1}{2}, \frac{1}{2})$ being related by

$q_i = P_i U'(\frac{1}{2} + \frac{1}{2}\lambda^i)/[P_{-1}U'(\frac{1}{2} + \frac{1}{2}\lambda^{-1}) + P_1 U'(\frac{1}{2} + \frac{1}{2}\lambda)]$

$= \frac{1}{2} [\frac{1}{\frac{1}{2} + \frac{1}{2}\lambda^i}] / [\frac{1}{2} (\frac{1}{\frac{1}{2} + \frac{1}{2}\lambda^{-1}}) + \frac{1}{2} (\frac{1}{\frac{1}{2} + \frac{1}{2}\lambda})]$

$= (1 + \lambda^i)^{-1}$, for $i = \pm 1$.

As in the 1965 paper, we convert (38) into a standard random-walk stochastic process by means of a logarithmic or exponential transformation in which $X = \lambda^k$, $k = \log_\lambda X$. It will suffice for an example to consider only integer values of k. Finally, write $F_n(\lambda^k) = F_{k,n}$. Then (38) becomes the familiar partial difference equation[22] of the classical random walk, $F_{k,n+1} = q_1 F_{k+1,n} + q_{-1}F_{k-1,n}$, $q_1 + q_{-1} = 1$ (40)

					k				
	−4	−3	−2	−1	0	1	2	3	4
n									
0	0	0	0	0	0	.1000	.2100	.3300	.4600
1		0	0	0	.0476	.1000	.2100	.3300	
2			0	.0363	.0476	.1250	.2100		
3				.0363	.0684	.1250			
4					.0684				

Table I

Table I illustrates, in the familiar form of Pascal's triangle, calculation of the warrant prices for our special case. The arrows in the table illustrate the step-by-step calculations: thus, $F_1(1) = F_1(\lambda^0) = F_{01}$, is for $\lambda = 1.1$, calculated as $F_{01} = \dfrac{1}{(1 + 1.1)}$

$F_{10} = .0476$, and $F_{13} = F_3(1.1)$ is calculated as $F_{13} = (\dfrac{1}{2.1}) F_{22} + (\dfrac{1.1}{2.1}) F_{02} = .1250$.

From Table I, we calculate

$$q_1 = \frac{1}{2.1} = .4762; \quad q_{-1} = \frac{1.1}{2.1} = .5238.$$

Note that there are several re-occurring patterns within the table which are not due to the particular choice of λ. For example, in the $k = 0$ column, successive odd and even entries repeat themselves: $F_{01} = F_{02}$; $F_{03} = F_{04}, \ldots, F_{0,2n+1} = F_{0,2n+2}$ for all λ.

What is the profitability of holding the warrant as against holding the common or holding. cash? We can compute this from our table, using the actual dP probabilities of $(\frac{1}{2}, \frac{1}{2})$. Thus, the outcomes $F_0(\lambda^{+1})$ that emerge from buying $F_1(1)$, have a mean yield of $\frac{1}{2} \cdot (2.1) + \frac{1}{2} \cdot (0) - 1 = .05$ per cent per month.

This turns out to be a higher actual yield than the postulated $\alpha = .04545$ per cent per month of the common stock. (We are here speaking of actual α_P and β_P yields and not of the hypothetical $\alpha_Q = r$ and $\beta_Q = r$ yields referred to in earlier sections.) One can easily verify from any other entry in the table that in every case, the warrant's β yield exceeds the fixed α yield of the common. Indeed, from the general formulas for any λ and not just for $\lambda = 1.1$, one finds $\beta > \alpha$. Thus, to find the mean yield from buying a 1-period warrant at $X_t = 1$ at the rational price $F_1(1)$ for any $\lambda > 1$, we calculate from (38) the price $F_1(1)$:

$$F_1(1) = (1 + \lambda)^{-1} F_0(\lambda) + (1 + \lambda^{-1})^{-1} F_0(\lambda^{-1})$$
$$= \frac{\lambda - 1}{\lambda + 1} \qquad\qquad + 0$$

Our mean gain per dollar, b, is:

$$E\left[\frac{F_0(X_{t+1})}{F_1(1)}\,\Big|\,X_t = 1\right] = \tfrac{1}{2}\,\frac{(\lambda - 1)}{(1+\lambda)^{-1}\,(\lambda - 1)} - 1$$

$$= \frac{\lambda - 1}{2} = b$$

For $\lambda > 1$, $\dfrac{\lambda - 1}{2} > \dfrac{\lambda + \lambda^{-1}}{2} = a$, from (35)

or $b > a$, and $\beta > \alpha$.

Is this a surprising finding? When one reflects that the warrant has higher "volatility" than does the common, it would seem intuitively reasonable that they should have to afford a higher yield than the common if they are to be held in the same portfolio. More-over, since the degree of volatility can be expected to vary with the price of the common and the duration of the warrant, there is no *a priori* reason to expect that the actual β should be a constant; instead it is reasonable to expect that it must be written as a function of X and n, namely, $\beta(X, n)$.

Actually, this expectation that $\beta(X,n) > \alpha$, which was based on our illustrative case and on *a priori* reasoning, turns out to be true for even the most general case. In the next section, by means of an important lemma, we shall prove the above inequality. Of course, in the limit when the perpetual warrant approaches the value of the common stock, the divergence $\beta(X,n) - \alpha$ will go to zero as $n \to \infty$.

Proof of the Superiority of Yield of Warrants Over Yield of Common Stock

First we wish to state an important lemma upon which this proof and other results rest. Proof of this lemma and indeed of a wider lemma of which this is a special case is rele-gated to Appendix A. Broadly speaking, what we wish to show is that if two perfectly positively correlated securities are to be held in the same portfolio, with the outcome of one being a monotone-increasing function of the other, but with its possessing greater "volatility" in the sense of its elasticity with respect to the other exceeding one, the mean yield of the volatile security must exceed the mean yield of the less volatile one.

We define the elasticity of the function $\Psi(Y)$ with respect to Y, E_Ψ, in the usual fashion as,

$$E_\Psi \equiv \frac{d(\log\Psi)}{d(\log Y)} = \frac{Y\Psi'(Y)}{\Psi(Y)}$$

Although we work here with functions possessing a derivative, this could be dispensed with and be replaced by working with finite-difference arc elasticities.

Lemma (a) Let $\Psi(Y)$ be a differentiable, non-negative function whose elasticity, E_Ψ, is strictly greater than one for all $Y \in (0, \infty)$.
(b) Let $v(Y)$ be a positive, monotone-decreasing, differentiable weighting function (i.e., $v(Y) > 0$, $v'(Y) < 0$) and $dP(Y)$ be a probability distribution function over non-negative Y such that its cumulative distribution function must grow at more than one positive point (so that P(Y) takes on at least three positive values for positive Y's).

If $\int_0^\infty \Psi(Y)v(Y)dP(Y) = \int_0^\infty Yv(Y)dP(Y)$

Then $\int_0^\infty \Psi(Y)dP(Y) > \int_0^\infty YdP(Y)$

With this Lemma, we can then proceed to state and prove the following theorem.

Theorem If $F_n(X)$ is generated by the process described in equations (20) and (21), or in (29), (30), and (31) and if the actual yield $\beta(X,n)$ is defined by $e^{\beta(X,n)} = \int_0^\infty F_n(XZ)/F_{n+1}(X)dP(Z;1)$, then for all finite n, $\beta(X,n) > \alpha$.

Now, writing $F_n(XZ)/F_{n+1}(X) = \Psi(Z)$, we must show that Ψ has the properties hypothesized by part (a) of the Lemma, i.e., $\Psi \geq 0$ and $E\Psi > 1$. Clearly, $\Psi(z) \geq 0$ and, even more, because F_n is an increasing function of its argument, $\Psi'(Z) > 0$ for all $Z > 0$. From equation (30) and the definition of $F_0(X)$, for all $X > 0$ such that $F_n(X) > 0$, we have:

$$0 \leq \frac{F_n'(X)}{F_n(X)} = \frac{\int_{1/X}^\infty ZdQ_n(Z)}{\int_{1/X}^\infty (XZ - 1)dQ_n(z)} = \frac{1}{X - \dfrac{\int_{1/X}^\infty xdQ_n(Z)}{\int_{1/X}^\infty ZdQ_n(Z)}} > \frac{1}{X} \tag{41}$$

So, for $X > 0$ such that $F_n(X) > 0$,

$$\frac{XF_n'(X)}{F_n(X)} > 1 \tag{42}$$

Therefore, from (42),

$$E_\Psi = \frac{Z[\dfrac{F_n'(XZ)X}{F_{n+1}(X)}]}{[\dfrac{F_n(XZ)}{F_{n+1}(X)}]} = \frac{(XZ)F_n'(XZ)}{F_n(XZ)} > 1$$

If we write $v(Z) = U'[(1 - w_2^*)e^r + w_2^*Z]$, we must show that U' satisfies condition (b) of the Lemma. Clearly, by the definition of U, $U' > 0$ and $U'' < 0$, condition (b) is satisfied. From (29), (30), and (31), with $n = 1$, all the conditions for the hypothesis of the Lemma are satisfied:

$$\int_0^\infty \frac{F_n(XZ)}{F_{n+1}(X)}dQ(Z;1) = e^r = \int_0^\infty ZdQ(Z;1).$$

Therefore, by the Lemma,

$$\int_0^\infty \frac{F_n(XZ)}{F_{n+1}(X)} dP(Z;1) > \int_0^\infty ZdP(Z;1)$$

or,

$$e^{\beta(x,n)} > e^\alpha$$

therefore,

$$\beta(X,n) > \alpha.$$

So the theorem is proved. Using the Lemma, as generalized in Appendix A, one could give a second proof that the common itself, being more "volatile" than the safe asset, must have a greater expected yield: namely $\alpha > r$ as expressed earlier in equation (21).

Conclusion

This completes the theory of utility-warranted warrant pricing. We leave to another occasion the calculation by a computer o˙ tables of values for $F_n(X)$ based upon certain empirical assumptions about the volatility and trend of the $P(X_{t+n}/X_t;n)$ process. Using the general mathematical methods of the 1965 paper, but with different economic interpretations, we can also prepare tables of $F_n(X)$ for the Appendix B case of dividend-paying stocks.

Appendix A

The generalization and proof of the Lemma to prove the theorem that $\beta(X,n) > \alpha$ is as follows:[23]

Lemma   Let Ψ, ϕ, and v be Reimann-Steiltjes integrable with respect to P where $dP(Y)$ is a probability distribution function and v is a monotone-decreasing function on $[0,\infty)$ and $v(Y) > 0$ for $Y > 0$. Suppose:

(a) there exists $\bar{Y}\epsilon(0,\infty)$ such that $\Psi(Y) \leq \phi(Y)$ for all $Y < \bar{Y}$ and $\phi(Y) \leq \Psi(Y)$, for all $Y > \bar{Y}$, and

(b) $\int_0^\infty \Psi(Y)v(Y)dP(Y) = \int_0^\infty \phi(Y)v(Y)dP(Y)$.

Then $\int_0^\infty \Psi(Y)dP(Y) \geq \int_0^\infty \phi(Y)dP(Y)$.

Proof:

1 $\int_0^{\bar{Y}} [\Psi(Y) - \phi(Y)]v(Y)dP(Y) \leq 0$

$\int_{\bar{Y}}^\infty [\Psi(Y) - \phi(Y)]v(Y)dP(Y) \geq 0$, because $v(Y) \geq 0$

2 $-\int_0^{\bar{Y}} [\Psi(Y) - \phi(Y)]v(Y)dP(Y) = \int_{\bar{Y}}^\infty [\Psi(Y) - \phi(Y)]v(Y)dP(Y)$, from (b)

3 Let $\bar{v} = v(\bar{Y}) > 0$

Then $v(Y) \geq \bar{v}$　　　for $Y \leq \bar{Y}$

$v(Y) \leq \bar{v}$　　　for $Y \geq \bar{Y}$, by hypothesis

4 Then

$-\int_0^{\bar{Y}} [\Psi(Y) - \phi(Y)]\bar{v}dP(Y) \leq \int_{\bar{Y}}^\infty [\Psi(Y) - \phi(Y)]\bar{v}dP(Y)$, from 2 and 3

5 Therefore,

$\int_0^\infty \Psi(Y)dP(Y) \geq \int_0^\infty \phi(Y)dP(Y)$　　　Q.E.D.

To show the Lemma stated in the text is a special case of this general Lemma and to get the sharper inequality result of that Lemma, it is necessary to prove a corollary to the general Lemma and also another lemma to the corollary. (The lemma to the corollary will be referred to with a lower case l to distinguish it from the general Lemma.)

Corollary   Let Ψ, ϕ, and dP be as in the Lemma, and let dP not have the property:

$dP = \begin{Bmatrix} p, & Y = 0 \\ 1 - p, & Y = \bar{Y} \\ 0, & \text{otherwise} \end{Bmatrix}$; suppose $v(Y)$ is *strictly* monotone-decreasing and non-negative on $[0,\infty]$. Suppose:

(a') there exists $\bar{Y}\epsilon(0,\infty)$ such that $\Psi(Y) < \phi(Y)$, for all $Y\epsilon(0,\bar{Y})$ and $\phi(Y) < \Psi(Y)$, for all $Y\epsilon(\bar{Y},\infty)$, and

(b) $\int_0^\infty \Psi(Y)v(Y)dP(Y) = \int_0^\infty \phi(Y)v(Y)dP(Y)$.

Then $\int_0^\infty \Psi(Y)dP(Y) > \int_0^\infty \phi(Y)dP(Y)$.

Proof:

1   $\int_0^{\bar{Y}} [\Psi(Y) - \phi(Y)]v(Y)dP(Y) < 0$

   $\int_{\bar{Y}}^\infty [\Psi(Y) - \phi(Y)]v(Y)dP(Y) > 0$, by the property of dP and $v \geq 0$.

2   $-\int_0^{\bar{Y}} [\Psi(Y) - \phi(Y)]v(Y)dP(Y) = \int_{\bar{Y}}^\infty [\Psi(Y) - \phi(Y)]v(Y)dP(Y)$ from (b).

3   Let $\bar{v} = v(\bar{Y}) > 0$

     Then $v(Y) > \bar{v}, Y < \bar{Y}$

        $v(Y) < \bar{v}, Y > \bar{Y}$, by hypothesis

4   Then

$$-\int_0^{\bar{Y}} [\Psi(Y) - \phi(Y)]\bar{v}dP(Y) < \int_{\bar{Y}}^\infty [\Psi(Y) - \phi(Y)]\bar{v}dP(Y)$$

(Note: the posited property of dP was needed for this step.)

5   Therefore,

$$\int_0^\infty \Psi(Y)dP(Y) > \int_0^\infty \phi(Y)dP(Y) \qquad \text{Q.E.D.}$$

Thus, the strict inequality form of the Lemma used in the text is proved.

Although it is clear that the strict inequality of the corollary would not hold for the pathological dP(Y) case ruled out in the hypothesis of the corollary and of the Lemma in the text, it is instructive to give an example of this case.

Let dP(Y) be such that
Prob $\{Z = 0\} = \frac{1}{2}$
Prob $\{Z = 3\} = \frac{1}{2}$ (Note: $\Psi(3) = 3$, from below.)
and suppose that we have Bernoulli logarithmic utility. Then we have
$1 + a = 1.5$ or $a = .5$, the mean yield of the stock. From the utility maximum equation, for $n = 1$,

$$F_1(X) = \tfrac{1}{3}F_0(3X)$$

and by the usual recursive process, we get:

$$F_n(X) = \tfrac{1}{3}{}^n F_0(3^n X).$$

The mean warrant yield, b, is defined as follows:

$$b = E[F_n(XZ)/F_{n+1}(X)] - 1$$

$$= \tfrac{1}{2}[\tfrac{1}{3}{}^n F_0(3^n X \cdot 3)/\frac{1}{3^{n+1}}X)] - 1$$

$$= 1.5 - 1 = .5$$

So, $b = a$ or $\beta(X,n) \equiv \alpha$ in this singular case.

In retrospect, the reason for $\beta(X,n) = \alpha$ for this type of distribution is that in it the stock and warrant are equally "volatile" with the chance of losing everything being the same for both stock and warrant.

We must show now the equivalence of the elasticity hypothesis of the Lemma in the text to the hypotheses of the general Lemma. To do so, we prove the following lemma to the corollary.

Lemma Let Ψ, ϕ, and dP be as in the general Lemma, and, in addition, Ψ and ϕ are continuous. Suppose either: (i) there exists an $\Sigma > 0$ such that $\Psi(Y) = 0$, $Y \leq \Sigma$; $\phi(0) \geq 0$; $E_\Psi > E_\phi > 0$, for all $Y > \Sigma$; $E_\phi > 0$ for all $Y > 0$ and (b) holds; or (ii) $E_\Psi > E_\phi > 0$, for all $Y > 0$ and (b) holds. Then condition (a') of the corollary holds.

Proof

(I) If $\phi(Y) = \Psi(\bar{Y})$ for some $\bar{Y} > 0$, then there does not exist $\tilde{Y} \neq \bar{Y}$, $\tilde{Y} > 0$ such that $\phi(\tilde{Y}) = \Psi(\tilde{Y})$.

Proof: Consider any point $Y > 0$ where $\phi(Y) = \Psi(Y)$. Under condition (i), $Y > \Sigma$ because $\phi(0) \geq 0$, $E_\phi > 0$, for all $Y > 0$. Thus Y is such that $E_\Psi(Y) > E_\phi(Y)$, i.e., Ψ cuts ϕ from below at Y. But since $E_\Psi > E_\phi$, for all $Y > \Sigma$, ϕ can cut Ψ from below only once.

(II) There exists a $\delta > 0$ such that $\Psi(Y) < \phi(Y)$ for all $Y \epsilon (0, \delta)$.

Proof: 1) For (i) this holds trivially by setting $\delta = \Sigma$, in view of the restrictions on ϕ and Ψ. 2) For (ii), suppose such a δ does not exist. Then, given any $\Sigma > 0$, there exists a Y such that $Y\epsilon(0, \Sigma)$ and $\Psi(Y) > \phi(Y)$. But since $E_\Psi > E_\phi$, for all $Y > 0$, this implies that $\Psi(Y) > \phi(Y)$, for all $Y > 0$.
But this contradicts (b).

Thus, $\int_0^\delta [\Psi(Y) - \phi(Y)]v(Y)dP(Y) < 0$, and therefore

$$\int_\delta^\infty [\Psi(Y) - \phi(Y)]v(Y)dP(Y) > 0$$

Thus $\Psi(Y) < \phi(Y)$ for some $y\epsilon(0, \delta)$

$\qquad \Psi(Y) > \phi(Y)$ for some $y\epsilon(\delta, \infty)$

This implies, since Ψ and ϕ are assumed continuous, that there exists $\bar{Y} > 0$ such that $\phi(\bar{Y}) = \Psi(\bar{Y})$. By (I) we know $\bar{Y}$ is unique in $(0, \infty)$.
Therefore $\Psi(Y) < \phi(Y)$, $0 < Y \leq \Sigma$ and $E_\Psi > E_\phi$ for $Y > \Sigma$ so that $\bar{Y}$ is such that for $Y\Sigma(0, \infty)$ and $\Psi(Y) < \phi(Y)$, for all $Y < \bar{Y}$ and $\phi(Y) < \Psi(Y)$, for all $Y > \bar{Y}$.

$\qquad\qquad\qquad\qquad\qquad\qquad\qquad\qquad\qquad\qquad\qquad\qquad$ Q.E.D.

Thus, from the corollary and the lemma to the corollary and by taking $\phi(Y) = Y$ (and therefore, $E_\phi \equiv 1$), we have proved the Lemma used in the text. It was necessary in the lemma to the corollary to include the alternative hypothesis (i) because in the case where

$$\Psi(Z) = F_n(XZ)/F_{n+1}(X),$$

it is possible that $F_n(XZ) \equiv 0$ for positive XZ in the neighborhood of $XZ = 0$, in which case E_Ψ will not be properly defined. One can see that this has no effect on the Lemma because

$$\int_0^\infty \Psi(Y)v(Y)dP(Y) = \int_R \Psi(Y)v(Y)dP(Y)$$

where $R = \{Y | Y \epsilon (0, \infty) \text{ and } \Psi(Y) > 0\}$ and similarly,
$$\int_0^\infty \Psi(Y) dP(Y) = \int_R \Psi(Y) dP(Y).$$

Thus, we could go through the entire derivation considering only $Y \epsilon R$ where E_Ψ is well-defined and then at the end substitute the integrals over all non-negative Y.

It should be emphasized that the proof of the general Lemma did not even require continuity of Ψ, ϕ, and v and that the probability distribution dP can be discrete, entailing corners in the $F_n(X)$ functions. Thus, it holds for quite general types of assets and probability distributions. A simple extension of the corollary would prove the following general theorem of portfolio analysis.

Theorem: Let $\Psi_1, \Psi_2, \ldots, \Psi_n$ be the set of price ratios for n perfectly-correlated assets and let their elasticities, E_{Ψ_i}, be such that $E_{\Psi_1} > E_{\Psi_2} > \ldots > E_{\Psi_n}$. Let Ψ_i, v, dP be as defined in the corollary. If
$$\int_0^\infty \Psi_i(Y) v(Y) dP(Y) = \int_0^\infty \Psi_j(Y) v(Y) dP(Y)$$

for $i,j = 1, \ldots, n$, then $E[\Psi_1] > E[\Psi_2] > \ldots > E[\Psi_n]$

Appendix B

If a common stock permanently pays no dividend, the theory of the text is applicable. If it does pay a dividend, the nice simplifications of the 1965 non-conversion special case is lost and we are back in all the 1965 complex inequalities. If we work with continuous rather than discrete time, the complicated McKean 1965 appendix methods are needed; and many unsolvable problems remain, problems that can be solved to any degree of accuracy only by taking smaller and smaller discrete time intervals. Here we shall sidestep all complexities stemming from continuous time, and can do so with a clearer conscience since the utility maximization is taken always to be over some prescribed finite interval (e.g. six months and a day to achieve capital gains tax privileges).

The simplest assumption about dividends is that the common priced at X_t will after any prescribed period, say T, pay a dividend proportional to its price X_{t+T}. The dividend will then be $X_{t+T}(e^{\delta T} - 1)$ where δ is the "force" or instantaneous rate of dividend yield. By convention, we may set $T = 1$; and each common that costs us X_t today brings us

$$X_{t+1} + X_{t+1}(e^\delta - 1) = X_{t+1}e^\delta$$

after one period. (We neglect all taxation throughout, despite the earlier remark about six-month holding periods.)

Now our maximum problem becomes

$$\underset{\{w_j\}}{\text{Max }} \bar{U}(w_1, w_2, w_3) = \underset{\{w_j\}}{\text{Max }} \int_0^\infty U[w_1 e^r + w_2 e^\delta Z + w_3 \frac{F_n(XZ)}{F_{n+1}(X)}] dP(Z;1)$$

subject to $w_1 + w_2 + w_3 = 1$.

The conditions for the critical point of the Lagrangian, $L = U + \gamma (1 - \Sigma^3_i w_i)$ are exactly as in (14), (15a,) and (16a) except that w_2*e^δ always appears where previously w_2* alone appeared. Hence, the basic equations of the present theory, (15a) and (16a), become

$$F_{n+1}(X) = e^{-r} \int_0^\infty F_n(XZ)dQ(Z;1) \tag{43}$$

$$\int_0^\infty ZdQ(Z;1) = e^{-\delta} \tag{44}$$

where of course dQ now involves δ along with its other suppressed parameters. Now $\beta_Q = r$ as before; but $\alpha_Q = r - \delta < \beta_Q$ and we are in the difficult $\beta > \alpha$ area of the 1965 analysis.

Now the values deduced from (43) will fall below $F_0(X)$ conversion levels for large enough X, and conversion will be mandatory. Hence, the recursion relation (43) above must be superseded by the inequalities

$$F_1(X) = Max [0,X - 1, e^{-r} \int_0^\infty F_0(XZ)dQ(Z;1)] \tag{45}$$

$$F_2(X) = Max [0,X - 1, e^{-r} \int_0^\infty F_1(XZ)dQ(Z;1)]$$

. . . .

. . . .

$$F_{n+1}(X) = Max [0,X - 1, e^{-r} \int_0^\infty F_n(XZ)dQ(Z;1)]$$

. . . .

. . . .

$$F_\infty(X) = F(X) = Max [0,X - 1, e^{-r} \int_0^\infty F(XZ)dQ(Z;1)]$$

By the 1965 methods, one can show that for given $r = \beta$, and $\delta = \beta - \alpha$, we can find conversion values $(X* = c_1, c_2, \ldots, c_\infty)$, which are in ascending order and for which

$$F_n(X) > F_0(X), X < c_n$$

$$\equiv X - 1, X > c_n$$

Actually, for the perpetual warrant case, we have the following Fredholm-like integral equation of the second kind to solve for $F_\infty(X) = F(X)$, namely, for $X<C =C_\infty$,

$$F(X) = e^{-r} \int_0^\infty F(XZ)dQ(Z;1)$$

$$= e^{-r} \int_0^{c/x} F(XZ)dQ(Z;1) + \int_{c/x}^\infty (XZ - 1)dQ(Z;1)$$

$$= e^{-r} \int_0^{c/x} F(XZ)dQ(Z;1) + \phi(X;c), \text{ where } \phi \text{ is a known function.} \tag{46}$$

If dQ corresponds to a probability density q(Z)dZ, we can transform this to

$$F(X) = e^{-r} \int_0^c \frac{1}{X} q(v/X)F(v)dv + \phi(X;c)$$

Suppose this is solved by any of the well-known methods, for each possible c, and let $F(X;c)$ be the solution. Then we can solve for the unknown $c = c_\infty$ as the root of the joining-up equation

$$F(X;c) = X-1 \text{ at } X = c_\infty, \text{ or} \tag{47}$$

$$F(c_\infty;c_\infty) = c_\infty - 1$$

Thus, the perpetual warrant case can be solved without going through the calculations of $F_n(X)$.

Actually, if the probabilities of price changes are bunched around $Z = 1$ with a finite range so that $P(Z;1) = Q(Z;1) = 0$ for $Z < \lambda^* < 1$ and $P(Z;1) = Q(Z;1) = 1$ for $Z > \lambda^{**} > 1$, this Fredholm-type equation can be solved as a Volterra-like equation, which, after a logarithmic transformation, becomes almost of the Poisson or Wiener-Hopf type. This can be seen as follows: consider an X small enough so that $(c_\infty/\lambda^{**}) > X$. Such an X exists because λ^{**} is finite. For X's satisfying this inequality, we have

$$F(X) = e^{-r} \int_{\lambda^*}^{\lambda^{**}} F(XZ)dQ(Z;1) > X - 1 \tag{48}$$

and we can now use the method of analysis shown in the section on utility-maximizing warrant pricing. There is an infinite number of solutions to the homogeneous integral equation (48) of the form cX^m. Substituting in (48), we have

$$\cdot cX^m = e^{-r}cX^m \int_{\lambda^*}^{\lambda^{**}} Z^m dQ(Z;1)$$

$$1 = e^{-r} \int_{\lambda^*}^{\lambda^{**}} Z^m dQ(Z;1) = \phi(m) \tag{49}$$

This is the same as the transcendental equation (23). However, in this case, because $r = \beta_Q > \alpha_Q = r - \delta$, $m = 1$ is no longer a solution. The relevant real root, satisfying the boundary conditions, is $m > 1$, giving us the power formula of the 1965 paper:

$$F_\infty(X) = aX^m = (c_\infty - 1) \left(\frac{X}{c_\infty}\right)^{\frac{c_\infty}{(c_\infty - 1)}}$$

Footnotes

[1]See Samuelson [6].

[2]See Kassouf [2].

[3]See Samuelson [5], where theorems like this one are proved without making the mean-variance approximations of the now classical Markowitz-Tobin type.

Since units are arbitrary, we can take any prescribed wealth level and by dimensional convention make it unity in all of our formulas. This enables expressions like wW to be written simply as w where W = total wealth. As will be specified later, working with isoelastic marginal utility functions that are uniform for all investors will make the scale of prescribed wealth of no importance.

[4]The concavity of U is sufficient to achieve the negative semi-definiteness of the constrained quadratic forms and bordered Hessian minors of L needed to insure that any solution to the first-order conditions does provide a global as well as local maximum. Although the maximum is unique, the portfolio proportions could take on more than one set of optimizing values in singular cases where the quadratic forms were semi-definite rather than definite, e.g., where a perpetual warrant and its common stock are perfectly linearly correlated, making the choice between them indifferent and not unique. This example will be presented later.

[5]At a Washington conference in 1953, the first author once shocked the late J. M. Clark by saying, "Although the probability of a serious 1954 recession is only one-third, that probability should be treated as though it were two-thirds." This was a crude and non-marginal use of a util-prob notion akin to dQ.

[6]In the 1965 paper [6], pp. 30–31, it was mentioned that the possibility of hedges, in which the common stock is sold short in some proportion and the warrant is bought long, would be likely to set limits on the discrepancies that, in the absence of dividend payments, could prevail between β and α. In a forthcoming paper, "Restrictions on Rational Option Pricing: A Set of Arbitrage Conditions," the second author develops arbitrage formulas on warrants and puts and calls which show how severely limited are such β-α discrepancies as a result of instantaneous, almost sure-thing arbitrage transformations.

[7]If the probability of good and bad crops were not equal or if the safe investment process had a non-zero yield, the proportion of the risk asset held would be a function of the λ yield factor; and for utility functions other than the Bernoulli log-form and a probability distribution different from the simple binomial, w^* would be a more complicated calculable function.

[8]Strictly speaking, a will probably be a function of time, a_{t-1} being high in the period following a generally poor crop when the λ_t^{-1} yield factor, rather than λ_t, has just occurred and the investable surplus is small. We have here a stationary time series in which total output vibrates around an equilibrium level. Spelling all this out would be another story: here a will be taken as a constant.

[9]For the family

$$U(X) = a + \frac{bX^{\frac{e-1}{e}}}{\frac{e-1}{e}}, \ 0 < e \neq 1, \ \frac{-U'(X)}{XU''(X)} = e.$$

The singular case where $e = 1$ can be found by L'Hôpital's evaluation of an indeterminate form to correspond to the Bernoulli case, $U(X) = a + b \log X$. As Arrow [1], Pratt [4], and others have shown, optimal portfolio proportions are independent of the absolute size of wealth for any function that is a member of this utility family.

Actually, we can free our analysis from the assumption of isoelastic marginal utility if we are willing to apply it to any single individual and determine from it the critical warrant price patterns at which he would be neither a buyer nor seller, or would hold some specified proportion of his wealth in the form of warrants. By pitting the algebraic excess demands of one set of individuals against the other, we could determine the market clearing pattern.

[10]U being concave assures a maximum. The problem could be formulated with Kuhn-Tucker inequalities to cover the no-borrowing restriction, $w_i \leq 1$, and the no-short-selling restriction, $w_i \geq 0$.

[11]The F_n function in (13) is the "utility-warranted" price of the warrant, which is not the same as the "rational" warrant price of the 1965 theory discussed above, even though we use the same symbol for both.

[12]This would be a generalization of the analysis above to three rather than only two assets. In the next section, we digress to discuss briefly in these terms the simplest case of pricing a given supply of 1-period warrants. This illustrates a general theory.

[13]Thorp and Kassouf [7] advocate hedged short sales of overpriced warrants about to expire. The analysis here defines the levels at which one who holds the stock long can just benefit in the maximizing expected utility sense from short-sale hedges in the warrant.

[14]Strictly speaking, F_1 is a function of more than X alone; it can be written as $F_1 (X;r;V/M)$. Likewise, the equilibrium S is of the form $G(X;r;V/M)M$, where both G and F_1 are functionals of the probability-distribution function $P(Z;1)$. There is a formal similarity here to the quantity theory of money and prices, due, of course, to the "homogeneity" assumption made about tastes. It should be fairly evident that in the same fashion by which we have here deduced the $F_1(\cdot)$ function from the known $F_0(\cdot)$ function, one could in general deduce recursively $F_{n+1}(\cdot)$ in terms of a known $F_n(\cdot)$ function. Similar homogeneity properties in terms of (V,M) and V/M would hold. Finally, instead of assuming completely inelastic V supply and completely elastic common stock supply dependent on a hard parameter, one could formulate a completely general equilibrium model in which r, α, and the probability distribution $P(Z;1)$ were all determined simultaneously.

[15]We will show later that $\beta_p > \alpha_p$ for finite-duration warrants, falling toward equality as the duration time becomes perpetual.

[16]The Hertz-Herglotz-Lotka methods of renewal theory are closely related, once we replace X and Z by their logarithms. However, the fact that our dQ involves Z's on *both* sides of unity with positive weights introduces some new complications. Later, without regard to formal expansions of this type, we prove that $F_n(X) \rightarrow F_\infty(X) \equiv X$. For references to this literature, including work by Fellner, see Lopez [3].

[17]There is a further complication. If decisions are frozen for n periods, then (26) is valid, superseding (24) and (20). Or put differently, n of the old time periods are now equivalent to one new time period; and in terms of this new time period, (20) would be rewritten to have exactly the same content as (26). Now (24) or (25) would simply be irrelevant. One must not suppose that this change in time units is merely a representational shift to new dimensional units, as from seconds to minutes. If our portfolio is to be frozen for six months, that differs substantially from its being frozen for six weeks, even though we may choose to write six months as twenty-six weeks. But now for the complication: one would not expect the U(W) function relevant for a six-week frozen-decision period to be relevant for a six-month period as well. Strictly speaking then, in using (26) for a long-frozen-period analysis, we should require that the U'(W) function which enters into $dQ(Z;n)$ be written as dependent on n, or as $\partial U[W;n]/\partial W$. . Two papers showing proper lifetime portfolio decisions are forthcoming: P. A. Samuelson, "Lifetime Portfolio Selection by Dynamic Stochastic Programming" and R. C. Merton, "Lifetime Portfolio Selection Under Uncertainty: The Continuous-Time Case."

One further remark. Consider the "incipient-cash" case, where $w_1^* = 0$ because the common stock dominates the safe asset, with $\alpha >> r$. Combining this case with our incipient-warrant case, w_2^* remains at unity in every period, no matter what we learn about the outcomes within any larger period. In this case, the results of (20) and those of (26) are compatible and the latter does give us by mere quadrature a one-step solution to the problem. The 1965 proof that $F_n(X) \rightarrow X$ as $n \rightarrow \infty$ can then be applied directly.

[18]If, as mentioned in footnote 9, we free the analysis from the assumption of isoelastic marginal utility, the definitions of (29) must be generalized to take account of the changing (w_i^*) optimizing decisions, which will now be different depending on changing wealth levels that are passed through.

[19]The results of this section hold also for calls. See Appendix B for the results for dividend-paying stocks.

[20]This is the limiting case where equations (30) and (31) become identical. The bordered Hessian becomes singular and w_2^* and w_3^* become indistinguishable, i.e., the warrant and the stock cease to be distinguishable assets.

[21]See Samuelson [6], p. 17. The paradox of almost-certain, almost-total ruin for fair-game betters who re-bet their proceeds is involved here. Consider a hypothetical multiplicative probability process $Y_0 = X$, $Y_1 = XZ_1$, $Y_2 = XZ_1Z_2, \ldots, Y_n = XZ_1 \ldots Z_n$ where X is a constant and each Z_i is independently distributed according to the probability distribution Prob $\{Z_i \leq Z\} = Q_1(Z)$. Then it directly follows that Prob $\{XZ_1Z_2 \leq XZ\} = Q_2(Z)$, and $\ldots$ Prob $\{XZ_1 \ldots Z_n \leq XZ\} = Q_n(Z)$. Since $E[Z] = \int_0^\infty ZQ_1(Z)dZ = e^0 = 1$, and $P(X;1)$ and $Q_1(Z)$ involve some positive dispersion, the geometric mean of $dQ_1(Z)$ lies below the arithmetic mean of $1 = E[Z]$. Hence, $E[logZ_i] = \int_0^\infty logZdQ_1(Z) = \nu < 0$. By the central limit theorem applied to $logX + \Sigma^n logZ_i = logY_n$, $E(logY_n) = logX + n\nu$ and $E[logY_n] \rightarrow - \infty$ as $n \rightarrow \infty$, so that all the probability becomes spread out to the left of any fixed number Z. Thus, $Q_n(Z) \rightarrow 1$ as $n \rightarrow \infty$ for all $Z > 0$. (Note: A fair-game (r = 0) in Q-space implies a better-than-fair game ($\alpha > 0$) in P-space from equation (21).)
Warning: Although $Q_\infty(Z)$ becomes a log-normal distribution, say, $L(Z;\nu,\delta,n)$, it is quite wrong to think that necessarily

$$X = F_\infty(X) = \lim_{n \to \infty} e^{-rn} \int_0^\infty F_0(XZ) dQ_n(Z)$$

$$= \int_0^\infty F_0(X) \lim_{n \to \infty} e^{-rn} dL(Z; \nu, \delta, n)$$

$$= \int_0^\infty F_0(XZ) dQ^*(Z)$$

Such interchanging of limits will generally not be permissible.

[22]This partial difference equation can presumably be solved by the methods of Lagrange and Laplace, but there are complexities involved due to the boundary conditions of arbitrage which we do not wish to go into at this time.

[23]The proofs of the general Lemma, the corollary, and the lemma to the corollary are by David T. Scheffman, Ph.D. candidate at MIT.

References

[1]   Arrow, K. J. *Aspects of the Theory of Risk-Bearing.* Helsinki, Yrjo Jahnssonin Saatio, 1965.

[2]   Kassouf, S. T. "Stock Price Random Walks: Some Supporting Evidence," *Review of Economics and Statistics,* Vol. 50 (1968), pp. 275-278.

[3]   Lopez, A. *Problems in Stable Population Theory.* Princeton, Office of Population Research, Princeton University, 1961.

[4]   Pratt, J. W. "Risk Aversion in the Small and in the Large," *Econometrica,* Vol. 32 (January 1964), pp. 122-136.

[5]   Samuelson, P. A. "General Proof that Diversification Pays," *Journal of Financial and Quantitative Analysis,* Vol. 3 (1967), pp. 1-13.

[6]   Samuelson, P. A. "Rational Theory of Warrant Pricing," *Industrial Management Review,* Vol. 6, no. 2 (Spring 1965), pp. 13-32; Mathematical Appendix by H. P. McKean, Jr., pp. 32-39.

[7]   Thorp, E. O., and Kassouf, S. T. *Beat the Market.* New York, Random House, 1967.

201

GENERAL PROOF THAT DIVERSIFICATION PAYS **

Paul A. Samuelson *

"Don't put all your eggs in one basket," is a familiar adage. Economists, such as Marschak, Markowitz, and Tobin,[1] who work only with mean income and its variance, can give specific content to this rule-- namely, putting a fixed total of wealth equally into independently, identically distributed investments will leave the mean gain unchanged and will minimize the variance.

However, there are many grounds for being dissatisfied with an analysis dependent upon but two moments, the mean and variance, of a statistical distribution. I have long used the following, almost obvious, theorem in lectures. When challenged to find it in the literature, I was unable to produce a reference--even though I should think it must have been stated more than once.

Theorem I: If $U(X)$ is a strictly concave and smooth function that is monotonic for non-negative X, and $(X_1,\ldots,X_n)$ are independently, identically distributed variates with joint frequency distribution

$$\text{Prob}\{X_1 \le x_1,\ldots,X_n \le x_n\} = F(x_1)F(x_2)\ldots F(x_n)$$

$$\text{with } E[x_i] = \int_{-\infty}^{\infty} X_i dF(X_i) = \mu_1$$

$$E[x_i - \mu_1]^2 = \int_{-\infty}^{\infty} (X_i - \mu_1)^2 dF(X_i) = \mu_2$$

$$\text{with } 0 < \mu_2 < \infty ,$$

---

* Massachusetts Institute of Technology.

** My thanks go to the Carnegie Corporation for providing me with a reflective year and to Mrs. F. Skidmore for research assistance.

then

$$E\left[U\left[\sum_1^n \lambda_j X_j\right]\right] = \int_{-\infty}^{\infty} \cdots \int_{-\infty}^{\infty} U\left[\sum_1^n \lambda_j X_j\right] dF(X_1) \cdots dF(X_n)$$

$$= \Psi(\lambda_1, \ldots, \lambda_n)$$

is a strictly concave symmetric function that attains its

unique maximum, subject to

$$\lambda_1 + \lambda_2 + \cdots + \lambda_n = 1 , \quad \lambda_i \geq 0$$

at $\Psi\left(\dfrac{1}{n}, \ldots, \dfrac{1}{n}\right)$.

The proof is along the lines of a proof[2] used to show that equal distribution of income among identical Benthamites will maximize the sum of social utility.

$$\frac{\partial \Psi(\lambda_1, \ldots, \lambda_n)}{\partial \lambda_i} = \int_{-\infty}^{\infty} \cdots \int_{-\infty}^{\infty} X_i \, U'\left[\sum_1^n \lambda_j X_j\right] dF(X_1) \ldots dF(X_n)$$

is independent of i at $(\lambda_1, \ldots \lambda_n) = (1/n, \ldots 1/n)$ by symmetry.

The Hessian matrix with elements

$$\frac{\partial^2 \Psi}{\partial \lambda_i \partial \lambda_j} = \int_{-\infty}^{\infty} \cdots \int_{-\infty}^{\infty} X_i X_j U''\left[\sum_1^n \lambda_k X_k\right] dF(X_1) \ldots dF(X_n)$$

is a Grammian negative definite matrix if $-U'' > 0$, $0 < \mu_2 < \infty$.

Hence , sufficient maximum conditions for a unique maximum are

satisfied, namely

$$\frac{\partial \Psi\left(\dfrac{1}{n}, \ldots, \dfrac{1}{n}\right)}{\partial \lambda_1} = \cdots = \frac{\partial \Psi\left(\dfrac{1}{n}, \ldots, \dfrac{1}{n}\right)}{\partial \lambda_n}$$

$$\sum_1^n \sum_1^n \frac{\partial^2 \Psi}{\partial \lambda_i \partial \lambda_j} y_i y_j < 0 \text{ for all non-negative } \lambda\text{'s and not all y's}$$

vanishing.

Remarks: Differentiability assumptions could be lightened.
It is not true, by the way, that $\frac{1}{2} X_1 + \frac{1}{2} X_2$ has a "uniformly more-bunched distribution" than X_1 or X_2 separately, as simple examples (even with finite μ_2) can show: still the risk averter will always benefit from diversification. The finiteness of μ_2 is important. Thus, for a Cauchy distribution $\frac{1}{2} X_1 + \frac{1}{2} X_2$ has the same distribution as either X_1 or X_2 separately; for the arc-sine Pareto-Lévy case, it has a worse distribution. The proof fails because the postulated $E[U]$ cannot exist (be finite) for any concave U.

The General Case of Symmetric Interdependence

We can now drop the assumption of independence of distribution, replacing it by the less restrictive postulate of a symmetric joint distribution. I.e., we replace $F(x_1) \ldots F(x_n)$ by

$$\text{Prob}\{X_1 \leq x_1, \ X_2 \leq x_2, \ldots, X_n \leq x_n\} = P(x_1, x_2, \ldots, x_n)$$

where P is a symmetric function in its arguments. We can rule out, as trivial, the case where the x's are connected by an exact functional relation, which in view of symmetry would have to take the form

$$x_1 = x_2 = \ldots = x_n = x$$

$$\text{Prob}\{X \leq x\} = P(x) = P(x, \ldots, x) \quad .$$

We do stipulate finite means, variances, and covariances

$$E[x_i] = \int_{-\infty}^{\infty} \cdots \int_{-\infty}^{\infty} X_i \, dP(X_1, \ldots, X_n) = \mu$$

$$E[(x_i - \mu)\ (x_j - \mu)] = \int_{-\infty}^{\infty} \cdots \int_{-\infty}^{\infty} (X_i - \mu)(X_j - \mu) \, dP(X_1, \ldots, X_n)$$

$$= \sigma_{ij}$$

the elements of a positive definite Grammian matrix. A generalization of our earlier theory on diversification can now be stated.

Theorem II: For U(x) a smooth, strictly concave function, the maximum of the symmetric, concave function

$$E[U\left(\sum_1^n \lambda_j x_j\right)] = \int_{-\infty}^{\infty} \cdots \int_{-\infty}^{\infty} U\left(\sum_1^n \lambda_j X_j\right) dP(X_1, \ldots, X_n)$$

$$= \phi(\lambda_1, \ldots, \lambda_n) \quad ,$$

subject to

$$\lambda_1 + \lambda_2 + \ldots \lambda_n = 1, \quad \lambda_i \geq 0 \;,$$

is given by $\phi\left(\frac{1}{n}, \ldots, \frac{1}{n}\right)$. Thus, diversification always pays.

The proof is exactly as before. By symmetry

$$\frac{\partial\phi\left(\frac{1}{n}, \ldots, \frac{1}{n}\right)}{\partial\lambda_1} = \ldots = \frac{\partial\phi\left(\frac{1}{n}, \ldots, \frac{1}{n}\right)}{\partial\lambda_n} \;,$$

the necessary first-order conditions for the constrained maximum.

The Hessian matrix has elements

$$\frac{\partial^2\phi}{\partial\lambda_i \partial\lambda_j} = \int_{-\infty}^{\infty} \ldots \int_{-\infty}^{\infty} X_i X_j U'' \left(\sum_1^n \lambda_k X_k\right) dP(X_1, \ldots, X_n)$$

which, being the coefficients of a negative-definite Grammian matrix, do confirm the concavity of ϕ and therefore the maximum value at $\phi(1/n, \ldots, 1/n)$.

If equal diversification is to be mandatory, symmetry or some assumption like it is of course needed. To verify this obvious fact, suppose (x_1, x_2, x_3) to be independently distributed, with x_2 and x_3 having the same distribution $P(x_i)$, but with x_1 having a distribution that is identical with that of $\frac{1}{2} x_2 + \frac{1}{2} x_3$, namely

$$\text{Prob}\{X_1 \leq x_1\} = Q(x_1) = \int_{-\infty}^{\infty} P(2x_1 - 2s) dP(2s) \;.$$

In this case, symmetry tells us that wealth should be divided equally between the investments x_1 and $\frac{1}{2} x_2 + \frac{1}{2} x_3$, which is equivalent to investing in the (x_1, x_2, x_3) in the fractions $\left(\frac{1}{2}, \frac{1}{4}, \frac{1}{4}\right)$. Those who work with two moments, mean and covariance matrix, will find that minimum variance does not come at $(\lambda_1, \ldots, \lambda_n) = (1/n, \ldots, 1/n)$ when $\sigma_{ii} \neq \sigma_{jj}, \sigma_{ij} \neq \sigma_{rs}$.

It is possible, though, to prove that _some_ positive diversification is mandatory under fairly general circumstances. Thus, in $(x_1, \ldots, x_n)$ let each have a common mean and each have finite but nonzero variance. Finally, suppose that one of the variables, say x_1, is independently distributed from the rest. Then an optimal portfolio <u>must</u> involve $\lambda_1^* > 0$, with some positive investment in x_1, as shown in the following.

<u>Theorem III.</u> Let $(x_1, x_2, \ldots, x_n)$ be jointly distributed as $P(x_1)Q(x_2, \ldots, x_n)$ with common mean and finite positive variances

$$E[x_i] = \int_{-\infty}^{\infty} \cdots \int_{-\infty}^{\infty} X_i \, dP(X_1) \, dQ(X_2, \ldots, X_n) = \mu$$

$$0 < E[(x_i - \mu)^2] < \infty$$

and

$$E[U] = \int_{-\infty}^{\infty} \cdots \int_{-\infty}^{\infty} U\left(\sum_1^n \lambda_j X_j\right) dP(X_1) \, dQ(X_2, \ldots, X_n)$$

$$= \theta \,(\lambda_1, \lambda_2, \ldots, \lambda_n)$$

where, for $U'' < 0$, θ is a strictly concave function.

Then if

$$\theta(\lambda_1^*, \lambda_2^*, \ldots, \lambda_n^*) = \underset{\{\lambda_i\}}{\text{Max}} \; \theta(\lambda_1, \ldots, \lambda_n) \; \text{s.t.} \; \sum_1^n \lambda_j = 1, \; \lambda_i \geq 0,$$

necessarily $\lambda_1^* > 0$ and $\lambda_1^* < 1$.

This will first be proved for n = 2, since the general case can be reduced down to that case. Denoting $\partial\theta(\lambda_1, \lambda_2)/\partial\lambda_i$ by $\theta_i(\lambda_1, \lambda_2)$, we need only show the following to be positive

$$\theta_1(0,1) - \theta_2(0,1) = \int_{-\infty}^{\infty} X_1 dP(X_1) \int_{-\infty}^{\infty} U'(X_2) \, dQ(X_2)$$

$$- \int_{-\infty}^{\infty} X_2 U'(X_2) \, dQ(X_2)$$

$$= E[x_2]E[U'(x_2)] - E[x_2 U'(x_2)]$$

$$= -E\left[\{x_2 - \mu\}\{U'(x_2) - E[U'(x_2)]\}\right] > 0$$

if $U''(x_2) < 0$, since the Pearsonian correlation coefficient between any monotone-decreasing function and its argument is negative.

We reduce n > 2 to the n = 2 case by defining

$$\lambda_1 x_1 + \sum_2^n \lambda_j x_j = \lambda_1 x_1 + \lambda_{II} x_{II}$$

where

$$x_{II} = \sum_2^n \frac{\lambda_i}{\lambda_{II}} x_j \;, \quad \sum_2^n \frac{\lambda_i}{\lambda_{II}} = 1, \; \text{as definition of } \lambda_{II}.$$

To show that the optimal portfolio has the property

$$\theta(\lambda_1^*,\lambda_2^*,\ldots,\lambda_n^*) > \theta(0,\lambda_2,\ldots,\lambda_n) \text{ for } \sum_2^n \lambda_j = 1,$$

it suffices to show that

$$\theta(\lambda_1^*,\lambda_2^*,\ldots,\lambda_n^*) > \theta(0,\lambda_2^{**} \cdots \lambda_n^{**})$$

$$= \underset{\{\lambda_2,\ldots,\lambda_n\}}{\text{Max}} \theta(0,\lambda_2,\ldots,\lambda_n) \text{ for } \sum_2^n \lambda_j = 1$$

But now if we define

$$\theta(\lambda_1,\lambda_{II}) = \theta(\lambda_i,\lambda_{II}\lambda_2^{**},\ldots,\lambda_{II}\lambda_n^{**}),$$

we have an ordinary n=2 case, for which we have shown that

$$\lambda_1^* > 0 \text{ and } \lambda_{II}^* > 0.$$

Having completed the proof of Theorem III, we can enunciate two easy corollaries that apply to risky investments.

Corollary I. If any investment has a mean at least as good as any other investment, and is independently distributed from all other investments, it must enter positively in the optimal portfolio.

Corollary II. If all investments have a common mean and are independently distributed, all must enter positively in the optimum portfolio.

Can one drop the strict independence assumption and still show that every investment, in a group with identical mean, must enter positively in the optimum portfolio? The answer is, in general, no. Only if, so to speak, the component of an investment that is orthogonal to the rest has an attractive mean can we be sure of wanting it. Since a single counterexample suffices, consider joint normal-distributions (x_1,x_2), with common mean and where optimality requires merely the minimization of the variance of $\lambda_1 x_1 + \lambda_2 x_2, \Sigma\Sigma\sigma_{ij} \lambda_i\lambda_j$, subject to $\Sigma\lambda_j = 1, \lambda_i \geq 0$. If one neglects the non-negativity constraints and minimizes the quadratic expression, one finds for the optimum

$$\lambda_1^* = \frac{\sigma_{22} - \sigma_{12}}{(\sigma_{22} - \sigma_{12}) + (\sigma_{11} - \sigma_{21})} \ .$$

If $\sigma_{12} = \sigma_{21} < 0$, λ_1^* is definitely a positive fraction. But, if σ_{12} is sufficiently positive, as in the admissible case $(\sigma_{11}, \sigma_{12}, \sigma_{22}) = (2, 1.1, 1)$, λ_1^* would want to take on an absurd negative value and would, of course, in the feasible optimum be zero, even though x_1's mean is equal to x_2's. Naturally this is a case of positive intercorrelation.

If the assumption of independence is abandoned in favor of positive correlation, we have seen that positive diversification need not be mandatory. However, as Professor Solow pointed out to me, abandoning independence in favor of negative correlation ought to improve the case for diversification. We saw that this was true in the case of negative linear correlation between two investments. It is easy to prove for any number of investments with common mean, among which all the inter-correlations are negative, that total variance is at a minimum when each investment appears with positive weight in the portfolio. (Although there is no limit on the degree to which all investments can be positively intercorrelated, it is impossible for all to be strongly negatively correlated. If A and B are both strongly negatively correlated with C, how can A and B fail to be positively intercorrelated with each other? For 3 variables, the maximum common negative correlation coefficient is $- 1/2$; for 4 variables, $- 1/3$;....for n variables $-1/(n-1)$.)

The whole point of this paper is to free the analysis from dependence on means, variances, and covariances. What is now needed is the gener-alization of the concept of negative linear correlation of the Pearsonian type. The natural tool is found in the concept of conditional probability of each variable, say x_i, and the requirement that increasing all or any other variables x_j be postulated to increase this conditional probability. Thus, define

$$\text{Prob}\{X_i \leq x_i | \text{each other } X_j = x_j\} = P(x_i | \underline{x}_i),$$

where $\underline{x}_i$ is the vector $(x_1, x_2, \ldots, x_{i-1}, x_{i+1}, \ldots, x_n)$

As always with conditional probabilities

$$\int_{-\infty}^{x_i} dP(x_1, x_2, \ldots, X_i, \ldots, x_n) \div \int_{-\infty}^{\infty} dP(x_1, x_2, \ldots, X_i, \ldots, x_n)$$

where the last divisor $Q(\underline{x}_i) = Q(x_1, \ldots, x_{i-1}, x_{i+1}, \ldots, x_n)$ is assumed not to vanish.

The appropriate generalization of pair-wise negative correlation or negative interdependence is the requirement

$$\frac{P(x_i | \underline{x}_i)}{\partial x_j} < 0 \qquad j \neq i$$

Theorem IV, which I shall not prove, states that where the joint probability distribution has the property of negative interdependence as thus defined, and has a common mean expectation for every investment, $E[x_i] = \mu$, every investment must enter with positive weight in the optimal portfolio of a risk-averter with strictly concave $U(x)$. Buying shares in a coal and in an ice company is a familiar example of such diversification strategy.

Having now shown that quite general conclusions can be rigorously proved for models that are free of the restrictive assumption that only two moments count, I ought to say a few words about how objectionably special the 2-moment theories are (except for textbook illustrations and simple proofs). To do this, I must review critically the conditions under which it is believed the mean-variance theories are valid.

1. If the utility to be maximized is a quadratic function of x, $U(x) = a_0 + a_1 x - a_2 x^2$,

$$E[U(x)] = a_0 + a_1 E[x] + a_2 E[x]^2 - a_2 V(x)$$
$$= a_0 + a_1 \mu + a_2 \mu^2 - a_2 \sigma_x^2,$$
$$= f(\mu, \sigma)$$

where μ = mean of x and σ^2 = variance of x

However, as Raiffa, Richter, Hicks, and other writers[3] have noted, the behavior resulting from quadratic utility contradicts familiar empirical patterns. [E.g., the more wealth I begin with the _less_ will I pay for the chance of winning ($0,$K) with probabilities (1/2,1/2) if I have to maximize quadratic utility. Moreover, for large enough x, U begins to decline -- as if having more money available begins to hurt a person.]

Anyone who uses quadratic utility should take care to ascertain which of his results depend critically upon its special (and empirically objectionable) features.

2. A quite different defense of 2-moment models can be given. Suppose we consider investment with less and less dispersion -- e.g., let

$$P(y_1,\ldots,y_n) \text{ have property } E[y_i] = 0 = \int_{-\infty}^{\infty} \cdots \int_{-\infty}^{\infty} Y_i dP(Y_1,\ldots,Y_n)$$

and

$$\text{Prob}\{X_1 \leq x_1,\ldots,X_n \leq x_n\} = P\left(\frac{x_1 - \mu_1}{\alpha},\ldots,\frac{x_n - \mu_n}{\alpha}\right)_n$$

Then in the limit as $\alpha \to 0$, only the first 2 moments of $\Sigma_1 \lambda_j x_j$ will turn out to count in $E[U(x)] = f(\mu,\sigma,\ldots)$. In the extreme limit, even the second moment will count for less and less: for α small enough the mean money outcome will dominate in decision making. Similarly, when α is small, but not limitingly small, the third moment of skewness will still count along with the mean and variance; then the third-degree polynomial form of $U(x)$ (its Taylor's expansion up to that point) will count. As Dr. M. Richter has shown in the cited paper, an nth degree polynomial for $U(x)$ implies, and is implied, by the condition that only the first n statistical moments count.

3. If each of the constituent elements of $(x_1,\ldots,x_n)$ is normally distributed, then so will be $z = \Sigma \lambda_j x_j$ and then it will be the case that only the mean and variance of z matter for $E[U(z)]$. However, with limited liability, no x_j can become negative as is required by the normal distribution. So some element of approximation would seem to be involved. Is the element of approximation, or rather of lack of approximation, ignorable? No, would seem to be the answer if there is some minimum of subsistence of z or x at which marginal utility becomes infinite. Thus, consider $U = \log x$, the Bernoulli form of logarithmic utility

$$E[U(x)] = \int_{-\infty}^{\infty} \log X dN\left(\frac{X-\mu}{\sigma}\right) = \lim_{a \to b} \int_a^{\infty} \log X dN\left(\frac{X-\mu}{\sigma}\right)$$

$$= -\infty \text{ for } b \leq 0,$$

where N(t) stands for the normal distribution with zero mean and unit variance.

Suppose that each constituent x_i takes on only non-negative values with variances all bounded by $M < \infty$. The central-limit theorem will still apply, so that $\Sigma_1^n x_j$ or $z_n = \Sigma \lambda_j x_j$, with certain weak restrictions on the spread of the λ's around $1/n$, will approach a Gaussian distribution. Thus, let z_n have the distribution $P_n(z_n)$, with

$$\lim_{n \to \infty} P_n(z_n) = N\left(\frac{z_n - a_n}{b_n}\right) .$$

Knowing how treacherous are double limits, we dare not infer

$$\lim_{n \to \infty} E[\log z_n] = \int_{-\infty}^{\infty} \log Z \lim_{n \to \infty} P_n(Z_n) .$$

Actually, as $n \to \infty$ and each investment has its $\lambda_j > a/n$, each $\lambda_j x_j$ does have a smaller and smaller dispersion so that we might switch from reliance on the central limit theorem of normality to the 2-moment Taylor-expansion justification given in paragraph 2 above. The law of large numbers, which is even more basic than the central limit theorem involving normality, assures us that z_n becomes more and more tightly bunched around some positive value and this fact will make the quadratic approximation applicable in the limit.

4. A final defense of the mean-variance formulation, in which $E[U(x)]$ is replaced by $f(\mu, \sigma)$, comes when x belongs to a 2-parameter probability distribution $P(x; \theta_1, \theta_2)$.

Then

$$E[U(x)] = \int_{-\infty}^{\infty} U(X) dP(X; \theta_1, \theta_2) = g(\theta_1, \theta_2) ,$$

$$\mu = \int_{-\infty}^{\infty} X dP(X; \theta_1, \theta_2) = h_1(\theta_1, \theta_2) ,$$

$$\sigma = \left[\int_{-\infty}^{\infty} (X-\mu)^2 dP(X; \theta_1, \theta_2)\right]^{1/2} = h_2(\theta_1, \theta_2) .$$

Then, provided the Jacobian $\partial(\mu, \sigma)/\partial(\theta_1, \theta_2) \neq 0$, each θ_i can be solved for as a function $\theta_i(\mu,\sigma)$, with

$$f(\mu,\sigma) = g[\theta_1(\mu,\sigma), \theta_2(\mu,\sigma)] \quad .$$

So far so good, although even here one has to take care to verify that $P(x;\theta_1,\theta_2)$ has the properties needed to give $f(\mu,\sigma)$ the quasi-concavity properties used by the practitioners of the mean-variance techniques. And furthermore one cannot draw up the $f(\mu,\sigma)$ indifference contours once and for all from knowledge of the decision-makers risk preferences, but instead must redraw them for each new probability distribution $P(x;\theta_1,\theta_2)$ upon which the f functional depends.

But waiving these last matters, we must point out that the Markowitz efficient-portfolio frontier need not work to screen out (or rather in!) optimal portfolios. For even when each constituent x_i belongs to a common 2-parameter family, the resulting $z = \Sigma\lambda_j x_j$ will not belong to that family or to any 2-parameter family that is independent of the λ weightings. It suffices to show this in the case of statistical independencies. Thus, define the rectangular distribution

$$R(x;a,b) = \frac{x-a}{b-a} \quad , \qquad a \leq x \leq b$$
$$= 0 \quad , \qquad x \leq a$$
$$= 1 \quad , \qquad x \geq b$$

and

$$P(x_1,\ldots,x_n) = \prod_{i=1}^{n} R(x_i;a_i,b_i)$$

Then, of course, $\Sigma\lambda_j x_j = z$ does not satisfy an R distribution but rather a 3n parameter distribution $P(z;\lambda_1,\ldots,\lambda_n;a_1,\ldots,a_n,b_1,\ldots,b_n)$. Let $(\lambda_1^{\dagger},\ldots,\lambda_n^{\dagger})$ be a point on the Markowitz efficiency frontier, with minimum variance $\Sigma\lambda_j^2\sigma_j^2$ subject to $\Sigma\lambda_j\mu_j = \mu$, $\Sigma\lambda_j = 1$. Then it need not be the case that the optimum $(\lambda_1^{*},\ldots,\lambda_n^{*})$ that maximizes $E[U(z)]$ will belong to the efficiency set $(\lambda_1^{\dagger},\ldots,\lambda_n^{\dagger})$! I do not recall this fact's being mentioned by those who speak of 2-parameter-family justifications of mean-variance analysis. Some quite different argument, such as that $n \to \infty$ and quadratic approximation to U then becomes increasingly good, will be needed to bring back the Markowitz frontier into more general applicability.

I do not wish to end on a nihilistic note. My objections are those of a purist, and my demonstrations in this paper have shown that even a purist can develop diversification theorems of great generality. But in practice, where crude approximations may be better than none, the 2-moment models may be found to have pragmatic usefulness.

FOOTNOTES

1. H. Makower and J. Marschak, "Assets, Prices, and Monetary Theory,"
   Economica N.S. (Vol. V, 1938), pp. 261-88. Harry M. Markowitz,
   "Portfolio Selection," The Journal of Finance (Vol. VII, 1952),
   pp. 77-91 and Portfolio Selection: Efficient Diversification of
   Investments (New York: John Wiley & Sons, 1959); James Tobin,
   "Liquidity Preference as Behavior Towards Risk," Review of Economic
   Studies (Vol. XXV, 1958), pp. 65-86. The path-breaking article,
   E. D. Domar and R. A. Musgrave, "Proportional Income Tax and Risk-
   taking," Quarterly Journal of Economics (Vol. LVII, 1944), pp.
   389-422 replaces variance by risk of loss (mean absolute loss) as
   dispersion parameters to be avoided. (This paper is reprinted in
   A.E.A. Selected Readings in Fiscal Policy and Taxation (Homewood,
   Ill.: Irwin, 1959).

2. P. A. Samuelson, "A Fallacy in the Interpretation of Pareto's Law of
   Alleged Constancy of Income Distribution," Essays in Honor of
   Marco Fanno, ed., Tullio Bagiotti, (Padua, Cedam-Casa Editrice Dott.
   Antonio Milani, 1966), pp. 580-584.

3. Howard Raiffa, unpublished Harvard Business School memos; Marcel K.
   Richter, "Cardinal Utility, Portfolio Selection and Taxation,"
   Review of Economic Studies (Vol. XXVII, 1959), pp. 152-66; E. C.
   Brown, "Mr. Kaldor on Taxation and Risk Bearing," Review of
   Economic Studies (Vol. XXV, 1957), pp. 49-52; J. R. Hicks,
   "Liquidity," Economic Journal (Vol. LXXII, 1962), pp. 787-802,
   depicts a rediscovery of some of the Markowitz theory. Also see
   John Lintner, "Valuation of Risk Assets," Review of Economics and
   Statistics (Vol. XLVII, 1965), pp. 13-37, and "Optimum Dividends
   and Uncertainty," Quarterly Journal of Economics (Vol. LXXVIII,
   1964), pp. 49-95 and unpublished appendix.

202

EFFICIENT PORTFOLIO SELECTION FOR PARETO-LEVY INVESTMENTS**

Paul A. Samuelson*

The Markowitz analysis of efficient portfolio selection, which can be interpreted as solving the quadratic-programming problem of minimizing the variance of a normal variate subject to each prescribed mean value, easily can be generalized (in the special case of independently distributed investments) to the concave-programming problem of minimizing the "dispersion" of a stable Pareto-Lévy variate subject to each prescribed mean value. Some further generalizations involving interdependent distributions will also be presented here.

Pareto-Lévy Investments

Let each investment $(X_1 \ldots, X_n)$ be subject to the Pareto-Lévy distribution

$$(1) \qquad \text{Prob} \left\{ X_j \le x_j \right\} = P \left(\frac{x_j - \mu_j}{\varepsilon_j} \right),$$

where P has the characteristic function

---

*Massachusetts Institute of Technology.

**Acknowledgement is made to the Carnegie Corporation for providing me with a reflective year; and to Mrs. F. Skidmore for the numerical computations. Since writing this, I have learned of the similar paper, Eugene F. Fama, "Portfolio Analysis in a Stable Paretian Market", Management Science, Vol. 11 (January 1965), pp. 404-419. While our results overlap, our papers do complement each other in providing generalizations both to the Markowitz general analysis and the Sharpe-Markowitz variant of it. See Harry M. Markowitz, "Portfolio Selection", The Journal of Finance, Vol. 7, 1952, pp. 77-91 and Portfolio Selection: Efficient Diversification of Investments, (New York, John Wiley & Sons, 1959). W. F. Sharpe, "A Simplified Model for Portfolio Analysis", Management Science, Vol. 9, (1963), pp. 277-293. For a rediscovery of the Markowitz theory see J. R. Hicks, "Liquidity", Economic Journal, Vol. 72, 1962, pp. 787-802. For technique, see H. W. Kuhn and A. W. Tucker, "Nonlinear Programming", in J. Neyman (ed.), Second Berkeley Symposium on Mathematical Statistics and Probability (Berkeley, Calif. University of California Press, 1951).

$$(2) \qquad E\left[e^{itx_j}\right] = \int_{-\infty}^{\infty} e^{itX_j} \, dP\left(\frac{X_j - \mu_j}{\varepsilon_j}\right)$$

$$= \exp\{i\mu_j t - |\varepsilon|^{\alpha}|t|^{\alpha}[1 + i\beta(t/|t|)\tan\pi\alpha/2]\}$$

where β is a skewness parameter common to all X_j and α is a kurtosis or "peakedness" parameter common to all X_j, with $-1 \le \beta \le +1$, $0 < \alpha \le 2$. (If $\alpha=1$, replace $\tan\pi\alpha/2$ by $(2/\pi)\log|t|$.)

For $\beta=0$ and $\alpha=2$, $P(x) = N(x)$, the well-known normal distribution of deMoivre and Laplace. For $\beta=0$ and $\alpha=1$, $P(x)$ is the familiar Cauchy distribution that lacks a convergent mean. If $\beta=0$ and $\alpha=1/2$, $P(x)$ is the arc-sine distribution relevant to the difference between the number of heads and tails turned up in repeated coin tossings.

For other values of α, the form of $P(x)$ was not until recently tabulated: but B. Mandelbrot[1] and others have presented evidence that

---

[1] B. Mandelbrot, "New Methods in Statistical Economics", Journal of Political Economy, Vol. 61, (October, 1963), pp. 421-40; "The Variation of Certain Speculative Prices", Journal of Business, Vol. 36, (October 1963), pp. 394-419; with F. Zarnfaller, "Five Place Tables of Certain Stable Distributions", Research note, Thomas J. Watson Research Center, Yorktown Heights, N.Y., December 31, 1959; E. F. Fama, "Mandelbrot and the Stable Paretian Hypothesis", Journal of Business, Vol. 36, (October 1963), pp. 420-29; "The Behavior of Stock-Market Prices", Journal of Business of the University of Chicago, Vol. 38, No. 1, (January 1965), pp. 34-105; Fama gives a useful bibliography with reference to P. Lévy, Calcul des Probabilités, (Paris, Gauthier-Villars, 1925), and B. V. Gnedenko and A. N. Kolmogorov, Limit Distributions for Sums of Independent Random Variables, (Addison-Wesley, 1954).
Actually, the Mandelbrot-Fama data refer to Pareto-Lévy distribution of the logarithms of price changes, not of arithmetic price changes. If $\log P_{t+1} - \log P_t$ is Pareto-Lévy with $1 < \alpha < 2$, $P_{t+1} - P_t$ has no finite mean and this would then be true of the investments $(X_1, \ldots, X_n)$, which would not themselves follow a Pareto-Lévy distribution. Similarly, if $\log P_{t+1} - \log P_t$ follows the normal distribution, X_j will be log-normal not normal and the Markowitz methods cannot be applied without serious modifications. Here I waive these difficulties, with due warning. For some progress in this matter, see J. Lintner, "Valuation of Risk Assets", Review of Economics and Statistics, Vol. 47, 1965, pp. 13-37, and "Optimum Dividends and Uncertainty", Quarterly Journal of Economics, Vol. 78, 1964, pp. 49-95 and unpublished appendix.

incomes, price changes, and other phenomena satisfy Pareto-Lévy distributions with $1 < \alpha < 2$, so that the mean is finite, while the variance (in contrast to other measures of dispersion, such as the mean absolute deviation or the interquartile range) is infinite.

The Pareto-Lévy functions are interesting because they have the following property:

Stable reproduction property: If $(X_1,\ldots,X_n)$ have a joint distribution

$$P\left(\frac{x_1 - \mu_1}{\varepsilon_1}\right) P\left(\frac{x_2 - \mu_2}{\varepsilon_2}\right) \ldots P\left(\frac{x_n - \mu_n}{\varepsilon_n}\right), \quad \varepsilon_i > 0$$

the linear sum

$$x = \lambda_1 x_1 + \ldots + \lambda_n x_n$$

has the distribution

$$P\left(\frac{x - \mu}{\varepsilon}\right),$$

(3)
$$\mu = \lambda_1 \mu_1 + \ldots + \lambda_n \mu_n$$

$$\varepsilon = \left(\lambda_1^\alpha \varepsilon_1^\alpha + \ldots \lambda_n^\alpha \varepsilon_n^\alpha\right)^{1/\alpha}$$

This of course includes the familiar property of the normal distribution as the special case when $\alpha=2$ and ε can be interpreted as the standard- or root-mean-square deviation. For $1 < \alpha < 2$, μ_j and μ can be interpreted as arithmetic means if we follow the convention that

(4)
$$E[\,x\,] = \int_{-\infty}^{\infty} X dP(X) = 0$$

A specific interpretation can be given to ε as proportional to the mean absolute deviation, dispersion or scale parameter around the mean, if we follow some convention, such as

(5)
$$E[\,|x - \mu|\,] = \int_{-\infty}^{\infty} |X - \mu| dP\,(X) = k$$

or a similar convention with respect to interquartile range or specified fractile difference.

Portfolio Efficiency

Let you as an investor begin with initial money wealth, W, which by conventional choice of units can be set equal to unity. You can allocate it among investments $(X_1, \ldots, X_n)$ at constant-returns-to-scale, so that each dollar invested in X_j brings the same return as any other dollar. (Commissions are proportional to value; you do not push prices by the size of your transactions.) The joint distribution of investment outcomes is that of independent Pareto-Lévy variates

$$P\left(\frac{x_1 - \mu_1}{\varepsilon_1}\right) P\left(\frac{x_2 - \mu_2}{\varepsilon_2}\right) \cdots P\left(\frac{x_n - \mu_n}{\varepsilon_n}\right) ,$$

and when you allocate your wealth among them in proportions $(\lambda_1, \ldots, \lambda_n)$, your final outcome is given by

$$x = \lambda_1 x_1 + \ldots + \lambda_n x_n, \qquad \lambda_1 + \ldots + \lambda_n = 1, \quad \lambda_j \geq 0$$

$$\text{Prob } \{X \leq x\} = P\left(\frac{x - \mu}{\varepsilon}\right), \qquad \mu = \sum_1^n \lambda_j \mu_j \text{ and } \qquad \varepsilon^\alpha = \sum_1^n \lambda_j^\alpha \varepsilon_j^\alpha$$

If some ε_j, say $\varepsilon_1 = 0$ depicting a riskless asset, then by proper convention all the above formulas hold with ε_1 set equal to zero in the expression for ε.

Any investor who maximizes the expected value of his utility

$$(6) \qquad E[U(x)] = \int_{-\infty}^\infty U(X) dP\left(\frac{X - \mu}{\varepsilon}\right) = u(\mu, \varepsilon)$$

will, if $U'' < 0$ and the integrals are all convergent, prefer large μ and small ε; i.e.

$$(7) \qquad \frac{\partial u(\mu, \varepsilon)}{\partial \mu} > 0, \qquad \frac{\partial u(\mu, \varepsilon)}{\partial \varepsilon} < 0 \quad .$$

Hence, it is a necessary condition for optimality that the following efficiency-frontier problem be solved:

Subject to $\lambda_1 + \ldots + \lambda_n = 1$, $\mu_1\lambda_1 + \ldots + \mu_n\lambda_n = \mu, \lambda_i \geq 0$

Minimize $\left[\varepsilon_1^{\alpha}\lambda_1^{\alpha} + \ldots + \varepsilon_n^{\alpha}\lambda_n^{\alpha}\right]^{1/\alpha} = \varepsilon =$

$$\phi[\lambda_1^*(\mu), \ldots, \lambda_n^*(\mu); \mu] = \phi(\mu)$$

This is a problem in non-linear programming, solvable by the Kuhn-Tucker techniques. In the above constraints, the = signs can, without alteration of the solution, be replaced by $\geq$ signs. (So long as one $\varepsilon_j > 0$, you will not end up making $\Sigma\lambda_j$ exceed 1; nor, for $\text{Min}(\mu_j) < \mu < \text{Max}(\mu_j)$ will you want to end up with $\Sigma\mu_j\lambda_j > \mu$.) Note that short-selling or borrowing to buy securities is ruled out by the non-negativity restriction $\lambda_i \geq 0$.

Solution of the Problem

Because the constraints are linear inequalities, and ε is a convex function, necessary and sufficient conditions for the efficient portfolio $(\lambda_1^*, \ldots, \lambda_n^*)$ are provided by the Kuhn-Tucker inequalities

$$\frac{\partial L}{\partial \lambda_i} = \alpha\varepsilon_i^{\alpha}\lambda_i^{\alpha-1} - v_1 - v_2\mu_i \geq 0; \quad \lambda_i \frac{\partial L}{\partial \lambda_i} = 0 \quad (i=1,2,\ldots n)$$

(8)

$$\frac{\partial L}{\partial v_1} = -\Sigma_1^n \lambda_j + 1 \leq 0; \quad v_1 \frac{\partial L}{\partial v_1} = 0$$

$$\frac{\partial L}{\partial v_2} = -\Sigma_1^n \mu_j\lambda_j + \mu \leq 0; \quad v_2 \frac{\partial L}{\partial v_2} = 0$$

where L is the Lagrangian expression,

(9)

$$L(\lambda_1, \ldots, \lambda_n; v_1, v_2) = \varepsilon^{\alpha} + v_1\left(1 - \Sigma_1^n \lambda_j\right) + v_2\left(\mu - \Sigma_1^n \mu_j\lambda_j\right)$$

and the v's are non-negative Lagrangian or dual variables, subject to the saddlepoint property

$$(10) \qquad L(\lambda^*;v) \leq L(\lambda^*;v^*) \leq L(\lambda;v^*) \ .$$

For $1 < \alpha < 2$, some $\varepsilon_j > 0$, and $\text{Min}(\mu_j) < \mu < \text{Max}(\mu_j)$, it can be proved that the solution $(\lambda^*;v^*)$ is unique, giving $\varepsilon^\alpha = \psi(\mu)$, with $\psi'(\mu) = a_2 \geq 0$. Elsewhere[2], I have proved that whenever an independent investment X_j with μ_j and some risk is being bought, it is mandatory that you buy a positive amount of an alternative independent investment X_i that has at least as great a mean, $\mu_i \geq \mu_j$. (This is true for much wider probability distributions than Pareto-Lévy.) Hence, all investments with equal means can be treated by themselves and considered already blended optimally to form a new Pareto-Lévy single (composite) investment. Thus, let

$$\mu_1 = \ldots = \mu_m = \mu_I, \ 0 < \varepsilon_1 \leq \varepsilon_2 \leq \ldots \leq \varepsilon_m.$$

Then $(X_1,\ldots,X_m)$ are optimally blended when,

Subject to $\lambda_1 + \ldots + \lambda_m = 1, \ \lambda_i \geq 0$

$$(11) \qquad \varepsilon^\alpha = \varepsilon_1^\alpha \lambda_1^\alpha + \ldots + \varepsilon_m^\alpha \lambda_m^\alpha \text{ is at a minimum.}$$

This requires that

$$\alpha \varepsilon_i^\alpha \lambda_i^{\alpha-1} = v_1 \qquad (i=1,\ldots,m)$$

---

[2]P.A. Samuelson, "General Proof That Diversification Pays", <u>Journal of Financial and Quantitative Analysis</u>, Vol. II, No. 1 (March, 1967), pp. 1-13.

$$(12) \qquad \lambda_i^* = \frac{\varepsilon_i^{(\frac{\alpha}{1-\alpha})}}{\sum\limits_1^m \varepsilon_j^{(\frac{\alpha}{1-\alpha})}}$$

$$\varepsilon^* = \left[\sum_1^m \varepsilon_j^\alpha \lambda_j^{*\alpha}\right]^{\frac{1}{\alpha}} = \frac{\left[\sum\limits_{-1}^m \varepsilon_j^\alpha \varepsilon_j^{(\frac{\alpha}{1-\alpha})}\right]^{\frac{1}{\alpha}}}{\sum\limits_1^m \varepsilon_j^{(\frac{\alpha}{1-\alpha})}} = \frac{\left[\sum\limits_{-1}^m \varepsilon_j^{(\frac{\alpha}{1-\alpha})}\right]^{\frac{1}{\alpha}}}{\sum\limits_1^m \varepsilon_j^{(\frac{\alpha}{1-\alpha})}} =$$

$$\left[\sum\limits_{-1}^m \varepsilon_j^{(\frac{\alpha}{1-\alpha})}\right]^{\frac{1-\alpha}{\alpha}}$$

Evidently, we can treat the composite investment of equal mean investments

$$x_I = \sum_1^m \lambda_j^* x_j$$

as if it were a simple investment with distribution

$$P\left(\frac{x_I - \mu_I}{\varepsilon_I}\right), \text{ where } \varepsilon_I = \varepsilon^* \text{ above.}$$

Hence, from now on we may assume all investments have different means and can follow the convention

$$(13) \qquad \mu_1 > \mu_2 > \ldots > \mu_n$$

Because of the cited general theorem, we can never invest in X_j and not in X_{j-1}: hence $\lambda_j > 0$ implies $\lambda_{j-k} > 0$.

This assures us that the only pattern of zeros in optimal $(\lambda_1,\ldots,\lambda_n)$ must be of the form $(\lambda_1,\ldots,\lambda_r,0,\ldots,0)$, $r \le n$. For a prescribed μ, we do not know in advance what r will be. But if we did know r, we could solve $(\lambda_1^*,\ldots,\lambda_r^*)$ from the equalities

(14)
$$\alpha\varepsilon_i^\alpha\lambda_i^{\alpha-1} - \mu_i v_1 - v_2 = 0 \qquad (i=1,\ldots,r)$$

$$\sum_1^r \lambda_j = 1$$

$$\sum_1^r \mu_j \lambda_j = \mu;$$

Since $\mu_1 - \mu_2 > 0$, we can eliminate (λ_1,λ_2) from the last two linear relations, and (v_1, v_2) from the first two equations, to attain the following $(r-2)$ non-linear relations to determine the $r-2$ unknowns $(\lambda_3,\ldots,\lambda_r)$:

(15)
$$\varepsilon_i^\alpha\lambda_i^{\alpha-1} - a_{i1}\varepsilon_1^\alpha(b_1\mu + \sum_3^r b_{1j}\lambda_j)^\alpha -$$

$$a_{i2}\varepsilon_2^\alpha(b_2\mu + \sum_3^r b_{2j}\lambda_j)^\alpha = 0 \qquad (i=3,\ldots,r)$$

where $(a_{i1},a_{i2},b_1,b_2,b_{1j},b_{2j})$ are rational functions of (μ_1,μ_2). Only non-negative $(\lambda_1^*,\ldots,\lambda_r^*)$ are relevant. As μ becomes lower, a larger r can be tolerated and for $\mu = \min_j(\mu_j)$, $r = n$.

Graphical Results

The accompanying diagrams in Figure I depict the nature of the efficiency frontiers. The first five, a through e, refer to two-investment portfolios; the remainder to the general case of three or more.

Figure I-a involves safe cash at A_1, with $\varepsilon_1 = 0$; investment 2, at A_2, offers a higher mean yield, $\mu_2 > \mu_1$, but at the cost of risk or dispersion, $\varepsilon_2 > 0 = \varepsilon_1$. The dark line segment $\underline{A_1A_2}$ shows the tradeoff

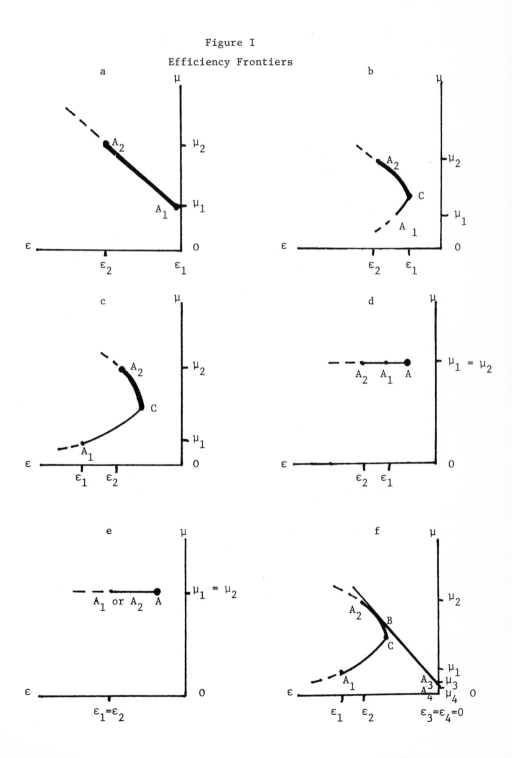

Figure I

Efficiency Frontiers

frontier between μ and ε, attainable by blending safe cash and the risky security. The broken line beyond A_2 is not feasible so long as we rule out borrowing or short-selling, and insist that $\lambda_i \geq 0$.

Figure I-b shows a choice between riskier higher-yielding X_2 at A_2 and a less-risky lower-yielding X_1 at A_1, with $\mu_2 \geq \mu_1$, $\varepsilon_2 > \varepsilon_1 > 0$. Now that no cash is being held, the dark efficiency frontier $\overline{CA_2}$ is concave rather than a straight line. The A_1C branch of $\overline{A_1A_2}$ is not efficient since every point on it is "dominated" by a point on $\overline{CA_2}$ that is northeast of it, providing less risk and higher yield. Blending independent dispersions results in gratifying cancellation of risk. Again the broken-line extensions beyond A_1 or A_2 are not feasible. In Markowitz quadratic programming, the frontier in the (variance, mean) space is a quadratic parabola, and the square root of this in the (standard deviation, mean) space. For Pareto-Lévy distributions, with $1 < \alpha < 2$, Figure I-b's A_1A_2 locus is given by the simple parametric equations

$$\mu = \mu_1\lambda_1 + \mu_2(1-\lambda_1), \quad 0 \leq \lambda_1 \leq 1$$

(16)
$$\varepsilon = \left[\varepsilon_1^{\alpha}\lambda_1^{\alpha} + \varepsilon_2^{\alpha}(1-\lambda_1)^{\alpha}\right]^{\frac{1}{\alpha}} = \left[\varepsilon_1^{\alpha}\left(\frac{\mu_2 - \mu}{\mu_2 - \mu_1}\right)^{\alpha} + \varepsilon_2^{\alpha}\left(\frac{\mu_1 - \mu}{\mu_1 - \mu_2}\right)^{\alpha}\right]^{\frac{1}{\alpha}}$$

$$= \frac{\left[\varepsilon_1^{\alpha}(\mu_2 - \mu)^{\alpha} - \varepsilon_2^{\alpha}(\mu - \mu_1)^{\alpha}\right]^{\frac{1}{\alpha}}}{\mu_2 - \mu_1}, \quad \mu_1 \leq \mu \leq \mu_2$$

In Figure I-c, X_1 has both a lower mean and a higher dispersion than X_2. Nevertheless, it can pay to invest in a little X_1, because its variation is independent of X_2's, permitting reduction of total dispersion. The efficiency frontier is shown by the dark $\underline{CA_2}$ segment of the total $\underline{A_1A_2}$ arc. All the points on the light A_1C branch are feasible, but again are dominated by the points northeast of them on the $\underline{CA_2}$ branch -- points which promise higher yield with less dispersion.

The point C is found where $\varepsilon = \Phi(\mu)$ of Equation (16) reaches its minimum, at $\Phi'(\mu_c) = 0$, which from (12) we know to be at

$$(17) \qquad \lambda_1^* = \frac{\varepsilon_1^{\gamma}}{\varepsilon_1^{\gamma} + \varepsilon_2^{\gamma}} \ , \quad \gamma = -\frac{\alpha}{\alpha-1} < -\alpha$$

In Figure I-d, both investments have equal means but X_2 has greater dispersion. It still pays to buy some X_2 for its independent, and hence cancelling, dispersion. Only the eastmost point A is efficient, dominating all the other points on the horizontal line A_2A_1A. Figure I-e is like I-d, except that $\mu_1 = \mu_2$ and A_1 coincides with $\overline{A_2}$. On the horizontal line $\underline{A_1A}$, only the eastmost A is efficient. From our last formula, we realize that equal investment shares are optimal among 2 or more identically (but independently) distributed investments. If each has dispersion ε_1, the resulting dispersion from equal diversification among n investments is

$$(18) \qquad \varepsilon = \varepsilon_1 \left[\sum_1^n \left(\frac{1}{n}\right)^{\alpha} \right]^{\frac{1}{\alpha}} = \frac{\varepsilon_1}{n^{\frac{\alpha-1}{\alpha}}} < \varepsilon_1, \ 1 < \alpha < 2$$

If $\alpha=2$, dispersion is reduced by the factor $n^{\frac{1}{2}}$. If $\alpha=1$, since the mean of independent Cauchy variates, is no better distributed than each separately, there is no benefit from diversification. If α is near to 2, say $\alpha=1.9$ as E. Fama's study of the 30 Dow Jones stocks indicates, diversifying among 2 independent investments will cut down dispersion by 28 percent; diversifying among n=20 investments will cut it down by 76 percent. Table 1 shows the reduced dispersion obtainable for different values of n and α.

TABLE 1

Ratio of dispersion from diversification among n independent
investments to single-investment dispersion for various α.

n \ α	2.0	1.9	1.5	1.1	1.0
1	1.00	1.00	1.00	1.00	1.00
2	.71	.72	.79	.94	1.00
5	.45	.47	.58	.86	1.00
10	.32	.34	.46	.81	1.00
20	.22	.24	.37	.76	1.00
100	.10	.11	.22	.66	1.00

Figure I-f goes beyond the two-investment case. X_1 and X_2 are
again like X_1 and X_2 of Figure I-c, both involving risk. X_3 involves
no risk -- say cash, or perhaps call-money known to be safe in principal
and yet with a positive yield. X_4 is also perfectly safe, with
$\varepsilon_4 = \varepsilon_3 = 0$, but with a lower yield, $\mu_4 < \mu_3$. Obviously X_4 is dominated by
X_3 and will never be used: i.e. $\lambda_4 = 0$ and we can treat this as a three-
investment case. By combining the insights of Figures I-a and I-c, we
can discern the optimal frontier of I-f, namely the dark locus A_3BA_2. To
derive this, first derive the A_2A_1 locus by considering blends of X_1 and
X_2 alone. Recognize that CA_2 is the only relevant branch of this locus.
Note that any point on CA_2 is feasible and, together with X_3 at A_3, can
be used to generate a feasible straight-line segment like that in
Figure I-a. Which is the best of the feasible line segments? Obviously,
the one shown as A_3B, which is tangential to CA_2, and represents the
line of steepest slope joining A_3 and the feasible points on CA_2. This
suggests the general rule: To blend a safe asset like cash (whose mean
is μ_c) with m alternative risky investments, first blend them so as to
produce a maximum $\dfrac{(\mu - \mu_c)}{\varepsilon}$ ratio at $\varepsilon*, \mu*$. Then the straight line

$(\varepsilon - \varepsilon^*) = \left[\varepsilon^*/(\mu^* - \mu_c)\right](\mu - \mu^*)$ will form the lowest branch of the efficiency frontier.

Figure I-f shows how the frontier for any three investments can be generated as the outer-envelope of the arcs connecting any two investments or the arcs connecting any two points on such arcs. The resulting frontier will always be concave.

Interdependent Investments

Independent normal variates generalize nicely into multivariate distributions, characterized by the positive definite quadratic form variance

$$V\left[\sum_{1}^{n}\lambda_j x_j\right] = \sum_{11}^{nn}\sigma_{ij}\lambda_i\lambda_j \quad ,$$

where the covariance matrix of $(x_1, \ldots, x_n)$ has for its elements

$$\sigma_{ij} = E[x_i x_j] \quad .$$

No such simple theory applicable to Pareto-Lévy distributions is known to me. However, the case of $n=2$ suggests a model of interdependence that can be handled fairly easily.[3] Thus, let

(19)
$$X_1 = a_1 Y + z_1$$
$$X_2 = a_2 Y + z_2$$

---

[3]This model turns out to coincide with the cited Sharpe-Fama model if Y represents a business-cycle component common to most stocks.

where (Y, z_1, z_2) satisfy independent Pareto-Lévy distributions with the same α and β. Then, if

$$P(Y, z_1, z_2) = P\left(\frac{Y - \mu(y)}{\varepsilon(y)}\right) P\left(\frac{z_1 - \mu(z_1)}{\varepsilon(z_1)}\right) P\left(\frac{z_2 - \mu(z_2)}{\varepsilon(z_2)}\right)$$

$$= P\left(\frac{Y - \mu_0'}{\varepsilon_0'}\right) P\left(\frac{z_1 - \mu_1'}{\varepsilon_1'}\right) P\left(\frac{z_2 - \mu_2'}{\varepsilon_2'}\right)$$

then the portfolio

$$X = \lambda_1 X_1 + \lambda_2 X_2 \quad ,$$

will have the Pareto-Lévy distribution

$$\text{Prob}\{X \leq x\} = P\left(\frac{x - \mu}{\varepsilon}\right) \quad , \qquad \text{where}$$

(20)
$$\mu = \lambda_1 \mu_1 + \lambda_2 \mu_2 = (\lambda_1 a_1 + \lambda_2 a_2)\mu_0' + \lambda_1 \mu_1' + \lambda_2 \mu_2'$$

$$\varepsilon^\alpha = (\lambda_1 a_1 + \lambda_2 a_2)^\alpha (\varepsilon_0')^\alpha + \lambda_1^\alpha (\varepsilon_1')^\alpha + \lambda_2^\alpha (\varepsilon_2')^\alpha$$

It is again a problem in convex programming to pick λ's to

$$\text{Minimize } \varepsilon \text{ or } \varepsilon^\alpha \text{ subject to } \sum_1^n \lambda_j \geq 1, \ \sum_1^n \mu_j \lambda_j \geq \mu.$$

But now ε^α does not have the simple property of being the sum of independent functions of each λ_j; i.e. ε^α is not equal to $\sum f_j(\lambda_j)$.

The solution can be indicated for the special symmetric case where $\mu_0' = 1$, $\epsilon_0' = 1$, $a_1 = a_2 = 1$, $\mu_1' = \mu_2'$, $\epsilon_1' = \epsilon_2' = 1$. Then $1/2 = \lambda_1^* = \lambda_2^*$ and

$$\epsilon^* = \left[1 + 2\left(\frac{1}{2}\right)^\alpha\right]^{\frac{1}{\alpha}} < 2 = \epsilon_1 = \epsilon_2 \ .$$

Even better is the case of negative interdependence, where

$$a_1 = -a_2 = 1, \ \mu_0' = 0, \ \epsilon_0' = 1, \ \mu_1' = \mu_2', \ \epsilon_1' = \epsilon_2' = 1.$$

Again symmetry requires $1/2 = \lambda_1^* = \lambda_2^*$, and

$$\epsilon^* = 0 + \left[2\left(\frac{1}{2}\right)^\alpha\right]^{\frac{1}{\alpha}} = \frac{2}{2} = \frac{\epsilon_1}{2} = \frac{\epsilon_2}{2}$$

Thus, for all α, as well as for $\alpha = 2$, the dispersions of the single investments are reduced by half through diversification among these particular negatively-interdependent investments.

This suggests how to handle interdependence among n investments that can be written as

(21) $\qquad X_i = \sum_{j=1}^{m} a_{ij} Y_j \qquad\qquad (i = 1,\ldots,n \lessgtr m)$

where

(22) $\qquad P(Y_1,\ldots,Y_m) = \prod_{j=1}^{m} P\left(\dfrac{Y_j - \mu_j'}{\epsilon_j'}\right)$

and

$$x = \sum_{i=1}^{n} \lambda_i x_i = \sum_{j=1}^{m}\sum_{i=1}^{n} \lambda_i a_{ij} Y_j = \sum_{i=1}^{n}\left(\sum_{j=1}^{m} a_{ij} Y_j\right)\lambda_i$$

has the Pareto-Lévy distribution

$$P\left(\frac{x - \mu}{\epsilon}\right) \quad \text{where}$$

(23) $\qquad \mu = \sum_{j=1}^{m}\left(\sum_{i=1}^{n} \lambda_i a_{ij}\right)\mu_j$

$$\varepsilon^\alpha = \sum_{j=1}^{m} \left(\sum_{1}^{n} \lambda_i a_{ij} \right)^\alpha \left(\varepsilon_j^{\cdot\cdot} \right)^\alpha$$

This leads to the general convex programming problem:

Subject to
$$\sum_{i=1}^{n} \left(\sum_{j=1}^{m} a_{ij} \mu_j' \right) \lambda_i \geq \mu, \sum_{1}^{n} \lambda_i \geq 1, \lambda_i \geq 0$$

Minimize
$$\varepsilon^\alpha = \sum_{j=1}^{m} \left(\varepsilon_j' \right)^\alpha \left(\sum_{i=1}^{n} \lambda_i a_{ij} \right)^\alpha$$

The necessary and sufficient conditions for the solution to the problem are identical to those of (8), but of course taking recognition of the fact that ε^α is not a sum of independent functions of the form $\sum_1^n \varepsilon_j^\alpha \lambda_j^\alpha$, so that $\partial \varepsilon^\alpha / \partial \lambda$ in (8) will be a function involving all the λ's in the form $\alpha \sum_1^m (\varepsilon_j')^\alpha a_{ij} (\sum_1^n \lambda_i a_{ik})^{\alpha - 1}$.

203

The Fundamental Approximation Theorem of Portfolio Analysis in terms of Means, Variances and Higher Moments[1]

I

James Tobin [7, 8], Harry Markowitz [3, 4], and many other writers have made valuable contributions to the problem of optimal risk decisions by emphasizing analyses of means and variances. These writers have realized that the results can be only approximate, but have also realized that approximate and computable results are better than none.

Recently, Karl Borch [1] and Martin Feldstein [2] have re-emphasized the lack of generality of mean-variance analysis and evoked a reply from Tobin [9]. None of the writers in this symposium refer to a paper of mine (Samuelson, [6]) which suggested that most of the interesting propositions of risk theory can be proved for the general case with no approximations being involved. This same paper pointed out all the realms of applicability of mean-variance analysis and also its realms of non-applicability.

There is no need here to redescribe these arguments. But I think it important to re-emphasize an aspect of the mean-variance model that seems not to have received sufficient attention in the recent controversy, namely the usefulness of mean and variance in situations involving less and less risk—what I call " compact " probabilities. The present paper states and proves the two general theorems involved. In a sense, therefore, it provides a defence of mean-variance analysis—in my judgement the most weighty defence yet given. (In economics, the relevant probability distributions are *not* nearly Gaussian, and quadratic utility in the large leads to well-known absurdities). But since I improve on mean-variance analysis and show its exact limitations—along with those for any *r*-moment model—the paper can also be regarded as a critique of the mean-variance approach. In any case, the theorems here provide valuable insight into the properties of the general case. I should add that their general content has long been sensed as true by most experts in this field, even though I am unable to cite publications that quite cover this ground.

II

The Tobin-Markowitz analysis of risk-taking in terms of mean and variance alone is rigorously applicable only in the restrictive cases where the statistical distributions are normally Gaussian or where the utility-function to be maximized is quadratic. In only a limited number of cases will the central limit law be applicable so that an approximation to normality of distribution becomes tenable; and it is well known that quadratic utility has anomalous properties in the large—such as reduced absolute and relative risk-taking as wealth increases, to say nothing of ultimate satiation.

1 Aid from the National Science Foundation is gratefully acknowledged, and from my M.I.T. students and co-researchers: Robert C. Merton, from whose conversations I have again benefited, and Dr. Stanley Fischer (now of the University of Chicago) whose 1969 M.I.T. doctoral dissertation, *Essays on Assets and Contingent Commodities* contains independently-derived results on compact distributions.

However, a defence for mean-variance analysis can be given (Samuelson, [6; p. 8]) along other lines—namely, when riskiness is " limited ", the quadratic solution " approximates " the true general solution. The present note states the underlying approximation theorems, and shows the exact limit of their accuracy.

III

Let the return from investing \$1 in each of " securities " 1, 2, ..., n be respectively the random variable $(X_1, ..., X_n)$, subject to the joint probability distribution

$$\text{prob}\{X_1 \leq x_1 \text{ and } X_2 \leq x_2 \text{ and } ...X_n \leq x_n\} = F(x_1, ..., x_n). \qquad ...(1)$$

Let initial wealth W be set (by dimensional-unit choice) at unity and $(w_1, w_2, ..., w_n)$ be the fractions of wealth invested in each security, where $\sum_1^n w_j = 1$. Then the investment outcome is the random variable $\sum_1^n w_j X_j$, and if $U[W]$ is the decision maker's concave utility, he is postulated as acting to choose $[w_j]$ to maximize expected utility, namely

$$\max_{\{w_i\}} \overline{U}[w_1, ..., w_n] = \int_0^\infty ... \int_0^\infty U\left[\sum_1^n w_j X_j\right] dF(X_1, ..., X_n). \qquad ...(2)$$

In general, the solution to this problem will *not* be the same as the solution to the quadratic case

$$\max_{\{w_i\}} \int_0^\infty ... \int_0^\infty \left\{U[1] + U'[1]\left[\sum_1^n w_j X_j - 1\right] + \tfrac{1}{2}U''[1]\left[\sum_1^n w_j X_j - 1\right]^2\right\} dF(X_1, ..., X_n). \qquad ...(3)$$

But now let us suppose that $F(\cdot, ..., \cdot)$ belongs to a family of " compact " or " small-risk " distributions, defined so that as some specified parameter goes to zero, all our distributions converge to a sure outcome. An appropriate family would be

$$F(x_1, ..., x_n) = P\left(\frac{x_1 - \mu - \sigma^2 a_1}{\sigma \sigma_1}, \frac{x_2 - \mu - \sigma^2 a_2}{\sigma \sigma_2}, ..., \frac{x_n - \mu - \sigma^2 a_n}{\sigma \sigma_n}\right). \qquad ...(4)$$

Here, the variables have been defined so that, as the parameter $\sigma \to 0$, it becomes ever more certain that the outcome for $(X_1, ..., X_n) = (\mu, \mu, ..., \mu)$, where μ might be $1 +$ the " safe " rate of interest. Fig. 1 illustrates for the one-dimensional case, $n = 1$, the meaning of such a " compact family ". As $\sigma \to 0$ all the probability piles up at μ. Note that no normality of distributions is involved—originally or (in any non-trivial sense) asymptotically.

By convention, $P(y_1, ..., y_n)$ is defined to have the properties

$$E[Y_i] = \int_0^\infty ... \int_0^\infty Y_i dP(Y_1, ..., Y_n) = 0,$$

$$E[Y_i^2] = \int_0^\infty ... \int_0^\infty Y_i^2 dP(Y_1, ..., Y_n) = 1, \qquad ...(5)$$

$$E[Y_i Y_j] = \int_0^\infty ... \int_0^\infty Y_i Y_j dP(Y_1, ..., Y_n) = r_{ij},$$

where $[r_{ij}]$ is a symmetric positive definite correlation matrix. Similarly higher moments $E[Y_i^{k_i} Y_j^{k_j}...]$, for k's integers, can be defined. It follows then that

$$E[X_i] = \mu + \sigma^2 a_i, \quad E[X_i - E[X_i]]^2 = \sigma_i^2 \sigma^2, \text{ etc.} \qquad ...(6)$$

An explanation may be needed to motivate our putting the σ parameter in the numerator of P's arguments. If $[\mu + \sigma^2 a_i]$ had been replaced by the simple constants $[\mu_i]$, and if they were not all equal, then the securities with the largest μ_i would dominate the rest as $\sigma \to 0$. All other w's would either go to zero, or if borrowing and selling short were freely permitted—so that the w's need not be non-negative—infinitely profitable arbitrage would be possible. This bizarre, infinite case is of trivial interest. Hence, $\mu_i(\sigma)$ must as $\sigma \to 0$ approach a common limit.

Anyone familiar with Wiener's Brownian motion will identify σ with the square root of time, $\sqrt{t}$: in the numerator σ^2 appears because means grow linearly with time in Brownian motion; in the denominator σ appears because standard deviations grow like $\sqrt{t}$, with variance growing linearly. Dimensionally $a_i\sigma^2$ has the same dimension, namely dollars, as does X_i and $\sigma\sigma_i$; in Brownian terms a_i would be " dollars/time ". The inequality of instantaneous mean gains in Brownian motion is indicated by inequalities among the a_i, not among the μ_i. Although I have couched this heuristic explanation in terms of Brownian motion in time, the concept of a compact family is an independent and completely general one. Fortunately, it gains in importance because it does throw light on the reasons why enormous " quadratic " simplicities occur in continuous-time models, as the cited Fischer thesis make clear and as is evident in Merton [5].

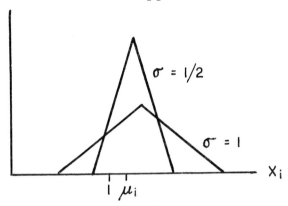

FIGURE 1

Example of family of compact probability densities.

Actually our family can be defined more generally than in terms of $[x_i - \mu - \sigma^2 a_i]/(\sigma\sigma_i)$. All that is required—and it *is* required if $[w_i(\sigma)]$, the optimal portfolio proportion as a function of the parameter σ, is to approach a unique and smooth limit $[w_i(0)]$—is that for the standardized variables $Z_i = X_i - \mu$

$$\lim_{\sigma \to 0} \frac{E[Z_i]}{E[Z_i^2]} = \frac{A}{B}, \quad \lim_{\sigma \to 0} \frac{E[Z_i^r]}{E[Z_i^2]} = \sigma^{r-2}C_r, \quad (r = 3, 4, \ldots). \qquad \ldots(7)$$

The P family defined above does have this property, as can now be verified for the one-dimensional case, $X_1 = X$,

$$E[X] = \int_0^\infty X dP\left(\frac{X - \mu - \sigma^2 a}{\sigma\sigma_1}\right) = \mu + \sigma^2 a,$$

$$E[(X - \mu - \sigma^2 a)^2] = \sigma^2 \sigma_1^2,$$

$$E[Z] = \int_0^\infty (X - \mu) dP\left(\frac{X - \mu - \sigma^2 a}{\sigma\sigma_1}\right) = \sigma^2 a,$$

$$E[Z^2] = E[(X - \mu - \sigma^2 a)^2] + (\sigma^2 a)^2, \qquad \ldots(8)$$

$$= \sigma_1^2 \sigma^2 + \sigma^4 a^2 = \sigma^2(\sigma_1^2 + \sigma^2 a^2),$$

$$E[Z^3] = E[\{(X - \mu - \sigma^2 a) + \sigma^2 a\}^3],$$

$$= \sigma^3 \sigma_1^3 \mu_3 + \sigma\psi_3,$$

where μ_3 is the third moment around the mean of $P(y)$ and $\sigma\psi_3$ involves powers of σ higher than 3. Similarly, it can be shown that

$$E[Z^4] = \sigma^4\sigma_1^4\mu_4 + \sigma\psi_4, \ldots, E[Z^r] = \sigma^r\sigma_1^r\mu_r + \sigma\psi_r, \quad r > 2. \qquad \ldots(9)$$

An example of an admissible compact family that cannot quite be written in the $P(\cdot)$ form is

$$\text{prob}\,\{X_1 = 1+\sigma\} = \text{prob}\,\{X_1 = (1+\sigma)^{-1}\} = \tfrac{1}{2}, \qquad \ldots(10)$$

Here,

$$E[X-1] = \frac{\sigma^2}{2} + \text{higher powers of } \sigma,$$

$$E[(X-1)^2] = 2\sigma^2 + \text{higher powers of } \sigma.$$

But this does satisfy our needed asymptotic conditions as defined in (7). We can now state our fundamental approximation theorem

Theorem 1. *The solution to the general problem, $[w_i(\sigma)]$, does, as $\sigma \to 0$ have the property that $[w_i(0)]$ is the exact solution to the quadratic problem*

$$\max_{\{w_i^*\}} \int_0^\infty \cdots \int_0^\infty \left\{ U[\mu] + U'[\mu]\left[\sum_1^n w_j^* X_j - \mu \right] + \frac{U''(\mu)}{2} \right.$$

$$\left. \cdot \left[\sum_1^n w_j^* X_j - \mu \right]^2 \right\} dP\left(\frac{X_1 - \mu - \sigma^2 a_1}{\sigma\sigma_1}, \ldots, \frac{X_n - \mu - \sigma^2 a_n}{\sigma\sigma_n} \right),$$

i.e.,

$$\lim_{\sigma \to 0} w_i^*(\sigma) = w_i^*(0) = w_i(0) = \lim_{\sigma \to 0} w_i(\sigma).$$

But it is definitely *not* the case that the higher approximation implied by $w_i'(0) = w_i^{*'}(0)$ will hold. Theorem 2 will show that one must use cubic-utility 3-moment theory to achieve this higher degree of approximation, and that in general (r-moment, rth degree) utility theory must be used in order to get agreement between $[w_i(0), w_i'(0), \ldots, w_i^{[r-2]}(0)]$ and $[w_i^*(0), w_i^{*'}(0), \ldots, w_i^{*[r-2]}(0)]$.

Theorem 2. *The solution to the general problem above is related asymptotically to that of the r-moment problem*

$$\max_{\{w_i^*\}} \int_0^\infty \cdots \int_0^\infty \left\{ \sum_0^r U^{[j]}(\mu) \frac{\left[\sum_1^n w_i X_i - \mu \right]^j}{j!} \right\} dP\left[\frac{X_1 - \mu - \sigma^2 a_1}{\sigma\sigma_1}, \ldots, \frac{X_n - \mu - \sigma^2 a_n}{\sigma\sigma_n} \right]$$

by the high-contact equivalences

$$w_i(0) = w_i^{**}(0), \ w_i'(0) = w_i^{**'}(0), \ldots, w_i^{[r-2]}(0) = w_i^{**[r-2]}(0).$$

To prove the theorems most rapidly, note that if U possesses an exact Taylor's expansion, $[w_i(\sigma)] \equiv [w_i^{**}(\sigma)]$ is for $r = \infty$ trivially identical. Hence, $w_i(\sigma)$ is formally defined from the power series

$$\bar{U}(\sigma) = \max_{\{w_i\}} \sum_0^\infty U^{[j]}(\mu) \frac{E\left[\left(\sum_1^n w_i Z_i \right)^j \right]}{j!}. \qquad \ldots(11)$$

The first-order conditions for a regular optimum are

$$\frac{\partial \bar{U}}{\partial w_1} = \frac{\partial \bar{U}}{\partial w_2} = \cdots = \frac{\partial \bar{U}}{\partial w_n}, \qquad \ldots(12)$$

where each of these is a power series in all the w's, with coefficients that depend on the moments $E[Z_1^{k_1} Z_2^{k_2}...]$. However, the moments in the infinite series that are involved if we truncate the series at $r-1 < \infty$ will be seen to be only the " lower " moments, in which $k_1 + k_2 + ... \leqq r$. Also straightforward but tedious formal algebra shows that in the infinite power series for $w_i(\sigma)$, the coefficients of the terms of order σ^{r-2} or less do depend only on the coefficients of the $\bar{U}(\sigma)$ power series only up to the rth degree terms and rth moments. Hence, the indicated agreement of derivatives in Theorem 2 does hold. Theorem 1 is of course only a special, but important, sub-case of Theorem 2.

There are a number of obvious corollaries of the theorems. Thus, the well-known Tobin separation theorem, which is valid for quadratic utilities, will necessarily be asymptotically valid in the sense of becoming true as $\sigma \to 0$. I.e. $w_i(0)/w_j(0)$ for assets held along with cash will be independent of the form of $U[\cdot]$.

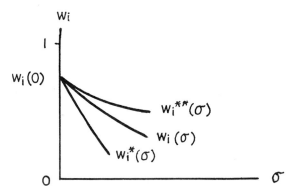

FIGURE 2

Although the quadratic mean-variance solution, $w_i^*(0)$, approaches the same intercept as the true solution, $w_i(0)$ the 3-moment cubic solution, $w_i^{**}(0)$, has higher contact with the true solution.

The exposition here has been heuristic, but can, subject to some hypotheses on the utility U and probability P functions, be made quite rigorous. The kind of formal algebra involved can be illustrated by the important case of cash versus one risky-asset (say a stock). Call cash X_0 and call the stock $X_1 = X$. Then the outcome for initial unit wealth is $(1-w) + wX = w(X-1) + 1 = wZ + 1$, where $w = w_1 = 1 - w_0$, and our general problem becomes

$$\bar{U}(w) = \max_{\{w\}} \int_0^\infty U[wZ+1]dP\left(\frac{Z-\sigma^2 a}{\sigma}\right),$$

$$\bar{U}'(w) = 0 = \int_0^\infty ZU'[wZ+1]dP \qquad ...(13)$$

$$= U'[1]\int_0^\infty ZdP + U''[1]\frac{w}{1}\int_0^\infty Z^2 dP + U'''[1]\frac{w^2}{2!}\int_0^\infty Z^3 dP + w^3 R_3,$$

where dP is short for $dP[\sigma^{-1}(Z-\sigma^2 a)]$ and $w^3 R_3$ involves higher powers of w than w^2.

If we truncate the series before the $U'''[1]$ term, we have the Tobin-Markowitz mean-variance approximation, with solution

$$w^*(0) = \lim_{\sigma \to 0} -\frac{a\sigma^2 U'[1]}{\sigma^2(\sigma_1^2 + a^2\sigma^2)U''[1]} = \frac{a}{\sigma_1^2}\left(\frac{U'[1]}{-U''[1]}\right), \qquad ...(14)$$

a not-surprising result. If from the above expression for $w^*(\sigma)$ we calculate $w^{*\prime}(0)$, we will not get the same result as if we had carried one more term in our truncated infinite expansion. Call this last value $w^{**}(\sigma)$ and define it as the root of the equation

$$0 = U'[1](a\sigma^2) + U''[1]w\sigma^2(\sigma_1^2 + a^2\sigma^2) + U'''(1)\frac{w^2}{2}\sigma^3(\sigma_1^3\mu_3 + \sigma\psi_3), \qquad ...(15)$$

where $\sigma^3\sigma\psi_3$ involves powers of σ beyond σ^3 and where the third moment of $P(y)$ has been earlier defined in (8). Then ignoring $\sigma^4\psi_3$, as we may, we find that $w^{**}(0)$ most definitely *is* affected by the value of $U'''[1]\sigma_1^3\mu_3$. Hence, the quadratic approximation is not locally of " high " contact. Fig. 2 illustrates the phenomenon. Notice how higher-than second moments do improve the solution. But it also needs emphasizing that near to $\sigma = 0$, when " risk is quite limited ", the mean-variance result is a very good approximation. When the heat of the controversy dissipates, that I think will be generally agreed on.[1]

Massachusetts Institute of Technology   PAUL A. SAMUELSON

First version received January 1970; *final version received March* 1970

REFERENCES

[1] Borch, K. " A Note on Uncertainty and Indifference Curves ", *Review of Economic Studies*, 36 (1969).

[2] Feldstein, M. S. " Mean-Variance Analysis in the Theory of Liquidity Preference and Portfolio Selection ", *Review of Economic Studies*, 36 (1969).

[3] Markowitz, H. " Portfolio Selection ", *The Journal of Finance*, 7 (1952).

[4] Markowitz, H. *Portfolio Selection: Efficient Diversification of Investments* (New York, John Wiley & Sons, 1959).

[5] Merton, R. C. " Lifetime Portfolio Selection under Uncertainty: the Continuous-Time Case ", *Review of Economics and Statistics*, 51 (1969).

[6] Samuelson, P. A. " General Proof that Diversification Pays ", *Journal of Financial and Quantitative Analysis*, 2 (1967).

[7] Tobin, J. " Liquidity Preference as Behaviour Towards Risk ", *Review of Economic Studies*, 25 (1958).

[8] Tobin, J. " The Theory of Portfolio Selection ", in F. H. Hahn and F. P. R. Brechling (eds.), *The Theory of Interest Rates* (London, Macmillan, 1965).

[9] Tobin, J. " Comment on Borch and Feldstein ", *Review of Economic Studies*, 36 (1969).

[1] See Markowitz [4] p. 121 for an argument that can be related closely to that here.

204

LIFETIME PORTFOLIO SELECTION
BY DYNAMIC STOCHASTIC PROGRAMMING

Paul A. Samuelson *

Introduction

MOST analyses of portfolio selection, whether they are of the Markowitz-Tobin mean-variance or of more general type, maximize over one period.[1] I shall here formulate and solve a many-period generalization, corresponding to lifetime planning of consumption and investment decisions. For simplicity of exposition I shall confine my explicit discussion to special and easy cases that suffice to illustrate the general principles involved.

As an example of topics that can be investigated within the framework of the present model, consider the question of a "businessman risk" kind of investment. In the literature of finance, one often reads; "Security A should be avoided by widows as too risky, but is highly suitable as a businessman's risk." What is involved in this distinction? Many things.

First, the "businessman" is more affluent than the widow; and being further removed from the threat of falling below some subsistence level, he has a high propensity to embrace variance for the sake of better yield.

Second, he can look forward to a high salary in the future; and with so high a present discounted value of wealth, it is only prudent for him to put more into common stocks compared to his present tangible wealth, borrowing if necessary for the purpose, or accomplishing the same thing by selecting volatile stocks that widows shun.

Third, being still in the prime of life, the businessman can "recoup" any present losses in the future. The widow or retired man nearing life's end has no such "second or nth chance."

Fourth (and apparently related to the last point), since the businessman will be investing for so many periods, "the law of averages will even out for him," and he can afford to act almost as if he were not subject to diminishing marginal utility.

What are we to make of these arguments? It will be realized that the first could be purely a one-period argument. Arrow, Pratt, and others [2] have shown that any investor who faces a range of wealth in which the elasticity of his marginal utility schedule is great will have high risk tolerance; and most writers seem to believe that the elasticity is at its highest for rich — but not ultra-rich! — people. Since the present model has no new insight to offer in connection with statical risk tolerance, I shall ignore the first point here and confine almost all my attention to utility functions with the same relative risk aversion at all levels of wealth. Is it then still true that lifetime considerations justify the concept of a businessman's risk in his prime of life?

Point two above does justify leveraged investment financed by borrowing against future earnings. But it does not really involve any increase in relative risk-taking once we have related what is at risk to the proper larger base. (Admittedly, if market imperfections make loans difficult or costly, recourse to volatile, "leveraged" securities may be a rational procedure.)

The fourth point can easily involve the innumerable fallacies connected with the "law of large numbers." I have commented elsewhere [3] on the mistaken notion that multiplying the same kind of risk leads to cancellation rather

* Aid from the National Science Foundation is gratefully acknowledged. Robert C. Merton has provided me with much stimulus; and in a companion paper in this issue of the REVIEW he is tackling the much harder problem of optimal control in the presence of continuous-time stochastic variation. I owe thanks also to Stanley Fischer.

[1] See for example Harry Markowitz [5]; James Tobin [14], Paul A. Samuelson [10]; Paul A. Samuelson and Robert C. Merton [13]. See, however, James Tobin [15], for a pioneering treatment of the multi-period portfolio problem; and Jan Mossin [7] which overlaps with the present analysis in showing how to solve the basic dynamic stochastic program recursively by working backward from the end in the Bellman fashion, and which proves the theorem that portfolio proportions will be invariant only if the marginal utility function is iso-elastic.

[2] See K. Arrow [1]; J. Pratt [9]; P. A. Samuelson and R. C. Merton [13].

[3] P. A. Samuelson [11].

than augmentation of risk. I.e., insuring many ships adds to risk (but only as $\sqrt{n}$); hence, only by insuring more ships and by *also* subdividing those risks among more people is risk on each brought down (in ratio $1/\sqrt{n}$).

However, before writing this paper, I had thought that points three and four could be reformulated so as to give a valid demonstration of businessman's risk, my thought being that investing for each period is akin to agreeing to take a $1/n^{\text{th}}$ interest in insuring n independent ships.

The present lifetime model reveals that investing for many periods does not *itself* introduce extra tolerance for riskiness at early, or any, stages of life.

Basic Assumptions

The familiar Ramsey model may be used as a point of departure. Let an individual maximize

$$\int_0^T e^{-\rho t} U[C(t)]dt \tag{1}$$

subject to initial wealth W_0 that can always be invested for an exogeneously-given certain rate of yield r; or subject to the constraint

$$C(t) = rW(t) - \dot{W}(t) \tag{2}$$

If there is no bequest at death, terminal wealth is zero.

This leads to the standard calculus-of-variations problem

$$J = \max_{\{W(t)\}} \int_0^T e^{-\rho t} U[rW - \dot{W}]dt \tag{3}$$

This can be easily related [4] to a discrete-time formulation

$$\max \sum_{t=0}^T (1+\rho)^{-t} U[C_t] \tag{4}$$

subject to

$$C_t = W_t - \frac{W_{t+1}}{1+r} \tag{5}$$

or,

$$\max_{\{W_t\}} \sum_{t=0}^T (1+\rho)^{-t} U\left[W_t - \frac{W_{t+1}}{1+r}\right] \tag{6}$$

[4] See P. A. Samuelson [12], p. 273 for an exposition of discrete-time analogues to calculus-of-variations models. Note: here I assume that consumption, C_t, takes place at the beginning rather than at the end of the period. This change alters slightly the appearance of the equilibrium conditions, but not their substance.

for prescribed (W_0, W_{T+1}). Differentiating partially with respect to each W_t in turn, we derive recursion conditions for a regular interior maximum

$$\frac{(1+\rho)}{1+r} U'\left[W_{t-1} - \frac{W_t}{1+r}\right]$$
$$= U'\left[W_t - \frac{W_{t+1}}{1+r}\right] \tag{7}$$

If U is concave, solving these second-order difference equations with boundary conditions (W_0, W_{T+1}) will suffice to give us an optimal lifetime consumption-investment program.

Since there has thus far been one asset, and that a safe one, the time has come to introduce a stochastically-risky alternative asset and to face up to a portfolio problem. Let us postulate the existence, alongside the safe asset that makes \$1 invested in it at time t return to you at the end of the period \$1$(1 + r)$, a risk asset that makes \$1 invested in, at time t, return to you after one period \$1Z_t, where Z_t is a random variable subject to the probability distribution

$$\text{Prob } \{Z_t \le z\} = P(z). \qquad z \ge 0 \tag{8}$$

Hence, $Z_{t+1} - 1$ is the percentage "yield" of each outcome. The most general probability distribution is admissible: i.e., a probability density over continuous z's, or finite positive probabilities at discrete values of z. Also I shall usually assume independence between yields at different times so that $P(z_0, z_1, \ldots, z_t, \ldots, z_T) = P(z_t)P(z_1) \ldots P(z_T)$.

For simplicity, the reader might care to deal with the easy case

$$\text{Prob } \{Z = \lambda\} = 1/2$$
$$= \text{Prob } \{Z = \lambda^{-1}\}, \qquad \lambda > 1 \tag{9}$$

In order that risk averters with concave utility should not shun this risk asset when maximizing the expected value of their portfolio, λ must be large enough so that the expected value of the risk asset exceeds that of the safe asset, i.e.,

$$\frac{1}{2}\lambda + \frac{1}{2}\lambda^{-1} > 1 + r, \text{ or}$$
$$\lambda > 1 + r + \sqrt{2r + r^2}.$$

Thus, for $\lambda = 1.4$, the risk asset has a mean yield of 0.057, which is greater than a safe asset's certain yield of $r = .04$.

At each instant of time, what will be the optimal fraction, w_t, that you should put in the risky asset, with $1 - w_t$ going into the safe asset? Once these optimal portfolio fractions are known, the constraint of (5) must be written

$$C_t = \left[W_t - \frac{W_{t+1}}{[(1-w_t)(1+r) + w_t Z_t]} \right].$$
(10)

Now we use (10) instead of (4), and recognizing the stochastic nature of our problem, specify that we maximize the expected value of total utility over time. This gives us the stochastic generalizations of (4) and (5) or (6)

$$\begin{array}{c} \text{Max} \\ \{C_t, w_t\} \end{array} E \sum_{t=0}^{T} (1+\rho)^{-t} U[C_t]$$
(11)

subject to

$$C_t = \left[W_t - \frac{W_{t+1}}{(1+r)(1-w_t) + w_t Z_t} \right]$$

W_0 given, W_{T+1} prescribed.

If there is no bequeathing of wealth at death, presumably $W_{T+1} = 0$. Alternatively, we could replace a prescribed W_{T+1} by a final bequest function added to (11), of the form $B(W_{T+1})$, and with W_{T+1} a free decision variable to be chosen so as to maximize (11) $+ B(W_{T+1})$. For the most part, I shall consider $C_T = W_T$ and $W_{T+1} = 0$.

In (11), E stands for the "expected value of," so that, for example,

$$E Z_t = \int_0^\infty z_t dP(z_t) .$$

In our simple case of (9),

$$E Z_t = \frac{1}{2}\lambda + \frac{1}{2}\lambda^{-1}.$$

Equation (11) is our basic stochastic programming problem that needs to be solved simultaneously for optimal saving-consumption and portfolio-selection decisions over time.

Before proceeding to solve this problem, reference may be made to similar problems that seem to have been dealt with explicitly in the economics literature. First, there is the valuable paper by Phelps on the Ramsey problem in which capital's yield is a prescribed random variable. This corresponds, in my notation, to the $\{w_t\}$ strategy being frozen at some fractional level, there being no portfolio selection problem. (My analysis could be amplified to

consider Phelps'[5] wage income, and even in the stochastic form that he cites Martin Beckmann as having analyzed.) More recently, Levhari and Srinivasan [4] have also treated the Phelps problem for $T = \infty$ by means of the Bellman functional equations of dynamic programming, and have indicated a proof that concavity of U is sufficient for a maximum. Then, there is Professor Mirrlees' important work on the Ramsey problem with Harrod-neutral technological change as a random variable.[6] Our problems become equivalent if I replace $W_t - W_{t+1}[(1+r)(1-w_t) + w_t Z_t]^{-1}$ in (10) by $A_t f(W_t/A_t) - nW_t - (W_{t+1} - W_t)$ let technical change be governed by the probability distribution

Prob $\{A_t \leqq A_{t-1}Z\} = P(Z);$

reinterpret my W_t to be Mirrlees' per capita capital, K_t/L_t, where L_t is growing at the natural rate of growth n; and posit that $A_t f(W_t/A_t)$ is a homogeneous first degree, concave, neoclassical production function in terms of capital and efficiency-units of labor.

It should be remarked that I am confirming myself here to regular interior maxima, and not going into the Kuhn-Tucker inequalities that easily handle boundary maxima.

Solution of the Problem

The meaning of our basic problem

$$J_T(W_0) = \begin{array}{c} \text{Max} \\ \{C_t, w_t\} \end{array} E \sum_{t=0}^{T} (1+\rho)^{-t} U[C_t]$$
(11)

subject to $C_t = W_t - W_{t+1}[(1-w_t)(1+r) + w_t Z_t]^{-1}$ is not easy to grasp. I act now at $t = 0$ to select C_0 and w_0, knowing W_0 but not yet knowing how Z_0 will turn out. I must act now, knowing that one period later, knowledge of Z_0's outcome will be known and that W_1 will then be known. Depending upon knowledge of W_1, a new decision will be made for C_1 and w_1. Now I can only guess what that decision will be.

As so often is the case in dynamic programming, it helps to begin at the end of the planning period. This brings us to the well-known

[5] E. S. Phelps [8].

[6] J. A. Mirrlees [6]. I have converted his treatment into a discrete-time version. Robert Merton's companion paper throws light on Mirrlees' Brownian-motion model for A_t.

one-period portfolio problem. In our terms, this becomes

$$J_1(W_{T-1}) = \underset{\{C_{T-1},w_{T-1}\}}{\text{Max}} U[C_{T-1}]$$
$$+ E(1+\rho)^{-1}U[(W_{T-1}-C_{T-1})$$
$$\{(1-w_{T-1})(1+r)$$
$$+ w_{T-1}Z_{T-1}\}^{-1}]. \quad (12)$$

Here the expected value operator E operates only on the random variable of the next period since current consumption C_{T-1} is known once we have made our decision. Writing the second term as $EF(Z_T)$, this becomes

$$EF(Z_T) = \int_0^\infty F(Z_T)dP(Z_T|Z_{T-1},Z_{T-2},\ldots,Z_0)$$
$$= \int_0^\infty F(Z_T)dP(Z_T), \text{ by our independence}$$

postulate.

In the general case, at a later stage of decision making, say $t = T-1$, knowledge will be available of the outcomes of earlier random variables, $Z_{t-2},\ldots$; since these might be relevant to the distribution of subsequent random variables, conditional probabilities of the form $P(Z_{T-1}|Z_{T-2},\ldots)$ are thus involved. However, in cases like the present one, where independence of distributions is posited, conditional probabilities can be dispensed within favor of simple distributions.

Note that in (12) we have substituted for C_T its value as given by the constraint in (11) or (10).

To determine this optimum (C_{T-1}, w_{T-1}), we differentiate with respect to each separately, to get

$$0 = U'[C_{T-1}] - (1+\rho)^{-1} EU'[C_T]$$
$$\{(1-w_{T-1})(1+r) + w_{T-1}Z_{T-1}\} \quad (12')$$
$$0 = EU'[C_T](W_{T-1}-C_{T-1})(Z_{T-1}-1-r)$$
$$= \int_0^\infty U'[(W_{T-1}-C_{T-1})$$
$$\{(1-w_{T-1}(1+r))+w_{T-1}Z_{T-1}\}]$$
$$(W_{T-1}-C_{T-1})(Z_{T-1}-1-r)dP(Z_{T-1})$$
$$(12'')$$

Solving these simultaneously, we get our optimal decisions (C^*_{T-1}, w^*_{T-1}) as functions of initial wealth W_{T-1} alone. Note that if somehow C^*_{T-1} were known, (12'') would by itself be the familiar one-period portfolio optimality condition, and could trivially be rewritten to handle any number of alternative assets.

Substituting (C^*_{T-1}, w^*_{T-1}) into the expression to be maximized gives us $J_1(W_{T-1})$ explicitly. From the equations in (12), we can, by standard calculus methods, relate the derivatives of U to those of J, namely, by the envelope relation

$$J_1'(W_{T-1}) = U'[C_{T-1}]. \quad (13)$$

Now that we know $J_1[W_{T-1}]$, it is easy to determine optimal behavior one period earlier, namely by

$$J_2(W_{T-2}) = \underset{\{C_{T-2},w_{T-2}\}}{\text{Max}} U[C_{T-2}]$$
$$+ E(1+\rho)^{-1} J_1[(W_{T-2}-C_{T-2})$$
$$\{(1-w_{T-2})(1+r) + w_{T-2}Z_{T-2}\}]. \quad (14)$$

Differentiating (14) just as we did in (11) gives the following equations like those of (12)

$$0 = U'[C_{T-2}] - (1+\rho)^{-1} EJ_1'[W_{T-2}]$$
$$\{(1-w_{T-2})(1+r) + w_{T-2}Z_{T-2}\} \quad (15')$$
$$0 = EJ_1'[W_{T-1}](W_{T-2}-C_{T-2})(Z_{T-2}-1-r)$$
$$= \int_0^\infty J_1'[(W_{T-2}-C_{T-2})\{(1-w_{T-2})(1+r)$$
$$+ w_{T-2}Z_{T-2}\}](W_{T-2}-C_{T-2})(Z_{T-2}-1-r)$$
$$dP(Z_{T-2}).$$
$$(15'')$$

These equations, which could by (13) be related to $U'[C_{T-1}]$, can be solved simultaneously to determine optimal (C^*_{T-2}, w^*_{T-2}) and $J_2(W_{T-2})$.

Continuing recursively in this way for $T-3$, $T-4,\ldots,2, 1, 0$, we finally have our problem solved. The general recursive optimality equations can be written as

$$\begin{cases} 0 = U'[C_0] - (1+\rho)^{-1} EJ'_{T-1}[W_0] \\ \quad \{(1-w_0)(1+r) + w_0Z_0\} \\ 0 = EJ'_{T-1}[W_1](W_0 - C_0)(Z_0 - 1-r) \end{cases}$$
$$\cdots \cdots \cdots \cdots$$
$$0 = U'[C_{t-1}] - (1+\rho)^{-1} EJ'_{T-t}[W_t]$$
$$\{(1-w_{t-1})(1+r) + w_{t-1}Z_{t-1}\} \quad (16')$$
$$0 = EJ'_{T-t}[W_{t-1}-C_{t-1}](Z_{t-1}-1-r),$$
$$(t = 1,\ldots,T-1). \quad (16'')$$

In (16'), of course, the proper substitutions must be made and the E operators must be over the proper probability distributions. Solving (16'') at any stage will give the optimal decision rules for consumption-saving and for portfolio selection, in the form

$$C^*_t = f[W_t; Z_{t-1},\ldots,Z_0]$$
$$= f_{T-t}[W_t] \text{ if the } Z\text{'s are independently distributed}$$

$$w*_t = g[W_t; Z_{t-1}, \ldots, Z_0]$$
$$= g_{T-t}[W_t] \text{ if the } Z\text{'s are independently distributed.}$$

Our problem is now solved for every case but the important case of infinite-time horizon. For well-behaved cases, one can simply let $T \to \infty$ in the above formulas. Or, as often happens, the infinite case may be the easiest of all to solve, since for it $C*_t = f(W_t)$, $w*_t = g(W_t)$, independently of time and both these unknown functions can be deduced as solutions to the following functional equations:

$$0 = U'[f(W)] - (1+\rho)^{-1}$$
$$\int_0^\infty f'[(W - f(W))\{(1+r)$$
$$- g(W)(Z - 1 - r)\}][(1+r)$$
$$- g(W)(Z - 1 - r)]dP(Z) \qquad (17')$$
$$0 = \int_0^\infty U'[\{W - f(W)\}$$
$$\{1 + r - g(W)(Z - 1 - r)\}]$$
$$[Z - 1 - r]. \qquad (17'')$$

Equation $(17')$, by itself with $g(W)$ pretended to be known, would be equivalent to equation (13) of Levhari and Srinivasan [4, p. f]. In deriving $(17')-(17'')$, I have utilized the envelope relation of my (13), which is equivalent to Levhari and Srinivasan's equation (12) [4, p. 5].

Bernoulli and Isoelastic Cases

To apply our results, let us consider the interesting Bernoulli case where $U = \log C$. This does not have the bounded utility that Arrow [1] and many writers have convinced themselves is desirable for an axiom system. Since I do not believe that Karl Menger paradoxes of the generalized St. Petersburg type hold any terrors for the economist, I have no particular interest in boundedness of utility and consider $\log C$ to be interesting and admissible. For this case, we have, from (12),

$$J_1(W) = \underset{\{C, w\}}{\text{Max}} \log C$$
$$+ E(1+\rho)^{-1} \log [(W - C)$$
$$\{(1-w)(1+r) + wZ\}]$$
$$= \underset{\{C\}}{\text{Max}} \log C + (1+\rho)^{-1} \log [W-C]$$
$$+ \underset{\{w\}}{\text{Max}} \int_0^\infty \log [(1-w)(1+r)$$
$$+ wZ]dP(Z). \qquad (18)$$

Hence, equations (12) and $(16')-(16'')$ split into two independent parts and the Ramsey-Phelps saving problem becomes quite independent of the lifetime portfolio selection problem. Now we have

$$0 = (1/C) - (1+\rho)^{-1}(W - C)^{-1} \text{ or}$$
$$C_{T-1} = (1+\rho)(2+\rho)^{-1}W_{T-1} \qquad (19')$$
$$0 = \int_0^\infty (Z-1-r)[(1-w)(1+r)$$
$$+ wZ]^{-1} dP(Z) \text{ or}$$
$$w_{T-1} = w* \text{ independently of } W_{T-1}. \qquad (19'')$$

These independence results, of the C_{T-1} and w_{T-1} decisions and of the dependence of w_{T-1} on W_{T-1}, hold for all U functions with isoelastic marginal utility. I.e., $(16')$ and $(16'')$ become decomposable conditions for all

$$U(C) = 1/\gamma \, C^\gamma, \qquad \gamma < 1 \qquad (20)$$

as well as for $U(C) = \log C$, corresponding by L'Hôpital's rule to $\gamma = 0$.

To see this, write (12) or (18) as

$$J_1(W) = \underset{\{C, w\}}{\text{Max}} \frac{C^\gamma}{\gamma} + (1+\rho)^{-1}\frac{(W-C)^\gamma}{\gamma}$$
$$\int_0^\infty [(1-w)(1+r) + wZ]^\gamma \, dP(Z)$$
$$= \underset{\{C\}}{\text{Max}} \frac{C^\gamma}{\gamma} + (1+\rho)^{-1}\frac{(W-C)^\gamma}{\gamma} \times$$
$$\underset{w}{\text{Max}} \int_0^\infty [(1-w)(1+r)$$
$$+ wZ]^\gamma \, dp(Z). \qquad (21)$$

Hence, $(12'')$ or $(15'')$ or $(16'')$ becomes

$$\int_0^\infty [(1-w)(1+r)$$
$$+ wZ]^{\gamma-1}(Z-r-1) \, dP(Z) = 0, \qquad (22'')$$

which defines optimal $w*$ and gives

$$\underset{\{w\}}{\text{Max}} \int_0^\infty [(1-w)(1+r) + wZ]^\gamma \, dP(Z)$$
$$= \int_0^\infty [(1-w*)(1+r) + w*Z]^\gamma \, dP(Z)$$
$$= [1 + r*]^\gamma, \text{ for short.}$$

Here, $r*$ is the subjective or util-prob mean return of the portfolio, where diminishing marginal utility has been taken into account.[7] To get optimal consumption-saving, differentiate (21) to get the new form of $(12')$, $(15')$, or $(16')$

[7] See Samuelson and Merton for the util-prob concept [13].

$$0 = C^{\gamma-1} - (1+\rho)^{-1}(1+r^*)^\gamma (W-C)^{\gamma-1}. \tag{22'}$$

Solving, we have the consumption decision rule

$$C^*_{T-1} = \frac{a_1}{1+a_1} W_{T-1} \tag{23}$$

where

$$a_1 = [(1+r^*)^\gamma/(1+\rho)]^{1/\gamma-1}. \tag{24}$$

Hence, by substitution, we find

$$J_1(W_{T-1}) = b_1 W^\gamma_{T-1}/\gamma \tag{25}$$

where

$$b_1 = a_1{}^\gamma (1+a_1)^{-\gamma} \\ + (1+\rho)^{-1}(1+r^*)^\gamma (1+a_1)^{-\gamma}. \tag{26}$$

Thus, $J_1(\cdot)$ is of the same elasticity form as $U(\cdot)$ was. Evaluating indeterminate forms for $\gamma = 0$, we find J_1 to be of log form if U was.

Now, by mathematical induction, it is easy to show that this isoelastic property must also hold for $J_2(W_{T-2})$, $J_3(W_{T-3}), \ldots,$ since, whenever it holds for $J_n(W_{T-n})$ it is deducible that it holds for $J_{n+1}(W_{T-n-1})$. Hence, at every stage, solving the general equations (16') and (16''), they decompose into two parts in the case of isoelastic utility. Hence,

Theorem:

For isoelastic marginal utility functions, $U'(C) = C^{\gamma-1}$, $\gamma < 1$, the optimal portfolio decision is independent of wealth at each stage and independent of all consumption-saving decisions, leading to a constant w^*, the solution to

$$0 = \int_0^\infty [(1-w)(1+r)+wZ]^{\gamma-1}(Z-1-r)dP(Z).$$

Then optimal consumption decisions at each stage are, for a no-bequest model, of the form

$$C^*_{T-i} = c_i W_{T-i}$$

where one can deduce the recursion relations

$$c_1 = \frac{a_1}{1+w_1},$$
$$a_1 = [(1+\rho)/(1+r^*)^\gamma]^{1/1-\gamma}$$
$$(1+r^*)^\gamma = \int_0^\infty [(1-w^*)(1+r) \\ + w^* Z]^\gamma dP(Z)$$
$$c_i = \frac{a_1 c_{i-1}}{1+a_1 c_{i-1}}$$
$$= \frac{a^i{}_1}{1+a_1+a^2{}_1+\ldots+a^i{}_1} < c_{i-1}$$
$$= \frac{a^i{}_1(a_1-1)}{a^{i+1}{}_1-1}, \qquad a_1 \neq 1$$
$$= \frac{1}{1+i}, \qquad a_1 = 1 .$$

In the limiting case, as $\gamma \to 0$ and we have Bernoulli's logarithmic function, $a_1 = (1+\rho)$, independent of r^*, and all saving propensities depend on subjective time preference ρ only, being independent of technological investment opportunities (except to the degree that W_t will itself definitely depend on those opportunities).

We can interpret $1+r^*$ as kind of a "risk-corrected" mean yield; and behavior of a long-lived man depends critically on whether

$$(1+r^*)^\gamma \gtrless (1+\rho), \text{ corresponding to } a_1 \lessgtr 1.$$

(i) For $(1+r^*)^\gamma = (1+\rho)$, one plans always to consume at a uniform rate, dividing current W_{T-i} evenly by remaining life, $1/(1+i)$. If young enough, one saves on the average; in the familiar "hump saving" fashion, one dissaves later as the end comes sufficiently close into sight.

(ii) For $(1+r^*)^\gamma > (1+\rho)$, $a_1 < 1$, and investment opportunities are, so to speak, so tempting compared to psychological time preference that one consumes nothing at the beginning of a long-long life, i.e., rigorously

$$\underset{i \to \infty}{\text{Lim }} c_i = 0, \qquad a_1 < 1$$

and again hump saving must take place. For $(1+r^*)^\gamma > (1+\rho)$, the *perpetual* lifetime problem, with $T = \infty$, is divergent and ill-defined, i.e., $J_i(W) \to \infty$ as $i \to \infty$. For $\gamma \leq 0$ and $\rho > 0$, this case cannot arise.

(iii) For $(1+r^*)^\gamma < (1+\rho)$, $a_1 > 1$, consumption at very early ages drops only to a limiting positive fraction (rather than zero), namely

$$\underset{i \to \infty}{\text{Lim }} c_i = 1 - 1/a_1 < 1, a_1 > 1.$$

Now whether there will be, on the average, initial hump saving depends upon the size of $r^* - c_\infty$, or whether

$$r^* - 1 - \frac{(1+r^*)^{\gamma/1-\gamma}}{(1+\rho)^{1/1-\gamma}} > 0.$$

This ends the *Theorem*. Although many of the results depend upon the no-bequest assumption, $W_{T+1} = 0$, as Merton's companion paper shows (p. 247, this *Review*) we can easily generalize to the cases where a bequest function $B_T(W_{T+1})$ is added to $\Sigma^T_0 (1+\rho)^{-t}U(C_t)$. If B_T is itself of isoelastic form,

$$B_T \equiv b_T(W_{T+1})^\gamma/\gamma,$$

the algebra is little changed. Also, the same comparative statics put forward in Merton's continuous-time case will be applicable here, e.g., the Bernoulli $\gamma = 0$ case is a watershed between cases where thrift is enhanced by riskiness rather than reduced; etc.

Since proof of the theorem is straightforward, I skip all details except to indicate how the recursion relations for c_i and b_i are derived, namely from the identities

$$b_{i+1}W^\gamma/\gamma = J_{i+1}(W)$$
$$= \underset{C}{\text{Max}} \{C^\gamma/\gamma$$
$$+ b_i(1+r^*)^\gamma(1+\rho)^{-1}(W-C)^\gamma/\gamma\}$$
$$= \{c^\gamma_{i+1} + b_i(1+r^*)^\gamma$$
$$(1+\rho)^{-1}(1-c_{i+1})^\gamma\} W^\gamma/\gamma$$

and the optimality condition

$$0 = C^{\gamma-1} - b_i(1+r^*)^\gamma(1+\rho)^{-1}(W-C)^{\gamma-1}$$
$$= (c_{i+1}W)^{\gamma-1} - b_i(1+r^*)^\gamma(1+\rho)^{-1}$$
$$(1-c_{i+1})^{\gamma-1}W^{\gamma-1},$$

which defines c_{i+1} in terms of b_i.

What if we relax the assumption of isoelastic marginal utility functions? Then w_{T-j} becomes a function of W_{T-j-1} (and, of course, of r, ρ, and a functional of the probability distribution P). Now the Phelps-Ramsey optimal stochastic saving decisions do interact with the optimal portfolio decisions, and these have to be arrived at by simultaneous solution of the nondecomposable equations (16') and (16'').

What if we have more than one alternative asset to safe cash? Then merely interpret Z_t as a (column) vector of returns $(Z^2_t, Z^3_t, \ldots)$ on the respective risky assets; also interpret w_t as a (row) vector $(w^2_t, w^3_t, \ldots)$, interpret $P(Z)$ as vector notation for

Prob $\{Z^2_t \leqq Z^2, Z^3_t \leqq Z^3, \ldots\}$
$= P(Z^2, Z^3, \ldots) = P(Z),$

interpret all integrals of the form $\int G(Z)dP(Z)$ as multiple integrals $\int G(Z^2, Z^3, \ldots)dP(Z^2, Z^3, \ldots)$. Then (16'') becomes a vector-set of equations, one for each component of the vector Z_t, and these can be solved simultaneously for the unknown w_t vector.

If there are many consumption items, we can handle the general problem by giving a similar vector interpretation to C_t.

Thus, the most general portfolio lifetime problem is handled by our equations or obvious extensions thereof.

Conclusion

We have now come full circle. Our model denies the validity of the concept of businessman's risk; for isoelastic marginal utilities, in your prime of life you have the same relative risk-tolerance as toward the end of life! The "chance to recoup" and tendency for the law of large numbers to operate in the case of repeated investments is not relevant. (Note: if the elasticity of marginal utility, $-U'(W)/WU''(W)$, rises empirically with wealth, and if the capital market is imperfect as far as lending and borrowing against future earnings is concerned, then it seems to me to be likely that a doctor of age 35–50 might rationally have his highest consumption then, and certainly show greatest risk tolerance then — in other words be open to a "businessman's risk." But not in the frictionless isoelastic model!)

As usual, one expects w^* and risk tolerance to be higher with algebraically large γ. One expects C_t to be higher late in life when r and r^* is high relative to ρ. As in a one-period model, one expects any increase in "riskiness" of Z_t, for the same mean, to decrease w^*. One expects a similar increase in riskiness to lower or raise consumption depending upon whether marginal utility is greater or less than unity in its elasticity.[8]

Our analysis enables us to dispel a fallacy that has been borrowed into portfolio theory from information theory of the Shannon type. Associated with independent discoveries by J. B. Williams [16], John Kelly [2], and H. A. Latané [3] is the notion that if one is investing for many periods, the proper behavior is to maximize the *geometric* mean of return rather than the arithmetic mean. I believe this to be incorrect (except in the Bernoulli logarithmic case where it happens [9] to be correct for reasons

---

[8] See Merton's cited companion paper in this issue, for explicit discussion of the comparative statical shifts of (16)'s C^*_t and w^*_t functions as the parameters (ρ, γ, r, r^*, and $P(Z)$ or $B(W_T)$ functions change. Similar results hold in the discrete-and-continuous-time models.

[9] See Latané [3, p. 151] for explicit recognition of this point. I find somewhat mystifying his footnote there which says, "As pointed out to me by Professor L. J. Savage (in correspondence), not only is the maximization of G [the geometric mean] the rule for maximum expected utility in connection with Bernoulli's function but (in so far as certain approximations are permissible) this same rule is approximately valid for all utility functions." [Latané, p. 151, n.13.] The geometric mean criterion is definitely too conservative to maximize an isoelastic utility function corresponding to positive γ in my equation (20), and it is definitely too daring to maximize expected utility when $\gamma < 0$. Professor Savage has informed me recently that his 1969 position differs from the view attributed to him in 1959.

quite distinct from the Williams-Kelly-Latané reasoning).

These writers must have in mind reasoning that goes something like the following: If one maximizes for a distant goal, investing and reinvesting (all one's proceeds) many times on the way, then the probability becomes great that with a portfolio that maximizes the geometric mean at each stage you will end up with a larger terminal wealth than with any other decision strategy.

This is indeed a valid consequence of the central limit theorem as applied to the additive logarithms of portfolio outcomes. (I.e., maximizing the geometric mean is the same thing as maximizing the arithmetic mean of the logarithm of outcome at each stage; if at each stage, we get a mean log of $m^{**} > m^*$, then after a large number of stages we will have $m^{**}T >> m^*T$, and the properly normalized probabilities will cluster around a higher value.)

There is nothing wrong with the logical deduction from premise to theorem. But the implicit premise is faulty to begin with, as I have shown elsewhere in another connection [Samuelson, 10, p. 3]. It is a mistake to think that, just because a w^{**} decision ends up with almost-certain probability to be better than a w^* decision, this implies that w^{**} must yield a better expected value of utility. Our analysis for marginal utility with elasticity differing from that of Bernoulli provides an effective counter example, if indeed a counter example is needed to refute a gratuitous assertion. Moreover, as I showed elsewhere, the ordering principle of selecting between two actions in terms of which has the greater probability of producing a higher result does not even possess the property of being transitive.[10] By that principle, we could have w^{***} better than w^{**}, and w^{**} better than w^*, and also have w^* better than w^{***}

[10] See Samuelson [11].

REFERENCES

[1] Arrow, K. J., "Aspects of the Theory of Risk-Bearing" (Helsinki, Finland: Yrjö Jahnssonin Säätiö, 1965).

[2] Kelly, J., "A New Interpretation of Information Rate," *Bell System Technical Journal* (Aug. 1956), 917–926.

[3] Latané, H. A., "Criteria for Choice Among Risky Ventures," *Journal of Political Economy* 67 (Apr. 1959), 144–155.

[4] Levhari, D. and T. N. Srinivasan, "Optimal Savings Under Uncertainty," Institute for Mathematical Studies in the Social Sciences, Technical Report No. 8, Stanford University, Dec. 1967.

[5] Markowitz, H., *Portfolio Selection: Efficient Diversification of Investment* (New York: John Wiley & Sons, 1959).

[6] Mirrlees, J. A., "Optimum Accumulation Under Uncertainty," Dec. 1965, unpublished.

[7] Mossin, J., "Optimal Multiperiod Portfolio Policies," *Journal of Business* 41, 2 (Apr. 1968), 215–229.

[8] Phelps, E. S., "The Accumulation of Risky Capital: A Sequential Utility Analysis," *Econometrica* 30, 4 (1962), 729–743.

[9] Pratt, J., "Risk Aversion in the Small and in the Large," *Econometrica* 32 (Jan. 1964).

[10] Samuelson, P. A., "General Proof that Diversification Pays," *Journal of Financial and Quantitative Analysis* II (Mar. 1967), 1–13.

[11] ———, "Risk and Uncertainty: A Fallacy of Large Numbers," *Scientia*, 6th Series, 57th year (April-May, 1963).

[12] ———, "A Turnpike Refutation of the Golden Rule in a Welfare Maximizing Many-Year Plan," Essay XIV *Essays on the Theory of Optimal Economic Growth*, Karl Shell (ed.) (Cambridge, Mass.: MIT Press, 1967).

[13] ———, and R. C. Merton, "A Complete Model of Warrant Pricing that Maximizes Utility," *Industrial Management Review* (in press).

[14] Tobin, J., "Liquidity Preference as Behavior Towards Risk," *Review of Economic Studies*, XXV, 67, Feb. 1958, 65–86.

[15] ———, "The Theory of Portfolio Selection," *The Theory of Interest Rates*, F. H. Hahn and F. P. R. Brechling (eds.) (London: Macmillan, 1965).

[16] Williams, J. B., "Speculation and the Carryover," *Quarterly Journal of Economics* 50 (May 1936), 436–455.

205

Foreword

PAUL A. SAMUELSON

Scientific research should be devoted to important questions. Here is one important question: Do organized speculative markets perform a socially useful function? There are two *standard* answers offered to this question: (1) A speculator is a fat man with a penchant for arithmetic who garners gobs of money for no good reason. (2) A speculator is a noble soul who takes risk upon his own shoulders so that producers of a chancy commodity can slough off risk by hedging operations and thereby reduce the cost to the consumer of goods that are subject to unpredictable acts of God, the weatherman, and the king's enemies.

These, I have been careful to say, are standard and hence rather superficial reactions. But they are replicated at a deeper scientific level of discourse. Maynard Keynes was a scientific genius. He was also a highly successful speculator. Therefore when he speaks on the subject of what organized bourses accomplish, his is a voice worth listening to. Keynes left us many memorable passages of prose: "In the long run we are all dead." Or the cadenza ending his classic *General Theory:* "the ideas of economists and political philosophers, both when they are right and when they are wrong are more powerful . . . ." And, among connoisseurs, there is the pre-Galbraithian prophecy of Keynes (in 1930) of affluence ahead and the problem of leisure that this would bring for humans, whose bodies and temperaments have developed through eons of evolution, equipped to earn their daily bread. His concern that release from the struggle for existence might result in a "nervous breakdown" perhaps provides insight into the quandary of affluent youth on our college campuses.

But among his *bons mots* are the following passages, highly relevant to appraisal of speculative markets:

> the energies and skill of the professional investor and speculator are mainly occupied . . . , not with making superior long-term forecasts of the probable yield of an investment over its whole life, but with foreseeing changes in the conventional basis of valuation a short time ahead of the general public . . . . The social object of skilled investment should be to defeat the dark forces of time and ignorance which envelop our future. The actual, private object of the most skilled investment to-day is "to beat the gun," as the Americans so well express it, to outwit the crowd, and to pass the bad, or depreciating, half-crown to the other fellow . . . it is, so to speak, a game of Snap, of Old Maid, of Musical Chairs—a pastime in which he is victor who says *Snap* neither too soon nor too late, who passes the Old Maid to his neighbour before the game is over, who secures a chair for himself when the music stops . . . . Or, to change the metaphor slightly, professional investment may be likened to those news-paper competitions in which the competitors have to pick out the six prettiest faces from a hundred photographs, the prize being awarded to the competitor whose choice most nearly corresponds to the average preferences of the competitors as a whole; so that each competitor has to pick, not those faces which he himself finds prettiest, but those which he thinks likeliest to catch the fancy of the other competitors . . . .[1]

Since Keynes was a notoriously successful investor, this adverse judgment on competitive markets is deemed worthy of special weight. And yet, a lifetime of scientific research by Holbrook Working at Stanford's Research Institute led him to the finding that prices quoted on the Board of Trade produced that pattern of carry-over from years of dearth to years of plenty which a technocrat would prescribe as optimal. This is a far cry from the Keynes witticism: "It is said, for example, that the shares of American companies which manufacture ice tend to sell at a higher price in summer when their profits are seasonally high than in winter when no one wants ice."[2]

And so we have, at a more sophisticated level, a reprise of the polar contentions that the ticker tape reveals God's wisdom, or that it spins a tale, told by an idiot, full of sound and fury, signifying nothing. The present book by Richard Roll offers a significant contribution to this important debate. Roll measures the facts against plausible theoretical models. I shall not presume to interpret his findings. That is a privilege reserved for the reader. But I hope it will be in order to call attention to Roll's grappling with a fascinating problem that once challenged my own research efforts. "How can the market price of a stock—say General Motors—ever be other than 'correct'? For if it were quoted at *patently* bargain levels, sharpeyed speculators would already have turned to it and bid up its price." This bit of wisdom undulates tantalizingly between irrefutable (and hence uninteresting) truism and gratuitous assertion. My own offering in the matter was to prove the deductive theorem: For very general stochastic processes, the changes in the expected value of a future variable, as new random data become available, cancel out to zero, or to a systematic bias inherent in investor risk aversion. Dr. Roll has, happily, gone beyond deduction to hypothesis formation and verification and I commend his vintage.

NOTES

1. John Maynard Keynes, *General Theory of Employment, Interest, and Money* (New York: Harcourt, Brace and World, 1936), pp. 154-156.

2. *Ibid.*, p. 154.

206

Stochastic Speculative Price

PAUL A. SAMUELSON

Department of Economics, Massachusetts Institute of Technology, Cambridge, Mass. 02139

Communicated October 27, 1970

ABSTRACT   Because a commodity like wheat can be carried forward from one period to the next, speculative arbitrage serves to link its prices at different points of time. Since, however, the size of the harvest depends on complicated probability processes impossible to forecast with certainty, the minimal model for understanding market behavior must involve stochastic processes. The present study, on the basis of the axiom that it is the *expected* rather than the known-for-certain prices which enter into all arbitrage relations and carryover decisions, determines the behavior of price as the solution to a stochastic-dynamic-programming problem. The resulting stationary time series possesses an ergodic state and normative properties like those often observed for real-world bourses.

CERTAINTY RELATIONS

The simplest formal theory of speculative price [1] assumes that demands of different periods are independent functions relating consumption, c_t, to p_t, $p_t = P[c_t]$, $P' < 0$, and that costs of carryover consist only of interest and "shrinkage" charges. The equation of price then becomes

$$p_t = P[H_t + aq_{t-1} - q_t], \qquad (t = 0,1,2,\dots) \qquad (1)$$

where a is the fraction of grain carried over at a time, $t - 1$, which is left after shrinkage to be available at time t, q_t is the amount of grain carried over at time t for availability at time $t + 1$, r is the interest rate, and H_t is the harvest at time t. When $[H_t]$ is foreseeable with certainty, competitive arbitrage would enforce the intertemporal-equilibrium conditions

$$(1 + r)^{-1}aP[H_{t+1} + aq_t - q_{t+1}] - P[H_t + aq_{t-1} - q_t] \le 0$$

$$q_t\{(1 + r)^{-1}aP[H_{t+1} + aq_t - q_{t+1}] -$$

$$P[H_t + aq_{t-1} - q_t]\} = 0, \qquad (t = 0,1\dots,T)$$

$[q_{-1},q_T]$ specified. $\qquad (2)$

These second-order dynamic difference equations and inequalities can be solved for the unknowns $[q_0, q_1, \dots q_{T-1}; c_0, \dots c_T; p_0, \dots p_T]$. It can be shown that these unknowns are obtainable as the maximizing solution to a variational problem of optimal-control type, namely

$$\underset{q_0,\dots q_{T-1}}{\text{Max}} \sum_0^T (1 + r)^{-t}U[H_t + aq_{t-1} - q_t] \qquad (3)$$

where the $[H_0,\dots,H_T; q_{-1},q_T]$ are prescribed and all the decision variables are restricted to being nonnegative, $q_t \ge 0$, and where

$$U[c] = \int_b^c P[x]dx, P[c] = U'[c], U'' < 0 \qquad (4)$$

Applying the Kuhn-Tucker conditions to the solution of (3) is seen to yield the market behavior conditions of (2).

PROBABILITY MODEL

It is assumed that the harvests $[H_t]$ are not foreseeable with certainty but can be taken as subject to known probability distributions that are uniform through time and independent, namely

$$\text{Prob}\{H_t \le h\} = F(h),$$

$$\text{Prob}\{H_t \le h_0 \text{ and } H_{t+1} \le h_1\} = F(h_0)F(h_1) \qquad (5)$$

Since exact arbitrage relations like (2) are no longer valid, some new hypothesis is needed. The present model postulates that the mathematical expectation of price plays the role in the decisions of the stochastic model about carryover that known-future-price plays in the deterministic model.

Postulate: Positive carryover will take place only if interest and shrinkage costs are just covered by expected future price:

$$(1 + r)^{-1}aEp_{t+1} - p_t \le 0$$

$$q_t\{(1 + r)^{-1}aEp_{t+1} - p_t\} = 0 \qquad (6)$$

where E stands for the expected value operator: e.g.,

$$EH_t = \int_0^\infty hdF(h)$$

a Stieltjes integral that handles both discrete probabilities and densities.

Just as (2) was obtainable as the optimizing solution to (3), the conditions of (4) are deducible as the optimizing solution to the following stochastic-dynamic-programming problem: for prescribed $[q_{-1},q_T]$

$$J_T[H_0 + aq_{-1}] = \underset{q_0,\dots,q_{T-1}}{\text{Max}} E\sum_0^T (1 + r)^{-t}U[H_t +$$

$$aq_{t-1} - q_t], \qquad q_t \ge 0 \quad (7)$$

The usual Bellman [2] technique solves such a programming problem by recursive sequence

$$J_n[H_{T-n} + aq_{T-n-1}] =$$

$$\underset{q_{T-n}}{\text{Max}} \{U[H_{T-n} + aq_{T-n-1} - q_{T-n}] +$$

$$(1 + r)^{-1}EJ_{n-1}[H_{T-n+1} + aq_{T-n}]\}, \qquad q_{T-n} \ge 0,$$

$$(n = 1,2,\dots,T) \quad (8)$$

$$J_0[H_T + aq_{T-1}] = U[H_T + aq_{T-1} - q_T]$$

Each of these concave programming problems can be solved by Kuhn-Tucker programming for one (or in case of ties, more than one) optimal carryover strategy

$$q_{T-n}^* = f_n(H_{T-n} + aq_{T-n-1}), \qquad 0 \leqslant f_n' \leqslant 1 \quad (9)$$

The dependence of these functions on terminal q_T is not indicated explicitly.

To solve for the q_t^*, we write out the (Kuhn-Tucker) necessary conditions for the maxima

$$0 \geqslant -U'[H_{T-n} + aq_{T-n-1} - q_{T-n}] +$$
$$(1 + r)^{-1} aE J_{n-1}'[H_{T-n+1} + aq_{T-n}],$$
$$0 = q_{T-n} \{ -U'[H_{T-n} + aq_{T-n-1} - q_{T-n}] + $$
$$(1 + r)^{-1} aE J_{n-1}'[H_{T-n+1} + aq_{T-n}] \} \quad (10)$$

Because the maximands are all concave, these necessary conditions are also sufficient. Their equivalence with the basic postulate of the model, (6), is obvious upon recalling the definitional identity $P[c] \equiv U'[c]$. Worth noting also is the envelope condition implied by the maximum

$$J_n'[H_{T-n} + aq_{T-n-1}]$$
$$= U'[H_{T-n} + aq_{T-n-1} - f_n(H_{T-n} + aq_{T-n-1})] \quad (11)$$

This completes the solution for fixed horizon T, permitting derivation of all economic magnitudes as random variables, whose laws of behavior depend upon the exogenous random variable $[H_t]$ and the form of the various functions involved. For unlimited horizon, $T = \infty$, the variables will form a stationary time series.

Unlimited horizon

As T, the length of the horizon becomes ever larger, the dependence on terminal q_T becomes ever weaker. Actually, $f_n(\cdot)$ approaches a limiting function $f(\cdot)$, and also $J_n(\cdot)$ approaches $J[\cdot]$ as $n \to \infty$,

$$\underset{T \to \infty}{\text{Lim}} q_t^* = \underset{T \to \infty}{\text{Lim}} f_{T-t}(H_t + aq_{t-1})$$
$$= \underset{n \to \infty}{\text{Lim}} f_n(H_t + aq_{t-1}) = f(H_t + aq_{t-1}) \quad (12)$$

$$\underset{T \to \infty}{\text{Lim}} J_{T-t}[H_t + aq_{t-1}] = J[H_t + aq_{t-1}]$$

These presuppose that regularity conditions and well-behaved transversality conditions are satisfied, such as

$$\underset{T \to \infty}{\text{Lim}} (1 + r)^{-T} q_T = 0, \quad \underset{T \to \infty}{\text{Lim}} (1 + r)^{-T} E p_T = 0$$

The limiting functions themselves satisfy time-free functional equations of Bellman type

$$0 \geqslant -U'[x - f(x)] + (1 + r)^{-1} a \int_0^\infty U'[h + af(x)] dF(h)$$
$$0 = f(x) \{ -U'[x - f(x)] +$$
$$(1 + r)^{-1} a \int_0^\infty U'[h + af(x)] dF(h) \} \quad (13)$$

$$J[x] = U[x - f(x)] + (1 + r)^{-1} \int_0^\infty J'[h + af(x)] dF(h)$$

These are derived by taking T limits in (10), using the envelope relation (11), and recalling the definition of the expectation operator. In principle, they can be solved for $f(x)$ and $J(x)$ by

a variety of methods of successive approximation; in the absence of $U(c)$ and $F(h)$ taking specially simple analytic forms, one natural method of solution would be to set q_T at some reasonable level, between $\int_0^\infty h dF(h)$ and zero, actually solve recursively for $f_n(x)$, $J_n[x]$, and then let n become large.

Conditional probabilities

Once the decision rule for carryover, $f(x)$, becomes known, $[q_t]$, $[p_t]$, and $[c_t]$ become random variables subject to known probability laws. For brevity, denote $H_t + aq_{t-1} = x_t$, the stock of grain available after the harvest is in. This also is a random variable.

Economic intuition about how an organized market both does and should work suggests certain reasonable properties for the carryover function $f(x)$.

1. When, because of a run of recent harvests "above normal," the stock of available inventory is "high," one expects the carryover to be high: i.e., $f(x)$ increases with x.

2. Each increment of inventory, additional to already high inventory, can be expected to be divided between abnormally high consumption today (high c_t and low p_t) and incremental carryover for higher future consumptions: i.e., $c(x) = x - f(x)$ and $f(x)$ have the properties, $0 \leqslant f'(x) \leqslant 1$, $0 \leqslant c'(x) \leqslant 1$.

3. When, because of a run of recent harvests "below normal," available inventory, x, is below some critical level, one would expect carryover to drop down to zero, since the price now will be too high relative to the price expected for the next period to permit grain that is carried over to earn the interest and shrinkage charges involved in the process: i.e., for $x < x^*$, $f(x) \equiv 0$, and the price inequalities of (6) will hold.

4. In summary, the lower is present price, p_t, the lower the conditional expectation of future prices, but with a quantitative strength that attenuates with time.

Solving $p = P[x - f(x)]$ inversely for $x = X\{p\}$ and $q = f(X\{p\}) = q\{p\}$, we have the following recursion relation connecting p_{t+1} with p_t and the intervening random harvest

$$p_{t+1} = P[H_{t+1} + aq\{p_t\} - f(H_{t+1} + aq\{p_t\})],$$
$$0 \leqslant \partial p_{t+1} / \partial p_t \leqslant 1 \quad (14)$$

From this we can calculate the conditional probabilities

$$\text{Prob}\{p_{t+1} \leqslant p \,|\, p_t = p_0\} = \pi_1(p;p_0)$$
$$\text{Prob}\{p_{t+2} \leqslant p \,|\, p_t = p_0\} = \pi_2(p;p_0)$$
$$\dots\dots\dots\dots\dots\dots\dots\dots\dots\dots\dots \quad (15)$$
$$\text{Prob}\{p_{t+n} \leqslant p \,|\, p_t = p_0\} = \pi_n(p;p_0)$$

Since p_t can affect p_{t+2} or p_{t+n} only through the effect of its $q\{p_t\}$ on p_{t+1}, we have here a Markov process with

$$\text{Prob}\{p_{t+n} \leqslant p \,|\, p_t = p_0, \, p_{t+m} = p_m\} =$$
$$\pi_n(p;p_0) \text{ independently of } p_m, \qquad n > m > 0$$

Hence, the Markov transitional probabilities will satisfy the Chapman-Kolmogorov relations

$$\pi_{n+m}(p;p_0) = \int_0^\infty \pi_n(p;y) d\pi_m(y;p_0) \quad (16)$$

The conditional probabilities of (15) necessarily have the properties

$$\partial \pi_n(p;p_0) / \partial p_0 \geqslant 0, \qquad \partial E[p_{t+n} \,|\, p_0] / \partial p_0 \geqslant 0 \quad (17)$$

in consequence of (14).

Finally, under weak regularity conditions, an ergodic state is assured, with

$$\text{Lim}_{n \to \infty} \pi_n(p;p_0) = \pi(p) \text{ independently of } p_0$$

$$\text{Lim}_{n \to \infty} E[p_{t+n}|p_0] = \int_0^\infty p \, d\pi(p) \qquad (18)$$

CONCLUSION

A model of (nonindependent) Brownian vibration for stochastic speculative price has been rigorously deduced. It has quantitative properties like those observed for historical organized markets (Board of Trade, Cotton Exchange, etc.), and also broad properties that a technocratic planner would prescribe for well-functioning carryovers. This simple model is readily capable of being generalized—to consider $[H_t]$ sub-ject to a periodic seasonal stochastic fluctuation, to allow serial dependence of harvests in different crop years, to let plantings vary in function of current price (and conditionally expected future prices) by deleting H_t as a variable and making a a random variable over the nonnegative range. The model is inadequate to explain the empirical facts of negative carrying charges and "normal backwardation," and therefore needs further amplification.

* I owe thanks to the National Science Foundation for financial assistance, and Mrs. Jillian Pappas for editorial help.

1. Samuelson, P. A., in "Intertemporal Price Equilibrium: A Prologue to the Theory of Speculation," *Collected Scientific Papers* (The M.I.T. Press, Cambridge, Mass., 1966), Ch. 13, pp. 946–984.

2. Bellman, R., *Dynamic Programming* (Princeton University Press, Princeton, N.J., 1957).

207

The "Fallacy" of Maximizing the Geometric Mean in Long Sequences of Investing or Gambling

(maximum geometric mean strategy/uniform strategies/asymptotically sufficient parameters)

PAUL A. SAMUELSON

Department of Economics, Massachusetts Institute of Technology, Cambridge, Mass. 02139

Contributed by Paul A. Samuelson, July 26, 1971

ABSTRACT   Because the outcomes of repeated investments or gambles involve products of variables, authorities have repeatedly been tempted to the belief that, in a long sequence, maximization of the expected value of terminal utility can be achieved or well-approximated by a strategy of maximizing at each stage the geometric mean of outcome (or its equivalent, the expected value of the logarithm of principal plus return). The law of large numbers or of the central limit theorem as applied to the logs can validate the conclusion that a maximum-geometric-mean strategy does indeed make it "virtually certain" that, in a "long" sequence, one will end with a higher terminal wealth and utility. However, this does not imply the false corollary that the geometric-mean strategy is optimal for any finite number of periods, however long, or that it becomes asymptotically a good approximation. As a trivial counter-example, it is shown that for utility proportional to x^γ/γ, whenever $\gamma \neq 0$, the geometric strategy is suboptimal for all T and never a good approximation. For utility bounded above, as when $\gamma < 0$, the same conclusion holds. If utility is bounded above and finite at zero wealth, *no* uniform strategy can be optimal, even though it can be that the best uniform strategy will be that of the maximum geometric mean. However, asymptotically the same level of utility can be reached by an infinity of nearby uniform strategies. The true optimum in the bounded case involves nonuniform strategies, usually being more risky than the geometric-mean maximizer's strategy at low wealths and less risky at high wealths. The novel criterion of maximizing the expected average compound return, which asymptotically leads to maximizing of geometric mean, is shown to be arbitrary.

BACKGROUND

Suppose one begins with initial wealth, X_0, and after a series of decisions one is left with terminal wealth, X_T, subject to a conditional probability distribution

$$\text{prob}\left\{ X_T \leqslant X | X_0 = A \right\} = P_T(X,A) \qquad (1)$$

Then an "expected utility" maximizer, by definition, will choose his decisions to

$$\max E\{u(X_T)\} = \max \int_{-\infty}^{\infty} u(X)P_T(dX,A), \qquad (2)$$

where E stands for the "expected value" and where $u(x)$ is a specified utility function that is unique except for arbitrary scale and origin parameters, b and a, in $a + bu(x)$, $b > 0$.

In a portfolio, or gambling situation, at each period one can make investments or bets proportional to wealth at the beginning of that period, X_t, so that the outcome of wealth for the next period is the random variable

$$X_{t+1} = X_t\{w_1Y_1 + \ldots + w_nY_n\}, \ \sum_1^n w_j = 1 \qquad (3)$$

where the w's are the proportions decided upon for investment in the different securities (or gambling games). The returns per dollar invested in each alternative, respectively, are subject to known probability distributions.

$$\text{prob}\left\{ Y_1 \leq y_1, \ldots, Y_n \leq y_n \right\} = F(y_1, \ldots, y_n), \qquad (4)$$

where for simplicity the vector outcomes at any t are assumed each to be independent of outcomes at any other time periods, and to remain the same distribution over all time periods. Usually Y_t is restricted to being nonnegative to avoid bankruptcy. A complete decision involves selecting over the interval of time $t = 1,2,\ldots,T$, all the vectors $[w_j(t)]$, which will be nonnegative if short-selling and bankruptcy are ruled out.

In particular, if the same strategy is followed at all times, so that $w_j(t) \equiv w_j$, the variables become

$$
\begin{aligned}
X_1 &= X_0x_1, \ X_2 = X_1x_2 = X_0x_1x_2 \\
X_t &= X_{t-1}x_t = X_0x_1x_2 \ldots x_t
\end{aligned}
\qquad (5)
$$

and all x_t are independently distributed according to the same distribution, which we may write as

$$\text{prob}\left\{ x_t \leqslant x \right\} = \Pi(x). \qquad (6)$$

Of course, $\Pi(x)$ will depend on the w strategy chosen, and is short for $\Pi(x; w_1, \ldots, w_n)$ in this particular case, and on the assumed $F(y_1, \ldots, y_n)$ function.

It can be easily shown that

$$\text{prob}\left\{ X_t \leq X | X_0 = Z \right\} = P_t(X,Z)$$

$$P_t(X,Z) = P_t(X/Z,1) \qquad (7)$$

$$= P_t(X/Z) \text{ for short}$$

and

$$P_1(x) \equiv \Pi(x)$$

$$P_2(x) = \int_{-\infty}^{\infty} P_1(x/s)dP_1(s)$$

$$\ldots \ldots \ldots \ldots \ldots \ldots \qquad (8)$$

$$P_T(x) = \int_{-\infty}^{\infty} P_{T-1}(x/s)dP_1(s)$$

EXACT SOLUTIONS

For general $u(.)$ functions, a different decision-vector $[w_j(t)]$ is called for at each intermediate time period, $t = 1, 2, \ldots, T - 1$. This is tedious, but both inevitable and feasible. It is well known that for one, and only one, family of utility functions, namely

$$u(x; \gamma) = x^\gamma/\gamma \qquad \gamma \neq 0$$
$$= \log x \qquad \gamma = 0 \qquad (9)$$

it is optimal to use the same repeated strategy. For this case the common optimal strategy is that of a $T = 1$ period problem, namely

$$X_0{}^\gamma \max_{w_i} Ex^\gamma/\gamma = X_0{}^\gamma \max_{w_i} \int_0^\infty (x^\gamma/\gamma) dP_1(x; w_1, \ldots, w_n) \qquad (10)$$

The $\log x$ case is included in this formulation, since as $\gamma \to 0$, the indeterminate form is easily evaluated.

PROPOSED CRITERION

Often in probability problems, as the number of variables becomes large, $T \to \infty$. In this case, certain asymptotic simplifications become feasible. Repeatedly, authorities (1–3) have proposed a drastic simplification of the decision problem whenever T is large.

Rule. Act in each period to maximize the geometric mean or the expected value of $\log x_t$.

The plausibility of such a procedure comes from recognition of the following valid asymptotic result.

Theorem. If one acts to maximize the geometric mean at every step, if the period is "sufficiently long," "almost certainly" higher terminal wealth and terminal utility will result than from any other decision rule.

To prove this obvious truth, one need only apply the central-limit theorem, or even the weaker law of large numbers, to the sum of independent variables

$$\log X_T = \log X_0 + \sum_1^T \log x_t \qquad (11)$$

We may note the following fact about $P_T(x; \max \text{ g.m.}) = Q_T{}^*(x)$ and $P_T(x; \text{ other rule}) = Q_T(x)$.

$$Q_T{}^*(x) < Q_T(x) \qquad \text{for } T > M(x) \qquad (12)$$

The crucial point is that M is a function of x that is unbounded in x.

From this indisputable fact, it is tempting to believe in the truth of the following false corollary:

False Corollary. If maximizing the geometric mean almost certainly leads to a better outcome, then the expected utility of its outcomes exceeds that of any other rule, provided T is sufficiently large.

The temptation to error is compounded by the consideration that both distributions approach asymptotically log normal distributions.

Since $\mu^* > \mu$ by hypothesis, it follows at once that, for T large enough $L_T{}^*(x)$ can be made smaller than $L_T(x)$ for *any* x. From this it is thought, apparently, that one can validly deduce that $\int_0^\infty u(x) dQ_T{}^* > \int_0^\infty u(x) dQ_T(x)$.

FALSITY OF COROLLARY

A single example can show that the needed corollary is not generally valid. Suppose $\gamma = 1$, and one acts, in the fashion recommended by Pascal, to maximize expected money wealth itself. Let the gambler–investor face a choice between investing completely in safe cash, Y_1, or completely in a "security" that yields for each dollar invested, $2.70 with probability $1/2$ or only $0.30 with probability $1/2$. To maximize the geometric mean, one must stick only to cash, since $[(2.7)(.3)]^{1/2} = .9 < 1$. But, Pascal will always put all his wealth into the risky gamble.

Isn't he a fool? If he wins and loses an equal number of bets, and in the long run that will be his median position, he ends up with

$$(2.7)^T(.3)^T = (.9)^T \to 0 \text{ as } T \to \infty \qquad (14)$$

"Almost certainly," he will be "virtually ruined" in a "long enough" sequence of play.

No, Pascal is not a fool according to *his* criterion. In those rare long sequences (and remember *all* sequences are *finite*, albeit very large) when he does experience relatively many wins, he makes more than enough to compensate him, according to the $\max EX_T$ criterion, for the more frequent times when he is ruined.

Actually,

$$E\{X_T\} = E\left\{X_0 \prod_1^T x_t\right\}$$
$$= X_0 \prod_1^n E\{x_t\}, \text{ for independent variates} \qquad (15)$$
$$= X_0\{Ex_1\}^T$$
$$= X_0 1.5^T > X_0 1^T \text{ for } all\ T$$

But, you may say, Pascal is foolish to court ruin just for a large money gain. A dollar he wins is surely worth less in utility than the dollar he loses. Very well, as with eighteenth-century writers on the St. Petersburg Paradox, let us assume a concave utility-function, $u(x)$, with $u''(x) < 0$. Let us now test the false corollary for $u(x) = x^\gamma/\gamma$, $1 > \gamma \neq 0$. Let the decision according to the geometric mean rule lead to

$$E\{\log x_1{}^*\} > E \log x_1 \qquad (16)$$

But let the alternative decision produce

$$E\{x_1{}^\gamma/\gamma\} > E\{x_1{}^\gamma/\gamma\} \qquad (17)$$

Then, as before, except for the changed value of the γ exponent

$$E\{X_T{}^\gamma/\gamma\} > E\{X_T{}^{*\gamma}/\gamma\}, \qquad (18)$$

$$\lim_{T \to \infty} Q_T{}^*(x) \cong \frac{1}{\sqrt{2\pi}\sigma^* T^{1/2}} \int_{-\infty}^{\log x} \left\{\exp -\frac{1}{2}[s - \mu^* T]^2/(\sigma^*)^2 T\right\} ds = L_T{}^*(x)$$

$$\lim_{T \to \infty} Q_T(x) \cong \frac{1}{\sqrt{2\pi}\sigma T^{1/2}} \int_{-\infty}^{\log x} \left\{\exp -\frac{1}{2}[s - \mu T]^2/\sigma^2 T\right\} ds = L_T(x) \qquad (13)$$

since

$$E\{X_T{}^\gamma/\gamma\} = X_0{}^\gamma \prod_1^T E\{x_1{}^\gamma/\gamma\}$$

$$= X_0{}^\gamma [E\{x_1{}^\gamma/\gamma\}]^T \qquad (19)$$

$$> X^\gamma [E\{x_1{}^{*\gamma}/\gamma\}]^T = EX_T{}^{*\gamma}/\gamma$$

This strong inequality holds for all T, however large. Thus, the false corollary is seen to be invalid in general, even for concave utilities.

BOUNDED UTILITIES

Most geometric-mean maximizers are convinced by this reasoning (5). But not all. Thus, Markowitz, in the new 1971 preface to the reissue of his classic work on portfolio analysis (4), says that "boundedness" of the utility function will save the geometric-mean rule. For $\gamma < 0$, $u = x^\gamma/\gamma$ will be bounded from above, and a run of favorable gains will not bring the decision maker a utility gain of more than a finite amount. But, as the case $\gamma = -1$ shows, that cannot save the false corollary. For in all cases when $\gamma < 0$, the false rule leads to *over-riskiness*, just as for $\gamma > 0$ it leads to *under-riskiness*. Those few times, and they will happen for all T, however large, with a positive (albeit diminishing probability), whenever the false rule brings you closer to zero terminal wealth (or ruin), the unboundedness of u as $x \to 0$ and $u \to -\infty$ puts a prohibitive penalty against the false rule.

What about the case where utility is bounded above and is finite at $X_T = 0$ or ruin? It is easy to show that *no* uniform decision rule can be optimal for such a case, where

$$-\infty < u(0) \leqslant u(X) \leqslant M < \infty \qquad (20)$$

But suppose we choose among all suboptimal uniform strategies that have the property of "limited liability," so that each x_t is confined to the range of nonnegative numbers. Then the following theorem, which seems to contain the germ of truth the geometric mean maximizers are groping for, is valid.

Theorem. For $u(x)$ bounded above and below in the range of nonnegative numbers, the uniform rule of maximizing the geometric mean $E\{\log X_T{}^*\}$, will asymptotically outperform any other uniform strategy's result, $E\{u(X_T)\}$, in the following sense

$$E\{u(X_T{}^*)\} > E\{u(X_T)\}, \ T > \boldsymbol{T}(X_0) \qquad (21)$$

The limited worth of this theorem is weakened a bit further by the consideration that an infinite number of blends of a suboptimal strategy with the geometric mean rule, of the form $vx^* + (1 - v)x$, v sufficiently small and positive, will do negligibly worse as $T \to \infty$.

Thus for all X_0,

$$\lim_{T \to \infty} E\{u(X_T{}^*)\} = u(0) \text{ or } M = \sup_X u(X), \qquad (22)$$

depending upon whether

$$E(\log x_1{}^*) \leqslant 0 \text{ or } > 0$$

For a range of v's, the same utility level will be approached as $T \to \infty$.

OPTIMAL NONUNIFORM STRATEGY

To illustrate that no uniform strategy can be optimal when utility is bounded, consider the well-known case of $u = -e^{-bx}$.

Suppose X_t can be invested at each stage into Z_t dollars of a risky Y_2 such that $E\{Y_2\} > 1$, or into $X_t - Z_t$ dollars of safe cash. Under "limited liability," if the lowest Y_2 could get were r, Z_t could not exceed $X_t/(1 - r)$.

First, disregard limited liability and permit negative X_T. Then a well-known result of Pfansangl (6) shows that at every stage, it is optimal to set $Z_t = Z^*$, where

$$\max_z \int_{-\infty}^\infty - \exp[-b(X-Z) - \boldsymbol{b}Y_2Z]dF_2(Y_2)$$

$$= -[\exp - b(X - Z^*)] \int_{-\infty}^\infty \exp - [bY_2Z^*]dF_2(Y_2) \qquad (23)$$

Then optimally

$$X_T = X_0 - TZ^* + (Y_2{}^{(1)} + Y_2{}^{(2)} + \ldots + Y_2{}^{(T)})Z^* \qquad (24)$$

As $T \to \infty$, X_T approaches a normal distribution, not a log-normal distribution as in the case of uniform strategies. However, the utility level itself will approach a log-normal distribution.

$$U_t \equiv \exp - b[X_0 - TZ^*] \prod_1^T (\exp - bY_2{}^{(t)}Z^*)$$

$$\lim_{T \to \infty} E\{U_T\} = 0 = M \qquad (25)$$

For this option of cash or a risky asset with positive return, it will necessarily be the case that

$$\max_w E\{\log[w + (1 - w)Y_2]\} > 1$$

$$\lim_{T \to \infty} E\{U_T{}^*\} = 0 = M$$

Nonetheless, at every wealth level, above or below a critical number, the optimal policy will generally differ from that of maximum geometric mean.

When we reintroduce limited liability in the problem and never permit an investor to take a position that could leave him bankrupt with negative wealth, the optimal strategy at each X_t will be to put min (X_t, Z^*) into the risky asset and an exact solution becomes more tedious. But clearly the optimal strategy is nonuniform and will outperform any and all uniform strategies, including that of the geometric-mean maximizer.

MAXIMIZING EXPECTED AVERAGE COMPOUND GROWTH

Hakansson (7) has presented an analysis with a bearing on geometric-mean maximization by the long-run investor. Defining the rate of return in any period as x_t and the average compound rate of return as $(x_1x_2 \ldots x_T)^{1/T}$, one can propose as a criterion of portfolio selection maximizing the expected value of this magnitude. After the conventional scaling-factor T is introduced, this gives

$$\max_{w_i} TX_0 E(x_1x_2 \ldots x_T)^{1/T} = X_0\{\max_{w_i} E[x_j{}^{1/T}/(1/T)]\}^T \qquad (26)$$

This problem we have already met in (19) for $\gamma = 1/T$. For finite T, this new criterion leads to slightly more risk-taking than does geometric-mean or expected-logarithm maximizing: for $T = 1$, it leads to Pascal's maximizing of expected money gain; for $T = 2$, it leads to the eighteenth century square-root utility function proposed by Cramer to resolve the St. Petersburg Paradox.

However, as $T \rightarrow \infty$ and $\gamma = 1/T \rightarrow 0$,

$$\lim_{\gamma \to 0} x^\gamma/\gamma = \log x \qquad (27)$$

and we asymptotically approach the geometric-mean maximizing.

Thus, one wedded psychologically to a utility function $-x^{-1}$ will find the new criterion leads to rash investing. Example: modify the numerical example of (14) above so that 2.7 and .3 are replaced by 2.4 and .6. Because the geometric mean of these numbers equals $1.2 > 1$, none in cash is better for such an investor than is all in cash. But, since the harmonic means of these numbers equals $.96 < 1$, our hypothesized investor would prefer to satisfy his own psychological tastes and choose to invest all in cash rather than none in cash—no matter how great T is and in the full recognition that he is violating the new criterion. The few times that following that criterion leads him to comparative losses are important enough in his eyes to scare him off from use of that criterion.

Indeed, if commissions were literally zero, then no matter how short were T in years, the number of transaction periods would become indefinitely large: Hence, with $\gamma = 0$, the novel criterion would lead to geometric-mean maximization, not just asymptotically for long-lived investors, but for any T. To be sure, as one shortens the time period between transactions, my assertion of independence of probabilities between periods might become unrealistic. This opens a Pandora's Box of difficulties. Fortuitously, the utility function $\log x$ is the one case that is least complicated to handle when probabilities are intertemporally dependent. This makes $\log x$ an attractive candidate for Santa Claus examples in textbooks, but will not endear it to anyone whose psychological tastes deviate significantly from $\log x$. (For what it is worth, I may mention that I do not fall into that category, but that does not affect the logic of the problem.)

These remarks critical of the criterion of maximum expected average compound growth do not deny that this criterion, arbitrary as it is, still avoids some of the even greater arbitrariness of conventional mean-variance analysis. Its essential defect is that it attempts to replace the pair of "asymptotically sufficient parameters" $[E\{\log x_t\}, \text{Variance}\{\log x_t\}]$ by the first of these alone, thereby gratuitously ruling out arbitrary γ in the family $u(x) = x^\gamma/\gamma$ in favor of $u(x) = \log x$. This diagnosis can be substantiated by the valuable discussion in the cited Hakansson paper of the efficiency properties of the pair $[E\{\text{average–compound–return}\}, \text{Variance}\{\text{average–compound–return}\}]$, which are asymptotically surrogates for the above sufficient parameters.

Financial aid from the National Science Foundation and editorial assistance from Mrs. Jillian Pappas are gratefully acknowledged. I have benefited from conversations with H. M. Markowitz, H. A. Latané, and L. J. Savage, but cannot claim that they would hold my views. N. H. Hakansson has explicitly warned that the purpose of his paper was not to favor maximizing the expected average–compound–return criterion.

1. Williams, J. B., "Speculation and Carryover," *Quarterly Journal of Economics,* **50,** 436–455 (1936).
2. Kelley, J. L., Jr., "A New Interpretation of Information Rate," *Bell System Technical Journal,* 917–926 (1956).
3. Latané, H. A., "Criteria for Choice Among Risky Ventures," *Journal of Political Economy,* **67,** 144–155 (1956); Kelley, J. L., Jr., and L. Breiman, "Investment Policies for Expanding Business Optimal in a Long-Run Sense," *Naval Research Logistics Quarterly,* **7** (4), 647–651 (1960); Breiman, L., "Optimal Gambling Systems for Favorable Games," ed. J. Neyman, *Proceedings of the Fourth Berkeley Symposium on Mathematical Statistics and Probability* (University of California Press, Berkeley, Calif., 1961).
4. Markowitz, H. M., *Portfolio Selection. Efficient Diversification of Investments* (John Wiley & Sons, New York, 1959), Ch. 6.
5. Samuelson, P. A., "Lifetime Portfolio Selection by Dynamic Stochastic Programming," *Review of Economics and Statistics,* **51,** 239–246 (1969).
6. Pfanzagl, J., "A General Theory of Measurement-Applications to Utility," *Naval Research Logistics Quarterly,* **6,** 283–294 (1959).
7. Hakansson, N. H., "Multi-period Mean-variance Analysis: Toward a General Theory of Portfolio Choice," *Journal of Finance,* **26,** 4 (September, 1971).

CONTENTS

Volume I

Book One

Problems in Pure Theory: The Theory of Consumer's Behavior and Capital Theory

Contents

Contents of Volume II

Acknowledgments

CONTENTS

Volume II

Book Three

Trade, Welfare, and Fiscal Policy

Contents

Book Five

Economics — Past and Present

Contents of Volume I

Acknowledgments

Index

ACKNOWLEDGMENTS

The author, editor, and The MIT Press wish to thank the publishers of the following essays for permission to reprint them here. The selections are arranged chronologically, with cross references in brackets to the chapter numbers used in this collection.

"Personal Freedoms and Economic Freedoms in the Mixed Economy," in E. F. Cheit, ed., *The Business Establishment* (New York: John Wiley & Sons, Inc., 1964), Ch. 6, pp. 193–227. [Chapter 181]

"Principles of Efficiency — Discussion," *American Economic Review* (Papers and Proceedings of the 76th Annual Meeting of the American Economic Association), Vol. 54, No. 3 (May 1964), pp. 93–96. [Chapter 164]

"Problems of the American Economy — Hard and Easy," in L. H. Seltzer, ed., *New Horizons of Economic Progress*, The Franklin Memorial Lectures, Vol. XII (Detroit, Michigan: Wayne State University Press, 1964), pp. 13–36. [Chapter 192]

"Reply" to "D. H. Robertson: Comment," *Quarterly Journal of Economics*, Vol. 78, (May 1964), pp. 328–330. Copyright 1964 by the President and Fellows of Harvard College. [Chapter 182]

"A. P. Lerner at Sixty," *Review of Economic Studies*, Vol. XXXI (3), No. 87 (June 1964), pp. 169–178. [Chapter 183]

"Theory and Realism: A Reply," *American Economic Review*, Vol. LIV, No. 5 (September 1964), pp. 736–739. [Chapter 195]

Acknowledgments

"Public Goods and Subscription TV: Correction of the Record," *Journal of Law and Economics*, Vol. VII (October 1964), pp. 81–83. [Chapter 173]

"Tax Deductibility of Economic Depreciation to Insure Invariant Valuations," *Journal of Political Economy*, Vol. LXXII, No. 6 (December 1964), pp. 604–606. Copyright 1964 by the University of Chicago. [Chapter 179]

"A Fallacy in the Interpretation of Pareto's Law of Alleged Constancy of Income Distribution," *Rivista Internazionale di Scienze Economiche e Commerciali*, Vol. XII, No. 3 (April 1965), pp. 246–253. [Chapter 165]

"Proof that Properly Anticipated Prices Fluctuate Randomly," *Industrial Management Review*, Vol. 6, No. 2 (Spring 1965), pp. 41–49. [Chapter 198]

"Rational Theory of Warrant Pricing" and "Appendix: A Free Boundary Problem for the Heat Equation Arising from a Problem in Mathematical Economics," by H. P. McKean, Jr., *Industrial Management Review*, Vol. 6, No. 2 (Spring 1965), pp. 13–39. [Chapter 199]

"A Catenary Turnpike Theorem Involving Consumption and the Golden Rule," *American Economic Review*, Vol. LV, No. 3 (June 1965), pp. 486–496. [Chapter 136]

"Some Notions on Causality and Teleology in Economics," in Daniel Lerner, ed., *Cause and Effect* (New York: The Free Press, 1965), pp. 99–143. [Chapter 169]

"Using Full Duality to Show that Simultaneously Additive Direct and Indirect Utilities Implies Unitary Price Elasticity of Demand," *Econometrica*, Vol. 33, No. 4 (October 1965), pp. 781–796. [Chapter 134]

"Economic Forecasting and Science," *Michigan Quarterly Review*, Vol. IV, No. 4 (October 1965) pp. 274–280. [Chapter 197]

"A Theory of Induced Innovation Along Kennedy-Weizsäcker Lines," *Review of Economics and Statistics*, Vol. XLVII, No. 4 (November 1965), pp. 343–356. [Chapter 143]

"Professor Samuelson on Theory and Realism: Reply," *American Economic Review*, Vol. LV, No. 5 (December 1965), pp. 1164–1172. [Chapter 196]

"The Fundamental Singularity Theorem for Non-Joint Production," *International Economic Review*, Vol. 7, No. 1 (January 1966), pp. 34–41. [Chapter 145]

"A Negative Report on Hertz's Program for Reformulating Mechanics," *Scientia*, Vol. LX, Series VII (January-February 1966), pp. 32–39. [Chapter 156]

With F. Modigliani, "The Pasinetti Paradox in Neoclassical and More General Models," *Review of Economic Studies*, Vol. XXXIII, No. 4 (October 1966), pp. 269–301. [Chapter 146]

With F. Modigliani, "Reply to Pasinetti and Robinson," *Review of Economic Studies*, Vol. XXXIII, No. 4 (October 1966), pp. 321–330. [Chapter 147]

"Rejoinder: Agreements, Disagreements, Doubts, and the Case of Induced Harrod-Neutral Technical Change," *Review of Economics and Statistics,* Vol. XLVIII, No. 4 (November 1966), pp. 444–448. [Chapter 144]

"A Summing Up," *Quarterly Journal of Economics,* Vol. LXXX, No. 4 (November 1966) pp. 568–583. Copyright 1966 by the President and Fellows of Harvard College. [Chapter 148]

With D. Levhari, "The Non-Switching Theorem is False," *Quarterly Journal of Economics,* Vol. LXXX, No. 4 (November 1966), pp. 518–519. Copyright 1966 by the President and Fellows of Harvard College. [Chapter 149]

"The Monopolistic Competition Revolution," in R. E. Kuenne, ed., *Monopolistic Competition Theory: Studies in Impact. Essays in Honor of Edward H. Chamberlin* (New York: John Wiley & Sons, Inc., 1967), Ch. 5, pp. 105–138. [Chapter 131]

"General Proof that Diversification Pays," *Journal of Financial and Quantitative Analysis,* Vol. II, No. 1 (March 1967), pp. 1–13. [Chapter 201]

"Marxian Economics as Economics," *American Economic Review,* Vol. LVII, No. 2 (May 1967), pp. 616–623. [Chapter 152]

"A Universal Cycle?" in Rudolf Henn, ed., *Methods of Operations Research* (Meisenheim: Verlag Anton Hain, 1967), Vol. III, pp. 307–320. [Chapter 170]

"Stabilization Policies in the Contemporary U. S. Economy," in George Horwich, ed., *Monetary Process and Policy* (Homewood, Illinois: Richard D. Irwin, Inc., 1967), pp. 3–11. Copyright © Purdue University. [Chapter 193]

"Foreword," in P. A. Samuelson, *Foundations of Economic Analysis,* Japanese Edition, translated by Ryuzo Sato (Tokyo: Keiso-Shobo Ltd., July 1967), pp. vi–x. Copyright 1947 by the President and Fellows of Harvard College. [Chapter 187]

"Efficient Portfolio Selection for Pareto-Levy Investments," *Journal of Financial and Quantitative Analysis,* Vol. II, No. 2 (June 1967), pp. 107–122. [Chapter 202]

"A Turnpike Refutation of the Golden Rule in a Welfare-Maximizing Many-Year Plan," in K. Shell, ed., *Essays on the Theory of Optimal Economic Growth* (Cambridge, Massachusetts: MIT Press, 1967), Ch. XIV, pp. 269–280. [Chapter 137]

"Indeterminacy of Development in a Hetereogeneous-Capital Model with Constant Saving Propensity," in Karl Shell, ed., *Essays on the Theory of Optimal Economic Growth* (Cambridge, Massachusetts: MIT Press, 1967), Ch. XII, pp. 219–231. [Chapter 150]

"Money, Interest Rates, and Economic Activity: Their Interrelationship in a Market Economy," *Proceedings of a Symposium on Money, Interest Rates, and Economic Activity* (New York: American Bankers Association, 1967), pp. 40–60. [Chapter 178]

Acknowledgments

"Indeterminacy of Governmental Role in Public-Good Theory," *Papers on Non-Market Decision Making*, Vol. III (Fall 1967), p. 47. [Chapter 174]

"Summary on Factor-Price Equalization," *International Economic Review*, Vol. 8, No. 3 (October 1967), pp. 286–295. [Chapter 161]

"Foreword," in J. de V. Graaff, *Theoretical Welfare Economics* (Cambridge, U. K.: Cambridge University Press, 1967), pp. vii–viii. [Chapter 166]

"Irving Fisher and the Theory of Capital," in W. Fellner *et al.*, *Ten Economic Studies in the Tradition of Irving Fisher* (New York: John Wiley & Sons, Inc., 1967), Ch. 2, pp. 17–39. [Chapter 184]

"Arrow's Mathematical Politics," in S. Hook, ed., *Human Values and Economic Policy: A* Symposium (New York: New York University Press, 1967), pp. 41–52. [Chapter 167]

"Pitfalls in the Analysis of Public Goods," *Journal of Law and Economics*, Vol. 10 (January 1968), pp. 199–204. [Chapter 175]

"What Classical and Neoclassical Monetary Theory Really Was," *Canadian Journal of Economics*, Vol. I, No. 1 (February 1968), pp. 1–15. [Chapter 176]

"The Two-Part Golden Rule Deduced as the Asymptotic Turnpike of Catenary Motions," *Western Economic Journal*, Vol. VI, No. 2 (March 1968), pp. 85–89. [Chapter 138]

"Reciprocal Characteristic Root Property of Discrete-Time Maxima," *Western Economic Journal*, Vol. VI, No. 2 (March 1968), pp. 90–93. [Chapter 157]

"Two Generalizations of the Elasticity of Substitution," in J. N. Wolfe, ed., *Value, Capital and Growth: Papers in Honour of Sir John Hicks* (Edinburgh: Edinburgh University Press, 1968), pp. 467–480. [Chapter 133]

"Constructing an Unbiased Random Sequence," *Journal of the American Statistical Association*, Vol. 63 (December 1968), pp. 1526–1527. [Chapter 159]

"How Deviant Can You Be?" *Journal of the American Statistical Association*, Vol. 63 (December 1968), pp. 1522–1525. [Chapter 160]

With R. C. Merton, "A Complete Model of Warrant Pricing that Maximizes Utility," *Industrial Management Review*, Vol. 10, No. 2 (Winter 1969), pp. 17–46. [Chapter 200]

"Contrast between Welfare Conditions for Joint Supply and for Public Goods," *Review of Economics and Statistics*, Vol. LI, No. 1 (February 1969) pp. 26–30. [Chapter 168]

"Local Proof of the Turnpike Theorem," *Western Economic Journal*, Vol. VII, No. 1 (March 1969) pp. 1–8. [Chapter 139]

"Corrected Formulation of Direct and Indirect Additivity," *Econometrica*, Vol. 37, No. 2 (April 1969), pp. 355–359. [Chapter 135]

"Nonoptimality of Moneyholding under *Laissez Faire*," *Canadian Journal of Economics*, Vol. II, No. 2 (May 1969), pp. 303–308. [Chapter 177]

"Memories," *Newsweek* June 2, 1969), p. 83. [Chapter 191]

"An Analytic Evaluation of Interest Rate Ceilings for Savings and Loan Associations and Competitive Institutions," in *Study of the Savings and Loan Industry* (Washington, D.C.: Federal Home Loan Bank Board, July 1969) pp. 1563–1590. [Chapter 180]

"Money and History," from *Documentary History of Banking and Currency in the United States,* edited by Herman K. Krooss (1969) published by Chelsea House in association with McGraw-Hill Book Company, pp. xxxi–xlii. [Chapter 189]

"The Way of an Economist," in P. A. Samuelson, ed., *International Economic Relations: Proceedings of the Third Congress of the International Economic Association* (London: Macmillan, 1969), pp. 1–11. [Chapter 186]

"Lifetime Portfolio Selection by Dynamic Stochastic Programming," *Review of Economics and Statistics,* Vol. LI, No. 4 (August 1969) pp. 239–246. Copyright by the President and Fellows of Harvard College. [Chapter 204]

"Pure Theory of Public Expenditure and Taxation," in J. Margolis and H. Guitton, eds., *Public Economics: An Analysis of Public Production and Consumption and their Relations to the Private Sectors: Proceedings of a Conference Held by the International Economics Association* (London: Macmillan, 1969), pp. 98–123. [Chapter 172]

"Foreword," in S. Chakrovarty, *Capital and Development Planning* (Cambridge, Massachusetts: MIT Press, 1969), pp. vii–xii. Reprinted as "What Makes for a Beautiful Problem in Science?" *Journal of Political Economy,* Vol. 78, No. 6 (December 1970) pp. 1372–1377. [Chapter 151]

With N. Liviatan, "Notes on Turnpikes: Stable and Unstable," *Journal of Economic Theory,* Vol. 1, No. 4 (December 1969), pp. 454–475. [Chapter 141]

"Reflections on Recent Federal Reserve Policy," by Paul A. Samuelson, is reprinted from the *Journal of Money, Credit, and Banking,* Vol. II, No. 1 (February 1970), pp. 33–44. Copyright © 1970 by the Ohio State University Press. All Rights Reserved. [Chapter 194]

"Joseph Schumpeter," *Newsweek* (April 13, 1970), p. 75. [Chapter 185]

"Reply," *Quarterly Journal of Economics,* Vol. LXXXIV, No. 2 (May 1970), pp. 341–345. Copyright 1970 by the President and Fellows of Harvard College. [Chapter 132]

"Classical Orbital Stability Deduced for Discrete-Time Maximum Systems," *Western Economic Journal,* Vol. VIII, No. 2 (June 1970), pp. 110–119. [Chapter 158]

"The 'Transformation' from Marxian 'Values' to Competitive 'Prices': A Process of Rejection and Replacement," *Proceedings of the National Academy of Sciences, U.S.A.,* Vol. 67, No. 1 (September 1970), pp. 423–425. [Chapter 154]

Acknowledgments

"The Fundamental Approximation Theorem of Portfolio Analysis in Terms of Means, Variances, and Higher Moments," *Review of Economic Studies*, Vol. XXXVII, No. 4 (October 1970), pp. 537–542. [Chapter 203]

"Foreword," in R. Roll, *The Behavior of Interest Rates: An Application of the Efficient Market Model to U.S. Treasury Bills* (New York: Basic Books, Inc., 1970), pp. ix–xi. Copyright © 1970 by Basic Books, Inc., Publishers, New York. [Chapter 205]

"Law of Conservation of the Capital-Output Ratio," *Proceedings of the National Academy of Sciences, U.S.A.*, Vol. 67, No. 3 (November 1970), pp. 1477–1479. [Chapter 142]

"Economic Growth," in *Gendaisekai Hyakka Daijiten*, Vol. I (Tokyo: Kodansha Ltd, 1971). [Chapter 190]

"An Exact Hume-Ricardo-Marshall Model of International Trade," *Journal of International Economics*, Vol. 1, No. 1 (February 1971), pp. 1–18. [Chapter 162]

"Stochastic Speculative Price," *Proceedings of the National Academy of Sciences, U.S.A.*, Vol. 68, No. 2 (February 1971), pp. 335–337. [Chapter 206]

"Turnpike Theorems Even Though Tastes Are Intertemporally Dependent," *Western Economic Journal*, Vol. IX, No. 1 (March 1971), pp. 21–26. [Chapter 140]

"Generalized Predator-Prey Oscillations in Ecological and Economic Equilibrium," *Proceedings of the National Academy of Sciences, U.S.A.*, Vol. 68, No. 5 (May 1971), pp. 980–983. [Chapter 171]

"Understanding the Marxian Notion of Exploitation: A Summary of the So-Called Transformation Problem Between Marxian Values and Competitive Prices," *Journal of Economic Literature*, Vol. IX, No. 2 (June 1971), pp. 399–431. [Chapter 153]

With C. C. von Weizsäcker, "A New Labor Theory of Value for Rational Planning Through Use of the Bourgeois Profit Rate," *Proceedings of the National Academy of Sciences, U.S.A.*, Vol. 68, No. 6 (June 1971), pp. 1192–1194. [Chapter 155]

"Maximum Principles in Analytical Economics," in *Les Prix Nobel en 1970* (Stockholm: The Nobel Foundation, 1971), pp. 273–288. Copyright © by The Nobel Foundation, 1971. [Chapter 130]

"On the Trail of Conventional Beliefs about the Transfer Problem," in J. Bhagwati *et al.*, eds., *Trade, Balance of Payments, and Growth: Papers in International Economics in Honor of Charles P. Kindleberger* (Amsterdam: North-Holland Publishing Company, 1971), Ch. 15, pp. 327–351. [Chapter 163]

"The 'Fallacy' of Maximizing the Geometric Mean in Long Sequences of Investing or Gambling," *Proceedings of the National Academy of Sciences, U.S.A.*, Vol. 68, No. 10 (October 1971), pp. 2493–2496. [Chapter 207]

INDEX